Motif Programming Manual

Volume Six A

Motif Programming Manual

---

by Dan Heller and Paula M. Ferguson

UIL Material by David Brennan

O'Reilly & Associates, Inc.

Motif Programming Manual
by Dan Heller and Paula M. Ferguson
UIL Material by David Brennan

Editor: Tim O'Reilly

Production Editors: Eileen Kramer
Stephen Spainhour

Printing History:

September 1991:	First Edition.
July 1992:	Minor corrections. New Chapter 20 added.
February 1994:	Second Edition. Updated to cover Motif 1.2 and UIL.

ISBN 1-56592-016-3
[M]

Table of Contents

Chapter 6 Selection Dialogs 167

Chapter 7 Custom Dialogs 195

Chapter 8 Manager Widgets 235

Chapter 9 ScrolledWindows and ScrollBars 297

Chapter 10 The DrawingArea Widget 337

Chapter 11 Labels and Buttons 363

Chapter 15 Menus 519

Chapter 16 Interacting With the Window Manager 567

Chapter 25 Building an Application With UIL

Chapter 26 Advanced UIL Programming

Figures

Examples

Tables

Preface

By convention, a preface describes the book itself, while the introduction describes the subject matter. You should read through the preface to get an idea of how the book is organized, the conventions it follows, and so on.

In the Preface:

Preface

This book describes how to write applications using the Motif toolkit from the Open Software Foundation (OSF). The Motif toolkit is based on the X Toolkit Intrinsics (Xt), which is the standard mechanism on which many of the toolkits written for the X Window System are based. Xt provides a library of user-interface objects called *widgets* and *gadgets*, which provide a convenient interface for creating and manipulating X windows, colormaps, events, and other cosmetic attributes of the display. In short, widgets can be thought of as building blocks that the programmer uses to construct a complete application.

However, the widgets that Xt provides are generic in nature and impose no user-interface policy whatsoever. That is the job of a user-interface toolkit such as Motif. Motif provides a complete set of widgets designed to implement the application look and feel specified in the *Motif Style Guide* and the *Motif Application Environment Specification*.

The book provides a complete programmer's guide to the Motif toolkit. While the OSF/Motif toolkit is based on Xt, the focus of the book is on Motif itself, not on the Intrinsics. Detailed information about Xt is provided by Volume Four, *X Toolkit Intrinsics Programming Manual*, and references are made to that volume throughout the course of this book. You are not required to have Volume Four in order to use this book effectively, as the books are not companion volumes, but complementary ones. However, truly robust applications require a depth of knowledge about Xt and Xlib, the layer on which Xt itself is based, that is not addressed in this book alone. We never leave you completely in the dark about Xt or Xlib functions that we use or reference, but you won't learn everything there is to know about them through this particular volume.

This book covers Motif 1.2, which is the latest major release of the Motif toolkit. Motif 1.2 is based on Release 5 of the Xlib and Xt specifications (X11R5). This release of Motif provides many new features, as well as a number of enhancements to existing functionality. All of the changes in Motif 1.2 are summarized in Section 3.5, which provides references to other sections that describe the changes in more detail.

The Plot

There are several plots and subplots in this book and the stories told are intertwined. Our primary goal is to help you learn about the Motif environment from both the programmer's and the user's perspectives. However, we are talking to you as a programmer, not as a user. We treat the user as a third party who is not with us now. In order to create an application for the user, you sometimes have to assume her role, so at times we may ask you to play such a role to help you think about things from the user's perspective rather than the programmer's.

Each chapter begins by discussing the goals that Motif is trying to achieve using a particular widget or gadget. For example, before we describe how to create a FileSelectionDialog, we introduce the object visually and conceptually, discuss its features and drawbacks, and put you in the role of the user. Once you understand what the user is working with, you should have a better perspective on the task of presenting it to her.

The next subplot is that of application design. Many design concepts transcend the graphical user interface (GUI) and are common to all programs that interact with users. You could even interpret this book as a programmer's guide that happens to use Motif as an example. As you read the material, you should stop and think about how you might approach a particular interface method if you were using another toolkit instead of Motif. A wild concept, perhaps, but this approach is the key to better application design and to toolkit independence. If Motif changes in a later release, or if you decide to port your application to another toolkit or even another windowing system, the more generalized your code is, the easier it will be to bring it into a new realm successfully.

The last story we are telling is that of general programming technique. By providing you with examples of good programming habits, styles, and usages, we hope to propagate a programming methodology that has proven to be successful over the years. These techniques have been applied to applications that have been ported to multiple architectures and operating systems. As an added bonus, we have thrown in a number of interesting programming tricks. No, these are not hacks, but conveniences that are particular to C, to UNIX, or even to the X Window System. We don't focus on these things, but they are made available to you in passing, so you should have no problem identifying them when they come up.

This book is intended to be used as a programmer's manual, not a reference manual. Volume Six B, *Motif Reference Manual*, contains reference material for all of the Motif library functions and widget classes. We have tried to identify those features of the toolkit that are most important for general discussion, so we do not discuss every aspect of the Motif toolkit in the body of this book.

Any major software development effort, especially in its early stages, has bugs that prevent certain features from being used and the Motif toolkit is no exception. There are some bugs in the Motif toolkit that have not yet been worked out, but this does not imply that the toolkit is poorly written or riddled with errors. Throughout the book, we try to alert you to any potential problems you may encounter due to bugs. In some cases, there are things that work in Motif, but they are poorly designed, and we don't recommend that you use them. Again, we provide an explanation of what's going on and sometimes describe an alternative solution. There are also some features, resources, and functions available in the toolkit that are not supported by OSF. OSF reserves the right to change anything not publicly documented, so rather than discuss undocumented features, we simply ignore them.

We should also point out that this book is not intended to solve all your problems or answer all your questions concerning Motif or its toolkit. It is not going to spoon feed you by giving you step-by-step instructions on how to achieve a particular task. You are encouraged, and even expected, to experiment on your own with the example applications or, better yet, with your own programs. We want to provide you with discussion and examples that provoke you into asking questions like, "What would happen if I changed this program to do this?" It would be unrealistic to believe that we could address every problem that might come up. Rather than approaching situations using overly specific examples, we discuss them in a generalized way that should be applicable to many different scenarios.

Assumptions

The basic method for creating simple applications in Motif is conceptually simple and straightforward. Even if you only dabble in C, you can probably understand the concepts well enough to do most things. However, unless you have a strong handle on the C programming language, there is an upper limit to what you will be able to do when you try to create a full-featured, functioning application. After all, the user-interface portion of most applications should make up no more than 30-40% of the total code. The functionality of an application is up to you and is not discussed here. Without a strong background with C, or some other structured programming language, you might have a problem keeping up with the material presented here.

This book also assumes that you are familiar with the concepts and architecture of the X Toolkit Intrinsics, which are presented in Volume Four, *X Toolkit Intrinsics Programming Manual, Motif Edition*, and Volume Five, *X Toolkit Intrinsics Reference Manual*. A basic understanding of the X Window System is also useful. For some advanced topics, the reader may need to consult Volume One, *Xlib Programming Manual*, and Volume Two, *Xlib Reference Manual*.

How This Book Is Organized

While this book attempts to serve the widest possible audience, that does not imply that the material is so simple that it is only useful to novice programmers. In fact, this book can be considered an advanced programmer's handbook, since in many places, it assumes a fairly sophisticated knowledge of many features of the X Window System.

Each chapter is organized so that it gets more demanding as you read through it. Each chapter begins with a short introduction to the particular Motif element that is the subject of the chapter. The basic mechanics involved in creating and manipulating the object are addressed next, followed by the resources and other configurable aspects of the object. If there is any advanced material about the object, it is presented at the end of the chapter. Many chapters also include exercises that suggest how the material can be adapted for uses not discussed explicitly in the text.

While the chapters may be read sequentially, it is certainly not required or expected that you do so. As you will soon discover, there are many circular dependencies that justify skipping around between chapters. Since there is no organization that would eliminate this problem, the material is not organized so that you "learn as you go." Instead, we organized the material in a top-down manner, starting with several chapters that provide an introduction to the Motif look and feel, followed by chapters organized on a widget-by-widget basis. The higher-level manager widgets are discussed first, followed by the primitive widgets and gadgets. Advanced material is positioned at the end of the book, since the details are not of paramount importance to the earlier material. The last four chaapters are devoted to UIL.

In short, everything is used everywhere. Starting at the beginning, however, means that we won't necessarily assume you know about the material that is referenced in later chapters. On the other hand, the later chapters may make the assumption that you are aware of material in earlier chapters.

The book is broken down into twenty six chapters and one appendix as follows:

Chapter 1   *Introduction to Motif* answers the question "Why Motif?" and suggests some of the complexities that the programmer has to master in order to make an application easy to use.

Chapter 2   *The Motif Programming Model* teaches the fundamentals of Motif by example. It presents a simple "Hello, World" program that shows the structure and style common to all Motif programs. Much of this material is already covered in detail in Volume Four, *X Toolkit Intrinsics Programming Manual, Motif Edition*, so the chapter can be read as a refresher, or a light introduction for those who haven't read the earlier book. The chapter references Volume Four and Volume One, *Xlib Programming Manual*, to point out areas that the programmer needs to understand before progressing with Motif.

Chapter 3   *Overview of the Motif Toolkit* explains what is involved in creating a real application. The chapter discusses the arrangement of primitive widgets in an interface, the use of dialog boxes and menus, and the relationship between an application and the window manager. The chapter also describes all of the changes in Release 1.2 of the Motif toolkit. After reading this chapter, the programmer should have a solid overview of Motif application programming and be able to read the remaining chapters in any order.

Chapter 4   *The Main Window* describes the Motif MainWindow widget, which can be used to frame many types of applications. The MainWindow is a manager widget that provides a MenuBar, a scrollable work area, and various other optional display and control areas.

Chapter 5   *Introduction to Dialogs* describes the fundamental concepts that underly all Motif dialogs. It provides a foundation for the more advanced material in the following chapters. In the course of the introduction, this chapter also provides details on Motif's predefined MessageDialog classes.

Chapter 6   *Selection Dialogs* presents the more complex Motif-supplied dialogs for displaying selectable items, such as lists of files or commands, to the user.

Chapter 7   *Custom Dialogs* describes how to create new dialog types, either by customizing Motif dialogs or by creating entirely new dialogs.

Chapter 8   *Manager Widgets* provides detailed descriptions of the various classes of Motif manager widgets. Useful examples explore the various methods of positioning components in Form and RowColumn widgets.

Chapter 9   *ScrolledWindows and ScrollBars* describes the ins and outs of scrolling, with particular attention to application-defined scrolling, which is often required when the simple scrolling provided by the ScrolledWindow widget is insufficient.

Chapter 10   *The DrawingArea Widget* describes the Motif DrawingArea widget, which provides a canvas for interactive drawing. The chapter simply highlights, with numerous code examples, the difficulties that may be encountered when working with this widget, rather than trying to teach Xlib drawing techniques. Some knowledge of Xlib is assumed; we direct the reader to Volume One, *Xlib Programming Manual*, for additional information.

Chapter 11   *Labels and Buttons* provides an in-depth look at labels and buttons, the most commonly-used primitive widgets. The chapter discusses the Label, PushButton, ToggleButton, ArrowButton, and DrawnButton widget classes.

Chapter 12   *The List Widget* describes yet another method for the user to exert control over an application. A List widget displays a group of items from which the user can make a selection.

Chapter 13   *The Scale Widget* describes how to use the Scale to display a range of values.

Chapter 14   *Text Widgets* explains how the Text and TextField widgets can be used to provide text entry in an application, from a single data-entry field to a full-fledged text editor. Special attention is paid to problems such as how to mask or convert data input by the user so as to control its format. The chapter also discusses the internationalization features of the widgets provided in Motif 1.2.

Chapter 15   *Menus* describes the menus provided by the Motif toolkit. The chapter examines how menus are created and presents some generalized menu creation routines.

Chapter 16   *Interacting With the Window Manager* provides additional information on the relationship between an application and the Motif Window Manager (*mwm*). It discusses the shell widget resources and window manager protocols that can be used to communicate with the window manager.

Chapter 17   *The Clipboard* describes a way for the application to interact with other applications. Data is placed on the clipboard, where it can be accessed by other windows on the desktop, regardless of the applications with which they are associated.

Chapter 18   *Drag and Drop* presents the drag and drop mechanism for transferring data that is provided in Motif 1.2. The chapter describes the built-in drag and drop features of the Motif toolkit and provides examples of adding drag and drop functionality to an application.

Chapter 19   *Compound Strings* describes Motif's technology for encoding font and directional information in the strings that are used by almost all Motif widgets. It discusses how to use compound strings in an internationalized application.

Chapter 20   *Signal Handling* presents the problems that can be encountered when mixing UNIX signals with X applications. It explains how signals work and why they can wreak such havoc with X, and suggests workarounds that can help you to minimize the damage.

Chapter 21   *Advanced Dialog Programming* describes the issues involved in creating multi-stage help systems, using WorkingDialogs that allow the user to interrupt long-running tasks, and dynamically changing the pixmaps displayed in a dialog.

Chapter 22   *Introduction to UIL* introduces Motif's User Interface Language (UIL) and the Motif Resource Manager (Mrm). It presents a "Hello, World" program that shows the basic structure of an application that uses UIL and Mrm.

Chapter 23   *Using the UIL Compiler* describes how to use the UIL compiler.

Chapter 24   *Creating a User Interface With UIL* presents details about the syntax and usage of UIL, as well as the various Mrm functions that are associated with the different UIL constructs.

Chapter 25   *Building an Application With UIL* describes how the various components of UIL and Mrm come together in a real application by presenting a text-editor program.

Chapter 26   *Advanced UIL Programming* describes some advanced UIL programming techniques that can make it easier to use UIL to prototype a user interface.

Appendix   *Additional Example Programs* provides several additional examples that illustrate techniques not discussed in the body of the book.

Related Documents

The following books on the X Window System are available from O'Reilly & Associates:

Volume Zero   *X Protocol Reference Manual*

Volume One   *Xlib Programming Manual*

Volume Two   *Xlib Reference Manual*

Volume Three   *X Window System User's Guide, Motif Edition*

Volume Four   *X Toolkit Intrinsics Programming Manual, Motif Edition*

Volume Five	*X Toolkit Intrinsics Reference Manual*
Volume Six B	*Motif Reference Manual*
Volume Seven	*XView Programming Manual* (with accompanying reference volume)
Volume Eight	*X Window System Administrator's Guide*

PHIGS Programming Manual

PHIGS Reference Manual

PEXlib Programming Manual

PEXlib Reference Manual

Quick Reference *The X Window System in a Nutshell*

Conventions Used in This Book

Italic is used for:

*   UNIX pathnames, filenames, program names, user command names, options for user commands, and variable expressions in syntax sections.

*   New terms where they are defined.

`Typewriter Font` is used for:

*   Anything that would be typed verbatim into code, such as examples of source code and text on the screen.

*   Variables, data structures (and fields), symbols (defined constants and bit flags), functions, macros, and a general assortment of anything relating to the C programming language.

*   All functions relating to Motif, Xt, and Xlib.

*   Names of subroutines in example programs.

Italic Typewriter Font is used for:

*   Arguments to functions, since they could be typed in code as shown but are arbitrary names that could be changed.

Boldface is used for:

*   Names of buttons and menus.

Obtaining Motif

If your hardware vendor is an OSF member, they may be able to provide Motif binaries for your machine. Various independent vendors also provide binaries for some machines. Source licenses must be obtained directly from OSF:

OSF Direct
Open Software Foundation
11 Cambridge Center
Cambridge, MA 02142
USA
+1 617 621-7300
Internet: direct@osf.org

Obtaining the Example Programs

The example programs in this book are available electronically in a number of ways: by FTP, FTPMAIL, BITFTP, and UUCP. The cheapest, fastest, and easiest ways are listed first. If you read from the top down, the first one that works for you is probably the best. Use FTP if you are directly on the Internet. Use FTPMAIL if you are not on the Internet but can send and receive electronic mail to internet sites (this includes CompuServe users). Use BITFTP if you send electronic mail via BITNET. Use UUCP if none of the above works.

Versions of the example programs for both Motif 1.2 and Motif 1.1 are available electronically. If you want the Motif 1.2 version, use the filename *examples12.tar.Z*, as shown in the sample sessions below. The filename for the Motif 1.1 version is *examples11.tar.Z*.

FTP

To use FTP, you need a machine with direct access to the Internet. A sample session is shown, with what you should type in boldface.

```
% ftp ftp.uu.net
Connected to ftp.uu.net.
220 FTP server (Version 6.21 Tue Mar 10 22:09:55 EST 1992) ready.
Name (ftp.uu.net:paula): anonymous
331 Guest login ok, send domain style e-mail address as password.
Password: paula@ora.com (use your user name and host here)
230 Guest login ok, access restrictions apply.
ftp> cd /published/oreilly/xbook/motif
250 CWD command successful.
ftp> binary (Very important! You must specify binary transfer for compressed files.)
200 Type set to I.
ftp> get examples12.tar.Z
200 PORT command successful.
150 Opening BINARY mode data connection for examples12.tar.Z.
226 Transfer complete.
ftp> quit
```

```
221 Goodbye.
%
```

If the file is a compressed tar archive, extract the files from the archive by typing:

```
% zcat examples12.tar.Z | tar xf -
```

System V systems require the following *tar* command instead:

```
% zcat examples12.tar.Z | tar xof -
```

If *zcat* is not available on your system, use separate *uncompress* and *tar* commands.

FTPMAIL

FTPMAIL is a mail server available to anyone who can send electronic mail to and receive it from Internet sites. This includes any company or service provider that allows email connections to the Internet. Here's how you do it.

You send mail to *ftpmail@online.ora.com*. In the message body, give the FTP commands you want to run. The server will run anonymous FTP for you and mail the files back to you. To get a complete help file, send a message with no subject and the single word "help" in the body. The following is an example mail session that should get you the examples. This command sends you a listing of the files in the selected directory, and the requested example files. The listing is useful if there's a later version of the examples you're interested in.

```
% mail ftpmail@online.ora.com
Subject:
reply-to paula@ora.com        Where you want files mailed
open
cd /published/oreilly/xbook/motif
dir
mode binary
uuencode
get examples12.tar.Z
quit
```

A signature at the end of the message is acceptable as long as it appears after "quit."

All retrieved files will be split into 60KB chunks and mailed to you. You then remove the mail headers and concatenate them into one file, and then *uudecode* or *atob* it. Once you've got the desired file, follow the directions under FTP to extract the files from the archive.

VMS, DOS, and Mac versions of *uudecode*, *atob*, *uncompress*, and *tar* are available.

BITFTP

BITFTP is a mail server for BITNET users. You send it electronic mail messages requesting files, and it sends you back the files by electronic mail. BITFTP currently serves only users who send it mail from nodes that are directly on BITNET, EARN, or NetNorth. BITFTP is a public service of Princeton University. Here's how it works.

To use BITFTP, send mail containing your ftp commands to *BITFTP@PUCC*. For a complete help file, send HELP as the message body.

The following is the message body you should send to BITFTP:

```
FTP  ftp.uu.net  NETDATA
USER  anonymous
PASS your Internet email address (not your bitnet address)
CD  /published/oreilly/xbook/motif
DIR
BINARY
GET  examples12.tar.Z
QUIT
```

Once you've got the desired file, follow the directions under FTP to extract the files from the archive. Since you are probably not on a UNIX system, you may need to get versions of *uudecode*, *uncompress*, *atob*, and *tar* for your system. VMS, DOS, and Mac versions are available. The VMS versions are on *gatekeeper.dec.com* in */archive/pub/VMS*.

Questions about BITFTP can be directed to Melinda Varian, *MAINT@PUCC* on BITNET.

UUCP

UUCP is standard on virtually all UNIX systems, and is available for IBM-compatible PCs and Apple Macintoshes. The examples are available by UUCP via modem from UUNET; UUNET's connect-time charges apply.

You can get the examples from UUNET whether you have an account or not. If you or your company has an account with UUNET, you will have a system with a direct UUCP connection to UUNET. Find that system, and type:

```
uucp uunet\!~/published/oreilly/xbook/motif/examples12.tar.Z yourhost\!~/yourname/
```

The backslashes can be omitted if you use the Bourne shell (*sh*) instead of *csh*. The file should appear some time later (up to a day or more) in the directory */usr/spool/uucppublic/yourname*. If you don't have an account but would like one so that you can get electronic mail, then contact UUNET at 703-204-8000.

It's a good idea to get the file */published/oreilly/xbook/motif/ls-lR.Z* as a short test file containing the filenames and sizes of all the files in the directory.

Once you've got the desired file, follow the directions under FTP to extract the files from the archive.

Copyright

The example programs are written by Dan Heller and Paula Ferguson for the *Motif Programming Manual*, Copyright 1994 O'Reilly & Associates, Inc. Permission to use, copy, and modify these programs without restriction is hereby granted, as long as this copyright notice appears in each copy of the program source code.

For the purposes of making the book easier to read, the above copyright notice does not appear in the program examples. However, the copyright does exist in the electronic form of the programs available on the Internet.

Compiling the Example Programs

Once you have the examples and you've unpacked the archive as described above, you're ready to compile them. The easiest way is to use *imake*, a program supplied with the X11 distribution that generates proper Makefiles on a wide variety of systems. *imake* uses configuration files called Imakefiles that are included with the examples. If you have *imake*, you should go to the top-level directory containing the examples, and type:

```
% xmkmf
% make Makefiles
% make
```

The examples all have the same application class for purposes of the app-defaults file. The class name is "Demos" and the app-defaults file (*Demos*) in the main examples directory should be placed in */usr/lib/X11/app-defaults/Demos* on a UNIX system. If you can't write to that directory, or if your normal X11 directory tree is installed elsewhere, you should set the environment variable XAPPLRESDIR to the directory where you installed the examples.

Notes on Z-Mail

Many of the screenshots in this book that are not based on the example programs are of Z-Mail, an electronic mail program. Z-Mail is the culmination of years of work, starting with a freely-distributed program called Mail User's Shell (Mush). Mush's only GUI interface was SunView, although it also supported tty and curses interfaces. Over the course of writing this book, I developed the Motif interface for Z-Mail that you see here, which was my reality-check that what I preach really does work.

It should be mentioned that Z-Mail also supports an OPEN LOOK interface. To do the OPEN LOOK version, I chose to use OLIT (OPEN LOOK Intrinsics Toolkit) because, like Motif, it is based on the X Toolkit Intrinsics. Xt is a great environment for developing applications for the X environment. I also believe that the best applications are those whose user interfaces can be abstracted, generalized, and modularized so that you can unplug one interface and plug in another. My approach to doing that is also reflected in this book, although not as a major topic.

Since the first writing of this book, I'm happy to say that Z-Mail has become a great success. It has been ported to Microsoft Windows and to the Apple Macintosh, both of which have graphical user environments that are substantially different from Motif in look, feel, and API implementations. However, the models described in this book, namely the abstraction and generalization of core components from one another, were maintained throughout the course of the porting processes.

Dan Heller

Acknowledgments

Second Edition. The current edition of this book was updated to cover Motif 1.2, including drag and drop and internationalization, by Paula Ferguson. Dave Brennan, of HaL Computer Systems, took on the unenviable task of learning everything he could about UIL and Mrm, in order to write the UIL programming material for this edition. He did a great job of covering a complex subject.

Adrian Nye deserves recognition for allowing me to work on this project, when I'm sure that he had other projects he would have liked to send my way. I don't think either one of us had any idea how involved this update project would become. He also provided editorial support that helped keep me on track in the final stages of the work on the book.

The other writers at O'Reilly & Associates in Cambridge, Valerie Quercia and Linda Mui, provided support that kept me sane while I was working on the book. Their willingness to listen and offer advice is greatly appreciated. Extra gratitude goes to Valerie Quercia for her help with the screen dumps for the book.

David Flanagan deserves credit for always being willing to answer my questions about the technical details of Motif and X. Douglas Rand, Scott Meeks, and David Brooks at OSF answered questions and helped review the new material. Daniel Jahn, of SAS Institute, Inc., also provided valuable review comments for this edition.

Special thanks go to the people who worked on the production of this book. The final form of this book is the work of the staff at O'Reilly & Associates. The authors would like to thank Chris Reilly for the figures, Donna Woonteiler, Chris Tong, and Ellie Cutler for indexing, Lenny Muellner for tools support, and Stephen Spainhour, Clairemarie Fisher O'Leary, Kismet McDonough, and Eileen Kramer for copyediting and production of the final copy. Thanks also to Donna Woonteiler for her patience in helping me understand the production process.

Finally, I'd like to thank my friends for putting up with me when I kept telling them that I'd be done working non-stop in a month or two. Special thanks to my housemate, Meredith Hunt, who put up with me when I was stressed out and not much fun to live with, and who took care of the cats when I wasn't around. My friends Karen Lewis and Liz Bradley opened their house to me when I needed to escape and be someplace where there are mountains. And thanks to the great people at the Boston Rock Gym, who provided me with a much-needed outlet for climbing the walls.

Despite the efforts of all of these people, the authors alone are responsible for any errors or omissions that remain.

Paula M. Ferguson

First Edition. The first edition of this book took over a year and a half to write and compile from the beginning. But when I look back on the entire effort, and I think about what it takes to do things like this (and other difficult things in life), I realize that what it *really* requires is a state of mind and a mental model that lends itself to seeing the big picture and choosing to do what's necessary to get the job done.

To this, I can only credit one person, Tim O'Reilly, my friend and editor of this book. It's his approach to life, his values, his way of thinking about things, and his talent for expressing them is what has influenced me more than anything else in adopting the kind of mental framework necessary to write a book like this (or to start my company, Z-Code Software, or to do anything I do in life). He never gives me advice when I ask for it, nor does he tell me what to do. Instead, he uses quotes, cites anecdotes, or just describes an abstract thought that always seems to be appropriate to every situation. In short, he's shown me a way of thinking about things that appreciates the big picture. I take this with me wherever I go, and in whatever I do. Without it, I couldn't have written this book.

Those who worked most closely with me on the project include Irene Jacobson, who dedicated long hours to meticulous editing and support. Her intuition and insistence on proper use of words saved many cuts of Tim O'Reilly's scalpel. David Lewis also gets super-high marks for his excellent feedback, for his technical expertise, and for helping take care of certain Z-Mail ports while I was busy hunched over this computer. More thanks go to the great folks at Z-Code Software, Bart Schaefer and Don Hatch, for not laughing at me when I told people for at least six months that the book would take "just two more weeks now." (I really meant it, too!) Actually, they helped quite a bit with reading nroff'd manuscripts, and by taking care of the business whenever I was at O'Reilly & Associates' offices in "Bahston."

The figures in this book come in two forms: screendumps and hand-generated figures done by Chris Reilly. What a super job he did—and always on time. And how can I thank Kismet McDonough, Lenny Muellner, Rosanne Wagger, Mike Sierra, Eileen Kramer, and the other production folks at O'Reilly & Associates, who did a wonderful job of copyediting, proofing, page layout, and all the other things that make the difference between a manuscript and a finished book. And that's not all: Ellie Cutler wrote the index. Tony Marotto of Cambridge Computer Associates figured out how to convert our screen dumps into PostScript files and how to scale screen dumps without the moire and plaid patterns you see in many books. He used Jeff Poskanzer's *pmbplus* to convert *xwd* dumps to *gif* format, and then wrote a set of image-processing programs that shift and enhance the tones. Daniel Gilly took on the enormous job of developing the reference appendices when it became clear that I wouldn't have time.

Enthusiastic applause goes to Libby Hanna (do I get a *real* official OSF/Motif decoder ring now!!??), David Brooks, Scott Meeks, Susan Thompson, Carl Scholz, Benjamin Ellsworth, and the entire cast at OSF in Cambridge for their support. And, of course, *everyone* on the motif-talk mailing list. (I wish I could remember all your names!)

People I can't forget: Bill "Rock" Petro, Akkana, Mike Harrigan at NCD for the terminal, Danny Backx at BIM (sorry I didn't get you any review copies!), John Harkin, and certain folks at Sun that I'd love to mention, but I can't because they're into that *OL-thang* and they wouldn't want to be associated with the *M-word*, Jordan Hayes, Paula Ferguson, and Kee

Hinckley (just because he's cool). Also thanks to Ralph Swick and Donna Converse at the X Consortium for being somewhat patient with me.

Added thanks to Lynn Vaughn at CNN for keeping me informed about what's going on in the world, since I have no time to look out the window; to Short Attention-Span Theatre, for keeping me amused; and to Yogurt World, for keeping me fed.

This book was written using a Sun workstation, the *vi* editor (for which I guess I ought to thank Bill Joy), SoftQuad's *sqtroff*, X11R4 and various versions of Motif (1.0 through 1.1.3).

For catching and reporting errors that have been fixed in the second printing, I'd like to thank Akkana, Wayne Robertz, Glen Shute, Scott Strool, Trevor Taylor, Peter Wagner, Andrew Wason, Tim Weinrich, and Bill Wohler.

Dan Heller

We'd Like to Hear From You

We have tested and verified all of the information in this book to the best of our ability, but you may find that features have changed (or even that we have made mistakes!). Please let us know about any errors you find, as well as your suggestions for future editions, by writing:

```
O'Reilly & Associates, Inc.
103 Morris Street, Suite A
Sebastopol, CA 95472
1-800-998-9938 (in the US or Canada)
1-707-829-0515 (international/local)
1-707-829-0104 (FAX)
```

You can also send us messages electronically. To be put on the mailing list or request a catalog, send email to:

> *info@ora.com*   (via the Internet)
> *uunet!ora!info*   (via UUCP)

To ask technical questions or comment on the book, send email to:

> *bookquestions@ora.com*   (via the Internet)

1

Introduction to Motif

This chapter answers the question "Why Motif?" in terms of the development of applications that are "easy enough for your mother to use." It suggests some of the complexities that the programmer has to master in order to make an application simple.

In This Chapter:

Introduction to Motif

Congratulations! After slaving behind the computer for months, fighting a deadline that seemed impossible to meet, you've finished your software product and it's a big hit. The critics love it, you're in the money, and everyone, including your mother, is buying your new product. Just as everything seems to be going your way, your worst nightmare comes true: your mother calls and asks you how to use it.

An unlikely scenario? Not if you're developing applications to run under the Motif graphical user interface (GUI). As a proposed standard for graphical user interfaces, Motif may be implemented on a wide range of computer platforms, from large IBM mainframes right down to the PC that your mom may be using. The Open Software Foundation (OSF), developer of the Motif GUI, hopes to reach all kinds of computers and computer users no matter how advanced (or limited) their computer skills may be.

So, will your mom really call you for help? Well, mine did. In fact, she did something worse. She wanted me to explain how to use a software product I didn't write. I didn't know how her software worked or even what it was. Fortunately, though, the software was based on Microsoft Windows, which has more than a passing similarity to Motif. The experience of providing technical support to my mother reminded me of some of the fundamental concepts behind the design of a user interface and the role of the application programmer in carrying out that design.

1.1 A True Story

Before I tell my story, let me start with a little background. I have been developing software for the X Window System for several years. Every now and then, when the family gets together for dinner, someone always asks the same thing, "So, explain it to me again: just what *is* it that you do?" I launch into my usual speech: "It's called *X Windows*, dad ... uh, no, mom, it's computer software ... it's rather hard to explain, but ..." The attention span lasts only until the next course is served, at which time the discussion turns to new ways for cooking eggplant. Little did I realize that something actually registered with someone in my family, because shortly thereafter, I got a call from my mom.

Mom: Guess what?!

Me: What?

Mom: Our company is switching to a new line of software based on *your* work!

Me: Really? You're going to use electronic mail?

Mom: No, all of our insurance packages use this new software that runs under *Windows*. You wrote that, didn't you?

Me: No, mom. I write software using *X Windows* — and I didn't write X, I just use it. I think you're talking about *Microsoft Windows*. You're using it with your PC, right?

Mom: That's right, but it looks exactly like your software, so I figured you could show me how to use it. I have never seen this stuff before.

(Uh, oh . . . I see it coming now. Last time she wanted me to help her explain her computer to her, I ended up translating the entire DOS 2.0 user's guide into English, which she conveniently forgot in about a week.)

Me: Mom, I don't know Microsoft Windows, I know *X Windows* and they're not the same . . .

Mom: You mean you won't help me?

Me: You don't understand — I *can't* help you. MS-Windows has nothing to do with X . . .

Silence.

Me: I don't think I'm getting through to you.

Silence.

Me: Ok, I'll be right over . . .

Despite all my explanations of the X Window System, the only keyword my mom remembered was *Windows*. I had high hopes, though, because I was actually going to teach her something related to what I do for a living. And this time she had to listen because her job depended on it.

After some fidgeting with diskettes and other necessary start-up procedures, I finally got Microsoft Windows 3.0 up and running. Sure enough, it looked just like Motif. Several applications came up by default: a clock, an editor of some sort, and a little calendar program. Immediately, the questions started flying at me:

Mom: How do you access those buttons at the top of the window?

Me: Those are called Pulldown Menus and every application has them. They are located in what is called a MenuBar.

Mom: What does "F1" mean?

Me: The "F" denotes a function key and the "1" indicates it's the first function key. Pressing it gives you help depending on where the cursor is. For example . . .

Mom (*interrupting*): Why are these keys labeled "ALT?" What do they do?

Me: Oh, those are used in conjunction with other keys. You press "ALT" and then some other key and you get special attention, like . . .

Mom (*growing frustrated*): Look what you did. Now there are too many windows up. How do I get back to the one I was using?

Me (*fighting for words*): Well, you see, you can move from one window to the next or between elements within a window by using the Tab key and possibly some other key like the Control key, the Shift key, or the Alt key, or maybe a combination of several of these keys depending on where you want to go . . .

Mom (*sitting back and sighing*): Oh, that's way too complicated, I'll never remember all that. And just *look* at those colors—they're awful.

Me (*trying to sound encouraging*): You can change them using this tool . . .

It was a long grueling day, but she eventually figured out how to do most of what she had to do. After she memorized those actions she used most frequently, she seemed quite capable and no longer needed my supervision. Her favorite trick was **Alt-F3**, which closed a window and terminated a program. Because she had several things figured out, I thought I'd dare teach her something new.

Me: You know, if you don't want to use that key sequence, you can define it yourself by . . .

Mom (*protecting the computer like it was her only child*): NO! Don't touch anything! I know how to use it now, so don't confuse me any more!

My fault. I figured that since she was pleased that she could change window colors, she'd be eager to make other aesthetic alterations. Her reaction to my offer to teach her how to change keyboard input foreshadowed what was about to come. I was in the other room when I heard a screech: "The computer is broken! The Alt-F3 thingy you showed me doesn't work any more!" Sure enough, it didn't work on the window she was trying to use it on, but as we discovered, that was the only window on the screen where it didn't work. It turned out that the program she tried it on didn't understand the Alt-F3 thingy. It was devastating for my mom and, needless to say, she will never run *that* program again.

We never did get to her new insurance software; we didn't have to. All she needed to learn was how to use the graphical user interface. She now reports having figured out her company's software "all by herself" and I can't take credit for teaching her.

1.2 Basic User-interface Concepts

There are many lessons an application designer can learn from this story. As it so happens, the designer and the application programmer are often the same person. But whether you are the designer of the software or an engineer responsible for implementing someone else's design, there are still some basic principles that will benefit you in your work. Let's begin with the basics drawn from this particular story:

- All applications running on a user's workstation should have a consistent interface design. Programs that deviate from the expected design will almost assuredly confuse the user even if the changes were intended for the user's benefit. Chances are also high that the user will not want to use the questionable software again.

- Users rely on rote memory; they will remember seemingly complicated interface interaction techniques provided that the functions they perform are useful and are invoked frequently. There is a limit, however, to how much users want to remember. It is important that essential or frequently used functions follow memorable patterns.

- Users, especially novices, will probably not want to customize or alter their applications in any way. If they do, the available methods must be as easy and painless as possible.

If you are a cast-in-stone UNIX software engineer, you may be quite skeptical about this last point. It is true that, traditionally, UNIX applications are extremely flexible, offering the user many options for modifying functional or aesthetic details. One of the first things the hardcore X programmer learns is that "the user is always right; if he wants to customize his interface, by God you had better let him."

This principle is absolutely correct. Unfortunately, many early X applications carry it too far and end up "spineless." Many such programs actually require the user to make certain customizations in order for the program to be usable or attractive. For some programs, the problem worsens if unreasonable customization settings are given, since there is no sanity-checking for unreasonable configurations.

So far, such customization issues have not gotten out of hand because UNIX and X applications are used almost exclusively by technical people who understand the environment and know how to work within it. But it is now time to consider users who know absolutely nothing about computers and who don't want to—they are only using your software because they have to.

1.3 What Is Motif?

So, back to Motif. What is it and how can it help you solve your user-interface design goals? To start, Motif is a set of guidelines that specifies how a user interface for graphical computers should *look and feel*. This term describes how an application appears on the screen (the look) and how the user interacts with it (the feel).

Figure 1-1 shows a Motif application.

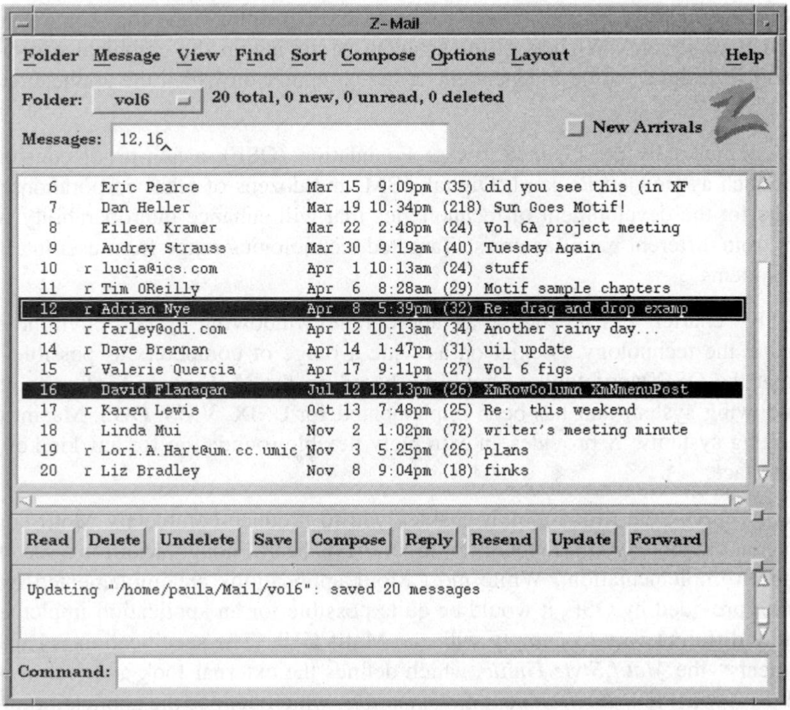

Figure 1-1. A Motif application

The user interacts with the application by typing at the keyboard, and by clicking, selecting, and dragging various graphic elements of the application with the mouse. For example, any application window can be moved on the screen by moving the pointer to the top of the window's frame (the title bar), pressing and holding down a button on the mouse, and dragging the window to a new location. The window can be made larger or smaller by pressing a mouse button on any of the resize corners and dragging.

Most applications sport buttons that can be clicked with the mouse to initiate application actions. Motif uses clever highlighting and shadowing to make buttons, and other components, look three-dimensional. When a button is clicked on, it actually appears to be pressed in and released.

A row of buttons across the top of most applications forms a *menu bar*. Clicking on any of the titles in the menu bar pops up a menu of additional buttons. Buttons can also be arranged in palettes that are always visible on the screen. When a button is clicked, the application can take immediate action or it can pop up an additional window called a *dialog box*. A dialog box can ask the user for more information or present additional options.

This style of application interaction isn't new to most people, since the Apple MacIntosh popularized it years ago. What is different about Motif is that the graphical user interface specification is designed to be independent of the computer on which the application is running.

Motif was designed by the Open Software Foundation (OSF), a non-profit consortium of companies such as Hewlett-Packard, Digital, IBM, and dozens of other corporations. OSF's charter calls for the development of technologies that will enhance interoperability between computers from different manufacturers. Targeted technologies range from user interfaces to operating systems.

Part of OSF's charter was to choose an appropriate windowing system environment that would enable the technology to exist on as wide a range of computers as possible. It was decided that the OSF/Motif toolkit should be based on the X Window System, a network-based windowing system that has been implemented for UNIX, VMS, DOS, Macintosh, and other operating systems. X provides an extremely flexible foundation for any kind of graphical user interface.

When used properly, the Motif toolkit enables you to produce completely Motif-compliant applications in a relatively short amount of time. At its heart, though, Motif is a specification rather than an implementation. While most Motif applications are implemented using the Motif toolkit provided by OSF, it would be quite possible for an application implemented in a completely different way to comply with the Motif GUI. The specification is captured in two documents: the *Motif Style Guide*, which defines the external look and feel of applications, and the *Application Environment Specification*, which defines the application programmer's interface (API).†

The Motif specifications don't have a whole lot to say about the overall layout of applications. Instead, they focus mainly on the design of the objects that make up a user interface—the menus, buttons, dialog boxes, text entry, and display areas. There are some general rules, but for the most part, the consistency of the user interface relies on the consistent behavior of the objects used to make it up, rather than their precise arrangement.

The Motif specification is broken down into two basic parts:

- The output model describes what the objects on the screen look like. This model includes the shapes of buttons, the use of three-dimensional effects, the use of cursors and bitmaps, and the positioning of windows and subwindows. Although some recommendations are

---

† Both books have been published for OSF by Prentice-Hall and are available in most technical bookstores.

given concerning the use of fonts and other visual features of the desktop's, Motif is flexible in most of these recommendations.

- The input model specifies how the user interacts with the elements on the screen.

The key point of the specification is that consistency should be maintained across all applications. Similar user-interface elements should look and act similarly regardless of the application that contains them.

Motif can be used for virtually any application that interacts with a computer user. Programs as conceptually different as a CAD/CAM package or an electronic mail application still use the same types of user-interface elements. When the user interface is standardized, the user gets more quickly to the point where he is working with the application, rather than just mastering its mechanics.

My experience with Microsoft Windows and my mother's new software demonstrates how far Motif has come in reaching this goal. I was faced with a window system that I had literally never seen before and an operating system I rarely use (DOS), but that didn't prevent me from using the application. This is not a coincidence; I knew how to use MS-Windows because its user-interface is based on the same principles as Motif. Motif can be seen as a superset of both MS-Windows and Presentation Manager. Even though the others came first, Motif views them as specific implementations of an abstract specification.

The Motif interface was intentionally modeled after IBM's Common User Access (CUA) specification, which defines the interface for OS/2 and Microsoft Windows. The reason for this is twofold: first, there is a proven business model for profiting from an "open systems" philosophy; second, the level of success and acceptance of Microsoft Windows in the PC world is expected to be quite substantial. As a result, more and more vendors are jumping on the bandwagon and are supporting Motif as their native graphical interface environment.

Just as my mom becomes more and more familiar with how to use Windows-based software, so too are thousands of other PC users. As the PC world migrates to UNIX and other larger-scale computers, so too will their applications. In order to keep their customer base, the developers of those PC applications will adopt Motif as the GUI for the UNIX versions of their software. As a result, the next few years will see the number of Motif users and developers grow astronomically as Motif becomes the focal point for software and hardware companies alike.

You have two options for making applications Motif-compliant. You can write the entire application yourself, and make sure that all your user-interface features conform to the Motif GUI specifications, or you can use a programming toolkit, which is a more realistic option. A toolkit is a collection of prewritten functions that implement all the features and specifications of a particular GUI.

However, a toolkit cannot write an application for you, nor can it enforce good programming techniques. It isn't going to tell you that there are too many objects on the screen or that your use of colors is outrageous. The job of Motif is solely to provide a consistent appearance and behavior for user-interface controls. So, before we jump into the mechanics of the Motif toolkit, let's take a moment longer with the philosophy of graphical user interfaces.

1.4 Designing User Interfaces

The principles behind an effective user interface cannot be captured in the specifications for Motif or any other GUI. Even though the Motif toolkit specifies how to create and use its interface elements, there is still quite a bit left unsaid. As the programmer, you must take the responsibility of using those elements effectively and helping the user to be as productive as possible. You must take care to keep things simple for the beginner and, at the same time, not restrict the more experienced user. This task is perhaps the most difficult one facing the programmer in application design.

There is frequently no right or wrong way to design an interface. Good user-interface design is usually a result of years of practice: you throw something at a user, he plays with it, complains, and throws it back at you. Experience will teach you many lessons, although we hope to guide you in the right direction, so that you can avoid many common mistakes and so that the ones that you do make are less painful.

So, rather than having absolute commandments, we rely on heuristics, or rules of thumb. Here is a rough list to start with:

- Keep the interface as simple as possible.

- Make direct connections to real-world objects or concepts.

- If real-world metaphors are not available, improvise.

- Don't forget to keep the interface simple.

- Don't restrict functionality to accommodate simplicity.

This list may sound flippant, but it is precisely what makes designing an interface so frustrating. Keeping an interface as simple as possible relies on various other factors, the most basic of which is intuition. The user is working with your application because he wants to solve a particular problem or accomplish a specific task. He is going to be looking for clues to spark that connection between the user interface and the preconceived task in his mind. Strive to make the use of an application obvious by helping the user form a mental mapping between the application and real-world concepts or objects. For example, a calculator program can use buttons and text areas to graphically represent the keypad and the one-line display on a calculator. Most simple calculators have the common digit and arithmetic operator keys; a graphical display can easily mimic this appearance. Other examples include a programmatic interface to a cassette player, telephone, or FAX machine. All of these could have graphical equivalents to their real-world counterparts.

The reason these seemingly obvious examples are successful interface approaches is because they take advantage of the fact that most people are already familiar with their real-life counterparts. But there is another, less obvious quality inherent in those objects: they are simple. The major problem concerning interface design is that not everything is simple. There isn't always a real-world counterpart to use as a crutch. In the most frustrating cases, the concept itself may be simple, but there may not be an obvious way to present the interaction. Of course, once someone thinks of the obvious solution, it seems odd that it could have been difficult in the first place.

Consider the VCR. Conceptually, a VCR is a simple device, yet statistics say that 70% of VCR owners don't know how to program one. How many times have you seen the familiar **12:00-AM** flashing in someone's living room? Researchers say that this situation occurs because most VCRs are poorly designed and are "too featureful." They're half-right; the problem is not that they are too featureful, but that the ways to control those features are too complicated. Reducing the capabilities of a VCR isn't going to make it easier to use; it's just going to make it less useful. The problem with VCRs is that their designers focused too much on functionality and not enough on usability.

So, how do you design an interface for a VCR when there is no other object like it? You improvise. Sure, the VCR is a simple device; everyone understands how one is supposed to work, but few people have actually designed one that is easy to use until recently. Maybe you've heard about the new device that, when connected to your VCR, enables you to have a complete TV program guide displayed on your screen in the bar-graph layout similar to the nightly newspaper listings. All you have to do is point and click on the program you want to record and that's it—you're done. No more buttons to press, levels of features to browse through, dials to adjust or manuals to read. At last, the right interface has been constructed. None of the machine's features have been removed. It's just that they are now organized in an intuitive way and are accessible in an simple manner.

This method for programming VCRs satisfies the last two heuristics. Functionality has not been reduced, yet simplicity has been heightened because a creative person thought of a new way to approach the interface. The lesson here is that no object should be difficult to use no matter how featureful it is or how complex it may seem. You must rely heavily on your intuition and creativity to produce truly innovative interfaces.

Let's return to computer software and how these principles apply to the user-interface design model. The first heuristic is simplicity, which typically involves fewer, rather than more, user-interface elements on the screen. Buttons, popup menus, colors, and fonts should all be used sparingly in an application. Often, the availability of hundreds of colors and font styles along with the attractiveness of a three-dimensional interface compels many application programmers to feel prompted, and even justified, in using all of the bells and whistles. Unfortunately, overuse of these resources quickly fatigues the user and overloads his ability to recognize useful and important information.

Ironically, the potential drawbacks to simplicity are those that are also found in complexity. By oversimplifying an interface, you may introduce ambiguity. If you reduce the number of elements on your screen or make your iconic representations too simple, you may be providing too little information to the user about what a particular interface element is supposed to do. Underuse of visual cues may make an application look bland and uninteresting.

One of Motif's strengths is the degree of configurability that you can pass on to the end user. Colors, fonts, and a wide variety of other resources can be set specifically by the user. You should be aware, however, that once your application ships, its default state is likely to be the interface most people use, no matter how customizable it may be. While it is true that more sophisticated users may customize their environment, you are ultimately in control of how flexible it is. Also, novice users quickly become experts in a well-designed system, so you must not restrict the user from growth.

Simplicity may not always be the goal of a user interface. In some cases, an application may be intentionally complex. Such applications are only supposed to be used by sophisticated users. For example, consider a 747 aircraft. Obviously, these planes are intended to be flown by experts who have years of experience. In this case, aesthetics is not the goal of the interior design of a cockpit; the goal is that of functionality.

In order to design an effective graphical user interface for an application, you must evaluate both the goals of your particular application and your intended audience. Only with a complete understanding of these issues will you be able to determine the best interface to use. And remember, your mom just might call you for help.

2

The Motif Programming Model

This chapter teaches the fundamentals of Motif by example. It dissects a simple "Hello, World" program, showing the program structure and style common to all Motif programs. Because much of this material is already covered in detail in Volume Four, X Toolkit Intrinsics Programming Manual, Motif Edition, this chapter can be used as a refresher or a light introduction for those who haven't read the earlier book. It makes reference to Volume One, Xlib Programming Manual, and Volume Four to point out areas that the programmer needs to understand (windows, widgets, events, callbacks, resources, translations) before progressing with Motif.

In This Chapter:

2

The Motif Programming Model

Though we expect most readers of this book to be familiar with the X Toolkit Intrinsics (Xt), this chapter briefly reviews the foundations of Motif in Xt. This review serves a variety of purposes. First, for completeness, we define our terms, so if you are unfamiliar with Xt, you will not be completely at sea if you forge ahead. Second, there are many important aspects of the X Toolkit Intrinsics that we aren't going to cover in this book; this review gives us a chance to direct you to other sources of information about these areas. Third, Motif diverges from Xt in some important ways, and we point out these differences up front. Finally, we point out some of the particular choices you can make when Xt or Motif provides more than one way to accomplish the same task.

If you are unfamiliar with any of the concepts introduced in this chapter, please read the first few chapters of Volume Four, *X Toolkit Intrinsics Programming Manual*. Portions of Volume One, *Xlib Programming Manual*, and Volume Three, *X Window System User's Guide, Motif Edition*, may also be appropriate.

2.1 Basic X Toolkit Terminology and Concepts

As discussed in Chapter 1, *Introduction to Motif*, the Motif user-interface specification is completely independent of how it is implemented. In other words, you do not have to use the X Window System to implement a Motif-style graphical user interface (GUI). However, to enhance portability and robustness, the Open Software Foundation (OSF) chose to implement the Motif GUI using X as the window system and the X Toolkit Intrinsics as the platform for the Application Programmer's Interface (API).

Xt provides an object-oriented framework for creating reusable, configurable user-interface components called *widgets*. Motif provides widgets for such common user-interface elements as labels, buttons, menus, dialog boxes, scrollbars, and text-entry or display areas. In addition, there are widgets called managers, whose only job is to control the layout of other widgets, so the application doesn't have to worry about details of widget placement when the application is moved or resized.

A widget operates independently of the application, except through prearranged interactions. For example, a button widget knows how to draw itself, how to highlight itself when it is clicked on with the mouse, and how to respond to that mouse click.

The general behavior of a widget, such as a PushButton, is defined as part of the Motif library. Xt defines certain base classes of widgets, whose behavior can be inherited and augmented or modified by other widget classes (subclasses). The base widget classes provide a common foundation for all Xt-based widget sets. A *widget set*, such as Motif's Xm library, defines a complete set of widget classes, sufficient for most user-interface needs. Xt also supports mechanisms for creating new widgets or for modifying existing ones.

Xt also supports lighter-weight objects called *gadgets*, which for the most part look and act just like widgets, but their behavior is actually provided by the manager widget that contains them. For example, a pulldown menu pane can be made up of button gadgets rather than button widgets, with the menu pane doing much of the work that would normally be done by the button widgets.

Most widgets and gadgets inherit characteristics from objects above them in the class hierarchy. For example, the Motif PushButton class inherits the ability to display a label from the Label widget class, which in turn inherits even more basic widget behavior from its own superclasses. See Volume Four, *X Toolkit Intrinsics Programming Manual*, for a complete discussion of Xt's classing mechanisms; see Chapter 3, *Overview of the Motif Toolkit*, for details about the Motif widget class hierarchy.

The object-oriented approach of Xt completely insulates the application programmer from the code inside of widgets. As a programmer, you only have access to functions that create, manage, and destroy widgets, plus certain public widget variables known as *resources*. As a result, the internal implementation of a widget can change without requiring changes to the API. A further benefit of the object-oriented approach is that it forces you to think about an application in a more abstract and generalized fashion, which leads to fewer bugs in the short run and to a better design in the long run.

Creating a widget is referred to as instantiating it. You ask the toolkit for an *instance* of a particular widget class, which can be customized by setting its resources. All Motif Push-Button widgets have the ability to display a label; an instance of the PushButton widget class actually has a label that can be set with a resource.

Creating widgets is a lot like buying a car: first you choose the model (class) of car you want, then you choose the options you want, and then you drive an actual car off the lot. There may exist many cars exactly like yours, others that are similar, and still others that are completely different. You can create widgets, destroy them, and even change their attributes just as you can buy, sell, or modify a car by painting it, adding a new stereo, and so on.

Widgets are designed so that many of their resources can be modified by the user at run-time. When an application is run, Xt automatically loads data from a number of system and user-specific files. The data from these files is used to build the *resource database*, which is used to configure the widgets in the application. If you want to keep the user from modifying resources, you can set their values when you create the widget. This practice is commonly referred to as *hard-coding* resources.

It is considered good practice to hard-code only those resource values that are essential to program operation and to leave the rest of the resources configurable. Default values for configurable resources are typically specified in an application defaults file, which is more colloquially referred to as the app-defaults file. By convention, this file is stored in the directory */usr/lib/X11/app-defaults* and it has the same name as the application with the first letter capitalized. The app-defaults file is loaded into the resource database along with other files that may contain different values set by the system administrator or the user. In the event of a conflict between different settings, a complex set of precedence rules determines the value actually assigned to a resource. See Volume Four, *X Toolkit Intrinsics Programming Manual*, for more information on how to set resources using the various resource files.

Motif widgets are prolific in their use of resources. For each widget class, there are many resources that neither the application nor the user should ever need to change. Some of these resources provide fine control over the three-dimensional appearance of Motif widgets; these resources should not be modified, since that would interfere with the visual consistency of Motif applications. Other resources are used internally by Motif to make one large, complex widget appear to the user in a variety of guises.

The *callback resources* for a widget are a particularly important class of resources that must be set in the application code. A widget that expects to interact with an application provides a callback resource for each type of interaction it supports. An application associates a function with the callback resources in which it is interested; the function is invoked when the user performs certain actions in the widget. For example, a PushButton provides a callback for when the user activates the button.

Note, however, that not every event that occurs in a widget results in a callback to an application function. Widgets are designed to handle many events themselves, with no interaction from the application. All widgets know how to draw themselves, for example. A widget may even provide application-like functionality. For example, a Text widget typically provides a complete set of editing commands via internal widget functions called *actions*. Actions are mapped to events in a *translation table*. This table can be augmented, selectively overridden, or completely replaced by settings contained in the implementation of a widget class, in application code, or in a user's resource files.

In the basic Xt design, translations are intended to be configurable by the user. However, the purpose of Xt is to provide mechanism, not impose user-interface policy. In Motif, translations are typically not modified by either the user or the application programmer. While it is possible for an application to install event handlers or new translations and actions for a widget, most Motif widgets expect application interaction to occur only through callbacks.

Since the Motif widgets are designed to allow application interaction through callbacks, we don't discuss translations very often in this book. Some of the Motif widgets, particularly buttons when they are used in menus, have undefined behavior when their translations are augmented or overiddden. An experienced Xt programmer may feel that Motif's limitations on the configurability of translations violates Xt. But consider that Xt is a library for building toolkits, not a toolkit itself. Motif has the further job of ensuring consistent user-interface behavior across applications.

Whether the goal of consistency is sufficient justification for OSF's implementation is a matter of judgement, but it should at least be taken into account. At any rate, you should be aware of the limitations when configuring Motif widgets. Motif widgets provide callback resources to support their expected behavior. If a widget does not have a callback associated with an event to which you want your application to respond, you should be cautious about adding actions to the widget or modifying its translations.

2.2 The Xm and Xt Libraries

A Motif user interface is created using both the Motif Xm library and the Intrinsics' Xt library. Xt provides functions for creating and setting resources on widgets. Xm provides the widgets themselves, plus an array of utility routines and convenience functions for creating groups of widgets that are used collectively as single user-interface components. For example, the Motif MenuBar is not implemented as one particular widget, but as a collection of smaller widgets put together by a convenience function.

An application may also need to make calls to the Xlib layer to render graphics or get events from the window system. In the application itself, rather than in the user interface, you may also be expected to make lower-level system calls into the operating system, filesystem, or hardware-specific drivers. Thus, the whole application may have calls to various libraries within the system. Figure 2-1 represents the model for interfacing to these libraries.

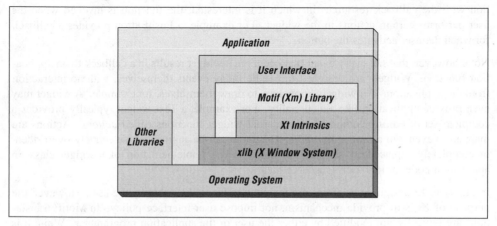

Figure 2-1. User-interface library model

As illustrated above, the application itself may interact with all layers of the windowing system, the operating system, and other libraries (math libraries, rpc, database) as needed. On the other hand, the user-interface portion of the application should restrict itself to the Motif, Xt, and Xlib libraries whenever possible. This restriction aids in the portability of the user-interface across multiple computers and operating systems. Since X is a distributed windowing system, once the application runs on a particular computer, it can be displayed on any computer running X—even across a local or wide-area network.

In addition to restricting yourself to using the Motif, Xt, and Xlib libraries, you should try to use the higher-level libraries whenever possible. Focus on using Motif-specific widgets and functions, rather than trying to implement equivalent functionality using Xt or Xlib.†
Higher-level libraries hide a great number of details that you would otherwise have to handle

---

† An exception to this guideline is the use of Xt creation routines rather than Motif convenience functions for creating simple widgets, as discussed later in the chapter.

yourself. By following these guidelines, you can reduce code complexity and size, creating applications that are easier to maintain.

In situations where the Motif library does not provide the functionality you need, you may attempt to borrow widgets from other toolkits or write your own. This technique is possible and made relatively simple because Motif is based on Xt.† For example, an application might make good use of a general-purpose graphing widget.

Whatever libraries you use, be sure to keep your application modular. The first and most important step in the development of an application is its design. You should always identify the parts of the application that are functional and the parts that make up the user interface. Well-designed applications keep the user-interface code separate from the functional code. You should be able to unplug the Motif code and replace it with another user-interface widget set based on Xt merely by writing corresponding code that mirrors the Motif implementation.

2.3 Programming With Xt and Motif

The quickest way to understand the basic Motif programming model is to examine a simple application. Example 2-1 is a version of the classic "hello world" program that uses the Motif toolkit.‡

Example 2-1. The hello.c program

```
/* hello.c -- initialize the toolkit using an application context and a
 * toplevel shell widget, then create a pushbutton that says Hello using
 * the varargs interface.
 */
#include <Xm/PushB.h>

main(argc, argv)
int argc;
char *argv[];
{
    Widget         toplevel, button;
    XtAppContext   app;
    void           button_pushed();
    XmString       label;

    XtSetLanguageProc (NULL, NULL, NULL);

    toplevel = XtVaAppInitialize (&app, "Hello", NULL, 0,
        &argc, argv, NULL, NULL);

    label = XmStringCreateLocalized ("Push here to say hello");
    button = XtVaCreateManagedWidget ("pushme",
        xmPushButtonWidgetClass, toplevel,
```

---

†While this book discusses certain methods for extending the Motif library, you should refer to Volume Four, *X Toolkit Intrinsics Programming Manual*, for a general discussion of how to build your own widgets.

‡XtSetLanguageProc() is only available in X11R5; there is no corresponding function in X11R4. XmStringCreateLocalized() is only available in Motif 1.2; XmStringCreateSimple() is the corresponding function in Motif 1.1.

Example 2-1. The hello.c program (continued)

```
        XmNlabelString, label,
        NULL);
    XmStringFree (label);
    XtAddCallback (button, XmNactivateCallback, button_pushed, NULL);

    XtRealizeWidget (toplevel);
    XtAppMainLoop (app);
}

void
button_pushed(widget, client_data, call_data)
Widget widget;
XtPointer client_data;
XtPointer call_data;
{
    printf ("Hello Yourself!\n");
}
```

The output of the program is shown in Figure 2-2.

Figure 2-2. Output of hello.c

You can get the source code for *hello.c* and the rest of the examples in this book via anonymous *ftp* or other methods that are described in the Preface. It is a good idea to compile and run each example as it is presented.

The example programs come with Imakefiles that should make building them easy if you have the *imake* program. This program should already be in */usr/bin/X11* on UNIX-based systems that have X11 Release 4 or Release 5 installed. You also need the configuration files for *imake*; they are in */usr/lib/X11/config* on most UNIX-based systems. An Imakefile is a system-independent makefile that is used by *imake* to generate a Makefile. This process is necessary because it is impossible to write a Makefile that works on all systems. You invoke *imake* using the *xmkmf* program. Complete instructions for compiling the examples using *imake* are provided in the *README* file included with the source code.

As explained in the Preface, there are versions of the example programs for both Motif 1.2 and Motif 1.1 available electronically. However, all of the example code in this book is designed to work with Motif 1.2 (and X11R5); the programs use functions that are not available in Motif 1.1 (and X11R4). Where we use Motif 1.2 functions, we try to mention how to perform the same tasks using Motif 1.1, usually in a footnote. To use the example programs with Motif 1.1, make the changes we describe. When the necessary changes are significant, we may explain both versions of the program. For a description of the changes that we made to convert the example programs to Motif 1.2, see Section 3.5.

To compile any of the examples on a UNIX system without using *imake*, use the following command line:

```
cc –O –o filename filename.c –lXm –lXt –lX11
```

If you want to do debugging, replace –O with –g in this command line. The order of the libraries is important. Xm relies on Xt, and both Xm and Xt rely on Xlib (the –lX11 link flag specifies Xlib).

Now let's take a look at this program step by step, noting elements of the underlying Xt model and where Motif differs from it.

2.3.1 Header Files

An application that uses the Motif toolkit must include a header file for each widget that it uses. For example, *hello.c* uses a PushButton widget, so we include *<Xm/PushB.h>*. The appropriate header file for each Motif widget class is included on the reference page for the widget in Volume Six B, *Motif Reference Manual*.

If you simply browse through */usr/include/Xm* (or wherever you have installed your Motif distribution) trying to find the appropriate header file, you will find that each widget class actually has two header files. The one with the name ending in a "P" (e.g. *PushBP.h*) is the widget's private header file and should never be included directly by an application. Private header files are used only by the code that implements a widget class and its subclasses.

Xt uses public and private header files to hide the details of widget implementation from applications. This technique provides object-oriented encapsulation and data hiding in the C language, which is not designed to support object-oriented programming. (See Volume Four, *X Toolkit Intrinsics Programming Manual*, for additional information on the object-oriented design of widgets.)

For some types of objects, you may see another pair of header files, each containing a capital "G" at the end of their names (for example, *PushBG.h* and *PushBGP.h*). These files are for the gadget version of the object. For the most part, when we talk about widgets, we include gadgets. Later chapters make it clear when to use gadgets and when to use widgets.

A quick examination of the #include directives in each of the Motif widget or gadget header files reveals that each of them includes *<Xm/Xm.h>*, the general header file for the Motif library. *<Xm/Xm.h>* in turn includes the following files:

```
#include <X11/Intrinsic.h>
#include <X11/Shell.h>
#include <X11/Xatom.h>
#include <Xm/XmStrDefs.h>
#include <Xm/VirtKeys.h>
```

Therefore, none of these files ever need to be included by your application, as long as you include *<Xm/Xm.h>*. Since *<Xm/Xm.h>* is included by each widget header file, you do not need to include it directly either. If you look closely at the code, you'll see that just about every necessary header file is included the moment you include your widget header file. This method of using header files contrasts with the way other Xt-based toolkits, like the Athena toolkit or the OPEN LOOK Intrinsics Toolkit (OLIT), use header files.

Release 1.2 of the Motif toolkit provides a new header file, *<Xm/XmAll.h>*, that simply includes all of the public header files. The *<Xm/ExtObject.h>*, *<Xm/Traversal.h>*, *<Xm/VaSimple.h>*, and *<Xm/VendorE.h>* header files are present in Motif 1.1, but they are obsolete in Motif 1.2.

We recommend that you not duplicate the inclusion of header files. One reason is that if you include only the header files that you need, whoever has to maintain your code can see which widgets you are dealing with in your source files. Another reason is that duplicating header files is generally bad practice, as you run the risk of redeclaring macros, functions, and variables.

However, it isn't always easy to prevent multiple inclusions. For example, *<Xm/Xm.h>* is included by each widget header file that you include. All of the Motif, Xt and X header files are protected from multiple inclusion using a technique called *ifdef-wrapping*. We recommend that you use this method in your own header files as well. The ifdef-wrapper for *<X11/Intrinsic.h>* is written as follows:

```
#ifndef _XtIntrinsic_h
#define _XtIntrinsic_h

/* Include whatever is necessary for the file... */
#endif /* _XtIntrinsic_h */
```

The wrapper defines `_XtIntrinsic_h` when a file is first included. If the file is ever included again during the course of compiling the same source (*.c*) file, the `#ifdef` prevents anything from being redeclared or redefined.

Of course, the wrapper prevents multiple inclusion only within a single source file; the next source file that gets compiled goes through the same test. If the same files are included, the same macros, data types, and functions are declared again for the benefit of the new file. For this reason, you should never write functions in a header file, since it would be equivalent to having the same function exist in every source file. Function declarations, however, are acceptable and expected.

In addition to the widget header files, you will most likely need other include files specific to your application, such as *<stdio.h>* or *<ctype.h>*.

The order of inclusion is generally not important unless certain types or declarations required by one file are declared in another. In this case, you should include the files in the necessary order. Otherwise, application-specific header files are usually included first, followed by UI-specific header files (with Xt header files, if any, preceding Motif header files), followed by system-specific header files.

2.3.2 Setting the Language Procedure

For Release 5 of the X Window System, the X Toolkit was modified to better support internationalization. An internationalized application retrieves the user's language (called a *locale*) from the environment or a resource file and operates in that language without changes to the binary. An internationalized application must display all of its text in the user's language and accept textual input in that same language. It must also display dates, times, and numbers in the appropriate format for the language environment.

X internationalization is based on the ANSI-C internationalization model. This approach is based on the concept of *localization*, whereby an application uses a library that reads a customizing database at startup time. This database contains information about the characteristics of every locale that is supported by the system. When an application establishes its locale by calling `setlocale()`, the library customizes the behavior of various routines based on the locale. See the Third Edition of Volume One, *Xlib Programming Manual*, for a complete description of the concepts and implementation of X internationalization.

Xt support of internationalization is trivial in most applications; the only additional code needed is a call to `XtSetLanguageProc()` before the toolkit is initialized. `XtSetLanguageProc()` sets the *language procedure* that is used to set the locale of an application. The first argument to the routine specifies an application context, the second argument specifies the language procedure, and the third parameter specifies additional data that is passed to the language procedure when it is called. Since the language procedure is responsible for setting the locale, an Xt application does not call `setlocale()` directly. The language procedure is called by `XtDisplayInitialize()`.

If the second argument to `XtSetLanguageProc()` is NULL, the routine registers a default language procedure. Here's the call that we used in Example 2-1 to set the default language procedure:

```
XtSetLanguageProc (NULL, NULL, NULL);
```

The default language procedure sets the locale according to the LANG environment variable, verifies that the current locale is supported, and returns the value of the current locale. For more information about establishing the locale in an Xt application, see Volume Four, *X Toolkit Intrinsics Programming Manual*.

Most of the support for internationalization in Motif 1.2 is provided by Xlib and Xt. Xlib provides support for internationalized text output, interclient communication, and localization of the resource database, while Xt handles establishing the locale. The Motif Text and TextField widgets have been modified to support internationalized text input and output; see Section 14.6 for more information. The Motif routines that work with compound strings and font lists have also been updated in Motif 1.2. See Chapter 19, *Compound Strings*, for details on the new API for `XmString` and `XmFontList` values.

2.3.3 Initializing the Toolkit

Before an application creates any widgets, it must initialize the toolkit. There are many ways to perform this task, most of which also perform a number of related tasks, such as opening a connection to the X server and loading the resource database. Here's a list of some of the things that are almost always done:

- Open the application's connection to the X server.

- Parse the command line for the standard X Toolkit command-line options plus any custom command-line options that have been defined for the application.

- Create the resource database using the app-defaults file, if any, as well as any user, host, and locale-specific resource files.

- Create the application's top-level window, a Shell class widget that handles interaction with the window manager and acts as the parent of all of the other widgets in the application.

There are several functions available to perform toolkit initialization. The one we use most often is XtVaAppInitialize(), since it performs all of the functions listed above in one convenient call. Here's the call we used in Example 2-1:

```
Widget        toplevel;
XtAppContext  app;

toplevel = XtVaAppInitialize (&app, "Hello", NULL, 0,
    &argc, argv, NULL, NULL);
```

The widget returned by XtVaAppInitialize() is a shell widget. The shell widget acts as the top-level window of the application and handles the application's interaction with the window manager. All of the other widgets created by the application are created as descendents of the shell, which we'll talk about more later in this chapter.

The Application Context

The first argument to XtVaAppInitialize() is the address of an application context, which is a structure that Xt uses to manage some internal data associated with an application. Most applications do not manipulate the application context directly. Most often, an application receives an opaque pointer to an application context in the toolkit initialization call and merely passes that pointer to a few other toolkit functions that require it as an argument. The fact that the application context is a public variable, rather than hidden in the toolkit internals, is a forward-looking feature of Xt, designed to support multiple threads of control.

The simpler X11R3 initialization call, XtInitialize(), is still supported by later versions of the toolkit. Its use is discouraged because the new initialization calls provide a greater degree of upward compatibility with future Xt-based applications. The simpler function creates an application context that is stored internally by Xt.

The Application Class

The second argument to XtVaAppInitialize() is a string that defines the *class name* of the application. A class name is used in resource files to specify resource values that apply to all instances of an application, a widget, or a resource. (See Volume Three, *X Window System User's Guide, Motif Edition*, and Volume Four, *X Toolkit Intrinsics Programming Manual*, for details.) For many applications, the application class is rarely used and the class name is important only because it is also used as the name of the application's app-defaults file.

Whenever a widget is created in Xt, its resources must have certain initial (or default) values. You can either hard-code the values, allow them to default to widget-defined values, or specify the default values in the app-defaults file. These default values are used unless the user has provided his own default settings in another resource file.

By convention, the class name is the same as the name of the application itself, except that the first letter is capitalized.† For example, a program named *draw* would have a class name of *Draw* and an app-defaults filename of */usr/lib/X11/app-defaults/Draw*. Note, however, that there is no requirement that an app-defaults file with this name actually be installed.

Exceptions can be made to this convention, as long as you document it. For example, all the example programs in this book have the class name of *Demos*, which allows us to set certain common defaults in a single file. This technique can be useful whenever you have a large collection of independent programs that are part of the same suite of applications.

Command-line Arguments

The third and fourth arguments specify an array of objects that describe the command-line arguments for your program, if any, and the number of arguments in the array. These arguments are unused in most of the examples in this book and are specified as NULL and 0, respectively. The program *xshowbitmap.c* in the Appendix, *Additional Example Programs*, provides an example of using command-line arguments. See Volume Four, *X Toolkit Intrinsics Programming Manual*, for a more complete discussion of application-specific command-line arguments.

The fifth and sixth arguments contain the value (argv) and count (argc) of any actual command-line arguments. The initialization call actually removes and acts on any arguments it recognizes, such as the standard X Toolkit command-line options and any options that you have defined in the third argument. After this call, argv should contain only the application name and any expected arguments such as filenames. You may want to check the argument count at this point and issue an error message if any spurious arguments are found.

Fallback Resources

The seventh argument is the start of a NULL-terminated list of *fallback resources* for the top-level shell widget created by the initialization call. Fallback resources provide a kind of "belt and suspenders" protection against the possibility that an app-defaults file is not installed. They are ignored if the app-defaults file or any other explicit resource settings are found. When no fallback resources are specified, the seventh argument should be NULL.

It is generally a good idea to provide fallbacks for resources that are essential to the operation of your application. An example of how fallback resources can be used by an application is shown in the following code fragment:

```
String fallbacks[] = {
    "Demos*background: grey",
    "Demos*XmList.fontList: -*-courier-medium-r-*--12-*",
    "Demos*XmText.fontList: -*-courier-medium-r-*--12-*",
    /* list the rest of the app-defaults resources here ... */
    NULL
};
...
```

---

† Some applications follow the convention that if the application's name begins with an "X", the X is silent and so the second letter is capitalized as well. For example, the class name of *xterm* is *XTerm*.

```
toplevel = XtVaAppInitialize (&app, "Demos", NULL, 0,
         &argc, argv, fallbacks, NULL);
    . . .
```

Fallback resources protect your application against a missing app-defaults file, but they do not guard against one that is modified incorrectly or otherwise corrupted, since they are not used if the app-defaults file is present in any form. A better fallback mechanism would provide protection against these types of problems. Fortunately, X11 Release 5 introduces a new function, XrmCombineDatabases(), that allows you to provide real fallbacks in case the user or the system administrator misconfigures the app-defaults file.

Additional Initialization Parameters

The eighth parameter is the start of a NULL-terminated list of resource/value pairs that are applied to the top-level widget returned by XtVaAppInitialize(). If there are no resource settings, which is often the case for this function, you can pass NULL as the eighth parameter. If you do pass any parameters, it should be done just as we describe for Xt-VaCreateWidget() later in this chapter. All of the functions whose names begin with XtVa support the same type of varargs-style (variadic) argument lists.

The X11 Release 4 implementation of XtVaAppInitialize() and other varargs functions may not work entirely as expected for some non-ANSI-C compilers due to a bug in the way that Xt declares variadic functions. This problem only arises for some compilers that do not understand function prototypes. The problem is rare since it is compiler-dependent and it only happens on older compilers. It is not a compiler error but an Xt error, since functions are not supposed to mix fixed parameter declarations with variadic declarations. XtVaApp-Initialize() mixes these declarations; the first seven parameters are fixed while the eighth through nth arguments are variadic. ANSI-C allows, and even requires, this type of specification.

If you experience problems such as segmentation faults or bus errors as a result of using Xt-VaAppInitialize(), you can try passing an extra NULL parameter after the final NULL. Another option is to use XtAppInitialize(), which is identical to XtVaApp-Initialize(), but does not contain a variable argument list of resource/values pairs. Instead, it uses the old-style args and num_args method of specifying resource values, which we describe later in this chapter.

2.3.4 Creating Widgets

There is a convenience function for creating every class of widget and gadget supported by the Motif toolkit. For example, to create a PushButton widget, you can use the function Xm-CreatePushButton(). To create the corresponding gadget, you can use XmCreate-PushButtonGadget(). In addition, there are convenience functions for creating *compound objects*. A compound object is a collection of widgets that is treated like a single object. For example, a ScrolledList object is really a List widget inside a ScrolledWindow widget. XmCreateScrolledList() creates the compound object consisting of both widgets.

The convenience functions for creating all of the different types of widgets are described in Volume Six B, *Motif Reference Manual*. In the examples in this book, however, we typically use the Xt functions `XtVaCreateWidget()` and `XtVaCreateManaged-Widget()` for creating simple widgets. These functions allow you to decide whether to create a widget as managed or unmanaged, while the Motif convenience functions always create unmanaged widgets. The Xt routines also allow you to set resources for a widget using the varargs interface, which is more convenient than the `args` and `num_args` method used by the Motif creation routines.

X nests windows using a parent-child model. A display screen is defined as the root window; every application has a top-level window that is a child of the root window. A top-level window in turn has subwindows, which overlay it but cannot extend beyond its boundaries. If a window extends beyond the boundaries of its parent, it is clipped.

Because every widget has its own X window, widgets follow a similar parent-child model. Whenever a widget is created, it is created as the child of another widget. The shell widget returned by the call to `XtVaAppInitialize()` is the top-level widget of an application. It is usually overlaid with a special class of widget called a *manager widget*, which implements rules for controlling the size and placement of widget children. For example, the Motif RowColumn widget is a manager that allows widgets to be laid out in regular rows and columns, while the Form widget is a manager that allows widgets to be placed at precise positions relative to one another. A manager widget can contain other manager widgets as well as *primitive widgets*, which are used to implement actual user-interface controls. Managers also support gadgets. A gadget is a lighter-weight object that is identical to its corresponding widget in appearance, but does not have its own window.

In Example 2-1, the button was created as a child of the top-level shell window. This simple application contains only one visible widget, so it does not use a manager. Actually, shells are extremely simple managers. A shell can only have one child; the shell makes itself exactly the same size as the child so the shell remains invisible behind the child. Here's the call we used to create the button:

```
button = XtVaCreateManagedWidget ("pushme",
    xmPushButtonWidgetClass, toplevel,
    XmNlabelString, label,
    NULL);
```

The first argument is a string that is used as the name of the widget in the resource database. If a user wants to specify the color of the button label for the application, he can use the following specification in a resource file:

```
hello.pushme.foreground:  blue
```

The name is different from the variable name that is used to refer to the widget in application code. The following resource specification is not correct:

```
hello.button.foreground:  blue
```

The resource name does not need to be identical to the variable name given to the widget inside the program, though to minimize confusion, many programmers make the two names the same. If you want users to be able to configure widget resources, be sure to include the names of the widgets in your documentation.

The second argument is the class of the widget to be created. This name is defined in the public header file for the widget. The widget reference pages in Volume Six B list the widget class name for each Motif and Xt widget class.

The third argument is the parent of the widget, which must be a manager widget that has already been created. In this example, the parent of the PushButton widget is `toplevel`, the shell widget returned by the call to `XtVaAppInitialize()`. The remainder of the argument list is a variable-length list of resource settings. We'll talk about the format of these resource settings in the next section.

2.3.5 Setting and Getting Widget Resources

A widget class defines resources of its own and it inherits resources from its superclasses. The names of the resources provided by each widget class (new and inherited) are documented in the widget reference pages in Volume Six B, *Motif Reference Manual*. The most useful resources are described in detail in the individual chapters on each of the Motif widget classes.

When resources are set in a program, each resource name begins with the prefix XmN. These names are mnemonic constants that correspond to actual C strings that have the same name without the XmN prefix. For example, the actual resource name associated with `XmNlabel-String` is `labelString`. The XmN identifies the resource as being Motif-related. Motif also uses the XmC prefix to identify resource class symbols. Xt uses the prefix XtN for any resources defined by its base widget classes. Motif also provides corresponding XmN names for most of these resources.† When you are specifying resources in a resource file or when you are using the `-xrm` option to specify resources on the command line, omit the XmN prefix.

The main purpose of the constant definitions for resource names is to allow the C preprocessor to catch spelling errors. If you use the string `width` rather than the constant `XmNwidth`, the program still works. However, if you type `widdth`, the compiler happily compiles the application, but your program won't work and you'll have a difficult time trying to figure out why. Because resource names are strings, there is no way for Xt or Motif to report an error when an unknown resource name is encountered. On the other hand, if you use `XmN-widdth`, then the compiler complains that the token is an undefined variable.

---

† Some toolkits use the XtN prefix, even though its resource are not common to all Xt toolkits. The resource naming convention has not been used long enough for all vendors to conform to it. If you need access to an Xt-based resource that does not have a corresponding XmN constant, you need to include the file *<X11/StringDefs.h>*.

Setting Resources During Widget Creation

The Motif convenience functions, as well as the Xt functions `XtCreateWidget()` and `XtCreateManagedWidget()`, require you to declare resource settings in a static array. You pass this array to the function, along with the number of items in the array. By contrast, the varargs-style functions introduced in X11R4 allow you to specify resources directly in a creation call, as a NULL-terminated list of resource/value pairs.

In the call to `XtVaCreateManagedWidget()` in *hello.c*, the only resource set was the string displayed as the PushButton's label. Other resources could have been set in the same call, as shown in the following code:

```
button = XtVaCreateManagedWidget ("pushme",
    xmPushButtonWidgetClass, toplevel,
    XmNlabelString, label,
    XmNwidth, 200,
    XmNheight, 50,
    NULL);
```

These settings specify that the widget is 200 pixels wide by 50 pixels high, rather than its default size, which would be just big enough to display its label.

When you set resources in the creation call for the widget, those resources can no longer be configured by the user. Such resources are said to be hard-coded. For example, since we've set the width and height of the PushButton in the call to `XtVaCreateManaged-Widget()`, a user resource specification of the following form is ignored:

```
*pushme.width:   250
*pushme.height:  100
```

It is recommended that you hard-code only those resource values that are absolutely required by your program. Most widgets have reasonable default values for their resources. If you need to modify the default values, specify the necessary resource values in an app-defaults file, instead of in the application code.

Every resource has a data type that is specified by the widget class defining the resource. When a resource is specified in a resource file, Xt automatically converts the resource value from a string to the appropriate type. However, when you set a resource in your program, you must specify the value as the appropriate type. For example, the Motif PushButton widget expects its label to be a compound string (see Chapter 19, *Compound Strings*), so we create a compound string, use it to specify the resource value, and free it when we were done.

Rather than specifying a value of the appropriate type, you can invoke Xt's resource converters in a varargs list using the keyword `XtVaTypedArg`, followed by four additional parameters: the resource name, the type of value you are providing, the value itself, and the size of the value in bytes. Xt figures out the type of value that is needed and performs the necessary conversion. For example, to specify the background color of the button directly in our program without calling an Xlib routine to allocate a colormap entry, we can use the following code:

```
button = XtVaCreateManagedWidget ("pushme",
    xmPushButtonWidgetClass, toplevel,
    XmNlabelString, label,
```

```
XtVaTypedArg, XmNbackground, XmRString, "red", strlen ("red") + 1,
NULL);
```

The data type in this construct is specified using a special symbol called a *representation type*, rather than the C type. An XmR prefix identifies the symbol as a representation type. See Volume Four, *X Toolkit Intrinsics Programming Manual*, for more information on resource type conversion and the possible values for representation types. These symbols are defined in the same way as the XmN symbols that are used for resource names.

Setting Resources After Widget Creation

After a widget has been created, you can set resources for it using XtVaSetValues(). The values set by this function override any values that are set either in the widget creation call or in a resource file. The syntax for using XtVaSetValues() is:

```
XtVaSetValues (widget_id,
    resource-value-list,
    NULL);
```

The widget_id is the value returned from a widget creation call, and *resource-value-list* is a NULL-terminated list of resource/value pairs.

Some Motif widget classes also provide convenience routines for setting certain resources. For example, XmToggleButtonSetState() sets the XmNset resource of a Toggle-Button to either True or False. The available convenience functions are described in Volume Six B, *Motif Reference Manual*, and in the chapters on each widget class in this book. A convenience function has direct access to the internal fields in a widget's data structures, so it might have slightly better performance than XtVaSetValues(). Functionally, however, the two methods are interchangeable.

Getting Resource Values

The routine used to get widget resource values is XtVaGetValues(). The syntax of this routine is exactly the same as XtVaSetValues(), except that the value part of the resource/value pair is the address of a variable that stores the resource value. For example, the following code gets the label string and the width for a Label widget:

```
extern Widget    label;
XmString         str;
Dimension        width;
    . . .
XtVaGetValues (label,
    XmNlabelString, &str,
    XmNwidth,          &width,
    NULL);
```

Notice that the value for XmNlabelString is an XmString, which is a Motif compound string. Almost all of the Motif widget resources that specify textual information use compound strings rather than regular character strings. The XmNvalue and XmNvalueWcs resources for Text and TextField widgets are the only exceptions to this policy. When you are retrieving a string resource from a widget, make sure that you pass the address of a compound string, not a character string, as in the following incorrect example:

```
extern Widget    label;
char             *buf;
Dimension        width;
    ...
XtVaGetValues (label,
    XmNlabelString, &buf, /* do not do this */
    XmNwidth,        &width,
    NULL);
```

If you try to get a compound string resource value with a character string variable, the program still works, but the value of the character string is meaningless. The correct way to handle a compound string resource is to retrieve it with an XmString variable and then get the character string from the compound string using XmStringGetLtoR(). See Chapter 19, *Compound Strings*, for more information.

There are some things to be careful about when you are getting resource values from a widget. First, always pass the address of the variable that is being used to store the retrieved value. A value represented by a pointer is not copied into the address space. Instead, the routine sets the value for the address of the pointer to the position of the internal variable that contains the desired value. If you pass an array, rather than a pointer to the array, the routine cannot move its address. If you pass the address of a pointer, XtVaGetValues() is able to reset the pointer to the correct internal value.† For values that are not represented by pointers, such as integers, the value is simply copied. For example, the width value is an int, so the resource value is copied into the variable.

You should also be careful about changing the value of a variable returned by XtVaGet-Values(). In the case of a variable that is not a pointer, the value can be changed because the variable contains a copy of the value and does not point to internal data for the widget. However, if the variable is a pointer to a string or a data structure, it does point to internal data for the widget. If you dereference the pointer and change the resulting value, you are changing the internal contents of the widget. This technique should not be used to change the value of a resource. To modify a resource value, you should use XtVaSetValues() with a defined resource name, as this routine ensures that the widget redraws and manages itself appropriately.

Motif also provides convenience routines for getting certain resource values from particular widget classes. Most of these functions correspond to the convenience routines for setting resource values. Many of the functions allocate memory for the value that is returned. For example, XmTextGetString() allocates space for and returns a pointer to the text in a Text widget. When a convenience function for retrieving a resource value is available, we generally recommend using it.

━━━━━━━━━━━━━━

†The Motif toolkit sometimes sets the given address to allocated data, which must be freed when it is no longer needed. This situation occurs when a compound string resource is retrieved from a widget and when the text value of a Text widget is retrieved. These cases are discussed in Chapter 14, *Text Widgets*, and Chapter 19, *Compound Strings*.

Using Argument Lists

While we use the variadic functions almost exclusively in this book, you should know how to use the old-style argument lists needed by the Motif widget creation functions. The Motif convenience functions, and some Xt functions like `XtCreateWidget()` and `XtCreate-ManagedWidget()`, require you to set resources using a separately-declared array of objects of type `Arg`. You pass this array to the appropriate function along with the number of items in the array.

For example, the following code fragment creates a PushButton widget like the one in *hello.c*, but it uses a Motif convenience routine:

```
Arg args[5];
int n = 0;

XtSetArg (args[n], XmNlabelString, label); n++;
button = XmCreatePushButton (toplevel, "pushme", args, n);
XtManageChild (button);
```

For all of the Motif convenience routines, the first argument is the parent of the widget being created, the second argument is the widget's name, and the third and fourth arguments are the array of resource specifications and the number of resources in the array. Since the class of the widget being created is reflected in the name of the convenience function, it does not need to be specified as an argument to the routine. For example, `XmCreateLabel()` creates a Label widget, while `XmCreatePushButton()` creates a PushButton widget.

Xt also provides some generic widget creation functions that use the old-style argument lists for specifying widget resources. The following code fragment shows the use of `XtCreate-Widget()`:

```
Arg args[5];
int n = 0;

XtSetArg (args[n], XmNlabelString, label); n++;
button = XtCreateWidget ("pushme",
    xmPushButtonWidgetClass, toplevel, args, n);
XtManageChild (button);
```

With this routine, the name of the widget is the first parameter, the widget class is the second parameter, and the parent is the third parameter. The fourth and fifth parameters specify the resources, as in the Motif convenience routines.

The argument-list style of setting resources is quite clumsy and error-prone, since it requires you to declare an array (either locally or statically) and to make sure that it has enough elements. It is a common programming mistake to forget to increase the size of the array when new resource/value pairs are added; this error usually results in a segmentation fault.

In spite of the disadvantages of this method of setting resources, there are still cases where the convenience routines may be useful. One such case is when the routine creates several widgets and arranges them in a predefined way consistent with the *Motif Style Guide*. The argument-list style functions also can be useful when you have different resources that should be set depending on run-time constraints. For example, the following code fragment creates a widget whose foreground color is set only if the application knows it is using a color display:

```
extern Widget parent;
Arg args[5];
Pixel red;
int n = 0;

XtSetArg (args[n], XmNlabelString, label); n++;
if (using_color) {
    XtSetArg (args[n], XmNforeground, red); n++;
}
. . .
widget = XtCreateManagedWidget ("name", xmLabelWidgetClass, parent,
    args, n);
```

The old-style routines also allow you to pass the exact same set of resources to more than one widget. Since the contents are unchanged, you can reuse the array for as long as it is still available. Be careful of scoping problems, such as using a local variable outside of the function where it is declared. The following code fragment creates a number of widgets that all have the same hard-coded resources:

```
static char *labels[] = { "A Label", "Another Label", "Yet a third" };
XmString label;
Widget widget, rc;
Arg args[3];
int i, n = 0;

/* Create an unmanaged RowColumn widget parent */
rc = XtCreateWidget ("rc", xmRowColumnWidgetClass, parent, NULL, 0);

/* Create RowColumn's children -- all 50x50 with different labels */
XtSetArg (args[n], XmNwidth, 50); n++;
XtSetArg (args[n], XmNheight, 50); n++;
for (i = 0; i < XtNumber (labels); i++) {
    xm_label = XmStringCreateLocalized (labels[i]);
    XtSetArg (args[n], XmNlabelString, xm_label);
    widget = XtCreateManagedWidget ("label", xmLabelWidgetClass, rc,
        args, n + 1);
    XmStringFree (xm_label);
}

/* Now that all the children are created, manage RowColumn */
XtManageChild (rc);
```

Each Label widget is created with the same width and height resource settings, while each `XmNlabelString` resource is distinct. All other resource settings for the widgets can be set in a resource file.

To set resources in a resource file, you need to specify the names of the widgets, which in this case are all set to *label*. It is perfectly legal to give the same name to more than one widget. As a result, a resource specification in a resource file that uses a particular name affects all of the widgets with that name, provided that the widget tree matches the resource specification. For example, you could set the foreground color of all of the Labels using the following resource specification:

```
*rc.label.foreground: red
```

Other widgets in the application that have the widget name *label*, but are not children of the widget named *rc*, are not affected by this specification. Obviously, whether you really want to use the same name for a number of widgets is dependent on your application. This technique makes it easier to maintain a consistent interface, but it also limits the extent to which the application can be customized.

We could have used the elements of the `labels` array as widget names, but in this example, these strings contain spaces, which are "illegal" widget names. If you want to allow the user to specify resources on a per-widget basis, you cannot use spaces or other non-alphanumeric characters, except the hyphen (`-`) and the underscore (`_`), in widget names. If per-widget resource specification is not a concern, you can use any widget name you like, including `NULL` or the null string (`" "`).

Even if a widget has an illegal name, the user can still specify resources for it using the widget class, as in the following example:

```
*rc.XmLabel.foreground: red
```

This resource setting causes each Label widget to have a foreground color of red, regardless of the name of the widget (and provided that the resource value is not hard-coded for the widget). See Volume Four, *X Toolkit Intrinsics Programming Manual*, for a discussion of appropriate widget names and further details on resource specification syntax.

2.3.6 Event Handling for Widgets

Once we have created and configured the widgets for an application, they must be hooked up to application functions via callback resources. Before we can talk about callback resources and callback functions, we need to discuss events and event handling. In one sense, the essence of X programming is the handling of asynchronous events. Events can occur in any order, in any window, as the user moves the pointer, switches between the mouse and the keyboard, moves and resizes windows, and invokes functions available through user interface components. X handles events by dispatching them to the appropriate application and to the separate windows that make up each application.

Xlib provides many low-level functions for handling events. In special cases, which are described later in this book, you may need to dip down to this level to handle events. However, Xt simplifies event handling by having widgets handle many events for you, without any application interaction. For example, widgets know how to redraw themselves, so they respond automatically to `WExpose` events, which are generated when one window is covered up by another and then uncovered. These "widget survival skills" are handled by functions called *methods* deep in the widget internals. Some typical methods redraw the widget, respond to changes in resource settings that result from calls to `XtVaSet-Values()`, and free any allocated storage when the widget is destroyed.

The functionality of a widget also encompasses its behavior in response to user events. This type of functionality is typically handled by action routines. Each widget defines a table of events, called a translation table, to which it responds. The translation table maps each event, or sequence of events, to one or more actions.

Consider the PushButton in *hello.c*. Run the program and note how the widget highlights its border as the pointer moves into it, displays in reverse-video when you click on it, and switches back when you release the button. Watch how the highlighting disappears when you move the pointer out of the widget. Also, notice how pressing the SPACEBAR while the pointer is in the widget has the same effect as clicking on it. These behaviors are the kinds of things that are captured in the widget's translation table:

```
<Btn1Down>:                       Arm()
<Btn1Down>,<Btn1Up>:              Activate() Disarm()
<Btn1Down>(2+):                   MultiArm()
<Btn1Up>(2+):                     MultiActivate()
<Btn1Up>:                         Activate() Disarm()
<Btn2Down>:                       ProcessDrag()
<Key>osfSelect:                   ArmAndActivate()
<Key>osfActivate:                 PrimitiveParentActivate()
<Key>osfCancel:                   PrimitiveParentCancel()
<Key>osfHelp:                     Help()
~Shift ~Meta ~Alt <Key>Return:   PrimitiveParentActivate()
~Shift ~Meta ~Alt <Key>space:    ArmAndActivate()
<EnterWindow>:                    Enter()
<LeaveWindow>:                    Leave()
```

The translation table contains a list of event translations on the left side, with a set of action functions on the right side. When an event specified on the left occurs, the action routine on the right is invoked. As we just described, moving the pointer in and out of the PushButton causes some visual feedback. The `EnterWindow` and `LeaveWindow` events generated by the pointer motion cause the `Enter()` and `Leave()` actions to be invoked.

As another example, when the first mouse button is pressed down inside the PushButton, the `Arm()` action routine is called. This routine contains the code that displays the button as if it were "pushed in," as opposed to "pushed out." When the mouse button is released, both the `Activate()` and `Disarm()` routines are invoked in that order. Here is where your application actually steps in. If you have provided an appropriate callback function, the `Activate()` action calls it. The `Disarm()` routine causes the button to be redrawn so that it appears "pushed out" again.

Event Specification

In the Xt syntax, events are specified using symbols that are tied fairly closely to pure X hardware events, such as `ButtonPress` or `EnterWindow`. For example, `<Btn1Down>` specifies a button press for the first mouse button. `KeyPress` events are indicated by symbols called *keysyms*, which are hardware-independent symbols that represent individual keystrokes. Different keyboards may produce different hardware *keycodes* for the same key; the X server uses keysyms as a portable representation, based on the common labels found on the tops of keys.

Motif provides a further level of indirection in the form of *virtual keysyms*, which describe key events in a completely device-independent manner. For example, `osfActivate` indicates that the user invoked an action that Motif considers to be an activating action. An activating action typically corresponds to the RETURN key being pressed or the left mouse button being clicked. Similarly, `osfHelp` corresponds to a user request for help, such as the HELP or F1 key being pressed.

Virtual keysyms are supposed to be provided by the vendor of the user's hardware, based on the keys on the keyboard, but some X vendors also provide keysym databases to support multiple keyboards. As of X11 Releaase 5, the X Consortium provides a virtual keysym database in the file */usr/lib/X11/XKeysymDB*. This file contains a number of predefined key bindings that OSF has registered with the X Consortium to support actions in the Motif toolkit.

Virtual keysyms can be invoked by physical events, but the Motif toolkit goes one step further and defines them in the form of *virtual bindings*. Here's the translation table for the PushButton widget expressed using virtual bindings:

```
BSelect Press:          Arm()
BSelect Click:          Activate() Disarm()
BSelect Release:        Activate() Disarm()
BSelect Press 2+:       MultiArm()
BSelect Release 2+:     MultiActivate() Disarm()
BTranserPress:          ProcessDrag()
KSelect:                ArmAndActivate()
KHelp:                  Help()
```

Examples of virtual bindings are `BSelect`, which corresponds to the first mouse button, and `KHelp`, which is usually the HELP key on the keyboard. The rule of thumb is that any virtual binding beginning with a "B" corresponds to a mouse button event, while any binding beginning with a "K" corresponds to a keyboard event. More than one event can be bound to a single virtual keysym. For example, the *Motif Style Guide* permits F1 to be a help key, so that key is also virtually bound to `KHelp`.

Virtual bindings can be specified by a system administrator, a user, or an application. One common use of virtual bindings is to reconfigure the operation of the BACKSPACE and DELETE keys. On some keyboards, the BACKSPACE key is in a particularly difficult location for frequent access. Users of this type of keyboard may prefer to use the DELETE key for backspacing. These people may find the default operation of the Motif Text widget annoying, since it does not allow them to backspace using their "normal" backspace key.

Since Xt allows applications and users to override, augment, or replace translation tables, many people familiar with Xt try to specify a new translation for the DELETE key to make it act like a backspace. The translation invokes the action routine that backspaces in a Text widget. However, this approach is limited, in that it only works for a single Text widget. The Text widget has the following translation:

```
<Key>osfBackSpace:  delete-previous-char()
```

The virtual keysym `osfBackSpace` is bound to `delete-previous-char()`, which is the backspace action. Rather than changing the translation table to specify that `<Key>Delete` should invoke this action, a user can redefine the virtual binding of the `osfBackSpace` keysym. A user can configure his own bindings by specifying the new virtual keysym bindings in a *.motifbind* file in his home directory. The following virtual binding specifies that the DELETE key is mapped to `osfBackSpace`:

```
osfBackSpace : <Key>Delete
```

As a result of this specification, the DELETE key performs the backspace action in the Text widget, as well as any other widgets in the Motif toolkit that use the `osfBackSpace` keysym. The advantage of using virtual bindings is that the interface remains consistent and nothing in the toolkit or the application needs to change.

Virtual keysym bindings can also be set in a resource file, using the `XmNdefault-VirtualBindings` resource. The resource can be specified for all applications or on a per-application basis. To map the DELETE key to `osfBackSpace`, use the following specification:

```
*defaultVirtualBindings: \
    osfBackSpace : <Key>Delete    \n\
    other bindings
```

The only difference between the syntax for the resource specification and for the *.motifbind* file is that the resource specification must have a newline character (`\n`) between each entry. The complete syntax of Motif virtual bindings is explained in Volume Six B, *Motif Reference Manual*.

Motif 1.2 includes a new client, *xmbind*, that configures the virtual key bindings for Motif applications. This action is performed by the Motif Window Manager (*mwm*) or any application that uses the Motif toolkit at startup, so you really only need to use *xmbind* if you want to reconfigure the bindings without restarting *mwm* or a Motif application. Motif 1.2 also provides a new function, `XmTranslateKey()`, to translate a keycode into a virtual keysym. This function allows applications that override the default `XtKeyProc` to handle Motif's virtual key bindings.

Callbacks

Translations and actions allow a widget class to define associations between events and widget functions. A complex widget, such as the Motif Text widget, is almost an application in itself, since its actions provide a complete set of editing functions. But beyond a certain point, a widget is helpless unless control is passed from the widget to the application. A widget that expects to call application functions defines one or more callback resources, which are the hooks on which an application can hang its functions. For example, the PushButton widget defines the `XmNactivateCallback`, `XmNarmCallback`, and `XmNdisarmCallback` callback resources.

It is no accident that the callback resource names bear a resemblance to the names of widget action routines. In addition to highlighting the widget, the action routines call any application functions associated with the callbacks of the same name. There is no reason why a callback has to be called by an action; a widget could install a low-level event handler to perform the same task. However, this convention is followed by most widgets.

Figure 2-3 illustrates the event-handling path that results in an application callback being invoked. The widget's translation table registers the widget's interest in a particular type of event. When Xt receives an event that happened in the widget's window, it tests the event against the translation table. If there is no match, the event is thrown away. If there is a match, the event is passed to the widget and an action routine is invoked. The action routine may perform a function internal to the widget, such as changing the widget's appearance by highlighting it. Depending on the design of the widget, the action routine may then pass control to an application callback function. If the action is associated with a callback resource, it checks to see if a callback function has been registered for that resource, and if so, it dispatches the callback.

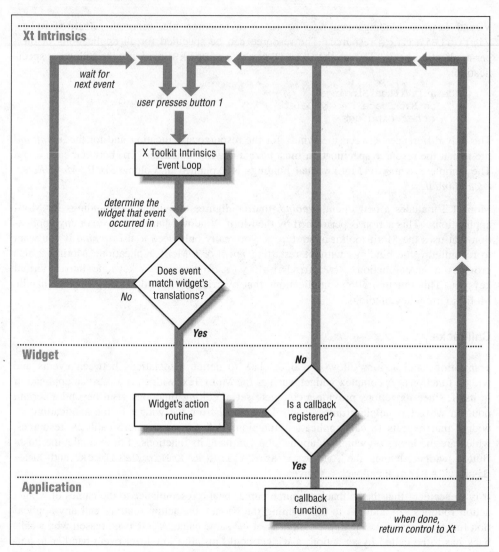

Figure 2-3. Event-handling using action routines and callbacks

There are several ways to connect an application function to a callback resource. The most common is to call XtAddCallback(), as demonstrated in *hello.c*:

```
void button_pushed();
. . .
XtAddCallback(button, XmNactivateCallback, button_pushed, NULL);
```

The first argument specifies the widget for which the callback is installed. The second parameter is the name of the callback resource, while the third is a pointer to the callback function. The fourth argument is referred to as *client data*. If this parameter is specified, its value is passed to the callback function when it is called. Here, the client data is NULL.

The client data can be a value of any type that has the same size as an XtPointer. An Xt-Pointer is usually the same as a char pointer; it is typically represented by a 32-bit value. You can pass pointers to variables, data structures, and arrays as client data. You cannot pass actual data structures; the result of passing a data structure is undefined. You can pass variables of type int or char, but understand that you are passing the data by value, not by reference. If you want to pass a variable so that the callback routine can change its value, you must pass the address of the variable. In this case, you need to make sure that the variable is global, rather than local, since a local variable loses its scope outside of the routine that calls XtAddCallback().

The callback function itself is passed the widget, the client data, if any, and a third argument that is referred to as *call data*. The signature of a callback function can be expressed in one of two ways: using an ANSI-compliant function prototype or using the older style conventions of K&R C. The ANSI-style function declaration is as follows:

```
button_pushed (Widget widget, XtPointer client_data, XtPointer call_data)
```

In the strictest sense, declaring the types of the parameters to the function is the proper way to handle function declarations and signatures. While this convention is good style and recommended for upwards compatibility, most compilers today still understand the older style conventions:

```
button_pushed (widget, client_data, call_data)
    Widget widget;
    XtPointer client_data;
    XtPointer call_data;
```

Since this style is the least common denominator, your best bet is to use the second, more portable method. In the course of the book, we make a habit of declaring client_data and call_data as XtPointers, even though we usually know the actual types of the parameters being passed to the function. Before referencing these parameters, we cast the values to the appropriate types.

The third parameter in a Motif-based callback function is always a structure that contains information specific to the widget class that invoked the callback function, as well as information about the event that triggered the callback. There is a generic callback structure, Xm-AnyCallbackStruct, as well as variations for specific widget classes and callback resources. The XmAnyCallbackStruct is defined as follows:

```
typedef struct {
    int     reason;
    XEvent *event;
} XmAnyCallbackStruct;
```

The callback structure for the PushButton widget class, XmPushButtonCallback-Struct, is defined as follows:

```
typedef struct {
    int     reason;
    XEvent *event;
    int     click_count;
} XmPushButtonCallbackStruct;
```

We discuss the callback structures for a widget class in this book (see the chapter corresponding to the specific widget type). The callback structures are also documented in the widget reference pages in Volume Six B, *Motif Reference Manual*.

All of the callback structures contain at least the two fields found in `XmAnyCallback-Struct`. The `reason` field always contains a symbolic value that indicates why the callback was called. These values are defined in */usr/include/Xm/Xm.h* and are usually self-explanatory. For example, when a callback function associated with a PushButton's `XmN-activateCallback` resource is called, the `reason` is `XmCR_ACTIVATE`. The different values for `reason` make it easier to write callback routines that are called by more than one type of widget. By testing the `reason` field, you can determine the appropriate action to take in the callback. Because the widget is always passed to the callback function, you can also find out what widget caused the function to be invoked.

The `event` field contains the actual event that triggered the callback, which can provide a great deal of useful information. See Volume Four, *X Toolkit Intrinsics Programming Manual*, for information on how to interpret the contents of an event. That subject is not discussed at length in this book, although our examples frequently use the events in callback structures to control processing.

2.3.7 The Event Loop

Once all of the widgets for an application have been created and managed and all of the callbacks have been registered, it's time to start the application running. The final two function calls in *hello.c* perform this task:

```
XtRealizeWidget (toplevel);
XtAppMainLoop (app);
```

Realizing a widget creates the actual window for the widget. When you call `XtRealize-Widget()` on the top-level widget of an application (the one returned by the call to `Xt-VaAppInitialize()`), Xt recursively traverses the hierarchy of widgets in the application and creates a window for each widget. Before this point, the widgets existed only as data structures on the client side of the X connection. After the call, the widgets are fully instantiated, with windows, fonts, and other X server data in place. The first `Expose` event is also generated, which causes the application to be displayed.

The call to `XtAppMainLoop()` turns control of the application over to the X Toolkit Intrinsics. Xt handles the dispatching of events to the appropriate widgets, which in turn pass them to the application via callbacks. The application code is idle until summoned to life by user-generated events.

2.4 Summary

We've looked at the skeleton of a simple Motif program. Every application follows more or less the same plan:

1. Initialize the X Toolkit Intrinsics.

2. Create and manage widgets.

3. Configure widgets by setting their resources.

4. Register callbacks to application functions.

5. Realize the widgets and turn control over to Xt's event loop.

How this skeleton is fleshed out in a real application is the subject of the next chapter. Chapter 3, *Overview of the Motif Toolkit*, addresses the role of manager widgets in laying out a user interface, the use of dialog boxes and other popups for transient interactions with the user, the many specialized types of widgets available in Motif, and other essential concepts. Once you have read that chapter, you should have a sufficient foundation for reading the remaining chapters in any order.

3

Overview of the Motif Toolkit

This chapter helps the reader understand the components of a real Motif application. It discusses how to handle the geometry management of primitive widgets within a manager widget, when to put components into the main window, when to use dialog boxes and menus, and how to relate to the window manager. After reading this chapter, the programmer should have a solid overview of Motif application programming, and she should be able to read the remaining chapters in any order.

In This Chapter:

3

Overview of the Motif Toolkit

In Chapter 2, *The Motif Programming Model*, we talked about the basic structure of an Xt-based program. We described how to initialize the toolkit, create and configure widgets, link them to the application, and turn control over to Xt's main loop. In this chapter, we discuss the widgets in the Motif toolkit and how you can put them together to create an effective user interface for an application.

If you already have a basic understanding of the Motif widgets, you can jump ahead to any of the later chapters in the book that focus on individual widget classes. This chapter provides some insight into the design of the widgets and a general overview of the Motif style and methodology, which you may find useful when developing your own applications.

This chapter also describes all of the new features in Release 1.2 of Motif. If you are familiar with Motif 1.1 but need to get up to speed with Motif 1.2, you should read Section 3.5. In this section, we summarize the new features and tell you where to find more information about them. We also describe all the changes made to the example programs in this book to make them up-to-date with Motif 1.2. While Motif 1.2 is backwards-compatible with Motif 1.1, there are a number of functions and resources in Motif 1.2 that replace obsolete functions and resources in Motif 1.1.

3.1 The Motif Style

You don't build a house just by nailing together a bunch of boards; you have to design it from the ground up before you really get started. Even with a prefabricated house, where many of the components have already been built, you need a master plan for putting the pieces together. Similarly, when you are designing a graphical user interface for an application, you have to think about the tasks your application is going to perform. You must envision the interface and then learn to use your tools effectively in order to create what you've envisioned.

The Motif toolkit provides basic components that you can assemble into a graphical user interface. However, without design schematics, the process of assembling the user-interface elements may become ad hoc or inconsistent. Here is where the *Motif Style Guide* comes in. It presents a set of guidelines for how widgets should be assembled and grouped, as well as how they should function and interact with the user.

All Motif programmers should be intimately familiar with the *Style Guide*. While we make recommendations for Motif style from time to time, this book is not a replacement for the *Style Guide*. There are many aspects of Motif style that are not covered in detail here, as they involve the content of an application rather than just the mechanics. On the other hand, the *Motif Style Guide* is not an instructional manual for the Motif toolkit. In fact, many of the objects described in the *Style Guide* are not even widgets, but higher-level, more complex objects that are composed of many widgets.

For example, the *Style Guide* describes an object called a MenuBar, which spans the top of the main window of an application. The MenuBar contains menu titles that, when clicked on, display PulldownMenus. The Motif toolkit does not implement MenuBars or Pulldown-Menus as distinct widget classes, nor does the *Style Guide* make any recommendations about how menu objects should be implemented. What the *Style Guide* does talk about (albeit somewhat loosely) is the actions that can be taken by an item on a menu: it can invoke an application function, pop up a dialog box containing yet more options and commands, or display a cascading menu (also known as a pullright menu).

The *Style Guide* also makes recommendations about the menus that an application should provide. For example, most applications should have a **File** menu that provides items such as an **Exit** button to exit the application and a **Save** button to save file. It also specifies details of presentation, such as that you should provide an ellipsis (. . .) as part of the label for a menu item that requires the user to provide more information before action is taken.

How the Motif toolkit goes about supporting, and in some cases enforcing, the guidelines of the *Motif Style Guide* brings up some interesting points, particularly in relation to some of the underlying principles of the X Toolkit Intrinsics. In Xt, a widget is envisioned as a self-contained object that is designed to serve a specific, clearly-defined function. Many of the Motif widgets, such as Labels, PushButtons, ScrollBars, and other common interface objects, are implemented as separate widgets.

In other cases, however, Motif steps outside of the Xt model by creating compound objects out of several widgets and then expecting you to treat them as if they were a single object. For example, Motif provides the ScrolledText and ScrolledList objects, which combine a Text or List widget with a ScrolledWindow widget, which in turn automatically manages horizontal and vertical ScrollBars.

In another case, the Motif toolkit provides a complex, general-purpose widget that can be configured to appear in several guises. There is no MenuBar widget class and no Pulldown-Menu widget class. Instead, the RowColumn widget, which also serves as a general-purpose manager widget, has resources that allow it to be configured as either a MenuBar or a PulldownMenu pane. Those familiar with Xt may find this widget design to be a breach of Xt's design goals, though.

In order to allow the programmer to think of ScrolledText objects, MenuBars, and Pulldown-Menus as distinct objects, the Motif toolkit provides convenience creation functions. These routines make it appear as though you are creating discrete objects when, in fact, you are not. For example, `XmCreateMenuBar()` and `XmCreateSimplePulldownMenu()` automatically create and configure a RowColumn widget as a MenuBar and a PulldownMenu, respectively. There are also convenience routines for creating various types of predefined dialog boxes, which are actually composed of widgets from four or five separate widget classes.

Convenience routines emphasize the functional side of user-interface objects while hiding their implementation. However, since Motif is a truly object-oriented system, it behooves you to understand what you're really dealing with. For example, if you want to use resource classes to configure all MenuBars to be one color and all PulldownMenus another, you cannot do so because they are not actually distinct widget classes. The class name for both objects is XmRowColumn.

In the remainder of this chapter, we look at Motif user-interface objects from the perspective of both the functional object illusion and the actual widget implementation. In the body of the book, we use the Motif convenience routines for creating most compound objects, but stick to the underlying Xt routines for creating simple widgets or gadgets. With the compound objects, we show you how to pierce the veil of Motif's convenience functions and work directly with the underlying widgets when necessary. Figure 3-1 shows the entire class hierarchy of the Motif widget set.

We begin by taking a closer look at the Motif user-interface components with which the user typically interacts. Then we examine how the manager widget classes are used to arrange the more visible application controls. And finally, we explore the use of all of these objects to create functional windows and dialogs that make up a real application.

3.2 Application Controls

In many ways, application controls are the heart of a graphical user interface. Rather than controlling an application by typing commands, the user is presented with choices using graphical elements. The user no longer needs to remember the syntax of commands, since her choices are presented to her as she goes along. As we've discussed, some of Motif's application controls (such as menus) are compound objects assembled by convenience routines. Others are simple, single-purpose widgets that you can create directly.

The widgets in this latter group are collectively referred to as *primitive* widgets — not because they are simple, but because they are designed to work alone. The contrast is not between primitive and sophisticated widgets, but between primitive and manager widgets. Some of the primitive Motif widget classes have corresponding gadget classes. The following sections describe the different types of primitive application controls available in the Motif toolkit.

The compound objects in the Motif toolkit are composed of primitive widgets and gadgets. Because an understanding of these objects relies on an understanding of the primitive widgets, as well as the Motif manager and shell widgets, we are going to postpone discussing compound objects until later in the chapter.

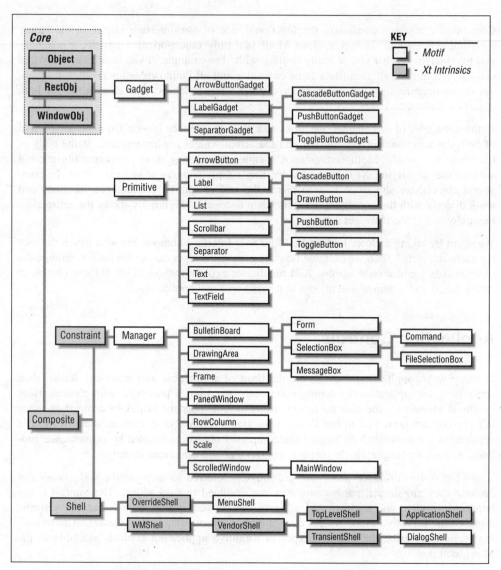

Figure 3-1. The class hierarchy of the Motif widget set

3.2.1 The Primitive Widget Class

The Primitive widget class is a superclass for all of the Motif primitive widgets. This widget class is a metaclass; it serves only to define certain common behavior used by all its subclasses, so one never instantiates a widget directly from the Primitive class. This statement is somewhat like saying that hammer is a class of object, but that you never really have a generic hammer. You can only have a specific type of hammer, like a claw hammer, a ball peen hammer, or a sledge hammer.†

Just as all hammers have particular characteristics that qualify them as hammers, the Primitive widget class provides its subclasses with common resources such as window border attributes, highlighting, and help with keyboard traversal (so the user can avoid the mouse and navigate through the controls in a window using the keyboard). The actual widget classes that you use are subclassed from the Primitive class, as shown in Figure 3-2.

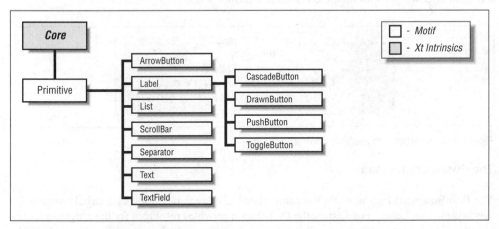

Figure 3-2. The Primitive widget class hierarchy

The Primitive class itself inherits even more basic widget behavior from the Xt-defined Core widget class, which establishes the basic nature of "widgetness." The Core class provides widgets with the capability to have windows and background colors, as well as translations, actions, and so on. You could actually use a simple Core widget as an instance and define your own translations and action routines, although this technique is not used frequently. Complete details are provided in Volume Four, *X Toolkit Intrinsics Programming Manual*.

The Label Class

The Label widget provides a visual label either as text or as an image in the form of a `Pixmap`. The text of a Label is an `XmString`, or compound string, not a character string (`char *`). A compound string can be oriented from left-to-right or right-to-left and it can also contain multiple lines and multiple fonts. Chapter 19, *Compound Strings*, discusses functions that manipulate compound strings, as well as functions that convert between character strings and compound strings.

---

† A claw hammer has the prongs in the back behind the hammer-head that allow you to pull nails out of a wall; a ball peen hammer has a round corner where the claw would be otherwise be; a sledge hammer is the large, heavyweight hammer used to drive thick nails through concrete or to destroy things.

The Label widget does not provide any callback routines, since it does not have any specified behavior. Using Xt, you could install event translations and action routines to make a Label respond to user input, but the Label widget is not intended to be used this way. It is only meant to be used to display labels or other visual aids. In Motif 1.2, instances of Label and all of its subclasses are automatically registered as drag sources for drag and drop operations by the toolkit.

Label widgets are described in detail in Chapter 11, *Labels and Buttons*. Figure 3-3 displays a single Label widget with multiple lines and multiple fonts.

Figure 3-3. A Label with multiple lines and fonts

The PushButton Class

The PushButton widget supports the same visual display capabilities as a Label, since it is subclassed from Label. In addition, the PushButton provides resources for the programmer to install callback routines that are called when the user arms, activates, or disarms the button. The PushButton also displays a shadow border that changes in appearance to indicate when the pointer is in the widget and when it has been activated.

When a PushButton is not selected, it appears to project out towards the user. When the pointer moves into the button, its border is highlighted. When the user actually selects the button by pressing the first mouse button on it, the button appears to be pushed in and is said to be armed. The user activates a PushButton by releasing the mouse button while the button is armed. PushButton widgets are also covered in detail in Chapter 11, *Labels and Buttons*. Figure 3-4 shows some examples of PushButtons.

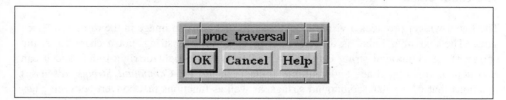

Figure 3-4. PushButton widgets

The DrawnButton Class

The DrawnButton widget is similar to a PushButton in its functionality and its three-dimensional appearance. However, the DrawnButton is used when an application wants to draw the text or image directly into the widget's window, rather than have the widget handle the drawing. If the image is dynamic and changes frequently during the course of an application, you may want to handle the drawing yourself. The DrawnButton provides additional callback resources that are called when the button is resized or exposed and additional ways to draw an outlined border. The DrawnButton widget is discussed in Chapter 11, *Labels and Buttons*. Figure 3-5 shows some DrawnButtons.

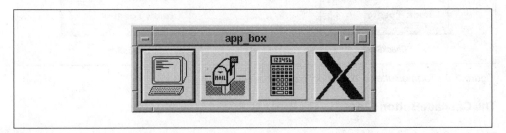

Figure 3-5. DrawnButtons widgets

The ToggleButton Class

The ToggleButton widget displays text or graphics like a Label widget, but it has an additional indicator graphic (a square or diamond shape) to the left of the label. The indicator shows the state of the ToggleButton: on or off. When the ToggleButton is on, the indicator is colored and appears to be pushed in. When the button is off, the indicator appears to project outward. The ToggleButton provides a additional resource for specifying a callback routine that is called when the user changes the state of the ToggleButton.

One common use of ToggleButtons is to set the application state. In this case, the callback routines typically set simple `Boolean` variables internal to the application. ToggleButtons can also be arranged in two different kinds of groups. In one configuration, known as a RadioBox, only one button in the group of buttons can be chosen at a time. The other configuration, a CheckBox, allows the user to select any number of buttons. When ToggleButtons are grouped as a RadioBox, the indicators are diamond-shaped; otherwise, they are square-shaped. ToggleButton widgets are described in detail in Chapter 11. Figure 3-6 shows the two different ways that ToggleButtons can be grouped.

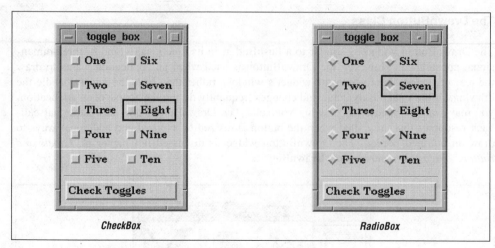

Figure 3-6. ToggleButtons in a CheckBox and a RadioBox

The CascadeButton Class

The CascadeButton widget is a special kind of button that is used to pop up menus. A CascadeButton can only be used as a child of a RowColumn widget, such as: in a MenuBar as the title of a PulldownMenu, in a PulldownMenu pane as an item that has a cascading menu associated with it, or as the button in an OptionMenu. The menu that is posted by a CascadeButton is not a part of the widget itself; the menu is associated with the button through a resource. A CascadeButton merely provides the label and other visual aids that support the appearance that a menu can pop up from the object. Even though the Cascade-Button widget class is subclassed from Label and could inherit all of its functionality, Motif imposes restrictions on the labels that a CascadeButton can display. CascadeButton labels cannot contain multiple lines or multiple fonts. Because CascadeButtons are typically used in menus, they do not display border shadows like other buttons. They do have similar high-lighting behavior when selected, however. CascadeButton widgets are explained in both Chapter 4, *The Main Window*, and Chapter 15, *Menus*.

The ArrowButton Class

Despite the similarity in its name, the ArrowButton widget is not subclassed from Label like the other button widgets. Like the remaining widgets described in this section, it is sub-classed directly from the Primitive widget class. The ArrowButton widget contains an image of an arrow pointing in one of four directions: up, down, left, or right. When the user selects this widget, the ArrowButton provides visual feedback giving the illusion that the button is pressed in and invokes a callback routine that an application can use to perform application-specific positioning.

In most respects, an ArrowButton can be considered identical to a PushButton, as it is easy enough to provide an arrow pixmap for a PushButton. Since directional arrows are a com-mon user-interface element, the ArrowButton is provided as a separate widget class for simplicity. ArrowButton widgets are covered in detail in Chapter 11, *Labels and Buttons*. Figure 3-7 shows the four variations of the ArrowButton widget.

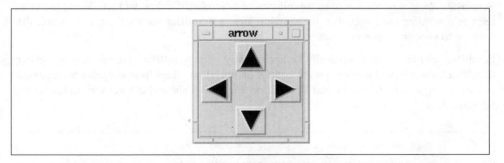

Figure 3-7. ArrowButton widgets

The List Class

The List widget provides a mechanism for the programmer to make a list of text items available to the user for selection. The user selects items from a List using the mouse or the keyboard. The List widget allows you to specify whether the user can select a single item or multiple items. While List is a Primitive widget, it is typically created as part of a Scrolled-List compound object using a Motif convenience function. The advantage of the ScrolledList object is that it provides a ScrollBar when the List grows bigger than the size of its visible area. In Motif 1.2, instances of the List widget are automatically registered as drag sources for drag and drop operations by the toolkit. We explore the List widget in detail in Chapter 12, *The List Widget*. Figure 3-8 shows a List widget in context with other interface elements.

			Z-Mail		

Folder Message View Find Sort Compose Options Layout   Help

Folder: vol6 | 20 total, 0 new, 0 unread, 0 deleted

Messages: 6, 11   □ New Arrivals

```
    1   r Karen Lewis       Oct 24   6:42pm  (36) hullo
    2     dbrooks@osf.org   Oct 28   3:27pm  (49) mwm segfault
    3     Adrian Nye        Nov 12   5:42pm  (65) Re: some thought about
    4     David Flanagan    Feb 16 10:18am   (74) building motif 1.2.2
    5   r Liz Bradley       Feb 18   3:01pm  (23) Everest talk
    6     Eric Pearce       Mar 15   9:09pm  (35) did you see this (in XF
    7     Dan Heller        Mar 19 10:34pm  (218) Sun Goes Motif!
    8   f Eileen Kramer     Mar 22   2:48pm  (24) Vol 6A project meeting
    9     Audrey Strauss     Mar 30   9:19am  (40) Tuesday Again
   10   r lucia@ics.com     Apr  1 10:13am   (24) stuff
   11   r Tim OReilly       Apr  6   8:28am   (29) Motif sample chapters
```

Figure 3-8. A List widget in an application

The ScrollBar Class

The ScrollBar widget is one of the more intuitive user-interface elements in the Motif toolkit. ScrollBars are almost always used as children of a ScrolledWindow widget. When the contents of a window are larger than the viewing area, a ScrollBar allows the user to scroll the window to view the entire contents.

ScrollBars can be oriented vertically or horizontally. The ScrollBar also provides a number of callback resources that allow you to control its operation. ScrollBar widgets are discussed in Chapter 9, *ScrolledWindows and ScrollBars*. Figure 3-9 shows both vertical and horizontal ScrollBars.

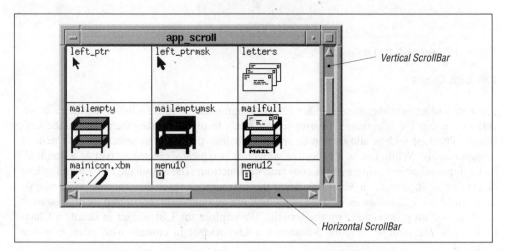

Figure 3-9. Horizontal and vertical ScrollBar widgets in a ScrolledWindow

The Separator Class

The Separator widget is used as a visual aid to separate adjacent items in a display. A Separator appears as a line between the objects it is separating; it can be oriented vertically or horizontally. Separators can be used in menus to separate menu items, in dialog boxes to separate discrete areas of control, and at various points in an interface for purely aesthetic reasons.

The Text and TextField Classes

The Text widget is a complete text editor contained in a widget. The Text widget provides resources to configure the editing style of the widget, as well as callback resources that allow text verification. The widget can be configured as a multiline text entry area or as a single-line data entry field. The TextField widget class is available as a somewhat lighter-weight text entry area. The TextField widget is limited to a single-line, but in all other respects there is little difference between the two classes. In Motif 1.2, instances of the Text and TextField widgets are automatically registered as drag sources and drop sites for drag and drop operations by the toolkit.

The Text and TextField widgets can be used in many different ways to support the text entry requirements of an application. The two widgets are described in detail in Chapter 14, *Text Widgets*. Figure 3-10 shows an application that uses various forms of the Text widget.

```
┌──────────────────────────────────────────────────────────────────┐
│ ─                              editor                            □ │
│  File  Edit  Search                                               │
│                                                                    │
│  Search Pattern:  xwud            Replace Pattern:  I             │
│  ┌──────────────────────────────────────────────────────────┐ ▲  │
│  │ XWUD(1)              USER COMMANDS              XWUD(1)    │    │
│  │                                                           │    │
│  │ NAME                                                      │    │
│  │      xwud - image displayer for X                        │    │
│  │                                                           │    │
│  │ SYNOPSIS                                                  │    │
│  │      xwud [-in file] [-noclick] [-geometry geom] [-display│    │
│  │      display] [-new] [-std <maptype>] [-raw] [-vis <vis-type-or-│ │
│  │      id>] [-help] [-rv] [-plane number] [-fg color] [-bg color]│ │
│  │                                                           │ ▼  │
│  └──────────────────────────────────────────────────────────┘    │
│  ◁                                                           ▷    │
│  Found 2 occurrences.                                             │
└──────────────────────────────────────────────────────────────────┘
```

Figure 3-10. Text and TextField widgets

3.2.2 Gadgets

Another set of application controls is provided in the form of gadgets. There are gadgets that are equivalent to many of the primitive widgets: LabelGadgets, SeparatorGadgets, Push-ButtonGadgets, CascadeButtonGadgets, ToggleButtonGadgets, and ArrowButtonGadgets. The appearance and behavior of the gadgets is mostly identical to that of the corresponding widgets. A further understanding of how gadgets work depends on an understanding of the manager widgets that support them, so we are going to return to this topic later in the chapter.

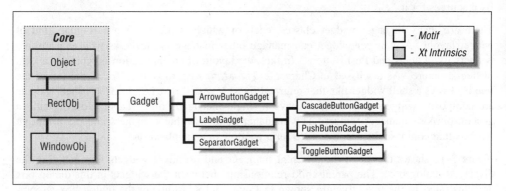

Figure 3-11. The Gadget class hierarchy

The Gadget class is a superclass for all of the Motif gadgets. Like Primitive, this class is a metaclass that is never instantiated. However, gadgets are not widgets. The Gadget class is subclassed from the RectObj class, not from the Core widget class. Figure 3-11 shows the class hierarchy for gadgets.

3.3 Application Layout

While the controls are the most obvious part of a graphical user interface, these elements alone do not make an effective interface. A random arrangement of buttons or a collection of nested menus can make an application as obscure and as difficult to use as one with a command-line interface. The arrangement of the controls in an application makes all the difference.

To help you lay out your application, Motif provides you with a set of manager widgets. You can think of manager widgets as boxes in which you can put things. These boxes, however, can grow or shrink as necessary to provide the best fit possible for the items that they contain. You can place boxes inside of other boxes, whether or not they contain other items. By using different size boxes, you can organize things in many different ways.

Manager widgets are so named because they manage the size and position of other widgets. The relationship between a manager widget and the widgets that it manages is commonly referred to as the *parent-child* model. The manager acts as the parent, and the other widgets are its children.

Unlike primitive widgets, such as PushButtons, ScrollBars, and Labels, whose usefulness depends on their visual appearance and interaction with the user, manager widgets provide no visual feedback and have few callback routines that react to user input. Manager widgets have two basic purposes: they manage the sizes and positions of their children, and they provide support for gadgets. Like other widgets, manager widgets have windows, they can receive events, and they can be manipulated directly with Motif and Xt functions. You can draw directly into the window of a manager widget, look for events in the widget, and specify resources for it.

There are many manager widget classes, each of which is tuned for a particular kind of widget layout. A manager widget can manage other manager widgets, as well as primitive widgets like Labels and PushButtons. In fact, the layout of an application is typically a kind of tree structure. As discussed in Chapter 2, *The Motif Programming Model*, the top of the tree is always a shell widget like that returned by `XtVaAppInitialize()`. Shell widgets are composite widgets that can only have a single managed child. This child is usually a general-purpose manager widget. This manager contains other managers and the primitive widgets that compose the user interface for a window in an application.

Figure 3-12 shows the all of the different manager and primitive widgets that make up the displayed dialog box. The parent-child relationships between the widgets in this dialog box are illustrated in the tree structure shown in Figure 3-13. Although the dialog box is composed of many different components, it appears to the user as a single, conceptually focused user-interface object.

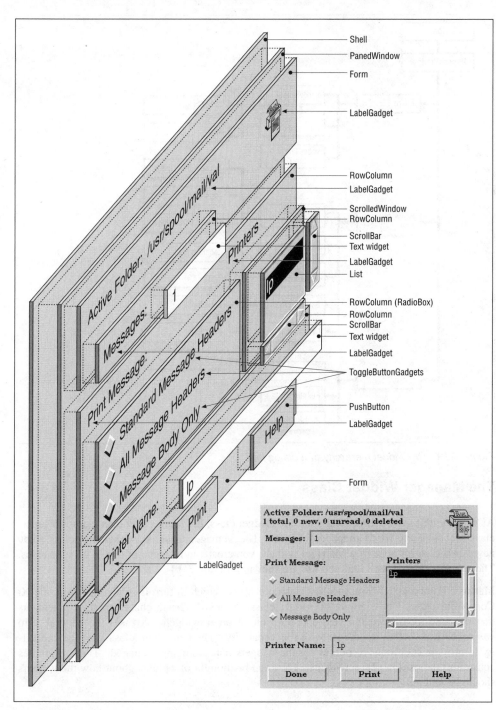

Figure 3-12. The layout of a dialog box

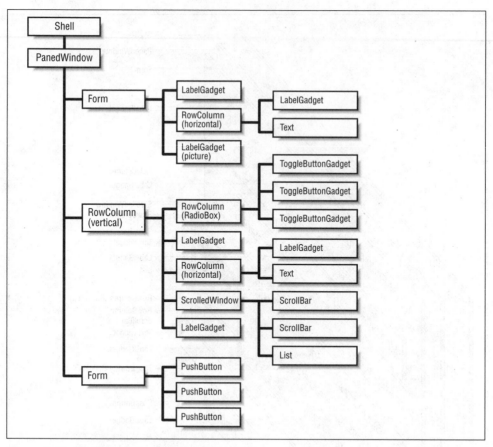

Figure 3-13. The widget hierarchy of a dialog box

3.3.1 The Manager Widget Class

As with the Primitive widget class and the Gadget class, the Manager widget class is a super-class for all of the Motif manager widgets. The Manager class is another metaclass. You never create an instance of a Manager widget; you create an instance of one of its subclasses. The actual widget classes that you use are shown in Figure 3-14.

Manager is subclassed from the Xt Constraint class, which in turn is subclassed from the Xt Composite class. The Composite widget class defines the basic characteristics of widgets that are able to manage the size and position of other widgets. Xt uses the general term *composite widget* for any widget with this capability. The Constraint class adds the capability to provide additional resources for the widgets that are being managed. These resources constrain the position of the widgets. They can be thought of as hints about how the widgets should be laid out.

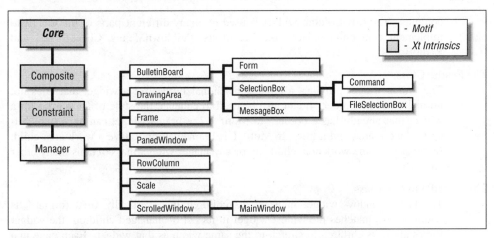

Figure 3-14. The Manager widget class hierarchy

Motif provides a number of general-purpose manager widgets that allow the programmer to manage the size and arrangement of an arbitrary number of children. In some ways, the art of Motif programming is the design of effective widget layouts, using these particular manager widgets. Motif also provides some narrowly-focused manager widgets, such as certain dialog classes, that can almost be treated as if they were single user-interface components. These widgets create and manage their children with minimal help from an application. We some-times refer to these widgets as compound objects, since they include both a manager widget and one or more children. This section describes the different manager widgets briefly; a more detailed description of the widgets is given in Chapter 8, *Manager Widgets*.

The DrawingArea Class

The DrawingArea widget provides an area in which an application can display graphics. Callback routines can be used to notify the application when expose and resize events take place and when there is input from the keyboard or mouse. The DrawingArea can also be used to manage the geometry layout for child widgets, but its functionality in this area is quite limited.

The ScrolledWindow Class

The ScrolledWindow widget provides a viewport for data such as text or graphics. If the data that is being viewed is larger than the ScrolledWindow, ScrollBars allow the user to view the entire contents of the window interactively.

The MainWindow Class

The MainWindow widget acts as the standard layout manager for the main window of an application. It is specifically tuned to pay attention to the existence of a MenuBar, a command area, a message area, a work region, and ScrollBars, although all of these areas are optional.

The RowColumn Class

The RowColumn widget is perhaps the most widely used and robust of all of the manager widgets. As its name suggests, the widget lays out its children in rows and columns. The RowColumn widget is used by many different parts of the toolkit to implement compound objects like MenuBars, PulldownMenus, CheckBoxes, and RadioBoxes.

The Frame Class

The Frame widget provides a three-dimensional border for a widget that does not normally have a border. It can also be used to enhance the style of the border for a widget that already has a border. In Motif 1.2, a Frame widget can have two children: a work area and a title. In Motif 1.1, Frame can only have a work area child. In either case, the work area child can be a manager widget that contains many other children.

The PanedWindow Class

The PanedWindow widget manages its children in a vertically tiled format. Its width always matches the widest widget in its list of managed children; the widget forces all of its children to stretch to the same width as that widget. Each pane in a PanedWindow contains a child widget; every pane has an associated sash (or grip) that allows the user to change the height of the pane interactively. Resizing a pane with the grip can cause the widgets in other panes to change size.

The BulletinBoard Class

The BulletinBoard widget does not impose much of a layout policy for the widgets that it manages. The widget acts like a real bulletin board, in that an application pins a widget on the bulletin board, and it sticks where it is placed. The Bulletin-Board does impose margins and has a resource that controls whether or not its children can overlap. However, when a BulletinBoard is resized, it does not move or resize its children based on its new size. The BulletinBoard is useful mostly for the layout of dialog boxes and other windows that are rarely resized. The predefined Motif dialog widget classes use BulletinBoard widgets for this reason.

The Form Class

The Form widget provides a great deal of control over the placement and sizing of the widgets it manages. A Form can lay out its children in a grid-like manner or it can allow its children to link themselves to one another in a chain-like fashion. Form uses constraint resources to specify how children are resized and positioned relative to each other and the Form as a whole.

The Scale Class

The Scale widget is a slider object that is somewhat similar in appearance and functionality to a ScrollBar. A Scale is typically used to provide feedback to the user about the value of a state variable in an application. This widget class is not intended to be used as a general manager. The Scale creates and manages its own widgets, which are needed to construct the Scale object. The only children that you can add to a Scale widget are Label widgets that represent tick marks.

3.3.2 Geometry Management

The process by which a manager widget controls the layout of its children is known as *geometry management*. A child widget is always placed within the boundaries of its parent. A child cannot move or resize itself without requesting permission from its parent, which can deny the request. The manager, acting as the parent, can even force the child into an arbitrary size or position. However, like any good parent, a manager widget should be fair at all times and not deny reasonable requests made by its children. As you might expect, geometry management can be quite complex in an application with several levels of managers.

As an example, consider adding a new item to a List widget. In order to display the new item, the List widget must grow vertically, so it requests a new size from its manager parent. If that parent can accomodate the larger size, or it has another mechanism for satisfying the request, such as ScrollBars, it can approve the request. However, if the manager itself must grow to honor the List widget's request, it has to negotiate with its own parent. This chain reaction may go all the way up to the shell widget, in which case the shell must communicate with the window manager about the new size. If the window manager and the shell agree to the new size, the acknowledgement filters back down through the widget tree to the List widget, which can now grow to its requested size. If any of the composite widgets in the hierarchy refuse to resize, the List widget's request is either denied or only partially fulfilled.

Most of the time, this type of interaction completes successfully, as there are rarely disputes among children about resizing negotiations or positional boundaries. Children usually go where their managers put them and make very few requests of their own. One exception is a RowColumn widget that is acting as a MenuBar, since it must be situated at the top of the window, and it must span the window horizontally. ScrollBars are another possible exception, since they are typically positioned at the edges of ScrolledWindow widgets.

So, how do children request geometry changes from their parents? The answer to this question is rather complicated, since the X Toolkit Intrinsics supports a large selection of functions that enable two-way communication about geometry management. For example, a child can use `XtMakeGeometryRequest()` to request permission to be made a specific size or to be placed in a particular location. A parent can use a function like `XtQuery-Geometry()` to give a child the opportunity to announce its preferred geometry.

Some of these functions and methods are described in Chapter 8, *Manager Widgets*, but a detailed treatment of custom geometry management techniques is beyond the scope of this book. These functions are mostly used by the internals of composite and constraint widgets. See Volume Four, *X Toolkit Intrinsics Programming Manual*, for a more detailed discussion of geometry management techniques.

In the Motif toolkit, geometry management cannot work without cooperation. The easiest way for a child to cooperate with its parents and siblings is simply to comply with whatever layout policy is supported by its manager widget parent. A child should not try to force itself into a size or a position that is not supported by its parent. Each of the manager widget classes described above is designed to support a specific layout style. For example, the Row-Column widget lays out its children in rows and columns, the Form widget allows its children to specify positions relative to other widgets within the Form, and the PanedWindow widget lets its children specify their desired maximum and minimum heights.

Manager widgets use constraint resources to support their layout policies. Constraint resources are defined by Xt's Constraint widget class, which is a superclass for the Manager widget class and thus all of the Motif manager widgets. Unlike other resources, constraint resources apply to the *children* of a manager widget, not to the manager itself. Examples of constraint resources include maximum and minimum heights, relative sizes and positions, specific positional constraints, and even absolute x,y coordinates. While these examples deal exclusively with size and position, constraint resources can be used for any arbitrary information that needs to be kept on a per-child basis.

Here's how constraint resources work. When a manager needs to size or position its children, it deals only with the children that are managed; unmanaged children are ignored in geometry management negotiations. For each managed child, the manager examines the child's constraint resources. Depending on the constraints that are specified, the manager either enforces the geometry changes or negotiates with its own parent to see if it can comply with the changes. This process uses an extra internal data structure for each child. The data structure stores the constraints that are used by the widget's parent to aid it in geometry management.

3.3.3 Gadget Management

In addition to handling geometry management, manager widgets are responsible for their gadget children. In order to understand how managers support gadgets, we need to define more clearly what a gadget is. Every widget has its own X window, which simplifies many aspects of programming, since each widget can take responsibility for repainting itself, selecting its own events, and in general being as self-sufficient as possible. Historically, however, windows have been perceived as heavyweight objects. The concern is that system performance will be degraded if an application uses too many windows. Since an application with a graphical user interface frequently uses hundreds of widgets, or perhaps even thousands for a very large program, the performance issue is an important one.

Gadgets, or windowless widgets, were originally developed as a part of Motif. They were added to Xt as of X11 Release 4. Motif provides gadget versions of many common primitive widgets, such as PushButtons and Labels. Like widgets, gadgets can be created using either Motif convenience functions or XtCreateManagedWidget(). While the widget and gadget versions of an object are functionally very similar, there are some small but important differences.

Because a gadget does not have its own window, it is entirely dependent on its parent, a manager widget, for its basic functionality. For example, the manager must handle redrawing the gadget on exposure, highlighting it as a result of keyboard traversal, and notifying it of event activity. Without a window, a gadget has no control over the colors that it uses or any other window-based attributes normally associated with a widget. For this reason, gadgets can only be used in managers that support them. How closely a gadget emulates its widget counterpart is largely dependent on the capabilities of the manager widget parent.

The Motif Manager class limits the colors that can be used by gadgets. A gadget uses the same background, foreground, and shadow colors as its manager widget parent. These restrictions are not inherent in the Xt Composite widget class or in Xt-based gadgets; they are specific to the Motif Manager and Gadget classes. Hypothetically, you could write a Composite widget that allows its gadget children to specify their own background colors. Such a widget would have to paint the area of its window occupied by the gadget with the specified color to give the user the impression that the gadget is indeed a separately-colored widget.

You can use the color restrictions of the Motif managers and gadgets to provide a consistent interface for your application. For example, by using PushButton gadgets instead of PushButton widgets, you can ensure that all of the buttons in particular window are the same color. In this situation, the user can specify color resources for the manager widget, but not the PushButtons themselves.

Although gadgets were originally developed to improve performance, it is no longer necessary to automatically use them if you are looking for performance improvements in an application with many widgets. In both X11 Release 4 and Release 5, windows have become substantially lighter-weight objects than they were when gadgets were first developed. If anything, gadgets are worse than widgets at this point from a performance perspective because the Motif managers take a very simplistic approach to the way they handle events for gadgets. A manager tracks all events, even `MotionNotify`, whether or not its gadgets have expressed interest in the events. As a result, gadgets typically generate a great deal of network traffic. X terminal users are especially likely to notice a network performance drop. There are some other complications that surround the use of gadgets, which we discuss when they come up in the course of this book.

3.3.4 Keyboard Traversal

Keyboard traversal is a mechanism that allows a user to navigate through the components in a user interface using only the keyboard. The *Motif Style Guide* specifies that all applications must support keyboard traversal for all application functionality. Support of keyboard traversal is important because not every display provides a mouse or other pointing device. For some applications, such as data entry, using keyboard traversal is more convenient than using a pointing device. All of the Motif widgets support keyboard-based navigation.

Keyboard traversal is based on the concept of a *tab group*. A tab group is a group of widgets that are related for the purpose of keyboard traversal. For example, all the items in a menu are considered a tab group, since they are grouped together and perform related functions.

At any given time, only one component on a display can be "listening" to the keyboard for keyboard events. The widget that is listening to the keyboard is said to have the keyboard focus, or input focus. The widget that has the input focus identifies itself by displaying a location cursor. The location cursor is often a highlighted border that surrounds the widget. A user can move the input focus to another widget using the mouse or the keyboard.

The user can move the keyboard focus between items in the same tab group using the arrow keys. When the user finds the item that she wants, she can activate it with the RETURN key or the SPACEBAR. If the user wants to move from one tab group to another, she uses the TAB key. (In a multiline Text widget, CTRL-TAB is used because otherwise there would be no way to insert a tab character.) To traverse the tab groups in reverse, the SHIFT key is used with the TAB key. Keyboard traversal wraps from the last item to the first item, both within a tab group and between tab groups.

Although keyboard traversal is not completely controlled by manager widgets, they do play a pivotal role in implementing it. A manager widget is typically initialized as a tab group; its primitive widget children are members of the tab group. The Text and List widgets are exceptions to this rule. These widgets are set up as their own tab groups, so that keyboard traversal can be used to move among the text in a Text widget or the items in a List widget. Within a tab group, there is no sense of a manager-within-manager structure. The widget hierarchy is flattened out so that it appears to the user that all of the controls in a window are at the same level.

Keyboard traversal only works if each widget in an interface cooperates. If a PushButton has the keyboard focus and the user presses the TAB key, the internals of the PushButton widget are responsible for directing the focus to the next tab group. Manager widgets play a key role in keyboard traversal because they are responsible for the keyboard events that take place within gadgets. If an event occurs within a PushButton gadget, its manager parent is responsible for directing the input focus to the next tab group.

Although the whole process of keyboard traversal may seem complex and difficult, it is automated by the Motif toolkit and does not require application intervention. However, the toolkit does provide mechanisms that allow you to control keyboard navigation. There are resources that allow you to specify widgets that are tab groups, widgets that are in tab groups, and widgets that do not participate in keyboard navigation. There are also functions that allow you to specify explicitly the direction of keyboard traversal. Fortunately, such fine-tuning is rarely necessary:

3.4 Putting Together a Complete Application

Managers and primitive widgets provide the basic tools with which you can build a graphical user interface from the ground up. Motif also provides several components that address the large-scale organization of an application. The specialized MainWindow manager widget is intended to be used as the organizing frame for an application. Motif also provides different types of menus and dialog boxes that can be used to organize application functionality.

Since an application is always used in conjuction with a window manager, we need to discuss the role played by the window manager. In the course of this discussion, we also need to take a closer look at shell widgets, since they provide the communication link between an application and the window manager.

Both pixmaps and colors play an important role in a graphical user interface. Motif provides routines that cache pixmaps so that they can be reused throughout an application. The three-dimensional appearance of Motif components is implemented using a variety of color resources. It is important to understand these resources so that the 3D shadows are an effective part of the user interface.

3.4.1 The Main Window

Every application is different. A word processor, paint program, or spreadsheet typically has a single main work area, with controls taking on a peripheral role, perhaps in Pulldown-Menus. More sophisticated programs, on the other hand, may have several main work areas. For example, an electronic mail program may have a work area in which the user reviews and selects from a list of incoming messages, another where she reads and responds to messages, and yet another where she issues commands to organize, delete, or otherwise affect groups of messages. Still other applications, such as data-entry programs, don't really have a separate work area. The work area is really just a collection of controls, such as CheckBoxes and text entry areas, that are filled in by the user.

It is quite conceivable that an application could provide multiple windows for performing different tasks. For example, an order entry program might use one window for looking up a customer record, another for checking stock on hand, and yet another for entering the current order. Motif allows for the creation of multiple top-level application windows, as well as transient dialog boxes that ask for additional information or confirmation before carrying out a command.

Nonetheless, every application has at least one main window. The main window is the most visible window in an application. It is the first window the user sees and also the place where the user interacts with most application functionality. No matter how small or large an application may be, there needs to be a focal point that ties it all together. As a program grows more complex, the main window may grow more abstract and perform fewer functions, but it always exists. In a sophisticated application, the main window is transformed into a hub where the user starts, finishes, and returns again and again as she goes from one function to the next.

The *Motif Style Guide* suggests a particular layout for the main window. Applications should use this layout unless they have a compelling reason not to. The recommended layout is shown in Figure 3-15.

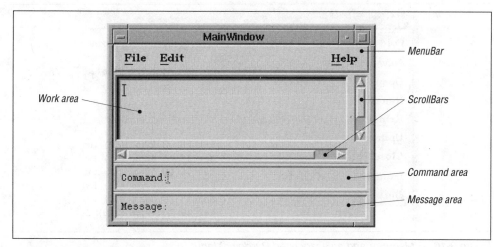

Figure 3-15. Recommended layout for a main window

A main window should have a menu bar across the top, with the work area immediately below it. The work area usually contains the main interface object of the application. For example, a paint or draw application might provide a DrawingArea widget as a canvas, an electronic mail application might provide a ScrolledList of message summaries from which the user can make selections, and a Text editor might place a Text widget in the work area. An application work area might require a custom widget or a non-widget-based X window instead.

The work area can have both horizontal and vertical scrollbars allowing the user to view its entire contents if they are too large to be displayed all at once. The main window can also contain an optional *command area* below the work area, where the user can enter typed commands. This area is most helpful for porting character-based applications to a Motif GUI, but it can be useful for other applications as well. At the bottom of the main window is an optional *message area*. This area should be used for status and informational messages only, not for error messages or any other type of message that requires a response from the user.

While it is possible to construct your own main window, the Motif toolkit provides the special-purpose MainWindow widget, which supports the recommended style. All of the elements in the MainWindow are optional, so an application can use it to display just the areas that it requires. The MainWindow widget is described in detail in Chapter 4, *The Main Window*.

3.4.2 Menus

Motif supports three different styles of menus. PulldownMenus that are displayed from the MenuBar in a MainWindow are the most common type of menu. A PulldownMenu is displayed when the user selects a CascadeButton in the MenuBar. The menu pane is displayed below the CascadeButton. Figure 3-16 shows a typical MenuBar and Pulldown-Menu.

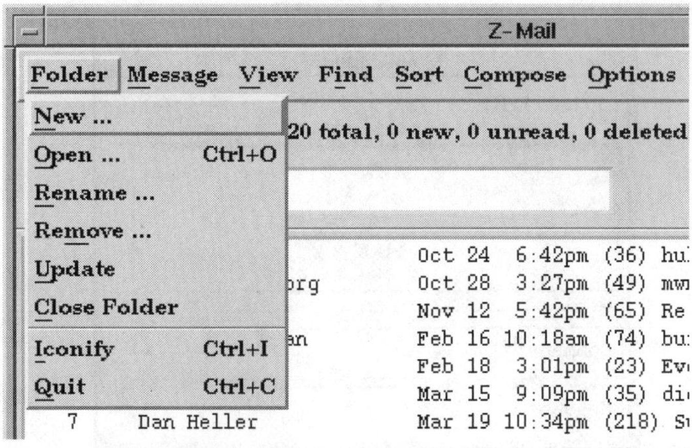

Figure 3-16. A MenuBar and an associated PulldownMenu

An item in a PulldownMenu can have a *cascading menu* associated with it. The cascading menu is displayed to the right of the menu item as shown in Figure 3-17, so these menus are sometimes referred to as *pullright menus*.

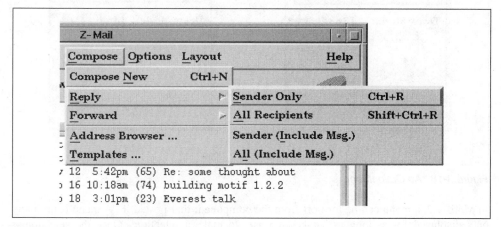

Figure 3-17. A cascading menu

MenuBars, PulldownMenus, and cascading menus are all created in a similar way. Motif provides convenience functions that create specially configured RowColumn widgets for these menu objects. The RowColumn widget is then populated with PushButtons, Cascade-Buttons, ToggleButtons, and Separators, or their gadget equivalents. In the case of a Menu-Bar, all of the children must be CascadeButtons, since each button brings up a separate menu. In a PulldownMenu pane, most of the items are PushButtons or ToggleButtons, although Separators can be used for clarity. If an item posts a cascading menu, it must be a Cascade-Button. The additional menu is created separately, populated with its own buttons, and attached to the CascadeButton.

Motif also supports a construct called an OptionMenu. An OptionMenu is another specially-configured RowColumn widget, but in this case the behavior is quite different. An Option-Menu is typically used to prompt the user to choose a value. The RowColumn widget displays a Label and a CascadeButton that shows the current value. When the user clicks on the button, a menu that contains the rest of the choices is popped up directly on top of the CascadeButton. Choosing an item from the menu modifies the label of the CascadeButton so that it shows the currently-selected item. Figure 3-18 shows an OptionMenu, both before and after it is popped up.

Additionally, Motif provides PopupMenus. Unlike the other types of menus, a PopupMenu is not attached to a visible interface element. A PopupMenu can be popped up at any arbitrary location in an application, usually as a result of the user pressing the third mouse button. PopupMenus are meant to provide shortcuts to application functionality, so an application can use different PopupMenus in different contexts and for different components in an interface.

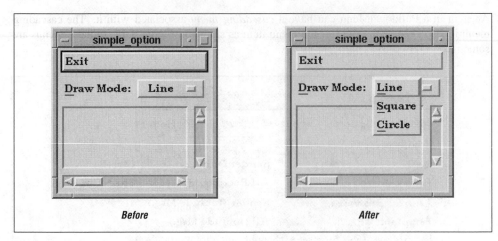

Figure 3-18. An OptionMenu

In Motif 1.2, a menu can be torn off from the component that posted it. A menu is normally only displayed for as long as it takes the user to make a selection. Once the selection is made, the menu is closed. When a menu is torn off, it remains posted in its own window. Now the user can make as many selections from the menu as she would like without having to repost the menu each time. For more information on tear-off menu functionality, as well as the different types of Motif menus, see Chapter 15, *Menus*.

3.4.3 The Window Manager

To the user, the MainWindow looks like the top-level window of an application. In window-system talk, a top-level window resides at the top of the window hierarchy for an application. Its parent is the *root window*, which is what the user perceives as the background behind all the windows on the desktop. In the Xt-world, however, things are a little different. Behind every visible top-level application window is a special kind of widget known as a shell widget.

Every window that can be placed independently on the screen, including top-level windows and dialog boxes, has a shell widget as its parent. The user does not see the shell because it is obscured by all of the other widgets in the window. A shell widget can only contain one managed child widget; the shell does not perform any geometry management except to shrink-wrap itself around this child. The child is typically a manager widget, such as a Main-Window, that is responsible for managing the layout of the primitive components, such as Labels, Text widgets, ScrollBars, and PushButtons. The items that the user actually sees and interacts with are descendants of the shell widget because they are contained within its boundaries.

Aside from managing its single child, the main job of the shell is to communicate with the *window manager* on behalf of the application. Without the shell, the application has no idea what else is happening on the desktop. It is very important for you to understand that the window manager is a separate application from your own. The visual and physical interaction between an application and the window manager is usually so close that most users cannot tell the difference between the two, but the distinction is important from a programming perspective.

To get an idea of the relationship between the window manager and an application, let's compare it with the way a bed is built and how it fits into a room. A bed is made up of a frame, a mattress, and as many accessories as you want to pile on top of it. The main window is the mattress; the sheets, pillows, blankets, and stuffed animals you throw on it represent the user-interface controls inside the main window. The whole lot sits on top of the bed frame, which is the shell widget. When you push a bed around the room, you're really pushing the bed's frame. The rest just happens to go along with it. The same is true for windows on the screen. The user never moves an application window, she moves the shell widget using the window manager frame. The application just happens to move with it.

You may have to stretch your imagination a little to visualize a bed resizing itself with its frame, but this is precisely what happens when the user resizes an application. It is the window manager that the user interacts with during a resizing operation. The window manager only informs the application about the new size when the user is done resizing. The window manager tells the shell, the shell communicates the new size to its child, and the change filters down to the rest of the widgets in the application.

The window manager frame is composed of *window decorations* that the window manager places on all top-level windows. These controls allow the user to interactively move a window, resize it, cause it to redraw itself, or even to close it. Figure 3-19 shows the standard Motif window manager (*mwm*) decorations. For information on how to use *mwm*, see Volume Three, *X Window System User's Guide, Motif Edition*.

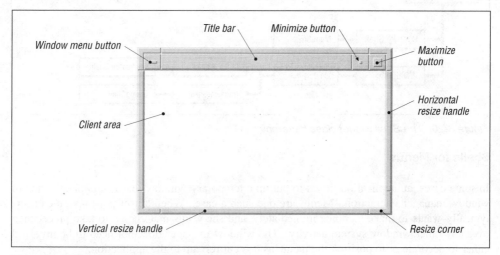

Figure 3-19. Motif window manager decorations

The *window menu* displays a list of window manager functions that allow the user to move, resize, and exit the application. An application does not have access to the menu itself or the items within it; similarly, it cannot get handles to the minimize and maximize buttons. These objects belong to the window manager and act independently from an application.

Motif provides *window manager protocols* that allow menu items like these to affect an application. An application can also interact with the window manager using many of the same types of protocols. You can specify which of the items in the window menu you want to appear, whether or not there are resize handles on the window frame, and whether or not you want to allow the user to iconify the window. However, the user is expecting all of the applications on her desktop to interact consistently with the window manager. This expectation is magnified by the fact that the user has probably set quite a few resources for the window manager. Since unexpected interference from an application rarely makes users happy, you should leave the window manager alone. A technical discussion of the window manager can be found in Chapter 16, *Interacting With the Window Manager*.

As we pointed out earlier, it is possible for an application to have more than one independent window. In addition to the main window, there may be one or more dialog boxes, as well as popup windows, and even independent application windows that co-exist with the main window. Each of these cases requires different handling by the window manager, and as a result, there are several different classes of shell widgets. Figure 3-20 shows the class hierarchy of the different types of shell widgets available in the Motif toolkit. The Shell widget class is another metaclass that specifies resources and behaviors inherited by all of its subclasses.

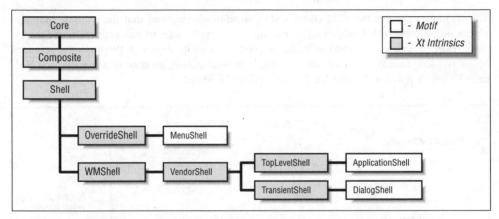

Figure 3-20. The Shell widget class hierarchy

Shells for Menus

In some cases, an application needs to put up a temporary window that is completely free of window manager interaction. Menus are one such a case. When a user pops up a menu, she typically wants to make a choice immediately, and she wants that choice to take precedence over any other window system activity. The window manager does not need to be involved either to decorate or to position the menu, as it is entirely up to the application.

As its name suggests, the OverrideShell widget class is provided for windows that bypass the window manager. OverrideShells are like futons; you can place them on the floor without using a bed-frame (and without being tasteless). It doesn't make much sense to use an OverrideShell as the main window for an application, except possibly for a screen-locking application. The purpose of this type of application is to prevent other applications from appearing on the screen while the computer is left unattended. Because the window manager is unaware of the OverrideShell, it does not provide window manager controls, and it does not interpret window manager accelerators and other methods for bypassing the lock.

The OverrideShell is a generic Xt-based widget class, so the Motif toolkit provides the MenuShell to service the special interface needs required by the *Motif Style Guide*. The MenuShell's translation table is set to support keyboard traversal, its XmNfocusPolicy is set to XmPOINTER, and its XmNallowShellResize resource is set to True. The Menu-Shell also makes sure that its child is a RowColumn widget. There is little more to be said about MenuShells, but for an in-depth discussion on the various types of menus you can use in Motif, see Chapter 15, *Menus*.

Shells for Window Manager Communication

Shell widgets must communicate with the window manager to negotiate screen real estate and a wide variety of other properties. The information that is exchanged is defined by the X Consortium's *Inter-Client Communications Conventions Manual* (ICCCM). The WMShell widget class implements ICCCM-compliant behavior as a standard part of the X Toolkit Intrinsics, so that it is available to all vendors providing Xt-based widget sets and window managers. This shell widget is what allows Motif applications to work correctly with virtually any ICCCM-compliant window manager. In our analogy, a WMShell is a simple, wire bed-frame that doesn't have any special attributes, like wheels or rollers.

The VendorShell widget class is subclassed from the WMShell class; it allows vendors, such as OSF, to define attributes that are specific to their own window managers. In our analogy, this widget class is like having a bed frame that has attached cabinets, shelves above the headboard, or nice wheels that glide on the carpet. The Motif VendorShell is aware of special features of *mwm*. The widget does not actually add any functionality to the window manager, but it is designed for applications that wish to interact with it. For example, all the attributes of window manager decorations can be modified or controlled through resources specific to the VendorShell.

WMShells and VendorShells are never instantiated directly by an application, but the features they provide are available to an application. For example, the Motif VendorShell allows an application to specify the items in the window menu and to control what happens when the user closes the window from the window menu. Chapter 16, *Interacting With the Window Manager*, discusses window manager interactions in more detail.

Shells for Dialogs

You can think of dialog boxes as an application's *secondary windows*. Since dialogs are not meant to remain on the screen for very long, they do not need all of the decorations that are typically provided by the window manager. However, dialogs are not completely independent like menus, so they do need to be controlled by the window manager. For example, if an application is iconified, its dialog boxes are typically iconified as well. Dialog boxes are usually implemented in Xt using TransientShells.

The DialogShell is a Motif-defined widget class subclassed from the TransientShell and VendorShell classes. Motif functions for creating dialog boxes tend to hide the shell widget side of the dialog. When you make a call like `XmCreateMessageDialog()`, you are actually creating a MessageBox widget as a child of a DialogShell widget. See Chapter 5, *Introduction to Dialogs*, for details on Motif dialogs.

Shells for Application Windows

When you initialize the X Toolkit with a call such as `XtAppInitialize()`, you are automatically returned an ApplicationShell widget to use as the top-level widget in your application. If an application uses additional top-level windows, they are typically TopLevelShells. The differences between these two classes are subtle and deal mostly with how resources are specified in a resource file. In Chapter 7, *Custom Dialogs*, we explore some ways in which TopLevelShells can be used as primary windows apart from the main window.

3.4.4 Dialogs

Some applications can get all their work done in one main window. Others may require multiple windows, so Motif allows an application to have multiple top-level windows. However, even applications without this level of complexity need to display transient windows called dialog boxes. Motif provides two main types of dialog boxes: message dialogs and selection dialogs. Message dialogs are designed to allow an application to communicate with the user, while selection dialogs prompt the user to enter different types of information. It is also possible to create custom dialogs for specialized application functionality.

Message Dialogs

Message dialogs simply communicate some kind of message to the user and include buttons that allow the user to respond to the message. For example, a menu item to delete a file might issue a dialog with the message, "Are you sure?" with PushButtons labeled **Yes**, **No**, and **Cancel**.

The Motif MessageBox widget that is used to create message dialogs actually comes in seven different guises. The different styles are meant to be used for different types of messages; some of the styles also display a symbol defined by the *Motif Style Guide*. Motif provides convenience routines for creating all of the different styles, so they are often referred to as if they are distinct widget classes.

ErrorDialog
> The ErrorDialog shows a "do not enter" symbol along with a message that the user has made an error. For example, she may have pressed a PushButton at the wrong time, made an invalid selection in a List widget, or entered an unknown filename for a Text widget.

InformationDialog
> The InformationDialog displays an "i" along with an informational message. These dialogs are usually displayed in response to a request for help.

MessageDialog

The MessageDialog does not display a symbol by default, although a symbol can be specified using the `XmNsymbolPixmap` resource. These dialogs can be used to display any kind of message.

QuestionDialog

The QuestionDialog shows a question mark symbol with a question that the user needs to answer. Questions are typically of the yes/no form, so the possible answers typically include **Yes** and **No**. A QuestionDialog should not be used for a question that requires an answer in the form of text or a selection from a list of some kind.

TemplateDialog

Motif 1.2 provides a TemplateDialog to allow an application to create a custom dialog. By default, the TemplateDialog does not display a symbol or a message, but these items can be added to the dialog.

WarningDialog

The WarningDialog displays an exclamation mark along with a message that warns the user about a particular situation. These dialogs are commonly used to make sure that the user wants to do something destructive, like delete a file or exit an application without saving data.

WorkingDialog

The WorkingDialog displays an hourglass with a message indicating that the application is busy processing a lengthy computation or anything else that requires the user to wait.

Figure 3-21 shows a typical QuestionDialog in an application. For more information on message dialogs, see Chapter 5, *Introduction to Dialogs*.

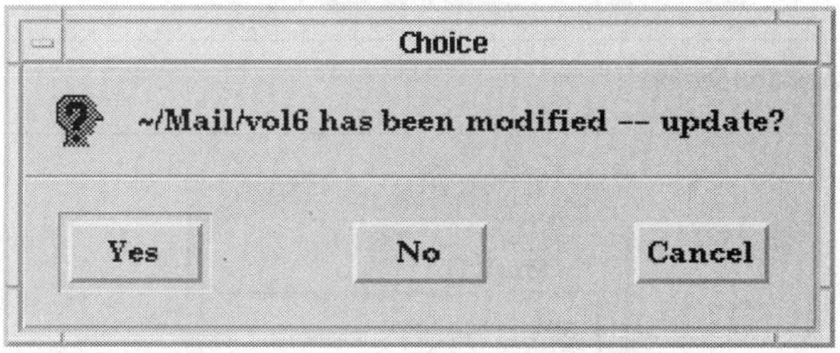

Figure 3-21. A QuestionDialog

Selection Dialogs

Selection dialogs are meant to provide the user with a list of choices of some sort. Motif provides different styles of selection dialogs for different purposes. For example, a SelectionDialog presents a ScrolledList containing an arbitrary list of choices that can be selected with the mouse. The dialog also contains a TextField widget that can be used to type in a choice which may or may not also be on the list. Figure 3-22 shows a SelectionDialog.

The PromptDialog, as shown in Figure 3-23, is useful for prompting the user to enter some information.

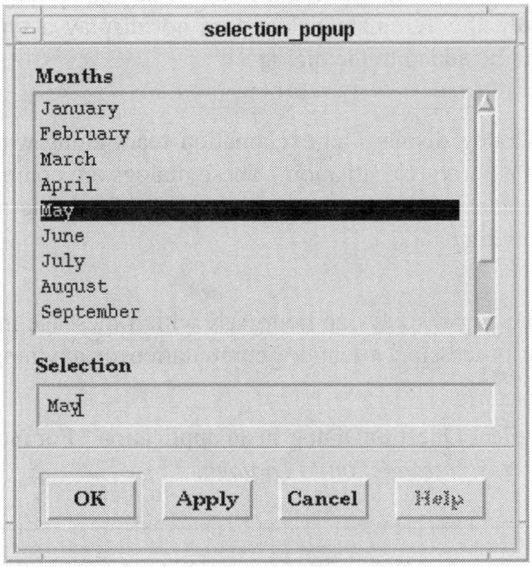

Figure 3-22. A SelectionDialog

Figure 3-23. A PromptDialog

The FileSelectionDialog is a more complex cousin to the SelectionDialog. It is used to select a file in the directory structure. A FileSelectionDialog is shown in Figure 3-24.

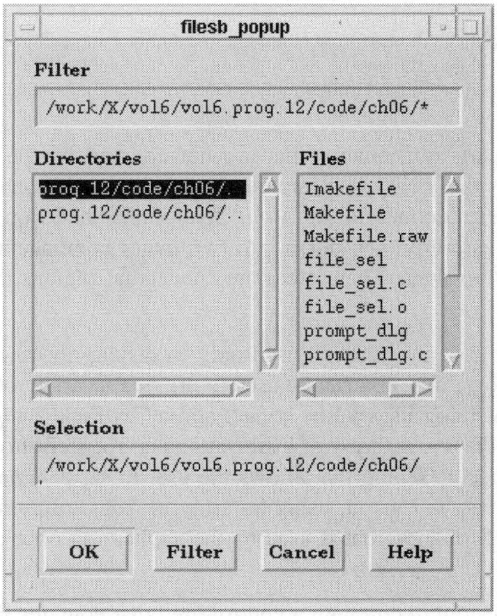

Figure 3-24. A FileSelectionDialog

The CommandDialog is an extension of the PromptDialog in that items input to the text entry field are stored in a ScrolledList. The intent is for the user to provide the application with commands; the list region contains a history of the commands that have already been typed. The user can select an item in the history list to reissue a previous command. Figure 3-25 shows an example of a CommandDialog.

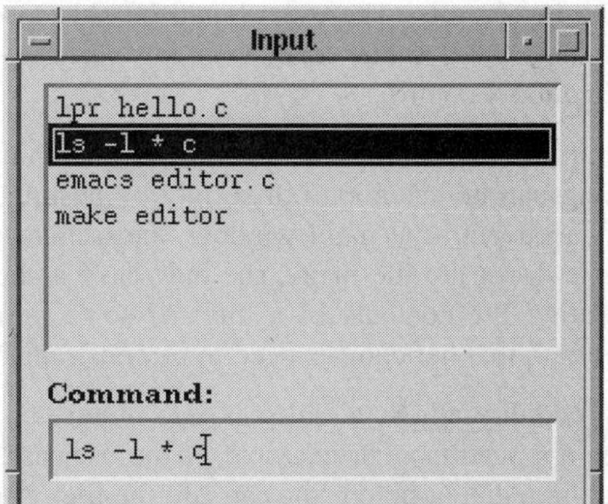

Figure 3-25. A CommandDialog

Overview of
the Motif Toolkit

For detailed information about all of the different Motif selection dialogs, see Chapter 6, *Selection Dialogs*.

Custom Dialogs

There are many types of functionality that are not covered by the standard Motif dialog types. Fortunately, it is fairly easy to create your own dialogs. If you need to create a custom dialog, there are some guidelines in the *Motif Style Guide* that you should follow. At the highest level, all dialogs are broken down into two major components: the *control area* (or work area) and the *action area*. These areas are conceptual regions that may be represented by multiple widgets.

In a message dialog, the control area is used only to display messages, but as you can see from the selection dialogs, this area can be used to provide a variety of control elements. For example, the SelectionDialog uses a List widget and a TextField widget. It is also common for a custom dialog to display an array of PushButtons or ToggleButtons. A communications program might have a setup dialog that allows the user to set parameters such as baud rate, parity, start and stop bits, and so on, using an array of ToggleButtons. The controls in the control area provide information that is used by the application once an action area button is pressed.

Figure 3-26 shows a custom dialog with a control area that contains many items. Chapter 7, *Custom Dialogs*, discusses how to build customized dialogs, which may require the direct creation of widgets in the control area. Motif dialogs, on the other hand, do not require you to create any of the objects in the control area. The widgets displayed in that part of the dialog are always predefined and automatically created.

Dialog Modality

One important concept to be aware of when it comes to dialogs is *modality*. In general, GUI-based programs are expected to be modeless. What this ultimately means is that the user, not the application, should be in control. The user should be able to choose from an array of application functions at any time, rather than stepping through them in a prearranged sequence, under the application's control.

Of course, there are limits to modelessness. Sometimes one thing has to happen before another. Often, sequencing can be taken care of simply by nesting graphical user interface elements. For example, faced with the main window, the user may have only a choice of menu titles; once she pulls down the file menu, she may have a choice of opening, closing, saving, renaming, or printing the contents of a file. At some point, though, she goes far enough down a particular path that her choices need to be constrained.

With respect to dialogs, modality allows a dialog box to require and before the user can go back to working with the application. For example, if the user asks to load a file, she may need to specify a filename in a dialog before she can edit the file. A modal dialog requires an answer immediately, by disallowing input to any other part of the application until it is either satisfied or cancelled. There may be other cases, though, where dialogs are modeless. They can be left up on the screen without an immediate response, while the user interacts with the main application window or another dialog.

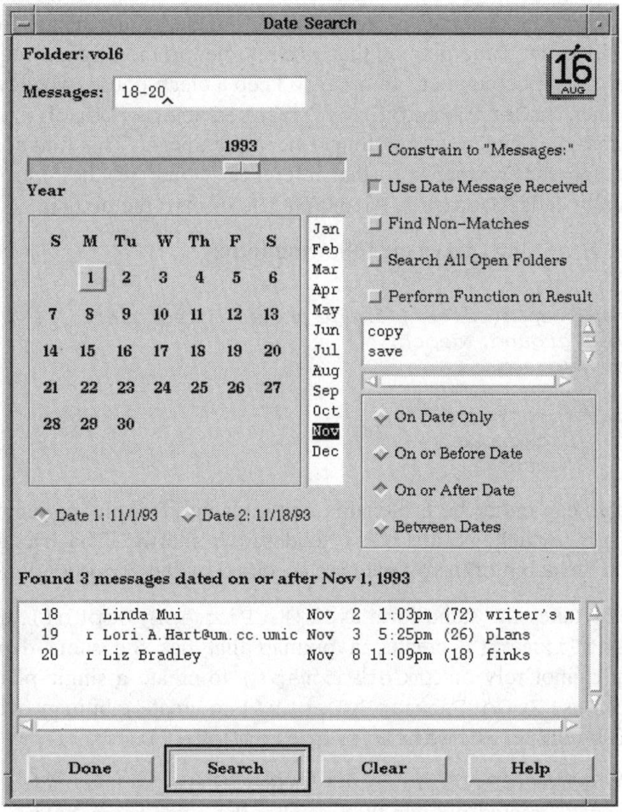

Figure 3-26. A custom dialog

3.4.5 Pixmaps

In this section, we are going to take a closer look at how Motif supports graphic images. The Motif Label widget and all of its subclasses can display pixmaps as their labels. The MessageBox provides the XmNsymbolPixmap resource for specifying the image that is displayed in a dialog.

The Motif toolkit provides a number of routines for manipulating pixmaps. XmGet-PixmapByDepth() and XmGetPixmap() both create a pixmap and cache it, so that it can be reused by an application. XmGetPixmapByDepth() is new in Motif 1.2; it provides a way to specify the depth of the pixmap that is created. XmGetPixmap() always creates a pixmap that has the same depth as the screen on which image is created. The caching mechanism provided by these routines is on a per-client basis; different processes cannot share pixmaps.

Whenever a new pixmap is created using one of these functions, the toolkit retains a handle to the pixmap in case another call is made requesting the same image. If this occurs, the function returns the exact same pixmap that was returned to the original requestor and increments an internal reference counter. In order to keep a clean house, whenever you retrieve a pixmap using either XmGetPixmap() or XmGetPixmapByDepth(), you should call XmDestroyPixmap() when you no longer need the image. This function decrements the reference count for the pixmap. If the reference count reaches zero, XmDestroy-Pixmap() actually calls XDestroyPixmap() to discard the pixmap.

XmGetPixmapByDepth() takes the following form:

```
Pixmap
XmGetPixmapByDepth(screen, image_name, foreground,
        background, depth)
    Screen *screen;
    char    *image_name;
    Pixel   foreground;
    Pixel   background;
    int     depth;
```

The *image_name* can either be a filename or the name of an image registered using Xm-InstallImage(), which we are going to describe shortly. The background and foreground colors and the depth of the pixmap are specified by the corresponding parameters.

XmGetPixmap() takes the same form as XmGetPixmapByDepth(), minus the *depth* parameter. XmGetPixmap() creates a pixmap that has the same depth as the given *screen*, so you cannot rely on XmGetPixmap() to create a single-plane pixmap.† In Motif 1.2, you can use XmGetPixmapByDepth() to create a bitmap; with Motif 1.1 you have to use an Xlib routine, XCreateBitmapFromData().

Whenever XmGetPixmapByDepth() or XmGetPixmap() is called, it looks in the cache for a previously-created pixmap that matches the given name, colors, and depth. If the routine finds a match, it returns the cached pixmap and increments the reference count for the image. Since the pixmaps are cached, two separate parts of an application could have a handle to the same pixmap.

The *image_name* parameter is the key to where the routines get the data for the pixmap. As we just mentioned, this parameter can either be a filename or a symbolic name previously registered using XmInstallImage(). Both XmGetPixmap() and XmGetPixmap-ByDepth() use the following algorithm to determine what pixmap to return or create:

1. Look in the pixmap cache for an image that has the same *screen*, *image_name*, *foreground*, *background*, and *depth* as the specified image. If there is a match, return the pixmap.

2. If there is no match in the pixmap cache, look in the image cache for an image that matches the specified *image_name*. If there is a match, use the image to create the pixmap that is returned.

---

† The terms single-bit and single-plane are interchangeable; they imply a pixmap with only two colors: 0 and 1. While the term *bitmap* usually refers to a single-plane pixmap, this is not necessarily true outside of the X social culture.

3. Otherwise, interpret the *image_name* as a filename, read the pixmap data directly out of that file, and create the pixmap.

The first step is fairly straightforward. The second step checks the image cache that is used internally by the Motif toolkit. Motif defines a number of images that you can use in an application. Table 3-1 lists the image names predefined by the toolkit.

Table 3-1. Predefined Image Names in the Motif Toolkit

Image Name	Description
background	Solid background tile
25_foreground	A 25% foreground, 75% background tile
50_foreground	A 50% foreground, 50% background tile
75_foreground	A 75% foreground, 25% background tile
horizontal	Horizontal lines tile
vertical	Vertical lines tile
slant_left	Left slanting lines tile
slant_right	Right slanting lines tile

Motif also installs a number of images at run-time to support dialog images and other random pixmaps. None of these image names are publicly available. You can install your own images by predefining them and loading them into the image cache using XmInstall-Image(), which takes the following form:

```
Boolean
XmInstallImage(image, image_name)
    XImage  *image;
    char    *image_name;
```

The *image* parameter is a pointer to an XImage data structure that has been previously created or, more commonly, statically initialized by the application. It is possible to create an image dynamically from an existing window or pixmap using XGetImage(), but this is not the way the function is typically used.

If you attempt to install an image using an *image_name* that matches one already in the cache, the function returns False and the image is not installed. Otherwise, the function returns True. You can uninstall an image by calling XmUninstallImage(). Once the image is uninstalled, it cannot be referenced by name anymore and a new image may be installed with the same name. The XImage structure is not copied by XmInstall-Image(), so if the image pointer you pass has been allocated using XCreateImage() or XGetImage(), you must not free the data until after you call XmUninstallImage().

If XmGetPixmap() or XmGetPixmapByDepth() finds a match in the image cache, it creates the pixmap based on the image data, not on the image itself. As a result, the pixmap that is created is not affected by the image being uninstalled by XmUninstallImage().

If the pixmap retrieval routines do not find a match in the image cache, the pixmap is loaded from a file. If *image_name* starts with a slash character (/), it is taken as a full pathname. Otherwise, the routines look for the file using a search path. On POSIX systems, the environment variable XBMLANGPATH can be set to specify a desired directory in which to search for bitmap files. If this variable is not set, the pathname used is based on the values of the XAPPLRESDIR, HOME, and LANG environment variables. See the reference page in Volume Six B, *Motif Reference Manual*, for complete details on the search path that is used.

When XmGetPixmap() or XmGetPixmapByDepth() looks in the pixmap cache for a image name, the pathname must match completely for the routine to return a cached image. The file *xlogo64* will not match a previously-loaded pixmap that has the name */usr/include/X11/bitmaps/xlogo64*. If you do not need to worry about using different pixmaps for different environments, we recommended that you always specify a full pathname to these routines to be assured that you get the desired file.

3.4.6 Color

Color plays an important role in a graphical user interface. It appeals to the senses, so it can provide an aesthetic quality, while at the same time it can be used to convey information to the user. However, for all the power of color, it is frequently abused by applications. A color combination that appeals to some people may offend others. The safest bet with color is to avoid hard-coding any use of color in your application and provide enough flexibility so that the user can configure colors in a resource file or interactively using the application. Of course, many applications are based on the use of color, so this sweeping generalization only applies to those parts of an application that are not dependent on color.

The Motif widget set provides a number of widget resources that specify colors. All of the Motif widgets use the XmNforeground and XmNbackground resources. However, Motif gadgets do not use these resources because they are rendered using the foreground and background colors of their parent. Although every widget class makes different use of the XmNbackground and foreground resources, text is typically rendered in the foreground color and everything else is shown using the background color. Some widgets provide additional color resources for particular aspects of their appearance. For example, ToggleButtons use the XmNselectColor resource for the square/diamond selection indicator, PushButtons use XmNarmColor as their background when they are armed, and ScrollBars use XmNtroughColor to set the color of the area behind the slider and directional arrows.

The XmNborderColor resource is another resource that can be specified for any widget, as it is defined by the Core widget class. Since Motif widgets typically have a border width of 0, this resource is rarely used. The XmNhighlightColor resource specifies the color of the highlighting rectangle that is displayed around the interface component that has the keyboard focus. This resource is defined by the Gadget, Manager, and Primitive metaclasses, so it can be specified for any Motif component.

Perhaps the most troublesome of all the color resources are XmNtopShadowColor and XmNbottomShadowColor. These are the colors that give Motif widgets their 3D appearance on a color display. If set inappropriately, these colors can ruin the aesthetics of a interface. These resources are set automatically by the toolkit based on the background color of the object, so the colors are not normally a problem. If the background color of a PushButton is blue when it is created, the toolkit automatically calculates the XmNtopShadowColor to be a slightly lighter shade of blue and the `XmNbottomShadowColor` to be a slightly darker shade.

The problems arise if you want to change the background color of a widget dynamically because the toolkit does not automatically change the shadow colors for you. So if you change the `XmNbackground` of the PushButton to red, the top and bottom shadow colors remain the different shades of blue. It is important to note that the shadow resources are only used by widgets, not gadgets. If you dynamically change the background color of a manager widget, it automatically recalculates the top and bottom shadow colors and redisplays its gadgets correctly. Many consider the fact that this process is not automated for widgets to be a design flaw in the Motif toolkit.

If you need to change the background color of a widget dynamically, you can recalculate the shadow colors and set the resources yourself. If you are using Motif 1.2, you can use the new `XmChangeColor()` routine, which takes the following form:

```
void
XmChangeColor(widget, background)
    Widget   widget;
    Pixel    background;
```

This routine changes all the foreground color, shadow colors, and select color for the specified *widget* based on the *background* color. The select color only applies to Toggle-Buttons (`XmNselectColor`) and PushButtons (`XmNarmColor`).

If you are using Motif 1.1, you have to do a bit more work to change the colors for a widget. In this case, you need to use `XmGetColors()`, which takes the following form:

```
void
XmGetColors(screen, colormap, bg, fg, top_shadow,
        bottom_shadow, select)
    Screen   *screen;
    Colormap colormap;
    Pixel    bg;
    Pixel    *fg;
    Pixel    *top_shadow;
    Pixel    *bottom_shadow;
    Pixel    *select;
```

This routine takes a colormap and a background color and calculates and returns an appropriate foreground color, top and bottom shadow colors, and select color. Once you have the colors, you need to specify the appropriate resources for the widget. The following code fragment demonstrates how to set the background of a PushButton to red:

```
Pixel bg, top_shadow, bottom_shadow, fg, select_color;
Colormap cmap;
Widget pb;

/* First, set the background color to red... */
XtVaSetValues (pb,
    XtVaTypedArg, XmNbackground, XmRString, "red", 4,/* strlen("red")+1 */
    NULL);

/* Once set, get it again, so we know what pixel value it got.
 * Also get the widget's colormap, since we'll be setting its new
 * colors based on the same colormap.
 */
```

```
XtVaGetValues (pb,
    XmNbackground, &bg,
    XmNcolormap,    &cmap,
    NULL);

/* Let Motif calculate the new colors based on that one color */
XmGetColors (XtScreen (pb), cmap, bg, &fg,
    &top_shadow, &bottom_shadow, &select_color);

/* Set the colors accordingly. */
XtVaSetValues (pb,
    XmNtopShadowColor,    top_shadow,
    XmNbottomShadowColor, bottom_shadow,
    XmNarmColor,          select_color,
    XmNborderColor,       fg,
    NULL);
```

A basic problem behind setting and getting colors for widgets is that what you get for a given pixel value depends on the colormap. A pixel is simply an index value into an array of color definitions (a colormap). The problem with colormaps is that you never know what colormap is associated with any particular widget.

By calling `XtVaSetValues()` using the type-converting resource, `XtVaTypedArg`, we defer the problem to the toolkit and its string-to-color type converter. The toolkit allocates the color out of the colormap already owned by the toolkit and sets the background color accordingly. Then we can get the actual pixel value and the colormap using `XtVaGet-Values()`. We pass the colormap and the background pixel value to `XmGetColors()` to calculate the rest of the colors. Once we have obtained all of the colors, we can set them using `XtVaSetValues()`.

The Label widget and its subclasses cannot display text using more than one color. However, you can create a multi-plane pixmap and render various strings directly into it using `XDraw-String()`. You can use multiple colors by changing the foreground color in the GC using `XSetForeground()` or `XChangeGC()`. Once you have the pixmap, you can use it to set the `XmNlabelPixmap` resource for the widget.

The text of the entries in a List widget is rendered using the widget's `XmNforeground` color. You cannot change the color of individual items in a List widget. The `XmN-background` of the List affects all areas of the widget not associated with the entries themselves. The text in a Text widget or a TextField widget is also displayed using the `XmN-foreground` color; there is no way to display text using different colors in these widgets. When a List widget or Text widget is the direct child of a ScrolledWindow, the ScrollBars automatically match the background color of the List or Text widget.

3.5 Changes in Motif 1.2

Release 1.2 of the Motif toolkit introduces a number of new features, as well as many enhancements to existing functionality. This section summarizes all of the changes in Motif 1.2 and refers you to other sections in the book for more detailed information on specific changes. We also describe the changes that we made to the example programs in the book to make them accurate with respect to Motif 1.2.

3.5.1 General Toolkit Changes

Many of the changes in Motif 1.2 affect the functionality of the toolkit as whole, rather than individual widget classes. This release demonstrates performance improvements, as the code has been reorganized to improve locality and dynamic memory usage has been reduced. The toolkit also benefits from the improved performance of the X11R5 translation manager. Motif 1.2 provides a new header file, *<Xm/XmAll.h>*, that includes all of the public header files for the toolkit. The *<Xm/ExtObject.h>*, *<Xm/Traversal.h>*, *<Xm/VaSimple.h>*, and *<Xm/VendorE.h>* header files that are present in Motif 1.1 are obsolete in Motif 1.2.

Internationalization

The addition of internationalization capabilities is one of the major enhancements provided by Motif 1.2. An internationalized application can run in different language environments without any modification. Most of the support for developing internationalized applications in Motif is based on features provided by X11R5. Xlib provides support for internationalized text output, interclient communication, and localization of the resource database, while Xt handles establishing the locale. See Section 2.3.2 in Chapter 2, *The Motif Programming Model*, for more information on establishing the language environment in an Xt-based application; refer to Volume One, *Xlib Programming Manual*, for a description of the internationalization features in X11R5.

The Text and TextField widgets have been modified to support internationalized text input and output; see Section 14.6 in Chapter 14, *Text Widgets*, for more information. The Motif routines that manipulate compound strings and font lists have also been updated for Motif 1.2. See Chapter 19, *Compound Strings*, for details on the new API for XmString and Xm-FontList values.

Drag and Drop

The ability to transfer data using the drag and drop metaphor is another major new feature in Motif 1.2. Drag and drop allows the user to select a data source, drag the data around on the display, and drop the data on a new location. The drag and drop mechanism handles data transfer both within and between applications. The Label widget and its subclasses, the List widget, and the Text and TextField widgets all provide built-in drag and drop capabilities. The toolkit also provides some new objects and routines that can be used to implement custom drag and drop functionality. In Chapter 18, *Drag and Drop*, we describe the Motif drag and drop model and the objects that implement it, and we present some examples of providing custom drag and drop functionality in an application.

Tear-Off Menus

Motif provides a new feature in menus that allows them to be torn off and displayed in separate windows. Tear-off menus make it easy for the user to make repeated selections from a menu. Normally, when a menu is posted, it is only displayed until a selection is made, and then it is removed. If the menu has been torn off, it is placed in its own window and remains available for the user to make multiple selections. The tear-off functionality is activated by a special tear-off button in the menu. The button displays a dashed line to indicate that the menu can be torn off, much as a coupon is torn out of a newspaper. Tear-off functionality is provided for all of the Motif menu types; it is controlled by the XmNtearOffModel resource of the RowColumn widget. See Section 15.3.7 in Chapter 15, *Menus*, for a more complete description of tear-off menus.

Display and Screen Objects

The new Display and Screen objects store per-display and per-screen resources and data. These objects essentially provide a way for the toolkit to keep track of information about the display and the screen that it needs to access frequently. When Motif creates the first shell on a particular display or screen, it creates a Display or Screen object automatically. An application can retrieve the Display and Screen objects using XmGetXmDisplay() and XmGetXmScreen(), respectively. Values for the resources defined by the Display and Screen objects can be set in a resource file or in a program using XtVaSetValues(), and they can be retrieved using XtVaGetValues().

The Display object defines resources that an application can set to control the behavior of the application on the display. The XmNdragInitiatorProtocolStyle and XmNdragReceiverProtocolStyle resources specify the protocol used during a drag and drop transfer, as described in Section 18.3.1, while XmNdefaultVirtualBindings sets the default virtual bindings for the display. For a complete description of the Display object, see the reference page in Volume Six B, *Motif Reference Manual*.

The Screen object defines a number of resources that control the default drag icons used during drag and drop; see Section 18.3.3 for a discussion of these resources. The XmNdarkThreshold, XmNforegroundThreshold, and XmNlightThreshold resources specify values that affect the default color calculation algorithm, as we describe shortly.

The XmNfont, XmNhorizontalFontUnit, and XmNverticalFontUnit resources specify the font units that are used to convert geometry values when the Xm100TH_FONT_UNITS value is being used for units. These resources make the XmSetFontUnit() and XmSetFontUnits() routines in Motif 1.1 obsolete.

The XmNmenuCursor resource controls the pointer shape that is used when a menu is posted; the resource supercedes the XmGetMenuCursor() and XmSetMenuCursor() functions in Motif 1.1. The XmNunpostBehavior resource indicates the behavior of a menu when the mouse button is pressed outside of the menu. The value XmUNPOST_AND_REPLAY unposts the menu hierarchy and replays the event, while

XmUNPOST just unposts the menu. For more information on the various Screen resources, see the reference page in Volume Six B, *Motif Reference Manual*.

Keyboard Traversal

Motif provides a number of new functions that support better control of keyboard traversal. The XmGetFocusWidget() routine returns the widget that has the input focus, while XmGetTabGroup() returns the widget that is the tab group for the specified widget. An application can also call XmIsTraversable() to determine whether or not a particular widget is eligible to receive the input focus. See Section 8.8 in Chapter 8, *Manager Widgets*, for more information about keyboard traversal.

The Manager widget class defines the XmNinitialFocus resource to allow an application to specify the widget that has the initial keyboard focus in a dialog. This resource can be used for both MessageDialogs and SelectionDialogs, although it is normally only used for SelectionDialogs. The resource specifies the widget that has the keyboard focus the first time that the dialog is popped up, as described in Section 5.4.2 in Chapter 5, *Introduction to Dialogs*.

The XmTrackingEvent() routine in Motif 1.2 replaces the existing XmTracking-Locate() routine for implementing context-sensitive help. XmTrackingEvent() works for both keyboard and mouse events, and it returns the widget selected by the user, regardless of whether or not the widget is sensitive to input. The routine also returns the actual event performed by the user, as explained in Section 21.1.2 in Chapter 21, *Advanced Dialog Programming*.

Resource Management

Motif 1.2 provides a representation type manager to handle many of the tasks related to enumerated values, such as installing resource converters that convert string values to their numerical representations. The toolkit provides following functions for managing representation types:

```
XmRepTypeAddReverse()
XmRepTypeGetId()
XmRepTypeGetNameList()
XmRepTypeGetRecord()
XmRepTypeGetRegistered()
XmRepTypeRegister()
XmRepTypeValidValue()
```

For more information about these routines, see the appropriate reference pages in Volume Six B, *Motif Reference Manual*.

Motif also provides a name-to-widget converter in this release so that widgets can be specified in resource files. This converter is most useful for specifying Form attachments in a resource file. The converter uses XtNameToWidget() from the parent of the widget specified on the left-hand side of the resource specification.

Overview of the Motif Toolkit

Virtual Bindings

Motif includes the new *xmbind* client that configures the virtual key bindings for Motif applications. This action is performed at startup by the Motif Window Manager (*mwm*) or any application that uses the Motif toolkit, so an application only needs to use *xmbind* if it wants to reconfigure the bindings without restarting *mwm* or a Motif application. The toolkit also provides a new function, XmTranslateKey(), to translate a keycode into a virtual keysym. This function allows an application that overrides the default XtKeyProc to handle Motif's virtual key bindings. See Section 2.3.6 in Chapter 2, *The Motif Programming Model*, for more information on virtual bindings.

Color

The new XmChangeColor() routine changes the foreground color, shadow colors, and select color for a widget based on a background color. The XmNdarkThreshold, XmNforegroundThreshold, and XmNlightThreshold resources of the Screen object allow the application or the user to set values that affect the default color calculation algorithm. The values for these resources indicate the levels of perceived brightness (between 0 and 100) that distinguish between a light color and a dark color. The XmNforeground-Threshold value is used in calculating the default foreground and highlight colors, while the other two resources are used in calculating the default shadow and select colors. See Section 3.4.6 for a discussion of color resources in Motif.

Layout

An application can use the new XmWidgetGetBaselines() routine to get the position of the text baseline in a widget, while XmWidgetGetDisplayRect() can be used to get the size and position of the bounding box for the widget. These routines provide information that is useful in laying out and aligning components in an interface.

3.5.2 Specific Widget Changes

Motif 1.2 also introduces a number of new features, including resources and callback routines, for individual widget classes.

Frame

In Motif 1.2, the Frame widget can have two children: a work area and a title. The Frame draws a border around its work area child and adds space for a title if one is specified. The XmNchildType constraint resource specifies whether a child is the work area or the title. This resource can have either the value XmFRAME_WORKAREA_CHILD or Xm-FRAME_TITLE_CHILD. The XmNchildHorizontalAlignment, XmNchild-HorizontalSpacing, and XmNchildVerticalAlignment constraint resources control the positioning of the title child. For more information on these resources, see Section 8.6 in Chapter 8, *Manager Widgets*.

Label

The Label widget functions as a drag source for drag and drop, as described in Chapter 18, *Drag and Drop*. The `ProcessDrag()` action routine, which is bound to the second mouse button, handles this functionality.

List

The List widget provides the following new functions for managing list items:

```
XmListAddItemUnselected()
XmListDeletePositions()
XmListGetKbdItemPos()
XmListPosSelected()
XmListPosToBounds()
XmListReplaceItemsPosUnselected()
XmListReplaceItemsUnselected()
XmListReplacePositions()
XmListSetKbdItemPos()
XmListUpdateSelectedList()
XmListYToPos()
```

For more information on these routines, see Chapter 12, *The List Widget*, and the appropriate reference pages in Volume Six B, *Motif Reference Manual*.

When a List widget is set insensitive, it provides visual indication by greying out all of its items. The default value of the `XmNvisibleItemCount` resource is now set dynamically, based on the item count and the height of the List.

The List widget functions as a drag source for drag and drop, as described in Chapter 18, *Drag and Drop*. The `ListProcessDrag()` action routine, which is bound to the second mouse button, handles this functionality. The List also has a `ListCopyToClipboard()` action routine for copying the selected items to the clipboard, as well as a `ListScroll-CursorVertically()` routine for scrolling the cursor vertically based on a y-position.

MessageBox

The MessageBox widget supports the addition of a MenuBar child, a work area child, and multiple PushButton children. The `XmNdialogType` resource can also be set to the value `XmDIALOG_TEMPLATE` to create a MessageBox that can be used as a template for creating a custom dialog. Section 7.1.1 in Chapter 7, *Custom Dialogs*, describes the template dialog in more detail.

PanedWindow

The PanedWindow defines a new constraint resource, XmNpositionIndex, for specifying the position of a child widget in the PanedWindow's list of children. The children are positioned vertically in the PanedWindow according to this list. The list of children does not include the Sashes. A value of 0 indicates the beginning of the list, while XmLAST_POSITION places the child at the end of the list.

RowColumn

The RowColumn widget provides a new resource for controlling the alignment of its children. The XmNentryVerticalAlignment resource controls the vertical positioning of children that are subclasses of Label, LabelGadget, and Text, as described in Section 8.5 in Chapter 8, *Manager Widgets*.

The RowColumn widget also defines the XmNpositionIndex constraint resource for specifying the position of a child widget in the RowColumn's list of children. The children are positioned in the RowColumn according to this list. A value of 0 indicates the beginning of the list, while XmLAST_POSITION places the child at the end of the list.

The XmNtearOffModel resource of the RowColumn widget controls tear-off functionality in Motif menus. The widget also defines the XmNtearOffMenuActivateCallback and XmNtearOffMenuDeactivateCallback callback routines for performing any special processing that is necessary for handling tear-off menus. Tear-off functionality is described in detail in Section 15.3.7 in Chapter 15, *Menus*.

ScrollBar

When a ScrollBar is set insensitive, it provides a visual indication of this state by dimming itself. The ScrollBar also has new action routine, CancelDrag(), that cancels the current slider drag. When the user presses the ESCAPE key while the slider is being dragged, the action is invoked.

ScrolledWindow

In Motif 1.2, the ScrolledWindow has a new callback that supports keyboard traversal. The XmNtraverseObscuredCallback is invoked when the user attempts to traverse to a widget that is not visible in a ScrolledWindow. An application can use this callback to make a widget visible in a ScrolledWindow so that the widget can receive the input focus. The XmScrollVisible() routine makes an obscured child of a ScrolledWindow visible, while XmGetVisibility() determines whether or not a widget is visible. See Section 9.5 in Chapter 9, *ScrolledWindows and ScrollBars*, for more information on keyboard traversal in ScrolledWindows.

SelectionBox and FileSelectionBox

The SelectionBox and FileSelectionBox widgets now support the addition of a MenuBar child and multiple PushButton children in addition to the work area child that was supported in Motif 1.1. The new `XmNchildPlacement` resource controls the location of the work area child, as described in Section 7.1.2 in Chapter 7, *Custom Dialogs*.

Text and TextField

The Text and TextField widgets have a number of new resources and callback routines that support wide-character strings. These changes have been made for internationalization purposes and are described in Section 14.6 in Chapter 14, *Text Widgets*. The widgets function as drag sources and drop sites for drag and drop, as described in Chapter 18, *Drag and Drop*.

The insertion position in the Text and TextField widgets is marked by an I-beam cursor. The destination cursor now follows the insertion cursor, so it is no longer drawn independently as a caret (^). When a Text or TextField widget is set insensitive, it provides a visual indication of this state by greying out its text and its insertion cursor. Both the Text and TextField widgets provide the `toggle-overstrike()` action routine for switching between insert and overstrike modes. The Text widget also provides the `scroll-cursor-vertically()` action to scroll the cursor based on a y position. When the user moves the pointer outside of a Text widget while selecting text, the widget continues selecting text by scrolling automatically after a time delay.

The new `XmTextDisableRedisplay()` and `XmTextEnableRedisplay()` routines provide a way to control visual updating in a Text widget. The `XmTextFindString()`, `XmTextGetSubstring()`, and `XmTextFieldGetSubstring()` functions make string manipulation easier. For more information on these routines, see the appropriate reference pages in Volume Six B, *Motif Reference Manual*. The TextField widget also has an `XmNfocusCallback` in Motif 1.2. The performance of scrolling in the ScrolledText object has been improved in Motif 1.2. One unfortunate side-effect of this improvement is that it introduces a new data structure, which means that subclasses of the Motif 1.1 Text widget may break under Motif 1.2.

ToggleButton

If `XmNfillOnSelect` is explicitly set to `True` when `XmNindicatorOn` is `False`, the background of the ToggleButton is set to the `XmNselectColor` when the button is on.

VendorShell

The VendorShell provides the `XmNaudibleWarning` resource to specify whether or not an audible cue accompanies a warning message. The default value is `XmBELL`, but the resource can also be set to `XmNONE`. The value of the `XmNverifyBell` resource of the Text and TextField widgets is based on the new VendorShell resource.

The VendorShell defines the XmNbuttonFontList, XmNlabelFontList, and XmN-textFontList resources to replace the existing XmNdefaultFontList resource. The new resources specify the font lists for the specific types of children of the VendorShell.

The VendorShell also defines the XmNinputMethod and XmNpreeditType resources for controlling internationalized text input. XmNinputMethod specifies the input method for the application, while XmNpreeditType indicates the input method styles that are available. The syntax and possible values of both of these resources are vendor-specific, as discussed in Section 14.6 in Chapter 14, *Text Widgets*.

3.5.3 Changes to the Example Programs

All of the example programs in this book have been updated to Motif 1.2 and X11R5. Some of the changes are quite repetitive and are described in the following list:

- A call to XtSetLanguageProc() has been added to the beginning of each example program, as described in Section 2.3.2.

- Any calls to XmStringCreateSimple() have been replaced with calls to Xm-StringCreateLocalized(), as explained in Section 19.2.1.

- Any references to XmSTRING_DEFAULT_CHARSET have been replaced with references to XmFONTLIST_DEFAULT_TAG, as discussed in Section 19.2.2.

- Any calls to XmFontListAdd() and XmFontListCreate() have been replaced with calls to XmFontListAppendEntry(), as described in Section 19.4.

The rest of the changes involve using new Motif 1.2 functions and resources. These changes are described in detail when each example is presented.

3.6 Summary

The Motif widget set gives you a great deal of flexibility in designing an application. But with this flexibility can come indecision, or even confusion, about the most effective way to use these objects. If you want to give a user a set of exclusive choices, should you use a PulldownMenu, a dialog box that contains ToggleButtons arranged in a CheckBox, or a List widget? There is no right answer—or perhaps it is better to say that the right answer depends on the nature of the choices and the flow of control in your application.

Designing an effective user-interface is an art. Only experience and experimentation can teach you the most effective way to organize an application. What we can do in this book is teach you how to use each widget class and give you a sense of the tradeoffs involved in using different widgets. In this chapter, we've given you a broad overview of the Motif toolkit. Subsequent chapters delve into each widget class in detail. You should be able to read the chapters in any order, as the needs of your application dictate.

4

The Main Window

This chapter describes the Motif MainWindow widget, which can be used to frame many types of applications. The MainWindow is a manager widget that provides a menu bar, a scrollable work area, and various other optional display and control areas.

In This Chapter:

The Main Window

As discussed in Chapter 3, *Overview of the Motif Toolkit*, the main window of an application is the most visible and the most used of all the windows in an application. It is the focal point of the user's interactions with the program, and it is typically the place where the application provides most of its visual feedback. To encourage consistency across the desktop, the *Motif Style Guide* suggests a generic main window layout, which can vary from application to application, but is generally followed by most Motif applications. Such a layout is shown in Figure 4-1. As described in Section 3.4.1, a main window can provide a menu bar, a work area, horizontal and vertical scrollbars, a command area, and a message area.

In an effort to facilitate the task of building a main window, the Motif toolkit provides the MainWindow widget. This widget supports the different areas of the generic main window layout. However, the MainWindow widget is not the only way to handle the layout of the main window of your application. You are not required to use the MainWindow widget and you should not feel that you need to follow the Motif specifications to the letter. While the *Style Guide* strongly recommends using the main window layout, many applications simply do not fit the standard GUI design model. For example, a clock application, a terminal emulator, a calculator, and a host of other desktop applications do not follow the Motif specifications in this regard, but they can still have Motif elements within them and can still be regarded as Motif-compliant. If you already have an application in mind, chances are you already know whether or not the main window layout is suited to the application; if you are in doubt, your best bet is to comply with the *Motif Style Guide*.

Before we start discussing the MainWindow widget, you should realize that this widget class does not create any of the widgets it manages. It merely facilitates managing the widgets in a way that is consistent with the *Style Guide*. In order to discuss the MainWindow widget, we are going to have to discuss a number of other widget classes and use them in examples. As a beginning chapter in a large book on Motif programming, this may seem like a bit much to handle, especially if you are completely unfamiliar with the Motif toolkit. We encourage you to branch off into other chapters whenever you find it necessary to do so. However, it is not our intention to explain these other widgets ahead of time, nor is it our assumption that you already understand them. The lack of an understanding of the other widgets should not interfere with our goal of describing the MainWindow widget and how it fits into the design of an application.

The Main Window

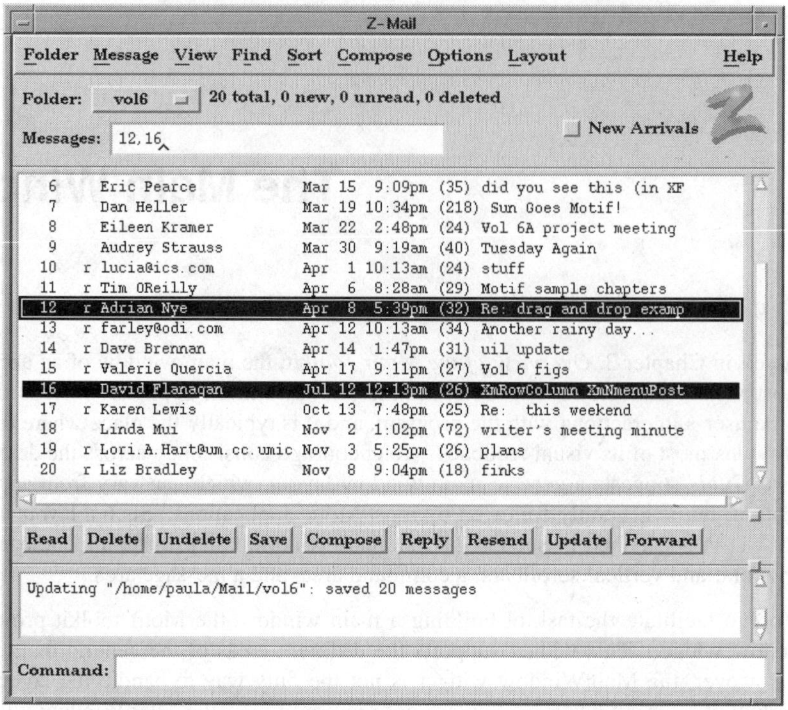

Figure 4-1. The main window of a Motif program

4.1 Creating a MainWindow

The MainWindow widget class is defined in *<Xm/MainW.h>*, which must be included whenever you create a MainWindow widget. As mentioned in Chapter 2, *The Motif Programming Model*, you should probably use an ApplicationShell or TopLevelShell widget as the parent of a MainWindow. If the MainWindow is being used as the main application window, the ApplicationShell returned by XtVaAppInitialize() (or another similar toolkit initialization function) is typically used as the parent. The function XtVaCreateManaged-Widget() can be used to create an instance of a MainWindow widget, as shown in the following code fragment:

```
#include <Xm/MainW.h>
...
main(argc, argv)
int argc;
char *argv[];
{
    Widget toplevel, main_w;
    XtAppContext app;

    XtSetLanguageProc (NULL, NULL, NULL);
    toplevel = XtAppInitialize (&app, "App-Class",
        NULL, 0, &argc, argv, NULL, NULL);
```

```
        main_w = XtVaCreateManagedWidget ("mw",
            xmMainWindowWidgetClass, toplevel,
            resource-value-list,
            NULL);

        XtRealizeWidget(toplevel);
        XtAppMainLoop(app);
    }
```

The MainWindow class is subclassed from the ScrolledWindow class, which means that it inherits all the attributes of a ScrolledWindow, including its resources. A ScrolledWindow allows the user to view an arbitrary widget of any size by attaching horizontal and vertical ScrollBars to it. You can think of a MainWindow as a ScrolledWindow with the additional ability to have an optional menu bar, command area, and message area. Because the Main-Window is subclassed from the ScrolledWindow widget, we will be referring to some ScrolledWindow resources and disclosing some facts about the ScrolledWindow. For more information about the ScrolledWindow, see Chapter 9, *ScrolledWindows and ScrollBars*. You may eventually need to learn more about the ScrolledWindow widget to best make use of the MainWindow, but this chapter tries to present the fundamentals of the MainWindow widget, rather than focus on the ScrolledWindow.

While a MainWindow does control the sizes and positions of its widget children like any manager widget, the geometry management it performs is not the classic management style of other manager widgets. The MainWindow is a special-case object that handles only certain types of children and performs only simple widget positioning. It is designed to support the generic main window layout specified by the *Motif Style Guide*.

Let's take a look at how the MainWindow can be used in an actual application. Example 4-1 demonstrates how the MainWindow widget fits into a typical application design.†

Example 4-1. The show_pix.c program

```
/* show_pix.c -- A minimal example of a MainWindow. Use a Label as the
 * workWindow to display a bitmap specified on the command line.
 */
#include <Xm/MainW.h>
#include <Xm/Label.h>

main(argc, argv)
int argc;
char *argv[];
{
    Widget toplevel, main_w, label;
    XtAppContext app;
    Pixmap pixmap;

    XtSetLanguageProc (NULL, NULL, NULL);

    toplevel = XtVaAppInitialize (&app, "Demos",
        NULL, 0, &argc, argv, NULL, NULL);

    if (!argv[1]) {
        printf ("usage: %s bitmap-file\n", *argv);
        exit (1);
```

_____

†XtSetLanguageProc() is only available in X11R5; there is no corresponding function in X11R4.

Example 4-1. The show_pix.c program (continued)

```
    }

    main_w = XtVaCreateManagedWidget ("main_window",
        xmMainWindowWidgetClass, toplevel,
        XmNscrollBarDisplayPolicy, XmAS_NEEDED,
        XmNscrollingPolicy,        XmAUTOMATIC,
        NULL);

    /* Load bitmap given in argv[1] */
    pixmap = XmGetPixmap (XtScreen (toplevel), argv[1],
        BlackPixelOfScreen (XtScreen (toplevel)),
        WhitePixelOfScreen (XtScreen (toplevel)));

    if (pixmap == XmUNSPECIFIED_PIXMAP) {
        printf ("can't create pixmap from %s\n", argv[1]);
        exit (1);
    }

    /* Now create label using pixmap */
    label = XtVaCreateManagedWidget ("label", xmLabelWidgetClass, main_w,
        XmNlabelType,    XmPIXMAP,
        XmNlabelPixmap, pixmap,
        NULL);

    /* set the label as the "work area" of the main window */
    XtVaSetValues (main_w,
        XmNworkWindow, label,
        NULL);

    XtRealizeWidget (toplevel);
    XtAppMainLoop (app);
}
```

In this example, the MainWindow widget is not used to its full potential. It only contains one other widget, a Label widget, that is used to display a bitmap from the file specified as the first argument on the command line (argv[1]).† The Label widget is used as the work area window for the MainWindow. We did this intentionally to focus your attention on the scrolled-window aspect of the MainWindow widget. The following command line:

    % show_pix /usr/include/X11/bitmaps/xlogo64

produces the output shown in Figure 4-2.

The file specified on the command line should contain X11 bitmap data, so that the application can create a pixmap. The pixmap is displayed in a Label widget, which has been specified as the XmNworkWindow of the MainWindow. As shown in Figure 4-1, the bitmap is simply displayed in the window. However, if a larger bitmap is specified, only a portion of the bitmap can be displayed, so ScrollBars are provided to allow the user to view the entire bitmap. The output of the command:

    % show_pix /usr/include/X11/bitmaps/escherknot

is shown in Figure 4-3.

---

† XtVaAppInitialize ( ) parses the command-line arguments that are used when the program is run. The command-line options that are specific to Xlib or Xt are evaluated and removed from the argument list. What is not parsed is left in argv; our program reads argv[1] as the name of a bitmap to display in the MainWindow.

Figure 4-2. Output of show_pix xlogo64

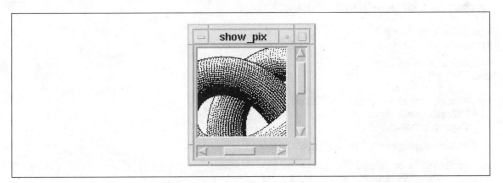

Figure 4-3. Output of show_pix escherknot

The bitmap is obviously too large to be displayed in the MainWindow without either clipping the image or enlarging the window. Rather than resize its own window to an unreasonable size, the MainWindow can display ScrollBars. This behavior is enabled by setting the Main-Window resources `XmNscrollBarDisplayPolicy` to `XmAS_NEEDED` and `XmN-scrollingPolicy` to `XmAUTOMATIC`. These values automate the process whereby ScrollBars are managed when they are needed. If there is enough room for the entire bitmap to be displayed, the ScrollBars are not provided. Try resizing the *show_pix* window and see how the ScrollBars appear and disappear as needed. This behavior occurs as a result of set-ting `XmNscrollBarDisplayPolicy` to `XmAS_NEEDED`.

Since we do not specify a size for the MainWindow, the toolkit sets both the width and height to be `100` pixels. These default values are not a documented feature. Both the MainWindow and the ScrolledWindow suffer from the same problem: if you do not specifically set the `XmNwidth` and `XmNheight` resources, the default size of the widget is not very useful.

The `XmNscrollBarDisplayPolicy` and `XmNscrollingPolicy` resources are inher-ited from the ScrolledWindow widget class. Because `XmNscrollingPolicy` is set to `XmAUTOMATIC`, the toolkit creates and manages the ScrollBars automatically. Another pos-sible value for the resource is `XmAPPLICATION_DEFINED`, which implies that the applica-tion is going to create and manage the ScrollBars for the MainWindow and control all of the aspects of their functionality. Application-defined scrolling is the default style for the

The Main Window

MainWindow widget, but it is unlikely that you will want to leave it that way, since automatic scrolling is far easier to manage at this stage of the game. For complete details on the different scrolling styles, see Chapter 9, *ScrolledWindows and ScrollBars*.

Using the application-defined scrolling policy does not necessarily require you to provide your own scrolling mechanisms. It simply relieves the MainWindow widget of the responsibility of handling the scrolling mechanisms. If you use a ScrolledList or ScrolledText widget as the work area, you should definitely leave the XmNscrollingPolicy as Xm-APPLICATION_DEFINED, since these widgets manage their own ScrollBars. They will handle the scrolling behavior instead of the MainWindow. Example 4-2 shows an example of a program that uses a ScrolledList for the work area in a MainWindow widget.†

Example 4-2. The main_list.c program

```
/* main_list.c -- Use the ScrolledList window as the feature
 * component of a MainWindow widget.
 */
#include <Xm/MainW.h>
#include <Xm/List.h>

main(argc, argv)
char *argv[];
{
    Widget toplevel, main_w, list_w;
    XtAppContext app;
    Pixmap pixmap;

    XtSetLanguageProc (NULL, NULL, NULL);

    toplevel = XtVaAppInitialize (&app, "Demos",
        NULL, 0, &argc, argv, NULL, NULL);

    main_w = XtVaCreateManagedWidget ("main_window",
        xmMainWindowWidgetClass,   toplevel,
        NULL);

    list_w = XmCreateScrolledList (main_w, "main_list", NULL, 0);
    XtVaSetValues (list_w,
        XtVaTypedArg, XmNitems, XmRString,
            "Red, Green, Blue, Orange, Maroon, Grey, Black, White", 53,
        XmNitemCount,           8,
        XmNvisibleItemCount,    5,
        NULL);
    XtManageChild (list_w);

    /* set the list_w as the "work area" of the main window */
    XtVaSetValues (main_w, XmNworkWindow, XtParent (list_w), NULL);

    XtRealizeWidget (toplevel);
    XtAppMainLoop (app);
}
```

---

† XtSetLanguageProc() is only available in X11R5; there is no corresponding function in X11R4.

In order to simplify the application, we specified the items in the ScrolledList as a single string:

```
XtVaSetValues(list_w,
    XtVaTypedArg, XmNitems, XmRString,
        "Red, Green, Blue, Orange, Maroon, Grey, Black, White", 53,
    XmNitemCount,           8,
    XmNvisibleItemCount,    5,
    NULL);
```

This technique provides the easiest way to specify a list for a List widget. The items in a List widget must be specified as an array of compound strings. If we took the time to create each list item separately, we would have to create each compound string, assemble the array of XmString objects and specify it as the XmNitems resource, and then free each string separately after the widget was created. By using XtVaTypedArg, the whole list can be created in one line using the List widget's type converter to convert the string into a list of compound strings. We use this form of resource specification frequently in the book to simplify examples. See Volume Four, *X Toolkit Intrinsics Programming Manual*, for a complete discussion on how this kind of type conversion is done. See Chapter 12, *The List Widget*, for details on the List widget; see Chapter 19, *Compound Strings*, for details on compound strings.

It is important to note that while XmCreateScrolledList() creates both a Scrolled-Window widget and a List widget, it returns the List widget. As a result, we must use Xt-Parent() to get access to the ScrolledWindow widget, so that it can be specified as the work area of the MainWindow. A common programming error with a ScrolledText or a ScrolledList widget is using the actual Text or List widget rather than its ScrolledWindow parent. Again, we refer you to Chapter 9, *ScrolledWindows and ScrollBars*, for a complete discussion of the use of ScrolledText and ScrolledList compound objects.

4.2 The MenuBar

Creating a MenuBar is a fairly complex operation, and one that is completely independent of the MainWindow itself. However, one of the principal reasons for using the MainWindow widget is that it manages the layout of a MenuBar. In this section, we demonstrate the simplest means of creating a MenuBar. Once a MenuBar has been created, you simply tell the MainWindow to include it in the window layout by specifying the MenuBar as the value of the XmNmenuBar resource for the MainWindow.

In the Motif toolkit, a MenuBar is not implemented as a separate widget, but as a set of CascadeButtons arranged horizontally in a RowColumn widget. Each CascadeButton is associated with a PulldownMenu that can contain PushButtons, ToggleButtons, Labels, and Separators. The managing RowColumn widget has a resource setting indicating that it is being used as a MenuBar. You do not need to know any specific details about any of these widgets in order to create a functional MenuBar, since Motif provides convenience routines that allow you to create self-sufficient menu systems. While the specifics on creating Popup-Menus, PulldownMenus, and MenuBars are covered in more detail in Chapter 15, *Menus*, the basic case that we present in this section is quite simple.

There are a variety of methods that you can use to create and manage a MenuBar, but the easiest method is to use the convenience menu creation routine provided by the Motif toolkit: XmVaCreateSimpleMenuBar().† This function is demonstrated in the following code fragment:

```
XmString file, edit, help;
Widget menubar, main_w;
. . .
/* Create a simple MenuBar that contains three menus */
file = XmStringCreateLocalized ("File");
edit = XmStringCreateLocalized ("Edit");
help = XmStringCreateLocalized ("Help");
menubar = XmVaCreateSimpleMenuBar (main_w, "menubar",
    XmVaCASCADEBUTTON, file, 'F',
    XmVaCASCADEBUTTON, edit, 'E',
    XmVaCASCADEBUTTON, help, 'H',
    NULL);
XmStringFree (file);
XmStringFree (edit);
XmStringFree (help);
. . .
```

The output generated by this code is shown in Figure 4-4.

Like XtVaSetValues() and XtVaCreateWidget(), XmVaCreateSimpleMenu-Bar() takes a variable-length argument list of configuration parameters. In addition to resource/value pairs, it also takes special arguments that specify the items in the MenuBar. You can specify RowColumn-specific resource/value pairs just as you would for any varargs routine. Once all the items in a MenuBar have been created, it must be managed using Xt-ManageChild().

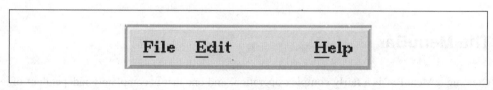

Figure 4-4. A simple MenuBar

If you are specifying an item in the MenuBar, the first parameter is a symbolic constant that identifies the type of the item. Since CascadeButtons are the only elements that can display PulldownMenus, the first parameter should always be set to XmVaCASCADEBUTTON. The label of the CascadeButton is given by the second parameter, which must be a compound string. In the above example, the variable file contains a compound string that contains the text File. The third parameter specifies an optional mnemonic character for the CascadeButton that can be used to post the menu from the keyboard. The mnemonic for the **File** menu is F. By convention, the first letter of a menu or menu item label is used as the mnemonic.

---

† There is also a non-varargs version of this function. It requires you to create each of the buttons in the MenuBar individually and associate it with a PulldownMenu via resources. The varargs function is much easier to use.

We use the compound string creation function, `XmStringCreateLocalized()`, to create the compound strings for the menu labels. This function creates a compound string with the text encoded in the current locale. `XmStringCreateLocalized()` is a new routine in Motif 1.2; it replaces `XmStringCreateSimple()`, which creates a compound string using the default character set associated with the widget in which the string is rendered. For a complete discussion of compound strings, see Chapter 19, *Compound Strings*.

Since you are not creating each CascadeButton using the normal creation routines, you are not returned a handle to each button. You might think that the label string that you assign to each button is used as the widget's name, but this is not the case. The buttons are created sequentially, so the MenuBar assigns the name `button_n` to each button. The value *n* is the position of the button in the MenuBar, where positions are numbered starting with 0 (zero). We will discuss how you can specify resources for items on the MenuBar later in the chapter.

Do not attempt to install callback routines on the CascadeButtons themselves. If you need to know when a particular menu is popped up, you should use the `XmNpopupCallback` on the MenuShell that contains the PulldownMenu associated with the CascadeButton. The popup and popdown callback lists are described briefly in Chapter 7, *Custom Dialogs*; for more information, see Volume Four, *X Toolkit Intrinsics Programming Manual*.

4.2.1 Creating a PulldownMenu

Every CascadeButton in a MenuBar must have a PulldownMenu associated with it. You can create the items in a PulldownMenu using a method that is similar to the one for creating a MenuBar. A PulldownMenu can be created using the function `XmVaCreateSimplePulldownMenu()`. This routine is slightly more involved than `XmVaCreateSimpleMenuBar()`. The routine takes the following form:

```
Widget
XmVaCreateSimplePulldownMenu (parent, name, post_from_button,
                              callback, ...)
    Widget          parent;
    String          name;
    int             post_from_button;
    XtCallbackProc  callback;
    ...
```

The *post_from_button* parameter specifies the CascadeButton that posts the Pulldown-Menu. This parameter is an index (starting at zero) into the array of CascadeButtons in the *parent* widget, which should be a MenuBar. The *name* parameter specifies the widget name for the RowColumn widget that is the PulldownMenu. This name is not the title of the CascadeButton associated with the menu. The MenuShell that contains the PulldownMenu uses the same name with `_popup` appended to it. The *callback* parameter specifies a function that is invoked whenever the user activates any of the items in the menu. The rest of the arguments to `XmVaCreateSimplePulldownMenu()` are either RowColumn resource/value pairs or special arguments that specify the items in the PulldownMenu.

You should not manage a PulldownMenu after you create it because you do not want it to appear until it is posted by the user. The CascadeButton that posts the menu handles managing the menu when it needs to be displayed. The following code fragment shows the use of `XmVaCreateSimplePulldownMenu()` to create a PulldownMenu:

```
XmString open, save, quit, quit_acc;
Widget menubar, menu;
...
/* First menu is the File menu -- callback is file_cb() */
open = XmStringCreateLocalized ("Open...");
save = XmStringCreateLocalized ("Save...");
quit = XmStringCreateLocalized ("Quit");
quit_acc = XmStringCreateLocalized ("Ctrl-C");
menu = XmVaCreateSimplePulldownMenu (menubar, "file_menu", 0, file_cb,
    XmVaPUSHBUTTON, open, 'O', NULL, NULL,
    XmVaPUSHBUTTON, save, 'S', NULL, NULL,
    XmVaSEPARATOR,
    XmVaPUSHBUTTON, quit, 'Q', "Ctrl<Key>c", quit_acc,
    NULL);
XmStringFree (open);
XmStringFree (save);
XmStringFree (quit);
XmStringFree (quit_acc);
...
```

Unlike a MenuBar, which can only contain CascadeButtons, a PulldownMenu can contain a number of different types of elements. As with `XmVaCreateSimpleMenuBar()`, these elements are specified by a symbolic constant that identifies the type of the item. The symbolic constant is followed by a variable number of additional parameters that depend on the type of the menu item. You can use the following values to specify the items in a Pulldown-Menu:

XmVaPUSHBUTTON

> The item is a PushButton. It takes four additional parameters: a compound string label, a mnemonic, an accelerator, and a compound string that contains a text representation of the accelerator. When the PushButton is selected, the *callback* routine is called. It is passed an integer value as `client_data` that indicates the item on the PulldownMenu that was activated. The value is an index into the menu that ranges from 0 to `n-1`; if `client_data` is two, then the third item in the menu was selected.

XmVaTOGGLEBUTTON

> The item is a ToggleButton. It takes the same four additional parameters as described for `XmVaPUSHBUTTON`. When the ToggleButton is selected, the value of the button is toggled and the *callback* routine is called. The `client_data` that is passed to the callback routine is handled the same as for PushButtons.

XmVaCHECKBUTTON

> This value is identical to `XmVaTOGGLEBUTTON`.

XmVaRADIOBUTTON

> The item is a ToggleButton with RadioBox characteristics, which means that only one item in the menu can be set at a time. The PulldownMenu does not enforce this

behavior, so you must either handle it yourself or specify other RowColumn resources to make the menu function like a RadioBox. We demonstrate creating a menu with RadioBox behavior later in the chapter. This value takes the same additional parameters and deals with the callback routine in the same way as Toggle-Buttons.

XmVaCASCADEBUTTON

> The item is a CascadeButton, which is usually associated with a pullright menu. The value takes two additional parameters: a compound string label and a mnemonic. Pullright menus are, ironically, easier to implement and manage using the not-so-simple menu creation routines described in Chapter 15, *Menus*.

XmVaSEPARATOR

> The item is a Separator and it does not take any additional parameters. Since separators cannot be selected, the callback routine is not called for this item. Adding a separator does not affect the item count with respect to the client_data values that are passed to the callback routine for other menu items.

XmVaSINGLE_SEPARATOR

> This value is identical to XmVaSEPARATOR.

XmVaDOUBLE_SEPARATOR

> This value is identical to XmVaSEPARATOR, except that the separator widget displays a double line instead of a single line.

XmVaTITLE

> The item is a Label that is used to create a title in a menu. It takes one additional parameter: a compound string label. The item is not selectable, so it does not have a mnemonic associated with it and it does not call the callback routine. Adding a title does not affect the item count with respect to the client_data values that are passed to the callback routine for other menu items.

Just as with the CascadeButtons in a MenuBar, the labels associated with each menu item are not the names of the widgets themselves. The names of the buttons are button_*n*, where *n* is the position of the button in the menu (starting with zero). Similarly, the names of the separators and the titles are separator_*n* and label_*n*, respectively. We will discuss how you can use resources to specify labels, mnemonics, and accelerators for menus and menu items later in the chapter.

Menus are not intended to be changed dynamically. You should not add, delete, or modify the menus on the MenuBar or the menu items in PulldownMenus once an application is running. Rather than delete an item on a menu when it is not appropriate, you should change the sensitivity of the item using XmNsensitive. The menus in an application should be static in the user's eyes; changing the menus would be like changing the functionality of the program while the user is running it. The one exception to this guideline involves menu items that correspond to dynamic objects. For example, if you have a menu that contains an item for each application that is running on a display, it is acceptable for the items on the menu to change to reflect the current state of the display.

4.2.2 SimpleMenu Callback Routines

The callback routine associated with the **File** menu shown earlier is invoked whenever the user selects any of the buttons in the menu. Just like any callback, the routine takes the form of an XtCallbackProc:

```
void
file_cb (widget, client_data, call_data)
    Widget widget;
    XtPointer client_data;
    XtPointer call_data;
```

The widget parameter is a handle to the widget that was selected in the menu. The client_data parameter is the index of the menu item in the menu. The call_data parameter is a pointer to a callback structure that contains data about callback. Both the client_data and call_data parameters should be cast to their appropriate types before the data that they contain is accessed.

Every Motif callback routine has a callback structure associated with it. The simplest such structure is of type XmAnyCallbackStruct, which has the following form:

```
typedef struct {
    int     reason;
    XEvent *event;
} XmAnyCallbackStruct;
```

All of the Motif callback structures have these two fields, but they also contain more detailed information about why the callback function was invoked. The callback routine for the **File** menu would be passed an XmPushButtonCallbackStruct, since all of the menu items are PushButtons. This structure has the following form:

```
typedef struct {
    int     reason;
    XEvent *event;
    int     click_count;
} XmPushButtonCallbackStruct;
```

The click_count field is not normally used when a PushButton is in a menu. If one of the items in the menu were a ToggleButton, the call_data parameter would be of type Xm-ToggleButtonCallbackStruct, which has the following form:

```
typedef struct {
    int     reason;
    XEvent *event;
    int     set;
} XmToggleButtonCallbackStruct;
```

The set field indicates whether the item was selected (turned on) or deselected (turned off).

When a menu contains both PushButtons and ToggleButtons, you can determine which of the two callback structures the call_data parameter points to by examining the reason field. Since all callback structures have this field, it is always safe to query it. As its name implies, this field indicates why the callback routine was invoked. The value of this field may also indicate the type of the widget that invoked the callback. While we can always determine the type of the widget parameter by using the macro XtIsSubClass(), using the reason field is more straightforward. The PushButton widget uses the value

XmCR_ACTIVATE to indicate that it has been activated, while the ToggleButton uses Xm-CR_VALUE_CHANGED to indicate that its value has been changed. In our example, the reason will always be XmCR_ACTIVATE, since there are only PushButtons in the menu. If there were also ToggleButtons in the menu, we would know that the callback was invoked by a ToggleButton if the value were XmCR_VALUE_CHANGED.

The event field in all of the callback structures is a pointer to an XEvent structure. The XEvent identifies the actual event that caused the callback routine to be invoked. In this example, the event is not of particular interest.

In the callback function, you can choose to do whatever is appropriate for the item that was selected. The callback structure is probably not going to be of that much help in most cases. However, the client_data passed to the function can be used to identify which of the menu items was selected. The following code fragment demonstrates the use of client_data:

```
/* a menu item from the "File" pulldown menu was selected */
void
file_cb(widget, client_data, call_data)
Widget widget;
XtPointer client_data;
XtPointer call_data;
{
    extern void OpenNewFile(), SaveFile();
    int item_no = (int) client_data;

    if (item_no == 0)          /* the "new" button */
        OpenNewFile ();
    else if (item_no == 1)     /* the "save" button */
        SaveFile();
    else                /* the "Quit" button */
        exit (0);
}
```

The callback routines for menu items should be as simple as possible from a structural point of view. A well-designed application should have application-specific entry points such as OpenNewFile() and SaveFile(), as shown in the previous example. These routines should be defined in separate files that are not necessarily associated with the user-interface portion of the program. The use of modular programming techniques helps considerably when an application is being maintained by a large group of people or when it needs to be ported to other user-interface platforms.

4.2.3 A Sample Application

Let's examine an example program that integrates what we have discussed so far. Example 4-3 modifies the behavior of our first example, which displayed an arbitrary pixmap, by allowing the user to change the bitmap dynamically using a Motif FileSelectionDialog. The program also allows the user to dynamically change the color of the bitmap using a PulldownMenu. As you can see by the size of the program, adding these two simple features is not trivial. Many functions and widgets are required in order to make the program functional. As you read the example, don't worry about unknown widgets or details that we haven't addressed just yet; we will discuss them afterwards. For now, just try to identify the familiar parts and see how everything works together.†

Example 4-3. The dynapix.c program

```
/* dynapix.c -- Display a bitmap in a MainWindow, but allow the user
 * to change the bitmap and its color dynamically.  The design of the
 * program is structured on the pulldown menus of the menubar and the
 * callback routines associated with them.  To allow the user to choose
 * a new bitmap, the "Open" button pops up a FileSelectionDialog where
 * a new bitmap file can be chosen.
 */
#include <Xm/MainW.h>
#include <Xm/Label.h>
#include <Xm/MessageB.h>
#include <Xm/FileSB.h>

/* Globals: the toplevel window/widget and the label for the bitmap.
 * "colors" defines the colors we use, "cur_color" is the current
 * color being used, and "cur_bitmap" references the current bitmap file.
 */
Widget toplevel, label;
String colors[] = { "Black", "Red", "Green", "Blue" };
Pixel cur_color;
char cur_bitmap[1024] = "xlogo64"; /* make large enough for full pathnames */

main(argc, argv)
int argc;
char *argv[];
{
    Widget main_w, menubar, menu, widget;
    XtAppContext app;
    Pixmap pixmap;
    XmString file, edit, help, open, quit, red, green, blue, black;
    void file_cb(), change_color(), help_cb();

    XtSetLanguageProc (NULL, NULL, NULL);

    /* Initialize toolkit and parse command line options. */
    toplevel = XtVaAppInitialize (&app, "Demos",
        NULL, 0, &argc, argv, NULL, NULL);

    /* main window contains a MenuBar and a Label displaying a pixmap */
    main_w = XtVaCreateManagedWidget ("main_window",
        xmMainWindowWidgetClass,    toplevel,
        XmNscrollBarDisplayPolicy, XmAS_NEEDED,
        XmNscrollingPolicy,        XmAUTOMATIC,
        NULL);

    /* Create a simple MenuBar that contains three menus */
    file = XmStringCreateLocalized ("File");
    edit = XmStringCreateLocalized ("Edit");
    help = XmStringCreateLocalized ("Help");
    menubar = XmVaCreateSimpleMenuBar (main_w, "menubar",
```

---

†XtSetLanguageProc() is only available in X11R5; there is no corresponding function in X11R4. Xm-StringCreateLocalized() is only available in Motif 1.2; XmStringCreateSimple() is the corresponding function in Motif 1.1. XmFONTLIST_DEFAULT_TAG replaces XmSTRING_DEFAULT_CHARSET in Motif 1.2.

Example 4-3. The dynapix.c program (continued)

```
        XmVaCASCADEBUTTON, file, 'F',
        XmVaCASCADEBUTTON, edit, 'E',
        XmVaCASCADEBUTTON, help, 'H',
        NULL);
    XmStringFree (file);
    XmStringFree (edit);
    /* don't free "help" compound string yet -- reuse it later */

    /* Tell the menubar which button is the help menu  */
    if (widget = XtNameToWidget (menubar, "button_2"))
        XtVaSetValues (menubar, XmNmenuHelpWidget, widget, NULL);

    /* First menu is the File menu -- callback is file_cb() */
    open = XmStringCreateLocalized ("Open...");
    quit = XmStringCreateLocalized ("Quit");
    XmVaCreateSimplePulldownMenu (menubar, "file_menu", 0, file_cb,
        XmVaPUSHBUTTON, open, 'N', NULL, NULL,
        XmVaSEPARATOR,
        XmVaPUSHBUTTON, quit, 'Q', NULL, NULL,
        NULL);
    XmStringFree (open);
    XmStringFree (quit);

    /* Second menu is the Edit menu -- callback is change_color() */
    black = XmStringCreateLocalized (colors[0]);
    red = XmStringCreateLocalized (colors[1]);
    green = XmStringCreateLocalized (colors[2]);
    blue = XmStringCreateLocalized (colors[3]);
    menu = XmVaCreateSimplePulldownMenu (menubar, "edit_menu", 1, change_color,
        XmVaRADIOBUTTON, black, 'k', NULL, NULL,
        XmVaRADIOBUTTON, red, 'R', NULL, NULL,
        XmVaRADIOBUTTON, green, 'G', NULL, NULL,
        XmVaRADIOBUTTON, blue, 'B', NULL, NULL,
        XmNradioBehavior, True,      /* RowColumn resources to enforce */
        XmNradioAlwaysOne, True,     /* radio behavior in Menu */
        NULL);
    XmStringFree (black);
    XmStringFree (red);
    XmStringFree (green);
    XmStringFree (blue);

    /* Initialize menu so that "black" is selected. */
    if (widget = XtNameToWidget (menu, "button_0"))
        XtVaSetValues (widget, XmNset, True, NULL);

    /* Third menu is the help menu -- callback is help_cb() */
    XmVaCreateSimplePulldownMenu (menubar, "help_menu", 2, help_cb,
        XmVaPUSHBUTTON, help, 'H', NULL, NULL,
        NULL);
    XmStringFree (help); /* we're done with it; now we can free it */

    XtManageChild (menubar);

    /* user can still specify the initial bitmap */
    if (argv[1])
        strcpy (cur_bitmap, argv[1]);
    /* initialize color */
    cur_color = BlackPixelOfScreen (XtScreen (toplevel)),
```

Example 4-3. The dynapix.c program (continued)

```
        /* create initial bitmap */
        pixmap = XmGetPixmap (XtScreen (toplevel), cur_bitmap,
            cur_color, WhitePixelOfScreen (XtScreen (toplevel)));

        if (pixmap == XmUNSPECIFIED_PIXMAP) {
            puts ("can't create initial pixmap");
            exit (1);
        }

        /* Now create label using pixmap */
        label = XtVaCreateManagedWidget ("label", xmLabelWidgetClass, main_w,
            XmNlabelType,    XmPIXMAP,
            XmNlabelPixmap, pixmap,
            NULL);

        /* set the label as the "work area" of the main window */
        XtVaSetValues (main_w,
            XmNmenuBar,     menubar,
            XmNworkWindow, label,
            NULL);

        XtRealizeWidget (toplevel);
        XtAppMainLoop (app);
}

/* Any item the user selects from the File menu calls this function.
 * It will either be "Open" (item_no == 0) or "Quit" (item_no == 1).
 */
void
file_cb(widget, client_data, call_data)
Widget widget;          /* menu item that was selected */
XtPointer client_data;  /* the index into the menu */
XtPointer call_data; /* unused */
{
    static Widget dialog; /* make it static for reuse */
    extern void load_pixmap();
    int item_no = (int) client_data;

    if (item_no == 1) /* the "quit" item */
        exit (0);

    /* "Open" was selected.  Create a Motif FileSelectionDialog w/callback */
    if (!dialog) {
        dialog = XmCreateFileSelectionDialog (toplevel, "file_sel", NULL, 0);
        XtAddCallback (dialog, XmNokCallback, load_pixmap, NULL);
        XtAddCallback (dialog, XmNcancelCallback, XtUnmanageChild, NULL);
    }
    XtManageChild (dialog);
    XtPopup (XtParent (dialog), XtGrabNone);
}

/* The OK button was selected from the FileSelectionDialog (or, the user
 * double-clicked on a file selection).  Try to read the file as a bitmap.
 * If the user changed colors, we call this function directly from change_color()
 * to reload the pixmap.  In this case, we pass NULL as the callback struct
 * so we can identify this special case.
 */
void
load_pixmap(dialog, client_data, call_data)
```

Example 4-3. The dynapix.c program (continued)

```
Widget dialog;
XtPointer client_data;
XtPointer call_data;
{
    Pixmap pixmap;
    char *file = NULL;
    XmFileSelectionBoxCallbackStruct *cbs =
        (XmFileSelectionBoxCallbackStruct *) call_data;

    if (cbs) {
        if (!XmStringGetLtoR (cbs->value, XmFONTLIST_DEFAULT_TAG, &file))
            return; /* internal error */
        (void) strcpy (cur_bitmap, file);
        XtFree (file); /* free allocated data from XmStringGetLtoR() */
    }

    pixmap = XmGetPixmap (XtScreen (toplevel), cur_bitmap,
        cur_color, WhitePixelOfScreen (XtScreen (toplevel)));

    if (pixmap == XmUNSPECIFIED_PIXMAP)
        printf ("Can't create pixmap from %s\n", cur_bitmap);
    else {
        Pixmap old;
        XtVaGetValues (label, XmNlabelPixmap, &old, NULL);
        XmDestroyPixmap (XtScreen (toplevel), old);
        XtVaSetValues (label,
            XmNlabelType,   XmPIXMAP,
            XmNlabelPixmap, pixmap,
            NULL);
    }
}

/* called from any of the "Edit" menu items.  Change the color of the
 * current bitmap being displayed.  Do this by calling load_pixmap().
 */
void
change_color(widget, client_data, call_data)
Widget widget;          /* menu item that was selected */
XtPointer client_data;      /* the index into the menu */
XtPointer call_data; /* unused */
{
    XColor xcolor, unused;
    Display *dpy = XtDisplay (label);
    Colormap cmap = DefaultColormapOfScreen (XtScreen (label));
    int item_no = (int) client_data;

    if (XAllocNamedColor (dpy, cmap, colors[item_no], &xcolor, &unused) == 0 ||
        cur_color == xcolor.pixel)
        return;

    cur_color = xcolor.pixel;
    load_pixmap (widget, NULL, NULL);
}

#define MSG \
"Use the FileSelection dialog to find bitmap files to\n\
display in the scrolling area in the main window.  Use\n\
the edit menu to display the bitmap in different colors."
```

Example 4-3. The dynapix.c program (continued)

```
/* The help button in the help menu from the menubar was selected.
 * Display help information defined above for how to use the program.
 * This is done by creating a Motif information dialog box.  Again,
 * make the dialog static so we can reuse it.
 */
void
help_cb(widget, client_data, call_data)
Widget widget;
XtPointer client_data;
XtPointer call_data;
{
    static Widget dialog;

    if (!dialog) {
        Arg args[5];
        int n = 0;
        XmString msg = XmStringCreateLtoR (MSG, XmFONTLIST_DEFAULT_TAG);
        XtSetArg (args[n], XmNmessageString, msg); n++;
        dialog = XmCreateInformationDialog (toplevel, "help_dialog", args, n);
    }
    XtManageChild (dialog);
    XtPopup (XtParent (dialog), XtGrabNone);
}
```

The output of the program is shown in Figure 4-5.

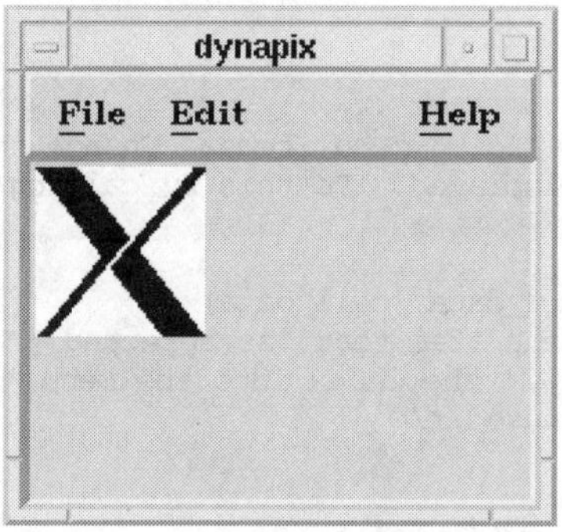

Figure 4-5. Output of dynapix.c

The beginning of the program is pretty much as expected. After the toolkit is initialized, the MainWindow and the MenuBar are created the same way as in the previous examples. Just after the MenuBar is created, however, we make the following calls:

```
    if (widget = XtNameToWidget (menubar, "button_2"))
        XtVaSetValues(menubar, XmNmenuHelpWidget, widget, NULL);
```

The purpose of these statements is to inform the MenuBar which of its CascadeButtons contains the **Help** menu. Setting the MenuBar's XmNmenuHelpWidget resource to the CascadeButton returned by XtNameToWidget() causes the MenuBar to position the menu specially. The **Help** menu is placed at the far right on the MenuBar; this position is necessary for the application to conform to Motif sytle guidelines. For details on how to support a help system, see Chapter 7, *Custom Dialogs*, and Chapter 21, *Advanced Dialog Programming*.

PulldownMenus are created next in the expected manner. The only variation is for the **Edit** menu, where each item in the menu represents a color. Since only one color can be used at a time, the color that is currently being used is marked with a diamond-shape indicator. In order to get this radio-box behavior, each menu item in the PulldownMenu is a `Xm-VaRADIOBUTTON` and the menu is told to treat the items as a RadioBox. The analogy is that of an old car radio, where selecting a new station causes the other selectors to pop out. Just as you can only have the radio tuned to one station at a time, you may only have one color set at a time. The RadioBox functionality is managed automatically by the RowColumn widget that is used to implement the PulldownMenu. Setting the `XmNradioBehavior` and `XmN-radioAlwaysOne` RowColumn resources to `True` provides the RadioBox behavior. See Chapter 11, *Labels and Buttons*, for a complete description and further examples of this type of behavior. Figure 4-6 shows the RadioBox-style **Edit** menu.

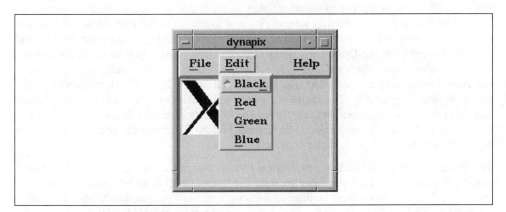

Figure 4-6. The Edit menu for dynapix.c

Although the RowColumn manages the RadioBox automatically, we need to turn the radio on by setting the initial color. After the PulldownMenu is created, the menu (RadioBox) is initialized so that its first item is selected, since we know that we are using black as the initial color. `XtNameToWidget()` is used again to get the appropriate button from the menu. Since the menu items were created using `XmVaRADIOBUTTON`, the widget that is returned is a ToggleButton. The `XmNset` resource is used to turn the button on. Once the menu has been initialized, the Motif toolkit handles everything automatically.

Note that when we create the **Help** menu, there is only one item in the menu. You might think that it is redundant to have a single **Help** item in the **Help** menu, but this design is an element of Motif style. The *Motif Style Guide* states that items on the MenuBar should always post PulldownMenu, not perform application actions directly.

It is important to note that `XmVaCreateSimplePulldownMenu()` returns the Row-Column widget that contains the items in the menu, even though the routine creates both the RowColumn widget and its MenuShell parent. The routine does not return the MenuShell widget that is actually popped up and down when the menu posted. To get a handle to that widget, you need to use XtParent() on the RowColumn widget. This design makes sense, since you need access to the RowColumn widget much more often than you need access to the MenuShell.

Once all of the items have been installed, the MenuBar is managed using XtManage-Child(). The approach to creating MenuBars, PulldownMenus, menu items, and their associated callback routines that we have described here is meant to be simple and straightforward. In some cases, you may find that these techniques are too limiting. For example, you cannot specify different callback routines for different items in the same menu, you cannot pass different client data for different items, and you cannot name the widgets individually. The most inconvenient aspect of this method, however, is that it requires so much redundant code in order to build a realistically sized MenuBar. Our intent here is to introduce the basic concepts of menus and to demonstrate the recommended design approach for applications. We describe how the menu creation process can be generalized for large menu systems in Chapter 15, *Menus*.

The rest of Example 4-3 is composed of callback routines that are used by the PulldownMenu items. For example, when the user selects either of the items in the **File** menu, the function file_cb() is called. If the **Quit** item is selected, the client_data parameter is 1 and the program exits. If the **Open** item is selected, client_data is 0 and a FileSelection-Dialog is popped up to allow the user to select a new bitmap file. The dialog is created using the convenience routine XmCreateFileSelectionDialog(), which produces the results shown in Figure 4-7. Two callback routines are installed for the dialog: load_pixmap(), which is called when the user presses the **OK** button, and XtUnmanageChild(), which is called when the user selects the **Cancel** button. For more detailed information on the FileSelectionDialog, see Chapter 6, *Selection Dialogs*.

The load_pixmap() function loads a new bitmap from a file and displays it in the Label widget. This function uses the same method for loading a pixmap as was used earlier in main(). Since the function is invoked as a callback by the FileSelectionDialog, we need to get the value of the file selection. The value is taken from the value field of the File-SelectionDialog's callback structure, XmFileSelectionBoxCallbackStruct. Since the filename is represented as a compound string, it must be converted to a character string. The conversion is done using XmStringGetLtoR(), which creates a regular C string for use by XmGetPixmap(). The load_pixmap() routine is also called directly from change_color(), so we need to check the call_data parameter. This parameter is NULL if the routine is not invoked as a callback.

If XmGetPixmap() succeeds, we get the old pixmap and destroy it using XmDestroy-Pixmap() before we install the new pixmap. XmGetPixmap() loads and caches a pixmap. If the function is called more than once for a given image, it returns the cached image, which saves space because a new version of the pixmap is not allocated for each call. Xm-DestroyPixmap() decrements the reference count for the image; if the reference count reaches to zero, the pixmap is actually destroyed. Otherwise, another reference to it may exist, so nothing is done. It is important to use these two functions in conjunction with each other. However, if you use other pixmap-loading functions to create pixmaps, you cannot use XmDestroyPixmap() to free them.

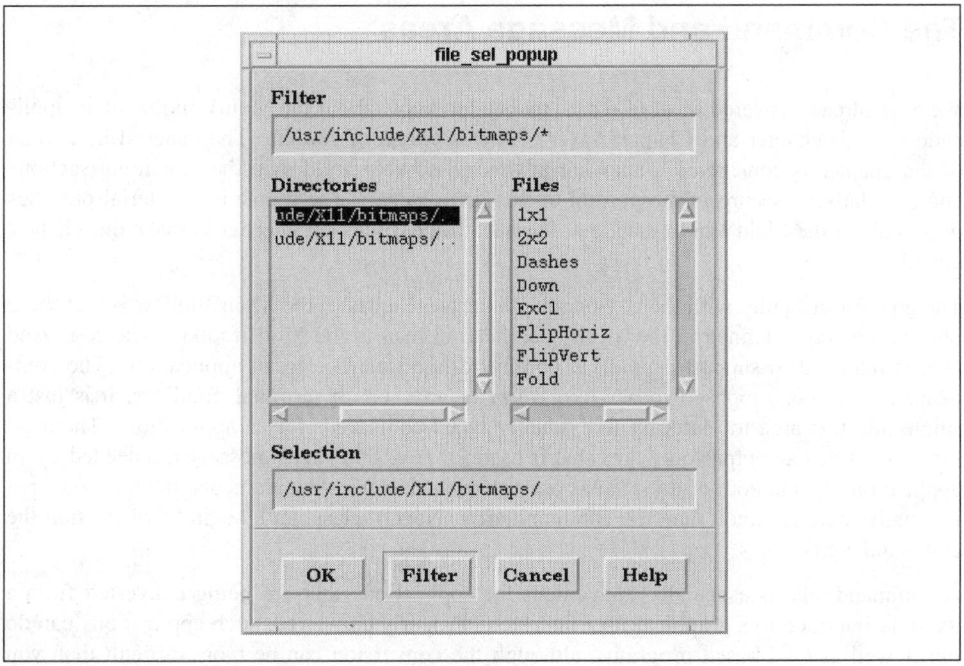

Figure 4-7. The FileSelectionDialog for dynapix.c

The function change_color() is used as the callback routine for items in the **Edit** menu. The names of the colors are stored in the colors array. The index of a color in this array is the same as the index of the corresponding menu item in the menu. The color name is parsed and loaded using XAllocNamedColor(), provided that the string exists in the RGB database (usually */usr/lib/X11/rgb.txt*). If the routine is successful, it returns a non-zero status and the XColor structure is filled with the RGB data and pixel value. In this case, load_pixmap() is called to reload the pixmap with the new color. If XAllocNamed-Color() returns zero, or if the returned pixel value is the same as the current one, change_color() returns, as there is no point in reloading an identical pixmap. For additional information about loading and using colors, see Volume One, *Xlib Programming Manual*, and Volume Two, *Xlib Reference Manual*.

The help_cb() function is the callback routine for the **Help** menu item on the **Help** menu. It simply displays an InformationDialog that contains a message describing how to use the program. See Chapter 5, *Introduction to Dialogs*, and Chapter 21, *Advanced Dialog Programming*, for a complete description of these dialogs and suggestions on implementing a functional help system.

The Main Window

4.3 The Command and Message Areas

We have already covered most of what you need to know about the MainWindow of an application in this chapter and Chapter 3, *Overview of the Motif Toolkit*. The material in the rest of the chapter is considered somewhat advanced, so you could skip the remaining sections and be relatively secure in moving on to the next chapter. The remaining material provides details about the MainWindow widget that need to be discussed in order to make this chapter complete.

The greatest difficulty with the command and message areas of the MainWindow is that these objects are better defined in the Motif specification than in the Motif toolkit. The command area is intended to support a tty-style command-line interface to an application. The command area is not supposed to act like *xterm* or any sort of terminal emulator; it is just a single-line text area for entering individually typed commands for an application. The message area is just an output-only area that is used for error and status messages as needed by an application. While both of these areas are optional MainWindow elements, the message area is usually more common than the command area. Nevertheless, let's begin by discussing the command area.

A command area is especially convenient for applications that are being converted from a tty-style interface to a graphical user interface. Properly converted, such applications can do rather well as GUI-based programs, although the conversion can be more difficult than you might expect. For example, a PostScript interpreter could be implemented using a command area in the MainWindow. However, since PostScript is a verbose language, it does not work well with single-line text entry fields.

Example 4-4 shows how the command area can be used to allow the user to input standard UNIX commands. The output of the commands is displayed in the ScrolledText object, which is the work area of the MainWindow. For simplicity, we've kept the MenuBar small so as to dedicate most of the program to the use of the command area.†

Example 4-4. The cmd_area.c program

```
/* cmd_area.c -- use a ScrolledText object to view the
 * output of commands input by the user in a Command window.
 */
#include <Xm/Text.h>
#include <Xm/MainW.h>
#include <Xm/Command.h>
#include <stdio.h>            /* For popen() */

/* main() -- initialize toolkit, create a main window, menubar,
 * a Command Area and a ScrolledText to view the output of commands.
 */
main(argc, argv)
int argc;
char *argv[];
```

---

† XtSetLanguageProc() is only available in X11R5; there is no corresponding function in X11R4. Xm-StringCreateLocalized() is only available in Motif 1.2; XmStringCreateSimple() is the corresponding function in Motif 1.1. XmFONTLIST_DEFAULT_TAG replaces XmSTRING_DEFAULT_CHARSET in Motif 1.2.

Example 4-4. The cmd_area.c program (continued)

```
{
    Widget        top, main_w, menubar, menu, command_w, text_w;
    XtAppContext  app;
    XmString      file, quit;
    extern void   exec_cmd(), exit();
    Arg           args[5];
    int           n = 0;

    XtSetLanguageProc (NULL, NULL, NULL);

    /* initialize toolkit and create toplevel shell */
    top = XtVaAppInitialize (&app, "Demos",
        NULL, 0, &argc, argv, NULL, NULL);

    (void) close (0); /* don't let commands read from stdin */

    /* MainWindow for the application -- contains menubar, ScrolledText
     * and CommandArea (which prompts for filename).
     */
    main_w = XtVaCreateManagedWidget ("main_w",
        xmMainWindowWidgetClass, top,
        XmNcommandWindowLocation, XmCOMMAND_BELOW_WORKSPACE,
        NULL);

    /* Create a simple MenuBar that contains one menu */
    file = XmStringCreateLocalized ("File");
    menubar = XmVaCreateSimpleMenuBar (main_w, "menubar",
        XmVaCASCADEBUTTON, file, 'F',
        NULL);
    XmStringFree (file);

    /* "File" menu has only one item (Quit), so make callback exit() */
    quit = XmStringCreateLocalized ("Quit");
    menu = XmVaCreateSimplePulldownMenu (menubar, "file_menu", 0, exit,
        XmVaPUSHBUTTON, quit, 'Q', NULL, NULL,
        NULL);
    XmStringFree (quit);

    /* Menubar is done -- manage it */
    XtManageChild (menubar);

    /* Create ScrolledText -- this is work area for the MainWindow */
    XtSetArg (args[n], XmNrows,      24); n++;
    XtSetArg (args[n], XmNcolumns,   80); n++;
    XtSetArg (args[n], XmNeditable,  False); n++;
    XtSetArg (args[n], XmNeditMode,  XmMULTI_LINE_EDIT); n++;
    text_w = XmCreateScrolledText (main_w, "text_w", args, n);
    XtManageChild (text_w);

    /* store text_w as user data in "File" menu for file_cb() callback */
    XtVaSetValues (menu, XmNuserData, text_w, NULL);

    /* Create the command area -- this must be a Command class widget */
    file = XmStringCreateLocalized ("Command:");
    command_w = XtVaCreateWidget ("command_w", xmCommandWidgetClass, main_w,
        XmNpromptString, file,
        NULL);
    XmStringFree (file);
    XtAddCallback (command_w, XmNcommandEnteredCallback, exec_cmd, text_w);
    XtManageChild (command_w);
```

Example 4-4. The cmd_area.c program (continued)

```
    XmMainWindowSetAreas (main_w, menubar, command_w,
        NULL, NULL, XtParent (text_w));
    XtRealizeWidget (top);
    XtAppMainLoop (app);
}

/* execute the command and redirect output to the ScrolledText window */
void
exec_cmd (cmd_widget, client_data, call_data)
Widget cmd_widget;   /* the command widget itself, not its Text widget */
XtPointer client_data; /* passed the text_w as client_data */
XtPointer call_data;
{
    char *cmd, buf[BUFSIZ];
    XmTextPosition pos;
    FILE *pp, *popen();
    Widget text_w = (Widget) client_data;
    XmCommandCallbackStruct *cbs =
        (XmCommandCallbackStruct *) call_data;

    XmStringGetLtoR (cbs->value, XmFONTLIST_DEFAULT_TAG, &cmd);

    if (!cmd || !*cmd) { /* nothing typed? */
        if (cmd)
            XtFree (cmd);
        return;
    }

    /* make sure the file is a regular text file and open it */
    if (!(pp = popen (cmd, "r")))
        perror (cmd);
    XtFree (cmd);
    if (!pp)
        return;

    /* put the output of the command in the Text widget by reading
     * until EOF (meaning that the command has terminated).
     */
    for (pos = 0; fgets (buf, sizeof buf, pp); pos += strlen (buf))
        XmTextReplace (text_w, pos, pos, buf);

    pclose (pp);
}
```

This example uses a Command widget for the command area. The output of the program is shown in Figure 4-8. The Command widget provides a command entry area and a command history area. However, you do not necessarily have to use a Command widget for the command area. A TextField widget can be used instead to provide a simple command area.

When we created the MainWindow, we set the XmNcommandWindowLocation resource to XmCOMMAND_BELOW_WORKSPACE, which caused the command area to be placed below the work window. Although the default value of the resource is XmCOMMAND_ABOVE_WORKSPACE, the *Style Guide* recommends that the command area be positioned beneath the work window, rather than above it. You need to explicitly set the value of XmNcommandWindowLocation to ensure that the command area is positioned appropriately.

Note that we use the ScrolledWindow that is created by `XmCreateScrolledText()` for the work window, rather than the scrolling area provided by the MainWindow. Since `Xm-CreateScrolledText()` returns a Text widget, we are careful to use the parent of the Text widget for the `XmNworkWindow` resource of the MainWindow. We set the areas of the MainWindow using `XmMainWindowSetAreas()`, which is a convenience function that tells the MainWindow which of its child widgets should be used for its different predefined areas. The routine takes the following form:

```
void
XmMainWindowSetAreas (main_w, menubar, cmd_w, h_scroll,
                      v_scroll, work_w)
    Widget  main_w;
    Widget  menubar;
    Widget  cmd_w;
    Widget  h_scroll;
    Widget  v_scroll;
    Widget  work_w;
```

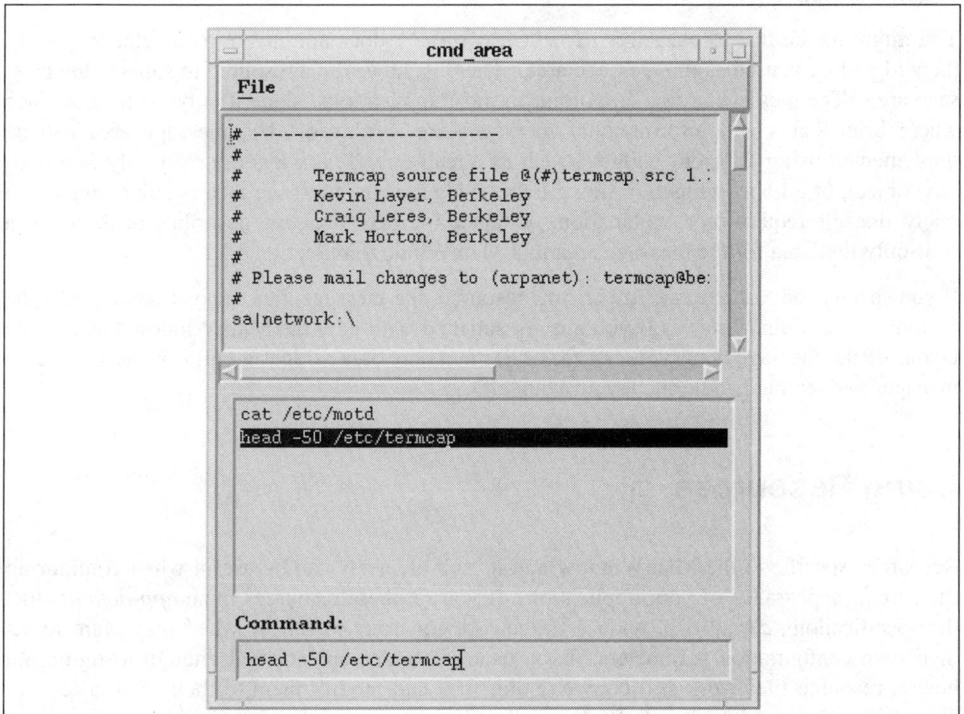

Figure 4-8. Output of cmd_area.c

The function is really a front end for `XmScrolledWindowSetAreas()`. Basically, both of these functions manage the appropriate widgets so that they appear in the correct locations in the MainWindow, while making sure there is enough space for all of them to be visible. Neither function is entirely necessary, though. When you create a widget as a child of a

MainWindow widget, the MainWindow checks the type of the widget you are adding. If the new widget is a RowColumn that is being used as a MenuBar (XmNrowColumnType is XmMENU_BAR), the MainWindow automatically uses it for the menu bar. This same check is performed for a Command widget, which is automatically used as the command area. The MainWindow also provides resources for its different areas that you can set using Xt-VaSetValues(). The resources you can use are:

```
XmNmenuBar
XmNcommandWindow
XmNverticalScrollBar
XmNhorizonalScrollBar
XmNworkWindow
XmNmessageWindow
```

Once one of these values is set, it cannot be reset to NULL, although it can be reset to another widget. However, XmMainWindowSetAreas() can be used to set the different areas to NULL. You should only use this routine when you are doing the initial layout of your application; changing the major elements of the MainWindow while an application is running would be quite disruptive.

You might notice that XmMainWindowSetAreas() does not have a parameter to specify the widget that is used as the message area. There is, however, a resource to support the message area. The message area is important in most applications, since it is typically the place where brief status and informational messages are displayed. The message area can be implemented using different widgets, such as a read-only Text widget, a read-only Scrolled-Text object, or a Label widget. Using a Label widget as the message area is quite simple and really doesn't require any explanation. Chapter 14, *Text Widgets*, describes how to use a read-only text area for the message area in a MainWindow in Section 14.2.5.

If you specify the XmNmessageWindow resource, the message area is positioned across the bottom of the MainWindow. If you are not satisfied with how the MainWindow handles the layout of the message area, you can make the message area widget a child of the work area manager widget and handle the layout yourself.

4.4 Using Resources

Resources specific to the MainWindow and its sub-elements can be useful when configuring the default appearance of your application. If you set these resources in an *app-defaults* file, the specifications can also provide a framework for users to follow when they want to set their own configuration parameters. Even users who are sophisticated enough to figure out how X resource files work still copy existing files and modify them to their own tastes. To assist users, the app-defaults file for an application should be informative and complete, even though it might be lengthy.

Of course, the first step in specifying resources in an app-defaults file is to determine exactly which aspects of the program you want to be configurable. Remember, consistency is the only way to keep from completely confusing a user. Once you have decided which portions of the application are going to be configurable, you can set resource values by specifying complete widget hierarchies. As an example, let's specify some resources for the menu system from *dynapix.c*. The application creates the **File** menu in the following way:

```
XmVaCreateSimplePulldownMenu(menubar, "file_menu", 0, file_cb,
    XmVaPUSHBUTTON, open, 'O', NULL, NULL,
    XmVaSEPARATOR,
    XmVaPUSHBUTTON, quit, 'Q', NULL, NULL,
    NULL);
```

We can add accelerators to both the **Open** and **Quit** menu items using the following resource specifications:

```
dynapix.main_window.menubar*button_0.accelerator: Ctrl<Key>O
dynapix.main_window.menubar*button_0.acceleratorText: Ctrl+O
dynapix.main_window.menubar*button_1.accelerator: Ctrl<Key>C
dynapix.main_window.menubar*button_1.acceleratorText: Ctrl+C
```

The result is shown in Figure 4-9.

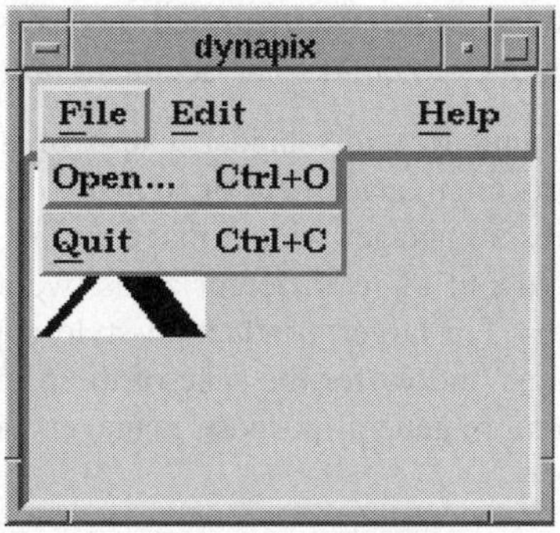

Figure 4-9. The File menu for dynapix.c with accelerators

These resource settings work because `XmNaccelerator` and `XmNacceleratorText` were not hard-coded by the application. By the same token, the labels of the MenuBar titles and the menu items in the PulldownMenus are hard-coded values that cannot be modified through resources. To relax this restriction, you could try setting the `label` and `mnemonic` parameters to `NULL` in calls to `XmVaCreateSimplePulldownMenu()`. Unfortunately, this technique makes resource specification awfully messy, since the CascadeButtons in the MenuBar and the various PulldownMenus all have names of the form `button_n`. The other alternative is to use the more advanced methods of menu creation that are described in Chapter 15, *Menus*.

The MainWindow provides a few other resources that control different visual attributes: `XmNshowSeparator`, `XmNmainWindowMarginWidth`, and `XmNmainWindow-MarginHeight`. The `XmNshowSeparator` resource controls whether or not Separator widgets are displayed between the different areas of a MainWindow. The margin resources specify the width and height of the MainWindow's margins. Generally, these resources should not be set by the application, but left to the user to specify. For example:

```
*XmMainWindow.showSeparator: True
*XmMainWindow.mainWindowMarginWidth: 10
*XmMainWindow.mainWindowMarginHeight: 10
```

The class name for the MainWindow widget is XmMainWindow. If these resource settings were specified in an app-defaults file, they would affect all of the MainWindow widgets in the application. If a user makes these specifications in his *.Xdefaults* file, they would apply to all MainWindow widgets in all applications.

4.5 Summary

This chapter introduced you to the concepts involved in creating the main window of an application. To a lesser degree, we showed you how the MainWindow widget can be used to accomplish some of the necessary tasks. We identified the areas involved in a MainWindow and used some convenience routines to build some adequate prototypes.

The MainWindow can be difficult to understand because of its capabilities as a Scrolled-Window and because it supports the management of so many other objects. The work area of a MainWindow usually contains a manager widget that contains other widgets. Although the MainWindow can handle the layout of its different areas, we do not necessarily encourage you to use all its of its features. For larger, production-style applications, you would probably be better off using the MainWindow for the sake of the MenuBar, while placing the rest of the layout in the hands of a more general-purpose manager widget. These are described in Chapter 8, *Manager Widgets*.

You could also decide not to use the MainWindow widget at all. If done properly, you could probably use one of the manager widget classes described in Chapter 8 and still be Motif-compliant. Depending on your application, you might find this technique easier to deal with than the MainWindow widget.

4.6 Exercises

Based on the material in this chapter, you should be able to do the following exercises:

1. Modify *dynapix.c* to have a new PulldownMenu that controls the background color of the pixmap.

2. Modify *dynapix.c* so that it has a command area. The callback for the Command widget should understand either filenames or color names. If you feel adventurous, try to have it understand both the command `file` and the command `color`. Each command would take a second argument indicating the file or color to use.

5

Introduction to Dialogs

This chapter describes the fundamental concepts that underly all Motif dialogs. It provides a foundation for the more advanced material in the following chapters. In the course of the introduction, the chapter also provides information about Motif's predefined MessageDialog classes.

In This Chapter:

5

Introduction to Dialogs

In Chapter 4, *The Main Window*, we discussed the top-level windows that are managed by the window manager and that provide the overall framework for an application. Most applications are too complex to do everything in one main top-level window. Situations arise that call for secondary windows, or *transient windows*, that serve specific purposes. These windows are commonly referred to as *dialog boxes*, or more simply as dialogs.

Dialog boxes play an integral role in a GUI-based interface such as Motif. The examples in this book use dialogs in many ways, so just about every chapter can be used to learn more about dialogs. We've already explored some of the basic concepts in Chapter 2, *The Motif Programming Model*, and Chapter 3, *Overview of the Motif Toolkit*. However, the use of dialogs in Motif is quite complex, so we need more detail to proceed further.

The *Motif Style Guide* makes a set of generic recommendations about how all dialogs should look. The *Style Guide* also specifies precisely how certain dialogs should look, how they should respond to user events, and under what circumstances the dialogs should be used. We refer to these dialogs as predefined Motif dialogs, since the Motif toolkit implements each of them for you. These dialogs are completely self-sufficient, opaque objects that require very little interaction from your application. In most situations, you can create the necessary dialog using a single convenience routine and you're done. If you need more functionality than what is provided by a predefined Motif dialog, you may have to create your own customized dialog. In this case, building and handling the dialog requires a completely different approach.

There are three chapters on basic dialog usage in this book—two on the predefined Motif dialogs and one on customized dialogs. There is also an additional chapter later in the book that deals with more advanced dialog topics. This first chapter discusses the most common class of Motif dialogs, called MessageDialogs. These are the simplest kinds of dialogs; they typically display a short message and use a small set of standard responses, such as **OK**, **Yes**, or **No**. These dialogs are transient, in that they are intended to be used immediately and then dismissed. MessageDialogs define resources and attributes that are shared by most of the other dialogs in the Motif toolkit, so they provide a foundation for us to build upon in the later dialog chapters. Although Motif dialogs are meant to be opaque objects, we will examine their implementation and behavior in order to understand how they really work. This information can help you understand not only what is happening in your application, but also how to create customized dialogs.

Chapter 6, *Selection Dialogs*, describes another set of predefined Motif dialogs, called SelectionDialogs. Since these dialogs are the next step in the evolution of dialogs, most of the material in this chapter is applicable there as well. SelectionDialogs typically provide the user with a list of choices. These dialogs can remain displayed on the screen so that they can be used repeatedly. Chapter 7, *Custom Dialogs*, addresses the issues of creating customized dialogs, and Chapter 21, *Advanced Dialog Programming*, discusses some advanced topics in X and Motif programming using dialogs as a backdrop.

5.1 The Purpose of Dialogs

For most applications, it is impossible to develop an interface that provides the full functionality of the application in a single main window. As a result, the interface is typically broken up into discrete functional modules, where the interface for each module is provided in a separate dialog box.

As an example, consider an electronic mail application. The broad range of different functions includes searching for messages according to patterns, composing messages, editing an address book, reporting error messages, and so on. Dialog boxes are used to display simple messages, as shown in Figure 5-1. They are also used to prompt the user to answer simple questions, as shown in Figure 5-2. A dialog box can also present a more complicated interaction, as shown in Figure 5-3.

Figure 5-1. A message dialog

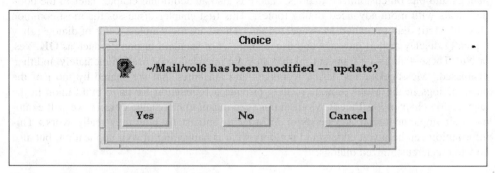

Figure 5-2. A question dialog

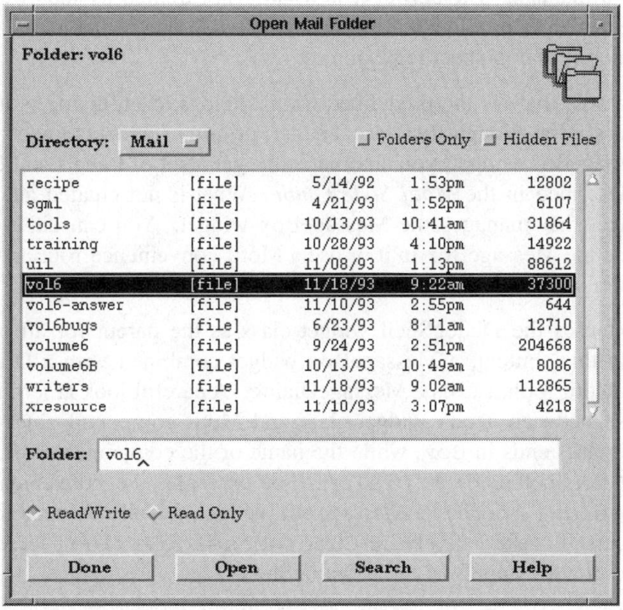

```
┌─────────────────────────────────────────────────────────┐
│  ─                  Open Mail Folder                  ▫  │
│  Folder: vol6                                            │
│                                                          │
│  Directory:  Mail ⌐           ⌐ Folders Only ⌐ Hidden Files │
│  recipe        [file]      5/14/92    1:53pm     12802   │
│  sgml          [file]      4/21/93    1:52pm      6107   │
│  tools         [file]     10/13/93   10:41am     31864   │
│  training      [file]     10/28/93    4:10pm     14922   │
│  uil           [file]     11/08/93    1:13pm     88612   │
│  vol6          [file]     11/18/93    9:22am     37300   │
│  vol6-answer   [file]     11/10/93    2:55pm       644   │
│  vol6bugs      [file]      6/23/93    8:11am     12710   │
│  volume6       [file]      9/24/93    2:51pm    204668   │
│  volume6B      [file]     10/13/93   10:49am      8086   │
│  writers       [file]     11/18/93    9:02am    112865   │
│  xresource     [file]     11/10/93    3:07pm      4218   │
│                                                          │
│  Folder:  vol6                                           │
│                                                          │
│   ◇ Read/Write  ◇ Read Only                              │
│                                                          │
│   │  Done  │   │  Open  │   │  Search  │   │  Help  │    │
└─────────────────────────────────────────────────────────┘
```

Figure 5-3. A custom dialog box

In Figure 5-3, many different widget classes are used to provide an interface that allows the user to save e-mail messages in different folders. The purpose of a dialog is to focus on one particular task in an application. Since the scope of these tasks is usually quite limited, an application usually provides them in dialog boxes, rather than in its main window.

There is actually no such thing as a dialog widget class in the Motif toolkit. A dialog is actually made up of a DialogShell widget and a manager widget child that implements the visible part of the dialog. The DialogShell interacts with the window manager to provide the transient window behavior required of dialogs. When we refer to a dialog widget, we are really talking about the manager widget and all of its children collectively.

When you write a custom dialog, you simply create and manage the children of the Dialog-Shell in the same way that you create and manage the children of a top-level application shell. The predefined Motif dialogs follow the same approach, except that the toolkit creates the manager widget and all of its children internally. Most of the standard Motif dialogs are composed of a DialogShell and either a MessageBox or SelectionBox widget. Each of these widget classes creates and manages a number of internal widgets without application intervention. See Chapter 3, *Overview of the Motif Toolkit*, to review the various types of predefined Motif dialogs.

All of the predefined Motif dialogs are subclassed from the BulletinBoard widget class. As such, a BulletinBoard can be thought of as the generic dialog widget class, although it can certainly be used as generic manager widget (see Chapter 8, *Manager Widgets*). Indeed, a dialog widget is a manager widget, but it is usually not treated as such by the application. The BulletinBoard widget provides the keyboard traversal mechanisms that support gadgets, as well as a number of dialog-specific resources.

It is important to note that for the predefined Motif dialogs, each dialog is implemented as a single widget class, even though there are smaller, primitive widgets under the hood. When you create a MessageBox widget, you automatically get a set of Labels and PushButtons that are laid out as described in the *Motif Style Guide*. What is not created automatically is the DialogShell widget that manages the MessageBox widget. You can either create the shell yourself and place the MessageBox in it or use a Motif convenience routine that creates both the shell and its dialog widget child.

The Motif toolkit uses the DialogShell widget class as the parent for all of the predefined Motif dialogs. In this context, a MessageBox widget combined with a DialogShell widget creates what the Motif toolkit calls a MessageDialog. A careful look at terminology can help you to distinguish between actual widget class and Motif compound objects. The name of the actual widget class ends in `Box`, while the name of the compound object made up of the widget and a DialogShell ends in `Dialog`. For example, the convenience routine `Xm-CreateMessageBox()` creates a MessageBox widget, which you need to place inside of a DialogShell yourself. Alternatively, `XmCreateMessageDialog()` creates a Message-Dialog composed of a MessageBox and a DialogShell.

Another point about terminology involves the commonly-used term dialog box. When we say dialog box, we are referring to a compound object composed of a DialogShell and a dialog widget, not the dialog widget alone. This terminology can be confusing, since the Motif toolkit also provides widget classes that end in `box`.

One subtlety in the use of MessageBox and SelectionBox widgets is that certain types of behavior depend on whether or not the widget is a direct child of a DialogShell. For example, the *Motif Style Guide* says that clicking on the **OK** button in the action area of a MessageDialog invokes the action of the dialog and then dismisses the dialog. Furthermore, pressing the RETURN key anywhere in the dialog is equivalent to clicking on the **OK** button. However, none of this takes place when the MessageBox widget is not a direct child of a DialogShell.

Perhaps the most important thing to remember is how the Motif toolkit treats dialogs. Once a dialog widget is placed in a DialogShell, the toolkit tends to treat the entire combination as a single entity. In fact, as we move on, you'll find that the toolkit's use of convenience routines, callback functions, and popup widget techniques all hide the fact that the dialog is composed of these discrete elements. While the Motif dialogs are really composed of many primitive widgets, such as PushButtons and TextFields, the single-entity approach implies that you never access the subwidgets directly. If you want to change the label for a button, you set a resource specific to the dialog class, rather than getting a handle to the button widget and changing its resource. Similarly, you always install callbacks on the dialog widget itself, instead of installing them directly on buttons in the control or action areas.

This approach may be confusing for those already familiar with Xt programming, but not yet familiar with the Motif toolkit. Similarly, those who learn Xt programming through experiences with the Motif toolkit might get a misconception of what Xt programming is all about. We try to point out the inconsistencies between the two approaches so that you will understand the boundaries between the Motif toolkit and its Xt foundations.

5.2 The Anatomy of a Dialog

As described in Chapter 3, *Overview of the Motif Toolkit*, dialogs are typically broken down into two regions known as the control and action areas. The control area is also referred to as the work area. The control area contains the widgets that provide the functionality of the dialog, such as Labels, ToggleButtons, and List widgets. The action area contains PushButtons whose callback routines actually perform the action of the dialog box. While most dialogs follow this pattern, it is important to realize that these two regions represent user-interface concepts and do not necessarily reflect how Motif dialogs are implemented.

Figure 5-4 shows these areas in a sample dialog box.

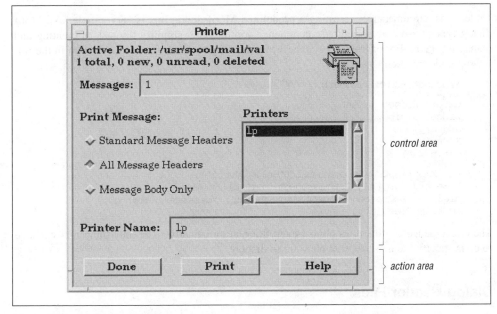

Figure 5-4. A sample dialog box

The *Motif Style Guide* describes in a general fashion how the control and action areas for all dialogs should be laid out. For predefined Motif dialogs, the control area is rigidly specified. For customized dialogs, there is only a general set of guidelines to follow. The guidelines for the action area specify a number of common actions that can be used in both predefined Motif dialogs and customized dialogs. These actions have standard meanings that help ensure consistency between different Motif applications.

By default, the predefined Motif MessageDialogs provide three action buttons, which are normally labeled **OK**, **Cancel**, and **Help**, respectively. SelectionDialogs provide a fourth button, normally labeled **Apply**, which is placed between the **OK** and **Cancel** buttons. This button is created but not managed, so it is not visible unless the application explicitly manages it. The *Style Guide* specifies that the **OK** button applies the action of the dialog and dismisses it, while the **Apply** button applies the action but does not dismiss the dialog. The

Cancel button dismisses the dialog without performing any action and the **Help** button provides any help that is available for the dialog. When you are creating custom dialogs, or even when you are using the predefined Motif dialogs, you may need to provide actions other than the default ones. If so, you should change the labels on the buttons so that the actions are obvious. You should try to use the common actions defined by the *Motif Style Guide* if they are appropriate, since these actions have standard meanings. We will address this issue further as it comes up in discussion; it is not usually a problem until you create your own customized dialogs, as described in Chapter 7, *Custom Dialogs*.

5.3 Creating Motif Dialogs

Under most circumstances, creating a predefined Motif dialog box is very simple. All Motif dialog types have corresponding convenience routines that simplify the task of creating and managing them. For example, a standard MessageDialog can be created as shown in the following code fragment:

```
#include <Xm/MessageB.h>

extern Widget parent;
Widget dialog;
Arg arg[5];
XmString t;
int n = 0;

t = XmStringCreateLocalized ("Hello World");
XtSetArg (arg[n], XmNmessageString, t); n++;
dialog = XmCreateMessageDialog (parent, "message", arg, n);
XmStringFree (t);
```

The convenience routine does almost everything automatically. The only thing that we have to do is specify the message that we want to display.

5.3.1 Dialog Header Files

As we mentioned earlier, there are two basic types of predefined Motif dialog boxes: MessageDialogs and SelectionDialogs. MessageDialogs present a simple message, to which a yes (**OK**) or no (**Cancel**) response usually suffices. There are six types of MessageDialogs: ErrorDialog, InformationDialog, QuestionDialog, TemplateDialog, WarningDialog, and WorkingDialog. These types are not actually separate widget classes, but rather instances of the generic MessageDialog that are configured to display different graphic symbols. All of the MessageDialogs are compound objects that are composed of a MessageBox widget and a DialogShell. When using MessageDialogs, you must include the file *<Xm/MessageB.h>*.

SelectionDialogs allow for more complicated interactions. The user can select an item from a list or type an entry into a TextField widget before acting on the dialog. There are essentially four types of SelectionDialogs, although the situation is a bit more complex than for MessageDialogs. The PromptDialog is a specially configured SelectionDialog; both of these dialogs are compound objects that are composed of a SelectionBox widget and a DialogShell. The Command widget and the FileSelectionDialog are based on separate widget classes. However, they are both subclassed from the SelectionBox and share many of its features. When we use the general term "selection dialogs," we are referring to these three widget classes plus their associated dialog shells. To use a SelectionDialog, you must include the file *<Xm/SelectioB.h>*.† For FileSelectionDialogs, the appropriate include file is *<Xm/FileSB.h>*, and for the Command widget it is *<Xm/Command.h>*.

5.3.2 Creating a Dialog

You can use any of the following convenience routines to create a dialog box. They are listed according to the header file in which they are declared:

<Xm/MessageB.h>:

```
XmCreateMessageBox()
XmCreateMessageDialog()
XmCreateErrorDialog()
XmCreateInformationDialog()
XmCreateQuestionDialog()
XmCreateTemplateDialog()
XmCreateWarningDialog()
XmCreateWorkingDialog()
```

<Xm/SelectioB.h>:

```
XmCreateSelectionBox()
XmCreateSelectionDialog()
XmCreatePromptDialog()
```

<Xm/FileSB.h>:

```
XmCreateFileSelectionBox()
XmCreateFileSelectionDialog()
```

<Xm/Command.h>:

```
XmCreateCommand()
```

Each of these routines creates a dialog widget. In addition, the routines that end in `Dialog` automatically create a DialogShell as the parent of the dialog widget. All of the convenience functions for creating dialogs use the standard Motif creation routine format. For example, `XmCreateMessageDialog()` takes the following form:

```
Widget
XmCreateMessageDialog(parent, name, arglist, argcount)
    Widget      parent;
    String      *name;
    ArgList     arglist;
    Cardinal    argcount;
```

In this case, we are creating a common MessageDialog, which is a MessageBox with a DialogShell parent. The `parent` parameter specifies the widget that acts as the owner or parent of the DialogShell. Note that the parent must not be a gadget, since the parent must

---

† Yes, you read that right. It does, in fact, read *SelectioB.h*. The reason for the missing *n* is there is a fourteen-character filename limit on UNIX System V machines.

have a window associated with it. The dialog widget itself is a child of the DialogShell. You are returned a handle to the newly created dialog widget, not the DialogShell parent. For the routines that just create a dialog widget, the *parent* parameter is simply a manager widget that contains the dialog.

The *arglist* and *argcount* parameters for the convenience routines specify resources using the old-style ArgList format, just like the rest of the Motif convenience routines. A varargs-style interface is not available for creating dialogs. However, you can use the varargs-style interface for setting resources on a dialog after is has been created by using XtVaSetValues().

5.3.3 Setting Resources

There are a number of resources and callback functions that apply to almost all of the Motif dialogs. These resources deal with the action area buttons in the dialogs. Other resources only apply to specific types of dialogs; they deal with the different control area components such as Labels, TextFields, and List widgets. The different resources are listed below, grouped according to the type of dialogs that they affect:

General dialog resources:

    XmNokLabelString   XmNokCallback
    XmNcancelLabelString   XmNcancelCallback
    XmNhelpLabelString   XmNhelpCallback

MessageDialog resources:

    XmNmessageString   XmNsymbolPixmap

SelectionDialog resources:

    XmNapplyLabelString   XmNapplyCallback
    XmNselectionLabelString   XmNlistLabelString

FileSelectionDialog resources:

    XmNfilterLabelString   XmNdirListLabelString
    XmNfileListLabelString

Command resources:

    XmNpromptString

The labels and callbacks of the various buttons in the action area are specified by resources based on the standard Motif dialog button names. For example, the XmNokLabelString resource is used to set the label for the **OK** button. XmNokCallback is used to specify the callback routine that the dialog should call when that button is activated. As discussed earlier, it may be appropriate to change the labels of these buttons, but the resource and callback names will always have names that correspond to their default labels.

The XmNmessageString resource specifies the message that is displayed by the Message-Dialog. The XmNsymbolPixmap resource specifies the iconic symbol that is associated with each of the MessageDialog types. This resource is rarely changed, so discussion of it is deferred until Chapter 21, *Advanced Dialog Programming*.

The other resources apply to the different types of selection dialogs. For example, XmNselectionLabelString sets the label that is placed above the list area in SelectionDialog. These resources are discussed in Chapter 6, *Selection Dialogs*.

All of these resources apply to the Labels and PushButtons in the different dialogs. It is important to note that they are different from the usual resources for Labels and PushButtons. For example, the Label resource XmNlabelString would normally be used to specify the label for both Label and PushButton widgets. Dialogs use their own resources to maintain the abstraction of the dialog widget as a discrete user-interface object.

Another important thing to remember about the resources that refer to widget labels is that their values must be specified as compound strings. Compound strings allow labels to be rendered in arbitrary fonts and to span multiple lines. See Chapter 19, *Compound Strings*, for more information.

The following code fragment demonstrates how to specify dialog resources and callback routines:

```
Widget dialog;
XmString msg, yes, no;
extern void my_callback();

dialog = XmCreateQuestionDialog (parent, "dialog", NULL, 0);
yes = XmStringCreateLocalized ("Yes");
no = XmStringCreateLocalized ("No");
msg = XmStringCreateLocalized ("Do you want to quit?");

XtVaSetValues (dialog,
    XmNmessageString,       msg,
    XmNokLabelString,       yes,
    XmNcancelLabelString,   no,
    NULL);
XtAddCallback (dialog, XmNokCallback, my_callback, NULL);
XtAddCallback (dialog, XmNcancelCallback, my_callback, NULL);

XmStringFree (yes);
XmStringFree (no);
XmStringFree (msg);
```

5.3.4 Dialog Management

None of the Motif toolkit convenience functions manage the widgets that they create, so the application must call XtManageChild() explicitly. It just so happens that managing a dialog widget that is the immediate child of a DialogShell causes the entire dialog to pop up. Similarly, unmanaging the same dialog widget causes it and its DialogShell parent to pop down. This behavior is consistent with the Motif toolkit's treatment of the dialog/shell combination as a single object abstraction. The toolkit is treating its own dialog widgets as opaque objects and trying to hide the fact that there are DialogShells associated with them. The toolkit is also making the assumption that when the programmer manages a dialog, she wants it to pop up immediately.

This practice is somewhat presumptuous and it conflicts directly with the specifications for the X Toolkit Intrinsics. These specifications say that when the programmer wants to display a popup shell on the screen, she should use XtPopup(). Similarly, when the dialog is to be dismissed, the programmer should call XtPopdown(). The fact that XtManageChild() happens to pop up the shell and XtUnmanageChild() causes it to pop down is misleading to the new Motif programmer and confusing to the experienced Xt programmer.

You should understand that this discussion of managing dialogs does not apply to customized dialogs that you create yourself. It only applies to the predefined Motif dialog widgets that are created as immediate children of DialogShells. The Motif toolkit uses this method because it has been around for a long time and it must be supported for backwards compatibility with older versions. Furthermore, using XtPopup() requires access to the Dialog-Shell parent of a dialog widget, which breaks the single-object abstraction.

There are two ways to manage Motif dialogs. You can follow the Motif toolkit conventions of using XtManageChild() and XtUnmanageChild() to pop up and pop down dialog widgets or you can use XtPopup() and XtPopdown() on the dialog's parent to do the same job. Whatever you do, it is good practice to pick one method and be consistent throughout an application. It is possible to mix and match the methods, but there may be some undesirable side effects, which we will address in the next few sections.

In an effort to make our applications easier to port to other Xt-based toolkits, we follow the established convention of using XtPopup(). This technique can coexist easily with Xt-ManageChild(), since popping up an already popped-up shell has no effect. Xt-Popup() takes the following form:

```
void
XtPopup(shell, grab_kind)
    Widget shell;
    XtGrabKind grab_kind;
```

The *shell* parameter to the function must be a shell widget; in this case it happens to be a DialogShell. If you created the dialog using one of the Motif convenience routines, you can get a handle to the DialogShell by calling XtParent() on the dialog widget.

The *grab_kind* parameter can be one of XtGrabNone, XtGrabNonexclusive, or XtGrabExclusive. We almost always use XtGrabNone, since the other values imply a *server grab*, which means that other windows on the desktop are locked out. Grabbing the server results in what is called *modality*; it implies that the user cannot interact with anything but the dialog. While a grab may be desirable in some cases, the Motif toolkit provides some predefined resources that handle the grab for you automatically. The advantage of using this alternate method is that it allows the client to communicate more closely with the Motif Window Manager (*mwm*) and it provides for different kinds of modality. These methods are discussed in Section 5.7.1. For detailed information on XtPopup() and the different uses of *grab_kind*, see Volume Four, *X Toolkit Intrinsics Programming Manual*.

If you call XtPopup() on a dialog widget that has already been popped up using Xt-ManageChild(), the routine has no effect. As a result, if you attempt to specify *grab_kind* as something other than XtGrabNone, it also has no effect.

The counterpart to XtPopup() is XtPopdown(). Any time you want to pop down a shell, you can use this function, which has the following form:

```
void
XtPopdown(shell)
    Widget shell;
```

Again, the *shell* parameter should be the XtParent() of the dialog widget. If you use XtUnmanageChild() to pop down a dialog, it is not necessary to call XtPopdown(), although we advise it for correctness and good form. However, it is important to note that if you use XtUnmanageChild() to pop down a dialog, you must use XtManageChild() to redisplay it again. Don't forget that the dialog widget itself is not a shell, so managing or unmanaging it still takes place when you use the manage and unmanage functions.

Let's take a closer look at how dialogs are really used in an application. Examining the overall design and the mechanics that are involved will help to clarify a number of issues about managing and unmanaging dialogs and DialogShells. The program listed in Example 5-1 displays an InformationDialog when the user presses a PushButton in the application's main window.†

Example 5-1. The hello_dialog.c program

```
/* hello_dialog.c -- your typical Hello World program using
 * an InformationDialog.
 */
#include <Xm/RowColumn.h>
#include <Xm/MessageB.h>
#include <Xm/PushB.h>

main(argc, argv)
int argc;
char *argv[ ];
{
    XtAppContext app;
    Widget toplevel, rc, pb;
    extern void popup(); /* callback for the pushbuttons -- pops up dialog */
    extern void exit();

    XtSetLanguageProc (NULL, NULL, NULL);

    toplevel = XtVaAppInitialize (&app, "Demos", NULL, 0,
        &argc, argv, NULL, NULL);

    rc = XtVaCreateWidget ("rowcol",
        xmRowColumnWidgetClass, toplevel, NULL);
    pb = XtVaCreateManagedWidget ("Hello",
        xmPushButtonWidgetClass, rc, NULL);
    XtAddCallback (pb, XmNactivateCallback, popup, "Hello World");
    pb = XtVaCreateManagedWidget ("Goodbye",
        xmPushButtonWidgetClass, rc, NULL);
    XtAddCallback (pb, XmNactivateCallback, exit, NULL);

    XtManageChild (rc);
```

---

†XtSetLanguageProc() is only available in X11R5; there is no corresponding function in X11R4. XmStringCreateLocalized() is only available in Motif 1.2; XmStringCreateSimple() is the corresponding function in Motif 1.1.

Example 5-1. The hello_dialog.c program (continued)

```
        XtRealizeWidget (toplevel);
        XtAppMainLoop (app);
}

/* callback for the PushButtons.  Popup an InformationDialog displaying
 * the text passed as the client data parameter.
 */
void
popup(button, client_data, call_data)
Widget button;
XtPointer client_data;
XtPointer call_data;
{
        Widget dialog;
        XmString xm_string;
        extern void activate();
        Arg args[5];
        int n = 0;
        char *text = (char *) client_data;

        /* set the label for the dialog */
        xm_string = XmStringCreateLocalized (text);
        XtSetArg (args[n], XmNmessageString, xm_string); n++;

        /* Create the InformationDialog as child of button */
        dialog = XmCreateInformationDialog (button, "info", args, n);

        /* no longer need the compound string, free it */
        XmStringFree (xm_string);

        /* add the callback routine */
        XtAddCallback (dialog, XmNokCallback, activate, NULL);

        /* manage the dialog */
        XtManageChild (dialog);
        XtPopup (XtParent (dialog), XtGrabNone);
}

/* callback routine for when the user presses the OK button.
 * Yes, despite the fact that the OK button was pressed, the
 * widget passed to this callback routine is the dialog!
 */
void
activate(dialog, client_data, call_data)
Widget dialog;
XtPointer client_data;
XtPointer call_data;
{
        puts ("OK was pressed.");
}
```

The output of this program is shown in Figure 5-5.

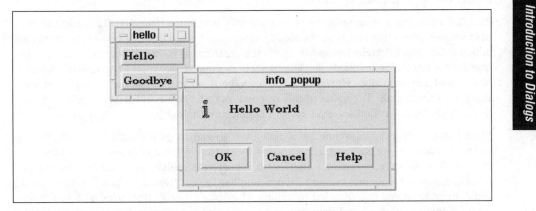

Figure 5-5. Output of hello_dialog.c

Dialogs are often invoked from callback routines attached to PushButtons or other interactive widgets. Once the dialog is created and popped up, control of the program is returned to the main event-handling loop (XtAppMainLoop()), where normal event processing resumes. At this point, if the user interacts with the dialog by selecting a control or activating one of the action buttons, a callback routine for the dialog is invoked. In Example 5-1, we happen to use an InformationDialog, but the type of dialog used is irrelevant to the model.

When the PushButton in the main window is pressed, popup() is called. A text string that is used as the message to display in the InformationDialog is passed as client data. The dialog uses a single callback routine, activate(), for the XmNokCallback resource. This function is invoked when the user presses the **OK** button. The callback simply prints a message to standard output that the button has been pressed. Similar callback routines could be installed for the **Cancel** and **Help** buttons through the XmNcancelCallback and XmNhelpCallback resources.

5.3.5 Closing Dialogs

You might notice that activating either the **OK** or the **Cancel** button in the previous example causes the dialog to be automatically popped down. The *Motif Style Guide* says that when any button in the action area of a predefined Motif dialog is pressed, except for the **Help** button, the dialog should be dismissed. The Motif toolkit takes this specification at face value and enforces the behavior, which is consistent with the idea that Motif dialogs are self-contained, self-sufficient objects. They manage everything about themselves from their displays to their interactions with the user. And when it's time to go away, they unmanage themselves. Your application does not have to do anything to cause any of the behavior to occur.

Unfortunately, this behavior does not take into account error conditions or other exceptional events that may not necessarily justify the dialog's dismissal. For example, if pressing **OK** causes a file to be updated, but the operation fails, you may not want the dialog to be dismissed. If the dialog is still displayed, the user can try again without having to repeat the actions that led to popping up the dialog.

The XmNautoUnmanage resource provides a way around the situation. This resource controls whether the dialog box is automatically unmanaged when the user selects an action area button other than the **Help** button. If XmNautoUnmanage is True, after the callback routine for the button is invoked, the DialogShell is popped down and the dialog widget is unmanaged automatically. However, if the resource is set to False, the dialog is not automatically unmanaged. The value of this resource defaults to True for MessageDialogs and SelectionDialogs; it defaults to False for FileSelectionDialogs.

Since it is not always appropriate for a dialog box to unmanage itself automatically, it turns out to be easier to set XmNautoUnmanage to False in most circumstances. This technique makes dialog management easier, since it keeps the toolkit from indiscriminately dismissing a dialog simply because an action button has been activated. While it is true that we could program around this situation by calling XtPopup() or XtManageChild() from a callback routine in error conditions, this type of activity is confusing because of the double-negative action it implies. In other words, programming around the situation is just undoing something that should not have been done in the first place.

This discussion brings up some issues about when a dialog should be unmanaged and when it should be destroyed. If you expect the user to have an abundant supply of computer memory, you may reuse a dialog by retaining a handle to the dialog, as shown in Example 5-4 later in this chapter. There are also performance considerations that may affect whether you choose to destroy or reuse dialogs. It takes less time to reuse a dialog than it does to create a new one, provided that your application is not so large that it is consuming all of the system's resources. If you do not retain a handle to a dialog, and if you need to conserve memory and other resources, you should destroy the dialog whenever you pop it down.

Another method the user might use to close a dialog is to select the **Close** item from the window menu. This menu can be pulled down from the title bar of a window. Since the menu belongs to the window manager, rather than the shell widget or the application, you cannot install any callback routines for its menu items. However, you can use the XmNdelete-Response resource to control how the DialogShell responds to a **Close** action.† It can have one of the following values:

XmUNMAP

> This value causes the dialog to be unmapped. The dialog disappears from the screen, but it is not destroyed, nor is it iconified. The dialog widget and its windows are still intact and can be redisplayed using XtPopup(). This value is the default for DialogShells.

XmDESTROY

> This value destroys the DialogShell and calls its XmNdestroyCallback. Note that all of the shell's children are also destroyed, including the dialog widget and its subwidgets. When the dialog is destroyed, you cannot redisplay the dialog or reference its handle again. If you need the dialog again, you have to create another one.

---

† The Motif VendorShell, from which the DialogShell is subclassed, is responsible for trapping the notification and determining what to do next, based on the value of the resource.

Examples of using the `XmNdestroyCallback` are presented in Chapter 21, *Advanced Dialog Programming*.

`XmDO_NOTHING`

This value causes the toolkit to take no action. The value should only be specified in circumstances where you want to handle the event on your own. However, handling the event involves much more than installing a simple callback routine. It requires building a lower-level mechanism that interprets the proper events when they are sent by the window manager. The most common thing to do in such cases is to activate the default action of the dialog or to interpose a prompting mechanism to verify the user's action. This topic is discussed in Chapter 16, *Interacting With the Window Manager*.

It may be convenient for your application to know when a dialog has been popped up or down. If so, you can install callbacks that are invoked whenever either of these events take place. The actions of popping up and down dialogs can be monitored through the `XmNpopupCallback` and `XmNpopdownCallback` callback routines. For example, when the function associated with a `XmNpopupCallback` is invoked, you could position the dialog automatically, rather than allowing the window manager to control the placement. See Chapter 7, *Custom Dialogs*, for more information on these callbacks.

5.3.6 Generalizing Dialog Creation

Posting dialogs that display informative messages is something just about every application is going to do frequently. Rather than write a separate routine for each case where a message needs to be displayed, we can generalize the process by writing a single routine that handles most, if not all, cases. Example 5-2 shows the `PostDialog()` routine. This routine creates a MessageDialog of a given type and displays an arbitrary message. Rather than use the convenience functions provided by Motif for each of the MessageDialog types, the routine uses the generic function `XmCreateMessageDialog()` and configures the symbol to be displayed by setting the `XmNdialogType` resource.†

Example 5-2. The PostDialog() routine

```
/*
 * PostDialog() -- a generalized routine that allows the programmer
 * to specify a dialog type (message, information, error, help, etc..),
 * and the message to display.
 */
Widget
PostDialog(parent, dialog_type, msg)
Widget parent;
int dialog_type;
char *msg;
{
    Widget dialog;
    XmString text;
```

---

†`XmStringCreateLocalized()` is only available in Motif 1.2; `XmStringCreateSimple()` is the corresponding function in Motif 1.1.

Example 5-2. The PostDialog( ) routine (continued)

```
    dialog = XmCreateMessageDialog (parent, "dialog", NULL, 0);
    text = XmStringCreateLocalized (msg);
    XtVaSetValues (dialog,
        XmNdialogType,     dialog_type,
        XmNmessageString, text,
        NULL);
    XmStringFree (text);

    XtManageChild (dialog);
    XtPopup (XtParent (dialog), XtGrabNone);

    return dialog;
}
```

This routine allows the programmer to specify several parameters: the parent widget, the type of dialog that is to be used, and the message that is to be displayed. The function returns the new dialog widget, so that the calling routine can modify it, unmanage it, or keep a handle to it. You may have additional requirements that this simplified example does not satisfy. For instance, the routine does not allow you to specify callback functions for the buttons in the action area and it does not handle the destruction of the widget when it is no longer needed. You could extend the routine to handle these issues, or you could control them outside the context of the function. You may also want to extend the routine so that it reuses the same dialog each time it is called and so that it allows you to disable the different action area buttons. All of these issues are discussed again in Chapter 6, *Selection Dialogs*, and in Chapter 21, *Advanced Dialog Programming*.

5.4 Dialog Resources

The following sections discuss resources that are specific to Motif dialogs. In most cases, these resources are BulletinBoard widget resources, since all Motif dialogs are subclassed from this class. However, they are not intended to be used by generic BulletinBoard widgets. The resources only apply when the widget is an immediate child of a DialogShell widget; they are really intended to be used exclusively by the predefined Motif dialog classes. Remember that the resources must be set on the dialog widget, not the DialogShell. See Chapter 8, *Manager Widgets*, for details on the generic BulletinBoard resources.

5.4.1 The Default Button

All predefined Motif dialogs have a *default button* in their action area. The default button is activated when the user presses the RETURN key in the dialog. The **OK** button is normally the default button, but once the dialog is displayed, the user can change the default button by using the arrow keys to traverse the action buttons. The action button with the keyboard focus is always the default button. Since the default button can be changed by the user, the button that is the default is only important when the dialog is initially popped up. The importance of the default button lies in its ability to influence the user's default response to the dialog.

You can change the default button for a MessageDialog by setting the XmNdefault-ButtonType resource on the dialog widget. This resource is specific to MessageDialogs; it cannot be set for the various types of selection dialogs. The resource can have one of the following values:

XmDIALOG_OK_BUTTON
>   This value specifies that the default button is the furthest button on the left of the dialog. By default, this button is the **OK** button, although its label may have been changed to another string.

XmDIALOG_CANCEL_BUTTON
>   This value specifies that the **Cancel** button is the default button. This value is appropriate in situations where the action of the dialog is destructive, such as for a WarningDialog that is posted in order to warn the user of a possibly dangerous action.

XmDIALOG_HELP_BUTTON
>   This value specifies the **Help** button, which is always the furthest button on the right of a Motif dialog. This button is rarely set as the default button.

XmDIALOG_NONE
>   This value specifies that there is no default button.

The values for XmNdefaultButtonType come up again later, when we discuss Xm-MessageBoxGetChild() and again in Chapter 6, *Selection Dialogs*, for Xm-SelectionBoxGetChild(). An example of how the default button type can be used is shown in Example 5-3.†

Example 5-3. The WarningMsg() function

```
/*
 * WarningMsg() -- Inform the user that she is about to embark on a
 * dangerous mission and give her the opportunity to back out.
 */
void
WarningMsg(parent, client_data, call_data)
Widget parent;
XtPointer client_data;
XtPointer call_data;
{
    static Widget dialog;
    XmString text, ok_str, cancel_str;
    char *msg = (char *) client_data;

    if (!dialog)
        dialog = XmCreateWarningDialog (parent, "warning", NULL, 0);
    text = XmStringCreateLtoR (msg, XmFONTLIST_DEFAULT_TAG);
    ok_str = XmStringCreateLocalized ("Yes");
    cancel_str = XmStringCreateLocalized ("No");
    XtVaSetValues (dialog,
        XmNmessageString,       text,
```

---

†XmStringCreateLocalized() is only available in Motif 1.2; XmStringCreateSimple() is the corresponding function in Motif 1.1.

Example 5-3. The WarningMsg( ) function (continued)

```
            XmNokLabelString,      ok_str,
            XmNcancelLabelString,  cancel_str,
            XmNdefaultButtonType, XmDIALOG_CANCEL_BUTTON,
            NULL);
    XmStringFree (text);
    XmStringFree (ok_str);
    XmStringFree (cancel_str);

    XtManageChild (dialog);
    XtPopup (XtParent (dialog), XtGrabNone);
}
```

The intent of this function is to create a dialog that tries to discourage the user from performing a destructive action. By using a WarningDialog and by making the **Cancel** button the default choice, we have given the user adequate warning that the action may have dangerous consequences. The output of a program running this code fragment is shown in Figure 5-6.

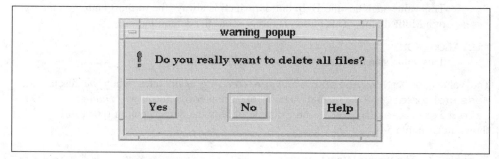

Figure 5-6. Output of WarningMsg( )

You can also set the default button for a dialog by the setting the BulletinBoard resource `XmNdefaultButton`. This technique works for both MessageDialogs and Selection-Dialogs. The resource value must be a widget ID, which means that you have to get a handle to a subwidget in the dialog to set the resource. You can get the handle to subwidgets using `XmMessageBoxGetChild()` or `XmSelectionBoxGetChild()`. Since this method breaks the Motif dialog abstraction, we describe it later in Section 5.6.3.

5.4.2 Initial Keyboard Focus

When a dialog widget is popped up, one of the internal widgets in the dialog has the keyboard focus. This widget is typically the default button for the dialog, which makes sense in most cases. However, there are situations where it is appropriate for another widget to have the initial keyboard focus. For example, when a PromptDialog is popped up, it makes sense for the TextField to have the keyboard focus so that the user can immediately start typing a response.

In Motif 1.1, it is not easy to set the initial keyboard focus in a dialog widget to anything other than a button in the action area. Motif 1.2 has introduced the XmNinitialFocus resource to deal with this situation. Since this resource is a Manager widget resource, it can be used for both MessageDialogs and SelectionDialogs, although it is normally only used for SelectionDialogs. The resource specifies the subwidget that has the keyboard focus the first time that the dialog is popped up. If the dialog is popped down and popped up again later, it remembers the widget that had the keyboard focus when it was popped down and that widget is given the keyboard focus again. The resource value must again be a widget ID. The default value of XmNinitialFocus for MessageDialogs is the subwidget that is also the XmNdefaultButton for the dialog. For SelectionDialogs, the text entry area is the default value for the resource.

5.4.3 Button Sizes

The XmNminimizeButtons resource controls how the dialog sets the widths of the action area buttons. If the resource is set to True, the width of each button is set so that it is as small as possible while still enclosing the entire label, which means that each button will have a different width. The default value of False specifies that the width of each button is set to the width of the widest button, so that all buttons have the same width.

5.4.4 The Dialog Title

When a new shell widget is mapped to the screen, the window manager creates its own window that contains the title bar, resize handles, and other window decorations and makes the window of the DialogShell the child of this new window. This technique is called reparenting a window; it is only done by the window manager in order to add window decorations to a shell window. The window manager reparents instances of all of the shell widget classes except OverrideShell. These shells are used for menus and thus should not have window manager decorations.

Most window managers that reparent shell windows display titles in the title bars of their windows. For predefined Motif dialogs, the Motif toolkit sets the default title to the name of the dialog widget with the string _popup appended. Since this string is almost certainly not an appropriate title for the window, you can change the title explicitly using the XmNdialogTitle BulletinBoard resource. (Do not confuse this title with the message displayed in MessageDialog, which is set by XmNmessageString.) The value for XmNdialogTitle must be a compound string. The BulletinBoard in turn sets the XmNtitle resource of the DialogShell; the value of this resource is a regular C string.

So, you can set the title for a dialog window in one of two ways. The following code fragment shows how to set the title using the `XmNdialogTitle` resource:

```
XmString title_string;

title_string = XmStringCreateLocalized ("Dialog Box");
dialog = XmCreateMessageDialog (parent, "dialog_name", NULL, 0);
XtVaSetValues (dialog,
    XmNdialogTitle, title_string,
    NULL);
XmStringFree (title_string);
```

This technique requires creating a compound string. If you set the `XmNtitle` resource directly on the DialogShell, you can use a regular C string, as in the following code fragment:

```
dialog = XmCreateMessageDialog (parent, "dialog_name", NULL, 0);
XtVaSetValues (XtParent (dialog),
    XmNtitle, "Dialog Box",
    NULL);
```

While the latter method is easier and does not require creating and freeing a compound string, it does break the abstraction of treating the dialog as a single entity.

5.4.5 Dialog Resizing

The `XmNnoResize` resource controls whether or not the window manager allows the dialog to be resized. If the resource is set to `True`, the window manager does not display resize handles in the window manager frame for the dialog. The default value of `False` specifies that the window manager should provide resize handles. Since some dialogs cannot handle resize events very well, you may find it better aesthetically to prevent the user from resizing them.

This resource is an attribute of the BulletinBoard widget, even though it only affects the shell widget parent of a dialog widget. The resource is provided as a convenience to the programmer, so that she is not required to get a handle to the DialogShell. The resource only affects the presence of resize handles in the window manager frame; it does not deal with other window manager controls. See Chapter 16, *Interacting With the Window Manager*, for details on how to specify the window manager controls for a DialogShell, or any shell widget, directly.

5.4.6 Dialog Fonts

The BulletinBoard widget provides resources that enable you to specify the fonts that are used for all of the button, Label, and Text widget descendants of the BulletinBoard. Since Motif dialog widgets are subclassed from the BulletinBoard, you can use these resources to make sure that the fonts that are used within a dialog are consistent. The `XmNbutton-FontList` resource specifies the font list that is used for all of the button descendants of the dialog. The resource is set on the dialog widget itself, not on its individual children. Similarly, the `XmNlabelFontList` resource is used to set the font list for all of the Label descendants of the dialog and `XmNtextFontList` is used for all of the Text and TextField descendants.

If one of these resources is not set, the toolkit determines the font list by searching up the widget hierarchy for an ancestor that is a subclass of BulletinBoard, VendorShell, or Menu-Shell. If an ancestor is found, the font list resource is set to the value of that font list resource in the ancestor widget. See Chapter 19, *Compound Strings*, for more information on font lists.

You can override the `XmNbuttonFontList`, `XmNlabelFontList`, and `XmNtext-FontList` resources on a per-widget basis by setting the `XmNfontList` resource directly on individual widgets. Of course, you must break the dialog abstraction and retrieve the widgets internal to the dialog itself to set this resource. While we describe how to do this in the following section, we do not recommend configuring dialogs down to this level of detail.

5.5 Dialog Callback Routines

As mentioned earlier, the predefined Motif dialogs have their own resources to reference the labels and callback routines for the action area PushButtons. Instead of accessing the Push-Button widgets in the action area to install callbacks, you use the resources `XmNok-Callback`, `XmNcancelCallback`, and `XmNhelpCallback` on the dialog widget itself. These callbacks correspond to each of the three buttons, **OK**, **Cancel**, and **Help**.

Installing callbacks for a dialog is no different than installing them for any other type of Motif widget; it may just seem different because the dialog widgets contain so many subwidgets. The following code fragment demonstrates the installation of simple callback for all of the buttons in a MessageDialog:

```
    ...
    dialog = XmCreateMessageDialog (w, "notice", NULL, 0);
    ...
    XtAddCallback (dialog, XmNokCallback, ok_pushed, "Hi");
    XtAddCallback (dialog, XmNcancelCallback, cancel_pushed, "Foo");
    XtAddCallback (dialog, XmNhelpCallback, help_pushed, NULL);
    XtManageChild (dialog);
    ...

/* ok_pushed() --the OK button was selected.  */
void
ok_pushed(widget, client_data, call_data)
Widget widget;
XtPointer client_data;
XtPointer call_data;
{
    char *message = (char *) client_data;

    printf ("OK was selected: %s\n", message);
}

/* cancel_pushed() --the Cancel button was selected.  */
void
cancel_pushed(widget, client_data, call_data)
Widget widget;
XtPointer client_data;
```

```
        XtPointer call_data;
        {
            char *message = (char *) client_data;

            printf ("Cancel was selected: %s\n", message);
        }

        /* help_pushed() --the Help button was selected.   */
        void
        help_pushed(widget, client_data, call_data)
        Widget widget;
        XtPointer client_data;
        XtPointer call_data;
        {
            printf ("Help was selected\n");
        }
```

In this example, a dialog is created and callback routines for each of the three responses are
added using XtAddCallback(). We also provide simple client data to demonstrate how
the data is passed to the callback routines. These callback routines simply print the fact that
they have been activated; the messages they print are taken from the client data.

All of the dialog callback routines take three parameters, just like any standard callback routine. The widget parameter is the dialog widget that contains the button that was selected;
it is not the DialogShell widget or the PushButton that the user selected from the action area.
The second parameter is the client_data, which is supplied to XtAddCallback(),
and the third is the call_data, which is provided by the internals of the widget that
invoked the callback.

The client_data parameter is of type XtPointer, which means that you can pass arbitrary values to the function, depending on what is necessary. However, you cannot pass a
float or a double value or an actual data structure. If you need to pass such values, you
must pass the address of the variable or a pointer to the data structure. In keeping with the
philosophy of abstracting and generalizing code, you should use the client_data parameter as much as possible because it eliminates the need for some global variables and it keeps
the structure of an application modular.

For the predefined Motif dialogs, the call_data parameter is a pointer to a data structure
that is filled in by the dialog box when the callback is invoked. The data structure contains a
callback reason and the event that invoked the callback. The structure is of type XmAny-
CallbackStruct, which is declared as follows:

```
        typedef struct {
            int      reason;
            XEvent  *event;
        } XmAnyCallbackStruct;
```

The value of the reason field is an integer value that can be any one of XmCR_HELP, Xm-
CR_OK, or XmCR_CANCEL. The value specifies the button that the user pressed in the dialog
box. The values for the reason field remain the same, no matter how you change the button
labels for a dialog. For example, you can change the label for the **OK** button to say **Help**,
using the resource XmNokLabelString, but the reason parameter will still be Xm-
CR_OK when the button is activated.

Because the `reason` field provides information about the user's response to the dialog in terms of the button that was pushed, we can simplify the previous code fragment and use one callback function for all of the possible actions. The callback function can determine which button was selected by examining `reason`. Example 5-4 demonstrates this simplification.†

Example 5-4. The reason.c program

```
/* reason.c -- examine the reason field of the callback structure
 * passed as the call_data of the callback function.  This field
 * indicates which action area button in the dialog was pressed.
 */
#include <Xm/RowColumn.h>
#include <Xm/MessageB.h>
#include <Xm/PushB.h>

/* main() --create a pushbutton whose callback pops up a dialog box */
main(argc, argv)
char *argv[ ];
{
    XtAppContext app;
    Widget toplevel, rc, pb;
    extern void pushed();

    XtSetLanguageProc (NULL, NULL, NULL);

    toplevel = XtVaAppInitialize (&app, "Demos", NULL, 0,
        &argc, argv, NULL, NULL);

    rc = XtVaCreateWidget ("rowcol", xmRowColumnWidgetClass, toplevel, NULL);

    pb = XtVaCreateManagedWidget ("Hello",
        xmPushButtonWidgetClass, rc, NULL);
    XtAddCallback (pb, XmNactivateCallback, pushed, "Hello World");

    pb = XtVaCreateManagedWidget ("Goodbye",
        xmPushButtonWidgetClass, rc, NULL);
    XtAddCallback (pb, XmNactivateCallback, pushed, "Goodbye World");

    XtManageChild (rc);
    XtRealizeWidget (toplevel);
    XtAppMainLoop (app);
}

/* pushed() --the callback routine for the main app's pushbuttons.
 * Create and popup a dialog box that has callback functions for
 * the OK, Cancel and Help buttons.
 */
void
pushed(widget, client_data, call_data)
Widget widget;
XtPointer client_data;
XtPointer call_data;
{
    static Widget dialog;
    char *message = (char *) client_data;
```

---

†XtSetLanguageProc() is only available in X11R5; there is no corresponding function in X11R4. Xm-StringCreateLocalized() is only available in Motif 1.2; XmStringCreateSimple() is the corresponding function in Motif 1.1.

Example 5-4. The reason.c program (continued)

```
    XmString t = XmStringCreateLocalized (message);

    /* See if we've already created this dialog -- if so,
     * we don't need to create it again.  Just set the message
     * and manage it (repop it up).
     */
    if (!dialog) {
        extern void callback();
        Arg args[5];
        int n = 0;

        XtSetArg (args[n], XmNautoUnmanage, False); n++;
        dialog = XmCreateMessageDialog (widget, "notice", args, n);
        XtAddCallback (dialog, XmNokCallback, callback, "Hi");
        XtAddCallback (dialog, XmNcancelCallback, callback, "Foo");
        XtAddCallback (dialog, XmNhelpCallback, callback, "Bar");
    }
    XtVaSetValues (dialog, XmNmessageString, t, NULL);
    XmStringFree (t);
    XtManageChild (dialog);

    XtPopup (XtParent (dialog), XtGrabNone);
}

/* callback() --One of the dialog buttons was selected.
 * Determine which one by examining the "reason" parameter.
 */
void
callback(widget, client_data, call_data)
Widget widget;
XtPointer client_data;
XtPointer call_data;
{
    char *button;
    char *message = (char *) client_data;
    XmAnyCallbackStruct *cbs = (XmAnyCallbackStruct *) call_data;

    switch (cbs->reason) {
        case XmCR_OK : button = "OK"; break;
        case XmCR_CANCEL : button = "Cancel"; break;
        case XmCR_HELP : button = "Help";
    }
    printf ("%s was selected: %s\n", button, message);
    if (cbs->reason != XmCR_HELP) {
        /* the ok and cancel buttons "close" the widget */
        XtPopdown (XtParent (widget));
    }
}
```

Another interesting change in this application is the way `pushed()` determines if the dialog has already been created. By making the dialog widget handle `static` to the `pushed()` callback function, we retain a handle to this object across multiple button presses. For each invocation of the callback, the dialog's message is reset and it is popped up again.

Considering style guide issues again, it is important to know when it is appropriate to dismiss a dialog. As noted earlier, the toolkit automatically unmanages a dialog whenever any of the action area buttons are activated, except for the **Help** button. This behavior is controlled by

XmNautoUnmanage, which defaults to True. However, if you set this resource to False, the callback routines for the buttons in the action area have to control the behavior on their own. In Example 5-4, the callback routine pops down the dialog when the reason is Xm-CR_OK or XmCR_CANCEL, but not when it is XmCR_HELP.

5.6 Piercing the Dialog Abstraction

As described earlier, Motif treats dialogs as if they are single user-interface objects. However, there are times when you need to break this abstraction and work with some of the individual widgets that make up a dialog. This section describes how the dialog convenience routines work, how to work directly with the DialogShell, and how to access the widgets that are internal to dialogs.

5.6.1 Convenience Routines

The fact that Motif dialogs are self-sufficient does not imply that they are black boxes that perform magic that you cannot perform yourself. For example, the convenience routines for the MessageDialog types follow these basic steps:

1. Create a popup widget of type xmDialogShellWidgetClass using XtCreate-PopupShell().

2. Create a widget of type xmMessageBoxWidgetClass as the child of the DialogShell.

3. Set the XmNdialogType resource for the dialog.

4. Install a callback routine for the XmNdestroyCallback resource of the MessageBox, so that it automatically destroys its DialogShell parent.

The XmNdialogType resource can be set to one of the following values:

```
XmDIALOG_ERROR
XmDIALOG_INFORMATION
XmDIALOG_MESSAGE
XmDIALOG_QUESTION
XmDIALOG_TEMPLATE
XmDIALOG_WARNING
XmDIALOG_WORKING
```

The type of the dialog does not affect the kind of widget that is created. The only thing the type affects is the graphical symbol that is displayed in the control area of the dialog. The convenience routines set the resource based on the routine that is called (e.g. XmCreate-ErrorDialog() sets the resource to XmDIALOG_ERROR). The widget automatically sets the graphical symbol based on the dialog type. You can change the type of a dialog after it is created using XtVaSetValues(); modifying the type also changes the dialog symbol that is displayed.

The Motif dialog convenience routines create DialogShells internally to support the single-object dialog abstraction. With these routines, the toolkit is responsible for the DialogShell, so the dialog widget uses its `XmNdestroyCallback` to destroy its parent upon its own destruction. If the dialog is unmapped or unmanaged, so is its DialogShell parent. The convenience routines do not add any resources or call any functions to support the special relationship between the dialog widget and the DialogShell, since most of the code that handles the interaction is written into the internals of the BulletinBoard.

5.6.2 The DialogShell

As your programs become more complex, you may eventually have to access the DialogShell parent of a dialog widget in order to get certain things done. This section examines Dialog-Shells as independent widgets and describes how they are different from other shell widgets. There are three main features of a DialogShell that differentiate it from an ApplicationShell and a TopLevelShell.

- A DialogShell cannot be iconified by the user or by the application.

- When the parent of a DialogShell is iconified, withdrawn, unmapped, or destroyed, the DialogShell children of that window are withdrawn or destroyed.

- A DialogShell is always placed on top of the shell widget that owns the parent of the DialogShell.

The DialogShell is subclassed from the TransientShell and VendorShell classes. A shell that is subclassed from TransientShell cannot be iconified independently of its parent. However, if the parent of a DialogShell is iconified or unmapped, the DialogShell is unmapped as well. If the parent is destroyed, so is the DialogShell and the dialog within it. Remember, the parent of the DialogShell is another widget somewhere in the application, such as a Label, a PushButton, as ApplicationShell, or even another DialogShell. For example, if the callback for PushButton creates a dialog, the PushButton might be designated as the owner of the dialog. If the shell that contains the PushButton is iconified, the dialog is also withdrawn from the screen. If the PushButton's shell or the PushButton itself is destroyed, the dialog is destroyed as well.

The parent-child relationship between a DialogShell and its parent is different from the classic case, where the parent actually contains the child within its geometrical bounds. The DialogShell widget is a popup child of its parent, which means that the usual geometry-management relationship does not apply. Nonetheless, the parent widget must be managed in order for the child to be displayed. If a widget has popup children, those children are not mapped to the screen if the parent is not managed, which means that you must never make a menu item the parent of a DialogShell.

Assuming that the parent is displayed, the window manager attempts to place the DialogShell based on the value of the `XmNdefaultPosition` BulletinBoard resource. The default value of this resource is `True`, which means that the window manager positions the Dialog-Shell so that it is centered on top of its parent. If the resource is set to `False`, the application and the window manager negotiate about where the dialog is placed. This resource is only relevant when the BulletinBoard is the immediate child of a DialogShell, which is always the case for Motif dialogs. If you want, you can position the dialog by setting the XmNx and XmNy resources for the dialog widget. Positioning the dialog on the screen must be done through a XmNmapCallback routine, which is called whenever the application calls XtManageChild(). See Chapter 7, *Custom Dialogs*, for a discussion about dialog positioning.

The Motif Window Manager imposes an additional constraint on the stacking order of the DialogShell and its parent. *mwm* always forces the DialogShell to be directly on top of its parent in the stacking order. The result is that the shell that contains the widget acting as the parent of the DialogShell cannot be placed on top of the dialog. This behavior is defined by the *Motif Style Guide* and is enforced by the Motif Window Manager and the Motif toolkit. Many end-users have been known to report the behavior as an application-design bug, so you may want to describe this behavior explicitly in the documentation for your application, in order to prepare the user ahead of time.

Internally, DialogShell widgets communicate frequently with dialog widgets in order to support the single-entity abstraction promoted by the Motif toolkit. However, you may find that you need to access the DialogShell part of a Motif dialog in order to query information from the shell or to perform certain actions on it. The include file *<Xm/DialogS.h>* provides a convenient macro for identifying whether or not a particular widget is a DialogShell:

```
#define XmIsDialogShell(w)   XtIsSubclass(w, xmDialogShellWidgetClass)
```

If you need to use this macro, or you want to create a DialogShell using XmCreate-DialogShell(), you need to include *<Xm/DialogS.h>*.

The macro is useful if you want to determine whether or not a dialog widget is the direct child of a DialogShell. For example, earlier in this chapter, we mentioned that the *Motif Style Guide* suggests that if the user activates the **OK** button in a MessageDialog, the entire dialog should be popped down. If you have created a MessageDialog without using Xm-CreateMessageDialog() and you want to be sure that the same thing happens when the user presses the **OK** button in that dialog, you need to test whether or not the parent is a DialogShell before you pop down the dialog. The following code fragment shows the use of the macro in this type of situation:

```
/* traverse up widget tree till we find a window manager shell */
Widget
GetTopShell(widget)
Widget widget;
{
    while (widget && !XmIsWMShell (widget))
        widget = XtParent (widget));

    return widget;
}

void
ok_callback(dialog, client_data, call_data)
Widget dialog;
XtPointer client_data;
XtPointer call_data;
{
    /*  do whatever the callback needs to do ... */
```

```
            /* if immediate parent is not a DialogShell, mimic the same
             * behavior as if it were (i.e., pop down the parent.)
             */
            if (!XmIsDialogShell (XtParent (dialog)))
                XtPopdown (GetTopShell (dialog));
        }
```

The Motif toolkit defines similar macros for all of its widget classes. For example,
<Xm/MessageB.h> defines the macro `XmIsMessageBox()`:

```
        #define XmIsMessageBox(w)   XtIsSubclass (w, xmMessageBoxWidgetClass)
```

This macro determines whether or not a particular widget is subclassed from the MessageBox
widget class. Since all of the MessageDialogs are really instances of the MessageBox class,
the macro covers all of the different types of MessageDialogs. If the widget is a Message-
Box, the macro returns `True` whether or not the widget is an immediate child of a Dialog-
Shell. Note that this macro does not return `True` if the widget is a DialogShell.

5.6.3 Internal Widgets

All of the Motif dialog widgets are composed of primitive subwidgets such as Labels, Push-
Buttons, and TextField widgets. For most tasks, it is possible to treat a dialog as a single
entity. However, there are some situations when it is useful to be able to get a handle to the
widgets internal to the dialog. For example, one way to set the default button for a dialog is
to use the `XmNdefaultButton` resource. The value that you specify for this resource must
be a widget ID, so this is one of those times when it is necessary to get a handle to the actual
subwidgets contained within a dialog.

The Motif toolkit provides routines that allow you to access the internal widgets. For
MessageDialogs, you can retrieve the subwidgets using `XmMessageBoxGetChild()`,
which has the following form:

```
        Widget
        XmMessageBoxGetChild(widget, child)
            Widget          widget;
            unsigned char   child;
```

The *widget* parameter is a handle to a dialog widget, not its DialogShell parent. The
child parameter is an enumerated value that specifies a particular subwidget in the dialog.
The parameter can have any one of the following values:

```
        XmDIALOG_OK_BUTTON
        XmDIALOG_CANCEL_BUTTON
        XmDIALOG_HELP_BUTTON
        XmDIALOG_DEFAULT_BUTTON
        XmDIALOG_MESSAGE_LABEL
        XmDIALOG_SEPARATOR
        XmDIALOG_SYMBOL_LABEL
```

The values refer to the different widgets in a MessageDialog and they should be self-explanatory. For SelectionDialogs, the toolkit provides the `XmSelectionBoxGetChild()` routine. This routine is identical to `XmMessageBoxGetChild()`, except that it takes different values for the different widgets in a SelectionDialog. The routine is discussed in Chapter 6, *Selection Dialogs*.

One method that you can use to customize the predefined Motif dialogs is to unmanage the subwidgets that are inappropriate for your purposes. To get the widget ID for a widget, so that you can pass it to `XtUnmanageChild()`, you need to call `XmMessageBoxGet-Child()`. You can also use this routine to get a handle to a widget that you want to temporarily disable. These techniques are demonstrated in the following code fragment:

```
text = XmStringCreateLocalized ("You have new mail.");
XtSetArg (args[0], XmNmessageString, text);
dialog = XmCreateInformationDialog (parent, "message", args, 1);
XmStringFree (text);

XtSetSensitive (
    XmMessageBoxGetChild (dialog, XmDIALOG_HELP_BUTTON), False);
XtUnmanageChild (
    XmMessageBoxGetChild (dialog, XmDIALOG_CANCEL_BUTTON));
```

The output of a program using this code fragment is shown in Figure 5-7.

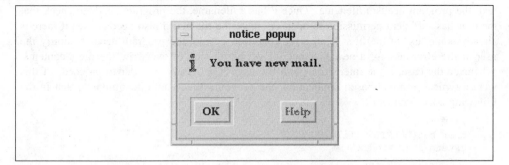

Figure 5-7. MessageDialog with an unmanaged Cancel button and an insensitive Help button

Since the message in this dialog is so simple, it does not make sense to have both an **OK** and a **Cancel** button, so we unmanage the latter. On the other hand, it does make sense to have a **Help** button. However, there is currently no help available, so we make the button unselectable by desensitizing it using `XtSetSensitive()`.

5.7 Dialog Modality

The concept of forcing the user to respond to a dialog is known as *modality*. Modality governs whether or not the user can interact with other windows on the desktop while a particular dialog is active. Dialogs are either modal or modeless. There are three levels of modality: primary application modal, full application modal, and system modal. In all cases, the user must interact with a modal dialog before control is released and normal input is resumed. In a system modal dialog, the user is prevented from interacting with any other window on the display. Full application modal dialogs allow the user to interact with any window on the desktop except those that are part of the same application as the modal window. Primary application modal dialogs allow the user to interact with any other window on the display except for the window that is acting as the parent for this particular dialog.

For example, if the user selected an action that caused an error dialog to be displayed, the dialog could be primary application modal, so that the user would have to acknowledge the error before she interacts with the same window again. This type of modality does not restrict her ability to interact with another window in the same application, provided that the other window is not the one acting as the parent for the modal dialog.

Modal dialogs are perhaps the most frequently misused feature of a graphical user interface. Programmers who fail to grasp the concept of event-driven programming and design, whereby the user is in control, often fall into the convenient escape route that modal dialogs provide. This problem is difficult to detect, let alone cure, because there are just as many right ways to invoke modal dialogs as there are wrong ways. Modality should be used in moderation, but it should also be used consistently. Let's examine a common scenario. Note that this example does not necessarily favor using modal dialogs; it is presented as a reference point for the types of things that people are used to doing in tty-based programs.

A text editor has a function that allows the user to save its text to a file. In order to save the text, the program needs a filename. Once it has a filename, the program needs to check that the user has sufficient permission to open or create the file and it also needs to see if there is already some text in the file. If an error condition occurs, the program needs to notify the user of the error, ask for a new filename, or get permission to overwrite the file's contents. Whatever the case, some interaction with the user is necessary in order to proceed. If this were a typical terminal-based application, the program flow would be similar to that in the following code fragment:

```
FILE *fp;
char buf[BUFSIZ], file[BUFSIZ];
extern char *index();

printf ("What file would you like to use? ");
if (!(fgets (file, sizeof file, stdin)) || file[0] == 0) {
    puts ("Cancelled.");
    return;
}

*(index (file, '\n')) = 0; /* get rid of newline terminator */

/* "a+" creates file if it doesn't exist */
if (!(fp = fopen (file, "a+"))) {
    perror (file);
    return;
}

if (ftell (fp) > 0) { /* There's junk in the file already */
    printf ("Overwrite contents of %s? ", file);
    buf[0] = 0;
    if (!(fgets (buf, sizeof buf, stdin)) || buf[0] == 0 ||
            buf[0] == 'n' || buf[0] == 'N') {
        puts ("Cancelled.");
        fclose (fp);
        return;
    }
}

rewind (fp);
```

This style of program flow is still possible with a graphical user interface system using modal dialogs. In fact, the style is frequently used by engineers who are trying to port tty-based applications to Motif. It is also a logical approach to programming, since it does one task followed by another, asking only for information that it needs when it needs it.

However, in an event-driven environment, where the user can interact with many different parts of the program simultaneously, displaying a series of modal dialogs is not the best way to handle input and frequently it's just plain wrong as a design approach. You must adopt a new paradigm in interface design that conforms to the capabilities of the window system and meets the expectations of the user. It is essential that you understand the event-driven model if you want to create well-written, easy-to-use applications.

Window-based applications should be modeled on the behavior of a person filling out a form, such as an employment application or a medical questionnaire. Under this scenario, you are given a form asking various questions. You take it to your seat and fill it out however you choose. If it asks for your license number, you can get out your driver's license and copy down the number. If it asks for your checking account number, you can examine your checkbook for that information. The order in which you fill out the application is entirely up to you. You are free to examine the entire form and fill out whatever portions you like, in whatever order you like.

When the form is complete, you return it to the person who gave it to you. The attendant can check it over to see if you forgot something. If there are errors, you typically take it back and continue until it's right. The attendant can simply ask you the question straight out and write down whatever you say, but this prevents him from doing other work or dealing with other people. Furthermore, if you don't know the answer to the question right away, then you have to take the form back and fill it out the way you were doing it before. No matter how you look at it, this process is not an interview where you are asked questions in sequence and must answer them that way. You are supposed to prepare the form off-line, without requiring interaction from anyone else.

Window-based applications should be treated no differently. Each window, or dialog, can be considered to be a form of some sort. Allow the user to fill out the form at her own convenience and however she chooses. If she wants to interact with other parts of the application or other programs on the desktop, she should be allowed to do so. When the user selects one of the buttons in the action area, this action is her way of returning the form. At this time, you may either accept it or reject it. At no point in the process so far have we needed a modal dialog.

Once the form has been submitted, you can take whatever action is appropriate. If there are errors in any section of the dialog, you may need to notify the user of the error. Here is where a modal dialog can be used legitimately. For example, if the user is using a FileSelectionDialog to specify the file she wants to read and the file is unreadable, then you must notify her so that she can make another selection. In this case, the notification is usually in the form of an ErrorDialog, with a message that explains the error and an **OK** button. The user can read the message and press the button to acknowledge the error.

It is often difficult to judge what types of questions or how much information is appropriate in modal dialogs. The rule of thumb is that questions in modal dialogs should be limited to simple, yes/no questions. You should not prompt for any information that is already available through an existing dialog, but instead bring up that dialog and instruct the user to provide the necessary information there. You should also avoid posting modal dialogs that prompt for a filename or anything else that requires typing. You should be requesting this type of information through the text fields of modeless dialog boxes.

As for the issue of forcing the user to fill out forms in a particular order, it may be perfectly reasonable to require this type of interaction. You should implement these restrictions by managing and unmanaging separate dialogs, rather than by using modal dialogs to prevent interaction with all but a single dialog.

All of these admonitions are not to suggest that modal dialogs are rare or that you should avoid using them at all costs. On the contrary, they are extremely useful in certain situations, are quite common, and are used in a wide variety of ways—even those that we might not recommend. We have presented all of these warnings because modal dialogs are frequently misused and programs that use fewer of them are usually better than those that use more of them. Modal dialogs interrupt the user and disrupt the flow of work in an application. There is no sanity checking to prevent you from misusing dialogs so it is up to you to keep the use of modal dialogs to a minimum.

5.7.1 Implementing Modal Dialogs

Once you have determined that you need to implement a modal dialog, you can use the `XmNdialogStyle` resource to set the modality of the dialog. This resource is defined by the BulletinBoard widget class; it is only relevant when the widget is an immediate child of a DialogShell. The resource can be set to one of the following values:†

```
XmDIALOG_MODELESS
XmDIALOG_PRIMARY_APPLICATION_MODAL
XmDIALOG_FULL_APPLICATION_MODAL
XmDIALOG_SYSTEM_MODAL
```

`XmDIALOG_MODELESS` is the default value for the resource, so unless you change the value any dialog that you create will be modeless.

When you use one of the modal values, the user has no choice but to respond to your dialog box before continuing to interact with the application. If you use modality at all, you should probably avoid using `XmDIALOG_SYSTEM_MODAL`, since it is rarely necessary to restrict the user from interacting with all of the other applications on the desktop. This style of modality is typically reserved for system-level interactions. Under the Motif Window Manager, when a system modal dialog is popped up, if the user moves the mouse outside of the modal dialog, the cursor turns into the international "do not enter" symbol. Attempts to interact with other windows cause the server to beep.

Example 5-5 shows a sample program that displays a dialog box that the user must reply to before continuing to interact with the application.‡

---

†The value `XmDIALOG_APPLICATION_MODAL` is used for backwards compatibility with Motif 1.0; it is defined to be the same as `XmDIALOG_PRIMARY_APPLICATION_MODAL`.

‡`XtSetLanguageProc()` is only available in X11R5; there is no corresponding function in X11R4. `XmStringCreateLocalized()` is only available in Motif 1.2; `XmStringCreateSimple()` is the corresponding function in Motif 1.1.

Example 5-5. The modal.c program

```
/* modal.c -- demonstrate modal dialogs.  Display two pushbuttons
 * each activating a modal dialog.
 */
#include <Xm/RowColumn.h>
#include <Xm/MessageB.h>
#include <Xm/PushB.h>

/* main() --create a pushbutton whose callback pops up a dialog box */
main(argc, argv)
char *argv[];
{
    XtAppContext app;
    Widget toplevel, button, rowcolumn;
    void pushed();

    XtSetLanguageProc (NULL, NULL, NULL);

    toplevel = XtVaAppInitialize (&app, "Demos",
        NULL, 0, &argc, argv, NULL, NULL);

    rowcolumn = XtCreateManagedWidget ("rowcolumn",
        xmRowColumnWidgetClass, toplevel, NULL, 0);

    button = XtCreateManagedWidget ("Application Modal",
        xmPushButtonWidgetClass, rowcolumn, NULL, 0);
    XtAddCallback (button, XmNactivateCallback,
        pushed, XmDIALOG_FULL_APPLICATION_MODAL);
    button = XtCreateManagedWidget ("System Modal",
        xmPushButtonWidgetClass, rowcolumn, NULL, 0);
    XtAddCallback (button, XmNactivateCallback, pushed,
        XmDIALOG_SYSTEM_MODAL);

    XtRealizeWidget (toplevel);
    XtAppMainLoop (app);
}

/* pushed() --the callback routine for the main app's pushbutton.
 * Create either a full-application or system modal dialog box.
 */
void
pushed(widget, client_data, call_data)
Widget widget;
XtPointer client_data;
XtPointer call_data;
{
    static Widget dialog;
    XmString t;
    extern void dlg_callback();
    unsigned char modality = (unsigned char) client_data;

    /* See if we've already created this dialog -- if so,
     * we don't need to create it again.  Just re-pop it up.
     */
    if (!dialog) {
        Arg args[5];
        int n = 0;
        XmString ok = XmStringCreateLocalized ("OK");
        XtSetArg(args[n], XmNautoUnmanage, False); n++;
        XtSetArg(args[n], XmNcancelLabelString, ok); n++;
```

Example 5-5. The modal.c program (continued)

```
        dialog = XmCreateInformationDialog (widget, "notice", args, n);
        XtAddCallback (dialog, XmNcancelCallback, dlg_callback, NULL);
        XtUnmanageChild (
            XmMessageBoxGetChild (dialog, XmDIALOG_OK_BUTTON));
        XtUnmanageChild (
            XmMessageBoxGetChild (dialog, XmDIALOG_HELP_BUTTON));
    }
    t = XmStringCreateLocalized ("You must reply to this message now!");
    XtVaSetValues (dialog,
        XmNmessageString,    t,
        XmNdialogStyle,      modality,
        NULL);
    XmStringFree (t);
    XtManageChild (dialog);
    XtPopup  (XtParent (dialog), XtGrabNone);
}

void
dlg_callback(dialog, client_data, call_data)
Widget dialog;
XtPointer client_data;
XtPointer call_data;
{
    XtPopdown (XtParent (dialog));
}
```

The output of this program is shown in Figure 5-8.

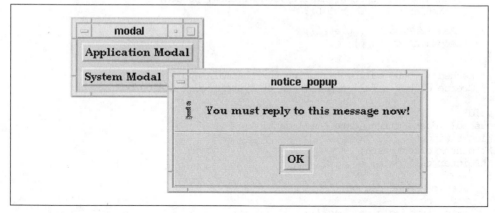

Figure 5-8. Output of modal.c

This program demonstrates both application modal and system modal dialogs. The value for the XmNdialogType resource is passed as client data to the callback routine that posts the dialog.

5.7.2 Forcing an Immediate Response

In Example 5-5, once the dialog is posted, the function returns so that `XtAppMainLoop()` can continue to process the events. If the function does not return, the application will not respond to user events and, for that matter, the dialog will not even be displayed. Just because a dialog is realized and managed does not mean that it is displayed on the screen, as events must be processed in order for it to appear. See Chapter 21, *Advanced Dialog Programming*, for a discussion of this phenomenon. (See Volume One, *Xlib Programming Manual*, for more information on event processing.)

However, there are situations where it would be nice not to have to return from the function and break its flow of control. As an example, consider a function that allows the user to perform a particularly dangerous action, such as removing or overwriting a file. What you'd like to do is prompt the user first and allow her to reconsider the action before proceeding. If she confirms the action, you'd like to continue from within the same function without having to return in order to process events.

In order to write this type of function, we need to find a way to process the events that display and manage the dialog without returning to the main loop. The user also needs to be able to respond to the dialog, so we really need to allow normal event processing to continue in the context of the function. Let's assume that there is a hypothetical function, `AskUser()`, that we can use in the following way:

```
if (AskUser ("Are you sure you want to do this?") == YES) {
    /* proceed with action... */
}
```

The function `AskUser()` should post a full application modal MessageDialog, wait for the user to respond to the dialog, and return a predefined value for either YES or NO. The magic of the function is to get around the requirement that events can only be read and processed directly from `XtAppMainLoop()`. The code for such a function is shown in Example 5-6.†

Example 5-6. The AskUser() routine

```
#define YES  1
#define NO   2

/*
 * AskUser() -- a generalized routine that asks the user a question
 * and returns the Yes/No response.
 */
int
AskUser(parent, question)
Widget parent;
char *question;
{
    static Widget dialog;
    XmString text, yes, no;
    static int answer;
```

†`XmStringCreateLocalized()` is only available in Motif 1.2; `XmStringCreateSimple()` is the corresponding function in Motif 1.1.

Example 5-6. The AskUser() routine (continued)

```
    extern void response();
    extern XtAppContext app;

    if (!dialog) {
        dialog = XmCreateQuestionDialog (parent, "dialog", NULL, 0);
        yes = XmStringCreateLocalized ("Yes");
        no = XmStringCreateLocalized ("No");
        XtVaSetValues (dialog,
            XmNdialogStyle,         XmDIALOG_FULL_APPLICATION_MODAL,
            XmNokLabelString,       yes,
            XmNcancelLabelString,   no,
            NULL);
        XtSetSensitive (
            XmMessageBoxGetChild (dialog, XmDIALOG_HELP_BUTTON),
            False);
        XtAddCallback (dialog, XmNokCallback, response, &answer);
        XtAddCallback (dialog, XmNcancelCallback, response, &answer);
        XmStringFree (yes);
        XmStringFree (no);
    }
    answer = 0;
    text = XmStringCreateLocalized (question);
    XtVaSetValues (dialog,
        XmNmessageString,       text,
        NULL);
    XmStringFree (text);
    XtManageChild (dialog);
    XtPopup (XtParent (dialog), XtGrabNone);

    /* while the user hasn't provided an answer, simulate main loop.
     * The answer changes as soon as the user selects one of the
     * buttons and the callback routine changes its value.
     */
    while (answer == 0)
        XtAppProcessEvent (app, XtIMAll);

    XtPopdown (XtParent (dialog));
    return answer;
}

/* response() --The user made some sort of response to the
 * question posed in AskUser().  Set the answer (client_data)
 * accordingly and destroy the dialog.
 */
void
response(widget, client_data, call_data)
Widget widget;
XtPointer client_data;
XtPointer call_data;
{
    int *answer = (int *) client_data;
    XmAnyCallbackStruct *cbs = (XmAnyCallbackStruct *) call_data;

    switch (cbs->reason) {
        case XmCR_OK:
            *answer = YES;
            break;
        case XmCR_CANCEL:
```

Example 5-6. The AskUser( ) routine (continued)

```
            *answer = NO;
            break;
    default:
        return;
    },
}
```

The first parameter to the function is the widget that acts as the parent of the new dialog. It is important to choose this widget wisely. The parent widget must not be a gadget or an unrealized widget; it should be a widget that is currently mapped to the screen. Widgets that are menu items are not good candidates, since they are not mapped to the screen for very long. The top-level shell widget of the widget that caused the callback function to be invoked is typically a good choice. The second parameter is the string that is displayed in the dialog.

The routine is intended to be used to display a dialog that asks a Yes/No question, so we change the **OK** and **Cancel** labels to say **Yes** and **No**, respectively. The routine creates a QuestionDialog as a static `Widget`, which allows us to reuse the dialog, rather than create it each time the function is called. This technique may improve performance on some machines. The modality of the dialog and the labels for the PushButtons in the action area are set at creation time, but the actual message string is set each time that the function is called, since the message can change. When we install the callback routines for the buttons, we use the address of the `answer` variable as the client data. As a result, when the user responds to the question by selecting the **Yes** or **No** button, the callback routine has access to the variable and can change its value accordingly.

The `while` loop is where the application waits for the user to make a selection. The loop exits when the variable `answer` is changed from its initial value (0) to either `YES` (1) or `NO` (2) by the callback routine. By using `XtAppProcessEvent()`, we have effectively reproduced the `XtAppMainLoop()` function that is used in the main application. Rather than returning to that level and breaking our flow of control, we have introduced a miniature main loop in the function itself.

While the `AskUser()` routine in Example 5-6 is useful as it is written, there are a number of enhancements that will make it even more useful. By using what we've learned in this chapter, we can come up with a simple, yet extremely robust interface for prompting the user for responses to questions without breaking the natural flow of control in the application. Example 5-7 demonstrates a generalized version of `AskUser()` in a complete application. The program *ask_user.c* allows the user to execute UNIX commands that create and remove a temporary file.†

Example 5-7. The ask_user.c program

```
/* ask_user.c -- the user is presented with two pushbuttons.
 * The first creates a file (/tmp/foo) and the second removes it.
 * In each case, a dialog pops up asking for verification of the action.
 *
```

---

†`XtSetLanguageProc()` is only available in X11R5; there is no corresponding function in X11R4. `XmStringCreateLocalized()` is only available in Motif 1.2; `XmStringCreateSimple()` is the corresponding function in Motif 1.1.

Example 5-7. The ask_user.c program (continued)

```
 * This program is intended to demonstrate an advanced implementation
 * of the AskUser() function.  This time, the function is passed the
 * strings to use for the OK button and the Cancel button as well as
 * the button to use as the default value.
 */
#include <Xm/DialogS.h>
#include <Xm/SelectioB.h>
#include <Xm/RowColumn.h>
#include <Xm/MessageB.h>
#include <Xm/PushB.h>

#define YES 1
#define NO  2

/* Generalize the question/answer process by creating a data structure
 * that has the necessary labels, questions and everything needed to
 * execute a command.
 */
typedef struct {
        char *label;     /* label for pushbutton used to invoke cmd */
        char *question;  /* question for dialog box to confirm cmd */
        char *yes;       /* what the "OK" button says */
        char *no;        /* what the "Cancel" button says */
        int   dflt;      /* which should be the default answer */
        char *cmd;       /* actual command to execute (using system()) */
} QandA;

QandA touch_foo = {
        "Create", "Create /tmp/foo?", "Yes", "No", YES, "touch /tmp/foo"
};
QandA rm_foo = {
        "Remove", "Remove /tmp/foo?", "Yes", "No", NO, "rm /tmp/foo"
};

XtAppContext app;

main(argc, argv)
int argc;
char *argv[];
{
        Widget toplevel, button, rowcolumn;
        XmString label;
        void pushed();

        XtSetLanguageProc (NULL, NULL, NULL);

        toplevel = XtVaAppInitialize (&app, "Demos",
            NULL, 0, &argc, argv, NULL, NULL);

        rowcolumn = XtVaCreateManagedWidget ("rowcolumn",
            xmRowColumnWidgetClass, toplevel, NULL);

        label = XmStringCreateLocalized (touch_foo.label);
        button = XtVaCreateManagedWidget ("button",
            xmPushButtonWidgetClass, rowcolumn,
            XmNlabelString,          label,
            NULL);
        XtAddCallback (button, XmNactivateCallback, pushed, &touch_foo);
        XmStringFree (label);
```

Example 5-7. The ask_user.c program (continued)

```
        label = XmStringCreateLocalized (rm_foo.label);
        button = XtVaCreateManagedWidget ("button",
            xmPushButtonWidgetClass, rowcolumn,
            XmNlabelString,          label,
            NULL);
        XtAddCallback (button, XmNactivateCallback, pushed, &rm_foo);
        XmStringFree (label);

        XtManageChild (rowcolumn);
        XtRealizeWidget (toplevel);
        XtAppMainLoop (app);
}

/* pushed() --when a button is pressed, ask the question described
 * by the QandA parameter (client_data).  Execute the cmd if YES.
 */
void
pushed(widget, client_data, call_data)
Widget widget;
XtPointer client_data;
XtPointer call_data;
{
        QandA *quest = (QandA *) client_data;

        if (AskUser (widget, quest->question, quest->yes, quest->no,
                quest->dflt) == YES) {
            printf ("Executing: %s\n", quest->cmd);
            system (quest->cmd);
        } else
            printf ("Not executing: %s\n", quest->cmd);
}

/*
 * AskUser() -- a generalized routine that asks the user a question
 * and returns a response.  Parameters are: the question, the labels
 * for the "Yes" and "No" buttons, and the default selection to use.
 */
AskUser(parent, question, ans1, ans2, default_ans)
Widget parent;
char *question, *ans1, *ans2;
int default_ans;
{
        static Widget dialog; /* static to avoid multiple creation */
        XmString text, yes, no;
        static int answer;
        extern void response();

        if (!dialog) {
            dialog = XmCreateQuestionDialog (parent, "dialog", NULL, 0);
            XtVaSetValues (dialog,
                XmNdialogStyle,          XmDIALOG_FULL_APPLICATION_MODAL,
                NULL);
            XtSetSensitive (
                XmMessageBoxGetChild (dialog, XmDIALOG_HELP_BUTTON),
                False);
            XtAddCallback (dialog, XmNokCallback, response, &answer);
            XtAddCallback (dialog, XmNcancelCallback, response, &answer);
        }
```

Example 5-7. The ask_user.c program (continued)

```
        answer = 0;
        text = XmStringCreateLocalized (question);
        yes = XmStringCreateLocalized (ans1);
        no = XmStringCreateLocalized (ans2);
        XtVaSetValues (dialog,
            XmNmessageString,      text,
            XmNokLabelString,      yes,
            XmNcancelLabelString,  no,
            XmNdefaultButtonType,  default_ans == YES ?
                XmDIALOG_OK_BUTTON : XmDIALOG_CANCEL_BUTTON,
            NULL);
        XmStringFree (text);
        XmStringFree (yes);
        XmStringFree (no);
        XtManageChild (dialog);
        XtPopup (XtParent (dialog), XtGrabNone);

        while (answer == 0)
            XtAppProcessEvent (app, XtIMAll);

        XtPopdown (XtParent (dialog));
        /* make sure the dialog goes away before returning. Sync with server
         * and update the display.
         */
        XSync (XtDisplay (dialog), 0);
        XmUpdateDisplay (parent);

        return answer;
}

/* response() --The user made some sort of response to the
 * question posed in AskUser().  Set the answer (client_data)
 * accordingly.
 */
void
response(widget, client_data, call_data)
Widget widget;
XtPointer client_data;
XtPointer call_data;
{
    int *answer = (int *) client_data;
    XmAnyCallbackStruct *cbs = (XmAnyCallbackStruct *) call_data;

    if (cbs->reason == XmCR_OK)
        *answer = YES;
    else if (cbs->reason == XmCR_CANCEL)
        *answer = NO;
}
```

The new version of AskUser() is more dynamic than before, since more of the dialog is configurable upon each invocation of the function. The routine now allows you to specify the message, the labels for the **OK** and **Cancel** buttons, and the default button for the dialog. The flexibility of the routine is achieved at the cost of a few more lines of source code and additional parameters to the function. The performance of the function is completely unaffected.

One case that the new version of AskUser() does not deal with is the need for additional buttons in the action area of the dialog. For example, what if you need to provide a **Cancel** button in addition to the **Yes** and **No** answers? Let's say that the user has selected the **Quit** menu item in a text editor application. Since the user has yet to update the changes to the file that she has been editing, the application posts a dialog that asks her if she wants to update her changes before exiting. There are three possible responses:

- Yes, update the changes and exit (**Yes**).

- No, don't update the changes, but exit anyway (**No**).

- Don't update the changes and don't exit the application (**Cancel**).

One easy way to provide these three choices is to set the label for the **Help** button to **Cancel** using the XmNhelpLabelString resource. Then you just need to modify the callback function so that it handles the XmCR_HELP reason and returns a new value for the **Cancel** button.

However, this solution does not work if you want to provide help in addition to these choices. The default MessageDialog only provides three buttons in the action area, although in Motif 1.2 you can add additional action area buttons to the dialog. For more information on how to handle this situation, see Chapter 7, *Custom Dialogs*.

5.8 Summary

Dialogs are used extensively in all window-oriented applications and their uses are quite diverse. As a result, it is impossible to provide numerous examples of the use of any one particular style of dialog. This chapter introduced the implementation of Motif dialogs by using the predefined MessageDialogs as examples. We described how to create the dialogs, how to set various dialog resources, how to handle dialog callback routines, and how to implement modal dialogs. Although our examples used MessageDialogs, much of the discussion is applicable to other types of Motif dialogs.

The next chapter deals with the predefined Motif selection dialogs. These dialogs allow you to provide the user with a group of choices from which to make a selection. Chapter 7, *Custom Dialogs*, discusses how you can break away from the predefined Motif dialogs and build dialogs on your own. Chapter 21, *Advanced Dialog Programming*, gets into advanced topics in Xt and Motif programming, using various types of MessageDialogs as examples.

6

Selection Dialogs

This chapter describes the predefined Motif selection-style dialogs. These dialogs display a list of items, such as files or commands, and allow the user to select items.

In This Chapter:

Selection Dialogs

6

Selection Dialogs

In Chapter 5, *Introduction to Dialogs*, we introduced the idea that dialogs are transient windows that perform a single task in an application. Dialogs may perform tasks that range from displaying a simple message, to asking a question, to providing a highly interactive window that obtains information from the user. The previous chapter also introduced Message-Dialogs and discussed how they are used by the Motif toolkit. This chapter discusses SelectionDialogs, which are at the next level of complexity in predefined Motif dialogs.

In general, SelectionDialogs are used to present the user with a list of choices. The user can also enter a new selection or edit an existing one by typing in a text area in the dialog. SelectionDialogs are appropriate when the user is supposed to respond to the dialog with more than just a simple yes or no answer. With respect to the action area, SelectionDialogs have the same default buttons as MessageBoxes (e.g., **OK**, **Cancel**, and **Help**). The dialogs also provide an **Apply** button, but the button is not always managed by default. Selection-Dialogs are meant to be less transient than MessageDialogs, since the user is expected to do more than read a message.

6.1 Types of SelectionDialogs

As explained in Chapter 5, *Introduction to Dialogs*, there are four kinds of SelectionDialogs. The SelectionDialog and the PromptDialog are compound objects composed of a Selection-Box and a DialogShell. To use these objects, you need to include the header file *<Xm/SelectioB.h>*. The FileSelectionDialog is another compound object made up of a File-SelectionBox and a DialogShell. The include file for this object is *<Xm/FileSB.h>*. The Command widget is somewhat different, in that it is typically used as part of a larger interface, rather than as a dialog. To use the Command widget, include the file *<Xm/Command.h>*. You can create each of these dialogs using the associated convenience routines:

```
XmCreateSelectionBox()
XmCreateSelectionDialog()
XmCreatePromptDialog()
XmCreateFileSelectionBox()
XmCreateFileSelectionDialog()
XmCreateCommand()
```

Like the MessageDialog convenience routines, each of the SelectionDialog routines creates a dialog widget. In addition, routines that end in `Dialog` automatically create a DialogShell as the parent of the dialog widget. Note that the Command widget does not provide a convenience routine that creates a DialogShell; to put a Command widget in a DialogShell, you must create the DialogShell yourself. All of the convenience functions use the standard format for Motif creation routines.

The SelectionBox resource XmNdialogType specifies the type of dialog that has been created. The resource is set automatically by the dialog convenience routines. Unlike the XmNdialogType resource for MessageDialogs, the SelectionBox resource cannot be changed once the dialog has been created. The resource can have one of the following values:

```
XmDIALOG_WORK_AREA
XmDIALOG_PROMPT
XmDIALOG_SELECTION
XmDIALOG_COMMAND
XmDIALOG_FILE_SELECTION
```

These values should be self-explanatory, with the exception of XmDIALOG_WORK_AREA. This value is set when a SelectionBox is not the child of a DialogShell and it is not one of the other types of dialogs. In other words, if you create a SelectionDialog using XmCreateSelectionDialog(), the value is XmDIALOG_SELECTION, but if you use XmCreateSelectionBox(), the value is XmDIALOG_WORK_AREA. When a SelectionBox is created as the child of a DialogShell, the **Apply** button is automatically managed, except if XmNdialogType is set to XmDIALOG_PROMPT. Otherwise, the button is created but not managed.

The different types of SelectionDialogs are meant to be used for unique purposes. Each dialog provides different components that the user can interact with to perform a task. In the following sections, we examine each of the SelectionDialogs in turn.

6.2 SelectionDialogs

The SelectionDialog provides a ScrolledList that allows the user to select from a list of choices, as well as a TextField where the user can type in choices. When the user makes a selection from the list, the selected item is displayed in the text entry area. The user can also type new or existing choices into the text entry area directly. The dialog does not take any action until the user activates one of the buttons in the action area or presses the RETURN key. If the user double-clicks on an item in the List, the item is displayed in the text area and the **OK** button is automatically activated. Example 6-1 demonstrates the use of a SelectionDialog.†

---

†XtSetLanguageProc() is only available in X11R5; there is no corresponding function in X11R4. XmStringCreateLocalized() is only available in Motif 1.2; XmStringCreateSimple() is the corresponding function in Motif 1.1. XmFONTLIST_DEFAULT_TAG replaces XmSTRING_DEFAULT_CHARSET in Motif 1.2.

Example 6-1. The select_dlg.c program

```
/* select_dlg.c -- display two pushbuttons: days and months.
 * When the user selections one of them, post a selection
 * dialog that displays the actual days or months accordingly.
 * When the user selects or types a selection, post a dialog
 * the identifies which item was selected and whether or not
 * the item is in the list.
 *
 * This program demonstrates how to use selection boxes,
 * methods for creating generic callbacks for action area
 * selections, abstraction of data structures, and a generic
 * MessageDialog posting routine.
 */
#include <Xm/SelectioB.h>
#include <Xm/RowColumn.h>
#include <Xm/MessageB.h>
#include <Xm/PushB.h>

Widget PostDialog();

char *days[] = {
    "Sunday", "Monday", "Tuesday", "Wednesday",
    "Thursday", "Friday", "Saturday"
};
char *months[] = {
    "January", "February", "March", "April", "May", "June",
    "July", "August", "September", "October", "November", "December"
};
typedef struct {
    char *label;
    char **strings;
    int size;
} ListItem;

ListItem month_items = { "Months", months, XtNumber (months) };
ListItem days_items = { "Days", days, XtNumber (days) };

/* main() --create two pushbuttons whose callbacks pop up a dialog */
main(argc, argv)
char *argv[];
{
    Widget toplevel, button, rc;
    XtAppContext app;
    void pushed();

    XtSetLanguageProc (NULL, NULL, NULL);

    toplevel = XtVaAppInitialize (&app, "Demos", NULL, 0,
        &argc, argv, NULL, NULL);

    rc = XtVaCreateWidget ("rowcolumn",
        xmRowColumnWidgetClass, toplevel, NULL);

    button = XtVaCreateManagedWidget (month_items.label,
        xmPushButtonWidgetClass, rc, NULL);
    XtAddCallback (button, XmNactivateCallback, pushed, &month_items);

    button = XtVaCreateManagedWidget (days_items.label,
        xmPushButtonWidgetClass, rc, NULL);
    XtAddCallback (button, XmNactivateCallback, pushed, &days_items);
```

Example 6-1. The select_dlg.c program (continued)

```
        XtManageChild (rc);
        XtRealizeWidget (toplevel);
        XtAppMainLoop (app);
}

/* pushed() --the callback routine for the main app's pushbutton.
 * Create a dialog containing the list in the items parameter.
 */
void
pushed(widget, client_data, call_data)
Widget widget;
XtPointer client_data;
XtPointer call_data;
{
    Widget dialog;
    XmString t, *str;
    int i;
    extern void dialog_callback();
    ListItem *items = (ListItem *) client_data;

    str = (XmString *) XtMalloc (items->size * sizeof (XmString));
    t = XmStringCreateLocalized (items->label);
    for (i = 0; i < items->size; i++)
        str[i] = XmStringCreateLocalized (items->strings[i]);
    dialog = XmCreateSelectionDialog (widget, "selection", NULL, 0);
    XtVaSetValues (dialog,
        XmNlistLabelString, t,
        XmNlistItems,       str,
        XmNlistItemCount,   items->size,
        XmNmustMatch,       True,
        NULL);
    XtSetSensitive (
        XmSelectionBoxGetChild (dialog, XmDIALOG_HELP_BUTTON), False);
    XtAddCallback (dialog, XmNokCallback, dialog_callback, NULL);
    XtAddCallback (dialog, XmNnoMatchCallback, dialog_callback, NULL);
    XmStringFree (t);
    while (--i >= 0)
        XmStringFree (str[i]); /* free elements of array */
    XtFree (str); /* now free array pointer */
    XtManageChild (dialog);

    XtPopup (XtParent (dialog), XtGrabNone);
}

/* dialog_callback() --The OK button was selected or the user
 * input a name by himself.  Determine whether the result is
 * a valid name by looking at the "reason" field.
 */
void
dialog_callback(widget, client_data, call_data)
Widget widget;
XtPointer client_data;
XtPointer call_data;
{
    char msg[256], *prompt, *value;
    int dialog_type;
    XmSelectionBoxCallbackStruct *cbs =
        (XmSelectionBoxCallbackStruct *) call_data;
```

Example 6-1. The select_dlg.c program (continued)

```
    switch (cbs->reason) {
        case XmCR_OK:
            prompt = "Selection: ";
            dialog_type = XmDIALOG_MESSAGE;
            break;
        case XmCR_NO_MATCH:
            prompt = "Not a valid selection: ";
            dialog_type = XmDIALOG_ERROR;
            break;
        default:
            prompt = "Unknown selection: ";
            dialog_type = XmDIALOG_ERROR;
    }
    XmStringGetLtoR (cbs->value, XmFONTLIST_DEFAULT_TAG, &value);
    sprintf (msg, "%s%s", prompt, value);
    XtFree (value);
    (void) PostDialog (XtParent (XtParent (widget)), dialog_type, msg);
    if (cbs->reason != XmCR_NO_MATCH) {
        XtPopdown (XtParent (widget));
        XtDestroyWidget (widget);
    }
}

/*
 * PostDialog() -- a generalized routine that allows the programmer
 * to specify a dialog type (message, information, error, help,
 * etc..), and the message to show.
 */
Widget
PostDialog(parent, dialog_type, msg)
Widget parent;
int dialog_type;
char *msg;
{
    Widget dialog;
    XmString text;

    dialog = XmCreateMessageDialog (parent, "dialog", NULL, 0);
    text = XmStringCreateLocalized (msg);
    XtVaSetValues (dialog,
        XmNdialogType,    dialog_type,
        XmNmessageString, text,
        NULL);
    XmStringFree (text);
    XtUnmanageChild (
        XmMessageBoxGetChild (dialog, XmDIALOG_CANCEL_BUTTON));
    XtSetSensitive (
        XmMessageBoxGetChild (dialog, XmDIALOG_HELP_BUTTON), False);
    XtAddCallback (dialog, XmNokCallback, XtDestroyWidget, NULL);
    XtManageChild (dialog);
    return dialog;
}
```

The output of the program is shown in Figure 6-1. The program displays two PushButtons, one for months and one for the days of the week. When either button is activated, a SelectionDialog that displays the list of items corresponding to the button is popped up. In

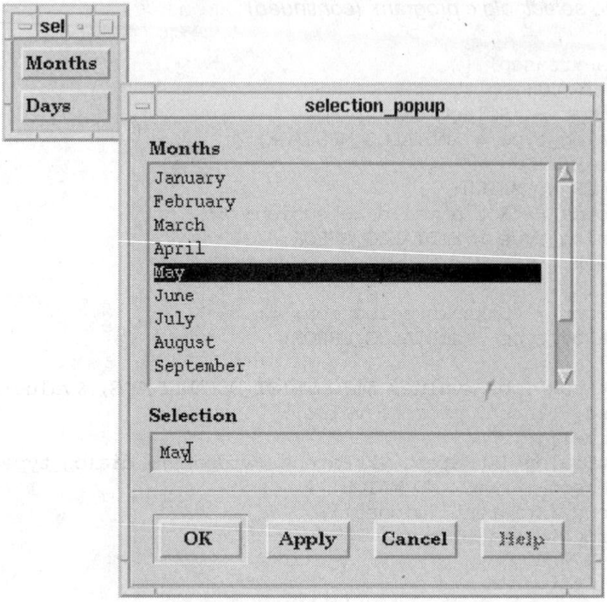

Figure 6-1. Output of select_dlg.c

keeping with the philosophy of modular programming techniques, we have broken the application into three routines — two callbacks and one general-purpose message posting function. The lists of day and month names are stored as arrays of strings. We have declared a data structure, `ListItem`, to store the label and the items for a list. Two instances of this data structure are initialized to the correct values for the lists of months and days. We pass these data structures as the `client_data` to the callback function `pushed()`. This callback routine is associated with both of the PushButtons.

The `pushed()` callback function creates the SelectionDialogs. Since the list of items for a SelectionDialog must be specified as an array of `XmString` values, the list passed in the `client_data` parameter must be converted. We create an array of compound strings the size of the list and copy each item into the new array using `XmStringCreate-Localized()`. The resulting list is used as the value for the `XmNlistItems` resource. The number of items in the list is specified as the value of the `XmNlistItemCount` resource. This value must be given for the list to be displayed. It must be less than or equal to the actual number of items in the list. We also set the `XmNlistLabelString` resource to specify the label for the list of items in the dialog. The SelectionDialog also provides the `XmNlistVisibleItemCount` resource for specifying the number of visible items in the list. We let the dialog use the default value for this resource.

The final resource that we set for the SelectionDialog is `XmNmustMatch`. This resource controls whether an item that the user types in the text entry area must match one of the items in the list. By setting the resource to `True`, we are specifying that the user cannot make up a month or day name. When the user activates the **OK** button or presses the RETURN key, the widget checks the item in the text entry area against those in the list. If the selection doesn't match any of the items in the list, the program pops up a dialog that indicates the error.

Once the dialog is created, we desensitize its **Help** button because we are not providing help. We install a callback routine for the **OK** button using the XmNokCallback. To handle the case when the user types an item that does not match, we also install a callback routine for the XmNnoMatchCallback. The dialog_callback() routine is used to handle both cases. We use the reason field of the callback structure to determine why the callback was called and act accordingly. The value field of the callback structure contains the selected item. If the item is valid, we use the value to create a dialog that confirms the selection. Otherwise, we post an error dialog that indicates the invalid selection. In both cases we use the generalized function, PostDialog(), to display the MessageDialog. If the selection is valid, the routine pops down and destroys the SelectionDialog. Otherwise, we leave the dialog posted so that the user can make another selection.

Just as a point of discussion, you should realize that it was an arbitrary decision to have the PostDialog() function accept a char strings rather than an XmString. The routine could be modified to use an XmString, but doing so doesn't buy us anything. If you find that your application deals with one string format more often than the other, you may want to modify your routines accordingly. You should be aware that converting from one type of string to the other is expensive; if it is done frequently, you may see an effect on performance. Another option is for your routine to accept both string types as different parameters. You can pass a valid value for one parameter and NULL for the other parameter and deal with them accordingly. For more information on handling compound strings, see Chapter 19, *Compound Strings*.

6.2.1 Callback Routines

The SelectionDialog provides callbacks for its action buttons in the same way as the MessageDialog. Instead of accessing the PushButton widgets to install callbacks, you use the resources XmNokCallback, XmNapplyCallback, XmNcancelCallback, and XmNhelpCallback on the dialog widget itself. These callbacks correspond to each of the four buttons, **OK**, **Apply**, **Cancel**, and **Help**. The SelectionDialog also provides the XmNno-MatchCallback for handling the case when the item in the text entry area does not match an item in the list.

All of these callback routines take three parameters, just like any standard callback routine. The callback structure that is passed to all of the callback routines in the call_data parameter is of type XmSelectionBoxCallbackStruct. This structure is similar to the one used by MessageDialogs, but it has more fields. The structure is declared as follows:

```
typedef struct {
    int         reason;
    XEvent      *event;
    XmString    value;
    int         length;
} XmSelectionBoxCallbackStruct;
```

The value of the `reason` field is an integer value that specifies the reason that the callback routine was invoked. The field can be one of the following values:

```
XmCR_OK
XmCR_APPLY
XmCR_CANCEL
XmCR_HELP
XmCR_NO_MATCH
```

The `value` and `length` fields represent the compound string version of the item that the user selected from the list or typed into the text entry area. In order to get the actual character string for the item, you have to use `XmStringGetLtoR()` to convert the compound string into a character string. (See Chapter 19, *Compound Strings*, for a discussion of compound strings.)

6.2.2 Internal Widgets

The SelectionDialog is obviously composed of primitive subwidgets, like PushButtons, Labels, a ScrolledList, and a TextField widget. For most tasks, it is possible to treat the dialog as a single entity because the dialog provides resources that manage the different components. However, there are some situations where it is useful to be able to get a handle to the widgets internal to the dialog. The Motif toolkit provides the `XmSelectionBoxGet-Child()` routine to allow you to access the internal widgets. This routine takes the following form:

```
Widget
XmSelectionBoxGetChild(widget, child)
    Widget          widget;
    unsigned char   child;
```

The *widget* parameter is a handle to a dialog widget, not its DialogShell parent. The *child* parameter is an enumerated value that specifies a particular subwidget in the dialog. The parameter can have any one of the following values:

```
XmDIALOG_OK_BUTTON
XmDIALOG_APPLY_BUTTON
XmDIALOG_CANCEL_BUTTON
XmDIALOG_HELP_BUTTON
XmDIALOG_DEFAULT_BUTTONX
XmDIALOG_LIST
XmDIALOG_LIST_LABEL
XmDIALOG_SELECTION_LABEL
XmDIALOG_TEXT
XmDIALOG_WORK_AREA
XmDIALOG_SEPARATOR
```

The values refer to the different widgets in a SelectionDialog and they should be self-explanatory, with the exception of `XmDIALOG_WORK_AREA`. A SelectionDialog can manage a work area child; this value returns the work area child. You can customize the operation of a SelectionDialog by adding a work area that contains other components. For a detailed discussion of this technique, see Chapter 7, *Custom Dialogs*.

One use of `XmSelectionBoxGetChild()` is to get a handle to the **Apply** button so that you can manage it. When you create a SelectionBox that is not a child of a DialogShell, the toolkit creates the **Apply** button, but it is unmanaged by default. The **Apply** button is available to the PromptDialog, but it is unmanaged by default. To use the button, you must manage it and specify a callback routine, as in the following code fragment:

```
XtAddCallback (dialog, XmNapplyCallback, dialog_callback, NULL);
XtManageChild (XmSelectionBoxGetChild (dialog, XmDIALOG_APPLY_BUTTON));
```

The callback routine is the same as the one we set for the **OK** button, but the `reason` field in the callback structure will indicate that it was called as a result of the **Apply** button being activated.

6.3 PromptDialogs

The PromptDialog is unique among the SelectionDialogs, in that it does not create a ScrolledList object. This dialog allows the user to type a text string in the text entry area and then enter it by selecting the **OK** button or by pressing the RETURN key. Example 6-2 shows an example of creating and using a PromptDialog.†

Example 6-2. The prompt_dlg.c program

```
/* prompt_dlg.c -- prompt the user for a string.  Two PushButtons
 * are displayed.  When one is selected, a PromptDialog is displayed
 * allowing the user to type a string.  When done, the PushButton's
 * label changes to the string.
 */
#include <Xm/SelectioB.h>
#include <Xm/RowColumn.h>
#include <Xm/PushB.h>

main(argc, argv)
char *argv[];
{
    XtAppContext app;
    Widget toplevel, rc, button;
    void pushed();

    XtSetLanguageProc (NULL, NULL, NULL);

    /* Initialize toolkit and create toplevel shell */
    toplevel = XtVaAppInitialize (&app, "Demos", NULL, 0,
        &argc, argv, NULL, NULL);

    /* RowColumn managed both PushButtons */
    rc = XtVaCreateWidget ("rowcol", xmRowColumnWidgetClass, toplevel,
        NULL);
    /* Create two pushbuttons -- both have the same callback */
    button = XtVaCreateManagedWidget ("PushMe 1",
        xmPushButtonWidgetClass, rc, NULL);
```

---

†`XtSetLanguageProc()` is only available in X11R5; there is no corresponding function in X11R4. `XmStringCreateLocalized()` is only available in Motif 1.2; `XmStringCreateSimple()` is the corresponding function in Motif 1.1.

Example 6-2. The prompt_dlg.c program (continued)

```
        XtAddCallback (button, XmNactivateCallback, pushed, NULL);
        button = XtVaCreateManagedWidget ("PushMe 2",
            xmPushButtonWidgetClass, rc, NULL);
        XtAddCallback (button, XmNactivateCallback, pushed, NULL);

        XtManageChild (rc);
        XtRealizeWidget (toplevel);
        XtAppMainLoop (app);
}

/* pushed() --the callback routine for the main app's pushbuttons.
 * Create a dialog that prompts for a new button name.
 */
void
pushed(widget, client_data, call_data)
Widget widget;
XtPointer client_data;
XtPointer call_data;
{
        Widget dialog;
        XmString t = XmStringCreateLocalized ("Enter New Button Name:");
        extern void read_name();
        Arg args[5];
        int n = 0;

        /* Create the dialog -- the PushButton acts as the DialogShell's
         * parent (not the parent of the PromptDialog).
         */
        XtSetArg (args[n], XmNselectionLabelString, t); n++;
        XtSetArg (args[n], XmNautoUnmanage, False); n++;
        dialog = XmCreatePromptDialog (widget, "prompt", args, n);
        XmStringFree (t); /* always destroy compound strings when done */

        /* When the user types the name, call read_name() ... */
        XtAddCallback (dialog, XmNokCallback, read_name, widget);

        /* If the user selects cancel, just destroy the dialog */
        XtAddCallback (dialog, XmNcancelCallback, XtDestroyWidget, NULL);

        /* No help is available... */
        XtSetSensitive (
            XmSelectionBoxGetChild (dialog, XmDIALOG_HELP_BUTTON), False);
        XtManageChild (dialog);

        XtPopup (XtParent (dialog), XtGrabNone);
}

/* read_name() --the text field has been filled in. */
void
read_name(widget, client_data, call_data)
Widget widget;
XtPointer client_data;
XtPointer call_data;
{
        Widget push_button = (Widget) client_data;
        XmSelectionBoxCallbackStruct *cbs =
            (XmSelectionBoxCallbackStruct *) call_data;

        XtVaSetValues (push_button, XmNlabelString, cbs->value, NULL);
        /* Name's fine -- go ahead and enter it */
```

Example 6-2. The prompt_dlg.c program (continued)

```
    XtDestroyWidget(widget);
}
```

The output of the program is shown in Figure 6-2.

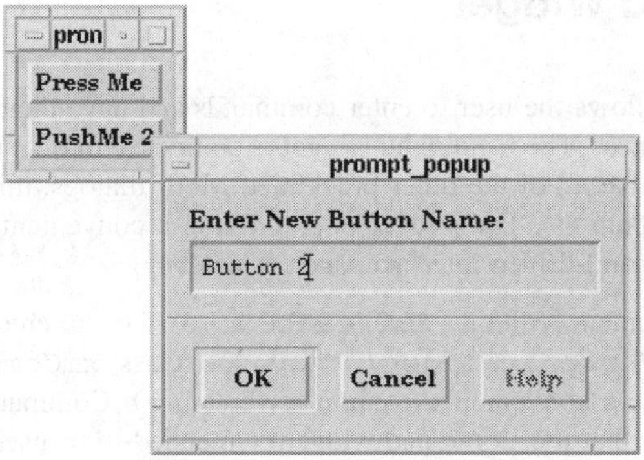

Figure 6-2. Output of prompt_dlg.c

The callback routine for each of the PushButtons, `pushed()`, creates a PromptDialog that prompts the user to enter a new name for the PushButton. The PushButton is passed as the `client_data` to the `XmNokCallback` routine, `read_name()`, so that the routine can set the label of the PushButton directly from inside the callback. The `read_name()` function destroys the dialog once it has set the label, since the dialog is no longer needed.

If the **Cancel** button is pressed, the text is not needed, so we can simply destroy the dialog. Since the first parameter to a dialog callback routine is the dialog widget, we can use `Xt-DestroyWidget` as the callback routine. Since the function only takes one parameter, and the widget that is to be destroyed is passed as the first parameter, no client data is needed. We set `XmNautoUnmanage` to `False` for the dialog because the application is assuming the responsibility of managing the dialog. There is no help for the dialog so the **Help** button is disabled by setting it insensitive.

The text area in the PromptDialog is a TextField widget, so you can get a handle to it and set TextField widget resources accordingly. Use `XmSelectionBoxGetChild()` to access the widget. In order to promote the single-entity abstraction, the dialog provides two resources that affect the TextField widget. You can set the `XmNtextString` resource to change the value of the text string in the widget. Like other string resources, the value for this resource must be a compound string. The `XmNtextColumns` resource specifies the width of the TextField in columns.

In Motif 1.1, one frustrating feature of the predefined SelectionDialogs is that when they are popped up, the TextField widget does not receive the keyboard focus by default. If the user is not paying attention, starts typing, and then presses the RETURN key, all of the keystrokes will be thrown away except the RETURN, which will activate the **OK** button. Motif 1.2 solves this problem by introducing the `XmNinitialFocus` resource. This resource specifies the widget that has the keyboard focus the first time that the dialog is popped up. The text entry area is the default value of the resource for SelectionDialogs. If you are using Motif 1.1, you need to warn your users about the problem. You can also program around the problem by using `XmProcessTraversal()` to set the focus to a particular widget.

6.4 The Command Widget

A Command widget allows the user to enter commands and have them saved in a history list widget for later reference. The Command widget is composed of a text entry area and a command history list. Unlike all of the other predefined Motif dialogs, this widget does not provide any action area buttons. The widget does provide a convenient interface for applications that have a command-driven interface, such as a debugger.

You can use the convenience routine `XmCreateCommand()` to create a Command widget or you can use `XtVaCreateWidget()` with the class `xmCommandWidgetClass`. Motif does not provide a convenience routine for creating a Command widget in a Dialog-Shell. The rationale is that the Command widget is intended to be used on a more permanent basis, since it accumulates a history of command input. A Command widget is typically used as part of a larger interface, such as in a MainWindow, which is why it does not have action buttons. (See Chapter 4, *The Main Window*, for an example.) If you want to create a CommandDialog, you will have to create the DialogShell widget yourself and make the Command widget its immediate child. See Section 5.6.2 in Chapter 5, *Introduction to Dialogs*, for more information about DialogShells.

The Command widget class is subclassed from SelectionBox. There are similarities between the two widgets, in that the user has the ability to select items from a list. However, the list is composed of the commands that have been previously entered. When the user enters a command, it is added to the list. If the user selects an item from the command history list, the command is displayed in the text entry area. Although the Command widget inherits resources from the SelectionBox, many of the resources are not applicable since the Command widget does not have any action area buttons. All of the SelectionBox resources for setting the labels and callbacks of the buttons do not apply to the Command widget.

The Command widget provides a number of resources that can be used to control the command history list. The `XmNhistoryItems` and `XmNhistoryItemCount` resources specify the list of commands and the number of commands in the list. The `XmNhistory-VisibleItemCount` resource controls the number of items that are visible in the command history. `XmNhistoryMaxItems` specifies the maximum number of items in the history list. When the maximum value is reached, a command is removed from the beginning of the list to make room for each new command that is entered.

The Command widget provides two callback resources, `XmNcommandEnteredCallback` and `XmNcommandChangedCallback`, for the text entry area. When the user changes the text in the command entry area, the `XmNcommandChangedCallback` is invoked. If the user presses the RETURN key or double-clicks on an item in the command history list, the `XmNcommandEnteredCallback` is called. The callback routine for each of the callbacks takes the usual three parameters. The callback structure passed to the routines in the `call_data` parameter is of type `XmCommandCallbackStruct`, which is identical to the `XmSelectionBoxCallbackStruct`. The possible values for the `reason` field in the structure are `XmCR_COMMAND_ENTERED` and `XmCR_COMMAND_CHANGED`.

You can get a handle to the subwidgets of the Command widget using function `XmCommandGetChild()`. The function takes the following form:

```
Widget
XmCommandGetChild(widget, child)
    Widget          widget;
    unsigned char   child;
```

The *widget* parameter is a handle to a dialog widget. The *child* parameter is an enumerated value that specifies a particular subwidget in the dialog. The parameter can have any one of the following values:

```
XmDIALOG_COMMAND_TEXT
XmDIALOG_HISTORY_LIST
XmDIALOG_PROMPT_LABEL
XmDIALOG_WORK_AREA
```

The values refer to the different widgets in the Command widget and they should be self-explanatory.

In order to support the idea that the dialog is a single widget, the toolkit also provides a number of convenience routines that you can use to modify the Command widget. The function `XmCommandSetValue()` sets the text in the command entry area of the dialog. The function takes the following form:

```
void
XmCommandSetValue(widget, command)
    Widget          widget;
    XmString        command;
```

The *command* is displayed in the command entry area. The Command widget resource `XmNcommand` specifies the text for the command entry area, so you can also set this resource directly. Alternatively, you can use `XmTextSetString()` on the Text widget in the dialog to set the command. However, note that the string you specify to this function is a regular character string, not a compound string.

If you want to append some text to the string in the command entry area, you can use the routine `XmCommandAppendValue()`, which takes the following form:

```
void
XmCommandAppendValue(widget, command)
    Widget          widget;
    XmString        command;
```

The *command* is added to the end of the string in the command entry area. The function XmCommandError() displays an error message in the history area of the Command widget. The function takes the following form:

```
void
XmCommandError(widget, message)
    Widget          widget;
    XmString        message;
```

The error message is displayed until the user enters the next command.

6.5 FileSelectionDialogs

Like the Command widget, the FileSelectionBox is subclassed from SelectionBox. The FileSelectionDialog looks somewhat different than the other selection dialogs because of its complexity and its unusual widget layout and architecture. Functionally, the FileSelectionDialog allows the user to move through the file system and select a file or a directory for use by the application. The dialog also lets the user specify a filter that controls the files that are displayed in the dialog. This filter is generally specified as a regular expression reminiscent of the classic UNIX meta-characters (e.g., * matches all files, while *.c matches all files that end in .c). Figure 6-3 shows a FileSelectionDialog.

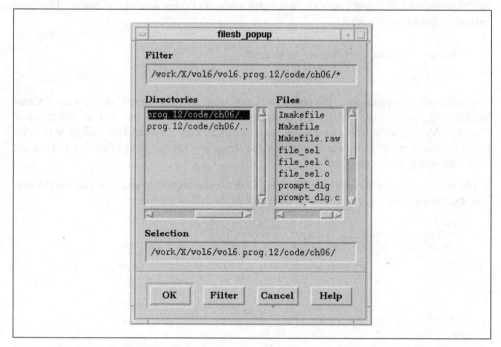

Figure 6-3. A typical FileSelectionDialog

The control area of the FileSelectionDialog has four components. The filter text entry area specifies the directory and the filter. The directories list displays the directories in the current directory specified by the filter. If the user selects a directory, the filter is modified to reflect the selection. The files list shows the files in the current directory. The selection text entry area specifies the file selected by the user. If the user selects a file from the file list, the full pathname is displayed in the selection text entry area.

The FileSelectionDialog has four buttons in its action area. The **OK**, **Cancel**, and **Help** buttons are the same as for other SelectionDialogs. The **Filter** button acts on the directory and pattern specified in the filter text entry area. For example, the user could enter */usr/src/motif/lib/Xm/** as the filter. In this case, the directory is */usr/src/motif/lib/Xm* and the pattern is the "*". When the user selects the **Filter** button or presses RETURN in the Text widget, the directory part of the filter is searched and all of the directories within that directory are displayed in the directories list. The pattern part is then used to find all of the matching files in the directory and the files are shown in the files list. Only files are placed in this list; directories are excluded since they are listed separately.

While this process seems straightforward, it can become confusing for users and programmers alike because of the way that the widget parses the filter. For example, consider the following string: */usr/src/motif/lib/Xm*. This pathname appears to be a common directory path, but in fact, the widget interprets the filter so that the directory is */usr/src/motif/lib* and the pattern is *Xm*. If searched, the directories list will contain all the directories in */usr/src/motif/lib* and the files list won't contain anything because Xm is a directory, not a pattern that matches any files. Since users frequently make this mistake when using the FileSelectionDialog, you should be sure to explain the operation of the dialog in the documentation for your application.

The convention that the widget follows is to use the last / in the filter to separate the directory part from the pattern part. Fortunately, the FileSelectionDialog provides resources and other mechanisms to retrieve the proper parts of the filter specification. We will demonstrate how to use these mechanisms in the next few subsections.

6.5.1 Creating a FileSelectionDialog

The convenience function for creating a FileSelectionDialog is `XmCreateFileSelectionDialog()`. The routine is declared in *<Xm/FileSB.h>*. The function creates a FileSelectionBox widget and its DialogShell parent and returns the FileSelectionBox. Alternatively, you can create a FileSelectionBox widget using either `XmCreateFileSelectionBox()` or `XtVaCreateWidget()` with the widget class specified as `xmFileSelectionBoxWidgetClass`. In this case, you could use the widget as part of a larger interface, or put it in a DialogShell yourself.

Example 6-3 demonstrates how a FileSelectionDialog can be created. This program produces the dialog shown in Figure 6-3. The intent of the program is to display a single FileSelectionDialog and print the selection that is made. We will provide a more realistic example shortly. For now, you should notice how little code is actually required to create the dialog.†

Example 6-3. The show_files.c program

```
/* show_files.c -- introduce FileSelectionDialog; print the file
 * selected by the user.
 */
#include <Xm/FileSB.h>

main(argc, argv)
int argc;
char *argv[];
{
    Widget          toplevel, text_w, dialog;
    XtAppContext    app;
    extern void     exit(), echo_file();

    XtSetLanguageProc (NULL, NULL, NULL);

    toplevel = XtVaAppInitialize (&app, "Demos",
        NULL, 0, &argc, argv, NULL, NULL);

    /* Create a simple FileSelectionDialog -- no frills */
    dialog = XmCreateFileSelectionDialog (toplevel, "filesb", NULL, 0);
    XtAddCallback (dialog, XmNcancelCallback, exit, NULL);
    XtAddCallback (dialog, XmNokCallback, echo_file, NULL);
    XtManageChild (dialog);

    XtAppMainLoop (app);
}

/* callback routine when the user selects OK in the FileSelection
 * Dialog.  Just print the file name selected.
 */
void
echo_file(widget, client_data, call_data)
Widget widget;   /* file selection box */
XtPointer client_data;
XtPointer call_data;
{
    char *filename;
    XmFileSelectionBoxCallbackStruct *cbs =
        (XmFileSelectionBoxCallbackStruct *) call_data;

    if (!XmStringGetLtoR (cbs->value, XmFONTLIST_DEFAULT_TAG, &filename))
        return; /* must have been an internal error */

    if (!*filename) { /* nothing typed? */
        puts ("No file selected.");
        XtFree( filename); /* even "" is an allocated byte */
        return;
    }
```

---

†XtSetLanguageProc() is only available in X11R5; there is no corresponding function in X11R4. Xm-
StringCreateLocalized() is only available in Motif 1.2; XmStringCreateSimple() is the corre-
sponding function in Motif 1.1. XmFONTLIST_DEFAULT_TAG replaces XmSTRING_DEFAULT_CHARSET in
Motif 1.2.

Example 6-3. The show_files.c program (continued)

```
    printf ("Filename given: \"%s\"\n", filename);
    XtFree (filename);
}
```

The program simply prints the selected file when the user activates the **OK** button. The user can change the file by selecting an item from the files list or by typing directly in the selection text entry area. The user can also activate the dialog by double-clicking on an item in the files list. The FileSelectionDialog itself is very simple to create; most of the work in the program is done by the callback routine for the **OK** button.

6.5.2 Internal Widgets

A FileSelectionDialog is made up of a number of subwidgets, including Text, List, and Push-Button widgets. You can get the handles to these children using the routine XmFile-SelectionBoxGetChild(), which takes the following form:

```
    Widget
    XmFileSelectionBoxGetChild(widget, child)
        XmFileSelectionBox  widget;
        unsigned char       child;
```

The *widget* parameter is a handle to a dialog widget, not its DialogShell parent. The *child* parameter is an enumerated value that specifies a particular subwidget in the dialog. The parameter can have any one of the following values:

```
    XmDIALOG_APPLY_BUTTON
    XmDIALOG_CANCEL_BUTTON
    XmDIALOG_DEFAULT_BUTTON
    XmDIALOG_DIR_LIST
    XmDIALOG_DIR_LIST_LABEL
    XmDIALOG_FILTER_LABEL
    XmDIALOG_FILTER_TEXT
    XmDIALOG_HELP_BUTTON
    XmDIALOG_LIST
    XmDIALOG_LIST_LABEL
    XmDIALOG_OK_BUTTON
    XmDIALOG_SELECTION_LABEL
    XmDIALOG_SEPARATOR
    XmDIALOG_TEXT
    XmDIALOG_WORK_AREA
```

The values refer to the different widgets in a FileSelectionDialog and they should be self-explanatory, with the exception of XmDIALOG_WORK_AREA. A FileSelectionDialog can manage a work area child; this value returns the work area child. You can customize the operation of a FileSelectionDialog by adding a work area that contains other components. For a detailed discussion of this technique, see Chapter 7, *Custom Dialogs*.

When you use XmFileSelectionBoxGetChild(), you should not assume that the returned widget is of any particular class, so you should treat it as an opaque object as much as possible. Getting the children of a FileSelectionDialog is not necessary in most cases because the Motif toolkit provides FileSelectionDialog resources that access most of the important resources of the children. You should only get handles to the children if you need to change resources that are not involved in the file selection mechanisms.

6.5.3 Callback Routines

The XmNokCallback, XmNcancelCallback, XmNapplyCallback, XmNhelp-Callback, and XmNnoMatchCallback callbacks can be specified for a FileSelection-Dialog as they are for SelectionDialog. The callback routines take the usual parameters, but the callback structure passed in the call_data parameter is of type XmFile-SelectionBoxCallbackStruct. The structure is declared as follows:

```
typedef struct {
        int         reason;
        XEvent      *event;
        XmString    value;
        int         length;
        XmString    mask;
        int         mask_length;
        XmString    dir;
        int         dir_length;
        XmString    pattern;
        int         pattern_length;
} XmFileSelectionBoxCallbackStruct;
```

The value of the reason field is an integer value that specifies the reason that the callback routine was invoked. The possible values are the same as those for a SelectionDialog:

```
XmCR_OK
XmCR_APPLY
XmCR_CANCEL
XmCR_HELP
XmCR_NO_MATCH
```

The value field contains the item that the user selected from the files list or typed into the selection text entry area. The value corresponds to the XmNdirSpec resource and it does not necessarily have to match an item in the directories or files lists. The mask field corresponds to the XmNdirMask resource; it represents a combination of the entire pathname specification in the filter. The dir and pattern fields represent the two components that make up the mask. All of these fields are compound strings; they can be converted to character strings using XmStringGetLtoR().

6.5.4 File Searching

You can force a FileSelectionDialog to reinitialize the directory and file lists by calling Xm-FileSelectionDoSearch(). This routine reads the directory filter and scans the specified directory, which is useful if you set the mask directly. The function takes the following form:

```
void
XmFileSelectionDoSearch(widget, dirmask)
    XmFileSelectionBoxWidget  widget;
    XmString                  dirmask;
```

When the routine is called, the widget invokes its directory search procedure and sets the text in the filter text entry area to the *dirmask* parameter. Calling XmFileSelection-DoSearch() has the same effect as setting the filter and selecting the **Filter** button.

By default, the FileSelectionDialog searches the directory specified in the mask according to its internal searching algorithm. You can replace this file searching procedure with your own routine by specifying a callback routine for the XmNfileSearchProc resource. This resource is not a callback list, so you do not install it by calling XtAddCallback(). Since the resource is just a single procedure, you specify it as a value like you would any other resource, as shown in the following code fragment:

```
extern void my_search_proc();

XtVaSetValues (file_selection_dialog,
    XmNfileSearchProc, my_search_proc,
    NULL);
```

If you specify a search procedure, it is used to generate the list of filenames for the files list. A file search routine takes the following form:

```
void
(* XmSearchProc) (widget, search_data)
    Widget      widget;
    XtPointer  *search_data;
```

The *widget* parameter is the actual FileSelectionBox widget and *search_data* is a callback structure of type XmFileSelectionBoxCallbackStruct. This structure is just like the one used in the callback routines discussed in the previous section. Do not be concerned with the value of the reason field in this situation because none of the routines along the way use the value. The search function should scan the directory specified by the dir field of the *search_data* parameter. The pattern should be used to filter the files within the directory. You can get the complete filter from the mask field.

After the search procedure has determined the new list of files that it is going to use, it must set the XmNfileListItems and XmNfileListItemCount resources to store the list into the List widget used by the FileSelectionDialog. The routine must also set the XmNlistUpdated resource to True to indicate that it has indeed done something, whether or not any files are found. The function can also set the XmNdirSpec resource to reflect the full file specification in the selection text entry area, so that if the user selects the **OK** button, the specified file is used. Although this step is optional, we recommend doing it in case the old value is no longer valid.

To understand why it may be necessary to have your own file search procedure, consider how you would customize a FileSelectionDialog so that it only displays the writable files in an arbitrary directory. This customization might come in handy for a save operation in an electronic mail application, where the user invokes a **Save** action that displays a FileSelection-Dialog that lists the files in which the user can save messages. Files that are not writable should not be displayed in the dialog. Example 6-4 shows an example of how a file search procedure can be used to implement this type of dialog.†

Example 6-4. The file_sel.c program

```
/* file_sel.c -- file selection dialog displays a list of all the writable
 * files in the directory described by the XmNmask of the dialog.
 * This program demonstrates how to use the XmNfileSearchProc for
 * file selection dialog widgets.
 */
#include <stdio.h>
#include <Xm/Xm.h>
#include <Xm/FileSB.h>
#include <Xm/DialogS.h>
#include <Xm/PushBG.h>
#include <Xm/PushB.h>
#include <X11/Xos.h>
#include <sys/stat.h>

void do_search(), new_file_cb();

/* routine to determine if a file is accessible, a directory,
 * or writable.  Return -1 on all errors or if the file is not
 * writable.  Return 0 if it's a directory or 1 if it's a plain
 * writable file.
 */
int
is_writable(file)
char *file;
{
    struct stat s_buf;

    /* if file can't be accessed (via stat()) return. */
    if (stat (file, &s_buf) == -1)
        return -1;
    else if ((s_buf.st_mode & S_IFMT) == S_IFDIR)
        return 0; /* a directory */
    else if (!(s_buf.st_mode & S_IFREG) || access (file, W_OK) == -1)
        /* not a normal file or it is not writable */
        return -1;
    /* legitimate file */
    return 1;
}

/* main() -- create a FileSelectionDialog */
main(argc, argv)
int argc;
char *argv[];
{
    Widget toplevel, dialog;
    XtAppContext app;
    extern void exit();
    Arg args[5];
```

---

†XtSetLanguageProc() is only available in X11R5; there is no corresponding function in X11R4. Xm-StringCreateLocalized() is only available in Motif 1.2; XmStringCreateSimple() is the corresponding function in Motif 1.1. XmFONTLIST_DEFAULT_TAG replaces XmSTRING_DEFAULT_CHARSET in Motif 1.2.

Example 6-4. The file_sel.c program (continued)

```
    int n = 0;

    XtSetLanguageProc (NULL, NULL, NULL);

    toplevel = XtVaAppInitialize (&app, "Demos",
        NULL, 0, &argc, argv, NULL, NULL);

    XtSetArg (args[n], XmNfileSearchProc, do_search); n++;
    dialog = XmCreateFileSelectionDialog (toplevel, "Files", args, n);
    XtSetSensitive (
        XmFileSelectionBoxGetChild (dialog, XmDIALOG_HELP_BUTTON), False);
    /* if user presses OK button, call new_file_cb() */
    XtAddCallback (dialog, XmNokCallback, new_file_cb, NULL);
    /* if user presses Cancel button, exit program */
    XtAddCallback (dialog, XmNcancelCallback, exit, NULL);

    XtManageChild (dialog);

    XtAppMainLoop (app);
}

/* a new file was selected -- check to see if it's readable and not
 * a directory.  If it's not readable, report an error.  If it's a
 * directory, scan it just as tho the user had typed it in the mask
 * Text field and selected "Search".
 */
void
new_file_cb(widget, client_data, call_data)
Widget widget;
XtPointer client_data;
XtPointer call_data;
{
    char *file;
    XmFileSelectionBoxCallbackStruct *cbs =
        (XmFileSelectionBoxCallbackStruct *) call_data;

    /* get the string typed in the text field in char * format */
    if (!XmStringGetLtoR (cbs->value, XmFONTLIST_DEFAULT_TAG, &file))
        return;
    if (*file != '/') {
        /* if it's not a directory, determine the full pathname
         * of the selection by concatenating it to the "dir" part
         */
        char *dir, *newfile;
        if (XmStringGetLtoR (cbs->dir, XmFONTLIST_DEFAULT_TAG, &dir)) {
            newfile = XtMalloc (strlen (dir) + 1 + strlen (file) + 1);
            sprintf (newfile, "%s/%s", dir, file);
            XtFree( file);
            XtFree (dir);
            file = newfile;
        }
    }
    switch (is_writable (file)) {
        case 1 :
            puts (file); /* or do anything you want */
            break;
        case 0 : {
            /* a directory was selected, scan it */
```

Example 6-4. The file_sel.c program (continued)

```
                XmString str = XmStringCreateLocalized (file);
                XmFileSelectionDoSearch (widget, str);
                XmStringFree (str);
                break;
        }
        case -1 :
                /* a system error on this file */
                perror (file);
        }
    XtFree (file);
}

/* do_search() -- scan a directory and report only those files that
 * are writable.  Here, we let the shell expand the (possible)
 * wildcards and return a directory listing by using popen().
 * A *real* application should -not- do this; it should use the
 * system's directory routines: opendir(), readdir() and closedir().
 */
void
do_search(widget, search_data)
Widget widget; /* file selection box widget */
XtPointer search_data;
{
    char            *mask, buf[BUFSIZ], *p;
    XmString        names[256]; /* maximum of 256 files in dir */
    int             i = 0;
    FILE            *pp, *popen();
    XmFileSelectionBoxCallbackStruct *cbs =
        (XmFileSelectionBoxCallbackStruct *) search_data;

    if (!XmStringGetLtoR (cbs->mask, XmFONTLIST_DEFAULT_TAG, &mask))
        return; /* can't do anything */

    sprintf (buf, "/bin/ls %s", mask);
    XtFree (mask);
    /* let the shell read the directory and expand the filenames */
    if (!(pp = popen (buf, "r")))
        return;
    /* read output from popen() -- this will be the list of files */
    while (fgets (buf, sizeof buf, pp)) {
        if (p = index (buf, '\n'))
            *p = 0;
        /* only list files that are writable and not directories */
        if (is_writable (buf) == 1 &&
            (names[i] = XmStringCreateLocalized (buf)))
            i++;
    }
    pclose (pp);
    if (i) {
        XtVaSetValues (widget,
            XmNfileListItems,       names,
            XmNfileListItemCount,   i,
            XmNdirSpec,             names[0],
            XmNlistUpdated,         True,
            NULL);
        while (i > 0)
            XmStringFree (names[--i]);
```

Example 6-4. The file_sel.c program (continued)

```
    } else
        XtVaSetValues (widget,
            XmNfileListItems,      NULL,
            XmNfileListItemCount,  0,
            XmNlistUpdated,        True,
            NULL);
}
```

The program simply displays a FileSelectionDialog that only lists the files that are writable by the user. The directories listed may or may not be writable. We are not testing that case here as it is handled by another routine that deals specifically with directories, which are discussed in the next section. The XmNfileSearchProc is set to do_search(), which is our own routine that creates the list of files for the files List widget. The function calls is_writable() to determine if a file is accessible and if it is a directory or a regular file that is writable.

The callback routine for the **OK** button is set to new_file_cb() through the XmNok-Callback resource. This routine is called when a new file is selected in from the files list or new text is entered in the selection text entry area and the **OK** button is pressed. The specified file is evaluated using is_writable() and acted on accordingly. If it is a directory, the directory is scanned as if it had been entered in the filter text entry area. If the file cannot be read, an error message is printed. Otherwise, the file is a legitimate selection and, for demonstration purposes, the filename is printed to stdout.

Obviously, a real application would do something more appropriate in each case; errors would be reported using ErrorDialogs and legitimate values would be used by the application. An example of such a program is given in Chapter 14, *Text Widgets*, as *file_browser.c*. This program is an extension of Example 6-4 that takes a more realistic approach to using a FileSelectionDialog. Of course, the intent of that program is to show how Text widgets work, but its use of dialogs is consistent with the approach we are taking here.

Directory Searching

The FileSelectionDialog also provides a directory searching function that is analogous to the file searching function. While file searching may be necessary for some applications, it is less likely that customized directory searching will be as useful, since the default action taken by the toolkit should cover all common usages. However, since it is impossible to second-guess the requirements of all applications, Motif allows you to specify a directory searching function through the XmNdirSearchProc resource.

The procedure is used to create the list of directories. The method used by the procedure is virtually identical to the one used for files, except that the routine must set different resources. The routine must set the XmNdirListItems and XmNdirListItemCount resources to store the list of directories in the List widget. The value for XmNlistUpdated must be set just as it was for the file selection routine and XmNdirectoryValid must also be set to either True or False. If the directory cannot be read, XmNdirectoryValid is set to False to prevent the XmNfileSearchProc from being called. In this way, the file searching procedure is protected from getting invalid directories from the directory searching procedure.

The Search Process

In order to fully customize the directory and file searching functions in a FileSelection-Dialog, it is important to understand exactly how the dialog works. This material is advanced and is intended for programmers who need to write advanced file and/or directory searching routines. When the user or the application invokes a directory search, the FileSelection-Dialog performs the following tasks:

1. The List widgets are unmapped to give the user immediate feedback that something is happening. So, if a file and/or directory search takes a long time, the user has a visual cue that the application is not waiting for input.

2. All of the items are deleted from the List widgets.

3. The widget calls its qualify search procedure to construct a proper directory mask, base directory, and file search pattern based on the text in the filter text entry area. The procedure creates a callback structure of type `XmFileSelectionBoxCallbackStruct` for use by the directory and file search routines.

4. The `XmNdirSearchProc` function is called with the callback structure constructed by the qualify search procedure. The directory search routine checks to be sure that it can search the specified directory and if it can, it creates the list of directories for the dialog. If the directory cannot be searched, the routine sets `XmNdirectoryValid` to `False`.

5. The `XmNfileSearchProc` function is called if `XmNdirectoryValid` has been set to `True`. This routine creates the list of files for the dialog. If `XmNdirectoryValid` has been set to `False`, the file list remains empty.

Just as for the directory and file search routines, you can write your own qualify search procedure and install it as the value for the `XmNqualifySearchProc` resource. The routine takes the following form:

```
void
(* XmQualifyProc) (widget, input_data, output_data)
    Widget      widget;
    XtPointer   *input_data;
    XtPointer   *output_data;
```

The *widget* parameter is the actual FileSelectionBox widget; *input_data* and *output_data* are callback structures of type `XmFileSelectionBoxCallbackStruct`. *input_data* contains the directory information that needs to be qualified. The routine uses this information to fill in the *output_data* callback structure that is then passed to the directory and file search procedures.

The `XmNfileTypeMask` resource indicates the types of files for which a particular search routine should be looking. The resource can be set to one of the following values:

```
XmFILE_REGULAR
XmFILE_DIRECTORY
XmFILE_ANY_TYPE
```

If you are using the same routine for both the `XmNdirSearchProc` and the `XmNfile-SearchProc`, you can query this resource to determine the type of file to search for.

6.6 Summary

This chapter described the different types of selection dialogs provided by the Motif toolkit. These dialogs implement some common functionality that is needed by many different applications. This chapter builds on the material in Chapter 5, *Introduction to Dialogs*, which introduced the concept of dialogs and discussed the basic mechanisms that implement them. While the dialogs are designed to be used as single-entity abstractions, they can be customized to provide additional functionality as necessary. We describe how to customize the dialogs and how to create your own dialogs in Chapter 7, *Custom Dialogs*.

7

Custom Dialogs

This chapter describes how to create new types of dialogs, either by customizing Motif dialogs or by creating entirely new dialogs.

In This Chapter:

Custom Dialogs

In this chapter we examine methods for creating your own dialogs. The need for such dialogs exists when those provided by Motif are too limited in functionality or are not specialized enough for your application. Sometimes it is not clear when you need to create your own dialog. In some situations, you may find that a Motif dialog would be just fine if only they did this one little thing. Fortunately, you can often make small adjustments to a predefined Motif dialog, rather than building an entirely new dialog box from scratch.

There are some issues to consider before you decide how you want to approach the problem of developing custom dialogs. For example, do you want to use your own widget layout or is the layout of one of the predefined dialogs sufficient? Do you have specialized user--interface appearance and functionality needs that go beyond what is provided by Motif? The answers to these questions affect the design of your dialogs. The discussion and examples provided in this chapter address both scenarios. We provide information on how to create dialogs that are based on the predefined Motif dialogs, as well as how to design completely new dialogs.

Before we get started, we should mention that creating your own dialogs makes heavy use of manager widgets, such as the Form, BulletinBoard, RowColumn, and PanedWindow widgets. While we use and describe the manager widgets in context, you may want to consult Chapter 8, *Manager Widgets*, for specific details about these widgets.

7.1 Modifying Motif Dialogs

We begin by discussing the simpler case of modifying existing Motif dialogs. In Chapter 5, *Introduction to Dialogs*, we showed you how to modify a dialog to some extent by changing the default labels on the buttons in the action area or by unmanaging or desensitizing certain components in the dialog. What we did not mention is that you can also add new components to a dialog box to expand its functionality. All of the predefined Motif dialog widgets let you add children. In this sense, you can treat a dialog as a manager widget. In Motif 1.1, you can only add a single work area child to a Motif dialog, which limits the amount of customization that is possible. Motif 1.2 allows you to add multiple children to an existing dialog, so you can provide additional controls, action area buttons, and even a MenuBar.

7.1.1 Modifying MessageDialogs

At the end of Chapter 5, *Introduction to Dialogs*, we described a scenario where an application might want to have more than three action area buttons in a MessageDialog. If the user has selected the **Quit** button in a text editor but has not saved her changes, an application might want to post a dialog that asks about saving the changes before exiting. The user could want to save the changes and exit, not save the changes and exit anyway, cancel the exit operation, or get help.

In Motif 1.1, the MessageDialog only supported three action area buttons, so creating a dialog with four buttons required designing a custom dialog. However, in Motif 1.2, the MessageDialog allows you to provide additional action area buttons. Example 7-1 demonstrates how to create a QuestionDialog with four action area buttons.†

Example 7-1. The question.c program

```
/* question.c -- create a QuestionDialog with four action buttons
 */
#include <Xm/MessageB.h>
#include <Xm/PushB.h>

main(argc, argv)
int argc;
char *argv[];
{
    XtAppContext app;
    Widget toplevel, pb;
    extern void pushed();

    toplevel = XtVaAppInitialize (&app, "Demos", NULL, 0,
        &argc, argv, NULL, NULL);
    pb = XtVaCreateManagedWidget ("Button",
        xmPushButtonWidgetClass, toplevel, NULL);
    XtAddCallback (pb, XmNactivateCallback, pushed, NULL);

    XtRealizeWidget (toplevel);
    XtAppMainLoop (app);
}

void
pushed(w, client_data, call_data)
Widget w;
XtPointer client_data;
XtPointer call_data;
{
    Widget dialog, no_button;
    extern void dlg_callback();
    Arg args[5];
    int n = 0;
    XmString m = XmStringCreateLocalized
        ("Do you want to update your changes?");
    XmString yes = XmStringCreateLocalized ("Yes");
    XmString no = XmStringCreateLocalized ("No");
```

---

† This example uses functionality that is new in Motif 1.2, so it only works with the 1.2 version of the Motif toolkit.

Example 7-1. The question.c program (continued)

```
        XtSetArg (args[n], XmNautoUnmanage, False); n++;
        XtSetArg (args[n], XmNmessageString, m); n++;
        XtSetArg (args[n], XmNokLabelString, yes); n++;
        dialog = XmCreateQuestionDialog (w, "notice", args, n);
        XtAddCallback (dialog, XmNokCallback, dlg_callback, NULL);
        XtAddCallback (dialog, XmNcancelCallback, dlg_callback, NULL);
        XtAddCallback (dialog, XmNhelpCallback, dlg_callback, NULL);
        XmStringFree (m);
        XmStringFree (yes);

        no_button = XtVaCreateManagedWidget ("no",
            xmPushButtonWidgetClass, dialog,
            XmNlabelString, no,
            NULL);
        XtAddCallback (no_button, XmNactivateCallback, dlg_callback, NULL);

        XtManageChild (dialog);
        XtPopup (XtParent (dialog), XtGrabNone);
}

void
dlg_callback(w, client_data, call_data)
Widget w;
XtPointer client_data;
XtPointer call_data;
{
        XmAnyCallbackStruct *cbs = (XmAnyCallbackStruct *) call_data;

        switch (cbs->reason) {
            case XmCR_OK :
            case XmCR_CANCEL :
                XtPopdown (XtParent (w));
                break;
            case XmCR_ACTIVATE :
                XtPopdown (XtParent (XtParent (w)));
                break;
            case XmCR_HELP :
                puts ("Help selected");
        }
}
```

The dialog box from the program is shown in Figure 7-1. The extra button is added to the dialog by creating a PushButton as a child of the dialog. We are treating the MessageDialog just like any other manager widget. The MessageDialog inserts any additional PushButton children into the action area after the **OK** button, which is why we added a **No** button. If you add more than one button, they are all put after the **OK** button, in the order that you create them. We have also changed the label of the **OK** button so that it is now the **Yes** button.

Since the **No** button is not part of the standard MessageDialog, we have to set the callback routine on its XmNactivateCallback. For the rest of the buttons, we use the callbacks defined by the dialog. The dialog callback routine, dlg_callback(), has to handle the various callbacks in different ways. By checking the reason field of the callback structure, the routine can determine which button was selected. For the **Yes** and **Cancel** buttons, the routine unposts the dialog by popping down the DialogShell parent of the dialog. For the **No** button, we need to be a bit more careful about popping down the right widget. Since the

Custom Dialogs (side tab)

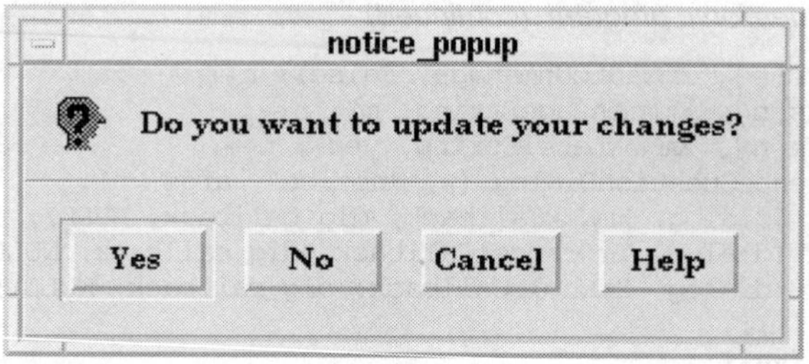

Figure 7-1. Output of question.c

widget in this case is the PushButton, we need to call XtParent() twice to get the DialogShell.

With Motif 1.2, the MessageDialog also supports the addition of other children besides Push-Buttons. If you add a MenuBar child, it is placed across the top of the dialog, although it is not clear why you would want a MenuBar in a MessageDialog. Any other type of widget child is considered the work area. The work area is placed below the message text if it exists. If there is a symbol, but no message, the work area is placed to the right of the symbol. The MessageDialog only supports the addition of one work area; the layout of multiple work area children is undefined. In Motif 1.1, only a single work area child can be added to a Message-Dialog. This child is always placed below the message text.

The XmNdialogType resource can take the value XmDIALOG_TEMPLATE in Motif 1.2. This value creates a TemplateDialog, which is basically an empty MessageDialog that can be modified by the programmer. By default, the dialog only contains a Separator child. By setting various resources on a TemplateDialog when it is created, you can cause the dialog to create other standard children. If you set a string or callback resource for an action area button, the button is created. If you set the XmNmessageString resource, the message is displayed in the standard location. If you set the XmNsymbolPixmap resource, the specified symbol appears in its normal location. If you don't set a particular resource, then that child is not created, which means that you cannot modify the resource later with XtSet-Values(), set a callback for the child with XtAddCallback(), or retrieve the child with XmMessageBoxGetChild().

7.1.2 Modifying SelectionDialogs

The Motif SelectionDialog supports the same types of modifications as the MessageDialog. With Motif 1.2, you can provide additional action area buttons, a work area child, and a MenuBar. Unlike the MessageDialog, the first widget that is added is taken as the work area, regardless of whether it is a PushButton or a MenuBar.† If you want to add a PushButton to the action area of a SelectionDialog, you need to add an unmanaged work area widget first, so that the PushButton is placed in the action area, rather than used as the work area. After

---

† The fact that the first child is always considered the work area is a bug. As a result of the bug, you need to be careful about the order in which you add children to a SelectionDialog.

you add a work area, if you add a MenuBar, it is placed along the top of the dialog, and Push-Button children are inserted after the **OK** button. The position of the work area child is controlled by the XmNchildPlacement resource, which can take the following values:

```
XmPLACE_ABOVE_SELECTION
XmPLACE_BELOW_SELECTION
XmPLACE_TOP
```

The SelectionDialog only supports the addition of one work area; the layout of multiple work area children is undefined. In Motif 1.1, only a single work area child can be added to a SelectionDialog. This child is always placed between the list and the text entry area.

Consider providing additional controls in a PromptDialog like the one used in the program *prompt_dlg* from Chapter 6, *Selection Dialogs*. In this program, the dialog prompts the user for a new label for the PushButton that activated the dialog. By adding another widget to the dialog, we can expand its functionality to prompt for either a label name or a button color. The user enters either value in the same text input area and the RadioBox controls how the text is evaluated. Example 7-2 shows the new program.†

Example 7-2. The modify_btn.c program

```
/* modify_btn.c -- demonstrate how a default Motif dialog can be
 * modified to support additional items that extend the usability
 * of the dialog itself.  This is a modification of the prompt_dlg.c
 * program.
 */
#include <Xm/SelectioB.h>
#include <Xm/RowColumn.h>
#include <Xm/PushB.h>

main(argc, argv)
char *argv[];
{
    XtAppContext app;
    Widget toplevel, rc, button;
    void pushed();

    XtSetLanguageProc (NULL, NULL, NULL);

    /* Initialize toolkit and create toplevel shell */
    toplevel = XtVaAppInitialize (&app, "Demos", NULL, 0,
        &argc, argv, NULL, NULL);

    /* RowColumn managed both PushButtons */
    rc = XtVaCreateWidget ("rowcol", xmRowColumnWidgetClass, toplevel,
        NULL);
    /* Create two pushbuttons -- both have the same callback */
    button = XtVaCreateManagedWidget ("PushMe 1",
        xmPushButtonWidgetClass, rc, NULL);
    XtAddCallback (button, XmNactivateCallback, pushed, NULL);
    button = XtVaCreateManagedWidget ("PushMe 2",
        xmPushButtonWidgetClass, rc, NULL);
```

---

†XtSetLanguageProc() is only available in X11R5; there is no corresponding function in X11R4. Xm-StringCreateLocalized() is only available in Motif 1.2; XmStringCreateSimple() is the corresponding function in Motif 1.1. XmFONTLIST_DEFAULT_TAG replaces XmSTRING_DEFAULT_CHARSET in Motif 1.2.

Example 7-2. The modify_btn.c program (continued)

```
    XtAddCallback (button, XmNactivateCallback, pushed, NULL);

    XtManageChild (rc);
    XtRealizeWidget (toplevel);
    XtAppMainLoop (app);
}

/* pushed() --the callback routine for the main app's pushbuttons.
 * Create a dialog that prompts for a new button name or color.
 * A RadioBox is attached to the dialog.  Which button is selected
 * in this box is held as an int (0 or 1) in the XmNuserData resource
 * of the dialog itself.  This value is changed when selecting either
 * of the buttons in the ToggleBox and is queried in the dialog's
 * XmNokCallback function.
 */
void
pushed(pb, client_data, call_data)
Widget pb;
XtPointer client_data;
XtPointer call_data;
{
    Widget dialog, toggle_box;
    XmString t, btn1, btn2;
    extern void read_name(), toggle_callback();
    Arg args[5];
    int n = 0;

    /* Create the dialog -- the PushButton acts as the DialogShell's
     * parent (not the parent of the PromptDialog).  The "userData"
     * is used to store the value
     */
    t = XmStringCreateLocalized ("Enter New Button Name:");
    XtSetArg (args[n], XmNselectionLabelString, t); n++;
    XtSetArg (args[n], XmNautoUnmanage, False); n++;
    XtSetArg (args[n], XmNuserData, 0); n++;
    dialog = XmCreatePromptDialog (pb, "notice_popup", args, n);
    XmStringFree (t); /* always destroy compound strings when done */

    /* When the user types the name, call read_name() ... */
    XtAddCallback (dialog, XmNokCallback, read_name, pb);

    /* If the user selects cancel, just destroy the dialog */
    XtAddCallback (dialog, XmNcancelCallback, XtDestroyWidget, NULL);

    /* No help is available... */
    XtUnmanageChild (XmSelectionBoxGetChild (dialog, XmDIALOG_HELP_BUTTON));

    /* Create a toggle box -- callback routine is toggle_callback() */
    btn1 = XmStringCreateLocalized ("Change Name");
    btn2 = XmStringCreateLocalized ("Change Color");
    toggle_box = XmVaCreateSimpleRadioBox (dialog,
        "radio_box", 0 /* inital value */, toggle_callback,
        XmVaRADIOBUTTON, btn1, 0, NULL, NULL,
        XmVaRADIOBUTTON, btn2, 0, NULL, NULL,
        NULL);
    XtManageChild (toggle_box);

    XtManageChild (dialog);
```

Example 7-2. The modify_btn.c program (continued)

```
    XtPopup (XtParent (dialog), XtGrabNone);
}

/* callback for the items in the toggle box -- the "client data" is
 * the item number selected.  Since the function gets called whenever
 * either of the buttons changes from true to false or back again,
 * it will always be called in pairs -- ignore the "False" settings.
 * When cbs->set is true, set the dialog's label string accordingly.
 */
void
toggle_callback(toggle_box, client_data, call_data)
Widget toggle_box;
XtPointer client_data;
XtPointer call_data;
{
    Widget dialog = XtParent(XtParent(toggle_box));
    XmString str;
    int n = (int) client_data;
    XmToggleButtonCallbackStruct *cbs =
        (XmToggleButtonCallbackStruct *) call_data;

    if (cbs->set == False)
        return; /* wait for the one that toggles "on" */
    if (n == 0)
        str = XmStringCreateLocalized ("Enter New Button Name:");
    else
        str = XmStringCreateLocalized ("Enter Text Color:");
    XtVaSetValues (dialog,
        XmNselectionLabelString, str,
        XmNuserData, n, /* reset the user data to reflect new value */
        NULL);
    XmStringFree (str);
}

/* read_name() --the text field has been filled in.  Get the userData
 * from the dialog widget and set the PushButton's name or color.
 */
void
read_name(dialog, client_data, call_data)
Widget dialog;
XtPointer client_data;
XtPointer call_data;
{
    char *text;
    int n;
    Widget push_button = (Widget) client_data;
    XmSelectionBoxCallbackStruct *cbs =
        (XmSelectionBoxCallbackStruct *) call_data;

    /* userData: n == 0 -> Button Label, n == 1 -> Button Color */
    XtVaGetValues (dialog, XmNuserData, &n, NULL);

    if (n == 0)
        XtVaSetValues (push_button, XmNlabelString, cbs->value, NULL);
    else {
        /* convert compound string into regular text string */
        XmStringGetLtoR (cbs->value, XmFONTLIST_DEFAULT_TAG, &text);
        XtVaSetValues (push_button,
```

Example 7-2. The modify_btn.c program (continued)

```
            XtVaTypedArg, XmNforeground,
                XmRString, text, strlen (text) + 1,
            NULL);
        XtFree (text); /* must free text gotten from XmStringGetLtoR() */
    }
}
```

The new dialog is shown in Figure 7-2.

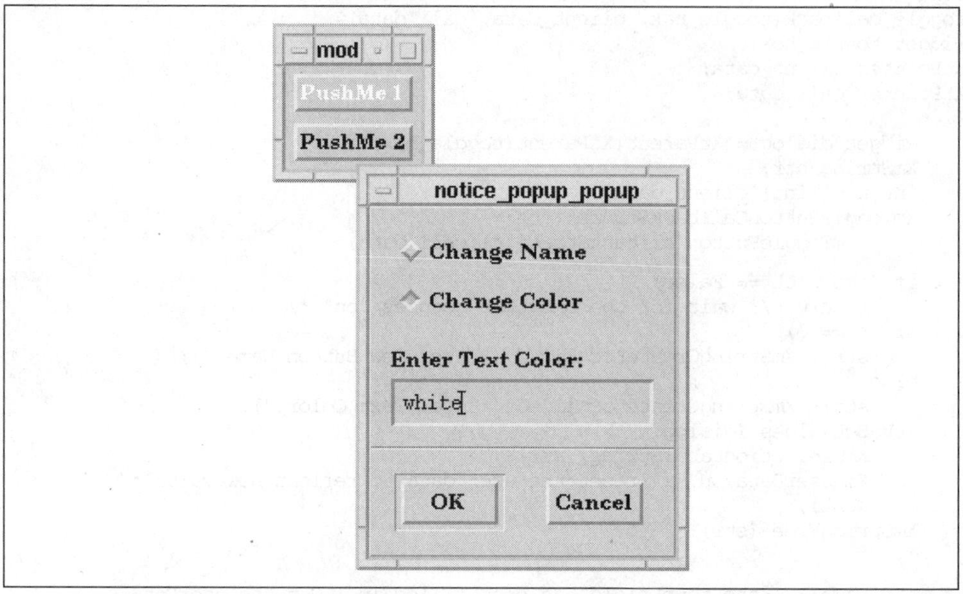

Figure 7-2. Output of modify_btn.c

We add a RadioBox as the work area child of the PromptDialog. The ToggleButtons in the RadioBox indicate whether the input text is supposed to change the label of the PushButton or its text color. To determine which of these attributes to change, we use the callback routine toggle_callback().

Rather than storing the state of the RadioBox in a global variable, we store the value in the XmNuserData resource of the dialog widget. Using this technique, we can retrieve the value anytime we wish and minimize the number of global variables in the program. The XmNuserData resource is available for all Motif widgets except shells, so it is a convenient storage area for arbitrary values. The type of value that XmNuserData takes is any type whose size is less than or equal to the size of an XtPointer, which is typically defined as a char pointer. As a result, storing an int works just fine. If you want to store a data structure in this resource, you need to store a pointer to the structure. The size or type of the structure is irrelevant, since pointers are the same size.†

When the user enters new text and presses RETURN or activates the **OK** button, read_name() is called. This callback routine gets the XmNuserData from the dialog widget. If the value is 0, the label of the PushButton is reset using the XmNlabelString resource. Since the callback routine provides the text in compound string format, it is already in the correct format for the label. If the XmNuserData is 1, then the text describes a color name for the PushButton.

Rather than converting the string into a color explicitly, we use the XtVaTypedArg feature of XtVaSetValues() to do the conversion for us. This feature converts a value to the format needed by the specified resource. The XmNforeground resource takes a variable of type Pixel as a value. The conversion works provided there is an underlying conversion function to support it.‡ Motif does not supply a conversion function to change a compound string into a Pixel value, but there is one for converting a C string into a Pixel. We convert the compound string into a C string using XmStringGetLtoR() and then set the foreground color as follows:

```
XtVaSetValues (push_button,
    XtVaTypedArg, XmNforeground,
        XmRString, text, strlen (text) + 1,
    NULL);
```

The amount of customization that is possible with the predefined Motif dialogs varies greatly between Motif 1.1 and Motif 1.2. We've described the possibilities for both MessageDialogs and SelectionDialogs using the two versions of the toolkit. If the layouts that are possible do not meet your needs, you should consider building your own dialogs from scratch.

7.2 Designing New Dialogs

In this section, we introduce the methods for building a dialog entirely from scratch. To create a new dialog, you need to follow basically the same steps that are used by the Motif convenience routines, which we described in Section 5.6.1. We've modified the list a bit to reflect the flexibility that you have in controlling the kind of dialog that you make. Here are the steps that you need to follow:

1. Choose a shell widget that best fits the needs of your dialog. You may continue to use a DialogShell if you like.

---

† You might run into problems with unusual architectures where pointers of different types are not the same size, like DOS.

‡ For more information on conversion functions, how to write them, or how to install your own, see Volume Four, *X Toolkit Intrinsics Programming Manual*.

2. Choose an appropriate manager widget to control the layout of the components of the dialog. This manager is a child of the shell widget. The manager widget you choose greatly affects how the dialog is laid out. You do not have to use a BulletinBoard or Form widget, but you can if you like.†

3. Create the control area, which may include any of the Motif primitive or manager widgets. This step is the one that gives you the most flexibility, as you have complete control over the contents and layout of the control area.

4. Create an action area with PushButtons such as **OK**, **Cancel**, and **Help**. Since you are creating the control area yourself, you cannot use `XmNokCallback` and the other resources specific to the predefined Motif dialogs. Instead, you use the callback resources appropriate for the widgets that you use in the dialog.

5. Pop up the shell created in the first step.

7.2.1 The Shell

In Chapter 4, *The Main Window*, we demonstrated the purpose of a main window in an application and the kinds of widgets that you use in a top-level window. Dialog boxes, as introduced in Chapter 5, *Introduction to Dialogs*, are thought of as transient windows that act as satellites to a top-level shell. A transient dialog should use a DialogShell widget. However, not all dialogs are transient. A dialog may act as a secondary application window that remains on display for an extended period of time. This usage is especially common in large applications. The MainWindow widget can even be used in a dialog box. For dialogs of this type, you may want to use a TopLevelShell or an ApplicationShell.

Choosing the appropriate shell widget for a dialog depends on the activities carried out in the dialog, so it is difficult to provide rules or even heuristics to guide you in your choice. As discussed in Chapter 5, a DialogShell cannot be iconified, it is always placed on top of the shell widget that owns the parent of the dialog, and it is always destroyed or withdrawn from the screen if its parent is destroyed or withdrawn. These three characteristics may influence your decision to use a DialogShell. An ApplicationShell or a TopLevelShell, on the other hand, is always independent of other windows, so you can change its stacking order, iconify it separately, and not worry about it being withdrawn because of another widget. The main difference between an ApplicationShell and a TopLevelShell is that an ApplicationShell is designed to start a completely new widget tree, as if it were a completely separate application. It is recommended that an application only have one ApplicationShell.

For some applications, you may want a shell with characteristics of several of the available shell classes. Unfortunately, it is difficult to intermix the capabilities of a DialogShell with those of an ApplicationShell or a TopLevelShell because it involves doing quite a bit of intricate window manager interaction. Having ultimate control over the activities of a shell

---

† If you do want to use a DialogShell with either a Form or a BulletinBoard widget as the manager, you can use one of the Motif convenience routines: `XmCreateBulletinBoardDialog()` or `XmCreateFormDialog()`. These routines give you a starting point for creating a custom dialog. However, in this chapter, we create each of the widgets explicitly, so that you have a complete sense of what goes into a dialog.

widget requires setting up a number of event handlers on the shell and monitoring certain window property event state changes. Aside from being very complicated, you run the risk of breaking Motif compliance. See Chapter 16, *Interacting With the Window Manager*, for details on how you might handle this situation.

Once you have chosen the shell widget that you want to use, you need to decide how to create it. A DialogShell can be created using `XtCreatePopupShell()`, `XtVaCreate-PopupShell()`, or the Motif convenience routine, `XmCreateDialogShell()`. An ApplicationShell or a TopLevelShell can be created using either of the popup shell routines, `XtAppCreateShell()` or `XtVaAppCreateShell()`. The difference between the two types of routines involves whether the newly-created shell is treated like a popup shell or as a more permanent window on the desktop. If you create the shell as a popup shell, you need to select an adequate parent. The parent for a popup shell must be an initialized and realized widget. It can be any kind of widget, but it may not be a gadget because the parent must have a window. A dialog that uses a popup shell inherits certain attributes from its parent. For example, if the parent is insensitive (`XmNsensitive` is set to `False`), the entire dialog is insensitive as well.

7.2.2 The Manager Child

The manager widget that you choose for a dialog is the only managed child of the shell widget, which means that the widget must contain both the control area and the action area of the dialog and manage the relationship between them. Recall that the *Motif Style Guide* suggests that a dialog be composed of two main areas: the control area and the action area. Both of these areas extend to the left and right sides of a dialog and are stacked vertically, with the control area on the top. The action area usually does not fluctuate in size as the shell is resized, while the control area may be resized in any way. Figure 7-3 illustrates the general layout of a dialog.

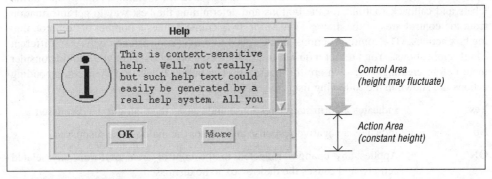

Figure 7-3. Layout of a dialog

Motif dialog widgets handle this layout automatically. When you create your own dialog, you are responsible for managing the layout. We recommend using the PanedWindow widget as the manager widget for a dialog. The PanedWindow supports vertically stacked windows, each of which may or may not be resizable, which allows you to create the suggested layout. If you use a PanedWindow as the manager widget for a dialog, it can manage two other managers that act as the control and action areas. The control area can be resizable, while the action area is not. The PanedWindow also provides a separator between the panes, which fulfills the *Style Guide* recommendation that there be a Separator widget between the control and action areas.

Of course you can use whatever manager widget you like for a dialog. If you use a Bulletin-Board or a Form widget, you may be able to take advantage of the special interaction these widgets have with a DialogShell. The RowColumn widget can also lay out its children vertically, so you could use one to manage the control and action areas of a dialog. The difficulty with using a RowColumn involves resizing, in that there is no way to tell the widget to keep the bottom partition a constant height while allowing the top to fluctuate as necessary. The same problem can also arise with other manager widgets, so you need to be sure that the resizing behavior is appropriate.

7.2.3 The Control Area

The control area of a dialog box contains the widgets that provide the functionality of the dialog, such as Labels, ToggleButtons, and List widgets. Creating the control area of a dialog is entirely application-defined. You can use any of the Motif primitive and manager widgets in the control area to implement the functionality of the dialog. The ability to design your own control area is the main reason to create your own dialog as opposed to using one of the predefined Motif dialogs.

7.2.4 The Action Area

The action area of a dialog contains PushButtons whose callback routines actually perform the action of the dialog box. Constructing the action area for a dialog involves specifying labels and callback routines for the buttons and determining the best way to get information from the control area of the dialog. The *Motif Style Guide* defines a number of common dialog box actions. The common actions are designed to provide consistency betweeen different Motif applications. You are not required to use the common actions, but you should consider them before creating your own arbitrary actions. The button labels and their corresponding actions are shown in the following list.

Yes   Indicates an affirmative response and causes the dialog to be dismissed.

No   Indicates a negative response and vauses the dialog to be dismissed.

OK   Applies any changes reflected in the control area, performs any related actions, and causes the dialog box to be dismissed.

Close   Closes the dialog box without performing any action.

Apply   Applies any changes reflected in the control area, performs any related actions, and leaves the dialog open for further interaction.

Retry	Tries the task in progress again. This action is commonly found in dialog boxes that report errors.
Stop	Stops the task in progress at the next possible breaking prioint. This action is often found in dialog boxes that indicate that the application is "busy."
Pause	Pauses the task in progress. This action is used in combination with **Resume**.
Resume	Resumes the task in progress. This action is used in combination with **Pause**.
Reset	Resets the controls in the work area to the values they had at the time the dialog was originally opened.
Cancel	Resets the controls in the work area and causes the dialog to be dismissed.
Help	Provides help for the dialog box.

The following heuristics can help in designing the action area for a dialog box:

- Lay out the action area as a single horizontal row at the bottom of the dialog.

- Set the action area apart from the rest of the dialog using a Separator.

- Use single-word button labels.

- Choose command-style verbs over nouns when possible. Since some words can be interpreted in more than one way, be careful to avoid ambiguity.

- Affirmative actions should be placed farthest to the left (in a left-to-right language environment), followed by negative actions, followed by cancelling actions. For example, **Yes** should always be placed to the left of **No**.

- **Help**, if available, should always be placed farthest to the right (in a left-to-right language environment).

Depending on your application, you may want to create your own actions and overlook some of these guidelines. Figure 7-4 shows a custom dialog from an e-mail application that demonstrates some of the issues involved in designing an action area. In this dialog, the **Help** button is the only one with a label recommended by Motif. Since the other common actions did not effectively represent the actions of the dialog, we chose our own labels. We decided not to use the **Cancel** action because we didn't want to combine the actions of **Reset** and **Close** in one button. Instead, we separated the functionality into two actions. The **Clear** button resets the controls without closing the window and the **Done** button closes the window. While **Cancel**, the recommended Motif label, implies that the action specified by the dialog should not be taken, **Done** merely suggests that the dialog be dismissed. Selecting **Done** does not cancel anything, it just dismisses the dialog. **Close** might be more appropriate, but since the dialog is part of an electronic mail application where the term "close" is used to describe the action of closing a folder, we are not using that label to avoid ambiguity.

We do not use the **OK** action in the dialog because it doesn't work with the desired usage of the dialog. Let's say the user selects a date to search for messages and then presses the **OK** button to start the search. By definition, **OK** should perform the action and dismiss the dialog. If that were to happen here, the user would never see the results of the search. While

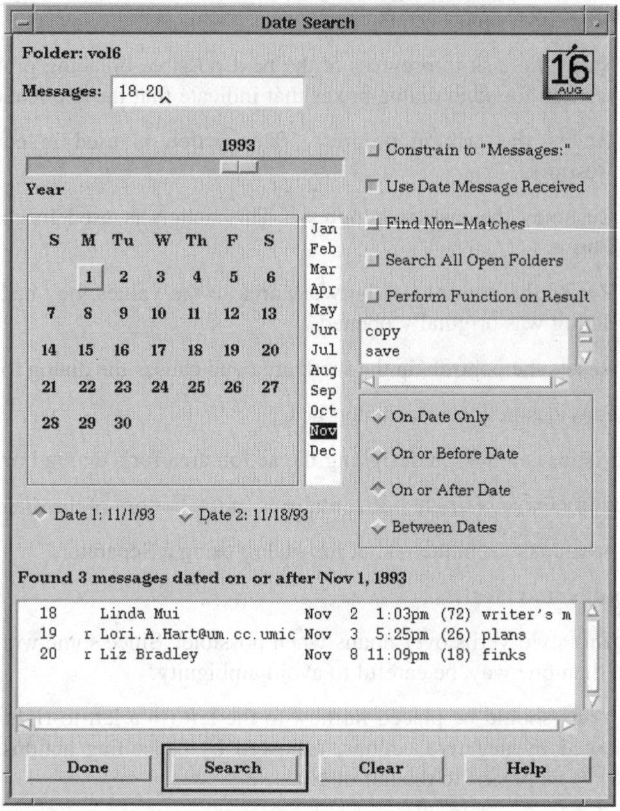

Figure 7-4. A custom dialog

Apply might be more appropriate for our desired action, we decided to use **Search** instead because it is more descriptive of the action being taken by the dialog.

7.3 Building a Dialog

Now that we've explained the design process for a dialog, let's create a real dialog and identify each of the steps in the process. Consider the problem of providing help. While the Motif InformationDialog is adequate for brief help messages, a customized dialog may be more appropriate for displaying large amounts of text. Our custom dialog displays the text in a scrolling region which is capable of handling arbitrarily large amounts of data.

Example 7-3 shows a program that uses a main application window as a generic backdrop. The MainWindow widget contains a MenuBar that has two menus: **File** and **Help**. The **Help** menu contains several items that, when selected, pop up a dialog window that displays the

associated help text. The text that we provide happens to be predefined in the program, but
you could incorporate information from other sources, such as a database or an external file.†

Example 7-3. The help_text.c program

```
/* help_text.c:
 * Create a simple main window that contains a sample (dummy) work
 * area and a menubar.  The menubar contains two items: File and Help.
 * The items in the Help pulldown call help_cb(), which pops up a
 * home-made dialog that displays predefined help texts.  The purpose
 * of this program is to demonstrate how one might approach the
 * problem displaying a large amount of text in a dialog box.
 */
#include <stdio.h>
#include <ctype.h>
#include <Xm/DialogS.h>
#include <Xm/MainW.h>
#include <Xm/RowColumn.h>
#include <Xm/Form.h>
#include <Xm/Text.h>
#include <Xm/PushBG.h>
#include <Xm/LabelG.h>
#include <Xm/PanedW.h>

/* The following help text information is a continuous stream of characters
 * that will all be placed in a single ScrolledText object.  If a specific
 * newline is desired, you must do that yourself.  See "index_help" below.
 */
String context_help[] = {
    "This is context-sensitive help.  Well, not really, but such",
    "help text could easily be generated by a real help system.",
    "All you really need to do is obtain information from the user",
    "about the widget from which he needs help, or perhaps prompt",
    "for other application-specific contexts.",
    NULL
};

String window_help[] = {
    "Each of the windows in your application should have an",
    "XmNhelpCallback associated with it so you can monitor when",
    "the user presses the Help key over any particular widget.",
    "This is another way to provide context-sensitive help.",
    "The MenuBar should always have a Help entry at the far right",
    "that provides help for most aspects of the program, including",
    "the user interface.  By providing different levels of help",
    "indexing, you can provide multiple stages of help, making the",
    "entire help system easier to use.",
    NULL
};

String index_help[] = {
    "This is a small demonstration program, so there is very little",
    "material to provide an index.  However, an index should contain",
```

---

†XtSetLanguageProc() is only available in X11R5; there is no corresponding function in X11R4. Xm-
StringCreateLocalized() is only available in Motif 1.2; XmStringCreateSimple() is the correspond-
ing function in Motif 1.1. XmFONTLIST_DEFAULT_TAG replaces XmSTRING_DEFAULT_CHARSET in
Motif 1.2.

Example 7-3. The help_text.c program (continued)

```
    "a summary of the type of help available.  For example, we have:\n",
    "    Help On Context\n",
    "    Help On Windows\n",
    "    This Index\n",
    "\n",
    "Higher-end applications might also provide a tutorial.",
    NULL
};

String *help_texts[] = {
    context_help,
    window_help,
    index_help
};

main(argc, argv)
int argc;
char *argv[];
{
    XtAppContext app;
    Widget toplevel, rc, main_w, menubar, w;
    extern void help_cb(), file_cb();
    XmString str1, str2, str3;
    Widget *cascade_btns;
    int num_btns;

    XtSetLanguageProc (NULL, NULL, NULL);

    toplevel = XtVaAppInitialize (&app, "Demos", NULL, 0,
        &argc, argv, NULL, NULL);

    /* the main window contains the work area and the menubar */
    main_w = XtVaCreateWidget ("main_w",
        xmMainWindowWidgetClass, toplevel, NULL);

    /* Create a simple MenuBar that contains two cascade buttons */
    str1 = XmStringCreateLocalized ("File");
    str2 = XmStringCreateLocalized ("Help");
    menubar = XmVaCreateSimpleMenuBar (main_w, "main_w",
        XmVaCASCADEBUTTON, str1, 'F',
        XmVaCASCADEBUTTON, str2, 'H',
        NULL);
    XmStringFree (str1);
    XmStringFree (str2);

    /* create the "File" pulldown menu -- callback is file_cb() */
    str1 = XmStringCreateLocalized ("New");
    str2 = XmStringCreateLocalized ("Open");
    str3 = XmStringCreateLocalized ("Quit");
    XmVaCreateSimplePulldownMenu (menubar, "file_menu", 0, file_cb,
        XmVaPUSHBUTTON, str1, 'N', NULL, NULL,
        XmVaPUSHBUTTON, str2, 'O', NULL, NULL,
        XmVaSEPARATOR,
        XmVaPUSHBUTTON, str3, 'Q', NULL, NULL,
        NULL);
    XmStringFree (str1);
    XmStringFree (str2);
    XmStringFree (str3);
```

Example 7-3. The help_text.c program (continued)

```
    /* create the "Help" menu -- callback is help_cb() */
    str1 = XmStringCreateLocalized ("On Context");
    str2 = XmStringCreateLocalized ("On Window");
    str3 = XmStringCreateLocalized ("Index");
    w = XmVaCreateSimplePulldownMenu (menubar, "help_menu", 1, help_cb,
        XmVaPUSHBUTTON, str1, 'C', NULL, NULL,
        XmVaPUSHBUTTON, str2, 'W', NULL, NULL,
        XmVaPUSHBUTTON, str3, 'I', NULL, NULL,
        NULL);
    XmStringFree (str1);
    XmStringFree (str2);
    XmStringFree (str3);

    /* Identify the Help Menu for the MenuBar */
    XtVaGetValues (menubar,
        XmNchildren,        &cascade_btns,
        XmNnumChildren,     &num_btns,
        NULL);
    XtVaSetValues (menubar,
        XmNmenuHelpWidget, cascade_btns[num_btns-1],
        NULL);
    XtManageChild (menubar);

    /* the work area for the main window -- just create dummy stuff */
    rc = XtVaCreateWidget ("rc", xmRowColumnWidgetClass, main_w, NULL);
    str1 = XmStringCreateLtoR ("\n  This is an Empty\nSample Control Area\n ",
        XmFONTLIST_DEFAULT_TAG);
    XtVaCreateManagedWidget ("label", xmLabelGadgetClass, rc,
        XmNlabelString,  str1,
        NULL);
    XmStringFree (str1);
    XtManageChild (rc);
    XtManageChild (main_w);

    XtRealizeWidget (toplevel);
    XtAppMainLoop (app);
}

/* callback for all the entries in the File pulldown menu. */
void
file_cb(w, client_data, call_data)
Widget w;
XtPointer client_data;
XtPointer call_data;
{
    int item_no = (int) client_data;

    if (item_no == 2) /* the Quit menu button */
        exit (0);
    printf ("Item %d (%s) selected\n", item_no + 1, XtName (w));
}

/* climb widget tree until we get to the top.  Return the Shell */
Widget
GetTopShell(w)
Widget w;
{
    while (w && !XtIsWMShell (w))
```

Example 7-3. The help_text.c program (continued)

```
            w = XtParent (w);
    return w;
}

#include "info.xbm"   /* bitmap data used by our dialog */

/* callback for all the entries in the Help pulldown menu.
 * Create a dialog box that contains control and action areas.
 */
void
help_cb(w, client_data, call_data)
Widget w;
XtPointer client_data;
XtPointer call_data;
{
    Widget help_dialog, pane, text_w, form, sep, widget, label;
    extern void DestroyShell();
    Pixmap pixmap;
    Pixel fg, bg;
    Arg args[10];
    int n = 0;
    int i;
    char *p, buf[BUFSIZ];
    int item_no = (int) client_data;
    Dimension h;

    /* Set up a DialogShell as a popup window.  Set the delete
     * window protocol response to XmDESTROY to make sure that
     * the window goes away appropriately.  Otherwise, it's XmUNMAP
     * which means it'd be lost forever, since we're not storing
     * the widget globally or statically to this function.
     */
    help_dialog = XtVaCreatePopupShell ("Help",
        xmDialogShellWidgetClass, GetTopShell (w),
        XmNdeleteResponse, XmDESTROY,
        NULL);

    /* Create a PanedWindow to manage the stuff in this dialog. */
    pane = XtVaCreateWidget ("pane", xmPanedWindowWidgetClass, help_dialog,
        XmNsashWidth,  1, /* PanedWindow won't let us set these to 0! */
        XmNsashHeight, 1, /* Make small so user doesn't try to resize */
        NULL);

    /* Create a RowColumn in the form for Label and Text widgets.
     * This is the control area.
     */
    form = XtVaCreateWidget ("form1", xmFormWidgetClass, pane, NULL);
    XtVaGetValues (form,  /* once created, we can get its colors */
        XmNforeground, &fg,
        XmNbackground, &bg,
        NULL);

    /* create the pixmap of the appropriate depth using the colors
     * that will be used by the parent (form).
     */
    pixmap = XCreatePixmapFromBitmapData (XtDisplay (form),
        RootWindowOfScreen (XtScreen (form)),
        info_bits, info_width, info_height,
```

Example 7-3. The help_text.c program (continued)

```
                 fg, bg, DefaultDepthOfScreen (XtScreen (form)));

    /* Create a label gadget using this pixmap */
    label = XtVaCreateManagedWidget ("label", xmLabelGadgetClass, form,
        XmNlabelType,        XmPIXMAP,
        XmNlabelPixmap,      pixmap,
        XmNleftAttachment,   XmATTACH_FORM,
        XmNtopAttachment,    XmATTACH_FORM,
        XmNbottomAttachment, XmATTACH_FORM,
        NULL);

    /* prepare the text for display in the ScrolledText object
     * we are about to create.
     */
    for (p = buf, i = 0; help_texts[item_no][i]; i++) {
        p += strlen (strcpy (p, help_texts[item_no][i]));
        if (!isspace (p[-1])) /* spaces, tabs and newlines are spaces.. */
            *p++ = ' '; /* lines are concatenated together, insert a space */
    }
    *--p = 0; /* get rid of trailing space... */

    XtSetArg (args[n], XmNscrollVertical,        True); n++;
    XtSetArg (args[n], XmNscrollHorizontal,      False); n++;
    XtSetArg (args[n], XmNeditMode,              XmMULTI_LINE_EDIT); n++;
    XtSetArg (args[n], XmNeditable,              False); n++;
    XtSetArg (args[n], XmNcursorPositionVisible, False); n++;
    XtSetArg (args[n], XmNwordWrap,              True); n++;
    XtSetArg (args[n], XmNvalue,                 buf); n++;
    XtSetArg (args[n], XmNrows,                  5); n++;
    text_w = XmCreateScrolledText(form, "help_text", args, n);
    /* Attachment values must be set on the Text widget's PARENT,
     * the ScrolledWindow. This is the object that is positioned.
     */
    XtVaSetValues (XtParent (text_w),
        XmNleftAttachment,   XmATTACH_WIDGET,
        XmNleftWidget,       label,
        XmNtopAttachment,    XmATTACH_FORM,
        XmNrightAttachment,  XmATTACH_FORM,
        XmNbottomAttachment, XmATTACH_FORM,
        NULL);
    XtManageChild (text_w);
    XtManageChild (form);

    /* Create another form to act as the action area for the dialog */
    form = XtVaCreateWidget ("form2", xmFormWidgetClass, pane,
        XmNfractionBase,     5,
        NULL);

    /* The OK button is under the pane's separator and is
     * attached to the left edge of the form.  It spreads from
     * position 0 to 1 along the bottom (the form is split into
     * 5 separate grids via XmNfractionBase upon creation).
     */
    widget = XtVaCreateManagedWidget ("OK",
        xmPushButtonGadgetClass, form,
        XmNtopAttachment,            XmATTACH_FORM,
        XmNbottomAttachment,         XmATTACH_FORM,
        XmNleftAttachment,           XmATTACH_POSITION,
```

Example 7-3. The help_text.c program (continued)

```
                XmNleftPosition,            1,
                XmNrightAttachment,         XmATTACH_POSITION,
                XmNrightPosition,           2,
                XmNshowAsDefault,           True,
                XmNdefaultButtonShadowThickness, 1,
                NULL);
        XtAddCallback (widget, XmNactivateCallback, DestroyShell, help_dialog);

        /* This is created with its XmNsensitive resource set to False
         * because we don't support "more" help.  However, this is the
         * place to attach it to if there were any more.
         */
        widget = XtVaCreateManagedWidget ("More",
                xmPushButtonGadgetClass, form,
                XmNsensitive,               False,
                XmNtopAttachment,           XmATTACH_FORM,
                XmNbottomAttachment,        XmATTACH_FORM,
                XmNleftAttachment,          XmATTACH_POSITION,
                XmNleftPosition,            3,
                XmNrightAttachment,         XmATTACH_POSITION,
                XmNrightPosition,           4,
                XmNshowAsDefault,           False,
                XmNdefaultButtonShadowThickness, 1,
                NULL);

        /* Fix the action area pane to its current height -- never let it resize */
        XtManageChild (form);

        XtVaGetValues (widget, XmNheight, &h, NULL);
        XtVaSetValues (form, XmNpaneMaximum, h, XmNpaneMinimum, h, NULL);

        XtManageChild (pane);

        XtPopup (help_dialog, XtGrabNone);
}

/* The callback function for the "OK" button.  Since this is not a
 * predefined Motif dialog, the "widget" parameter is not the dialog
 * itself.  That is only done by Motif dialog callbacks.  Here in the
 * real world, the callback routine is called directly by the widget
 * that was invoked.  Thus, we must pass the dialog as the client
 * data to get its handle.  (We could get it using GetTopShell(),
 * but this way is quicker, since it's immediately available.)
 */
void
DestroyShell(widget, client_data, call_data)
Widget widget;
XtPointer client_data;
XtPointer call_data;
{
    Widget shell = (Widget) client_data;

    XtDestroyWidget(shell);
}
```

The output of the program is shown in Figure 7-5. The function help_cb ( ) is the callback routine that is invoked by all of the **Help** menu items. This routine follows the steps that we outlined earlier to create the dialog box.

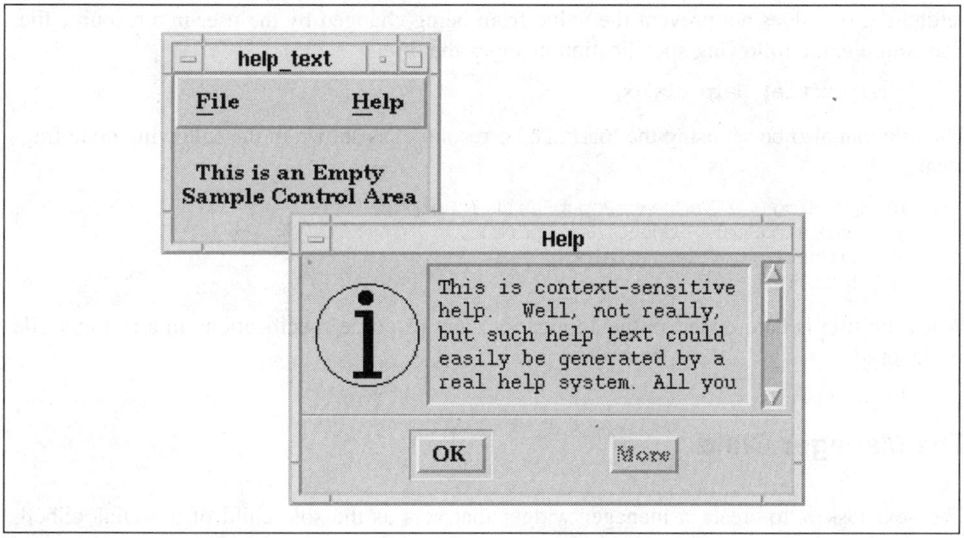

Figure 7-5. Output of help_text.c

7.3.1 The Shell

Since the dialog is a transient dialog, we use a DialogShell widget for the shell. We create the shell as follows:

```
help_dialog = XtVaCreatePopupShell ("Help",
    xmDialogShellWidgetClass, GetTopShell (w),
    XmNdeleteResponse, XmDESTROY,
    NULL);
```

Instead of using XtVaCreatePopupShell(), we could have used a Motif convenience routine as shown in the following code fragment:

```
n = 0;
XtSetArg (args[n], XmNdeleteResponse, XmDESTROY); n++;
help_dialog = XmCreateDialogShell (GetTopShell (w), "Help", args, n);
```

Both methods return a DialogShell. The XmNdeleteResponse resource is set to Xm-DESTROY because we want the **Close** item from the window menu in the window manager's titlebar for the shell to destroy the shell and its children. The default value for this resource is XmUNMAP; had we wanted to reuse the same dialog upon each invocation, we would have used XmUNMAP and retained a handle to the dialog widget.

The name of the dialog is *Help*, since that is the first parameter in the call to XtVaCreate-PopupShell(). Resource specifications in a resource file that pertain to this dialog should use *Help* as the widget name, as shown below:

```
*Help*foreground: green
```

The string displayed in the title bar of a dialog defaults to the name of the dialog. Since the name of the dialog is *Help*, the title defaults to the same value. However, this method of setting the title does not prevent the value from being changed by the user in a resource file. For example, the following specification changes the title:

```
*Help.title: Help Dialog
```

The title can also be set using the XmNtitle resource, as shown in the following code fragment:†

```
help_dialog = XtVaCreatePopupShell ("Help",
    xmDialogShellWidgetClass, parent,
    XmNtitle,   "Help Dialog",
    NULL);
```

When the title is hard-coded in the application, any resource specifications in a resource file are ignored.

7.3.2 The Manager Child

The next task is to create a manager widget that acts as the sole child of the DialogShell, since shell widgets can have only one managed child. This section deals heavily with manager widget issues, so if you have problems keeping up, you should look ahead to Chapter 8, *Manager Widgets*. However, the main point of the section is to provide enough context for you to understand Example 7-3. We are using a PanedWindow widget as the child of the DialogShell, as per our earlier recommendations. The PanedWindow is created as follows:

```
pane = XtVaCreateWidget ("pane",
    xmPanedWindowWidgetClass, help_dialog,
    XmNsashWidth,  1,
    XmNsashHeight, 1,
    NULL);
```

The PanedWindow manages two Form widget children, one each for the control area and the action area. These children are also called the PanedWindow's panes. Normally, in a Paned-Window, the user can resize the panes by moving the control sashes that are placed between the panes. Because the action area is not supposed to grow or shrink in size, we don't want to allow the user to adjust the sizes of the panes. There are really two issues involved here: the user might try to resize the panes individually or she might resize the entire dialog, which would cause the PanedWindow itself to resize them.

You can prevent the PanedWindow from resizing the action area when it is itself resized by setting the pane's XmNskipAdjust resource to True. However, this technique still allows the user to resize the individual panes, which means that you need to disable the control sashes. The best way to prevent both undesirable resize possibilities is to set the action area pane's maximum and minimum allowed heights to the same value. These settings should cause the PanedWindow to disable the sashes for that particular pane, but due to a bug in the PanedWindow widget class, the sashes are rarely disabled. To compensate, we try to make the sashes invisible by setting their sizes to a minimum value. Unfortunately, the

---

† XmNtitle is defined identically to XtNtitle, which is an Xt resource, which means that the value is a regular character string, not a compound string.

PanedWindow won't let you set the size of a sash to 0 (a design error), so we set the values for XmNsashWidth and XmNsashHeight to 1.†

The PanedWindow widget is created unmanaged using XtVaCreateWidget(). As pointed out in Chapter 8, *Manager Widgets*, manager widgets should not be managed until all of their children have been created and managed. Using this order allows the children's desired sizes and positions to be specified before the manager widget tries to negotiate other sizes and positions.

7.3.3 The Control Area

The Form widget is the control area, so it is created as a child of the PanedWindow, as shown in the following fragment:

```
form = XtVaCreateWidget ("form1", xmFormWidgetClass, pane, NULL);
```

As far as the PanedWindow is concerned, the Form widget is a single child whose width is stretched to the left and right edges of the shell. Within the Form, we add two widgets: a Label widget that contains the help pixmap and a ScrolledText for the help information.

In order to create the Label, we must first create the pixmap it is going to use. The following code fragment shows how we create the pixmap and then create the Label:

```
XtVaGetValues (form,
    XmNforeground, &fg,
    XmNbackground, &bg,
    NULL);

pixmap = XCreatePixmapFromBitmapData (XtDisplay (form),
    RootWindowOfScreen (XtScreen (form)),
    bitmap_bits, bitmap_width, bitmap_height,
    fg, bg, DefaultDepthOfScreen (XtScreen (form)));

label = XtVaCreateManagedWidget ("label", xmLabelGadgetClass, form,
    XmNlabelType,        XmPIXMAP,
    XmNlabelPixmap,      pixmap,
    XmNleftAttachment,   XmATTACH_FORM,
    XmNtopAttachment,    XmATTACH_FORM,
    XmNbottomAttachment, XmATTACH_FORM,
    NULL);
```

We cannot create the pixmap until we know the foreground and background colors, so we retrieve these colors from the Form, since it has a valid window and colormap. This approach works for either monochrome or color screens. We use these values as the foreground and background for the pixmap we create in the call to XCreatePixmapFrom-BitmapData().‡ The bits for the bitmap, the width, and the height are predefined in the

---

† The only other problem that might arise is that keyboard traversal still allows the user to reach the sashes, so you may want to remove them from the traversal list by setting their XmNtraversalOn resources to False. This issue is described in detail in Chapter 8, *Manager Widgets*.

‡ We could have used XmGetPixmap() to create a pixmap, but this routine does not allow us to load a pixmap directly from bitmap data, as we have done here. For us to use XmGetPixmap(), the file that contains the bitmap data would have to exist at run-time, or we would have to load the bitmap data directly into a static XImage. For more information on this technique, see Section 3.4.5 in Chapter 3, *Overview of the Motif Toolkit*.

X bitmap file included earlier in the program (*info.xbm*). The Label uses the pixmap by setting the `XmNlabelType` and `XmNlabelPixmap` resources (see Chapter 11, *Labels and Buttons*, for more information on these resources).

The attachment resources we specified for the Label are constraint resources for the Form widget that describe how the Form should lay out its children. These constraint resources are ignored by the Label widget itself. See Chapter 8, *Manager Widgets*, for a complete description of how constraint resources are handled by widgets. In this case, the top, bottom, and left sides of the Label are all attached to the edge of the Form, which causes the Label to position itself relative to the Form.

Next, we create a ScrolledText compound object to display the help text, as shown in the following fragment:

```
n = 0;
XtSetArg (args[n], XmNscrollVertical,       True); n++;
XtSetArg (args[n], XmNscrollHorizontal,     False); n++;
XtSetArg (args[n], XmNeditMode,             XmMULTI_LINE_EDIT); n++;
XtSetArg (args[n], XmNeditable,             False); n++;
XtSetArg (args[n], XmNcursorPositionVisible, False); n++;
XtSetArg (args[n], XmNwordWrap,             True); n++;
XtSetArg (args[n], XmNvalue,                buf); n++;
XtSetArg (args[n], XmNrows,                 5); n++;
text_w = XmCreateScrolledText(form, "help_text", args, n);

XtVaSetValues (XtParent (text_w),
    XmNleftAttachment,    XmATTACH_WIDGET,
    XmNleftWidget,        label,
    XmNtopAttachment,     XmATTACH_FORM,
    XmNrightAttachment,   XmATTACH_FORM,
    XmNbottomAttachment,  XmATTACH_FORM,
    NULL);

XtManageChild (text_w);
```

In order to use `XmCreateScrolledText()`, we must use the old-style `XtSetArg()` method of setting the resources that are passed to the function. The routine actually creates two widgets that appear to be a single interface object. A ScrolledWindow widget and a Text widget are created so that the Text widget is a child of the ScrolledWindow. The toolkit returns a handle to the Text widget, but since the ScrolledWindow widget is the direct child of the Form, we set the constraint resources on the ScrolledWindow, not the Text widget. The top, right, and bottom sides of the ScrolledWindow are attached to the Form, while the left side is attached to the Label widget, so that the two widgets are always positioned next to each other.

We could have passed these resource/value pairs in the `args` list, but then the resources would have been set on both the ScrolledWindow widget and the Text widget. Since the attachment constraints would be ignored by the Text widget, there would be no real harm in setting them on both widgets. However, it is better programming style to set the resources directly on the ScrolledWindow. Details on the Text widget and the ScrolledText object can be found in Chapter 14, *Text Widgets*. Chapter 9, *ScrolledWindows and ScrollBars*, discusses the ScrolledWindow widget and its resources.

The text for the widget is set using the `XmNvalue` resource. The value for this resource is the appropriate help text taken from the `help_texts` array declared at the beginning of the program. We set the `XmNeditable` resource to `False` so that the user cannot edit the help text.

The Text and Label widgets are the only two items in the Form widget. Once these children are created and managed, the Form can be managed using `XtManageChild()`.

7.3.4 The Action Area

At this point, the control area of the dialog has been created, so it is time to create the action area. In our example, the action area is pretty simple, as the only action needed is to close the dialog. We use the **OK** button for this action. For completeness, we have also provided a **More** button to support additional or extended help. Since we don't provide any additional help, we set this button insensitive (although you can extend this example by providing it).

The action area does not have to be contained in a separate widget, although it is generally much easier to do so. We use a Form widget in order to position the buttons evenly across the width of the dialog. We create the Form as follows:

```
form = XtVaCreateWidget ("form2", xmFormWidgetClass, pane,
    XmNfractionBase,    5,
    NULL);
```

The `XmNfractionBase` resource of the Form widget is set to five, so that the Form is broked down into five equal units, as shown in Figure 7-6.

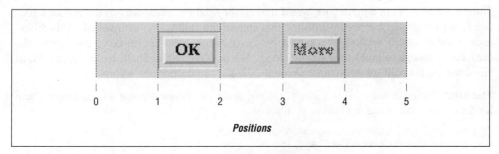

Figure 7-6. The XmNfractionBase resource divides the Form into equal units

Position zero is the left edge of the form and position five is the right edge of the form. We chose five because it gave us the best layout aesthetically. The region is divided up equally, so you can think of the sections as percentages of the total width (or height) of the Form. By using this layout method, we don't have to be concerned with the width of the Form or of the DialogShell itself, since we know that the placement of the buttons will always be proportional. We create the **OK** button as shown in the following code fragment:

```
widget = XtVaCreateManagedWidget ("OK",
    xmPushButtonGadgetClass, form,
    XmNtopAttachment,       XmATTACH_FORM,
    XmNbottomAttachment,    XmATTACH_FORM,
```

```
        XmNleftAttachment,      XmATTACH_POSITION,
        XmNleftPosition,        1,
        XmNrightAttachment,     XmATTACH_POSITION,
        XmNrightPosition,       2,
        XmNshowAsDefault,       True,
        XmNdefaultButtonShadowThickness, 1,
        NULL);
```

The left and right sides of the button are placed at positions one and two, respectively. Since this button is the default button for the dialog, we want the button to be displayed as such. We set XmNshowAsDefault to True and XmNdefaultButtonShadowThickness to 1. The value for the latter resource is a pixel value that specifies the width of an extra three-dimensional border that is placed around the default button to distinguish it from the other buttons. If the value for XmNshowAsDefault is False, the button is not shown as the default, regardless of the value of the default shadow thickness.†

Because the dialog is not reused, we want the callback for the **OK** button to destroy the DialogShell. We use the XmNactivateCallback of the PushButton to implement the functionality. The callback routine is DestroyShell(), which is shown below:

```
static void
DestroyShell(widget, client_data, call_data)
Widget widget;
XtPointer client_data;
XtPointer call_data;
{
    Widget shell = (Widget) client_data;

    XtDestroyWidget(shell);
}
```

Since the dialog is not a predefined Motif dialog, the widget parameter to the callback routine is not the dialog, but the PushButton that caused the callback to be invoked. This difference is subtle and it is often overlooked by programmers who are breaking away from the predefined dialogs to build their own dialogs. We pass the DialogShell, help_dialog, as client data to the callback routine, so that the callback can destroy the widget.

The **More** button is not used in the application, since we do not provide any additional help for the dialog. We create the button as follows:

```
widget = XtVaCreateManagedWidget ("More",
        xmPushButtonGadgetClass, form,
        XmNsensitive,           False,
        XmNtopAttachment,       XmATTACH_FORM,
        XmNbottomAttachment,    XmATTACH_FORM,
        XmNleftAttachment,      XmATTACH_POSITION,
        XmNleftPosition,        3,
        XmNrightAttachment,     XmATTACH_POSITION,
        XmNrightPosition,       4,
        XmNshowAsDefault,       False,
        XmNdefaultButtonShadowThickness,   1,
        NULL);
```

---

† The XmNshowAsDefault resource can also take a numeric value that indicates the shadow thickness to use, but its value is only interpreted in this way if XmNdefaultButtonShadowThickness is set to 0. This functionality is for backwards compatibility with Motif 1.0 and should not be used.

In this case, the `XmNshowAsDefault` resource is set to `False`. We have also set `XmN-sensitive` to `False` so that the widget is insensitive to user input.

Once the buttons in the action area have been created, we need to fix the size of the action area. We manage the Form and then we retrieve the height of one of the action area buttons, so that we can use the value as the minimum and maximum height of the pane. We set the `XmNpaneMaximum` and `XmNpaneMinimum` constraint resources on the Form, so that the PanedWindow sets the action area to a constant height.

Once the control area and the action area have been created and managed, the PanedWindow is managed using `XtManageChild()` and the dialog is popped up using `XtPopup()`. This last step is necessary because the DialogShell is not automatically popped up when you manage the PanedWindow widget. This special behavior only happens when the immediate child of the DialogShell is a BulletinBoard or Form widget. This program provides an example of why you should never rely on this behavior or expect it to happen. See Chapter 5, *Introduction to Dialogs*, for a complete discussion of the posting of dialogs.

7.4 Generalizing the Action Area

While dialogs can vary in many respects, the structure of the action area usually remains consistent for all dialogs. Most large programs are going to make use of many customized dialogs. In the general case, you do not want to rewrite the code to generate an action area for each special case. It is much easier and more efficient to write a generalized routine that creates an action area for any dialog.

Whenever we generalize any procedure, we first identify how the situation may change from one case to the next. For example, not all action areas have only two buttons; you may have any number from one to, say, ten. As a result, you need to be able to change the number of partitions in the Form widget to an arbitrary value depending on the number of actions in the dialog. The positions to which the left and right sides of each action button are attached also need to be adjusted.

Some known quantities in this equation are that the action area must be at the bottom of a dialog and it must contains PushButtons. While the PushButtons may be either widgets or gadgets, you should probably choose one or the other and use them consistently throughout your application. Since gadgets use the colors of their parent, one advantage of using them is that you can set the colors of all of the buttons quite easily, as shown in the following resource specification:

```
*action_area.foreground: red
```

On the other hand, since widgets have windows, you can specify different colors for different buttons. For example, you could use blue for the **OK** button and red for the **Cancel** button, as shown in the following specifications:

```
*action_area.ok_button.foreground: blue
*action_area.cancel_button.foreground: red
```

In general, all of the buttons in the action area should be from the same class, and all of the action areas in an application should be consistent with one another.

Each button in an action area has its own label, its own callback routine, and its own associated client data. To create a general action area, we need a data structure that abstracts this information. The `ActionAreaItem` structure is defined as follows:

```
typedef struct {
    char *label;          /* PushButton's Label */
    void (*callback)();  /* pointer to a callback routine */
    XtPointer data;       /* client data for the callback routine */
} ActionAreaItem;
```

This data structure contains all of the information that we need to know in order to create an action area; the rest of the information is known or it can be derived.

Now we can write a routine that creates an action area. The purpose of the function is to create and return a composite widget that contains the specified number of PushButtons, where the buttons are arranged horizontally and evenly spaced. The `CreateActionArea()` routine is used in Example 7-4. This program does not do anything substantial, but it does present a generalized architecture for creating dialogs for an application.†

Example 7-4. The action_area.c program

```
/* action_area.c -- demonstrate how CreateActionArea() can be used
 * in a real application.  Create what would otherwise be identified
 * as a PromptDialog, only this is of our own creation.  As such,
 * we provide a TextField widget for input.  When the user presses
 * Return, the OK button is activated.
 */
#include <Xm/DialogS.h>
#include <Xm/PushBG.h>
#include <Xm/PushB.h>
#include <Xm/LabelG.h>
#include <Xm/PanedW.h>
#include <Xm/Form.h>
#include <Xm/RowColumn.h>
#include <Xm/TextF.h>

typedef struct {
    char *label;
    void (*callback)();
    XtPointer data;
} ActionAreaItem;

static void
    do_dialog(), close_dialog(), activate_cb(),
    ok_pushed(), clear_pushed(), help();

main(argc, argv)
int argc;
char *argv[];
{
    Widget toplevel, button;
    XtAppContext app;
```

---

†`XtSetLanguageProc()` is only available in X11R5; there is no corresponding function in X11R4. `Xm-StringCreateLocalized()` is only available in Motif 1.2; `XmStringCreateSimple()` is the corresponding function in Motif 1.1.

Motif Programming Manual

Example 7-4. The action_area.c program (continued)

```
    XtSetLanguageProc (NULL, NULL, NULL);

    toplevel = XtVaAppInitialize (&app, "Demos",
        NULL, 0, &argc, argv, NULL, NULL);

    button = XtVaCreateManagedWidget ("Push Me",
        xmPushButtonWidgetClass, toplevel, NULL);
    XtAddCallback (button, XmNactivateCallback, do_dialog, NULL);

    XtRealizeWidget (toplevel);
    XtAppMainLoop (app);
}

/* callback routine for "Push Me" button.  Actually, this represents
 * a function that could be invoked by any arbitrary callback.  Here,
 * we demonstrate how one can build a standard customized dialog box.
 * The control area is created here and the action area is created in
 * a separate, generic routine: CreateActionArea().
 */
static void
do_dialog(w, client_data, call_data)
Widget w; /* will act as dialog's parent */
XtPointer client_data;
XtPointer call_data;
{
    Widget dialog, pane, rc, text_w, action_a;
    XmString string;
    extern Widget CreateActionArea();
    static ActionAreaItem action_items[] = {
        { "OK",     ok_pushed,      NULL            },
        { "Clear",  clear_pushed,   NULL            },
        { "Cancel", close_dialog,   NULL            },
        { "Help",   help,           "Help Button" },
    };

    /* The DialogShell is the Shell for this dialog.  Set it up so
     * that the "Close" button in the window manager's system menu
     * destroys the shell (it only unmaps it by default).
     */
    dialog = XtVaCreatePopupShell ("dialog",
        xmDialogShellWidgetClass, XtParent (w),
        XmNtitle,  "Dialog Shell",      /* give arbitrary title in wm */
        XmNdeleteResponse, XmDESTROY,  /* system menu "Close" action */
        NULL);

    /* now that the dialog is created, set the Cancel button's
     * client data, so close_dialog() will know what to destroy.
     */
    action_items[2].data = (XtPointer) dialog;

    /* Create the paned window as a child of the dialog.  This will
     * contain the control area and the action area
     * (created by CreateActionArea() using the action_items above).
     */
    pane = XtVaCreateWidget ("pane", xmPanedWindowWidgetClass, dialog,
        XmNsashWidth,  1,
        XmNsashHeight, 1,
        NULL);
```

Example 7-4. The action_area.c program (continued)

```
        /* create the control area which contains a
         * Label gadget and a TextField widget.
         */
        rc = XtVaCreateWidget ("control_area", xmRowColumnWidgetClass, pane, NULL);
        string = XmStringCreateLocalized ("Type Something:");
        XtVaCreateManagedWidget ("label", xmLabelGadgetClass, rc,
            XmNlabelString,     string,
            NULL);
        XmStringFree (string);

        text_w = XtVaCreateManagedWidget ("text-field",
            xmTextFieldWidgetClass, rc, NULL);

        /* RowColumn is full -- now manage */
        XtManageChild (rc);

        /* Set the client data for the "OK" and "Cancel" buttons */
        action_items[0].data = (XtPointer) text_w;
        action_items[1].data = (XtPointer) text_w;

        /* Create the action area. */
        action_a = CreateActionArea (pane, action_items, XtNumber (action_items));

        /* callback for Return in TextField.  Use action_a as client data */
        XtAddCallback (text_w, XmNactivateCallback, activate_cb, action_a);

        XtManageChild (pane);
        XtPopup (dialog, XtGrabNone);
}

/* The next four functions are the callback routines for the buttons
 * in the action area for the dialog created above.  Again, they are
 * simple examples, yet they demonstrate the fundamental design approach.
 */
static void
close_dialog(w, client_data, call_data)
Widget w;
XtPointer client_data;
XtPointer call_data;
{
    Widget shell = (Widget) client_data;

    XtDestroyWidget (shell);
}

/* The "ok" button was pushed or the user pressed Return */
static void
ok_pushed(w, client_data, call_data)
Widget w;
XtPointer client_data;
XtPointer call_data;
{
    Widget text_w = (Widget) client_data;
    XmAnyCallbackStruct *cbs = (XmAnyCallbackStruct *) call_data;
    char *text = XmTextFieldGetString (text_w);

    printf ("String = %s\n", text);
    XtFree (text);
}

static void
```

Example 7-4. The action_area.c program (continued)

```
clear_pushed(w, client_data, call_data)
Widget w;
XtPointer client_data;
XtPointer call_data;
{
    Widget text_w = (Widget) client_data;
    XmAnyCallbackStruct *cbs = (XmAnyCallbackStruct *) call_data;

    /* cancel the whole operation; reset to NULL. */
    XmTextFieldSetString (text_w, "");
}

static void
help(w, client_data, call_data)
Widget w;
XtPointer client_data;
XtPointer call_data;
{
    String string = (String) client_data;

    puts(string);
}

/* When Return is pressed in TextField widget, respond by getting
 * the designated "default button" in the action area and activate
 * it as if the user had selected it.
 */
static void
activate_cb(text_w, client_data, call_data)
Widget text_w;                /* user pressed Return in this widget */
XtPointer client_data;        /* action_area passed as client data */
XtPointer call_data;
{
    XmAnyCallbackStruct *cbs = (XmAnyCallbackStruct *) call_data;
    Widget dflt, action_area = (Widget) client_data;

    /* get the "default button" from the action area... */
    XtVaGetValues (action_area, XmNdefaultButton, &dflt, NULL);
    if (dflt) /* sanity check -- this better work */
        /* make the default button think it got pushed using
         * XtCallActionProc().  This function causes the button
         * to appear to be activated as if the user pressed it.
         */
        XtCallActionProc (dflt, "ArmAndActivate", cbs->event, NULL, 0);
}

#define TIGHTNESS 20

Widget
CreateActionArea(parent, actions, num_actions)
Widget parent;
ActionAreaItem *actions;
int num_actions;
{
    Widget action_area, widget;
    int i;

    action_area = XtVaCreateWidget ("action_area", xmFormWidgetClass, parent,
        XmNfractionBase, TIGHTNESS*num_actions - 1,
```

Example 7-4. The action_area.c program (continued)

```
            XmNleftOffset,    10,
            XmNrightOffset,   10,
            NULL);

    for (i = 0; i < num_actions; i++) {
        widget = XtVaCreateManagedWidget (actions[i].label,
            xmPushButtonWidgetClass, action_area,
            XmNleftAttachment,        i? XmATTACH_POSITION : XmATTACH_FORM,
            XmNleftPosition,          TIGHTNESS*i,
            XmNtopAttachment,         XmATTACH_FORM,
            XmNbottomAttachment,      XmATTACH_FORM,
            XmNrightAttachment,
                i != num_actions - 1 ? XmATTACH_POSITION : XmATTACH_FORM,
            XmNrightPosition,         TIGHTNESS * i + (TIGHTNESS - 1),
            XmNshowAsDefault,         i == 0,
            XmNdefaultButtonShadowThickness, 1,
            NULL);
        if (actions[i].callback)
            XtAddCallback (widget, XmNactivateCallback,
                actions[i].callback, actions[i].data);
        if (i == 0) {
            /* Set the action_area's default button to the first widget
             * created (or, make the index a parameter to the function
             * or have it be part of the data structure). Also, set the
             * pane window constraint for max and min heights so this
             * particular pane in the PanedWindow is not resizable.
             */
            Dimension height, h;
            XtVaGetValues (action_area, XmNmarginHeight, &h, NULL);
            XtVaGetValues (widget, XmNheight, &height, NULL);
            height += 2 * h;
            XtVaSetValues (action_area,
                XmNdefaultButton, widget,
                XmNpaneMaximum,   height,
                XmNpaneMinimum,   height,
                NULL);
        }
    }

    XtManageChild (action_area);

    return action_area;
}
```

The application uses a PushButton to create and pop up a customized dialog. The control area is composed of a RowColumn widget that contains a Label gadget and a TextField widget. The action area is created using `CreateActionArea()`. The actions and the number of actions are specified in the `actions` and `num_actions` parameters. We use a

Form widget to lay out the actions. We give the Form the name *action_area*, since it is descriptive and it makes it easy for the user to specify the area in a resource file. The output of the program in shown in Figure 7-7.

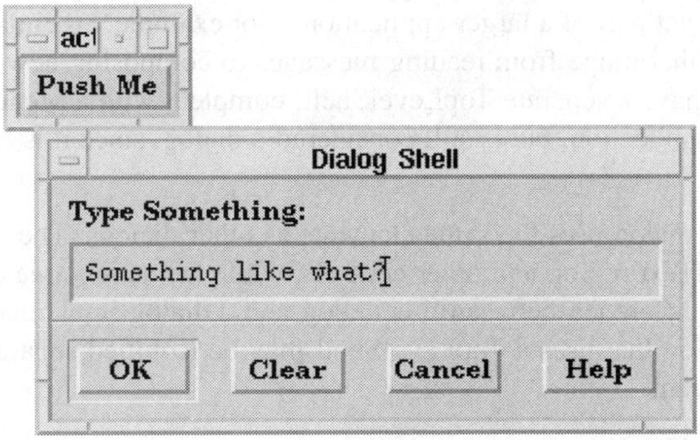

Figure 7-7. Output of action_area.c

In order to distribute the PushButtons evenly across the action area, we use the XmN-fractionBase resource of the Form widget to segment the widget into equal portions. The value of the resource is based on the value of the TIGHTNESS definition, which controls the spacing between buttons. A higher value causes the PushButtons to be closer together, while a lower value spaces them further apart. We use the value 20 for purely aesthetic reasons. As each button is created, its attachments are set. The left side of the first button and right side of the last button are attached to the left and right edges of the Form, respectively, while all of the other left and right edges are attached to positions.

The callback routine and associated client data for each button are added using XtAdd-Callback(). The first button in the action area is specified as the default button for the dialog. The XmNdefaultButton resource indicates which button is designated as the default button for certain actions that take place in the control area of the dialog. The XmN-activateCallback of the TextField widget in the control area uses the resource to activate the default button when the user presses the RETURN key in the TextField.

The CreateActionArea() function also sets XmNpaneMaximum and XmNpane-Minimum constraint resources on the action area. These are PanedWindow constraint resources that are used to specify the height of the action area. The assumption, of course, is that the parent of the action area is a PanedWindow. If that is not true, these resource specifications have no effect.

7.5 Using a TopLevelShell for a Dialog

You don't have to use a DialogShell widget to implement a dialog. In fact, it is quite common to use a TopLevelShell or even an ApplicationShell in cases where the particular functionality is an important part of a larger application. For example, an e-mail application has a variety of functions that range from reading messages to composing new ones. As shown in Figure 7-8, you can have a separate TopLevelShell, complete with a MenuBar, that looks and acts like a separate application, but is still considered a dialog, since it is only a subpart of the whole application.

As you can see, this dialog uses the same elements as other dialogs. The control area is complete with a ScrolledText region and other controls, while the action area contains action buttons. The principal difference between this dialog and a dialog implemented with a DialogShell is that this dialog that uses a TopLevelShell may be iconified separately from the other windows in the program.

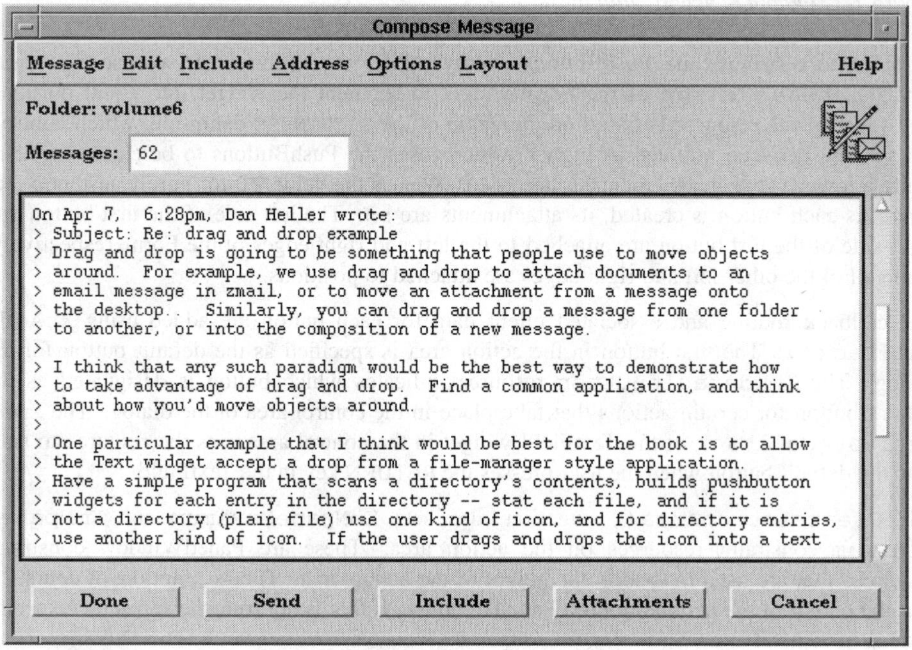

Figure 7-8. A message composition dialog from an e-mail application

When you need to implement a dialog with a TopLevelShell, you should not regard or implement it as a popup dialog. But for the most part, there is little difference from this approach and the method discussed for regular dialogs. You may still use BulletinBoards, Forms, and RowColumns to manage the inner controls. You still need an action area (provided you want to look and act like a dialog), and you still need to handle the cases where the dialog is popped up and down. You can create the TopLevelShell with `XtVaAppCreateShell()`. The shell is automatically mapped onto the screen when you call `XtPopup()`. You may also want to call `XMapRaised()` on the shell, in case it is already popped up but is not at the top of the window hierarchy.

In direct contrast to the DialogShell widget, managing the immediate child of a TopLevel-Shell does not cause the dialog to pop up automatically. Even if that child is subclassed from the BulletinBoard widget, this type of behavior only happens if the shell is a DialogShell widget. Because you are using a TopLevelShell, you cannot rely on the special communication that happens between a DialogShell and a BulletinBoard or Form widget. As a result, many resources such as `XmNautoUnmanage` and `XmNdialogTitle` no longer apply. To achieve the effects of these resources, you have to implement the functionality yourself.

If you want to use one of the standard Motif dialogs, such as a MessageDialog or a File-SelectionDialog, in a shell widget that can be iconified iconified separately from its primary window shell, you can put the dialog in a TopLevelShell. Create the shell using `XtVaApp-CreateShell()` and then use one of the Motif convenience routines to create a Message-Box or a FileSelectionBox, rather than the corresponding dialog widget. The following code fragment shows an example of this usage:

```
shell = XtVaAppCreateShell (NULL, "Class",
    topLevelShellWidgetClass, dpy,
    XtNtitle, "Dialog Shell Title",
    NULL);

dialog = XmCreateMessageBox (shell, "MessageDialog", NULL, 0);

XtAddCallback (dialog, XmNokCallback, callback_func, NULL);
XtAddCallback (dialog, XmNcancelCallback, callback_func, NULL);
XtAddCallback (dialog, XmNhelpCallback, help_func, NULL);
```

7.6 Positioning Dialogs

In all of the dialog examples that you have seen so far, the toolkit has handled the positioning of the dialog. For dialogs that use the DialogShell widget with a subclass of BulletinBoard as the immediate child, the `XmNdefaultPosition` resource controls this behavior. If the resource is `True`, the dialog is centered relative to the parent of the DialogShell and placed on top of the parent. If the resource is set to `False`, the application is responsible for positioning the dialog. It is easy to position a dialog using the `XmNmapCallback` resource that is supported by all of the Motif manager widgets, as shown in Example 7-5.

Example 7-5. The map_dlg.c program

```
/* map_dlg.c -- Use the XmNmapCallback to automatically position
 * a dialog on the screen.  Each time the dialog is displayed, it
 * is mapped down and to the right by 200 pixels in each direction.
 */
#include <Xm/MessageB.h>
#include <Xm/PushB.h>

/* main() --create a pushbutton whose callback pops up a dialog box */
```

Example 7-5. The map_dlg.c program (continued)

```
main(argc, argv)
int argc;
char *argv[];
{
    Widget toplevel, button;
    XtAppContext app;
    void pushed();

    toplevel = XtVaAppInitialize (&app, "Demos",
        NULL, 0, &argc, argv, NULL, NULL);

    button = XtVaCreateManagedWidget ("Push Me",
        xmPushButtonWidgetClass, toplevel,
        NULL);

    XtAddCallback (button, XmNactivateCallback, pushed, "Hello World");

    XtRealizeWidget (toplevel);
    XtAppMainLoop (app);
}

/* callback function for XmNmapCallback.  Position dialog in 200 pixel
 * "steps".  When the edge of the screen is hit, start over.
 */
static void
map_dialog(dialog, client_data, call_data)
Widget dialog;
XtPointer client_data;
XtPointer call_data;
{
    static Position x, y;
    Dimension w, h;

    XtVaGetValues(dialog,
        XmNwidth, &w,
        XmNheight, &h,
        NULL);

    if ((x + w) >= WidthOfScreen (XtScreen (dialog)))
        x = 0;
    if ((y + h) >= HeightOfScreen (XtScreen (dialog)))
        y = 0;
    XtVaSetValues (dialog,
        XmNx, x,
        XmNy, y,
        NULL);

    x += 200;
    y += 200;
}

/* pushed() --the callback routine for the main app's pushbutton.
 * Create and popup a dialog box that has callback functions for
 * the Ok, Cancel and Help buttons.
 */
void
pushed(w, client_data, call_data)
Widget w;
XtPointer client_data;
```

Example 7-5. The map_dlg.c program (continued)

```
XtPointer call_data;
{
    extern void response();
    Widget dialog;
    Arg arg[5];
    int n = 0;
    char *message = (char *) client_data;
    XmString t = XmStringCreateLocalized (message);

    XtSetArg (arg[n], XmNmessageString, t); n++;
    XtSetArg (arg[n], XmNdefaultPosition, False); n++;
    dialog = XmCreateMessageDialog (w, "notice", arg, n);
    XmStringFree (t);

    XtAddCallback (dialog, XmNmapCallback, map_dialog, NULL);

    XtManageChild (dialog);
    XtPopup (XtParent (dialog), XtGrabNone);
}
```

Each time the dialog is mapped to the screen, the map_dialog() routine is invoked. The routine merely places the dialog at a location that is 200 pixels from its previous position. Obviously, this example is meant to demonstrate the technique of positioning a dialog, rather than providing any useful functionality. The XmNwidth, XmNheight, XmNx, and XmNy resources are retrieved from the DialogShell widget since the dialog is a predefined Motif dialog. Similarly, the position of the DialogShell is set by calling XtVaSetValues() using the same resources.

If you are using an ApplicationShell or a TopLevelShell, rather than a DialogShell, the position of the dialog is subject to various resources that are controlled by the user and/or the window manager. For example, if the user is using *mwm*, she can set the resource interactivePlacement, which allows her to position the shell interactively. While it is acceptable for an application to control the placement of a DialogShell, it should not try to control the placement of a TopLevelShell or an ApplicationShell because that is the user's domain. However, if you feel you must, you can position any shell widget directly by setting its XmNx and XmNy resources to the desired position when the shell is created or later using XtVaSetValues(). The Motif toolkit passes the coordinate values to the window manager and allows it to position the dialog at the intended location.

This issue is an important dilemma in user-interface design. If you are going to hard-code the position of a dialog on the screen, you probably do not want to position the dialog at that location each time that it is popped up. Imagine that you pop up a dialog, move it to an uncluttered area on your screen, interact with it for a while, and then pop it down. If you use the dialog again, you would probably like it to reappear in the location where you put it previously. The best way to handle this dilemma is to avoid doing any of your own dialog placement, with the possible exception of the first time that a dialog is popped up.

Whether or not you want to position a dialog when it is displayed, you may still find it useful to be informed about when a dialog is popped up or down. The XmNmapCallback is not the best tool for this purpose, since it is not called each time the popped-up state of the dialog changes. The XmNpopupCallback and XmNpopdownCallback callbacks are meant for this purpose. These resources are defined and implemented by X Toolkit Intrinsics for all shell widgets. The `XmNpopupCallback` is invoked each time `XtPopup()` is called on a shell widget, while the `XmNpopdownCallback` is called for `XtPopdown()`.

People often get confused by the terminology of a dialog being popped down and a shell being iconified. Remember that whether or not a shell is popped up is independent of its iconic state. Although a DialogShell cannot be iconified separately, other shells can. These shells may also be popped up and down using `XtPopup()` and `XtPopdown()` independent of their iconic state. `XtPopup()` causes a shell to be deiconified, while `XtPopdown()` causes the dialog and its icon to be withdrawn from the screen, regardless of its iconic state. The subject of window iconification is discussed in Chapter 16, *Interacting With the Window Manager*.

7.7 Summary

Obviously, it is impossible to cover all of the possible scenarios of how dialogs can and should be used in an application. If nothing else, you should come away from the chapters on dialogs with a general feeling for the design approach that we encourage. You should also understand the steps that are necessary to create and use both predefined Motif dialogs and customized dialogs. For a final look at some particularly thorny issues in using dialogs, see Chapter 21, *Advanced Dialog Programming*.

8

Manager Widgets

This chapter provides detailed descriptions of the various classes of Motif manager widgets. Examples explore the various methods of positioning children within the BulletinBoard, Form, and RowColumn widgets.

In This Chapter:

8
Manager Widgets

As their name implies, manager widgets manage other widgets, which means that they control the size and location (geometry) and input focus policy for one or more widget children. The relationship between managers and the widgets that they manage is commonly referred to as the parent-child model. The manager acts as the parent and the other widgets are its children. Since manager widgets can also be children of other managers, this model produces the widget hierarchy, which is a framework for how widgets are laid out visually on the screen and how resources are specified in the resource database.

While managers are used and explained in different contexts throughout this book, this chapter discusses the details of the different manager widget classes. Chapter 3, *Overview of the Motif Toolkit*, discusses the general concepts behind manager widgets and how they fit into the broader application model. You are encouraged to review the material in this and other chapters for a wider range of examples, since it is impossible to deal with all of the possibilities here. For an in-depth discussion of the X Toolkit Composite and Constraint widget classes, from which managers are subclassed, see Volume Four, *X Toolkit Intrinsics Programming Manual*.

8.1 Types of Manager Widgets

The Manager widget class is a metaclass for a number of functional subclasses. The Manager widget class is never instantiated; the functionality it provides is inherited by each of its subclasses. In this chapter, we describe the general-purpose Motif manager widgets, which are introduced below:

BulletinBoard

The BulletinBoard is the most basic of the manager widgets. The geometry management is, as the class name implies, like a bulletin board. A child is pinned up on the BulletinBoard in a particular location and remains there until it moves itself or someone else moves it. The BulletinBoard widget does not impose any layout policy on its children, but it does support keyboard traversal. The BulletinBoard is a superclass for more sophisticated and useful managers. The BulletinBoard is also designed to be used as the container for dialog boxes, so it has translation tables and callback routines for this purpose. The predefined Motif dialogs use the BulletinBoard widget class to handle all of their input mechanisms; each dialog widget class handles its own geometry management. See Chapter 5, *Introduction to Dialogs*, for a complete discussion of dialogs.

Form

The Form widget is subclassed from the BulletinBoard. The Form extends the capabilities of the BulletinBoard by introducing a sophisticated geometry management policy that involves both absolute and relative positioning and sizing of its children. For example, a Form may lay out its children in a grid-like manner, anchoring the edges of each child to specific positions on the grid, or it may attach the children to one another in a chain-like fashion.

RowColumn

The RowColumn widget lays out its children in rows and columns. Resources control the number of rows or columns and the packing of widgets into those rows and columns. The Motif toolkit uses the RowColumn internally to implement many objects that are not implemented as individual widgets, such as PopupMenus, PulldownMenus, MenuBars, RadioBoxes, and CheckBoxes. There are a number of RowColumn resources that are specific to these objects.

Frame

The purpose of the Frame widget is to provide a visible, three-dimensional border for objects such as RowColumns or Labels that do not provide a border for themselves. In Motif 1.2, the Frame widget may have two children: a work area child and a label child. With Motif 1.1, the Frame widget may have only one child. In either case, the Frame sizes itself just big enough to contain its children.

PanedWindow

The PanedWindow manages its children in a vertically-tiled format. The widget takes its width from the widest widget in its list of children. The PanedWindow also provides control sashes or grips that enable the user to adjust the individual heights of the PanedWindow's children. Constraint resources for the PanedWindow allow each child to specify its desired maximum and minimum height and whether it may be resized.

DrawingArea

Although the DrawingArea widget is subclassed from the Manager widget class, it is not generally used in the way that conventional managers are used. The widget does not do any drawing and it doesn't define any keyboard or mouse behavior, although it does provide callbacks for user input. It is basically a free-form widget that can be used for application-specific purposes. The widget provides callback resources to handle keyboard, mouse, exposure, and resize events. While the DrawingArea widget can have children, it does not manage them in any defined way. Since the DrawingArea widget is typically used for drawing, rather than for managing other widgets, it is discussed separately in Chapter 10, *The DrawingArea Widget*.

ScrolledWindow

The ScrolledWindow widget provides a viewing area into another widget. The user can adjust the viewing area using ScrollBars that are attached to the ScrolledWindow. The ScrolledWindow can handle scrolling automatically, so that the application does not have to do any work. The widget also has an application-defined mode, which allows an application to control all of the aspects of scrolling. Since the operation of the ScrolledWindow is tied to the operation of ScrollBars, the two widgets are discussed together in Chapter 9, *ScrolledWindows and ScrollBars*.

MainWindow

The MainWindow widget is subclassed from the ScrolledWindow widget. The MainWindow is the standard layout manager for the main application window in a Motif application. The widget is designed to lay out a MenuBar, a work area, ScrollBars, a command area, and a message area. Since the MainWindow is central to any real Motif application, it is discussed separately in Chapter 4, *The Main Window*.

Scale

The Scale widget displays a slider object that has a specific value in a range of values. The user can adjust the value of the widget by moving the slider. The Scale creates and manages its own widgets; the only children that you can add to a Scale are Label widgets that represent tickmarks. The widget class is not meant to be a general-purpose manager, so it is described separately in Chapter 13, *The Scale Widget*.

The MessageBox, SelectionBox, FileSelectionBox, and Command widgets are also Motif manager widgets. These widgets are used for predefined Motif dialogs and are discussed in Chapter 5, *Introduction to Dialogs*; Chapter 6, *Selection Dialogs*; and Chapter 7, *Custom Dialogs*.

8.2 Creating Manager Widgets

A manager widget may be created and destroyed like any other widget. The main difference between using a manager and other widgets involves when the widget is declared to be managed in the creation process. While we normally suggest that you create widgets using XtVaCreateManagedWidget(), we recommend that you create a manager widget using XtVaCreateWidget() instead, and then manage it later using XtManageChild(). To understand why this technique can be important, you need to understand how a manager widget manages its children.

A manager widget manages its children by controlling the sizes and positions of the children. The process of widget layout only happens when the child and the parent are both in the managed state. If a child is created as an unmanaged widget, the parent skips over that widget when it is determining the layout until such time as the child is managed. However, if a manager widget is not itself managed, it does not perform geometry management on any of its children regardless of whether those children are managed.†

---

† To be precise, a manager does not actually manage its children until it is both managed and realized. If you realize all of your widgets at once, by calling XtRealizeWidget() on the top-level widget of the application, as described in Chapter 2, *The Motif Programming Model*, it should not make a difference whether a manager is managed before or after its children are created. However, if you are adding widgets to a tree of already-realized widgets, the principles set forth in this section are important. If you are adding children to an already-realized parent, the child is automatically realized when it is managed. If you are adding a manager widget as a child of a realized widget, you should explicitly realize the widget before you manage it. Otherwise, the resize calculations may be performed in the wrong order. In a case such as this, it is essential to use XtManageChild() rather than XtVaCreateManaged-Widget(), since doing so allows you to make the explicit realize call before managing the widget.

To demonstrate the problems that you are trying to avoid, consider creating a manager as a managed widget before any of its children are created. The manager is going to have a set of PushButtons as its children. When the first child is added using `XtVaCreateManaged-Widget()`, the manager widget negotiates the size and position of the PushButton. Depending on the type of manager widget being used, the parent either changes its size to accommodate the new child or it changes the size of the child to its own size. In either case, these calculations are not necessary because the geometry needs to change as more buttons are added. The problem becomes complicated by the fact that when the manager's size changes, it must also negotiate its new size with its own parent, which causes that parent to negotiate with its parent all the way up to the highest-level shell. If the new size is accepted, the result goes back down the widget tree with each manager widget resizing itself on the way down. Repeating this process each time a child is added almost certainly affects performance.

Because of the different geometry management methods used by the different manager widgets, there is the possibility that all of this premature negotiation can result in a different layout than you intended. For example, as children are added to a RowColumn widget, the RowColumn checks to see if there is enough room to place the new child on the same row or column. If there isn't, then a new row or column is created. This behavior depends heavily on whether the RowColumn is managed and also on whether its size has been established by being realized. If the manager parent is not managed when the children are added, the whole process can be avoided, yet you still have the convenience of using `XtVaCreate-ManagedWidget()` for all of the widget children. When the manager is itself managed, it queries its children for their size and position requests, calculates its own size requirements, and communicates that size back up the widget tree.

For best results, you should use `XtVaCreateWidget()` to create manager widgets and `XtVaCreateManagedWidget()` to create primitive widgets. Creating a primitive widget as an unmanaged widget serves no purpose, unless you explicitly want the widget's parent to ignore it for some reason. If you are adding another manager as a child, the same principle applies; you should also create it as an unmanaged widget until all its children are added as well. The idea is to descend as deeply into the widget tree and create as many children as possible before managing the manager parents as you ascend back up. Once all the children have been added, `XtManageChild()` can be called for the managers so that they only have to negotiate with their parents once, thus saving time, improving performance, and probably producing better results.

Despite all we've just said, realize that the entire motivating factor behind this principle is to optimize the method by which managers negotiate sizes and positions of their children. If a manager only has one child, it does not matter if you create the manager widget as managed or not. Also, the geometry management constraints of some widgets are such that no negotiation is required between the parent and the children. In these situations, it is not necessary to create the manager as an unmanaged widget, even though it has children. We will explain these cases as they arise.

In the rest of this chapter, we examine the basic manager widget classes and present examples of how they can be used. While geometry management is the most obvious and widely used aspect of the widget class, managers are also responsible for keyboard traversal, gadget display, and gadget event handling. Many of the resources of the Manager metaclass are inherited by each of its subclasses for handling these tasks.

8.3 The BulletinBoard Widget

The BulletinBoard is the most basic of the manager widget subclasses. The BulletinBoard widget does not enforce position or size policies on its children, so it is rarely used by applications as a general geometry manager for widgets. The BulletinBoard is the superclass for the Form widget and all of the predefined Motif dialog widgets. To support these roles, the BulletinBoard has a number of resources that are used specifically for communicating with DialogShells.

The BulletinBoard has callback resources for `FocusIn`, `FocusOut`, and `MapNotify` events. These callbacks are invoked when the user moves the mouse or uses the TAB key to traverse the widget hierarchy. The events do not require much visual feedback and they only require application-specific callback routines when an application needs to set internal states based on the events. The `XmNfocusCallback` and `XmNmapCallback` resources are used extensively by DialogShells.

Despite the low profile of the BulletinBoard as a manager widget, there is a lot to be learned from it, since the principles also apply to most other manager widgets. In this spirit, let's take a closer look at the BulletinBoard widget and examine the different things that can be done with it as a manager widget. If you want to use a BulletinBoard directly in an application, you must include the file *<Xm/BulletinB.h>*. The following code fragment shows the recommended way to create a BulletinBoard:

```
Widget  bboard;

bboard = XtVaCreateWidget ("name",
    xmBulletinBoardWidgetClass, parent,
    resource-value-list,
    NULL);

/* Create children */

XtManageChild (bboard);
```

The `parent` parameter is the parent of the BulletinBoard, which may be another manager widget or a shell widget. You can specify any of the resources that are specific to the BulletinBoard, but unless you are using the widget as a dialog box, your choices are quite limited.

8.3.1 Resources

Of the few BulletinBoard resources not tied to DialogShells, the only visual one is XmN-shadowType. When used in conjunction with the `XmNshadowThickness` resource, you can control the three-dimensional appearance of the widget. There are four possible values for XmNshadowType:

```
XmSHADOW_IN
XmSHADOW_OUT
XmSHADOW_ETCHED_IN
XmSHADOW_ETCHED_OUT
```

The default value for XmNshadowThickness is 0, except when the BulletinBoard is the child of a DialogShell, in which case the default value is 1. In either case, the value can be changed by the application or by the user.

The XmNbuttonFontList resource may be set to a font list as described in Chapter 19, *Compound Strings*. This font list is used for each of the button children of the BulletinBoard, when the button does not specify its own font. If the resource is not specified, its value is taken from the XmNbuttonFontList of the nearest ancestor that is a subclass of Bulletin-Board, VendorShell, or MenuShell. Similarly, the XmNlabelFontList and XmNtext-FontList resources can be set for the Labels and Text widgets, respectively, that are direct children of the BulletinBoard.

8.3.2 Geometry Management

Since the BulletinBoard does not provide any geometry management by default, you must be prepared to manage the positions and sizes of the widgets within a BulletinBoard. As a result, you must set the XmNx and XmNy resources for each child. You may also have to set the XmNwidth and XmNheight resources if you need consistent or predetermined sizes for the children. In order to maintain the layout, you must add an event handler for resize (ConfigureNotify) events, so that the new sizes and positions of the children can be calculated. Example 8-1 shows the use of an event handler with the BulletinBoard.†

Example 8-1. The corners.c program

```
/* corners.c -- demonstrate widget layout management for a
 * BulletinBoard widget.  There are four widgets each labeled
 * top-left, top-right, bottom-left and bottom-right.  Their
 * positions in the bulletin board correspond to their names.
 * Only when the widget is resized does the geometry management
 * kick in and position the children in their correct locations.
 */
#include <Xm/BulletinB.h>
#include <Xm/PushB.h>

char *corners[] = {
    "Top Left", "Top Right", "Bottom Left", "Bottom Right",
};

static void resize();

main(argc, argv)
int argc;
char *argv[];
{
    Widget toplevel, bboard;
    XtAppContext app;
    XtActionsRec rec;
    int i;

    XtSetLanguageProc (NULL, NULL, NULL);
```

---

†XtSetLanguageProc() is only available in X11R5; there is no corresponding function in X11R4.

Example 8-1. The corners.c program (continued)

```
    /* Initialize toolkit and create toplevel shell */
    toplevel = XtVaAppInitialize (&app, "Demos", NULL, 0,
        &argc, argv, NULL, NULL);

    /* Create your standard BulletinBoard widget */
    bboard = XtVaCreateManagedWidget ("bboard",
        xmBulletinBoardWidgetClass, toplevel, NULL);

    /* Set up a translation table that captures "Resize" events
     * (also called ConfigureNotify or Configure events).  If the
     * event is generated, call the function resize().
     */
    rec.string = "resize";
    rec.proc = resize;
    XtAppAddActions (app, &rec, 1);
    XtOverrideTranslations (bboard,
        XtParseTranslationTable ("<Configure>: resize()"));

    /* Create children of the dialog -- a PushButton in each corner. */
    for (i = 0; i < XtNumber (corners); i++)
        XtVaCreateManagedWidget (corners[i],
            xmPushButtonWidgetClass, bboard, NULL);

    XtRealizeWidget (toplevel);
    XtAppMainLoop (app);
}

/* resize(), the routine that is automatically called by Xt upon the
 * delivery of a Configure event.  This happens whenever the widget
 * gets resized.
 */
static void
resize(w, event, args, num_args)
Widget w;    /* The widget (BulletinBoard) that got resized */
XEvent *event;  /* The event struct associated with the event */
String args[]; /* unused */
int *num_args; /* unused */
{
    WidgetList children;
    Dimension w_width, w_height;
    short margin_w, margin_h;
    XConfigureEvent *cevent = (XConfigureEvent *) event;
    int width = cevent->width;
    int height = cevent->height;

    /* get handle to BulletinBoard's children and marginal spacing */
    XtVaGetValues (w,
        XmNchildren, &children,
        XmNmarginWidth, &margin_w,
        XmNmarginHeight, &margin_h,
        NULL);

    /* place the top left widget */
    XtVaSetValues (children[0],
        XmNx, margin_w,
        XmNy, margin_h,
        NULL);
    /* top right */
    XtVaGetValues (children[1], XmNwidth, &w_width, NULL);
```

Manager Widgets

Example 8-1. The corners.c program (continued)

```
    XtVaSetValues (children[1],
        XmNx, width - margin_w - w_width,
        XmNy, margin_h,
        NULL);
    /* bottom left */
    XtVaGetValues (children[2], XmNheight, &w_height, NULL);
    XtVaSetValues (children[2],
        XmNx, margin_w,
        XmNy, height - margin_h - w_height,
        NULL);
    /* bottom right */
    XtVaGetValues (children[3],
        XmNheight, &w_height,
        XmNwidth, &w_width,
        NULL);
    XtVaSetValues (children[3],
        XmNx, width - margin_w - w_width,
        XmNy, height - margin_h - w_height,
        NULL);
}
```

The program uses four widgets, labeled **Top Left**, **Top Right**, **Bottom Left**, and **Bottom Right**. The positions of the buttons in the BulletinBoard correspond to their names. Since the widgets are not positioned when they are created, the geometry management only happens when the widget is resized. Figure 8-1 shows the application before and after a resize event.

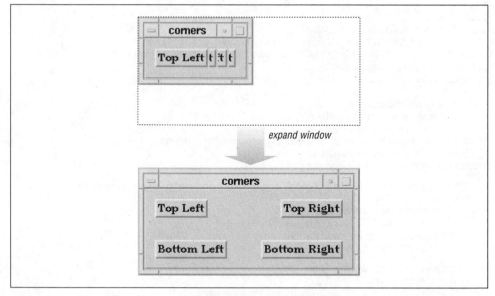

Figure 8-1. Output of corners.c before and after a resize event

When a resize event occurs, X generates a ConfigureNotify event. This event is interpreted by Xt and the translation table of the widget corresponding to the resized window is searched to see if the application is interested in being notified of the event. We have indicated interest in this event by calling `XtAppAddActions()` and `XtOverride-Translations()`, as shown below:

```
XtActionsRec rec;
...
rec.string = "resize";
rec.proc = resize;
XtAppAddActions (app, &rec, 1);
XtOverrideTranslations (bboard,
    XtParseTranslationTable ("<Configure>: resize()"));
```

As described in Volume Four, *X Toolkit Intrinsics Programming Manual*, a translation table pairs a sequence of one or more events with a sequence of one or more functions that are called when the event sequence occurs. In this case, the event is a `ConfigureNotify` event and the function is `resize()`. Translations are specified as strings and then parsed into an internal format with the function `XtParseTranslationTable()`. The routine creates an internal structure of events and the functions to which they correspond. Xt provides the table for translating event strings such as `<Configure>` to the actual `ConfigureNotify` event, but Xt cannot convert the string `resize()` to an actual function unless we provide a lookup table. The `XtActionsRec` type performs this task. The structure is defined as follows:

```
typedef struct {
    String      string;
    XtActionProc proc;
} XtActionsRec;
```

The action list is initialized to map the string `resize` to the actual function `resize()` using `XtAppAddActions()`. We install the translation table on the widget using `Xt-OverrideTranslations()` so that when a `ConfigureNotify` event occurs, the `resize()` function is called.

The `resize()` function takes four arguments. The first two arguments are a pointer to the widget in which the event occurred and the event structure. The `args` and `num_args` parameters are ignored because we did not specify any extra parameters to be passed to the function when we installed it. Since the function is called as a result of the event happening on the BulletinBoard widget, we know that we are dealing with a composite widget. We also know that there is only one event type that could have caused the function to be called, so we cast the `event` parameter accordingly.

The task of the function is to position the children so that there is one per corner in the BulletinBoard. We get a handle to all of the children of the BulletinBoard. Since we are going to place the children around the perimeter of the widget, we also need to know how far from the edge to place them. This distance is taken from the values for `XmNmarginWidth` and `XmNmarginHeight`. All three resource values are retrieved in the following call:

```
XtVaGetValues (w,
    XmNchildren,    &children,
    XmNmarginWidth, &margin_w,
    XmNmarginHeight, &margin_h,
    NULL);
```

The remainder of the function simply places the children at the appropriate positions within the BulletinBoard. The routine uses a very simple method for geometry management, but it does demonstrate the process.

The general issue of geometry management for composite widgets is not trivial. If you plan on doing your own geometry management for a BulletinBoard or any other composite widget, you should be very careful to consider all the resources that could possibly affect layout. In our example, we considered the margin width and height, but there is also `XmNallow-Overlap`, `XmNborderWidth` (which is a general Core widget resource), `XmNshadow-Thickness` (a general manager widget resource) and the same values associated with the children of the BulletinBoard.

There are also issues about what to do if a child decides to resize itself, such as if a label widget gets wider. In this case, you must first evaluate what the geometry layout of the widgets would be if you were to grant the Label permission to resize itself as it wants. This evaluation is done by asking each of the children how big they want to be and calculating the hypothetical layout. The BulletinBoard either accepts or rejects the new layout. Of course, the BulletinBoard may have to make itself bigger too, which requires asking its parent for a new size, and so on. If the BulletinBoard cannot resize itself, then you have to decide whether to force other children to be certain sizes or to reject the resize request of the child that started all the negotiation. Geometry management is by no means a simple task; it is explained more completely in Volume Four, *X Toolkit Intrinsics Programming Manual*.

8.4 The Form Widget

The Form widget is subclassed from the BulletinBoard class, so it inherits all of the resources that the BulletinBoard has to offer. Accordingly, the children of a Form can be placed at specific x,y coordinates and geometry management can be performed as in Example 8-1. However, the Form provides additional geometry management features that allow its children to be positioned relative to one another and relative to specific locations in the Form.

In order to use a Form, you must include the file *<Xm/Form.h>*. A Form is created in a similar way to other manager widgets, as shown below:

```
Widget form;

form = XtVaCreateWidget ("name",
    xmFormWidgetClass, parent,
    resource-value-list,
    NULL);

/* create children */

XtManageChild (form);
```

8.4.1 Form Attachments

Geometry management in a Form is done using attachment resources. These resources are constraint resources, which means that they are specified for the children of the Form. The resources provide various ways of specifying the position of a child of a Form by attaching each of the four sides of the child to another entity. The side of a widget can be attached to another widget, to a fixed position in the Form, to a flexible position in the Form, to the Form itself, or to nothing at all. These attachments can be considered hooks, rods, and anchor points, as shown in Figure 8-2.

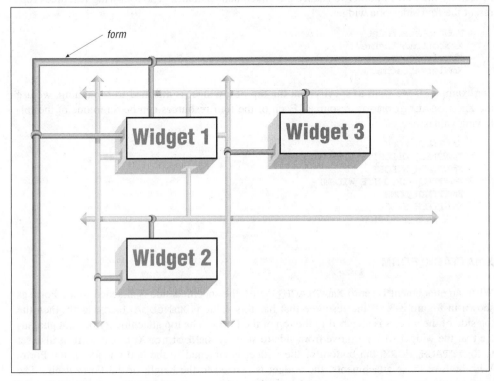

Figure 8-2. Attachments in a Form

In this figure, there are three widgets. The sizes and types of the widgets are not important. What is important is the relationship between the widgets with respect to their positions in the Form. **Widget 1** is attached to the top and left sides of the Form by creating two attachments. The top side of the widget is hooked to the top of the Form. It can slide from side to side, but it cannot be moved up or down (just like a shower curtain). The left side can slide up and down, but not to the right or to the left. Given these two attachment constraints, the top and left sides of the widget are fixed. The right and bottom edges of the widget are not attached to anything, but other widgets are attached to those edges.

The left side of **Widget 2** is attached to the right side of **Widget 1**. Similarly, the top side of **Widget 2** is attached to the top side of **Widget 1**. As a result, the top and left sides of the widget cannot be moved unless **Widget 1** moves. The same kind of attachments hold for **Widget 3**. The top side of this widget is attached to the bottom of **Widget 1** and its left side is attached to the left side of **Widget 1**. Given these constraints, no matter how large each of the widgets may be, or how the Form may be resized, the positional relationship of the widgets is maintained.

In general, you must attach at least two adjacent edges of a widget to keep it from moving unpredictably. If you attach opposing sides of the widget, the widget will probably be resized by the Form in order to satisfy the attachment policies. The following resources represent the four sides of a widget:

```
XmNtopAttachment
XmNbottomAttachment
XmNrightAttachment
XmNleftAttachment
```

For example, if we want to specify that the top of a widget is attached to something, we use the XmNtopAttachment resource. Each of the four resources can be set to one of the following values:

```
XmATTACH_FORM
XmATTACH_OPPOSITE_FORM
XmATTACH_WIDGET
XmATTACH_OPPOSITE_WIDGET
XmATTACH_NONE
XmATTACH_SELF
XmATTACH_POSITION
```

XmATTACH_FORM

When an attachment is set to XmATTACH_FORM, the specified side is attached to the Form as shown in Figure 8-3. If the resource that has this value is XmNtopAttachment, then the top side of the widget is attached to the top of the Form. The top attachment does not guarantee that the widget will not move from side to side. If XmNbottomAttachment is also set to XmATTACH_FORM, the bottom of the widget is attached to the bottom side of the Form. With both of these attachments, the widget is resized to the height of the Form itself. The same would be true for the right and left edges of the widget if they were attached to the Form.

XmATTACH_OPPOSITE_FORM

When an attachment is set to XmATTACH_OPPOSITE_FORM, the specified side of the widget is attached to the opposite side of the Form. For example, if XmNtopAttachment is set to XmATTACH_OPPOSITE_FORM, the top side of the widget is attached to the bottom side of the Form. This value must be used with a negative offset value (discussed in the next section) or the widget is placed off of the edge of the Form and it is not visible. While it may seem confusing, this value is the only one that can be applied to an attachment resource that allows you to specify a constant offset from the edge of a Form.

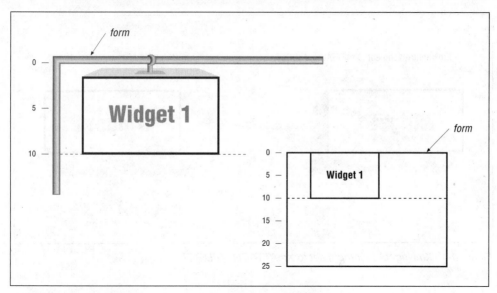

Figure 8-3. XmNtopAttachment set to XmATTACH_FORM

XmATTACH_WIDGET

The XmATTACH_WIDGET value indicates that the side of a widget is attached to another widget. The other widget must be specified using the appropriate resource from the following list:

```
XmNtopWidget
XmNbottomWidget
XmNleftWidget
XmNrightWidget
```

The value for one of these resources must be the widget ID. For example, Figure 8-4 shows how to attach the right side of **Widget 1** to the left side of **Widget 2**. This attachment method is commonly used to chain together a series of adjacent widgets. Chaining widgets horizontally does not guarantee that the widgets will be aligned vertically, or vice versa.

XmATTACH_OPPOSITE_WIDGET

The XmATTACH_OPPOSITE_WIDGET value is just like XmATTACH_WIDGET, except that the widget is attached to the same edge of the specified widget, as shown in Figure 8-5. In this case, the right side of **Widget 1** is attached to the right side of **Widget 3**. This attachment method allows you to align the edges of a group of widgets. As with Xm-ATTACH_WIDGET, the other widget must be specified using XmNtopWidget, XmN-bottomWidget, XmNleftWidget, or XmNrightWidget.

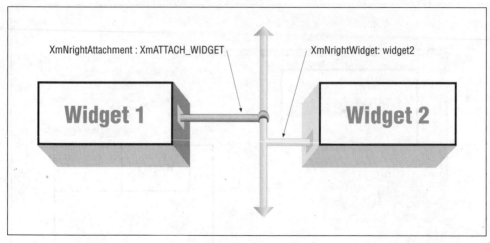

Figure 8-4. XmNrightAttachment set to XmATTACH_WIDGET

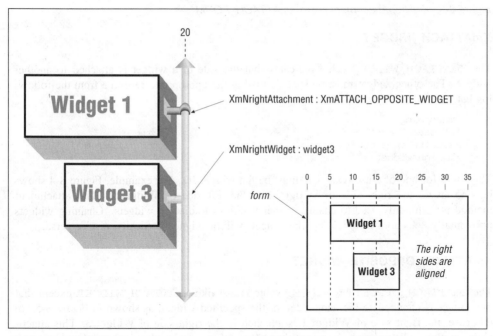

Figure 8-5. XmNrightAttachment set to XmATTACH_OPPOSITE_WIDGET

XmATTACH_NONE

XmATTACH_NONE specifies that the side of a widget is not attached to anything, which is the default value. This case could be represented by a dangling hook that is not attached to anything. If the entire widget moves because another side is attached to something, then this side gets dragged along with it so that the widget does not need resizing. Unless a particular side of a widget is attached to something, that side of the widget is free-floating and moves proportionally with the other parts of the widget.

XmATTACH_POSITION

When the side of a widget is attached using XmATTACH_POSITION, the side is anchored to a relative position in the Form. This value works by segmenting the Form into a fixed number of equally-spaced horizontal and vertical positions, based on the value of the XmN-fractionBase resource. The position of the side must be specified using the appropriate resource from the following list:

```
XmNtopPosition
XmNbottomPosition
XmNleftPosition
XmNrightPosition
```

See Section 8.4.3 for a complete discussion of position attachments.

XmATTACH_SELF

When an attachment is set to XmATTACH_SELF, the side of the widget is attached to its initial position in the Form. You position the widget initially by specifying its x,y location in the Form. After the widget has been placed in the Form, the attachment for the side reverts to XmATTACH_POSITION, with the corresponding position resource set to the relative position of the x,y coordinate in the Form.

Some Examples

Now that we have explained the concept of Form attachments, we can reimplement the four corners example from the previous section. Unlike in the previous version, we no longer need a resize procedure to calculate the positions of the widgets. By specifying the correct attachments, as shown in Example 8-2, the widgets are placed and managed correctly by the Form when it is resized.†

Example 8-2. The form_corners.c program

```
/* form_corners.c -- demonstrate form layout management.  Just as
 * in corners.c, there are four widgets each labeled top-left,
 * top-right, bottom-left and bottom-right.  Their positions in the
 * form correspond to their names.  As opposed to the BulletinBoard
 * widget, the Form manages this layout management automatically by
 * specifying attachment types for each of the widgets.
 */
#include <Xm/PushB.h>
#include <Xm/Form.h>

char *corners[] = {
    "Top Left", "Top Right", "Bottom Left", "Bottom Right",
```

---

† XtSetLanguageProc() is only available in X11R5; there is no corresponding function in X11R4.

Example 8-2. The form_corners.c program (continued)

```
};

main(argc, argv)
char *argv[];
{
    Widget toplevel, form;
    XtAppContext app;

    XtSetLanguageProc (NULL, NULL, NULL);

    toplevel = XtVaAppInitialize (&app, "Demos", NULL, 0,
        &argc, argv, NULL, NULL);

    form = XtVaCreateManagedWidget ("form",
        xmFormWidgetClass, toplevel, NULL);

    /* Attach the edges of the widgets to the Form.  Which edge of
     * the widget that's attached is relative to where the widget is
     * positioned in the Form.  Edges not attached default to having
     * an attachment type of XmATTACH_NONE.
     */
    XtVaCreateManagedWidget (corners[0],
        xmPushButtonWidgetClass, form,
        XmNtopAttachment,         XmATTACH_FORM,
        XmNleftAttachment,        XmATTACH_FORM,
        NULL);

    XtVaCreateManagedWidget (corners[1],
        xmPushButtonWidgetClass, form,
        XmNtopAttachment,         XmATTACH_FORM,
        XmNrightAttachment,       XmATTACH_FORM,
        NULL);

    XtVaCreateManagedWidget (corners[2],
        xmPushButtonWidgetClass, form,
        XmNbottomAttachment,      XmATTACH_FORM,
        XmNleftAttachment,        XmATTACH_FORM,
        NULL);

    XtVaCreateManagedWidget (corners[3],
        xmPushButtonWidgetClass, form,
        XmNbottomAttachment,      XmATTACH_FORM,
        XmNrightAttachment,       XmATTACH_FORM,
        NULL);

    XtRealizeWidget (toplevel);
    XtAppMainLoop (app);
}
```

In this example, two sides of each widget are attached to the Form. It is not necessary to attach the other sides of the widgets to anything else. If we attach the other sides to each other, the widgets would have to be resized so that they could stretch to meet each other. With the specified attachments, the output of the program looks just like the output in Figure 8-1.

A more complex example of Form attachments is shown in Example 8-3. This example implements the layout shown in Figure 8-2.†

---

† XtSetLanguageProc() is only available in X11R5; there is no corresponding function in X11R4.

Example 8-3. The attach.c program

```
/* attach.c -- demonstrate how attachments work in Form widgets. */

#include <Xm/PushB.h>
#include <Xm/Form.h>

main(argc, argv)
int argc;
char *argv[ ];
{
    Widget toplevel, parent, one, two, three;
    XtAppContext app;

    XtSetLanguageProc (NULL, NULL, NULL);

    toplevel = XtVaAppInitialize (&app, "Demos", NULL, 0,
        &argc, argv, NULL, NULL);

    parent = XtVaCreateManagedWidget ("form",
        xmFormWidgetClass, toplevel, NULL);
    one = XtVaCreateManagedWidget ("One",
        xmPushButtonWidgetClass, parent,
        XmNtopAttachment,    XmATTACH_FORM,
        XmNleftAttachment,   XmATTACH_FORM,
        NULL);
    two = XtVaCreateManagedWidget ("Two",
        xmPushButtonWidgetClass, parent,
        XmNleftAttachment,   XmATTACH_WIDGET,
        XmNleftWidget,       one,
        /* attach top of widget to same y coordinate as top of "one" */
        XmNtopAttachment,    XmATTACH_OPPOSITE_WIDGET,
        XmNtopWidget,        one,
        NULL);
    three = XtVaCreateManagedWidget ("Three",
        xmPushButtonWidgetClass, parent,
        XmNtopAttachment,    XmATTACH_WIDGET,
        XmNtopWidget,        one,
        /* attach left of widget to same x coordinate as left side of "one" */
        XmNleftAttachment,   XmATTACH_OPPOSITE_WIDGET,
        XmNleftWidget,       one,
        NULL);

    XtRealizeWidget (toplevel);
    XtAppMainLoop (app);
}
```

The example uses three PushButton gadgets inside of a Form widget. The output of the program is shown in Figure 8-6.

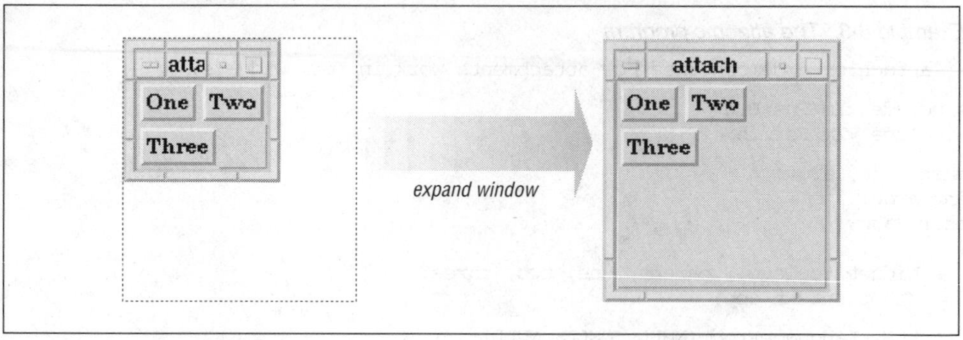

Figure 8-6. Output of attach.c

You should notice that the widgets are packed together quite tightly, which might not be how you expected them to appear. In order to space the widgets more reasonably, we need to specify some distance between them using attachment offsets.

8.4.2 Attachment Offsets

Attachment offsets control the spacing between widgets and the objects to which they are attached. The following resources represent the attachment offsets for the four sides of a widget:

```
XmNleftOffset
XmNrightOffset
XmNtopOffset
XmNbottomOffset
```

Figure 8-7 shows the graphic representation of attachment offsets.

By default, offsets are set to 0 (zero), which means that there is no offset, as shown in the output for Example 8-3. To make the output more reasonable, we need only to set the left offset between widgets **One** and **Two** and the top offset to between widgets **One** and **Three**. The resources values can be hard-coded in the application or set in a resource file, using the following specification:

```
*form.One.leftOffset:    10
*form.One.topOffset:     10
*form.Two.leftOffset:    10
*form.Three.topOffset:   10
```

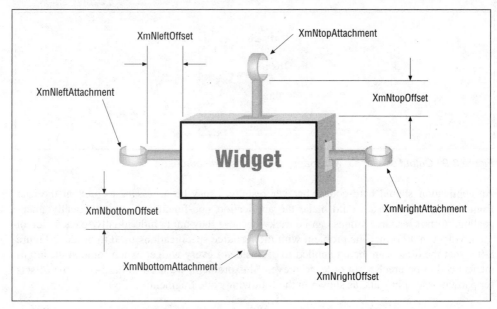

Figure 8-7. Attachment offsets

Our choice of the value 10 was arbitrary. The widgets are now spaced more appropriately, as shown in Figure 8-8.

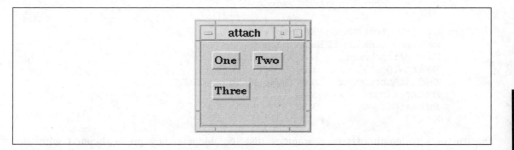

Figure 8-8. Output of attach.c with offset resources set to 10

While the layout of the widgets can be improved by setting offset resources, it is also possible to disrupt the layout. Consider the following resource specifications:

```
*form*leftOffset: 10
*form*topOffset:  10
```

While it might seem that these resource values are simply a terser way to specify the offsets shown earlier, Figure 8-9 makes it clear that these specifications do not produce the desired effect.

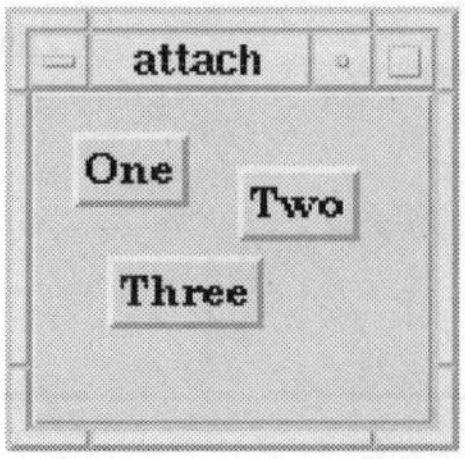

Figure 8-9. Output of attach.c with inappropriate offset resources

An application should hard-code whatever resources may be necessary to prevent the user from setting values that would make the application non-functional or aesthetically unappealing. Offset resource values can be tricky because they apply individually to each side of each widget in a Form. The problem with the resource specifications used to produce Figure 8-9 is that the offsets are being applied to each side of every widget, when some of the alignments need to be precise. In order to prevent this problem, we need to hard-code the offsets for particular attachments, as shown in the following code fragment:

```
two = XtVaCreateManagedWidget ("Two",
    xmPushButtonWidgetClass, parent,
    XmNleftAttachment,   XmATTACH_WIDGET,
    XmNleftWidget,       one,
    XmNtopAttachment,    XmATTACH_OPPOSITE_WIDGET,
    XmNtopWidget,        one,
    XmNtopOffset,        0,
    NULL);
three = XtVaCreateManagedWidget ("Three",
    xmPushButtonWidgetClass, parent,
    XmNtopAttachment,    XmATTACH_WIDGET,
    XmNtopWidget,        one,
    XmNleftAttachment,   XmATTACH_OPPOSITE_WIDGET,
    XmNleftWidget,       one,
    XmNleftOffset,       0,
    NULL);
```

The use of zero-length offsets guarantees that the widgets they are associated with are aligned exactly with the widgets to which they are attached, regardless of any resource specifications made by the user. A general rule of thumb is that whenever you use Xm-ATTACH_OPPOSITE_WIDGET, you should also set the appropriate offset to zero so that the alignment remains consistent.

In some situations it is necessary to use negative offsets to properly arrange widgets in a Form. The most common example of this situation occurs when using the Xm-ATTACH_OPPOSITE_FORM attachment. Unless you use a negative offset, as shown in Figure 8-10, the widgets are placed off the edge of the Form and are not visible.

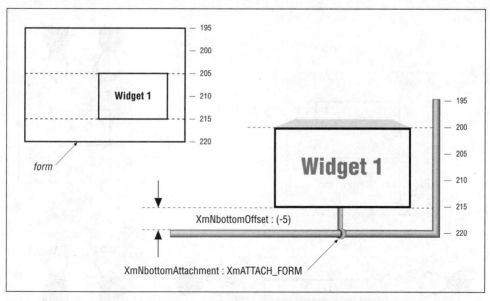

Figure 8-10. *XmNleftAttachment set to XmATTACH_OPPOSITE_FORM with negative offset*

8.4.3 Position Attachments

Form positions provide another way to position widgets within a Form. The concept is similar to the hook and rod principle described earlier, but in this case the widgets are anchored on at positions that are based on imaginary longitude and latitude lines that are used to segment the Form into equal pieces. The resource used to partition the Form into segments is XmNfractionBase. Although the name of this resource may suggest complicated calculations, you just need to know that the Form is divided horizontally and vertically into the number of partitions represented by its value. For example, Figure 8-11 shows how a Form is partitioned if XmNfractionBase is set to 5. As you can see, there are an equal number of horizontal and vertical partitions, but the size of the horizontal partitions is not the same as the size of the vertical partitions. It is currently not possible to set the number of horizontal partitions separately from the number of vertical ones, although it is possible to work around this shortcoming, as we will describe shortly.

Widgets are placed at the coordinates that represent the partitions by specifying Xm-ATTACH_POSITION for the attachment resource and by specifying a coordinate value for the corresponding position resource. The position resources are XmNtopPosition, XmNbottomPosition, XmNleftPosition, and XmNrightPosition. For example, if we wanted to attach the top and left sides of a PushButton to position 1, we could use the following code fragment:

```
XtVaCreateManagedWidget ("name",
    xmPushButtonWidgetClass, form,
    XmNtopAttachment,    XmATTACH_POSITION,
    XmNtopPosition,      1,
    XmNleftAttachment,   XmATTACH_POSITION,
    XmNleftPosition,     1,
    NULL);
```

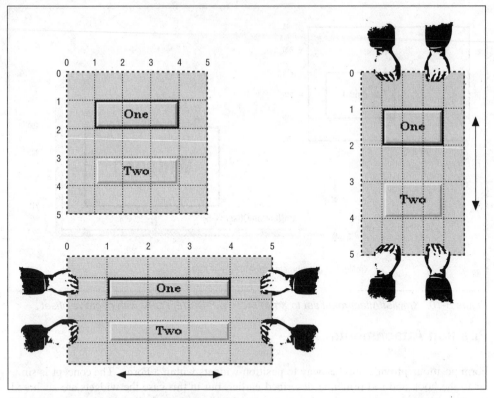

Figure 8-11. Form with XmNfractionBase set to 5

The right and bottom attachments are left unspecified, so those edges of the widget are not explicitly positioned by the Form. If attachments had been specified for these edges, the widget would have to be resized by the Form in order to satisfy all the attachment constraints.

One obvious example of using position attachments is to create a tic-tac-toe board layout, as is done in Example 8-4.†

Example 8-4. The tictactoe.c program

```
/* tictactoe.c -- demonstrate how fractionBase and XmATTACH_POSITIONs
 * work in Form widgets.
 */
#include <Xm/PushB.h>
#include <Xm/Form.h>

main(argc, argv)
int argc;
char *argv[];
{
```

---

†XtSetLanguageProc() is only available in X11R5; there is no corresponding function in X11R4. XmStringCreateLocalized() is only available in Motif 1.2; XmStringCreateSimple() is the corresponding function in Motif 1.1.

Example 8-4. The tictactoe.c program (continued)

```
    XtAppContext app;
    Widget toplevel, parent, w;
    int x, y;
    extern void pushed();   /* callback for each PushButton */

    XtSetLanguageProc (NULL, NULL, NULL);

    toplevel = XtVaAppInitialize (&app, "Demos", NULL, 0,
        &argc, argv, NULL, NULL);

    parent = XtVaCreateManagedWidget ("form",
        xmFormWidgetClass, toplevel,
        XmNfractionBase,    3,
        NULL);

    for (x = 0; x < 3; x++)
        for (y = 0; y < 3; y++) {
            w = XtVaCreateManagedWidget ("   ",
                xmPushButtonWidgetClass, parent,
                XmNtopAttachment,     XmATTACH_POSITION,
                XmNtopPosition,       y,
                XmNleftAttachment,    XmATTACH_POSITION,
                XmNleftPosition,      x,
                XmNrightAttachment,   XmATTACH_POSITION,
                XmNrightPosition,     x+1,
                XmNbottomAttachment, XmATTACH_POSITION,
                XmNbottomPosition,    y+1,
                NULL);
            XtAddCallback (w, XmNactivateCallback, pushed, NULL);
        }
    XtRealizeWidget (toplevel);
    XtAppMainLoop (app);
}
void
pushed(w, client_data, call_data)
Widget     w;              /* The PushButton that got activated */
XtPointer  client_data; /* unused -- NULL was passed to XtAddCallback() */
XtPointer  call_data;
{
    char buf[2];
    XmString str;
    XmPushButtonCallbackStruct *cbs =
        (XmPushButtonCallbackStruct *) call_data;

    /* Shift key gets an O.   (xbutton and xkey happen to be similar) */
    if (cbs->event->xbutton.state & ShiftMask)
        buf[0] = 'O';
    else
        buf[0] = 'X';
    buf[1] = 0;
    str = XmStringCreateLocalized (buf);
    XtVaSetValues (w, XmNlabelString, str, NULL);
    XmStringFree (str);
}
```

The output of this program is shown in Figure 8-12.

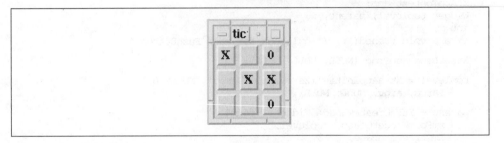

Figure 8-12. Output of tictactoe.c

As you can see, the children of the Form are equally sized because their attachment positions are segmented equally. If the user resizes the Form, all of the children maintain their relationship to one another. The PushButtons simply grow or shrink to fill the form.

One common use of positional attachments is to lay out a number of widgets that need to be of equal size and equal spacing. For example, you might use this technique to arrange the buttons in the action area of a dialog. Chapter 7, *Custom Dialogs*, provides a detailed discussion of how to arrange buttons in this manner.

There may be situations where you would like to attach widgets to horizontal positions that do not match up with how you'd like to attach their vertical positions. Since the fraction base cannot be set differently for the horizontal and vertical orientations, you have to use the least common multiple as the fraction base value. For example, say you want to position the tops and bottoms of all of your widgets to the 2nd and 4th positions, as if the Form were segmented vertically into 5 parts. But, you also want to position the left and right edges of those same widgets to the 3rd, 5th, 7th, and 9th positions, as if it were segmented into 11 parts. You would have to apply some simple arithmetic and set the value for XmNfractionBase to 55 (5x11). The top and bottom edges would be set to the 22nd (2x11) and 44th (4x11) positions and the left and right edges would be set to the 15th (3x5), 25th (5x5), 35th (7x5), and 45th (9x5) positions.

8.4.4 Additional Resources

There are a few other useful Form resources that we have not covered so far. The XmN-horizontalSpacing resource can be used to specify the distance between horizontally adjacent widgets, while XmNverticalSpacing specifies the distance between vertically adjacent widgets. These values only apply when the left and right offset values are not specified, so they are intended to be used as global offset values global for a Form. The following resource specification:

```
*horizontalSpacing: 10
```

is equivalent to:

```
*leftOffset:    10
*rightOffset:   10
```

The `XmNrubberPositioning` resource specifies the default attachments for widgets in the Form. The default value of `False` indicates that the top and left edges are attached to the form by default. If `XmNrubberPositioning` is set to `True`, the top and left attachments are set to `XmATTACH_POSITION` by default. If the `XmNtopAttachment` or `XmNleftAttachment` resource is explicitly set for a widget, then the default attachment has no effect.

The `XmNresizable` resource is another constraint resource that can be set on the children of a Form widget. This resource indicates whether or not the Form tries to grant resize requests from the child.

8.4.5 Nested Forms

Some widget layouts are difficult to create using a single Form widget. Since a manager widget can contain other managers, it is often possible to generate the desired layout by using a Form within a Form. One common problem is that there are no Form attachments available to align two widgets horizontally if they have different heights. We need a middle attachment resource, but one doesn't exist. For example, if you have a series of Labels and Text widgets that you want to pair off and stack vertically, it would be nice to align each pair of widgets at their midsections.

To solve this problem, we can place each Label-Text widget pair in a separate Form. If the top and bottom edges of the widgets are attached to the Form, the widgets are stretched to satisfy the constraints, which means that they are aligned horizontally. All of these smaller Form widgets can be placed inside of a larger Form widget. Example 8-5 shows an implementation of this idea.†

Example 8-5. The text_form.c program

```
/* text_form.c -- demonstrate how attachments work in Form widgets
 * by creating a text-entry form type application.
 */

#include <Xm/LabelG.h>
#include <Xm/Text.h>
#include <Xm/Form.h>

char *prompts[] = {
    "Name:", "Phone:", "Address:",
    "City:", "State:", "Zip Code:",
};

main(argc, argv)
int argc;
char *argv[];
{
    Widget toplevel, mainform, subform, label, text;
    XtAppContext app;
    char buf[32];
    int i;
```

†`XtSetLanguageProc()` is only available in X11R5; there is no corresponding function in X11R4.

Example 8-5. The text_form.c program (continued)

```
    XtSetLanguageProc (NULL, NULL, NULL);

    toplevel = XtVaAppInitialize (&app, "Demos", NULL, 0,
        &argc, argv, NULL, NULL);

    mainform = XtVaCreateWidget ("mainform",
        xmFormWidgetClass, toplevel,
        NULL);

    for (i = 0; i < XtNumber (prompts); i++) {
        subform = XtVaCreateWidget ("subform",
            xmFormWidgetClass,   mainform,
            /* first one should be attached for form */
            XmNtopAttachment,    i ? XmATTACH_WIDGET : XmATTACH_FORM,
            /* others are attached to the previous subform */
            XmNtopWidget,        subform,
            XmNleftAttachment,   XmATTACH_FORM,
            XmNrightAttachment,  XmATTACH_FORM,
            NULL);
    /* Note that the label here contains a colon from the prompts
     * array above.  This makes it impossible for external resources
     * to be set on these widgets.  Here, that is intentional, but
     * be careful in the general case.
     */
        label = XtVaCreateManagedWidget (prompts[i],
            xmLabelGadgetClass,  subform,
            XmNtopAttachment,    XmATTACH_FORM,
            XmNbottomAttachment, XmATTACH_FORM,
            XmNleftAttachment,   XmATTACH_FORM,
            XmNalignment,        XmALIGNMENT_BEGINNING,
            NULL);
        sprintf (buf, "text_%d", i);
        text = XtVaCreateManagedWidget (buf,
            xmTextWidgetClass,   subform,
            XmNtopAttachment,    XmATTACH_FORM,
            XmNbottomAttachment, XmATTACH_FORM,
            XmNrightAttachment,  XmATTACH_FORM,
            XmNleftAttachment,   XmATTACH_WIDGET,
            XmNleftWidget,       label,
            NULL);
        XtManageChild (subform);
    }
    /* Now that all the forms are added, manage the main form */
    XtManageChild (mainform);

    XtRealizeWidget (toplevel);
    XtAppMainLoop (app);
}
```

The output of the program is shown in Figure 8-13.

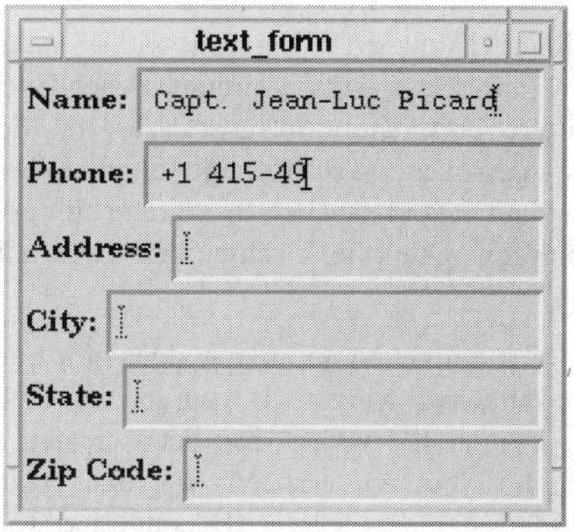

Figure 8-13. Output of text_form.c

Notice that the Labels are centered vertically with respect to their corresponding Text widgets. This arrangement happened because each Label was stretched vertically in order to attach it to the top and bottom of the respective Form. Of course, if the Labels were higher than the Text widgets, the Text widgets would be stretched instead.

Later, we'll show another version of this program that gives better results. As you can imagine, there are many different ways for a Form, or any other manager widget, to manage the geometry of its children to produce the same layout. Later, when we discuss the RowColumn widget, we will show you another solution to the problem of horizontal alignment. It is important to remember that there is no right or wrong way to create a layout, as long as it works for your application. However, you should be very careful to experiment with resizing issues as well as with resources that can be set by the user that might affect widget layout, such as fonts and strings.

8.4.6 Common Problems

With a Form widget, you can specify a virtually unlimited number of attachments for its children. The dependencies inherent in these attachments can lead to various errors in the layout of the widgets. One common problem involves circular dependencies. The following code fragment shows a very simple example of a circular dependency:

```
w1 = XtVaCreateManagedWidget ("w1", xmLabelGadgetClass, form, NULL);
w2 = XtVaCreateManagedWidget ("w2", xmLabelGadgetClass, form, NULL);

XtVaSetValues (w1,
    XmNrightAttachment, XmATTACH_WIDGET,
    XmNrightWidget,     w2,
    NULL);
```

```
XtVaSetValues (w2,
     XmNleftAttachment, XmATTACH_WIDGET,
     XmNleftWidget,     w1,
     NULL);
```

In this example, the left widget is attached to the right widget and the right widget is attached to the left one. If you do mistakenly specify a circular dependency, it is unlikely that it will be as obvious as this example. Fortunately, in most cases, the Motif toolkit catches circular dependencies and displays an error message if one is found. When this situation occurs, you need to reconsider your widget layout and try to arrange things such that the relationship between widgets is less complex. One rule to remember is that adjacent widgets should only be attached in one direction.

When you attach the side of a widget to another widget in a Form, you need to be careful about how you specify the attached widget. If you specify this widget in the application code, you need to make sure that the widget has been created before you specify it as a resource value. With Motif 1.1, you cannot specify a widget ID in a resource file unless you have installed your own widget-name-to-widget-ID converter. (See Volume Four, *X Toolkit Intrinsics Programming Manual*, for information about resource converters.) In Motif 1.2, the toolkit provides a name-to-widget converter, so you can specify widget IDs in a resource file.

Another common problem arises with certain Motif compound objects, such as ScrolledList and ScrolledText objects. `XmCreateScrolledText()` and `XmCreateScrolled-List()` return the corresponding Text or List widget, but it is the parent of this widget that needs to be positioned within a Form. The following code fragment shows an example of positioning a ScrolledList incorrectly:

```
form = XmCreateForm (parent, "form", NULL, 0);

list = XmCreateScrolledList (form, "scrolled_list", NULL, 0);

XtVaSetValues(list,    /* <- WRONG */
    XmNleftAttachment, XmATTACH_FORM,
    XmNtopAttachment,  XmATTACH_FORM,
    NULL);
```

Since the List is a child of the ScrolledWindow, not the Form, specifying attachments for the List has no effect on the position of the List in the Form. The attachments need to be specified on the ScrolledWindow, as shown in the following code fragment:

```
XtVaSetValues (XtParent (list),
    XmNleftAttachment, XmATTACH_FORM,
    XmNtopAttachment,  XmATTACH_FORM,
    NULL);
```

If you specify attachments for two opposing sides of a widget, the Form resizes the widget as needed, so that the default size of the widget is ignored. In most cases, the Form can resize the widget without a problem. However, one particular case that can cause a problem is a List widget that has its XmNvisibleItemCount resource set. This resource implies a specific size requirement, so that when the List is laid out in the Form widget, the negotiation process between the Form and the List may not be resolved. See Chapter 12, *The List Widget*, for a complete discussion of the List widget.

Attachments in Form widgets can be delicate specifications, which means that you must be specific and, above all, complete in your descriptions of how widgets should be aligned and positioned. Since resources can be set from many different places, the only way to guarantee that you get the layout you want is to hard-code these resource values explicitly. Even though it is important to allow the user to specify as many resources as possible, you do not want to compromise the integrity of your application. Attachments and attachment offsets are probably not in the set of resources that should be user-definable.

Although attachments can be delicate, they are also provide a powerful, convenient, and flexible way to lay out widgets within a Form, especially when the widgets are grouped together in some abstract way. Attachments make it easy to chain widgets together, to bind them to the edge of a Form, and to allow them to be fixed on specific locations. You do not need to use a single attachment type exclusively; it is perfectly reasonable, and in most cases necessary, to use a variety of different types of attachments to achieve a particular layout. If you specify too few attachments, you may end up with misplaced widgets or widgets that drift when the Form is resized, while too many attachments may cause the Form to be too inflexible. In order to determine the best way to attach widgets to one another, you may find it helpful to a draw picture first, with all of the hooks and offset values considered.

8.5 The RowColumn Widget

The RowColumn widget is a manager widget that, as its name implies, lays out its children in a row and/or column format. The widget is also used internally by the Motif toolkit to implement a number of special objects, such as the Motif menus, including PopupMenus, PulldownMenus, MenuBars, and OptionMenus. Many of the resources for the RowColumn widget are used to control different aspects of these objects. The Motif convenience functions for creating these objects set most of these resources automatically, so they are generally hidden from the programmer. The resources are not useful when you are using the Row-Column as a simple manager widget anyway, so we do not discuss them here.

The `XmNrowColumnType` resource controls how a particular instance of the RowColumn is used. The resource can be set to the following values:

    XmWORK_AREA
    XmMENU_BAR
    XmPULLDOWN
    XmMENU_POPUP
    XmMENU_OPTION

The default value is `XmWORK_AREA`; this value is also the one that you should use whenever you want to use a RowColumn widget as a manager. The rest of the values are for the different types of Motif menus. If you want to create a particular menu object, you should use the appropriate convenience function, rather than try to create the menu yourself using a Row-Column directly. We discuss menu creation in in Chapter 4, *The Main Window*, and Chapter 15, *Menus*. The RowColumn widget is also used to implement RadioBoxes and Check-Boxes, which are collections of ToggleButtons. See Chapter 11, *Labels and Buttons*, for more information on these objects.

The RowColumn is useful for generic geometry management because it requires less fine tuning than is necessary for a Form or a BulletinBoard widget. Although the RowColumn has a number of resources, you can create a usable layout without specifying any resources. In this case, the children of the RowColumn are automatically laid out vertically. In Example 8-6, we create several PushButtons as children of a RowColumn, without specifying any RowColumn resources.†

Example 8-6. The rowcol.c program

```
/* rowcol.c -- demonstrate a simple RowColumn widget.  Create one
 * with 3 pushbutton gadgets.  Once created, resize the thing in
 * all sorts of contortions to get a feel for what RowColumns can
 * do with its children.
 */
#include <Xm/PushB.h>
#include <Xm/RowColumn.h>

main(argc, argv)
int argc;
char *argv[];
{
    Widget toplevel, rowcol;
    XtAppContext app;

    XtSetLanguageProc (NULL, NULL, NULL);

    toplevel = XtVaAppInitialize (&app, "Demos", NULL, 0,
        &argc, argv, NULL, NULL);

    rowcol = XtVaCreateManagedWidget ("rowcolumn",
        xmRowColumnWidgetClass, toplevel, NULL);

    (void) XtVaCreateManagedWidget ("One",
        xmPushButtonWidgetClass, rowcol, NULL);

    (void) XtVaCreateManagedWidget ("Two",
        xmPushButtonWidgetClass, rowcol, NULL);

    (void) XtVaCreateManagedWidget ("Three",
        xmPushButtonWidgetClass, rowcol, NULL);

    XtRealizeWidget (toplevel);
    XtAppMainLoop (app);
}
```

What makes the RowColumn widget unique is that it automates much of the process of widget layout and management. If you display the application and resize it in a number of ways, you can get a better feel for how the RowColumn works. Figure 8-14 shows a few configurations of the application; the first configuration is the initial layout of the application. As you can see, if the application is resized just so, the widgets are oriented horizontally rather than vertically.

The orientation of the widgets in a RowColumn is controlled by the XmNorientation resource. The default value of the resource is XmVERTICAL. If we want to arrange the widgets horizontally, we can set the resource to XmHORIZONTAL. The orientation can be

---

†XtSetLanguageProc() is only available in X11R5; there is no corresponding function in X11R4.

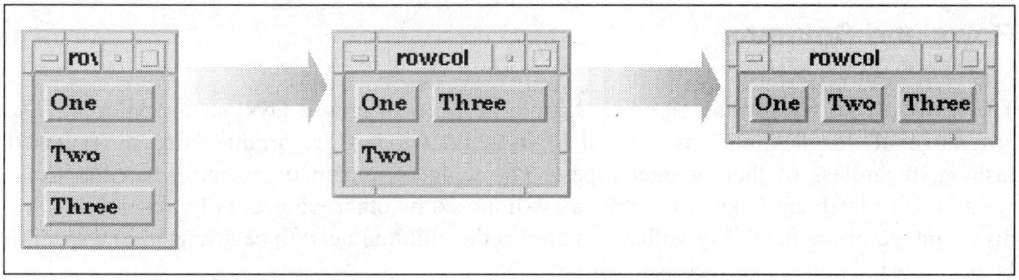

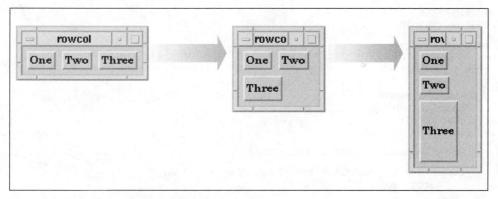

Figure 8-14. Output of rowcol.c

hard-coded in the application, or we can specify the value of the resource in a resource file. The following resource specification sets the orientation to horizontal:

```
*RowColumn.orientation: horizontal
```

Alternatively, we can specify the resource on the command line as follows:

```
% rowcol -xrm "*orientation: horizontal"
```

Figure 8-15 shows the output of Example 8-6 with a horizontal orientation. As before, the figure shows a few different configurations of the application, with the first configuration being the initial one.

Figure 8-15. Output of rowcol.c with a horizontal orientation

If you use a RowColumn widget to manage more objects than can be arranged in a single row or column, you can specify that the widgets should be arranged in both rows and columns. You can also specify whether the widgets should be packed together tightly, so that the rows and columns are not necessarily the same size, or whether the objects should be placed in identically-sized boxes. As with the Form and BulletinBoard widgets, objects can also be placed at specific x, y locations in a RowColumn widget. The RowColumn widget does not provide a three-dimensional border, so if you want to provide a visual border for the widget, you should create it as a child of a Frame widget.

8.5.1 Rows and Columns

The RowColumn widget can be quite flexible in terms of how it lays out its children. The advantage of this flexibility is that all of its child widgets are arranged in an organized fashion, regardless of their widget types. The widgets remain organized when the Row-Column is resized and in spite of constraints imposed by other widgets or by resources. One disadvantage of the flexibility is that sometimes the children need to be arranged in a specific layout so that the user interface is intuitive.

Example 8-7 shows how to lay out widgets in a spreadsheet-style format using a Row-Column. This layout requires that each of the widgets be the same size and be spaced equally in a predetermined number of rows and columns.†

Example 8-7. The spreadsheet.c program

```
/* spreadsheet.c -- This demo shows the most basic use of the RowColumn
 * It displays a table of widgets in a row-column format similar to a
 * spreadsheet.  This is accomplished by setting the number ROWS and
 * COLS and setting the appropriate resources correctly.
 */
#include <Xm/LabelG.h>
#include <Xm/PushB.h>
#include <Xm/RowColumn.h>

#define ROWS  8
#define COLS 10

main(argc, argv)
int argc;
char *argv[];
{
    Widget toplevel, parent;
    XtAppContext app;
    char buf[16];
    int i, j;

    XtSetLanguageProc (NULL, NULL, NULL);

    toplevel = XtVaAppInitialize (&app, "Demos", NULL, 0,
        &argc, argv, NULL, NULL);

    parent = XtVaCreateManagedWidget ("rowcolumn",
        xmRowColumnWidgetClass, toplevel,
        XmNpacking,      XmPACK_COLUMN,
        XmNnumColumns,   COLS,
        XmNorientation, XmVERTICAL,
        NULL);

    /* simply loop thru the strings creating a widget for each one */
    for (i = 0; i < COLS; i++)
        for (j = 0; j < ROWS; j++) {
            sprintf (buf, "%d-%d", i+1, j+1);
            if (i == 0 || j == 0)
                XtVaCreateManagedWidget (buf,
                    xmLabelGadgetClass, parent, NULL);
```

†XtSetLanguageProc() is only available in X11R5; there is no corresponding function in X11R4.

Motif Programming Manual

Example 8-7. The spreadsheet.c program (continued)

```
            else
                XtVaCreateManagedWidget ("",
                    xmPushButtonWidgetClass, parent, NULL);
        }

    XtRealizeWidget (toplevel);
    XtAppMainLoop (app);
}
```

The output of this example is shown in Figure 8-16.

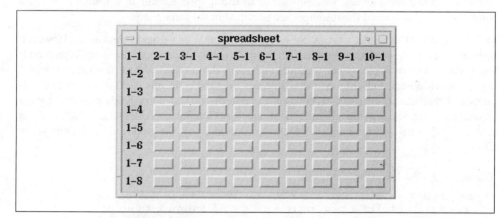

Figure 8-16. Output of spreadsheet.c

The number of rows is specified by the ROWS definition and the number of columns is specified by COLS. In order to force the RowColumn to lay out its children in the spreadsheet format, we set the XmNpacking, XmNnumColumns, and XmNorientation resources.

The value for XmNpacking is set to XmPACK_COLUMN, which specifies that each of the cells should be the same size. The heights and widths of the widgets are evaluated and the largest height and width are used to determine the size of the rows and columns. All of the widgets are resized to this size. If you are mixing different widget types in a RowColumn, you may not want to use XmPACK_COLUMN because of size variations. XmPACK_COLUMN is typically used when the widgets are exactly the same, or at least similar in nature. The default value of XmPACK_TIGHT for XmNpacking allows each widget to keep its specified size and packs the widgets into rows and columns based on the size of the RowColumn widget.

Since we are packing the widgets in a row/column format, we need to specify how many columns (or rows) we are using by setting the value of XmNnumColumns to the number of columns. In this case, the program defines COLS to be 10, which indicates that the RowColumn should pack its children such that there are 10 columns. The widget creates as many rows as necessary to provide enough space for all of the child widgets.

Whether XmNnumColumns specifies the number of columns or the number of rows depends on the orientation of the RowColumn. In this program, XmNorientation is set to XmVERTICAL to indicate that the value of XmNnumColumns specifies the number of columns

Manager Widgets

to use. If `XmNorientation` is set to `XmHORIZONTAL`, `XmNnumColumns` indicates the number of rows. If we wanted to use a horizontal orientation in our example, we would set `XmNnumColumns` to `ROWS` and `XmNorientation` to `XmHORIZONTAL`. The orientation also dictates how children are added to the RowColumn; when the orientation is vertical, children are added vertically so that each column is filled up before the next one is started.†

In our example, we explicitly set the value of `XmNorientation` to the default value of `XmVERTICAL`. If we do not hard-code this resource, an external resource specification can reset it. Since the orientation and the value for `XmNnumColumns` need to be consistent, you should always specify these resources together. Whether you choose to hard-code the resources, to use the fallback mechanism, or to use a specification in a resource file, you should be sure that both of the resources are specified in the same place.

In the spreadsheet example, we can use either a horizontal or vertical orientation. However, orientation may be significant in other situations, since it affects how the RowColumn adds its children. For example, if we want to implement the text-entry form from Example 8-5 using a RowColumn, the order of the widgets is important. In this case, there are two columns and the number of rows depends on the number of text entry fields provided by the application. We specify the orientation of the RowColumn as `XmHORIZONTAL` and set `XmNnumColumns` to the number of entries provided by the application, as shown in Example 8-8.‡

Example 8-8. The text_entry.c program

```
/* text_entry.c -- This demo shows how the RowColumn widget can be
 * configured to build a text entry form.  It displays a table of
 * right-justified Labels and Text widgets that extend to the right
 * edge of the Form.
 */
#include <Xm/LabelG.h>
#include <Xm/RowColumn.h>
#include <Xm/Text.h>

char *text_labels[] = {
    "Name:", "Phone:", "Address:", "City:", "State:", "Zip Code:",
};

main(argc, argv)
int argc;
char *argv[];
{
    Widget toplevel, rowcol;
    XtAppContext app;
    char buf[8];
    int i;

    XtSetLanguageProc (NULL, NULL, NULL);

    toplevel = XtVaAppInitialize (&app, "Demos", NULL, 0,
        &argc, argv, NULL, NULL);
```

---

† If you need to insert a child in the middle of an existing RowColumn layout, you can use the `XmNposition-Index` constraint resource to specify the position of the child. Since this resource is used most often with menus, it is discussed in Chapter 15, *Menus*.

‡ `XtSetLanguageProc()` is only available in X11R5; there is no corresponding function in X11R4.

Example 8-8. The text_entry.c program (continued)

```
    rowcol = XtVaCreateWidget ("rowcolumn",
        xmRowColumnWidgetClass, toplevel,
        XmNpacking,         XmPACK_COLUMN,
        XmNnumColumns,      XtNumber (text_labels),
        XmNorientation,     XmHORIZONTAL,
        XmNisAligned,       True,
        XmNentryAlignment, XmALIGNMENT_END,
        NULL);

    /* simply loop thru the strings creating a widget for each one */
    for (i = 0; i < XtNumber (text_labels); i++) {
        XtVaCreateManagedWidget (text_labels[i],
            xmLabelGadgetClass, rowcol,
            NULL);
        sprintf (buf, "text_%d", i);
        XtVaCreateManagedWidget (buf,
            xmTextWidgetClass, rowcol,
            NULL);
    }

    XtManageChild (rowcol);
    XtRealizeWidget (toplevel);
    XtAppMainLoop (app);
}
```

The output of this example is shown in Figure 8-17.

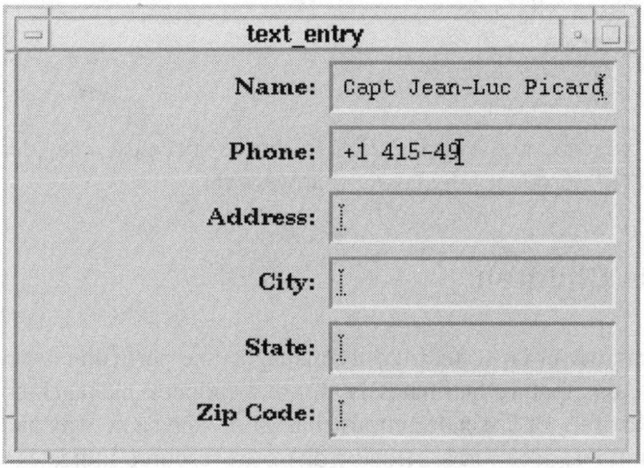

Figure 8-17. Output of text_entry.c

The labels for the text fields are initialized by the `text_labels` string array. When the RowColumn is created, it is set to a horizontal orientation and the number of rows is set to the number of items in `text_labels`. As you can see, the output of this program is slightly different from the output for the *text_form* example.

The example uses the `XmNisAligned` and `XmNentryAlignment` resources to control the positioning of the Labels in the RowColumn. These resources control the alignment of widgets that are subclasses of Label and LabelGadget. When `XmNisAligned` is `True` (the default), the alignment is taken from the `XmNentryAlignment` resource. The possible alignment values are the same as those that can be set for the Label's `XmNalignment` resource:

```
XmALIGNMENT_BEGINNING
XmALIGNMENT_CENTER
XmALIGNMENT_END
```

By default, the text is left justified. While the alignment of the Labels could also be specified using the `XmNalignment` resource for each widget, it is convenient to be able to set the alignment for the RowColumn and have it propagate automatically to its children. In our example, we use `XmALIGNMENT_END` to right justify the Labels so that they appear to be attached to the Text widgets.

In Motif 1.2, there is an additional resource for controlling the alignment of various children. The `XmNentryVerticalAlignment` resource controls the vertical positioning of children that are subclasses of Label, LabelGadget, and Text. The possible values for this resource are:

```
XmALIGNMENT_BASELINE_BOTTOM
XmALIGNMENT_BASELINE_TOP
XmALIGNMENT_CENTER
XmALIGNMENT_CONTENTS_BOTTOM
XmALIGNMENT_CONTENTS_TOP
```

In the example, we do not specify this resource because the default value, `Xm-ALIGNMENT_CENTER`, produces the layout that we want.

8.5.2 Homogeneous Children

The RowColumn can be set up so that it only manages one particular type of widget or gadget. In many cases, this feature facilitates layout and callback management. For example, a MenuBar consists entirely of CascadeButtons that all act the same way and a RadioBox contains only ToggleButtons. The `XmNisHomogeneous` resource indicates whether or not the RowColumn should only allow one type of widget child. The widget class that is allowed to be managed is specified by the `XmNentryClass` resource. `XmNisHomogeneous` can be set at creation-time only. Once a RowColumn is created, you cannot reset this resource, although you can always get its value. These resources are useful for ensuring consistency; if you attempt to add a widget as a child of a RowColumn that does not permit that widget class, an error message is printed and the widget is not accepted.

The Motif toolkit uses these mechanisms to ensure consistency in certain compound objects, to prevent you from doing something like adding a List widget to a MenuBar, for example. In this case, the XmNentryClass is set to xmCascadeButtonWidgetClass. As another example, when XmNradioBehavior is set, the RowColumn only allows Toggle-Button widgets and gadgets to be added. The XmCreateRadioBox() convenience function creates a RowColumn widget with the appropriate resources set automatically. (See Chapter 11, *Labels and Buttons*.)

You probably do not need to use XmNisHomogeneous unless you are providing a mechanism that is exported to other programmers. If you are writing an interactive user-interface builder or a program that creates widgets by scanning text files, you may want to ensure that new widgets are of a particular type before they are added to a RowColumn widget. In such cases, you may want to use XmNisHomogeneous and XmNentryClass. Unless there is some way for a user to to dynamically create widgets while an application is running, these resources are not particularly useful.

8.5.3 Callbacks

The RowColumn does not provide any specific callback routines that react to user input. While there are no callbacks for FocusIn and FocusOut events, the widget does have XmNmapCallback and XmNunmapCallback callback resources. These callbacks are invoked when the window for the RowColumn is mapped and unmapped. The callbacks are similar to those for the BulletinBoard, but since the RowColumn is not designed specifically to be a child of a DialogShell, the routines are invoked regardless of whether the parent of the RowColumn is a DialogShell.

The XmNentryCallback is the only other callback that is associated specifically with the RowColumn widget. This callback resource makes it possible to install a single callback function that acts as the activation callback for each of the children of a RowColumn widget. The routine specified for the XmNentryCallback overrides the XmNactivate-Callback functions for any PushButton or CascadeButton children and the XmNvalue-ChangedCallback functions for ToggleButtons. The XmNentryCallback is a convenience to the programmer; if you use it, you don't have to install separate callbacks for each widget in the RowColumn. XmNentryCallback functions must be installed before children are added to the RowColumn, so be sure you call XtAddCallback() before you create any child widgets.

The callback procedure takes the standard form of an XtCallbackProc. The call_data parameter is an XmRowColumnCallbackStruct, which is defined as follows:

```
typedef struct {
    int      reason;
    XEvent   *event;
    Widget   widget;
    char     *data;
    char     *callbackstruct;
} XmRowColumnCallbackStruct;
```

The reason field of this data structure is set to XmCR_ACTIVATE when the XmNentry-Callback is invoked. The event indicates the event that caused the notification. The entry callback function is called regardless of which widget within the RowColumn was activated. Since an entry callback overrides any previously-set callback lists for Push-Buttons, CascadeButtons, and ToggleButtons, the parameters that would have been passed to these callback routines are provided in the RowColumn callback structure. The widget field specifies the child that was activated, the widget-specific callback structure is placed in the callbackstruct field, and the client data that was set for the widget is passed in the data field.

Example 8-9 shows the installation of an entry callback and demonstrates how the normal callback functions are overridden.†

Example 8-9. The entry_cb.c program

```
/* entry_cb.c -- demonstrate how the XmNentryCallback resource works
 * in RowColumn widgets.  When a callback function is set for this
 * resource, all the callbacks for the RowColumn's children are reset
 * to point to this function.  Their original functions are no longer
 * called had they been set in favor of the entry-callback function.
 */
#include <Xm/PushBG.h>
#include <Xm/RowColumn.h>

char *strings[] = {
    "One", "Two", "Three", "Four", "Five",
    "Six", "Seven", "Eight", "Nine", "Ten",
};

void
called(widget, client_data, call_data)
Widget widget;
XtPointer client_data;
XtPointer call_data;
{
    XmRowColumnCallbackStruct *cbs =
        (XmRowColumnCallbackStruct *) call_data;
    Widget pb = cbs->widget;

    printf ("%s: %d\n", XtName (pb), cbs->data);
}

static void
never_called(widget, client_data, call_data)
Widget widget;
XtPointer client_data;
XtPointer call_data;
{
    puts ("This function is never called");
}

main(argc, argv)
int argc;
char *argv[];
```

---

†XtSetLanguageProc() is only available in X11R5; there is no corresponding function in X11R4.

Example 8-9. The entry_cb.c program (continued)

```
{
    Widget toplevel, parent, w;
    XtAppContext app;
    int i;

    XtSetLanguageProc (NULL, NULL, NULL);

    toplevel = XtVaAppInitialize (&app, "Demos",
        NULL, 0, &argc, argv, NULL, NULL);

    parent = XtVaCreateManagedWidget ("rowcolumn",
        xmRowColumnWidgetClass, toplevel,
        NULL);
    XtAddCallback (parent, XmNentryCallback, called, NULL);

    /* simply loop thru the strings creating a widget for each one */
    for (i = 0; i < XtNumber (strings); i++) {
        w = XtVaCreateManagedWidget (strings[i],
            xmPushButtonGadgetClass, parent, NULL);
        /* Call XtAddCallback() to install client_data only! */
        XtAddCallback (w, XmNactivateCallback, never_called, i+1);
    }

    XtRealizeWidget (toplevel);
    XtAppMainLoop (app);
}
```

The RowColumn is created and its XmNentryCallback is set to called(). This routine ignores the client_data parameter, as none is provided. However, we do use the data field of the cbs because this is the data that is specified in the call to XtAdd-Callback() for each of the children. We install the never_called() routine for each PushButton and pass the position of the button in the RowColumn as the client_data. Even though the entry callback overrides the activate callback, the client_data is preserved.

Our example is a bit contrived, so it may seem pointless to call XtAddCallback() for each PushButton and specify an XmNentryCallback as well. The most compelling reason for using an entry callback is that you may want to provide client data for the Row-Column as a whole, as well as for each child widget.

Remember that the RowColumn widget is also used for a number of objects implemented internally by the Motif toolkit, such as the Motif menu system, RadioBoxes, and Check-Boxes. Many of the resources for the widget are specific to these objects, so they are not discussed here. For more information on menus, see Chapter 4, *The Main Window*, and Chapter 15, *Menus*; for information on RadioBoxes and CheckBoxes, see Chapter 11, *Labels and Buttons*.

Manager Widgets

8.6 The Frame Widget

The Frame is a simple manager widget; the purpose of the Frame is to draw a three-dimensional border around its child. In Motif 1.1, a Frame can contain only one child. With Motif 1.2, the widget can have two children: a work area child and a title child. The Frame shrink wraps itself around its work area child, adding space for a title if one is specified. The children are responsible for setting the size of the Frame.

The Frame is useful for grouping related control elements, so that they are separated visually from other elements in a window. The Frame is commonly used as the parent of RadioBoxes and CheckBoxes, since the RowColumn widget does not provide a three-dimensional border. Figure 8-18 shows a portion of a dialog box that uses Frames to segregate three groups of ToggleButtons.

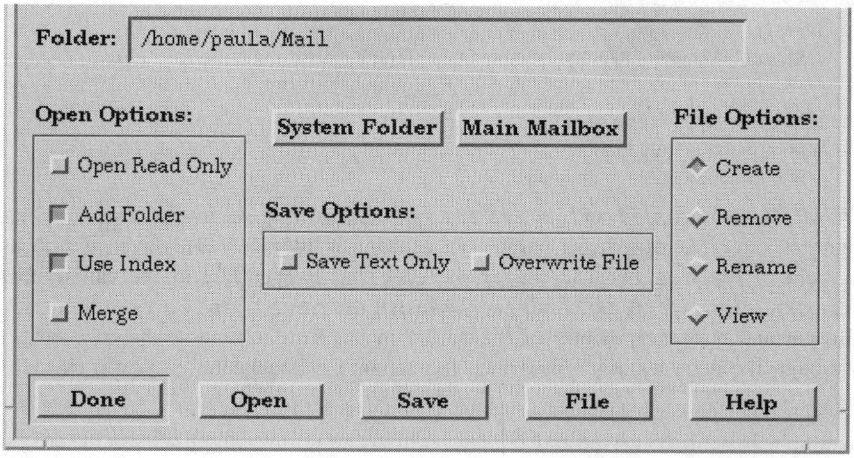

Figure 8-18. Frame widgets used to provide borders around RowColumn widgets

To use Frame widgets in an application, you must include the file *<Xm/Frame.h>*. Creating a Frame widget is just like creating any other manager widget, as shown in the following code fragment:

```
Widget frame;

frame = XtVaCreateManagedWidget ("name",
    xmFrameWidgetClass, parent,
    resource-value-list,
    NULL);
```

Since the Frame performs only simple geometry management, you can create a Frame widget as managed using XtVaCreateManagedWidget() and not worry about a performance loss. The Frame widget is an exception to the guidelines about creating manager widgets that we presented earlier in the chapter.

The principal resource used by the Frame widget is XmNshadowType. This resource specifies the style of the three-dimensional border that is placed around the work area child of the Frame. The value may be any of the following:

```
XmSHADOW_IN
XmSHADOW_OUT
XmSHADOW_ETCHED_IN
XmSHADOW_ETCHED_OUT
```

If the parent of the Frame is a shell widget, the default value for XmNshadowType is set to XmSHADOW_OUT and the value for XmNshadowThickness is set to 1. Otherwise, the default shadow type is XmSHADOW_ETCHED_IN and the thickness is 2. Of course, these values may be overridden by the application or the user.

In Motif 1.2, the Frame provides some constraint resources that can be specified for its children. The XmNchildType resource indicates whether the child is the work area or the title child for the Frame. The default value is XmFRAME_WORKAREA_CHILD. To specify that a child is the title child, use the value XmFRAME_TITLE_CHILD.

The XmNchildHorizontalAlignment and XmNchildHorizontalSpacing resources control the horizontal positioning of the title. The possible values for horizontal alignment are:

```
XmALIGNMENT_BEGINNING
XmALIGNMENT_END
XmALIGNMENT_CENTER
```

The XmNchildVerticalAlignment resource specifies the vertical positioning of the title child relative to the top shadow of the Frame. The possible values for this resource are:

```
XmALIGNMENT_BASELINE_BOTTOM
XmALIGNMENT_BASELINE_TOP
XmALIGNMENT_CENTER
XmALIGNMENT_WIDGET_TOP
XmALIGNMENT_WIDGET_BOTTOM
```

Example 8-10 demonstrates many of the different shadow and alignment styles that are possible with the Frame widget.†

Example 8-10. The frame.c program

```
/* frame.c -- demonstrate the Frame widget by creating
 * four Labels with Frame widget parents.
 */
#include <Xm/LabelG.h>
#include <Xm/RowColumn.h>
#include <Xm/Frame.h>

main(argc, argv)
int argc;
char *argv[];
```

---

†XtSetLanguageProc() is only available in X11R5; there is no corresponding function in X11R4. This example also uses functionality that is new in Motif 1.2; to take advantage of this functionality, define the symbol MOTIF_1_2 when you compile the program.

Example 8-10. The frame.c program (continued)

```
{
    Widget toplevel, rowcol, frame;
    XtAppContext app;

    XtSetLanguageProc (NULL, NULL, NULL);

    /* Initialize toolkit and create TopLevel shell widget */
    toplevel = XtVaAppInitialize (&app, "Demos",
        NULL, 0, &argc, argv, NULL, NULL);

    /* Make a RowColumn to contain all the Frames */
    rowcol = XtVaCreateWidget ("rowcolumn",
        xmRowColumnWidgetClass, toplevel,
        XmNspacing, 5,
        NULL);

    /* Create different Frames each containing a unique shadow type */
    XtVaCreateManagedWidget ("Frame Types:",
        xmLabelGadgetClass, rowcol, NULL);
    frame = XtVaCreateManagedWidget ("frame1",
        xmFrameWidgetClass, rowcol,
        XmNshadowType,      XmSHADOW_IN,
        NULL);
    XtVaCreateManagedWidget ("XmSHADOW_IN",
        xmLabelGadgetClass, frame,
        NULL);
#ifdef MOTIF_1_2
    XtVaCreateManagedWidget ("XmALIGNMENT_CENTER",
        xmLabelGadgetClass, frame,
        XmNchildType, XmFRAME_TITLE_CHILD,
        XmNchildVerticalAlignment, XmALIGNMENT_CENTER,
        NULL);
#endif

    frame = XtVaCreateManagedWidget ("frame2",
        xmFrameWidgetClass, rowcol,
        XmNshadowType,      XmSHADOW_OUT,
        NULL);
    XtVaCreateManagedWidget ("XmSHADOW_OUT",
        xmLabelGadgetClass, frame,
        NULL);
#ifdef MOTIF_1_2
    XtVaCreateManagedWidget ("XmALIGNMENT_BASELINE_TOP",
        xmLabelGadgetClass, frame,
        XmNchildType, XmFRAME_TITLE_CHILD,
        XmNchildVerticalAlignment, XmALIGNMENT_BASELINE_TOP,
        NULL);
#endif

    frame = XtVaCreateManagedWidget ("frame3",
        xmFrameWidgetClass, rowcol,
        XmNshadowType,      XmSHADOW_ETCHED_IN,
        NULL);
    XtVaCreateManagedWidget ("XmSHADOW_ETCHED_IN",
        xmLabelGadgetClass, frame,
        NULL);
#ifdef MOTIF_1_2
    XtVaCreateManagedWidget ("XmALIGNMENT_WIDGET_TOP",
```

Example 8-10. The frame.c program (continued)

```
            xmLabelGadgetClass, frame,
            XmNchildType, XmFRAME_TITLE_CHILD,
            XmNchildVerticalAlignment, XmALIGNMENT_WIDGET_TOP,
        NULL);
#endif

    frame = XtVaCreateManagedWidget ("frame4",
        xmFrameWidgetClass, rowcol,
        XmNshadowType,        XmSHADOW_ETCHED_OUT,
        NULL);
    XtVaCreateManagedWidget ("XmSHADOW_ETCHED_OUT",
        xmLabelGadgetClass, frame,
        NULL);
#ifdef MOTIF_1_2
    XtVaCreateManagedWidget ("XmALIGNMENT_WIDGET_BOTTOM",
        xmLabelGadgetClass, frame,
        XmNchildType, XmFRAME_TITLE_CHILD,
        XmNchildVerticalAlignment, XmALIGNMENT_WIDGET_BOTTOM,
        NULL);
#endif

    XtManageChild (rowcol);
    XtRealizeWidget (toplevel);
    XtAppMainLoop (app);
}
```

The output of this example is shown in Figure 8-19.

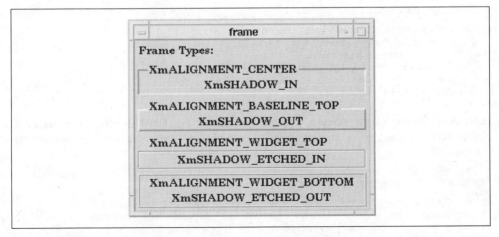

Figure 8-19. Output of frame.c

The program creates four Frame widgets. Each Frame has two Label children, one for the work area and one for the title. Each Frame uses a different value for the XmNshadowType and XmNchildVerticalPlacement resources, where these values are indicated by the text of the Labels. Although we have used a Label as the work area child of a Frame in this example, it is not a good idea to put a border around a Label. The shadow border implies selectability, which can confuse the user.

8.7 The PanedWindow Widget

The PanedWindow widget lays out its children in a vertically-tiled format.† The idea behind the PanedWindow is that the user can adjust the individual panes to provide more or less space as needed on a per-child basis. For example, if the user wants to see more text in a Text widget, he can use the control sashes (sometimes called grips) to resize the area for the Text widget. When the user moves the sash, the widget above or below the one being resized is resized smaller to compensate for the size change.

The width of the widget expands to that of its widest managed child and all of the other children are resized to match that width. The height of the PanedWindow is set to the sum of the heights of all of its children, plus the spacing between them and the size of the top and bottom margins. In Motif 1.1, widgets are placed in a PanedWindow in the order that you create them, with the first child being placed at the top of the PanedWindow. With Motif 1.2, you can set the XmNpositionIndex constraint resource to control the position of a child in a PanedWindow if you do not want to use the default order.

An application that wants to use the PanedWindow must include the file *<Xm/PanedW.h>*. An instance of the widget may be created as usual for manager widgets, as shown in the following code fragment:

```
Widget paned_w;

paned_w = XtVaCreateWidget ("name",
    xmPanedWindowWidgetClass, parent,
    resource-value-list,
    NULL);
...
XtManageChild (paned_w);
```

The PanedWindow widget provides constraint resources that allow its children to indicate their preferred maximum and minimum sizes. Example 8-11 shows three widgets that are set in a PanedWindow.‡

Example 8-11. The paned_win1.c program

```
/* paned_wind1.c --there are two Label widgets that are positioned
 * above and below a Text widget. The Labels' minimum and maximum
 * sizes are set to 25 and 45 respectively, preventing those
 * panes from growing beyond those bounds. The Text widget has its
 * minimum size set to 35 preventing it from becoming so small that
 * its text cannot be read.
 */
```

---

† The *Motif Style Guide* also provides for a horizontally-oriented paned window, but the Motif toolkit does not yet support it.

‡ XtSetLanguageProc() is only available in X11R5; there is no corresponding function in X11R4.

Motif Programming Manual

Example 8-11. The paned_win1.c program (continued)

```
#include <Xm/Label.h>
#include <Xm/PanedW.h>
#include <Xm/Text.h>

main(argc, argv)
char *argv[];
{
    Widget          toplevel, pane;
    XtAppContext    app;

    XtSetLanguageProc (NULL, NULL, NULL);

    toplevel = XtVaAppInitialize (&app, "Demos", NULL, 0,
        &argc, argv, NULL, NULL);

    pane = XtVaCreateWidget ("pane",
        xmPanedWindowWidgetClass, toplevel,
        NULL);

    XtVaCreateManagedWidget ("Hello", xmLabelWidgetClass, pane,
        XmNpaneMinimum,    25,
        XmNpaneMaximum,    45,
        NULL);

    XtVaCreateManagedWidget ("text", xmTextWidgetClass, pane,
        XmNrows,           5,
        XmNcolumns,        80,
        XmNpaneMinimum,    35,
        XmNeditMode,       XmMULTI_LINE_EDIT,
        XmNvalue,    "This is a test of the paned window widget.",
        NULL);

    XtVaCreateManagedWidget ("Goodbye", xmLabelWidgetClass, pane,
        XmNpaneMinimum,    25,
        XmNpaneMaximum,    45,
        NULL);

    XtManageChild (pane);

    XtRealizeWidget (toplevel);
    XtAppMainLoop (app);
}
```

The two Label widgets are positioned above and below a Text widget in a PanedWindow. The minimum and maximum sizes of the Labels are set to 25 and 45 pixels respectively, using the resources XmNpaneMinimum and XmNpaneMaximum. No matter how the PanedWindow or any of the other widgets are resized, the two Labels cannot grow or shrink beyond these bounds. The Text widget, however, only has a minimum size restriction, so it may be resized as large or as small as the user prefers, provided that it does not get smaller than the 35-pixel minimum. Figure 8-20 shows two configurations of this application.

Manager Widgets

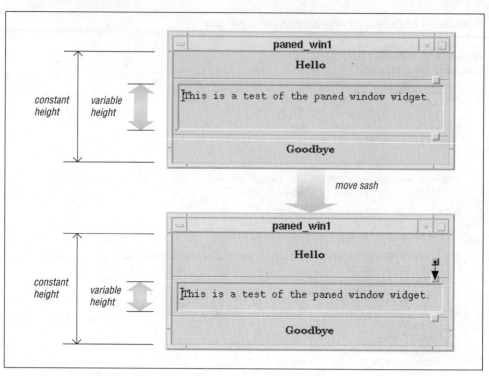

Figure 8-20. Output of paned_win1.c

8.7.1 Pane Constraints

One problem with setting the maximum and minimum resources for a widget involves determining exactly what those extents should be. The maximum size of 45 for the Label widgets
in Example 8-11 is an arbitrary value that was selected for demonstration purposes only. If
other resources had been set on one of the Labels such that the widget needed to be larger,
the application would definitely look unbalanced. For example, an extremely high resolution
monitor might require the use of unusually large fonts in order for text to appear normal.
There are two choices available at this point. One is to specify the maximum and minimum
values in a resolution-independent way and the other is to ask the Label widget itself what
height it wants to be.

Specifying resolution-independent dimensions requires you to carefully consider the type of
application you are creating. When you specify resolution-independent values, you must
specify the values in either millimeters, inches, points, or font units. The value of the XmN-
unitType Manager resource controls the type of units that are used. Example 8-12 demonstrates the use of resolution-independent dimensions.†

---

†XtSetLanguageProc() is only available in X11R5; there is no corresponding function in X11R4.

Example 8-12. The unit_types.c program

```
/* unit_types.c --the same as paned_win1.c except that the
 * Labels' minimum and maximum sizes are set to 1/4 inch and
 * 1/2 inch respectively.  These measurements are retained
 * regardless of the pixels-per-inch resolution of the user's
 * display.
 */
#include <Xm/Label.h>
#include <Xm/PanedW.h>
#include <Xm/Text.h>

main(argc, argv)
char *argv[ ];
{
    Widget          toplevel, pane;
    XtAppContext    app;

    XtSetLanguageProc (NULL, NULL, NULL);

    toplevel = XtVaAppInitialize (&app, "Demos", NULL, 0,
        &argc, argv, NULL, NULL);

    pane = XtVaCreateWidget ("pane",
        xmPanedWindowWidgetClass, toplevel,
        XmNunitType, Xm1000TH_INCHES,
        NULL);

    XtVaCreateManagedWidget ("Hello", xmLabelWidgetClass, pane,
        XmNpaneMinimum,     250, /* quarter inch */
        XmNpaneMaximum,     500, /* half inch */
        NULL);

    XtVaCreateManagedWidget ("text", xmTextWidgetClass, pane,
        XmNrows,            5,
        XmNcolumns,         80,
        XmNpaneMinimum,     250,
        XmNeditMode,        XmMULTI_LINE_EDIT,
        XmNvalue,    "This is a test of the paned window widget.",
        NULL);

    XtVaCreateManagedWidget ("Goodbye", xmLabelWidgetClass, pane,
        XmNpaneMinimum,     250, /* quarter inch */
        XmNpaneMaximum,     500, /* half inch */
        NULL);

    XtManageChild (pane);

    XtRealizeWidget (toplevel);
    XtAppMainLoop (app);
}
```

The second technique that we can use is to query the Label widgets about their heights. This technique requires the use of the Xt function XtQueryGeometry(), as shown in Example 8-13.†

---

†XtSetLanguageProc() is only available in X11R5; there is no corresponding function in X11R4.

Example 8-13. The paned_win2.c program

```c
/* paned_wind2.c --there are two label widgets that are positioned
 * above and below a Text widget.  The labels' desired heights are
 * queried using XtQueryGeometry() and their corresponding maximum
 * and minimum sizes are set to the same value.  This effectively
 * prevents those panes from being resized.  The Text widget has its
 * minimum size set to 35 preventing it from becoming so small that
 * its text cannot be read.
 */
#include <Xm/Label.h>
#include <Xm/PanedW.h>
#include <Xm/Text.h>

main(argc, argv)
char *argv[];
{
    Widget          toplevel, pane, label;
    XtWidgetGeometry  size;
    XtAppContext    app;

    XtSetLanguageProc (NULL, NULL, NULL);

    toplevel = XtVaAppInitialize (&app, "Demos", NULL, 0,
        &argc, argv, NULL, NULL);

    pane = XtVaCreateWidget ("pane",
        xmPanedWindowWidgetClass, toplevel, NULL);

    label = XtVaCreateManagedWidget ("Hello",
        xmLabelWidgetClass, pane, NULL);
    size.request_mode = CWHeight;
    XtQueryGeometry (label, NULL, &size);
    XtVaSetValues (label,
        XmNpaneMaximum, size.height,
        XmNpaneMinimum, size.height,
        NULL);
    printf ("hello's height: %d\n", size.height);

    XtVaCreateManagedWidget ("text", xmTextWidgetClass, pane,
        XmNrows,            5,
        XmNcolumns,         80,
        XmNresizeWidth,     False,
        XmNresizeHeight,    False,
        XmNpaneMinimum,     35,
        XmNeditMode,        XmMULTI_LINE_EDIT,
        XmNvalue,           "This is a test of the paned window widget.",
        NULL);

    label = XtVaCreateManagedWidget ("Goodbye",
        xmLabelWidgetClass, pane, NULL);
    size.request_mode = CWHeight;
    XtQueryGeometry (label, NULL, &size);
    XtVaSetValues (label,
        XmNpaneMaximum, size.height,
        XmNpaneMinimum, size.height,
        NULL);
    printf ("goodbye's height: %d\n", size.height);

    XtManageChild (pane);

    XtRealizeWidget (toplevel);
```

Example 8-13. The paned_win2.c program (continued)

```
    XtAppMainLoop (app);
}
```

`XtQueryGeometry()` asks a widget what size it would like to be. This routine takes the following form:

```
XtGeometryResult
XtQueryGeometry(widget, intended, preferred_return)
    Widget widget;
    XtWidgetGeometry *intended;
    XtWidgetGeometry *preferred_return;
```

Since we do not want to resize the widget, we pass NULL for the *intended* parameter. We are not interested in the return value of the function, since the information that we want is returned in the `preferred_return` parameter. This parameter is of type `XtWidget-Geometry`, which is defined as follows:

```
typedef struct {
    XtGeometryMask request_mode;
    Position x, y;
    Dimension width, height, border_width;
    Widget sibling;
    int stack_mode;
} XtWidgetGeometry;
```

We tell the widget what we want to know by setting the `request_mode` field of the `size` variable that we pass to the routine. The `request_mode` field is checked by the `query_geometry` function within the called widget. Depending on which bits that are specified, the appropriate fields are set within the returned data structure. In Example 8-13, we set `request_mode` to `CWHeight`, which tells the Label widget's `query_geometry` method to return the desired height in the `height` field of the data structure. If we had wanted to know the width as well, we could have set `request_mode` as follows:

```
    size.request_mode = (CWHeight | CWWidth);
```

In this case, the `width` and `height` fields would be filled in by the Label widget.

Once we have the Label's desired height, we can set the constraint resources `XmNpane-Maximum` and `XmNpaneMinimum` to the height of the Label. By making these two values the same, the pane associated with the Label cannot be resized. In most cases, the `Xt-QueryGeometry()` method can be used reliably to determine proper values for minimum and maximum pane extents.† Setting extents is useful, since without them, the user can adjust a PanedWindow so that the size of a widget is unreasonable or unaesthetic. If you are setting the extents for a scrolled object (ScrolledText or ScrolledList), you do not need to be as concerned about the maximum extent, since these objects handle larger sizes appropriately. Minimum states are certainly legitimate though. For example, you could use the height of a font as a minimum extent for Text or a List.

---

† In Motif 1.1, many of the Motif widgets do not have `query_geometry` methods, so they do not return sensible values when `XtQueryGeometry()` is called. In Motif 1.2, the `query_geometry` method has been implemented for all Motif widgets.

The PanedWindow widget can be useful for building your own dialogs because you can control the size of the action area. The action area is always at the bottom of the dialog and its size should never be changed. See Chapter 7, *Custom Dialogs*, for a complete discussion of how a PanedWindow can be used in in this manner.

8.7.2 Sashes

The Sashes in a PanedWindow widget are in fact widgets, even though they are not described or defined publicly. While the *Motif Style Guide* says that the Sash is part of the Paned-Window widget, the Motif toolkit defines the object privately, which means that technically the Sash is not supported and it may change in the future. However, it is possible to get a handle to a Sash if you absolutely need one. In order to retrieve a Sash, you need to include the header file *<Xm/SashP.h>*. The fact that the file ends in an uppercase *P* indicates that it is a private header file, which means that an application program should not include it. However, there is no public header file for the Sash widget, so unless you include the private header file, you cannot access the Sashes in a PanedWindow.

If you retrieve all of the children from a PanedWindow using `XtVaGetValues()` on the `XmNchildren` resource, you can use the `XmIsSash()` macro to locate the Sash children. This macro is defined as follows:

```
#define XmIsSash(w)     XtIsSubclass(w, xmSashWidgetClass)
```

Although `XtIsSubclass()` is a public function, `xmSashWidgetClass` is not declared publicly. One reason that you might want to get handles to the Sashes in a PanedWindow is to turn off keyboard traversal to the Sashes, as described in the next section.

8.8 Keyboard Traversal

The *Motif Style Guide* specifies methods by which the user can interact with an application without using the mouse. These methods provide a way for the user to navigate through an application and activate user-interface elements on the desktop using only the keyboard. Such activity is known as *keyboard traversal* and is based on the Common User Access (CUA) interface specifications from Microsoft Windows and Presentation Manager.

These specifications make heavy use of the TAB key to move between elements in a user interface; related interface controls are grouped into what are called *tab groups*. Some examples of tab groups are a set of ToggleButtons or a collection of PushButtons. Just as only one shell on the screen can have the keyboard focus, only one widget at a time can have the input focus. When keyboard activity occurs in a window, the toolkit knows which tab group is current and directs the input focus to the active item within that group.

The user can move from one item to the next within a tab group using the arrow keys. The user can move from one tab group to the next using the TAB key. To traverse the tab groups in the reverse direction, the user can use SHIFT-TAB. The CTRL key can be used with the TAB key in a Text widget to differentiate between a traversal operation and the use of the TAB key for input. The SPACEBAR activates the item that has the keyboard focus.

To illustrate the keyboard traversal mechanisms, let's examine *tictactoe.c* from Example 8-4. This program contains one tab group, the Form widget. Because the PushButtons inside of it are elements in the tab group, the user can move between the items in the tic-tac-toe board using the arrow keys on the keyboard, as illustrated in Figure 8-21.

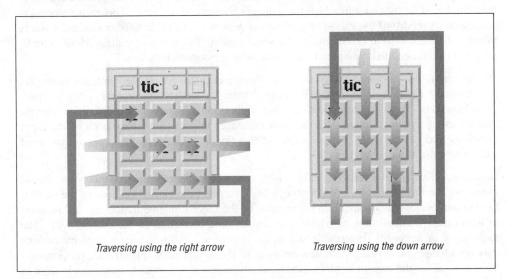

Traversing using the right arrow   Traversing using the down arrow

Figure 8-21. Keyboard traversal for tictactoe.c

Pressing the TAB key causes the input focus to be directed to the next tab group and set to the first item in the group, which is known as the *home* element. Since there is only one tab group in this application, the traversal mechanism moves the input focus to the first element in the same group. Thus, pressing the TAB key in this program always causes the home item to become the current input item.

The conceptual model of the tab group mechanism corresponds to the user's view of an application. With tab groups, the widget tree is flattened out into two simple layers: the first layer contains tab groups and the second layer contains the elements of those groups. In this model, there is no concept of managers and children or any sort of widget hierarchy. But as you know, an application is based on a very structured widget hierarchy. The implementation of tab groups is based on lists of widget pointers that refer to existing widgets in the widget tree. These lists, known as navigation groups, are maintained by the VendorShell and MenuShell widgets and are accessed by the input-handling mechanisms of the Motif toolkit.

Each widget class in the Motif toolkit is initialized either as a tab group itself or as a member of a tab group. Manager widgets, Lists, and Text widgets are usually tagged as tab groups, since they typically contain subelements that can be traversed. For example, the elements in a List can be traversed using the arrow keys on the keyboard; the up arrow moves the selection to the previous element in the List widget. In a Text widget, the arrow keys move the insertion cursor. The other primitive widgets, such as PushButtons and ToggleButtons, are usually tagged as tab group members. Output-only widgets are not tagged at all and are excluded from the tab group mechanism, since you cannot traverse to an output-only widget. These default settings are not permanent. For example, a PushButton or a ToggleButton can be a tab group, although this setting is uncommon and should only be done when you have a special reason for forcing the widget to be recognized as a separate tab group.

When the TAB key is pressed, the next tab group in the list of tab groups becomes the current tab group. Since manager widgets are normally tab groups, the order of tab group traversal is typically based on the order in which the manager widgets are created. This entire process is automated by the Motif toolkit, so an application does not have to do anything unless it wants to use a different system of tab groups for some reason. In order to maintain Motif compliance, we recommend that you avoid interfering with the default behavior.

We are discussing keyboard traversal in the chapter on manager widgets because managers play the most visible role in keyboard traversal from the application programmer's perspective. Managers, by their nature, contain other widgets, which are typically primitive widgets that act as tab group members. Furthermore, manager widgets must handle all of the input events for gadgets, so there is a great deal of functionality that supports keyboard traversal written into the Manager widget class.

Before we discuss the details of dealing with tab groups, there are a few things we should mention. The implementation of tab groups has changed from earlier versions of the toolkit; to maintain backwards compatibility, remnants of the older implementation are still resident in the current implementation, which may cause some confusion in the current API. The technology of keyboard traversal is still being improved. Although later implementations may not change the existing API, new versions of the toolkit may optimize the process substantially. Since the current implementation of tab groups is not perfect, some people want to change the default behavior and control it entirely on their own. We do not recommend this approach. You should avoid interfering with the keyboard traversal mechanisms, as it will make it easier to maintain compatibility with other Motif applications and it won't require any changes for new versions of the toolkit. If you are going to modify the operation of keyboard traversal, you should be careful and test your changes thoroughly.

8.8.1 Turning Traversal Off

You can prevent a widget from participating in keyboard traversal by removing the widget from the traversal list. To remove a widget from the traversal list, set its XmNtraversalOn resource to False. If the widget is a member of a tab group, it is simply removed from the list and the user cannot traverse to it. If the widget is a tab group, it is removed and all of its elements are also all removed.

Let's experiment with tab group members by modifying *tictactoe.c*. We can modify the pushed() callback routine to remove the selected PushButton from the traversal list when it is selected. If the keyboard is used to traverse and select the items on the tic-tac-toe board, the toolkit automatically skips over those that have already been selected. The new callback routine is shown in Example 8-14.†

---

† XtSetLanguageProc() is only available in X11R5; there is no corresponding function in X11R4.

Example 8-14. The pushed() routine

```
void
pushed(w, client_data, call_data)
Widget      w;
XtPointer   client_data;
XtPointer   call_data;
{
    char buf[2];
    XmString str;
    int letter;
    XmPushButtonCallbackStruct *cbs =
        (XmPushButtonCallbackStruct *) call_data;

    XtVaGetValues (w, XmNuserData, &letter, NULL);
    if (letter) {
        XBell (XtDisplayOfObject (w), 50);
        return;
    }
    /* Shift key gets an O.  (xbutton and xkey happen to be similar) */
    if (cbs->event->xbutton.state & ShiftMask)
        letter = buf[0] = 'O';
    else
        letter = buf[0] = 'X';
    buf[1] = 0;
    str = XmStringCreateLocalized (buf);
    XtVaSetValues (w,
        XmNlabelString,    str,
        XmNuserData,       letter,
        XmNshadowThickness, 0,
        XmNtraversalOn,    False,
        NULL);
    XmStringFree (str);
}
```

The user can still click on a previously-selected item with the mouse button, but the routine causes an error bell to sound in this situation.

Output-only widgets, like Labels and Separators, always have their XmNtraversalOn resource initialized to False. In most cases, setting the value to True would be annoying to the user, since these objects cannot respond to keyboard input anyway. The user would have to traverse many unimportant widgets to get to a desired item. However, it is commonly overlooked that a Label can have a XmNhelpCallback routine associated with it. If the keyboard traversal mechanism allows the user to traverse to Labels, he could get help on them by pressing the HELP or F1 keys. It may be considered a design flaw in Motif that a non-mouse-driven interface is not supported for getting help for these objects. However, this situation is not generally a problem, since most people do not try to get help on Labels and most programmers do not install help for them.

A general problem that people tend to have with the PanedWindow widget is that the Sashes are included in the traversal list. Since the PanedWindow is a manager widget, it is a tab group, which means that all of its children are members of the tab group. If you run the program from Example 8-13 and use the TAB key to move from one widget to the next, you'll find that the traversal also includes the Sash widgets. Many users find it annoying to traverse to Sashes, since it is more likely that they want to skip the Sashes when using keyboard

Manager Widgets

traversal, rather than use them to resize any of the panes. While it is common to resize panes, people usually do so using the mouse, not the keyboard.

As of Motif 1.2, it is possible to turn off Sash traversal using the following resource specification in a resource file:

```
*XmSash.traversalOn: False
```

Prior to this release, the PanedWindow and its Sashes were created in such a way that you could not override the traversability of the Sashes using hard-coded values in the widget creation call or using a resource specification in a resource file. In fact, the internals of the PanedWindow widget hard-coded its Sash widgets' XmNtraversalOn resources to True as they were created, thus eliminating the possibility of turning traversal off using resources. The only way to turn off traversal for Sashes in this case was to reset the resource values after all of the Sashes were created. Example 8-15 demonstrates a routine that handles this task.

Example 8-15. The TurnOffSashTraversal() routine

```
#include <Xm/SashP.h>

void
TurnOffSashTraversal (panedw)
Widget panedw;
{
    Widget *children;
    int num_children;

    XtVaGetValues (panedw,
        XmNchildren,    &children,
        XmNnumChildren, &num_children,
        NULL);
    while (num_children-- > 0)
        if (XmIsSash (children[num_children]))
            XtVaSetValues (children[num_children],
                XmNtraversalOn, False,
                NULL);
}
```

There are some applications that might actually have to be used without a mouse, just as there are some users who prefer to use the keyboard, so you should be careful about turning off keyboard traversal for the Sashes in a PanedWindow widget. If you do turn off Sash traversal, we recommend that you document the behavior and provide a way for the user to control this behavior. For example, you could provide an application-specific resource that controls whether or not Sashes can be traversed using the keyboard.

As noted earlier, XmNtraversalOn can be set on tab groups (which tend to be manager widgets) as well as tab group members. If traversal is off for a tab group, none of its members can be traversed. If keyboard traversal is something that you need to modify in your application, you should probably hard-code XmNtraversalOn values directly into individual widgets as you create them. Turning off traversal is typically not something that is done on a per-widget-class basis. When you turn traversal off in application code, be careful to make sure that there is no reason that a user would want to traverse to the particular widgets because once you hard-code the resource values, they cannot be modified by the user in a resource file.

8.8.2 Modifying Tab Groups

The XmNnavigationType resource controls whether a widget is a tab group itself or is a member of a tab group. When this resource is set to XmNONE, the widget is not a tab group, so it defaults to being a member of one. As a member, its XmNtraversalOn resource indicates whether or not the user can direct the input focus to the widget using the keyboard. This value is the default for most primitive widgets. When the resource is set to Xm-TAB_GROUP, the widget is a tab group itself, so it is included in keyboard navigation. This value is the default for managers, Lists, and Text widgets. By modifying the default value of the XmNnavigationType resource for a widget, you can specify that a primitive widget is a tab group. As a result, the user traverses to the widget using the TAB key rather than one of the arrow keys. For example, you can modify *tictactoe.c* by setting the XmNnavigation-Type to XmTAB_GROUP for each PushButton.

There are two other values for XmNnavigationType that are used for backwards compatibility with older versions of the toolkit. They are not generally used unless you are porting programs from Motif 1.0. In this version of the toolkit, there is an application called Xm-AddTabGroup() to make a widget a tab group. With Motif 1.0, the programmer was required to specify precisely which widgets were tab groups, which were members of a tab group, and which were not traversable. As a result, XmAddTabGroup() had to be called for all manager widgets. To maintain backwards compatibility, whenever XmAddTab-Group() is called, the toolkit assumes the programmer is using the old Motif 1.0 specifications and disables the new, automatic behavior. Unless your application is currently using the old API, you can probably skip to the next section.

Calling XmAddTabGroup() is equivalent to setting XmNnavigationType to Xm-EXCLUSIVE_TAB_GROUP. If this value is set on a widget or if XmAddTabGroup() is called, new widgets are no longer added as tab groups automatically. Basically, the toolkit reverts to the old behavior. An exclusive tab group is much the same as a normal tab group, but Motif recognizes this special value and ignores all widgets that have the newer Xm-TAB_GROUP value set. You can think of this value as setting exclusivity on the tab group behavior.

The value XmSTICKY_TAB_GROUP can also be used for XmNnavigationType in Motif 1.0. If this value is used on a widget, the widget is included automatically in keyboard traversal, even if another widget has its navigation type set to XmEXCLUSIVE_TAB_GROUP or if XmAddTabGroup() has been called. This value provides a partial workaround for the new behavior, but not exactly. You can set a widget to be a sticky tab group without completely eliminating the old behavior and without interfering with the new behavior.

You can ignore these two values for all intents and purposes. If you need to port an old application to a newer version of the Motif toolkit, you should consider removing all of the calls to XmAddTabGroup() and just going with the new behavior. If you need to change the default behavior, you should use XmNONE and XmTAB_GROUP to control whether or not a widget is a tab group or a member of one. To control whether the widget is part of the whole keyboard traversal mechanism, use the XmNtraversalOn resource.

8.8.3 Handling Event Translations

In order for manager widgets to implement keyboard traversal, they have their own event translation tables that specify what happens when certain events occur. As discussed in Chapter 2, *The Motif Programming Model*, a translation table specifies a series of one or more events and an action that is invoked if the event occurs. The X Toolkit Intrinsics handles event translations automatically; when the user presses the TAB key, Xt looks up the event <Key>Tab in the table and invokes the corresponding action procedure. In this case, the procedure changes the input focus from the current tab group to the next one on the list.

This mechanism is dependent on the window hierarchy of the widget tree. Events are first delivered to the widget associated with the window where the event took place. If that widget (or its window) does not handle the type of event delivered, it passes the event up the window tree to its parent, which then has the option of dealing with the event. Assuming that the parent is a manager widget of some kind, it now has the option to process the event. If the event is a keyboard traversal event, the appropriate action routine moves the input focus. The default event translations that manager widgets use to handle keyboard traversal are currently specified as follows:

```
<Key>osfBeginLine:            ManagerGadgetTraverseHome()
<Key>osfUp:                   ManagerGadgetTraverseUp()
<Key>osfDown:                 ManagerGadgetTraverseDown()
<Key>osfLeft:                 ManagerGadgetTraverseLeft()
<Key>osfRight:                ManagerGadgetTraverseRight()
Shift ~Meta ~Alt <Key>Tab:   ManagerGadgetPrevTabGroup()
~Meta ~Alt <Key>Tab:         ManagerGadgetNextTabGroup()
<EnterWindow>:               ManagerEnter()
<LeaveWindow>:               ManagerLeave()
<FocusOut>:                  ManagerFocusOut()
<FocusIn>:                   ManagerFocusIn()
```

The OSF-specific keysyms are vendor-defined, which means that the directional arrows must be defined by the user's system at run-time. Values like <Key>osfUp and <Key>osf-Down may not be the same as <Key>Up and <Key>Down.

The routines that handle keyboard traversal are prefixed by ManagerGadget. Despite their names, these functions are not specific to gadgets; they are used to handle keyboard traversal for all of the children in the manager. If a primitive widget inside of a manager widget specifies an event translation that conflicts with one of the manager's translations, the primitive widget can interfere with keyboard traversal. If the primitive widget has the input focus, the user cannot use the specified event to move the input focus with the keyboard. The following code fragment shows how the translation table for a PushButton can interfere with the keyboard traversal mechanism in its parent:

```
Widget pb;
XtActionRec action;
extern void do_tab();

actions.string = "do_tab";
actions.proc = do_tab;
XtAddActions (&actions, 1);

pb = XtVaCreateManagedWidget ("name",
    xmPushButtonWidgetClass, parent,
```

```
              resource-value-list,
           NULL);
     XtOverrideTranslations (pb, XtParseTranslationTable ("<Key>Tab: do_tab"));
```

The translation table is merged into the existing translations for the PushButton widget. This translation table does not interfere with the translation table in the manager widget, but it does interfere with event propagation to the manager. When the TAB key is pressed, the action routine do_tab() is called and the event is consumed by the PushButton widget. The event is not propagated up to the manager widget so that it can perform the appropriate keyboard traversal action. The workaround for this problem is to have do_tab() process the keyboard traversal action on its own, in addition to performing its own action. This technique is discussed in the next section.

Since a manager can also contain gadgets, the manager widget must also handle input that is destined for gadgets. Since gadgets do not have windows, they cannot receive events. Only the manager widget that is the parent of a gadget can receive events for the gadget. The manager widget has the following additional translations to handle input on behalf of gadgets:

```
    <Key>osfActivate:              ManagerParentActivate()
    <Key>osfCancel:                ManagerParentCancel()
    <Key>osfSelect:                ManagerGadgetSelect()
    <Key>osfHelp:                  ManagerGadgetHelp()
    ~Shift ~Meta ~Alt <Key>Return: ManagerParentActivate()
    ~Shift ~Meta ~Alt <Key>space:  ManagerGadgetSelect()
    <Key>:                         ManagerGadgetKeyInput()
    <BtnMotion>:                   ManagerGadgetButtonMotion()
    <Btn1Down>:                    ManagerGadgetArm()
    <Btn1Down>,<Btn1Up>:           ManagerGadgetActivate()
    <Btn1Up>:                      ManagerGadgetActivate()
    <Btn1Down>(2+):                ManagerGadgetMultiArm()
    <Btn1Up>(2+):                  ManagerGadgetMultiActivate()
    <Btn2Down>:                    ManagerGadgetDrag()
```

Unlike with keyboard traversal translations, widget translations cannot interfere with the manager translations that handle events destined for gadgets. If a widget had the input focus, the user's actions cannot be destined for a gadget, since the user would have to traverse to the gadget first, in which case the manager would really have the input focus.

In Chapter 10, *The DrawingArea Widget*, we discuss the problems involved in handling input events on the DrawingArea widget. The problems arise because the widget can be used for interactive drawing, as well as serve as a manager. There may be events that you want to process in your application, but they could also be processed by the DrawingArea itself. The problem is really a semantic one, as there is no way to determine which action procedure should be invoked for each event if the DrawingArea has a manager-based action and the application defines its own action. For more information on translation tables and action routines, see Chapter 2, *The Motif Programming Model*, and Volume Four, *X Toolkit Intrinsics Programming Manual*.

8.8.4 Processing Traversal Manually

At times, an application may want to move the input focus as a result of something that the user has done. For example, you might have an action area where each PushButton invokes a callback function and then sets the input focus to the home item in the tab group, presumably to protect the user from inadvertently selecting the same item twice. Example 8-16 demonstrates how this operation can be accomplished.

Example 8-16. The proc_traversal.c program

```
/* proc_traverse.c -- demonstrate how to process keyboard traversal
 * from a PushButton's callback routine.  This simple demo contains
 * a RowColumn (a tab group) and three PushButtons.  If any of the
 * PushButtons are activated (selected), the input focus traverses
 * to the "home" item.
 */
#include <Xm/PushB.h>
#include <Xm/RowColumn.h>

main(argc, argv)
int argc;
char *argv[];
{
    Widget toplevel, rowcol, pb;
    XtAppContext app;
    void do_it();

    XtSetLanguageProc (NULL, NULL, NULL);

    toplevel = XtVaAppInitialize (&app, "Demos", NULL, 0,
        &argc, argv, NULL, NULL);

    rowcol = XtVaCreateManagedWidget ("rowcolumn",
        xmRowColumnWidgetClass, toplevel,
        XmNorientation, XmHORIZONTAL,
        NULL);

    (void) XtVaCreateManagedWidget ("OK",
        xmPushButtonWidgetClass, rowcol, NULL);

    pb = XtVaCreateManagedWidget ("Cancel",
        xmPushButtonWidgetClass, rowcol, NULL);
    XtAddCallback (pb, XmNactivateCallback, do_it, NULL);

    pb = XtVaCreateManagedWidget ("Help",
        xmPushButtonWidgetClass, rowcol, NULL);
    XtAddCallback (pb, XmNactivateCallback, do_it, NULL);

    XtRealizeWidget (toplevel);
    XtAppMainLoop (app);
}

/* callback for pushbuttons */
void
do_it(widget, client_data, call_data)
Widget widget;
XtPointer client_data;
XtPointer call_data;
```

Example 8-16. The proc_traversal.c program (continued)

```
{
    /* do stuff here for PushButton widget */
    (void) XmProcessTraversal(widget, XmTRAVERSE_HOME);
}
```

The three frames in Figure 8-22 show the movement of keyboard focus in the program. In the figure, the current input focus is on the **Cancel** button; when it is selected, the input focus is changed to the **OK** button.

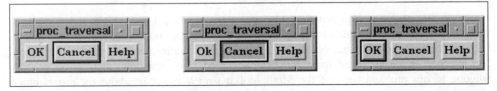

Figure 8-22. Output of proc_traversal.c

The callback routine associated with the PushButtons does whatever it needs and then calls `XmProcessTraversal()` to change the input item to the home item, which happens to be the **OK** button. This function can be used when an application needs to set the current item in the tab group to another widget or gadget or it can be used to traverse to a new tab group. The function takes the following form:

```
Boolean
XmProcessTraversal(widget, direction)
    Widget widget;
    int    direction;
```

The function returns `False` if the VendorShell associated with the widget has no tab groups, the input focus policy doesn't make sense, or if there are other extenuating circumstances that would be considered unusual. It is unlikely that you'll ever have this problem.

The *direction* parameter specifies where the input focus should be moved. This parameter can take any of the following values:

```
XmTRAVERSE_CURRENT
XmTRAVERSE_NEXT
XmTRAVERSE_PREV
XmTRAVERSE_HOME
XmTRAVERSE_UP
XmTRAVERSE_DOWN
XmTRAVERSE_LEFT
XmTRAVERSE_RIGHT
XmTRAVERSE_NEXT_TAB_GROUP
XmTRAVERSE_PREV_TAB_GROUP
```

All but the last two values are for traversing to items within the current tab group; the last two are for traversing to the next or previous tab group relative to the current one. In the case of Example 8-16, the call to `XmProcessTraversal()` forces the home element to be the current item in the current tab group. For a more sophisticated example of manipulating the input focus, see Section 14.5.1 in Chapter 14, *Text Widgets*. One problem with Xm-`ProcessTraversal()` is that you can only move in a relative direction from the item that has the input focus. This functionality is sufficient in most cases, since the logic of your application should not rely on the user following any particular input sequence. If you need to traverse to a specific widget regardless of the current item, in most cases you can make the following call:

```
XmProcessTraversal (desired_widget, XmTRAVERSE_CURRENT);
```

This calling sequence specifies that the desired_widget takes the input focus, but only if the shell that contains the widget already has the keyboard focus. If the shell does not have the focus, nothing happens until the shell obtains the keyboard focus. When it does, the desired_widget should have the input focus.

Under certain conditions, this function may appear not to work. For example, if you create a dialog and want to set the input focus to one of its subwidgets, you may or may not get this to happen, depending on whether or not the dialog has been realized and mapped to the screen and whether or not keyboard focus has been accepted. Unfortunately, there is no general solution to this problem because the Motif toolkit isn't very robust about the programmer changing input focus out from under it. You cannot call generic X functions like XSet-InputFocus() to force a widget to take input focus or you will undermine Motif's attempt at monitoring and controlling the input policy on its own.

In Motif 1.2, there are some new functions that make it easier for an application to control keyboard traversal. The XmGetFocusWidget() routine returns the widget that has the input focus, while XmGetTabGroup() returns the widget that is the tab group for the specified widget. You can also call XmIsTraversable() to determine whether or not a particular widget is eligible to receive the input focus. With Motif 1.1, you often cannot determine which widget has the input focus or where a particular widget is in the widget tree relative to the current input item.

8.9 Summary

Manager widgets are the backbone of an application. Without them, primitive widgets have no way of controlling their size, layout, and input focus. While the Motif toolkit provides many different manager widget classes, you may find that there are some things that you cannot do with them. Experienced toolkit programmers have found that it is possible to port Constraint class widgets from other toolkits to the Motif toolkit, by subclassing them from the generic Manager widget class. This topic is beyond the scope of this book.

This chapter introduces the Motif manager widgets, but it does not discuss in detail some of the basic issues of geometry management. If the basic concepts presented in this chapter are still somewhat foreign to you, see Volume Four, *X Toolkit Intrinsics Programming Manual*, for a more in-depth discussion of composite widgets and geometry management.

9

ScrolledWindows and ScrollBars

This chapter describes the ins and outs of scrolling. It pays particular attention to application-defined scrolling, which is often required when the simple scrolling provided by the ScrolledWindow widget is insufficient.

In This Chapter:

ScrolledWindows and ScrollBars

The ScrolledWindow widget provides a viewing area into another, usually larger, visual object. The viewport may be adjusted by the user through the use of ScrollBars that are attached to the ScrolledWindow. The Motif MainWindow, ScrolledList, and ScrolledText objects use ScrolledWindows to implement scrolling for their respective contents. The ScrolledWindow can also be used independently to provide a viewport into another large object, such as a DrawingArea or a manager widget that contains a large group of widgets. All of these scenarios are explored in this chapter.

9.1 The ScrolledWindow Design Model

The user always interacts with a ScrolledWindow through ScrollBars. Internally, however, there are several ways to implement what the user sees. These methods are based on two different scrolling models: automatic scrolling and application-defined scrolling. In either case, the application gives the ScrolledWindow a *work window* that contains the visual data to be viewed. Although the two models are different, they share many of the same concepts and features.

In automatic scrolling mode, the ScrolledWindow operates entirely on its own, adjusting the viewport as necessary in response to ScrollBar activity. The application simply creates the desired data, such as a Label widget that contains a large pixmap, and makes that widget the work window for the ScrolledWindow. When the user operates the ScrollBars to change the visible area, the ScrolledWindow adjusts the Label so that the appropriate portion is visible. This design is demonstrated in Chapter 4, *The Main Window*, and Chapter 10, *The DrawingArea Widget*.

With application-defined scrolling, the ScrolledWindow operates under the assumption that the work window is not complete. The widget assumes that another entity, such as the application or the internals of another widget, controls the data within the work window and that the data may change dynamically as the user scrolls. In order to control scrolling, the application must control all aspects of the ScrollBars. This level of control is necessary when it is impossible or impractical for an application to provide the ScrolledWindow with a sufficiently large work window (or the data for it) at any one time.

ScrolledWindows and ScrollBars

9.1.1 The Automatic Scrolling Model

Most of the time, the ScrolledWindow widget is used in automatic scrolling mode. When it is used in this mode, the ScrolledWindow contains at most three internal widgets: two Scroll-Bars and a *clip window*.† The ScrolledWindow creates these widgets automatically. The work area is an external widget (specified by the XmNworkWindow resource) that is clipped by the clip window. This work window is a child of the ScrolledWindow that is provided by the application; it is not created automatically by the ScrolledWindow. When the user interacts with the ScrollBars, the work window is adjusted so that the appropriate part is visible through the clip window. The general design of the ScrolledWindow in automatic scrolling mode is illustrated in Figure 9-1.

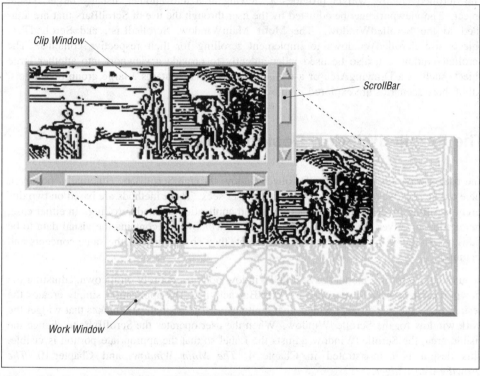

Figure 9-1. Design of an automatic ScrolledWindow

The work window can be almost any widget, but there can be only one work window per ScrolledWindow. If you want to have more than one widget inside of a ScrolledWindow, you can place all of the widgets in a manager widget and make that manager the work window. The clip window is always the size of the viewport portion of the ScrolledWindow, which is the size of the ScrolledWindow minus the size of the ScrollBars and any borders and margins. The clip window is not adjusted in size unless the ScrolledWindow is resized. The clip

---

† The clip window is implemented as a DrawingArea widget.

window is always positioned at the origin, which means that you cannot use `XtMove-Widget()` or change its `XmNx` and `XmNy` resources to reposition it in the ScrolledWindow. The internals of the ScrolledWindow are solely responsible for changing the view in the clip window, although you can affect this behavior. While you can get a handle to the clip window, you cannot remove it or replace it with another window.

9.1.2 The Application-defined Scrolling Model

In the application-defined scrolling model, which is the default model, the ScrolledWindow always makes itself the same size as the work window. Just as for automatic scrolling, the application must provide the work window as a child of the ScrolledWindow. The main reason to use application-defined scrolling is if the work window contains more data than can possibly be loaded in the automatic scrolling mode. An application may also require different scrolling behavior than the default pixel-by-pixel increments provided by the automatic scrolling mode. Application-defined scrolling is also the best option when the contents of the work window changes dynamically and the application does not want to rely on the Scrolled-Window to scroll new data into view.

The disadvantage of application-defined scrolling is that the application, not the Scrolled-Window, is responsible for the ScrollBars. The application must create and manage the ScrollBars, as well as respond to the scrolling actions initiated by the user. Since what is displayed in the clip window and the work window are identical, the ScrolledWindow widget does not bother to create a clip window. However, there are still some limitations as to what the ScrolledWindow can support. It is important that you understand the limitations before designing your application, so let's look at two examples.

A Text widget that displays the contents of an arbitrarily large file provides a classic example of application-defined scrolling. Under the automatic scrolling model, the application might have to provide the ScrolledWindow with a work window that is large enough to render thousands of lines of text, so that all of the text is immediately available to the user. An object of such proportions is prohibitive for reasonable performance and resource consumption. Since the work window cannot be as large as it would need to be for automatic scrolling, it might as well be as small as possible, which is the size of the clip window. When the Text widget is a child of a ScrolledWindow, the Text widget creates its own ScrollBars and attaches callback routines to them so that it can be notified of scrolling actions. When the user scrolls, the Text widget changes the text in the work window to the text that corresponds to the new region that just scrolled into view. The user has the illusion that scrolling is taking place, but in reality, the data in the work window has simply changed, thereby saving a great deal of overhead in system and server resources. The List widget uses the same method when it is the child of a ScrolledWindow. The Text and List widgets are the only examples of application-defined scrolling that are supported by the current implementation of the ScrolledWindow.

There is another scenario in which a large amount of data is retrieved dynamically and is not all available at the same time. Even though the ScrolledWindow does not really support this scenario, you should be familiar with the situation, since it may come up in a large application. There are some possible workarounds that we'll discuss later in the chapter. Let's say that the Pacific Gas and Electric Company has an online database that contains all of the pipeline information for California and that an operator wants to view the data for San

Francisco county. To display this information, the application must read the data from the database and convert that data into an image that can be presented in a ScrolledWindow.

Although the database cannot get all the information for the whole county all at once, it can get more information than the window can display. Let's say that the window can display 10% of the county and the database can return information on 20% of the county in a reasonable amount of time. The application needs to use the application-defined mechanisms because 100% of the data is not available for automatic scrolling. The fact that more than what can be displayed is available just means that the application could optimize performance by avoiding unnecessary retrieval of data from the database whenever scrolling takes place. The application could reuse the existing work window as a cache, so that if the user scrolls by an amount that is small enough, the work window is redisplayed in a way similar to the automatic scrolling mechanism. The application would still have to control this behavior manually, though.

Unfortunately, the ScrolledWindow does not support this type of behavior. The Scrolled-Window always expands to the size of its work window in application-defined scrolling mode. In other words, you cannot have a work window that is a different size from the clip window. This situation leaves you with several design decisions. You could reduce the amount of data obtained from a database query, throw away excess information not used in your display, or make the viewport of an automatic ScrolledWindow large enough for each query. In any case, the best approach is to use some method that makes the size of the work window the same as the clip window. While this requirement may present some logistical problems with the design of your application, we'll discuss some workarounds for the situation later in the chapter.

In the two preceding examples, we have defined two fundamentally similar methods of scrolling: semi-automatic scrolling and true application-defined scrolling. In the first case, Text and List widgets handle their own scrolling internally through special-case routines attached to the ScrollBars. We call this method semi-automatic scrolling, since the application programmer is not responsible for the scrolling of these widgets. Nevertheless, the Scrolled-Window is in the application-defined scrolling mode. This situation is in contrast to true application-defined scrolling, where you must handle the ScrollBars and the associated scrolling actions entirely on your own. This method is more intricate and requires a significant amount of code to be implemented properly.

Obviously, the automatic scrolling mechanism provided by the ScrolledWindow is much simpler than the application-defined mechanism and it requires much less application intervention. However, there are some drawbacks in the implementation of automatic scrolling. Automatic ScrolledWindows only scroll in single-pixel increments. If other scrolling behavior is required, you must use application-defined scrolling. And while application-defined scrolling is far more complicated, the advantage is that it provides more flexibility in the ways that the object is scrolled.

9.2 Creating a ScrolledWindow

Creating a ScrolledWindow is no different from creating other kinds of Motif widgets. Applications that wish to use ScrolledWindows must include the header file *<Xm/Scrolled-W.h>*. The process of creating a ScrolledWindow is shown in the following code fragment:

```
Widget  scrollw;

scrollw = XtVaCreateManagedWidget ("name",
    xmScrolledWindowWidgetClass, parent,
    resource-value-list,
    NULL);
```

The `parent` can be a Shell or any manager widget. The ScrolledWindow can be created as a managed widget, since the addition of its child does not cause it to renegotiate its size. (See Chapter 8, *Manager Widgets*, for a discussion of when manager widgets should be created as managed or unmanaged widgets.) The resource-value pairs control the behavior of the ScrolledWindow, as well as its visual effects. The most important resources are `XmN-scrollingPolicy`, `XmNvisualPolicy`, and `XmNscrollBarDisplayPolicy`. The value for `XmNscrollingPolicy` can be set to either `XmAUTOMATIC` or `Xm-APPLICATION_DEFINED`, depending on which scrolling method you want to use. The use of other ScrolledWindow resources varies depending on the scrolling behavior that is specified.

9.2.1 Automatic Scrolling

In automatic scrolling mode, the ScrolledWindow assumes that all of the data is already available in the work window and that the size of the work window represents the entire size of the viewable data. Even if the data changes and the size of work window is modified, the ScrolledWindow can still manage its display automatically. The ScrolledWindow should never resize itself due to changes in the work windows, so `XmNvisualPolicy` is typically set to `XmCONSTANT`. This value tells the ScrolledWindow not to resize itself when the work window grows or shrinks. If `XmNvisualPolicy` is set to `XmVARIABLE`, the Scrolled-Window always sizes itself to contain the entire work window, which nullifies the need for an automatic ScrolledWindow. Like any other widget, the only time that a ScrolledWindow should change size is when the parent resizes it, presumably for one of the following reasons:

- The shell has been resized.

- The ScrolledWindow is a child of a PanedWindow that the user has resized.

- Adjacent, sibling widgets have been resized, added, removed, etc.

- Application-controlled changes in widget size have been made.

The default size of the ScrolledWindow is never the same size as the work area, unless it's a coincidence.† The default size is not very useful, so you should probably specify the

---

† The internals to the ScrolledWindow widget happen to set the width and height to 100 pixels, although this fact is not officially documented by OSF.

XmNwidth and XmNheight resources for a ScrolledWindow. A problem arises if you want the ScrolledWindow to initialize itself to the size of the work window and have it be in automatic scrolling mode. To make the ScrolledWindow the same size as the work window, you must use application-defined scrolling.

For automatic scrolling, the only thing left to decide is how you want the ScrollBars to be displayed if the work window dynamically grows or shrinks. There may be situations where the work window is the same size as or smaller than the clip window. In this case, you may not want to display the ScrollBars, since they are not needed. If so, you can set XmNscrollBarDisplayPolicy to XmAS_NEEDED. If you always want the ScrollBars to be visible, whether or not they are needed, you can set the resource to XmSTATIC. Some people prefer static ScrollBars, so that consistency is maintained in the interface; having ScrollBars appear and disappear frequently may be confusing. Perhaps the best thing to do is to allow the user to specify the XmNscrollBarDisplayPolicy. You can always set your preference in the application defaults file, as shown below:

```
*XmScrolledWindow.scrollBarDisplayPolicy: static
```

9.2.2 Application-defined Scrolling

In the application-defined scrolling mode, XmNscrollingPolicy is set to Xm-APPLICATION_DEFINED. In this case, the work window must be the same size as the clip window, so the size of the work window is set by the toolkit. As a result, the XmNvisual-Policy resource has the value of XmVARIABLE, which indicates that the work window grows and shrinks with the ScrolledWindow. Since the two windows are the same size, the ScrolledWindow doesn't need to have a clip window, so it doesn't create one.

Because application-defined scrolling implies that you are responsible for the creation and management of the ScrollBars, the toolkit forces the XmNscrollBarDisplayPolicy to XmSTATIC. which means that the ScrolledWindow always displays the ScrollBars if they are managed. Since the ScrolledWindow cannot know the size of the entire data, it cannot automate the visibility of the ScrollBars. If you want your application to emulate the Xm-AS_NEEDED behavior, you must monitor the size of the ScrolledWindow and the work area and manage the ScrollBars manually.

9.2.3 Additional Resources

Another ScrolledWindow resource is the XmNworkWindow, which is used to identify the widget that acts as the ScrolledWindow's work window. A ScrolledWindow can have only one work window and a work window can be associated with only one ScrolledWindow. In other words, you cannot assign the same widget ID to multiple ScrolledWindows to get multiple views into the same object. There are ways of achieving this effect, though, that will become apparent as we go through the chapter.

The XmNclipWindow resource specifies the widget ID for the clip window. This resource is read-only, so it is illegal to set the clip window manually or to reset it to NULL. For practical purposes, this resource should be left alone. The XmNverticalScrollBar and

`XmNhorizontalScrollBar` resources specify the widget IDs of the ScrollBars in the ScrolledWindow. These resources allow you to set and retrieve the ScrollBars, which is useful for monitoring scrolling actions and setting up application-defined scrolling. Like any other manager, the ScrolledWindow also has resources that control the margin height and width and other visual attributes.

9.2.4 An Automatic ScrolledWindow Example

Automatic scrolling is the simpler of the two types of scrolling policies available. Fortunately, it is also the more common of the two. You shouldn't let this simplicity sway you too much, though, as it is a common design error for programmers to use the automatic scrolling mechanisms for designs that are better suited to the application-defined model. On the other hand, if you merely want to monitor scrolling without necessarily controlling it, you can install your own callback routines on the ScrollBars in an automatic ScrolledWindow, as we'll describe in the next section

In automatic mode, a ScrolledWindow automatically creates its own ScrollBars and handles their callback procedures to position the work window in the clip window. All of the examples that use ScrolledWindows in the rest of the chapters in this book (such as those in Chapter 4, *The Main Window*, and Chapter 10, *The DrawingArea Widget*) use the automatic scrolling mode. The only exceptions are the ScrolledList and ScrolledText objects, but the List and Text widgets handle application-defined scrolling internally.

Example 9-1 shows a large panel of Labels, ToggleButtons, and Text widgets that are arranged in a collection of Form and RowColumn widgets and managed by a Scrolled-Window widget.†

Example 9-1. The getusers.c program

```
/* getusers.c -- demonstrate a simple ScrolledWindow by showing
 * how it can manage a RowColumn that contains a vertical stack of
 * Form widgets, each of which contains a Toggle, two Labels and
 * a Text widget.  The program fills the values of the widgets
 * using various pieces of information from the password file.
 * Note: there are no callback routines associated with any of the
 * widgets created here -- this is for demonstration purposes only.
 */
#include <Xm/PushBG.h>
#include <Xm/LabelG.h>
#include <Xm/ToggleB.h>
#include <Xm/ScrolledW.h>
#include <Xm/RowColumn.h>
#include <Xm/Form.h>
#include <Xm/Text.h>
#include <pwd.h>

typedef struct {
    String      login;
    int         uid;
```

---

†`XtSetLanguageProc()` is only available in X11R5; there is no corresponding function in X11R4.

Example 9-1. The getusers.c program (continued)

```
    String      name;
    String      homedir;
} UserInfo;

/* use getpwent() to read data in the password file to store
 * information about all the users on the system.  The list is
 * a dynamically grown array, the last of which has a NULL login.
 */
UserInfo *
getusers()
{
    /* extern struct *passwd getpwent(); */
    extern char *strcpy();
    struct passwd *pw;
    UserInfo *users = NULL;
    int n;

    setpwent();

    /* getpwent() returns NULL when there are no more users */
    for (n = 0; pw = getpwent(); n++) {
        /* reallocate the pointer to contain one more entry.  You may choose
         * to optimize by adding 10 entries at a time, or perhaps more?
         */
        users = (UserInfo *) XtRealloc (users, (n+1) * sizeof (UserInfo));
        users[n].login = strcpy (XtMalloc
            (strlen (pw->pw_name)+1), pw->pw_name);
        users[n].name = strcpy (XtMalloc
            (strlen (pw->pw_gecos)+1), pw->pw_gecos);
        users[n].homedir = strcpy (XtMalloc
            (strlen (pw->pw_dir)+1), pw->pw_dir);
        users[n].uid = pw->pw_uid;
    }
    /* allocate one more item and set its login string to NULL */
    users = (UserInfo *) XtRealloc (users, (n+1) * sizeof (UserInfo));
    users[n].login = NULL;
    endpwent();
    return users; /* return new array */
}

main(argc, argv)
int argc;
char *argv[];
{
    Widget toplevel, sw, main_rc, form, toggle;
    XtAppContext app;
    UserInfo *users;

    XtSetLanguageProc (NULL, NULL, NULL);

    toplevel = XtVaAppInitialize (&app, "Demos", NULL, 0,
        &argc, argv, NULL, NULL);

    /* Create a 500x300 scrolled window.  This value is arbitrary,
     * but happens to look good initially.  It is resizable by the user.
     */
    sw = XtVaCreateManagedWidget ("scrolled_w",
        xmScrolledWindowWidgetClass, toplevel,
        XmNwidth,               500,
```

Example 9-1. The getusers.c program (continued)

```
        XmNheight,              300,
        XmNscrollingPolicy, XmAUTOMATIC,
        NULL);

    /* RowColumn is the work window for the widget */
    main_rc = XtVaCreateWidget ("main_rc", xmRowColumnWidgetClass, sw, NULL);
    /* load the users from the passwd file */
    if (!(users = getusers())) {
        perror ("Can't read user data info");
        exit (1);
    }
    /* for each login entry found in the password file, create a
     * form containing a toggle button, two labels and a text widget.
     */
    while (users->login) { /* NULL login terminates list */
        char uid[8];
        form = XtVaCreateWidget (NULL, xmFormWidgetClass, main_rc, NULL);
        XtVaCreateManagedWidget (users->login, xmToggleButtonWidgetClass, form,
            XmNalignment,           XmALIGNMENT_BEGINNING,
            XmNtopAttachment,       XmATTACH_FORM,
            XmNbottomAttachment,    XmATTACH_FORM,
            XmNleftAttachment,      XmATTACH_FORM,
            XmNrightAttachment,     XmATTACH_POSITION,
            XmNrightPosition,       15,
            NULL);
        sprintf (uid, "%d", users->uid);
        XtVaCreateManagedWidget (uid, xmLabelGadgetClass, form,
            XmNalignment,           XmALIGNMENT_END,
            XmNtopAttachment,       XmATTACH_FORM,
            XmNbottomAttachment,    XmATTACH_FORM,
            XmNleftAttachment,      XmATTACH_POSITION,
            XmNleftPosition,        15,
            XmNrightAttachment,     XmATTACH_POSITION,
            XmNrightPosition,       20,
            NULL);
        XtVaCreateManagedWidget (users->name, xmLabelGadgetClass, form,
            XmNalignment,           XmALIGNMENT_BEGINNING,
            XmNtopAttachment,       XmATTACH_FORM,
            XmNbottomAttachment,    XmATTACH_FORM,
            XmNleftAttachment,      XmATTACH_POSITION,
            XmNleftPosition,        20,
            XmNrightAttachment,     XmATTACH_POSITION,
            XmNrightPosition,       50,
            NULL);
        /* Although the home directory is readonly, it may be longer
         * than expected, so don't use a Label widget.  Use a Text widget
         * so that left-right scrolling can take place.
         */
        XtVaCreateManagedWidget (users->homedir, xmTextWidgetClass, form,
            XmNeditable,            False,
            XmNcursorPositionVisible, False,
            XmNtopAttachment,       XmATTACH_FORM,
            XmNbottomAttachment,    XmATTACH_FORM,
            XmNleftAttachment,      XmATTACH_POSITION,
            XmNleftPosition,        50,
            XmNrightAttachment,     XmATTACH_FORM,
```

Example 9-1. The getusers.c program (continued)

```
            XmNvalue,                users->homedir,
            NULL);
        XtManageChild (form);
        users++;
    }
    XtManageChild (main_rc);

    XtRealizeWidget (toplevel);
    XtAppMainLoop (app);
}
```

Those of you who are familiar with UNIX programming techniques should find the use of
getpwent() and endpwent() quite familiar. If you are not aware of these functions,
you should consult the documentation for your UNIX system. In short, they can be used to
return information about the contents of the password file (typically */etc/passwd*), which contains information about all of the users on the system. The first call to getpwent() opens
the password file and returns a data structure describing the first entry. Subsequent calls
return consecutive entries. When the entries have been exhausted, getpwent() returns
NULL and endpwent() closes the password file. In Example 9-1, the information from the
password file is represented using ToggleButtons, Labels, and Text widgets, as shown in Figure 9-2.

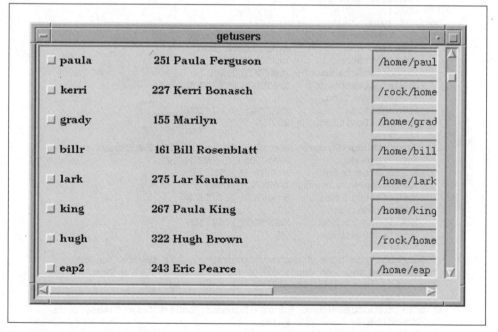

Figure 9-2. Output of getusers.c

The components in the program do not have any functionality; the program is used solely to
demonstrate how panels of arbitrary widgets can be displayed in a ScrolledWindow. The
widget hierarchy is irrelevant to the operation of the ScrolledWindow. In this particular case,

the ScrolledWindow is a child of the top-level shell. We could have used a MainWindow widget in place of a ScrolledWindow; these two components are interchangeable because the MainWindow is subclassed from the ScrolledWindow. See Chapter 4, *The Main Window*, for more details on how the MainWindow widget fits into the design of an application.

We used arbitrary values for the width and height of the ScrolledWindow; they were chosen because they seemed to work best. If you are using a ScrolledWindow with a number of other widgets in an interface, you do not need to specify an initial size for the Scrolled-Window. Since the ScrolledWindow is extremely flexible, you can allow its parent or its siblings to control its size. ScrolledWindows work well with PanedWindows because they can be adjusted easily. However, the ScrolledWindow does not have a sensible default size, so you should provide an initial geometry if the ScrolledWindow is going to control its own size. In this case, the size that you choose for the widget should be based on the aesthetics of the data that is being displayed.

In the example, the child of the ScrolledWindow is the main_rc widget, which is a Row-Column that contains all of the children that represent the password file information. After getusers() is called, the program loops through each item in the array of UserInfo structures and creates a Form widget that contains a ToggleButton, two Labels, and a Text widget. All of the Forms are stacked vertically on top of one another in the RowColumn. Once complete, the user can scroll around and access any of the elements without the application having to support any of the scrolling mechanisms because they are completely automated by the toolkit. In most cases, an application does not need to do anything other than what we described in this section to take advantage of automatic scrolling.

9.3 Working Directly With ScrollBars

The ScrollBar is the backbone of the ScrolledWindow. Although the ScrollBar is a stand-alone widget that can be created and manipulated without being the child of a Scrolled-Window, we are not going to discuss this usage because it is not consistent with the *Motif Style Guide*. The kinds of things that you can do with a ScrollBar individually are no more interesting than the sorts of things that you can do with them as children of Scrolled-Windows, anyway. We are going to discuss how to control a ScrollBar directly from an application in the context of a ScrolledWindow widget. This information is useful if you want to monitor scrolling, if you want to fine-tune the way that automatic scrolling is handled, or if you want to implement application-defined scrolling.

Before we begin, it is important to understand that the ScrollBar does *not* handle scrolling itself. The widget merely reports scrolling actions through its callback routines. It is up to the internals of an application or a widget to install callback procedures on the ScrollBar that adjust the work window appropriately. The ScrollBar manages its own display in accordance with scrolling actions, so you do not need to update the ScrollBar's display unless the underlying data of the object being scrolled changes. To change the display, you can set resources that are associated with the different elements of the ScrollBar. Figure 9-3 illustrates the design of a ScrollBar and identifies its elements. This figure represents a vertical ScrollBar; a ScrollBar can also be oriented horizontally. The appearance and behavior of a ScrollBar is directly related to the object that it scrolls. The relationship between the ScrollBar and the

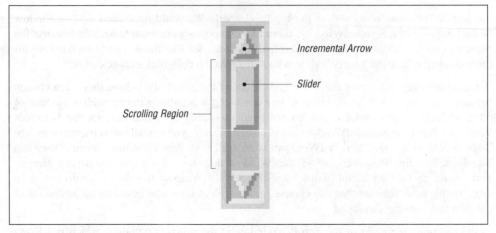

Incremental Arrow

Slider

Scrolling Region

Figure 9-3. Elements of a ScrollBar

object it scrolls is proportional, so that the size of the slider in the ScrollBar represents how much of the object that is being scrolled is visible in the clip window. The size of the object being scrolled is broken down into equally sized units; the size of the units is called the *unit length*. When the user clicks on one of the incremental arrows (also called directional arrows), the ScrollBar scrolls in the direction indicated by the arrow in unit increments. It is important to realize that the unit length is stored and interpreted internally by the object being scrolled; it is of no interest to the ScrollBar itself, since it does not affect the display of the ScrollBar. While this value is not set on the ScrollBar itself, it plays a key role in understanding how ScrollBars work.

All of the other resource values for the ScrollBar are measured in terms of the unit length. A Text widget might set its unit length for the vertical ScrollBar to the height of the tallest character in the widget's font set, plus some margin for whitespace on the top and bottom of the character. As a result, vertical scrolling adjusts the window so that the text is always displayed without lines being partially obscured. However, it is the Text widget's responsibility to know the unit length value. The unit length for the horizontal ScrollBar unit length might be the average width of the characters in the font that is being used.

The *value* of a ScrollBar is the offset, measured in unit lengths, of the data in the clip window from the object's origin. For example, if the top of the clip window displays the fourth line of text in a Text widget, the ScrollBar is said to have a value of 3, since it is offset from 0. Clicking and dragging the slider directly changes the ScrollBar's value to an absolute number; clicking on either of the directional arrows changes the ScrollBar's value incrementally; clicking in the scrolling region, but not on the slider itself changes the ScrollBar's value by page lengths. The value is measured in units, not pixels.

The *view length* is the size of the viewable area (clip window), as measured in unit lengths. The vertical ScrollBar for a Text widget that is displaying 15 lines of text would have a view length of 15. The horizontal ScrollBar's view length would be the number of columns that the clip window can display.

The *page length* is measured in unit lengths and is usually one less than the view length. If the user scrolls the window by a page increment, the first line from the old view is retained as the last line in the new view for visual reference because otherwise, the user might lose her orientation.

9.3.1 Resources

Figure 9-4 illustrates the relationship between the elements listed above and introduces the ScrollBar resources that correspond to these values.

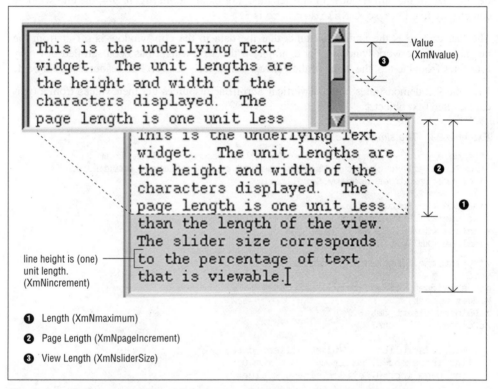

Figure 9-4. Conceptual relationship between a ScrollBar and the object it scrolls

The XmNincrement resource represents the number of units that the ScrollBar reports having scrolled when the user clicks on its incremental arrows. The value for XmNincrement in Figure 9-4 is 1 because each incremental scroll on the vertical ScrollBar should scroll the text one line. Internally, the Text widget knows that the number of pixels associated with XmNincrement is the height of a line. For an automatic ScrolledWindow, it is rare to set the resource to any value other than 1.

The XmNpageIncrement resource specifies the number of units that the ScrollBar should report having scrolled when the user moves the ScrollBar by a page. Again, the ScrollBar doesn't actually perform the scrolling, it just reports the scrolling action. However, the ScrollBar does use this value to calculate the new visual position for the slider within the scrolling area and to update its display. The application can use this value, multiplied by pixels-per-unit, to determine the new data to display in the work window.

The XmNmaximum resource is the largest size, measured in unit increments, that the object can have. For the Text widget shown above, the value for XmNmaximum is 9.† The XmNminimum resource is the smallest size, measured in unit increments, that the object will ever have. The XmNsliderSize resource corresponds to the view length. The resource specifies the size of the clip window in unit lengths. For example, in Figure 9-4, the clip window can display five lines, so XmNsliderSize is 5.

The XmNvalue is the number of units that the data in the clip window is offset from the beginning of the work window. For example, if the Text widget has been scrolled down by four lines from the top, the value of the vertical ScrollBar's XmNvalue resource would be 4.

Example 9-2 demonstrates how the vertical ScrollBar resources get their values from a typical ScrolledText object.‡

Example 9-2. The simple_sb.c program

```
/* simple_sb.c -- demonstrate the Scrollbar resource values from
 * a ScrolledText object.  This is used as an introductory examination
 * of the resources used by Scrollbars.
 */
#include <Xm/ScrolledW.h>
#include <Xm/RowColumn.h>
#include <Xm/PushBG.h>
#include <Xm/Text.h>

/* print the "interesting" resource values of a scrollbar */
void
get_sb(widget, client_data, call_data)
Widget widget;
XtPointer client_data;
XtPointer call_data;
{
    Widget scrollbar = (Widget) client_data;
    int increment=0, maximum=0, minimum=0;
    int page_incr=0, slider_size=0, value=0;

    XtVaGetValues (scrollbar,
        XmNincrement,     &increment,
        XmNmaximum,       &maximum,
        XmNminimum,       &minimum,
        XmNpageIncrement, &page_incr,
        XmNsliderSize,    &slider_size,
        XmNvalue,         &value,
        NULL);
```

---

† The Motif Text widget sets its horizontal ScrollBar's XmNmaximum to the number of characters in its widest visible line, rather than the widest of all of its lines.

‡ XtSetLanguageProc() is only available in X11R5; there is no corresponding function in X11R4.

Example 9-2. The simple_sb.c program (continued)

```
    printf ("increment=%d, max=%d, min=%d, page=%d, slider=%d, value=%d\n",
        increment, maximum, minimum, page_incr, slider_size, value);
}

main(argc, argv)
int argc;
char *argv[];
{
    Widget          toplevel, rowcol, text_w, pb, sb;
    XtAppContext    app;
    Arg             args[10];
    int             n = 0;

    XtSetLanguageProc (NULL, NULL, NULL);

    toplevel = XtVaAppInitialize (&app, "Demos",
        NULL, 0, &argc, argv, NULL, NULL);

    /* RowColumn contains ScrolledText and PushButton */
    rowcol = XtVaCreateWidget ("rowcol",
        xmRowColumnWidgetClass, toplevel, NULL);

    XtSetArg (args[n], XmNrows,            10); n++;
    XtSetArg (args[n], XmNcolumns,         80); n++;
    XtSetArg (args[n], XmNeditMode,    XmMULTI_LINE_EDIT); n++;
    XtSetArg (args[n], XmNscrollHorizontal,  False); n++;
    XtSetArg (args[n], XmNwordWrap,    True); n++;
    text_w = XmCreateScrolledText (rowcol, "text_w", args, n);
    XtManageChild (text_w);

    /* get the scrollbar from ScrolledWindow associated with Text widget */
    XtVaGetValues (XtParent (text_w), XmNverticalScrollBar, &sb, NULL);

    /* provide a pushbutton to obtain the scrollbar's resource values */
    pb = XtVaCreateManagedWidget ("Print ScrollBar Values",
        xmPushButtonGadgetClass, rowcol, NULL);
    XtAddCallback (pb, XmNactivateCallback, get_sb, sb);

    XtManageChild (rowcol);

    XtRealizeWidget (toplevel);
    XtAppMainLoop (app);
}
```

This program simply displays a ScrolledText object and a PushButton. The ScrolledText object does not contain any text by default; you can cut and paste some text into the object. The graphical output of the program is displayed in Figure 9-5.

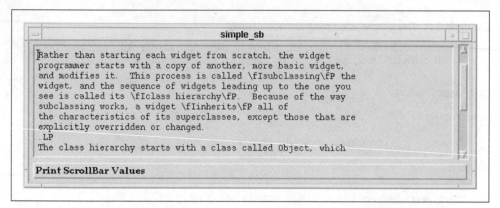

Figure 9-5. Output of simple_sb.c

When the PushButton is activated, it retrieves some resource values from the vertical Scroll-Bar of the Text widget's ScrolledWindow. These values are output to *stdout*. The following output shows some possible values for the different resources:

```
increment=1, max=12, min=0, page=9, slider=10, value=0
increment=1, max=12, min=0, page=9, slider=10, value=1
increment=1, max=25, min=0, page=9, slider=10, value=6
increment=1, max=25, min=0, page=9, slider=10, value=12
increment=1, max=25, min=0, page=9, slider=10, value=15
```

The value for XmNincrement is always 1, which indicates that the incremental arrow buttons scroll the text by one unit in either direction. The value for XmNmaximum changes according to the number of lines of text that there are in the window. The value of XmNminimum is always 0 because this object can have as few as zero lines of text.

The values for XmNsliderSize and XmNpageIncrement are 10 and 9, respectively. The values never changed because the ScrolledWindow was not resized. If it had been, the slider size and page increment values would have changed to match the new number of lines displayed in the window. The page increment is one less than the number of lines that can be displayed in the clip window, so that if the user scrolls by a page, the new view contains at least one of the previously-viewed lines for reference.

The value for XmNvalue varies depending on the line that is displayed at the top of the clip window. If the beginning of the text is displayed, XmNvalue is 0. As the user scrolls through the text, the value for XmNvalue increases or decreases, but it is always a positive value.

Incidentally, you can adjust these resource values to get some different results. For example, you could set the XmNincrement resource to 2 in order to modify the number of lines that are scrolled when the user selects the incremental arrows. However, you should not change these resources arbitrarily, as you could really confuse the user.

As mentioned at the beginning of this section, the most important thing to remember about the ScrollBar widget is that it does not cause any actual scrolling of the object in the work window. The widget merely reports scrolling activity through its callback routines. When scrolling occurs, it is the callback routines that are responsible for modifying the data in the work window, by adjusting elements or redrawing the image. The ScrollBar updates its own display according to the scrolling action. If the widget or the application that owns the callback routines fails to modify the display, the user will see an inconsistency between the ScrollBar display and the data in the clip window.

9.3.2 Orientation

Two ScrollBar resources that are closely related are `XmNorientation` and `XmNprocessingDirection`. These resources specify the horizontal or vertical orientation of the ScrollBar and its normal processing direction. The value for `XmNorientation` can be either `XmHORIZONTAL` or `XmVERTICAL`. When a ScrollBar is oriented horizontally, the normal processing direction for it is such that the minimum value is on the left and the maximum is on the right. When the orientation is vertical, the minimum is on the bottom and the maximum is on the top. You can change the processing direction using the `XmNprocessingDirection` resource. This resource can have the following values:

```
XmMAX_ON_LEFT
XmMAX_ON_RIGHT
XmMAX_ON_TOP
XmMAX_ON_BOTTOM
```

These values only need to be changed when the user's environment is such that the natural language for the locale is read from right-to-left. In this case, The `XmNscrollBarPlacement` resource for the ScrolledWindow needs to be changed to match the processing direction. This resource can have the following values:

```
XmTOP_LEFT
XmTOP_RIGHT
XmBOTTOM_LEFT
XmBOTTOM_RIGHT
```

9.3.3 Callback Routines

The callback routines associated with the ScrollBar are its only links into the internal mechanisms that actually scroll the data. You can use these callback routines in various contexts, depending on what you want to accomplish. For example, you can monitor scrolling in an automatic or semi-automatic ScrolledWindow, such as a ScrolledText or ScrolledList object. These two activities are identical when it comes to the implementation of what we are about to describe. You can also implement application-defined scrolling, which requires intimate knowledge of the internals of the object being scrolled.

There are different parts of a ScrollBar that the user can manipulate to cause a scrolling action. In fact, each part of the ScrollBar has a separate callback routine associated with it. These callback routines are used both to monitor automatic (or semi-automatic) scrolling and to implement application-defined scrolling. As with all Motif callbacks, the callback routines take the form of an `XtCallbackProc`. All of the ScrollBar callbacks pass a structure of type `XmScrollBarCallbackStruct` for the third parameter. This structure takes the following form:

```
typedef struct {
    int      reason;
    XEvent   *event;
    int      value;
    int      pixel;
} XmScrollBarCallbackStruct;
```

The `reason` field specifies the scrolling action performed by the user. Each callback has a corresponding reason that indicates the action. Table 9-1 lists the callback name, reason, and scrolling action for each ScrollBar callback resource.

Table 9-1. Callback Resources for the ScrollBar Widget

Resource Name	Reason	Action
XmNincrementCallback	XmCR_INCREMENT	Top or right directional arrow clicked
XmNdecrementCallback	XmCR_DECREMENT	Bottom or left directional arrow clicked
XmNpageIncrementCallback	XmCR_PAGE_INCREMENT	Area above or right of slider clicked
XmNpageDecrementCallback	XmCR_PAGE_DECREMENT	Area below or left of slider clicked
XmNtoTopCallback	XmCR_TO_TOP	Top or right directional arrow CTRL-clicked
XmNtoBottomCallback	XmCR_TO_BOTTOM	Bottom or left directional arrow CTRL-clicked
XmNdragCallback	XmCR_DRAG	Slider dragged
XmNvalueChangedCallback	XmCR_VALUE_CHANGED	Value changed (see explanation)

The scrolling action that invokes the various increment and decrement callbacks depends on the value of the `XmNprocessingDirection` resource; the table shows the actions for a left-to-right environment. The `XmNvalueChangedCallback` is invoked when the user releases the mouse button after dragging the slider. The callback is also invoked for any of the other scrolling actions if the corresponding callback resource is not set, with the exception of the `XmNdragCallback`. This feature is convenient for cases where you are handling your own scrolling and you are not concerned with the type of scrolling the user invoked.

The `value` field of the callback structure indicates the new position of the ScrollBar. This value can range from `XmNminimum` to `XmNmaximum`. The `pixel` field indicates the *x* or *y* coordinate of the mouse location relative to the origin of the ScrollBar for the `XmNtoTop-Callback`, `XmNtoBottomCallback`, and `XmNdragCallback` routines. The origin is the top of a vertical ScrollBar or the left side of a horizontal ScrollBar, regardless of the value of `XmNprocessingDirection`.

Example 9-3 demonstrates how a callback routine can be hooked up to each of the callback resources to allow you to monitor the scrolling in a List widget more precisely. For Text and List widgets, you really should not be using the callback routines to change the default scrolling behavior.†

Example 9-3. The monitor_sb.c program

```
/* monitor_sb.c -- demonstrate the ScrollBar callback routines by
 * monitoring the ScrollBar for a ScrolledList.  Functionally, this
 * program does nothing.  However, by tinkering with the Scrolled
 * List and watching the output from the ScrollBar's callback routine,
 * you'll see some interesting behavioral patterns.  By interacting
 * with the *List* widget to cause scrolling, the ScrollBar's callback
 * routine is never called.  Thus, monitoring the scrolling actions
 * of a ScrollBar should not be used to keep tabs on exactly when
 * the ScrollBar's value changes!
 */
#include <Xm/List.h>

/* print the interesting resource values of a scrollbar */
void
scroll_action(scrollbar, client_data, call_data)
Widget scrollbar;
XtPointer client_data;
XtPointer call_data;
{
    XmScrollBarCallbackStruct *cbs =
        (XmScrollBarCallbackStruct *) call_data;

    printf ("cbs->reason: %s, cbs->value = %d, cbs->pixel = %d\n",
        cbs->reason == XmCR_DRAG? "drag" :
        cbs->reason == XmCR_VALUE_CHANGED? "value changed" :
        cbs->reason == XmCR_INCREMENT? "increment" :
        cbs->reason == XmCR_DECREMENT? "decrement" :
        cbs->reason == XmCR_PAGE_INCREMENT? "page increment" :
        cbs->reason == XmCR_PAGE_DECREMENT? "page decrement" :
        cbs->reason == XmCR_TO_TOP? "top" :
        cbs->reason == XmCR_TO_BOTTOM? "bottom" : "unknown",
        cbs->value, cbs->pixel);
}

main(argc, argv)
int argc;
char *argv[];
{
    Widget        toplevel, list_w, sb;
    XtAppContext  app;
    char *items = "choice0, choice1, choice2, choice3, choice4, \
                    choice5, choice6, choice7, choice8, choice9, \
                    choice10, choice11, choice12, choice13, choice14";

    XtSetLanguageProc (NULL, NULL, NULL);

    toplevel = XtAppInitialize(&app, "Demos",
        NULL, 0, &argc, argv, NULL, NULL, 0);
```

---

†XtSetLanguageProc() is only available in X11R5; there is no corresponding function in X11R4.

Example 9-3. The monitor_sb.c program (continued)

```
    list_w = XmCreateScrolledList (toplevel, "list_w", NULL, 0);
    XtVaSetValues (list_w,
        /* Rather than convert the entire list of items into an array
         * of compound strings, let's just let Motif's type converter
         * do it for us and save lots of effort (altho not much time).
         */
        XtVaTypedArg, XmNitems, XmRString, items, strlen (items)+1,
        XmNitemCount, 15,
        XmNvisibleItemCount, 5,
        NULL);
    XtManageChild (list_w);

    /* get the scrollbar from ScrolledWindow associated with Text widget */
    XtVaGetValues (XtParent (list_w), XmNverticalScrollBar, &sb, NULL);
    XtAddCallback (sb, XmNvalueChangedCallback, scroll_action, NULL);
    XtAddCallback (sb, XmNdragCallback, scroll_action, NULL);
    XtAddCallback (sb, XmNincrementCallback, scroll_action, NULL);
    XtAddCallback (sb, XmNdecrementCallback, scroll_action, NULL);
    XtAddCallback (sb, XmNpageIncrementCallback, scroll_action, NULL);
    XtAddCallback (sb, XmNpageDecrementCallback, scroll_action, NULL);
    XtAddCallback (sb, XmNtoTopCallback, scroll_action, NULL);
    XtAddCallback (sb, XmNtoBottomCallback, scroll_action, NULL);

    XtRealizeWidget (toplevel);
    XtAppMainLoop (app);
}
```

The program displays a simple ScrolledList that contains 15 entries, as shown in Figure 9-6.

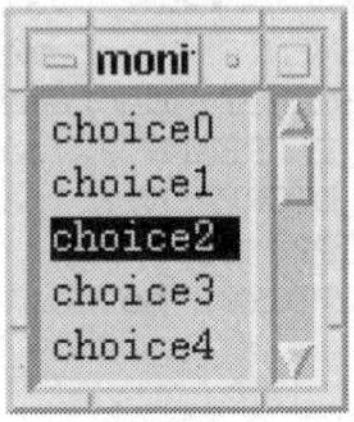

Figure 9-6. Output of monitor_sb.c

The entries in the List are not important; the way that the ScrollBar reacts to the user's interaction is what is interesting. The following output shows what happens when the user scrolls the List:

```
    cbs->reason: increment, cbs->value = 1, cbs->pixel = 0
    cbs->reason: page increment, cbs->value = 5, cbs->pixel = 0
    cbs->reason: drag, cbs->value = 6, cbs->pixel = 46
    cbs->reason: drag, cbs->value = 7, cbs->pixel = 50
    cbs->reason: value changed, cbs->value = 7, cbs->pixel = 50
    cbs->reason: decrement, cbs->value = 6, cbs->pixel = 0
    cbs->reason: top, cbs->value = 0, cbs->pixel = 11
```

If you use the keyboard to select elements or scroll around in the list, you'll notice that the callbacks for the ScrollBar are not invoked because the List widget is taking all of the keyboard events from the ScrollBar. Like any other widget, the ScrollBar can receive keyboard events, and it even has translations to map certain key sequences to scrolling actions. However, the List widget sets XmNtraversalOn to False for the ScrollBar, so that the List can process its own keyboard actions, some of which scroll the window. The Text widget does the same thing with its ScrollBars. As a result, there is a limit to what you can accomplish by monitoring ScrollBar actions on semi-automatic scrolling objects like List and Text widgets.

9.4 Implementing True Application-defined Scrolling

In this section, we pull together what we've learned in this chapter and put it to work to implement application-defined scrolling. We are going to use an example that displays a large number of individual bitmaps in a ScrolledWindow, so that the user can view all of the bitmaps by scrolling the window. The intent is to make the appearance and functionality of the ScrolledWindow mimic the automatic scrolling mode as much as possible.

There are actually several ways to go about writing this program, depending on the constraints that we impose. The simplest method is to render each bitmap into one large pixmap and use that pixmap as the XmNlabelPixmap for a Label widget. The Label widget can then be used as the work window for an automatic ScrolledWindow. This design is similar to most of the other examples of ScrolledWindows used throughout the book. However, we want to add a constraint such that each incremental scrolling action causes the display to shift by one bitmap cell, so that the top and left sides of the viewport always show a full bitmap. In other words, no partially-displayed bitmaps are allowed. Furthermore, when the user drags the slider, we want the display to scroll in cell-increments, not pixel-by-pixel.

The constraints that we just described define the behavior that the List and Text widgets use for their own displays. Like those widgets, our example program has a conceptual unit size that is represented by the object being scrolled. For the Text and List widgets, the unit size is the height and width of the font used by the entries. For our bitmap viewer, the heights and widths of the bitmaps vary more dramatically than the characters in a font, so for consistency, the unit size is set to the largest of all of the bitmaps. The design of our program is based on the same principles used by the ScrolledWindow's automatic scrolling method. Only in this case, we are going to do the work ourselves. The reason that we need to use application-defined scrolling is that the automatic scrolling method cannot support the scrolling constraints described above; there is no way to change the number of pixels per scrolling unit with an automatic ScrolledWindow.

In our implementation, the work window is a DrawingArea widget whose size is constrained by the size of the viewport in the ScrolledWindow. Initially, the ScrolledWindow sizes itself to the size of the DrawingArea widget, but once the program is running, the size of the DrawingArea is changed by the ScrolledWindow as it is resized. The bitmaps are rendered into a large pixmap, which is rendered into the DrawingArea in connection with scrolling actions. The offset of the pixmap and how much of it is copied into the DrawingArea is controlled by the application, following the same algorithm that the ScrolledWindow uses in automatic scrolling mode. The only difference is that we can adjust for the pixels-per-unit value, whereas the automatic ScrolledWindow is only aware of single-pixel units.

Proper scrolling is not a particularly difficult problem to solve, as it only involves simple arithmetic. The real problem is handling the case where the user or the application causes the ScrolledWindow to resize, since this action changes all of the variables in the calculation. When resizing happens, the ScrolledWindow passes that resizing onto the DrawingArea widget, which must recalculate its size and update the ScrollBar resources so that the display and the graphic representation match. Basically, the program has to solve four independent problems:

1. Read the bitmaps and load them into a sufficiently large pixmap.

2. Create the ScrolledWindow, a DrawingArea widget, and two ScrollBars; the program must initialize each of these widgets' resources so that the ratio between their sizes and the size of the pixmap is consistent.

3. Set up a callback routine for the ScrollBars to respond to scrolling actions.

4. Provide a callback routine for the DrawingArea widget's XmNresizeCallback that updates all of the widgets' resources according to the new ratio between the widgets and the pixmap.

Although each of these problems has a simple solution, when combined the general solution becomes quite complex. Rather than trying to solve each problem individually, a well-designed application integrates the solutions to the problems into a single, elegant design. Example 9-4 demonstrates our implementation of the bitmap viewer. Although the program is quite long, you can follow along with the comments embedded in the code to understand what is going on.†

Example 9-4. The app_scroll.c program

```
/* app_scroll.c - Displays bitmaps specified on the command line.  All
 * bitmaps are drawn into a pixmap, which is rendered into a DrawingArea
 * widget, which is used as the work window for a ScrolledWindow.  This
 * method is only used to demonstrate application-defined scrolling for
 * the motif ScrolledWindow.  Automatic scrolling is much simpler, but
 * does not allow the programmer to impose incremental scrolling units.
 *
 * The bitmaps are displayed in an equal number of rows and columns if
 * possible.
 *
 * Example:
 *   app_scroll /usr/include/X11/bitmaps/*
 */

#include <stdio.h>
#include <strings.h>
#include <Xm/ScrolledW.h>
#include <Xm/DrawingA.h>
#include <Xm/ScrollBar.h>
```

---

†XtSetLanguageProc() is only available in X11R5; there is no corresponding function in X11R4.

Example 9-4. The app_scroll.c program (continued)

```
#ifdef max   /* just in case--we don't know, but these are commonly set */
#undef max   /* by arbitrary unix systems.  Also, we cast to int! */
#endif
/* redefine "max" and "min" macros to take into account "unsigned" values */
#define max(a,b)  ((int)(a)>(int)(b)?(int)(a):(int)(b))
#define min(a,b)  ((int)(a)<(int)(b)?(int)(a):(int)(b))

/* don't accept bitmaps larger than 100x100 .. This value is arbitrarily
 * chosen, but is sufficiently large for most images.  Handling extremely
 * large bitmaps would eat too much memory and make the interface awkward.
 */
#define MAX_WIDTH  100
#define MAX_HEIGHT 100

typedef struct {
    char *name;
    int len; /* strlen(name) */
    unsigned int width, height;
    Pixmap bitmap;
} Bitmap;

/* get the integer square root of n -- used to calculate an equal
 * number of rows and colums for a given number of elements.
 */
int_sqrt(n)
register int n;
{
    register int i, s = 0, t;
    for (i = 15; i >= 0; i--) {
        t = (s | (1L << i));
        if (t * t <= n)
            s = t;
    }
    return s;
}

/* Global variables */
Widget drawing_a, vsb, hsb;
Pixmap pixmap; /* used as the image for DrawingArea widget */
Display *dpy;
Dimension view_width = 300, view_height = 300;
int rows, cols;
unsigned int cell_width, cell_height;
unsigned int pix_hoffset, pix_voffset, sw_hoffset, sw_voffset;
void redraw();

main(argc, argv)
int argc;
char *argv[];
{
    extern char *strcpy();
    XtAppContext app;
    Widget toplevel, scrolled_w;
    Bitmap *list = (Bitmap *) NULL;
    GC gc;
    char *p;
    XFontStruct *font;
```

Example 9-4. The app_scroll.c program (continued)

```
    int i = 0, total = 0;
    unsigned int bitmap_error;
    int j, k;
    void scrolled(), expose_resize();

    XtSetLanguageProc (NULL, NULL, NULL);

    toplevel = XtAppInitialize (&app, argv[0], NULL, 0,
        &argc, argv, NULL, NULL, 0);
    dpy = XtDisplay (toplevel);

    font = XLoadQueryFont (dpy, "fixed");

    /* load bitmaps from filenames specified on command line */
    while (*++argv) {
        printf ("Loading \"%s\"...", *argv), fflush (stdout);
        if (i == total) {
            total += 10; /* allocate bitmap structures in groups of 10 */
            if (!(list = (Bitmap *) XtRealloc (list, total * sizeof (Bitmap))))
                XtError ("Not enough memory for bitmap data");
        }
        /* read bitmap file using standard X routine.  Save the resulting
         * image if the file isn't too big.
         */
        if ((bitmap_error = XReadBitmapFile (dpy, DefaultRootWindow (dpy),
                *argv, &list[i].width, &list[i].height, &list[i].bitmap,
                &j, &k)) == BitmapSuccess) {
            /* Get just the base filename (minus leading pathname)
             * We save this value for later use when we caption the bitmap.
             */
            if (p = rindex (*argv, '/'))
                p++;
            else
                p = *argv;
            if (list[i].width > MAX_WIDTH || list[i].height > MAX_HEIGHT) {
                printf ("%s: bitmap too big\n", p);
                XFreePixmap (dpy, list[i].bitmap);
                continue;
            }
            list[i].len = strlen (p);
            list[i].name = p;  /* we'll be getting it later */
            printf ("Size: %dx%d\n", list[i].width, list[i].height);
            i++;
        } else {
            printf ("Couldn't load bitmap: \"%s\": ", *argv);
            switch (bitmap_error) {
                case BitmapOpenFailed : puts ("Open failed."); break;
                case BitmapFileInvalid : puts ("Bad file format."); break;
                case BitmapNoMemory : puts ("Not enough memory."); break;
            }
        }
    }
    if ((total = i) == 0) {
        puts ("Couldn't load any bitmaps.");
        exit (1);
    }
    printf ("Total bitmaps loaded: %d\n", total);
    /* calculate size for pixmap by getting the dimensions of each. */
```

Example 9-4. The app_scroll.c program (continued)

```
    printf ("Calculating sizes for pixmap..."), fflush (stdout);
    for (i = 0; i < total; i++) {
        if (list[i].width > cell_width)
            cell_width = list[i].width;
        if (list[i].height > cell_height)
            cell_height = list[i].height;
        /* the bitmap's size is one thing, but its caption may exceed it */
        if ((j = XTextWidth (font, list[i].name, list[i].len)) > cell_width)
            cell_width = j;
    }
    /* compensate for font in the vertical dimension; add a 6 pixel padding */
    cell_height += 6 + font->ascent + font->descent;
    cell_width += 6;
    cols = int_sqrt (total);
    rows = (total + cols-1)/cols;

    printf ("Creating pixmap area of size %dx%d (%d rows, %d cols)\n",
        cols * cell_width, rows * cell_height, rows, cols);

    /* Create a single, 1-bit deep pixmap */
    if (!(pixmap = XCreatePixmap (dpy, DefaultRootWindow (dpy),
            cols * cell_width + 1, rows * cell_height + 1, 1)))
        XtError ("Can't Create pixmap");

    if (!(gc = XCreateGC (dpy, pixmap, NULL, 0)))
        XtError ("Can't create gc");
    XSetForeground(dpy, gc, 0); /* 1-bit deep pixmaps use 0 as background */
    /* Clear the pixmap by setting the entire image to 0's */
    XFillRectangle (dpy, pixmap, gc, 0, 0,
        cols * cell_width, rows * cell_height);
    XSetForeground (dpy, gc, 1); /* Set the foreground to 1 (1-bit deep) */
    XSetFont (dpy, gc, font->fid); /* to print bitmap filenames (captions) */

    /* Draw the grid lines between bitmaps */
    for (j = 0; j <= rows * cell_height; j += cell_height)
        XDrawLine (dpy, pixmap, gc, 0, j, cols * cell_width, j);
    for (j = 0; j <= cols * cell_width; j += cell_width)
        XDrawLine (dpy, pixmap, gc, j, 0, j, rows*cell_height);

    /* Draw each of the bitmaps into the big picture */
    for (i = 0; i < total; i++) {
        int x = cell_width * (i % cols);
        int y = cell_height * (i / cols);
        XDrawString (dpy, pixmap, gc, x + 5, y + font->ascent,
            list[i].name, list[i].len);
        XCopyArea (dpy, list[i].bitmap, pixmap, gc,
            0, 0, list[i].width, list[i].height,
            x + 5, y + font->ascent + font->descent);
        /* Once we copy it into the big picture, we don't need the bitmap */
        XFreePixmap (dpy, list[i].bitmap);
    }
    XtFree (list); /* don't need the array of structs anymore */
    XFreeGC (dpy, gc); /* nor do we need this GC */

    /* Create automatic Scrolled Window */
    scrolled_w = XtVaCreateManagedWidget ("scrolled_w",
        xmScrolledWindowWidgetClass, toplevel,
        XmNscrollingPolicy, XmAPPLICATION_DEFINED, /* default values */
```

ScrolledWindows and ScrollBars

Example 9-4. The app_scroll.c program (continued)

```
                XmNvisualPolicy,    XmVARIABLE,              /* specified for clarity */
            NULL);

        /* Create a drawing area as a child of the ScrolledWindow.
         * The DA's size is initialized (arbitrarily) to view_width and
         * view_height.  The ScrolledWindow will expand to this size.
         */
        drawing_a = XtVaCreateManagedWidget ("drawing_a",
            xmDrawingAreaWidgetClass, scrolled_w,
            XmNwidth,       view_width,
            XmNheight,      view_height,
            NULL);

        XtAddCallback (drawing_a, XmNexposeCallback, expose_resize, NULL);
        XtAddCallback (drawing_a, XmNresizeCallback, expose_resize, NULL);

        /* Application-defined ScrolledWindows won't create their own
         * ScrollBars.  So, we create them ourselves as children of the
         * ScrolledWindow widget.  The vertical ScrollBar's maximum size is
         * the number of rows that exist (in unit values).  The horizontal
         * ScrollBar's maximum width is represented by the number of columns.
         */
        vsb = XtVaCreateManagedWidget ("vsb", xmScrollBarWidgetClass, scrolled_w,
            XmNorientation, XmVERTICAL,
            XmNmaximum,     rows,
            XmNsliderSize,  min (view_height / cell_height, rows),
            XmNpageIncrement, max ((view_height / cell_height) - 1, 1),
            NULL);
        if (view_height / cell_height > rows)
            sw_voffset = (view_height - rows * cell_height) / 2;
        hsb = XtVaCreateManagedWidget ("hsb", xmScrollBarWidgetClass, scrolled_w,
            XmNorientation, XmHORIZONTAL,
            XmNmaximum,     cols,
            XmNsliderSize,  min (view_width / cell_width, cols),
            XmNpageIncrement, max ((view_width / cell_width) - 1, 1),
            NULL);
        if (view_width / cell_width > cols)
            sw_hoffset = (view_width - cols * cell_width) / 2;

        /* Allow the ScrolledWindow to initialize itself accordingly...*/
        XmScrolledWindowSetAreas (scrolled_w, hsb, vsb, drawing_a);

        /* use same callback for both ScrollBars and all callback reasons */
        XtAddCallback (vsb, XmNvalueChangedCallback, scrolled, XmVERTICAL);
        XtAddCallback (hsb, XmNvalueChangedCallback, scrolled, XmHORIZONTAL);
        XtAddCallback (vsb, XmNdragCallback, scrolled, XmVERTICAL);
        XtAddCallback (hsb, XmNdragCallback, scrolled, XmHORIZONTAL);

        XtRealizeWidget (toplevel);
        XtAppMainLoop (app);
    }

    /* React to scrolling actions.  Reset position of ScrollBars; call redraw()
     * to do actual scrolling.  cbs->value is ScrollBar's new position.
     */
    void
    scrolled(scrollbar, client_data, call_data)
    Widget scrollbar;
    XtPointer client_data;
```

Example 9-4. The app_scroll.c program (continued)

```
XtPointer call_data;
{
    int orientation = (int) client_data; /* XmVERTICAL or XmHORIZONTAL */
    XmScrollBarCallbackStruct *cbs =
        (XmScrollBarCallbackStruct *) call_data;

    if (orientation == XmVERTICAL) {
        pix_voffset = cbs->value * cell_height;
        if (((rows * cell_height) - pix_voffset) > view_height)
            XClearWindow (dpy, XtWindow (drawing_a));
    } else {
        pix_hoffset = cbs->value * cell_width;
        if (((cols * cell_width) - pix_hoffset) > view_width)
            XClearWindow (dpy, XtWindow (drawing_a));
    }
    redraw (XtWindow (drawing_a));
}

/* This function handles both expose and resize (configure) events.
 * For XmCR_EXPOSE, just call redraw() and return.  For resizing,
 * we must calculate the new size of the viewable area and possibly
 * reposition the pixmap's display and position offsets.  Since we
 * are also responsible for the ScrollBars, adjust them accordingly.
 */
void
expose_resize(drawing_a, client_data, call_data)
Widget drawing_a;
XtPointer client_data;
XtPointer call_data;
{
    Dimension new_width, new_height, oldw, oldh;
    Boolean do_clear = False;
    XmDrawingAreaCallbackStruct *cbs =
        (XmDrawingAreaCallbackStruct *) call_data;

    if (cbs->reason == XmCR_EXPOSE) {
        redraw (cbs->window);
        return;
    }
    oldw = view_width;
    oldh = view_height;

    /* Unfortunately, the cbs->event field is NULL, so we have to have
     * get the size of the drawing area manually.  A misdesign of
     * the DrawingArea widget--not a bug (technically).
     */
    XtVaGetValues (drawing_a,
        XmNwidth,   &view_width,
        XmNheight,  &view_height,
        NULL);

    /* Get the size of the viewable area in "units lengths" where
     * each unit is the cell size for each dimension.  This prevents
     * rounding error for the pix_voffset and pix_hoffset values later.
     */
    new_width = view_width / cell_width;
    new_height = view_height / cell_height;
```

Example 9-4. The app_scroll.c program (continued)

```
/* When the user resizes the frame bigger, expose events are generated,
 * so that's not a problem, since the expose handler will repaint the
 * whole viewport.  However, when the window resizes smaller, no
 * expose event is generated.  The window does not need to be
 * redisplayed if the old viewport was smaller than the pixmap.
 * (The existing image is still valid--no redisplay is necessary.)
 * The window WILL need to be redisplayed if:
 * 1) new view size is larger than pixmap (pixmap needs to be centered).
 * 2) new view size is smaller than pixmap, but the OLD view size was
 *     larger than pixmap.
 */
if ((int) new_height >= rows) {
    /* The height of the viewport is taller than the pixmap, so set
     * pix_voffset = 0, so the top origin of the pixmap is shown,
     * and the pixmap is centered vertically in viewport.
     */
    pix_voffset = 0;
    sw_voffset = (view_height - rows * cell_height)/2;
    /* Case 1 above */
    do_clear = True;
    /* scrollbar is maximum size */
    new_height = rows;
} else {
    /* Pixmap is larger than viewport, so viewport will be completely
     * redrawn on the redisplay.  (So, we don't need to clear window.)
     * Make sure upper side has origin of a cell (bitmap).
     */
    pix_voffset = min (pix_voffset, (rows-new_height) * cell_height);
    sw_voffset = 0; /* no centering is done */
    /* Case 2 above */
    if (oldh > rows * cell_height)
        do_clear = True;
}
XtVaSetValues (vsb,
    XmNsliderSize,     max (new_height, 1),
    XmNvalue,          pix_voffset / cell_height,
    XmNpageIncrement, max (new_height-1, 1),
    NULL);

/* identical to vertical case above */
if ((int) new_width >= cols) {
    /* The width of the viewport is wider than the pixmap, so set
     * pix_hoffset = 0, so the left origin of the pixmap is shown,
     * and the pixmap is centered horizontally in viewport.
     */
    pix_hoffset = 0;
    sw_hoffset = (view_width - cols * cell_width)/2;
    /* Case 1 above */
    do_clear = True;
    /* scrollbar is maximum size */
    new_width = cols;
} else {
    /* Pixmap is larger than viewport, so viewport will be completely
     * redrawn on the redisplay.  (So, we don't need to clear window.)
     * Make sure left side has origin of a cell (bitmap).
     */
```

Example 9-4. The app_scroll.c program (continued)

```
            pix_hoffset = min (pix_hoffset, (cols-new_width)*cell_width);
            sw_hoffset = 0;
            /* Case 2 above */
            if (oldw > cols * cell_width)
                do_clear = True;
        }
        XtVaSetValues (hsb,
            XmNsliderSize,    max (new_width, 1),
            XmNvalue,         pix_hoffset / cell_width,
            XmNpageIncrement, max (new_width-1, 1),
            NULL);

        if (do_clear) {
            /* XClearWindow() doesn't generate an ExposeEvent */
            XClearArea (dpy, cbs->window, 0, 0, 0, 0, True);
                                /* all 0's means the whole window */
        }
}

void
redraw(window)
Window window;
{
    static GC gc; /* static variables are *ALWAYS* initialized to NULL */
    if (!gc) { /* !gc means that this GC hasn't yet been created. */
        /* We create our own gc because the other one is based on a 1-bit
         * bitmap and the drawing area window might be color (multiplane).
         * Remember, we're rendering a multiplane pixmap, not the original
         * single-plane bitmaps!
         */
        gc = XCreateGC (dpy, window, NULL, 0);
        XSetForeground (dpy, gc, BlackPixelOfScreen (XtScreen (drawing_a)));
        XSetBackground (dpy, gc, WhitePixelOfScreen (XtScreen (drawing_a)));
    }
    if (DefaultDepthOfScreen (XtScreen (drawing_a)) > 1)
        XCopyPlane (dpy, pixmap, window, gc, pix_hoffset, pix_voffset,
            view_width, view_height, sw_hoffset, sw_voffset, 1L);
    else
        XCopyArea (dpy, pixmap, window, gc, pix_hoffset, pix_voffset,
            view_width, view_height, sw_hoffset, sw_voffset);
}
```

The bitmaps to be displayed are specified on the command line, as shown in the following command:

```
% app_scroll /usr/include/X11/bitmaps/*
```

The output of this command is shown in Figure 9-7. The program begins by loading the bit-maps into an array of Bitmap structures that are specially designed for this application. Since each bitmap can have a different size, we save all of the information about them for comparison after they are all loaded. At that time, the largest bitmap is found and its size is used as the cell size for the viewer. The pixmap is created with a single-plane (a bitmap), since color is not used to render the standard X11 bitmaps when they are created. This pix-map is used as a virtual work window; its contents are rendered into the real DrawingArea work window.

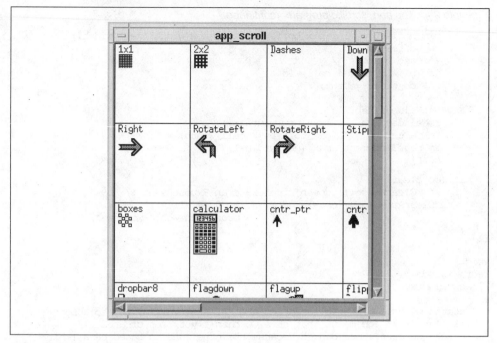

Figure 9-7. Output of app_scroll.c

After the bitmaps are loaded, the ScrolledWindow and DrawingArea are created. The
DrawingArea has XmNexposeCallback and XmNresizeCallback callbacks installed
so that the pixmap can be rendered or repositioned within the DrawingArea at any time.
Resizing does not change the pixmap, but it may cause its origin to be repositioned relative to
the DrawingArea widget. We create the ScrollBars explicitly, since they are not created
automatically when XmNscrollingPolicy is set to XmAPPLICATION_DEFINED. The
ScrollBars are created as children of the ScrolledWindow, as shown in the following fragment:

```
vsb = XtVaCreateManagedWidget ("vsb",
    xmScrollBarWidgetClass, scrolled_w,
    XmNorientation, XmVERTICAL,
    XmNmaximum,      rows,
    XmNsliderSize,   min (view_height / cell_height, rows),
    XmNpageIncrement, max ((view_height / cell_height) - 1, 1),
    NULL);
if (view_height / cell_height > rows)
    sw_voffset = (view_height - rows * cell_height) / 2;
```

The ScrollBars are initialized so that the XmNmaximum values are set to the number of rows
and columns in the pixmap. Similarly, XmNsliderSize is set to the number of bitmap
cells that can fit in the viewport in the horizontal and vertical dimensions. Internally, the
application knows how many pixels each scrolling unit represents, since there is no ScrollBar
resource for this value. The variables sw_hoffset and sw_voffset are used when the
pixmap is smaller than the actual ScrolledWindow. In this case, the variables indicate the

origin of the pixmap in the DrawingArea, so that the pixmap appears centered, as shown in Figure 9-8.

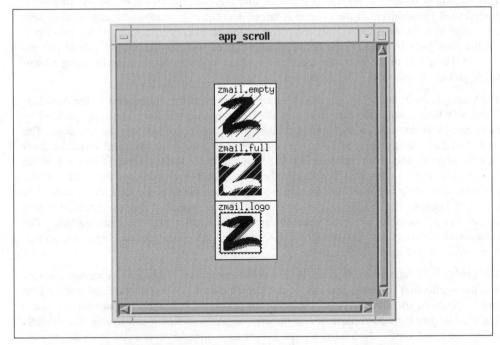

Figure 9-8. Output of app_scroll.c when the viewport is larger than the pixmap

The call to `XmScrolledWindowSetAreas()` initializes the ScrolledWindow appropriately. This function assigns the ScrollBars and the DrawingArea widget to internal variables within the ScrolledWindow, so that the widget functions properly. While this call is opaque for automatic scrolling, it must be done for application-defined scrolling.

The ScrollBars are assigned a callback routine for the `XmNvalueChangedCallback` and `XmNdragCallback` callbacks. The `scrolled()` routine handles all of the scrolling actions, including incremental and page scrolling, that cause the value of the ScrollBar to change. We pass the values `XmHORIZONTAL` and `XmVERTICAL` as `client_data`, so that the routine knows which of the two ScrollBars invoked it. The routine determines the portion of the pixmap that should be rendered in the DrawingArea by calculating offsets into the pixmap. These offsets are calculated by multiplying the value of the ScrollBar by the pixels-per-unit value for the pixmap.

Finally, the top-level widget is realized and the main loop is started. At this point, the DrawingArea is realized, so the `XmNexposeCallback` is activated, which causes the DrawingArea to draw itself and display the first image of the pixmap. The function `expose_resize()` handles both the Expose and ConfigureNotify (resize) events. The function determines which event was delivered by checking the `reason` field of the callback structure passed to the function. When the DrawingArea is resized, we need to adjust a number of resources so that the pixmap is scrolled properly. For Expose events, no recalculation of variables is necessary, so all we need to do is redraw the display using `redraw()`.

The position at which the pixmap is rendered into the DrawingArea's window is somewhat complicated to calculate. If the pixmap is larger than the clip window, the clip window acts as a view into the pixmap, so only a portion of the pixmap can be seen. If the pixmap is smaller than the clip window, the entire pixmap can be seen, so the pixmap should be centered in the middle of the viewable area. The application controls this behavior using a number of global variables.

The `view_width` and `view_height` variables represent the dimensions of the Scrolled-Window, which are also the dimensions of the DrawingArea window. The area specified by these values is the area of the pixmap that is going to be copied into the window. The `pix_hoffset` and `pix_voffset` variables represent the horizontal and vertical offsets into the pixmap when it is rendered into the DrawingArea. If the pixmap is larger than the clip window, these values are calculated in the `scrolled()` callback routine when the user performs a scrolling action. If the pixmap is smaller than the DrawingArea, these values are set to 0 because the origin of the pixmap is always visible. The `sw_hoffset` and `sw_voffset` variables are used when the pixmap is smaller than the DrawingArea. The values indicate the offsets into the DrawingArea where the entire pixmap is rendered so that it appears centered in the viewport.

The `redraw()` routine depends on these variables being set. In order to maintain the values, the application monitors the size of the DrawingArea. When a `ConfigureNotify` event occurs on the DrawingArea, the `expose_resize()` callback routine is invoked. The routine gets the new dimensions of the DrawingArea so that it can update the six variables mentioned above. Normally, we can get the new dimensions directly from the `event` field of the callback structure. However, the DrawingArea widget invokes the `XmNresize-Callback` from within the `Resize()` method, instead of from an action routine, so the callback does not have an `XEvent` structure associated with it.† Since the `event` field of the callback structure is set to `NULL`, we have to get the window's size in another way. We use `XtVaGetValues()`, as shown in the following code fragment:

```
XtVaGetValues (drawing_a,
    XmNwidth,  &view_width,
    XmNheight, &view_height,
    NULL);
```

Once we have the dimensions, we need to recalculate the value of the other four variables. Since our variables represent pixel values, while the ScrollBar resources that we need to set use an abstract unit size, we must convert between the two types of values using the `cell_width` and `cell_height` values. The variables `new_width` and `new_height` represent the new viewport width and height in ScrollBar units.

If the new viewport height exceeds the number of rows in the pixmap, we know that the height of the viewport exceeds the height of the pixmap. In this case, the value for `sw_voffset` is calculated to determine the offset that causes the pixmap to be centered

---

† All widget internals have methods that are invoked automatically by the X Toolkit Intrinsics and are not associated with the translation tables normally used to handle events. `Resize()` is one such method. See Volume Four, *X Toolkit Intrinsics Programming Manual*, for more information.

vertically in the viewport. Since the viewport needs to be completely redisplayed, we set the local variable `do_clear` to `True`. We use this variable instead of calling `XClear-Window()` directly because we may have to do it again later when we calculate the values for the horizontal ScrollBar. The value for `new_height` is going to be used to set the `XmN-sliderSize` for the vertical ScrollBar, so we make sure that it does not exceed its `XmN-maximum` value.

On the other hand, if the new viewport height does not exceed the total number of rows, we know that the pixmap is larger than the viewport vertically. The pixmap is not going to be centered in the DrawingArea, so `sw_voffset` is set to 0. `pix_voffset` is set to the minimum of its existing value and the difference between the total number of rows and the new height of the viewport. If the viewport used to be bigger than the pixmap, but is now smaller, we need to clear the window and do a complete redisplay. If the pixmap was bigger than the viewport and it still is, then we do not need to clear the window because the current view is still accurate. The different between these two cases is subtle and it is the sort of thing that you catch only when you test your program thoroughly.

After the calculations are performed, the application sets the `XmNsliderSize`, `XmN-value`, and `XmNpageIncrement` resources for the vertical ScrollBar. The exact same calculations are done for the horizontal dimension and the same resources are set on the horizontal ScrollBar. With these resources set, scrolling continues to function properly when the DrawingArea is resized. When `redraw()` is called, it uses the global variables to copy the relevant portion of the full pixmap directly into the DrawingArea. If the program is running on a color screen, the routine uses `XCopyPlane()` because the DrawingArea cannot create a 1-bit deep window on a color screen. (Motif widgets always create windows of the same depth as the screen on which they reside.) If the application is run on a monochrome screen, the routine uses `XCopyArea()`. We determine the depth of the screen using `Default-DepthOfScreen()`.

Incidentally, while we did not use it, `XmScrollBarSetValues()` could have been used to set the resources on the ScrollBars. This function takes the following form:

```
void
XmScrollBarSetValues(widget, value, slider_size, increment,
                                    page_increment, notify)
    Widget widget;
    int value;
    int slider_size;
    int increment;
    int page_increment;
    Boolean notify;
```

The *notify* parameter specifies whether you want the `XmNvalueChangedCallback` for the ScrollBar to be invoked. Using this interface is probably slightly faster than using the `XtVaSetValues()` method, but only by a small margin, so we chose to maintain consistency with our own style. The companion function for `XmScrollBarSetValues()` is `XmScrollBarGetValues()`. This function retrieves the values from the ScrollBar widget and takes the following form:

```
void
XmScrollBarGetValues(widget, value, slider_size, increment,
                                    page_increment)
    Widget widget;
```

```
int *value;
int *slider_size;
int *increment;
int *page_increment;
```

Before closing this section, let's examine what the Text and List widgets do and compare it with what we have done in Example 9-4. We stated earlier that while we mimic much of what these widgets do internally, the implementation is quite different. The major difference is that we are fortunate enough to have all of the bitmaps loaded into a large, statically-sized pixmap that we can render at will using the `redraw()` function. This function is clearly a convenience, since it simply calls `XCopyArea()` or `XCopyPlane()` to copy the pixmap into the DrawingArea using pre-calculated internal variables. The Text and List widgets do not have this luxury; they must redraw their respective data directly into the work windows each time they need to redisplay.

If we were to implement the bitmap viewer using this technique, we would have to move the functionality of the main `for` loop in `main()` into `redraw()` and calculate the location of each individual bitmap in the DrawingArea. This process is quite painstaking and very error-prone. If you do not take into account multiple exposures, exposure regions, and other low-level Xlib functionality, you might run into X performance issues. We didn't even take these issues into account in our program. For example, our `redraw()` routine completely repaints the entire window for every Expose event. Strictly speaking, repainting is inefficient and may not perform adequately for all applications, especially graphic-intensive ones. To avoid this problem, you could come up with a generic set of routines to handle exposures, so that of all your applications could use the same methodology, but that's the point of a toolkit.

Let's take another look at the PG&E scenario that we discussed at the beginning of the chapter. As you recall, the problem with that particular situation was that the database could retrieve 20% of the county (the work window), but the graphic resolution was such that only 10% of it could be displayed at one time (the viewport). The fundamental problem with the application-defined scrolling mode is that the work window cannot be a different size from the viewport. However, we can work around this problem by complying with the restriction that the work window and viewport are the same size, but we can use the enlarged pixmap idea from Example 9-4 to accomplish the task. Each database query can be converted and rendered into a sufficiently large pixmap, which can then be rendered into the work window as necessary. If the scrolling is small enough, another part of the pixmap can be rendered into the work window, instead of performing a completely new database lookup.

9.5 Working With Keyboard Traversal in ScrolledWindows

As we described in Chapter 8, *Manager Widgets*, manager widgets play a significant role in handling keyboard traversal mechanisms. As a manager, the ScrolledWindow supports keyboard traversal. However, one significant difference is that the widgets in a ScrolledWindow may not be visible at all times. In Motif 1.1, the toolkit does not provide a mechanism to allow keyboard traversal to widgets that are not visible. While it might be possible to implement this feature, it certainly would not be an easy task. By default, the ScrolledWindow only allows the user to traverse to widgets that are visible.

In Motif 1.2, there is a new callback for the ScrolledWindow that supports keyboard traversal in a ScrolledWindow. The `XmNtraverseObscuredCallback` is invoked when the user attempts to traverse to a widget that is not visible in a ScrolledWindow. If there is no routine specified for this callback, the keyboard traversal functionality is the same as in Motif 1.1. An application can use the callback to cause the ScrolledWindow to make a widget visible, so that it can receive the input focus. Example 9-5 shows the use of the `XmNtraverse-ObscuredCallback`.†

Example 9-5. The traversal.c program

```
/* traversal.c -- demonstrate keyboard traversal in a ScrolledWindow
 * using the XmNtraverseObscuredCallback.
 */
#include <Xm/PushB.h>
#include <Xm/ToggleB.h>
#include <Xm/ScrolledW.h>
#include <Xm/RowColumn.h>

main(argc, argv)
int argc;
char *argv[];
{
    Widget toplevel, sw, rc;
    XtAppContext app;
    void traverse();
    int i;
    char name[10];

    XtSetLanguageProc (NULL, NULL, NULL);

    toplevel = XtVaAppInitialize (&app, "Demos", NULL, 0,
        &argc, argv, NULL, NULL);

    sw = XtVaCreateManagedWidget ("scrolled_w",
        xmScrolledWindowWidgetClass, toplevel,
        XmNscrollingPolicy, XmAUTOMATIC,
        NULL);

    XtAddCallback (sw, XmNtraverseObscuredCallback, traverse, NULL);

    /* RowColumn is the work window for the widget */
    rc = XtVaCreateWidget ("rc",
        xmRowColumnWidgetClass, sw,
```

_____

† This example uses functionality that is new in Motif 1.2, so it only works with the 1.2 version of the Motif toolkit.

Example 9-5. The traversal.c program (continued)

```
            XmNorientation, XmHORIZONTAL,
                XmNpacking, XmPACK_COLUMN,
            XmNnumColumns, 10,
                NULL);

        for ( i = 0; i < 10; i++ ) {
            sprintf (name, "Toggle %d", i);
            XtVaCreateManagedWidget (name, xmToggleButtonWidgetClass, rc, NULL);
            sprintf (name, "Button %d", i);
            XtVaCreateManagedWidget (name, xmPushButtonWidgetClass, rc, NULL);
        }
        XtManageChild (rc);

        XtRealizeWidget (toplevel);
        XtAppMainLoop (app);
}

void
traverse(widget, client_data, call_data)
Widget widget;
XtPointer client_data;
XtPointer call_data;
{
    XmTraverseObscuredCallbackStruct *cbs =
        (XmTraverseObscuredCallbackStruct *) call_data;

    XmScrollVisible (widget, cbs->traversal_destination, 10, 10);
}
```

This program creates a bunch of ToggleButtons and PushButtons in a RowColumn widget that is the work area for a ScrolledWindow. The `traverse()` routine is installed as the `XmNtraverseObscuredCallback`. The `call_data` parameter is an `XmTraverse-ObscuredCallbackStruct`, which is defined as follows:

```
    typedef struct {
        int                  reason;
        XEvent               *event;
        Widget               traversal_destination;
        XmTraversalDirection direction;
    } XmTraverseObscuredCallbackStruct;
```

The `reason` field contains the value `XmCR_OBSCURED_TRAVERSAL`. The `traversal_destination` field specifies the widget that is to receive the input focus and `direction` specifies the direction of traversal. The `traverse()` routine calls `XmScrollVisible()` to make the `traversal_destination` widget visible. This routine takes the following form:

```
    void
    XmScrollVisible(scrollw, widget, hor_margin, ver_margin)
        Widget scrollw;
        Widget widget;
        Dimension hor_margin;
        Dimension ver_margin;
```

The `scrollw` parameter specifies the ScrolledWindow widget, while the `widget` parameter specifies the widget that is to be made visible. The `hor_margin` and `ver_margin` arguments indicate the margins that are used if the viewport of the ScrolledWindow needs to be adjusted to make the widget visible.† If you run the program in Example 9-5, you can use the arrow keys to traverse all of the widgets in the ScrolledWindow.

9.6 Summary

The ScrolledWindow provides a convenient interface for displaying large amounts of data when you have limited screen real estate. For most situations, the automatic scrolling mode is all that you really need. In this mode, a ScrolledWindow requires very little care and feeding. By installing callback routines on the ScrollBars, you can even monitor the scrolling actions. However, there are some drawbacks to the automatic scrolling mode: all of the data must be rendered into the work window widget and scrolling occurs in single-pixel increments. If the size of the work window that you need is prohibitively large or if you need to support scrolling in other than single-pixel increments, you must use application-defined scrolling.

As demonstrated in Example 9-4, there is quite a bit of work involved in supporting real application-defined scrolling because of the different states in the relationship between the size of the work window and the underlying data. You must be able to support not only the underlying data, but also the way it is rendered into the work window, the ScrollBars, and all of the auxiliary variables required for the scrolling calculations. And that work is just to support the scrolling functionality. When you introduce the complexity of a real application, there is a greater chance of a poor design model. The *xshowbitmap.c* program in the Appendix, *Additional Example Programs*, is fundamentally the same program as *app_scroll.c*, but it has been enhanced into more of a real-world program.

9.7 Exercises

The following exercises focus on the concepts and methods described in this chapter.

1. In Chapter 10, *The DrawingArea Widget*, the program *color_draw.c* used a Scrolled-Window to support a DrawingArea widget that allows the user to draw different colored lines. Although this program uses an automatic ScrolledWindow, the work window is constantly updated as new lines are drawn. However, the lines are actually drawn into a background pixmap, rather than into the drawing area. The pixmap is copied into the DrawingArea dynamically, which gives the illusion that the user is drawing directly into it. This method of indirection can be used to provide a way for the user to have two different views into the same pixmap. Write a program that uses two automatic Scrolled-Windows and two DrawingArea widgets to draw into a single pixmap.

---

† In early versions of the Motif 1.2 toolkit, there is a bug in `XmScrollVisible()` that may cause it to function incorrectly when the margins are set to any value other than 0.

2. The *getusers.c* example uses an automatic ScrolledWindow to display a manager widget that contains many widgets and gadgets. Modify the program to use application-defined scrolling, so that the scrolling increment for the vertical ScrollBar is the size of the height of one of the Forms. The Forms all have the same height.

10

The DrawingArea Widget

This chapter describes the Motif DrawingArea widget, which provides a canvas for interactive drawing. The chapter does not try to teach Xlib drawing, but rather it highlights, with numerous code examples, the difficulties that may be encountered when working with this widget. The chapter assumes some knowledge of Xlib. See Volume One, Xlib Programming Manual, for additional information.

In This Chapter:

10
The DrawingArea Widget

The DrawingArea widget provides a blank canvas for interactive drawing using basic Xlib drawing primitives. The widget does no drawing of its own, nor does it define or support any Motif user-interface design style. Since it is subclassed from the Manager widget class, the DrawingArea widget may also contain other widgets as children, although there is no regimented layout policy. In short, the DrawingArea is a free-form widget that you can use for interactive drawing or object placement when conventional user-interface rules do not apply.

The most intuitive use of the DrawingArea is for a drawing or painting program. Here, the user can interactively draw geometric objects and paint arbitrary colors. Another interesting application demonstrated at a recent trade show used a DrawingArea widget to display a map of the United States with dynamically-drawn line segments representing the flight paths taken by airplanes. The actual airplanes were represented by PushButton widgets displaying pixmaps. Each airplane icon moved dynamically along its flight path unless the user grabbed and moved it interactively in order to change the flight path. Both of these examples demonstrate how certain applications require visual or interactive interfaces that go beyond the scope of the structured interface provided by Motif.

In order to support the widest range of uses for the DrawingArea widget, the toolkit provides callback resources for exposure, configure (resize), and input (button and key presses) events. Each of these callbacks allows you to install very simple drawing routines without doing substantial event-handling of your own. Unfortunately, this level of event-handling support is usually insufficient for most robust applications. As a result, most applications install direct event handlers or action routines to manage user input. The free-form nature of the DrawingArea makes it one of the few Motif widgets where you can do handle events at this level without risking non-compliance with the *Motif Style Guide*. (Most Motif widgets either do not allow programmer-installed translations or (silently) accept only a few override translations for fear that you might inadvertently interfere with Motif GUI specifications.)

If you are using a DrawingArea as a manager widget, there are two important things to keep in mind: translation tables and widget layout management. As a Manager widget subclass, the DrawingArea inherits certain translation and action tables that pass events to gadget children and handle tab group traversal. Because of the inherited translations, you must be careful about application-specific translations that you may introduce into particular instances of the DrawingArea. If you are planning to use the DrawingArea to contain children and to have those children follow the standard Motif keyboard traversal motions, you must be careful not to override the existing translations.

However, if you need a manager widget in the conventional sense, you should probably choose something other than a DrawingArea widget, since the widget has no geometry management policy of its own. The DrawingArea should probably only be used to manage children when no structured widget layout policy is needed, as in the airline application from the trade show. In this situation, the widget assumes the dual responsibility of managing children and allowing for application-defined interaction. As a result, there are going to be some complexities and inconveniences with event handling, since the application is trying to take advantage of both aspects of the widget simultaneously.

10.1 Creating a DrawingArea Widget

Applications that wish to create DrawingArea widgets must include the file *<Xm/Drawing-A.h>*. To create a DrawingArea widget, you can use the following call:

```
Widget drawing_a;

drawing_a = XtVaCreateManagedWidget ("name",
    xmDrawingAreaWidgetClass, parent,
    resource-value-list,
    NULL);
```

The parent of a DrawingArea must be either some type of Shell or a manager widget. It is quite common to find a DrawingArea widget as a child of a ScrolledWindow or a Main-Window, since drawing surfaces tend to be quite large, or at least dynamic in their growth potential.

If the DrawingArea widget is to have children, you might want to follow the guidelines set forth in Chapter 8, *Manager Widgets*, about creating the widget in an unmanaged state. The widget can be managed with a call to XtManageChild() after its children have been created. We do not demonstrate this technique, since we are not going to use the widget as a traditional manager and there is not going to be a great deal of parent-child interaction involving geometry management.

10.2 Using DrawingArea Callback Functions

The DrawingArea widget provides virtually no visual resources and very few functional ones. The most important resources are those that allow you to provide callback functions for handling expose, resize, and input events. The DrawingArea is typically input-intensive and, unlike most of the other Motif widgets, requires the application to provide all of the necessary redrawing.

The callback routine for the XmNexposeCallback is invoked whenever an Expose event is generated for the widget. In this callback function, an application must repaint all or part of the contents of the DrawingArea widget. If an application does not redraw the contents of the widget, it appears empty, as the widget is cleared automatically. Similarly, the XmNresizeCallback is called whenever a ConfigureNotify event occurs as a result of the DrawingArea being resized. The generalized XmNinputCallback is invoked as a result of every keyboard and button event except button motion events.

As discussed in Chapter 2, *The Motif Programming Model*, callback routines are invoked by internal action routines that are an integral part of all Motif widgets. Translation tables are used to specify X event sequences that invoke the action routines. Action functions typically invoke the appropriate application callback functions associated with the widget's resources.

Most Motif widgets do not allow the application to override or replace their default translations; the input model that allows the application to conform to the Motif specifications is not to be overridden by the application. However, because of the free-form nature of the DrawingArea widget, you are free to override or replace the default translation tables used for event-handling and notification without non-compliant behavior. If you install your own translation tables, you can have your action routines invoke callback routines as is done by the existing DrawingArea actions, or you can have your action functions do the drawing directly. For even tighter control over event-handling, you can install event handlers at the X Toolkit Intrinsics level.

There are a number of techniques available for doing event management and we only demonstrate a few of them in this chapter. The technique you choose is a matter of personal preference and the intended extensibility of your application. Event handlers involve less overhead, but translations are user-configurable. Either approach provides more flexibility than using the default translation table and callback resources of the DrawingArea. See Volume Four, *X Toolkit Intrinsics Programming Manual*, for a detailed discussion of translation tables and action routines and how they are associated with callback functions.

10.2.1 Handling Input Events

Since the callback approach to event handling is the simplest, we'll begin by discussing that approach. Example 10-1 shows an extremely simple drawing program that associates a line drawing function with the XmNinputCallback resource. Pressing any of the pointer buttons marks the starting point of a line; releasing the button marks the endpoint. You can only draw straight lines. Even though the default translation table for the DrawingArea widget selects key events and these events are passed to the callback function, the callback function itself ignores them and thus key events have no effect.

To demonstrate the complications inherent in using the DrawingArea widget as a manager, the program also displays a PushButton gadget that clears the window. A single callback function, drawing_area_callback(), uses both the reason and the event fields of the XmDrawingAreaCallbackStruct to determine whether to draw a line or to clear the window.

This simple application draws directly into the DrawingArea widget; the contents of its window is not saved anywhere. The program does not support redrawing, since its purpose is strictly to demonstrate the way input handling can be managed using the XmNinput-Callback. If the window is exposed due to the movement of other windows, the contents of the window is not redrawn. A more realistic drawing application would need code to handle both expose and resize actions. The current application simply clears the window on resize to further illustrate that the DrawingArea does not retain what is in its window.†

---

† XtSetLanguageProc() is only available in X11R5; there is no corresponding function in X11R4.

Example 10-1. The drawing.c program

```
/* drawing.c -- extremely simple drawing program that introduces
 * the DrawingArea widget.  This widget provides a window for
 * drawing and some callbacks for getting input and other misc
 * events.  It's also a manager, so it can have children.
 * There is no geometry management, tho.
 */
#include <Xm/DrawingA.h>
#include <Xm/PushBG.h>
#include <Xm/RowColumn.h>

main(argc, argv)
int argc;
char *argv[];
{
    Widget toplevel, drawing_a, pb;
    XtAppContext app;
    XGCValues gcv;
    GC gc;
    void drawing_area_callback();

    XtSetLanguageProc (NULL, NULL, NULL);

    toplevel = XtVaAppInitialize (&app, "Demos", NULL, 0,
        &argc, argv, NULL,
        XmNwidth,  400,
        XmNheight, 300,
        NULL);

    /* Create a DrawingArea widget. */
    drawing_a = XtVaCreateWidget ("drawing_a",
        xmDrawingAreaWidgetClass, toplevel,
        NULL);
    /* add callback for all mouse and keyboard input events */
    XtAddCallback (drawing_a, XmNinputCallback, drawing_area_callback, NULL);

    /* Since we're going to be drawing, we will be using Xlib routines
     * and therefore need a graphics context.  Create a GC and attach
     * to the DrawingArea's XmNuserData to avoid having to make global
     * variable. (Avoiding globals is a good design principle to follow.)
     */
    gcv.foreground = BlackPixelOfScreen (XtScreen (drawing_a));
    gc = XCreateGC (XtDisplay (drawing_a),
        RootWindowOfScreen (XtScreen (drawing_a)), GCForeground, &gcv);
    XtVaSetValues (drawing_a, XmNuserData, gc, NULL);

    /* add a pushbutton the user can use to clear the canvas */
    pb = XtVaCreateManagedWidget ("Clear",
        xmPushButtonGadgetClass, drawing_a,
        NULL);
    /* if activated, call same callback as XmNinputCallback. */
    XtAddCallback (pb, XmNactivateCallback, drawing_area_callback, NULL);

    XtManageChild (drawing_a);
    XtRealizeWidget (toplevel);
    XtAppMainLoop (app);
}

/* Callback routine for DrawingArea's input callbacks and the
 * PushButton's activate callback.  Determine which it is by
```

Example 10-1. The drawing.c program (continued)

```
 * testing the cbs->reason field.
 */
void
drawing_area_callback(widget, client_data, call_data)
Widget widget;
XtPointer client_data;
XtPointer call_data;
{
    static Position x, y;
    XmDrawingAreaCallbackStruct *cbs =
        (XmDrawingAreaCallbackStruct *) call_data;
    XEvent *event = cbs->event;

    if (cbs->reason == XmCR_INPUT) {
        /* activated by DrawingArea input event -- draw lines.
         * Button Down events anchor the initial point and Button
         * Up draws from the anchor point to the button-up point.
         */
        if (event->xany.type == ButtonPress) {
            /* anchor initial point (i.e., save its value) */
            x = event->xbutton.x;
            y = event->xbutton.y;
        } else if (event->xany.type == ButtonRelease) {
            /* draw full line; get GC and use in XDrawLine() */
            GC gc;
            XtVaGetValues (widget, XmNuserData, &gc, NULL);
            XDrawLine (event->xany.display, cbs->window, gc, x, y,
                event->xbutton.x, event->xbutton.y);
            x = event->xbutton.x;
            y = event->xbutton.y;
        }
    }

    if (cbs->reason == XmCR_ACTIVATE)
        /* activated by pushbutton -- clear parent's window */
        XClearWindow (event->xany.display, XtWindow (XtParent (widget)));
}
```

The output of the program is shown in Figure 10-1. The callback routine that is used for the XmNinputCallback takes the form of a standard callback routine. The DrawingArea provides a XmDrawingAreaCallbackStruct for all of its callbacks. This structure is defined as follows:

```
typedef struct {
    int      reason;
    XEvent   *event;
    Window   window;
} XmDrawingAreaCallbackStruct;
```

The reason field identifies the type of occurrence that caused the callback to be invoked. For the XmNinputCallback, the value is XmCR_INPUT. The event field of the callback structure describes the event that caused the callback to be invoked.† The window

---

† In older versions of the Motif toolkit, the pointer may be NULL if reason is XmCR_RESIZE.

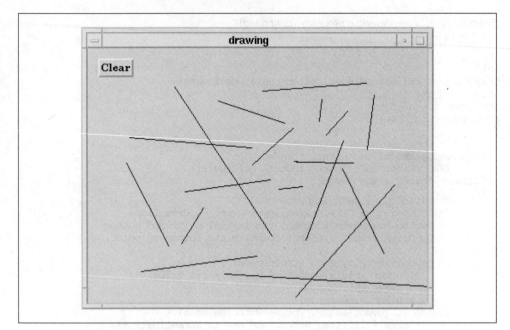

Figure 10-1. Output of drawing.c

field is the window associated with the DrawingArea widget—this is the same value returned by calling XtWindow() on the widget.

Since the event itself is passed in as part of the callback structure, we can look at the type field of the event for more information than is provided by the callback reason alone. (See Volume One, *Xlib Programming Manual*, for a detailed description of XEvent structures and how to use them.) In fact, since there are many possible events that can be associated with the reason XmCR_INPUT, you have to look at the event structure if you need any detail about what actually happened. Table 10-1 shows the possible event types for each of the DrawingArea callbacks.

Table 10-1. Callback Reasons and Event Types

Callback	Reason	Event Type(s)
XmNexposeCallback	XmCR_EXPOSE	Expose
XmNresizeCallback	XmCR_RESIZE	ConfigureNotify
XmNinputCallback	XmCR_INPUT	ButtonPress, ButtonRelease, KeyPress, KeyRelease

A common convention we've included in this program is the double use of the draw-ing_area_callback() function. This technique is known as *function overloading*, since the same function is used by more than one source. We are using the routine as the input callback for the DrawingArea widget, as well as the activate callback for the Push-Button gadget. Whenever the PushButton is activated, the callback function is invoked and passed an `XmPushButtonCallbackStruct` with the `reason` field set to `XmCR_ACTI-VATE`.

It is beyond the scope of this book to discuss at length or even introduce the use of Xlib; for that, see Volume One, *Xlib Programming Manual*. However, there are a couple of details concerning the use of Xlib functions that are noteworthy. For efficiency in use of the X protocol, Xlib drawing calls typically do not carry a lot of information about the drawing to be done. Instead, drawing characteristics such as the foreground and background colors, fill style, line weight, and so on, are defined in a graphics context (GC), which is cached in the X server. Any drawing function that wishes to use a particular GC must include the handle returned by a GC creation call.

If many different routines are going to use the same GC, the programmer should try to make the handle to it generally available. The natural tendency is to declare the GC as a global variable. However, as a program gets large, it is easy to get carried away with the use of global variables. As a result, programs tend to get overly complicated and decentralized. To avoid this problem, you can use the `XmNuserData` resource (inherited from the Manager widget class) as a temporary holding area for arbitrary pointers and values. Since this program is small, it may not be worth the overhead of a call to `XtGetValues()` to avoid a global variable. It is up to you if you want to use the `XmNuserData` resource; this particular example just shows one way of avoiding global variables.

If you play with the program a little, you will soon find that you can draw right through the PushButton gadget in the DrawingArea. Because gadgets do not have windows, the DrawingArea widget indiscriminately allows you to draw through any gadget children it may be managing. Similarly, activating the PushButton clears the DrawingArea window, but it does not repaint the PushButton. None of the manager widgets, including the DrawingArea, check if the user (or the application) is overwriting or erasing gadgets. Changing the Push-Button from a gadget to a widget solves the immediate problem. However, it is generally not a good idea to use a DrawingArea widget as both a drawing canvas and as a place to have user-interface elements such as PushButtons.

For conventional geometry management involving DrawingArea widgets, you have two choices. You can write your own geometry management routine (as demonstrated for BulletinBoard widgets in Section 8.3 in Chapter 8, *Manager Widgets*) or you can place the DrawingArea inside another manager that does more intelligent geometry management. The nice part about this alternative is that the other manager widgets are no more or less intelligent about graphics and repainting than the DrawingArea widget. They don't provide a callback for `Expose` events, but you can always add translations for those events, if you need them.

10.2.2 Redrawing a DrawingArea

In Example 10-1, when an `Expose` event or a `Resize` event occurs, the drawing is not retained and as a result the DrawingArea is always cleared. This problem was intentional for the first example because we wanted to focus on the use of the input callback routine.

However, when you use the DrawingArea widget, you must always be prepared to repaint whatever is supposed to be displayed in the widget at any time.

As you may already know, most X servers support a feature called *backing store*, which saves the contents of windows, even when they are obscured by other windows, and repaints them when they are exposed. When backing store is enabled and there is enough memory available for the server, X will repaint all damaged windows without ever notifying the application that anything happened. However, you should never rely on this behavior, since you never know if the X server supports backing store, or if it has enough memory to save the contents of your windows. All applications are ultimately responsible for redrawing their windows' contents whenever necessary.

For a painting application like that in Example 10-1, the easiest way to make sure that a window can be repainted whenever necessary is to draw both into the window and into an off-screen pixmap. The contents of the pixmap can be copied back into the window as needed. Example 10-2 demonstrates such a program. The offscreen pixmap is copied back to the window with XCopyArea() to redisplay the drawing when the XmNexposeCallback is called.†

Example 10-2. The draw2.c program

```
/* draw2.c -- extremely simple drawing program that demonstrates
 * how to draw into an off screen pixmap in order to retain the
 * contents of the DrawingArea widget.  This allows us to redisplay
 * the widget if it needs repainting (expose events).
 */
#include <Xm/DrawingA.h>
#include <Xm/PushBG.h>
#include <Xm/RowColumn.h>

#define WIDTH 400    /* arbitrary width and height values */
#define HEIGHT 300

Pixmap pixmap; /* used to redraw the DrawingArea */

main(argc, argv)
int argc;
char *argv[];
{
    Widget toplevel, drawing_a, pb;
    XtAppContext app;
    GC gc;
    void drawing_area_callback();

    XtSetLanguageProc (NULL, NULL, NULL);

    toplevel = XtVaAppInitialize (&app, "Demos", NULL, 0,
        &argc, argv, NULL,
        XmNwidth,   WIDTH,
        XmNheight, HEIGHT,
        NULL);

    /* Create a DrawingArea widget. */
    drawing_a = XtVaCreateWidget ("drawing_a",
```

---

†XtSetLanguageProc() is only available in X11R5; there is no corresponding function in X11R4.

Example 10-2. The draw2.c program (continued)

```
                xmDrawingAreaWidgetClass, toplevel,
                NULL);
        /* add callback for all mouse and keyboard input events */
        XtAddCallback (drawing_a, XmNinputCallback, drawing_area_callback, NULL);
        XtAddCallback (drawing_a, XmNexposeCallback, drawing_area_callback, NULL);

        gc = XCreateGC (XtDisplay (drawing_a),
                RootWindowOfScreen (XtScreen (drawing_a)), 0, NULL);
        XtVaSetValues (drawing_a, XmNuserData, gc, NULL);

        XSetForeground (XtDisplay (drawing_a), gc,
                WhitePixelOfScreen (XtScreen (drawing_a)));
        /* create a pixmap the same size as the drawing area. */
        pixmap = XCreatePixmap (XtDisplay (drawing_a),
                RootWindowOfScreen (XtScreen (drawing_a)), WIDTH, HEIGHT,
                DefaultDepthOfScreen (XtScreen (drawing_a)));
        /* clear pixmap with white */
        XFillRectangle (XtDisplay (drawing_a), pixmap, gc, 0, 0, WIDTH, HEIGHT);
        /* drawing is now drawn into with "black"; change the gc for future */
        XSetForeground (XtDisplay (drawing_a), gc,
                BlackPixelOfScreen (XtScreen (drawing_a)));

        /* add a pushbutton the user can use to clear the canvas */
        pb = XtVaCreateManagedWidget ("Clear",
                xmPushButtonGadgetClass, drawing_a,
                NULL);
        /* if activated, call same callback as XmNinputCallback. */
        XtAddCallback (pb, XmNactivateCallback, drawing_area_callback, NULL);

        XtManageChild (drawing_a);
        XtRealizeWidget (toplevel);
        XtAppMainLoop (app);
}

/* Callback routine for DrawingArea's input and expose callbacks
 * as well as the PushButton's activate callback.  Determine which
 * it is by testing the cbs->reason field.
 */
void
drawing_area_callback(widget, client_data, call_data)
Widget widget;
XtPointer client_data;
XtPointer call_data;
{
        static Position x, y;
        XmDrawingAreaCallbackStruct *cbs =
                (XmDrawingAreaCallbackStruct *) call_data;
        XEvent *event = cbs->event;
        Display *dpy = event->xany.display;

        if (cbs->reason == XmCR_INPUT) {
                /* activated by DrawingArea input event -- draw lines.
                 * Button Down events anchor the initial point and Button
                 * Up draws from the anchor point to the button-up point.
                 */
                if (event->xany.type == ButtonPress) {
                        /* anchor initial point (i.e., save its value) */
                        x = event->xbutton.x;
```

Example 10-2. The draw2.c program (continued)

```
            y = event->xbutton.y;
        } else if (event->xany.type == ButtonRelease) {
            /* draw full line; get GC and use in XDrawLine() */
            GC gc;
            XtVaGetValues (widget, XmNuserData, &gc, NULL);
            XDrawLine (dpy, cbs->window, gc, x, y,
                event->xbutton.x, event->xbutton.y);
            /* draw into the pixmap as well for redrawing later */
            XDrawLine (dpy, pixmap, gc, x, y,
                event->xbutton.x, event->xbutton.y);
            x = event->xbutton.x;
            y = event->xbutton.y;
        }
    }

    if (cbs->reason == XmCR_EXPOSE || cbs->reason == XmCR_ACTIVATE) {
        GC gc;
        if (cbs->reason == XmCR_ACTIVATE) /* Clear button pushed */
            widget = XtParent (widget); /* get the DrawingArea widget */
        XtVaGetValues (widget, XmNuserData, &gc, NULL);
        if (cbs->reason == XmCR_ACTIVATE) { /* Clear button pushed */
            /* to clear a pixmap, reverse foreground and background */
            XSetForeground (dpy, gc, WhitePixelOfScreen (XtScreen (widget)));
            /* ...and fill rectangle the size of the pixmap */
            XFillRectangle (dpy, pixmap, gc, 0, 0, WIDTH, HEIGHT);
            /* don't foreget to reset */
            XSetForeground (dpy, gc, BlackPixelOfScreen (XtScreen (widget)));
        }
        /* Note: we don't have to use WIDTH and HEIGHT--we could pull the
         * exposed area out of the event structure, but only if the reason
         * was XmCR_EXPOSE... make it simple for the demo; optimize as needed.
         */
        XCopyArea (dpy, pixmap, event->xany.window, gc,
            0, 0, WIDTH, HEIGHT, 0, 0);
    }
}
```

A frequent problem encountered in using the DrawingArea widget is the need to redraw after every `Resize` event. When you enlarge the DrawingArea window, an `Expose` event is automatically generated since more of the window becomes exposed. But, if you shrink the window, no `Expose` event is generated since no new part of the window is being exposed.

The reason why no `Expose` event is generated when you shrink a DrawingArea widget is deep inside Xlib. The bit gravity of a window indicates where new bits are placed automatically by X when a window is resized. If you resize a window larger, then the data in the window remains in the top-left corner and the application gets a `Resize` event and an `Expose` event. The `Expose` event just identifies the newly exposed area, not the entire window. If you make the window smaller, all of the data in the window gets pushed to the top left; there is no newly exposed area, so there is no `Expose` event.

The solution is to make the window forget about bit gravity, so every `Resize` event causes all of the bits to be cleared. As a result, the `Expose` event identifies the entire window as being exposed, instead of just the newly exposed region. This technique has the side effect of generating an `Expose` event even when the window is resized smaller.

There is no routine to set the bit gravity of a window individually. It can be set only with `XChangeWindowAttributes()`, as in the following code fragment:

```
XSetWindowAttributes attrs;
attrs.bit_gravity = ForgetGravity;
XChangeWindowAttributes (XtDisplay (drawing_area),
    XtWindow (drawing_area), CWBitGravity, &attrs);
```

Once you do this, the DrawingArea widget gets `Expose` events when you resize it to be smaller.

10.3 Using Translations on a DrawingArea

As mentioned earlier, it is generally permissible to override or replace the default translation table of the DrawingArea widget with new translations. The only potential problem is if you plan to use the DrawingArea as a manager for other widgets and you expect it to follow the keyboard traversal mechanisms described by the *Motif Style Guide*. In fact, handling keyboard traversal is pretty much all that the default translations for the DrawingArea do. For example, the following is a subset of the default translations for the DrawingArea widget:†

```
<Key>osfSelect:          DrawingAreaInput() ManagerGadgetSelect()
<Key>osfActivate:        DrawingAreaInput() ManagerParentActivate()
<Key>osfHelp:            DrawingAreaInput() ManagerGadgetHelp()
<KeyDown>:               DrawingAreaInput() ManagerGadgetKeyInput()
<KeyUp>:                 DrawingAreaInput()
<BtnMotion>:             ManagerGadgetButtonMotion()
<Btn1Down>:              DrawingAreaInput() ManagerGadgetArm()
<Btn1Down>,<Btn1Up>:     DrawingAreaInput() ManagerGadgetActivate()
```

These translations show that the manager widget part of the DrawingArea is responsible for tracking events for its gadget children. It is not necessary to support these translations if you are not going to use the DrawingArea to manage children. Most user-generated events also invoke `DrawingAreaInput()`, which does not do any drawing, but simply invokes the `XmNinputCallback`.

As you can see, the `BtnMotion` translation is not passed to `DrawingAreaInput()`, which means that the `XmNinputCallback` is not called for pointer motion events. When it comes to more complex drawing than that done in Example 10-2, this omission is a serious deficiency. To support rubberbanding or free-hand drawing techniques, which require pointer motion events, you must install either an event handler or a translation entry to handle motion events.

---

† This translation table lists only a subset of the current translations in the DrawingArea widget; there is no guarantee that the translations will remain the same in future revisions of the toolkit.

The simplest approach would be to replace the translation table entry for <BtnMotion> events. However, this is not possible, due to a bug in the X Toolkit Intrinsics. The correct thing to do is the following:

```
String translations =
    "<Btn1Motion>: DrawingAreaInput() ManagerGadgetButtonMotion()";
 . . .
drawing_a = XtVaCreateManagedWidget ("drawing_a",
    xmDrawingAreaWidgetClass, main_w,
    . . .
    NULL);
XtOverrideTranslations (drawing_a, XtParseTranslationTable (translations));
XtAddCallback (drawing_a, XmNinputCallback, draw, NULL);
```

With this new translation, the XmNinputCallback function (draw()) would be notified of pointer motion while Button 1 is down.

XtOverrideTranslations() is the preferred method for installing a new translation into the DrawingArea widget because it is nondestructive. The routine only replaces translations for which identical events are specified and leaves all other translations in place. However, this routine does not work in this case because there is already a translation for the Button 1 down-up sequence in the DrawingArea translation table. In the current implementation, once Button 1 goes down, the Xt event translator waits for the Button 1 up event to match the partially finished translation. Therefore, no Button 1 motion events can be caught. If we want to get pointer motion events while the button is down, we have to resort to other alternatives.

One such alternative is to replace the entire translation table, regardless of whether we are adding new entries or overriding existing ones. This is known as a destructive override because the existing translation table is thrown out. This action has the desired effect because the offending Button 1 translation is thrown out. However, we must then take steps to re-install any other default translations that are still required. To completely replace the existing translations, the XmNtranslations resource can be set as shown in the following code fragment:

```
String translations =
    "<Btn1Motion>: DrawingAreaInput() ManagerGadgetButtonMotion()";
 . . .
drawing_a = XtVaCreateManagedWidget ("drawing_a",
    xmDrawingAreaWidgetClass, main_w,
    XmNtranslations,  XtParseTranslationTable (translations),
    NULL);
XtAddCallback (drawing_a, XmNinputCallback, draw, NULL);
```

Once you go to the trouble of replacing the translation table, you may as well install your own action functions as well. Doing so allows you to do the drawing directly from the action functions, rather than using it as an intermediate function to call an application callback. This direct-drawing approach is demonstrated in Example 10-3. The program uses pointer motion to draw lines as the pointer is dragged with the button down, rather than when the button is pressed and released. You'll notice that we have used much the same design as in Example 10-2, but have moved some of the code into different callback routines and have placed the DrawingArea widget into a MainWindow widget for flexibility. None of these changes are required nor do they enhance performance in any way. They merely point out different ways of providing the same functionality.†

---

† XtSetLanguageProc() is only available in X11R5; there is no corresponding function in X11R4.

Example 10-3. The free_hand.c program

```
/* free_hand.c -- simple drawing program that does freehand
 * drawing.  We use translations to do all the event handling
 * for us rather than using the drawing area's XmNinputCallback.
 */
#include <Xm/MainW.h>
#include <Xm/DrawingA.h>
#include <Xm/PushBG.h>
#include <Xm/RowColumn.h>

/* Global variables */
GC gc;
Pixmap pixmap;
Dimension width, height;

main(argc, argv)
int argc;
char *argv[];
{
    Widget toplevel, main_w, drawing_a, pb;
    XtAppContext app;
    XGCValues gcv;
    void draw(), redraw(), clear_it();
    XtActionsRec actions;
    String translations = /* for the DrawingArea widget */
        /* ManagerGadget* functions are necessary for DrawingArea widgets
         * that steal away button events from the normal translation tables.
         */
        "<Btn1Down>:    draw(down) ManagerGadgetArm()  \n\
         <Btn1Up>:      draw(up)   ManagerGadgetActivate()  \n\
         <Btn1Motion>: draw(motion) ManagerGadgetButtonMotion()";

    XtSetLanguageProc (NULL, NULL, NULL);

    toplevel = XtVaAppInitialize (&app, "Demos", NULL, 0,
        &argc, argv, NULL, NULL);

    /* Create a MainWindow to contain the drawing area */
    main_w = XtVaCreateManagedWidget ("main_w",
        xmMainWindowWidgetClass, toplevel,
        XmNscrollingPolicy, XmAUTOMATIC,
        NULL);

    /* Add the "draw" action/function used by the translation table */
    actions.string = "draw";
    actions.proc = draw;
    XtAppAddActions (app, &actions, 1);

    /* Create a DrawingArea widget.  Make it 5 inches wide by 6 inches tall.
     * Don't let it resize so the Clear Button doesn't force a resize.
     */
    drawing_a = XtVaCreateManagedWidget ("drawing_a",
        xmDrawingAreaWidgetClass, main_w,
        XmNtranslations, XtParseTranslationTable (translations),
        XmNunitType,     Xm1000TH_INCHES,
        XmNwidth,         5000, /* 5 inches */
        XmNheight,        6000, /* 6 inches */
        XmNresizePolicy, XmNONE,  /* remain this a fixed size */
        NULL);
    /* When scrolled, the drawing area will get expose events */
```

Example 10-3. The free_hand.c program (continued)

```
    XtAddCallback (drawing_a, XmNexposeCallback, redraw, NULL);

    /* convert drawing area back to pixels to get its width and height */
    XtVaSetValues (drawing_a, XmNunitType, XmPIXELS, NULL);
    XtVaGetValues (drawing_a, XmNwidth, &width, XmNheight, &height, NULL);
    /* create a pixmap the same size as the drawing area. */
    pixmap = XCreatePixmap (XtDisplay (drawing_a),
        RootWindowOfScreen (XtScreen (drawing_a)), width, height,
        DefaultDepthOfScreen (XtScreen (drawing_a)));

    /* Create a GC for drawing (callback).  Used a lot -- make global */
    gcv.foreground = WhitePixelOfScreen (XtScreen (drawing_a));
    gc = XCreateGC (XtDisplay (drawing_a),
        RootWindowOfScreen (XtScreen (drawing_a)), GCForeground, &gcv);
    /* clear pixmap with white */
    XFillRectangle (XtDisplay (drawing_a), pixmap, gc, 0, 0, width, height);
    /* drawing is now drawn into with "black"; change the gc */
    XSetForeground (XtDisplay (drawing_a), gc,
        BlackPixelOfScreen (XtScreen (drawing_a)));

    pb = XtVaCreateManagedWidget ("Clear",
        xmPushButtonGadgetClass, drawing_a, NULL);
    /* Pushing the clear button calls clear_it() */
    XtAddCallback (pb, XmNactivateCallback, clear_it, drawing_a);

    XtRealizeWidget (toplevel);
    XtAppMainLoop (app);
}

/* Action procedure to respond to any of the events from the
 * translation table declared in main().  This function is called
 * in response to Button1 Down, Up and Motion events.  Basically,
 * we're just doing a freehand draw -- not lines or anything.
 */
void
draw(widget, event, args, num_args)
Widget widget;
XEvent *event;
String *args;
int *num_args;
{
    static Position x, y;
    XButtonEvent *bevent = (XButtonEvent *) event;

    if (*num_args != 1)
        XtError ("Wrong number of args!");

    if (strcmp (args[0], "down")) {
        /* if it's not "down", it must either be "up" or "motion"
         * draw full line from anchor point to new point.
         */
        XDrawLine (bevent->display, bevent->window, gc, x, y,
            bevent->x, bevent->y);
        XDrawLine (bevent->display, pixmap, gc, x, y, bevent->x, bevent->y);
    }

    /* freehand is really a bunch of line segments; save this point */
    x = bevent->x;
    y = bevent->y;
```

Example 10-3. The free_hand.c program (continued)

```
}

/* Clear the window by clearing the pixmap and calling XCopyArea() */
void
clear_it(pb, client_data, call_data)
Widget pb;
XtPointer client_data;
XtPointer call_data;
{
    Widget drawing_a = (Widget) client_data;
    XmPushButtonCallbackStruct *cbs =
        (XmPushButtonCallbackStruct *) call_data;

    /* clear pixmap with white */
    XSetForeground (XtDisplay (drawing_a), gc,
        WhitePixelOfScreen (XtScreen (drawing_a)));
    XFillRectangle (XtDisplay (drawing_a), pixmap, gc, 0, 0, width, height);
    /* drawing is now done using black; change the gc */
    XSetForeground (XtDisplay (drawing_a), gc,
        BlackPixelOfScreen (XtScreen (drawing_a)));
    XCopyArea (cbs->event->xbutton.display, pixmap, XtWindow (drawing_a), gc,
        0, 0, width, height, 0, 0);
}

/* redraw is called whenever all or portions of the drawing area is
 * exposed.  This includes newly exposed portions of the widget resulting
 * from the user's interaction with the scrollbars.
 */
void
redraw(drawing_a, client_data, call_data)
Widget      drawing_a;
XtPointer client_data;
XtPointer call_data;
{
    XmDrawingAreaCallbackStruct *cbs =
        (XmDrawingAreaCallbackStruct *) call_data;

    XCopyArea (cbs->event->xexpose.display, pixmap, cbs->window, gc,
        0, 0, width, height, 0, 0);
}
```

The output of the program is shown in Figure 10-2. In Example 10-3, the DrawingArea widget uses the following translation string:

```
String translations =
    "<Btn1Down>:   draw(down) ManagerGadgetArm()        \n\
     <Btn1Up>:     draw(up)   ManagerGadgetActivate() \n\
     <Btn1Motion>: draw(motion) ManagerGadgetButtonMotion()";
```

For each of the specified events, the translation describes two actions. The draw() action is our own function that actually draws into the DrawingArea. The ManagerGadget actions are standard DrawingArea actions (inherited from the Manager widget class) for passing events to a gadget child, as described earlier. We keep them in place because we are still using the PushButton gadget. We are not keeping the routines for managing keyboard traversal, but simply those required to arm and activate the button.

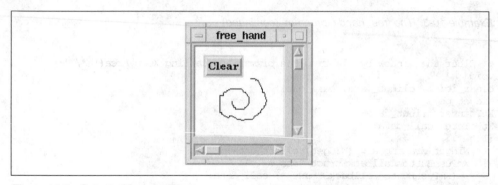

Figure 10-2. Output of free_hand.c.

The draw() action routine tests whether it has been called from a button up event, a button down event, or a motion event. Since the action function is passed the event that invoked it, we could simply test the type field of the event. However, this example gives us a chance to exercise the Xt feature that supports string arguments passed to action functions. Accordingly, the draw() function determines what action to take by examining its args[0] parameter, which contains the string passed as the single parameter in the translation table. For example, draw(up) passes the string "up" as the args[0] parameter in response to a <Btn1Up> event.

Lines are drawn for both ButtonRelease and ButtonMotion events, but not for ButtonPress events. A line is drawn from the last anchor point to the current location of the mouse. As the pointer moves from one point to the next, the anchor point is always one step behind, so a line segment is drawn from that location to the current location. The only time that a line segment is not drawn is on the initial button press (and any motion events that occur while the button is not down). The coordinate values are relative to the current location of the pointer within the DrawingArea widget, no matter how it is positioned in the MainWindow.

The draw() function draws into the window and also into a pixmap. The MainWindow widget is configured to have its XmNscrollingPolicy set to XmAUTOMATIC, so Scroll-Bars are automatically installed over the DrawingArea when it is larger than the Main-Window, which allows the user to view different parts of the canvas interactively. Scrolling actions cause the contents of the newly exposed portions of the canvas to be erased by default. Unless we provide a mechanism by which the DrawingArea can redraw itself, scrolling the DrawingArea loses previously drawn contents. To handle this problem, we employ the same principle we used in Example 10-2. We install a pixmap that is used by both the draw() and redraw() functions.

The redraw() routine is installed as the callback function for the XmNexpose-Callback. The function merely uses XCopyArea() to copy the pixmap onto the window of the DrawingArea. We are not concerned with the position of the DrawingArea with respect to the MainWindow in this routine. All we need to do is copy the pixmap directly into the window. X ensures that the visible portion of the window is clipped as necessary.

In this example, the ManagerGadget actions don't do anything unless the pointer is inside the **Clear** button, so the translation is relatively safe. However, you should be sure to remember that both actions are called. If you press Button 1 inside the PushButton and doodle around a bit before releasing it, the drawing is still done, even though the result is hidden by the gadget. In another application, the fact that actions for both the drawing area itself and its gadget children are both called might lead to indeterminate results.

The `draw()` action does not (and cannot) know if the gadget is also going to react to the button event. This problem does not exist with the standard `DrawingAreaInput()` action routine used in the previous examples because that routine is implemented by the Motif toolkit and it uses its own internal mechanisms to determine if the gadget is activated as well. If the DrawingArea does process the event on the gadget, the `DrawingArea-Input()` action knows that it should not invoke the callback function. However, this internal mechanism is not available outside of the widget code. Reordering the action functions does not help, since there is still no way to know, without making an educated guess, whether or not the DrawingArea acted upon an event on behalf of a gadget child.

As a result of this problem, `draw()` starts drawing a line, even if it starts in the middle of the PushButton, because the DrawingArea processes all of the action functions in the list. If you drag the pointer out of the gadget before releasing the mouse button, the starting point of the line is inside the gadget, but it is hidden when the gadget repaints itself. However, in this particular situation, you can do some guesswork. By installing an `XmNarmCallback` function, you can tell whether or not the DrawingArea activated a button, and by setting an internal state variable, you can decide whether or not the `draw()` action routine should do its drawing.

This confusing behavior is yet another reason why it is best not to include children in DrawingArea widgets that are intended for interactive graphics. If the DrawingArea does not have any gadget children, installing these auxiliary actions in the translation table is not necessary.

10.4 Using Color in a DrawingArea

In this section, we expand on our previous examples by incorporating color. The choice of colors is primarily supported by a function we define called `set_color()`, which takes a widget and an arbitrary color name and sets the global GC's foreground color. By providing an array of colors in the form of colored PushButtons, we've got a color paint program. We have removed the PushButton gadget from the DrawingArea and created a proper control panel to the left of the DrawingArea. The program uses a RowColumn widget (see Section 8.5 in Chapter 8, *Manager Widgets*) to manage a set of eighteen colored PushButtons.†
The program that demonstrates these techniques is shown in Example 10-4.‡

---

† On a monochrome screen, the program runs, but the buttons are either black or white, depending on which is closer to their RGB values corresponding to the color names chosen. You can only draw with the black buttons, since the background is already white.

‡ `XtSetLanguageProc()` is only available in X11R5; there is no corresponding function in X11R4.

Example 10-4. The color_draw.c program

```
/* color_draw.c -- simple drawing program using predefined colors.  */
#include <Xm/MainW.h>
#include <Xm/DrawingA.h>
#include <Xm/PushBG.h>
#include <Xm/PushB.h>
#include <Xm/RowColumn.h>
#include <Xm/ScrolledW.h>
#include <Xm/Form.h>

GC gc;
Pixmap pixmap;
/* dimensions of drawing area (pixmap) */
Dimension width, height;

String colors[] = {
    "Black", "Red", "Green", "Blue", "White", "Navy", "Orange", "Yellow",
    "Pink", "Magenta", "Cyan", "Brown", "Grey", "LimeGreen", "Turquoise",
    "Violet", "Wheat", "Purple"
};

main(argc, argv)
int argc;
char *argv[];
{
    Widget toplevel, main_w, sw, rc, form, drawing_a, pb;
    XtAppContext app;
    XGCValues gcv;
    void draw(), redraw(), set_color(), exit(), clear_it();
    int i;
    XtActionsRec actions;
    String translations = /* for the DrawingArea widget */
        "<Btn1Down>:    draw(down)\n\
         <Btn1Up>:      draw(up)  \n\
         <Btn1Motion>: draw(motion)";

    XtSetLanguageProc (NULL, NULL, NULL);

    toplevel = XtVaAppInitialize (&app, "Demos", NULL, 0,
        &argc, argv, NULL, NULL);

    /* Create a MainWindow to contain the drawing area */
    main_w = XtVaCreateManagedWidget ("main_w",
        xmFormWidgetClass, toplevel, NULL);

    /* Create a GC for drawing (callback).  Used a lot -- make global */
    gcv.foreground = WhitePixelOfScreen (XtScreen (main_w));
    gc = XCreateGC (XtDisplay (main_w),
        RootWindowOfScreen (XtScreen (main_w)), GCForeground, &gcv);

    /* Create a 3-column array of color tiles */
    rc = XtVaCreateWidget ("rc", xmRowColumnWidgetClass, main_w,
        XmNnumColumns,       3,
        XmNpacking,          XmPACK_COLUMN,
        XmNleftAttachment,   XmATTACH_FORM,
        XmNtopAttachment,    XmATTACH_FORM,
        NULL);
    for (i = 0; i < XtNumber(colors); i++) {
        /* Create a single tile (pixmap) for each color */
        pixmap = XCreatePixmap (XtDisplay (rc),
```

Example 10-4. The color_draw.c program (continued)

```
            RootWindowOfScreen (XtScreen (rc)),
            16, 16, DefaultDepthOfScreen (XtScreen (rc)));
        set_color (rc, colors[i]); /* set the gc's color according to name */
        XFillRectangle (XtDisplay (main_w), pixmap, gc, 0, 0, 16, 16);
        pb = XtVaCreateManagedWidget (colors[i], xmPushButtonWidgetClass, rc,
            XmNlabelType, XmPIXMAP,
            XmNlabelPixmap, pixmap,
            NULL);
        /* callback for this pushbutton sets the current color */
        XtAddCallback (pb, XmNactivateCallback, set_color, colors[i]);
    }
    XtManageChild (rc);

    pb = XtVaCreateManagedWidget ("Quit",
        xmPushButtonGadgetClass, main_w,
        XmNleftAttachment,      XmATTACH_FORM,
        XmNtopAttachment,       XmATTACH_WIDGET,
        XmNtopWidget,           rc,
        NULL);
    XtAddCallback (pb, XmNactivateCallback, exit, NULL);

    /* Clear button -- wait till DrawingArea is created so we can use
     * it to pass as client data.
     */
    pb = XtVaCreateManagedWidget ("Clear",
        xmPushButtonGadgetClass, main_w,
        XmNleftAttachment,      XmATTACH_WIDGET,
        XmNleftWidget,          pb,
        XmNtopAttachment,       XmATTACH_WIDGET,
        XmNtopWidget,           rc,
        NULL);

    sw = XtVaCreateManagedWidget ("scrolled_win",
        xmScrolledWindowWidgetClass, main_w,
        XmNwidth,                   300,
        XmNscrollingPolicy,         XmAUTOMATIC,
        XmNscrollBarDisplayPolicy,  XmAS_NEEDED,
        XmNtopAttachment,           XmATTACH_FORM,
        XmNbottomAttachment,        XmATTACH_FORM,
        XmNleftAttachment,          XmATTACH_WIDGET,
        XmNleftWidget,              rc,
        XmNrightAttachment,         XmATTACH_FORM,
        NULL);

    /* Add the "draw" action/function used by the translation table
     * parsed by the translations resource below.
     */
    actions.string = "draw";
    actions.proc = draw;
    XtAppAddActions (app, &actions, 1);

    /* Create a DrawingArea widget. Make it 5 inches wide by 6 inches tall.
     * Don't let it resize so the Clear Button doesn't force a resize.
     */
    drawing_a = XtVaCreateManagedWidget ("drawing_a",
        xmDrawingAreaWidgetClass, sw,
        XmNtranslations, XtParseTranslationTable (translations),
        XmNunitType,     Xm1000TH_INCHES,
```

Example 10-4. The color_draw.c program (continued)

```
            XmNwidth,        5000, /* 5 inches */
            XmNheight,       6000, /* 6 inches */
            XmNresizePolicy, XmNONE,  /* remain this a fixed size */
            NULL);
    /* When scrolled, the drawing area will get expose events */
    XtAddCallback (drawing_a, XmNexposeCallback, redraw, NULL);
    /* Pushing the clear button clears the drawing area widget */
    XtAddCallback (pb, XmNactivateCallback, clear_it, drawing_a);

    /* convert drawing area back to pixels to get its width and height */
    XtVaSetValues (drawing_a, XmNunitType, XmPIXELS, NULL);
    XtVaGetValues (drawing_a, XmNwidth, &width, XmNheight, &height, NULL);
    /* create a pixmap the same size as the drawing area. */
    pixmap = XCreatePixmap (XtDisplay (drawing_a),
        RootWindowOfScreen (XtScreen (drawing_a)), width, height,
        DefaultDepthOfScreen (XtScreen (drawing_a)));
    /* clear pixmap with white */
    set_color (drawing_a, "White");
    XFillRectangle (XtDisplay (drawing_a), pixmap, gc, 0, 0, width, height);

    XtRealizeWidget (toplevel);
    XtAppMainLoop (app);
}

/* Action procedure to respond to any of the events from the
 * translation table declared in main().  This function is called
 * in response to Button1 Down, Up and Motion events.  Basically,
 * we're just doing a freehand draw -- not lines or anything.
 */
void
draw(widget, event, args, num_args)
Widget widget;
XEvent *event;
String *args;
int *num_args;
{
    static Position x, y;
    XButtonEvent *bevent = (XButtonEvent *) event;

    if (*num_args != 1)
        XtError ("Wrong number of args!");

    if (strcmp (args[0], "down")) {
        /* if it's not "down", it must either be "up" or "motion"
         * draw full line from anchor point to new point.
         */
        XDrawLine (bevent->display, bevent->window, gc, x, y,
            bevent->x, bevent->y);
        XDrawLine (bevent->display, pixmap, gc, x, y, bevent->x, bevent->y);
    }

    /* freehand is really a bunch of line segements; save this point */
    x = bevent->x;
    y = bevent->y;
}

/* Clear the window by clearing the pixmap and calling XCopyArea() */
void
clear_it(pb, client_data, call_data)
```

Example 10-4. The color_draw.c program (continued)

```
Widget pb;
XtPointer client_data;
XtPointer call_data;
{
    Widget drawing_a = (Widget) client_data;
    XmPushButtonCallbackStruct *cbs =
        (XmPushButtonCallbackStruct *) call_data;

    /* clear pixmap with white */
    XSetForeground (XtDisplay (drawing_a), gc,
        WhitePixelOfScreen (XtScreen (drawing_a)));
    /* this clears the pixmap */
    XFillRectangle (XtDisplay (drawing_a), pixmap, gc, 0, 0, width, height);
    /* drawing is now done using black; change the gc */
    XSetForeground (XtDisplay (drawing_a), gc,
        BlackPixelOfScreen (XtScreen (drawing_a)));
    /* render the newly cleared pixmap onto the window */
    XCopyArea (cbs->event->xbutton.display, pixmap, XtWindow (drawing_a), gc,
        0, 0, width, height, 0, 0);
}

/* redraw is called whenever all or portions of the drawing area is
 * exposed.  This includes newly exposed portions of the widget resulting
 * from the user's interaction with the scrollbars.
 */
void
redraw(drawing_a, client_data, call_data)
Widget     drawing_a;
XtPointer client_data;
XtPointer call_data;
{
    XmDrawingAreaCallbackStruct *cbs =
        (XmDrawingAreaCallbackStruct *) call_data;

    XCopyArea (cbs->event->xexpose.display, pixmap, cbs->window, gc,
        0, 0, width, height, 0, 0);
}

/* callback routine for when any of the color tiles are pressed.
 * This general function may also be used to set the global gc's
 * color directly.  Just provide a widget and a color name.
 */
void
set_color(widget, client_data, call_data)
 Widget widget;
XtPointer client_data;
XtPointer call_data;
{
    String color = (String) client_data;
    Display *dpy = XtDisplay (widget);
    Colormap cmap = DefaultColormapOfScreen (XtScreen (widget));
    XColor col, unused;

    if (!XAllocNamedColor (dpy, cmap, color, &col, &unused)) {
        char buf[32];
        sprintf (buf, "Can't alloc %s", color);
        XtWarning (buf);
```

Example 10-4. The color_draw.c program (continued)

```
        return;
    }
    XSetForeground (dpy, gc, col.pixel);
}
```

The output of the program in shown in Figure 10-3.

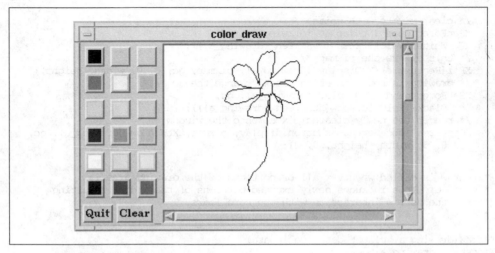

Figure 10-3. Output of color_draw.c

One thing to note about the program is that the callback routine for the **Clear** button is passed the DrawingArea widget as the client data. This technique saves us from having to declare a global variable, while still providing a handle to the DrawingArea in the callback routine.

10.5 Summary

The DrawingArea widget is probably most useful when it is used as a canvas for displaying raster images, animation, or a mixture of text and graphics. It is also well-suited for tasks that require interactive user input. The widget provides some rudimentary input mechanisms in the form of callbacks that are invoked by button events.

The translation and action tables supported by the X Toolkit Intrinsics provide a simple mechanism for notifying applications of user events such as double-mouse clicks, keyboard events, and so on. By creatively modifying the default translations and actions, you could build a rather intricate system of action functions that produces interesting graphics based on various forms of user input sequences.

However, what you can do with actions is simplistic given the complexities that are involved in true paint or draw applications. Applications that require a graphic front end should probably dig deeper into the lower levels of Xt for event handling and into Xlib for image rendering.

10.6 Exercises

There are a number of different possibilities you could explore in extending the DrawingArea widget. The following exercises are intended to shine the light down some interesting paths that you can take.

1. As we have demonstrated, a DrawingArea widget needs to be able to redisplay the contents of its window. For the programs in this chapter, we implemented redisplay by duplicating in a pixmap all of the drawing done in the window. When the window needs to be repainted, the pixmap is simply copied into it. However, this technique does not take resizing into account. If the *draw2* application is resized bigger, parts of the window are not properly redrawn because the pixmap is not resized. If you wanted to support a canvas that can grow dynamically, you also have to resize the off-screen pixmap. Modify *draw2.c* so that the pixmap resizes along with the DrawingArea. You need to add a callback for XmNresizeCallback. The callback should query the size of the DrawingArea, create a new pixmap, use XCopyArea() to copy the old pixmap into the new one, and destroy the old pixmap.

2. The resource XmNcolormap can be used to set and get the colormap associated with a DrawingArea widget, using XtVaSetValues() and XtVaGetValues(). Modify *color_draw.c* to use colormap values rather than predefined colors.

3. A paint program and a draw program differ in the way they internally represent their graphical displays. A paint program usually maintains a background pixmap as demonstrated by *free_hand*, whereas a draw program stores geometric information about the shapes that are drawn. For example, circles can be represented using a center (x,y coordinate) and a radius; rectangles can be represented by an origin coordinate with width and height values; and freehand drawings can be represented by a list of coordinates (line segments). Entire pictures can be represented by a list of geometric shape definitions.

   Modify *free_hand.c* or *color_draw.c* to use a list of XSegment structures to represent the lines that are drawn by the user. Instead of using a pixmap and XCopyArea() to repaint the DrawingArea widget on Expose events, repaint the picture by calling XDrawSegments() and using the data stored in the internal list of XSegment structures.

4. In the previous exercise, we gave you some hints about how you might build an interactive drawing application. For those of you who really want to dig into this subject, you can extend the program by giving the user a choice of geometric shapes to draw. You need to provide a user interface to support an array of object types: arcs, circles, squares, rectangles, lines, and freehand drawings. Based on the user's choice, you have to maintain a state machine that indicates how much of a geometric figure has been drawn. Use a translation table to monitor the events that correspond to the state machine and store the coordinates of key geometric points in internal data structures. Granted, this exercise is no small feat, but it is a great way to kill a weekend!

11

Labels and Buttons

This chapter contains an in-depth look at the label and button widgets provided by the Motif toolkit. These widgets are the most commonly used primitive widgets.

In This Chapter:

11
Labels and Buttons

Labels and buttons are among the most widely used interface objects in GUI-based applications. They are also the simplest in concept and design. Labels provide the basic resources necessary to render and manage text or images (pixmaps) by controlling color, alignment, and other visual attributes. PushButtons are subclassed from Label; they extend its capabilities by adding callback routines that respond to user interaction from the mouse or keyboard. These visual and interactive features provide the cornerstone for many widgets in the Motif toolkit, such as CascadeButtons, DrawnButtons, and ToggleButtons.

This chapter also discusses ArrowButtons. While the ArrowButton is not subclassed from Label like the other buttons, it does provide a subset of the interactive capabilities of the other buttons. ArrowButtons do not contain text or graphical labels; they simply display directional arrows that point up, down, left, or right. These widgets are meant to act as companions to other interface objects whose values or displays can be controlled or changed incrementally by the user. An example might be four ArrowButtons that are used to represent directional movement for the display of a bitmap editor.

Although CascadeButtons are subclassed from the Label widget, they are specifically used in Motif menus and are not addressed in this chapter. The menu systems that are provided by Motif are separate entities and are treated separately in Chapter 4, *The Main Window*, and Chapter 15, *Menus*. Since the Motif menus use Labels and PushButtons for menu items, these widgets have certain resources that only take effect when the widgets are used in menus. These resources are not discussed in this chapter either.

Labels and buttons have a wide range of uses and they are used in many of the compound objects provided by the Motif toolkit. As a result, these widgets are discussed throughout this book. This chapter provides a basic discussion of the main resources and callbacks used by the objects. It also provides examples of common usage and attempts to address problem areas.

11.1 Labels

Labels are simply props for the stage. They are not intended to respond to user interaction, although a help callback can be attached in case the HELP key is pressed. It is equally common to find Labels displaying either text or graphics, yet they cannot display both simultaneously in the conventional sense.

Since Labels can display text, it may not always be obvious whether to use a Label or a Text widget to display textual information. The *Motif Style Guide* suggests that Labels should always be used when noneditable text is displayed, even if the text is longer than what you might think of as a label. If a Label is large, you can always place it in the work area of an automatic ScrolledWindow widget, as discussed in Chapter 9, *ScrolledWindows and ScrollBars*. Even if the text is expected to change frequently, your needs can often be accommodated by a Label widget or gadget.

Another issue that affects the choice between a Label widget and a Text widget is the ability to select the text. Even if you have text that is not editable by the user, you may wish to allow the user to select all or part of the text. With Motif 1.2, the Label widget acts as a drag source for drag and drop operations, which means that the full text of a Label can be manipulated using drag and drop.† However, this capability does not allow the user to manipulate only part of the text. For that type of interaction, and with previous versions of the toolkit, you need to use a Text widget rather than a Label to provide selection capabilities.

Labels have a number of added visual advantages over Text widgets. The text in a Label can be greyed out when it is insensitive and it can display text using multiple fonts. The Text widgets do not support multiple fonts. In Motif 1.2, an insensitive Text widget greys out its text, while in Motif 1.1 it does not. Labels are also lighter-weight objects than Text widgets. There is little overhead in maintaining or displaying a Label and there is no need to handle event processing on a Label to the same degree as for a Text widget. All things considered, we would recommend using Label widgets over Text widgets.

However, when it comes to interactive objects, Labels are not the best choice. In most cases where you want to allow the user to click on a Label, it is more appropriate to use a Push-Button or a ToggleButton, since they are designed to support user interaction. Furthermore, users who are familiar with other Motif applications will not expect to have to interact with Labels. In short, the best thing to do with Label widgets is simple and obvious: use them to display labels.

There are a number of resources associated with Labels that are used by other Motif objects or by widget classes that are subclassed from Label. For example, since Labels (and Push-Buttons) are used extensively as menu items in menus, they can have accelerators, mnemonics, and other visual resources set to provide the appropriate functionality for menus. These resources do not apply to Labels (and PushButtons) that are not used as menu items, so we do not discuss them here.

---

† All of the button subclasses of Label inherit the drag source capability, so the text labels for PushButtons and ToggleButtons can also be manipulated using drag and drop.

The only callback routine for the Label widget is the `XmNhelpCallback` associated with all Primitive widgets. If the user presses the HELP key on a Label widget, its help callback is called.†

11.1.1 Creating a Label

Applications that use Labels must include the header file *<Xm/Label.h>*, which defines the `xmLabelWidgetClass` type. This type is a pointer to the actual widget structure used by `XtVaCreateManagedWidget()`. This routine can be used to create a Label as follows:

```
Widget label;

label = XtVaCreateManagedWidget ("name",
    xmLabelWidgetClass, parent,
    resource-value-list,
    NULL);
```

This code fragment shows the most common way to create a Label. Since Labels do not have children, there is no reason to create them as unmanaged widgets first and then manage them later. As for all widgets classes, the Motif toolkit also provides the `XmCreateLabel()` convenience routine for creating Labels.

Label gadgets are also available. Recall that a gadget is a windowless object that relies on its parent to display its visual attributes and to provide it with events generated either by the system or by the user. Since a gadget does not have a window, its background color and pattern cannot be set individually; they are provided by the parent.

The Label gadget is an entirely different class from its widget counterpart. To use the gadget variant, you must include the header file *<Xm/LabelG.h>* and use the `xmLabelGadgetClass` pointer in the call to `XtVaCreateManagedWidget()`, as in the following example:

```
Widget label;

label = XtVaCreateManagedWidget ("name",
    xmLabelGadgetClass, parent,
    resource-value-list,
    NULL);
```

11.1.2 Text Labels

A Label widget or gadget can display either text or an image. The `XmNlabelType` resource controls the type of label that is displayed; the resource can be set to `XmSTRING` or `XmPIXMAP`. The default value is `XmSTRING`, so if you want to display text in a Label, you do not need to set this resource explicitly.

---

† Whether a Label receives `Help` events depends on the input policy the user is using and whether or not keyboard traversal is on. Since it may not be possible for the user to use the HELP key on Labels, we don't recommend providing help callbacks for them.

The resource that specifies the string that is displayed in a Label is `XmNlabelString`. The value for this resource must be a Motif compound string; common C character strings are not allowed. The following code fragment shows the appropriate way to specify the text for a Label:

```
Widget    label;
XmString  str = XmStringCreateLocalized ("A Label");

label = XtVaCreateManagedWidget ("label",
    xmLabelWidgetClass, parent,
    XmNlabelString,  str,
    NULL);

XmStringFree (str);
```

If the `XmNlabelString` resource is not specified, the Label automatically converts its name into a compound string and uses that as its label. Therefore, the previous example could also be implemented as follows:

```
Widget label;

label = XtVaCreateManagedWidget ("A Label",
    xmLabelWidgetClass, parent,
    NULL);
```

This method of specifying the label string for the widget is much simpler than using a compound string. It avoids the overhead of creating and destroying a compound string, which is expensive in terms of allocating and freeing memory. The problem with the name of the widget shown above is that it is illegal as a widget name. Technically, widget names should only be composed of alphanumerics (letters and numbers), hyphens, and underscores. Characters such as space, dot (`.`), and the asterisk (`*`) are disallowed because they make it impossible for the user to specify these widgets in resource files. On the other hand, using names that contain these characters can be to your advantage if you want to try to prevent users from changing the resource values of certain widgets. You can achieve the same result by hard-coding the label or by using an illegal widget name. The first method is more elegant, so the decision you make here should be well-informed.

If you are going to hard-code the label string, you can avoid the overhead of creating a compound string by using the `XtVaTypedArg` feature of Xt, as shown in the following example:

```
label = XtVaCreateManagedWidget ("widget_name",
    xmLabelWidgetClass, parent,
    XtVaTypedArg, XmNlabelString, XmRString,
        "A Label", 8, /* 8 = strlen("A Label") + 1 */
    NULL);
```

The C string `"A Label"` (which is 7 chars long, plus 1 `NULL` byte) is automatically converted into a compound string by the toolkit using a pre-installed type converter. This method can also be used to change the label for a widget using `XtVaSetValues()`.

Since compound strings are dynamically created and destroyed, you cannot statically declare an argument list that contains a pointer to a compound string. For example, it would be an error to do the following:

```
static Arg list[] = {
    ...
    XmNlabelString, XmStringCreateLocalized ("A label"),
    ...
};

label = XtCreateManagedWidget ("name",
    xmLabelWidgetClass, parent,
    list, XtNumber (list));
```

This technique causes an error because you cannot create a compound string in a statically declared array. For a complete discussion of compound strings, see Chapter 19, *Compound Strings*.

11.1.3 Images as Labels

A Label widget or gadget can display an image instead of text by setting the XmNlabel-Type resource to XmPIXMAP. As a result of this resource setting, the Label displays the pixmap specified for the XmNlabelPixmap resource. Example 11-1 demonstrates how pixmaps can be used as labels.†

Example 11-1. The pixmaps.c program

```
/* pixmaps.c -- Demonstrate simple label gadgets in a row column.
 * Each command line argument represents a bitmap filename.  Try
 * to load the corresponding pixmap and store in a RowColumn.
 */
#include <Xm/LabelG.h>
#include <Xm/RowColumn.h>

main(argc, argv)
int argc;
char *argv[];
{
    XtAppContext app;
    Pixel fg, bg;
    Widget toplevel, rowcol;

    XtSetLanguageProc (NULL, NULL, NULL);

    toplevel = XtVaAppInitialize (&app, "Demos", NULL, 0,
        &argc, argv, NULL, NULL);

    if (argc < 2) {
        puts ("Specify bitmap filenames.");
        exit (1);
    }
    /* create a RowColumn that has an equal number of rows and
     * columns based on the number of pixmaps it is going to
```

---

†XtSetLanguageProc() is only available in X11R5; there is no corresponding function in X11R4.

Example 11-1. The pixmaps.c program (continued)

```
            * display (this value is in "argc").
            */
        rowcol = XtVaCreateWidget ("rowcol",
            xmRowColumnWidgetClass, toplevel,
            XmNnumColumns,  int_sqrt (argc),
            XmNpacking,     XmPACK_COLUMN,
            NULL);

        /* Get the foreground and background colors of the rowcol to make
         * all the pixmaps appear using a consistent color.
         */
        XtVaGetValues (rowcol,
            XmNforeground, &fg,
            XmNbackground, &bg,
            NULL);

        while (*++argv) {
            Pixmap pixmap = XmGetPixmap (XtScreen (rowcol), *argv, fg, bg);
            if (pixmap == XmUNSPECIFIED_PIXMAP)
                printf ("Couldn't load %s\n", *argv);
            else
                XtVaCreateManagedWidget (*argv, xmLabelGadgetClass, rowcol,
                    XmNlabelType, XmPIXMAP,
                    XmNlabelPixmap, pixmap,
                    NULL);
        }

        XtManageChild (rowcol);
        XtRealizeWidget (toplevel);
        XtAppMainLoop (app);
    }

/* get the integer square root of n -- used to determine the number
 * of rows and columns of pixmaps to use in the RowColumn widget.
 */
int_sqrt (n)
register int n;
{
    register int i, s = 0, t;
    for (i = 15; i >= 0; i--) {
        t = (s | (1 << i));
        if (t * t <= n)
            s = t;
    }
    return s;
}
```

The program displays a two-dimensional array of pixmaps based on the bitmap files listed on the command line. For example, the following command produces the output shown in Figure 11-1.

```
% pixmaps flagup letters wingdogs xlogo64 calculator tie_fighter
```

To optimize the use of space by the RowColumn widget, the number of rows and columns is set to the square root of the number of images. For example, if there are nine pixmaps to load, there should be a 3×3 grid of images. Since the number of files to be loaded corresponds to the number of arguments in argv, argc is passed to int_sqrt() to get the

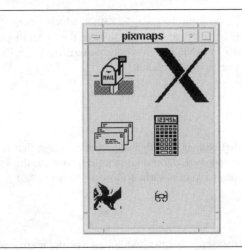

Figure 11-1. Output of pixmaps flagup letters wingdogs xlogo64 calculator tie_fighter

integer square root of its value. This value tells us the number of columns to specify for the
XmNnumColumns resource of the RowColumn.

The bitmap files are read using XmGetPixmap(), which is a function that creates a pixmap
from the specified file. This file must be in X11 bitmap format. Since the function needs
foreground and background colors for the pixmap, we use the colors of the RowColumn. If
the specified file cannot be found or if it does not contain a bitmap, the function returns the
constant XmUNSPECIFIED_PIXMAP.† If this error condition is returned, the program
skips the file and goes on to the next one. For more detailed information on XmGet-
Pixmap() and other supporting functions, see Section 3.4.5 in Chapter 3, *Overview of the
Motif Toolkit*.

11.1.4 Label Sensitivity

A Label can be made inactive by setting the XmNsensitive resource to False. While it
may seem frivolous to set a Label insensitive, since Labels are never really active, it is quite
common to associate a Label with another interactive element, such as a List, a TextField, or
even a composite item such as RadioBox. In these situations, it is useful to desensitize the
Label along with its corresponding user-interface element, to emphasive that the component
is inactive. In the same vein, if XtSetSensitive() is applied to a Manager widget, the
routine sensitizes or desensitizes all of the children of the widget, including Labels.

If a Label is displaying text, setting the widget insensitive causes the text to be greyed out.
This effect is achieved by stippling the text label. If a Label is displaying an image, you need
to specify the XmNlabelInsensitivePixmap resource to indicate the image that is
displayed when the Label is inactive; the Label does not stipple the image for you. By

---

† XmUNSPECIFIED_PIXMAP is not 0 or NULL. Many people have a tendency to test for these values upon return
of functions that return opaque objects. The literal value is 2.

default, the resource is set to XmUNSPECIFIED_PIXMAP, which means that the Label will not display a pixmap when it is insensitive. In order to have the Label display a stippled pixmap, you must create a bitmap by AND-ing a stipple pattern over the image and then set XmNlabelInsensitivePixmap to this value.

11.1.5 Label Alignment

Within the boundaries of a Label widget or gadget, the text or image that is displayed can be left justified, right justified, or centered. The alignment depends on the value of the XmNalignment resource, which can have one of the following values:

    XmALIGNMENT_BEGINNING
    XmALIGNMENT_END
    XmALIGNMENT_CENTER

The default value is XmALIGNMENT_CENTER, which causes the text or pixmap to be centered vertically and horizontally within the widget or gadget. The XmALIGNMENT_BEGINNING and XmALIGNMENT_END values refer to the left and right edges of the widget or gadget when the value for XmNstringDirection is set to XmSTRING_DIRECTION_L_TO_R. If the text used within a Label is read from left-to-right (the default), the beginning of the string is on the left. However, if the text used is read from right-to-left, the alignment values are inverted, as should be the value for XmNstringDirection. These values also apply to Labels that display pixmaps.

If you have a set of Labels that are associated with strings of text that are right justified, all of the Labels should use the same alignment and string direction settings for consistency. One way to handle this situation is to set the resources universally (as a class-based resource) for all Labels and subclasses of Labels. For example, if your application is written for a language that displays text from right-to-left, you may choose to have the following lines in the application defaults file:

    *XmLabel.stringDirection: string_direction_r_to_l
    *XmLabelGadget.stringDirection: string_direction_r_to_l

Note that the resource must be set for both the widget and gadget classes. You should also be aware that setting the string direction does not cause the compound strings for the Labels to be automatically converted to the right direction. Similarly, a Label that uses a compound string with a right-to-left string direction does not automatically set the XmNstringDirection resource appropriately. These are internationalization issues if you are thinking of supporting languages that are justified either left-to-right or right-to-left.

The RowColumn manager widget can also be used to enforce consistency by controlling the geometry management of its children. If you are using a RowColumn to lay out a group of Labels (or objects subclassed from Label, such as PushButtons), you can tell the RowColumn to align each of its children in a consistent manner using the XmNentryAlignment resource. This resource takes the same values as the XmNalignment resource for Labels. If the parent of a Label widget or gadget is a RowColumn with its XmNisAligned resource set to True, the alignment resource of each of the Label children is forced to the same value as the XmNentryAlignment resource.

You should note that the alignment is only enforced when the RowColumn resource XmN-rowColumnType is XmWORK_AREA. If you are using a RowColumn to arrange components in your application, its type should always be a work area. The other types of the widget are used by the internals of Motif for creating special objects like MenuBars and PulldownMenus. If you set the XmNentryAlignment resource for other types of Row-Column widgets, you may or may not see the alignment effects.

In Motif 1.2, there is a new RowColumn resource that affects the vertical alignment of its children that are Labels, subclasses of Label, and Text widgets. The XmNentry-VerticalAlignment resource can take one of the following values:

```
XmALIGNMENT_BASELINE_BOTTOM
XmALIGNMENT_BASELINE_TOP
XmALIGNMENT_CONTENTS_BOTTOM
XmALIGNMENT_CENTER
XmALIGNMENT_CONTENTS_TOP
```

The resource only takes effect when the children of the RowColumn are arranged in rows, which means that the XmNorientation is XmHORIZONTAL. The default value is Xm-ALIGNMENT_CENTER, which causes the center of all of the children in a row to be aligned.

11.1.6 Multi-line and Multi-font Labels

The fonts used within a Label are directly associated with the font list element tags used in the compound string specified for the XmNlabelString resource. The XmNfontList resource for a Label specifies the mapping between font list tags and font names that is used when displaying the text. Since a compound string may use multiple character sets, a Label can display any number of fonts, as specified in the XmNlabelString for the Label. A compound string may also contain embedded newlines. Example 11-2 shows the use of a Label to display a single compound string that contains a monthly calendar.†

Example 11-2. The xcal.c program

```
/* xcal.c -- display a monthly calendar.  The month displayed is a
 * single Label widget whose text is generated from the output of
 * the "cal" program found on any UNIX machine.  popen() is used
 * to run the program and read its output.  Although this is an
 * inefficient method for getting the output of a separate program,
 * it suffices for demonstration purposes.  A List widget displays
 * the months and the user can provide the year as argv[1].
 */
#include <stdio.h>
#include <X11/Xos.h>
#include <Xm/List.h>
#include <Xm/Frame.h>
#include <Xm/LabelG.h>
```

---

†XtSetLanguageProc() is only available in X11R5; there is no corresponding function in X11R4. XmFont-ListEntryCreate() is only available in Motif 1.2; there is no corresponding function in Motif 1.1. XmFont-ListAppendEntry() is only available in Motif 1.2; XmFontListCreate() and XmFontListAdd() are the corresponding functions in Motif 1.1. XmFONTLIST_DEFAULT_TAG replaces XmSTRING_DEFAULT_CHARSET in Motif 1.2.

Example 11-2. The xcal.c program (continued)

```
#include <Xm/RowColumn.h>
#include <Xm/SeparatoG.h>

int year;
XmStringTable ArgvToXmStringTable();
void FreeXmStringTable();

char *months[] = {
    "January", "February", "March", "April", "May", "June",
    "July", "August", "September", "October", "November", "December"
};

main(argc, argv)
int argc;
char *argv[];
{
    Widget toplevel, frame, rowcol, label, w;
    XtAppContext app;
    Display *dpy;
    extern void set_month();
    XmFontList fontlist;
    XmFontListEntry entry;
    XFontStruct *font;
    XmStringTable strs;
    int month_no;

    XtSetLanguageProc (NULL, NULL, NULL);

    toplevel = XtVaAppInitialize (&app, "Demos", NULL, 0,
        &argc, argv, NULL, NULL);

    /* Create a fontlist based on the fonts we're using.  These are the
     * fonts that are going to be hardcoded in the Label and List widgets.
     */
    dpy = XtDisplay (toplevel);
    font = XLoadQueryFont (dpy, "-*-courier-bold-r-*--18-*");
    entry = XmFontListEntryCreate ("tag1", XmFONT_IS_FONT, font);
    fontlist = XmFontListAppendEntry (NULL, entry);
    font = XLoadQueryFont (dpy, "-*-courier-medium-r-*--18-*");
    entry = XmFontListEntryCreate ("tag2", XmFONT_IS_FONT, font);
    fontlist = XmFontListAppendEntry (fontlist, entry);
    XtFree (entry);

    if (argc > 1) {
        month_no = 1;
     year = atoi (argv[1]);
    }
    else {
        long time(), t = time(0);
        struct tm *today = localtime (&t);
        year = 1900 + today->tm_year;
        month_no = today->tm_mon+1;
    }

    /* The RowColumn is the general layout manager for the application.
     * It contains two children: a Label gadget that displays the calendar
     * month, and a ScrolledList to allow the user to change the month.
     */
    rowcol = XtVaCreateWidget ("rowcol",
```

Example 11-2. The xcal.c program (continued)

```
            xmRowColumnWidgetClass, toplevel,
            XmNorientation, XmHORIZONTAL,
            NULL);

    /* enclose the month in a Frame for decoration. */
    frame = XtVaCreateManagedWidget ("frame",
        xmFrameWidgetClass, rowcol, NULL);
    label = XtVaCreateManagedWidget ("month",
        xmLabelGadgetClass, frame,
        XmNalignment, XmALIGNMENT_BEGINNING,
        XmNfontList,  fontlist,
        NULL);

    /* create a list of month names */
    strs = ArgvToXmStringTable (XtNumber (months), months);
    w = XmCreateScrolledList (rowcol, "list", NULL, 0);
    XtVaSetValues (w,
        XmNitems,        strs,
        XmNitemCount,    XtNumber(months),
        XmNfontList,     fontlist,
        NULL);
    FreeXmStringTable (strs);
    XmFontListFree (fontlist);
    XtAddCallback (w, XmNbrowseSelectionCallback, set_month, label);
    XtManageChild (w);
    XmListSelectPos (w, month_no, True); /* initialize month */

    XtManageChild (rowcol);
    XtRealizeWidget (toplevel);
    XtAppMainLoop (app);
}

/* callback function for the List widget -- change the month */
void
set_month(w, client_data, call_data)
Widget w;
XtPointer client_data;
XtPointer call_data;
{
    register FILE *pp;
    extern FILE *popen();
    char text[BUFSIZ];
    register char *p = text;
    XmString str;
    Widget label = (Widget) client_data;
    XmListCallbackStruct *list_cbs =
        (XmListCallbackStruct *) call_data;

    /* Ask UNIX to execute the "cal" command and read its output */
    sprintf (text, "cal %d %d", list_cbs->item_position, year);
    if (!(pp = popen (text, "r"))) {
        perror (text);
        return;
    }
    *p = 0;
    while (fgets (p, sizeof (text) - strlen (text), pp))
        p += strlen (p);
    pclose (pp);
```

Example 11-2. The xcal.c program (continued)

```
    /* display the month using the "tag1" font from the
     * Label gadget's XmNfontList.
     */
    str = XmStringCreateLtoR (text, "tag1");
    XtVaSetValues (label, XmNlabelString, str, NULL);
    XmStringFree (str);
}

/* Convert an array of string to an array of compound strings */
XmStringTable
ArgvToXmStringTable(argc, argv)
int argc;
char **argv;
{
    XmStringTable new =
        (XmStringTable) XtMalloc ((argc+1) * sizeof (XmString));

    if (!new)
        return (XmStringTable) NULL;

    new[argc] = 0;
    while (--argc >= 0)
        new[argc] = XmStringCreate (argv[argc], "tag2");
    return new;
}

/* Free the table created by ArgvToXmStringTable() */
void
FreeXmStringTable(argv)
XmStringTable argv;
{
    register int i;

    if (!argv)
        return;
    for (i = 0; argv[i]; i++)
        XmStringFree (argv[i]);
    XtFree (argv);
}
```

The output of this program is shown in Figure 11-2. The principal function in Example 11-2 is set_month(). In this function, we call popen() to run the UNIX program *cal* and read its input into a buffer. Since we know ahead of time about how much text we are going to read, text is declared with ample space (BUFSIZ). Each line is read consecutively until fgets() returns NULL, at which time we close the opened process using pclose() and convert the text buffer into a compound string. This compound string specifies a font list element tag and it includes newlines because fgets() does not strip newline characters from the strings it retrieves.

The program displays the calendar for the month corresponding to the selected item in the List, but only as a single Label widget. If we wanted to display individual days using different fonts (with Sundays grayed out, for example), then the text buffer would have to be parsed. In this case, separate compound strings would be created using a different font for the Sunday dates only. Since this exercise is more about manipulating compound strings than it is about Label widgets, we refer you to Chapter 19, *Compound Strings*, for a detailed

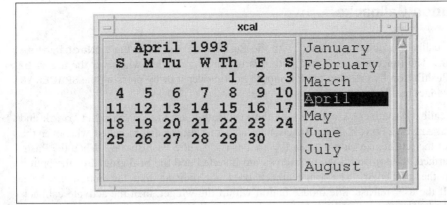

Figure 11-2. Output of xcal.c

discussion of the use of multiple fonts in compound strings. If you want to provide the user with the ability to select individual days from the month displayed, you must parse the dates from the text buffer and you probably want to use separate PushButton widgets for each date. See the Appendix, *Additional Example Programs*, for an example of this technique.

11.2 PushButtons

Since the PushButton is subclassed from Label, a PushButton can do everything that a Label can. However, unlike Labels, PushButtons can interact with the user and invoke functions internal to the underlying application through callback routines. This interactivity is the principal difference between PushButtons and Labels. There are other visual differences, but these are adjusted automatically by the PushButton widget using Label resources.

<Xm/PushB.h> and *<Xm/PushBG.h>* are the header files for PushButton widgets and gadgets, respectively. These objects can be created using XtVaCreateManagedWidget(), as in the following code fragment:

```
Widget pushb_w, pushb_g;

pushb_w = XtVaCreateManagedWidget ("name",
    xmPushButtonWidgetClass, parent,
    resource-value-list,
    NULL);

pushb_g = XtVaCreateManagedWidget ("name",
    xmPushButtonGadgetClass, parent,
    resource-value-list,
    NULL);
```

11.2.1 PushButton Callbacks

The major callback routine associated with the PushButton widget is the XmNactivate-Callback. The functions associated with this resource are called whenever the user activates the PushButton by pressing the left mouse button over it or by pressing the SPACEBAR when the widget has the keyboard focus.

The other callback routines associated with the PushButton are the XmNarmCallback and the XmNdisarmCallback. Each function in an arm callback list is called whenever the user presses the left mouse button when the pointer is over the PushButton. When the Push-Button is armed, the top and bottom shadows are inverted and the background of the button changes to the arm color. The arm callback does not indicate that the button has been released. If the user releases the mouse button within the widget, then the activate callback list is invoked. The arm callback is always called before the activate callback, whether or not the activate callback is even called.

When the user releases the button, the disarm callback list is invoked. When the button is disarmed, its shadow colors and the background return to their normal state. Like the arm callback, the disarm callback does not guarantee that the activate callback has been invoked. If the user changes her mind before releasing the mouse button, she can move the mouse outside of the widget area and then release the button. In this case, only the arm and disarm callbacks are called. However, the most common case is that the user actually selects and activates the button, in which case the arm callback is called first, followed by the activate callback and then the disarm callback.

The activate callback function is by far the most useful of the PushButton callbacks. It is generally unnecessary to register arm and disarm callback functions, unless your application has a specific need to know when the button is pushed and released, even if it is not activated. Example 11-3 demonstrates the use of the various PushButton callbacks.†

Example 11-3. The pushb.c program

```
/* pushb.c -- demonstrate the pushbutton widget.  Display one
 * PushButton with a single callback routine.  Print the name
 * of the widget and the number of "multiple clicks".  This
 * value is maintained by the toolkit.
 */
#include <Xm/PushB.h>

main(argc, argv)
int argc;
char *argv[];
{
    XtAppContext app;
    Widget toplevel, button;
    void my_callback();
    XmString btn_text;

    XtSetLanguageProc (NULL, NULL, NULL);
```

†XtSetLanguageProc() is only available in X11R5; there is no corresponding function in X11R4. Xm-StringCreateLocalized() is only available in Motif 1.2; XmStringCreateSimple() is the corresponding function in Motif 1.1.

Example 11-3. The pushb.c program (continued)

```
    toplevel = XtVaAppInitialize (&app, "Demos",
        NULL, 0, &argc, argv, NULL, NULL);

    btn_text = XmStringCreateLocalized ("Push Here");
    button = XtVaCreateManagedWidget ("button",
        xmPushButtonWidgetClass, toplevel,
        XmNlabelString, btn_text,
        NULL);
    XmStringFree (btn_text);
    XtAddCallback (button, XmNarmCallback, my_callback, NULL);
    XtAddCallback (button, XmNactivateCallback, my_callback, NULL);
    XtAddCallback (button, XmNdisarmCallback, my_callback, NULL);

    XtRealizeWidget (toplevel);
    XtAppMainLoop (app);
}

void
my_callback(w, client_data, call_data)
Widget w;
XtPointer client_data;
XtPointer call_data;
{
    XmPushButtonCallbackStruct *cbs =
        (XmPushButtonCallbackStruct *) call_data;

    if (cbs->reason == XmCR_ARM)
        printf ("%s: armed\n", XtName (w));
    else if (cbs->reason == XmCR_DISARM)
        printf ("%s: disarmed\n", XtName (w));
    else
        printf ("%s: pushed %d times\n", XtName (w), cbs->click_count);
}
```

The callback structure associated with the PushButton callback routines is `XmPush-`
`ButtonCallbackStruct`, which is defined as follows:

```
    typedef struct {
        int     reason;
        XEvent *event;
        int     click_count;
    } XmPushButtonCallbackStruct;
```

The `reason` parameter is set to `XmCR_ACTIVATE`, `XmCR_ARM`, or `XmCR_DISARM`
depending on the callback that invoked the callback routine. We use this value to decide
what action to take in the callback routine. The event that caused the callback routine to be
invoked is referenced by the `event` field.

The value of the `click_count` field reflects how many times the PushButton has been
clicked repeatedly. A repeated button click is one that occurs during a predefined time segment since the last button click. Repeated button clicks can only be done using the mouse.
The time segment that determines whether a button click is repeated is defined by the
resource `multiClickTime`. This resource is not defined by Motif but on a per-display
basis; the value should be left to the user to specify independently from the application. You
can get or set this value using the functions `XtGetMultiClickTime()` or `XtSet-`
`MultiClickTime()`. The time interval is used by Xt's translation manager to determine

when multiple events are interpreted as a repeat event. The default value is 200 milliseconds (1/5 of a second).

11.2.2 Multiple Button Clicks

Unfortunately, there is no way to determine whether you are about to receive multiple button clicks from a PushButton. Each time the user activates the PushButton, the arm callback is invoked, followed by the activate callback, followed by the disarm callback. These three callbacks are invoked regardless of whether multiple clicks have occurred.

The best way to determine whether multiple button clicks have occurred would be for the disarm callback to be called only when there are no more button clicks queued. Under this scenario, the same callback function can be used to determine the end of a multiple button click sequence. However, since the Motif toolkit does not operate this way, we must approach the task of handling multiple button clicks differently. We handle the situation by setting up our own timeout routines independently of Motif and handling multiple clicks through the timeout function. Even though we are going to use an alternate method for handling multiple clicks, we can still use the `click_count` parameter in the callback structure provided by the PushButton callback routine. Our technique is demonstrated in Example 11-4.†

Example 11-4. The multi_click.c program

```
/* multi_click.c -- demonstrate handling multiple PushButton clicks.
 * First, obtain the time interval of what constitutes a multiple
 * button click from the display and pass this as the client_data
 * for the button_click() callback function.  In the callback, single
 * button clicks set a timer to expire on that interval and call the
 * function process_clicks().  Double clicks remove the timer and
 * just call process_clicks() directly.
 */
#include <Xm/PushB.h>

XtAppContext app;

main(argc, argv)
int argc;
char *argv[];
{
    Widget toplevel, button;
    void button_click();
    XmString btn_text;
    int interval;

    XtSetLanguageProc (NULL, NULL, NULL);

    toplevel = XtVaAppInitialize (&app, "Demos",
        NULL, 0, &argc, argv, NULL, NULL);

    /* get how long for a double click */
```

---

†XtSetLanguageProc() is only available in X11R5; there is no corresponding function in X11R4. XmStringCreateLocalized() is only available in Motif 1.2; XmStringCreateSimple() is the corresponding function in Motif 1.1.

Example 11-4. The multi_click.c program (continued)

```
        interval = XtGetMultiClickTime (XtDisplay (toplevel));
        printf ("Interval = %d\n", interval);

        btn_text = XmStringCreateLocalized ("Push Here");
        button = XtVaCreateManagedWidget ("button",
            xmPushButtonWidgetClass, toplevel,
            XmNlabelString, btn_text,
            NULL);
        XmStringFree (btn_text);
        XtAddCallback (button, XmNactivateCallback, button_click, interval);

        XtRealizeWidget (toplevel);
        XtAppMainLoop (app);
}

/* Process button clicks.  Single clicks set a timer, double clicks
 * remove the timer, and extended clicks are ignored.
 */
void
button_click(w, client_data, call_data)
Widget w;
XtPointer client_data;
XtPointer call_data;
{
    static XtIntervalId id;
    void process_clicks();
    int interval = (int) client_data;
    XmPushButtonCallbackStruct *cbs =
        (XmPushButtonCallbackStruct *) call_data;

    if (cbs->click_count == 1)
        id = XtAppAddTimeOut (app, interval, process_clicks, False);
    else if (cbs->click_count == 2) {
        XtRemoveTimeOut (id);
        process_clicks (True);
    }
}

/* This function won't be called until we've established whether
 * or not a single or a double click has occured.
 */
void
process_clicks(client_data, id)
XtPointer client_data;
XtIntervalId id;
{
    int double_click = (int) client_data;

    if (double_click)
        puts ("Double click");
    else
        puts ("Single click");
}
```

The program displays the same basic PushButton widget. First, it obtains the time interval that constitutes a multiple button click from the display. This value is passed as the `client_data` to the PushButton's callback function, `button_click()`. When the user first clicks on the PushButton, the callback function is called, and since it is a single-click at this point, a timer is set to expire on the given time interval. If the timer expires, the function `process_clicks()` is called with `False` as its parameter, which means that a single-click has indeed occurred. However, if a second button click occurs before the timer expires, the timer is removed and `process_clicks()` is called directly with `True` as its data, to indicate that a double-click has occurred. The function `process_clicks()` can be any function that processes single, double, or multiple clicks, depending on how you modify the example we've provided.

If you run Example 11-4, you may find that you get mixed messages about whether an action is a single or double mouse click. A multiple mouse click means that the user has both pressed and released the mouse button more than once. It is very common for a user to intend to double click on a button only to find that she really invoked a double press; she quickly pressed the mouse button twice, but she failed to release it before the required time interval. This problem makes it difficult to interpret double (multiple) button clicks. It is important that you inform the user of the proper double-clicking method in any accompanying documentation you provide with your application, as attempting to program around this problem will definitely cause you great distress.

If you are going to use multiple button clicks for PushButtons, it is important that the multiple-click actions perform a more global version of the single-click actions. The reason for this recommendation is that if the user intends to perform a double click but doesn't click fast enough, the single-click action is invoked instead of the double-click action. If the two actions are completely different, it can make an application difficult to use. You might also consider displaying some visual cue to the user about the availability of double-click actions. For example, you could use a multi-lined label in a PushButton, where the first line indicates the single-click action and the second line specifies the double-click action. If you use this technique, make sure that your documentation informs the user how to invoke either of the two actions.

While double-clicking is a popular interface technique among application programmers and it is certainly useful for computers with single-button mice, it may not be the best interface for all occasions. Possible error conditions may arise when the user is unfamiliar with single and double-clicking techniques. Users often trip on mouse buttons, causing unintentional multiple clicks. Also, users frequently intend to do one double click yet succeed in doing two single clicks. As a result, they get very upset because the application invokes the wrong action twice as opposed to the right action once. Rather than subjecting your users to possible misinterpretation, it may be better to define an alternate method for providing separate actions for the same PushButton widget.

For example, you could define an action for a SHIFT-modified button click. This action is easy enough for the user to do, it is less subject to ambiguity or accidental usage, and it is much easier to program. The callback function only needs to check the `event` data structure and see if the SHIFT key is down when the button is activated.

The PushButton looks for and reports multiple button-click actions by default, so if you are not interested in multiple button clicks, you should set the resource `XmNmultiClick` to `XmMULTICLICK_DISCARD`. When multiple clicks are discarded, only the first of a series of clicks are processed; the rest are discarded without notifying the callback routine. To turn multiple clicks back on, set the resource to `XmMULTICLICK_KEEP`.

11.3 ToggleButtons

A ToggleButton is a simple user-interface element that represents a Boolean state. Usually, the widget consists of an indicator (a square or diamond) with either text or a pixmap on one side of it. The indicator is optional, however, since the text or pixmap itself can provide the state information of the button. The ToggleButton widget is subclassed from Label, so ToggleButtons can have their labels set to compound strings or pixmaps and can be aligned in the same ways and under the same restrictions as Label widgets.

Individually, a ToggleButton might be used to indicate whether a file should be opened in overwrite mode or append mode, or whether a mail application should update a folder upon process termination. But for the most part, it is when ToggleButtons are grouped together that they become interesting components of a user interface. A RadioBox is a group of ToggleButtons in which only one may be on at any given time. Like the old AM car radios, when one button is pressed in, all of the others are popped out. A CheckBox is a group of ToggleButtons in which each ToggleButton may be set independently of the others. In a RadioBox the selection indicator is represented by a diamond shape, and in a CheckBox it is represented by a square. In either case, when the button is on, the indicator is filled with a highlight color and appears to be pressed in, and when it is off, the indicator appears to be popped out.

A CheckBox or a RadioBox can often present a set of choices to the user more effectively than a List widget, a PopupMenu, or a row of PushButtons. In fact, these configurations are so common that Motif provides convenience routines for creating them: XmCreate-RadioBox() and XmCreateSimpleCheckBox(). RadioBoxes and CheckBoxes are really specialized instances of the RowColumn manager widget that contain ToggleButton children.

11.3.1 Creating ToggleButtons

Applications that use ToggleButtons must include the header file <Xm/ToggleB.h>. Toggle-Buttons may be created using XtVaCreateManagedWidget(), as in the following code fragment:

```
Widget toggle;

toggle = XtVaCreateManagedWidget ("name",
    xmToggleButtonWidgetClass, parent,
    resource-value-list,
    NULL);
```

ToggleButtons are also available in the form of gadgets. To use a ToggleButton gadget, you must include the header file <Xm/ToggleBG.h>. ToggleButton gadgets may be created using XtVaCreateManagedWidget() as follows:

```
Widget toggle;

toggle = XtVaCreateManagedWidget ("name",
    xmToggleButtonGadgetClass, parent,
    resource-value-list,
    NULL);
```

As we'll show you later in this section, it is also possible to create ToggleButtons at the same time as you create their RowColumn parent. This technique is commonly used when you create a RadioBox or a CheckBox.

Figure 11-3 shows an example of several different ToggleButtons in various states.

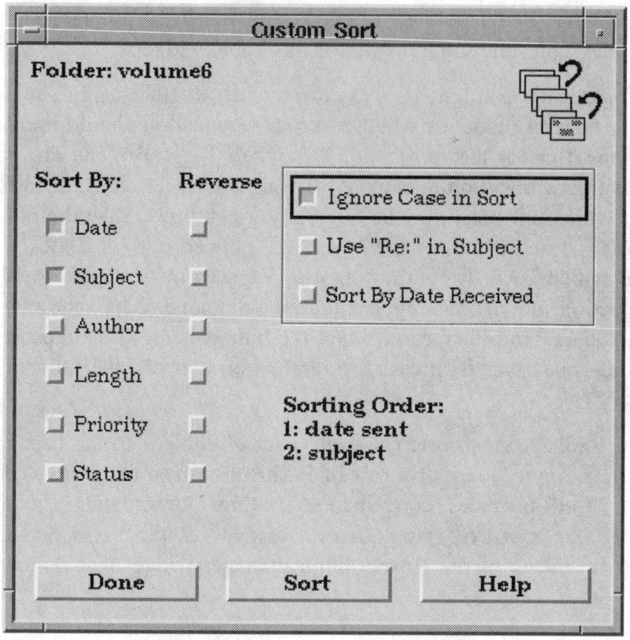

Figure 11-3. ToggleButton widgets and gadgets

11.3.2 ToggleButton Resources

Since ToggleButtons are fairly simple objects, there are only a few resources associated with them aside from those inherited from the Label class. Probably the most important of these resources is XmNindicatorType, which controls whether the selection indicator is a square or a diamond and indicates whether the ToggleButtons are part of a CheckBox or a RadioBox. The resource can be set to XmN_OF_MANY, which specifies a square-shaped indicator that indicates that multiple ToggleButtons in the same group can be selected, or Xm-ONE_OF_MANY, which specifies a diamond-shaped indicator that indicates that only one ToggleButton in the group may be set. Applications rarely set this resource directly, however, because the convenience routines that create RadioBoxes and CheckBoxes set the resource automatically.

When you are grouping ToggleButtons together in a single manager widget, the Motif toolkit expects you to use a RowColumn widget. The RowColumn widget has several resources intrinsic to its class that control the behavior of ToggleButton children. Setting the Row-Column resource XmNradioBehavior to True automatically changes the XmN-indicatorType resource of every ToggleButton managed by the RowColumn to Xm-ONE_OF_MANY, which provides the exclusive RadioBox behavior. Setting XmNradio-Behavior to False sets the XmNindicatorType to XmN_OF_MANY and gives the CheckBox behavior. If you want to use ToggleButtons in a manager widget other than a RowColumn, you need to set the XmNindicatorType resource for each ToggleButton individually, as well as manage the state of each button.

Many of the remaining resources are intended mostly for fine-tuning the details of the indicator square or diamond. These details are straightforward and do not require a great deal of discussion. For example, the XmNindicatorSize resource can be used to set the width and height of the indicator. There is nothing magical about these sorts of resources or their side effects, so most are either set automatically by the ToggleButton or they should be left to the user to configure for herself.

11.3.3 ToggleButton Pixmaps

The XmNselectPixmap resource specifies the pixmap to use when a ToggleButton is on (or selected). The XmNset resource specifies the state of a ToggleButton; the button is selected when the resource is set to True. The selected pixmap only applies if the XmN-labelType resource is set to XmPIXMAP. XmNlabelType is a Label class resource, but it applies to ToggleButtons since they are subclassed from Label. Example 11-5 demonstrates the creation of a ToggleButton and the use of the XmNselectPixmap resource.†

Example 11-5. The toggle.c program

```
/* toggle.c -- demonstrate a simple toggle button.  */
#include <Xm/ToggleB.h>
#include <Xm/RowColumn.h>

void
toggled(widget, client_data, call_data)
Widget widget;
XtPointer client_data;
XtPointer call_data;
{
    XmToggleButtonCallbackStruct *state =
        (XmToggleButtonCallbackStruct *) call_data;

    printf ("%s: %s\n", XtName (widget), state->set? "on" : "off");
}

main(argc, argv)
int argc;
char *argv[ ];
{
```

---

†XtSetLanguageProc() is only available in X11R5; there is no corresponding function in X11R4.

Example 11-5. The toggle.c program (continued)

```
    Widget toplevel, rowcol, toggle;
    XtAppContext app;
    Pixmap on, off;
    Pixel fg, bg;

    XtSetLanguageProc (NULL, NULL, NULL);

    toplevel = XtVaAppInitialize (&app, "Demos", NULL, 0,
        &argc, argv, NULL, NULL);

    rowcol = XtVaCreateWidget ("_rowcol",
        xmRowColumnWidgetClass, toplevel,
        XmNorientation, XmHORIZONTAL,
        NULL);

    XtVaGetValues (rowcol,
        XmNforeground, &fg,
        XmNbackground, &bg,
        NULL);
    on = XmGetPixmap (XtScreen (rowcol), "switch_on", fg, bg);
    off = XmGetPixmap (XtScreen (rowcol), "switch_off", fg, bg);
    if (on == XmUNSPECIFIED_PIXMAP || off == XmUNSPECIFIED_PIXMAP) {
        puts ("Couldn't load pixmaps");
        exit (1);
    }

    toggle = XtVaCreateManagedWidget ("toggle",
        xmToggleButtonWidgetClass, rowcol,
        XmNlabelType,    XmPIXMAP,
        XmNlabelPixmap,  off,
        XmNselectPixmap, on,
        NULL);
    XtAddCallback (toggle, XmNvalueChangedCallback, toggled, NULL);

    toggle = XtVaCreateManagedWidget ("toggle",
        xmToggleButtonWidgetClass, rowcol,
        XmNlabelType,    XmPIXMAP,
        XmNlabelPixmap,  off,
        XmNselectPixmap, on,
        NULL);
    XtAddCallback (toggle, XmNvalueChangedCallback, toggled, NULL);

    XtManageChild (rowcol);

    XtRealizeWidget (toplevel);
    XtAppMainLoop (app);
}
```

The output for this program is shown in Figure 11-4. The button on the left shows the
ToggleButton when it is in the off state and the button on the right shows it in the on state.
The pixmaps illustrate the movement of a simple mechanical switch. Since the pixmaps
make the state of the toggle clear, the square indicator is not really necessary. It can be
turned off by setting XmNindicatorOn to False (its default value is True).

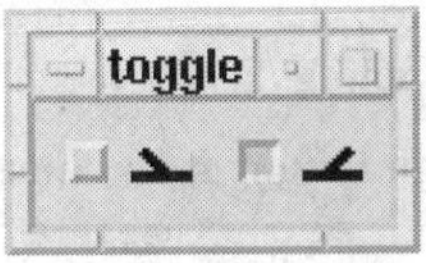

Figure 11-4. Output of toggle.c

In order to create the pixmaps for the ToggleButtons, we use the function XmGet-
Pixmap(), which is a general-purpose pixmap loading and caching function. The function
needs a foreground and background color for the pixmap it creates, so we retrieve and use the
colors from the RowColumn that is the parent of the ToggleButton. XmGetPixmap()
loads the pixmaps stored in the files *switch_on* and *switch_off* in the current directory.†
Those files contain the following bitmap definitions:

```
#define switch_on_width 16
#define switch_on_height 16
static char switch_on_bits[] = {
    0x00, 0x00, 0x00, 0x00, 0x00, 0x00, 0x00, 0x00, 0x00, 0x18, 0x00, 0x3c,
    0x00, 0x1e, 0x00, 0x0f, 0x80, 0x07, 0xc0, 0x03, 0xff, 0xff, 0xff, 0xff,
    0xff, 0xff, 0x00, 0x00, 0x00, 0x00, 0x00, 0x00};

#define switch_off_width 16
#define switch_off_height 16
static char switch_off_bits[] = {
    0x00, 0x00, 0x00, 0x00, 0x00, 0x00, 0x00, 0x00, 0x18, 0x00, 0x3c, 0x00,
    0x78, 0x00, 0xf0, 0x00, 0xe0, 0x01, 0xc0, 0x03, 0xff, 0xff, 0xff, 0xff,
    0xff, 0xff, 0x00, 0x00, 0x00, 0x00, 0x00, 0x00};
```

The XmNselectInsensitivePixmap resource can be used to specify a third pixmap to
be used when the widget or gadget is insensitive, but in a selected state. When a Toggle-
Button is insensitive, the user cannot change its value interactively.

11.3.4 ToggleButton Callbacks

The primary callback routine associated with the ToggleButton is the XmNvalueChanged-
Callback, which is invoked when the value of the ToggleButton changes. The Toggle-
Button also has arm and disarm callbacks that are analogous to the callbacks in PushButtons.
The callback structure associated with the ToggleButton callback routines is XmToggle-
ButtonCallbackStruct, which is defined as follows:

```
typedef struct {
    int     reason;
    XEvent *event;
    int     set;
} XmToggleButtonCallbackStruct;
```

---

†The fact that the pixmap files happen to reside in the current directory is not necessarily the recommended method
for using XmGetPixmap(). For a complete discussion of the function, see Section 3.4.5 in Chapter 3, *Overview of
the Motif Toolkit.*

When the value of the ToggleButton has changed, the `reason` field is set to `Xm-CR_VALUE_CHANGED` and the `set` field indicates the current state of the widget.

You can determine the state of a ToggleButton at any time using either `XmToggleButton-GetState()` or `XmToggleButtonGadgetGetState()`. These functions take the following form:

```
Boolean
XmToggleButtonGetState(toggle_w)
    Widget toggle_w;

Boolean
XmToggleButtonGadgetGetState(toggle_w)
    Widget toggle_w;
```

Both of the routines return the state of the specified ToggleButton. `XmToggleButton-GetState()` determines if the `toggle_w` parameter is a widget or a gadget, so you can use the routine on either a ToggleButton widget or a ToggleButton gadget. `XmToggle-ButtonGadgetSetState()` can only be used on a gadget.

You can explicitly set the state of a ToggleButton using similar functions: `XmToggle-ButtonSetState()` and `XmToggleButtonGadgetSetState()`. These functions take the following form:

```
void
XmToggleButtonSetState(toggle_w, state, notify)
    Widget    toggle_w;
    Boolean   state;
    Boolean   notify;

void
XmToggleButtonGadgetSetState(toggle_w, state, notify)
    Widget    toggle_w;
    Boolean   state;
    Boolean   notify;
```

The *state* argument specifies the state of the ToggleButton. The *notify* parameter allows you to specify whether or not the `XmNvalueChangedCallback` of the ToggleButton is called when the state is changed. Just like the corresponding get function, `Xm-ToggleButtonSetState()` determines if its parameter is a widget or gadget internally, so you can use it on either a ToggleButton widget or a ToggleButton gadget. `XmToggle-ButtonGadgetSetState()` can only be used on a gadget.

One important point to make about ToggleButtons is that, unlike PushButtons and Drawn-Buttons, the callback is not typically used to take an action in the application. This point becomes clearer with groups of ToggleButtons, which are commonly used to set the state of various variables. When the user has set the state as desired, she might tell the application to apply the settings by clicking on an associated PushButton. For this reason, the callback routine for a ToggleButton may simply set the state of a global variable; the value can then be used by other application functions.

Of course, like almost every object in Motif, a ToggleButton can be put to many uses. For example, a single ToggleButton could be used to swap the foreground and background colors of a window as soon as the user selects the button. An application that controls a CD player could have a **Pause** button represented by a ToggleButton.

11.3.5 RadioBoxes

When a group of ToggleButtons are used as part of an interface, it is in the form of a Radio-Box or a CheckBox. The primary difference between the two is the selection of the Toggle-Buttons within. In a RadioBox, only one item may be selected at a time (analogous to old-style AM car radios). You push one button and the previously set button pops out. Examples of exclusive settings in a RadioBox might be baud rate settings for a communications program or U.S. versus European paper sizes in the page setup dialog of a word processing program.

A RadioBox is implemented using a combination of ToggleButton widgets or gadgets and a RowColumn manager widget. As discussed in Chapter 8, *Manager Widgets*, the RowColumn widget is a general-purpose composite widget that manages the layout of its children. The RowColumn has special resources that allow it to act as a RadioBox for a group of Toggle-Buttons.

In a RadioBox, only one of the buttons may be set at any given time. This functionality is enforced by the RowColumn when the resource XmNradioBehavior is set to True. For true RadioBox effect, the XmNradioAlwaysOne resource can also be set to tell the Row-Column that one of the ToggleButtons should always be set.† Whenever XmNradio-Behavior is set, the RowColumn automatically sets the XmNindicatorType resource to XmONE_OF_MANY and the XmNvisibleWhenOff resource to True for all of its Toggle-Button children. Furthermore, the XmNisHomogeneous resource on the RowColumn is forced to True to ensure that no other kinds of widgets can be contained in that RowColumn instance.

Motif provides the convenience function XmCreateRadioBox() to automatically create a RowColumn widget that is configured as a RadioBox. This routine creates a RowColumn widget with XmNisHomogeneous set to True, XmNentryClass set to xmToggle-ButtonGadgetClass, XmNradioBehavior set to True, and XmNpacking set to XmPACK_COLUMN. Keep in mind that unless XmNisHomogeneous is set to True, there is nothing restricting a RadioBox from containing other classes as well as ToggleButtons. Whether the RowColumn is homogeneous or not, the toggle behavior is not affected. Although the Motif convenience function sets the homogeneity, it is not a requirement.‡ For example, you might want a RadioBox to contain a Label, or perhaps even some other control area, like a Command widget.

Example 11-6 contains a program that creates and uses a RadioBox.§

---

† Since you have the freedom to add or delete ToggleButtons from a RowColumn, regardless of their state, if you are not careful you can violate this aspect of radio behavior. Also, XmNradioBehavior is currently not a dynamically settable resource. If you want to use it, you should create the RowColumn widget with this resource set. Setting it using XtVaSetValues() after widget creation may not result in the desired behavior.

‡ Prior to Motif 1.1.1, XmCreateRadioBox() actually set XmNisHomogeneous to False rather than True, which is a bug. If your code relies on the bug and now breaks, all you need to do is add code to set XmNis-Homogeneous to False when you create your RadioBox.

§ XtSetLanguageProc() is only available in X11R5; there is no corresponding function in X11R4.

Example 11-6. The radio_box.c program

```
/* simple_radio.c -- demonstrate a simple radio box.  Create a
 * box with 3 toggles: "one", "two" and "three".  The callback
 * routine prints the most recently selected choice.  Maintain
 * a global variable that stores the most recently selected.
 */
#include <Xm/ToggleBG.h>
#include <Xm/RowColumn.h>

int toggle_item_set;

void
toggled(widget, client_data, call_data)
Widget widget;
XtPointer client_data;
XtPointer call_data;
{
    int which = (int) client_data;
    XmToggleButtonCallbackStruct *state =
        (XmToggleButtonCallbackStruct *) call_data;

    printf ("%s: %s\n", XtName (widget), state->set? "on" : "off");
    if (state->set)
        toggle_item_set = which;
    else
        toggle_item_set = 0;
}

main(argc, argv)
int argc;
char *argv[];
{
    Widget toplevel, radio_box, one, two, three;
    XtAppContext app;

    XtSetLanguageProc (NULL, NULL, NULL);

    toplevel = XtVaAppInitialize (&app, "Demos", NULL, 0,
        &argc, argv, NULL, NULL);

    radio_box = XmCreateRadioBox (toplevel, "radio_box", NULL, 0);

    one = XtVaCreateManagedWidget ("One",
        xmToggleButtonGadgetClass, radio_box, NULL);
    XtAddCallback (one, XmNvalueChangedCallback, toggled, 1);

    two = XtVaCreateManagedWidget ("Two",
        xmToggleButtonGadgetClass, radio_box, NULL);
    XtAddCallback (two, XmNvalueChangedCallback, toggled, 2);

    three = XtVaCreateManagedWidget ("Three",
        xmToggleButtonGadgetClass, radio_box, NULL);
    XtAddCallback (three, XmNvalueChangedCallback, toggled, 3);

    XtManageChild (radio_box);

    XtRealizeWidget (toplevel);
    XtAppMainLoop (app);
}
```

The program creates three ToggleButtons inside of a RadioBox. When the user selects one of the buttons, the previously-set widget is toggled off, and the `XmNvalueChanged-Callback` routine is called. Notice that the routine is called twice for each selection: the first time to notify that the previously set widget has been turned off, and the second time to notify that the newly set widget has been turned on. The output of the program is shown in Figure 11-5.

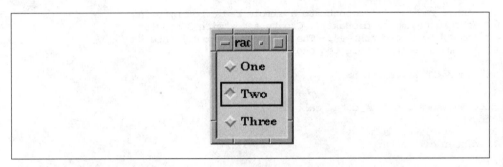

Figure 11-5. Output of radio_box.c

The global variable `toggle_item_set` indicates which of the three selections is on. The value of `toggle_item_set` is accurate at any given time because it is either set to the most currently selected object or it is set to 0. In a real application, this global variable would be used to store the state of the buttons, so that other application functions could reference them.

You should beware of lengthy callback lists, however. If you have more than one function in the callback list for the ToggleButtons (unlike the situation shown above), the entire list is going to be called twice. A zero value for `toggle_item_set` indicates that you are in the first of two phases of the toggling mechanism. In this case, you can fall through your callback lists, as the list is called again with the value set to the recently selected toggle item.

Motif provides another RadioBox creation routine, `XmVaCreateSimpleRadioBox()`, for creating simple RadioBoxes. If a RadioBox only has one callback associated with it and you only need to know which button has been selected, this routine may be used. The form of the function is:

```
XmVaCreateSimpleRadioBox(parent, name, button_set, callback, ..., NULL)
    Widget parent;
    String name;
    int    button_set;
    void   *callback;
```

In addition to the specified parameters, the function also accepts a NULL-terminated list of resource-value pairs that apply to the RowColumn widget that acts as the RadioBox. You can specify any normal RowColumn resources in this list, as well as the value Xm-VaRADIOBUTTON, which is a convenient method for specifying a button that is to be created inside the RadioBox. This parameter is followed by four additional arguments: a *label* of type XmString, a *mnemonic* of type XmKeySym, an *accelerator* of type String, and *accelerator_text* (also of type XmString) that is used to display the accelerator in the widget.† You can use XmVaRADIOBUTTON multiple times in the same

---

† Only the *label* argument has any effect through Motif 1.2 and all subreleases.

call to XmVaCreateSimpleRadioBox(), so that you can create an entire group of ToggleButtons in one function call.

Example 11-7 contains an example of XmVaCreateSimpleRadioBox(). This program is functionally identical to the previous example.†

Example 11-7. The simple_radio.c program

```
/* simple_radio.c -- demonstrate a simple radio box by using
 * XmVaCreateSimpleRadioBox().  Create a box with 3 toggles:
 * "one", "two" and "three".  The callback routine prints
 * the most recently selected choice.
 */
#include <Xm/RowColumn.h>

void
toggled(widget, client_data, call_data)
Widget widget;
XtPointer client_data;
XtPointer call_data;
{
    int which = (int) client_data;
    XmToggleButtonCallbackStruct *state =
        (XmToggleButtonCallbackStruct *) call_data;

    printf ("%s: %s\n", XtName (widget), state->set? "on" : "off");
}

main(argc, argv)
int argc;
char *argv[];
{
    Widget toplevel, radio_box;
    XtAppContext app;
    XmString one, two, three;

    XtSetLanguageProc (NULL, NULL, NULL);

    toplevel = XtVaAppInitialize (&app, "Demos", NULL, 0,
        &argc, argv, NULL, NULL);

    one   = XmStringCreateLocalized ("One");
    two   = XmStringCreateLocalized ("Two");
    three = XmStringCreateLocalized ("Three");
    radio_box = XmVaCreateSimpleRadioBox (toplevel, "radio_box",
        0,   /* the inital choice */
        toggled, /* the callback routine */
        XmVaRADIOBUTTON, one,  NULL, NULL, NULL,
        XmVaRADIOBUTTON, two,  NULL, NULL, NULL,
        XmVaRADIOBUTTON, three, NULL, NULL, NULL,
        NULL);
    XmStringFree (one);
    XmStringFree (two);
    XmStringFree (three);
```

---

†XtSetLanguageProc() is only available in X11R5; there is no corresponding function in X11R4. Xm-StringCreateLocalized() is only available in Motif 1.2; XmStringCreateSimple() is the corresponding function in Motif 1.1.

Example 11-7. The simple_radio.c program (continued)

```
    XtManageChild (radio_box);

    XtRealizeWidget (toplevel);
    XtAppMainLoop (app);
}
```

11.3.6 CheckBoxes

A CheckBox is similar to a RadioBox, except that there is no restriction on how many items may be selected at once. A word processing program might use a CheckBox for non-exclusive settings, such as whether font smoothing, bitmap smoothing, or both, should be applied.

Like RadioBoxes, CheckBoxes are implemented using RowColumn widgets and Toggle-Button children. To allow multiple items to be selected, the XmNradioBehavior resource is set to False. The convenience routine XmVaCreateSimpleCheckBox() works just like the radio box creation routine, except that it turns off the XmNradioBehavior resource. Rather than using this function, we can simply create a common RowColumn widget without the aid of convenience functions and add ToggleButton children. With this technique, we have more direct control over the resources that are set in the RowColumn, since we can specify exactly which ones we want using the varargs interface for creating the widget.

Example 11-8 demonstrates how to create a CheckBox with a regular RowColumn widget.†

Example 11-8. The toggle_box.c program

```
/* toggle_box.c -- demonstrate a homebrew ToggleBox.  A static
 * list of strings is used as the basis for a list of toggles.
 * The callback routine toggled() is set for each toggle item.
 * The client data for this routine is set to the enumerated
 * value of the item with respect to the entire list.  This value
 * is treated as a bit which is toggled in "toggles_set" -- a
 * mask that contains a complete list of all the selected items.
 * This list is printed when the PushButton is selected.
 */
#include <Xm/ToggleBG.h>
#include <Xm/PushBG.h>
#include <Xm/SeparatoG.h>
#include <Xm/RowColumn.h>

unsigned long toggles_set; /* has the bits of which toggles are set */

char *strings[] = {
    "One", "Two", "Three", "Four", "Five",
    "Six", "Seven", "Eight", "Nine", "Ten",
};

/* A RowColumn is used to manage a ToggleBox (also a RowColumn) and
```

---

†XtSetLanguageProc() is only available in X11R5; there is no corresponding function in X11R4.

Example 11-8. The toggle_box.c program (continued)

```
 * a PushButton with a separator gadget in between.
 */
main(argc, argv)
int argc;
char *argv[];
{
    Widget toplevel, rowcol, toggle_box, w;
    XtAppContext app;
    void toggled(), check_bits();
    int i;

    XtSetLanguageProc (NULL, NULL, NULL);

    toplevel = XtVaAppInitialize (&app, "Demos",
        NULL, 0, &argc, argv, NULL, NULL);

    rowcol = XtVaCreateManagedWidget ("rowcolumn",
        xmRowColumnWidgetClass, toplevel,
        NULL);

    toggle_box = XtVaCreateWidget ("togglebox",
        xmRowColumnWidgetClass, rowcol,
        XmNpacking,         XmPACK_COLUMN,
        XmNnumColumns,      2,
        NULL);

    /* simply loop thru the strings creating a widget for each one */
    for (i = 0; i < XtNumber (strings); i++) {
        w = XtVaCreateManagedWidget (strings[i],
            xmToggleButtonGadgetClass, toggle_box, NULL);
        XtAddCallback (w, XmNvalueChangedCallback, toggled, i);
    }

    XtVaCreateManagedWidget ("sep",
        xmSeparatorGadgetClass, rowcol, NULL);
    w = XtVaCreateManagedWidget ("Check Toggles",
        xmPushButtonGadgetClass, rowcol, NULL);
    XtAddCallback (w, XmNactivateCallback, check_bits, NULL);

    XtManageChild (rowcol);
    XtManageChild (toggle_box);

    XtRealizeWidget (toplevel);
    XtAppMainLoop (app);
}

/* callback for all ToggleButtons. */
void
toggled(widget, client_data, call_data)
Widget widget;
XtPointer client_data;
XtPointer call_data;
{
    int bit = (int) client_data;
    XmToggleButtonCallbackStruct *toggle_data =
        (XmToggleButtonCallbackStruct *) call_data;

    if (toggle_data->set) /* if the toggle button is set, flip its bit */
        toggles_set |= (1 << bit);
    else /* if the toggle is "off", turn off the bit. */
```

Example 11-8. The toggle_box.c program (continued)

```
        toggles_set &= ~(1 << bit);
}

void
check_bits(widget, client_data, call_data)
Widget widget;
XtPointer client_data;
XtPointer call_data;
{
    int i;

    printf ("Toggles set:");
    for (i = 0; i < XtNumber (strings); i++)
        if (toggles_set & (1<<i))
            printf (" %s", strings[i]);
    putchar ('\n');
}
```

The output of this program is shown in Figure 11-6.

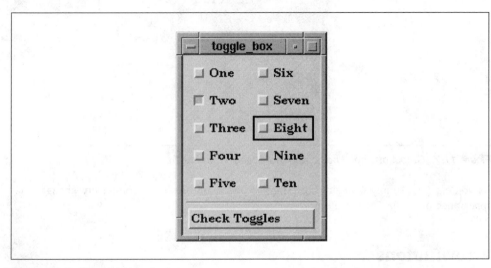

Figure 11-6. Output of toggle_box.c

This example is similar to the previous RadioBox examples, except that since more than one of the buttons may be set at a time in a CheckBox, we can no longer use `toggle_item_set` the way we did in the previous examples. Instead, we are going to change its name to `toggles_set` and its type to `unsigned long`. This time we are going to use the variable as a *mask*, which means that its individual bits have meaning, rather than the combined value of the variable. The bits indicate which of the ToggleButtons have been set. Each time a ToggleButton changes its value, the callback routine flips the corresponding bit in the mask. We can therefore determine at any given time which buttons are set and which are not.†

---

† The `unsigned long` type can only represent up to 32 ToggleButtons. If more buttons are used within the Check-Box, a new mechanism is needed, although the basic design presented here can still be used.

The PushButton in the program provides a way to check the state of all of the ToggleButtons. The callback routine for the PushButton prints the strings of those buttons that are selected by looping through the `toggles_set` variable and checking for bits that have been set.

One interesting aspect of this program is that it works just as well if the CheckBox is a RadioBox. To test this statement, we can run the program again with the `radioBehavior` resource set to `True` via the `-xrm` command-line option:

```
toggle_box -xrm "*radioBehavior: True"
```

The result is shown in Figure 11-7.

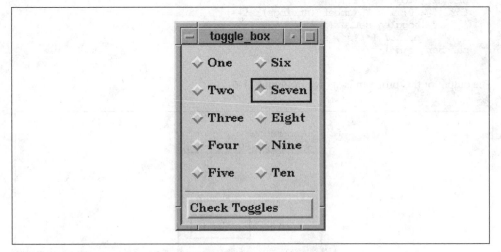

Figure 11-7. Output of toggle_box.c with radioBehavior set to True

As you can see, simply changing this single RowColumn resource completely changes the appearance of all the ToggleButtons.

11.4 ArrowButtons

An ArrowButton is just like a PushButton, except that it only displays a directional arrow symbol. The arrow can point up, down, left, or right. Motif provides both widget and gadget versions of the ArrowButton; the associated header files are *<Xm/ArrowB.h>* and *<Xm/ArrowBG.h>*. Example 11-9 shows a program that creates four ArrowButtons, one for each direction.†

Example 11-9. The arrow.c program
```
/* arrow.c -- demonstrate the ArrowButton widget.
 * Have a Form widget display 4 ArrowButtons in a
```

---

†`XtSetLanguageProc()` is only available in X11R5; there is no corresponding function in X11R4.

Example 11-9. The arrow.c program (continued)

```
 * familiar arrangement.
 */
#include <Xm/ArrowBG.h>
#include <Xm/Form.h>

main(argc, argv)
int argc;
char *argv[];
{
    XtAppContext app;
    Widget toplevel, form;
    Display *dpy;

    XtSetLanguageProc (NULL, NULL, NULL);

    toplevel = XtVaAppInitialize (&app, "Demos",
        NULL, 0, &argc, argv, NULL, NULL);

    dpy = XtDisplay (toplevel);
    /* Rather than listing all these resources in an app-defaults file,
     * add them directly to the database for this application only. This
     * would be virtually equivalent to hard-coding values, since these
     * resources will override any other specified external to this file.
     */
    XrmPutStringResource
        (&dpy->db, "*form*topAttachment", "attach_position");
    XrmPutStringResource
        (&dpy->db, "*form*leftAttachment", "attach_position");
    XrmPutStringResource
        (&dpy->db, "*form*rightAttachment", "attach_position");
    XrmPutStringResource
        (&dpy->db, "*form*bottomAttachment", "attach_position");

    form = XtVaCreateWidget ("form", xmFormWidgetClass, toplevel,
        XmNfractionBase,     3,
        NULL);

    XtVaCreateManagedWidget ("arrow1",
        xmArrowButtonGadgetClass, form,
        XmNtopPosition,      0,
        XmNbottomPosition,   1,
        XmNleftPosition,     1,
        XmNrightPosition,    2,
        XmNarrowDirection,   XmARROW_UP,
        NULL);

    XtVaCreateManagedWidget ("arrow2",
        xmArrowButtonGadgetClass, form,
        XmNtopPosition,      1,
        XmNbottomPosition,   2,
        XmNleftPosition,     0,
        XmNrightPosition,    1,
        XmNarrowDirection,   XmARROW_LEFT,
        NULL);

    XtVaCreateManagedWidget ("arrow3",
        xmArrowButtonGadgetClass, form,
        XmNtopPosition,      1,
        XmNbottomPosition,   2,
```

Example 11-9. The arrow.c program (continued)

```
            XmNleftPosition,      2,
            XmNrightPosition,     3,
            XmNarrowDirection,    XmARROW_RIGHT,
            NULL);

    XtVaCreateManagedWidget ("arrow4",
        xmArrowButtonGadgetClass, form,
        XmNtopPosition,       2,
        XmNbottomPosition,    3,
        XmNleftPosition,      1,
        XmNrightPosition,     2,
        XmNarrowDirection,    XmARROW_DOWN,
        NULL);

    XtManageChild (form);
    XtRealizeWidget (toplevel);
    XtAppMainLoop (app);
}
```

Figure 11-8 shows the output of this program.

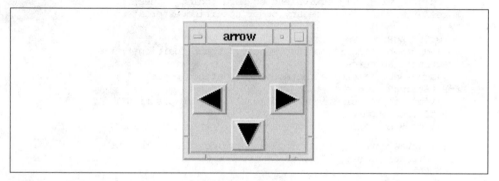

Figure 11-8. The four ArrowButton directions

The size of the arrow-shaped image is calculated dynamically based on the size of the widget itself. If the widget is resized for some reason, the directional arrow grows or shrinks to fill the widget. The `XmNarrowDirection` resource controls the direction of the arrow displayed by an ArrowButton. This resource may have one of the following values:

```
    XmARROW_UP
    XmARROW_DOWN
    XmARROW_LEFT
    XmARROW_RIGHT
```

ArrowButtons are useful if you want to provide redundant interface methods for certain widgets. For example, you could use ArrowButtons to move the viewport of a Scrolled-Window. Redundancy, when used appropriately, can be an important part of a graphical user interface. Many users may not adapt well to certain interface controls, such as Pulldown-Menus in MenuBars or keyboard accelerators, while they are perfectly comfortable with iconic controls such as ArrowButtons and PushButtons displaying pixmaps. ArrowButtons are also useful if you want to build your own interface for an object that is not part of the Motif widget set.

ArrowButton widgets and gadgets work in the same way as PushButtons. ArrowButtons have an `XmNactivateCallback`, an `XmNarmCallback`, an `XmNdisarmCallback`, and a `XmNmultiClick` resource. The callback routines all take a parameter of type `XmArrowButtonCallbackStruct`, which is defined as follows:

```
typedef struct {
    int     reason;
    XEvent  *event;
    int     click_count;
} XmArrowButtonCallbackStruct;
```

This callback structure is identical to the one used for PushButtons.

ArrowButtons are commonly used to increment and decrement a value, a position, or another type of data by some arbitrary amount. If the amount being incremented or decremented is sufficiently small in comparison to the total size of the object, it is convenient for the user if you give her the ability to change the value quickly. For example, we can emulate the activate callback routine being called continuously when the user holds down the mouse button over an ArrowButton widget. This functionality is not a feature of the ArrowButton; it is something we have to add ourselves. To implement this feature, we use an Xt timer as demonstrated in Example 11-10.†

Example 11-10. The arrow_timer.c program

```
/* arrow_timer.c -- demonstrate continuous callbacks using
 * ArrowButton widgets.  Display up and down ArrowButtons and
 * attach arm and disarm callbacks to them to start and stop timer
 * that is called repeatedly while the button is down.  A label
 * that has a value changes either positively or negatively
 * by single increments while the button is depressed.
 */
#include <Xm/ArrowBG.h>
#include <Xm/Form.h>
#include <Xm/RowColumn.h>
#include <Xm/LabelG.h>

XtAppContext app;
Widget label;
XtIntervalId arrow_timer_id;
typedef struct value_range {
    int value, min, max;
} ValueRange;

main(argc, argv)
int argc;
char *argv[];
{
    Widget w, toplevel, rowcol;
    void start_stop();
    ValueRange range;

    XtSetLanguageProc (NULL, NULL, NULL);

    toplevel = XtVaAppInitialize (&app, "Demos",
        NULL, 0, &argc, argv, NULL, NULL);
```

---

†`XtSetLanguageProc()` is only available in X11R5; there is no corresponding function in X11R4.

Example 11-10. The arrow_timer.c program (continued)

```
    rowcol = XtVaCreateWidget ("rowcol",
        xmRowColumnWidgetClass, toplevel,
        XmNorientation, XmHORIZONTAL,
        NULL);

    w = XtVaCreateManagedWidget ("arrow_up",
        xmArrowButtonGadgetClass, rowcol,
        XmNarrowDirection,   XmARROW_UP,
        NULL);
    XtAddCallback (w, XmNarmCallback, start_stop, 1);
    XtAddCallback (w, XmNdisarmCallback, start_stop, 1);

    w = XtVaCreateManagedWidget ("arrow_dn",
        xmArrowButtonGadgetClass, rowcol,
        XmNarrowDirection,   XmARROW_DOWN,
        NULL);
    XtAddCallback (w, XmNarmCallback, start_stop, -1);
    XtAddCallback (w, XmNdisarmCallback, start_stop, -1);

    range.value = 0;
    range.min = -50;
    range.max = 50;
    label = XtVaCreateManagedWidget ("label",
        xmLabelGadgetClass, rowcol,
        XtVaTypedArg, XmNlabelString, XmRString, "0   ", 3,
        XmNuserData, &range,
        NULL);

    XtManageChild (rowcol);
    XtRealizeWidget (toplevel);
    XtAppMainLoop (app);
}

/* start_stop is used to start or stop the incremental changes to
 * the label's value.  When the button goes down, the reason is
 * XmCR_ARM and the timer starts.  XmCR_DISARM disables the timer.
 */
void
start_stop(w, client_data, call_data)
Widget w;
XtPointer client_data;
XtPointer call_data;
{
    int incr = (int) client_data;
    XmArrowButtonCallbackStruct *cbs =
        (XmArrowButtonCallbackStruct *) call_data;
    void change_value();

    if (cbs->reason == XmCR_ARM)
        change_value (incr, 1 );
    else if (cbs->reason == XmCR_DISARM)
        XtRemoveTimeOut (arrow_timer_id);
}

/* change_value is called each time the timer expires.  This function
 * is also used to initiate the timer.  The "id" represents that timer
 * ID returned from the last call to XtAppAddTimeOut().  If id == 1,
 * the function was called from start_stop(), not a timeout.  If the value
```

Example 11-10. The arrow_timer.c program (continued)

```
 * has reached its maximum or minimum, don't restart timer, just return.
 * If id == 1, this is the first timeout so make it be longer to allow
 * the user to release the button and avoid getting into the "speedy"
 * part of the timeouts.
 */
void
change_value(client_data, id)
XtPointer client_data;
XtIntervalId id;
{
    ValueRange *range;
    char buf[8];
    int incr = (int) client_data;

    XtVaGetValues (label, XmNuserData, &range, NULL);
    if (range->value + incr > range->max ||
        range->value + incr < range->min)
        return;
    range->value += incr;
    sprintf (buf, "%d", range->value);
    XtVaSetValues (label,
        XtVaTypedArg, XmNlabelString, XmRString, buf, strlen(buf),
        NULL);
    arrow_timer_id =
        XtAppAddTimeOut (app, id==1? 500 : 100, change_value, incr);
}
```

The output of this program is shown in Figure 11-9.

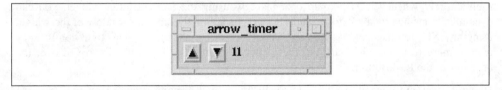

Figure 11-9. Output of arrow_timer.c

The program creates up and down ArrowButtons and attaches arm and disarm callbacks that start and stop an internal timer. Each time the timer expires, the value displayed by the Label changes incrementally by one. The timer remains on as long as the button is down. We know that the button has been released when the disarm event occurs.

The function responsible for this behavior is start_stop(); it is installed for both the arm and disarm callback. When the button is pressed, the reason is XmCR_ARM, and the timer starts. When the button is released, the disarm callback is invoked, the reason is Xm-CR_DISARM, and the timer is disabled. The start_stop() routine initiates the timer by calling change_value(). Each time the timer expires, change_value() is also called, which means that the function is called repeatedly while the button is pressed. The id represents the ID of the timer that recently expired from the last call to XtAppAdd-TimeOut(). If the value is one, the function was called from start_stop(), not as a timeout. We don't restart the timer if the value has reached its maximum or minimum value. If id is one, we know that this is the initiating call, so we make the first timeout last longer to allow the user to release the button before getting into the "speedy" timeouts. Otherwise, the time out occurs every 100 milliseconds.

If you experiment with the program, you can get a feel for how the functions work and modify some of the hard-coded values, such as the timeout values. While we demonstrate this technique with ArrowButtons, it can also be applied to a PushButton or any other widget that provides arm and disarm callbacks.

11.5 DrawnButtons

DrawnButtons are similar to PushButtons, except that they also have callback routines for Expose and ConfigureNotify events. Whenever a DrawnButton is exposed or resized, the corresponding callback routine is responsible for redisplaying the contents of the button. The widget does not handle its own repainting. These callbacks are invoked anytime the widget needs to redraw itself, even if it is a result of a change to a resource such as XmN-shadowType, XmNshadowThickness, or the foreground or background color of the widget.

The purpose of the DrawnButton is to allow you to draw into it while maintaining complete control over what the widget displays. Unlike with a PushButton, you are in control of the repainting of the surface area of the widget, not including the beveled edges that give it a 3D effect. To provide a dynamically changing pixmap using a PushButton widget, you would have to change the XmNlabelPixmap resource using XtVaSetValues(). Unfortunately, this method results in an annoying flickering effect because the PushButton redisplays itself entirely whenever its pixmap changes. By using the DrawnButton widget, you can dynamically change its display by rendering graphics directly onto the window of the widget using any Xlib routines such as XDrawLine() or XCopyArea(). This tight control may require more work on your part, but the feedback to the user is greatly improved over the behavior of the PushButton.

DrawnButtons are created similarly to PushButtons and ArrowButtons. However, because the widget provides you with its own drawing area, there is no corresponding gadget version of this object. The associated header file is *Xm/DrawnB.h* and it must be included by files that create the widget. Example 11-11 shows a simple example of how a DrawnButton can be created.†

Example 11-11. The drawn.c program

```
/* drawn.c -- demonstrate the DrawnButton widget by drawing a
 * common X logo into its window.  This is hardly much different
 * from a PushButton widget, but the DrawnButton isn't much
 * different, except for a couple more callback routines...
 */
#include <Xm/DrawnB.h>
#include <Xm/BulletinB.h>

Pixmap pixmap;
```

†XtSetLanguageProc() is only available in X11R5; there is no corresponding function in X11R4.

Example 11-11. The drawn.c program (continued)

```
main(argc, argv)
int argc;
char *argv[];
{
    XtAppContext app;
    Widget toplevel, bb, button;
    Pixel fg, bg;
    Dimension ht, st;
    void my_callback();

    XtSetLanguageProc (NULL, NULL, NULL);

    toplevel = XtVaAppInitialize (&app, "Demos",
        NULL, 0, &argc, argv, NULL, NULL);

    bb = XtVaCreateManagedWidget ("bb",
        xmBulletinBoardWidgetClass, toplevel, NULL);

    XtVaGetValues (bb,
        XmNforeground, &fg,
        XmNbackground, &bg,
        NULL);
    pixmap = XmGetPixmap (XtScreen (bb), "xlogo64", fg, bg);

    button = XtVaCreateManagedWidget ("button",
        xmDrawnButtonWidgetClass, bb,
        NULL);

    XtVaGetValues (button,
        XmNhighlightThickness, &ht,
        XmNshadowThickness, &st,
        NULL);

    XtVaSetValues (button,
        XmNwidth, 2 * ht + 2 * st + 64,
        XmNheight, 2 * ht + 2 * st + 64,
        NULL);

    XtAddCallback (button, XmNactivateCallback, my_callback, NULL);
    XtAddCallback (button, XmNexposeCallback, my_callback, NULL);
    XtAddCallback (button, XmNresizeCallback, my_callback, NULL);

    XtRealizeWidget (toplevel);
    XtAppMainLoop (app);
}

void
my_callback(w, client_data, call_data)
Widget w;
XtPointer client_data;
XtPointer call_data;
{
    XmDrawnButtonCallbackStruct *cbs =
        (XmDrawnButtonCallbackStruct *) call_data;
    if (cbs->reason == XmCR_ACTIVATE)
        printf ("%s: pushed %d times\n", XtName(w), cbs->click_count);
    else if (cbs->reason == XmCR_EXPOSE) {
        Dimension ht, st;

        XtVaGetValues (w,
```

Example 11-11. The drawn.c program (continued)

```
            XmNhighlightThickness, &ht,
            XmNshadowThickness, &st,
            NULL);

        XtVaSetValues (w,
            XmNwidth, 2 * ht + 2 * st + 64,
            XmNheight, 2 * ht + 2 * st + 64,
            NULL);

        XCopyArea (XtDisplay (w), pixmap, XtWindow (w),
            XDefaultGCOfScreen (XtScreen (w)), 0, 0, 64, 64,
            ht + st, ht + st);
    }
    else /* XmCR_RESIZE */
        puts ("Resize");
}
```

The program simply displays the X Window System logo as shown in Figure 11-10.

Figure 11-10. Output of drawn.c

A single callback routine, my_callback(), is specified for the XmNactivate-Callback, XmNexposeCallback, and XmNresizeCallback callbacks. The callback structure associated with the DrawnButton is called the XmDrawnButton-CallbackStruct, which is defined as follows:

```
    typedef struct {
        int     reason;
        XEvent  *event;
        Window  window;
        int     click_count;
    } XmDrawnButtonCallbackStruct;
```

The `window` field of the structure is the window ID of the DrawnButton widget. This value is the same as that returned by `XtWindow()`. The `my_callback()` callback routine checks the value of the `reason` field to determine which action to take. The `reason` can be one of the following values:†

```
XmCR_ACTIVATE
XmCR_ARM
XmCR_DISARM
XmCR_EXPOSE
XmCR_RESIZE
```

When the `reason` is `XmCR_EXPOSE`, the callback routine handles drawing the X Window System logo in the DrawnButton. Since the widget takes care of drawing its own highlight and shadow, we have to be careful not to draw over these areas.

Since all of the rendering in a DrawnButton is the responsibility of the application, you must decide whether you want to render the graphics differently when the button is insensitive. Since the DrawnButton is subclassed from the Label class, you can provide a `XmNlabel-Pixmap` and `XmNlabelInsensitivePixmap` if you like, but in this case you might as well use a PushButton instead of a DrawnButton.

In Chapter 20, *Signal Handling*, we present an example that shows how DrawnButtons can be used to construct an *application manager*. An application manager is a program that contains a set of icons, where each icon corresponds to a program. When the user pushes one of the buttons, the corresponding program is run. The button deactivates itself so that only one instance of each application can run at a time. There is no particular reason for this design restriction aside from the fact that it demonstrates the use of the visual resources of the DrawnButton widget.

The `XmNpushButtonEnabled` resource of the DrawnButton indicates whether or not the DrawnButton should look and act like a PushButton. When the value is `False` (the default), the DrawnButton displays whatever contents you put in it as well as a shadow border. The style of the shadow is specified by the `XmNshadowType` resource, which can be set to one of the following values:

```
XmSHADOW_IN
XmSHADOW_OUT
XmSHADOW_ETCHED_IN
XmSHADOW_ETCHED_OUT
```

When `XmNpushButtonEnabled` is `False`, the button does not provide any feedback to the user when the button is activated.

When the value of `XmNpushButtonEnabled` is set to `True`, the DrawnButton behaves like a PushButton and does provide feedback to the user when the button is activated. The shadow border for the button is always drawn in the `XmSHADOW_IN` style, regardless of the setting of the `XmNshadowType` resource. When the button is activated, the shadow is reversed, just as for a PushButton.

---

† In some versions of the Motif 1.1 toolkit, the `event` field of this callback structure is NULL when the reason is `Xm-CR_RESIZE`. As a result, you cannot use the `event` structure to provide you with the new dimensions of the widget. To query the widget's size, you must use `XtVaGetValues()` or possibly `XtQueryGeometry()`. The `event` field is also NULL when the user activates the button using the keyboard rather than the mouse.

11.6 Summary

The Label class acts as a superclass for more widgets than any other widget in the Motif toolkit and as a result, its use is rather broad. We have presented the fundamentals of Labels, PushButtons, ToggleButtons, ArrowButtons, and DrawnButtons in this chapter. For additional information on these widgets, especially their uses in menu systems, see Chapter 4, *The Main Window*, and Chapter 15, *Menus*. Examples of all these widgets are also liberally spread throughout the rest of the book.

11.7 Exercise

The following exercise is intended to stimulate and encourage other creative uses of labels and buttons.

1. Generic X windows have a background pixmap property that can be set using `XSet-WindowBackgroundPixmap()`.† Whenever the background pixmap is set, the image is tiled on the window. If the window is larger than the image, the image is replicated in a checkerboard fashion until the window's background is filled; if the window is the same size or smaller than the image, the image is centered in the window. The image is automatically rendered into the window appropriately by the server whenever necessary. Since widgets have windows, the X Toolkit Intrinsics provides a resource for the Core widget class that allows you to set the background pixmap using `XtN-backgroundPixmap`. (Motif's `XmNbackgroundPixmap` resource is identical except that the naming convention provides consistency among resource names.) Write a program that displays a Label that contains both graphics and a text label by setting both `XmNlabelString` and `XmNbackgroundPixmap` to appropriate values.

---

† See Volume One, *Xlib Programming Manual*, for details on `XSetWindowBackgroundPixmap()`.

12

The List Widget

This chapter describes another control that the user can manipulate. The List widget displays a number of text choices that the user can select interactively.

In This Chapter:

12
The List Widget

Almost every application needs to display lists of choices to the user. This task can be accomplished in many ways, depending on the nature of the choices. For example, a group of ToggleButtons is ideal for displaying configuration settings that can be individually set and unset and then applied all at once. A list of commands can be displayed in a Popup-Menu, or for a more permanent command palette, a RowColumn or Form widget can manage a group of PushButton widgets. But for displaying a list of text choices, such as a list of files to be opened or a list of fonts to be applied to text, nothing beats a List widget.

A List widget displays a single column of text choices that can be selected or deselected using either the mouse or the keyboard. Each choice is represented by a single-line text element specified as a compound string. Figure 12-1 shows a typical List widget.

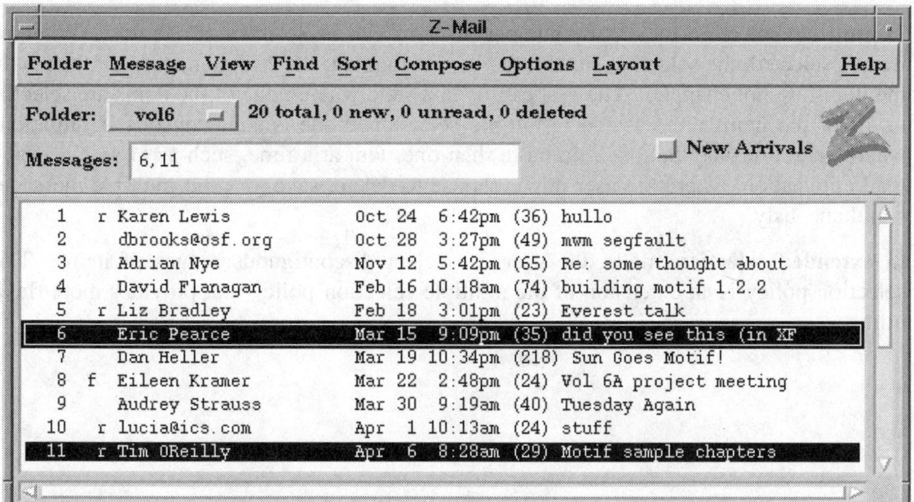

Figure 12-1. A List widget with two selected items

Internally, the List widget operates on an array of compound strings that are defined by the application. (See Chapter 19, *Compound Strings*, for a discussion of how to create and manage compound strings.†) Each string is an element of the array, with the first position starting at one, as opposed to position zero, which is used in C-style arrays. The user can select a particular choice by clicking and releasing the left mouse button on the item. All of the items in the list are available to the user for selection at all times; you cannot make individual items unselectable. What happens when an item is selected is up to the application callback routines invoked by the List widget.

A List widget is typically a child of a ScrolledWindow, so that the List is displayed with ScrollBars attached to it. The selection mechanism for the List does not change, so the user can still select items as before, but the user can now use the ScrollBars to adjust the items in the list that are visible.

The List widget supports four different selection policies:

- In **single selection** mode, selecting an item toggles its selection state and deselects any other selected item. Single selection Lists should be used when only one of many choices may be selected at a time, although under this policy there may also be no items selected. Some possible uses for a single selection List include choosing a font family or style for text input and choosing a color for a bitmap editor.

- In **browse selection** mode, selecting a new item deselects any other selected item, but there can never be a state where no items are selected. From the user's perspective, browse selection is similar to single selection, except that there is an initial selected item. There are also differences with respect to callback routines. This issue is addressed in Section 12.5.

- In **multiple selection** mode, any number of items can be selected at one time. When an item is selected, the selection state of the item is toggled; the selection states of the rest of the items are not changed. The List can be in a state where none of the items are selected or all of the items are selected. Multiple selection mode is advantageous in situations where an action may be taken on more than one item at a time, such as in an electronic mail application, where the user might choose to delete, save, or print multiple messages simultaneously.

- In **extended selection** mode, the user can select discontiguous ranges of items. This selection policy is an extension of the multiple selection policy that provides more flexibility.

---

† Compound strings that use multiple fonts are allowed, but the List widget does not render these items very well.

12.1 Creating a List Widget

Using List widgets is fairly straightforward. An application that uses the List widget must include the header file *<Xm/List.h>*. This header file declares the types of the public List functions and the widget class name `xmListWidgetClass`. A List widget can be created as shown in the following code fragment:

```
Widget list;

list = XtVaCreateManagedWidget ("name",
    xmListWidgetClass, parent,
    resource-value-list,
    NULL);
```

Example 12-1 shows a program that creates a simple List widget.†

Example 12-1. The simple_list.c program

```
/* simple_list.c -- introduce the List widget.  Lists present
 * a number of comound strings as choices.  Therefore, strings
 * must be converted before set in lists.  Also, the number of
 * visible items must be set or the List defaults to 1 item.
 */
#include <Xm/List.h>

char *months[] = {
    "January", "February", "March", "April", "May", "June", "July",
    "August", "September", "October", "November", "December"
};

main(argc, argv)
int argc;
char *argv[];
{
    Widget          toplevel;
    XtAppContext    app;
    int             i, n = XtNumber (months);
    XmStringTable   str_list;

    XtSetLanguageProc (NULL, NULL, NULL);

    toplevel = XtVaAppInitialize (&app, "Demos", NULL, 0,
        &argc, argv, NULL, NULL);

    str_list = (XmStringTable) XtMalloc (n * sizeof (XmString));

    for (i = 0; i < n; i++)
        str_list[i] = XmStringCreateLocalized (months[i]);

    XtVaCreateManagedWidget ("Hello",
        xmListWidgetClass,      toplevel,
        XmNvisibleItemCount,    n,
        XmNitemCount,           n,
        XmNitems,               str_list,
        NULL);
```

---

†XtSetLanguageProc() is only available in X11R5; there is no corresponding function in X11R4. XmStringCreateLocalized() is only available in Motif 1.2; XmStringCreateSimple() is the corresponding function in Motif 1.1.

The List Widget

Example 12-1. The simple_list.c program (continued)

```
    for (i = 0; i < n; i++)
        XmStringFree (str_list[i]);
    XtFree (str_list);

    XtRealizeWidget (toplevel);
    XtAppMainLoop (app);
}
```

The program simply creates a List widget as the child of the `toplevel` widget. The List contains the names of the months as its choices. The output of the program is shown in Figure 12-2.

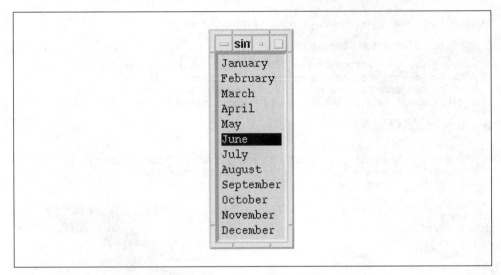

Figure 12-2. Output of simple_list.c

The selection policy of the List is controlled by the `XmNselectionPolicy` resource. The possible values for this resource are:

```
    XmSINGLE_SELECT
    XmBROWSE_SELECT
    XmMULTIPLE_SELECT
    XmEXTENDED_SELECT
```

`XmBROWSE_SELECT` is the default selection policy for the List widget. Since this policy is the one that we want to use, we do not need to set the `XmNselectionPolicy` resource. You should be aware that the user could change this policy with a resource specification. If you want to enforce this selection policy, you can program defensively and hard-code the value for `XmNselectionPolicy`, despite its default.

The program demonstrates the use of three basic elements of the List widget: the list of items, the number of items in the list, and the number of visible items. Because the items in a List must be compound strings, each of the choices must be converted from a C string to a compound string. The application allocates an array of `XmStrings`, creates a compound string for each month name, and stores the string in the `str_list`. The List widget is created with `str_list` as the value for the `XmNitems` resource and `XmNitemCount` is set to `n`.

Just like other widgets that use compound strings, the List widget copies the entire table of compound strings into its own internal storage. As a result, the list of strings needs to be freed after you have used it to set the `XmNitems` resource. When you set the items using this resource, you also need to set the `XmNitemCount` resource to specify the number of items in the list. If this resource is not set, the List does not know how many items to copy. The value of `XmNitemCount` should never be larger than the number of items in `XmN-items`. If the value for `XmNitemCount` is less than the number of items, the additional items are not put in the list.

To retrieve the list of items, you can call `XtVaGetValues()` on these resources, as shown in the following code fragment:

```
extern Widget    list;
XmStringTable    choices;
int              n_choices;

XtVaGetValues (list,
     XmNitems,       &choices,
     XmNitemCount,   &n_choices,
     NULL);
```

Since the items that the area returned are compound strings, you must convert them to C-style strings if you need to use any of the standard C library functions to view or manipulate the strings. You can also use any of the compound string functions described in Chapter 19, *Compound Strings*, for this purpose. Since we used `XtVaGetValues()` to obtain the values for the resources, the returned data should, as always, be considered read-only. You should not change any of the items in the list or attempt to free them (or the pointer to them) when you are done examining their values.

Example 12-1 also makes use of the `XmNvisibleItemCount` resource, which sets the height of the list to match the number of items that should be visible. If you want all the items to be visible, you simply set the value to the total number of items in the list. Setting the visible item count to a higher value is acceptable, assuming that the list is expected to grow to at least that size. If you want to set the number of visible items to be less than the number of items actually in the list, you should use a ScrolledList as described in the next section.

12.2 Using ScrolledLists

Most applications use List widgets in conjunction with ScrolledWindows. By creating a List widget as the child of a ScrolledWindow, we create what Motif calls a ScrolledList. The ScrolledList is not a widget, but a compound object. While this chapter describes most of the common resources and functions that deal with ScrolledLists, more detailed information about ScrolledWindows and ScrollBars can be found in Chapter 9, *ScrolledWindows and ScrollBars*.

A ScrolledList is built from two widget classes, so we could create and manage the widgets separately using two calls to `XtVaCreateManagedWidget()`. However, since Scrolled-Lists are used so frequently, Motif provides a convenience function to create this compound object. `XmCreateScrolledList()` takes the following form:

```
Widget
XmCreateScrolledList(parent, name, arglist, argcount)
     Widget    parent;
     char      *name;
     ArgList    arglist;
     Cardinal argcount;
```

The *arglist* parameter is an array of size *argcount* that contains resources to be passed to both the ScrolledWindow widget and the List widget. Generally, the two widgets use different resources that are specific to the widgets themselves, so there isn't any confusion about which resources apply to which widget. However, common resources, such as Core resources, are interpreted by both widgets, so caution is advised. If you want to set some resources on one widget, while ensuring that the values are not set on the other widget, you should avoid passing the values to the convenience routine. Instead, you can set resources separately by using `XtVaSetValues()` on each widget individually. `XmCreate-ScrolledList()` returns the List widget; if you need a handle to the ScrolledWindow, you can use `XtParent()` on the List widget. When you use the convenience routine, you need to manage the object explicitly with `XtManageChild()`.

ScrolledLists are useful because they can display a portion of the entire list provided by the widget. For example, we can modify the previous example, *simple_list.c*, to use a Scrolled-List by using the following code fragment:

```
. . .
/* Create the ScrolledList */
list_w = XmCreateScrolledList (toplevel, "Months", NULL, 0);

/* set the items, the item count, and the visible items */
XtVaSetValues (list_w,
     XmNitems,           str_list,
     XmNitemCount,       n,
     XmNvisibleItemCount, 5,
     NULL);

/* Convenience routines don't create managed children */
XtManageChild (list_w);
. . .
```

The size of the viewport into the entire List widget is controlled by the `XmNvisibleItem-Count` resource. In Motif 1.1, the value of this resource defaults to 1, while in Motif 1.2, the resource calculates its value based on the `XmNheight` of the List. We set the resource to 5. The output resulting from our changes is shown in Figure 12-3.

The `XmNscrollBarDisplayPolicy` and `XmNlistSizePolicy` resources control the display of the ScrollBars in a ScrolledList. The value for `XmNscrollBarDisplay-Policy` controls the display of the vertical ScrollBar; the resource can be set to either `Xm-AS_NEEDED` (the default) or `XmSTATIC`. If the policy is `XmAS_NEEDED`, when the entire list is visible, the vertical ScrollBar is not displayed. When the resource is set to `XmSTATIC`, the vertical ScrollBar is always displayed. The `XmNlistSizePolicy` resource reflects

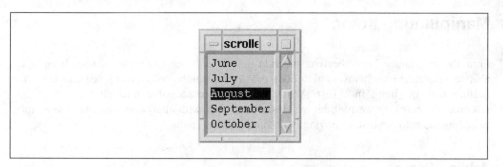

Figure 12-3. Output of simple_list.c modified to use a ScrolledList

how the ScrolledList manages its horizontal ScrollBar. The default setting is XmVARIABLE, which means that the ScrolledList attempts to grow horizontally to contain its widest item and a horizontal ScrollBar is not displayed. This policy may present a problem if the parent of the ScrolledList constrains its horizontal size. If the resource is set to XmRESIZE_IF_POSSIBLE, the ScrolledList displays a horizontal ScrollBar only if it cannot resize itself accordingly. If the value XmCONSTANT is used, the horizontal ScrollBar is displayed at all times, whether it is needed or not.

The size of a ScrolledList is ultimately controlled by its parent. In most cases, a manager widget such as a RowColumn or Form allows its children to be any size they request. If a ScrolledList is a child of a Form widget, its size is whatever you specify with either the XmNheight resource or the XmNvisibleItemCount. However, certain constraints, such as the XmNresizePolicy in a Form widget, may affect the height of its children unexpectedly. For example, if you set XmNresizePolicy to XmRESIZE_NONE, the ScrolledList widget's height request is ignored, which makes it look like XmNvisibleItemCount is not working.

The List widget accepts keyboard input to select items in the list, browse the list, and scroll the list. Like all other Motif widgets, the List has translation functions that facilitate this process. The translations are hard-coded into the widget and we do not recommend attempting to override this list with new translations. For ScrolledLists, the List widget automatically sets the ScrollBar's XmNtraversalOn resource to False so that the ScrollBar associated with the ScrolledList does not get keyboard input. Instead, the List widget handles the input that affects scrolling. We recommended that you do not interfere with this process, so users are not confused by different applications on the desktop behaving in different ways.

If a List widget is sensitive, all of the items in the List are selectable. If it is insensitive, none of them are selectable. You cannot set certain items to be insensitive to selection at any given time. Furthermore, you cannot set the entire List to be insensitive and allow the user to manipulate the ScrollBars. It is not entirely possible to make a read-only List widget; the user always has the ability to select items in the List, providing that it is sensitive. Of course, you can always choose not to hook up callback procedures to the widget, but this can lead to more confusion than anything else because if the user selects an object and the toolkit provides the visual feedback acknowledging the action, the user will expect the application to respond as well.

12.3 Manipulating Items

From the programmer's perspective, much of the power of the List widget comes from being able to manipulate its items. The toolkit provides a number of convenience functions for dealing with the items in a List. While the items are accesible through the XmNitems resource, the convenience routines are designed to deal with many common operations, such as adding items to the List, removing items, and locating items.

12.3.1 Adding Items

The entire list of choices may not always be available at the time the List is created. In fact, it is not uncommon to have no items available for a new list. In these situations, items can be added to the list dynamically using the following functions XmListAddItem(), Xm-ListAddItemUnselected(), XmListAddItems(), and XmListAddItems-Unselected(). XmListAddItemsUnselected() is a new routine in Motif 1.2. These functions take the following form:

```
void
XmListAddItem(list_w, item, position)
    Widget    list_w;
    XmString  item;
    int       position;

void
XmListAddItemUnselected(list_w, item, position)
    Widget    list_w;
    XmString  item;
    int       position;

void
XmListAddItems(list_w, items, item_count, position)
    Widget    list_w;
    XmString  *items;
    int       item_count;
    int       position;

void
XmListAddItemsUnselected(list_w, items, item_count, position)
    Widget    list_w;
    XmString  *items;
    int       item_count;
    int       position;
```

These routines allow you to add one or more items to a List widget at a specified position. Remember that list positions start at 1, not 0. The position 0 indicates the last position in the List; specifying this position appends the item or items to the end of the list. If the new item(s) are added to the list in between existing items, the rest of the items are moved down the list.

The difference between XmListAddItem() and XmListAddItemUnselected() is that XmListAddItem() compares each new item to each of the existing items. If a new item matches an existing item and if the existing item is selected, the new item is also selected. XmListAddItemUnselected() simply adds the new item without performing this check. In most situations, it is clear which routine you should use. If you know that the new item does not already exist, you should add it unselected. If the List is a single selection list, you should add new items as unselected. The only time that you should really add new items to the list using XmListAddItem() is when there could be duplicate entries, the list supports multiple selections, and you explicitly want to select all new items whose duplicates are already selected. The same is true of the routines that add multiple items.

Example 12-2 shows how items can be added to a ScrolledList dynamically using XmList-AddItemUnselected().†

Example 12-2. The alpha_list.c program

```
/* alpha_list.c -- insert items into a list in alphabetical order.  */

#include <Xm/List.h>
#include <Xm/RowColumn.h>
#include <Xm/TextF.h>

main(argc, argv)
int argc;
char *argv[];
{
    Widget        toplevel, rowcol, list_w, text_w;
    XtAppContext  app;
    Arg           args[5];
    int           n = 0;
    void          add_item();

    XtSetLanguageProc (NULL, NULL, NULL);

    toplevel = XtVaAppInitialize (&app, "Demos", NULL, 0,
        &argc, argv, NULL, NULL);

    rowcol = XtVaCreateWidget ("rowcol",
        xmRowColumnWidgetClass, toplevel, NULL);

    XtSetArg (args[n], XmNvisibleItemCount, 5); n++;
    list_w = XmCreateScrolledList (rowcol, "scrolled_list", args, n);
    XtManageChild (list_w);

    text_w = XtVaCreateManagedWidget ("text",
        xmTextFieldWidgetClass, rowcol,
```

---

†XtSetLanguageProc() is only available in X11R5; there is no corresponding function in X11R4. Xm-StringCreateLocalized() is only available in Motif 1.2; XmStringCreateSimple() is the corresponding function in Motif 1.1. XmFONTLIST_DEFAULT_TAG replaces XmSTRING_DEFAULT_CHARSET in Motif 1.2.

Example 12-2. The alpha_list.c program (continued)

```
            XmNcolumns,        25,
            NULL);
        XtAddCallback (text_w, XmNactivateCallback, add_item, list_w);

        XtManageChild (rowcol);
        XtRealizeWidget (toplevel);
        XtAppMainLoop (app);
}

/* Add item to the list in alphabetical order.  Perform binary
 * search to find the correct location for the new item position.
 * This is the callback routine for the TextField widget.
 */
void
add_item(text_w, client_data, call_data)
Widget text_w;
XtPointer client_data;
XtPointer call_data;
{
    Widget list_w = (Widget) client_data;
    char *text, *newtext = XmTextFieldGetString (text_w);
    XmString str, *strlist;
    int u_bound, l_bound = 0;

    /* newtext is the text typed in the TextField widget */
    if (!newtext || !*newtext) {
        /* non-null strings must be entered */
        XtFree (newtext); /* XtFree() checks for NULL */
        return;
    }
    /* get the current entries (and number of entries) from the List */
    XtVaGetValues (list_w,
        XmNitemCount, &u_bound,
        XmNitems,     &strlist,
        NULL);
    u_bound--;
    /* perform binary search */
    while (u_bound >= l_bound) {
        int i = l_bound + (u_bound - l_bound) / 2;
        /* convert the compound string into a regular C string */
        if (!XmStringGetLtoR (strlist[i], XmFONTLIST_DEFAULT_TAG, &text))
            break;
        if (strcmp (text, newtext) > 0)
            u_bound = i - 1; /* newtext comes before item */
        else
            l_bound = i + 1; /* newtext comes after item */
        XtFree (text); /* XmStringGetLtoR() allocates memory ... yuk */
    }
    str = XmStringCreateLocalized (newtext);
    XtFree (newtext);
    /* positions indexes start at 1, so increment accordingly */
    XmListAddItemUnselected (list_w, str, l_bound+1);
    XmStringFree (str);
    XmTextFieldSetString (text_w, "");
}
```

In Example 12-2, the ScrolledList is created with no items. However, we do specify XmN-visibleItemCount, in anticipation of items being added to the list. A TextField widget is used to prompt for strings that are added to the list using the add_item() callback. This function performs a binary search on the list to determine the position where the new item is to be added. A binary search can save time, as it is expensive to scan an entire List widget and convert each compound string into a C string. When the position for the new item is found, it is added using XmListAddItemUnselected(). The output of this program is shown in Figure 12-4.

Figure 12-4. Output of alpha_list.c

12.3.2 Finding Items

It is often useful to be able to determine whether or not a List contains a particular item. The simplest function for determining whether a particular item exists is XmListItem-Exists(), which takes the following form:

```
Boolean
XmListItemExists(list_w, item)
    Widget    list_w;
    XmString  item;
```

This function performs a linear search on the list for the specified item. If you are maintaining your list in a particular order, you may want to search the list yourself using another type of search to improve performance. The List's internal search function does not convert the compound strings to C strings. The search routine does a direct byte-by-byte comparison of the strings using XmStringByteCompare(), which is much more efficient than converting the compound strings to C strings for comparison. However, the linear search is still slower than a binary search by orders of magnitude. And unfortunately, XmStringByte-Compare() does not return which string is of greater or lesser value. The routine just returns whether the strings are different, so we cannot use it to alphabetize the items in a List.

If you need to know the position of an item in the List, you can use `XmListItemPos()`. This routine takes the following form:

```
int
XmListItemPos(list_w, item)
    Widget    list_w;
    XmString item;
```

This function returns the position of the first occurrence of *item* in the List, with 1 being the first position. If the function returns 0, the element is not in the List. If a List contains duplicate entries, you can find all of the positions of a particular item using `XmListGetMatchPos()`, which takes the following form:

```
Boolean
XmListGetMatchPos(list_w, item, pos_list, pos_cnt)
    Widget    list_w;
    XmString item;
    int      **pos_list;
    int      *pos_cnt;
```

This function returns `True` if the specified item is found in the List in one or more locations. The *pos_list* parameter is allocated to contain the array of positions of the item and the number of items found is returned in *pos_cnt*. When you are done using *pos_list*, you should free it using `XtFree()`. The function returns `False` if there are no items in the List, if memory cannot be allocated for *pos_list*, or if the specified item isn't in the List. In these cases, *pos_list* does not point to allocated space and should not be referenced or freed and the value of *pos_cnt* is not specified. The following code fragment shows the use of `XmListGetMatchPos()` to get the positions of an item in a List:

```
extern Widget  list_w;
int            *pos_list;
int            pos_cnt, i;
char           *choice = "A Sample Text String";
XmString       str = XmStringCreateLocalized (choice);

if (!XmListGetMatchPos (list_w, str, &pos_list, &pos_cnt))
    XtWarning ("Can't get items in list");
else {
    printf ("%s exists in positions %d:", choice, pos_cnt);
    for (i = 0; i < pos_cnt; i++)
        printf (" %d", pos_list[i]);
    puts ("");
    XtFree (pos_list);
}
```

12.3.3 Replacing Items

There are also a number of functions for replacing items in a List. To replace a contiguous sequence of items, use either `XmListReplaceItemsPos()` or `XmListReplace-ItemsPosUnselected()`. These functions take the following form:

```
void
XmListReplaceItemsPos(list_w, new_items, item_count, position)
    Widget    list_w;
    XmString *new_items;
    int       item_count;
    int       position;

void
XmListReplaceItemsPosUnselected(list_w, new_items, item_count,
                                position)
    Widget    list_w;
    XmString *new_items;
    int       item_count;
    int       position;
```

These functions replace the specified number of items with the new items starting at *position*. The difference between the two functions is the same as the difference between the List routines that add items selected and unselected. XmListReplaceItemsPos-Unselected() is a new routine in Motif 1.2.

You can also replace arbitrary elements in the list with new elements, using XmList-ReplaceItems() or XmListReplaceItemsUnselected. These routines take the following form:

```
void
XmListReplaceItems(list_w, old_items, item_count, new_items)
    Widget    list_w;
    XmString *old_items;
    int       item_count;
    XmString *new_items;


void
XmListReplaceItemsUnselected(list_w, old_items, item_count, new_items)
    Widget    list_w;
    XmString *old_items;
    int       item_count;
    XmString *new_items;
```

These functions work by searching the entire list for each element in *old_items*. Every occurrence of each element that is found is replaced with the corresponding element from *new_items*. The search continues for each element in *old_items* until *item_count* has been reached. The difference between the two functions is the same as the difference between the List routines that add items selected and unselected. XmListReplace-ItemsUnselected() is a new routine in Motif 1.2.

There is another new routine in Motif 1.2 that allows you to replace items in a List based upon position. The XmListReplacePositions() routine takes the following form:

```
void
XmListReplacePositions(list_w, pos_list, new_items, item_count)
    Widget    list_w;
    int      *pos_list;
    XmString *new_items;
    int       item_count;
```

This routine replaces the item at each position specified in *pos_list* with the corresponding item in *new_items* until *item_count* has been reached.

12.3.4 Deleting Items

You can delete items from a List widget in many ways. First, to delete a single item, you can use either `XmListDeleteItem()` or `XmListDeletePos()`. These functions take the following form:

```
void
XmListDeleteItem(list_w, item)
    Widget    list_w;
    XmString item;

void
XmListDeletePos(list_w, position)
    Widget list_w;
    int    position;
```

`XmListDeleteItem()` finds the given item and deletes it from the list, while `XmList-DeletePos()` removes an item directly from the given position. If you know the position of an item, you can avoid creating a compound string and use `XmListDeletePos()`. After an item is deleted, the items following it are moved up one position.

You can delete multiple items using either `XmListDeleteItems()`, `XmListDelete-ItemsPos()`, or `XmListDeletePositions()`. These routines take the following form:

```
void
XmListDeleteItems(list_w, items, item_count)
    Widget    list_w;
    XmString *items;
    int       item_count;

XmListDeleteItemsPos(list_w, item_count, position)
    Widget list_w;
    int    item_count;
    int    position;

XmListDeletePositions(list_w, pos_list, pos_count)
    Widget list_w;
    int   *pos_list;
    int    pos_count;
```

`XmListDeleteItems()` deletes each of the items in the *items* array from the List; there are *item_count* strings in the array. You must create and initialize this array before calling the function and you must free it afterwards. If you already know the positions of the items you want to delete, you can avoid creating an array of compound strings and use `XmListDeleteItemsPos()` or `XmListDeletePositions()`. `XmListDelete-ItemsPos()` deletes *item_count* items from the List starting at *position*. `XmList-DeletePositions()` deletes the item at each position specified in *pos_list* until *item_count* has been reached. This routine is new in Motif 1.2.

You can delete all of the items in a List widget using `XmListDeleteAllItems()`. This routine takes the following form:

```
void
XmListDeleteAllItems(list_w)
    Widget list_w;
```

12.3.5 Selecting Items

Since the main purpose of the List widget is to allow a user to make a selection from a set of choices, one of the most important tasks for the programmer is to determine which items have been selected by the user. In this section, we present an overview of the resources and functions available to set or get the actual items that are selected in the List widget. Later in Section 12.5, we discuss how to determine the items that are selected by the user when they are selected. The resources and functions used to set and get the selected items in the List widget are directly analogous to those that set the actual items in the list. Just as `XmNitems` represents the entire list, the `XmNselectedItems` resource represents the list of selected items. The `XmNselectedItemCount` resource specifies the number of items that are selected.

There are convenience routines that allow you to modify the items that are selected in a List. The functions `XmSelectItem()` and `XmSelectPos()` can be used to select individual items. These functions take the following form:

```
void
XmListSelectItem(list_w, item, notify)
    Widget     list_w;
    XmString   item;
    Boolean    notify;

void
XmListSelectPos(list_w, position, notify)
    Widget     list_w;
    int        position;
    Boolean    notify;
```

These functions cause the specified item to be selected. If you know the position in the list of the item to be selected, you should use `XmListSelectPos()` rather than `XmList-SelectItem()`. The latter routine uses a linear search to find the specified item. The search can take a long time in a large list, which can affect performance if you are performing frequent list operations.

When the specified item is selected, any other items that have been previously selected are deselected, except when `XmNselectionPolicy` is set to `XmMULTIPLE_SELECT`. In this case, the specified item is added to the list of selected items. Even though the extended selection policy allows multiple items to be selected, the previous selection is deselected when one of these routines is called. If you want to add an item to the list of selected items in an extended selection list, you can set the selection policy to `XmMULTIPLE_SELECT`, use one of the routines, and then set the selection policy back to `XmEXTENDED_SELECT`.

The *notify* parameter indicates whether or not the callback routine for the List widget should be called. If your callback routine does special processing of list items, then you can avoid having redundant code by passing True. As a result, the callback routine is called just as if the user had made the selection himself. If you are calling either of these functions from the callback routine, you probably want to pass False to avoid a possible infinite loop.

There are no functions available for selecting multiple items at the same time. To select multiple items, use XtVaSetValues() and set the XmNselectedItems and XmN-selectedItemCount resources to the entire list of selected items. Another alternative is to follow the suggestion made earlier and temporarily set XmNselectionPolicy to Xm-MULTIPLE_SELECT. You can call the above routines repeatedly to select the desired items individually and then set the selection policy back to XmEXTENDED_SELECT.

Items can be deselected in the same manner that they are selected using XmList-DeselectItem() and XmListDeselectPos(). These functions take the following form:

```
void
XmListDeselectItem(list_w, item)
    Widget    list_w;
    XmString item;


void
XmListDeselectPos(list_w, position)
    Widget    list_w;
    int       position;
```

These routines modify the list of selected items, but they do not have a *notify* parameter, so they do not invoke the callback routine for the List. You can deselect all items in the list by calling XmListDeselectAllItems(), which takes the following form:

```
void
XmListDeselectAllItems(list_w)
    Widget list_w;
```

There are also convenience routines that allow you to check on the selected items in a List. You can use XmListPosSelected() to determine whether an item is selected. This routine in new in Motif 1.2; it takes the following form:

```
Boolean
XmListPosSelected(list_w, position)
    Widget list_w;
    int    position;
```

The routine returns True if the item at the specified position is selected and False otherwise. You can get the positions of all of the selected items in a List using XmListGet-SelectedPos(), which takes the following form:

```
Boolean
XmListGetSelectedPos(list_w, pos_list, pos_cnt)
    Widget    list_w;
    int       **pos_list;
    int       *pos_cnt;
```

The use of this function is identical to that of XmListGetMatchPos(). The *pos_list* parameter is allocated to contain the array of positions of selected items and the number of items selected is returned in *pos_cnt*. When you are done using *pos_list*, you should free it using XtFree(). The function returns False if there are no selected items in the List or if memory cannot be allocated for *pos_list*. In these cases, *pos_list* does not point to allocated space and should not be referenced or freed and the value of *pos_cnt* is not specified.

12.3.6 An Example

In this section, we pull together all of the functions we have described in the preceding sections. This example builds on *alpha_list.c*, the program that adds items that are input by the user to a ScrolledList in alphabetical order. Using another Text widget, the user can also search for items in the list. The searching method uses regular expression pattern-matching functions intrinsic to UNIX systems. Example 12-3 shows the new application.†

Example 12-3. The search_list.c program

```
/* search_list.c -- search for items in a List and select them */

#include <stdio.h>
#include <Xm/List.h>
#include <Xm/LabelG.h>
#include <Xm/Label.h>
#include <Xm/RowColumn.h>
#include <Xm/PanedW.h>
#include <Xm/TextF.h>

main(argc, argv)
int argc;
char *argv[];
{
    Widget          toplevel, rowcol, list_w, text_w;
    XtAppContext    app;
    Arg             args[5];
    int             n = 0;
    XmString        label;
    void            add_item(), search_item();

    XtSetLanguageProc (NULL, NULL, NULL);

    toplevel = XtVaAppInitialize (&app, "Demos", NULL, 0,
        &argc, argv, NULL, NULL);

    rowcol = XtVaCreateWidget ("rowcol",
        xmPanedWindowWidgetClass, toplevel, NULL);

    label = XmStringCreateLocalized ("List:");
    XtVaCreateManagedWidget ("list_lable", xmLabelWidgetClass, rowcol,
        XmNlabelString,  label,
        NULL);
```

---

†XtSetLanguageProc() is only available in X11R5; there is no corresponding function in X11R4. XmStringCreateLocalized() is only available in Motif 1.2; XmStringCreateSimple() is the corresponding function in Motif 1.1. XmFONTLIST_DEFAULT_TAG replaces XmSTRING_DEFAULT_CHARSET in Motif 1.2.

Example 12-3. The search_list.c program (continued)

```
        XmStringFree (label);
        XtSetArg (args[n], XmNvisibleItemCount, 10); n++;
        XtSetArg (args[n], XmNselectionPolicy, XmEXTENDED_SELECT); n++;
        list_w = XmCreateScrolledList (rowcol, "scrolled_list", args, n);
        XtManageChild (list_w);

        label = XmStringCreateLocalized ("Add:");
        XtVaCreateManagedWidget ("add_label", xmLabelWidgetClass, rowcol,
            XmNlabelString,  label,
            NULL);
        XmStringFree (label);
        text_w = XtVaCreateManagedWidget ("add_text",
            xmTextFieldWidgetClass, rowcol,
            XmNcolumns,      25,
            NULL);
        XtAddCallback (text_w, XmNactivateCallback, add_item, list_w);

        label = XmStringCreateLocalized ("Search:");
        XtVaCreateManagedWidget ("search_label", xmLabelWidgetClass, rowcol,
            XmNlabelString,  label,
            NULL);
        XmStringFree (label);
        text_w = XtVaCreateManagedWidget ("search_text",
            xmTextFieldWidgetClass, rowcol,
            XmNcolumns,      25,
            NULL);
        XtAddCallback (text_w, XmNactivateCallback, search_item, list_w);

        XtManageChild (rowcol);
        XtRealizeWidget (toplevel);
        XtAppMainLoop (app);
}

/* Add item to the list in alphabetical order.  Perform binary
 * search to find the correct location for the new item position.
 * This is the callback routine for the Add: TextField widget.
 */
void
add_item(text_w, client_data, call_data)
Widget text_w;
XtPointer client_data;
XtPointer call_data;
{
    Widget list_w = (Widget) client_data;
    char *text, *newtext = XmTextFieldGetString (text_w);
    XmString str, *strlist;
    int u_bound, l_bound = 0;

    if (!newtext || !*newtext) {
        /* non-null strings must be entered */
        XtFree (newtext);
        return;
    }
    XtVaGetValues (list_w,
        XmNitemCount, &u_bound,
        XmNitems,     &strlist,
        NULL);
    u_bound--;
```

Example 12-3. The search_list.c program (continued)

```
    /* perform binary search */
    while (u_bound >= l_bound) {
        int i = l_bound + (u_bound - l_bound)/2;
        if (!XmStringGetLtoR (strlist[i], XmFONTLIST_DEFAULT_TAG, &text))
            break;
        if (strcmp (text, newtext) > 0)
            u_bound = i-1; /* newtext comes before item */
        else
            l_bound = i+1; /* newtext comes after item */
        XtFree (text);
    }
    str = XmStringCreateLocalized (newtext);
    XtFree (newtext);
    /* positions indexes start at 1, so increment accordingly */
    XmListAddItemUnselected (list_w, str, l_bound+1);
    XmStringFree (str);
    XmTextFieldSetString (text_w, "");
}

/* find the item in the list that matches the specified pattern */
void
search_item(text_w, client_data, call_data)
Widget text_w;
XtPointer client_data;
XtPointer call_data;
{
    Widget list_w = (Widget) client_data;
    char *exp, *text, *newtext = XmTextFieldGetString (text_w);
    XmString *strlist, *selectlist = NULL;
    int matched, cnt, j = 0;
#ifndef SYSV
    extern char *re_comp();
#endif /* SYSV */

    if (!newtext || !*newtext) {
        /* non-null strings must be entered */
        XtFree (newtext);
        return;
    }

    /* compile expression into pattern matching library */
#ifdef SYSV
    if (!(exp = regcmp (newtext, NULL))) {
        printf ("Error with regcmp(%s)\n", newtext);
        XtFree (newtext);
        return;
    }
#else /* BSD */
    if (exp = re_comp (newtext)) {
        printf ("Error with re_comp(%s): %s\n", newtext, exp);
        XtFree (newtext);
        return;
    }
#endif /* SYSV */

    /* get all the items in the list ... we're going to search each one */
    XtVaGetValues (list_w,
        XmNitemCount, &cnt,
```

Example 12-3. The search_list.c program (continued)

```
        XmNitems,       &strlist,
        NULL);
    while (cnt--) {
        /* convert item to C string */
        if (!XmStringGetLtoR (strlist[cnt], XmFONTLIST_DEFAULT_TAG, &text))
            break;
        /* do pattern match against search string */
#ifdef SYSV
        /* returns NULL if match failed */
        matched = regex (exp, text, NULL) != NULL;
#else /* BSD */
        /* -1 on error, 0 if no-match, 1 if match */
        matched = re_exec (text) > 0;
#endif /* SYSV */
        if (matched) {
            selectlist = (XmString *) XtRealloc (selectlist,
                (j+1) * (sizeof (XmString *)));
            selectlist[j++] = XmStringCopy (strlist[cnt]);
        }
        XtFree (text);
    }
#ifdef SYSV
    free (exp);  /* this must be freed for regcmp() */
#endif /* SYSV */
    XtFree (newtext);
    /* set the actual selected items to be those that matched */
    XtVaSetValues (list_w,
        XmNselectedItems,       selectlist,
        XmNselectedItemCount, j,
        NULL);
    while (j--)
        XmStringFree (selectlist[j]);
    XmTextFieldSetString (text_w, "");
}
```

The output of this program is shown in Figure 12-5. The TextField widget that is used to search for items in the List widget works identically to the one that is used to add new items. Its callback routine, search_item(), searches the list for the specified pattern. The version of UNIX you are running (System V or BSD) dictates which kind of regular expression matching is done. System V machines use the function regcmp() to compile the pattern and regex() to search for the pattern within another string, while BSD UNIX systems use the functions re_comp() and re_exec() to do the same thing.†

The items in the list are retrieved using XtVaGetValues() and the strlist parameter. This variable points to the internal list used by the List widget, so it is important that we do not change any of these elements or free these pointers when we are through with them. Changing the value of XmNselectedItems causes the internal list to change. Since the internal list is referenced by strlist, it is important to copy any values that we want to use elsewhere. If the pattern matches a list item, the item is copied using XmStringCopy() and is later added to the List's XmNselectedItems.

---

† Systems that support both BSD and System V may support one, the other, or both methods of regular expression handling. You should consult your system's documentation for more information on these functions.

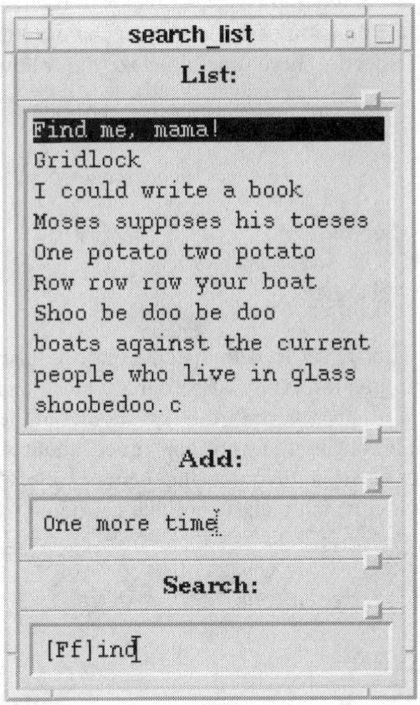

Figure 12-5. Output of search_list.c

12.4 Positioning the List

The items within a List can be positioned such that an arbitrary element is placed at the top or bottom of the List. If the List is being used as part of a ScrolledList, the item is placed at the top or bottom of the viewport of the ScrolledWindow. To position a particular item at the top or bottom of the window, use either `XmListSetItem()` or `XmListSetBottomItem()`. These routines take the following form:

```
void
XmListSetItem(list_w, item)
    Widget    list_w;
    XmString  item;

void
XmListBottomItem(list_w, item)
    Widget    list_w;
    XmString  item;
```

The List Widget   427

Both of these functions require an `XmString` parameter to reference a particular item in the list. However, if you know the position of the item, you can use `XmListSetPos()` or `Xm-ListSetBottomPos()` instead. These functions take the following form:

```
void
XmListSetPos(list_w, position)
    Widget      list_w;
    int         position;


void
XmListSetBottomPos(list_w, position)
    Widget      list_w;
    int         position;
```

The *position* parameter can be set to 0 to specify that the last item be positioned at the bottom of the viewport. Through a mixture of resource values and simple calculations, you can position any particular item anywhere in the list. For example, if you have an item that you want to be sure is visible, but you are not concerned about where in the viewport it is displayed, you can write a function to make the item visible. Example 12-4 shows the `MakePosVisible()` routine, which makes sure that the item at a specified position is visible.

Example 12-4. The MakePosVisible() routine

```
void
MakePosVisible(list_w, item_no)
Widget list_w;
int item_no;
{
    int top, visible;

    XtVaGetValues (list_w,
        XmNtopItemPosition,  &top,
        XmNvisibleItemCount, &visible,
        NULL);
    if (item_no < top)
        XmListSetPos (list_w, item_no);
    else if (item_no >= top + visible)
        XmListSetBottomPos (list_w, item_no);
}
```

The function gets the number of visible items and the position of the item at the top of the viewport. The `XmNtopItemPosition` resource stores this information. If the item comes before `top`, `item_no` is set to the top of the List using `XmListSetPos()`. If it comes after `top + visible`, the item is set at the bottom of the List using `XmListSet-BottomPos()`. If you don't know the position of the item in the List, you can write a function that makes a specified item visible, as shown in Example 12-5.

Example 12-5. The MakeItemVisible() routine

```
MakeItemVisible(list_w, item)
Widget list_w;
XmString item;
{
    int item_no = XmListItemPos (list_w, item);
```

Example 12-5. The MakeItemVisible() routine (continued)

```
    if (item_no > 0)
        MakePosVisible (list_w, item_no);
}
```

The `MakeItemVisible()` routine simple gets the position of the given item in the list using `XmListItemPos()` and calls `MakePosVisible()`.

In Motif 1.2, there are some new routines that deal with positions in a List. The `XmList-GetKbdItemPos()` and `XmListSetKbdItemPos()` routines retrieve and set the item in the List that has the location cursor. These routines take the following form:

```
    int
    XmListGetKbdItemPos(list_w)
        Widget    list_w;

    Boolean
    XmListSetKbdItemPos(list_w, position)
        Widget    list_w;
        int       position;
```

`XmListGetKbdItemPos()` returns the position of the item that has the location cursor, while `XmListSetKbdItemPos()` provides a way to specify the position of this item.

The `XmListPosToBounds()` and `XmListYToPos()` functions in Motif 1.2 provide a way to translate list items to x,y coordinates and vice versa. `XmListPosToBounds()` returns the bounding box of the item at a specified position in a List. This routine takes the following form:

```
    Boolean
    XmListPosToBounds(list_w, position, x, y, width, height)
        Widget     list_w;
        int        position;
        Position   *x;
        Position   *y;
        Dimension  *width;
        Dimension  *height;
```

This routine returns `True` if the item at the specified position is visible and `False` otherwise. If the item is visible, the return parameters specify the bounding box of the item. This information can be useful if you need to perform additional event processing or draw special graphics for the item. The `XmListYToPos()` routine returns the position of the List item at a specified y-coordinate. This function takes the following form:

```
    int
    XmListYToPos(list_w, y)
        Widget    list_w;
        Position  y;
```

The position information returned by this routine can be useful if you are processing events that report a pointer position and you need to convert the location of the event into an item position.

12.5 List Callback Routines

While the callback routines associated with the List widget are not affected by whether the List is scrollable, they do depend on the selection policy currently in use. There is a separate callback resource for each selection policy, plus a callback for the default action. The default action is invoked when the left mouse button is double-clicked on an item or the RETURN key is pressed. The callback resources are:

```
XmNbrowseSelectionCallback
XmNdefaultActionCallback
XmNextendedSelectionCallback
XmNmultipleSelectionCallback
XmNsingleSelectionCallback
```

12.5.1 The Default Action

In all of the selection modes there is the concept of the *default action*. This term refers to the action that is taken when the user double clicks the left mouse button on an item or presses the RETURN key when an item has the location cursor. The default action always indicates that the active item should be selected, regardless of the selection policy. The XmN-defaultActionCallback is invoked for the default action.

The default selection is activated when the user double clicks on a List item. The time interval between two consecutive button clicks determines whether the clicks are interpreted as individual clicks or as a double click. You can set or get the time interval using the XmN-doubleClickInterval resource. The value is stored as milliseconds, so a value of 500 is half a second. If the resource is not set, the value of the multiClickTime resource is used instead. This resource is a fundamental X resource that is understood by all X applications; it is not an Xt or Motif toolkit resource. You should let the user specify the double-click interval in a resource file; the value should be set using the more global multi-ClickTime resource.

12.5.2 Browse and Single Selection Callbacks

The browse and single selection modes only allow the selection of a single item. The browsing mode is regarded as a simpler interface for the user. Interactively, browse selection allows the user to drag the selection over many items; the selection is not made till the mouse button is released. In the single selection mode, the selection is made as soon as the mouse button is pressed. For browse selection, the callback list associated with the XmNbrowse-SelectionCallback is used, while the XmNsingleSelectionCallback is used for the single selection mode.

Keyboard traversal in the List is also different between the two modes. If the user uses the keyboard to move from one item to the next in single selection mode, the XmNsingle-SelectCallback is not invoked until the SPACEBAR is pressed. In browse selection, the XmNbrowseSelectionCallback is invoked for each item the user traverses. Since these two modes for the List widget are visually similar, your treatment of the callbacks is very important for maintaining consistency between Lists that use different selection modes.

A simple example of using callbacks with a List widget is shown in Example 12-6.†

Example 12-6. The browse.c program

```
/* browse.c -- specify a browse selection callback for a simple List.
 */
#include <Xm/List.h>

char *months[] = {
    "January", "February", "March", "April", "May", "June", "July",
    "August", "September", "October", "November", "December"
};

main(argc, argv)
int argc;
char *argv[];
{
    Widget          toplevel, list_w;
    XtAppContext    app;
    int             i, n = XtNumber (months);
    XmStringTable   str_list;
    void            sel_callback();

    XtSetLanguageProc (NULL, NULL, NULL);

    toplevel = XtVaAppInitialize (&app, "Demos", NULL, 0,
        &argc, argv, NULL, NULL);

    str_list = (XmStringTable) XtMalloc (n * sizeof (XmString *));

    for (i = 0; i < n; i++)
        str_list[i] = XmStringCreateLocalized (months[i]);

    list_w = XmCreateScrolledList (toplevel, "months", NULL, 0);
    XtVaSetValues (list_w,
        XmNvisibleItemCount,    n,
        XmNitemCount,           n,
        XmNitems,               str_list,
        NULL);
    XtManageChild (list_w);

    XtAddCallback (list_w, XmNdefaultActionCallback, sel_callback, NULL);
    XtAddCallback (list_w, XmNbrowseSelectionCallback, sel_callback, NULL);

    for (i = 0; i < n; i++)
        XmStringFree (str_list[i]);
    XtFree (str_list);

    XtRealizeWidget (toplevel);
    XtAppMainLoop (app);
}
```

---

†XtSetLanguageProc() is only available in X11R5; there is no corresponding function in X11R4. Xm-StringCreateLocalized() is only available in Motif 1.2; XmStringCreateSimple() is the corresponding function in Motif 1.1. XmFONTLIST_DEFAULT_TAG replaces XmSTRING_DEFAULT_CHARSET in Motif 1.2.

Example 12-6. The browse.c program (continued)

```
void
sel_callback(list_w, client_data, call_data)
Widget list_w;
XtPointer client_data;
XtPointer call_data;
{
    XmListCallbackStruct *cbs = (XmListCallbackStruct *) call_data;
    char *choice;

    if (cbs->reason == XmCR_BROWSE_SELECT)
        printf ("Browse selection -- ");
    else
        printf ("Default action -- ");

    XmStringGetLtoR (cbs->item, XmFONTLIST_DEFAULT_TAG, &choice);
    printf ("selected item: %s (%d)\n", choice, cbs->item_position);
    XtFree (choice);
}
```

For this example, we modified our previous example that uses a ScrolledList to display the
months of the year. We have added the same callback routine, `sel_callback()`, to the
`XmNbrowseSelectionCallback` and `XmNdefaultActionCallback` resources.
Since the default action may happen for any List widget, it is advisable to set this callback,
even if there are other callbacks. The callback routine prints the type of action performed by
the user and the selection that was made. The callback structure is used to get information
about the nature of the List widget and the selection made.

The List callbacks provide a callback structure of type `XmListCallbackStruct`, which
is defined as follows:

```
typedef struct {
    int         reason;
    XEvent      *event;
    XmString    item;
    int         item_length;
    int         item_position;
    XmString    *selected_items;
    int         selected_item_count;
    int         *selected_item_positions;
    char        selection_type;
} XmListCallbackStruct;
```

The `reason` field specifies the reason that the callback was invoked, which corresponds to
the type of action performed by the user. The possible values for this field are:

```
XmCR_BROWSE_SELECT
XmCR_DEFAULT_ACTION
XmCR_EXTENDED_SELECT
XmCR_MULTIPLE_SELECT
XmCR_SINGLE_SELECT
```

The `reason` field is important with List callbacks because not all of the fields in the callback structure are valid for every reason. For the browse and single selection policies, the
`reason`, `event`, `item`, `item_length`, and `item_position` fields are valid. For the

default action, all of the fields are valid. List items are stored as compound strings in the callback structure, so to print an item using `printf()`, we must convert the string with the compound string function `XmStringGetLtoR()`.

12.5.3 Multiple Selection Callback

When `XmNselectionPolicy` is set to `XmMULTIPLE_SELECT`, multiple items can be selected in the List widget. When the user selects an item, its selection state is toggled. Each time the user selects an item, the callback routine associated with the `XmNmultiple-SelectionCallback` is invoked. Example 12-7 shows the `sel_callback()` routine that could be used with a multiple selection List.†

Example 12-7. The sel_callback() routine for a multiple selection List

```
void
sel_callback(list_w, client_data, call_data)
Widget list_w;
XtPointer client_data;
XtPointer call_data;
{
    XmListCallbackStruct *cbs = (XmListCallbackStruct *) call_data;
    char *choice;
    int  i;

    if (cbs->reason == XmCR_MULTIPLE_SELECT) {
        printf ("Multiple selection -- %d items selected:\n",
            cbs->selected_item_count);
        for (i = 0; i < cbs->selected_item_count; i++) {
            XmStringGetLtoR (cbs->selected_items[i], XmFONTLIST_DEFAULT_TAG,
                &choice);
            printf ("%s (%d)\n", choice, cbs->selected_item_positions[i]);
            XtFree (choice);
        }
    }
    else {
        XmStringGetLtoR (cbs->item, XmFONTLIST_DEFAULT_TAG, &choice);
        printf ("Default action -- selected item %s (%d)\n",
            choice, cbs->item_position);
        XtFree (choice);
    }
}
```

The routine tests the callback structure's `reason` field to determine whether the callback was invoked as a result of a multiple selection action or the default action. When the `reason` is `XmCR_MULTIPLE_SELECT`, we print the list of selected items by looping through `selected_items` and `selected_item_positions`. With this reason, all of the fields in the callback structure except `selection_type` are valid. If the `reason` is `XmCR_DEFAULT_ACTION`, there is only one item selected, since the default selection action causes all of the other items to be deselected.

---

† `XmFONTLIST_DEFAULT_TAG` replaces `XmSTRING_DEFAULT_CHARSET` in Motif 1.2.

12.5.4 Extended Selection Callback

With the extended selection model, the user has the greatest flexibility to select and deselect individual items or ranges of items. The XmNextendedSelectionCallback is invoked whenever the user makes a selection or modifies the selection. Example 12-8 demonstrates the sel_callback() routine that could be used with an extended selection List.†

Example 12-8. The sel_callback() routine for an extended selection List

```
void
sel_callback(list_w, client_data, call_data)
Widget list_w;
XtPointer client_data;
XtPointer call_data;
{
    XmListCallbackStruct *cbs = (XmListCallbackStruct *) call_data;
    char *choice;
    int   i;

    if (cbs->reason == XmCR_EXTENDED_SELECT) {
        if (cbs->selection_type == XmINITIAL)
            printf ("Extended selection -- initial selection: ");
        else if (cbs->selection_type == XmMODIFICATION)
            printf ("Extended selction -- modification of selection: ");
        else /* selection type = XmADDITION */
            printf ("Extended selection -- additional selection: ");
        printf ("%d items selected\n", cbs->selected_item_count);
        for (i = 0; i < cbs->selected_item_count; i++) {
            XmStringGetLtoR (cbs->selected_items[i], XmFONTLIST_DEFAULT_TAG,
                &choice);
            printf ("%s (%d)\n", choice, cbs->selected_item_positions[i]);
            XtFree (choice);
        }
    }
    else {
        XmStringGetLtoR (cbs->item, XmFONTLIST_DEFAULT_TAG, &choice);
        printf ("Default action -- selected item %s (%d)\n",
            choice, cbs->item_position);
        XtFree (choice);
    }
}
```

Most of the callback routine is the same as it was for multiple selection mode. With an extended selection callback, the selection_type field is also valid. This field can have the following values:

```
    XmINITIAL
    XmMODIFICATION
    XmADDITION
```

The XmINITIAL value indicates that the selection is an initial selection for the List. All previously-selected items are deselected and the items selected with this action comprise the entire list of selected items. The value is XmMODIFICATION when the user modifies the

---

† XmFONTLIST_DEFAULT_TAG replaces XmSTRING_DEFAULT_CHARSET in Motif 1.2.

selected list by using the SHIFT key in combination with a selection action. In this case, the selected item list contains some items that were already selected before this action took place. XmADDITION indicates that the items that are selected are in addition to what was previously selected. The user can select additional items by using the CTRL key in combination with a selection action. Regardless of the value for selection_type, the selected_items and selected_item_positions fields always reflect the set of currently selected items.

12.6 Summary

The List widget is a powerful user interface tool that has a simple design. The programming interface to the widget is mostly mechanical. The List allows you to present a vast list of choices to the user, although the choices themselves must be textual in nature. Lists are not suitable for all situations however, as they cannot display choices other than text (pixmaps cannot be used as selection items) and there is no ability to set color on individual items. Even with these shortcomings, the List widget is still a visible and intuitive object that can be used in designing a graphical user interface.

12.7 Exercises

The following exercises expand on some of the concepts presented in this chapter.

1. Write a program that reads each word from the file */usr/dict/words* into a ScrolledList. Provide a TextField widget whose callback routine searches for the word typed into it from the entries in the List. Once found, make the List widget scroll so that each item is centered in the ScrolledList's viewport. (Hint: convert the C string from the TextField into a compound string and use one of the List search routines to find the element.)

2. ScrolledLists frequently confuse the unsuspecting programmer who forgets that the parent of the List widget is a ScrolledWindow. For example, if you create a ScrolledList as a child of a Form widget, and want to specify attachment constraints on the ScrolledList, you should set these resources on the ScrolledWindow, not the List widget. Write a program that places two ScrolledList widgets next to each other in a single Form widget. (For more information on the role of the ScrolledWindow widget in a ScrolledList object, see the similar discussion on ScrolledText objects in Chapter 14, *Text Widgets*, and more discussion in Chapter 9, *ScrolledWindows and ScrollBars*.)

3. Consider two List widgets whose items are somewhat dependent on one another. For example, the one List contains login names and the other List contains the corresponding user-IDs. Write a program where the XmNdefaultActionCallback routine for each list selects the dependent/corresponding item in the other list. Since the user ID for "root" is always 0, selecting "root" from the login name list should cause the item 0 in the user-ID list to be selected.

13

The Scale Widget

This chapter describes how to use the Scale widget to represent a range of values. The widget can be manipulated to change the value.

In This Chapter:

The Scale Widget

The Scale widget displays a numeric value that falls within upper and lower bounds. The widget allows the user to change that value interactively using a *slider* mechanism similar to that of a ScrollBar. This style of interface is useful when it is inconvenient or inappropriate to have the user change a value using the keyboard. The widget is also extremely intuitive to use; inexperienced users often understand how a Scale works when they first see one. Figure 13-1 shows how a Scale can be used with other widgets in an application.

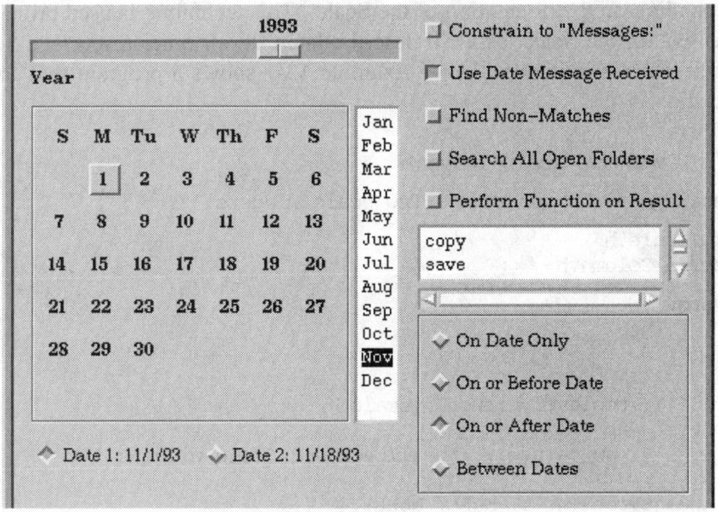

Figure 13-1. A Scale widget in an application

A Scale can be oriented either horizontally or vertically. The values given to a Scale are stored as integers, but decimal representation of values is possible through the use of a resource that allows you to place a decimal point in the value. A Scale can be put in output-only mode, in which it is sometimes called a *gauge*. When a Scale is read-only, it implies that the value is controlled by another widget or that it is being used to report status information specific to the application. The standard way to create a read-only Scale is to specify that it is insensitive. Unfortunately, this technique has the side-effect of graying out the widget. One workaround is to create a Scale widget that is sensitive, but that has a null translation table.

13.1 Creating a Scale Widget

Applications that use the Scale widget must include the header file *<Xm/Scale.h>*. You can then create a Scale widget as follows:

```
Widget scale;

scale = XtVaCreateManagedWidget ("name",
    xmScaleWidgetClass, parent,
    resource-value-list,
    NULL);
```

Even though the Scale widget functions as a primitive widget, it is actually subclassed from the Manager widget. All the parts of a Scale are really other primitive widgets, but these subwidgets are not accessible through the Motif toolkit. The fact that the Scale is a Manager widget means that you can create widgets that are children of a Scale. The children are arranged so that they are evenly distributed along the vertical or horizontal axis parallel to the slider, depending on the orientation of the Scale. This technique is used primarily to provide "tick marks" for the Scale, as we'll describe later. In all other respects, a Scale can be treated just like other primitive widgets. Example 13-1 shows a program that creates some Scale widgets.†

Example 13-1. The simple_scale.c program

```
/* simple_scale.c -- demonstrate a few scale widgets. */

#include <Xm/Scale.h>
#include <Xm/RowColumn.h>

main(argc, argv)
int argc;
char *argv[];
{
    Widget          toplevel, rowcol, scale;
    XtAppContext    app;
    void            new_value(); /* callback for Scale widgets */

    XtSetLanguageProc (NULL, NULL, NULL);

    toplevel = XtVaAppInitialize (&app, "Demos", NULL, 0,
        &argc, argv, NULL, NULL);

    rowcol = XtVaCreateWidget ("rowcol",
        xmRowColumnWidgetClass, toplevel,
        XmNorientation, XmHORIZONTAL,
        NULL);

    scale = XtVaCreateManagedWidget ("Days",
```

---

† XtSetLanguageProc() is only available in X11R5; there is no corresponding function in X11R4.

Motif Programming Manual

Example 13-1. The simple_scale.c program (continued)

```
            xmScaleWidgetClass, rowcol,
            XtVaTypedArg, XmNtitleString, XmRString, "Days", 5,
            XmNmaximum,   7,
            XmNminimum,   1,
            XmNvalue,     1,
            XmNshowValue, True,
            NULL);
    XtAddCallback (scale, XmNvalueChangedCallback, new_value, NULL);

    scale = XtVaCreateManagedWidget ("Weeks",
            xmScaleWidgetClass, rowcol,
            XtVaTypedArg, XmNtitleString, XmRString, "Weeks", 6,
            XmNmaximum,   52,
            XmNminimum,   1,
            XmNvalue,     1,
            XmNshowValue, True,
            NULL);
    XtAddCallback (scale, XmNvalueChangedCallback, new_value, NULL);

    scale = XtVaCreateManagedWidget ("Months",
            xmScaleWidgetClass, rowcol,
            XtVaTypedArg, XmNtitleString, XmRString, "Months", 7,
            XmNmaximum,   12,
            XmNminimum,   1,
            XmNvalue,     1,
            XmNshowValue, True,
            NULL);
    XtAddCallback (scale, XmNvalueChangedCallback, new_value, NULL);

    scale = XtVaCreateManagedWidget ("Years",
            xmScaleWidgetClass, rowcol,
            XtVaTypedArg, XmNtitleString, XmRString, "Years", 6,
            XmNmaximum,   20,
            XmNminimum,   1,
            XmNvalue,     1,
            XmNshowValue, True,
            NULL);
    XtAddCallback (scale, XmNvalueChangedCallback, new_value, NULL);

    XtManageChild (rowcol);

    XtRealizeWidget (toplevel);
    XtAppMainLoop (app);
}

void
new_value(scale_w, client_data, call_data)
Widget scale_w;
XtPointer client_data;
XtPointer call_data;
{
    XmScaleCallbackStruct *cbs = (XmScaleCallbackStruct *) call_data;

    printf("%s: %d\n", XtName(scale_w), cbs->value);
}
```

The output of this program is shown in Figure 13-2.

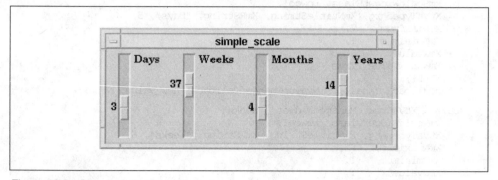

Figure 13-2. Output of simple_scale.c

The four Scales represent the number of days, weeks, months, and years, respectively. Each Scale displays a title that is specified by the XmNtitleString resource. Just as with other Motif widgets that display strings, the XmNtitleString must be set as a compound string, not a normal C string. The easiest way to make the conversion is to use the XtVaTypedArg feature, as we've done in this example. The use of this conversion method is described in detail in Chapter 19, *Compound Strings*.

A Scale cannot have a pixmap as its label. Since real estate for the label is limited in a Scale widget, you should take care to use small strings. If you need to use a longer string, you should include a separator so that the text is printed on two lines. If the string is too long, the label may be too wide and look awkward as a result. For a horizontal Scale, the label is displayed beneath the slider, while for a vertical Scale it is shown to the side of the slider.

The maximum and minimum values are set with the XmNmaximum and XmNminimum resources, respectively. The minimum values are set to 1 for the user's benefit; the minimum value of a Scale defaults to 0. Note that if you set a minimum value other than 0, you must also provide a default value for XmNvalue that is at least as large as the value of Xm-Nminimum, as we have done in our example. Each Scale displays its current value because the XmNshowValue resource is set to True.

13.2 Scale Values

The value of a Scale can only be stored as an integer. This restriction is largely based on the fact that variables of type float and double cannot be passed through XtVaSet-Values(), XtVaGetValues(), or any of the widget creation functions.† If you need to represent fractional values, you must use the XmNdecimalPoints resource. This resource specifies the number of places to move the decimal point to the left in the displayed value, which gives the user the impression that the value displayed is fractional.

---

† While the Xt functions mentioned do allow the passing of the address of a variable of type float or double, the Scale widget does not support this type of value representation.

For example, a Scale widget used to display the value of a barometer might range from 29 to 31, with a granularity of 1-100th. The necessary widget could be created as shown in the following code fragment:

```
XtVaCreateManagedWidget ("barometer", xmScaleWidgetClass, rowcol,
    XtVaTypedArg, XmNtitleString, XmRString,
        "Barometric\nPressure", 19,
    XmNmaximum,       3100,
    XmNminimum,       2900,
    XmNdecimalPoints, 2,
    XmNvalue,         3000,
    XmNshowValue,     True,
    NULL);
```

The value for XmNdecimalPoints is 2, so that the value displayed is 30.00, rather than 3000. If you are using a Scale to represent fractional values, it is probably a good idea to set XmNshowValue to True since fine tuning is probably necessary.

There is no limit to the values that can be specified for the XmNmaximum, XmNvalue, and XmNminimum resources, provided they can be represented by the int type, which includes negative numbers. In the previous example, the initial value of the Scale (XmNvalue) is set arbitrarily; the value must be set within the minimum and maximum values. If the value of the Scale is retrieved using XtVaGetValues() or through a callback routine, the integer value is returned. To get the appropriate decimal value, you need to divide the value by 10 to the power of the value of XmNdecimalPoints. For example, since XmNdecimal-Points is 2, the value needs to be divided by 10 to the power of 2, or 100.

The value of a Scale can be set and retrieved using XtVaSetValues() and XtVaGet-Values() on the XmNvalue resource. Motif also provides the functions XmScaleSet-Value() and XmScaleGetValue() to serve the same purpose. These functions take the following form:

```
void
XmScaleSetValue (scale_w, value)
    Widget  scale_w;
    int     value;

void
XmScaleGetValue (scale_w, value)
    Widget  scale_w;
    int     *value;
```

The advantage of using the Motif convenience routines, rather than the Xt routines, is that the Motif routines manipulate data in the widget directly, rather than using the set and get methods of the Scale. As a result, there is less overhead involved, although the added overhead of the Xt methods are negligible.

13.3 Scale Orientation and Movement

A Scale can be either vertical or horizontal and the maximum and minimum values can be on either end of the Scale. By default, as shown in the examples so far, the Scale is oriented vertically with the maximum on the top and the minimum on the bottom. The XmN-orientation resource can be set to XmHORIZONTAL to produce a horizontal Scale. The XmNprocessingDirection resource controls the location of the maximum and minimum values. The possible values for the resource are:

```
XmMAX_ON_TOP
XmMAX_ON_BOTTOM
XmMAX_ON_LEFT
XmMAX_ON_RIGHT
```

Unfortunately, you cannot set the processing direction unless you know the orientation of the Scale, so if you hard-code one resource, you should set both of them. If the Scale is oriented vertically, the default value is XmMAX_ON_TOP, but if it is horizontal, the default depends on the value of XmNstringDirection. If you use a font that is read from right to left, then the maximum value is displayed on the left rather than on the right.

As the user drags the slider, the value of the Scale changes incrementally in the direction of the movement. If the user clicks the middle mouse button inside the Scale widget, but not on the slider itself, the slider moves to the location of the click. Unfortunately, in a small Scale widget, the slider takes up a lot of space, so this method provides very poor control for moving the slider close to its current location.

If the user clicks the left mouse button inside the slider area, but not on the slider itself, the slider moves in increments determined by the value of XmNscaleMultiple. The value of this resource defaults to the difference between the maximum and minimum values divided by 10.† For example, a Scale widget whose maximum value is 250 has a scale increment of 25. If the user presses the left mouse button over the area above or below the slider, the Scale's value increases of decreases by 25. If the button is held down, the movement continues until the button is released, even if the slider moves past the location of the pointer.

13.4 Scale Callbacks

The Scale widget provides two callbacks that can be used to monitor the value of the Scale. The XmNdragCallback callback routines are invoked whenever the user drags the slider. This action does not mean that the value of the Scale has actually changed or that it will change; it just indicates that the slider is being moved.

The XmNvalueChangedCallback is invoked when the user releases the slider, which results in an actual change of the Scale's value. It is possible for the XmNvalueChanged-Callback to be called without the XmNdragCallback having been called. For example, when the user adjusts the Scale using the keyboard or moves the slider incrementally by

---

† As of Release 1.2 of the Motif toolkit, you should set XmNscaleMultiple explicitly if the difference between XmNmaximum and XmNminimum is less than 10. Otherwise, incremental scaling won't work.

clicking in the slider area, but not on the slider itself, only the XmNvalueChanged-Callback is invoked.

These callback routines take the form of an XtCallbackProc, just like any other callback. As with all Motif callback routines, Motif defines a callback structure for the Scale widget callbacks. The XmScaleCallbackStruct is defined as follows:

```
typedef struct {
    int       reason;
    XEvent    *event;
    int       value;
} XmScaleCallbackStruct;
```

The reason field of this structure is set to XmCR_DRAG or XmCR_VALUE_CHANGED, depending on the action that invoked the callback. The value field represents the current value of the Scale widget.

Example 13-2 shows another example of how the Scale widget can be used. In this case, we create a color previewer that uses Scales to control the red, green, and blue values of the color that is being edited. This example demonstrates how the XmNdragCallback can be used to automatically adjust colors as the slider is being dragged. The XmNvalue-ChangedCallback is also used to handle the cases where the user adjusts the Scale without dragging the slider. For a discussion of the Xlib color setting routines used in this program, see Volume One, *Xlib Programming Manual*.†

Example 13-2. The color_slide.c program

```
/* color_slide.c -- Use scale widgets to display the different
 * colors of a colormap.
 */
#include <Xm/LabelG.h>
#include <Xm/Scale.h>
#include <Xm/RowColumn.h>
#include <Xm/DrawingA.h>

Widget colorwindow; /* the window the displays a solid color */
XColor color;        /* the color in the colorwindow */

main(argc, argv)
int argc;
char *argv[];
{
    Widget         toplevel, rowcol, scale;
    XtAppContext   app;
    void           new_value();
    XtVarArgsList  arglist;

    XtSetLanguageProc (NULL, NULL, NULL);

    toplevel = XtVaAppInitialize (&app, "Demos", NULL, 0,
        &argc, argv, NULL, NULL);

    if (DefaultDepthOfScreen (XtScreen (toplevel)) < 2) {
        puts ("You must be using a color screen.");
        exit (1);
    }
```

---

†XtSetLanguageProc() is only available in X11R5; there is no corresponding function in X11R4.

Example 13-2. The color_slide.c program (continued)

```
    color.flags = DoRed | DoGreen | DoBlue;
    /* initialize first color */
    XAllocColor (XtDisplay (toplevel),
        DefaultColormapOfScreen (XtScreen (toplevel)), &color);

    rowcol = XtVaCreateManagedWidget ("rowcol",
        xmRowColumnWidgetClass, toplevel, NULL);

    colorwindow = XtVaCreateManagedWidget ("colorwindow",
        widgetClass,    rowcol,
        XmNheight,      100,
        XmNbackground, color.pixel,
        NULL);

    /* use rowcol again to create another RowColumn under the 1st */
    rowcol = XtVaCreateWidget ("rowcol", xmRowColumnWidgetClass, rowcol,
        XmNorientation, XmHORIZONTAL,
        NULL);

    arglist = XtVaCreateArgsList (NULL,
        XmNshowValue, True,
        XmNmaximum, 255,
        XmNscaleMultiple, 5,
        NULL);

    scale = XtVaCreateManagedWidget ("Red",
        xmScaleWidgetClass, rowcol,
        XtVaNestedList, arglist,
        XtVaTypedArg, XmNtitleString, XmRString, "Red", 4,
        XtVaTypedArg, XmNforeground, XmRString, "Red", 4,
        NULL);
    XtAddCallback (scale, XmNdragCallback, new_value, DoRed);
    XtAddCallback (scale, XmNvalueChangedCallback, new_value, DoRed);

    scale = XtVaCreateManagedWidget ("Green",
        xmScaleWidgetClass, rowcol,
        XtVaNestedList, arglist,
        XtVaTypedArg, XmNtitleString, XmRString, "Green", 6,
        XtVaTypedArg, XmNforeground, XmRString, "Green", 6,
        NULL);
    XtAddCallback (scale, XmNdragCallback, new_value, DoGreen);
    XtAddCallback (scale, XmNvalueChangedCallback, new_value, DoGreen);

    scale = XtVaCreateManagedWidget ("Blue",
        xmScaleWidgetClass, rowcol,
        XtVaNestedList, arglist,
        XtVaTypedArg, XmNtitleString, XmRString, "Blue", 5,
        XtVaTypedArg, XmNforeground, XmRString, "Blue", 5,
        NULL);
    XtAddCallback (scale, XmNdragCallback, new_value, DoBlue);
    XtAddCallback (scale, XmNvalueChangedCallback, new_value, DoBlue);

    XtFree (arglist);

    XtManageChild (rowcol);

    XtRealizeWidget (toplevel);
    XtAppMainLoop (app);
}
```

Example 13-2. The color_slide.c program (continued)

```
void
new_value(scale_w, client_data, call_data)
Widget scale_w;
XtPointer client_data;
XtPointer call_data;
{
    int rgb = (int) client_data;
    XmScaleCallbackStruct *cbs = (XmScaleCallbackStruct *) call_data;
    Colormap cmap = DefaultColormapOfScreen (XtScreen (scale_w));

    switch (rgb) {
        case DoRed :
            color.red = (cbs->value << 8);
            break;
        case DoGreen :
            color.green = (cbs->value << 8);
            break;
        case DoBlue :
            color.blue = (cbs->value << 8);
    }
    /* reuse the same color again and again */
    XFreeColors (XtDisplay (scale_w), cmap, &color.pixel, 1, 0);
    if (!XAllocColor (XtDisplay (scale_w), cmap, &color)) {
        puts ("Couldn't XAllocColor!");
      exit(1);
    }
    XtVaSetValues (colorwindow, XmNbackground, color.pixel, NULL);
}
```

The output of this program is shown in Figure 13-3. Obviously, a black and white book makes it difficult to show how this application really looks. However, when you run the program, you should get a feel for using Scale widgets.

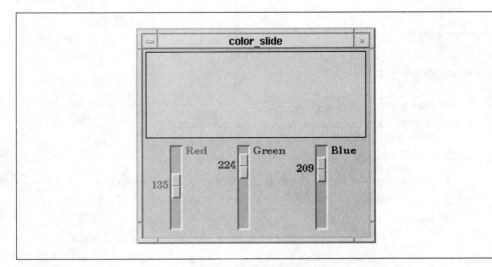

Figure 13-3. Output of color_slide.c

One interesting aspect of the *color_slide.c* program is the use of `XtVaCreateArgs-List()`. We use this function to build a single argument list that we use repeatedly. If we didn't use the function, we would have to duplicate the argument list for each call to `Xt-VaCreateManagedWidget()`. The function allocates and returns a pointer to an object of type `XtVarArgsList`. This type is an opaque pointer to an array of `XtVaTypedArg-List` objects, which means that you can specify normal resource-value pairs or the quadruplet used by `XtVaTypedArg`. We use the latter form to specify resource values that are not in the appropriate type, so that the toolkit handles the type conversion. For a discussion on type conversion and the use of `XtVaTypedArg`, see Volume Four, *X Toolkit Intrinsics Programming Manual*.

13.5 Scale Tick Marks

The *Motif Style Guide* suggests that a Scale widget can have "tick marks" that represent the incremental positions of the Scale. The Scale widget does not provide these marks by default, but you can add them yourself by creating Labels as children of a Scale widget, as demonstrated in Example 13-3. Each of the Label gadgets are given the same name (a dash), which is used as the actual label since the `XmNlabelString` resource is not set. Obviously, in a more complex application, the Labels should specify information that helps the user to read the Scale.†

Example 13-3. The tick_marks.c program

```
/* tick_marks.c -- demonstrate a scale widget with tick marks. */

#include <Xm/Scale.h>
#include <Xm/LabelG.h>

#define MAX_VAL 10 /* arbitrary value */

main(argc, argv)
int argc;
char *argv[];
{
    Widget          toplevel, scale;
    XtAppContext    app;
    int             i;

    XtSetLanguageProc (NULL, NULL, NULL);

    toplevel = XtVaAppInitialize (&app, "Demos", NULL, 0,
        &argc, argv, NULL, NULL);

    scale = XtVaCreateManagedWidget ("load",
        xmScaleWidgetClass, toplevel,
        XtVaTypedArg,       XmNtitleString, XmRString, "Process Load", 13,
        XmNmaximum,         MAX_VAL * 100,
        XmNminimum,         100,
        XmNvalue,           100,
        XmNdecimalPoints,   2,
```

---

†`XtSetLanguageProc()` is only available in X11R5; there is no corresponding function in X11R4.

Example 13-3. The tick_marks.c program (continued)

```
        XmNshowValue,        True,
        NULL);

    for (i = 0; i < MAX_VAL; i++)
        XtVaCreateManagedWidget ("-", xmLabelGadgetClass, scale, NULL);

    XtRealizeWidget (toplevel);
    XtAppMainLoop (app);
}
```

The output of this program is shown in Figure 13-4.

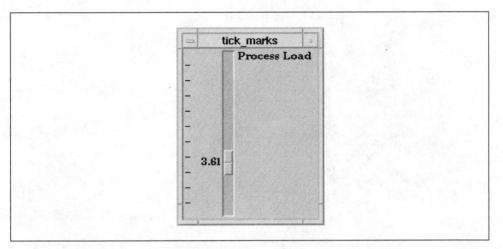

Figure 13-4. Output of tick_marks.c

The Scale can have any kind of widget as a child, but it is common to use Labels to represent tick marks. All of the children are evenly distributed along the axis of the slider; no other layout method is possible. As you can see in Figure 13-4, the tick marks are placed all the way to the left of the Scale widget to leave space for the value indicator. It is not possible to force the tick marks up against the Scale by using the XmNalignment resource of the Labels or to control the layout of the tick marks in any way.

13.6 Summary

The Scale widget is a simple widget, both in concept and in practical use. In this chapter, we have showed a few possible uses of the Scale to represent a range of values. The range of a Scale, as well as its orientation, are customizable. The widget also provides callbacks that allow an application to keep track of the value of the Scale as the user changes it. These features make the Scale quite versatile.

14

Text Widgets

This chapter explains how the Text and TextField widgets can be used to provide text-entry capabilities in an application. These widgets can be used for a variety of purposes, from a simple data-entry field to a full-fledged text editor. The chapter describes the selection mechanisms provided by the widgets and how they can be used to communicate with other applications via the clipboard. The widgets also allow the programmer to control the format of the data that is entered by the user.

In This Chapter:

14

Text Widgets

Despite all that can be done with menus, buttons, and lists, there are times when the user can best interact with an application by typing at the keyboard. The Text widget is usually the best choice for providing this style of interface, as it provides full-featured text editing capabilities. The Text widget can be used anywhere the user might be expected to type free-form text, such as in a compose window in a mail application. Unlike standard text editors, the Text widget supports the point-and-click model that people expect from GUI-based applications. The TextField widget provides a single-line data entry field with the same set of editing commands as the Text widget, but it requires less overhead. Text widgets can also be used in output-only mode to display more textual information than is practical with a label or a button.

Even though the text widgets allow for complex interaction, they still provide simple mechanisms for program control. The widgets have resources that access the text, as well as control their behavior. They also provide callback routines that allow an application to intervene on actions that add text, delete text, or move the insertion cursor. The widgets support keyboard management methods that control the editing style, paging style, character positioning, and line-wrapping. There are also convenience routines that enable quick and simple access to the clipboard.

The text widgets do have their limitations. For example, they do not support multiple colors or fonts, so a single widget can only use one color and one font. There is no support for text formatting such as paragraph specifications, automatic line numbering, or indentation, so you cannot create WYSIWYG documents.† The Text widget is not a terminal emulator; it cannot be used to run interactive programs. The widgets cannot display multi-media objects either, which means that it is not possible to insert graphics into the text stream.

There are some cases where a text widget is not the most appropriate user-interface element, even though you are displaying text. For example, a Text widget should not be used to display a list whose items can be individually selected; that is the job of the List widget. Text that cannot be edited, or selected should be displayed in a Label widget. Chapter 11, *Labels and Buttons*, and Chapter 12, *The List Widget*, describe the appropriate uses of these components.

---

† WYSIWYG stands for *What You See Is What You Get*. This term is used to describe page formatting programs that can produce camera-ready documents that match what is displayed on the screen.

If you have not used the Motif Text widget, you should familiarize yourself with one before getting too involved in this chapter. Running some of our introductory examples should provide an adequate platform for experimentation. Figure 14-1 shows an application that uses several Text widgets. Two widgets are used for single-line data entry. The widget with the ScrollBars attached to it is used for editing multiple lines.

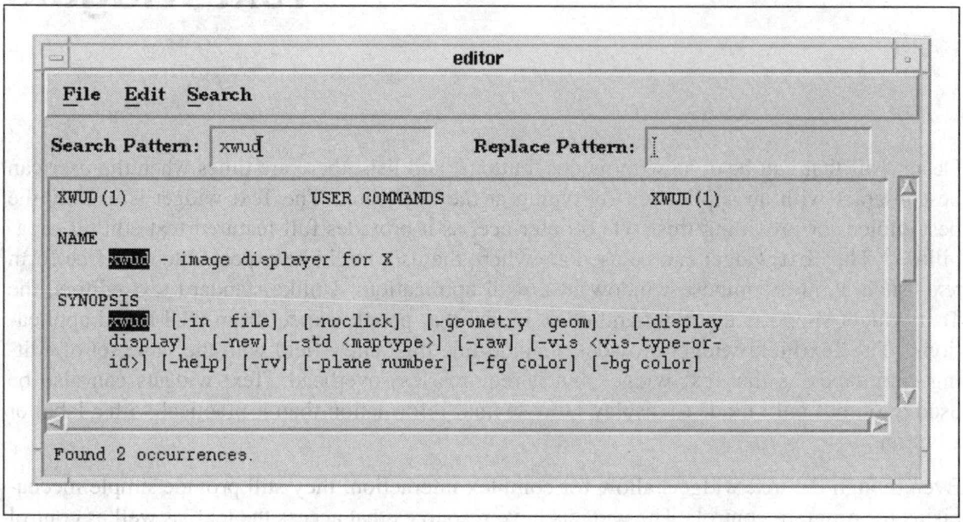

Figure 14-1. An editor application with two different styles of Text widgets

The Text widget supports both single-line and multiline editing. In single-line mode, which is the default mode, newlines are ignored. However, single-line text entry is usually done with the TextField widget class. This widget class is a completely separate class, not a subclass, of Text that is lighter-weight because it only supports single-line text editing.†
Although they are two separate widget classes, the Text and TextField widgets provide many of the same resources and convenience routines. We will point out the differences as we go, but keep in mind that there are two widget classes so you don't get confused as we discuss them throughout this chapter.

Since the TextField widget cannot handle multiline editing, you must use the Text widget for this purpose. When multiple lines are used for editing, the number of lines typically grows and shrinks dynamically as the user edits the text. The Text widget is often used in a scrollable window, so that the user can view different portions of the underlying text. The combination of a Text widget and a ScrolledWindow widget is called a ScrolledText object. This object is not a widget class, although there is a convenience routine, XmCreate-ScrolledText(), that allows you to create both widgets at once.

---

† The TextField widget was added to the toolkit in Motif 1.1; in early versions of that release the widget had a number of bugs that made it difficult to use. - These bugs have been fixed in later releases.

14.1 Interacting With Text Widgets

The Text and TextField widgets are highly configurable in terms of appearance and behavior. Given the level of sophistication for both the programmer and the user, the widgets should not be taken lightly or underestimated. The ease of configurability should not tempt you to enforce your personal ideas about how a text editor should work. The best thing to do with text widgets is configure them as minimally as possible to suit the needs of your program. You should let the user have control over as many details of their display and operation as possible. This laissez-faire approach ensures that your application is more compatible with other Motif programs.

14.1.1 Inserting Text

The user interface for the text widgets follows the point-and-click model of interaction. The insertion cursor indicates the position where the next character that is typed will be inserted. In Motif 1.2, the insertion position is marked by an I-beam cursor. Using the left mouse button, the user can click on a new location in the widget to move the insertion cursor there, so text may be inserted at any location in the widget.

In Motif 1.1, the text widgets used two different cursors. The I-beam was used to mark the insertion position, while a caret (^) was used as the destination cursor when it was separate from the insertion cursor. The destination cursor showed the last position that text was inserted, edited, or selected. Having two separate cursors was confusing for users and programmers, so the model has been simplified for Motif 1.2 to use only the I-beam cursor.

The text widgets have predefined action routines that allow the user to perform simple editing operations such as moving one character to the right or deleting backwards to the beginning of the line. The user can specify translations in a resource file that modify the input behavior of the widgets. The widgets are modeless, so they are always in text-insertion mode. In Motif 1.2, there is an action that puts the Text widget in overstrike mode, while in Motif 1.1, it is programmatically possible to emulate such a mode using multiple action routines.

The user can use the action routines provided by the widgets to set up the translation table to mimic an editor such as *emacs*. The Text widget does not insert nonprintable characters, so users typically bind control-character sequences to editing action routines. An editor like *vi* cannot be emulated because there is no distinction between command mode and text-entry mode.

14.1.2 Selecting Text

Users have become accustomed to the ability to cut and paste text between windows in GUI-based applications. Cut and paste is more difficult for the programmer to implement with the X Window System than a system where a single vendor controls all of the variables, because the nature of X requires a more general solution . For example, applications running on the same display may actually be executing on different systems; these systems may have different byte orders or other differences in the underlying data format.† In order to insulate cut and paste operations from dependencies like these, all communication between applications is implemented via the X server. Data that is cut is stored in a *property* on the X server. A property is simply a named piece of data associated with a window and stored on the server.

The *Interclient Communications Conventions Manual*‡ (ICCCM) defines a set of standard property names to be used for operations such as cut and paste and lays out rules for how applications should interact with these properties. According to the ICCCM, text that is selected is typically stored in the PRIMARY property. The SECONDARY property is defined as an alternate storage area for use by applications that wish to support more than one simultaneous selection operation or that wish to support operations requiring two selections, such as switching the contents of the two selections. The CLIPBOARD property is defined as a longer-term holding area for data that is actually cut (rather than simply copied) from the application's window. When we refer to the primary, secondary, or clipboard selection, we mean the property of the same name.

The most common implementation of the selection mechanism is provided by the X Toolkit Intrinsics. The low-level routines that are used to implement selections are described in detail in Volume Four, *X Toolkit Intrinsics Programming Manual*. In general, applications such as *xterm* and widgets such as the Motif Text widget encapsulate this functionality in action routines that are invoked by the user with mouse button or key combinations.

The user can select text in a Motif Text widget by pressing the left mouse button and dragging the pointer across the text. The selected text is displayed in reverse video. When the button is released, the text widget has ownership of the selection, but no text is copied. The selection can be extended either by pressing the SHIFT key and then dragging the pointer with the left mouse button down, or by pressing any of the arrow keys while holding down the SHIFT key. In addition to the click-and-drag technique for text selection, the Text widget also supports multiple-clicking techniques: double-clicking selects a word, triple-clicking selects the current line, and quadruple-clicking selects all of the text in the widget. An important constraint imposed by the ICCCM is that only one window may own a selection property at one time, which means that once the user makes another primary selection, the original selection is lost.

The user can copy text directly from the primary selection into the Text widget by clicking the middle mouse button at the location where the text is to be inserted. This action is sometimes called stuffing the selection into the widget. The user can stuff text at any location in the text stream, as long as the location is not inside the current selection. The text is copied only when the middle mouse button is clicked, which is defined as a quick succession of press and release actions. The operation does not take place simply because the middle mouse button is pressed, as this action is used for drag and drop operations.

In Motif 1.2, the Text and TextField widgets support the drag-and-drop model of transferring textual data. Once text has been selected in a widget, the selection can be dragged by pressing the middle mouse button over the selection and dragging the pointer. The text is

---

†Currently, only text selections are implemented, which makes byte order irrelevant. However, the mechanism is designed to allow transparent transfer of any kind of data.

‡Reprinted as Appendix L in Volume Zero, *X Protocol Reference Manual*.

transferred when the user releases the middle mouse button with the pointer over another location in the same widget or over another text widget. By default, the text is moved, which means that the original text is deleted once the transfer is complete. The user can force a copy operation by holding down the CONTROL key while dragging the pointer and releasing the mouse button. For more information on drag and drop, see Chapter 18, *Drag and Drop*.

The secondary selection is used by the Motif text widgets to copy text directly within a widget. The user performs this type of operation by first selecting the location where the copied text is to be placed; clicking the left mouse button places the insertion point. Then the text that is to be copied is selected by pressing and dragging the middle mouse button while the ALT key is pressed. The selected text is underlined rather than highlighted in reverse video. When the button is released, the selected text is immediately stuffed at the location of the insertion cursor. Unlike the primary selection, which may be retrieved many times, the secondary selection is immediate and can only be stuffed once.

The third location for holding text is the clipboard selection. The clipboard selection is designed to be used as a longer-term storage area for data. For example, MIT provides a client called *xclipboard* that asserts ownership of the CLIPBOARD property and provides a user interface to it. *xclipboard* not only allows a selection to survive the termination of the window where the data was originally selected, but it also allows for the storage of multiple selections. The user can view all of the selections before deciding which one to paste.

OSF's implementation of the clipboard is incompatible with *xclipboard*. If *xclipboard* is running, any Motif routines that attempt to store data on the clipboard will not succeed. The Motif routines temporarily try to lock the clipboard, and *xclipboard* will not give up its own lock. Motif treats the clipboard as a two-item cache. Only Motif applications that use the clipboard routines described in Chapter 17, *The Clipboard*, can interoperate using this selection. The advantage of the Motif implementation is that it provides functionality far beyond that provided by the standard MIT clients. With *xterm* and the Athena widgets, selections can really only be used for copy-and-paste operations; the selected text is unchanged. The Motif Text widget, by contrast, allows you to cut, copy, clear, or type over a selection. While there is a translation and action-based interface defined for these operations, it is typically not implemented.

As described in Chapter 2, *The Motif Programming Model*, Motif defines translations in terms of virtual key bindings. By default, the virtual keys **osfCut**, **osfCopy**, **osfPaste**, *et. al.*, are not bound to any actual keys. If a user wants to use these keys, he must specify the bindings in a *.motifbind* file in his home directory. The interface for these features is usually provided by menu items associated with the Text widget, as we will demonstrate in this chapter.

When text is selected in a Text widget, it is automatically stored in the primary selection. When one of the Text widget functions, such as XmTextCut(), is used, the text is also stored in the clipboard selection. Most users will be completely unaware that there are separate holding areas for selected text. If your application gets heavily into cutting and pasting, you may find that the fusion of the primary and clipboard selections in the convenience routines is confusing. You should be careful to implement the selection operations so that the different properties are transparent to the user.

The reference pages for the Text and TextField widgets (in Volume Six B, *Motif Reference Manual*; Section 2, *Motif and Xt Widget Classes*) lists the default translations for the widgets. See Volume Four, *X Toolkit Intrinsics Programming Manual*, for a description of how to programmatically alter translation tables; see Volume Three, *X Window System User's Guide*, for a description of how a user can customize widget translations. See Chapter 17, *The Clipboard*, for a discussion of the lower-level Motif clipboard functions.

14.2 Text Widget Basics

In order to understand the complexities of the Text and TextField widgets, you need to know about some of the basic resources and functions that they provide. This section describes the fundamentals of working with text widgets, including how to create the widgets, how to work with the textual data, and how to control simple aspects of appearance and behavior. Applications that wish to use the Text widget need to include the file *<Xm/Text.h>*. TextField widgets require the file *<Xm/TextF.h>*. You can create a Text widget using XtVaCreate-ManagedWidget() as usual:

```
Widget text_w;

text_w = XtVaCreateManagedWidget("name",
    xmTextWidgetClass, parent,
    resource-value-list,
    NULL);
```

To create a TextField widget instead, specify the class as xmTextFieldWidgetClass.

14.2.1 The Textual Data

The XmNvalue resource of the Text and TextField widgets provides the most basic means of access to the internal text storage for the widgets. Unlike the other widgets in the Motif toolkit that use text, the text widgets do not use compound strings for their values. Instead, the value is specified as a regular C string, as shown in Example 14-1.†

Example 14-1. The simple_text.c program

```
/* simple_text.c -- Create a minimally configured Text widget */
#include <Xm/Text.h>

main(argc, argv)
int argc;
char *argv[];
{
    Widget      toplevel;
    XtAppContext  app;

    XtSetLanguageProc (NULL, NULL, NULL);

    toplevel = XtVaAppInitialize (&app, "Demos",
        NULL, 0, &argc, argv, NULL, NULL);

    XtVaCreateManagedWidget ("text", xmTextWidgetClass, toplevel,
        XmNvalue,      "Now is the time...",
```

---

† XtSetLanguageProc() is only available in X11R5; there is no corresponding function in X11R4.

Example 14-1. The simple_text.c program (continued)

```
        NULL);

    XtRealizeWidget (toplevel);
    XtAppMainLoop (app);
}
```

This short program simply creates a Text widget with the initial value shown in Figure 14-2.

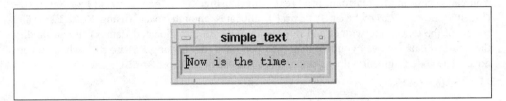

Figure 14-2. Output of simple_text.c

In Motif 1.2, both widgets also provide the XmNvalueWcs resource for storing a wide-character representation of the text value. For more information on using the text widgets in an internationalized application, see Section 14.6.

Specifying the Text

The initial value of the XmNvalue resource may be set either when the widget is created or by using XtVaSetValues() after the widget has been created. The value of the resource always represents the entire text of the widget. You can also use a Motif convenience routine, XmTextSetString(), to set the text value. This routine takes the following form:

```
    void
    XmTextSetString(text_w, value)
        Widget  text_w;
        char    *value;
```

This routine works for both Text and TextField widgets. The TextField widget has a corresponding routine, XmTextFieldSetString(), but it only works for TextField widgets. If you are using both types of text widgets in an application, we recommend using the Text widget routines to manipulate all of the widgets. Since these routines work with both types of widgets, you don't need to keep track of the widget types.

Although the convenience routine and XtVaSetValues() produce the same results, the convenience routine may be more efficient since it accesses the internals of the widget directly, while the XtVaSetValues() method involves going through Xt. On the other hand, if you are setting a number of resources at the same time, the XtVaSetValues() method is better because all of the resources can be set in a single function call. Whichever function you use, the text value is copied into the internals of the widget, and the displayed value is changed accordingly.

If, for whatever reason, you are making multiple changes in a short period of time to the text in a Text widget, you may have problems with visual flashing in the widget. With Motif 1.2, you can solve this problem by calling `XmTextDisableRedisplay()` to turn off visual updating in the widget. After the call, the appearance of the widget remains unchanged until `XmTextEnableRedisplay()` is called.

Retrieving the Text

You can access the textual data in a Text widget using `XtVaGetValues()` or `XmText-GetString()`. `XmTextGetString()` allocates enough space (using `XtMalloc()`) for all of the text in the widget and returns a pointer to the allocated data. You can modify the returned data any way you like, and then you must free it using `XtFree()` when you are done. The code fragment below demonstrates the use of `XmTextGetString()`:

```
char *text;

if (text = XmTextGetString (text_w)) {
    /* manipulate text in whatever way is necessary */
    . . .
    /* free text or there will be a memory leak */
    XtFree (text);
}
```

`XmTextGetString()` works with both Text and TextField widgets, while the corresponding TextField routine, `XmTextFieldGetString()`, only works with TextField widgets. In Motif 1.2, you can also use `XmTextGetSubstring()` to get a copy of a portion of the text in a Text widget.

The alternative to `XmTextGetString()` is the Xt function `XtVaGetValues()`. The Text widget responds to `XtVaGetValues()` by allocating memory and returning a copy of the text. As a result, this data must be freed after use. This use of the `GetValues()` method is different from most other resources. For most resources, `XtVaGetValues()` returns a pointer to internal data that should be treated as read-only data. In order to avoid memory leaks, you need to be sure to free the memory that is allocated by `XtVaGet-Values()` for the `XmNvalue` resource, as shown in the following code fragment:

```
char *text;

XtVaGetValues (text_w, XmNvalue, &text, NULL);
/* manipulate text in whatever way is necessary */
. . .
/* free text or there will be a memory leak */
XtFree (text);
```

Getting the value of a Text widget can be an expensive operation if the widget contains a large amount of text. In all situations, whenever text is retrieved from the Text widget with any function, the length of time the data is valid is only guaranteed until the next Xt call into the same Text widget; what any particular call might do to the internal text stream is undefined, and that information will not be reflected in the current character pointer handle you may have.

A Text widget may contain an arbitrarily large amount of text, assuming that there is enough memory on the computer running the client application. The text for a widget is not stored on the X server; only the client computer stores widget-specific information. The server displays a bitmap rendition of what the Text widget chooses to show. The XmNmaxLength resource specifies the upper limit on the number of characters the user can type into a Text widget. The default value of this resource is the largest integer for the particular system, so it is likely that the user's computer will run out of memory before the Text widget's maximum capacity is reached. You can lower the value of the resource to limit the number of characters that the user can input to a particular Text widget.

The Text widget does not use a temporary file to store its data. All of the data resides in memory on the machine, so you cannot use a Text widget to browse or edit a file directly. Instead, you load the contents of a file into a Text widget and allow the user to edit the internal buffer. The application controls when to rewrite files with updated data. An application can also provide an interface that allows the user to control this action. Applications that use Text widgets to edit vital information should make provisions for data recovery if the system fails or the application terminates unexpectedly. The Text widget does not support this type of recovery.

14.2.2 Single and Multiple Lines

In Example 14-1, the Text widget provides a single-line text entry area that is 20 columns wide; it is shown in Figure 14-2. Both the single-line editing style and the width are default values. The width of each column is based on the font that is used for the text. Since the widget uses the single-line editing style, nothing happens when the user presses RETURN in the widget. If the user types more text than the widget can display, the text scrolls to the left. Since newlines are not interpreted when they are typed by the user, textual data is always a single line.† The user can resize the widget to make it appear large enough to display multiple lines, but this action does not affect the operation of the widget or the way it handles input.

Multiline editing allows the user to enter newlines into a Text widget and provides the capability to edit a large amount of text. The switch from single-line to multiline causes a number of changes in the behavior of the widget. For example, now widget geometry must be considered in order to determine the amount of text that is visible at one time. The Text widget may need to be placed in a ScrolledWindow, so that the user can view all of the text.

Single or multiline editing is controlled through the XmNeditMode resource. The value of the resource can be either XmSINGLE_LINE_EDIT or XmMULTI_LINE_EDIT. While the two editing modes are quite different in concept, it should be quite intuitive when to use the different modes. Single-line text entry areas are commonly used to prompt for file and directory names, short phrases, or single words. They are also useful for command-line entry in applications that were originally based on a tty-style interface. Multiline editing is used for editing files or other large quantities of text.

---

† It is possible to set XmNvalue to a string that contains newline characters in a single-line Text widget, but the interaction with the user is undefined, and the widget produces confusing behavior.

14.2.3 Scrollable Text

The layout of a multiline Text widget can be difficult to manage, especially if the text is editable by the user. An application needs to decide how many lines of text are displayed, how to handle the layout when the user adds new text, and how to deal with resizing the Text widget. The easiest way to manage an editable multiline Text widget is to create it as part of a ScrolledText compound object. The ScrolledText object is not a widget class in and of itself, but rather a compound object that is composed of a Text widget and a ScrolledWindow widget.

When you create a ScrolledText object, the ScrolledWindow automatically handles scrolling the text in the Text widget. Basically, the two widget classes have hooks and procedures that allow them to cooperate intelligently with each other. As of Motif 1.2, the performance of the ScrolledText object has improved considerably.† In previous releases, scrolling operations could be quite slow when the Text widget contained a large amount of text.

You can create a ScrolledText object using the Motif convenience routine XmCreate-ScrolledText(), which takes the following form:

```
Widget
XmCreateScrolledText(parent, name, arglist, argcount)
    Widget   parent;
    char     *name;
    ArgList  arglist;
    Cardinal argcount;
```

This routine is not a variable-argument list function; it uses the argument-list style of setting resources with the XtSetArg() macro.

XmCreateScrolledText() creates a ScrolledWindow widget and a Text widget as its child. The routine returns a handle to the Text widget; you can get a handle to the Scrolled-Window using the function XtParent(). When you are laying out an application that uses ScrolledText objects, you should be sure to use XtParent() to get the ScrolledWindow widget, since that is the widget that you need to position.

For purposes of specifying resources, the ScrolledWindow takes the name of the Text widget with the suffix SW. For example, if the name of the Text widget is name, its ScrolledWindow parent widget has the name nameSW.

If you specify an argument list in a call to XmCreateScrolledText(), the resources are set for the Text widget or the ScrolledWindow as appropriate. The routine also sets some resources for the ScrolledWindow so that scrolling is handled automatically. You should be sure to set the XmNeditMode resource to XmMULTI_LINE_EDIT, since it doesn't make sense to have a single-line Text widget in a ScrolledWindow. If you don't set the resource, the Text widget defaults to single-line editing mode. The behavior of a single-line Text widget (or a TextField widget) in a ScrolledWindow is undefined.

---

† One unfortunate side-effect of the performance improvement is that subclasses of the Text widget may not work under Motif 1.2, due to the addition of a new data structure.

`XmCreateScrolledText()` is adequate for most situations, but you can also create the two widgets separately, as shown in the following code fragment:

```
Widget scrolled_w, text_w;

scrolled_w = XtVaCreateManagedWidget ("scrolled_w",
    xmScrolledWindowWidgetClass, parent,
    XmNscrollingPolicy,         XmAPPLICATION_DEFINED,
    XmNvisualPolicy,            XmVARIABLE,
    XmNscrollBarDisplayPolicy,  XmSTATIC,
    XmNshadowThickness,         0,
    NULL);

text_w = XtVaCreateManagedWidget ("text",
    xmTextWidgetClass, scrolled_w,
    XmNeditMode,                XmMULTI_LINE_EDIT,
    . . .
    NULL);
```

We create the ScrolledWindow widget with the same resource setting that the Motif function uses. Since we are creating the ScrolledWindow ourselves, we can give it our own name. The Text widget itself is created as a child of the ScrolledWindow. In this situation, it is clear that the parent of the ScrolledWindow controls the position of both of the widgets.

This creation method makes the programmer responsible for managing both of the widgets. You may also need to handle the case in which the widgets are destroyed. When you call `XmCreateScrolledText()`, the routine installs an `XmNdestroyCallback` on the Text widget that destroys the ScrolledWindow parent. When you create the widgets yourself, you also need to be sure that they are destroyed together, either by destroying them explicitly or installing a callback routine on the Text widget. Unless you are creating and destroying ScrolledText objects dynamically, this issue should not be a concern.

Example 14-2 shows a simple file browser that displays the contents of a file using a ScrolledText object. The user can specify a file by typing a filename in the TextField widget below the **Filename**: prompt. The user can also select a file from the FileSelectionDialog that is popped up by the **Open** entry on the **File** menu. The specified file is displayed immediately in the Text widget.†

Example 14-2. The file_browser.c program

```
/* file_browser.c -- use a ScrolledText object to view the
 * contents of arbitrary files chosen by the user from a
 * FileSelectionDialog or from a single-line text widget.
 */
#include <X11/Xos.h>
#include <Xm/Text.h>
#include <Xm/TextF.h>
#include <Xm/FileSB.h>
#include <Xm/MainW.h>
#include <Xm/RowColumn.h>
```

---

†XtSetLanguageProc() is only available in X11R5; there is no corresponding function in X11R4. Xm-StringCreateLocalized() is only available in Motif 1.2; XmStringCreateSimple() is the corresponding function in Motif 1.1. XmFONTLIST_DEFAULT_TAG replaces XmSTRING_DEFAULT_CHARSET in Motif 1.2.

Example 14-2. The file_browser.c program (continued)

```c
#include <Xm/LabelG.h>
#include <sys/types.h>
#include <sys/stat.h>
#include <stdio.h>

main(argc, argv)
int argc;
char *argv[];
{
    Widget          top, main_w, menubar, menu, rc, text_w, file_w;
    XtAppContext    app;
    XmString        file, open, exit;
    extern void     read_file(), file_cb();
    Arg             args[10];
    int             n;

    XtSetLanguageProc (NULL, NULL, NULL);

    /* initialize toolkit and create toplevel shell */
    top = XtVaAppInitialize (&app, "Demos",
        NULL, 0, &argc, argv, NULL, NULL);

    /* MainWindow for the application -- contains menubar
     * and ScrolledText/Prompt/TextField as WorkWindow.
     */
    main_w = XtVaCreateManagedWidget ("main_w",
        xmMainWindowWidgetClass, top, NULL);

    /* Create a simple MenuBar that contains one menu */
    file = XmStringCreateLocalized ("File");
    menubar = XmVaCreateSimpleMenuBar (main_w, "menubar",
        XmVaCASCADEBUTTON, file, 'F',
        NULL);
    XmStringFree (file);

    /* Menu is "File" -- callback is file_cb() */
    open = XmStringCreateLocalized ("Open...");
    exit = XmStringCreateLocalized ("Exit");
    menu = XmVaCreateSimplePulldownMenu (menubar, "file_menu", 0, file_cb,
        XmVaPUSHBUTTON, open, 'O', NULL, NULL,
        XmVaSEPARATOR,
        XmVaPUSHBUTTON, exit, 'x', NULL, NULL,
        NULL);
    XmStringFree (open);
    XmStringFree (exit);

    /* Menubar is done -- manage it */
    XtManageChild (menubar);

    rc = XtVaCreateWidget ("work_area", xmRowColumnWidgetClass, main_w, NULL);
    XtVaCreateManagedWidget ("Filename:", xmLabelGadgetClass, rc,
        XmNalignment, XmALIGNMENT_BEGINNING,
        NULL);
    file_w = XtVaCreateManagedWidget ("text_field",
        xmTextFieldWidgetClass, rc, NULL);

    /* Create ScrolledText -- this is work area for the MainWindow */
    n = 0;
    XtSetArg(args[n], XmNrows,      12); n++;
    XtSetArg(args[n], XmNcolumns,   70); n++;
```

Example 14-2. The file_browser.c program (continued)

```
    XtSetArg(args[n], XmNeditable,  False); n++;
    XtSetArg(args[n], XmNeditMode,  XmMULTI_LINE_EDIT); n++;
    XtSetArg(args[n], XmNcursorPositionVisible,  False); n++;
    text_w = XmCreateScrolledText (rc, "text_w", args, n);
    XtManageChild (text_w);

    /* store text_w as user data in "File" menu for file_cb() callback */
    XtVaSetValues (menu, XmNuserData, text_w, NULL);
    /* add callback for TextField widget passing "text_w" as client data */
    XtAddCallback (file_w, XmNactivateCallback, read_file, text_w);

    XtManageChild (rc);

    /* Store the filename text widget to ScrolledText object */
    XtVaSetValues (text_w, XmNuserData, file_w, NULL);

    XmMainWindowSetAreas (main_w, menubar, NULL, NULL, NULL, rc);
    XtRealizeWidget (top);
    XtAppMainLoop (app);
}

/* file_cb() -- "File" menu item was selected so popup a
 * FileSelectionDialog.
 */
void
file_cb(widget, client_data, call_data)
Widget widget;
XtPointer client_data;
XtPointer call_data;
{
    static Widget dialog;
    Widget text_w;
    extern void read_file();
    int item_no = (int) client_data;

    if (item_no == 1)
        exit (0);  /* user chose Exit */

    if (!dialog) {
        Widget menu = XtParent (widget);
        dialog = XmCreateFileSelectionDialog (menu, "file_sb", NULL, 0);

        /* Get the text widget handle stored as "user data" in File menu */
        XtVaGetValues (menu, XmNuserData, &text_w, NULL);
        XtAddCallback (dialog, XmNokCallback, read_file, text_w);
        XtAddCallback (dialog, XmNcancelCallback, XtUnmanageChild, NULL);
    }
    XtManageChild (dialog);

    XtPopup (XtParent (dialog), XtGrabNone);
    XMapRaised (XtDisplay (dialog), XtWindow (XtParent (dialog)));
}

/* read_file() -- callback routine when the user selects OK in the
 * FileSelection Dialog or presses Return in the single-line text widget.
 * The specified file must be a regular file and readable.
 * If so, it's contents are displayed in the text_w provided as the
 * client_data to this function.
 */
void
```

Example 14-2. The file_browser.c program (continued)

```
read_file(widget, client_data, call_data)
Widget widget;  /* file selection box or text field widget */
XtPointer client_data;
XtPointer call_data;
{
    char *filename, *text;
    struct stat statb;
    FILE *fp;
    Widget file_w;
    Widget text_w = (Widget) client_data;
    XmFileSelectionBoxCallbackStruct *cbs =
        (XmFileSelectionBoxCallbackStruct *) call_data;

    if (XtIsSubclass (widget, xmTextFieldWidgetClass)) {
        filename = XmTextFieldGetString (widget);
        file_w = widget; /* this *is* the file_w */
    }
    else {
        /* file was selected from FileSelectionDialog */
        XmStringGetLtoR (cbs->value, XmFONTLIST_DEFAULT_TAG, &filename);
        /* the user data stored the file_w widget in the text_w */
        XtVaGetValues (text_w, XmNuserData, &file_w, NULL);
    }

    if (!filename || !*filename) { /* nothing typed? */
        if (filename)
            XtFree (filename);
        return;
    }

    /* make sure the file is a regular text file and open it */
    if (stat (filename, &statb) == -1 ||
            (statb.st_mode & S_IFMT) != S_IFREG ||
            !(fp = fopen(filename, "r"))) {
        if ((statb.st_mode & S_IFMT) == S_IFREG)
            perror (filename); /* send to stderr why we can't read it */
        else
            fprintf (stderr, "%s: not a regular file\n", filename);
        XtFree (filename);
        return;
    }

    /* put the contents of the file in the Text widget by allocating
     * enough space for the entire file, reading the file into the
     * allocated space, and using XmTextFieldSetString() to show the file.
     */
    if (!(text = XtMalloc ((unsigned)(statb.st_size + 1)))) {
        fprintf (stderr, "Can't alloc enough space for %s", filename);
        XtFree (filename);
        fclose (fp);
        return;
    }

    if (!fread (text, sizeof (char), statb.st_size + 1, fp))
        fprintf (stderr, "Warning: may not have read entire file!\n");

    text[statb.st_size] = 0; /* be sure to NULL-terminate */

    /* insert file contents in Text widget */
```

Example 14-2. The file_browser.c program (continued)

```
        XmTextSetString (text_w, text);

        /* make sure text field is up to date */
        if (file_w != widget) {
            /* only necessary if activated from FileSelectionDialog */
            XmTextFieldSetString (file_w, filename);
            XmTextFieldSetCursorPosition (file_w, strlen(filename));
        }

        /* free all allocated space and */
        XtFree (text);
        XtFree (filename);
        fclose (fp);
}
```

The output of the program is shown in Figure 14-3.

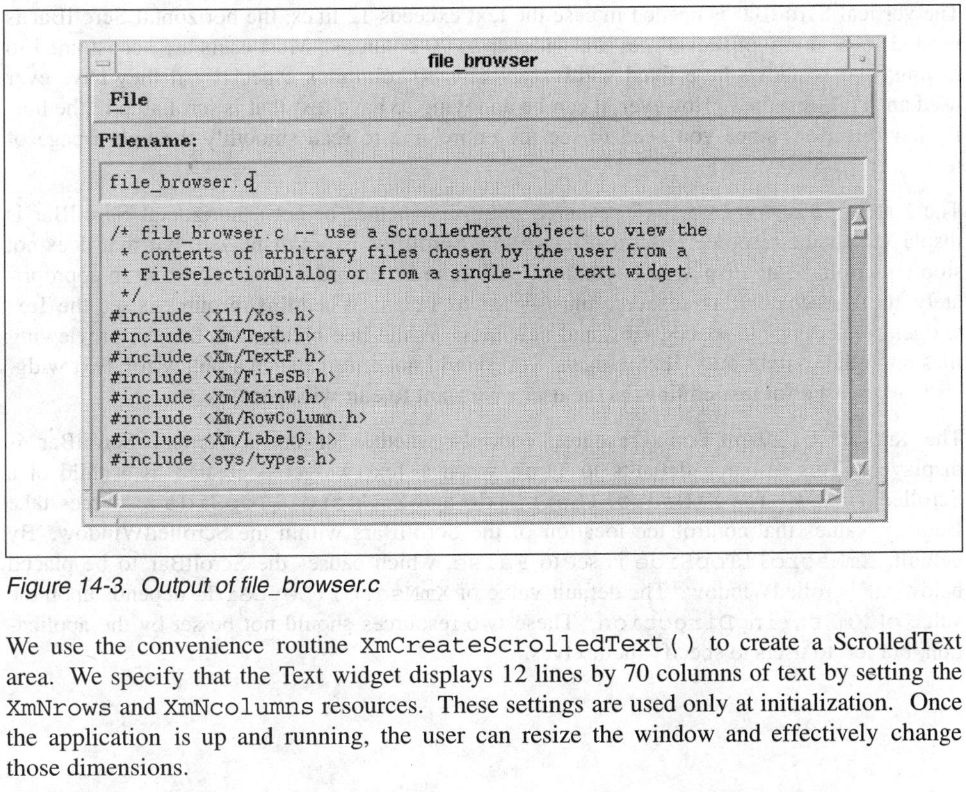

Figure 14-3. Output of file_browser.c

We use the convenience routine `XmCreateScrolledText()` to create a ScrolledText area. We specify that the Text widget displays 12 lines by 70 columns of text by setting the `XmNrows` and `XmNcolumns` resources. These settings are used only at initialization. Once the application is up and running, the user can resize the window and effectively change those dimensions.

The `XmNeditable` resource is set to `False` to prevent the user from editing the contents of the Text widget. Since we do not provide a way to write changes back to the file, we don't want to mislead the user into thinking that the file is editable. Since a noneditable Text widget should not display an insertion cursor, we remove it by setting `XmNcursorPositionVisible` to `False`.

The FileSelectionDialog is created and managed when the user selects the **Open** button from the **File** menu. The user can exit the program by selecting the **Exit** button from this menu. The `read_file()` routine is activated when the user presses the **OK** button in the File-SelectionDialog or enters RETURN in the TextField widget. This function gets the specified file and checks its type. If the file chosen is not a regular file (e.g., if it is a directory, device, tty, etc.) or if it cannot be opened, an error is reported and the function simply returns.†

Assuming that the file checks out, its contents are placed in the Text widget. Rather than loading the file by reading each line using a function like `fgets()`, we allocate enough space to contain the entire file and read it all in with one call to `fread()`. The text is then loaded into the Text widget using `XmTextSetString()`. The ScrollBars are updated automatically and the text is positioned so that the beginning of the file is displayed.

Line Wrapping and ScrollBar Placement

In *file_browser.c*, the ScrolledText object has two ScrollBars that are installed automatically. The vertical ScrollBar is needed in case the text exceeds 12 lines; the horizontal ScrollBar is needed in case any of those lines are wider than 70 columns. Most users are accustomed to having Text windows be a fixed width (typically 80 columns), especially if they have ever used an ASCII terminal. However, it can be annoying to have text that is scrollable in the horizontal direction, since you need to see the entire line to read smoothly through a page of text.

The `XmNscrollHorizontal` resource controls whether or not a horizontal ScrollBar is displayed. If the resource is set to `False`, the ScrollBar is not displayed, but that does not stop text from being displayed beyond the visible area. In order to have text wrap appropriately, the `XmNwordWrap` resource must be set to `True`. When this resource is set, the Text widget breaks lines at spaces, tabs, and newlines. While line breaking is fine for previewing files and other output-only Text widgets, you should not enforce such a policy for Text widgets that are used for text editing, as the user may want to edit wide files.

The `XmNscrollVertical` resource controls whether or not a vertical ScrollBar is displayed. This resource defaults to `True` when a Text widget is created as a child of a ScrolledWindow. The `XmNscrollLeftSide` and `XmNscrollTopSide` resources take Boolean values that control the location of the ScrollBars within the ScrolledWindow. By default, `XmNscrollTopSide` is set to `False`, which causes the ScrollBar to be placed below the ScrolledWindow. The default value of `XmNscrollLeftSide` depends upon the value of `XmNstringDirection`. These two resources should not be set by the application, but left to users to specify themselves.

---

† If you are unfamiliar with the use of the *stat( )* system call, or any other aspect of UNIX programming used in examples in this book, a good source of information is the Nutshell Handbook *Using C on the UNIX System*, by Dave Curry (O'Reilly & Associates, 1988).

Automatic Resizing

The `XmNresizeWidth` and `XmNresizeHeight` resources control whether or not a Text widget should resize itself vertically or horizontally in order to display the entire text stream. Both of the resources default to `False`. If `XmNresizeWidth` is set to `True` and new text is added such that the number of columns needs to grow, the width of the widget grows to contain the new text. Similarly, if `XmNresizeHeight` is set to `True` and the number of lines increases, the height of the widget increases so that it can display all of the lines. These resources have no effect in a ScrolledText object, since the ScrollBars are managing the widget's size. Also, if line breaking is active, `XmNresizeWidth` has no effect.

In most cases, it is not appropriate to set these resources, as it is regarded as poor user-interface design to have a Text widget that dynamically resizes as the text is being edited. It is also impolite for a window to resize itself except as the result of an explicit user action. One example of an acceptable use of these resources involves using a Text widget to display text for a help dialog. In this situation, the Text widget can resize itself silently before it is mapped to the screen, so that by the time it is visible, its size is constant.

14.2.4 Text Positions

A *position* in a Text widget specifies the number of characters from the beginning of the text in the widget, where the first character position is defined as zero (0). All whitespace and newline characters are considered part of the text and are counted as single characters. For example, in Figure 14-3, the insertion cursor in the TextField widget is at position 14. When the user types in a Text widget, the new text is always added at the position of the insertion cursor and the insertion cursor is advanced. If the user does not move the cursor, it is always positioned at the end of the text in the widget.

You can set the position of the insertion cursor explicitly using `XmTextSetInsertion-Position()`, which takes the following form:

```
void
XmTextSetInsertionPosition(text_w, position)
    Widget          text_w;
    XmTextPosition position;
```

This function is identical to `XmTextSetCursorPosition()`. The `XmTextPosition` type is a `long` value, so it can represent all of the positions in a Text widget. You can get the current cursor position using `XmTextGetInsertionPosition()` or `XmTextGet-CursorPosition()`. As with most of the Text widget functions, there are corresponding TextField functions for setting and getting the position of the insertion cursor. The TextField routines only work with TextField widgets, while the Text routines work with both Text and TextField widgets.

Example 14-3 shows an application that uses these routines as part of a search operation. The program searches the Text widget for a specified pattern and then positions the insertion cursor so that the pattern is displayed.†

---

†`XtSetLanguageProc()` is only available in X11R5; there is no corresponding function in X11R4.

Example 14-3. The search_text.c program

```
/* search_text.c -- demonstrate how to position a cursor at a
 * particular location.  The position is determined by a pattern
 * match search.
 */
#include <Xm/Text.h>
#include <Xm/TextF.h>
#include <Xm/LabelG.h>
#include <Xm/RowColumn.h>
#include <X11/Xos.h>   /* for the index() function */

Widget text_w, search_w, text_output;

main(argc, argv)
int argc;
char *argv[];
{
    Widget          toplevel, rowcol_v, rowcol_h;
    XtAppContext    app;
    int             i, n;
    void            search_text();
    Arg             args[10];

    XtSetLanguageProc (NULL, NULL, NULL);

    toplevel = XtVaAppInitialize (&app, "Demos",
        NULL, 0, &argc, argv, NULL, NULL);

    rowcol_v = XtVaCreateWidget ("rowcol_v",
        xmRowColumnWidgetClass, toplevel, NULL);

    rowcol_h = XtVaCreateWidget ("rowcol_h",
        xmRowColumnWidgetClass, rowcol_v,
        XmNorientation,  XmHORIZONTAL,
        NULL);
    XtVaCreateManagedWidget ("Search Pattern:",
        xmLabelGadgetClass, rowcol_h, NULL);
    search_w = XtVaCreateManagedWidget ("search_text",
        xmTextFieldWidgetClass, rowcol_h, NULL);
    XtManageChild (rowcol_h);

    text_output = XtVaCreateManagedWidget ("text_output",
        xmTextWidgetClass, rowcol_v,
        XmNeditable,              False,
        XmNcursorPositionVisible, False,
        XmNshadowThickness,       0,
        XmNhighlightThickness,    0,
        NULL);

    n = 0;
    XtSetArg (args[n], XmNrows,      10); n++;
    XtSetArg (args[n], XmNcolumns,   80); n++;
    XtSetArg (args[n], XmNeditMode,  XmMULTI_LINE_EDIT); n++;
    XtSetArg (args[n], XmNscrollHorizontal,  False); n++;
    XtSetArg (args[n], XmNwordWrap,  True); n++;
    text_w = XmCreateScrolledText (rowcol_v, "text_w", args, n);
    XtManageChild (text_w);

    XtAddCallback (search_w, XmNactivateCallback, search_text, NULL);

    XtManageChild (rowcol_v);
```

Example 14-3. The search_text.c program (continued)

```
    XtRealizeWidget (toplevel);
    XtAppMainLoop (app);
}

/* search_text() -- called when the user activates the TextField. */
void
search_text(widget, client_data, call_data)
Widget widget;
XtPointer client_data;
XtPointer call_data;
{
    char *search_pat, *p, *string, buf[32];
    XmTextPosition pos;
    int len;
    Boolean found = False;

    /* get the text that is about to be searched */
    if (!(string = XmTextGetString (text_w)) || !*string) {
        XmTextSetString (text_output, "No text to search.");
        XtFree (string); /* may have been ""; free it */
        return;
    }
    /* get the pattern we're going to search for in the text. */
    if (!(search_pat = XmTextGetString (search_w)) || !*search_pat) {
        XmTextSetString (text_output, "Specify a search pattern.");
        XtFree (string); /* this we know is a string; free it */
        XtFree (search_pat); /* this may be "", XtFree() checks.. */
        return;
    }
    len = strlen (search_pat);

    /* start searching at current cursor position + 1 to find
     * the -next- occurrance of string.  we may be sitting on it.
     */
    pos = XmTextGetCursorPosition (text_w);
    for (p = &string[pos+1]; p = index (p, *search_pat); p++)
        if (!strncmp (p, search_pat, len)) {
            found = True;
            break;
        }
    if (!found) { /* didn't find pattern? */
        /* search from beginning till we've passed "pos" */
        for (p = string;
                (p = index (p, *search_pat)) && p - string <= pos; p++)
            if (!strncmp (p, search_pat, len)) {
                found = True;
                break;
            }
    }
    if (!found)
        XmTextSetString (text_output, "Pattern not found.");
    else {
        pos = (XmTextPosition)(p - string);
        sprintf (buf, "Pattern found at position %ld.", pos);
        XmTextSetString (text_output, buf);
        XmTextSetInsertionPosition (text_w, pos);
    }
```

Text Widgets

Example 14-3. The search_text.c program (continued)

```
        XtFree (string);
        XtFree (search_pat);
}
```

In this example, the user can search for strings in a ScrolledText, as shown in Figure 14-4.

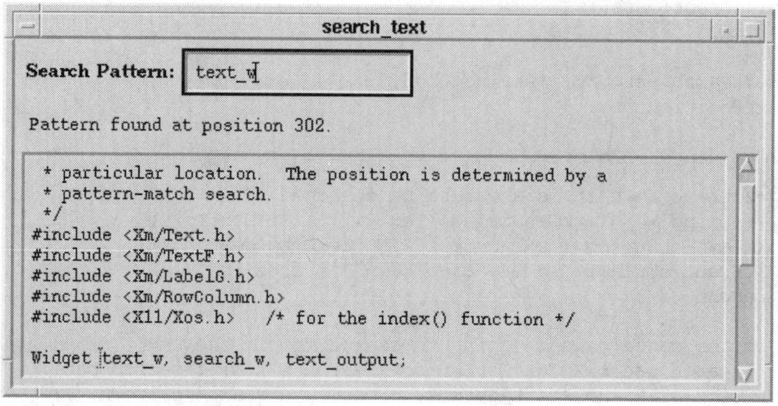

Figure 14-4. Output of search_text.c

This program doesn't provide a way to load a file, so if you want to experiment, you need to type or paste some text into the widget. Once there is some text in the widget, type a string pattern in the **Search Pattern** TextField widget and press RETURN to activate the search. The text is searched starting at the position immediately following the current cursor position. If the search routine reaches the end of the text before it finds the pattern, it resumes searching from the beginning of the text and continues until it finds the pattern or reaches the cursor position. If the routine finds the pattern, it moves the insertion point to that location using XmTextSetInsertionPosition(). Otherwise, the routine prints an error message and does not move the cursor.

The search_text() routine shown in Example 14-3 searches the text using various string routines. In Motif 1.2, there is a new Text routine that provides the same functionality. Xm-TextFindString() searches a Text widget for a specified string. This routine takes the following form:

```
    Boolean
    XmTextFindString(text_w, start, string, direction, position)
        Widget            text_w;
        XmTextPosition    start;
        char              *string;
        XmTextDirection   direction;
        XmTextPosition    *position;
```

The *start* argument specifies the starting position for the search, while *direction* indicates whether the routine searches forward or backward in the text. This parameter can have the value XmTEXT_FORWARD or XmTEXT_BACKWARD. The routine returns True if it finds the string, and in this case, the *position* parameter returns the position where the string starts in the text. If the string is not found, the routine returns False, and the value of *position* is undefined. It is easy to rewrite search_text() to take advantage of Xm-TextFindString(). In Section 14.4, we implement a full text editor and use XmText-FindString() to handle the various search operations.

The text_output widget in *search_text.c* is also a Text widget, even though it looks more like a Label widget. By setting XmNshadowThickness to 0 and XmNeditable to False, we create the Text widget that doesn't look like a normal Text widget, and the user cannot edit the text. We demonstrate this technique not to advocate such usage, but to point out the versatility of this widget class.

If you paste a large amount of text into the main Text widget and search repeatedly for a common pattern, you should notice that the Text widget may scroll automatically to make the specified text visible. This action is controlled by the XmNautoShowCursorPosition resource. This resource has a default value of True, which means that the Text widget adjusts the visible text to make sure that the cursor is always visible. When the resource is set to False, the widget does not scroll to compensate for the cursor's invisibility. This resource also works in single-line Text widgets and TextField widgets; these widgets may scroll their displays horizontally to display the insertion cursor.

It is easy to scroll a Text widget to a particular position in the text stream by setting the cursor position and then calling XmTextShowPosition(). This routine takes the following form:

```
void
XmTextShowPosition(text_w, position)
    Widget          text_w;
    XmTextPosition position;
```

To scroll to the end of the text, you need to scroll to the last position, which can be retrieved using XmTextGetLastPosition(). It is also possible to perform relative scrolling using the function XmTextScroll(), which takes the following form:

```
void
XmTextScroll(text_w, lines)
    Widget text_w;
    int    lines;
```

A positive value for lines causes a Text widget to scroll upward by that many lines, while a negative value causes downward scrolling. The Text widget does not have to be a child of ScrolledWindow for this routine to work; the widget simply adjusts the viewable text.

Now that we have a routine that searches for text, the next logical step is to implement a function that performs a search-and-replace operation. Motif makes this task fairly easy by providing the XmTextReplace() routine, which takes the following form:

```
void
XmTextReplace(text_w, from_pos, to_pos, value)
    Widget          text_w;
    XmTextPosition  from_pos;
    XmTextPosition  to_pos;
    char            *value;
```

This function identifies the text to be replaced in the Text widget starting at the position *from_pos* and ending at, but not including, the position *to_pos*. This text is replaced by the text in *value*. If *value* is NULL or an empty string, the text between the two positions is simply deleted. If you want to remove all of the text from the widget, call XmTextSet-String() with a NULL string as the text value.

To add search-and-replace functionality to the program in Example 14-3, we need to add a new TextField widget that prompts for the replacement text and provide a callback routine for the widget. Example 14-4 shows the additional code that is necessary.

Example 14-4. The search_and_replace() function

```
Widget text_w, search_w, replace_w, text_output;

main(argc, argv)
int argc;
char *argv[];
{
    ...
    replace_w = XtVaCreateManagedWidget ("replace_text",
        xmTextFieldWidgetClass, rowcol_h, NULL);

    XtAddCallback (replace_w, XmNactivateCallback, search_and_replace, NULL);
    ...
}

void
search_and_replace(widget, client_data, call_data)
Widget widget;
XtPointer client_data;
XtPointer call_data;
{
    char *search_pat, *p, *string, *new_pat, buf[32];
    XmTextPosition pos;
    int search_len, pattern_len;
    int nfound = 0;

    string = XmTextGetString (text_w);
    if (!*string) {
        XmTextSetString (text_output, "No text to search.");
        XtFree (string);
        return;
    }

    search_pat = XmTextGetString (search_w);
    if (!*search_pat) {
        XmTextSetString (text_output, "Specify a search pattern.");
        XtFree (string);
```

Example 14-4. The search_and_replace() function (continued)

```
                XtFree (search_pat);
                return;
        }

    new_pat = XmTextGetString (replace_w);
    search_len = strlen (search_pat);
    pattern_len = strlen (new_pat);
    /* start at beginning and search entire Text widget */
    for (p = string; p = index (p, *search_pat); p++)
            if (!strncmp (p, search_pat, search_len)) {
                    nfound++;
                    /* get the position where pattern was found */
                    pos = (XmTextPosition)(p-string);
                    /* replace the text from our position + strlen (new_pat) */
                    XmTextReplace (text_w, pos, pos + search_len, new_pat);
                    /* "string" has changed -- we must get the new version */
                XtFree (string); /* free the one we had first... */
                string = XmTextGetString (text_w);
                    /* continue search for next pattern -after- replacement */
                    p = &string[pos + pattern_len];
            }
    if (!nfound)
            strcpy (buf, "Pattern not found.");
    else
            sprintf (buf, "Made %d replacements.", nfound);
    XmTextSetString (text_output, buf);
    XtFree (string);
    XtFree (search_pat);
    XtFree (new_pat);
}
```

In this routine, the pattern search starts at the beginning of the text and searches all of the text in the widget. We are not interested in the cursor position and do not attempt to move it. The main loop of the function only needs to find the specified pattern and replace each occurrence with the new text. After each call to XmTextReplace(), we reread the text, since the old value is no longer valid. As with the search_text() routine, we could easily use Xm-TextFindString() to search for the pattern, as we do in the text editor in Section 14.4.

14.2.5 Output-only Text

The Text and TextField widgets can be used in an output-only mode by setting the XmN-editable resource to False. If the user tries to edit the text in a read-only widget, the widget beeps and does not allow the modification. We used an output-only Text widget in our file browsing application.

Our next example addresses a common need for many developers: a method for displaying text messages while an application is running. These messages may include status messages about application actions, as well as error messages from Xlib, Xt, and functions internal to the application. The message area is an important part of the main window of many applications, as discussed in Chapter 4, *The Main Window*. While a message area can be

Text Widgets

implemented using a Label widget, an output-only ScrolledText object is better suited for use as a message area because the user can scroll back to previous messages.

Example 14-5 shows the wprint() function that we wrote to handle displaying messages. The function acts like printf() in that it takes variable arguments and understands the standard string formatting characters. The output goes to a ScrolledText widget so the user can review previous messages. All new text is appended to the end of the output, so it is immediately visible and the user does not have to manually scroll to the end of the display.

Example 14-5. The wprint() function

```
#include <stdio.h>
#include <varargs.h> /* or <stdarg.h> */

/* global variable */
Widget text_output;

main(argc, argv)
int argc;
char *argv[];
{
    Arg          args[10];
    int          n;

    . . .

    /* Create output_text as a ScrolledText window */
    n = 0;
    XtSetArg(args[n], XmNrows,                  6); n++;
    XtSetArg(args[n], XmNcolumns,               80); n++;
    XtSetArg(args[n], XmNeditable,              False); n++;
    XtSetArg(args[n], XmNeditMode,              XmMULTI_LINE_EDIT); n++;
    XtSetArg(args[n], XmNwordWrap,              True); n++;
    XtSetArg(args[n], XmNscrollHorizontal, False); n++;
    XtSetArg(args[n], XmNcursorPositionVisible, False); n++;
    text_output = XmCreateScrolledText(rowcol, "text_output", args, n);
    XtManageChild (text_output);

    . . .

}
/*VARARGS*/
void
wprint(va_alist)
va_dcl
{
    char msgbuf[256];
    char *fmt;
    static XmTextPosition wpr_position;
    va_list args;

    va_start (args);
    fmt = va_arg (args, char *);
#ifndef NO_VPRINTF
    (void) vsprintf (msgbuf, fmt, args);
#else /* !NO_VPRINTF */
    {
        FILE foo;
        foo._cnt = 256;
        foo._base = foo._ptr = msgbuf; /* (unsigned char *) ?? */
```

Example 14-5. The wprint() function (continued)

```
            foo._flag = _IOWRT+_IOSTRG;
            (void) _doprnt (fmt, args, &foo);
            *foo._ptr = ' '; /* plant terminating null character */
    }
#endif /* NO_VPRINTF */
    va_end (args);

    XmTextInsert (text_output, wpr_position, msgbuf);
    wpr_position = wpr_position + strlen (msgbuf);
    XtVaSetValues (text_output, XmNcursorPosition, wpr_position, NULL);
    XmTextShowPosition (text_output, wpr_position);
}
```

Since the wprint () function acts like printf (), it takes a variable-length argument list, which requires the inclusion of either *<varargs.h>* or *<stdarg.h>*.† The function wprint () takes va_alist as its only parameter. This argument is a pointer to the first of a list of arguments passed to the function; it is declared as va_dcl in accordance with the standards for functions that take variable-length argument lists.

The va_start () and va_arg () macros are used to extract the first parameter from the argument list. Since wprint () is supposed to act like printf (), we know that the first parameter is going to be a char pointer. The call to va_arg () causes fmt to point to the format string, which may or may not contain % formatting characters that expand to other strings depending on the other arguments to the function.

The rest of the arguments are read and parsed by either vsprintf () or _doprnt (), depending on the C library that you are using. vsprintf () is a varargs version of sprintf () that exists on most modern UNIX machines.‡ If your machine does not have vsprintf (), you can use _doprnt () as shown in Example 14-5. Both of these functions consume all of the arguments in the list and leave the result in msgbuf.

Now that we have the complete string in msgbuf, we can append it to the existing text in the Text widget. We keep track of the end of text_output with wpr_position. Each time msgbuf is concatenated to the end of the text, the value of wpr_position is incremented appropriately. The new text is added using the convenience routine XmTextInsert (), which takes the following form:

```
void
XmTextInsert(text_w, position, string)
    Widget          text_w;
    XmTextPosition  position;
    char            *string;
```

The function simply inserts the given text at the specified position. Finally, we call Xm-TextShowPosition () to make the end position visible within the Text widget. This routine may cause the Text widget to adjust its text so that the new text is visible, as a convenience to the user so that he does not have to scroll the window to view new messages.

---

† If you have access to the source code for X, you could include *<X11/VarargsI.h>* instead. This file is used by the X Toolkit whenever variable-length argument lists are used; it includes the appropriate file for the current operating system.

‡ System V has vsprintf (), as does SunOS, but Ultrix and older BSD machines typically use _doprnt ().

The routines in Example 14-6 show how wprint() can be used to reset the error handling functions for Xlib and Xt so that the messages are printed in a Text widget rather than to stderr.

Example 14-6. The x_error() and xt_error() functions

```
extern void wprint();

static void
x_error(dpy, err_event)
Display     *dpy;
XErrorEvent *err_event;
{
    char                buf[256];

    XGetErrorText (dpy, err_event->error_code, buf, (sizeof buf));

    wprint("X Error: <%s>\n", buf);
}

static void
xt_error(message)
char *message;
{
    wprint ("Xt Error: %s\n", message);
}

main(argc, argv)
int argc;
char *argv[];
{
    XtAppContext app;

    . . .

    /* catch Xt errors */
    XtAppSetErrorHandler (app, xt_error);
    XtAppSetWarningHandler (app, xt_error);

    /* and Xlib errors */
    XSetErrorHandler (x_error);

    . . .
}
```

Using XtAppSetErrorHandler(), XtAppSetWarningHandler(), and XSet-ErrorHandler(), we send all X-related error messages to a Text widget through wprint(). You can also use wprint() to send any application-specific messages to the ScrolledText area.

14.3 Text Clipboard Functions

Both the Text widget and the TextField widget have convenience routines that support communication with the clipboard. Using these functions, you can implement the standard cut, copy, and paste functionality, as well as support communication with other windows or applications on the desktop. If you are not familiar with the clipboard and how it works, see Chapter 17, *The Clipboard*. Briefly, the clipboard is one of three transient locations where arbitrary data such as text can be stored so that other windows or applications can copy the data. For the Text widget, we are only interested in copying textual data and providing visual feedback within the widget. The Text widget can send and receive data from all three of the locations, depending on the interface style that you are using.

As described earlier in this chapter, the user typically selects text by pressing the first mouse button and dragging the pointer across the text. When text is selected, it is rendered in reverse video and automatically copied into the primary selection. Now the user can paste text from the primary selection into any Text widget on the desktop by pressing the middle mouse button. The insertion cursor is moved to the location of the button press, and the data is automatically copied into the Text widget at this position. This functionality works by default within the Text widget. However, the actions operate on the primary selection, not the clipboard selection. Furthermore, the actions only allow you to copy data to and from the selection, not cut it or clear it.

To provide these features, most applications provide other user-interface controls, such as a PulldownMenu and appropriate menu items, that call Text widget clipboard routines. These routines store text on the clipboard. They also allow the user to move text between the clipboard and the primary selection, as well as between windows that are interested only in the clipboard selection. Typical menu entries include **Cut**, **Copy**, **Paste**, and **Clear**. Example 14-7 demonstrates these common editing actions. The application creates a MenuBar with an **Edit** PulldownMenu that contains actions that operate on the Text widget.†

Example 14-7. The cut_paste.c program

```
/* cut_paste.c -- demonstrate the text functions that handle
 * clipboard operations.  These functions are convenience routines
 * that relieve the programmer of the need to use clipboard functions.
 * The functionality of these routines already exists in the Text
 * widget, yet it is common to place such features in the interface
 * via the MenuBar's "Edit" pulldown menu.
 */
#include <Xm/Text.h>
#include <Xm/LabelG.h>
#include <Xm/PushBG.h>
#include <Xm/RowColumn.h>
#include <Xm/MainW.h>

Widget text_w, text_output;

main(argc, argv)
```

---

†XtSetLanguageProc() is only available in X11R5; there is no corresponding function in X11R4. Xm-StringCreateLocalized() is only available in Motif 1.2; XmStringCreateSimple() is the corresponding function in Motif 1.1.

Example 14-7. The cut_paste.c program (continued)

```
int argc;
char *argv[];
{
    Widget         toplevel, main_w, menubar, rowcol_v;
    XtAppContext   app;
    void           cut_paste();
    XmString       label, cut, clear, copy, paste;
    Arg            args[10];
    int            n;

    XtSetLanguageProc (NULL, NULL, NULL);

    toplevel = XtVaAppInitialize (&app, "Demos",
        NULL, 0, &argc, argv, NULL, NULL);

    main_w = XtVaCreateWidget ("main_w",
        xmMainWindowWidgetClass, toplevel, NULL);

    /* Create a simple MenuBar that contains a single menu */
    label = XmStringCreateLocalized ("Edit");
    menubar = XmVaCreateSimpleMenuBar (main_w, "menubar",
        XmVaCASCADEBUTTON, label, 'E',
        NULL);
    XmStringFree (label);

    cut = XmStringCreateLocalized ("Cut");        /* create a simple    */
    copy = XmStringCreateLocalized ("Copy");      /* pulldown menu that  */
    clear = XmStringCreateLocalized ("Clear");    /* has these menu      */
    paste = XmStringCreateLocalized ("Paste");    /* items in it.        */
    XmVaCreateSimplePulldownMenu (menubar, "edit_menu", 0, cut_paste,
        XmVaPUSHBUTTON, cut, 't', NULL, NULL,
        XmVaPUSHBUTTON, copy, 'C', NULL, NULL,
        XmVaPUSHBUTTON, paste, 'P', NULL, NULL,
        XmVaSEPARATOR,
        XmVaPUSHBUTTON, clear, 'l', NULL, NULL,
        NULL);
    XmStringFree (cut);
    XmStringFree (clear);
    XmStringFree (copy);
    XmStringFree (paste);

    XtManageChild (menubar);

    /* create a standard vertical RowColumn... */
    rowcol_v = XtVaCreateWidget ("rowcol_v",
        xmRowColumnWidgetClass, main_w, NULL);

    text_output = XtVaCreateManagedWidget ("text_output",
        xmTextWidgetClass, rowcol_v,
        XmNeditable,                False,
        XmNcursorPositionVisible,   False,
        XmNshadowThickness,         0,
        XmNhighlightThickness,      0,
        NULL);

    n = 0;
    XtSetArg (args[n], XmNrows,          10); n++;
    XtSetArg (args[n], XmNcolumns,       80); n++;
    XtSetArg (args[n], XmNeditMode,   XmMULTI_LINE_EDIT); n++;
    XtSetArg (args[n], XmNscrollHorizontal,  False); n++;
```

Example 14-7. The cut_paste.c program (continued)

```
    XtSetArg (args[n], XmNwordWrap,   True); n++;
    text_w = XmCreateScrolledText (rowcol_v, "text_w", args, n);
    XtManageChild (text_w);

    XtManageChild (rowcol_v);
    XtManageChild (main_w);

    XtRealizeWidget (toplevel);
    XtAppMainLoop (app);
}

/* cut_paste() -- the callback routine for the items in the edit menu */
void
cut_paste(widget, client_data, call_data)
Widget widget;
XtPointer client_data;
XtPointer call_data;
{
    Boolean result = True;
    int reason = (int) client_data;
    XEvent *event = ((XmPushButtonCallbackStruct *) call_data)->event;
    Time when;

    XmTextSetString (text_output, NULL);    /* clear message area */

    if (event != NULL) {
        switch (event->type) {
            case ButtonRelease :
                when = event->xbutton.time;
                break;
            case KeyRelease :
                when = event->xkey.time;
                break;
            default:
                when = CurrentTime;
                break;
        }
    }

    switch (reason) {
        case 0 :
            result = XmTextCut (text_w, when);
            break;
        case 1 :
            result = XmTextCopy (text_w, when);
            break;
        case 2 :
            result = XmTextPaste (text_w);
        case 3 :
            XmTextClearSelection (text_w, when);
            break;
    }
    if (result == False)
        XmTextSetString (text_output, "There is no selection.");
    else
        XmTextSetString (text_output, NULL);
}
```

Text Widgets

The application creates a MainWindow widget, so that it can contain the MenuBar. The MenuBar and the PulldownMenu are created using their respective convenience routines, as described in Chapter 4, *The Main Window*, and Chapter 15, *Menus*. The output of the program is shown in Figure 14-5.

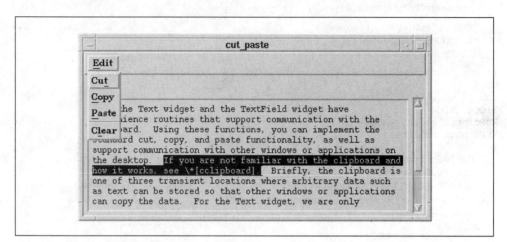

Figure 14-5. Output of cut_paste.c

Again, you need to enter some text or paste it from another window if you want to experiment with this application. The main window contains the same Text widgets used in previous examples. The **Edit** PulldownMmenu allows the user to interact with the clipboard. The cut_paste() routine is the callback function for all of the menu items in the **Edit** menu. This function uses four Text convenience routines to work with the clipboard: XmText-Cut(), XmTextCopy(), XmTextPaste(), and XmTextClearSelection(). These routines take the following form:

```
Boolean
XmTextCut(text_w, time)
    Widget   text_w;
    Time     time;

Boolean
XmTextCopy(text_w, time)
    Widget   text_w;
    Time     time;

Boolean
XmTextPaste(text_w)
    Widget   text_w;

void
XmTextClearSelection(text_w, time)
    Widget   text_w;
    Time     time;
```

`XmTextCopy()` copies the text that is selected in the Text widget and places it on the clipboard. `XmTextCut()` is similar to `XmTextCopy()`, except that the Text widget that owns the selection is instructed to delete the text once it has been copied to the clipboard.† The *time* parameters should not be set to `CurrentTime` to avoid race conditions with other clipboard operations that may be occurring at the same time. Since the clipboard routines are called by menu item callback routines, you can use the `time` field of the `XEvent` that is passed in the callback structure, as we do in Example 14-7. Both `XmTextCopy()` and `XmTextCut()` return `True` if the operation succeeds. `False` may be returned if there is no selected text or an error occurs in attempting to communicate with the clipboard.

`XmTextPaste()` gets the current selection from the clipboard and inserts it at the location of the insertion cursor. If there is some selected text in the Text widget, that text is replaced by the selection from the clipboard. `XmTextPaste()` returns `True` if there is a selection on the clipboard that can be retrieved.

`XmTextClearSelection()` deselects the text selection in the Text widget. If there is no selected text, nothing happens. The routine does not provide any feedback or return any value. Any text that is held on the clipboard or in a selection property remains.

One additional convenience routine that operates on the selection is `XmTextRemove()`. This function is like `XmTextCut()`, in that it removes the selected text from a Text widget, but it does not place the text on the clipboard.

14.3.1 Getting the Selection

You can get the selected text from a Text widget using `XmTextGetSelection()`, which takes the following form:

```
char *
XmTextGetSelection(text_w)
    Widget text_w;
```

This routine returns allocated data that contains the selected text. This text must be freed using `XtFree()` when you are through using it. The routine returns `NULL` if there is no text selected in the Text widget.

`XmTextGetSelectionPosition()` provides information about the selected text in a Text widget. This routine takes the following form:

```
Boolean
XmTextGetSelectionPosition(text_w, left, right)
    Widget          text_w;
    XmTextPosition *left;
    XmTextPosition *right;
```

If `XmTextGetSelectionPosition()` returns `True`, the values for *left* and *right* specify the boundaries of the selected text. If the routine returns `False`, the widget does not contain any selected text, and the values for *left* and *right* are undefined.

---

† The deletion is handled by sending a DELETE protocol request to the window holding the selection. This protocol is not the same as the WM_DELETE protocol, which indicates that a window is being deleted. See Chapter 16, *Interacting With the Window Manager*, for more information on window manager protocols.

14.3.2 Modifying the Selection Mechanisms

The Text widget supports multi-clicking techniques for selecting increasingly large chunks of text. The default multi-clicking actions in the Text widget are shown in Table 14-1.

Table 14-1. Default Selection Actions for Multiple Clicks

User Action	Text Widget Action
Single click	Resets insertion cursor to position
Double click	Selects a word (bounded by whitespace)
Triple click	Selects a line (bounded by newlines)
Quadruple click	Selects all of the text

These default actions can be modified using the XmNselectionArray and XmN-selectionArrayCount resources. The XmNselectionArray resource specifies an array of XmTextScanType values, where XmTextScanType is an enumerated type defined as follows:

```
typedef enum {
    XmSELECT_POSITION,
    XmSELECT_WHITESPACE, †
    XmSELECT_WORD,
    XmSELECT_LINE,
    XmSELECT_PARAGRAPH
    XmSELECT_ALL,
} XmTextScanType;
```

Each successive button click in a Text widget selects the text according to the corresponding item in the array. The default array is defined as follows:

```
static XmTextScanType sarray[] = {
    XmSELECT_POSITION, XmSELECT_WORD, XmSELECT_LINE, XmSELECT_ALL
};
```

You should keep the items in the array in ascending order, so as not to confuse the user. The following code fragment shows an acceptable change to the array:

```
static XmTextScanType sarray[] = {
    XmSELECT_POSITION, XmSELECT_WORD, XmSELECT_LINE, XmSELECT_PARAGRAPH,
    XmSELECT_ALL
};
...
XtVaSetValues (text_w,
    XmNselectionArray,        selectionArray,
    XmNselectionArrayCount, 5,
    NULL);
```

---

† XmSELECT_WHITESPACE works in the same way as XmSELECT_WORD.

The maximum time interval between button clicks in a multi-click action is specified by the multiClickTime resource. This resource is maintained by the X server and set for all applications; it is not a Motif resource. The value of the resource can be retrieved using Xt-GetMultiClickTime() and changed with XtSetMultiClickTime(). For more discussion on this value, see Chapter 11, *Labels and Buttons*.

The XmNselectThreshold resource can be used to modify the behavior of click-and-drag actions. This resource specifies the number of pixels that the user must move the pointer before a character can be selected. The default value is 5, which means that the user must move the mouse at least 5 pixels before the Text widget decides whether or not to select a character. This threshold is used throughout a selection operation to determine when characters are added or deleted from the selection. If you are using an extremely large font, you may want to increase the value of this resource to cut down on the number of calculations that are necessary to determine if a character should be added or deleted from the selection.

14.4 A Text Editor

Before we describe the Text widget callback routines, we are going to present an example that combines all the information covered so far. The example is a full-featured text editor built from the examples presented so far in this chapter. You should recognize most of the code in the example; the code that you don't recognize should be understandable from the context in which it is used. The output of the program is shown in Figure 14-6; the code is shown in Example 14-8.†

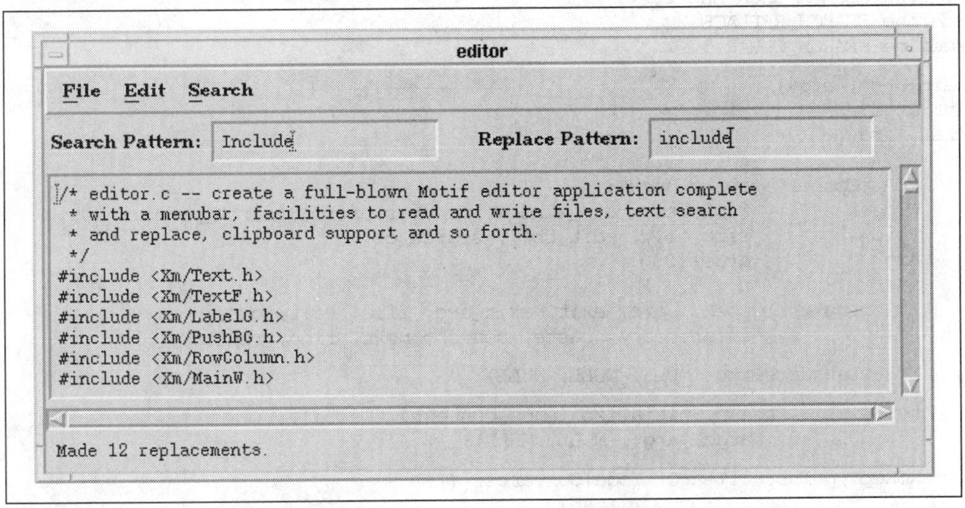

Figure 14-6. Output of editor.c

---

†XtSetLanguageProc() is only available in X11R5; there is no corresponding function in X11R4. Xm-StringCreateLocalized() is only available in Motif 1.2; XmStringCreateSimple() is the corresponding function in Motif 1.1. XmFONTLIST_DEFAULT_TAG replaces XmSTRING_DEFAULT_CHARSET in Motif 1.2. XmTextFindString() is only available in Motif 1.2; there is no corresponding function in Motif 1.1, so you have to implement your own search capabilities.

Example 14-8. The editor.c program

```
/* editor.c -- create a full-blown Motif editor application complete
 * with a menubar, facilities to read and write files, text search
 * and replace, clipboard support and so forth.
 */
#include <Xm/Text.h>
#include <Xm/TextF.h>
#include <Xm/LabelG.h>
#include <Xm/PushBG.h>
#include <Xm/RowColumn.h>
#include <Xm/MainW.h>
#include <Xm/Form.h>
#include <Xm/FileSB.h>
#include <X11/Xos.h>
#include <stdio.h>
#include <sys/types.h>
#include <sys/stat.h>

Widget text_edit, search_text, replace_text, text_output;

#define FILE_OPEN 0
#define FILE_SAVE 1
#define FILE_EXIT 2

#define EDIT_CUT 0
#define EDIT_COPY 1
#define EDIT_PASTE 2
#define EDIT_CLEAR 3

#define SEARCH_FIND_NEXT 0
#define SEARCH_SHOW_ALL 1
#define SEARCH_REPLACE 2
#define SEARCH_CLEAR 3

main(argc, argv)
int argc;
char *argv[];
{
    XtAppContext  app_context;
    Widget        toplevel, main_window, menubar, form, search_panel;
    void          file_cb(), edit_cb(), search_cb();
    Arg           args[10];
    int           n = 0;
    XmString      open, save, exit, exit_acc, file, edit, cut,
                  clear, copy, paste, search, next, find, replace;

    XtSetLanguageProc (NULL, NULL, NULL);

    toplevel = XtVaAppInitialize (&app_context, "Demos",
        NULL, 0, &argc, argv, NULL, NULL);

    XmRepTypeInstallTearOffModelConverter ();

    main_window = XtVaCreateWidget ("main_window",
        xmMainWindowWidgetClass, toplevel, NULL);

    /* Create a simple MenuBar that contains three menus */
    file = XmStringCreateLocalized ("File");
    edit = XmStringCreateLocalized ("Edit");
    search = XmStringCreateLocalized ("Search");
    menubar = XmVaCreateSimpleMenuBar (main_window, "menubar",
```

Example 14-8. The editor.c program (continued)

```
        XmVaCASCADEBUTTON, file, 'F',
        XmVaCASCADEBUTTON, edit, 'E',
        XmVaCASCADEBUTTON, search, 'S',
        NULL);
    XmStringFree (file);
    XmStringFree (edit);
    XmStringFree (search);

    /* First menu is the File menu -- callback is file_cb() */
    open = XmStringCreateLocalized ("Open...");
    save = XmStringCreateLocalized ("Save...");
    exit = XmStringCreateLocalized ("Exit");
    exit_acc = XmStringCreateLocalized ("Ctrl+C");
    XmVaCreateSimplePulldownMenu (menubar, "file_menu", 0, file_cb,
        XmVaPUSHBUTTON, open, 'O', NULL, NULL,
        XmVaPUSHBUTTON, save, 'S', NULL, NULL,
        XmVaSEPARATOR,
        XmVaPUSHBUTTON, exit, 'x', "Ctrl<Key>c", exit_acc,
        NULL);
    XmStringFree (open);
    XmStringFree (save);
    XmStringFree (exit);
    XmStringFree (exit_acc);

    /* ...create the "Edit" menu --  callback is edit_cb() */
    cut = XmStringCreateLocalized ("Cut");
    copy = XmStringCreateLocalized ("Copy");
    clear = XmStringCreateLocalized ("Clear");
    paste = XmStringCreateLocalized ("Paste");
    XmVaCreateSimplePulldownMenu (menubar, "edit_menu", 1, edit_cb,
        XmVaPUSHBUTTON, cut, 't', NULL, NULL,
        XmVaPUSHBUTTON, copy, 'C', NULL, NULL,
        XmVaPUSHBUTTON, paste, 'P', NULL, NULL,
        XmVaSEPARATOR,
        XmVaPUSHBUTTON, clear, 'l', NULL, NULL,
        NULL);
    XmStringFree (cut);
    XmStringFree (copy);
    XmStringFree (paste);

    /* create the "Search" menu -- callback is search_cb() */
    next = XmStringCreateLocalized ("Find Next");
    find = XmStringCreateLocalized ("Show All");
    replace = XmStringCreateLocalized ("Replace Text");
    XmVaCreateSimplePulldownMenu (menubar, "search_menu", 2, search_cb,
        XmVaPUSHBUTTON, next, 'N', NULL, NULL,
        XmVaPUSHBUTTON, find, 'A', NULL, NULL,
        XmVaPUSHBUTTON, replace, 'R', NULL, NULL,
        XmVaSEPARATOR,
        XmVaPUSHBUTTON, clear, 'C', NULL, NULL,
        NULL);
    XmStringFree (next);
    XmStringFree (find);
    XmStringFree (replace);
    XmStringFree (clear);

    XtManageChild (menubar);
```

Text Widgets

Example 14-8. The editor.c program (continued)

```
    /* create a form work are */
    form = XtVaCreateWidget ("form",
        xmFormWidgetClass, main_window, NULL);

    /* create horizontal RowColumn inside the form */
    search_panel = XtVaCreateWidget ("search_panel",
        xmRowColumnWidgetClass, form,
        XmNorientation,       XmHORIZONTAL,
        XmNpacking,           XmPACK_TIGHT,
        XmNtopAttachment,     XmATTACH_FORM,
        XmNleftAttachment,    XmATTACH_FORM,
        XmNrightAttachment,   XmATTACH_FORM,
        NULL);
    /* Create two TextField widgets with Labels... */
    XtVaCreateManagedWidget ("Search Pattern:",
        xmLabelGadgetClass, search_panel, NULL);
    search_text = XtVaCreateManagedWidget ("search_text",
        xmTextFieldWidgetClass, search_panel, NULL);
    XtVaCreateManagedWidget ("     Replace Pattern:",
        xmLabelGadgetClass, search_panel, NULL);
    replace_text = XtVaCreateManagedWidget ("replace_text",
        xmTextFieldWidgetClass, search_panel, NULL);
    XtManageChild (search_panel);

    text_output = XtVaCreateManagedWidget ("text_output",
        xmTextFieldWidgetClass, form,
        XmNeditable,              False,
        XmNcursorPositionVisible, False,
        XmNshadowThickness,       0,
        XmNleftAttachment,        XmATTACH_FORM,
        XmNrightAttachment,       XmATTACH_FORM,
        XmNbottomAttachment,      XmATTACH_FORM,
        NULL);

    n = 0;
    XtSetArg (args[n], XmNrows,             10); n++;
    XtSetArg (args[n], XmNcolumns,          80); n++;
    XtSetArg (args[n], XmNeditMode,         XmMULTI_LINE_EDIT); n++;
    XtSetArg (args[n], XmNtopAttachment,    XmATTACH_WIDGET); n++;
    XtSetArg (args[n], XmNtopWidget,        search_panel); n++;
    XtSetArg (args[n], XmNleftAttachment,   XmATTACH_FORM); n++;
    XtSetArg (args[n], XmNrightAttachment,  XmATTACH_FORM); n++;
    XtSetArg (args[n], XmNbottomAttachment, XmATTACH_WIDGET); n++;
    XtSetArg (args[n], XmNbottomWidget,     text_output); n++;
    text_edit = XmCreateScrolledText (form, "text_edit", args, n);
    XtManageChild (text_edit);

    XtManageChild (form);
    XtManageChild (main_window);

    XtRealizeWidget (toplevel);
    XtAppMainLoop (app_context);
}

/* file_select_cb() -- callback routine for "OK" button in
 * FileSelectionDialogs.
 */
void
```

Example 14-8. The editor.c program (continued)

```
file_select_cb(dialog, client_data, call_data)
Widget dialog;
XtPointer client_data;
XtPointer call_data;
{
    char buf[256], *filename, *text;
    struct stat statb;
    long len;
    FILE *fp;
    int reason = (int) client_data;
    XmFileSelectionBoxCallbackStruct *cbs =
        (XmFileSelectionBoxCallbackStruct *) call_data;

    if (!XmStringGetLtoR (cbs->value, XmFONTLIST_DEFAULT_TAG, &filename))
        return; /* must have been an internal error */

    if (*filename == NULL) {
        XtFree (filename);
        XBell (XtDisplay (text_edit), 50);
        XmTextSetString (text_output, "Choose a file.");
        return; /* nothing typed */
    }

    if (reason == FILE_SAVE) {
        if (!(fp = fopen (filename, "w"))) {
            perror (filename);
            sprintf (buf, "Can't save to %s.", filename);
            XmTextSetString (text_output, buf);
            XtFree (filename);
            return;
        }
        /* saving -- get text from Text widget... */
        text = XmTextGetString (text_edit);
        len = XmTextGetLastPosition (text_edit);
        /* write it to file (check for error) */
        if (fwrite (text, sizeof (char), len, fp) != len)
            strcpy (buf, "Warning: did not write entire file!");
        else {
            /* make sure a newline terminates file */
            if (text[len-1] != '\n')
                fputc ('\n', fp);
            sprintf (buf, "Saved %ld bytes to %s.", len, filename);
        }
    }
    else { /* reason == FILE_OPEN */
        /* make sure the file is a regular text file and open it */
        if (stat (filename, &statb) == -1 ||
                (statb.st_mode & S_IFMT) != S_IFREG ||
                !(fp = fopen (filename, "r"))) {
            perror (filename);
            sprintf (buf, "Can't read %s.", filename);
            XmTextSetString (text_output, buf);
            XtFree (filename);
            return;
        }
        /* put the contents of the file in the Text widget by
         * allocating enough space for the entire file, reading the
```

Example 14-8. The editor.c program (continued)

```
                * file into the space, and using XmTextSetString() to show
                * the file.
                */
              len = statb.st_size;
              if (!(text = XtMalloc ((unsigned)(len+1)))) /* +1 for NULL */
                  sprintf (buf, "%s: XtMalloc(%ld) failed", len, filename);
              else {
                  if (fread (text, sizeof (char), len, fp) != len)
                      sprintf (buf, "Warning: did not read entire file!");
                  else
                      sprintf (buf, "Loaded %ld bytes from %s.", len, filename);
                  text[len] = 0; /* NULL-terminate */
                  XmTextSetString (text_edit, text);
              }
          }
          XmTextSetString (text_output, buf); /* purge output message */

          /* free all allocated space. */
          XtFree (text);
          XtFree (filename);
          fclose (fp);
          XtUnmanageChild (dialog);
}

/* popdown_cb() -- callback routine for "Cancel" button. */
void
popdown_cb (w, client_data, call_data)
Widget w;
XtPointer client_data;
XtPointer call_data;
{
          XtUnmanageChild (w);
}

/* file_cb() -- a menu item from the "File" pulldown menu was selected */
void
file_cb(w, client_data, call_data)
Widget w;
XtPointer client_data;
XtPointer call_data;
{
          static Widget open_dialog, save_dialog;
          Widget dialog = NULL;
          XmString button, title;
          int reason = (int) client_data;

          if (reason == FILE_EXIT)
              exit (0);

          XmTextSetString (text_output, NULL);   /* clear message area */

          if (reason == FILE_OPEN && open_dialog)
              dialog = open_dialog;
          else if (reason == FILE_SAVE && save_dialog)
              dialog = save_dialog;

          if (dialog) {
              XtManageChild (dialog);
              /* make sure that dialog is raised to top of window stack */
```

Example 14-8. The editor.c program (continued)

```
            XMapRaised (XtDisplay (dialog), XtWindow (XtParent (dialog)));
            return;
        }

    dialog = XmCreateFileSelectionDialog (text_edit, "Files", NULL, 0);
    XtAddCallback (dialog, XmNcancelCallback, popdown_cb, NULL);
    XtAddCallback (dialog, XmNokCallback, file_select_cb, reason);
    if (reason == FILE_OPEN) {
        button = XmStringCreateLocalized ("Open");
        title = XmStringCreateLocalized ("Open File");
        open_dialog = dialog;
    }
    else { /* reason == FILE_SAVE */
        button = XmStringCreateLocalized ("Save");
        title = XmStringCreateLocalized ("Save File");
        save_dialog = dialog;
    }
    XtVaSetValues (dialog,
        XmNokLabelString, button,
        XmNdialogTitle,   title,
        NULL);
    XmStringFree (button);
    XmStringFree (title);
    XtManageChild (dialog);
}

/* search_cb() -- a menu item from the "Search" pulldown menu selected */
void
search_cb(w, client_data, call_data)
Widget w;
XtPointer client_data;
XtPointer call_data;
{
    char *search_pat, *p, *string, *new_pat, buf[256];
    XmTextPosition pos = 0;
    int len, nfound = 0;
    int search_len, pattern_len;
    int reason = (int) client_data;
    Boolean found = False;

    XmTextSetString (text_output, NULL);    /* clear message area */

    if (reason == SEARCH_CLEAR) {
        pos = XmTextGetLastPosition (text_edit);
        XmTextSetHighlight (text_edit, 0, pos, XmHIGHLIGHT_NORMAL);
        return;
    }

    if (!(string = XmTextGetString (text_edit)) || !*string) {
        XmTextSetString (text_output, "No text to search.");
        return;
    }
    if (!(search_pat = XmTextGetString (search_text)) || !*search_pat) {
        XmTextSetString (text_output, "Specify a search pattern.");
        XtFree (string);
        return;
    }
```

Example 14-8. The editor.c program (continued)

```
    new_pat = XmTextGetString (replace_text);
    search_len = strlen (search_pat);
    pattern_len = strlen (new_pat);

    if (reason == SEARCH_FIND_NEXT) {
        pos = XmTextGetCursorPosition (text_edit) + 1;
        found = XmTextFindString (text_edit, pos, search_pat,
            XmTEXT_FORWARD, &pos);
        if (!found)
            found = XmTextFindString (text_edit, 0, search_pat,
                XmTEXT_FORWARD, &pos);
        if (found)
            nfound++;
    }
    else { /* reason == SEARCH_SHOW_ALL || reason == SEARCH_REPLACE */
        do {
            found = XmTextFindString (text_edit, pos, search_pat,
                XmTEXT_FORWARD, &pos);
            if (found) {
                nfound++;
                if (reason == SEARCH_SHOW_ALL)
                    XmTextSetHighlight (text_edit, pos, pos + search_len,
                        XmHIGHLIGHT_SELECTED);
                else
                    XmTextReplace (text_edit, pos, pos + search_len, new_pat);
                pos++;
            }
        }
        while (found);
    }

    if (nfound == 0)
        XmTextSetString (text_output, "Pattern not found.");
    else {
        switch (reason) {
            case SEARCH_FIND_NEXT :
                sprintf (buf, "Pattern found at position %ld.", pos);
                XmTextSetInsertionPosition (text_edit, pos);
                break;
            case SEARCH_SHOW_ALL :
                sprintf (buf, "Found %d occurrences.", nfound);
                break;
            case SEARCH_REPLACE :
                sprintf (buf, "Made %d replacements.", nfound);
        }
        XmTextSetString (text_output, buf);
    }
    XtFree (string);
    XtFree (search_pat);
    XtFree (new_pat);
}

/* edit_cb() -- the callback routine for the items in the edit menu */
void
edit_cb(widget, client_data, call_data)
Widget widget;
XtPointer client_data;
```

Example 14-8. The editor.c program (continued)

```
XtPointer call_data;
{
    Boolean result = True;
    int reason = (int) client_data;
    XEvent *event = ((XmPushButtonCallbackStruct *) call_data)->event;
    Time when;

    XmTextSetString (text_output, NULL);   /* clear message area */

    if (event != NULL &&
        reason == EDIT_CUT || reason == EDIT_COPY || reason == EDIT_CLEAR) {
        switch (event->type) {
            case ButtonRelease :
                when = event->xbutton.time;
                break;
            case KeyRelease :
                when = event->xkey.time;
                break;
            default:
                when = CurrentTime;
                break;
        }
    }

    switch (reason) {
        case EDIT_CUT :
            result = XmTextCut (text_edit, when);
            break;
        case EDIT_COPY :
            result = XmTextCopy (text_edit, when);
            break;
        case EDIT_PASTE :
            result = XmTextPaste (text_edit);
        case EDIT_CLEAR :
            XmTextClearSelection (text_edit, when);
            break;
    }
    if (result == False)
        XmTextSetString (text_output, "There is no selection.");
}
```

14.5 Text Callbacks

The Text and TextField widgets use callback routines in the same way as other Motif widgets. The widgets provide callbacks for a number of different purposes, such as text modification, activation, and selection ownership. Some of the routines, such as those that monitor keyboard input, may be invoked rather frequently. In the next few sections, we introduce several of the callback routines for the widgets.

Text Widgets

14.5.1 The Activation Callback

We begin by exploring the callback routine that is most commonly used for single-line Text widgets and TextField widgets. This callback is the XmNactivateCallback, which is invoked when the user presses RETURN in a TextField widget or a single-line Text widget. The callback is not called for multiline Text widgets. The callback routine for an XmNactivateCallback receives the common XmAnyCallbackStruct as the call_data parameter to the function. The callback reason is always XmCR_ACTIVATE. Example 14-9 shows a callback function for some TextField widgets.†

Example 14-9. The text_box.c program

```
/* text_box.c -- demonstrate simple use of XmNactivateCallback
 * for TextField widgets.  Create a rowcolumn that has rows of Form
 * widgets, each containing a Label and a Text widget.  When
 * the user presses Return, print the value of the text widget
 * and move the focus to the next text widget.
 */
#include <Xm/TextF.h>
#include <Xm/LabelG.h>
#include <Xm/Form.h>
#include <Xm/RowColumn.h>

char *labels[] = { "Name:", "Address:", "City:", "State:", "Zip:" };

main(argc, argv)
int argc;
char *argv[];
{
    Widget        toplevel, text_w, form, rowcol;
    XtAppContext  app;
    int           i;
    void          print_result();

    XtSetLanguageProc (NULL, NULL, NULL);

    toplevel = XtVaAppInitialize (&app, "Demos",
        NULL, 0, &argc, argv, NULL, NULL);

    rowcol = XtVaCreateWidget ("rowcol",
        xmRowColumnWidgetClass, toplevel, NULL);

    for (i = 0; i < XtNumber (labels); i++) {
        form = XtVaCreateWidget ("form", xmFormWidgetClass, rowcol,
            XmNfractionBase,  10,
            NULL);
        XtVaCreateManagedWidget (labels[i],
            xmLabelGadgetClass, form,
            XmNtopAttachment,     XmATTACH_FORM,
            XmNbottomAttachment,  XmATTACH_FORM,
            XmNleftAttachment,    XmATTACH_FORM,
            XmNrightAttachment,   XmATTACH_POSITION,
            XmNrightPosition,     3,
            XmNalignment,         XmALIGNMENT_END,
            NULL);
```

---

† XtSetLanguageProc () is only available in X11R5; there is no corresponding function in X11R4.

Example 14-9. The text_box.c program (continued)

```
        text_w = XtVaCreateManagedWidget ("text_w",
            xmTextFieldWidgetClass, form,
            XmNtraversalOn,        True,
            XmNrightAttachment,    XmATTACH_FORM,
            XmNleftAttachment,     XmATTACH_POSITION,
            XmNleftPosition,       4,
            NULL);

        /* When user hits return, print the label+value of text_w */
        XtAddCallback (text_w, XmNactivateCallback,
            print_result, labels[i]);

        XtManageChild( form);
    }
    XtManageChild (rowcol);

    XtRealizeWidget (toplevel);
    XtAppMainLoop (app);
}
/* preint_result() -- callback for when the user hits return in the
 * TextField widget.
 */
void
print_result(text_w, client_data, call_data)
Widget text_w;
XtPointer client_data;
XtPointer call_data;
{
    char *value = XmTextFieldGetString (text_w);
    char *label = (char *) client_data;

    printf ("%s %s\n", label, value);
    XtFree (value);

    XmProcessTraversal (text_w, XmTRAVERSE_NEXT_TAB_GROUP);
}
```

The program displays a data form using a RowColumn widget that manages several rows of Form widgets. Each Form contains a Label and a TextField widget, as shown in Figure 14-7.

When the user enters a value for a field and presses RETURN, the `print_result()` callback routine is invoked. The routine prints the value of the field and advances the keyboard focus to the next widget using `XmProcessTraversal()`. This function takes a widget and a traversal direction as its two parameters. We use the `XmTRAVERSE_NEXT_TAB_GROUP` direction because each TextField widget is a tab group in and of itself, so we need to move to the next tab group, rather than to the next item in the same tab group. See Section 8.8, for more information on tab groups.

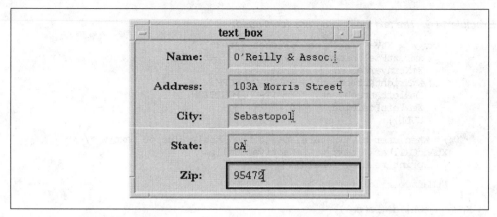

Figure 14-7. Output of text_box.c

When a single-line Text widget or a TextField widget is used as part of a predefined Motif dialog, the `XmNactivateCallback` for the widget is automatically hooked up to the **OK** button in the dialog. As a result, the same callback is called when the user presses RETURN in the widget or when the user selects the **OK** button. This convenience can confuse an unsuspecting programmer who may find that his callback is being invoked twice. It is also possible to overestimate what the Motif toolkit is going to do and expect a callback to be invoked when it isn't. The point is to be sure to verify that these callbacks are getting called at the appropriate times. See Chapter 6, *Selection Dialogs*, for examples of this feature in SelectionDialogs, PromptDialogs, and CommandDialogs.

14.5.2 Text Modification Callbacks

In this section, we discuss the callback routines that can be used to monitor and control text modification. Monitoring occurs both when the user types into a Text widget and when the text is changed using a convenience routine such as `XmTextInsert()`. These callbacks work for both single-line and multiline Text widgets, as well as TextField widgets. Since the text in a widget is modified by each keystroke, the modification callbacks are invoked quite frequently.

There are two callbacks for text modification: `XmNmodifyVerifyCallback` is called before the text is modified, and `XmNvalueChangedCallback` is called after the text has been changed. Depending on the needs of an application, either or both callbacks may be used on the same widget. You should never call `XtVaSetValues()` in one of these callbacks on the widget that is being modified because the state of the widget is unstable during these callbacks. Avoid adding or deleting callbacks or changing resources, especially the `XmNvalue` resource, in a callback routine. If a recursive loop occurs, you may get very unpredictable results.

Installing an `XmNmodifyVerifyCallback` function is useful when you need to monitor or change the user's input before it actually gets inserted into a Text widget. In Example 14-10, we demonstrate using this callback to convert text to uppercase.†

---

†`XtSetLanguageProc()` is only available in X11R5; there is no corresponding function in X11R4.

Example 14-10. The allcaps.c program

```
/* allcaps.c -- demonstrate the XmNmodifyVerifyCallback for
 * Text widgets by using one to convert all typed input to
 * capital letters.
 */
#include <Xm/Text.h>
#include <Xm/LabelG.h>
#include <Xm/RowColumn.h>
#include <ctype.h>

void allcaps();

main(argc, argv)
int argc;
char *argv[];
{
    Widget          toplevel, text_w, rowcol;
    XtAppContext   app;

    XtSetLanguageProc (NULL, NULL, NULL);

    toplevel = XtVaAppInitialize (&app, "Demos",
        NULL, 0, &argc, argv, NULL, NULL);

    rowcol = XtVaCreateWidget ("rowcol",
        xmRowColumnWidgetClass, toplevel,
        XmNorientation, XmHORIZONTAL,
        NULL);

    XtVaCreateManagedWidget ("Enter Text:",
        xmLabelGadgetClass, rowcol, NULL);
    text_w = XtVaCreateManagedWidget ("text_w",
        xmTextWidgetClass, rowcol, NULL);

    XtAddCallback (text_w, XmNmodifyVerifyCallback, allcaps, NULL);

    XtManageChild (rowcol);
    XtRealizeWidget (toplevel);
    XtAppMainLoop (app);
}

/* allcaps() -- convert inserted text to capital letters. */
void
allcaps(text_w, client_data, call_data)
Widget      text_w;
XtPointer   client_data;
XtPointer   call_data;
{
    int len;
    XmTextVerifyCallbackStruct *cbs =
        (XmTextVerifyCallbackStruct *) call_data;

    if (cbs->text->ptr == NULL)
        return;

    /* convert all input to upper-case if necessary */
    for (len = 0; len < cbs->text->length; len++)
        if (islower (cbs->text->ptr[len]))
            cbs->text->ptr[len] = toupper (cbs->text->ptr[len]);
}
```

The program creates a RowColumn widget that contains a Label and a Text widget, as shown in Figure 14-8.

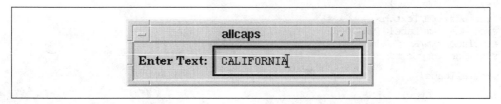

Figure 14-8. Output of allcaps.c

The Text widget uses the `allcaps()` routine as its `XmNmodifyVerifyCallback` function. The routine is actually quite simple, but there are a lot of details to examine. The `call_data` parameter to the function is of type `XmTextVerifyCallbackStruct`. This data structure provides information about the modification that may be done to the text. The data structure is defined as follows:

```
typedef struct {
    int              reason;
    XEvent           *event;
    Boolean          doit;
    XmTextPosition   currInsert, newInsert;
    XmTextPosition   startPos, endPos;
    XmTextBlock      text;
} XmTextVerifyCallbackStruct;
```

With an `XmNmodifyVerifyCallback`, the `reason` field has the value `XmCR_MODI-FYING_TEXT_VALUE`. The event field contains the `XEvent` that caused the callback to be invoked; this field is NULL if the modification is being done by a convenience routine that modifies the text. The values for `currInsert` and `newInsert` are always the same for a modification callback. These fields specify the location of the insertion cursor, so they are only different for the `XmNmotionVerifyCallback` when the user moves the insertion point.

The values for `startPos` and `endPos` indicate the range of text that is affected by the modification. For insertion, these values are always the same. However, for text deletion or replacement, the values specify the beginning and end of the text about to be deleted. For example, if the user selects some text and presses the BACKSPACE key, the `startPos` and `endPos` values indicate the boundaries of the text about to be deleted. We discuss text deletion in detail in an upcoming section.

The `text` field points to a data structure that describes the text about to be added to the widget. The field is a pointer of type `XmTextBlock`, which is defined as follows:

```
typedef struct {
    char         *ptr;
    int           length;
    XmTextFormat  format;
} XmTextBlockRec, *XmTextBlock;
```

The text being added is accessible through `ptr`; it is dynamically allocated using `Xt-Malloc()` for each callback invocation. The `ptr` field is not `NULL`-terminated, so you should not use `strlen()` or `strcpy()` to copy the data. The length is stored in the `length` field, so if you want to copy the text, you should use `strncpy()`. If the user is deleting text, `length` is `0`. While `ptr` should also be `NULL` in this case, the field isn't always set this way, so you shouldn't rely on it. The `format` field specifies the width of the text characters and can have the value `FMT8BIT` or `FMT16BIT`.

Let's review the simple case of adding new text, as demonstrated in Example 14-10. When new text is inserted into the Text widget, the values for `currInsert`, `newInsert`, `startPos`, and `endPos` all have the same value, which is the position in the widget where the new text will be added. Since the new text has not yet been added to the value of the widget, the application can change the value of `ptr` in the text block. In the `allcaps()` routine, we modify the input to be all capital letters by looping through the valid bytes in the `ptr` field of the text block that is going to be added, as shown in the following fragment:

```
for (len = 0; len < cbs->text->length; len++)
    if (islower (cbs->text->ptr[len]))
        cbs->text->ptr[len] = toupper (cbs->text->ptr[len]);
```

The `islower()` and `toupper()` macros are found in the *<ctype.h>* header file.

Since `allcaps()` is called each time new text is added to the widget, you might wonder how `length` can ever be more than one. If the user pastes a block of text into the widget, the entire block is added at once, so `ptr` points to that text, and `length` specifies the amount of text. Our loop handles both single-character typing and text-block paste operations.

Preventing Text Modification

Example 14-10 demonstrates how an application can modify the text that is entered by a user before it is displayed. An application may also want to filter the new text and prevent certain characters from being inserted. The easiest way to prevent a text modification is to set the `doit` field in the `XmTextVerifyCallbackStruct` to `False`. When the modification callback routine returns, the Text widget checks this field. If it has been set to `False`, the widget discards the new text, and the widget is left unmodified.

When a text modification is vetoed, the Text widget can sound the console bell to provide audio feedback informing the user that the input has been rejected. This action is dependent on the value of the `XmNverifyBell` resource. The default value is based on the value of the `XmNaudibleWarning` resource of the VendorShell, so it is set to `True` by default. You should allow a user to set this resource in a resource file, so he can turn off error notification if he doesn't want it. If you hard-code the resource value, users cannot control this feature. You should provide documentation with your application that explains how to set this resource or provide a way to set the value from the application.

Example 14-11 demonstrates a modification callback routine that filters input and prevents certain characters from being entered. The `check_zip()` routine would be used as the `XmNmodifyVerifyCallback` for a Text widget that prompts for a ZIP code. We want the user to type only digits; all other input should be ignored. We also want to keep the user from typing a string that is longer than five digits.

Example 14-11. The check_zip() function

```
/* check_zip() -- limit the user to entering a ZIP code. */
void
check_zip(text_w, client_data, call_data)
Widget text_w;
XtPointer client_data;
XtPointer call_data;
{
    XmTextVerifyCallbackStruct *cbs =
        (XmTextVerifyCallbackStruct *) call_data;
    int len = XmTextGetLastPosition (text_w);

    if (cbs->startPos < cbs->currInsert) /* backspace */
        return;

    if (len == 5) {
        cbs->doit = False;
        return;
    }
    /* check that the new additions won't put us over 5 */
    if (len + cbs->text->length > 5) {
        cbs->text->ptr[5 - len] = 0;
        cbs->text->length = strlen (cbs->text->ptr);
    }
    for (len = 0; len < cbs->text->length; len++) {
        /* make sure all additions are digits. */
        if (!isdigit (cbs->text->ptr[len])) {
            /* not a digit-- move all chars down one and
             * decrement cbs->text->length.
             */
            int i;
            for (i = len; (i+1) < cbs->text->length; i++)
                cbs->text->ptr[i] = cbs->text->ptr[i+1];
            cbs->text->length--;
            len--;
        }
    }
    if (cbs->text->length == 0)
        cbs->doit = False;
}
```

The first thing we do in check_zip() is to see if the user is backspacing, in which case we simply return. If text is not being deleted, then new text is definitely being added. Since the length of the current text is not available in the callback structure, we call XmTextGet- LastPosition() to determine it. If the string is already five digits long, we don't want to add more digits, so we set doit to False and return.

Otherwise, we loop through the length of the new text and check for characters that are not digits. If any exist, we remove them by shifting all of the characters that follow down one place, overwriting the undesirable character. If we loop through all of the characters and find that none of them are digits, the length ends up being zero, so we set doit to False.

Handling Text Deletion

A modification callback can determine if the user is backspacing or deleting a large block of text by checking to see if `startPos` is less than `currInsert`. Alternatively, the routine could check to see if `text->length` is 0. For backspacing, the values differ by one. If the user selects a large block of text and deletes the selection, the `XmNmodifyVerify-Callback` is invoked once to delete the text and may be invoked a second time if the user has typed new text to replace the selected text.

Our next example program demonstrates how to process character deletions in a text modification callback. Example 14-12 creates a single-line Text widget that prompts the user for a password. We don't provide any encryption for the password; we simply mask what the user is typing by displaying an asterisk (`*`) for each character. The actual text is stored in a separate internal variable. The challenge for this application is to capture the input text, store it internally, and modify the output, even for backspacing.†

Example 14-12. The password.c program

```
/* password.c -- prompt for a password. All input looks like
 * a series of *'s.  Store the actual data typed by the user in
 * an internal variable.  Don't allow paste operations.  Handle
 * backspacing by deleting all text from insertion point to the
 * end of text.
 */
#include <Xm/Text.h>
#include <Xm/LabelG.h>
#include <Xm/RowColumn.h>
#include <ctype.h>

void check_passwd();
char *passwd; /* store user-typed passwd here. */

main(argc, argv)
int argc;
char *argv[];
{
    Widget       toplevel, text_w, rowcol;
    XtAppContext app;

    XtSetLanguageProc (NULL, NULL, NULL);

    toplevel = XtVaAppInitialize (&app, "Demos",
        NULL, 0, &argc, argv, NULL, NULL);

    rowcol = XtVaCreateWidget ("rowcol",
        xmRowColumnWidgetClass, toplevel,
        XmNorientation, XmHORIZONTAL,
        NULL);

    XtVaCreateManagedWidget ("Password:",
        xmLabelGadgetClass, rowcol, NULL);
    text_w = XtVaCreateManagedWidget ("text_w",
        xmTextWidgetClass, rowcol, NULL);

    XtAddCallback(text_w, XmNmodifyVerifyCallback, check_passwd, NULL);
```

---

†`XtSetLanguageProc()` is only available in X11R5; there is no corresponding function in X11R4.

Example 14-12. The password.c program (continued)

```
    XtAddCallback(text_w, XmNactivateCallback, check_passwd, NULL);

    XtManageChild (rowcol);
    XtRealizeWidget (toplevel);
    XtAppMainLoop (app);
}

/* check_passwd() -- handle the input of a password. */
void
check_passwd(text_w, client_data, call_data)
Widget         text_w;
XtPointer      client_data;
XtPointer      call_data;
{
    char *new;
    int len;
    XmTextVerifyCallbackStruct *cbs =
        (XmTextVerifyCallbackStruct *) call_data;

    if (cbs->reason == XmCR_ACTIVATE) {
        printf ("Password: %s\n", passwd);
        return;
    }

    if (cbs->startPos < cbs->currInsert) {    /* backspace */
        cbs->endPos = strlen (passwd);        /* delete from here to end */
        passwd[cbs->startPos] = 0;            /* backspace--terminate */
        return;
    }

    if (cbs->text->length > 1) {
        cbs->doit = False;  /* don't allow "paste" operations */
        return;             /* make the user *type* the password! */
    }

    new = XtMalloc (cbs->endPos + 2); /* new char + NULL terminator */
    if (passwd) {
        strcpy (new, passwd);
        XtFree (passwd);
    } else
        new[0] = NULL;
    passwd = new;
    strncat (passwd, cbs->text->ptr, cbs->text->length);
    passwd[cbs->endPos + cbs->text->length] = 0;

    for (len = 0; len < cbs->text->length; len++)
        cbs->text->ptr[len] = '*';
}
```

As you can see in Figure 14-9, the Text widget only displays asterisks, no matter what the user has typed.

Figure 14-9. Output of password.c

We use the `check_passwd()` function for both the `XmNactivateCallback` and the `XmNmodifyVerifyCallback` callbacks. When the user presses RETURN, the routine prints what has been typed to `stdout`. If the user is not backspacing through the text, we know we can add the new text to `passwd`, which is the internal variable we use to store the text. Once the new text has been copied, we convert it into asterisks, so that the user cannot see what has been typed.

We need to handle two different cases for deletion. If the insertion cursor is at the end of the typed string and the user backspaces, we simply allow the action. If the user clicks somewhere in the middle of the string and then backspaces, we delete all of the characters from that point in the string to the end, since the user cannot see the characters that he is deleting.

To handle the different forms of text deletion, we test to see if `startPos` is less than `currInsert`. Since `startPos` and `endPos` specify the range of text that is being deleted, we can change these values and effectively delete more text than the user originally intended. By setting `endPos` to the string length of the internal variable `passwd`, we handle both of the cases that we just described. If we had wanted to, we could also have set `startPos` to 0 and deleted all of the text.

Extending Text Modification

We can expand on the ZIP code example that we used for filtering non-digits from typed input by providing an input field for an area code and phone number. The format for a US phone number is as follows:

    123-456-7890

We want to filter out all non-digits for a phone number, but we also want to add the dash character (-) automatically as it is needed. For example, after the user enters three digits, the Text widget should automatically insert a dash, so that the next character expected from the user is still a digit. Similarly, when the user backspaces and deletes a dash character, the widget should delete the preceding digit as well. Table 14-2 shows how the interaction should work.

Table 14-2. Phone Number Input Interaction

User Types	Text Widget Displays
4	4
1	41
5	415-
4	415-4
BACKSPACE	415-
BACKSPACE	41

We can continue to use the same type of algorithm that we used in check_zip() to filter digits, and we can use some of the code from check_passwd() to handle backspacing. The only remaining problem is adding the necessary dash characters. Since we are using US phone numbers, we know that the dashes should occur after the third and seventh digits. Therefore, when currInsert is either 2 or 6, the new digit should be added first, followed by the dash. Example 14-13 shows the program that implements this functionality.†

Example 14-13. The prompt_phone.c program

```
/* prompt_phone.c -- a complex problem for XmNmodifyVerifyCallback.
 * Prompt for a phone number by filtering digits only from input.
 * Don't allow paste operations and handle backspacing.
 */
#include <Xm/Text.h>
#include <Xm/LabelG.h>
#include <Xm/RowColumn.h>
#include <ctype.h>

void check_phone();

main(argc, argv)
int argc;
char *argv[];
{
    Widget          toplevel, text_w, rowcol;
    XtAppContext  app;

    XtSetLanguageProc (NULL, NULL, NULL);

    toplevel = XtVaAppInitialize (&app, "Demos",
        NULL, 0, &argc, argv, NULL, NULL);

    rowcol = XtVaCreateWidget ("rowcol",
        xmRowColumnWidgetClass, toplevel,
        XmNorientation, XmHORIZONTAL,
        NULL);

    XtVaCreateManagedWidget ("Phone Number:",
        xmLabelGadgetClass, rowcol, NULL);
    text_w = XtVaCreateManagedWidget ("text_w",
        xmTextWidgetClass, rowcol, NULL);
```

---

†XtSetLanguageProc() is only available in X11R5; there is no corresponding function in X11R4.

Example 14-13. The prompt_phone.c program (continued)

```
    XtAddCallback (text_w, XmNmodifyVerifyCallback, check_phone, NULL);

    XtManageChild (rowcol);
    XtRealizeWidget (toplevel);
    XtAppMainLoop (app);
}

/* check_phone() -- handle phone number input. */
void
check_phone(text_w, client_data, call_data)
Widget     text_w;
XtPointer  client_data;
XtPointer  call_data;
{
    char c;
    int len = XmTextGetLastPosition(text_w);
    XmTextVerifyCallbackStruct *cbs =
        (XmTextVerifyCallbackStruct *) call_data;

    /* no backspacing or typing in the middle of string */
    if (cbs->currInsert < len) {
        cbs->doit = False;
        return;
    }

    if (cbs->text->length == 0) {  /* backspace */
        if (cbs->startPos == 3 || cbs->startPos == 7)
            cbs->startPos--;          /* delete the hyphen too */
        return;
    }

    if (cbs->text->length > 1) { /* don't allow clipboard copies */
        cbs->doit = False;
        return;
    }

    /* don't allow non-digits or let the input exceed 12 chars */
    if (!isdigit (c = cbs->text->ptr[0]) || len >= 12)
        cbs->doit = False;
    else if (len == 2 || len == 6) {
        cbs->text->ptr = XtRealloc (cbs->text->ptr, 2);
        cbs->text->length = 2;
        cbs->text->ptr[0] = c;
        cbs->text->ptr[1] = '-';
    }
}
```

There are a couple of ways that you could think to add the dashes. One way would be to use the XmNvalueChangedCallback to keep track of the phone number after it has been entered and then use XmTextInsert() to add the dashes when appropriate. The problem with this approach is that XmTextInsert() activates the XmNmodifyVerifyCallback function again, so the dash would be subject to the input filtering.

As a result, the only way to handle the situation is to actually add the dashes in the XmNmodifyVerifyCallback routine at the same time the digits are added. This approach involves modifying the ptr and length fields of the XmTextBlock structure in the XmTextVerifyCallbackStruct. The check_phone() routine checks the current

Text Widgets

length of the phone number. If it is either two or six characters long, the routine reallocates `ptr` to hold two characters, adds the dash, and increments `length` to account for the dash.

When the Text widget adds the digit and the dash, it positions the insertion cursor at the end of the new text. Prior to Motif 1.2, the position of the insertion cursor was not affected by the amount of text that was added. The workaround to this problem was to use the `XmNvalue-ChangedCallback` and call `XmTextSetInsertionPosition()`. Although we haven't demonstrated its use, the `XmNvalueChangedCallback` is useful when you need to keep track of the changes in a Text widget, but you don't need to monitor or change the input before it is displayed. This callback is invoked after the text has been modified in any way, which means that it is called for each insertion and deletion. The `call_data` parameter to the routine is of type `XmAnyCallbackStruct`; the `reason` field is always `Xm-CR_VALUE_CHANGED`.

The `check_phone()` routine is fairly simple, in that it only allows text insertions and deletions that occur when the insertion cursor is at the end of the text. While it is possible to handle modifications in the middle of the text, the code quickly becomes a large bowl of spaghetti. We do not allow clipboard copies of more than one character at a time for the same reason. Our routine is sufficient for demonstration purposes, but for a real application, you should handle these cases.

14.5.3 The Cursor Movement Callback

The `XmNmotionVerifyCallback` can be used to monitor the position of the insertion cursor. This callback is invoked when the user moves the location cursor using the mouse or the arrow keys, when the user drags the mouse or multi-clicks to extend the text selection, or when the application calls a Text widget function that moves the cursor or adds, deletes, or replaces text. However, if the cursor does not move as a result of a function being called, the callback is not invoked. The `XmNmotionVerifyCallback` allows an application to intercept and prevent cursor movement.

The `XmNmotionVerifyCallback` uses the `XmTextVerifyCallbackStruct` as its callback structure, just like the `XmNmodifyVerifyCallback`. However, for motion callbacks, the `reason` is `XmCR_MOVING_INSERT_CURSOR` and the `startPos`, `endPos`, and `text` fields are invalid. The `doit` field can be set to `False` to reject requests to reposition the insertion cursor.

If the cursor motion occurs as a result of a user action, the `event` field should point to an XEvent structure describing the action that caused the cursor position to be modified, When the cursor moves as a result of an application action, the field should be set to `NULL`. However, the `event` field is currently set to `NULL` regardless of what caused the cursor motion. This bug makes it impossible to tell the difference between a cursor motion performed by the user and one caused by the application.

We can use the `XmNmotionVerifyCallback` to tie up a loose end in *prompt_phone.c*. To make the text verification simpler, we don't want to allow the user to move the insertion cursor except by entering digits or backspacing. Example 14-14 shows a new version of the `check_phone()` routine that prevents cursor movement.

Example 14-14. The new check_phone() routine

```
main(argc, argv)
int argc;
char *argv[ ];
{
    Widget text_w;

    . . .
    XtAddCallback (text_w, XmNmodifyVerifyCallback, check_phone, NULL);
    . . .
}
/* check_phone() -- handle phone number input. */
void
check_phone(text_w, client_data, call_data)
Widget      text_w;
XtPointer   client_data;
XtPointer   call_data;
{
    char c;
    int len = XmTextGetLastPosition (text_w);
    XmTextVerifyCallbackStruct *cbs =
        (XmTextVerifyCallbackStruct *) call_data;

    if (cbs->reason == XmCR_MOVING_INSERT_CURSOR) {
        if (cbs->newInsert != len)
          cbs->doit = False;
        return;
    }

    /* no backspacing, typing or stuffing in middle of string */
    if (cbs->currInsert < len) {
        cbs->doit = False;
        return;
    }

    if (cbs->text->length == 0) { /* backspace */
        if (cbs->startPos == 3 || cbs->startPos == 7)
            cbs->startPos--;       /* delete the hyphen too */
        return;
    }

    if (cbs->text->length > 1) { /* don't allow clipboard copies */
        cbs->doit = False;
        return;
    }

    /* don't allow non-digits or let the input exceed 12 chars */
    if (!isdigit (c = cbs->text->ptr[0]) || len >= 12)
        cbs->doit = False;
    else if (len == 2 || len == 6) {
        cbs->text->ptr = XtRealloc (cbs->text->ptr, 2);
        cbs->text->length = 2;
        cbs->text->ptr[0] = c;
        cbs->text->ptr[1] = '-';
    }
}
```

We check the value of newInsert against the length of the current string to determine whether or not the intended cursor position is at the end of the text string. If it is not, we set doit to False to prevent the cursor movement. The XmNmotionVerifyCallback function can also be used to monitor pointer dragging for text selections.

14.5.4 Focus Callbacks

The XmNfocusCallback and XmNlosingFocusCallback callback routines can be used to monitor when a Text widget gains and loses the keyboard focus. A Text widget can receive the input focus if the user intentionally shifts the focus to the widget or if the application moves the focus using XmProcessTraversal(). When a widget gains the input focus and the insertion cursor is not visible, we can make it visible and cause the widget to automatically scroll to the current cursor location by installing an XmNfocusCallback routine that calls XmTextShowCursorPosition(), as shown in the following code fragment:

```
{
    Widget text_w;
    extern void gain_focus();

    . . .
    text_w = XmCreateScrolledText(...);
    XtAddCallback(text_w, XmNfocusCallback, gain_focus, NULL);
    . . .
}

void
gain_focus(text_w, client_data, call_data)
Widget      text_w;
XtPointer client_data;
XtPointer call_data;
{
    XmTextShowCursorPosition (text_w, XmTextGetCursorPosition (text_w));
}
```

The XmNfocusCallback is passed a callback structure of type XmAnyCallback-Struct with the callback reason set to XmCR_FOCUS.

The XmNlosingFocusCallback callback can be used to monitor when the Text widget loses its focus. The callback structure passed to the callback function is an XmText-VerifyCallbackStruct. All of the fields except the text field are valid, and the reason field is set to XmCR_LOSING_FOCUS.

14.6 Text Widget Internationalization

In Motif 1.2, the Text and TextField widgets have been modified to support internationalized input and output. The internationalization capabilities of the widgets are layered on top of the functionality provided in X11R5, which is based on the ANSI-C locale model. An internationalized application uses a library that reads a locale database at runtime to get information about the user's language environment. An application that uses the X Toolkit establishes its language environment (or locale) by registering a language procedure using Xt-SetLanguageProc(), as explained in Section 2.3.2. See Volume Four, *X Toolkit Intrinsics Programming Manual*, for more information on the localization of an Xt-based application.

14.6.1 Text Representation

One of the important characteristics of a locale is the encoding used to represent the character set for the locale. A character set is simply a set of characters, while an encoding is a numeric representation of these characters. A charset (not the same as a character set) is an encoding in which all of the characters use the same number of bits. The Latin-1 charset (ISO8859-1) defines an encoding for all of the characters used in Western languages. However, not all languages can be represented by a single charset. Japanese text commonly contains words written using the Latin alphabet, as well as phonetic characters from the *katakana* and *hirigana* alphabets, and ideographic *kanji* characters. Each of these character sets has its own charset. The phonetic and Latin charsets are 8-bits wide, while the ideographic charset is 16-bits wide. Since the charsets must be combined into a single encoding for Japanese text, the encoding uses shift sequences to specify the character set for each character in a string.

When an encoding contains shift sequences and characters of nonuniform width, strings can still be stored in a standard NULL-terminated array of characters; this representation is known as a *multibyte string*. Strings can also be stored using a *wide-character* type (wchar_t in ANSI-C) in which each character has a fixed size and occupies one array element. ANSI-C provides functions that convert between multibyte and wide-character strings and the text output routines in X11R5 support both types of strings. Multibyte strings are usually more compact than wide-character strings, but wide-character strings are easier to work with. If an internationalized application performs any text manipulation, it must take care to handle all strings properly. Fortunately, many applications can do internationalized text input and output without performing any manipulations on the text.

Multibyte strings are NULL-terminated, while there is no single convention for the termination of wide-character strings. The following C string-handling routines are safe to use with multibyte strings: strcat(), strcmp(), strcpy(), strlen(), and strncmp(). The string comparison routines are only useful to check for byte-for-byte equality; use strcoll() to compare strings for sorting. None of the C string-handling routines work with wide-character strings.

Multibyte strings can be written to a file or an output stream. If the terminal is operating in the current locale, printing a multibyte string to `stdout` or `stderr` causes the correct text to be displayed. Multibyte strings can also be read from a file or the `stdin` input stream. If the file is encoded in the current locale, or the terminal is operating in the current locale, the strings that are read are meaningful. For a more complete description of working with multi-byte and wide-character strings, see Volume One, *Xlib Programming Manual*.

The Motif 1.2 Text and TextField widgets provide two resources for specifying their textual data: `XmNvalue` and `XmNvalueWcs`. The `XmNvalue` resource specifies the text string as a `char *` value, so it can be used to set the value of the widget to a multibyte string. `XmNvalueWcs` specifies the string as a `wchar_t *` value, so it is used to set the value to a wide-character string. This resource cannot be specified in a resource file. If `XmNvalue` and `XmNvalueWcs` are both defined, the value of `XmNvalueWcs` takes precedence.

Regardless of which resource you set, the widgets store the text internally as a multibyte string. The widgets take care of converting between multibyte strings and wide-character strings when necessary. As a result, you can set the text string using the `XmNvalue` resource and retrieve it with `XtVaGetValues()` using the `XmNvalueWcs` resource.

The Text widget provides the following convenience routines for manipulating the text value as a wide-character string:

```
XmTextFindStringWcs()
XmTextGetSelectionWcs()
XmTextGetStringWcs()
XmTextGetSubstringWcs()
XmTextInsertWcs()
XmTextReplaceWcs()
XmTextSetStringWcs()
```

These routines work for both Text and TextField widgets. The TextField also provides corresponding functions that only work with TextField widgets. All of these routines function identically to their regular character string counterparts, except that they take or return wide-character string values. If you have specified the text string using `XmNvalue`, you can still use the wide-character string routines because they handle any necessary string conversions. For more information on the different wide-character routines, see Volume Six B, *Motif Reference Manual*.

The widgets also provide a wide-character version of the text modification callback, `XmNmodifyVerifyCallbackWcs`. This callback is invoked before the value of the widget is modified, so an application can use it to monitor changes in the widget. The callback is passed a callback structure of type `XmTextVerifyCallbackStructWcs`, which is defined as follows:

```
typedef struct {
    int              reason;
    XEvent           *event;
    Boolean          doit;
    XmTextPosition   currInsert, newInsert;
    XmTextPosition   startPos, endPos;
    XmTextBlockWcs   text;
} XmTextVerifyCallbackStructWcs;
```

With this structure the `reason` field has the value `XmCR_MODIFYING_TEXT_VALUE`. All of the fields have the same meaning as the fields in the regular `XmTextVerify-CallbackStruct`, except that the `text` field is a pointer of type `XmTextBlockWcs`. This structure is defined as follows:

```
typedef struct {
    wchar_t     *wcsptr;
    int          length;
} XmTextBlockRecWcs, *XmTextBlockWcs;
```

If callback routines are registered for both the `XmNmodifyVerifyCallback` and the `XmNmodifyVerifyCallbackWcs`, the routines for the `XmNmodifyVerifyCallback` are invoked first. The resulting data, which may have been modified, is passed to the `XmN-modifyVerifyCallbackWcs` routines.

14.6.2 Text Output

The Text and TextField widgets do not use compound strings, so their text output functionality is based directly on Xlib's internationalized text output capabilities. To support languages that use multiple charsets, X11R5 introduced the `XFontSet` abstraction for its text output routines. An `XFontSet` contains all of the fonts necessary to display text in the current locale. The new text output routines work with font sets, so they can render text for locales that require multiple charsets. See Volume One, *Xlib Programming Manual*, for more information on internationalized text output.

Each of the widgets has a `XmNfontList` resource for specifying the font that it uses. Since the widgets do not use compound strings, they use font list tags to display text using different fonts as decribed in Section 19.2.2. However, the font list can specify a font set, so the widgets can display text using multiple character sets in a locale that requires them. The widgets pick a font by searching the font list for a font set that has the tag Xm-FONTLIST_DEFAULT_TAG. If the search finds such a font set, it is used. Otherwise, the widgets use the first font set specified in the font list. If the font list does not contain a font set, the first font is used. If you specify a font list entry with the tag Xm-FONTLIST_DEFAULT_TAG, make sure that it is appropriate for the encoding of the current locale.

14.6.3 Text Input

Converting user keystrokes into text in the encoding of the current locale is the most difficult task of internationalization. An internationalized program cannot assume any particular mapping between keystrokes and input characters, since it must run in any locale on a single workstation, using a single keyboard. The mapping between keystrokes and Japanese characters is very different and much more complex than the mapping between keystrokes and Latin characters, for example. When there are more characters in the codeset of a locale than there are keys on a keyboard, some sort of *input method* is required for mapping between multiple keystrokes and input characters.

All of the characters for English can be entered using the standard keyboard; the SHIFT key makes it possible to enter both lowercase and uppercase letters as well as the number and punctuation characters. For many European languages, the most common accented characters may appear directly on a keyboard, but there are still a number of other characters that cannot be entered with any single shifted or unshifted keystroke. In these cases, the input method is typically implemented in the keyboard hardware using a special key that puts the keyboard in "compose" mode in which one or more of the following keystrokes are combined into a single character.

The Asian ideographic languages are what make internationalized text input complicated. Japanese and Korean both have phonetic alphabets that are small enough to be mapped onto a keyboard. While it is sometimes adequate to leave text in this representation, the user usually wants the final text to be in the full ideographic language. Input methods for these languages often have the user type the phonetic symbols for a particular word or words and then signal that the composition or pre-editing is complete. At this point, the input method can look up the string of phonetic characters in a dictionary and convert it to the equivalent character or characters in the ideographic language. Multiple characters can have the same phonetic representation, so the user may still have to select the desired character.

Since input methods can be large and complex and they vary from locale to locale, it does not make sense to link every application with a generic input method that is localized at runtime. The X Input Method (XIM) abstraction in X11R5 supports the model of an *input manager* that is run as a separate process and that communicates with the X server and with the application. An application that needs to use an input method calls `XOpenIM()` to establish a connection to the input method that is appropriate for the current locale.

An input method needs to provide feedback to the user, so X defines three areas for interaction:

- The *status area* is an output-only window that displays information about the state of the input method interaction.

- The *pre-edit area* displays the intermediate text while the user is composing a character.

- The *auxiliary area* is used to display any dialog boxes or popup menus that are needed by the input method.

An application generally provides the status and pre-edit areas to the input method, which is responsible for their contents. The auxiliary area is managed entirely by the input method. The location of the pre-edit area depends on the interaction style used between the input method and the application. X defines the following four interaction styles:

- The *root-window* style, where the input method displays the pre-edit data in a window that is a child of the root window.

- The *off-the-spot* style, in which the input method displays the data at a fixed location in the application window, often at the bottom of the window.

- The *over-the-spot* style, where the input method displays the data in a window of its own that is placed over the current insertion point.

- The *on-the-spot* style, in which the input method directs the application to display the pre-edit data, so the application can display the data however it wants.

An application must choose an interaction style that is supported by the input method and it must provide the pre-edit and status areas as required by that style.

Just as the X server can display multiple windows for a single client, an input method can maintain multiple *input contexts* for an application. A text editor that supports multiple editing windows within a single top-level window could create an input context for each window or share a single context among all of the windows. The function `XCreateIC()` creates an X Input Context (`XIC`) that keeps track of information about the input context, such as the interaction style, the windows used for the pre-edit and status areas, and the font set for the text.

When an application gets a `KeyPress` event, it needs to use that event in a call to `Xmb-LookupString()` or `XwcLookupString()` to get the multibyte or wide-character string encoded in the current locale. These routines are analogous to `XLookupString()`, but this routine can only return Latin-1 strings, so it is not appropriate for internationalized input.

The support for input methods in Xlib is designed to be incorporated within toolkits and widgets. Accordingly, the internationalized text input capabilities of the Motif Text and TextField widgets are layered on top of the input method mechanism. Fortunately, the widgets encapsulate most of the lower-level functionality, so you don't need to understand the details of the Xlib implementation. For a more complete description of the Xlib functionality, see Volume One, *Xlib Programming Manual*.

Motif leaves it to the hardware vendors to supply input methods, so the toolkit does not provide any itself. If you need to provide internationalized text input, consult the documentation for your system for information about the input methods that it supports. Alternately, you can build one of the contributed input methods provided as part of X11R5. R5 as shipped from MIT contains two separate implementations of the input method facilities. The Xsi implementation is the default on all but Sony machines, which use the Ximp implementation. Each implementation defines its own protocol for communication between Xlib and input methods. Ximp and Xsi each come with contributed input methods that are not compatible with each other. For X11R6, the X Consortium is planning to standardize the input method implementation, so you may want to enquire about the status of that effort before putting any significant effort into a product that uses one of these implementations.

When you create an editable Text or TextField widget, it automatically provides a connection to the input method for the current locale. The VendorShell widget plays a role in internationalization as it defines the `XmNinputMethod` and `XmNpreeditType` resources for specifying the input method and the interaction style, respectively. A Text or TextField widget is always created as an ancestor of a VendorShell, so the widget can access these resources to set up the connection to the input method. The resources are defined by the VendorShell because it handles the geometry management of the pre-edit and status areas for the input method.

The `XmNinputMethod` resource specifies the input method portion of the locale modifier that is set before an input method is opened. The format of the value for this resource is vendor-defined. The `XmNpreeditType` resource sets the interaction style used by the input method. The syntax, possible values, and default value of this resource are also vendor-dependent.

Motif only supports the over-the-spot, off-the-spot, and root-window interaction styles. Under the off-the-spot style, the VendorShell positions the pre-edit and status areas below the application's main window but inside the shell. The VendorShell handles the geometry management for the areas and places a separator between the main window and the input method area. If the application sets or gets the XmNheight of the shell using XtVaSetValues() or XtVaGetValues(), the height includes the height of the input method area. With the over-the-spot style, the VendorShell still displays the status area at the bottom of the application's top-level window, but the pre-edit area is positioned over the insertion cursor in the Text widget. The Text widget passes the insertion position to the input method, so that the pre-edit area moves as with the insertion cursor.

The Motif toolkit implements its internationalized text input functionality using the following undocumented public routines:

```
XmImRegister()
XmImUnregister()
XmImSetFocusValues()
XmImSetValues()
XmImUnsetFocus()
XmImGetXIM()
XmImMbLookupString()
XmImVaSetFocusValues()
XmImVaSetValues()
```

These routines simplify the interaction with the lower-level XIM and XIC constructs provided by Xlib. If you need to provide text input in another widget, such as a DrawingArea, you have to handle opening an input method, creating an input context, and obtaining input from the input method yourself. If you have access to the source code, you may want to investigate these routines. The only danger is that because the routines are undocumented, they may change in the next release of Motif.

14.7 Summary

The Motif Text and TextField widgets can be used to provide an application with sophisticated text entry capabilities. The widgets come with a full set of convenience routines that make it easy to perform a number of standard text editing tasks. However, these widgets work best when they are left alone to do their jobs. While they are highly configurable, the little bits of fine tuning you add may cause your code to grow twice as much to accommodate the new features and the necessary error checking.

14.8 Exercises

The following exercises are designed to expand on the ideas described in this chapter and introduce some new directions for using Text widgets.

1. Using the XmNmodifyVerifyCallback, you can add more data to a Text widget than what is typed by the user. This technique is useful for supporting advanced editing features such as file or word completion. The user should be able to enter the leading part of a word and then type a special character that completes the word automatically, based on a predefined list of words in */usr/dict/words*. Write an XmNmodifyVerifyCallback routine that checks each character that is typed and, upon receipt of the special character, looks backwards in the text until it finds whitespace and checks this word against the words in the list. If there is a match, modify the text to complete the work.

2. The function XmTextHighlight() can be used to highlight text in the same fashion as if the user had selected it. This routine is useful for emphasizing different pieces of text. Based upon the previous exercise, write a simple spell-checker program. Use a PushButton or a menu item to get all of the text from a Text widget and check the words against */usr/dict/words*. Highlight all of the words that are not found in the dictionary so that the user can find them quickly.

3. Modify the *allcaps.c* program to use the XmNgainFocusCallback and XmN-losingFocusCallback callback routines. When the widget loses the focus, all of the characters should be converted to lowercase, and when the input focus is gained, the characters should revert to uppercase.

4. The XmNsource resource specifies an XmTextSource, which is an internal object that contains all of the information about the text in a Text widget. You can set or get the value for this resource using XtVaSetValues() and XtVaGetValues(). Since the data type is opaque to the programmer, you cannot create your own source, but you can get one from an existing Text widget. By getting the XmNsource from one Text widget and setting it in another, you can have two Text widgets that edit the same text. Write a program that does just that.

15

Menus

This chapter describes the different types of menus provided by the Motif toolkit. It also presents a number of ways to create menus in an application and talks about the issues involved in designing menu systems.

In This Chapter:

15
Menus

Menus provide the user with a set of choices in an application without complicating its normal visual appearance. These convenient mini-toolboxes are essential for the user who, like an auto mechanic that is busy working under the car, needs quick and convenient access to her tools without having to look or move away from her work. The *Motif Style Guide* provides for three different types of menus: PulldownMenus, PopupMenus, and OptionMenus. Despite the differences between the three types of menus, they all provide simple and convenient access to application functionality.

15.1 Menu Types

PulldownMenus that are posted from the MenuBar are the most common menus in an application. Figure 15-1 shows an example of a PulldownMenu. The menu pops up when the user presses the first mouse button on a CascadeButton.† As described in Chapter 4, *The Main Window*, CascadeButtons may be displayed as titles in a MenuBar or as menu items in a PulldownMenu. When the CascadeButton is a child of a MenuBar, the menu drops down below the button when the user clicks on it. When the CascadeButton is an item in an existing menu, the new menu pops up to the right of the item; it is sometimes referred to as a cascading menu or a pullright menu.

Under certain conditions, it may be inconvenient for the user to stop what she is doing, move the mouse to the MenuBar to pull down a menu, and then move the mouse back to where she was working. Having to move the mouse away, even to another part of the same window, can reduce productivity. A PopupMenu is one solution to this problem as it can provide immediate access to application functionality. PopupMenus are posted using the third mouse button and can be displayed anywhere in an application. Rather than having to move the mouse, the user can simply press the third mouse button to cause a PopupMenu to appear on the spot. This type of menu does not need to be associated with a visible user-interface element. In fact, PopupMenus are usually popped up from a work area or another region that is not affiliated with a user-interface component like a PushButton or CascadeButton. The only drawback to this design is that there is no indication to the novice user that the menu exists. Figure 15-2 shows a PopupMenu.

---

† The button that posts the menu is typically user-settable, since left-handed users may want to reverse the default button bindings.

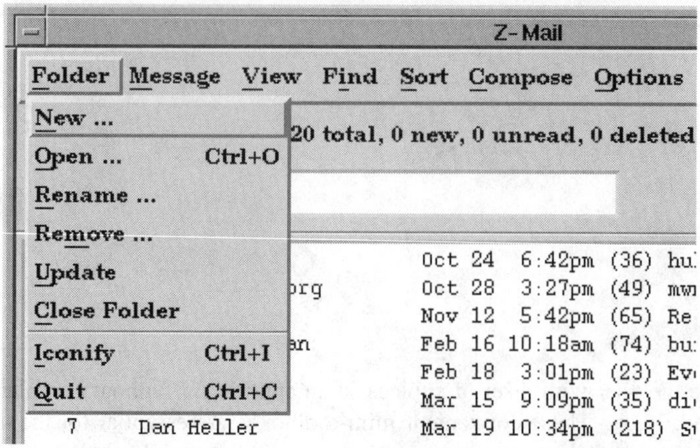

Figure 15-1. A PulldownMenu

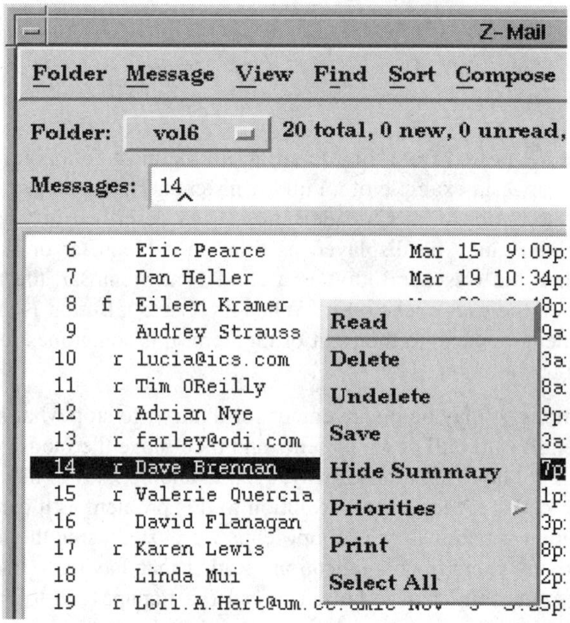

Figure 15-2. A PopupMenu

The OptionMenu combines the strengths of a PulldownMenu and a PopupMenu. Like a PulldownMenu, it is posted from a CascadeButton, but like a PopupMenu, it can be placed where it is needed. The CascadeButton is used to display the default choice for the menu. When the user presses the button, the alternate choices are displayed in a menu, as shown in

Figure 15-3. Like a PulldownMenu, an OptionMenu is invoked using the first mouse button, but it is displayed on top of its associated CascadeButton rather than below it.

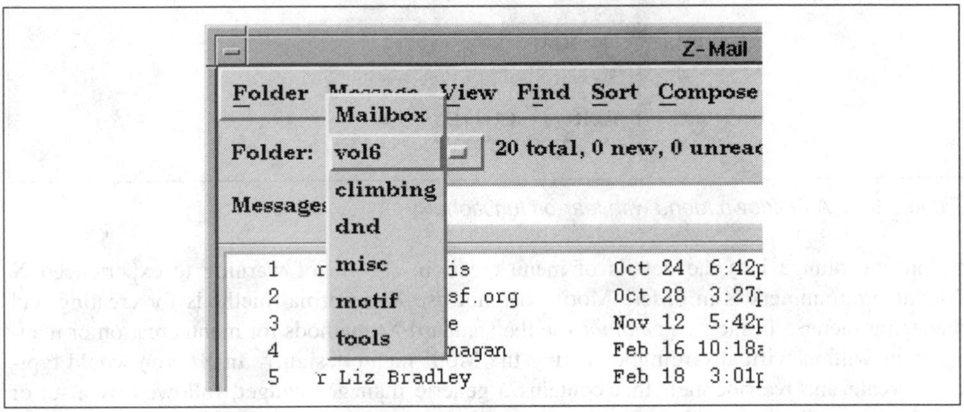

Figure 15-3. An OptionMenu

The use of the third mouse button to activate PopupMenus is in sharp contrast to Pulldown-Menus and OptionMenus, which are always invoked by the first mouse button. It may seem confusing to the user that some menus are invoked by the first button while others are invoked by the third. However, there is some consistency in the fact that PulldownMenus and OptionMenus are always attached to CascadeButtons, and buttons are always activated by the first mouse button. By specifying that PopupMenus use the third mouse button, the first mouse button is free to be used for other activities in an application work area, which is important since PopupMenus can be popped up anywhere in an application.

When the user posts a menu, it is only displayed until the user makes a selection, and then it is removed. In Motif 1.2, a menu can have an additional feature that allows it to be torn off, so that it remains posted in its own window. The tear-off functionality is activated by a special tear-off button in the menu. The button displays a dashed line to indicate that you can tear off the menu, like you would tear a coupon out of a newspaper. When the user presses the tear-off button, the menu is placed in a separate window, and the user can make as many selections as she would like. Figure 15-4 shows a PulldownMenu that provides the tear-off capability.

To make menus even more convenient to use, menu items can have *mnemonics* and *accelerators* associated with them. These devices are keyboard equivalents that allow the user to activate menu items using the keyboard rather than the mouse. For example, in Figure 15-1, the underlined letter in each menu item is its mnemonic. While the menu is posted, the user can type the specified character to activate that menu item. Accelerators are keystroke combinations that invoke a menu item even when the menu is not displayed. Accelerators typically use the CTRL or ALT key to distinguish them from ordinary keystrokes that are sent to the application. For example, again in Figure 15-1, the `Ctrl+C` accelerator allows the user to exit the application without accessing the menu.

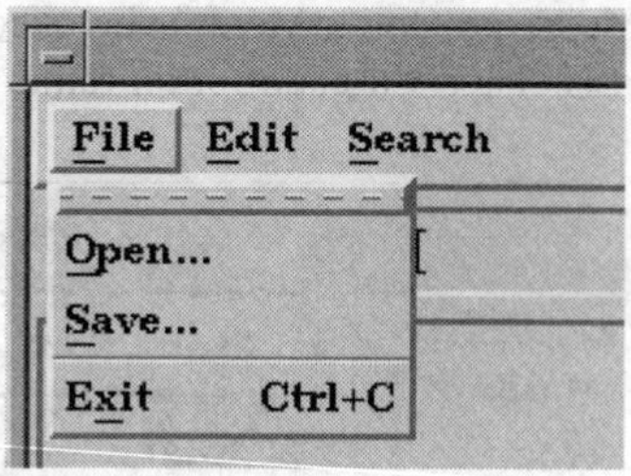

Figure 15-4. A Pulldown Menu with tear-off functionality

Before we plunge into the details of menu creation, a word of warning to experienced X Toolkit programmers is in order. Motif does not use Xt's normal methods for creating and managing menus. In fact, you *cannot* use the standard Xt methods for menu creation or management without virtually reimplementing the Motif menu design.† In Xt, you would typically create an OverrideShell that contains a generic manager widget, followed by a set of PushButtons. To display the menu, you would pop up the shell using XtPopup(). The Motif toolkit abstracts the menu creation and management process using routines that make the shell opaque to the programmer.

15.2 Creating Simple Menus

In Chapter 4, *The Main Window*, we used the simple menu creation routines to build the MenuBar and its associated PulldownMenus. These routines are designed to be plug-and-play convenience routines; their only requirements are compound strings for the menu labels and a single callback function that is invoked when the user activates any of the menu items.

XmVaCreateSimpleMenuBar() creates a MenuBar, while XmVaCreateSimple-PulldownMenu() generates a PulldownMenu and its associated items. These functions take a variable-length argument list of parameters that specify either the CascadeButtons for the MenuBar or the menu items for the PulldownMenu. You can also pass RowColumn-specific resource/value pairs to configure the RowColumn widget that manages the items in the menu. The functions are front ends for more primitive routines that actually create the underlying widgets, so they are convenient for many simple menu creation needs. You should review Chapter 4, *The Main Window*, for more information on how to use these functions.

Motif also provides simple creation routines for creating PopupMenus and OptionMenus. Both XmVaCreateSimplePopupMenu() and XmVaCreateSimpleOptionMenu() are very similar to the routines for creating PulldownMenus, so much of the information in Chapter 4 also applies to these functions.

---

† If you need to port an Athena or OPEN LOOK-based application to Motif, you will probably have to reimplement your menu design.

15.2.1 Popup Menus

The only difference between XmVaCreateSimplePulldownMenu() and XmVa-
CreateSimplePopupMenu() is that the latter routine does not have a *button* parameter for specifying the CascadeButton used to display the menu. Since PopupMenus are not
associated with CascadeButtons, this parameter isn't necessary. Example 15-1 demonstrates
the creation of a simple PopupMenu.†

Example 15-1. The simple_popup.c program

```
/* simple_popup.c -- demonstrate how to use a simple popup menu.
 * Create a main window that contains a DrawingArea widget, which
 * displays a popup menu when the user presses the third mouse button.
 */
#include <Xm/RowColumn.h>
#include <Xm/MainW.h>
#include <Xm/DrawingA.h>

main(argc, argv)
int argc;
char *argv[];
{
    XmString line, square, circle, exit, exit_acc;
    Widget toplevel, main_w, drawing_a, popup_menu;
    void popup_cb(), input();
    XtAppContext app;

    XtSetLanguageProc (NULL, NULL, NULL);

    toplevel = XtVaAppInitialize (&app, "Demos", NULL, 0,
        &argc, argv, NULL, NULL);

    /* Create a MainWindow widget that contains a DrawingArea in
     * its work window.
     */
    main_w = XtVaCreateManagedWidget ("main_w",
        xmMainWindowWidgetClass, toplevel,
        XmNscrollingPolicy,       XmAUTOMATIC,
        NULL);
    /* Create a DrawingArea -- no actual drawing will be done. */
    drawing_a = XtVaCreateManagedWidget ("drawing_a",
        xmDrawingAreaWidgetClass, main_w,
        XmNwidth,   500,
        XmNheight, 500,
        NULL);

    line = XmStringCreateLocalized ("Line");
    square = XmStringCreateLocalized ("Square");
    circle = XmStringCreateLocalized ("Circle");
    exit = XmStringCreateLocalized ("Exit");
    exit_acc = XmStringCreateLocalized ("Ctrl+C");
    popup_menu = XmVaCreateSimplePopupMenu (drawing_a, "popup", popup_cb,
        XmVaPUSHBUTTON, line, 'L', NULL, NULL,
```

---

†XtSetLanguageProc() is only available in X11R5; there is no corresponding function in X11R4. Xm-
StringCreateLocalized() is only available in Motif 1.2; XmStringCreateSimple() is the corresponding function in Motif 1.1.

Example 15-1. The simple_popup.c program (continued)

```
            XmVaPUSHBUTTON, square, 'S', NULL, NULL,
            XmVaPUSHBUTTON, circle, 'C', NULL, NULL,
            XmVaSEPARATOR,
            XmVaPUSHBUTTON, exit, 'x', "Ctrl<Key>c", exit_acc,
            NULL);
    XmStringFree (line);
    XmStringFree (square);
    XmStringFree (circle);
    XmStringFree (exit);
    XmStringFree (exit_acc);

    /* after popup menu is created, add callback for all input events */
    XtAddCallback (drawing_a, XmNinputCallback, input, popup_menu);

    XtRealizeWidget (toplevel);
    XtAppMainLoop (app);
}

/* input() -- called in responses to events in the DrawingArea;
 * button-3 pops up menu.
 */
void
input(widget, client_data, call_data)
Widget widget;
XtPointer client_data;
XtPointer call_data;
{
    Widget popup = (Widget) client_data;
    XmDrawingAreaCallbackStruct *cbs =
        (XmDrawingAreaCallbackStruct *) call_data;

    if (cbs->event->xany.type != ButtonPress ||
            cbs->event->xbutton.button != 3)
        return;

    /* Position the menu where the event occurred */
    XmMenuPosition (popup, (XButtonPressedEvent *) (cbs->event));
    XtManageChild (popup);
}

/* popup_cb() -- invoked when the user selects an item in the popup menu */
void
popup_cb(menu_item, client_data, call_data)
Widget menu_item;
XtPointer client_data;
XtPointer call_data;
{
    int item_no = (int) client_data;

    if (item_no == 3) /* Exit was selected -- exit */
        exit (0);
    puts (XtName (menu_item)); /* Otherwise, just print the selection */
}
```

This program creates a standard MainWindow widget that contains a DrawingArea widget. The program does not do any drawing; it is just a skeleton that demonstrates how to attach a PopupMenu. The PopupMenu is created using XmVaCreateSimplePopupMenu() with the DrawingArea widget as its parent. The menu is popped up when the user presses the third mouse button in the DrawingArea, as shown in Figure 15-5.

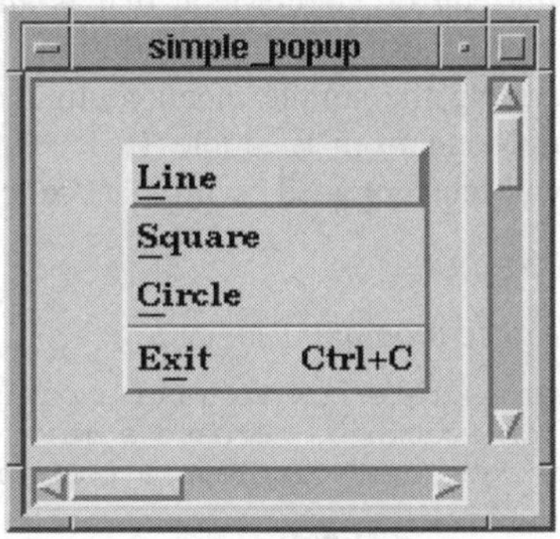

Figure 15-5. Output of simple_popup.c

The Motif toolkit does not handle posting a PopupMenu automatically, as it does with PulldownMenus and OptionMenus, so we must watch for the appropriate events ourselves. We use the `XmNinputCallback` resource of the DrawingArea widget to monitor events, as the routine is called whenever a keyboard or mouse action happens in the widget. In a real application, we would use this routine to handle drawing as well. However, in this case, the `input()` routine only looks for `ButtonPress` events for the third mouse button. The menu is passed as the client data to `input()`.

If `input()` sees an appropriate event, it uses the `XmMenuPosition()` routine to position the menu at the coordinates specified in the `event` data structure. The menu is then popped up using `XtManageChild()`.† The menu contains four items, the last of which has the accelerator `Ctrl<Key>C`. Any time the user presses CTRL-C in the application, the callback routine associated with the menu is called as if the menu had been popped up and the **Exit** item had been selected. The `popup_cb()` routine either prints the name of the menu item or exits, depending on which item the user selected. Note that the name of the menu item does not correspond to its label. As described in Chapter 4, *The Main Window*, menu items are automatically given names of the form `button_n`, where *n* is assigned in order of menu item creation, starting at 0 (zero).

---

† As far as Xt is concerned, this method for popping up a menu is technically incorrect. It is supported by the Motif toolkit to simplify the PopupMenu interface. For more information, see the discussion on popping up dialog boxes in Chapter 5, *Introduction to Dialogs*.

15.2.2 Cascading Menus

A cascading menu, or a pullright menu, is implemented as a PulldownMenu displayed from a menu item in another PulldownMenu or PopupMenu that is already displayed. The menu item that posts the cascading menu must be a CascadeButton. Example 15-2 demonstrates how to add a cascading menu using the simple menu routines. The program adds a **Line Width** menu item to the PopupMenu from Example 15-1. This menu item is a Cascade-Button that posts a PulldownMenu created with XmVaCreateSimplePulldown-Menu().†

Example 15-2. The simple_pullright.c program

```
/* simple_pullright.c -- demonstrate how to make a pullright menu
 * using simple menu creation routines.  Create a main window that
 * contains a DrawingArea widget that displays a popup menu when the
 * user presses the third mouse button.
 */
#include <Xm/RowColumn.h>
#include <Xm/MainW.h>
#include <Xm/DrawingA.h>

main(argc, argv)
int argc;
char *argv[];
{
    XmString line, square, circle, weight, exit, exit_acc;
    XmString w_one, w_two, w_four, w_eight;
    Widget toplevel, main_w, drawing_a, cascade, popup_menu, pullright;
    void popup_cb(), set_width(), input();
    XtAppContext app;

    XtSetLanguageProc (NULL, NULL, NULL);

    toplevel = XtVaAppInitialize (&app, "Demos", NULL, 0,
        &argc, argv, NULL, NULL);

    /* Create a MainWindow widget that contains a DrawingArea in
     * its work window.
     */
    main_w = XtVaCreateManagedWidget ("main_w",
        xmMainWindowWidgetClass, toplevel,
        XmNscrollingPolicy,      XmAUTOMATIC,
        NULL);
    /* Create a DrawingArea -- no actual drawing will be done. */
    drawing_a = XtVaCreateManagedWidget ("drawing_a",
        xmDrawingAreaWidgetClass, main_w,
        XmNwidth,   500,
        XmNheight, 500,
        NULL);

    line = XmStringCreateLocalized ("Line");
    square = XmStringCreateLocalized ("Square");
```

---

†XtSetLanguageProc() is only available in X11R5; there is no corresponding function in X11R4. Xm-StringCreateLocalized() is only available in Motif 1.2; XmStringCreateSimple() is the corresponding function in Motif 1.1.

Example 15-2. The simple_pullright.c program (continued)

```
        circle = XmStringCreateLocalized ("Circle");
        weight = XmStringCreateLocalized ("Line Width");
        exit = XmStringCreateLocalized ("Exit");
        exit_acc = XmStringCreateLocalized ("Ctrl+C");
        popup_menu = XmVaCreateSimplePopupMenu (drawing_a, "popup", popup_cb,
            XmVaPUSHBUTTON, line, 'L', NULL, NULL,
            XmVaPUSHBUTTON, square, 'S', NULL, NULL,
            XmVaPUSHBUTTON, circle, 'C', NULL, NULL,
            XmVaCASCADEBUTTON, weight, 'W',
            XmVaSEPARATOR,
            XmVaPUSHBUTTON, exit, 'x', "Ctrl<Key>c", exit_acc,
            NULL);
        XmStringFree (line);
        XmStringFree (square);
        XmStringFree (circle);
        XmStringFree (weight);
        XmStringFree (exit);

        /* create pullright for "Line Width" button -- this is the 4th item! */
        w_one = XmStringCreateLocalized (" 1 ");
        w_two = XmStringCreateLocalized (" 2 ");
        w_four = XmStringCreateLocalized (" 4 ");
        w_eight = XmStringCreateLocalized (" 8 ");
        pullright = XmVaCreateSimplePulldownMenu (popup_menu,
            "pullright", 3 /* menu item offset */, set_width,
            XmVaPUSHBUTTON, w_one, '1', NULL, NULL,
            XmVaPUSHBUTTON, w_two, '2', NULL, NULL,
            XmVaPUSHBUTTON, w_four, '4', NULL, NULL,
            XmVaPUSHBUTTON, w_eight, '8', NULL, NULL,
            NULL);
        XmStringFree (w_one);
        XmStringFree (w_two);
        XmStringFree (w_four);
        XmStringFree (w_eight);

        /* after popup menu is created, add callback for all input events */
        XtAddCallback (drawing_a, XmNinputCallback, input, popup_menu);

        XtRealizeWidget (toplevel);
        XtAppMainLoop (app);
}

/* input() -- called in responses to events in the DrawingArea;
 * button-3 pops up menu.
 */
void
input(widget, client_data, call_data)
Widget widget;
XtPointer client_data;
XtPointer call_data;
{
    Widget popup = (Widget) client_data;
    XmDrawingAreaCallbackStruct *cbs =
        (XmDrawingAreaCallbackStruct *) call_data;

    if (cbs->event->xany.type != ButtonPress ||
            cbs->event->xbutton.button != 3)
        return;
```

Example 15-2. The simple_pullright.c program (continued)

```
    /* Position the menu where the event occurred */
    XmMenuPosition (popup, (XButtonPressedEvent *) (cbs->event));
    XtManageChild (popup);
}

/* popup_cb() -- invoked when the user selects an item in the popup menu */
void
popup_cb(menu_item, client_data, call_data)
Widget menu_item;
XtPointer client_data;
XtPointer call_data;
{
    int item_no = (int) client_data;

    if (item_no == 4) /* Exit was selected -- exit */
        exit (0);
    puts (XtName (menu_item)); /* Otherwise, just print the selection */
}

/* set_width() -- called when items in the Line Width pullright menu
 * are selected.
 */
void
set_width(menu_item, client_data, call_data)
Widget menu_item;
XtPointer client_data;
XtPointer call_data;
{
    int item_no = (int) client_data;

    printf ("Line weight = %d\n", 1 << item_no);
}
```

In the call to `XmVaCreateSimplePulldownMenu()`, the PopupMenu is specified as the parent of the cascading menu. The *button* parameter is set to 3 to indicate that the fourth item in the PopupMenu posts the cascading menu. Figure 15-6 shows the output of the program.

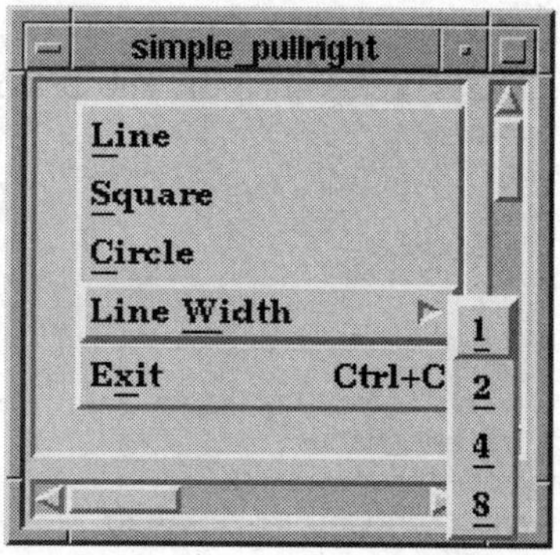

Figure 15-6. Output of simple_pullright.c

15.2.3   Option Menus

An OptionMenu is similar to a PulldownMenu in that they are both associated with Cascade-Buttons. However, there are also several major differences between the two types of menus. In an OptionMenu, the CascadeButton is not part of a MenuBar. Instead, it is created as the child of a RowColumn widget that also contains a Label.

Another difference is that the menu pops up on top of the CascadeButton, instead of dropping down from it. The label on the CascadeButton is one of the elements in the menu; the CascadeButton displays the current menu selection. The Motif toolkit handles the management of the PulldownMenu for the OptionMenu, so its handle is not available to you, nor does it need to be. Because of the design of the OptionMenu, it cannot have cascading menus.

Example 15-3 demonstrates the use of `XmVaCreateSimpleOptionMenu()`. The program uses a DrawingArea again, but now the user selects the drawing style from an Option-Menu that is displayed above the DrawingArea.

Example 15-3. The simple_option.c program

```
/* simple_option.c -- demonstrate how to use a simple option menu.
 * Display a drawing area.  The user selects the drawing style from
 * the option menu.
 */
#include <Xm/RowColumn.h>
#include <Xm/MainW.h>
#include <Xm/ScrolledW.h>
#include <Xm/DrawingA.h>
#include <Xm/PushB.h>

main(argc, argv)
int argc;
char *argv[];
{
    XmString draw_shape, line, square, circle;
    Widget toplevel, main_w, rc, sw, drawing_a, option_menu, pb;
    void option_cb(), exit();
    XtAppContext app;

    XtSetLanguageProc (NULL, NULL, NULL);

    toplevel = XtVaAppInitialize (&app, "Demos", NULL, 0,
        &argc, argv, NULL, NULL);

    /* Create a MainWindow widget that contains a RowColumn
     * widget as its work window.
     */
    main_w = XtVaCreateManagedWidget ("main_w",
        xmMainWindowWidgetClass, toplevel, NULL);
    rc = XtVaCreateWidget ("rowcol", xmRowColumnWidgetClass, main_w, NULL);

    /* Inside RowColumn is the Exit pushbutton, the option menu and the
     * scrolled window that contains the drawing area.
     */
    pb = XtVaCreateManagedWidget ("Exit", xmPushButtonWidgetClass, rc, NULL);
    XtAddCallback (pb, XmNactivateCallback, exit, NULL);
```

Example 15-3. The simple_option.c program (continued)

```
        draw_shape = XmStringCreateLocalized ("Draw Mode:");
        line = XmStringCreateLocalized ("Line");
        square = XmStringCreateLocalized ("Square");
        circle = XmStringCreateLocalized ("Circle");
        option_menu = XmVaCreateSimpleOptionMenu (rc, "option_menu",
            draw_shape, 'D', 0 /*initial menu selection*/, option_cb,
            XmVaPUSHBUTTON, line, 'L', NULL, NULL,
            XmVaPUSHBUTTON, square, 'S', NULL, NULL,
            XmVaPUSHBUTTON, circle, 'C', NULL, NULL,
            NULL);
        XmStringFree (line);
        XmStringFree (square);
        XmStringFree (circle);
        XmStringFree (draw_shape);

        XtManageChild (option_menu);

        /* Create a DrawingArea inside a ScrolledWindow */
        sw = XtVaCreateManagedWidget ("sw",
            xmScrolledWindowWidgetClass, rc,
            XmNscrollingPolicy, XmAUTOMATIC,
            NULL);
        drawing_a = XtVaCreateManagedWidget ("drawing_area",
            xmDrawingAreaWidgetClass, sw,
            XmNwidth,   500,
            XmNheight, 500,
            NULL);

        XtManageChild (rc);

        XtRealizeWidget (toplevel);
        XtAppMainLoop (app);
}

/* option_cb() -- invoked when the user selects an item in the
 * option menu
 */
void
option_cb(menu_item, client_data, call_data)
Widget menu_item;
XtPointer client_data;
XtPointer call_data;
{
    int item_no = (int) client_data;

    puts (XtName (menu_item));
}
```

The layout of the application is different from that in the previous examples because we use a separate ScrolledWindow for the DrawingArea. The RowColumn widget that contains the **Exit** button, the OptionMenu, and the ScrolledWindow is the work area for the Main-Window. Figure 15-7 shows the output of the program both before and after the OptionMenu is displayed. Notice how the label of the CascadeButton changes as you select alternate values from the menu.

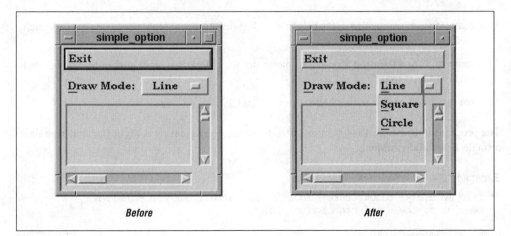

Figure 15-7. Output of simple_option.c

15.3 Designing Menu Systems

The advantages of the simple menu creation routines are clear. It is easy to create menus with them, the code is extremely readable, and the job gets done without much room for error. Once the code is written, it is easy to modify the callback function, labels, mnemonics, and accelerators used by a menu.

There are also some disadvantages to using the simple menu creation functions. One problem is that they require a great deal of bulk to create a single menu. If an application needs to create a large number of menus, it has to use a lot of redundant code because the simple creation routines make it difficult to build a looping construct or a function to automate the process. Since the creation routines name the widgets using non-unique names, it is difficult to specify labels, mnemonics, and accelerators in a resource file. If these values are set using a creation routine, this point is irrelevant because the routines hard-code the values. The simple creation routines also make it impossible to specify different callback functions for menu items.

To get around the shortcomings of the simple creation routines, we are going to build a new system that is just as simple to use, but more dynamic and easy to modify. Before we can build our new system, we need to examine the advanced Motif menu creation routines and discuss the overall design of a menu system. We are going to start with the MenuBar and PulldownMenus because almost every application uses these components. Furthermore, everything there is to know about menus can be adapted from the design of a menu system that uses these menus.

Let's begin by examining the steps that you need to take to create a MenuBar and its associated PulldownMenus:

1. Create a RowColumn widget for use as a MenuBar with `XmCreateMenuBar()`.

2. Create each PulldownMenu using `XmCreatePulldownMenu()`.

3. Create the menu items (PushButtons, ToggleButtons, Separators, etc.) for each PulldownMenu.

4. Create a CascadeButton for each menu in the MenuBar and attach the associated PulldownMenu to it.

5. Manage the MenuBar with `XtManageChild()`.

The program in Example 15-4 demonstrates these steps by creating a MenuBar that contains a single **File** PulldownMenu.†

Example 15-4. The file_menu.c program

```
/* file_menu.c -- demonstrate how to create a menu bar and pulldown
 * menu using the Motif creation routines.
 */
#include <Xm/RowColumn.h>
#include <Xm/MainW.h>
#include <Xm/CascadeB.h>
#include <Xm/SeparatoG.h>
#include <Xm/PushBG.h>

main(argc, argv)
int argc;
char *argv[];
{
    Widget toplevel, MainWindow, MenuBar, FilePullDown;
    XmString    label_str;
    XtAppContext app;

    XtSetLanguageProc (NULL, NULL, NULL);

    toplevel = XtVaAppInitialize (&app, "Demos", NULL, 0,
        &argc, argv, NULL, NULL);

    MainWindow = XtVaCreateManagedWidget ("main_w",
        xmMainWindowWidgetClass, toplevel,
        XmNscrollingPolicy,  XmAUTOMATIC,
        NULL);

    MenuBar = XmCreateMenuBar (MainWindow, "MenuBar", NULL, 0);

    /* create the "File" Menu */
    FilePullDown = XmCreatePulldownMenu (MenuBar, "FilePullDown", NULL, 0);

    /* create the "File" button (attach Menu via XmNsubMenuId) */
    label_str = XmStringCreateLocalized ("File");
    XtVaCreateManagedWidget ("File",
        xmCascadeButtonWidgetClass, MenuBar,
        XmNlabelString,   label_str,
        XmNmnemonic,      'F',
        XmNsubMenuId,     FilePullDown,
        NULL);
    XmStringFree (label_str);
```

---

†`XtSetLanguageProc()` is only available in X11R5; there is no corresponding function in X11R4. `XmStringCreateLocalized()` is only available in Motif 1.2; `XmStringCreateSimple()` is the corresponding function in Motif 1.1.

Example 15-4. The file_menu.c program (continued)

```
    /* Now add the menu items */
    XtVaCreateManagedWidget ("Open",
        xmPushButtonGadgetClass, FilePullDown, NULL);

    XtVaCreateManagedWidget ("Save",
        xmPushButtonGadgetClass, FilePullDown, NULL);

    XtVaCreateManagedWidget ("separator",
        xmSeparatorGadgetClass, FilePullDown, NULL);

    XtVaCreateManagedWidget ("Exit",
        xmPushButtonGadgetClass, FilePullDown, NULL);

    XtManageChild (MenuBar);

    XtRealizeWidget (toplevel);
    XtAppMainLoop (app);
}
```

The code follows the steps that we just outlined. The MenuBar is created as a child of the MainWindow, and the PulldownMenu is created as a child of the MenuBar. The Cascade-Button acts as the **File** title item in the MenuBar, so it is also created as the child of the MenuBar. Both the menu title and the PulldownMenu are children of the MenuBar. The CascadeButton sets its XmNsubMenuId resource to the PulldownMenu so that when the button is selected, it knows which PulldownMenu to display. When you create a Pulldown-Menu using the simple menu creation routine, it sets this resource behind the scenes.

We also set the label of the CascadeButton using the XmNlabelString resource. This value is a compound string, just as in the simple creation function. If we had not set the label directly, the name of the widget itself would appear as the label, and we could override it with a specification in a resource file. Since we are not using the simple creation routine, we can choose whether or not we hard-code the label for the CascadeButton. After we create the items in the menu, we manage the MenuBar using XtManageChild(). The output of Example 15-4, both before and after the PulldownMenu is posted, is shown in Figure 15-8.

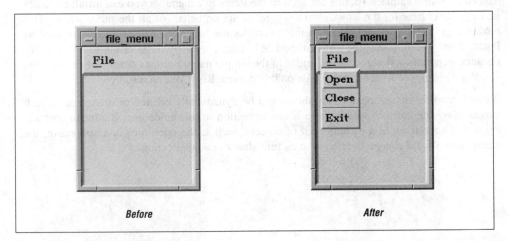

Before   *After*

Figure 15-8. Output of file_menu.c

15.3.1 Menu Titles

The titles in a MenuBar are actually the labels of the CascadeButtons. The labels can be specified using the XmNlabelString resource, either in the application code or in a resource file. Every CascadeButton must have a submenu associated with it via the XmNsubMenuId resource. When the user selects the CascadeButton, the associated PulldownMenu is displayed. You should never attach a callback function directly to a CascadeButton in the MenuBar as it would confuse the user. Callback functions should only be attached to menu items in PulldownMenus that are posted from the MenuBar.

The PulldownMenu that is associated with a CascadeButton is created using XmCreatePulldownMenu(). This routine returns the RowColumn widget that manages the menu items. The routine creates the RowColumn as a child of a MenuShell widget. Since the routine returns the RowColumn widget, the resource list provided to the function only sets resources for the RowColumn widget, not for the MenuShell that contains it.

Menu titles should not be dynamically created or destroyed. An application should not make the MenuBar disappear or add new titles to the MenuBar while the application is running. All of the titles in the MenuBar must be available to the user when the MainWindow is visible. You can, however, deactivate an entire menu by changing the XmNsensitive resource on the CascadeButton widget that acts as its title, as discussed in Section 15.3.6.

15.3.2 Menu Items

The items in a menu are actually the labels of the PushButtons that make up the menu. Unlike the **File** title item in the MenuBar, we chose not to use hard-coded values for the menu item strings, so the strings can be set in a resource file. While our menu only contains PushButton gadgets, a PulldownMenu can also contain ToggleButtons, Separators, and CascadeButtons.

You can install a callback routine for each of the items in a menu, or you can install an XmNentryCallback for the RowColumn widget to act on behalf of all the menu items. This resource specifies a callback function that overrides the XmNactivateCallback used by Pushbuttons and the XmNvalueChangedCallback used by ToggleButtons. Using this resource generates a design that is similar to the simple menu routines described earlier. See Chapter 8, *Manager Widgets*, for details on this generic RowColumn resource.

As with the title items, menu items should not be dynamically created or destroyed since it may confuse the user. However, there is one exception to this guideline. If a menu contains items that keep track of a dynamic list of objects, such as the open files in a text editor, the menu items should change to reflect the current state of the application.

15.3.3 Mnemonics

Mnemonics help users traverse the menu system and select actual menu items without having to use the mouse. In Example 15-4, we used the XmNmnemonic resource to attach the mnemonic "F" to the **File** menu, which allows the user to use the key sequence ALT-F to open or close the menu without using the mouse. The XmNmnemonic resource is defined by the Label class, but it is only used by PushButtons, ToggleButtons, and CascadeButtons when these objects are used in a menu system.

A mnemonic is represented visually by the underlining of the mnemonic character in the label string. In this case, the "F" in the word "File" is underlined. If the label does not contain the mnemonic character, there is no visual feedback for the mnemonic, but it still functions. When a mnemonic is specified, the character can be either uppercase or lowercase, but the distinction only affects which letter is underlined. For operational purposes, mnemonics are case insensitive.

Our example only provided a mnemonic for the entire menu, but mnemonics can be set on menu items as well. When a PulldownMenu is displayed, the user can activate a menu item simply by typing the letter represented by its mnemonic. (The ALT key is not used once the menu is displayed.) If the user activates a menu item using a mnemonic, the callback function for the menu is called just as if the user had selected it with the mouse.

Mnemonics are set on MenuBar titles and menu items in the same way. To illustrate, let's add a mnemonic to the **Exit** item in our **File** menu. We can set the mnemonic directly in the declaration of the item, as follows:

```
XtVaCreateManagedWidget ("Exit",
    xmPushButtonGadgetClass, FilePullDown,
    XmNmnemonic, 'x',
    NULL);
```

While this method accomplishes the task, one problem with it is that the mnemonic is hard-coded in the widget, while the label is not. Consider the following resource specification in a resource file:

```
*Exit.labelString: Quit
```

This resource sets the label for the item button to "Quit", but since the mnemonic for the button is hard-coded to "x", there is visual feedback, and the mnemonic itself is counterintuitive.

The best way to handle this situation is to specify both the label string and the mnemonic in the same place: a resource file or application code. For example:

```
*Exit.labelString: Exit
*Exit.mnemonic:    x
```

Setting both of these resources in the same way helps ensure that an application has a consistent interface.

15.3.4 Accelerators

The purpose of menu accelerators is to provide the user with the ability to activate menu items in a PulldownMenu without having to display the menu at all. In Figure 15-1, the **Quit** menu item displayed the accelerator `Ctrl+C` to indicate that the user could press the CTRL-C keyboard sequence to activate that menu item and quit the application.

To install a accelerator on a menu item, use the `XmNaccelerator` resource to specify the accelerator translation and `XmNacceleratorText` to provide visual feedback to the user.† These resources are defined by the Label class, but they only work for PushButtons and ToggleButtons in menus. The syntax for the accelerator is exactly the same as for a translation table, except that you do not specify an action function with the event sequence. The accelerator for the **Quit** button in Figure 15-1 is specified as `"Ctrl<Key>C"`. (For information on how to specify translation tables, see Volume Four, *X Toolkit Intrinsics Programming Manual*.

However, the string that is displayed for the accelerator is not the same as the accelerator translation because it would be confusing for most users. Instead, you should display something like `"^C"`, `"Ctrl-C"`, or `"Ctrl+C"`, as these make it reasonably clear what the user is expected to type. (The latter is the convention recommended by the *Motif Style Guide*, though all three forms are frequently used.) Since this resource specifies displayable text, you cannot use a common C string; the text must be given as a compound string.

For example, the following code demonstrates how to install an accelerator for the **Exit** button in Example 15-4.

```
char     *accel = "Ctrl<Key>C";
XmString  accel_text = XmStringCreateLocalized ("Ctrl+C");

XtVaCreateManagedWidget ("Exit",
    xmPushButtonGadgetClass, FilePullDown,
    XmNaccelerator,        accel,
    XmNacceleratorText,    accel_text,
    NULL);

XmStringFree (accel_text);
```

As with mnemonics, the resources for the accelerator itself and the text used to display the accelerator can either be set directly in application code or specified in a resource file. Both of the resources should be specified in the same way, so that they are always consistent.

---

† A side effect of the implementation of Motif accelerators is that you cannot install your own accelerators using the standard methods provided by the X Toolkit Intrinsics (such as `XtInstallAccelerators ()` or `XtInstall-AllAccelerators ()`). These functions will not work, and you may interfere with the Motif accelerator mechanism by attempting to use them.

15.3.5 The Help Menu

Motif specifies various ways for the user to get help. She can use the HELP or F1 keys on the keyboard, the **Help** button in a dialog box, or the **Help** title on the MenuBar. This title provides the highest level of help for your application, so it should not provide too much detail about lower-level functions in the program. When you create a PulldownMenu for this title, it should provide items that give the user access to the help system. Figure 15-9 shows a common **Help** menu.

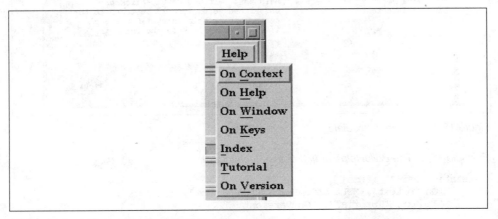

Figure 15-9. A Help menu from the MenuBar

The choices shown in Figure 15-9 are recommended by the *Motif Style Guide*; if they apply to your application, you should use them. There is usually an item on the **Help** menu that gives the user a brief overview of how to use the help system. You should consult the *Motif Style Guide* for details on what kind of help each of the above selections should provide. It is usually a good idea to have an item that displays an index of the type of help that is available in an application. An example of help index dialog is shown in Figure 15-10. See Chapter 21, *Advanced Dialog Programming*, for a discussion of help dialogs.

Creating a **Help** menu is just like creating any other menu, except that once you have created the CascadeButton, you should set the XmNmenuHelpWidget resource for the MenuBar. This resource specifies which CascadeButton is placed to the far right in the MenuBar, which is where the *Style Guide* states that the **Help** menu must be positioned. Example 15-5 contains a routine that demonstrates how to build a **Help** menu and attach it to the MenuBar. In this example, we present an alternate approach to creating MenuBar titles and their associated PulldownMenus.

Example 15-5. The BuildHelpMenu( ) routine

```
void
BuildHelpMenu(MenuBar)
Widget MenuBar;
{
    Widget HelpPullDown, widget;
    int i;
```

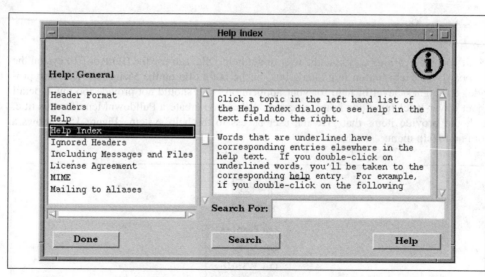

Figure 15-10. A help index dialog

Example 15-5. The BuildHelpMenu() routine (continued)

```
static char *h_items[] = {
    "On Context", NULL, "On Help", "On Window", "On Keys",
    "Index", "Tutorial", "On Version"
};

/* Help menu */
HelpPullDown = XmCreatePulldownMenu (MenuBar, "HelpPullDown", NULL, 0);
widget = XtVaCreateManagedWidget ("Help",
    xmCascadeButtonWidgetClass, MenuBar,
    XmNsubMenuId, HelpPullDown,
    NULL);
/* tell the MenuBar that this is the help widget */
XtVaSetValues (MenuBar, XmNmenuHelpWidget, widget, NULL);

/* Now add the menu items to the pulldown menu */
for (i = 0; i < XtNumber (h_items); i++) {
    if (h_items[i] != NULL) {
        widget = XtVaCreateManagedWidget (h_items[i],
            xmPushButtonGadgetClass, HelpPullDown, NULL);
        XtAddCallback (widget, XmNactivateCallback,
            do_help, h_items[i]);
    }
    else
        widget = XtVaCreateManagedWidget ("sep",
            xmSeparatorGadgetClass, HelpPullDown, NULL);
}
}
```

Much of the work required to create a PulldownMenu is involved in creating the menu items.
We can optimize the code by using a loop that creates individual items based on the names
provided in a static array. If you want to add a new help item to the list, you just need to add
its name to the h_items list. A NULL entry causes a Separator gadget to be added to the
menu. In Example 15-5, we specify the same callback function for each item in the menu;

the `client_data` is the same as the name of the menu item. In Section 15.4, we expand on this approach to build arbitrary menus for the MenuBar.

15.3.6 Sensitivity

As we mentioned earlier, MenuBar titles and menu items should not be dynamically created or destroyed. They may, however, be activated or deactivated using `XtSetSensitive()`. When a CascadeButton or a menu item is *insensitive*, it is grayed out, and the user is unable to display the associated menu or activate the menu item.

For CascadeButtons, insensitivity has the additional effect of preventing the user from accessing any of the items on the associated menu, including access through mnemonics and accelerators, since the menu cannot be displayed. The menu and all its items are completely unavailable until the sensitivity of the CascadeButton is reset. An alternate way to disable an entire menu is to set the PulldownMenu pane insensitive. This approach has the advantage of still allowing the user to display the menu and see all the items, while making the items unavailable.

For example, take an editor program. If the user is not editing a file, it doesn't make sense to have the **Save** item in the **File** menu be selectable. Once the user starts editing a file, the **Save** button is sensitized so that the user can select it. Since the user cannot select the item until its sensitivity is reset, it is important that the application do so at the appropriate time. Another less realistic example, but one that we can demonstrate, involves a menu item that pops up a dialog. As long as that dialog is up, the user cannot reselect the menu item again. For purposes of this demonstration, let's say that the **Open** item pops up a FileSelection-Dialog and desensitizes itself. When the dialog is dismissed, the menu item is resensitized.†

To implement this behavior, we specify a callback routine for the **Open** menu item that creates a FileSelectionDialog and sets the item insensitive. We also specify a callback routine for the dialog box that resets the menu item's sensitivity. The code fragment in Example 15-6 shows these callback routines.

Example 15-6. The reset_sensitive() and open_callback() routines

```
/* reset_sensitive() -- generalized routine that resets the
 * sensitivity on the widget passed as the client_data parameter
 * in a call to XtAddCallback().
 */
void
reset_sensitive(w, client_data, call_data)
Widget w;
XtPointer client_data;
XtPointer call_data;
{
    Widget reset_widget = (Widget) client_data;

    XtSetSensitive (reset_widget, True);
}
```

---

† This behavior is not a great design. The dialog really should be cached, and the menu item should remain sensitive. If the item is reselected, the dialog should be remapped or raised to the top of the window stack, if necessary.

Example 15-6. The reset_sensitive() and open_callback() routines (continued)

```
/* open_callback() -- the callback routine for when the "Open"
 * menu item is selected from the "File" title in the MenuBar.
 */
void
open_callback(menu_item, client_data, call_data)
Widget menu_item;
XtPointer client_data;
XtPointer call_data;
{
    Widget dialog, parent = menu_item;

    /* Get the window manager shell widget associated with item */
    while (!XtIsWMShell (parent))
        parent = XtParent (parent);

    /* turn off the sensitivity for the Open button ... */
    XtSetSensitive (menu_item, False);
    dialog = XmCreateFileSelectionDialog (parent, "files", NULL, 0);

    /* Add callback routines to respond to OK button selection here. */

    /* Make sure that if the dialog is popped down or destroyed, the
     * menu_item's sensitivity is reset.
     */
    XtAddCallback (XtParent(dialog),  /* dialog's _parent_ */
        XmNpopdownCallback, reset_sensitive, menu_item);
    XtAddCallback (dialog, XmNdestroyCallback, reset_sensitive, menu_item);

    XtManageChild (dialog);
    XtPopup (XtParent (dialog), XtGrabNone);
}
```

The `open_callback()` function is called whenever the user activates the **Open** menu item on the **File** menu. The first thing `open_callback()` does is find the nearest WMShell widget associated with the menu item. We do not want the MenuShell here, as we need a non-transient widget to act as the parent for the FileSelectionDialog. If the menu item is used as the parent for the dialog, when the menu is popped down, the dialog is also popped down because it is a secondary window.

We set the menu item's sensitivity to `False`, which prevents the user from selecting the item again. In order to be notified when the FileSelectionDialog is dismissed, we add callback routines for `XmNpopdownCallback` and `XmNdestroyCallback`. In both cases, the **Open** menu item needs to be reset so that the user can select it again. The only thing in `open_callback()` is a callback function that opens the selected file when the user selects the **OK** button. This functionality is beyond the scope of this chapter; see Chapter 6, *Selection Dialogs*, for details.

15.3.7 Tear-Off Menus

Motif 1.2 provides a new feature that allows menus to be torn off and placed in separate windows. From the user's perspective, tear-off menus make it easy to make repeated menu selections. Normally, when the user posts a menu, it is only displayed until she makes a selection, and then it is removed. If the menu has been torn off, however, it is displayed in a separate window, and the user can make as many selections as she wants without having to repost it each time.

Tear-off behavior is provided for all of the Motif menu types, but the behavior is disabled by default. When tear-off functionality is enabled in a menu, the first item in the menu is a tear-off button. The button displays a dashed line to indicate that the user can tear off the menu, much as she would tear a coupon out of a newspaper. If the user selects the tear-off button, the menu is placed in a separate window with limited window manager decorations. The window can be moved, so the user can position it in a convenient location. The menu remains torn off until the user cancels the menu by pressing the ESCAPE key within the window.

Tear-off functionality is controlled by the XmNtearOffModel resource of the RowColumn widget. This resource is only valid when the RowColumn is being used as a PulldownMenu or a PopupMenu. The resource can have one of the following values: Xm-TEAR_OFF_ENABLED or XmTEAR_OFF_DISABLED. By default, the resource is set to XmTEAR_OFF_DISABLED, so if you want to provide tear-off functionality in the menus in your application, you must set the resource for all of your menu panes. Figure 15-11 shows a PulldownMenu both before and after being torn off.

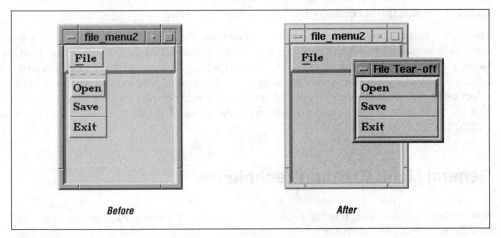

Figure 15-11. A PulldownMenu before and after being torn off

Motif does not install a resource converter for the XmNtearOffModel resource, but it does provide one that you can install if you want to specify the resource in a resource file. The XmRepTypeInstallTearOffModelConverter() routine installs the resource converter for XmNtearOffModel. This routine does not take any arguments, but it does win the award for the longest function name in the Motif toolkit. Once the converter is installed, you can use the following resource specification to enable tear-off functionality for all menus:

```
*tearOffModel: TEAR_OFF_ENABLED
```

The converter is not installed by default for backwards compatibility reasons.

Some applications use menus in such a way that they need to keep track of when the menu is popped up and popped down. For example, an application might use some ToggleButtons in a PulldownMenu to allow the user to set state variables for the program. If the application also provides another interface for changing the variables, such as a command-line, the application needs to know when the menu is popped up so that it can make sure the ToggleButtons are set appropriately.

Now let's say that this application is recompiled with Motif 1.2. If the resource converter for XmNtearOffModel were installed, the user could enable tear-off functionality, and that might cause the application to malfunction. If an application needs to keep track of the comings and goings of menus, it has to do extra work for tear-off menus. Since the converter is not installed by default, the programmer can decide whether or not to support tear-off functionality in this case. If the application is modified to support tear-off menus, then it can install the converter and allow the user to set the resource in a resource file. If your application does not require any special handling of menus, there is no reason not to enable tear-off functionality for all menus, as it really is a convenience to the user.

The RowColumn widget provides two new callback resources that allow an application to keep track of tear-off menus. The XmNtearOffMenuActivateCallback routine is called when a menu is torn off; XmNtearOffMenuDeactivateCallback is called when the torn-off menu is dismissed. These callbacks provide a way for you to perform any special processing that is necessary for handling tear-off menus.

Motif also provides access to the tear-off button with the XmGetTearOffControl() routine. This routine takes a menu pane and returns the widget ID of the tear-off button in the menu, if there is one. Otherwise the routine returns NULL. The tear-off button has a Separator-like appearance; you can specify its background, foreground, and top and bottom shadow colors using the standard resources, as well as the XmNseparatorType resource. You can also set these resources in a resource file using the name of the button, which is Tear-OffControl.

15.4 General Menu Creation Techniques

Now we have addressed each of the fundamental elements of the MenuBar and the resources used to provide the user with the appropriate feedback. Using this information, we can generalize the way we build MenuBars, enabling us to create arbitrarily large MenuBars and PulldownMenus using a substantially smaller amount of code.

In the examples that follow, we use many of the recommended elements for a standard Motif MenuBar. You can adjust the algorithms and data structures to fit the needs of your own application. Although we use hard-coded values for widget resources, this technique is by no means a requirement, nor should it be construed as recommended usage. If you choose to specify resources in a resource file, you should write an application defaults file that contains the appropriate resource values.

15.4.1 Building Pulldown Menus

Let's begin by identifying each of the attributes of a menu item:

- Label

- Mnemonic

- Accelerator

- Accelerator text

- Callback routine

- Callback data

Using this information, we can construct a data structure that describes all of the important aspects of a menu item. We define the `MenuItem` structure as follows:

```
typedef struct _menu_item {
    char        *label;        /* the label for the item */
    WidgetClass *class;        /* pushbutton, label, separator, ... */
    char        mnemonic;      /* mnemonic; NULL if none */
    char        *accelerator;  /* accelerator; NULL if none */
    char        *accel_text;   /* to be converted to compound string */
    void        (*callback)(); /* routine to call; NULL if none */
    XtPointer   callback_data; /* client_data for callback() */
} MenuItem;
```

To create a PulldownMenu, all we need to do is initialize an array of `MenuItem` structures and pass it to a routine that iterates through the array and creates the items using the appropriate information. For example, the following declaration describes the elements for a **File** menu:

```
MenuItem file_items[] = {
    { "New", &xmPushButtonGadgetClass, 'N',
        NULL, NULL, do_open, NEW },
    { "Open...", &xmPushButtonGadgetClass, 'O',
        NULL, NULL, do_open, OPEN },
    { "Save", &xmPushButtonGadgetClass, 'S',
        NULL, NULL, do_save, SAVE },
    { "Save As...", &xmPushButtonGadgetClass, 'A',
        NULL, NULL, do_save, SAVE_AS },
    { "Print...", &xmPushButtonGadgetClass, 'P',
        NULL, NULL, do_print, NULL },
    { "", &xmSeparatorGadgetClass, NULL,
        NULL, NULL, NULL, NULL },
    { "Exit", &xmPushButtonGadgetClass, 'x',
        "Ctrl<Key>C", "Ctrl+C", do_quit, NULL },
    NULL,
};
```

Each element in the `MenuItem` data structure is filled with default values for each menu item. If a resource value is not meaningful, or is not going to be hard-coded, we initialize the field to `NULL`. If you don't need a callback function or client data for an item, the field may be set to `NULL`. The only field that cannot be `NULL` is the widget class. The final terminating `NULL` in the `label` field indicates the end of the list.

We have not specified any accelerators except for the **Exit** item. The Separator gadget is completely unspecified, since none of the resources even apply to Separators. This design makes modification and maintenance very simple. If you want to add an accelerator for the **Save** item, all you need to do is change the appropriate fields in the data structure, instead of having to search through the source code looking for where that item is created.

One particular point of interest is the way the `WidgetClass` field is initialized. It is declared as a pointer to a widget class rather than just a widget class, so we initialize the field with the address of the widget class variable that is declared in the widget's header file. The use of `&xmPushButtonGadgetClass` is one such example. The structure must be initialized this way because the compiler requires a specific value in order to initialize a static data structure. The `xmPushButtonWidgetClass` pointer does not have a value until the program is actually running, but the address of the variable does have a value. Once the program is running, the pointer can be dereferenced to access the real PushButton widget class.

Now we can write a routine that uses the `MenuItem` data structure to create a Pulldown-Menu. The `BuildPulldownMenu()` function is shown in Example 15-7. The routine loops through each element in an array of pre-initialized `MenuItem` structures and creates menu items based on the information.†

Example 15-7. The BuildPulldownMenu() routine

```
Widget
BuildPulldownMenu(parent, menu_title, menu_mnemonic, tear_off, items)
Widget parent;
char *menu_title, menu_mnemonic;
Boolean tear_off;
MenuItem *items;
{
    Widget PullDown, cascade, widget;
    int i;
    XmString str;

    PullDown = XmCreatePulldownMenu (parent, "_pulldown", NULL, 0);
    if (tear_off)
        XtVaSetValues (PullDown, XmNtearOffModel, XmTEAR_OFF_ENABLED, NULL);
    str = XmStringCreateLocalized (menu_title);
    cascade = XtVaCreateManagedWidget (menu_title,
        xmCascadeButtonWidgetClass, parent,
        XmNsubMenuId,     PullDown,
        XmNlabelString,   str,
        XmNmnemonic,      menu_mnemonic,
        NULL);
    XmStringFree (str);
```

---

†`XmStringCreateLocalized()` is only available in Motif 1.2; `XmStringCreateSimple()` is the corresponding function in Motif 1.1. The `XmNtearOffModel` resource is only available in Motif 1.2; it should not be specified in Motif 1.1.

Example 15-7. The BuildPulldownMenu( ) routine (continued)

```
    /* Now add the menu items */
    for (i = 0; items[i].label != NULL; i++) {
        widget = XtVaCreateManagedWidget (items[i].label,
            *items[i].class, PullDown,
            NULL);
        if (items[i].mnemonic)
            XtVaSetValues (widget, XmNmnemonic, items[i].mnemonic, NULL);
        if (items[i].accelerator) {
            str = XmStringCreateLocalized (items[i].accel_text);
            XtVaSetValues (widget,
                XmNaccelerator, items[i].accelerator,
                XmNacceleratorText, str,
                NULL);
            XmStringFree (str);
        }
        if (items[i].callback)
            XtAddCallback (widget, XmNactivateCallback,
                items[i].callback, items[i].callback_data);
    }
    return cascade;
}
```

The function takes five parameters. `parent` is a handle to a MenuBar widget that must have already been created, `menu_title` indicates the title of the menu, `menu_mnemonic` specifies the mnemonic, `tear_off` indicates whether or not the menu can be torn off, and `items` is an array of `MenuItem` structures.

The first thing the routine does is create a PulldownMenu. Since the name of this widget is not terribly important, we use a predefined name, prefixed with an underscore, to indicate that the name is not intended to be referenced in a resource file. This use of the underscore is our own convention, by the way, not one adopted by the X Toolkit Intrinsics. We came up with this "unwritten rule" because Xt has no such naming conventions for widgets that do not wish to have their resources specified externally.

After creating the PulldownMenu, the routine creates the CascadeButton that acts as the title for the menu on the MenuBar. The name of the widget is taken from the second parameter, `menu_title`. The routine also sets the mnemonic and the `XmNtearOffModel` resource at this point. All MenuBar titles should have mnemonics associated with them.

Now the function loops through the array of `MenuItem` structures creating menu items until it finds an entry with a `NULL` label name. We use this value as an end-of-menu indicator in our initialization. When each widget is created, the mnemonic, accelerator, and callback function are added only if they are specified in the `MenuItem` structure.

`BuildPulldownMenu( )` must be called from another function that passes the appropriate data structures and other parameters. In our design, this would be the routine that creates the MenuBar itself. Example 15-8 shows the code for the `CreateMenuBar( )` routine. This simple function creates a MenuBar widget, calls `BuildPulldownMenu( )` for each menu, manages the MenuBar, and returns it to the calling function.

Example 15-8. The CreateMenuBar( ) function

```
Widget
CreateMenuBar(MainWindow)
Widget MainWindow;
{
    Widget MenuBar, widget, BuildPulldownMenu();

    MenuBar = XmCreateMenuBar (MainWindow, "MenuBar", NULL, 0);

    (void) BuildPulldownMenu (MenuBar, "File", 'F', True, file_items);
    (void) BuildPulldownMenu (MenuBar, "Edit", 'E', True, edit_items);
    (void) BuildPulldownMenu (MenuBar, "View", 'V', True, view_items);
    (void) BuildPulldownMenu (MenuBar, "Options", 'O', True, options_items);
    widget = BuildPulldownMenu (MenuBar, "Help", 'H', True, help_items);

    XtVaSetValues (MenuBar, XmNmenuHelpWidget, widget, NULL);

    XtManageChild (MenuBar);
    return MenuBar;
}
```

Each call to BuildPulldownMenu ( ) passes an array of pre-initialized MenuItem structures. The **Help** menu is a special case, so we set the XmNmenuHelpWidget resource to let the MenuBar know which item it is. By setting the resource to the CascadeButton returned by the function, the MenuBar knows that this button should be placed to the far right. The only parameter to the CreateMenuBar ( ) function is the MainWindow widget that is the parent of the MenuBar that is returned.

15.4.2 Building Cascading Menus

We can add pullright menus to our menu creation methodology quite easily by adding to the MenuItem data structure and making a slight modification to the CreatePulldown-Menu ( ) function. As we learned from the simple menu creation routines, a cascading menu is really a PulldownMenu that is associated with a CascadeButton. We also know that we can attach a menu to a CascadeButton by setting the XmNsubMenuId resource to the handle of the PulldownMenu. We begin by modifying the MenuItem structure as follows:

```
typedef struct _menu_item {
    char        *label;        /* the label for the item */
    WidgetClass *class;        /* pushbutton, label, separator... */
    char        mnemonic;      /* mnemonic; NULL if none */
    char        *accelerator;  /* accelerator; NULL if none */
    char        *accel_text;   /* to be converted to compound string */
    void        (*callback)(); /* routine to call; NULL if none */
    XtPointer   callback_data; /* client_data for callback() */
    struct _menu_item *subitems; /* pullright menu items, if not NULL */
} MenuItem;
```

The new field at the end of the structure is a pointer to another array of MenuItem structures. If this pointer is not NULL, the menu item has a cascading submenu that is described by subitems. Example 15-9 shows an example of creating a cascading menu. This program uses a modified version of `BuildPulldownMenu()` that calls itself to create cascading menus.†

Example 15-9. The build_menu.c program

```
/* build_menu.c -- Demonstrate the BuildPulldownMenu() routine and
 * how it can be used to build pulldown -and- pullright menus.
 * Menus are defined by declaring an array of MenuItem structures.
 */
#include <Xm/RowColumn.h>
#include <Xm/MainW.h>
#include <Xm/DrawingA.h>
#include <Xm/CascadeBG.h>
#include <Xm/PushB.h>
#include <Xm/PushBG.h>
#include <Xm/ToggleB.h>
#include <Xm/ToggleBG.h>

typedef struct _menu_item {
    char        *label;         /* the label for the item */
    WidgetClass *class;         /* pushbutton, label, separator... */
    char            mnemonic;   /* mnemonic; NULL if none */
    char        *accelerator;   /* accelerator; NULL if none */
    char        *accel_text;    /* to be converted to compound string */
    void        (*callback)();  /* routine to call; NULL if none */
    XtPointer   callback_data;  /* client_data for callback() */
    struct _menu_item *subitems; /* pullright menu items, if not NULL */
} MenuItem;

/* Pulldown menus are built from cascade buttons, so this function
 * also includes pullright menus.  Create the menu, the cascade button
 * that owns the menu, and then the submenu items.
 */
Widget
BuildPulldownMenu(parent, menu_title, menu_mnemonic, tear_off, items)
Widget parent;
char *menu_title, menu_mnemonic;
Boolean tear_off;
MenuItem *items;
{
    Widget PullDown, cascade, widget;
    int i;
    XmString str;

    PullDown = XmCreatePulldownMenu (parent, "_pulldown", NULL, 0);
    if (tear_off)
        XtVaSetValues (PullDown, XmNtearOffModel, XmTEAR_OFF_ENABLED, NULL);
    str = XmStringCreateLocalized (menu_title);
    cascade = XtVaCreateManagedWidget (menu_title,
        xmCascadeButtonGadgetClass, parent,
        XmNsubMenuId,   PullDown,
        XmNlabelString, str,
        XmNmnemonic,    menu_mnemonic,
```

---

†`XtSetLanguageProc()` is only available in X11R5; there is no corresponding function in X11R4. `Xm-StringCreateLocalized()` is only available in Motif 1.2; `XmStringCreateSimple()` is the corresponding function in Motif 1.1. The `XmNtearOffModel` resource is only available in Motif 1.2; it should not be specified in Motif 1.1.

Example 15-9. The build_menu.c program (continued)

```
            NULL);
        XmStringFree (str);

        /* Now add the menu items */
        for (i = 0; items[i].label != NULL; i++) {
            /* If subitems exist, create the pull-right menu by calling this
             * function recursively.  Since the function returns a cascade
             * button, the widget returned is used..
             */
            if (items[i].subitems)
                widget = BuildPulldownMenu (PullDown, items[i].label,
                    items[i].mnemonic, tear_off, items[i].subitems);
            else
                widget = XtVaCreateManagedWidget (items[i].label,
                    *items[i].class, PullDown,
                    NULL);
            /* Whether the item is a real item or a cascade button with a
             * menu, it can still have a mnemonic.
             */
            if (items[i].mnemonic)
                XtVaSetValues (widget, XmNmnemonic, items[i].mnemonic, NULL);
            /* any item can have an accelerator, except cascade menus. But,
             * we don't worry about that; we know better in our declarations.
             */
            if (items[i].accelerator) {
                str = XmStringCreateLocalized (items[i].accel_text);
                XtVaSetValues (widget,
                    XmNaccelerator, items[i].accelerator,
                    XmNacceleratorText, str,
                    NULL);
                XmStringFree (str);
            }
            if (items[i].callback)
                XtAddCallback(widget,
                    (items[i].class == &xmToggleButtonWidgetClass ||
                    items[i].class == &xmToggleButtonGadgetClass) ?
                        XmNvalueChangedCallback : /* ToggleButton class */
                        XmNactivateCallback,        /* PushButton class */
                    items[i].callback, items[i].callback_data);
        }
        return cascade;
}

/* callback functions for menu items declared later... */
void
set_weight(widget, client_data, call_data)
Widget widget;
XtPointer client_data;
XtPointer call_data;
{
    int weight = (int) client_data;

    printf ("Setting line weight to %d\n", weight);
}

set_color(widget, client_data, call_data)
Widget widget;
XtPointer client_data;
```

Example 15-9. The build_menu.c program (continued)

```
XtPointer call_data;
{
    char *color = (char *) client_data;

    printf ("Setting color to %s\n", color);
}

void
set_dot_dash(widget, client_data, call_data)
Widget widget;
XtPointer client_data;
XtPointer call_data;
{
    int dot_or_dash = (int) client_data;

    printf ("Setting line style to %s\n", dot_or_dash? "dot" : "dash");
}

MenuItem weight_menu[] = {
    { " 1 ", &xmPushButtonGadgetClass, '1', NULL, NULL,
        set_weight, (XtPointer) 1, (MenuItem *) NULL },
    { " 2 ", &xmPushButtonGadgetClass, '2', NULL, NULL,
        set_weight, (XtPointer) 2, (MenuItem *) NULL },
    { " 3 ", &xmPushButtonGadgetClass, '3', NULL, NULL,
        set_weight, (XtPointer) 3, (MenuItem *) NULL },
    { " 4 ", &xmPushButtonGadgetClass, '4', NULL, NULL,
        set_weight, (XtPointer) 4, (MenuItem *) NULL },
    NULL,
};

MenuItem color_menu[] = {
    { "Cyan", &xmPushButtonGadgetClass, 'C', "Alt<Key>C", "Alt+C",
        set_color, (XtPointer) "cyan", (MenuItem *) NULL },
    { "Yellow", &xmPushButtonGadgetClass, 'Y', "Alt<Key>Y", "Alt+Y",
        set_color, (XtPointer) "yellow", (MenuItem *) NULL },
    { "Magenta", &xmPushButtonGadgetClass, 'M', "Alt<Key>M", "Alt+M",
        set_color, (XtPointer) "magenta", (MenuItem *) NULL },
    { "Black", &xmPushButtonGadgetClass, 'B', "Alt<Key>B", "Alt+B",
        set_color, (XtPointer) "black", (MenuItem *) NULL },
    NULL,
};

MenuItem style_menu[] = {
    { "Dash", &xmPushButtonGadgetClass, 'D', NULL, NULL,
        set_dot_dash, (XtPointer) 0, (MenuItem *) NULL },
    { "Dot", &xmPushButtonGadgetClass, 'o', NULL, NULL,
        set_dot_dash, (XtPointer) 1, (MenuItem *) NULL },
    NULL,
};

MenuItem drawing_menus[] = {
    { "Line Weight", &xmCascadeButtonGadgetClass, 'W', NULL, NULL,
        0, 0, weight_menu },
    { "Line Color", &xmCascadeButtonGadgetClass, 'C', NULL, NULL,
        0, 0, color_menu },
    { "Line Style", &xmCascadeButtonGadgetClass, 'S', NULL, NULL,
        0, 0, style_menu },
    NULL,
};
```

Example 15-9. The build_menu.c program (continued)

```
main(argc, argv)
int argc;
char *argv[ ];
{
    Widget toplevel, main_w, menubar, drawing_a;
    XtAppContext app;

    XtSetLanguageProc (NULL, NULL, NULL);

    toplevel = XtVaAppInitialize (&app, "Demos", NULL, 0,
        &argc, argv, NULL, NULL);

    /* Create a MainWindow widget that contains a DrawingArea in
     * its work window.
     */
    main_w = XtVaCreateManagedWidget ("main_w",
        xmMainWindowWidgetClass, toplevel,
        XmNscrollingPolicy,  XmAUTOMATIC,
        NULL);

    menubar = XmCreateMenuBar (main_w, "menubar", NULL, 0);
    BuildPulldownMenu (menubar, "Lines", 'L', True, drawing_menus);
    XtManageChild (menubar);

    /* Create a DrawingArea -- no actual drawing will be done. */
    drawing_a = XtVaCreateManagedWidget ("drawing_a",
        xmDrawingAreaWidgetClass, main_w,
        XmNwidth, 500,
        XmNheight, 500,
        NULL);

    XtRealizeWidget (toplevel);
    XtAppMainLoop (app);
}
```

The majority of this program is composed of the new version of `BuildPulldownMenu ( )` and the menu and submenu declarations. All the menus and menu items are declared in reverse order because the cascading menu declaration must exist before the menu is actually referenced. The output of the program is shown in Figure 15-12.

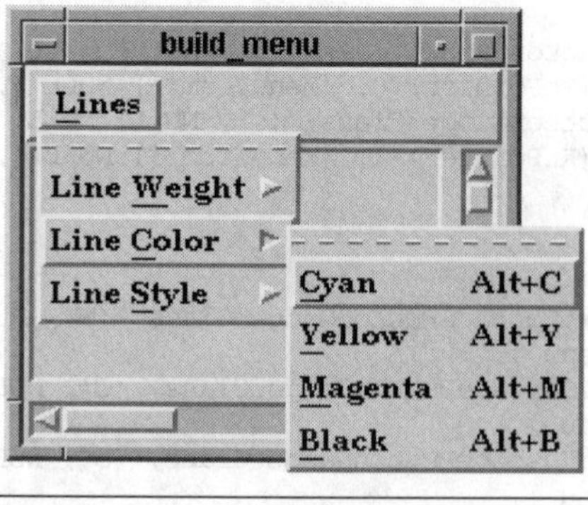

Figure 15-12. Output of build_menu.c

All we have to do to get `BuildPulldownMenu()` to create a cascading menu is add code that checks whether or not the current menu has a submenu. If it does, the routine calls itself to create the submenu. Because the function creates and returns a CascadeButton, the return value can be used as the menu item in the menu that is currently being built. We have to create the cascading menu first because it has to exist before it can be attached to a Cascade-Button. Recursion handles this problem for us by creating the deepest submenus first, which ensures that all the necessary submenus are built before their CascadeButtons require them.

We also added support for ToggleButtons to this version of `BuildPulldownMenu()`, even though our menus do not contain any ToggleButtons. The only change that we have to make here involves the callback function. Since ToggleButtons have an `XmNvalueChanged-Callback`, while PushButtons have an `XmNactivateCallback`, we check the class of the item being added and specify the appropriate callback resource in our call to `XtAdd-Callback()`.

15.4.3 Building Popup Menus

To further demonstrate the flexibility of our design and to exploit the similarities between PulldownMenus, PopupMenus, and cascading menus, we can easily modify the `Build-PulldownMenu()` routine to support any of these menu types. We only need to specify a new parameter indicating which of the two menu types to use. Since Motif already defines the values `XmMENU_PULLDOWN` and `XmMENU_POPUP` in *<Xm/Xm.h>*, we use those values. We have also given the function a more generic name, `BuildMenu()`, as shown in Example 15-10.†

Example 15-10. The BuildMenu() routine

```
Widget
BuildMenu(parent, menu_type, menu_title, menu_mnemonic, tear_off, items)
Widget parent;
int menu_type;
char *menu_title, menu_mnemonic;
Boolean tear_off;
MenuItem *items;
{
    Widget menu, cascade, widget;
    int i;
    XmString str;

    if (menu_type == XmMENU_PULLDOWN)
        menu = XmCreatePulldownMenu (parent, "_pulldown", NULL, 0);
    else
        menu = XmCreatePopupMenu (parent, "_popup", NULL, 0);
    if (tear_off)
        XtVaSetValues (menu, XmNtearOffModel, XmTEAR_OFF_ENABLED, NULL);

    if (menu_type == XmMENU_PULLDOWN) {
```

---

† `XmStringCreateLocalized()` is only available in Motif 1.2; `XmStringCreateSimple()` is the corresponding function in Motif 1.1. The `XmNtearOffModel` resource is only available in Motif 1.2; it should not be specified in Motif 1.1.

Example 15-10. The BuildMenu() routine (continued)

```
            str = XmStringCreateLocalized (menu_title);
            cascade = XtVaCreateManagedWidget (menu_title,
                xmCascadeButtonGadgetClass, parent,
                XmNsubMenuId,    menu,
                XmNlabelString,  str,
                XmNmnemonic,     menu_mnemonic,
                NULL);
            XmStringFree (str);
    }

    /* Now add the menu items */
    for (i = 0; items[i].label != NULL; i++) {
        /* If subitems exist, create the pull-right menu by calling this
         * function recursively.  Since the function returns a cascade
         * button, the widget returned is used..
         */
        if (items[i].subitems)
            widget = BuildMenu (menu, XmMENU_PULLDOWN, items[i].label,
                items[i].mnemonic, tear_off, items[i].subitems);
        else
            widget = XtVaCreateManagedWidget (items[i].label,
                *items[i].class, menu,
                NULL);
        /* Whether the item is a real item or a cascade button with a
         * menu, it can still have a mnemonic.
         */
        if (items[i].mnemonic)
            XtVaSetValues (widget, XmNmnemonic, items[i].mnemonic, NULL);
        /* any item can have an accelerator, except cascade menus. But,
         * we don't worry about that; we know better in our declarations.
         */
        if (items[i].accelerator) {
            str = XmStringCreateLocalized (items[i].accel_text);
            XtVaSetValues (widget,
                XmNaccelerator, items[i].accelerator,
                XmNacceleratorText, str,
                NULL);
            XmStringFree (str);
        }
        /* again, anyone can have a callback -- however, this is an
         * activate-callback.  This may not be appropriate for all items.
         */
        if (items[i].callback)
            XtAddCallback (widget,
                (items[i].class == &xmToggleButtonWidgetClass ||
                    items[i].class == &xmToggleButtonGadgetClass) ?
                        XmNvalueChangedCallback : /* ToggleButton class */
                        XmNactivateCallback,      /* PushButton class */
                    items[i].callback, items[i].callback_data);
    }
    return menu_type == XmMENU_POPUP ? menu : cascade;
}
```

All of the original functionality is maintained; we only added a couple of lines to support popup menus. Namely, when XmMENU_POPUP is passed as the menu_type parameter, the function XmCreatePopupMenu ( ) is called, and the menu itself is returned. Otherwise the routine returns a CascadeButton. If any of the menu items have cascading menus, we continue what we were doing before for submenus.

In order to use this routine in an application, we would have to create the PopupMenu as the child of another widget and set up a callback routine to post the menu, just as we did with the simple menu creation routine. Since mnemonics are not typically used for PopupMenus, the mnemonic fields in the data structure should be specified as NULL.

Now we can build PopupMenus, but what we really need to talk about is when you should use PopupMenus in an application. The *Motif Style Guide* has very little to say about when and how popup menus should be used. One guideline is that PopupMenus should only be used as a redundant means of activating application functionality, since they do not make themselves apparent to the user. The single requirement is that PopupMenus use the third mouse button, which leads to the question: how do you get the necessary events on an arbitrary widget so that you can pop up a menu?

In our previous PopupMenu examples, we have used the DrawingArea widget because of its ability to track such input events through a callback routine. However, for all other widgets, the solution is not so simple. Unfortunately, the design of PopupMenus in the Motif toolkit requires you to dig into lower-level Xt event-handling mechanisms in order to post a Popup-Menu. We can continue to build menus in the same way; it's just that we have to do a bit of work to pop them up.

Example 15-11 demonstrates how to display a PopupMenu for an arbitrary widget. Here, we use events in a PushButton widget to display a PopupMenu, but the menu could be triggered from any type of widget. This program uses the BuildMenu() routine from Example 15-10, so we do not show it in this example.†

Example 15-11. The popups.c program

```
/* popups.c -- demonstrate the use of a popup menus in an arbitrary
 * widget.  Display two PushButtons.  The second one has a popup
 * menu attached to it that is activated with the third
 * mouse button.
 */
#include <Xm/LabelG.h>
#include <Xm/PushBG.h>
#include <Xm/PushB.h>
#include <Xm/ToggleBG.h>
#include <Xm/ToggleB.h>
#include <Xm/SeparatoG.h>
#include <Xm/RowColumn.h>
#include <Xm/FileSB.h>
#include <Xm/CascadeBG.h>

Widget toplevel;
extern void exit();
void open_dialog_box();

/* callback for pushbutton activation */
void
put_string(w, client_data, call_data)
```

---

† XtSetLanguageProc() is only available in X11R5; there is no corresponding function in X11R4.

Example 15-11. The popups.c program (continued)

```
Widget w;
XtPointer client_data;
XtPointer call_data;
{
    String str = (String) client_data;

    puts (str);
}

typedef struct _menu_item {
    char        *label;
    WidgetClass *class;
    char         mnemonic;
    char        *accelerator;
    char        *accel_text;
    void        (*callback)();
    XtPointer    callback_data;
    struct _menu_item *subitems;
} MenuItem;

MenuItem file_items[] = {
    { "File Items", &xmLabelGadgetClass, NULL, NULL, NULL, NULL, NULL },
    { "_sep1", &xmSeparatorGadgetClass, NULL, NULL, NULL, NULL, NULL },
    { "New", &xmPushButtonGadgetClass, 'N', NULL, NULL,
        put_string, "New", NULL },
    { "Open...", &xmPushButtonGadgetClass, 'O', NULL, NULL,
        open_dialog_box, (XtPointer) XmCreateFileSelectionDialog, NULL },
    { "Save", &xmPushButtonGadgetClass, 'S', NULL, NULL,
        put_string, "Save", NULL },
    { "Save As...", &xmPushButtonGadgetClass, 'A', NULL, NULL,
        open_dialog_box, (XtPointer) XmCreateFileSelectionDialog, NULL },
    { "Exit", &xmPushButtonGadgetClass, 'x', "Ctrl<Key>C", "Ctrl+C",
        exit, NULL, NULL },
    NULL,
};

main(argc, argv)
int argc;
char *argv[];
{
    Widget BuildMenu(), button, rowcol, popup;
    XtAppContext app;
    extern void PostIt();

    XtSetLanguageProc (NULL, NULL, NULL);

    toplevel = XtVaAppInitialize (&app, "Demos", NULL, 0,
        &argc, argv, NULL, NULL);

    /* Build a RowColumn to contain two PushButtons */
    rowcol = XtVaCreateManagedWidget ("rowcol",
        xmRowColumnWidgetClass, toplevel,
        NULL);

    /* The first PushButton is a -gadget-, so we cannot popup a menu
     * from here!
     */
    button = XtVaCreateManagedWidget ("Button 1",
        xmPushButtonGadgetClass, rowcol, NULL);
```

Example 15-11. The popups.c program (continued)

```
    XtAddCallback (button, XmNactivateCallback, put_string, "Button 1");

    /* This PushButton is a widget, so it has its own window, so
     * we can pop up a menu from here by adding an event handler
     * specifically for the 3rd mouse button (motif compliance).
     */
    button = XtVaCreateManagedWidget ("Button 2",
        xmPushButtonWidgetClass, rowcol,
        NULL);
    /* it can still have its callback! */
    XtAddCallback (button, XmNactivateCallback, put_string, "Button 2");

    /* build the menu... */
    popup = BuildMenu(button, XmMENU_POPUP, "Stuff", NULL,
        True, file_items);
    /* Add the event handler (PostIt()) and pass the newly created menu
     * as the client_data.  This is done to avoid using unnecessary globals.
     */
    XtAddEventHandler (button, ButtonPressMask, False, PostIt, popup);

    XtRealizeWidget (toplevel);
    XtAppMainLoop (app);
}
/* PostIt() -- event handler for the 3rd mouse button on the
 * PushButton widget's window.
 */
void
PostIt(pb, client_data, event)
Widget pb;
XtPointer client_data;
XEvent *event;
{
    Widget popup = (Widget) client_data;
    XButtonPressedEvent *bevent = (XButtonPressedEvent *) event;

    if (bevent->button != 3)
        return;
    /* position the menu at the location of the button press.  If we wanted
     * to position it elsewhere, we could change the x,y fields of the
     * event structure.
     */
    XmMenuPosition (popup, bevent);
    XtManageChild (popup);
}

/* open_dialog_box() -- callback for some of the menu items declared
 * in the MenuItem struct.   The client data is the creation function
 * for the dialog.  Associate the dialog with the menu
 * item via XmNuserData so we don't have to keep a global and
 * don't have to repeatedly create one.
 */
void
open_dialog_box(w, client_data, call_data)
Widget w;
XtPointer client_data;
XtPointer call_data;
{
```

Example 15-11. The popups.c program (continued)

```
    Widget (*func)(); = client_data;
    Widget dialog = NULL;

    /* first see if this menu item's dialog has been created yet */
    XtVaGetValues(w, XmNuserData, &dialog, NULL);

    if (!dialog) {
        /* menu item hasn't been chosen yet -- create the dialog.
         * Use the toplevel as the parent because we don't want the
         * parent of a dialog to be a menu item.
         */
        dialog = (*func)(toplevel, "dialog", NULL, 0);

        XtVaSetValues (XtParent (dialog), XmNtitle, XtName (w), NULL);
    XtVaSetValues (dialog, XmNautoUnmanage, True, NULL);

        /* store the newly created dialog in the XmNuserData for the menu
         * item for easy retrieval next time. (see get-values above.)
         */
        XtVaSetValues (w, XmNuserData, dialog, NULL);
    }

    XtManageChild (dialog);
    XtPopup (XtParent (dialog), XtGrabNone);
    /* If the dialog was already open, XtPopup does nothing.  In
     * this case, at least make sure the window is raised to the top
     * of the window tree (or as high as it can get).
     */
    XRaiseWindow (XtDisplay (dialog), XtWindow (XtParent (dialog)));
}
```

The output of the program is shown in Figure 15-13.

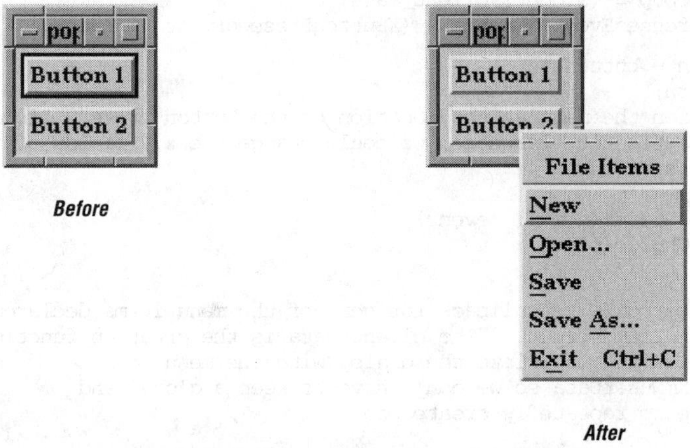

Figure 15-13. Output of popups.c

The program displays two PushButtons, one of which is a gadget and the other a widget. We get the `ButtonPress` event by specifically asking for it using `XtAddEventHandler()`.

This routine requires a widget because it needs a window. To add an event handler for a gadget, you would have to install it on the gadget's parent, which is a manager widget. Anytime a `ButtonPress` event occurs in the manager, the event handler would be called, so the event handler would have to check the coordinates of the event and see if it happened within the boundaries of the gadget. This technique would work, but it is beyond the scope of this simple demonstration.

`XtAddEventHandler()` takes the following form:

```
void XtAddEventHandler(w, event_mask, nonmaskable,
        proc, client_data)
    Widget w;
    EventMask event_mask;
    Boolean nonmaskable;
    XtEventHandler proc;
    XtPointer client_data;
```

The *widget* parameter specifies the widget on which the event handler is to be installed, while *event_mask* identifies the events that are being handled. We specify `Button-PressMask` to indicate that we are interested in `ButtonPress` events. The *nonmaskable* argument indicates whether or not the event handler should be called on non-maskable events. We specify `False` since we are not interested in the events. The final arguments specify the event handler routine and the client data that is passed to it. In our case, we specify the `PostIt()` routine and pass it the PopupMenu as client data. See Volume Four, *X Toolkit Intrinsics Programming Manual*, for a complete list of event masks and more detailed information about `XtAddEventHandler()`.

An event handler routine takes the following form:

```
void
event_handler(widget, client_data, event)
    Widget      widget;
    XtPointer   client_data;
    XEvent      *event;
```

In the `PostIt()` event handler, we check which button produced the `ButtonPress` event. If it wasn't the third button, we simply return. To pop up the menu, we need to position the menu and then manage the menu pane. To position it, we use `XmMenu-Position()`, which takes the following form:

```
void
XmMenuPosition(widget, event)
    Widget widget;
    XButtonPressedEvent *event;
```

Since the *event* parameter for this function is defined to be of type `XButtonPressed-Event`, you may run into problems if you try to use another type of event. The `x_root` and `y_root` fields in the event structure are used to position the menu appropriately, since these fields indicate the position where the mouse button was pressed. You could modify these fields to position the menu elsewhere, but we recommend restraint.

In order to actually pop up the menu, we call `XtManageChild()` on the PopupMenu. Motif treats PopupMenus just like dialog widgets with respect to their shell parents. Although the visible PopupMenu is a RowColumn widget, it has an invisible MenuShell parent. As with dialogs, when you call `XtManageChild()`, the RowColumn checks its

XmNrowColumnType resource to see if it is a PopupMenu. If it is, the widget checks to see if its parent is a MenuShell and if so, it automatically calls XtPopup() on the MenuShell.

The RowColumn widget has a resource that you can set on PopupMenus called XmNmenu-Post, which allows you to specify an alternate button to post the menu. As of Motif 1.2, if you specify this resource and then simply position and manage the menu in an event handler, the toolkit takes care of checking the event to make sure it matches the event description for the XmNmenuPost resource.†

You may have noticed that the PopupMenu shown in Figure 15-13 has accelerators associated with it. These accelerators only take effect if the input focus is in the widget that contains the menu.

The only time you should ever add an event handler to pop up a menu is when you are using a PopupMenu. You should not attach PulldownMenus or OptionMenus to arbitrary Motif widgets. It is also inappropriate to use a PopupMenu on a CascadeButton, since it already has a menu associated with it.

15.4.4 Building Option Menus

In this final section on generalized menu creation methods, we examine how to create OptionMenus using the BuildMenu() function. In this case, the underlying function is XmCreateOptionMenu(), which is another convenience routine provided by the Motif toolkit. The routine creates a RowColumn widget that manages the Label and Cascade-Button widgets that define the OptionMenu, but we must create the actual PulldownMenu ourselves. The final version of the BuildMenu() function is shown in Example 15-12.

Example 15-12. The build_option.c program

```
/* build_option.c -- The final version of BuildMenu() is used to
 * build popup, option, pulldown -and- pullright menus.  Menus are
 * defined by declaring an array of MenuItem structures as usual.
 */
#include <Xm/MainW.h>
#include <Xm/ScrolledW.h>
#include <Xm/PanedW.h>
#include <Xm/RowColumn.h>
#include <Xm/DrawingA.h>
#include <Xm/CascadeBG.h>
#include <Xm/ToggleB.h>
#include <Xm/ToggleBG.h>
#include <Xm/PushB.h>
#include <Xm/PushBG.h>

typedef struct _menu_item {
    char        *label;         /* the label for the item */
```

---

† In earlier releases of Motif, setting this resource could cause the server to hang, so we don't recommend using it unless you are using Motif 1.2.

Example 15-12. The build_option.c program (continued)

```
    WidgetClass *class;      /* pushbutton, label, separator... */
    char        mnemonic;    /* mnemonic; NULL if none */
    char        *accelerator; /* accelerator; NULL if none */
    char        *accel_text;  /* to be converted to compound string */
    void        (*callback)(); /* routine to call; NULL if none */
    XtPointer   callback_data; /* client_data for callback() */
    struct _menu_item *subitems; /* pullright menu items, if not NULL */
} MenuItem;

/* Build popup, option and pulldown menus, depending on the menu_type.
 * It may be XmMENU_PULLDOWN, XmMENU_OPTION or  XmMENU_POPUP.  Pulldowns
 * return the CascadeButton that pops up the menu.  Popups return the menu.
 * Option menus are created, but the RowColumn that acts as the option
 * "area" is returned unmanaged. (The user must manage it.)
 * Pulldown menus are built from cascade buttons, so this function
 * also builds pullright menus.  The function also adds the right
 * callback for PushButton or ToggleButton menu items.
 */
Widget
BuildMenu(parent, menu_type, menu_title, menu_mnemonic, tear_off, items)
Widget parent;
int menu_type;
char *menu_title, menu_mnemonic;
Boolean tear_off;
MenuItem *items;
{
    Widget menu, cascade, widget;
    int i;
    XmString str;

    if (menu_type == XmMENU_PULLDOWN || menu_type == XmMENU_OPTION)
        menu = XmCreatePulldownMenu (parent, "_pulldown", NULL, 0);
    else if (menu_type == XmMENU_POPUP)
        menu = XmCreatePopupMenu (parent, "_popup", NULL, 0);
    else {
        XtWarning ("Invalid menu type passed to BuildMenu()");
        return NULL;
    }
    if (tear_off)
        XtVaSetValues (menu, XmNtearOffModel, XmTEAR_OFF_ENABLED, NULL);

    /* Pulldown menus require a cascade button to be made */
    if (menu_type == XmMENU_PULLDOWN) {
        str = XmStringCreateLocalized (menu_title);
        cascade = XtVaCreateManagedWidget (menu_title,
            xmCascadeButtonGadgetClass, parent,
            XmNsubMenuId,   menu,
            XmNlabelString, str,
            XmNmnemonic,    menu_mnemonic,
            NULL);
        XmStringFree (str);
    }
    else if (menu_type == XmMENU_OPTION) {
        /* Option menus are a special case, but not hard to handle */
        Arg args[5];
        int n = 0;
        str = XmStringCreateLocalized (menu_title);
```

Example 15-12. The build_option.c program (continued)

```
        XtSetArg (args[n], XmNsubMenuId, menu); n++;
        XtSetArg (args[n], XmNlabelString, str); n++;
        /* This really isn't a cascade, but this is the widget handle
         * we're going to return at the end of the function.
         */
        cascade = XmCreateOptionMenu (parent, menu_title, args, n);
        XmStringFree (str);
    }

    /* Now add the menu items */
    for (i = 0; items[i].label != NULL; i++) {
        /* If subitems exist, create the pull-right menu by calling this
         * function recursively.  Since the function returns a cascade
         * button, the widget returned is used..
         */
        if (items[i].subitems)
            if (menu_type == XmMENU_OPTION) {
                XtWarning ("You can't have submenus from option menu items.");
                continue;
            }
            else
                widget = BuildMenu (menu, XmMENU_PULLDOWN, items[i].label,
                        items[i].mnemonic, tear_off, items[i].subitems);
        else
            widget = XtVaCreateManagedWidget (items[i].label,
                    *items[i].class, menu,
                    NULL);

        /* Whether the item is a real item or a cascade button with a
         * menu, it can still have a mnemonic.
         */
        if (items[i].mnemonic)
            XtVaSetValues (widget, XmNmnemonic, items[i].mnemonic, NULL);

        /* any item can have an accelerator, except cascade menus. But,
         * we don't worry about that; we know better in our declarations.
         */
        if (items[i].accelerator) {
            str = XmStringCreateLocalized (items[i].accel_text);
            XtVaSetValues (widget,
                    XmNaccelerator, items[i].accelerator,
                    XmNacceleratorText, str,
                    NULL);
            XmStringFree (str);
        }

        if (items[i].callback)
            XtAddCallback (widget,
                    (items[i].class == &xmToggleButtonWidgetClass ||
                     items[i].class == &xmToggleButtonGadgetClass) ?
                        XmNvalueChangedCallback : /* ToggleButton class */
                        XmNactivateCallback,      /* PushButton class */
                    items[i].callback, items[i].callback_data);
    }

    /* for popup menus, just return the menu; pulldown menus, return
     * the cascade button; option menus, return the thing returned
     * from XmCreateOptionMenu().  This isn't a menu, or a cascade button!
```

Example 15-12. The build_option.c program (continued)

```
    */
    return menu_type == XmMENU_POPUP ? menu : cascade;
}

MenuItem drawing_shapes[] = {
    { "Lines", &xmPushButtonGadgetClass, 'L', NULL, NULL, 0, 0, NULL },
    { "Circles", &xmPushButtonGadgetClass, 'C', NULL, NULL, 0, 0, NULL },
    { "Squares", &xmPushButtonGadgetClass, 'S', NULL, NULL, 0, 0, NULL },
    NULL,
};

main(argc, argv)
int argc;
char *argv[];
{
    Widget toplevel, main_w, pane, sw, drawing_a, menu, option_menu;
    void input();
    XtAppContext app;
    XtWidgetGeometry geom;

    XtSetLanguageProc (NULL, NULL, NULL);

    toplevel = XtVaAppInitialize (&app, "Demos", NULL, 0,
        &argc, argv, NULL, NULL);

    main_w = XtVaCreateManagedWidget ("main_w",
        xmMainWindowWidgetClass, toplevel, NULL);

    /* Use a PanedWindow widget as the work area of the main window */
    pane = XtVaCreateWidget ("pane", xmPanedWindowWidgetClass, main_w, NULL);

    /* create the option menu -- don't forget to manage it. */
    option_menu = BuildMenu (pane, XmMENU_OPTION, "Shapes",
        'S', True, drawing_shapes);
    XtManageChild (option_menu);

    /* Set the OptionMenu so that it can't be resized */
    geom.request_mode = CWHeight;
    XtQueryGeometry (option_menu, NULL, &geom);
    XtVaSetValues (option_menu,
        XmNpaneMinimum, geom.height,
        XmNpaneMaximum, geom.height,
        NULL);

    /* The scrolled window (which contains the drawing area) is a child
     * of the PanedWindow; its sibling, the option menu, cannot be resized,
     * so if the user resizes the toplevel shell, *this* window will resize.
     */
    sw = XtVaCreateManagedWidget ("sw",
        xmScrolledWindowWidgetClass, pane,
        XmNscrollingPolicy,  XmAUTOMATIC,
        NULL);
    /* Create a DrawingArea -- no actual drawing will be done. */
    drawing_a = XtVaCreateManagedWidget ("drawing_a",
        xmDrawingAreaWidgetClass, sw,
        XmNwidth, 500,
        XmNheight, 500,
        NULL);

    XtManageChild (pane);
```

Example 15-12. The build_option.c program (continued)

```
    XtRealizeWidget (toplevel);
    XtAppMainLoop (app);
}
```

There are two particularly interesting features of this program. First, of course, is the modifi-cation of the `BuildMenu()` function. As the comments in the code indicate, the function now fully supports all of the Motif menu types. We use `XmCreatePulldownMenu()` to create the menu pane that is posted from the CascadeButton of the OptionMenu. This menu pane is attached to the OptionMenu by setting the `XmNsubMenuId` as usual. As we loop through the menu items that are to be placed in the menu, we prevent the creation of a pullright menu in an OptionMenu, as cascading menus are not allowed in OptionMenus.

When `BuildMenu()` is used to create an OptionMenu, the function returns the Row-Column widget that is returned by `XmCreateOptionMenu()`, even though it is not really a CascadeButton as the variable name might indicate. The calling function needs the Row-Column widget so that it can manage the OptionMenu by calling `XtManageChild()`. (The call to `XtManageChild()` might be another automated part of `BuildMenu()` if you want to modify it.)

The other interesting feature of the program is the layout of the MainWindow. The Main-Window widget has a single PanedWindow widget as its child because we wish to retain the vertical stacking relationship between the OptionMenu and the DrawingArea. Another advantage of using the PanedWindow is that we can set the maximum and minimum height of each pane. The user can resize the entire window using the window manager, but we don't want the OptionMenu to change size, so we allow the ScrolledWindow to absorb the size fluctuations.

15.5 Summary

Menus are basically simple objects that provide the user with access to application func-tionality. While the simple menu creation routines are handy for basic prototyping and other simple application constructs, their usefulness is limited once you begin to develop larger-scale applications.

We have described the design of a general menu creation routine, so it should be clear that you only need two things to create an arbitrary number of menus: predefined arrays of `MenuItem` structures and the `BuildMenu()` function. Since initializing an array of `MenuItem` objects is very simple, our method is convenient and also more powerful than the simple menu creation routines. We have defined our own data type and generalized the rou-tine to build menus so that you can use and modify these functions however you like, to con-form to the needs of your application.

15.6 Exercises

This chapter could go on forever discussing more and more things you can do with menus. However, the goal was to present you with the fundamental concepts and design considerations behind menus. From this information, you should be able to teach yourself new techniques that we haven't touched upon. In that spirit, you should be able to do the following exercises based on the material covered in this chapter.

1. Create a MainWindow widget that has a MenuBar that contains at least the **File**, **Edit**, and **Help** menus, an OptionMenu, and a PopupMenu that pops up from a DrawingArea widget. First implement the menus using the simple menu creation routines, and then implement them using the `BuildMenu()` function.

2. Initialize a `MenuItem` structure whose fields are all set to NULL except for the menu items' names, callback routines, and widget classes, and then write a resource file that generates a usable menu.

3. Modify the `MenuItem` structure and the `BuildMenu` routine so that you can specify the initial sensitivity for menu items.

4. Modify `BuildMenu()` to recognize when the menu it is about to build is a RadioBox. You may choose to implement this behavior by passing a new parameter to the function or by examining the children in the `MenuItem` list to see if they are ToggleButtons. You will need to modify the `MenuItem` structure by adding another `Boolean` field to allow each element to indicate whether it is a radio button or a plain ToggleButton. See Chapter 4, *The Main Window*, for a discussion of RadioBoxes in menus.

16

Interacting With the
Window Manager

This chapter provides additional information on the relationship between shell widgets and the Motif window manager (mwm). It discusses shell widget resources and describes how to use functions in the Motif toolkit to add and modify window manager protocols.

In This Chapter:

Interacting With the Window Manager

This chapter provides technical details about how Motif applications can interact with the window manager. It discusses when and how to interpret special window manager events and client messages, how to set shell resources that act as hints to the window manager, and how to add protocols for communication between the application and the window manager. In the course of the discussion, we cover the major features of the X Toolkit Intrinsics' WMShell widget class, which handles basic window manager communication, and Motif's VendorShell widget, which handles window manager events that are specific to the Motif window manager (*mwm*).

The material in this chapter is advanced; you should typically not interfere with the predefined interactions between an application and the Motif window manager. When you do so, you risk interfering with the uniform look and feel that is at the heart of a graphical user interface such as Motif. However, the material in this chapter should provide you with an understanding of some important concepts that may allow you to make your applications more robust. This chapter also discusses the use of protocols and client messages for window manager communication. These techniques can be used for communication between instances of the same application or between suites of cooperating applications.

16.1 Interclient Communication

The X Window System is designed so that any user-interface style can be imposed on the display. The X libraries (Xlib and Xt) provide the mechanisms for applications to decide for themselves how to display information and how to react to user-generated actions. It is left up to graphical user interface specifications such as Motif to standardize most of these decisions. However, in order to preserve a baseline of interoperability, there are certain standards that an application must conform to if it is to be considered a "good citizen" of the desktop. These standards are referred to as interclient communication conventions. While X makes no suggestions about the way an application should look or act, it does have a lot to say about how it interacts with other applications on the user's display.

One such convention is that all applications must negotiate the sizes and positions of their windows with the window manager, rather than with one another. The window manager is, in essence, the ultimate ruler of the desktop. While it is mostly benevolent, its primary function is to prevent anarchy on the display. Communication with the window manager has various forms. Applications can talk directly to the window manager, or the window manager may initiate a conversation with an application. When the user selects a item from the window menu or issues other window manager commands, he or she initiates communication between the window manager and the application. Much of the communication between the window manager and the application is carried on in terms of *properties* and *protocols.*

A property is an arbitrary-length piece of data associated with a window. It is stored on the server identified by a unique integer value called an Atom.† An application sets properties on its windows as a way of communicating with the window manager or other applications. Some properties are referred to as "window manager hints" because the window manager doesn't have to obey them. For example, an application can specify the preferred size of its top-level window, but the window manager might use this value only in the absence of any other instructions from the user.

A window manager protocol is an agreed-upon procedure for the exchange of messages between the window manager and an application. Protocols are implemented with Client-Message events; the window manager sends an event to the application, and the application takes the appropriate action. For example, a protocol exchange occurs when the user selects **Close** from the window menu to close an application window.

There are low-level Xlib routines for setting and getting the value of window properties. However, the various shell widgets provided by Xt and Motif define resources that access most of the predefined properties of interest in window manager/application interaction. These resources are the preferred interface to window properties.

The WMShell widget defines many of the generic properties that are used for communication with the window manager. For example, you can use WMShell resources to specify an icon pixmap and resize increment values. The VendorShell widget class is defined by Xt as the widget class in which a vendor can define appearance and behavior resources specific to its own window manager. As such, this widget class is customized by every vendor of Xt-compatible toolkits. In the case of Motif, the VendorShell class provides resources that control the layout and operation of the Motif window manager decorations, and it supports the Motif window manager protocols.

You never instantiate WMShell or VendorShell widgets; they exist only as supporting classes for other shells, such as TopLevelShells, ApplicationShells, and DialogShells. However, you frequently need to set WMShell and VendorShell resources on other types of shell widgets. Remember that the MenuShell widget is not a subclass of VendorShell and WMShell, so it does not have the same provisions for window manager interaction. You can use the Xt-IsVendorShell() macro defined in *<X11/Intrinsic.h>*, to determine if a widget is a subclass of VendorShell. Similarly, the XtIsWMShell() macro indicates whether or not a widget is a subclass of WMShell. Once you have a handle to a shell widget, you can specify both generic and Motif-resources for it.

---

† Atoms are used to avoid the overhead of passing property names as arbitrary-length strings. See Volume One, *Xlib Programming Manual*, and Volume Four, *X Toolkit Intrinsics Programming Manual*, for a detailed discussion of properties and atoms.

16.2 Shell Resources

As discussed in Chapter 3, *Overview of the Motif Toolkit*, the WMShell widget class handles standard window manager/application communications as established by the *Inter-Client Communications Conventions Manual* (ICCCM). This document, which can be found in Appendix L of Volume Zero, *X Protocol Reference Manual*, describes the standards set forth by the X Consortium for all interclient communication. Such conventions are necessary because the window manager and a client application are two separate programs. Applications and window managers need to follow these standards to maintain order in the X world.

To give you an idea of the kinds of properties in which the window manager is interested, Table 16-1 shows a partial list of properties that are handled automatically by shells.

Table 16-1. Some Window Manager Properties

Atom	Meaning
WM_NAME	The name of the window
WM_CLASS	The class name of the window
WM_NORMAL_HINTS	Information about the size of the window
WM_ICON_NAME	The name of the icon for the window
WM_HINTS	Information about the icon pixmap, icon position, and input model for the window

Xlib provides functions for modifying the values of these atoms on a window so that you can change the visual appearance, size, position, or functionality of the window.† However, the job of the WMShell is to hide this interface from the programmer by providing resources that accomplish the same tasks. The next few sections describe how most of the common resources can be used. While we do not cover all of the WMShell resources here, most of the ones we have omitted are intuitive, so they do not require a great deal of explanation. See the WMShell reference page in Volume Six B, *Motif Reference Manual*, for a complete list of resources.

16.2.1 Shell Positions

You can position a shell at a specific location on the screen using the XmNx and XmNy resources. In addition, you can set the XmNx and XmNy resources of the immediate child of a shell widget to position the shell. This feature exists because Motif dialogs are designed to make their shell widgets invisible to the programmer. It is typically easier to set these resources directly on the child of a shell, as you are more likely to have a handle to that

---

† See Volume Zero, *X Protocol Reference Manual*, for complete details on the properties that can be set on windows; see Volume One, *Xlib Programming Manual*, for details on how to set or get these properties.

widget. The following code fragment shows how you can position a MessageDialog in the center of the screen:

```
Widget dialog, parent;
Dimension width, height;
Screen screen = XtScreen (parent);
Position x, y;

dialog = XmCreateMessageDialog (parent, "dialog", NULL, 0);

/* get width and height of dialog */
XtVaGetValues (dialog,
    XmNwidth, &width,
    XmNheight, &height,
    NULL);

/* center the dialog on the screen */
x = (WidthOfScreen (screen) / 2) - (width / 2);
y = (HeightOfScreen (screen) / 2) - (height / 2);
XtVaSetValues (dialog,
    XmNx, x,
    XmNy, y,
    NULL);
```

You can position a dialog in this way because the Motif BulletinBoard widget passes positional information to its shell parent. See Chapter 5, *Introduction to Dialogs*, and Chapter 7, *Custom Dialogs*, for further discussion. In most cases, you shouldn't be setting the XmNx and XmNy resources for a dialog because it is the job of the window manager to position shells. The user can also have some say in how placement should be handled. For example, if the user has set the `interactivePlacement` resource for *mwm* to True, he gets to place the window himself when it first appears. If you set the position of the window, then you are interfering with the positioning method preferred by the user.

16.2.2 Shell Sizes

In some situations, an application may want to prevent one of its windows from growing or shrinking beyond certain geometrical limits. For example, an application might want to keep a dialog box from getting so small that some of its elements are clipped. A paint application might want to restrict its top-level window from growing larger than the size of its canvas. An application can also constrain the increments by which the user can interactively resize the window. For example, *xterm* only allows itself to be resized in character-size increments, where the character size is defined by the font being used.

The WMShell defines the following resources that can be used to constrain the size of a window:

```
XmNminWidth
XmNmaxWidth
XmNminHeight
XmNmaxHeight
XmNwidthInc
XmNheightInc
XmNbaseWidth
XmNbaseHeight
```

The XmNminWidth, XmNmaxWidth, XmNminHeight, and XmNmaxHeight resources specify the minimum and maximum width and height for the shell. The XmNwidthInc and XmNheightInc resources control the pixel incrementals by which the window changes when it is being resized by the user. When *mwm* provides visual feedback during a resize operation, it specifies the width and height in terms of these increments, rather than pixels. The XmNbaseWidth and XmNbaseHeight resources specify the base values that are used when calculating the preferred size of the shell.

Example 16-1 demonstrates incremental resizing. The application displays a shell widget that contains a PushButton. When you click on the button, it displays the size of the window in pixels, but when you resize the window, the *mwm* feedback window displays the size in terms of XmNwidthInc and XmNheightInc.†

Example 16-1. The resize_shell.c program

```c
/* resize_shell.c -- demonstrate the max and min heights and widths.
 * This program should be run to really see how mwm displays the
 * size of the window as it is resized.
 */
#include <Xm/PushB.h>

main(argc, argv)
int argc;
char *argv[];
{
    Widget toplevel, button;
    XtAppContext app;
    extern void getsize();

    XtSetLanguageProc (NULL, NULL, NULL);

    toplevel = XtVaAppInitialize (&app, "Demos",
        NULL, 0, &argc, argv, NULL,
        XmNminWidth,    75,
        XmNminHeight,   25,
        XmNmaxWidth,    150,
        XmNmaxHeight,   100,
        XmNbaseWidth,   5,
        XmNbaseHeight,  5,
        XmNwidthInc,    5,
        XmNheightInc,   5,
        NULL);
```

---

†XtSetLanguageProc() is only available in X11R5; there is no corresponding function in X11R4.

Example 16-1. The resize_shell.c program (continued)

```
    /* Pushbutton's callback prints the dimensions of the shell. */
    button = XtVaCreateManagedWidget ("Print Size",
        xmPushButtonWidgetClass, toplevel, NULL);
    XtAddCallback (button, XmNactivateCallback, getsize, toplevel);

    XtRealizeWidget (toplevel);
    XtAppMainLoop (app);
}

void
getsize(widget, client_data, call_data)
Widget widget;
XtPointer client_data;
XtPointer call_data;
{
    Widget shell = (Widget) client_data;
    Dimension width, height;

    XtVaGetValues (shell,
        XmNwidth, &width,
        XmNheight, &height,
        NULL);
    printf ("Width = %d, Height = %d\n", width, height);
}
```

In our example, we arbitrarily specify the minimum and maximum extents of the shell. The width and height increments are each set to five, so the user can only resize the window in five-pixel increments. As the window is resized, the feedback window displays the size according to these incremental units, rather than using pixel values. If you run *resize_shell*, you can press the PushButton to print the size of the shell in pixels and compare that size with the size reported by the window manager. If you are going to specify the various size resources for a shell, it only makes sense to hard-code the values as we have done here. If you specify the resources in an app-defaults file, the user can override the settings, which defeats the whole point of setting them.

The problem with specifying minimum and maximum extents is that most real applications contain many components whose sizes cannot be computed easily, making it difficult to determine exactly how large or small the window should be. If the fonts and strings for Push-Buttons, Labels, and ToggleButtons can be set in a resource file, the equation becomes far too difficult to calculate before the window is actually created and displayed. Incremental width and height values are even more difficult to estimate because there are margins, border widths, and other resources to consider.

However, all is not lost. If you need to constrain the size of an application, you should consider whether the application's default initial size can be considered either its maximum or minimum size. If so, you can allow the window to come up using default size and trap for `ConfigureNotify` events on the shell widget. You can then use the default width and height reported in that event as your minimum or maximum size, as demonstrated in Example 16-2.†

---

†XtSetLanguageProc() is only available in X11R5; there is no corresponding function in X11R4.

Example 16-2. The set_minimum.c program

```
/* set_minimum.c -- demonstrate how to set the minimum size of a
 * window to its initial size.  This method is useful if your program
 * is initially displayed at its minimum size, but it would be too
 * difficult to try to calculate ahead of time what the initial size
 * would be.
 */
#include <Xm/PushB.h>

void getsize(), configure();

main(argc, argv)
int argc;
char *argv[];
{
    Widget toplevel, button;
    XtAppContext app;

    XtSetLanguageProc (NULL, NULL, NULL);

    toplevel = XtVaAppInitialize (&app, "Demos",
        NULL, 0, &argc, argv, NULL,
        XmNmaxWidth,     150,
        XmNmaxHeight,    100,
        XmNbaseWidth,    5,
        XmNbaseHeight,   5,
        XmNwidthInc,     5,
        XmNheightInc,    5,
        NULL);

    /* Add an event handler to trap the first configure event */
    XtAddEventHandler (toplevel, StructureNotifyMask, False, configure, NULL);

    /* Pushbutton's callback prints the dimensions of the shell. */
    button = XtVaCreateManagedWidget ("Print Size",
        xmPushButtonWidgetClass, toplevel, NULL);
    XtAddCallback (button, XmNactivateCallback, getsize, toplevel);

    XtRealizeWidget (toplevel);
    XtAppMainLoop (app);
}

void
getsize(widget, client_data, call_data)
Widget widget;
XtPointer client_data;
XtPointer call_data;
{
    Widget shell = (Widget) client_data;
    Dimension width, height;

    XtVaGetValues (shell,
        XmNwidth, &width,
        XmNheight, &height,
        NULL);
    printf ("Width = %d, Height = %d\n", width, height);
}

void
configure(shell, client_data, event)
Widget shell;
```

Example 16-2. The set_minimum.c program (continued)

```
XtPointer client_data;
XEvent *event;
{
    XConfigureEvent *cevent = (XConfigureEvent *) event;

    if (cevent->type != ConfigureNotify)
        return;
    printf ("Width = %d, Height = %d\n", cevent->width, cevent->height);
    XtVaSetValues (shell,
        XmNminWidth, cevent->width,
        XmNminHeight, cevent->height,
        NULL);
    XtRemoveEventHandler (shell, StructureNotifyMask, False, configure, NULL);
}
```

We use XtAddEventHandler() to add an event handler to the top-level shell for events that satisfy the StructureNotifyMask, which includes ConfigureNotify events indicating the window's dimensions. The configure() function is called when the window is initially sized, so we can use the width and height fields of the XConfigure-Event structure as values for the XmNminWidth and XmNminHeight resources for the shell. To prevent the event handler from being called each time the window is resized, the event handler removes itself using XtRemoveEventHandler().

One problem with this technique occurs when the user has the interactivePlacement resource for *mwm* set to True. This specification allows the user to set the initial size and position of an application. However, once the user sets the initial size, she will never be able to make the window any smaller. Although interactive placement adheres to the constraints we have set, it cannot enforce a minimum size because we have not set one. Unfortunately, there is no way to allow interactive placement without allowing the user to resize the window.

The Shell widget class defines the XmNallowShellResize resource that is inherited by all of its subclasses. This resource specifies whether or not the shell allows itself to be resized when its widget children are resized, but it does not affect whether the user can resize the window. For example, if the number of items in a List widget grows, the widget tries to increase its own size, which causes a rippling effect that eventually reaches the top-level window. If XmNallowShellResize is True for this shell, it grows, subject to the window manager's approval, of course. However, if the resource is False, the shell does not even consult the window manager because it knows that it doesn't want to resize. This resource only prevents the shell from resizing after it has been realized, so it does not interfere with the initial sizing of the shell.

16.2.3 The Shell's Icon

Shells can be in one of three states: normal, iconic, or withdrawn. When a shell is in its normal state, the user can interact with the user-interface elements in the expected way. If a shell is withdrawn, it is still active, but the user cannot interact with it directly. When a shell is iconic, its window is not mapped to the screen, but instead it displays a smaller image, or icon, that represents the entire window. The application is still running in this state, but the program does not expect any user interaction. The icon window usually displays a visual image that suggests some connection to the window from which it came. Some window managers, like *mwm*, also allow a label to be attached to the icon's window.

The `XmNiconPixmap` resource specifies the pixmap that is used when an application is in an iconic state. Example 16-3 shows a simple application that sets its icon pixmap.†

Example 16-3. The icon_pixmap.c program

```
#include <Xm/Xm.h>
#include <X11/bitmaps/mailfull>

main(argc, argv)
int argc;
char *argv[];
{
    Widget toplevel;
    XtAppContext app;
    Pixmap bitmap;

    XtSetLanguageProc (NULL, NULL, NULL);

    toplevel = XtVaAppInitialize (&app, "Demos",
        NULL, 0, &argc, argv, NULL,
        XmNwidth, 100, /* size is irrelevant -- toplevel is iconified */
        XmNheight, 100, /* it just can't be 0, or Xt complains */
        XmNiconic,      True,
        NULL);

    bitmap = XCreatePixmapFromBitmapData (XtDisplay (toplevel),
        RootWindowOfScreen (XtScreen (toplevel)),
        mailfull_bits, mailfull_width, mailfull_height, 1, 0, 1);

    XtVaSetValues (toplevel,
        XmNiconPixmap, bitmap,
        NULL);

    XtRealizeWidget (toplevel);
    XtAppMainLoop (app);
}
```

The program creates an ApplicationShell and sets the `XmNiconic` resource to `True` to cause the application to appear iconified. The `bitmap` variable is initialized to contain the bitmap described by the file */usr/include/X11/bitmaps/mailfull*, and the `XmNiconPixmap` resource for the shell is set to the bitmap.

When we set the `XmNiconPixmap` and `XmNiconic` resources, we are actually sending hints to the window manager that we would like the icon window to display the given pixmap and that we would like to be in the iconic state. These requests are called hints because the window manager does not have to comply with the requests. However, if the icon pixmap or iconic state is ignored, it is most likely a bug in the window manager, or an incomplete implementation of one, which is often the case for older versions of many window managers, including *mwm* (Version 1.0).

---

†`XtSetLanguageProc()` is only available in X11R5; there is no corresponding function in X11R4.

One workaround for a window manager that ignores the icon pixmap is to set the XmNicon-
Window resource. This resource sets the entire icon window, rather than just its image. In
environments where the user may not be running the most up-to-date window manager, it
may be best to create the icon window directly and then paint an image in that window.
Example 16-4 contains a routine that demonstrates this technique. This routine creates a
shell's icon window and can be called repeatedly to dynamically update its image.

Example 16-4. The SetIconWindow() routine

```
void
SetIconWindow(shell, image)
Widget shell;
Pixmap image;
{
    Window window, root;
    unsigned int width, height, border_width, depth;
    int x, y;
    Display *dpy = XtDisplay (shell);

    /* Get the current icon window associated with the shell */
    XtVaGetValues (shell, XmNiconWindow, &window, NULL);

    if (!window) {
        /* If there is no window associated with the shell, create one.
         * Make it at least as big as the pixmap we're
         * going to use.  The icon window only needs to be a simple window.
         */
        if (!XGetGeometry (dpy, image, &root, &x, &y,
                &width, &height, &border_width, &depth) ||
            !(window = XCreateSimpleWindow (dpy, root, 0, 0, width, height,
                (unsigned)0, CopyFromParent, CopyFromParent))) {
            XtVaSetValues (shell, XmNiconPixmap, image, NULL);
            return;
        }
        /* Now that the window is created, set it ... */
        XtVaSetValues (shell, XmNiconWindow, window, NULL);
    }
    /* Set the window's background pixmap to be the image. */
    XSetWindowBackgroundPixmap (dpy, window, image);
    /* cause a redisplay of this window, if exposed */
    XClearWindow (dpy, window);
}
```

SetIconWindow() takes two parameters: a shell and an image. If the icon window
for shell has not yet been set, we create a window using XCreateSimpleWindow().
The size of the window is set to the size of the image, which is retrieved with XGet-
Geometry(). This function is used to get the size of the image, but it can be used on windows as well. In the unlikely event that one of these routines fails, we fall back to using Xm-
NiconPixmap to specify the image and hope the window manager understands it. Otherwise, we set the XmNiconWindow resource to the window we just created.

We use the image pixmap to set the window's background pixmap, which saves us the
hassle of rendering it using XCopyArea() or XCopyPlane(). If the shell widget
already has an icon window, XSetWindowBackgroundPixmap() is still called so that
the specified image is displayed. The final call to XClearWindow() causes the icon to be

repainted. This call isn't necessary if the window has just been created, but it is necessary if the window is merely updated with a new image.

The `XmNiconX` and `XmNiconY` resources can be used to set the position of the icon window on the screen. However, you probably shouldn't set these resources arbitrarily without a really good reason. Most window managers deal with positioning icon windows, or leave the positioning for the user to specify, so it is best not to interfere.

The `XmNtitle` and `XmNiconName` resources specify the titles used for the application window and the icon window, respectively. These resources are set to regular character strings, not compound strings. These values are typically both set to the name of the program, `argv[0]`, by default. The values also affect the `WM_NAME` property for the top-level window, which is important for session managers and other applications that monitor all top-level windows on a desktop. These programs look for the `WM_NAME` property to provide menus or buttons that allow the user to control the desktop in a GUI-like fashion, rather than through tty-like shells such as *xterm* and *csh*. It is best to let the user set the `XmNtitle` and `XmNiconName` resources, especially since Xt provides command-line options such as `-name` that can be used to set the title of an application.

16.3 VendorShell Resources

The VendorShell widget class is subclassed from WMShell, so all of the shell widget classes subclassed from VendorShell can use the resources described in the previous section. All of the Motif shells except for MenuShell are subclassed from VendorShell. The VendorShell is designed to be implemented by individual vendors so that they can define resources specific to their own window manager. For example, *mwm* has some window manager features that are not found in other window managers. You need to be familiar with the Motif window manager in order to understand the discussion that follows.

16.3.1 Window Manager Decorations

The frame around an application's main window belongs to the window manager; the controls and window menu in it are not part of the application. The *mwm* window manager decorations for an application window are shown in Figure 16-1.

The user can set *mwm* resources to control which of these items are available for particular windows on the desktop. Also, *mwm* automatically controls which elements are visible for certain windows, in order to maintain compatibility with the *Motif Style Guide*. As such, we discourage you from modifiying the decorations that are available on specific windows. Nevertheless, the VendorShell does provide the `XmNmwmDecorations` resource for use in exceptional cases. The resource can be set to an integer value that is made up of any of the following values:

MWM_DECOR_BORDER
> This value enables the window manager borders for the frame. These borders are decorative only; they are not resize handles. Except for non-rectangular windows or programs like a clock, all Motif-style applications should have decorative borders.

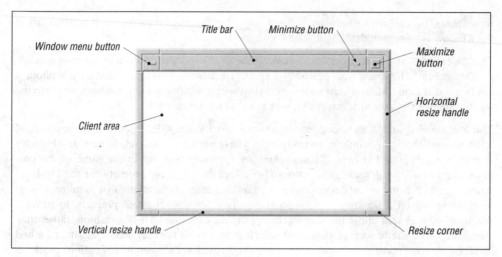

Figure 16-1. Motif window manager decorations

MWM_DECOR_RESIZEH
> This value enables the resize handles for the frame. If the resize handles are displayed, the decorative borders are forced to be displayed.

MWM_DECOR_TITLE
> This value enables the title bar for the window.

MWM_DECOR_MENU
> This value enables the window menu button on the title bar. If this item is on, the title bar is forced to be displayed.

MWM_DECOR_MAXIMIZE
> This value makes the maximize button visible. When this button is selected, the window is expanded to the largest size possible. The size of the window is constrained by the values for XmNmaxWidth and XmNmaxHeight. If these resources are not set, the window is expanded to the size of the screen.

MWM_DECOR_MINIMIZE
> This value makes the minimize button visible. This button does not shrink the window, but rather iconifies it. This item is turned off by default for TransientShell widgets (dialogs), since they cannot be iconified separately from their parent shells.

MWM_DECOR_ALL
> This value can be used to enable all of the window manager decorations.

All of these values are defined in *<Xm/MwmUtil.h>*, which must be included before any of them may be used. The values are bitmasks, so they are meant to be ORed together. For example, if you have a customized dialog that you do not want to have resize handles, you can turn them off as shown in the following code fragment:

```
Widget dialog_shell;
int decor;

XtVaGetValues (dialog_shell, XmNmwmDecorations, &decor, NULL);
decor &= ~MWM_DECOR_RESIZEH;
XtVaSetValues (dialog_shell, XmNmwmDecorations, decor, NULL);
```

While the programmatic interface is available to make changes in the form described above, you really don't have to resort to this level of complexity. If you want to do something that is allowed by the *Motif Style Guide*, chances are that the Motif toolkit provides a more convenient way of doing it. For example, you can turn off the resize handles for a Motif dialog by setting the XmNnoResize resource to True, as shown in the following code:

```
Widget dialog;
Arg args[5];
int n = 0;

XtSetArg (args[n], XmNnoResize, True); n++;
dialog = XmCreateFileSelectionDialog (parent, "dialog", args, n);
```

If Motif doesn't provide a convenience routine or a resource for doing what you want, chances are good that you shouldn't be doing it. On the other hand, you don't have to use the convenience method; if it seems appropriate, you can use the methods described here.

16.3.2 Window Menu Functions

The contents of the window menu can be modified using the XmNmwmFunctions resource defined by the VendorShell. This resource acts like XmNmwmDecorations, in that the value is an integer that may be set to one or more of the following values:

MWM_FUNC_RESIZE

> This value enables the **Size** item in the window menu. If this value isn't set, the resize handles for the window manager frame are disabled.

MWM_FUNC_MOVE

> This value enables the **Move** menu item. Disabling this item does not affect the window manager frame decorations for the window.

MWM_FUNC_MINIMIZE

> This value enables the **Minimize** menu item. Disabling this item causes the minimize button to be disabled as well.

MWM_FUNC_MAXIMIZE

> This value enables the **Maximize** menu item. Disabling this item causes the corresponding window frame decoration to be disabled.

MWM_FUNC_CLOSE

> This value enables the **Close** menu item. Disabling this item does not affect the window manager decorations for the window.

`MWM_FUNC_ALL`
> This value causes all of the standard items in the menu to be displayed and all the
> default functionality of the window manager to work.

It is important to remember that the user can specify these window menu functions, as well as
new functions, in an *.mwmrc* file. (See Volume Three, *X Window System User's Guide,
Motif Edition*.) While your settings override any user specifications, you should only modify
the window menu functions if it is absolutely necessary. A common misuse of this functionality is to disable the **Close** button. We strongly discourage disabling this button, as users
expect it to be in the window menu. Rather than disable the button, you should link its functionality to another control in your application that has the same meaning. For example, if
you are using a standard Motif dialog that provides **OK** and **Cancel** buttons, you can link the
Close menu item to the **Cancel** button. We explain how to connect the functionality of these
components in the next section.

16.4 Handling Window Manager Messages

A protocol is a set of rules that governs communication and data transfer. When the window
manager sends a message to an application that follows a predefined protocol, the client
application should respond accordingly. The ICCCM defines a number of protocols for window managers and applications to follow. One such protocol involves the **Close** item in the
window menu. When the user selects this item, the window manager sends the application a
protocol message, and the application must comply. The message is delivered through the
normal event-handling mechanisms provided by Xlib. The event that corresponds to this
message is called a `ClientMessage` event. The message itself is an `Atom`, which is
merely a unique integer that is used as an identifier. (The actual value is unimportant, since
you only need to reference the value through the preprocessor macro, `WM_PROTOCOLS`.) The
protocol itself takes the form of other atoms, depending on the nature of the message. Table
16-2 lists the atoms that are used as values for `WM_PROTOCOLS` client messages. Although
this table is currently complete, it is expected to grow in future editions of the ICCCM.

Table 16-2. Protocol Atoms Defined by the ICCCM

Atom	Meaning
`WM_TAKE_FOCUS`	The window is getting the input focus.
`WM_DELETE_WINDOW`	The window is about to be deleted.
`WM_SAVE_YOURSELF`	The application should save its internal state.

Example 16-5 demonstrates how to use the `WM_DELETE_YOURSELF` protocol to link the **Close**
item on the window menu with the **Cancel** button in a dialog.†

---

†`XtSetLanguageProc()` is only available in X11R5; there is no corresponding function in X11R4. `Xm-
StringCreateLocalized()` is only available in Motif 1.2; `XmStringCreateSimple()` is the correspond-
ing function in Motif 1.1.

Example 16-5. The wm_delete.c program

```c
/* wm_delete.c -- demonstrate how to bind the Close button in the
 * window manager's system menu to the "cancel" button in a dialog.
 */
#include <Xm/MessageB.h>
#include <Xm/PushB.h>
#include <Xm/Protocols.h>

main(argc, argv)
int argc;
char *argv[];
{
    Widget toplevel, button;
    XtAppContext app;
    void activate();

    XtSetLanguageProc (NULL, NULL, NULL);

    toplevel = XtVaAppInitialize  (&app, "Demos",
        NULL, 0, &argc, argv, NULL, NULL);

    button = XtCreateManagedWidget ("Push Me", xmPushButtonWidgetClass,
        toplevel, NULL, 0);
    XtAddCallback (button, XmNactivateCallback, activate, NULL);

    XtRealizeWidget (toplevel);
    XtAppMainLoop (app);
}

/* Create and popup an ErrorDialog indicating that the user may have
 * done something wrong.  The dialog contains an OK and Cancel button,
 * but he can still choose the Close button in the titlebar.
 */
void
activate(w, client_data, call_data)
Widget w;
XtPointer client_data;
XtPointer call_data;
{
    Widget dialog, shell;
    void response();
    XmString t = XmStringCreateLocalized ("Warning: Delete All Files?");
    Atom WM_DELETE_WINDOW;
    Arg args[5];
    int n;

    /* Make sure the VendorShell associated with the dialog does not
     * react to the user's selection of the Close system menu item.
     */
    n = 0;
    XtSetArg (args[n], XmNmessageString, t); n++;
    XtSetArg (args[n], XmNdeleteResponse, XmDO_NOTHING); n++;
    dialog = XmCreateWarningDialog (w, "notice", args, n);
    XmStringFree (t);

    /* add callback routines for ok and cancel -- desensitize help */
    XtAddCallback (dialog, XmNokCallback, response, NULL);
    XtAddCallback (dialog, XmNcancelCallback, response, NULL);
    XtSetSensitive (XmMessageBoxGetChild (dialog,
        XmDIALOG_HELP_BUTTON), False);
```

Example 16-5. The wm_delete.c program (continued)

```
    XtManageChild (dialog);

    /* Add a callback for the WM_DELETE_WINDOW protocol */
    shell = XtParent (dialog);
    WM_DELETE_WINDOW = XmInternAtom
        (XtDisplay (w), "WM_DELETE_WINDOW", False);
    XmAddWMProtocolCallback (shell, WM_DELETE_WINDOW, response, dialog);
}

/* callback for the OK and Cancel buttons in the dialog -- may also be
 * called from the WM_DELETE_WINDOW protocol message sent by the wm.
 */
void
response (widget, client_data, call_data)
Widget widget;
XtPointer client_data;
XtPointer call_data;
{
    XmAnyCallbackStruct *cbs = (XmAnyCallbackStruct *) call_data;
    Widget dialog;

    if (cbs->reason == XmCR_OK)
        puts ("Yes");
    else
        puts ("No");

    if (cbs->reason == XmCR_PROTOCOLS)
        /* we passed the dialog as client data for the protocol callback */
        dialog = (Widget) client_data;
    else
        dialog = widget;

    XtDestroyWidget (dialog);
}
```

When you run the application and click on the button, a dialog is displayed. All the application does is print "Yes" or "No" to standard output based on whether the **OK** or **Cancel** button is pressed. However, if you select **Close** from the window menu for the dialog, the dialog disappears, and the "No" message is printed.

When the user selects the **Close** item on the window menu, the application is sent a ClientMessage event by the window manager indicating that the window is about to be deleted. The value associated with the WM_PROTOCOLS message is WM_DELETE_WINDOW. The application is now responsible for complying with the protocol in some way.

At the highest level of abstraction, the VendorShell resource XmNdeleteResponse can be used to control what the application does in response to the user's selection of the **Close** button. The default behavior for a dialog is that the window is dismissed; the value XmUNMAP is used, and the window is unmapped from the screen. By setting XmNdeleteReponse to XmDESTROY, the window is destroyed; this value is the default for ApplicationShells. However, if the resource is set to XmDO_NOTHING, the application declares that it is going to handle the action itself.

In Example 16-5, we use this value to handle the WM_DELETE_WINDOW protocol ourselves by setting up a callback routine that is called whenever the protocol is sent. But before we can set up the callback, we have to get the atom associated with the WM_DELETE_WINDOW protocol. We retrieve the atom using XmInternAtom(), which takes the following form:

```
Atom
XmInternAtom(display, atom_name, dont_create)
    Display *display;
    char    *atom_name;
    Boolean dont_create;
```

If the atom name described by the string *atom_name* exists, then the Atom is returned. If it does not exist and if *dont_create* is True, the function returns None. Otherwise, the routine creates and returns the atom. This function is identical to XInternAtom(), with the exception that the Motif version maintains an internal cache of previously-accessed atoms. Since creating and returning atoms causes a round trip to the server, it is a nice performance improvement to have that cache available for frequently-accessed atoms.

Once we have the protocol atom, we can add a callback routine to respond to the client message event generated by that protocol. The function XmAddWMProtocolCallback() is used to install a callback routine invoked whenever the window manager sends a WM_PROTOCOLS client message to the application. If the protocol sent in the client message matches the protocol passed to XmAddWMProtocolCallback(), the associated function is called. In Example 16-5, we use the response() routine as the callback for the dialog buttons and the protocol. As a result, the **Close** item invokes the same callback as the **OK** and **Cancel** buttons.

The form of this callback routine is the same as any other Motif callback. The final parameter is a Motif-defined callback structure of some kind, where the reason field specifies why the callback was called. This field is provided because the same callback function may be invoked by more than one widget. In our example, the response() function's callback structure may have one of three different values for reason: XmCR_OK for the **OK** button, XmCR_CANCEL for the **Cancel** button, or XmCR_PROTOCOLS for the **Close** button in the window menu.† When the callback is invoked for the protocol message, the event field of the callback structure is an XClientMessageEvent.

The widget parameter passed to response() also varies depending on whether the routine is called from the dialog or from the **Close** button. When either **OK** or **Cancel** is pressed, the widget is the dialog itself. But the protocol callback routines are really processed by special *protocol widgets* that are attached to VendorShells.‡ When the protocol callback is invoked, the widget field is one of the special widgets, but this widget has no intrinsic meaning, so it can be ignored. We know that the activation of the WM_DELETE_WINDOW protocol causes a protocol widget to be passed as the widget parameter. Therefore, we pass a handle to the dialog widget as the client data to XmAddWMProtocolCallback() so that we have access to the dialog.

---

† In Motif 1.1, XmCR_PROTOCOLS was not publicly defined, but this problem has been fixed in Motif 1.2.

‡ A shell can actually have any number of widget children, as long as only one of them is managed at a time. In the case of the Motif VendorShell, these other widgets are not managed but are used to process and manage protocols that are exchanged between the window manager and the application.

The purpose, of course, is to destroy the window, but our function could just as easily veto the operation and render the **Close** button inoperable. However, this technique is really not appropriate, as users expect to be able to use the **Close** button to remove a window. If the **Close** button is not going to unmap the window for some good reason, like an error, you should report the error in another dialog. If you are going to modify the default behavior of standard user-interface controls, you should keep the user informed about what you are doing.

16.4.1 Adding New Protocols

In general, you can attach a callback routine to any of the published protocols using the mechanisms we just described. You may also assign new protocols to send yourself special messages that are pertinent only to your application, as protocol messages can be passed from application to application, not just between the window manager and other clients. Handling arbitrary protocols is basically a matter of following these simple steps:

1. Create an atom or retrieve one from the X server using XmInternAtom().

2. Register the atom on the shell with XmAddWMProtocols(), so the event-handling mechanism can recognize it if it should arrive.

3. Install a callback routine that is invoked when the protocol is sent to the application using XmAddWMProtocolCallback().

For the case of WM_DELETE_WINDOW, the second step has already been taken care of by the VendorShell, since it is an established and standardized ICCCM protocol. The VendorShell has already registered interest in the protocol so it can react to it in the method described by its XmNdeleteResponse resource. However, other protocols (customized or not) may not be registered. Since it doesn't hurt to register a protocol with a window more than once, it's always a good practice to register the protocol using XmAddWMProtocols(), which takes the following form:

```
void
XmAddWMProtocols(shell, protocols, num_protocols)
    Widget shell;
    Atom  *protocols;
    int    num_protocols;
```

This function takes a list of protocols, so you can use it to add as many protocols as you like at one time.

16.4.2 Saving Application State

A *session manager* is an application that acts something like a window manager. However, rather than controlling only the windows on a screen, it monitors the actual applications running on that screen. Frequently, session managers allow the user to start, terminate, or even restart any program automatically, through a variety of interface controls. Session managers may even cause a program to "sleep" by terminating all its keyboard and mouse input, so as far as the program is concerned, the user is just not interacting with it.

At the moment, there are not many full session managers available, so much of the possible functionality is uncharted. This section discusses one aspect of proposed session manager behavior and how it might be implemented. This behavior concerns the ability of an application running under the session manager to restart itself at the point where it left off in a previous session.

If the session manager decides that it might terminate (which might result in the entire X connection terminating), it may send a request to all its applications to save their internal state so they can be restarted later. In this case, the session manager sends a WM_SAVE_YOURSELF protocol message. According to the ICCCM, client applications that can save their current state and restart from that state should register the atom WM_SAVE_YOURSELF on the WM_PROTOCOLS property on one of their top-level windows.

The ICCCM states that after sending the WM_SAVE_YOURSELF message to the application, the session manager waits until the program updates its WM_COMMAND property on the same window that received the protocol message. The application is not permitted to interact with the user in any way at this time. You cannot prompt for filenames or ask if the user wants to save state. The callback routine must save its current state somehow, possibly in a predefined file that can be made known to the user through documentation, rather than a run-time message. It must then update the WM_COMMAND property to reflect the parameters that started the program, as well as any additional parameters that might be required to restart it.

For example, say your application is called *wm_save* and you want to be able to restart it from a previously-saved file. In this case, your application might parse the following command-line option:

```
% wm_save -restart filename
```

Example 16-6 contains a code fragment that demonstrates how you might implement this functionality.†

Example 16-6. The wm_save.c program

```
/* wm_save.c -- demonstrate how to save the state of an application
 * from a WM_SAVE_YOURSELF session manager protocol.  This is not a
 * real program -- just a template.
 */
#include <Xm/Xm.h>
#include <Xm/Protocols.h>
#include <stdio.h>

/* save the original argc and argv for possible WM_SAVE_YOURSELF messages */
int save_argc;
char **save_argv;

main(argc, argv)
int argc;
char *argv[];
```

---

†XtSetLanguageProc() is only available in X11R5; there is no corresponding function in X11R4.

Example 16-6. The wm_save.c program (continued)

```
{
    Widget toplevel;
    XtAppContext app;
    Atom WM_SAVE_YOURSELF;
    void save_state();
    char *restart_file;
    int i;

    /* save argc and argv values */
    save_argv = (char **) XtMalloc (argc * sizeof(char *));
    for (i = save_argc = 0; i < argc; i++)
        /* we don't need to save old -restart options */
        if (!strcmp (argv[i], "-restart"))
            i++; /* next arg is filename */
        else
            save_argv[save_argc++] =
                strcpy (XtMalloc (strlen(argv[i]) + 1), argv[i]);

    XtSetLanguageProc (NULL, NULL, NULL);

    /* initialize toolkit normally; argv has its Xt-specific args stripped */
    toplevel = XtVaAppInitialize (&app, "Demos",
        NULL, 0, &argc, argv, NULL,
        XmNwidth, 100,
        XmNheight, 100,
        NULL);

    /* get the WM_SAVE_YOURSELF protocol atom and register it with the
     * toplevel window's WM_PROTOCOLS property.  Also add a callback.
     */
    WM_SAVE_YOURSELF =
        XmInternAtom (XtDisplay (toplevel), "WM_SAVE_YOURSELF", False);
    XmAddWMProtocols (toplevel, &WM_SAVE_YOURSELF, 1);
    XmAddWMProtocolCallback (toplevel, WM_SAVE_YOURSELF,
        save_state, toplevel);

    /* create widgets... */

    /* now check to see if we are restarting from a previously run state */
    for (i = 0; i < argc; i++) {
        if (!strcmp (argv[i], "-restart")) {
            /* restarting from a previously saved state */
            restart_file = argv[++i];
        }

        /* possibly process other args here, too */
    }

    XtRealizeWidget (toplevel);
    XtAppMainLoop (app);
}

/* called if WM_SAVE_YOURSELF client message was sent... */
void
save_state(widget, client_data, call_data)
Widget widget;
XtPointer client_data;
XtPointer call_data;
{
    Widget toplevel = (Widget) client_data;
```

Example 16-6. The wm_save.c program (continued)

```
    extern char *SaveStateAndReturnFileName();  /* hypothetical function */
    char *filename = SaveStateAndReturnFileName ();
    puts("save_state()");

    save_argv = (char **) XtRealloc (save_argv,
        (save_argc+2) * sizeof (char *));

    save_argv[save_argc++] = "-restart";
    save_argv[save_argc++] = filename;

    XSetCommand (XtDisplay (toplevel), XtWindow (toplevel),
        save_argv, save_argc); /* notice the order of these args! */
}
```

This program registers the WM_SAVE_YOURSELF protocol using XmAddWMProtocols()
before it specifies the callback routine. If the session manager sends a WM_SAVE_YOURSELF
message to this program then the save_state() function is called, which causes the program to save its internal state using the function SaveStateAndReturnFileName().
This is a hypothetical function that you would write yourself to save the state of the program
and return the filename that contains the state information. The callback routine also adds
the -restart flag and the new filename to the saved argv from the beginning of the program. The function XSetCommand() is used to set the WM_COMMAND property on the window associated with the top-level shell, which fulfills the program's obligation to the session
manager.

For more information about session managers and the save-yourself communication protocol,
see Volume Zero, *X Protocol Reference Manual*. For more details on XSetCommand()
and other Xlib-based functions that set and get window manager properties on top-level windows, see Volume One, *Xlib Programming Manual*, and Volume Two, *Xlib Reference Manual*.

16.5 Customized Protocols

The previous section demonstrated how similar one protocol message is to the next in the
way they are added to a program. Adding a completely new protocol is not difficult either.
The only changes we have to make are those that would otherwise interfere with the standard
protocols and properties that are registered with the X protocol and ICCCM. To avoid conflicts, the convention is to begin the name of nonstandard atoms and window properties with
at least an underscore, and possibly a more detailed prefix that identifies the atom as a private
protocol or property. Accordingly, Motif provides the property _MOTIF_WM_MESSAGES as
a private atom specifically for Motif-based applications that wish to send private messages to
themselves or one another. Private does not mean that no one else can see the messages; it
just implies that the protocol is not publicly available for other third-party applications to
use, so don't expect other programs on the desktop to participate in the protocol.

Example 16-7 demonstrates how to register your own protocol with the shell and set up a callback routine that is invoked when that protocol is delivered. Like Example 16-6, this program is a skeletal frame only; it does not have any real functionality.†

Example 16-7. The wm_protocol.c program

```
/* wm_protocol.c -- demonstrate how to add your own protocol to a
 * shell.  The nature of the protocol isn't important; however, it
 * must be registered with the _MOTIF_WM_MESSAGES property on the
 * shell.  We also add a menu item to the window manager frame's
 * window menu to allow the user to activate the protocol, if desired.
 */
#include <Xm/Xm.h>
#include <Xm/Protocols.h>
#include <stdio.h>

main(argc, argv)
int argc;
char *argv[];
{
    Widget toplevel;
    XtAppContext app;
    Atom MOTIF_MSGS, MY_PROTOCOL;
    void my_proto_callback();
    char buf[64];

    toplevel = XtVaAppInitialize (&app, "Demos", NULL, 0,
        &argc, argv, NULL,
        XmNwidth, 100,
        XmNheight, 100,
        NULL);

    /* get the MOTIF_MSGS and MY_PROTOCOL atoms */
    MY_PROTOCOL = XmInternAtom (XtDisplay (toplevel),
        "_MY_PROTOCOL", False);
    MOTIF_MSGS = XmInternAtom (XtDisplay (toplevel),
        "_MOTIF_WM_MESSAGES", False);

    /* Add MY_PROTOCOL to the _MOTIF_WM_MESSAGES VendorShell-defined
     * property on the shell.  Add a callback for this protocol.
     */
    XmAddProtocols (toplevel, MOTIF_MSGS, &MY_PROTOCOL, 1);
    XmAddProtocolCallback (toplevel,
        MOTIF_MSGS, MY_PROTOCOL, my_proto_callback, NULL);

    /* allow the user to activate the protocol through the window manager's
     * window menu on the shell.
     */
    sprintf (buf, "MyProtocol _P Ctrl<Key>P f.send_msg %d", MY_PROTOCOL);
    XtVaSetValues (toplevel, XmNmwmMenu, buf, NULL);

    /* create widgets... */

    XtRealizeWidget (toplevel);
    XtAppMainLoop (app);
}
```

---

†XtSetLanguageProc() is only available in X11R5; there is no corresponding function in X11R4.

Example 16-7. The wm_protocol.c program (continued)

```
/* called if _MY_PROTOCOL was activated, a client message was sent... */
void
my_proto_callback(widget, client_data, call_data)
Widget widget;
XtPointer client_data;
XtPointer call_data;
{
    puts ("My protocol got activated!");
}
```

This program is set up to receive the protocol _MY_PROTOCOL. If the message is sent, the function my_proto_callback() is called, passing the appropriate client data and callback structure as before. However, since we just made up the protocol, the only way it can be delivered is by the window manager if (and only if) the user selects the new menu item that we attached to the window menu, as shown in Figure 16-2.

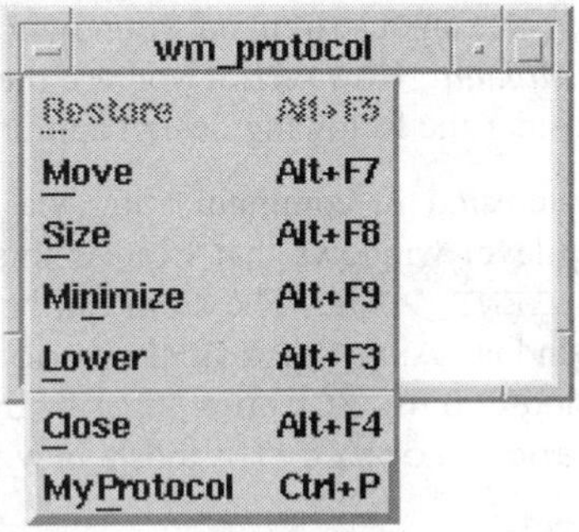

Figure 16-2. Output of wm_protocol.c

The menu item is added using the XmNmwmMenu resource in the call to XtVaSet-Values(). The syntax of the value for the string used by the XmNmwmMenu resource is described completely in the *mwm* documentation in Volume Six B, *Motif Reference Manual*. Briefly, each of the arguments refers to a single entry in the menu that is always added after the last standard protocol in the menu, which is usually the **Close** button. The syntax for the resource is:

```
label [mnemonic] [accelerator] function
```

Only the label and the window manager function (*mwm*-specific) are required. The label is always first; if a space needs to be embedded in the label, precede it by two backslashes. The next token is parsed as a mnemonic if it starts with an underscore. If an accelerator is given, the Motif toolkit parses this string and creates a corresponding accelerator text string for the menu. Finally, the parser looks for a window manager function as described by the *mwm* documentation. These include f.move, f.raise and f.send_msg, for example. We use f.send_msg to tell *mwm* to send the specified client message to the application.

It is possible to deactivate a protocol on the window menu using `XmDeactivate-WMProtocol()`. Deactivation makes a protocol insensitive (unselectable). Protocols may be reactivated by `XmActivateWMProtocol()`; new protocols are automatically activated when they are added. `XmActivateProtocol()` and `XmDeactivate-Protocol()` perform an analogous function for non-window manager protocols.

But what can you do with your own private protocol? These protocols can come in handy if you want to attach any application-specific functionality to a window so that it can communicate with similar applications on the desktop. For example, larger application suites that contain multiple programs might need to communicate with one another through this protocol. If a suite of painting, drawing, and desktop publishing products wanted to pass document information to one another, they could pass messages using their own protocol. Whether or not you allow the window manager (and thus the user) to participate in the protocol can be controlled by whether you make the protocol handle available in the window menu, as shown in Figure 16-2.

Advanced work with protocols is getting beyond the scope of this book. Further progress requires Xlib-level code that you can research on your own by reading portions of Volume One, *Xlib Programming Manual*. However, if you are interested in providing this kind of functionality, you might consider the following design approach:

- When an application is interested in communicating via a private protocol, it should place a property on its top-level windows that express this interest. For example, let's call this atom `_MYAPP_CLIENT_PROP`. The atom can be added to the `WM_PROTOCOLS` property already on the window using `XmAddWMProtocol()`, just as we did earlier. An application can also choose to use `XChangeProperty()` to actually use the atom as the property itself; `XChangeProperty()` adds a new property to a window's list of existing properties.

- An application interested in seeking out other windows that have expressed interest in `_MYAPP_CLIENT_PROP` can call `XQueryTree()` to start at the root window and search all of its immediate children for those windows that have that property. The function `XGetWindowProperty()` can be used to test for the existence of the property itself.

- When an application finds a window that contains the property, it can use `XSend-Event()` to send an `XClientMessageEvent` to that window. When sending a client message, the application can either do what the Motif toolkit does and send a `WM_PROTO-COLS` message, or it can just send the `_MYAPP_CLIENT_PROP` atom itself. If the program uses the first technique, the `data.l[0]` field of the `XClientMessageEvent` data structure contains the value `WM_PROTOCOLS`, and the the `data.l[1]` field contains `_MYAPP_CLIENT_PROP`. If the receiving window is part of a Motif application that has registered a callback function for this protocol, the function is invoked.†

- If the sending application wishes to send any additional data to the receiving application, it should either add or replace the receiving window's `_MYAPP_CLIENT_PROP` property and upgrade or change its value.

---

† Whether or not the receiving application is a Motif application, it can set up its own event handler to trap for the client message.

Remember, since this is your own private protocol, you can do whatever you like in the correspondence process. If you wanted, you could specify that the receiving window would always test for a newly-defined property on its window, and if that property is set, obtain further information from the primary selection. Using this process, you could write your own data transfer methods. However, whatever you come up with is strictly private, so no other application can participate in your protocol unless you tell the developer of the other application what to do.

You can place whatever information you like in properties: a string, an integer, or a data structure. Just make sure that it's not per-process information like a file descriptor. This type of data cannot be shared among separate processes. You should also try not to make the information host-specific because you are not guaranteed that both clients are going to be running on the same computer, although they will be running on the same server. It is also a good idea to avoid protocols that involve continuous chatting between programs. Protocols are not a good method for doing interactive talk programs because the network can't handle that kind of traffic. To do this kind of communication, it is typically better to establish your own TCP or STREAM connection between the two applications. You should attempt to be as network-portable as possible, but this is your own personal protocol, so you can do anything you like.

16.6 Summary

The best applications can still function adequately without a window manager. For portability reasons, you should not assume that the user is running *mwm*. Except for dealing with WM_DELETE_WINDOW protocol messages to handle the window menu's **Close** button, you should avoid interfering with the interaction between your applications and the window manager. Despite this advice, many developers believe they know better and attempt to redesign Motif on a per-application basis. If you attempt to go this route, be aware of the guidelines provided by the *Motif Style Guide* and the ICCCM.

Client messages can be an extremely powerful tool for a large application with many top-level windows that need to interact with each other. They can also be useful for larger groups of similar applications by the same vendor that need to talk to one another. The secret to making a private protocol work is establishing a good communication channel and being able to transfer a lot of information without having to transfer a lot of data.

16.7 Exercises

These exercises are designed to help you understand the material that was presented in this chapter.

1. Write a program that always places its error dialogs in the center of the screen.

2. Whenever a shell changes from normal state to iconic state, the window manager changes the shell's WM_STATE property. Write a program that gets the PropertyNotify event generated from this state change so that you can track when a shell is iconified and de-iconified. Use XtAddEventHandler() to register a routine that tracks for the event in the same way we tracked for ConfigureNotify events in *set_minimum.c*

3. Write a program so that when the user selects the **Close** button from a window menu, the shell iconifies itself if it is a TopLevelShell, and destroys itself if it is a DialogShell.

17

The Clipboard

This chapter describes a way for the application to interact with other applications. Data is placed on the clipboard, where it can be accessed by other windows on the desktop regardless of the applications with which they are associated.

In This Chapter:

Imagine a group of people in a room; the only way for them to communicate is by writing messages on paper, placing the paper on a clipboard, and passing the clipboard around. A single person acts as the moderator and holds the clipboard at all times. If someone wants to post a note, she writes the message on a slip of paper and hands the message to the moderator. The note is now available for anyone to read. However, those who read the message do not remove the message from the clipboard; rather, they copy what was written. There is no guarantee that anyone will want to look at any particular message, but it is there nonetheless and will remain there until someone writes a new one.

This scenario is the concept behind the Motif clipboard: a data transfer mechanism that enables widgets to make data available for other widgets, including those in separate applications. Information of any size or type can be passed using the clipboard interface. The most common example of this data transfer model is *cut and paste*, a method by which the user can move or copy text between windows. Here, the user interacts with a Text widget that contains some text that she wishes to transfer to another Text widget. The user first *selects* the text she wants to transfer by clicking the left mouse button and dragging it across the entire area to be copied. Then, she moves the pointer to the target widget and *pastes* the text by clicking the middle mouse button.†

This action causes the text to appear to be copied to the new window. However, the text does not actually move; it is copied to the clipboard, from which the second widget then copies it into its own window. The original data may have been changed or destroyed since it was sent to the clipboard, but that is of no concern to the second widget.

An object that wishes to place data on the clipboard or read data from it is called a *client* of the clipboard (one of the people in our imaginary room). Since only one client may access the clipboard at a time, whether it is storing or retrieving data, requesting access to the clipboard implies "locking" it. If another widget already has locked the clipboard, the client must wait and ask for it again later (after the current holder has "unlocked" it).

Now, imagine that the people in the room have all sorts of items besides text messages they wish to make available for copy. Some may have pictures, records, tapes—anything. Their "cargo" must be deliverable by the moderator to anyone who requests it. To deal with this situation, the moderator must know what type of cargo she will be handling. Therefore,

---

† This is the default cut and paste user model; the user may override it using resources or keyboard equivalents. The actual method for performing this task is not the point of discussion here.

certain information must be registered with the moderator before cargo may be sent or received through the clipboard mechanism. Once a particular cargo type is registered, anyone may post or request such cargo to or from the moderator.

In the Motif toolkit, different types of cargo are referred to as *formats*. With respect to the X server and client applications, text messages are the most commonly used format of clipboard messages and are therefore registered by default.† Application-specific data structures must be registered separately, perhaps on a per-application basis. Once a new data type is registered, even clients that exist on other computer architectures where data is not represented identically (e.g., due to byte swapping) can use that data type, since the clipboard registration handles the proper data conversion.

There are some situations where it is impractical to place complete information on the clipboard. Some people's cargo may be "too heavy" for the clipboard to hold indefinitely. Other people may have perishables that don't last very long. Still others may have information that varies with the state of the world. For these cases, the person with the special cargo may choose to leave only some information about their cargo rather than the cargo itself. This information might include its weight, type, name and/or reference number, for example. Potential recipients may then examine the clipboard and inquire about the cargo without having to get it or even look at it. Only in the event that someone else wishes to obtain the cargo is the original owner called upon to provide it.

In the Motif world, this scenario describes clipboard data that is available *by name*. For example, if a client wishes to place an entire file on the clipboard, it might choose to register the file by name without providing the actual contents unless someone requests it. This may save a lot of time and resources, since it's possible that no one will request it. Referencing data this way is very cheap and is not subject to expiration or obsolescence.

When posting messages by name, the client must provide the clipboard with a callback function that returns the actual data. This callback function may be called by the Motif toolkit at any time, provided another client requests the data. If the data is time-dependent or subject to other criteria (someone removed or changed the file), the callback routine may respond accordingly.

The Motif clipboard functions are based on X's Inter-Client Communications Conventions Manual (ICCCM). Knowledge of these conventions will aid greatly in your understanding of how these functions are implemented. However, knowledge of the implementation is not required in order to understand the concepts involved here or to be able to use the clipboard effectively through Motif's application interface. This chapter does not address many of the issues involved with the ICCCM and the lower-level Xlib properties that implement them. Rather, it only addresses the highest level of interaction provided by the Motif toolkit.

Also note that the clipboard is one of three commonly used mechanisms to support interclient communication. There are also the *primary* and *secondary* selections, which are similar in nature, but are handled differently at the application and user level. The Motif toolkit supports convenience routines that interact with clipboard selections only. To use the other selection mechanisms, you must use X Toolkit Intrinsics functions that were discussed in

---

† There are also other types that are automatically registered, such as integers. A complete list is given in Section 17.3.

Volume Four, *X Toolkit Intrinsics Programming Manual*. Note, however, that the Text widget supports both mechanisms.

17.1 Simple Clipboard Copy and Retrieval

To introduce the application programmer's interface (API) for the clipboard functions, we demonstrate how to handle simple copy and retrieval of text. The cut and paste functions provided by the Text widgets handle copy and retrieval from the clipboard in the manner we are about to describe; they also support interaction with the primary and secondary selection mechanisms. However, as pointed out in Chapter 14, *Text Widgets*, these functions are usually reserved for interactive actions taken by the user. Fortunately, Motif provides many convenience functions that facilitate the task of dealing with the clipboard for Text widgets. This section discusses the techniques used by the Text widget when it interacts with the clipboard.

Let's begin with the short program in Example 17-1. This program creates two PushButtons that have complementary callback routines: `to_clipbd()` copies text to the clipboard and `from_clipbd()` retrieves text from the clipboard. For this example, the text copied to the clipboard is arbitrary; we happen to use a string that represents the number of times the **Copy to Clipboard** button is pressed.†

Example 17-1. The copy_retrieve.c program

```
/* copy_retrieve.c -- simple copy and retrieve program.  Two
 * pushbuttons: the first places text in the clipboard, the other
 * receives text from the clipboard.  This just demonstrates the
 * API involved.
 */
#include <Xm/CutPaste.h>
#include <Xm/RowColumn.h>
#include <Xm/PushB.h>

static void to_clipbd(), from_clipbd();

main(argc, argv)
int argc;
char *argv[];
{
    Widget toplevel, rowcol, button;
    XtAppContext app;

    XtSetLanguageProc (NULL, NULL, NULL);

    /* Initialize toolkit, application context and toplevel shell */
    toplevel = XtVaAppInitialize (&app, "Demos", NULL, 0,
        &argc, argv, NULL, NULL);

    /* manage two buttons in a RowColumn widget */
    rowcol = XtVaCreateWidget ("rowcol", xmRowColumnWidgetClass,
```

---

†`XtSetLanguageProc()` is only available in X11R5; there is no corresponding function in X11R4. `Xm-StringCreateLocalized()` is only available in Motif 1.2; `XmStringCreateSimple()` is the corresponding function in Motif 1.1.

Example 17-1. The copy_retrieve.c program (continued)

```
        toplevel, NULL);

    /* button1 copies to the clipboard */
    button = XtVaCreateManagedWidget ("button1",
        xmPushButtonWidgetClass, rowcol,
        XtVaTypedArg, XmNlabelString, XmRString,
            "Copy To Clipboard", 18, /* strlen() + 1 */
        NULL);
    XtAddCallback (button, XmNactivateCallback, to_clipbd, "text");

    /* button2 retrieves text stored in the clipboard */
    button = XtVaCreateManagedWidget ("button2",
        xmPushButtonWidgetClass, rowcol,
        XtVaTypedArg, XmNlabelString, XmRString,
            "Retrieve From Clipboard", 24, /* strlen() + 1 */
        NULL);
    XtAddCallback (button, XmNactivateCallback, from_clipbd, NULL);

    /* manage RowColumn, realize toplevel shell and start main loop */
    XtManageChild (rowcol);
    XtRealizeWidget (toplevel);
    XtAppMainLoop (app);
}

/* copy data to clipboard. */
static void
to_clipbd(widget, client_data, call_data)
Widget widget;
XtPointer client_data;
XtPointer call_data;
{
    unsigned long item_id = 0;   /* clipboard item id */
    int          status;
    XmString     clip_label;
    char         buf[32];
    static int   cnt;
    Display      *dpy = XtDisplayOfObject (widget);
    Window       window = XtWindowOfObject (widget);
    char         *data = (char *) client_data;

    sprintf (buf, "%s-%d", data, ++cnt); /* make each copy unique */

    clip_label = XmStringCreateLocalized ("to_clipbd");

    /* start a copy -- retry till unlocked */
    do
        status = XmClipboardStartCopy (dpy, window,
            clip_label, CurrentTime, NULL, NULL, &item_id);
    while (status == ClipboardLocked);

    XmStringFree (clip_label);

    /* copy the data (buf) -- pass "cnt" as private id for kicks */
    do
        status = XmClipboardCopy (dpy, window, item_id, "STRING",
            buf, (long) strlen (buf)+1, cnt, NULL);
    while (status == ClipboardLocked);

    /* end the copy */
    do
```

Example 17-1. The copy_retrieve.c program (continued)

```
            status = XmClipboardEndCopy (dpy, window, item_id);
        while (status == ClipboardLocked);

        printf ("Copied \"%s\" to clipboard.\n", buf);
    }

static void
from_clipbd(widget, client_data, call_data)
Widget widget;
XtPointer client_data;
XtPointer call_data;
{
    int         status, private_id;
    char        buf[32];
    Display     *dpy = XtDisplayOfObject (widget);
    Window      window = XtWindowOfObject (widget);

    do
        status = XmClipboardRetrieve (dpy, window,
            "STRING", buf, sizeof (buf), NULL, &private_id);
    while (status == ClipboardLocked);

    if (status == ClipboardSuccess)
        printf ("Retrieved \"%s\" (private id = %d).\n", buf, private_id);
    }
```

The program uses the header file *<Xm/CutPaste.h>* to include the appropriate function declarations and various constants.† The to_clipbd() callback routine uses the following clipboard functions to copy data to the clipboard:

```
    XmClipboardStartCopy()
    XmClipboardCopy()
    XmClipboardEndCopy()
```

Copying data to the clipboard is a three-phase process. Each of the functions locks the clipboard so that other clients cannot access it. Since locking the clipboard is done on a per-window basis, the object that locks the clipboard should have an associated window, which means that gadgets may not work.‡ When the clipboard is locked, only requests from objects with the same window ID can access the clipboard. Each time an object requests a lock on the clipboard, a counter is incremented so that matching unlock requests can be honored.

XmClipboardStartCopy() sets up internal storage for the copy to take place, XmClipboardCopy() sends the data to the clipboard, and XmClipboardEndCopy() frees the internal supporting structures. When copying data to the clipboard, including copies by name, all three functions must be used.

The from_clipbd() callback routine uses XmClipboardRetrieveCopy() to retrieve data from the clipboard. Only a single call is needed for the retrieval of short items, as in this example. However, a three-step process similar to that for copying data to the

---

† Don't let the name of the file confuse you. *CutPaste.h* is derived from the phrase "cut and paste," which historically has been used to describe clipboard-type operations.

‡ Gadgets happen to work in some cases because of their window-based widget parents. However, some of the clipboard functions use XtWindow() rather than XtWindowOfObject() to get the window of an object. These functions do not work for gadgets.

clipboard is required for the incremental retrieval of large amounts of data. We will cover these functions shortly.

17.1.1 Copying Data

The syntax of the functions that copy data to the clipboard is outlined below. Due to the intricacies involved in providing data to the clipboard, these functions take a larger number of parameters than you might expect from the simple examples given so far. Later examples should clarify the intended usage of these functions and their corresponding parameters. Each of the routines takes a pointer to the Display and the Window associated with the object making the clipboard request. These parameters may be derived from any widget or gadget using XtDisplayOfObject() and XtWindowOfObject().

XmClipboardStartCopy() takes the following form:

```
int
XmClipboardStartCopy(display, window, label, timestamp,
                     widget, callback, item_id)
    Display        *display;
    Window         window;
    XmString       label;
    Time           timestamp;
    Widget         widget;
    XmCutPasteProc callback;
    long           *item_id;
```

The *widget* and *callback* parameters are only used when registering data by name (see Section 17.2). Although the *label* parameter is currently unused, its purpose is to label the data so that certain applications can view the contents of the clipboard. The *timestamp* identifies the server time when the cut took place (CurrentTime is the typical value). The *item_id* parameter is filled in by the toolkit and is returned to the client for use in subsequent clipboard function calls. This value identifies the item's entry in the clipboard.

XmClipboardCopy() has the following form:

```
int
XmClipboardCopy(display, window, item_id, format_name,
                buffer, length, private_id, data_id)
    Display        *display;
    Window         window;
    long           item_id;
    char           *format_name;
    XtPointer      buffer;
    unsigned long  length;
    int            private_id;
    int            *data_id;
```

`XmClipboardCopy()` copies the data in *buffer* to the clipboard. The format of the data is described by the *format_name* parameter. This value is not a type, but a string describing the type. For example, `"STRING"` indicates that the data is a text string. The *length* parameter is the size of the data. Text strings, can use `strlen (data)`.

The *item_id* parameter is the ID returned by `XmClipboardStartCopy()`. The *data_id* parameter returns the format ID. You may pass `NULL` for this parameter if you are not interested in the value, however you may need it for other functions. For example, you will need it if you wish to withdraw an item from the clipboard. We will discuss this issue later when we talk about registration by name. The *private_id* parameter is an arbitrary number that is application-defined. The value is passed back to various functions, including those that handle calling by name, so we will address it further in Section 17.2.

When copying is done, `XmClipboardEndCopy()` is called to free the internal data structures associated with the clipboard item. The routine takes the following form:

```
int
XmClipboardEndCopy(display, window, item_id)
     Display *display;
     Window   window;
     long     item_id;
```

The *item_id* parameter is the ID returned by the call to `XmClipboardStartCopy()`.

The clipboard copy functions return one of three status values: `ClipboardSuccess`, `ClipboardLocked`, or `ClipboardFail`. If the client is successful in gaining access to the clipboard, the routine returns `ClipboardSuccess`. If another client is already accessing the clipboard, the clipboard is locked and the client can loop repeatedly to attempt to gain access.

Motif keeps a stack of items that have been placed on the clipboard using any of the clipboard functions. As of Release 1.1, the stack depth is set to two. If a third item is added, the older of the other two is removed. Once a copy to the clipboard is complete, you can undo it using `XmClipboardUndoCopy()`, which takes the following form:

```
int
XmClipboardUndoCopy(display, window)
     Display *display;
     Window   window;
```

Calling `XmClipboardUndoCopy()` twice undoes the last undo. Thus, undoing a copy simply swaps the two elements on the clipboard stack. You can remove an item that you have placed on the clipboard using `XmClipboardWithdrawFormat()`. This routine is discussed in Section 17.2.

17.1.2 Retrieving Data

In Example 17-1, we retrieved the data stored on the clipboard using the function Xm-ClipboardRetrieve(). This function takes the following form:

```
int
XmClipboardRetrieve(display, window, format_name, buffer,
                    length, num_bytes, private_id)
    Display       *display;
    Window         window;
    char          *format_name;
    char          *buffer;
    unsigned long  length;
    unsigned long *num_bytes;
    int           *private_id;
```

When using XmClipboardRetrieve(), you must provide buffer space to retrieve the data. In our example, we know that the data is not very large, so we declared *buffer* to have 32 bytes, which is more than adequate. The *length* parameter tells the clipboard how much space is available in *buffer*. The *num_bytes* parameter is the address of an unsigned long variable. This value is filled in by XmClipboardRetrieve() to indicate how much data it gave us. The *private_id* parameter is the address of an int; its value is the same as the *private_id* parameter passed to XmClipboardCopy(). You can pass NULL as this parameter if you are not interested in it.

If the routine is successful in retrieving the data, it returns ClipboardSuccess. If the clipboard is locked, the function returns ClipboardLocked. A rare internal error may cause the function to return ClipboardFail. If the routine does not succeed, you can choose to loop repeatedly to attempt to retrieve data.

One problem with XmClipboardRetrieve() occurs when there is more data in the clipboard than buffer space to contain it. In this case, the function copies only *length* bytes into *buffer* and sets *num_bytes* to the number of bytes it copied, which should be the same value as *length* if not enough space is available. If this situation arises, the function returns ClipboardTruncate to indicate that it did not copy everything that is available. Since we cannot just arbitrarily specify a larger data space without knowing how much data there is, we have two choices: query the clipboard to find out how much data there is or copy the data incrementally. There are advantages and disadvantages to each method. Let's start by discussing incremental retrieval.

To do an incremental retrieval, we need to introduce two functions: XmClipboard-StartRetrieve() and XmClipboardEndRetrieve(). These functions are similar to the start and end copy functions discussed earlier. XmClipboardStartRetrieve() takes the following form:

```
int
XmClipboardStartRetrieve(display, window, timestamp)
    Display  *display;
    Window    window;
    Time      timestamp;
```

This function locks the clipboard and notes the *timestamp*. Data placed on the clipboard after this time is considered invalid and the function returns ClipboardFailed. The constant `CurrentTime` is typically used as this value.† `XmClipboardStart-Retrieve()` also allocates internal data structures to support the incremental retrieval operation. Once the function is called, multiple calls to `XmClipboardRetrieve()` can be made until it returns `ClipboardSuccess`. While the routine returns `Clipboard-Truncate`, more data needs to be read and you should continue to call the function. Be careful to save the data that has already been retrieved before the next call to the function, or you may overwrite the old data and lose information.

Once all of the data has been retrieved, call `XmClipboardEndRetrieve()`, which takes the following form:

```
int
XmClipboardEndRetrieve(display, window)
    Display    *display;
    Window     window;
```

This function unlocks the clipboard and frees the internal data structures. Example 17-2 shows a callback routine that retrieves data from the clipboard incrementally. The `from_clipbd_incr()` routine could replace the `from_clipbd()` callback routine in Example 17-1.

Example 17-2. The from_clipbd_incr() routine

```
static void
from_clipbd_incr(widget, client_data, call_data)
Widget widget;
XtPointer client_data;
XtPointer call_data;
{
    int            status;
    unsigned       total_bytes;
    unsigned long received;
    char           *data = NULL, buf[32];
    Display        *dpy = XtDisplayOfObject (widget);
    Window         window = XtWindowOfObject (widget);

    do
        status = XmClipboardStartRetrieve (dpy, window, CurrentTime);
    while (status == ClipboardLocked);

    /* initialize data to contain at least one byte. */
    data = XtMalloc (1);
    total_bytes = 1;
    do {
        /* retrieve data from clipboard -- if locked, try again */
        status = XmClipboardRetrieve (dpy, window, "STRING",
            buf, sizeof (buf), &received, NULL);

    /* reallocate data to contain enough space for everything */
    if (!(data = XtRealloc (data, total_bytes + received))) {
        XtError ("Can't allocate space for data");
        break; /* XtError may or may not return */
    }
```

---

† It is also common to provide the timestamp found in an event structure when available. This technique is typically used when the clipboard retrieval is initiated as a result of an action or callback routine where an event structure is available.

Example 17-2. The from_clipbd_incr() routine (continued)

```
        /* copy buf into data. strncpy() does not NULL terminate */
        strncpy (&data[total_bytes-1], buf, received);
        total_bytes += received;
    } while (status == ClipboardTruncate);

    if (data)
        data[total_bytes] = 0; /* NULL terminate */

    if (status == ClipboardSuccess)
        printf ("Retrieved \"%s\" from clipboard.\n", data);

    status = XmClipboardEndRetrieve (dpy, window);
}
```

The callback routine works regardless of the amount of data held by the clipboard. If the client placed an entire file on the clipboard, the routine would read all of it in 32-byte increments. It is probably wise to use a larger block size when retrieving data incrementally; the constant BUFSIZ† is a good default choice.

The primary advantage of using the incremental retrieval method is that you do not need to allocate a potentially large amount of memory at one time. By segmenting memory, you can reuse some of it, or even discard it as each increment is read. This technique is especially useful if you are scanning for specific data and you have no intention of actually saving everything that you retrieve.

17.1.3 Querying the Clipboard for Data Size

The problem with incremental retrieval is that numerous round trips to the server may be necessary in order to obtain the entire contents of the clipboard. If you intend to save every bit of information you retrieve, the most economical way to handle the retrieval is by reading everything in one fell swoop. A single call to XmClipboardRetrieve() is more convenient than the three-step process involving locking the clipboard.

However, as pointed out earlier, we have a problem since we do not know how much data there is to read. The solution to the problem is to determine exactly how much data there is by using XmClipboardInquireLength(). This routine has the following form:

```
int
XmClipboardInquireLength(display, window, format_name, length)
    Display       *display;
    Window         window;
    char          *format;
    unsigned long *length;
```

The function returns the amount of data being held by the clipboard under the specified *format_name*. In Example 17-3, we are looking for data in the "STRING" format. If any data on the clipboard is in this format, the function returns ClipboardSuccess and the

---

† BUFSIZ is defined in <*stdio.h*>.

length parameter is set to the number of bytes being held. If there is no data on the clipboard in the specified format, the function returns `ClipboardNoData`. If *length* is not set to a value other than 0, the data cannot be read from the clipboard.

If `XmClipboardInquireLength()` is successful, then the number of bytes specified by *length* can be allocated and the data can be retrieved in one call to `XmClipboard-Retrieve()`. Example 17-3 shows a callback routine that retrieves data from the clipboard after querying the size of the data. The `from_clipbd_query()` routine could replace the `from_clipbd()` callback routine in Example 17-1.

Example 17-3. The from_clipbd_query() routine

```
static void
from_clipbd_query(widget, client_data, call_data)
Widget widget;
XtPointer client_data;
XtPointer call_data;
{
    int         status, recvd, length;
    char        *data;
    Display     *dpy = XtDisplayOfObject (widget);
    Window      window = XtWindowOfObject (widget);

    do
        status = XmClipboardInquireLength (dpy, window, "STRING", &length);
    while (status == ClipboardLocked);

    if (length == 0)
        printf ("No data on clipboard in specified format.\n");

    data = XtMalloc (length+1);

    do
        status = XmClipboardRetrieve (dpy, window,
            "STRING", data, length+1, &recvd, NULL);
    while (status == ClipboardLocked);

    if (status != ClipboardSuccess || recvd != length) {
        printf ("Failed to receive all clipboard data\n");
      XtFree (data);
    }
    else
        printf ("Retrieved \"%s\" from clipboard.\n", data);
}
```

17.2 Copy by Name

As discussed earlier, there are cases where data should not be copied to the clipboard until it is requested. It is possible to copy data by name, so that the owner of the data is notified through a callback function when the data is needed by the clipboard. Since copying large amounts of data may be expensive, time-consuming, or even impossible due to other constraints in an application, copying data by name may be the only option available. The technique is especially advantageous if the data is never requested, since time and resources are saved.

The procedure for copying data by name is quite similar to the procedure for normal copying. The application first calls XmClipboardStartCopy(), but unlike a normal copy operation, the *callback* and *widget* parameters are specified. These values indicate that the data is to be copied by name. The *callback* parameter specifies the routine that is called when the data is requested by another client. The *widget* parameter specifies the widget that receives the messages requesting the data. Since the toolkit handles the messages, any valid widget ID can be used.

XmClipboardCopy() is then called with a *buffer* value of NULL. XmClipboard-EndCopy() is called as usual. When a client requests the data from the clipboard, the callback routine provided to XmClipboardStartCopy() is called and the application provides the actual data using XmClipboardCopyByName().

You can use the convenience function XmClipboardBeginCopy() instead of Xm-ClipboardStartCopy(). The only difference between the two routines is that the convenience function does not take a *timestamp* parameter; it simply uses CurrentTime as the timestamp value.

The program shown in Example 17-4 demonstrates copying data to the clipboard by name.

Example 17-4. The copy_by_name.c program

```
/* copy_by_name.c -- demonstrate clipboard copies "by-name".
 * Copying by name requires that the copy *to* clipboard
 * functions use the same window as the copy *from* clipboard
 * functions.  This is a restriction placed on the API by the
 * toolkit, not by the ICCCM.
 */
#include <Xm/CutPaste.h>
#include <Xm/RowColumn.h>
#include <Xm/PushB.h>

static void to_clipbd(), from_clipbd();
Widget toplevel;

main(argc, argv)
int argc;
char *argv[];
{
    Widget rowcol, button;
    XtAppContext app;

    XtSetLanguageProc (NULL, NULL, NULL);

    /* Initialize toolkit, application context and toplevel shell */
```

Example 17-4. The copy_by_name.c program (continued)

```
    toplevel = XtVaAppInitialize (&app, "Demos", NULL, 0,
        &argc, argv, NULL, NULL);

    /* manage two buttons in a RowColumn widget */
    rowcol = XtVaCreateWidget ("rowcol",
        xmRowColumnWidgetClass, toplevel,
        NULL);

    /* button1 copies to the clipboard */
    button = XtVaCreateManagedWidget ("button1",
        xmPushButtonWidgetClass, rowcol,
        XtVaTypedArg, XmNlabelString, XmRString,
            "Copy To Clipboard", sizeof (char *),
        NULL);
    XtAddCallback (button, XmNactivateCallback, to_clipbd, NULL);

    /* button2 retrieves text stored in the clipboard */
    button = XtVaCreateManagedWidget ("button2",
        xmPushButtonWidgetClass, rowcol,
        XtVaTypedArg, XmNlabelString, XmRString,
            "Retrieve From Clipboard", sizeof (char *),
        NULL);
    XtAddCallback (button, XmNactivateCallback, from_clipbd, NULL);

    /* manage RowColumn, realize toplevel shell and start main loop */
    XtManageChild (rowcol);
    XtRealizeWidget (toplevel);
    XtAppMainLoop (app);
}

static void
copy_by_name(widget, data_id, private_id, reason)
Widget widget;
int *data_id;
int *private_id;
int *reason;
{
    Display     *dpy = XtDisplay (toplevel);
    Window       window = XtWindow (toplevel);
    static int   cnt;
    int          status;
    char         buf[32];

    printf ("Copy by name called\n\treason: %s, private_id: %d, data_id: %d\n",
        *reason == XmCR_CLIPBOARD_DATA_REQUEST? "request" : "delete",
        *private_id, *data_id);

    if (*reason == XmCR_CLIPBOARD_DATA_REQUEST) {
        sprintf (buf, "stuff-%d", ++cnt); /* make each copy unique */

        do
            status = XmClipboardCopyByName (dpy, window, *data_id, buf,
                strlen (buf)+1, *private_id = cnt);
        while (status != ClipboardSuccess);
    }
}

/* copy data to clipboard */
static void
```

Example 17-4. The copy_by_name.c program (continued)

```
to_clipbd(widget, client_data, call_data)
Widget widget;
XtPointer client_data;
XtPointer call_data;
{
    unsigned long item_id = 0;  /* clipboard item id */
    int          status;
    XmString     clip_label;
    Display      *dpy = XtDisplay (toplevel);
    Window       window = XtWindow (toplevel);

    clip_label = XmStringCreateLocalized ("to_clipbd");

    /* start a copy.  retry till unlocked */
    do
        status = XmClipboardBeginCopy (dpy, window,
            clip_label, widget, copy_by_name, &item_id);
    while (status == ClipboardLocked);

    /* copy by name by passing NULL as the "data", copy_by_name() as
     * the callback and "widget" as the widget.
     */
    do
        status = XmClipboardCopy (dpy, window, item_id, "STRING",
            NULL, 8L, 0, NULL);
    while (status == ClipboardLocked);

    /* end the copy */
    do
        status = XmClipboardEndCopy (dpy, window, item_id);
    while (status == ClipboardLocked);
}

static void
from_clipbd(widget, client_data, call_data)
Widget widget;
XtPointer client_data;
XtPointer call_data;
{
    int          status;
    unsigned     total_bytes;
    unsigned long received;
    char         *data = NULL, buf[32];
    Display      *dpy = XtDisplay (toplevel);
    Window       window = XtWindow (toplevel);

    do
        status = XmClipboardStartRetrieve (dpy, window, CurrentTime);
    while (status == ClipboardLocked);

    /* initialize data to contain at least one byte. */
    data = XtMalloc (1);
    total_bytes = 1;
    do  {
        buf[0] = 0;
        /* retrieve data from clipboard -- if locked, try again */
        status = XmClipboardRetrieve (dpy, window, "STRING",
                buf, sizeof (buf), &received, NULL);
        if (status == ClipboardNoData) {
```

Example 17-4. The copy_by_name.c program (continued)

```
            puts ("No data on the clipboard");
            break;
        }
        /* reallocate data to contain enough space for everything */
        if (!(data = XtRealloc (data, total_bytes + received))) {
            XtError ("Can't allocate space for data");
            break; /* XtError may or may not return */
        }
        /* copy buf into data.  strncpy() does not NULL terminate */
        strncpy (&data[total_bytes-1], buf, received);
        total_bytes += received;
    } while (status == ClipboardTruncate);
    data[total_bytes-1] = 0; /* NULL terminate */

    if (status == ClipboardSuccess)
        printf ("Retrieved \"%s\" from clipboard (%d bytes)\n",
            data, total_bytes);

    status = XmClipboardEndRetrieve(dpy, window);
}
```

Just as in Example 17-1, the function `to_clipbd()` is used to initiate copying data to the clipboard. However, rather than passing actual data, we use:

```
    status = XmClipboardBeginCopy (dpy, window,
        clip_label, widget, copy_by_name, &item_id);
```

Passing a valid widget and a callback routine indicates that the copy-by-name method is being used. Here, the data is provided through the given callback routine when it is requested, rather than being provided immediately. The `item_id` parameter is filled in by the clipboard function to identify the particular data element. The parameter is then used in the call to copy data:

```
    status = XmClipboardCopy (dpy, window, item_id, "STRING",
        NULL, 8L, 0, NULL);
```

Passing `NULL` as the data also indicates that the data is passed by name. The value `8L` is passed as the *size* parameter to indicate how much data will be sent if the data is requested. This value is important in case other clients query the clipboard to find out how much data is available to copy.

The callback function `copy_by_name()` is called either when someone requests the data from the clipboard or when another client copies new data (by name or with actual data) to the clipboard. In the first case, the data must be copied to the clipboard; in the second case, the clipboard is telling the client that it can now free its data. The callback function is an `XmCutPasteProc`, which takes the following form:

```
    typedef void
    (*XmCutPasteProc) (Widget, * int, * int, * int)
        Widget widget;
        int *data_id;
        int *private_id;
        int *reason;
```

The *widget* parameter is the same as that passed to `XmClipboardStartCopy()`. The *data_id* arguemnt is the ID of the data item that is returned by `XmClipboardCopy()`, and *private_id* is the private data passed to XmClipboardCopy(). The *reason* parameter takes the value XmCR_CLIPBOARD_DATA_REQUEST, which indicates that the data must be copied to the clipboard, or XmCR_CLIPBOARD_DATA_DELETE, which indicates that the client can delete the data from the clipboard. Although the last three parameters are pointers to integer values, the values are read-only and changing them has no effect.

The purpose of the function is either to send the appropriate data to the clipboard or to free the data. The value of reason determines which action is taken. Since no data is passed to the clipboard until this callback function is called, either the data must be stored locally (in the application) or the function must be able to generate it dynamically. The example makes no assumptions or suggestions about how to create the data, since it is entirely subject to the nature of the data and/or the application.

Once the data is obtained, it is sent to the clipboard using XmClipboardCopyByName(). This function does not need to lock the clipboard since the clipboard is already being locked by the window that called XmClipboardRetrieve(). At this point in time, both routines are accessing the clipboard. If the same application is both retrieving the data and copying the data, the XmClipboardRetrieve() and XmClipboardCopyByName() routines must use the same window for their respective *window* parameters because otherwise deadlock will occur and the application will hang. There may be cases where you should copy data to the clipboard incrementally. The data may be large enough that allocating one large data space to handle the entire copy is unreasonable; its size may warrant sending it in smaller chunks. Moreover, data may be generated by a slow mechanism such as a database library. If the database only returns data in specific block sizes, then you need not buffer them all up and send to the clipboard with one call; you can send each block as it comes through.

Incremental copying requires multiple calls to XmClipboardCopyByName(). Since XmClipboardCopyByName() does not lock the clipboard, you need to do that yourself by calling XmClipboardLock(). However, you only need to call it once no matter how much data is transferred. When you are through copying the data, you need to call Xm-ClipboardUnlock(). In some cases, you may need to stop sending data before the copy is complete. For example, if the database is not responding to your application or there are other extenuating circumstances, you may want to terminate the copy operation using Xm-ClipboardCancelCopy(), which has the following form:

```
int
XmClipboardCancelCopy(display, window, item_id)
    Display *display;
    Window   window;
    long     item_id;
```

When using XmClipboardCancelCopy, you should not unlock the clipboard using Xm-ClipboardUnlock().

If you have copied data by name to the clipboard under a specific data format, you may withdraw it by calling XmClipboardWithdrawFormat(). The function takes the following form:

```
int
XmClipboardWithdrawFormat(display, window, data_id)
    Display *display;
    Window   window;
    int      data_id;
```

Despite the name of the procedure, its main purpose is not to remove a format specification, but to remove a data element in that format from the clipboard. The *data_id* parameter is the same value that is returned by XmClipboardCopy() when the data is initially copied by name. If the specified window holds the clipboard data but it is in a different format than that specified by *data_id*, then the data is not removed from the clipboard.

17.3 Clipboard Data Formats

As discussed in the introduction, the clipboard can contain data in arbitrary formats. While the most commonly used format is text, other formats include integers, pixmaps, and arbitrary data structures. Since all applications on the desktop have access to the clipboard, any of them may register a new format and place items of that type on the clipboard.

When registering a new format, you must also register a corresponding format name and the format length in bits (8, 16, and 32). Determining the type of data on the clipboard is much easier when there is a descriptive name associated with it. The length allows applications to send and receive data without suffering from byte-swapping problems due to differing computer architectures.

To register a new format, use XmClipboardRegisterFormat(), which takes the following form:

```
int
XmClipboardRegisterFormat(display, format_name, format_length)
    Display       *display;
    char          *format_name;
    unsigned long  format_length;
```

The function may return ClipboardBadFormat if the format name is NULL or the format length is other than 8, 16, or 32. The format length may be specified as 0, in which case Motif will attempt to look up the default length for the given name. Table 17-1 shows the format lengths for some predefined format names.

Table 17-1. Predefined Format Names and Lengths

Format Name	Format Length
"TARGETS"	32
"MULTIPLE"	32
"TIMESTAMP"	32
"STRING"	8
"LIST_LENGTH"	32
"PIXMAP"	32
"DRAWABLE"	32
"BITMAP"	32
"FOREGROUND"	32
"BACKGROUND"	32
"COLORMAP"	32
"ODIF"	8
"OWNER_OS"	8
"FILE_NAME"	8
"HOST_NAME"	8
"CHARACTER_POSITION"	32
"LINE_NUMBER"	32
"COLUMN_NUMBER"	32
"LENGTH"	32
"USER"	8
"PROCEDURE"	8
"MODULE"	8
"PROCESS"	32
"TASK"	32
"CLASS"	8
"NAME"	8
"CLIENT_WINDOW"	32

Although these format names are known, they are not necessarily registered automatically with the server; you may still need to register the one(s) you want to use. If you are specifying your own data structure as a format, you should choose an appropriate name for it and use 32 as the format size.

The following code fragment shows how you can register a data format and then copy data in that format to the clipboard:

```
unsigned long item_id;
int           data_id;
Display       *dpy = XtDisplay (widget);
Window        window = XtWindow (widget);
XmString      label = XmStringCreateLocalized ("my data");

/* register our own data structure with clipboard. */
XmClipboardRegisterFormat (dpy, "MY_DATA_STRUCT", 32);

/* use the copy-by-name method to transfer data to clipboard */
```

```
        do
            status = XmClipboardStartCopy (dpy, window, label, CurrentTime,
                my_data_callback, widget, &item_id);
        while (status == ClipboardLocked);

        XmStringFree (label); /* don't need this anymore */

        /* MY_DATA_SIZE is presumed to be the amount of data to transfer */
        do
            status = XmClipboardCopy (dpy, window, item_id, "MY_DATA+STRUCT",
                NULL, MY_DATA_SIZE, 0, &data_id); /* save the data_id! */
        while (status == ClipboardLocked);

        do
            status = XmClipboardEndCopy (dpy, window, item_id);
        while (status == ClipboardLocked);
```

Once the `"MY_DATA_STRUCT"` format has been registered with the server, we follow the standard procedure for copying data to the clipboard. Here, we chose to use the copy-by-name method discussed earlier. Note that we save the value of the data_id returned by Xm-ClipboardCopy(). This value is used so that we may withdraw the data later using Xm-ClipboardWithdrawFormat() if necessary. Note that formats are never removed from the clipboard; only data can be removed from the clipboard. Once a particular format is registered with the clipboard, it is there until the server goes down. If you plan on retrieving data held by the clipboard, you may wish to inquire about the format of the data it is holding. To do so, you must use two functions together: XmClipboardInquireCount() and XmClipboardInquireFormat(). They take the following form:

```
    int
    XmClipboardInquireCount(display, window, count, max_length)
        Display *display;
        Window  window;
        int     *count;
        int     *max_length;


    int
    XmClipboardInquireFormat(display, window, index,
                            format_name_buf, buffer_len, copied_len)
        Display         *display;
        Window          window;
        int             index;
        char            *format_name_buf;
        unsigned long   buffer_len;
        unsigned long   *copied_len;
```

XmClipboardInquireCount() returns the number of formats the clipboard knows about for the data item it is currently holding. Also returned is the string length of the longest format name. You can iterate through the formats starting from 1 (one) through count by calling XmClipboardInquireFormat(). The iteration number is passed as the index parameter. You should use this value to ensure that you can read all the format types in your search for the desired format.

Although there is only one data item stored on the clipboard at any one time, that item may have multiple formats associated with it. While this is unusual, it is possible to handle this case by providing different formats to successive calls to XmClipboardCopy() or Xm-ClipboardCopyByName().

17.4 The Primary Selection and the Clipboard

Since text is the most commonly used format in the clipboard, there is a natural interaction between the clipboard and windows that contain text. In most situations, it is usual (even expected) that when the user selects text, the selection should be placed on the clipboard, which is known as a copy operation. Retrieving text from the clipboard and placing it in another window is known as a paste operation. In some cases, after the data is pasted from the clipboard, the original window deletes the data it copied, which is classified as a cut operation. The clipboard uses what is commonly referred to as the cut and paste model.

The low-level implementation of the clipboard mechanism uses the X Toolkit selection mechanism. This model has additional properties that provide for more detailed communication between the clients involved. For example, cutting text from a Text widget and placing it in another widget involves more communication between the widgets than that of the clipboard copy and retrieval mechanism. When the text that was selected in the first widget is pasted in the other, the first widget may be notified to delete the selected text. This type of communication can be handled either automatically by the Text widgets or through low-level X calls where the corresponding windows of the widgets send real events called client messages to one another.

17.4.1 Clipboard Functions With Text Widgets

In most cases, you should not need to access the clipboard functions to perform simple text copy and retrieval (cut and paste) for Text widgets. If you need to access the clipboard above and beyond the normal selection mechanisms provided by the Text widgets, there are a number of convenience routines that deal with selections automatically. We present a brief overview of these functions here; see Chapter 14, *Text Widgets*, for detailed information.

The `XmTextCut()`, `XmTextCopy()`, and `XmTextPaste()` routines handles cutting, copying, and pasting operations for the Text widget. There are also corresponding functions for the TextField widget. `XmTextCut()` and `XmTextCopy()` take the following form:

```
Boolean
XmTextCut(widget, time)
    Widget widget;
    Time time;

Boolean
XmTextCopy(widget, time)
    Widget widget;
    Time time;
```

If there is text selected in the Text widget referred to by the `widget` parameter, the selected text is placed on the clipboard. For `XmTextCut()`, the selected text is also deleted from the Text widget, while for `XmTextCopy()` it is not. The functions return `True` if all of these things happen successfully. If `False` is returned, it is usually because the Text widget does not have any selected text.

The *time* parameter controls when the operation takes place and may be set to any server timestamp value. For example, if you are calling this function from a callback routine, you may wish to use the time field from the event pointer in the callback structure provided by the Motif toolkit. The value CurrentTime can also be used, but there is no guarantee that this value will prevent any race conditions between other clients wanting to use the clipboard. Although race conditions are not likely, the possibility does exist. The result of the race condition is that one widget may appear to have cut or copied selected text to the clipboard when in fact another Text widget got there first.

XmTextPaste() takes the following form:

```
Boolean
XmTextPaste(widget)
    Widget widget;
```

XmTextPaste() gets the current data from the clipboard and places it in the Text widget. The routine returns False if there is no data on the clipboard.

XmTextCut() and XmTextCopy() only work if there is a current selection in the specified Text widget, which may be dependent on whether or not the user has made a selection. However, you can force a selection in a Text widget using XmTextSetSelection(). This routine takes the following form:

```
void
XmTextSetSelection(widget, first, last, time)
    Widget          widget;
    XmTextPosition  first;
    XmTextPosition  last;
    Time            time;
```

XmTextSetSelection() selects the text between the specified positions in the Text widget. Once the text has been selected, either XmTextCut() or XmTextCopy() may be called to place the selection on the clipboard.

Although XmTextGetSelection() does not deal with the clipboard directly, it provides a convenient way to get the current selection from the corresponding Text widget. This routine takes the following form:

```
char *
XmTextGetSelection(widget)
    Widget widget;
```

Note that the text returned by the routine is allocated data and must be freed by the caller using XtFree(). The function returns NULL if the specified widget does not own the text selection.

To deselect the current selection in a Text widget, you can use XmTextClear-Selection(), which takes the following form:

```
void
XmTextClearSelection(widget, time)
    Widget  widget;
    Time    time;
```

17.4.2 The Owner of the Selection

Sometimes, if you have a large number of Text widgets, you may need to know which of the widgets has the text selection. You can determine this by using the Xlib function `XGet-SelectionOwner()`:

```
Window
XGetSelectionOwner(display, selection)
    Display *display;
    Atom    selection;
```

The *display* parameter can be taken from any widget using `XtDisplay()`. The *selection* argument represents the `Atom` associated with the kind of selection you are looking for. For example, you can determine the Text widget that has the current clipboard selection with the following calls:

```
Display *dpy = XtDisplay (widget);
Atom clipboard_atom = XmInternAtom (dpy, "CLIPBOARD", False);
Window win = XGetSelectionOwner (dpy, clipboard_atom);
Widget text_w = XtWindowToWidget (dpy, win);         \
```

17.5 Implementation Issues

The Motif clipboard mechanism relies on an underlying X mechanism referred to as properties. As you know, windows are data structures maintained by the X server; each window can have an arbitrary list of properties associated with it. Each property consists of a name (called an atom), an arbitrary amount of data, and a format. Property formats are not at all the same thing as the higher-level Motif formats—they simply indicate whether the data is a list of 8-bit, 16-bit, or 32-bit quantities, so that the server can perform byte-swapping, if appropriate. Properties are the underlying mechanism for all interclient communication, including interaction between applications and window managers, and interapplication interaction such as the transfer of selections.

In order to simplify communication over the network, property names are not passed as arbitrary-length strings, but as defined integers known as atoms. A number of standard properties (such as those used for communication between applications and window managers) are predefined and *interned*, or made known to, and cached by the server. However, application-defined atoms can also be interned with the server by calling the Xlib function `XInternAtom()` or the Motif function `XmInternAtom()`. Atoms are not only used to name properties, but to name any string data that may need to be passed back and forth between a client and the server.

We started this chapter with the analogy that the Motif toolkit is the moderator of the clipboard. In reality, the clipboard itself is a property (called CLIPBOARD) that is automatically maintained by the X server. A property is uniquely identified by both an atom and a window, which means that it is possible for there to be multiple copies of a given property. However, there should be only one CLIPBOARD property active at one time, based on conventions about the use of properties set forth in a document called the *Inter-Client Communication Conventions Manual*† (ICCCM) and followed by the deeper layers of X software. Among

---

† Reprinted as Appendix L of Volume Zero, *X Protocol Reference Manual*.

these conventions are that certain properties should only be set by application top-level windows and that only one window should own the CLIPBOARD property at any one time. When an application makes a call to `XmClipboardCopy()`, the data is actually stored in the CLIPBOARD property of the window that was identified in the call to `XmClipboard-Copy()`.

The format of the data stored in a property is defined by another property. The standard formats are based on those recommended by the ICCCM. For example, the FONT format might suggest that an application wants the font that the data string is rendered in, rather than the data string itself. At present, Motif does not support this functionality. You have to remember that formats (or targets, as they are referred to in the ICCCM) are not really things that have any functionality. They are simply names that are translated into integer atoms. The meaning of the formats to an application depends entirely on convention. At present, most applications only support the STRING format. But eventually, conventions will doubtless be articulated for doing far more with the selection mechanism.

A further complication that needs some mention is how the Motif clipboard implementation relates to the underlying X Toolkit implementation of selections. The ICCCM actually defines three separate properties that can be used for selections: PRIMARY, SECONDARY, and CLIPBOARD. Standard Xt applications, including all of the clients distributed by MIT, use the PRIMARY property for storing selections.

The SECONDARY property is designed for quicker, more transient selections. An application that makes use of this property usually copies data directly to another window instantly when the owner finishes copying data to the property. The Motif Text widget uses the SECONDARY property when the META key is down while the middle button is clicked and dragged. As soon as the selection is complete, the selected data is immediately sent to the window that has the input focus, which may be the same window.

In the standard MIT implementation, the CLIPBOARD property is used by an independent client called *xclipboard*. Keep in mind that a property stays around only as long as the window with which it is associated. When you terminate a client and close its windows, any data stored in a property on one of the client's windows is lost. If the CLIPBOARD property is associated with a client that is kept around between invocations of other applications, it embodies a consistent repository for information to be passed between applications.

The ICCCM blesses the use of both the PRIMARY and CLIPBOARD selection properties. However, you should be aware that the difference between the Motif use of the CLIPBOARD property and the use of the PRIMARY selection property by other Xt applications makes interoperability questionable, unless you take care to handle the PRIMARY selection in your application. The X Toolkit mechanisms for handling selections are described in Volume Four, *X Toolkit Intrinsics Programming Manual*. The Motif Text widgets support both the Xt mechanism, which uses the PRIMARY selection, and the Motif clipboard, depending on the interaction. You should probably do the same for your application.

While you can manipulate properties and atoms directly using Xlib, the higher-level API provided by Motif and Xt should insulate you from many of the details and ensure that your applications interoperate well with others. Eventually, toolkits and applications will doubtless support numerous extensions of the current clipboard and selection mechanisms.

17.6 Summary

The clipboard provides a convenient mechanism that allows applications to interact with one another in a way that is independent of the application, operating system, and system architecture. The clipboard is one of two common mechanisms used to handle data transfer between objects. The primary selection is still regarded as the most common method for data transfer between applications, mostly because it is the standard cut and paste method used to move textual data between terminal emulators like *xterm*. A secondary selection method is also available, but is not very widely used.

The Motif toolkit tries to compensate for the *de facto* standard use of the primary selection method by integrating both the primary and clipboard selections into the same set of functions. Although users seem to be oblivious to the differences, this technique has the unfortunate side effect of confusing programmers.

18

Drag and Drop

This chapter describes the drag and drop mechanism provided by the Motif toolkit. Drag and drop can be used to transfer data within and between applications on the desktop.

In This Chapter:

18
Drag and Drop

A graphical user interface provides objects that the user can manipulate and actions that can be performed on those objects. The drag and drop mechanism for transferring data is a natural one for a GUI, as drag and drop allows the user to transport data within and between applications by dragging an iconic representation of the data from one location to another. The ability to transfer data using drag and drop is new in Motif 1.2.

An important question that a developer needs to consider is whether or not drag and drop is appropriate for a particular application. You need to think about the data that is manipulated by the application, the actions that can be performed on the data, and whether the drag and drop metaphor makes sense in this context. This decision involves figuring out if drag and drop allows you to enhance the usability of your application by making it easier for the user to perform various tasks.

For example, an electronic mail application might allow the user to drag messages that have been received into folders for storage or into a text editor for composing a response. Perhaps the most common use of drag and drop functionality is for desktop-style applications. These programs allow the user to manipulate files in the directory structure and run other applications by dragging objects around on the desktop

18.1 Using Drag and Drop

From the user's perspective, drag and drop involves choosing a data source, dragging the data around on the desktop, and dropping the data on a new location. The mechanism is the same no matter what type of data is being manipulated. In most cases, the data is moved or copied to the new location. However, an application can also allow the user to drag an object and drop it to invoke an action. For example, dropping a file on a printer icon could cause the file to be printed.

The *Motif Style Guide* specifies that the middle mouse button is used for drag and drop. The user starts a drag and drop transfer by pressing the second button over the data, which is referred to as the *drag source*. While the user is dragging the data, the pointer shape is changed to a *drag icon* which is a picture that represents the type of data being dragged. The drag icon is meant to provide the user with feedback about the current data transfer, so different drag icons can be used to represent textual data and graphical data, for example.

The user can drag the data to another location within the same application or to a location within another application by moving the pointer with the middle button pressed. The data can be dropped in any location that has been registered as a *drop site*. The drop occurs when the user releases the mouse button. Figure 18-1 shows the conceptual model of drag and drop.

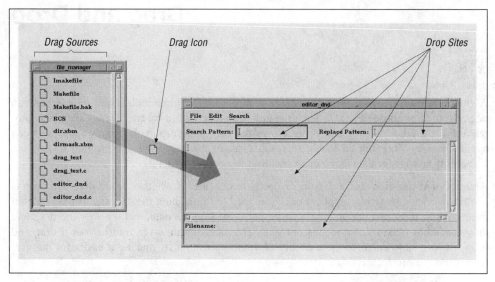

Figure 18-1. Drag and drop conceptual model

A drag and drop transfer can result in the data being moved, copied, or linked. A move operation copies the data to the drop site and then removes it from the drag source, while a copy operation copies the data to the drop site without removing it. A link operation allows the drop site access to the data in the drag source without copying it.

The default operation depends on the type of data that is being manipulated. In an editable text area, the default operation might be a move, while in a read-only area, the default operation should be a copy. A drag source can support multiple operations, in which case the user should be able to select the operation that is used. The *Style Guide* specifies that the SHIFT key selects a move operation, the CTRL key selects a copy operation, and CTRL-SHIFT selects a link operation.

The user can cancel a drag at any time by pressing the ESCAPE key. The user can also request help on a drop site by pressing the HELP or F1 key before dropping the data. The help information should tell the user what will happen if the data is dropped in the drop site.

Besides representing the type of data being manipulated, the drag icon can also indicate the current operation and whether the pointer is over a valid drop site, over an invalid drop site, or not over a drop site at all. For a drop site to be valid, the drag source and the drop site must understand at least one common data format. If a drag source only provides graphical data and a drop site only understands text, the data transfer cannot succeed.

The drag icon may change as it enters and leaves drop sites to provide this state information; these changes are called *drag-over* visuals. For example, the drag icon could be displayed without any modification when it is over a valid drop site, but be superimposed with a do-not-enter symbol when the drop site is invalid. A drop site may also change its appearance when the drag icon is within it; these effects are known as *drag-under* visuals. A "garbage can" drop site might use animation to show the lid opening when a drag icon moves into the drop site. When the user performs a drop, the drag icon melts into the drop site if the data transfer is successful or springs back to the drag source if the transfer fails.

18.2 The Drag and Drop Model

The Motif implementation of drag and drop introduces a number of new programming constructs. The interaction between the different components is complex, so it may be difficult to understand just what needs to be done to implement drag and drop functionality. Since you need to understand all of the different components before you can see what your application may need, we've decided to describe all of the components of drag and drop in a somewhat abstract way before we present any examples. Although this material may be a bit dry, we think that this approach works better than presenting an example early and then having to jump around a lot to explain all of its parts. Hopefully, once you see the big picture, it will be easier to understand the different pieces more fully.

From the programmer's perspective, providing drag and drop functionality in an application can be as simple as using the Motif widgets that support drag and drop. In Motif 1.2, the Text, TextField, and List widgets are all drag sources, which means that the textual data they contain can be dragged. The Label widget and its subclasses are also drag sources for both textual and pixmap data. The Text and TextField widgets are registered as drop sites, which means that textual data can be dropped in them. When you use these widgets in an application, you do not have to do any extra programming to provide their drag and drop capabilities since the functionality is built into the widgets.

The drag and drop capabilities provided by the Motif toolkit are highly customizable, so an application can also implement custom drag and drop transfers. Drag source and/or drop site functionality can be added to any widget. An application can provide custom drag icons and implement custom drag-under effects, such as animated drop sites. Drag and drop can be made to handle any type of data. The amount of programming required to implement custom drag and drop features varies depending on the degree of customization that is desired. While it is relatively easy to provide a new drop site for textual information, supporting drag and drop for graphical objects requires quite a bit of work.

The Motif toolkit layers the implementation of drag and drop on top of the selection mechanisms provided by the X Toolkit Intrinsics. If you are simply using the built-in drag and drop functionality, the implementation details are completely invisible. However, if you are customizing drag and drop in any way, you need to understand the underlying selection mechanisms because the drag and drop implementation is not a complete abstraction over the Xt mechanisms. For example, an application that uses custom drag sources and drop sites must provide certain selection conversion and transfer procedures in order for the data transfer to occur.

Drag and Drop

Since the Xt selection mechanisms are based on X's *Inter-Client Communications Conventions Manual* (ICCCM), the Motif implementation of drag and drop also adheres to the ICCCM. Data is transferred using properties on the server, where properties are referenced using atoms. Drag sources and drop sites also use atoms to specify the data formats, or targets, that they support. The ICCCM suggests a list of possible target types so that applications can understand each other. These targets and their meanings are shown in Table 18-1. You can also define your own targets, but unless you document them, other applications will not necessarily be able to communicate with your application using these targets.

Table 18-1. Target Types Defined by ICCCM

Atom	Type	Meaning
TARGETS	ATOM	List of valid target atoms
MULTIPLE	ATOM_PAIR	Multiple conversion requests
TIMESTAMP	INTEGER	Timestamp used to acquire selection
STRING	STRING	ISO Latin 1 text
COMPOUND_TEXT	COMPOUND_TEXT	Text in compound text encoding
TEXT	TEXT	Text in owner's encoding
LIST_LENGTH	INTEGER	Number of disjoint parts of selection
PIXMAP	DRAWABLE	Pixmap ID
DRAWABLE	DRAWABLE	Drawable ID
BITMAP	BITMAP	Bitmap ID
FOREGROUND	PIXEL	Pixel value
BACKGROUND	PIXEL	Pixel value
COLORMAP	COLORMAP	Colormap ID
ODIF	TEXT	ISO Office Document Interchange Format
OWNER_OS	TEXT	Operating system of owner
FILE_NAME	TEXT	Full path name of a file
HOST_NAME	TEXT	Hostname of machine of owner
CHARACTER_POSITION	SPAN	Start and end of selection in bytes
LINE_NUMBER	SPAN	Start and end line numbers
COLUMN_NUMBER	SPAN	Start and end column numbers
LENGTH	INTEGER	Number of bytes in selection
USER	TEXT	Name of user running owner
PROCEDURE	TEXT	Name of selected procedure
MODULE	TEXT	Name of selected module
PROCESS	INTEGER, TEXT	Process ID of owner
TASK	INTEGER, TEXT	Task ID of owner
CLASS	TEXT	Class of owner (WM_CLASS)
NAME	TEXT	Name of owner (WM_NAME)
CLIENT_WINDOW	WINDOW	Top-level window of owner
DELETE	NULL	True if owner deleted selection
INSERT_SELECTION	NULL	Insert specified selection
INSERT_PROPERTY	NULL	Insert specified property

Motif uses some new objects to encapsulate information about various aspects of a drag and drop transfer. These objects act like widgets, in that they are created by the programmer, they have resources that can be set and retrieved, and they interact with the application using callbacks. However, they are unlike traditional widgets in that they are not visible components of the user interface. The DragContext object is used to store information during a drag, while the DropTransfer object keeps track of information during a drop. The DragIcon object is used to represent the pointer shape that is used during a drag and drop transfer. The DropSite object maintains information about all of the drop sites in an application. The new Display and Screen objects also provide resources that control the behavior of drag and drop, although they are not specifically part of drag and drop.

The following sections describe all the components of a drag and drop transfer and present the Motif objects that are used to implement drag and drop. As we describe the objects, we mention many of their resources, callbacks, and related functions so that you can see how everything fits together. We describe each of the objects in much greater detail later in the chapter when we talk about how they can be used to customize different aspects of drag and drop. However, this chapter does not attempt to describe all of the possible ways in which drag and drop can be customized. We present some common situations and leave you to explore all of the details on your own. For complete information about each Motif object used to implement drag and drop, see the appropriate reference pages in Volume Six B, *Motif Reference Manual*.

18.2.1 The Drag Source

The widget that contains the data being manipulated with drag and drop is known as the drag source. When the user starts a drag, the application that contains the drag source is considered the initiator of the transfer. The data provided by a drag source depends on the type of object the source represents. For example, a Text widget provides textual data, while a DrawingArea could provide some form of graphical data.

A drag source can be designed to support and transfer any type of data. There can even be multiple formats for a given piece of data if appropriate. A drag source also specifies the operations (move, copy, or link) that it allows. The type of data, and in some cases the widget that contains the data, affects the operations that are supported. For example, the List widget only supports copy operations because it is a read-only component.

In order for a drag and drop transfer to work, the drag source and the drop site need to understand the same type of data. The drag source announces the data targets it can supply to the drop site. A drag source that supports textual data might offer the data using COMPOUND_TEXT, STRING, and TEXT targets, while a graphical drag source could provide PIXMAP, FOREGROUND, and BACKGROUND targets. When the drop occurs, the drop site can request the data in any of the targets supported by the drag source, so the drag source needs to know how to convert between supported types.

In order for a widget to be a drag source, the widget must be able to recognize a Button-Press event for the second mouse button. Essentially, you need to set up a translation and action or an event handler for this event that invokes a function that starts the drag. The following code fragment shows the definition of a translation and an action for a drag source:

```
static char dragTranslations[] =
    "#override <Btn2Down>: StartDrag()";

static XtActionsRec dragActions[] =
    { {"StartDrag", (XtActionProc) StartDrag} };
```

Just as with any translation and action, the application needs to call `XtParse-TranslationTable()` and `XtAppAddActions()`. The parsed translation table can be used to set the `XmNtranslations` resource for the drag source widget.

The Motif toolkit uses the DragContext object to store information about a drag source once a drag has started. This object also keeps track of state information about the transfer as it is happening. The routine that starts a drag calls `XmDragStart()` to create the DragContext and get things rolling. The DragContext object has resources that need to be set at creation time to provide information about the drag source. The `XmNdragOperations` resource specifies the operations supported by the drag source, while `XmNexportTargets` and `XmNnumExportTargets` indicate the data targets that are supported.

The DragContext also has a number of resources that control the visual effects used during the drag. Many of these resources specify various attributes of the drag icon for the transfer. For example, the `XmNsourceCursorIcon`, `XmNoperationCursorIcon`, and `XmN-stateCursorIcon` resources indicate the images that are used for different parts of the drag icon. If these resources are not specified, the DragContext uses default icons. There are also resources that allow you to specify different foreground and background colors for the drag icon. We describe the drag icon in more detail in Section 18.2.3.

The DragContext also provides callback routines that can be used to monitor the drag and provide custom visual effects. All of the routines use special callback structures that provide information about the current state of the drag. Section 18.4.5 provides more information about these callbacks.

The `XmNconvertProc` is a procedure that must be specified when a DragContext is created. This procedure is used to convert the drag source data to the format requested by the drop site when the drop occurs. The procedure is either an `XtConvertSelectionProc` or an `XtConvertSelectionIncrProc`, depending on whether or not the drag source is using incremental transfer. If the `XmNincremental` resource is set to `True`, the data is transferred incrementally. Both of these procedures are part of the underlying Xt selection mechanism that is not completely hidden by the Motif drag and drop abstraction. See Volume Four, *X Toolkit Intrinsics Programming Manual*, for more information on these procedures.

The following code fragment shows the creation of a DragContext object with a minimal set of resources:

```
Atom        exportList[1];
Widget      widget, dc;
Arg         args[5];
int         n;
Boolean     ConvertProc();
XEvent      *event;
```

```
    . . .
    n = 0;
    exportList[0] = COMPOUND_TEXT;
    XtSetArg (args[n], XmNexportTargets, exportList); n++;
    XtSetArg (args[n], XmNnumExportTargets, XtNumber (exportList)); n++;
    XtSetArg (args[n], XmNdragOperations, XmDROP_COPY); n++;
    XtSetArg (args[n], XmNconvertProc, ConvertProc); n++;
    dc = XmDragStart (widget, event, args, n);
```

In Section 18.4, we present an example that creates a custom drag source, and we describe the source code in detail.

Once a DragContext has been created, the Motif toolkit for the initiating application assumes control of the drag, so the application itself doesn't have to do anything during the drag. If any of the DragContext callbacks have been specified, they are called automatically by the Motif toolkit at the appropriate time.

When the drop occurs, the drop site determines whether or not the data transfer can succeed based on the operations and targets supported by the drag source and the drop site. If the transfer can succeed, the drop site initiates the transfer, which causes the XmNconvert-Proc to be called for each data target that the drop site has requested. This routine converts the data into the requested format and passes it back to the drop site, so the drop site can do whatever it needs with the data.

18.2.2 The Drop Site

Once the user starts a drag and drop transfer, the data can be dropped in any location that has been registered as a drop site, and if the drop site understands the data, the transfer will succeed. The application that contains the drop site where data is dropped is the receiving client in a drag and drop transfer. A drop site is always associated with a widget. Like a drag source, a drop site supports particular types of data, depending on the type of object it is.

A drop site can be designed to handle any type of data, or even multiple types if appropriate. A drop site also specifies the operations that it supports. The standard operations are to move, copy, and link data. However, a drop site can instead invoke an action as the result of a drop. For example, a "send message" drop site could send an electronic mail message when text is dropped in it. The type of object that functions as the drop site also has an effect on the supported operations. In most cases, it only makes sense for writable components to act as drop sites, since read-only components like Lists and Labels cannot be modified by the user.

Motif stores information about all of the drop sites in an application using DropSite objects. An application registers a widget as a drop site by calling XmDropSiteRegister() for the widget. The DropSite object uses resources to keep track of information about the drop site. This information can be set when the drop site is registered, or it can be specified later using XmDropSiteUpdate(); the values of the resources can be retrieved using Xm-DropSiteRetrieve(). Since a widget is being used as the handle to the drop site, you cannot use XtVaSetValues() and XtVaGetValues() to set and retrieve drop site information, as these routines manipulate the widget's resources.

Just as a drag source specifies the data types that it can process, a drop site also needs to provide this information. The XmNimportTargets and XmNnumImportTargets resources specify this information, while the XmNdropSiteOperations resource specifies the operations supported by the drop site.

A drop site provides visual effects when the drag icon passes through it; these effects are called drag-under effects. By default, the widget is highlighted. Other simple effects, such as a shadow border or a special pixmap, can be specified using the XmNanimationStyle resource. All of these effects are handled automatically by the toolkit on the initiating side once the resource is set. For more sophisticated effects, such as animation, a drop site must register an XmNdragProc. This callback is invoked whenever there is any drag activity in the drop site, so the application can do whatever it likes in terms of drag-under effects.

While the XmNdragProc is optional, every drop site must have a XmNdropProc registered. This routine is called when a drop occurs in the drop site. The procedure is responsible for determining whether the drop is successful or not, based on the targets and operations supported by the drag source and the drop site. The following code fragment shows how a widget that can handle compound text is registered as a drop site:

```
Arg          args[10];
int          n;
Widget       label;
Atom         importList[1];
void         HandleDrop();

. . .
n = 0;
importList[0] = COMPOUND_TEXT;
XtSetArg (args[n], XmNimportTargets, importList); n++;
XtSetArg (args[n], XmNnumImportTargets, XtNumber (importList)); n++;
XtSetArg (args[n], XmNdropSiteOperations, XmDROP_COPY); n++;
XtSetArg (args[n], XmNdropProc, HandleDrop); n++;
XmDropSiteRegister (label, args, n);
```

When a drop occurs in the drop site, the XmNdropProc is called automatically by the Motif toolkit. This routine must call XmDropTransferStart() whether or not the drop is successful. XmDropTransferStart() creates a DropTransfer object that maintains information about the data transfer. When The DropTransfer object is created, the XmNtransferStatus resource must be set to indicate the success or failure of the drop. If the resource is set to XmTRANSFER_FAILURE, XmDropTransferStart() does not transfer any data and merely cleans up after the drag and drop transfer.

If XmNtransferStatus is set to XmTRANSFER_SUCCESS when the DropTransfer object is created, some other resources must also be specified to cause the data to be transferred. The XmNdropTransfers and XmNnumDropTransfers resources specify the data targets to be processed, while XmNtransferProc indicates the procedure that receives the converted data from the drag source. This procedure is of type XtSelectionCallback-Proc. Once the data transfer has started, XmDropTransferAdd() can be used to request the processing of additional data targets. In Section 18.5, we discuss in detail the tasks involved in creating a drop site.

When a drop takes place, visual effects are used to indicate the status of the transfer. Unlike the different drag effects, these visuals are not customizable. When the drop occurs, the pointer shape is changed back to the standard cursor, while the drag icon sits over the drop site. If the drop succeeds, the icon melts into the drop site. If the transfer fails or is cancelled by the user, the icon snaps back to the drag source.

A drop site is normally the size and shape of the widget with which it is associated. However, a drop site can also be shaped. The `XmNdropRectangles` and `XmNnumDrop-Rectangles` resources control this feature. Drop sites can also be nested, so that a manager widget can be a drop site and can also contain children that are drop sites. The `XmNdropSiteType` resource controls whether the drop site is a simple drop site or a compound drop site. Drop sites have a stacking order, which means that they can overlap. When drop sites overlap, the drop site on the top of the stack obscures the drop sites beneath it, as you would expect. An application can control the stacking order of drop sites using `XmDropSiteQueryStackingOrder()` and `XmDropSiteConfigureStackingOrder()`.

18.2.3 The Drag Icon

During a drag, the pointer shape is changed into a drag icon that represents the data that is being dragged. One of the purposes of the special icon is to make it clear that a drag and drop transfer is in progress. The drag icon can also change during a drag to indicate the current status of the transfer. These visual effects are called drag-over visuals. Typical effects include changing the shape and changing the color of the icon.

A drag icon can be composed of three distinct parts, each of which is really a separate icon. The *source icon* represents the type of data that is being dragged; this icon is the only necessary component of a drag icon. The source icon for a drag that manipulates files might be an image of a piece of paper, for example. The *state icon* indicates whether the pointer is over a valid drop site, over an invalid drop site, or not over a drop site. The *operation icon* specifies the current operation. The source icon in a drag icon is static, while the state and operation icons can be dynamic. Figure 18-2 shows the components of a drag icon.

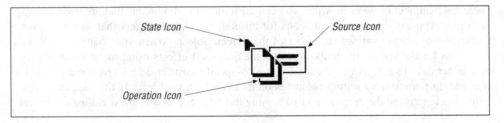

Figure 18-2. A drag icon

The Motif toolkit provides default icons for all of the different drag icon components. The default source icons for textual data and for generic data are shown in Figure 18-3.

Figure 18-3. Default source icons

The default state icon for all of the different states is an arrow, as shown in Figure 18-2, while the default operation icons for the move, copy, and link operations are shown in Figure 18-4.

Figure 18-4. Default operation icons

Motif uses DragIcon objects to represent the parts of a drag icon. In order to use a custom image, you need to create each part of the icon using `XmCreateDragIcon()`. The `XmN-blendModel` resource of the DragContext for a drag and drop transfer specifies the different pieces that are blended together to create the actual drag icon.

A drag icon is essentially a pixmap, and the DragIcon object encapsulates all of the information about the image. When you create a DragIcon, you specify resources that describe the image. The `XmNpixmap` and `XmNmask` resources represent the actual pixmap and its mask if you use one. Other resources include `XmNheight`, `XmNwidth`, and `XmNdepth` for specifying those attributes of the image, as well as `XmNhotX` and `XmNhotY` for indicating the x,y coordinate of the hotspot for the icon. The `XmNattachment`, `XmNoffsetX`, and `XmN-offsetY` resources specify how the icon is attached to the other parts of a drag icon.

There are a number of ways in which you can customize the drag icons that are used for drag and drop. You can specify default icons for all drag and drop transfers that start from your application by setting various resources of the Screen object. When you change the default drag icons for the Screen, the toolkit handles the drag-over effects using the icons, as we discuss in Section 18.3.3. An application can also specify custom drag icons for a particular drag and drop transfer by setting resources on its DragContext object. In this case, the application has to manage the drag-over visuals using the different DragContext callback routines.

18.2.4 Protocols

For drag and drop to work, the initiating and receiving applications must be able to talk to each other. The Motif toolkit supports two different mechanisms by which clients can communicate with each other during drag and drop. The main information that needs to be passed back and forth during a drag concerns the location of the drag icon relative to drop sites in the receiving application. The *dynamic* drag protocol requires messaging between the two applications, while the *preregister* drag protocol does not. During the drop, the Xt selection protocol is used to transfer the data from one application to the other.

Drag Protocols

An application can quite easily support both the dynamic and preregister drag protocols, although it can just support one or neither of the protocols if necessary. If an application does not support either of the protocols, it can still participate in drag and drop, but it does not provide any visual effects during the drag. The best approach is to support both protocols so that users can specify the protocol that is used based on their needs. By default the toolkit supports both protocols, so it is easy for an application to support both as well. The code for the initiating client is the same for both protocols, while the code for the receiver is the same except for an additional procedure that can be specified for use under the dynamic protocol.

With the preregister protocol, information about all of the drop sites in an application is stored in a database. This database is kept in a property on the top-level window of the application (or on each top-level window, if there is more than one) so that it can be read by an initiating application. During a drag, the initiator uses information in the database to manage both drag-over and drag-under visuals. Drop sites in the receiving application can set some resources to control the style of drag-under effect used, but the receiver does not participate directly in the drag.

One benefit of the preregister protocol is that it does not require dynamic communication between the initiating and receiving applications, so the performance of drag and drop does not suffer if the network is heavily loaded. However, a receiving application cannot provide sophisticated drag-under effects when the preregister protocol is being used. Under this protocol, the server is grabbed during the drag, which means that the drag icon can be any size (the size is not limited to the largest cursor size, as it is for the dynamic protocol).

Under the dynamic protocol, when the drag icon moves into a receiving application's window, the initiator sends a message to the application. Based on this message, the toolkit on the receiving side determines whether or not the drag icon is in a valid drop site. The toolkit also initializes state and operation information for the receiver, although the receiving application can update this information using its XmNdragProc. Based on the movement of the drag icon, the initiator receives the updated message back in one of its drag-related callbacks.

The benefit of the dynamic protocol is that the receiving application can provide sophisticated drag-under effects and drag processing using its XmNdragProc. However, the application does not have to provide these effects, as the toolkit provides some basic effects by default. The dynamic protocol also has some drawbacks. One drawback is that the messaging is expensive in terms of network traffic and may lead to unacceptable performance if the network is heavily loaded. Another limitation is that the image used for the drag icon can only be as large as the largest cursor supported by the system running the application.

The Display object provides two resources that can be set to indicate which protocol the toolkit should use when an application is the initiating or the receiving application in a drag and drop transfer. These resources are XmNdragInitiatorProtocolStyle and XmN-dragReceiverProtocolStyle. An application can set the resources if it needs to specify a particular protocol, or they can be set by the user in a resource file. We describe the different values for the resources and how the actual protocols are determined in Section 18.3.1, when we discuss how to customize drag and drop.

Drop Protocol

The protocol that is used to transfer data when the drop occurs encompasses the Xt incremental and non-incremental selection protocols. The DropTransfer object created by the receiving application handles the drop protocol. When the DropTransfer object is created using XmDropTransferStart(), the receiver specifies resources that indicate the list of desired targets, as well as an XmNtransferProc that handles the data once it has been converted by the initiator. The toolkit processes the requests one at a time by calling the XmNconvertProc of the initiating client. This procedure processes the request and passes the data back to the XmNtransferProc.

The DragContext and DropTransfer objects both have XmNincremental resources that specify whether or not the data transfer is incremental. Incremental transfers are used when the data is too large for a single X protocol request. No matter how the two resources are set, the toolkit handles the transfer of data using the underlying Xt selection mechanisms. Both the initiator and the receiver are informed about the completion of the entire transfer once all of the subtransfers are done, if there are any.

18.2.5 The Programming Model

If you review what we've just covered and put all of the pieces together, it creates a complex picture from the programmer's perspective. Fortunately, unless you are trying to do something really complicated, you can ignore many of the pieces and only use what you need. This section describes the complete picture by laying out the responsibilities of both the initiating and receiving applications for each step of a drag and drop operation. Figure 18-5 shows the steps graphically.

Even though most applications contain both drag sources and drop sites, it makes sense to think about the two roles separately, as the programming requirements for each are separate. If the initiator and receiver are in the same application, then the same toolkit is used by both parties. Otherwise, each application is using a separate toolkit.

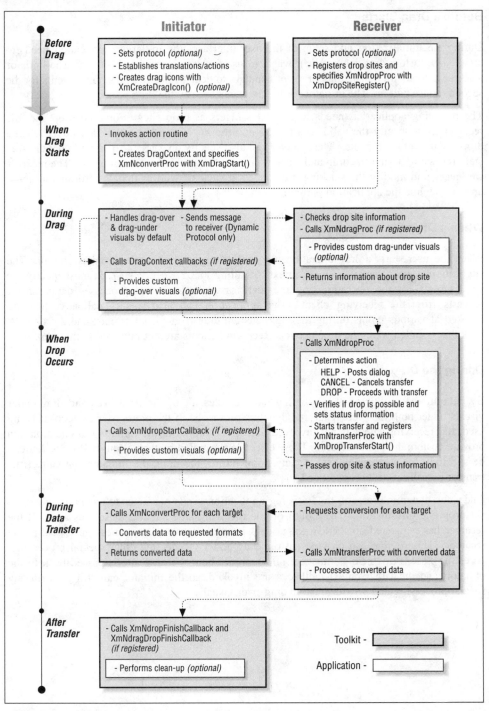

Figure 18-5. Drag and drop programming model

Drag and Drop

Before a Drag Starts

During the initialization and setup of the user interface, the initiating application needs to create any custom drag icons that it wants to use for drag-over visual effects. The initiator also needs to set up translations or event handlers to deal with `ButtonPress` events for the second mouse button. The initiator (or the user) can specify the drag protocol if necessary.

The receiving application needs to register widgets as drop sites. For each drop site, the receiver must specify the valid data targets and the `XmNdropProc` that takes over when a drop occurs in the drop site. The receiver can also specify an `XmNdragProc` to handle special processing during the drag and custom drag-under visuals for the drop site. The receiver can query and modify the stacking order of drop sites, as well as update information about drop sites while the application is running.

When a Drag Starts

When the user starts a drag operation, the toolkit on the initiating side takes control. The application needs to create a DragContext by calling `XmDragStart()`. It must specify the valid targets for the operation and the `XmNconvertProc` that processes data transfer requests from the receiving client. The application can also specify callbacks that are invoked at various points during the drag, custom drag-over visual effects, and a drop callback that is called when the drop occurs. Receiving clients are not involved in this step.

During the Drag

By default, the toolkit on the initiating side handles all of the drag-over and drag-under visuals under both the preregister and dynamic protocols. If the preregister protocol is being used, the receiving client is not involved during the drag, but the initiating application can provide custom drag-over effects. These effects are handled by the various callbacks that can be specified for a DragContext. At any point during the drag, the initiator can cancel the transfer by calling `XmDragCancel()`.

Under the dynamic protocol, the initiating application sends messages to receiving clients to get drop site information. The toolkit on the receiving side handles these messages. If the receiver has registered an `XmNdragProc`, it is invoked each time a message is sent to the receiver. This routine can provide custom drag-under visuals and other special processing. After the `XmNdragProc` is finished, information about the drop site is passed back to the initiator, and the DragContext callbacks are invoked, so the initiator can still perform any special processing and provide custom drag-over visuals.

When a Drop Occurs

When the user drops the data, the toolkit on the receiving side takes over from the toolkit on the initiating side. The XmNdropProc for the drop site determines what action the user has requested. If the user has requested help, the receiving application should display a help dialog and see if the user wants to proceed. If the user cancels the transfer, the drop does not proceed. Otherwise, the XmNdropProc determines if the transfer is possible by checking the targets supported by drag source.

If the drop is valid, the receiving client starts the transfer of data by calling XmDrop-TransferStart(). If the transfer is not valid, the routine still needs to be called to clean up the operation. If the initiator has registered an XmNdropStartCallback on its Drag-Context, it is invoked now. Other than this callback, the initiating client plays no role when the drop occurs.

During the Data Transfer

When the receiver calls XmDropTransferStart(), it must specify a list of data and target formats that it wants from the initiating application. The routine creates a DropTransfer object that can be updated during the transfer. The receiver must also specify an XmN-transferProc to handle the data once it has been converted by the initiator. The receiver can cancel the transfer at any point.

For each target requested by the receiver, the XmNconvertProc of the initiator is called to convert the data to the specified format. The formatted data is passed back to the receiver's XmNtransferProc. Once the entire transfer is complete, the XmNdropFinish-Callback and XmNdragDropFinishCallback callbacks of the initiating client's DragContext are invoked, if they have been specified.

18.3 Customizing Built-in Drag and Drop

In Motif 1.2, the Text and TextField widgets, the List widget, and the Label widget and its subclasses all support drag and drop functionality by default. When you use these widgets in an application, they provide built-in drag and drop capabilities. All of the widgets are drag sources for textual data, while just the Text and TextField widgets are registered as drop sites for text.

With a Label widget or a button, the user can drag the entire text string of the component by starting a drag in the component. The Label widget and its subclasses are also drag sources for graphical data, but there are no built-in drop sites for graphical data. However, when these components are in a menu, they do not function as drag sources. These components are not drop sites because they are meant to be read-only components in a user interface. Most applications would not want the user to be able to change the label on a button by dropping text on it. However, if you want to provide this type of functionality, it is easy to register a Label or a button as a drop site using the technique we describe in Section 18.5.

The user can drag the text of either a single item or the current selection in a List widget. If the pointer is over a selected item when the drag is started, the text of the selected item is used for the drag. If multiple items are selected, the text of all of the selected items is used, where the items are separated by newlines. If the drag is started over an unselected item, the text of that item is transferred by drag and drop. The List widget is not a drop site because its items are not meant to be modified by the user. If you want to allow the user to modify a List by dropping items in it, however, you can register the widget as a drop site.

The Text and TextField widgets are the only Motif widgets that have built-in drop site functionality. The user can drop textual data from any drag source in these widgets. The widgets also function as drag sources, so the user can move and copy the current selection within and between Text and TextField widgets.

Applications that simply use the built-in drag and drop capabilities of the Motif widgets can still customize various aspects of the functionality. This section explores the different types of customization that are possible.

18.3.1 Specifying the Drag Protocol

Motif supports two different protocols for communication between applications during a drag. The dynamic protocol passes messages between the two applications about the location of drop sites, while the preregister protocol keeps track of drop site information in a database. Since the preregister protocol does not require communication between applications, it can provide better performance on a heavily-loaded network. However, the dynamic protocol offers the advantage of sophisticated drag-under visual effects.

The programmer or the user can specify the drag protocol for an application by setting the XmNdragInitiatorProtocolStyle and XmNdragReceiverProtocolStyle resources defined by the Display object. Motif creates a Display object automatically for an application when it creates the first shell on a particular display. If an application uses multiple displays, it has a Display object for each one. An application can retrieve the Display object for a specified display using XmGetXmDisplay().

The XmNdragInitiatorProtocolStyle and XmNdragReceiverProtocol-Style resources indicate the preferred drag protocol for an application when it is acting as an initiator and as a receiver, respectively, in a drag and drop transfer. Each resource can be set to one of the following values:

XmDRAG_PREREGISTER
    This value means that the application can only support the preregister drag protocol.

XmDRAG_DYNAMIC
    This value indicates that the application can only support the dynamic drag protocol.

XmDRAG_NONE
    This value means that drag and drop is disabled for the application.

XmDRAG_DROP_ONLY

> This value specifies that the application does not support either drag protocol, but it does support drag and drop transfers. The user can transfer data using drag and drop, but there are no visual effects during the drag.

XmDRAG_PREFER_DYNAMIC

> This value means that the application supports both the preregister and dynamic protocols, but it prefers to use the dynamic protocol.

XmDRAG_PREFER_PREREGISTER

> This value means that the application supports both drag protocols, but it prefers to use the preregister protocol. The value is the default value for XmNdragReceiverProtocolStyle.

XmDRAG_PREFER_RECEIVER

> This value indicates that the application supports both the preregister and dynamic protocols, but it defers to the preference of the receiving application. The value can only be specified for the XmNdragInitiatorProtocolStyle resource, and it is the default value for the resource.

The actual protocol that is used during a drag and drop transfer is based on the preferences specified by the initiating and receiving applications. The protocol can change during a drag as the drag icon enters and leaves top-level windows. Table 18-2 shows how the protocol is resolved based on the preferred protocols for the initiator and the receiver.

Table 18-2. Drag Protocol Resolution

Initiator Protocol Style	Receiver Protocol Style			
	Preregister	Prefer Preregister	Prefer Dynamic	Dynamic
Preregister	Preregister	Preregister	Preregister	Drop Only
Prefer Preregister	Preregister	Preregister	Preregister	Dynamic
Prefer Receiver	Preregister	Preregister	Dynamic	Dynamic
Prefer Dynamic	Preregister	Dynamic	Dynamic	Dynamic
Dynamic	Drop Only	Dynamic	Dynamic	Dynamic

If two applications cannot find an agreeable protocol style, the XmDRAG_DROP_ONLY style is used. In this case, there are no drag-over or drag-under visuals except for the initial drag icon. An application can also explicitly set the protocol resources to XmDRAG_DROP_ONLY, in which case the application does not provide any visual effects during the drag.

If an application sets XmNdragInitiatorProtocolStyle or XmNdragReceiverProtocolStyle to XmDRAG_NONE, the application does not participate in drag and drop as an initiator or a receiver, respectively. This value is useful for disabling drag and drop functionality, as we discuss in the next section.

The actual protocol used for a drag and drop transfer controls the visual effects that the user sees during the drag. Under the preregister protocol, the server is grabbed so the drag icon can be a pixmap of arbitrary size. The drag icon uses the depth and colormap of the drag source widget, so it can be a color image. When the dynamic protocol is used, the drag icon is implemented using the X cursor, so it must be a bitmap and is limited in size (use `XQueryBestCursor()` to determine the largest size for a particular hardware configuration).

An application should support both the dynamic and preregister protocols so that the user can select the protocol based on his needs. Since the toolkit supports both protocols by default, an application can easily support both as well. The code for handling drag sources is the same under both protocols. Drop sites can specify an optional `XmNdragProc` routine that is invoked under the dynamic protocol and can be used to provide sophisticated drag-under effects.

The only reason that you should specify the `XmNdragInitiatorProtocolStyle` and `XmNdragReceiverProtocolStyle` resources in application code is if your application is going to support only one of the drag protocols. In this case, you should set the resources to force the application to use the supported protocol. You can retrieve the Display object for the application using `XmGetXmDisplay()` and then use `XtVaSetValues()` to specify the resources. You can also use `XtVaGetValues()` to check the values of the protocol resources.

If your application supports both drag protocols, you can specify the protocol resources in an app-defaults file to indicate the application's preferred protocol. By default, an application uses the preregister protocol because `XmNdragInitiatorProtocolStyle` is set to `XmDRAG_PREFER_RECEIVER` and `XmNdragReceiverProtocolStyle` is set to `XmDRAG_PREFER_PREREGISTER`. If you have implemented custom drag-under visuals with an `XmNdragProc`, you should set the protocol resources to `XmDRAG_PREFER_DYNAMIC` so that the dynamic protocol is used whenever possible. You can set these resources in an app-defaults file as follows:

```
*DragInitiatorProtocolStyle: DRAG_PREFER_DYNAMIC
*DragReceiverProtocolStyle: DRAG_PREFER_DYNAMIC
```

If you set the protocol resources in an app-defaults file, users can specify their own values in a resource file. Users that want to ensure good performance should specify a preference for the preregister protocol, while users that want sophisticated drag-under effects should indicate a preference for the dynamic protocol.

18.3.2 Turning Off Drag and Drop Functionality

If you do not want to provide drag and drop in an application, you can turn off the functionality in a number of ways. The most effective way to turn off the functionality is to set both `XmNdragInitiatorProtocolStyle` and `XmNdragReceiverProtocolStyle` to `XmDRAG_NONE`. These settings completely disable drag and drop for the application. You can also set just one of the resources to this value to prevent an application from participating in drag and drop as either an initiator or a receiver.

You can also selectively turn off individual drag sources in an application. To prevent a widget from providing its default drag source functionality, you need to override the translation for the second mouse button for the widget, as shown in the following code fragment:

```
static char dragTranslations[] =
    "#override <Btn2Down>: DoNothing()";

static XtActionsRec dragActions[] =
    { {"DoNothing", (XtActionProc) DoNothing} };
```

True to its name, the DoNothing() action routine does nothing. Once you parse the translation table and add the actions to the application, you can use the translation to set the XmN-translations resources of all of the widgets that you do not want to function as drag sources.

There are two different ways to disable the drop site functionality of a Text or TextField widget. If you want to turn off the drop site permanently, you can call XmDropSite-Unregister() for the widget. This routine removes the drop site associated with the widget, so you have to reregister it if you want to enable the drop site. To disable a drop site temporarily, it is easier to use the XmNdropSiteActivity resource defined by the Drop-Site object. This resource can be set to either XmDROP_SITE_ACTIVE or Xm-DROP_SITE_INACTIVE. When a drop site is inactive, it does not participate in drag and drop. You can set a drop site inactive using XmDropSiteUpdate(), as shown in the following code fragment:

```
Widget text_w;
Arg args[5];
int n = 0;

. . .

XtSetArg (args[n], XmNdropSiteActivity, XmDROP_SITE_INACTIVE); n++;
XmDropSiteUpdate (text_w, args, n);
. . .
```

Even though drop sites are associated with widgets, you have to set DropSite resources using XmDropSiteUpdate(), not XtVaSetValues().

One situation in which you would probably want to disable a built-in drop site is when the widget is designed to be output-only. If you set the XmNeditable resource of a Text or TextField widget to False, the user cannot drop data in the widget because it is uneditable. However, the toolkit still displays the default drag-under visual effects in this case, so the widget appears as though it functions as a drop site. To make it clear that the widget is not a drop site, you can disable the drop site using one of the techniques we just described. If the widget is always uneditable, it is fine to use XmDropSiteUnregister(), but if the widget changes state, you are better off setting XmNdropSiteActivity.

When you set a Text or TextField widget insensitive, the user cannot interact with the widget, so it doesn't make sense for the widget to function as a drop site. However, there is currently a bug in the implementation of drag and drop such that the user can drop text in an insensitive widget. To prevent this problem, whenever you change the sensitivity of a Text widget, you should set the XmNdropSiteActivity resource to match the sensitivity.

18.3.3 Modifying the Visual Effects

Motif provides resources that both the user and the programmer can use to change the default drag-over visual effects that are used during a drag and drop transfer. The Screen object provides the following resources:

```
XmNdefaultSourceCursorIcon
XmNdefaultMoveCursorIcon
XmNdefaultCopyCursorIcon
XmNdefaultLinkCursorIcon
XmNdefaultValidCursorIcon
XmNdefaultInvalidCursorIcon
XmNdefaultNoneCursorIcon
```

These resources specify the default icons for all the components of a drag icon, including the different operations and states.

Motif creates a Screen object automatically for an application when it creates the first shell on a particular screen. If an application accesses multiple screens, it has a Screen object for each one. An application can retrieve the Screen object for a specified screen using XmGet-XmScreen().

The drag icon resources defined by the Screen object only take effect when the XmN-sourceCursorIcon, XmNoperationCursorIcon, and XmNstateCursorIcon resources have not been specified for a particular DragContext. All Motif widgets with built-in drag source functionality set the XmNsourceCursorIcon resource, so the Screen resource cannot be used to specify a different source icon for these components. The widgets do not set the XmNoperationCursorIcon and XmNstateCursorIcon resources, so you can set the various default icons for these components.

If neither the DragContext resources nor the Screen resources are specified, Motif uses hard-coded default icons. For example, the running figure shown in Figure 18-3 is used as the source icon whenever a source icon has not been specified. Since this icon is rather arbitrary, you might want to set the XmNdefaultSourceCursorIcon resource to something more appropriate for your application.

Before you can set the Screen resources in application code, you must create DragIcon objects for the different resources. In Section 18.4.2 we describe how to create a drag icon using XmCreateDragIcon(). Once the drag icon exists, you can retrieve the Screen object using XmGetXmScreen() and set its resources, as shown in the following code fragment:

```
Widget drag_icon, screen, toplevel;
. . .
screen = XmGetXmScreen (XtScreen (toplevel));
XtVaSetValues (screen, XmNdefaultSourceCursorIcon, drag_icon, NULL);
. . .
```

The specified icon is used whenever the source icon has not been set for the DragContext for a drag and drop transfer.

The Screen resources can also be set in a resource file. In this case, the icons can be specified as bitmap files, so the application does not have to create DragIcon objects. Both the icon and an optional mask can be specified using resources as follows:

```
*defaultSourceCursorIcon.pixmap: icon.xbm
*defaultSourceCursorIcon.mask: icon_mask.xbm
```

Although it is convenient to be able to set the Screen resources in a resource file, this feature really isn't that useful since the Motif widgets and most applications specify their drag icons using DragContext resources.

The XmNvalidCursorForeground, XmNinvalidCursorForeground, and XmN-noneCursorForeground resources of the DragContext can be used to further distinguish between the different states in a drag and drop transfer. These resources can be specified in a resource file as follows:

```
*validCursorForeground: green
*invalidCursorForeground: red
*noneCursorForeground: yellow
```

In this case, the drag icon changes color as the user moves it between components that are valid drop sites, components that are invalid drop sites, and components that are not drop sites. While it is possible to modify some aspects of the drag-over effects using Screen and DragContext resources, if you really want to provide customized visual effects, you need to understand more about the implementation of drag and drop. In Section 18.4.5 we discuss how to provide custom drag-over effects.

18.4 Working With Drag Sources

Many applications work with data other than text. In order to provide drag and drop capabilities, these applications need to create drag sources for the data they manipulate. In this section, we describe the steps you need to follow to create a new drag source. We use an example program that displays all the files in a directory and allows the user to drag the files. However, in order for this drag to succeed, we need another application that understands files as objects and allows the user to drop files. In Section 18.5, we present a text editor that handles the dropping of file data, but for now we are just going to consider the ability to drag a file. Example 18-1 shows the *file_manager.c* application, which we are going to describe in detail in the following sections.†

Example 18-1. The file_manager.c program

```
/* file_manager.c -- displays all of the files in the current directory
 * and creates a drag source for each file.  The user can drag the
 * contents of the file to another application that understands
 * dropping file data.  Demonstrates creating a drag source, creating
 * drag icons, and handling data conversion.
 */
```

---

† This chapter describes functionality that is new in Motif 1.2, so this example only works with the 1.2 version of the Motif toolkit.

Example 18-1. The file_manager.c program (continued)

```
#include <Xm/Screen.h>
#include <Xm/ScrolledW.h>
#include <Xm/RowColumn.h>
#include <Xm/Form.h>
#include <Xm/Label.h>
#include <Xm/AtomMgr.h>
#include <Xm/DragDrop.h>
#include <X11/Xos.h>
#include <stdio.h>
#include <sys/stat.h>

typedef struct {
    char    *file_name;
    Boolean is_directory;
} FileInfo;

/* global variable -- arbitrarily limit number of files to 256 */
FileInfo                files[256];

void                    StartDrag();

/* translations and actions.  Pressing mouse button 2 calls
 * StartDrag to start a drag transaction */

static char dragTranslations[] =
    "#override <Btn2Down>: StartDrag()";

static XtActionsRec dragActions[] =
    { {"StartDrag", (XtActionProc) StartDrag} };

main (argc, argv)
int argc;
char *argv[];
{
    Arg                 args[10];
    int                 num_files, n, i = 0;
    Widget              toplevel, sw, panel, form;
    Display             *dpy;
    Atom                FILE_CONTENTS, FILE_NAME, DIRECTORY;
    XtAppContext        app;
    XtTranslations      parsed_trans;
    char                *p, *buf[256];
    FILE                *pp, *popen();
    struct stat         s_buf;
    Pixmap              file, dir;
    Pixel               fg, bg;

    XtSetLanguageProc (NULL, NULL, NULL);

    toplevel = XtAppInitialize (&app, "Demos", NULL, 0, &argc, argv,
        NULL, NULL, 0);

    /* intern the Atoms for data targets */
    dpy = XtDisplay (toplevel);
    FILE_CONTENTS = XmInternAtom (dpy, "FILE_CONTENTS", False);
    FILE_NAME = XmInternAtom (dpy, "FILE_NAME", False);
    DIRECTORY = XmInternAtom (dpy, "DIRECTORY", False);

    /* use popen to get the files in the directory */
    sprintf (buf, "/bin/ls .");
```

Example 18-1. The file_manager.c program (continued)

```
    if (!(pp = popen (buf, "r"))) {
        perror (buf);
        exit (1);
    }
    /* read output from popen -- store filename and type */
    while (fgets (buf, sizeof (buf), pp) && (i < 256)) {
        if (p = index (buf, '\n'))
            *p = 0;
        if (stat (buf, &s_buf) == -1)
            continue;
        else if ((s_buf.st_mode &S_IFMT) == S_IFDIR)
            files[i].is_directory = True;
        else if (!(s_buf.st_mode & S_IFREG))
            continue;
        else
            files[i].is_directory = False;
        files[i].file_name = XtNewString (buf);
        i++;
    }
    pclose (pp);
    num_files = i;

    /* create a scrolled window to contain the file labels */
    sw = XtVaCreateManagedWidget ("sw",
        xmScrolledWindowWidgetClass, toplevel,
        XmNwidth, 200,
        XmNheight, 300,
        XmNscrollingPolicy, XmAUTOMATIC,
        NULL);

    panel = XtVaCreateWidget ("panel", xmRowColumnWidgetClass, sw, NULL);

    /* get foreground and background colors and create label pixmaps */
    XtVaGetValues (panel,
        XmNforeground, &fg,
        XmNbackground, &bg,
        NULL);
    file = XmGetPixmap (XtScreen (panel), "file.xbm", fg, bg);
    dir = XmGetPixmap (XtScreen (panel), "dir.xbm", fg, bg);
    if (file == XmUNSPECIFIED_PIXMAP || dir == XmUNSPECIFIED_PIXMAP) {
        puts ("Couldn't load pixmaps");
        exit (1);
    }

    parsed_trans = XtParseTranslationTable (dragTranslations);
    XtAppAddActions (app, dragActions, XtNumber (dragActions));

    /* create image and filename Labels for each file */
    for (i = 0; i < num_files; i++) {
        form = XtVaCreateWidget ("form", xmFormWidgetClass, panel, NULL);
        XtVaCreateManagedWidget ("type", xmLabelWidgetClass, form,
            /* specify translation for drag and index into file array */
            XmNtranslations, parsed_trans,
            XmNuserData, i,
            XmNlabelType, XmPIXMAP,
            XmNlabelPixmap, files[i].is_directory ? dir : file,
            XmNtopAttachment, XmATTACH_FORM,
            XmNbottomAttachment, XmATTACH_FORM,
```

Example 18-1. The file_manager.c program (continued)

```
            XmNleftAttachment, XmATTACH_FORM,
            XmNrightAttachment, XmATTACH_POSITION,
            XmNrightPosition, 25,
            NULL);
        XtVaCreateManagedWidget (files[i].file_name,
            xmLabelWidgetClass, form,
            XmNalignment, XmALIGNMENT_BEGINNING,
            XmNtopAttachment, XmATTACH_FORM,
            XmNbottomAttachment, XmATTACH_FORM,
            XmNrightAttachment, XmATTACH_FORM,
            XmNleftAttachment, XmATTACH_POSITION,
            XmNleftPosition, 25,
            NULL);
        XtManageChild (form);
    }

    XtManageChild (panel);

    XtRealizeWidget (toplevel);
    XtAppMainLoop (app);
}

/* StartDrag() -- action routine called by the initiator when a drag starts
 * (in this case, when mouse button 2 is pressed).  It starts
 * the drag processing and establishes a drag context.
 */
void
StartDrag(widget, event, params, num_params)
Widget  widget;
XEvent  *event;
String  *params;
Cardinal *num_params;
{
    Arg             args[10];
    int             n, i;
    Display         *dpy;
    Atom            FILE_CONTENTS, FILE_NAME, DIRECTORY;
    Atom            exportList[2];
    Widget          drag_icon, dc;
    Pixel           fg, bg;
    Pixmap          icon, iconmask;
    XtPointer       ptr;
    Boolean         ConvertProc();
    void            DragDropFinish();

    /* intern the Atoms for data targets */
    dpy = XtDisplay (widget);
    FILE_CONTENTS = XmInternAtom (dpy, "FILE_CONTENTS", False);
    FILE_NAME = XmInternAtom (dpy, "FILE_NAME", False);
    DIRECTORY = XmInternAtom (dpy, "DIRECTORY", False);

    /* get background and foreground colors and fetch index into file
     * array from XmNuserData.
     */
    XtVaGetValues (widget,
        XmNbackground, &bg,
        XmNforeground, &fg,
        XmNuserData,   &ptr,
```

Example 18-1. The file_manager.c program (continued)

```
        NULL);

    /* create pixmaps for drag icon -- either file or directory */
    i = (int) ptr;
    if (files[i].is_directory) {
        icon = XmGetPixmapByDepth (XtScreen (widget), "dir.xbm", 1, 0, 1);
        iconmask = XmGetPixmapByDepth (XtScreen (widget), "dirmask.xbm",
            1, 0, 1);
    }
    else {
        icon = XmGetPixmapByDepth (XtScreen (widget), "file.xbm", 1, 0, 1);
        iconmask = XmGetPixmapByDepth (XtScreen (widget), "filemask.xbm",
            1, 0, 1);
    }
    if (icon == XmUNSPECIFIED_PIXMAP || iconmask == XmUNSPECIFIED_PIXMAP) {
        puts ("Couldn't load pixmaps");
        exit (1);
    }

    n = 0;
    XtSetArg (args[n], XmNpixmap, icon); n++;
    XtSetArg (args[n], XmNmask, iconmask); n++;
    drag_icon = XmCreateDragIcon (widget, "drag_icon", args, n);

    /* specify resources for DragContext for the transfer */
    n = 0;
    XtSetArg (args[n], XmNblendModel, XmBLEND_JUST_SOURCE); n++;
    XtSetArg (args[n], XmNcursorBackground, bg); n++;
    XtSetArg (args[n], XmNcursorForeground, fg); n++;
    XtSetArg (args[n], XmNsourceCursorIcon, drag_icon); n++;
    /* establish the list of valid target types */
    if (files[i].is_directory) {
        exportList[0] = DIRECTORY;
        XtSetArg (args[n], XmNexportTargets, exportList); n++;
        XtSetArg (args[n], XmNnumExportTargets, 1); n++;
    }
    else {
        exportList[0] = FILE_CONTENTS;
        exportList[1] = FILE_NAME;
        XtSetArg (args[n], XmNexportTargets, exportList); n++;
        XtSetArg (args[n], XmNnumExportTargets, 2); n++;
    }
    XtSetArg (args[n], XmNdragOperations, XmDROP_COPY); n++;
    XtSetArg (args[n], XmNconvertProc, ConvertProc); n++;
    XtSetArg (args[n], XmNclientData, widget); n++;

    /* start the drag and register a callback to clean up when done */
    dc = XmDragStart (widget, event, args, n);
    XtAddCallback (dc, XmNdragDropFinishCallback, DragDropFinish, NULL);
}

/* ConvertProc() -- convert the file data to the format requested
 * by the drop site.
 */
Boolean
ConvertProc(widget, selection, target, type_return, value_return,
        length_return, format_return)
Widget          widget;
```

Example 18-1. The file_manager.c program (continued)

```
Atom                *selection;
Atom                *target;
Atom                *type_return;
XtPointer           *value_return;
unsigned long       *length_return;
int                 *format_return;
{
    Display    *dpy;
    Atom        FILE_CONTENTS, FILE_NAME, MOTIF_DROP;
    XtPointer   ptr;
    Widget      label;
    int         i;
    char        *text;
    struct stat s_buf;
    FILE        *fp;
    long        length;
    String      str;

    /* intern the Atoms for data targets */
    dpy = XtDisplay (widget);
    FILE_CONTENTS = XmInternAtom (dpy, "FILE_CONTENTS", False);
    FILE_NAME = XmInternAtom (dpy, "FILE_NAME", False);
    MOTIF_DROP = XmInternAtom (dpy, "_MOTIF_DROP", False);

    /* check if we are dealing with a drop */
    if (*selection != MOTIF_DROP)
        return False;

    /* get the drag source widget */
    XtVaGetValues (widget, XmNclientData, &ptr, NULL);
    label = (Widget) ptr;

    if (label == NULL)
        return False;

    /* get the index into the file array from XmNuserData from the
     * drag source widget.
     */
    XtVaGetValues (label, XmNuserData, &ptr, NULL);
    i = (int) ptr;

    /* this routine processes only file contents and file name */
    if (*target == FILE_CONTENTS) {
        /* get the contents of the file */
        if (stat (files[i].file_name, &s_buf) == -1 ||
                (s_buf.st_mode & S_IFMT) != S_IFREG ||
                !(fp = fopen (files[i].file_name, "r")))
            return False;

        length = s_buf.st_size;
        if (!(text = XtMalloc ((unsigned) (length + 1))))
            return False;
        else if (fread (text, sizeof (char), length, fp) != length)
            return False;
        else
            text[length] = 0;
        fclose (fp);
```

Example 18-1. The file_manager.c program (continued)

```
            /* format the value for transfer */
            *type_return = FILE_CONTENTS;
            *value_return = (XtPointer) text;
            *length_return = length;
            *format_return = 8;
            return True;
        }
    else if (*target == FILE_NAME) {
        str = XtNewString (files[i].file_name);

            /* format the value for transfer */
            *type_return = FILE_NAME;
            *value_return = (XtPointer) str;
            *length_return = strlen (str) + 1;
            *format_return = 8;
            return True;
        }
    else
        return False;
}

/* DragDropFinish() -- clean up after a drag and drop transfer.
 */
void
DragDropFinish (widget, client_data, call_data)
Widget widget;
XtPointer client_data;
XtPointer call_data;
{
    Widget        source_icon = NULL;

    XtVaGetValues (widget, XmNsourceCursorIcon, &source_icon, NULL);

    if (source_icon)
        XtDestroyWidget (source_icon);
}
```

The output of this application is shown in Figure 18-6.

The application gets the names of all of the files in the current directory† and displays the filenames using Label widgets. Each file has a file or folder image next to it, depending on whether it is a regular file or a directory. The images are the drag sources for manipulating the files. If the user presses the middle mouse button over one of the symbols, the pointer changes to a drag icon and he can drag the file to another application that has a drop site that understands files.

---

† We use popen () here, but you should use opendir () and readdir ().

Drag and Drop

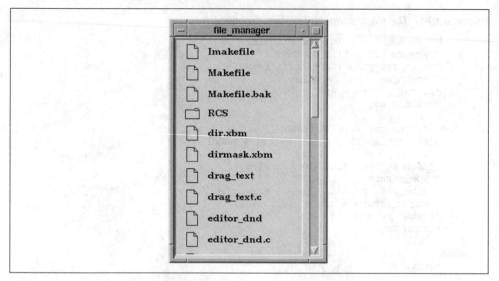

Figure 18-6. Output of file_manager.c

18.4.1 Creating a Drag Source

When the application reads the files in the directory, it creates a global array of structures that contain information about the files. This information is used to keep track of filenames and file types. For each file, the application creates two Label widgets: an image that represents the type of the file and a string that specifies the filename. To link the image Labels to the array, the application passes the index of each file in the array as the XmNuserData resource for the associated Label. This value can be retrieved and used to access the information in the array.

Depending on whether a file is a regular file or a directory, the application places an image of a file or a folder next to the filename Label. Each image is created using XmGetPixmap() and specified as the XmNlabelPixmap for the appropriate image Labels. The images are also used for drag icons during the drag operation, as we describe in the next section. For more information on XmGetPixmap(), see Section 3.4.5.

In order to specify that the file images are drag sources, we have to establish translations for the Label widgets that are used for the images. Label widgets already have drag source functionality, so we need to decide whether to override or augment this functionality. Since the existing translation merely allows the user to drag the pixmap image for the Label, we override the translation as shown in the following code fragment:

```
static char dragTranslations[] =
    "#override <Btn2Down>: StartDrag()";

static XtActionsRec dragActions[] =
    { {"StartDrag", (XtActionProc) StartDrag} };
```

The application parses the translation table and adds the action using XtParse-TranslationTable() and XtAppAddActions(), respectively. The new translation table is specified for the XmNtranslations resource for each of the image Labels.

The only other operation performed in `main()` that is relevant for the drag functionality is the interning of atoms for target types. We use the FILE_NAME target that is defined by the ICCCM, as well as two of our own targets, FILE_CONTENTS and DIRECTORY. We chose these target names ourselves because the ICCCM does not define any targets that are suitable for our purposes. We create atoms for these targets using `XmInternAtom()`, as shown in the following code fragment:

```
Widget    toplevel;
Display *dpy;
Atom      FILE_CONTENTS, FILE_NAME, DIRECTORY;

dpy = XtDisplay (toplevel);
FILE_CONTENTS = XmInternAtom (dpy, "FILE_CONTENTS", False);
FILE_NAME = XmInternAtom (dpy, "FILE_NAME", False);
DIRECTORY = XmInternAtom (dpy, "DIRECTORY", False);
```

Although we don't actually use the atoms in `main()`, we intern them so that they are cached by the Motif toolkit. When we intern the atoms in other routines in the application, they are retrieved from the cache.

18.4.2 Starting the Drag

When the user starts a drag, the `DragStart()` action routine is called. This routine creates a custom drag icon and calls `XmDragStart()` to start the drag. To create the appropriate drag icon, we need to know whether the drag source represents a file or a directory, so we fetch the `XmNuserData` from the Label widget that is the drag source. We use this value to access the appropriate structure in the `files` array and determine the type of file the user is manipulating.

Once we know what type of file we are dealing with, we can create the source icon for the drag. We use the same pixmap as for the image Label, so the drag icon is either a file image or a folder image. We use `XmGetPixmapByDepth()` to create both the icon and an icon-mask so that we can specify a depth of 1. We call `XmCreateDragIcon()` to create the drag icon, as shown in the following code fragment from Example 18-1:

```
n = 0;
XtSetArg (args[n], XmNpixmap, icon); n++;
XtSetArg (args[n], XmNmask, iconmask); n++;
drag_icon = XmCreateDragIcon (widget, "drag_icon", args, n);
```

The DragIcon is created as a child of the drag source widget. We only need to specify the `XmNpixmap` and `XmNmask` resources because the DragIcon sets its other attributes, such as width and height, based on the pixmap. The DragIcon takes its foreground and background colors from its parent, so we don't need to specify these resources either. The `XmNmask` resource must be set to a pixmap of depth 1, while the `XmNpixmap` can be any depth.

Now that we have a DragIcon object for the source icon, we can call `XmDragStart()` to start the drag as shown below:

```
n = 0;
XtSetArg (args[n], XmNblendModel, XmBLEND_JUST_SOURCE); n++;
XtSetArg (args[n], XmNcursorBackground, bg); n++;
XtSetArg (args[n], XmNcursorForeground, fg); n++;
```

```
    XtSetArg (args[n], XmNsourceCursorIcon, drag_icon); n++;
    if (files[i].directory) {
        exportList[0] = DIRECTORY;
        XtSetArg (args[n], XmNexportTargets, exportList); n++;
        XtSetArg (args[n], XmNnumExportTargets, 1); n++;
    }
    else {
        exportList[0] = FILE_CONTENTS;
        exportList[1] = FILE_NAME;
        XtSetArg (args[n], XmNexportTargets, exportList); n++;
        XtSetArg (args[n], XmNnumExportTargets, 2); n++;
    }
    XtSetArg (args[n], XmNdragOperations, XmDROP_COPY); n++;
    XtSetArg (args[n], XmNconvertProc, ConvertProc); n++;
    XtSetArg (args[n], XmNclientData, widget); n++;
    dc = XmDragStart (widget, event, args, n);
```

This routine creates a DragContext object for the drag and drop transfer and sets a number of resources for the DragContext. The `XmNsourceCursorIcon` specifies the source drag icon that we just created. We also specify the background and foreground colors for the icon. The DragContext also has `XmNoperationCursorIcon` and `XmNstateCursorIcon` resources for specifying the operation and state icons, but our drag icon does not use these parts, so we don't set the resources.

The `XmNblendModel` resource controls the components of the drag icon that are used during the drag. This resource can take one of the following values:

```
XmBLEND_ALL
XmBLEND_STATE_SOURCE
XmBLEND_JUST_SOURCE
XmBLEND_NONE
```

XmBLEND_ALL indicates that all three parts of the drag icon should be used, while Xm-BLEND_STATE_SOURCE causes only the state and source icons to be used. We specify the value XmBLEND_JUST_SOURCE since we only want the source icon to be used for the drag icon. XmBLEND_NONE means that the DragContext does not generate a drag icon.

Another important set of resources are the `XmNexportTargets` and `XmNnumExport-Targets` resources. These resources specify the data targets to which the drag source can convert the actual data. The `XmNexportTargets` resource contains a list of target atoms. If the file is a directory, we specify the DIRECTORY target. Otherwise, we specify both the FILE_CONTENTS and FILE_NAME targets, which means that the drag source can provide both a filename and the actual contents of the file to a drop site. In order for the drag to succeed, another application must use at least one of these targets for a drop site so that the user has some place to drop the data.

The `XmNdragOperations` resource specifies all of the operations that are supported by the application. This value is specified as a bitmask formed by combining the following possible values:

```
XmDROP_COPY
XmDROP_MOVE
XmDROP_LINK
XmDROP_NOOP
```

For the limited purpose of this application, we specify XmDROP_COPY because we only allow the user to copy the contents of a file. A fully-functional file manager application would probably also support moving and copying files within the directory structure, but that functionality is beyond the scope of our discussion. During the drag, the operations supported by the current drop site are matched against those supported by the drag source to see if the transfer is possible.

The final DragContext resource that we specify is the XmNconvertProc. This resource indicates the procedure that is called to convert the actual data into the format requested by the drop site when the drop occurs. We specify the ConvertProc() routine for our application; this routine is described in the next section. We also set XmNclientData to the Label widget that started the drag, so that we have access to the filename and file type data stored about that Label, as this information is needed to process the drop.

After we create the DragContext and start the drag with XmDragStart(), we register a callback routine for the XmNdragDropFinishCallback so that we can destroy the DragIcon that we created. This routine is discussed further in Section 18.4.6.

18.4.3 Converting the Data

When a drop occurs, a procedure that has been registered by the drop site is called to verify that the drop can take place. This procedure checks the status of the operation and then starts the data transfer. The receiving application requests the format that it wants to receive the data in; the receiver can even request the data in multiple formats, if they are available. For each requested data target, the initiating application's XmNconvertProc is invoked. In our case, this is the ConvertProc() routine. Since we are not using incremental transfer, this routine is of type XtConvertSelectionProc, which takes the following form:

```
typedef Boolean (*XtConvertSelectionProc)(Widget, Atom *, Atom *,
        Atom *, XtPointer *, unsigned long *, int *);
    Widget          widget;
    Atom            *selection;
    Atom            *target;
    Atom            *type_return;
    XtPointer        *value_return;
    unsigned long   *length_return;
    int             *format_return;
```

The *widget* parameter is the DragContext for the drag operation, *selection* is the selection atom, which in this case is _MOTIF_DROP, and *target* is the type of information requested about the selection. The *type_return*, *value_return*, *length_return*, and *format_return* parameters return the type, value, length, and format of the converted data. The routine should return True if the conversion succeeds and False otherwise. For more information about this procedure type, see Volume Four, *X Toolkit Intrinsics Programming Manual*, and the appropriate reference page in Volume Five, *X Toolkit Intrinsics Reference Manual*.

The ConvertProc() routine in Example 18-1 starts by retrieving the Label widget from the XmNclientData resource of the DragContext. The goal is to get an index into the files array so that we can access information about the file. The index is stored in the

XmNuserData resource of the Label widget. Once we have the index, we can use it to get the filename from the array.

Our conversion routine only handles requests for a filename or the contents of a file. If `tar-get` is set to FILE_CONTENTS, `ConvertProc()` retrieves the contents of the file and formats the data for transfer back to the receiving client. The contents of the file are passed as a pointer to the text, using the `value_return` parameter. If the drop site has requested the FILE_NAME target, the routine returns the filename in `value_return`. In either case, the `length_return` argument is set to the length of the text, and `format_return` is set to 8 to specify the length of each of the elements in `value_return`. The `return_type` parameter is set to the appropriate target. If the drop site has requested any other target, the routine returns `False` to indicate that the transfer has failed.

The conversion routine does not handle the DIRECTORY target, partly because we have not implemented any drop sites that understand the target. A real file manager application would want to support the dragging of directories to allow the user to modify the file system using drag and drop. In this case, the conversion procedure would need to have another branch for handling the DIRECTORY target.

Since the drag source only supports the copy operation, the conversion routine does not have to worry about deleting the existing data. With a copy operation, the XmNconvertProc returns a pointer to the data so that when the operation is done, both the initiator and the receiver have a copy of the data. With a move operation, the initiating application returns a pointer to the data and then waits for the receiver to tell it to delete the data. The receiving application gets the data, stores it, and then specifies the DELETE target to handle this situation. When the initiating client gets this target, it can safely delete the data. With a link operation, the initiator again passes a pointer to the data, but in this case the receiver uses the pointer to establish a link to the data.

18.4.4 Modifying an Existing Drag Source

In *file_manager.c*, we decided to replace the existing drag capabilities of the image Label widgets and provide our own functionality instead. By default, the Labels would function as graphical drag sources, but since there are no drop sites that support graphical data, there is no reason to preserve this functionality.

However, if you want to provide the default functionality for a drag source as well as your own functionality, the set up of the drag source becomes more complicated. Each Motif widget that acts as a drag source has a translation and action that starts the drag. Since the existing action calls `XmDragStart()` for the transfer, another action routine cannot call `XmDragStart()` again. The solution to this problem is to write an action routine that retrieves the DragContext for the transfer and modifies its resources.

In our application, we want to augment the drag source functionality of the filename Labels. If the user drags the Label to a drop site that understands file objects, the actual file is transferred. Otherwise, the default drag functionality for the Label causes the text of the Label to be passed to the drop site. The first thing that we need to do is modify the translations for the Label widgets. Since we want to provide the default functionality, the new translation calls the widget's existing drag action routine followed by our own action. The existing drag action routine for the Label widget is `ProcessDrag()`, so the translations and actions for the application can be defined as follows:

```
static char dragTranslations[] =
    "#override <Btn2Down>: StartDrag()";

static char newdragTranslations[] =
    "#override <Btn2Down>: ProcessDrag() UpdateDrag()";

static XtActionsRec dragActions[] =
    { {"StartDrag", (XtActionProc) StartDrag},
      {"UpdateDrag", (XtActionProc) UpdateDrag} };
```

As always, the translations need to be parsed using `XtParseTranslationTable()`, and the actions need to be registered using `XtAppAddActions()`. Now, when we create each of the filename Labels, we can specify the new translation for the `XmNtranslations` resource, as shown in the following code fragment:

```
parsed_trans_text = XtParseTranslationTable (newdragTranslations);
...
XtVaCreateManagedWidget (files[i].file_name,
    xmLabelWidgetClass, form,
    XmNtranslations, parsed_trans_text,
    XmNuserData, i,
    ...
    NULL);
```

Note that we also specify the index in the `files` array as the `XmNuserData` for these widgets, just as we did for the image Labels in Example 18-1.

The `UpdateDrag()` action routine is invoked after the Label's default drag action, which means that `XmDragStart()` has already been called for the operation. Our action routine retrieves the DragContext for the operation and modifies it, as shown in Example 18-2.

Example 18-2. The UpdateDrag() routine

```
void        (*convert_proc) ();

void
UpdateDrag(widget, event, params, num_params)
Widget  widget;
XEvent  *event;
String *params;
Cardinal *num_params;
{
    Arg             args[10];
    int             n, m, i;
    Display         *dpy;
    Atom            FILE_CONTENTS, FILE_NAME, DIRECTORY;
    Widget          drag_icon, dc;
    Pixel           fg, bg;
    Pixmap          icon, iconmask;
    XtPointer       ptr;
    Boolean         NewConvertProc();
    void            DragDropFinish();
    Cardinal        numExportTargets;
    Atom            *exportTargets, *newTargets;

    /* intern the Atoms for data targets */
```

Example 18-2. The UpdateDrag() routine (continued)

```
    dpy = XtDisplay (widget);
    FILE_CONTENTS = XmInternAtom (dpy, "FILE_CONTENTS", False);
    FILE_NAME = XmInternAtom (dpy, "FILE_NAME", False);
    DIRECTORY = XmInternAtom (dpy, "DIRECTORY", False);

    /* get background and foreground colors and fetch index into file
     * array from XmNuserData.
     */
    XtVaGetValues (widget,
        XmNforeground, &fg,
        XmNbackground, &bg,
        XmNuserData,  &ptr,
        NULL);

    /* create pixmaps for drag icon -- either file or directory */
    i = (int) ptr;
    if (files[i].is_directory) {
        icon = XmGetPixmapByDepth (XtScreen (widget), "dir.xbm", 1, 0, 1);
        iconmask = XmGetPixmapByDepth (XtScreen (widget), "dirmask.xbm",
            1, 0, 1);
    }
    else {
        icon = XmGetPixmapByDepth (XtScreen (widget), "file.xbm", 1, 0, 1);
        iconmask = XmGetPixmapByDepth (XtScreen (widget), "filemask.xbm",
            1, 0, 1);
    }
    if (icon == XmUNSPECIFIED_PIXMAP || iconmask == XmUNSPECIFIED_PIXMAP) {
        puts ("Couldn't load pixmaps");
        exit (1);
    }

    n = 0;
    XtSetArg(args[n], XmNpixmap, icon); n++;
    XtSetArg(args[n], XmNmask, iconmask); n++;
    drag_icon = XmCreateDragIcon (widget, "drag_icon", args, n);

    /* get the DragContext and retrive info about it */
    dc = XmGetDragContext (widget, event->xbutton.time);

    n = 0;
    XtSetArg (args[n], XmNexportTargets, &exportTargets); n++;
    XtSetArg (args[n], XmNnumExportTargets, &numExportTargets); n++;
    XtSetArg (args[n], XmNconvertProc, &convert_proc); n++;
    XtGetValues (dc, args, n);

    /* add new targets to the list of targets */
    n = 0;
    if (files[i].is_directory) {
        newTargets = (Atom *) XtMalloc
            (sizeof (Atom) * (numExportTargets + 1));
        for (m = 0; m < numExportTargets; m++)
            newTargets[m] = exportTargets[m];
        newTargets[m] = DIRECTORY;
        XtSetArg (args[n], XmNexportTargets, newTargets); n++;
        XtSetArg (args[n], XmNnumExportTargets, numExportTargets + 1); n++;
    }
    else {
        newTargets = (Atom *) XtMalloc
```

Example 18-2. The UpdateDrag() routine (continued)

```
                (sizeof (Atom) * (numExportTargets + 2));
        for (m = 0; m < numExportTargets; m++)
            newTargets[m] = exportTargets[m];
        newTargets[m] = FILE_CONTENTS;
        newTargets[m+1] = FILE_NAME;
        XtSetArg (args[n], XmNexportTargets, newTargets); n++;
        XtSetArg (args[n], XmNnumExportTargets, numExportTargets + 2); n++;
    }

    /* modify other DragContext resources */
    XtSetArg (args[n], XmNblendModel, XmBLEND_JUST_SOURCE); n++;
    XtSetArg (args[n], XmNcursorBackground, bg); n++;
    XtSetArg (args[n], XmNcursorForeground, fg); n++;
    XtSetArg (args[n], XmNsourceCursorIcon, drag_icon); n++;
    XtSetArg (args[n], XmNdragOperations, XmDROP_COPY); n++;
    XtSetArg (args[n], XmNconvertProc, NewConvertProc); n++;
    XtSetArg (args[n], XmNclientData, widget); n++;
    XtSetValues (dc, args, n);

    XtAddCallback (dc, XmNdragDropFinishCallback, DragDropFinish, NULL);
}
```

This routine performs many of the same tasks as the `StartDrag()` action routine, such as accessing the appropriate structure in the `files` array and creating a DragIcon for the source icon. The main difference is that we use `XmGetDragContext()` to retrieve the current DragContext object, rather than creating one using `XmStartDrag()`.

The routine retrieves the values of the `XmNexportTargets`, `XmNnumExportTargets`, and `XmNconvertProc` resources using `XtGetValues()` so that it can preserve the existing functionality. The appropriate new targets are added to the list of targets based on the type of the file, and `XmNexportTargets` is set to the new list. The `NewConvertProc()` routine is used for the `XmNconvertProc`. The rest of the DragContext resources are specified as in `StartDrag()`, and the DragContext is modified using `XtSetValues()`.

There is only one difference between the `NewConvertProc()` routine and `ConvertProc()` in *file_manager.c*. Instead of simply returning `False` if the requested target is not FILE_CONTENTS or FILE_NAME, `NewConvertProc()` calls the conversion procedure retrieved from the Label widget, as shown in the following fragment:

```
    (*convert_proc) (widget, selection, target, type_return,
        value_return, length_return, format_return);
```

Essentially, our conversion routine handles our data targets and passes other targets to the Label widget's default conversion procedure.

Drag and Drop

18.4.5 Providing Custom Drag-over Visuals

The DragContext has a number of callback routines that the initiating application can use to provide custom drag-over visuals. These callbacks are invoked when different events occur during the drag, like when the drag icon enters or leaves a drop site. The DragContext provides the following callback routines for monitoring the drag:

```
XmNdragMotionCallback
XmNdropSiteEnterCallback
XmNdropSiteLeaveCallback
XmNoperationChangedCallback
XmNtopLevelEnterCallback
XmNtopLevelLeaveCallback
```

The names of the routines are fairly self-explanatory. Each callback has its own special callback structure that contains the relevant information about the current state of the drag operation. For example, the XmNdropSiteEnterCallback uses a callback structure of type XmDropSiteEnterCallbackStruct, which is defined as follows:

```
typedef struct {
    int             reason;
    XEvent          *event;
    Time            timeStamp;
    unsigned char   operation;
    unsigned char   operations;
    unsigned char   dropSiteStatus;
    Position        x;
    Position        y;
} XmDropSiteEnterCallbackStruct, *XmDropSiteEnterCallback;
```

The reason field in this structure is always XmCR_DROP_SITE_ENTER. The operation and operations fields specify the current operation and the set of supported operations, respectively. The dropSiteStatus element indicates whether or not the current drop site is valid, based on the targets supported by the drag source and the drop site. This field can have one of the following values:

```
XmDROP_SITE_VALID
XmDROP_SITE_INVALID
XmNO_DROP_SITE
```

The operation, operations, and dropSiteStatus fields are initialized by the toolkit based on the values of different resources for both the drag source and the drop site. If the drop site has registered an XmNdragProc and the dynamic protocol is being used, this routine can update these fields as necessary before the data is passed to the callback routine. A drop site might want to update these fields if it is performing any special processing or simulating multiple drop sites.

All of the callback structures for the DragContext callback routines have a reason field that indicates why the callback was invoked. The callback structures also provide information that is relevant to the particular routine; they are all similar to the XmDropSiteEnter-CallbackStruct. See the DragContext reference page in Volume Six B, *Motif Reference Manual*, for complete information about the different callback structures.

When an application creates the DragContext for a drag, it can register routines for the different callback resources. These routines can perform any special processing that is necessary, as well as handle custom drag-over effects for the transfer. The typical way to handle drag-over effects is to modify the various drag icon resources of the DragContext during the drag. The XmNsourcePixmapIcon, XmNsourceCursorIcon, XmNoperationCursorIcon, and XmNstateCursorIcon resources specify the different components of the drag icon. The XmNvalidCursorForeground, XmNinvalidCursorForeground, and XmNnoneCursorForeground resources of the DragContext can be used to further distinguish between the different states during a drag.

The XmNsourcePixmapIcon is used under the preregister protocol and can be any size, while the XmNsourceCursorIcon is used for the dynamic protocol and is limited to the size of the largest cursor for a particular platform. If you want to specify a color icon, you must use the XmNsourcePixmapIcon resource. If XmNsourcePixmapIcon is not specified, the value of XmNsourceCursorIcon is used. If this resource has not been specified, the default source icon for the Screen object is used.

At any point during a drag, the initiating client can call XmDragCancel() to cancel the transfer. The user can also cancel the operation by pressing the ESCAPE key. The initiating client can retrieve additional information about the current drop site by calling XmDropSiteRetrieve() during the drag.

After the user drops the data in a drop site, the drag source has one last chance to check the status of the transfer and provide custom visual effects. After the receiving client's XmNdropProc completes, the DragContext's XmNdropStartCallback is invoked. This routine has a callback structure of type XmDropStartCallbackStruct, which is defined as follows:

```
typedef struct {
    int              reason;
    XEvent           *event;
    Time             timeStamp;
    unsigned char    operation;
    unsigned char    operations;
    unsigned char    dropSiteStatus;
    unsigned char    dropAction;
    Position         x;
    Position         y;
} XmDropStartCallbackStruct, *XmDropStartCallback;
```

The reason field is set to XmCR_DROP_START, while the operation, operations, and dropSiteStatus fields are set as described previously. The dropAction field is set to XmDROP if the user has simply dropped the data, XmDROP_HELP if the user has requested help on the drop site, or XmDROP_CANCEL if the user has cancelled the transfer.

Drag and Drop

18.4.6 Cleaning Up

The initiating client can also register callbacks that are invoked after a drag and drop transfer has completed. The `XmNdropFinishCallback` is called after the receiver's `XmNtransferProc` has finished processing all of the data targets requested by the receiver. This routine receives a callback structure of type `XmDropFinishCallbackStruct`, where the `reason` field is `XmCR_DROP_FINISH`.

The `XmNdragDropFinishCallback` is invoked when the entire operation has completed, which is immediately after the `XmNdropFinishCallback`. In this case, the callback structure is an `XmDragDropFinishCallbackStructure`, and `reason` is `XmCR_DRAG_DROP_FINISH`. Our application uses this callback to destroy the drag icon that we created, as shown below:

```
void
DragDropFinish (widget, client_data, call_data)
Widget widget;
XtPointer client_data;
XtPointer call_data;
{
        Widget        source_icon = NULL;

        XtVaGetValues (widget, XmNsourceCursorIcon, &source_icon, NULL);

        if (source_icon)
            XtDestroyWidget (source_icon);
}
```

The widget passed to the callback routine is the DragContext object for the drag and drop transfer. The routine retrieves the source icon from the DragContext and destroys it using `XtDestroyWidget()`.

18.5 Working With Drop Sites

In order to handle data from drag sources that provide something other than textual data, an application has to register drop sites that understand other types of data. To make the *file_manager.c* application useful, we need an application that has drop sites that can handle file objects. In this section, we are going to modify the text editor from Chapter 14, *Text Widgets*, so that it understands file data. The application contains two drop sites that handle files: the main text entry area and a filename status area. Example 18-3 shows the `main()`, `HandleDropLabel()`, `HandleDropText()`, and `TransferProc()` routines for *editor_dnd.c*. The rest of the routines in the application are the same as in Section 14.4, so we have not shown them here.

Example 18-3. The editor_dnd.c program

```
/* editor_dnd.c -- create an editor application that contains drop sites
 * that understand file data.  A file can be dragged from another
 * application and dropped in the text entry area or the filename status
 * area.
 */
```

Example 18-3. The editor_dnd.c program (continued)

```
#include <Xm/Text.h>
#include <Xm/TextF.h>
#include <Xm/LabelG.h>
#include <Xm/PushBG.h>
#include <Xm/RowColumn.h>
#include <Xm/MainW.h>
#include <Xm/Form.h>
#include <Xm/FileSB.h>
#include <Xm/SeparatoG.h>
#include <Xm/DragDrop.h>
#include <X11/Xos.h>
#include <stdio.h>
#include <sys/types.h>
#include <sys/stat.h>

#define FILE_OPEN 0
#define FILE_SAVE 1
#define FILE_EXIT 2

#define EDIT_CUT 0
#define EDIT_COPY 1
#define EDIT_PASTE 2
#define EDIT_CLEAR 3

#define SEARCH_FIND_NEXT 0
#define SEARCH_SHOW_ALL 1
#define SEARCH_REPLACE 2
#define SEARCH_CLEAR 3

/* global variables */
void            (*drop_proc) ();
Widget          text_edit, search_text, replace_text, text_output;
Widget          toplevel, file_label;

main(argc, argv)
int argc;
char *argv[];
{
    XtAppContext  app_context;
    Display       *dpy;
    Atom          FILE_CONTENTS, FILE_NAME;
    Widget        main_window, menubar, form, search_panel;
    Widget        sep1, sep2;
    void          file_cb(), edit_cb(), search_cb();
    Arg           args[10];
    int           n = 0;
    XmString      open, save, exit, exit_acc, file, edit, cut,
                  clear, copy, paste, search, next, find, replace;
    Cardinal      numImportTargets;
    Atom          *importTargets, *newTargets;
    Atom          importList[2];
    void          HandleDropLabel(), HandleDropText();

    XtSetLanguageProc (NULL, NULL, NULL);

    toplevel = XtVaAppInitialize (&app_context, "Demos",
        NULL, 0, &argc, argv, NULL, NULL);

    dpy = XtDisplay (toplevel);
```

Example 18-3. The editor_dnd.c program (continued)

```
    FILE_CONTENTS = XmInternAtom (dpy, "FILE_CONTENTS", False);
    FILE_NAME = XmInternAtom (dpy, "FILE_NAME", False);

    main_window = XtVaCreateWidget ("main_window",
        xmMainWindowWidgetClass, toplevel, NULL);

    /* Create a simple MenuBar that contains three menus */
    file = XmStringCreateLocalized ("File");
    edit = XmStringCreateLocalized ("Edit");
    search = XmStringCreateLocalized ("Search");
    menubar = XmVaCreateSimpleMenuBar (main_window, "menubar",
        XmVaCASCADEBUTTON, file, 'F',
        XmVaCASCADEBUTTON, edit, 'E',
        XmVaCASCADEBUTTON, search, 'S',
        NULL);
    XmStringFree (file);
    XmStringFree (edit);
    XmStringFree (search);

    /* First menu is the File menu -- callback is file_cb() */
    open = XmStringCreateLocalized ("Open...");
    save = XmStringCreateLocalized ("Save...");
    exit = XmStringCreateLocalized ("Exit");
    exit_acc = XmStringCreateLocalized ("Ctrl+C");
    XmVaCreateSimplePulldownMenu (menubar, "file_menu", 0, file_cb,
        XmVaPUSHBUTTON, open, 'O', NULL, NULL,
        XmVaPUSHBUTTON, save, 'S', NULL, NULL,
        XmVaSEPARATOR,
        XmVaPUSHBUTTON, exit, 'x', "Ctrl<Key>c", exit_acc,
        NULL);
    XmStringFree (open);
    XmStringFree (save);
    XmStringFree (exit);
    XmStringFree (exit_acc);

    /* ...create the "Edit" menu --  callback is edit_cb() */
    cut = XmStringCreateLocalized ("Cut");
    copy = XmStringCreateLocalized ("Copy");
    clear = XmStringCreateLocalized ("Clear");
    paste = XmStringCreateLocalized ("Paste");
    XmVaCreateSimplePulldownMenu (menubar, "edit_menu", 1, edit_cb,
        XmVaPUSHBUTTON, cut, 't', NULL, NULL,
        XmVaPUSHBUTTON, copy, 'C', NULL, NULL,
        XmVaPUSHBUTTON, paste, 'P', NULL, NULL,
        XmVaSEPARATOR,
        XmVaPUSHBUTTON, clear, 'l', NULL, NULL,
        NULL);
    XmStringFree (cut);
    XmStringFree (copy);
    XmStringFree (paste);

    /* create the "Search" menu -- callback is search_cb() */
    next = XmStringCreateLocalized ("Find Next");
    find = XmStringCreateLocalized ("Show All");
    replace = XmStringCreateLocalized ("Replace Text");
    XmVaCreateSimplePulldownMenu (menubar, "search_menu", 2, search_cb,
        XmVaPUSHBUTTON, next, 'N', NULL, NULL,
        XmVaPUSHBUTTON, find, 'A', NULL, NULL,
```

Example 18-3. The editor_dnd.c program (continued)

```
            XmVaPUSHBUTTON, replace, 'R', NULL, NULL,
            XmVaSEPARATOR,
            XmVaPUSHBUTTON, clear, 'C', NULL, NULL,
            NULL);
    XmStringFree (next);
    XmStringFree (find);
    XmStringFree (replace);
    XmStringFree (clear);

    XtManageChild (menubar);

    /* create a form work are */
    form = XtVaCreateWidget ("form",
        xmFormWidgetClass, main_window, NULL);

    /* create horizontal RowColumn inside the form */
    search_panel = XtVaCreateWidget ("search_panel",
        xmRowColumnWidgetClass, form,
        XmNorientation,        XmHORIZONTAL,
        XmNpacking,            XmPACK_TIGHT,
        XmNtopAttachment,      XmATTACH_FORM,
        XmNleftAttachment,     XmATTACH_FORM,
        XmNrightAttachment,    XmATTACH_FORM,
        NULL);

    /* Create two TextField widgets with Labels... */
    XtVaCreateManagedWidget ("Search Pattern:",
        xmLabelGadgetClass, search_panel, NULL);
    search_text = XtVaCreateManagedWidget ("search_text",
        xmTextFieldWidgetClass, search_panel, NULL);
    XtVaCreateManagedWidget ("    Replace Pattern:",
        xmLabelGadgetClass, search_panel, NULL);
    replace_text = XtVaCreateManagedWidget ("replace_text",
        xmTextFieldWidgetClass, search_panel, NULL);
    XtManageChild (search_panel);

    text_output = XtVaCreateManagedWidget ("text_output",
        xmTextFieldWidgetClass, form,
        XmNeditable,                False,
        XmNcursorPositionVisible,   False,
        XmNshadowThickness,         0,
        XmNleftAttachment,          XmATTACH_FORM,
        XmNrightAttachment,         XmATTACH_FORM,
        XmNbottomAttachment,        XmATTACH_FORM,
        NULL);

    sep2 = XtVaCreateManagedWidget ("sep2",
        xmSeparatorGadgetClass, form,
        XmNleftAttachment,          XmATTACH_FORM,
        XmNrightAttachment,         XmATTACH_FORM,
        XmNbottomAttachment,        XmATTACH_WIDGET,
        XmNbottomWidget,            text_output,
        NULL);

    /* create file status area */
    file_label = XtVaCreateManagedWidget ("Filename:",
        xmLabelGadgetClass, form,
        XmNalignment,               XmALIGNMENT_BEGINNING,
        XmNleftAttachment,          XmATTACH_FORM,
```

Example 18-3. The editor_dnd.c program (continued)

```
                XmNrightAttachment,         XmATTACH_FORM,
                XmNbottomAttachment,        XmATTACH_WIDGET,
                XmNbottomWidget,            sep2,
                NULL);

    /* register the file status label as a drop site */
    n = 0;
    importList[0] = FILE_CONTENTS;
    importList[1] = FILE_NAME;
    XtSetArg (args[n], XmNimportTargets, importList); n++;
    XtSetArg (args[n], XmNnumImportTargets, XtNumber (importList)); n++;
    XtSetArg (args[n], XmNdropSiteOperations, XmDROP_COPY); n++;
    XtSetArg (args[n], XmNdropProc, HandleDropLabel); n++;
    XmDropSiteRegister (file_label, args, n);

    sep1 = XtVaCreateManagedWidget ("sep1",
            xmSeparatorGadgetClass, form,
            XmNleftAttachment,          XmATTACH_FORM,
            XmNrightAttachment,         XmATTACH_FORM,
            XmNbottomAttachment,        XmATTACH_WIDGET,
            XmNbottomWidget,            file_label,
            NULL);

    /* create text entry area */
    n = 0;
    XtSetArg (args[n], XmNrows,                 10); n++;
    XtSetArg (args[n], XmNcolumns,              80); n++;
    XtSetArg (args[n], XmNeditMode,             XmMULTI_LINE_EDIT); n++;
    XtSetArg (args[n], XmNtopAttachment,        XmATTACH_WIDGET); n++;
    XtSetArg (args[n], XmNtopWidget,            search_panel); n++;
    XtSetArg (args[n], XmNleftAttachment,       XmATTACH_FORM); n++;
    XtSetArg (args[n], XmNrightAttachment,      XmATTACH_FORM); n++;
    XtSetArg (args[n], XmNbottomAttachment,     XmATTACH_WIDGET); n++;
    XtSetArg (args[n], XmNbottomWidget,         sep1); n++;
    text_edit = XmCreateScrolledText (form, "text_edit", args, n);
    XtManageChild (text_edit);

    /* retrieve drop site info so that we can modify it */
    n = 0;
    XtSetArg (args[n], XmNimportTargets, &importTargets); n++;
    XtSetArg (args[n], XmNnumImportTargets, &numImportTargets); n++;
    XtSetArg (args[n], XmNdropProc, &drop_proc); n++;
    XmDropSiteRetrieve (text_edit, args, n);

    /* add FILE_CONTENTS and FILE_NAME to the list of targets */
    newTargets = (Atom *) XtMalloc (sizeof (Atom) * (numImportTargets + 2));
    for (n = 0; n < numImportTargets; n++)
        newTargets[n] = importTargets[n];
    newTargets[n] = FILE_CONTENTS;
    newTargets[n+1] = FILE_NAME;

    /* update the drop site */
    n = 0;
    XtSetArg (args[n], XmNimportTargets, newTargets); n++;
    XtSetArg (args[n], XmNnumImportTargets, numImportTargets+2); n++;
    XtSetArg (args[n], XmNdropProc, HandleDropText); n++;
    XmDropSiteUpdate (text_edit, args, n);

    XtManageChild (form);
```

Example 18-3. The editor_dnd.c program (continued)

```
    XtManageChild (main_window);

    XtRealizeWidget (toplevel);
    XtAppMainLoop (app_context);
}
/* HandleDropLabel() -- start the data transfer when data is dropped in
 * the filename status area.
 */
void
HandleDropLabel(widget, client_data, call_data)
Widget          widget;
XtPointer        client_data;
XtPointer        call_data;
{
    Display               *dpy;
    Atom                   FILE_CONTENTS, FILE_NAME;
    XmDropProcCallback     DropData;
    XmDropTransferEntryRec transferEntries[2];
    XmDropTransferEntry    transferList;
    Arg                    args[10];
    int                    n, i;
    Widget                 dc;
    Cardinal               numExportTargets;
    Atom                   *exportTargets;
    Boolean                file_name = False;
    void                   TransferProc();

    /* intern the Atoms for data targets */
    dpy = XtDisplay (toplevel);
    FILE_CONTENTS = XmInternAtom (dpy, "FILE_CONTENTS", False);
    FILE_NAME = XmInternAtom (dpy, "FILE_NAME", False);

    DropData = (XmDropProcCallback) call_data;
    dc = DropData->dragContext;

    /* retrieve the data targets and search for FILE_NAME */
    n = 0;
    XtSetArg (args[n], XmNexportTargets, &exportTargets); n++;
    XtSetArg (args[n], XmNnumExportTargets, &numExportTargets); n++;
    XtGetValues (dc, args, n);

    for (i = 0; i < numExportTargets; i++) {
        if (exportTargets[i] == FILE_NAME) {
            file_name = True;
            break;
        }
    }

    /* make sure we have a drop that is a copy operation and one of
     * the targets is FILE_NAME.  if not, set the status to failure.
     */
    n = 0;
    if ((!file_name) || (DropData->dropAction != XmDROP) ||
        (DropData->operation != XmDROP_COPY)) {
        XtSetArg (args[n], XmNtransferStatus, XmTRANSFER_FAILURE); n++;
        XtSetArg (args[n], XmNnumDropTransfers, 0); n++;
    }
```

Example 18-3. The editor_dnd.c program (continued)

```
    else {
        /* set up transfer requests for drop site */
        transferEntries[0].target = FILE_CONTENTS;
        transferEntries[0].client_data = (XtPointer) text_edit;
        transferEntries[1].target = FILE_NAME;
        transferEntries[1].client_data = (XtPointer) file_label;
        transferList = transferEntries;
        XtSetArg (args[n], XmNdropTransfers, transferEntries); n++;
        XtSetArg (args[n], XmNnumDropTransfers,
            XtNumber (transferEntries)); n++;
        XtSetArg (args[n], XmNtransferProc, TransferProc); n++;
    }
    XmDropTransferStart (dc, args, n);
}

/* HandleDropText() -- start the data transfer when data is dropped in
 * the text entry area.
 */
void
HandleDropText(widget, client_data, call_data)
Widget          widget;
XtPointer       client_data;
XtPointer       call_data;
{
    Display             *dpy;
    Atom                FILE_CONTENTS, FILE_NAME;
    XmDropProcCallback  DropData;
    XmDropTransferEntryRec  transferEntries[2];
    XmDropTransferEntry     transferList;
    Arg                 args[10];
    int                 n, i;
    Widget              dc;
    Cardinal            numExportTargets;
    Atom                *exportTargets;
    Boolean             file_contents = False;
    void                TransferProc();

    /* intern the Atoms for data targets */
    dpy = XtDisplay (toplevel);
    FILE_CONTENTS = XmInternAtom (dpy, "FILE_CONTENTS", False);
    FILE_NAME = XmInternAtom (dpy, "FILE_NAME", False);

    DropData = (XmDropProcCallback) call_data;
    dc = DropData->dragContext;

    /* retrieve the data targets and search for FILE_CONTENTS */
    n = 0;
    XtSetArg (args[n], XmNexportTargets, &exportTargets); n++;
    XtSetArg (args[n], XmNnumExportTargets, &numExportTargets); n++;
    XtGetValues (dc, args, n);

    for (i = 0; i < numExportTargets; i++) {
        if (exportTargets[i] == FILE_CONTENTS) {
            file_contents = True;
            break;
        }
    }
```

Example 18-3. The editor_dnd.c program (continued)

```
        if (file_contents) {
            /* make sure we have a drop that is a copy operation.
             * if not, set the status to failure.
             */
            n = 0;
            if ((DropData->dropAction != XmDROP) ||
                (DropData->operation != XmDROP_COPY)) {
                XtSetArg (args[n], XmNtransferStatus, XmTRANSFER_FAILURE); n++;
                XtSetArg (args[n], XmNnumDropTransfers, 0); n++;
            }
            else {
                /* set up transfer requests for drop site */
                transferEntries[0].target = FILE_CONTENTS;
                transferEntries[0].client_data = (XtPointer) text_edit;
                transferEntries[1].target = FILE_NAME;
                transferEntries[1].client_data = (XtPointer) file_label;
                transferList = transferEntries;
                XtSetArg (args[n], XmNdropTransfers, transferEntries); n++;
                XtSetArg (args[n], XmNnumDropTransfers,
                    XtNumber (transferEntries)); n++;
                XtSetArg (args[n], XmNtransferProc, TransferProc); n++;
            }
            XmDropTransferStart (dc, args, n);
        }
    else
        (*drop_proc) (widget, client_data, call_data);
}

/* TransferProc() -- handle data transfer of converted data from drag
 * source to drop site.
 */
void
TransferProc(widget, client_data, seltype, type, value, length, format)
Widget          widget;
XtPointer       client_data;
Atom            *seltype;
Atom            *type;
XtPointer       value;
unsigned long   *length;
int             format;
{
    Display     *dpy;
    Atom        FILE_CONTENTS, FILE_NAME;
    Widget      w;
    XmString    string;
    char        *label[256];

    /* intern the Atoms for data targets */
    dpy = XtDisplay (toplevel);
    FILE_CONTENTS = XmInternAtom (dpy, "FILE_CONTENTS", False);
    FILE_NAME = XmInternAtom (dpy, "FILE_NAME", False);

    w = (Widget) client_data;

    if (*type == FILE_CONTENTS)
        XmTextSetString (w, value);
    else if (*type == FILE_NAME) {
```

Example 18-3. The editor_dnd.c program (continued)

```
        sprintf (label, "Filename: %s", value);
        string = XmStringCreateLocalized (label);
        XtVaSetValues (w, XmNlabelString, string, NULL);
        XmStringFree (string);
    }
}
```

The application basically has the same functionality as *editor.c* in Chapter 14. The only difference in the interface is the **Filename:** status area that displays the name of the current file.
This status area is also a drop site for file objects, so the user can drag a file from the
file_manager.c application and drop it in this area. When a file is dropped here, the filename
is displayed in the status area, and the contents of the file are copied into the ScrolledText
object. The ScrolledText object has also been modified to function as a drop site for file data,
so the user can drop a file in the text entry area. Figure 18-7 shows the output of the application before and after a file has been dropped in the file status area.

18.5.1 Creating a Drop Site

The file status area is a Label widget, so it does not have any drop site capabilities by default.
In order for the widget to function as a drop site, we have to register it using `XmDropSite-`
`Register()`, as shown below:

```
    n = 0;
    importList[0] = FILE_CONTENTS;
    importList[1] = FILE_NAME;
    XtSetArg (args[n], XmNimportTargets, importList); n++;
    XtSetArg (args[n], XmNnumImportTargets, XtNumber (importList)); n++;
    XtSetArg (args[n], XmNdropSiteOperations, XmDROP_COPY); n++;
    XtSetArg (args[n], XmNdropProc, HandleDropLabel); n++;
    XmDropSiteRegister (file_label, args, n);
```

This routine registers information about the drop site in a DropSite object using resources
that are specified as for a normal widget. Since drop sites are referenced by their associated
widget, however, the resources cannot be set using `XtVaSetValues()`.

The `XmNimportTargets` resource specifies the data targets that the drop site can handle.
We use the FILE_CONTENTS and FILE_NAME targets that we have interned using `Xm-`
`InternAtom()`. The drop site only supports copy operations, so `XmNdropSite-`
`Operations` is set to `XmDROP_COPY`. The final resource that we specify is the `XmN-`
`dropProc`. This callback is invoked when a drop occurs in the drop site; it is responsible
for starting the transfer of data from the drag source to the drop site. The `HandleDrop-`
`Label()` routine handles the drop for the file status area, as we describe in Section 18.5.3.

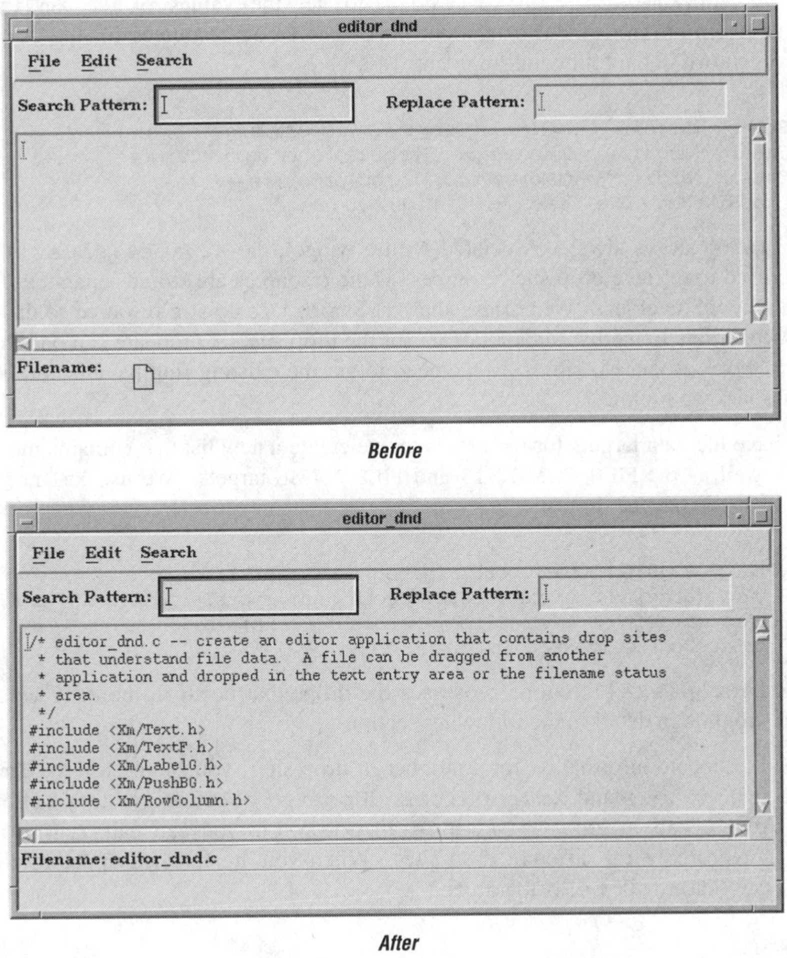

Figure 18-7. Output of editor_dnd.c

18.5.2 Modifying an Existing Drop Site

The *editor_dnd.c* application also allows the user to drag a file from *file_manager.c* to the main text entry area and drop it. This action causes the contents of the file to be copied to the Text widget. By default, the Text widget also has its own drop site functionality that allows the user to drop textual data. We want to modify the drop site to incorporate our own functionality but still allow the user to drag and drop textual data in the widget. The Text widget has already been registered as a drop site by the Motif toolkit, so we do not need to call Xm-DropSiteRegister(). In fact, if we did call that routine, we would override the default functionality.

Instead, we call `XmDropSiteRetrieve()` to get the values of the `XmNimport-Targets`, `XmNnumImportTargets`, and `XmNdropProc` resources for the Text widget drop site, as shown in the following fragment:

```
n = 0;
XtSetArg (args[n], XmNimportTargets, &importTargets); n++;
XtSetArg (args[n], XmNnumImportTargets, &numImportTargets); n++;
XtSetArg (args[n], XmNdropProc, &drop_proc); n++;
XmDropSiteRetrieve (text_edit, args, n);
```

Although a drop site is always associated with a widget, the `XtVaGetValues()` routine cannot be used to retrieve drop site resources, as the resources are stored separately from the widget in a DropSite object. We retrieve the `XmNimportTargets` resource so that we can add our own targets to the list of data targets for the drop site. A drop site can only have one `XmNdropProc` associated with it, so we need to get the existing routine and store it before we specify our own routine.

Once we have the data targets for the drop site, we create a new list that contains the existing targets, as well as the FILE_CONTENTS and FILE_NAME targets. We use `XmDropSite-Update()` to modify the drop site:

```
n = 0;
XtSetArg (args[n], XmNimportTargets, newTargets); n++;
XtSetArg (args[n], XmNnumImportTargets, numImportTargets + 2); n++;
XtSetArg (args[n], XmNdropProc, HandleDropText); n++;
XmDropSiteUpdate (text_edit, args, n);
```

The `HandleDropText()` routine processes the drops that occur in the Text widget. We explain this routine in detail in the following section.

If you need to update information for a number of drop sites, you should use the `XmDrop-SiteStartUpdate()` and `XmDropSiteEndUpdate()` routines, as they optimize the process. After a call to `XmDropSiteStartUpdate()`, you can call `XmDropSite-Update()` repeatedly for different drop sites. When you are finished updating all of the drop sites, call `XmDropSiteEndUpdate()`.

18.5.3 Handling the Drop

When a drop occurs, the receiving application takes over and the `XmNdropProc` for the drop site is called. This callback provides a callback structure of type `XmDropProc-CallbackStruct`, which is defined as follows:

```
typedef struct {
    int             reason;
    XEvent          *event;
    Time            timeStamp;
    Widget          dragContext;
    Position        x;
    Position        y;
    unsigned char   dropSiteStatus;
    unsigned char   operation;
    unsigned char   operations;
    unsigned char   dropAction;
} XmDropProcCallbackStruct, *XmDropProcCallback;
```

The `reason` field is always XmCR_DROP_MESSAGE, and `dragContext` specifies the DragContext object for the drag operation that caused the drop. The `dropSiteStatus` element is set to either XmDROP_SITE_VALID or XmDROP_SITE_INVALID, depending on the targets that are supported by the drop site and the drag source. The callback routine can change this value if necessary.

The `operations` and `operation` fields are set to the possible operations for the drag source data and the current operation, respectively. The `dropAction` field specifies the action requested by the user. If this field is set to XmDROP, the user has requested a normal drop; if it is set to XmDROP_HELP, the user has requested help for the drop site. We discuss providing help for a drop site in the next section.

The main task of the XmNdropProc is to determine whether or not the operation is possible and to start the data transfer by calling XmDropTransferStart(). This routine creates a DropTransfer object that keeps track of information about the data transfer. The Handle-DropLabel() routine initiates the data transfer for the file status drop site, as shown in the following code fragment from Example 18-3:

```
n = 0;
if ((!file_name) || (DropData->dropAction != XmDROP) ||
    (DropData->operation != XmDROP_COPY)) {
    XtSetArg (args[n], XmNtransferStatus, XmTRANSFER_FAILURE); n++;
    XtSetArg (args[n], XmNnumDropTransfers, 0); n++;
}
else {
    transferEntries[0].target = FILE_CONTENTS;
    transferEntries[0].client_data = (XtPointer) text_edit;
    transferEntries[1].target = FILE_NAME;
    transferEntries[1].client_data = (XtPointer) file_label;
    transferList = transferEntries;
    XtSetArg (args[n], XmNdropTransfers, transferEntries); n++;
    XtSetArg (args[n], XmNnumDropTransfers,
        XtNumber (transferEntries)); n++;
    XtSetArg (args[n], XmNtransferProc, TransferProc); n++;
}
XmDropTransferStart (dc, args, n);
```

If the action requested by the user is not a normal drop or if the operation is not a copy operation, we do not process the data transfer. However, we still have to call XmDropTransferStart() to clean up after the whole drag and drop operation. In this case, we set the XmNtransferStatus resource to XmTRANSFER_FAILURE to indicate that the transfer should not proceed. We also set XmNnumDropTransfers to 0.

Otherwise, the drop can proceed, so we establish a list of target data types that we want to receive using the XmNdropTransfers and XmNnumDropTransfer resources. Each entry in XmNdropTransfers is an XmDropTransferEntryRec, which is defined as follows:

```
typedef struct {
    XtPointer    client_data;
    Atom         target;
} XmDropTransferEntryRec, *XmDropTransferEntry;
```

The `target` field specifies the requested data target, and `client_data` passes any additional data that is necessary to the routine that processes the data transfer. We specify the

FILE_CONTENTS and FILE_NAME targets. For each target, we pass the widget that is modified by the data from the drag source as `client_data`. For the FILE_CONTENTS format, the widget is the text entry area `text_edit`, while for FILE_NAME, the widget is the file status area `file_label`.

The final resource that we specify for the DropTransfer is the `XmNtransferProc` routine. This routine is of type `XtSelectionCallbackProc`; it is responsible for actually processing the formatted data that is received from the drag source. The routine is called for each target data type requested by the drop site. This routine takes the following form:

```
typedef void (*XtSelectionCallbackProc)(Widget, XtPointer, Atom *,
        Atom *, XtPointer, unsigned long*, int *);
    Widget          widget;
    XtPointer       client_data;
    Atom            *selection;
    Atom            *type;
    XtPointer       value;
    unsigned long   *length;
    int             *format;
```

The *widget* parameter is the widget that requested the data, and *client_data* is the data specified in the `client_data` field of the `XmDropTransferEntryRec` that is being processed. The *type*, *value*, *length*, and *format* arguments contain the data that was converted by the drag source in its `XmNconvertProc`.

The `TransferProc()` routine in Example 18-3 checks the `type` to determine what needs to be done with the data. If the data is FILE_CONTENTS data, the text in `value` is placed in the Text widget with `XmTextSetString()`. Otherwise, the text is used to create a new value for `XmNlabelString` for the file status area. Since the file status area requests both target data types, both formats are processed by `TransferProc()`.

The `HandleDropText()` routine for the ScrolledText object is very similar to `Handle-DropLabel()`. The main difference is that the routine for the text area checks the `XmN-exportTargets` resource of the DragContext object to determine whether or not the drag source provides file data. If it does, `HandleDropText()` initiates the data transfer just as in `HandleDropLabel()`. Otherwise, the text routine calls the `XmNdropProc` that we retrieved from the Text widget when we modified the drop site. By calling the original drop routine, we allow the Text widget to process textual data as it would by default. As a result, the user can drop a file object in the text entry area, as well as manipulate textual data in the widget using drag and drop.

Once a data transfer is in progress, additional targets for the DropTransfer object can be specified using `XmDropTransferAdd()`. The primary use of this routine is for move operations. In this case, the drop site receives a copy of the data from the drag source and then requests that the source delete the data. Once the drop site has stored the data, it can call `XmDropTransferAdd()` to specify the DELETE target, which indicates to the initiating application that it should delete the data.

18.5.4 Providing Help

Since it is not always obvious what will happen when data is dropped on a particular drop site, the user can request help on a drop site by pressing the HELP or F1 key when the drag icon is over the drop site. An application should provide help information for its drop sites to assist users in understanding the drag and drop capabilities of the application. When the user requests help, the drop site should respond by posting an InformationDialog that explains what would happen and allows the user to proceed with the drop or cancel it.

When the user presses HELP while the drag icon is over a drop site, the XmNdropProc for the drop site is called with the dropAction field in the callback structure set to to Xm-DROP_HELP. Example 18-4 shows a new HandleDropLabel() routine for the *editor_dnd.c* application that provides help for the file status drop site. The example also shows the HandleDropOK() and HandleDropCancel() callback routines for the help dialog.

Example 18-4. The HandleDropLabel(), HandleDropOK(), and HandleDropCancel() routines

```
/* HandleDropLabel() -- start the data transfer when data is dropped in
 * the filename status area.
 */
void
HandleDropLabel(widget, client_data, call_data)
Widget          widget;
XtPointer       client_data;
XtPointer       call_data;
{
    Display               *dpy;
    Atom                  FILE_CONTENTS, FILE_NAME;
    XmDropProcCallback    DropData;
    XmDropTransferEntryRec transferEntries[2];
    XmDropTransferEntry   transferList;
    Arg                   args[10];
    int                   n, i;
    Widget                dc;
    Cardinal              numExportTargets;
    Atom                  *exportTargets;
    Boolean               file_name = False;
    static XmDropProcCallbackStruct client;
    static Widget         dialog = NULL;
    XmString              message;
    void                  HandleDropOK(), HandleDropCancel();
    void                  TransferProc();

    /* intern the Atoms for data targets */
    dpy = XtDisplay (toplevel);
    FILE_CONTENTS = XmInternAtom (dpy, "FILE_CONTENTS", False);
    FILE_NAME = XmInternAtom (dpy, "FILE_NAME", False);

    DropData = (XmDropProcCallback) call_data;
    dc = DropData->dragContext;

    /* retrieve the data targets and search for FILE_NAME */
    n = 0;
    XtSetArg (args[n], XmNexportTargets, &exportTargets); n++;
    XtSetArg (args[n], XmNnumExportTargets, &numExportTargets); n++;
    XtGetValues (dc, args, n);
```

```
    for (i = 0; i < numExportTargets; i++) {
        if (exportTargets[i] == FILE_NAME) {
            file_name = True;
            break;
        }
    }
    /* if one of the targets is not FILE_NAME, transfer fails */
    if (!file_name) {
        n = 0;
        XtSetArg (args[n], XmNtransferStatus, XmTRANSFER_FAILURE); n++;
        XtSetArg (args[n], XmNnumDropTransfers, 0); n++;
    }
    /* check if the user has requested help */
    else if (DropData->dropAction == XmDROP_HELP) {
        /* create a dialog if it doesn't already exist */
        if (!dialog) {
            n = 0;
            message = XmStringCreateLtoR (help_str, XmFONTLIST_DEFAULT_TAG);
            XtSetArg (args[n], XmNdialogStyle,
                XmDIALOG_FULL_APPLICATION_MODAL); n++;
            XtSetArg (args[n], XmNtitle, "Drop Help"); n++;
            XtSetArg (args[n], XmNmessageString, message); n++;
            dialog = XmCreateInformationDialog (toplevel, "help", args, n);
            XmStringFree (message);

            XtUnmanageChild (XmMessageBoxGetChild
                (dialog, XmDIALOG_HELP_BUTTON));

            XtAddCallback (dialog, XmNokCallback, HandleDropOK,
                (XtPointer) &client);
            XtAddCallback (dialog, XmNcancelCallback, HandleDropCancel,
                (XtPointer) &client);
        }

        /* set up the callback structure for when the user proceeds
         * with the drop and pass it as client data to the callbacks
         * for the buttons.
         */
        client.dragContext = dc;
        client.x = DropData->x;
        client.y = DropData->y;
        client.dropSiteStatus = DropData->dropSiteStatus;
        client.operation = DropData->operation;
        client.operations = DropData->operations;

        XtManageChild (dialog);
        return;
    }
    else if (DropData->operation != XmDROP_COPY) {
        /* if the operation is not a copy, the transfer fails */
        n = 0;
        XtSetArg (args[n], XmNtransferStatus, XmTRANSFER_FAILURE); n++;
        XtSetArg (args[n], XmNnumDropTransfers, 0); n++;
    }
    else {
```

```
        /* set up transfer requests since this is a normal drop */
        n = 0;
        transferEntries[0].target = FILE_CONTENTS;
        transferEntries[0].client_data = (XtPointer) text_edit;
        transferEntries[1].target = FILE_NAME;
        transferEntries[1].client_data = (XtPointer) file_label;
        transferList = transferEntries;
        XtSetArg (args[n], XmNdropTransfers, transferEntries); n++;
        XtSetArg (args[n], XmNnumDropTransfers,
            XtNumber (transferEntries)); n++;
        XtSetArg (args[n], XmNtransferProc, TransferProc); n++;
    }
    XmDropTransferStart (dc, args, n);
}

/* HandleDropOK() -- callback routine for OK button in drop site help
 * dialog that processes the drop as normal.
 */
void
HandleDropOK(widget, client_data, call_data)
Widget          widget;
XtPointer       client_data;
XtPointer       call_data;
{
    Display                     *dpy;
    Atom                        FILE_CONTENTS, FILE_NAME;
    XmDropProcCallbackStruct    *DropData;
    XmDropTransferEntryRec      transferEntries[2];
    XmDropTransferEntry         transferList;
    Arg                         args[10];
    int                         n;
    Widget                      dc;
    void                        TransferProc();

    /* intern the Atoms for data targets */
    dpy = XtDisplay (toplevel);
    FILE_CONTENTS = XmInternAtom (dpy, "FILE_CONTENTS", False);
    FILE_NAME = XmInternAtom (dpy, "FILE_NAME", False);

    /* get the callback structure passed via client data */
    DropData = (XmDropProcCallbackStruct *) client_data;
    dc = DropData->dragContext;

    n = 0;
    /* if operation is not a copy, the transfer fails */
    if (DropData->operation != XmDROP_COPY) {
        XtSetArg (args[n], XmNtransferStatus, XmTRANSFER_FAILURE); n++;
        XtSetArg (args[n], XmNnumDropTransfers, 0); n++;
    }
    else {
        /* set up transfer requests to process data transfer */
        transferEntries[0].target = FILE_CONTENTS;
        transferEntries[0].client_data = (XtPointer) text_edit;
        transferEntries[1].target = FILE_NAME;
        transferEntries[1].client_data = (XtPointer) file_label;
        transferList = transferEntries;
```

```
            XtSetArg (args[n], XmNdropTransfers, transferEntries); n++;
            XtSetArg (args[n], XmNnumDropTransfers,
                XtNumber (transferEntries)); n++;
            XtSetArg (args[n], XmNtransferProc, TransferProc); n++;
        }
        XmDropTransferStart (dc, args, n);
    }

/* HandleDropCancel() -- callback routine for Cancel button in drop site
 * help dialog that cancels the transfer.
 */
void
HandleDropCancel(widget, client_data, call_data)
Widget          widget;
XtPointer       client_data;
XtPointer       call_data;
{
    XmDropProcCallbackStruct        *DropData;
    Arg                             args[10];
    int                             n;
    Widget                          dc;

    /* get the callback structures passed via client data */
    DropData = (XmDropProcCallbackStruct *) client_data;
    dc = DropData->dragContext;

    /* user has canceled the transfer, so it fails */
    n = 0;
    XtSetArg (args[n], XmNtransferStatus, XmTRANSFER_FAILURE); n++;
    XtSetArg (args[n], XmNnumDropTransfers, 0); n++;
    XmDropTransferStart (dc, args, n);
}
```

When the user requests help on the file status drop site, the application displays a help dialog, as shown in Figure 18-8.

The new HandleDropLabel() routine handles the case when the dropAction field is set to XmDROP_HELP. In this case, the routine creates an InformationDialog if it has not already been created. The HandleDropOK() and HandleDropCancel() routines are registered for the **OK** and **Cancel** buttons in the dialog. If the dialog already exists, the necessary fields in the client structure are specified so that the callback structure information is passed to the callback routines as client data. If the user has performed a normal drop operation, the drop proceeds just as it did in *editor_dnd.c*.

The HandleDropOK() routine is invoked when the user presses the **OK** button in the help dialog. This routine proceeds with the drop by calling XmDropTransferStart(). The status of the transfer is based on whether the drop performs a copy operation or not. HandleDropCancel() cancels the drop when the user presses the **Cancel** button by calling XmDropTransferStart() with XmNtransferStatus set to XmTRANS-FER_FAILURE. One thing to note about both of these procedures is that they get the Xm-DropProcCallbackStruct from the client_data parameter, since the call_data parameter is the callback structure for the dialog.

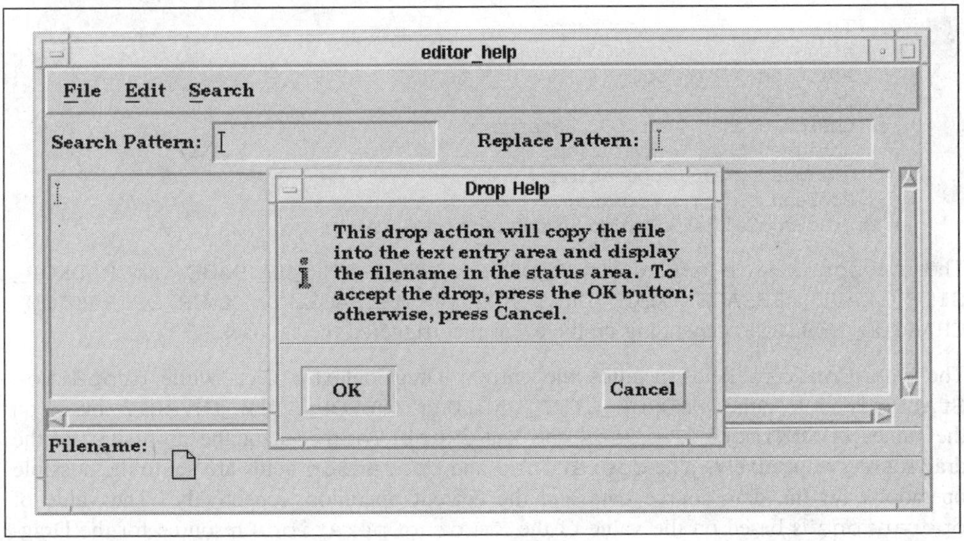

Figure 18-8. A drag and drop help dialog

18.5.5 Providing Custom Drag-under Visuals

Under the preregister protocol, the drop site does not participate during the drag. The initiating application handles the drag-under visual effects based on the value of the XmN-animationStyle resource for the drop site. This resource can have one of the following values:

```
XmDRAG_UNDER_HIGHLIGHT
XmDRAG_UNDER_SHADOW_OUT
XmDRAG_UNDER_SHADOW_IN
XmDRAG_UNDER_PIXMAP
XmDRAG_UNDER_NONE
```

The default value is XmDRAG_UNDER_HIGHLIGHT, which means that a highlighting rectangle is displayed around the drop site when the drag icon enters it. The drop site can also be displayed with an inset or outset shadow using XmDRAG_UNDER_SHADOW_OUT and Xm-DRAG_UNDER_SHADOW_IN, respectively. The XmDRAG_UNDER_PIXMAP value specifies that a special pixmap is displayed in the drop site when the drag icon is in it; the XmN-animationPixmap and XmNanimationMask resources indicate the pixmap that is used. If XmNanimationStyle is set to XmDRAG_UNDER_NONE, there are no animation effects unless they are provided by the XmNdragProc.

Under the dynamic protocol, the drop site can participate in the drag by specifying an XmN-dragProc. This callback routine is invoked when the drag icon enters or leaves the drop site, when the drag icon moves within the drop site, and when the operation changes while the icon is in the drop site. The callback receives a callback structure of the type XmDrag-ProcCallbackStruct, which is defined as follows:

```
typedef struct {
    int            reason;
    XEvent         *event;
```

```
    Time            timeStamp;
    Widget          dragContext;
    Position        x;
    Position        y;
    unsigned char   dropSiteStatus;
    unsigned char   operation;
    unsigned char   operations;
    Boolean         animate;
} XmDragProcCallbackStruct, *XmDragProcCallback;
```

The reason field is set to XmCR_DROP_SITE_ENTER_MESSAGE, XmCR_DROP_
SITE_LEAVE_MESSAGE, XmCR_DRAG_MOTION_MESSAGE, or XmCR_OPERATION_
CHANGED_MESSAGE, depending on the event that triggered the callback.

The dragContext field specifies the current DragContext object, while dropSite-
Status is set to either XmDROP_SITE_VALID or XmDROP_SITE_INVALID, based on
the values of XmNimportTargets and XmNexportTargets for the drop site and the
drag source, respectively. The operations and operation fields are set to the possible
operations for the drag source data and the current operation, repectively. The value of
operations is based on the value of the XmNdragOperations resource for the Drag-
Context, while the value of operation is based on operations and the value of XmN-
dropSiteOperations.

The XmNdragProc can change the values of these three fields based on any special processing it performs, such as handling simulated drop sites. When the routine is done, the toolkit
uses these values of the fields to initialize the fields in the callback structure that is passed to
the corresponding DragContext callback routine in the initiating application.

The animate field specifies whether the toolkit or the receiving client is handling drag-
under effects for the drop site. If the value is True, as it is by default, the toolkit handles the
effects based on the XmNanimationStyle resource. The receiving client can set the field
to False so that it is responsible for providing drag-under effects. The main use of the
XmNdragProc is for providing specialized drag-under effects, such as actual animation,
that the toolkit itself does not support.

18.6 Summary

The drag and drop capabilities provided by Motif 1.2 are highly customizable, so an application can use the toolkit to implement whatever functionality is necessary. The examples in
this chapter have demonstrated many of the techniques that an application needs to use to
provide drag and drop functionality, but they really just scratch the surface of what is possible.

Our examples implement the drag and drop features directly in application code because that
is sufficient for our purposes. However, if you are developing real applications, you should
think seriously about encapsulating drag and drop functionality in widgets, so that you can
reuse the components in all of the applications.

19

Compound Strings

This chapter describes Motif's technology for encoding font changes and character directions in the strings that are used by almost all of the Motif widgets.

In This Chapter:

19

19
Compound Strings

Compound strings are designed to address two issues frequently encountered by application designers: the use of foreign character sets to display text in other languages and the use of multiple fonts to render text. With the addition of internationalized string rendering capabilities in X11R5, the use of compound strings for internationalization purposes is theoretically no longer necessary. However, the Motif widget set still uses compound strings extensively, so applications have no choice but to create them to display text.

19.1 Internationalized Text Output

The internationalization features in X11R5 are based on the ANSI-C locale model. Under this model, an application uses a library that reads a customization database at run-time to get information about the user's language environment. An Xt-based application can establish its language environment (or locale) by registering a language procedure with `XtSet-LanguageProc()`, as described in Section 2.3.2. The language procedure returns a language string that is used by `XtResolvePathname()` to find locale-specific resource files. See Volume Four, *X Toolkit Intrinsics Programming Manual*, for more information on the localization of the resource database.

One of the important characteristics of a language environment is the *encoding* that is used to represent the *character set* for the particular language. In X, character set simply refers to a set of characters, while an encoding is a numeric representation of these characters.† A *charset* (not the same as a character set) is an encoding in which all of the characters have the same number of bits. Charsets are often defined by standards bodies such as the International Standards Organization (ISO). For example, the ISO Latin-1 charset (ISO8859-1) defines an encoding for the characters used in all Western languages. The first half of Latin-1 is standard ASCII, while the second half (with the eighth bit set) contains accented characters needed for Western languages other than English. Character 65 in ISO Latin-1 is an uppercase "A", while 246 is a lowercase "o" with an umlaut (ö).

---

† Both of these terms are different from the definition of a font, which is a collection of glyphs used to represent the characters in an encoding.

However, not all languages can be represented by a single charset. Japanese text commonly contains words written using the Latin alphabet, as well as phonetic characters from the *kata-kana* and *hirigana* alphabets, and ideographic *kanji* characters. Each of these character sets has its own charset; the phonetic and Latin charsets are 8-bits wide, while the ideographic charset is 16-bits wide. The charsets must be combined into a single encoding for Japanese text, so the encoding uses *shift sequences* to specify the character set for each character in a string.

Strings in an encoding that contains shift sequences and characters with non-uniform width can be stored in a standard `NULL`-terminated array of characters; this representation is known as a multibyte string. Strings can also be stored using a wide-character type in which each character has a fixed size and occupies one array element in the string. The text output routines in X11R5 support both multibyte and wide-character strings. To support languages that use multiple charsets, X developed the `XFontSet` abstraction for its text output routines. An `XFontSet` contains all of the fonts that are needed to display text in the current locale. The new text output routines work with font sets, so they can render text for languages that require multiple charsets. See Volume One, *Xlib Programming Manual*, for more information on internationalized text output.

With the addition of these features in X, a developer can write an internationalized application without using the internationalization features provided by compound strings. In an internationalized application, strings are interpreted using the encoding for the current locale. To support a number of locales, the application needs to store string data in separate files from the application code. The application must provide a separate file for each of the locales supported, so that the program can read the appropriate file during localization.

However, since most Motif widgets use compound strings for representing textual data, a Motif application has to use compound strings to display text. As we describe compound strings in this chapter, we'll discuss how to use them so as not to interfere with the lower-level X internationalization features.

19.2 Creating Compound Strings

Almost all of the Motif widgets use compound strings to specify textual data. Labels, Push-Buttons, and Lists, among others, all require their text to be given in compound string format, whether or not you require the additional flexibility compound strings provide. The only widgets that don't use compound strings are the Text and TextField widgets. As a result, you cannot use the compound string techniques for displaying text using multiple fonts. However, in Motif 1.2, these widgets do support internationalized text output, so they can display text using multiple character sets. For information on the internationalization capabilities of the Text and TextField widgets, see Section 14.6.

A compound string (`XmString`) is made of three components: a tag, a direction, and text. The tag is an arbitrary name that the programmer can use to associate a compound string with a particular font or font set. In Motif 1.1, the tag was referred to as a character set. Since the tag doesn't necessarily specify a character set, Motif 1.2 now refers to the entity as a font list tag; this change is strictly semantic. The tag-to-font mapping is done on a per-widget basis, so the same name can map to different fonts for different widgets.

An application can create a compound string that uses multiple fonts by concatenating separate compound strings with different tags to produce a single compound string. Concatenating compound strings with different fonts is a powerful way to create graphically interesting labels and captions. More importantly, because fonts are loosely bound to compound strings via resources, you can dynamically associate new fonts with a widget while an application is running and effectively change text styles on the fly.

19.2.1 The Simple Case

Many applications only need to use compound strings to specify various textual resources. In this case, all that is needed is a routine that converts a standard C-style NULL-terminated text string into a compound string. The most basic form of conversion can be done using the Xm-StringCreateLocalized() function, as demonstrated in examples throughout this book. This routine takes the following form:

```
XmString
XmStringCreateLocalized(text)
    char *text;
```

The *text* parameter is a common C char string. The value returned is of type XmString, which is an opaque type to the programmer.

XmStringCreateLocalized() is a new routine in Motif 1.2; it creates a compound string in the current locale, which is specified by the tag XmFONTLIST_DEFAULT_TAG. This routine interprets the *text* string in the current locale when creating the compound string. If you are writing an internationalized application that needs to support multiple locales, you should use XmStringCreateLocalized() to create compound strings. The routine allows you to take advantage of the lower-level internationalization features of X.

Most applications specify compound string resources in resource files. This technique is appropriate for an internationalized application, as there can be a separate resource file for each language environment that is supported. Motif automatically converts all strings that are specified in resource files into compound strings using XmStringCreate-Localized(), so the strings are handled correctly for the current locale. If an application needs to create a compound string programmatically, it should use XmStringCreate-Localized() to ensure that the string is interpreted in the current locale. All of the examples in this book use XmStringCreateLocalized() to demonstrate the appropriate technique, even though the examples are only designed to work in the C locale.

With Motif 1.1, you should use the XmStringCreateSimple() routine to create a compound string that uses the default character set and direction. This function is obsolete in Motif 1.2; it remains for backwards-compatibility purposes only. With both XmString-CreateLocalized() and XmStringCreateSimple(), you cannot explicitly specify the tag or the string direction that is used for the compound string, and the string cannot have multiple lines.

Both XmStringCreateLocalized() and XmStringCreateSimple() allocate memory to store the compound string that is returned. Widgets that have compound string resources always allocate their own space and store copies of the compound string values you give them. When you are done using a compound string to set widget resources, you must free it using `XmStringFree()`. The following code fragment demonstrates this usage:

```
XmString str = XmStringCreateLocalized ("Push Me");

XtVaCreateManagedWidget ("widget_name",
    xmPushButtonGadgetClass, parent,
    XmNlabelString,  str,
    NULL);

XmStringFree (str);
```

The process of creating a compound string, setting a widget resource, and then freeing the string is the most common use of compound strings. However, this process involves quite a bit of overhead, as memory operations are expensive. Memory is allocated by the string creation function and again by the internals of the widget for its own storage, and then your copy of the string must be deallocated.

The programmatic interface to the string creation process can be simplified by using the `Xt-VaTypedArg` feature in Xt. This special resource can be used in variable argument list specifications for functions such as `XtVaCreateManagedWidget()` and `XtVaSet-Values()`. It allows you to specify a resource using a convenient type and have Xt do the conversion for you. In the case of compound strings, we can use this method to convert a C string to a compound string. The following code fragment has the same effect as the previous example:

```
XtVaCreateManagedWidget ("widget_name",
    xmPushButtonWidgetClass, parent,
    XtVaTypedArg, XmNlabelString, XmRString,
        "Push Me", 8, /* or strlen ("Push Me") + 1 */
    NULL);
```

`XtVaTypedArg` takes four additional parameters: the name of the resource, the type of the value specified for the resource, the value itself, and the size of the value. We set the `XmNlabelString` resource. We want to avoid converting the character string to a compound string, so we specify a `char *` value and `XmRString` as its type.† The string `"Push Me"` is the string value; the length of the string, including the `NULL`-terminating byte, is 8.

The `XtVaTypedArg` method for specifying a compound string resource is only a programmatic convenience; it does not save time or improve performance. The three-step process of creating, setting, and freeing the compound string still takes place, but it happens within Motif's compound string resource converter. Using automatic conversion is actually slower than converting a string using `XmStringCreateLocalized()`. However, unless you are creating hundreds of strings, the difference is negligible. The convenience and elegance of the `XtVaTypedArg` method may be worth the performance tradeoff.

---

†This terminology may be confusing to a new Motif programmer. Xt uses the typedef `String` for `char *`. The representation type used by Xt resource converters for this type is `XtRString` (`XmRString` in Motif). A compound string, on the other hand, is of type `XmString`; its representation type is `XmRXmString`. You just have to read the symbols carefully. Resource converters are described in detail in Volume Four, *X Toolkit Intrinsics Programming Manual, Motif Edition*.

The reason most of the examples in this book do not make use of the feature is that we are trying to demonstrate good programming techniques tuned to a large-scale, production-size, and quality application. Using the XtVaTypedArg method for compound strings is painfully slow when repeated over hundreds of Labels, PushButtons, Lists, and other widgets. The XtVaTypedArg method is perfectly reasonable for converting other types of resources, however. If you are converting a lot of values from one type to another, it is in your own best interest to evaluate the conversion process yourself by testing the automatic versus the manual conversion methods.

19.2.2 Font List Tags

Motif provides two different compound string creation routines that allow you to specify a tag used to associate the compound string with a font or a font set. This tag is a programmer-specified identifier that enables a Motif widget to pick its font from a list of fonts at run-time. In Motif 1.1, the font list tag was referred to as a character set, but strictly speaking, it does not specify a character set.

The XmStringCreate() and XmStringCreateLtoR() routines allow you to specify a font list tag. These routines take the following form:

```
XmString
XmStringCreate(text, tag)
    char *text;
    char *tag;

XmString
XmStringCreateLtoR(text, tag)
    char *text;
    char *tag;
```

Both of these routines create and allocate a new compound string and associate the *tag* parameter with that string. As with any compound string, be sure to free it with XmString-Free() when you are done using it.

XmStringCreate() creates a compound string that has no specified direction. The default direction of a string may be taken from the XmNstringDirection resource. This resource is defined by manager widgets; it specifies the string direction for all the children of the manager. If the default direction is not adequate, XmStringDirectionCreate() can be used to create a compound string with an explicit direction, as we'll discuss shortly.

XmStringCreateLtoR() creates a compound string in which the direction is hard-coded as left-to-right.† This function is also useful for converting newline-separated strings into compound strings, as we explain later in this section. Unfortunately, Motif does not provide a corresponding right-to-left compound string creation function. If you need such a routine, it is not that difficult to write one.

---

†Motif also defines the XmStringLtoRCreate() routine; its functionality is identical to XmStringCreate-LtoR().

The actual font or font set that is associated with the compound string is dependent on the widget that renders the string. Every Motif widget that displays text has an XmNfontList resource. This resource specifies a list of fonts and/or font sets for the widget; each entry in the list may have an optional tag associated with it. For example, a resource file might specify a font list as follows:

```
*fontList: -*-courier-*-r-*--*-120-*=TAG1,\
           -*-courier-*-r-*--*-140-*=TAG2,\
           -*-courier-*-r-*--*-180-*=TAG3
```

At run-time, the compound string is rendered using the first font or font set in the widget's font list that matches the font list tag specified in the compound string creation function. In Motif 1.2, the compound string rendering functions use the new X11R5 text output functions, so compound strings are displayed appropriately for the current locale. If Motif cannot find a match, the compound string is rendered using the first item in the widget's font list, regardless of its tag. This loose binding between the compound string and the font or font set used to render it is useful in a number of ways:

- The same compound string can be rendered using different fonts in different widgets simply by specifying a different font list for each widget. For example:

```
*XmPushButton.fontList: -*-courier-*-r-*--*-120-*=TAG1
*XmPushButtonGadget.fontList: -*-courier-*-r-*--*-120-*=TAG1
*XmList.fontList: -*-helvetica-*-r-*--*-120-*=TAG1
```

These resource settings indicate that TAG1 maps to a 12-point Courier font for all Push-Button widgets and gadgets and maps to a 12-point Helvetica font for all List widgets.

- Compound strings rendered in different fonts can be concatenated to create a multi-font compound string. The font for each segment is selected from the widget's font list by means of a unique tag.

- Compound strings can be language-independent, with the tag used to select between fonts with different character set encodings. This is the least common use for compound strings, and as of X11R5, it is no longer needed to support internationalized text output.

Example 19-1 demonstrates how a compound string can be rendered using different fonts in different PushButton widgets.†

Example 19-1. The string.c program

```
/* string.c -- create a compound string with the "MY_TAG" tag.
 * The tag defaults to the "9x15" font.  Create three pushbuttons:
 * pb1, pb2, and pb3.  The user can specify resources so that each of the
 * widgets has a different font associated with the "MY_TAG" tag
 * specified in the compound string.
 */
#include <Xm/RowColumn.h>
#include <Xm/PushBG.h>
```

---

†XtSetLanguageProc() is only available in X11R5; there is no corresponding function in X11R4. Xm-StringCreateLocalized() is only available in Motif 1.2; XmStringCreateSimple() is the corresponding function in Motif 1.1.

Example 19-1. The string.c program (continued)

```
String fallbacks[] = { "*fontList:9x15=MY_TAG", NULL };

main(argc, argv)
int argc;
char *argv[];
{
    Widget          toplevel, rowcol;
    XtAppContext    app;
    XmString        text;
    Display         *dpy;

    XtSetLanguageProc (NULL, NULL, NULL);

    toplevel = XtVaAppInitialize (&app, "String", NULL, 0,
        &argc, argv, fallbacks, NULL);

    text = XmStringCreate ("Testing, testing...", "MY_TAG");

    rowcol = XtVaCreateWidget ("rowcol",
        xmRowColumnWidgetClass, toplevel,
        NULL);

    XtVaCreateManagedWidget ("pb1",
        xmPushButtonGadgetClass, rowcol,
        XmNlabelString, text,
        NULL);

    XtVaCreateManagedWidget ("pb2",
        xmPushButtonGadgetClass, rowcol,
        XmNlabelString, text,
        NULL);

    XtVaCreateManagedWidget ("pb3",
        xmPushButtonGadgetClass, rowcol,
        XmNlabelString, text,
        NULL);

    XmStringFree (text);
    XtManageChild (rowcol);
    XtRealizeWidget (toplevel);
    XtAppMainLoop (app);
}
```

This simple program creates three PushButton gadgets that all use the same compound string for their labels. The font list tag MY_TAG is associated with the 9x15 font in the fallback resources. By default, all of the buttons look the same, as shown in Figure 19-1.

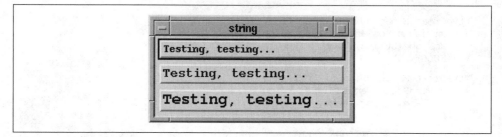

Figure 19-1. Output of string.c

However, Figure 19-2 shows what happens to the output when the following resources are specified:

```
*pb1.fontList: -*-courier-*-r-*--*-120-*=MY_TAG
*pb2.fontList: -*-courier-*-r-*--*-140-*=MY_TAG
*pb3.fontList: -*-courier-*-r-*--*-180-*=MY_TAG
```

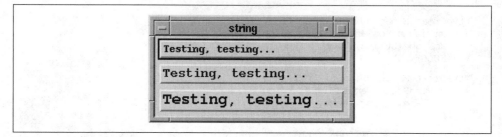

Figure 19-2. Output of string.c with font list resources set

The font associated with MY_TAG for each of the PushButtons is different, so the compound string for each one is rendered in a different font. This case isn't really that exciting, however, because we could have achieved the same effect without specifying a font list tag for each font. Since each font list only contains one font, Motif has no choice but to display the compound string using that font. The following resource specification creates the output shown in Figure 19-3:

```
*pb1.fontList: -*-courier-*-r-*--*-120-*
*pb2.fontList: fixed,-*-courier-*-r-*--*-140-*=ANOTHER_TAG
*pb3.fontList: fixed,-*-courier-*-r-*--*-180-*=MY_TAG
```

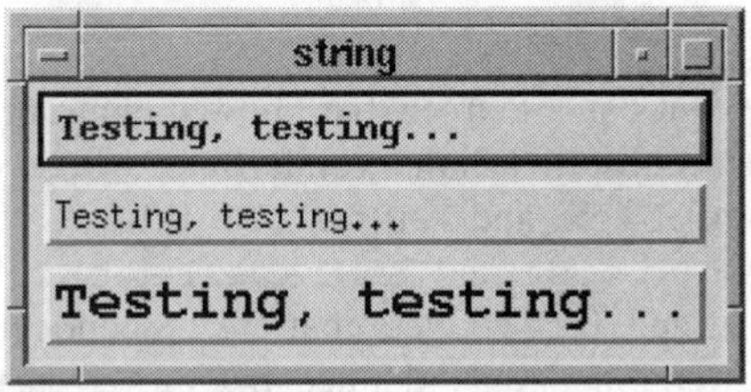

Figure 19-3. Output of string.c with multiple font list resources set

In this case, the compound string in the first PushButton uses a 12-point Courier font, since that is the only font in the font list. The second PushButton uses the `fixed` font because it is first in the list and neither of the fonts has MY_TAG associated with it. The third button uses the 18-point Courier font associated with MY_TAG.

The Default Font List Tag

In Motif 1.2, the constant XmFONTLIST_DEFAULT_TAG is used to tag compound strings that are created in the encoding of the current locale. When a compound string is created using XmStringCreateLocalized(), this tag is used. The equivalent compound string can also be created using XmStringCreate() with the tag explicitly set to Xm-FONTLIST_DEFAULT_TAG. Just as with other font list tags, Motif looks for a font or font set with a matching tag when it renders the compound string. This font list tag is used to identify the font or font set that is correct for the encoding of the current locale. If a font list does not use XmFONTLIST_DEFAULT_TAG, the first item in the font list is automatically associated with this tag.

An internationalized application should only use XmFONTLIST_DEFAULT_TAG in font lists to ensure that compound strings are rendered correctly for the current locale. However, it is possible to use explicit font list tags for locale-specific text. Explicit tags are necessary when an application wants to display compound strings using different point sizes or type styles. In this case, the compound string and the font list associated with it need to use the same tag, and the tag should be mapped to XmFONTLIST_DEFAULT_TAG using Xm-RegisterSegmentEncoding().

In Motif 1.1, the first font in widget's font list is the default character set for that widget. If the widget does not have a font list, it uses a default character set referred to by the constant XmSTRING_DEFAULT_CHARSET. If the user has set the LANG environment variable, its value is used for this character set. If this value is invalid or its associated font cannot be used, Motif uses the value of XmFALLBACK_CHARSET, which is vendor-defined but typically set to "ISO8859-1".

For backwards compatibility, Motif 1.2 essentially equates XmFONTLIST_DEFAULT_TAG with XmSTRING_DEFAULT_CHARSET when it cannot find an exact match between a compound string and a font list. XmFONTLIST_DEFAULT_TAG in a compound string or font list matches the tag used in creating a compound string or specifying a font list entry with the tag XmSTRING_DEFAULT_CHARSET.

Font List Resources

Some Motif widgets define font list resources that allow them to provide a consistent appearance for all of their children. In Motif 1.2, the VendorShell widget defines the XmNbuttonFontList, XmNlabelFontList, and XmNtextFontList resources, while the MenuShell defines XmNbuttonFontList and XmNlabelFontList. These resources apply to all of the buttons, Labels, and Text widgets that are descendents of the widget. In Motif 1.1, the VendorShell and MenuShell only defined the XmNdefaultFontList resource; this resource applied to all of the children of the widget. For backwards compatibility, if one of the more specific font list resources is not set, its value is taken from XmNdefaultFontList.

The BulletinBoard widget defines the XmNbuttonFontList, XmNlabelFontList, and XmNtextFontList resources primarily for use in dialog boxes. These font lists apply to the buttons, Labels, and Text widgets that descend from a BulletinBoard. For more information on the use of the resources in dialog boxes, see Chapter 5, *Introduction to Dialogs*.

All of these font list resources are designed to help you maintain a consistent interface. However, you can always specify the font for a particular button, Label, or Text widget using the widget's XmNfontList resource, as this resource overrides the more general ones.

19.2.3 Compound String Segments

A compound string is composed of *segments*, where each segment contains a continuous sequence of text with no change in font list tag or direction. A compound string segment can be terminated by a *separator*, which is the equivalent of a newline in a character string.†
Segments can be concatenated with other segments or compound strings to create longer strings; each segment can specify a different tag and direction to make a string that uses mutiple fonts and directions.

XmStringSegmentCreate() provides complete control over the creation of a compound string, as it allows you to specify the text, a font list tag, and a direction. This routine also lets you specify whether or not a separator is added to the compound string. The routine takes the following form:

```
XmString
XmStringSegmentCreate(text, tag, direction, separator)
    char              *text;
    char              *tag;
    XmStringDirection direction;
    Boolean           separator;
```

---

† Separators in compound strings should not be confused with the Separator widget and gadget class.

String Directions

Compound strings are rendered either from left-to-right or from right-to-left. If you are going to use left-to-right strings uniformly in your applications, you really don't need to read this section. There are several ways to build a compound string that is rendered from right-to-left; the best method is dependent on the nature of your application.

If your application uses right-to-left strings for all of its widgets, you may want to use the Manager `XmNstringDirection` resource. This resource specifies the direction for compound strings used by widgets that are immediate children of a Manager widget, provided that the string direction is not hard-coded in the compound strings. If you use this resource, you can continue to use `XmStringCreate()` or `XmStringCreateLocalized()` to create compound strings.

Most right-to-left languages display certain things, like numbers, from left-to-right, so it is not always possible to use the `XmNstringDirection` resource. In this case, you have to create compound string segments that hard-code their directional information. You can create individual string segments with a specific by direction using either `XmString-DirectionCreate()` or `XmStringSegmentCreate()`. Both of these routines take an argument of type `XmStringDirection`, which is defined as an unsigned char. You can specify either `XmSTRING_DIRECTION_R_TO_L` or `XmSTRING_DIRECTION_L_TO_R` for values of this type.

When using `XmStringSegmentCreate()`, you specify the string direction using the *direction* parameter. For example, we can change the call to `XmStringCreate()` in Example 19-1 to the following:

```
text = XmStringSegmentCreate ("Testing, testing...", "MY_TAG",
    XmSTRING_DIRECTION_R_TO_L, False);
```

Obviously, you would normally do this only if you were using a font that was meant to be read from right-to-left, such as Hebrew or Arabic. The output that results from this change is shown in Figure 19-4.

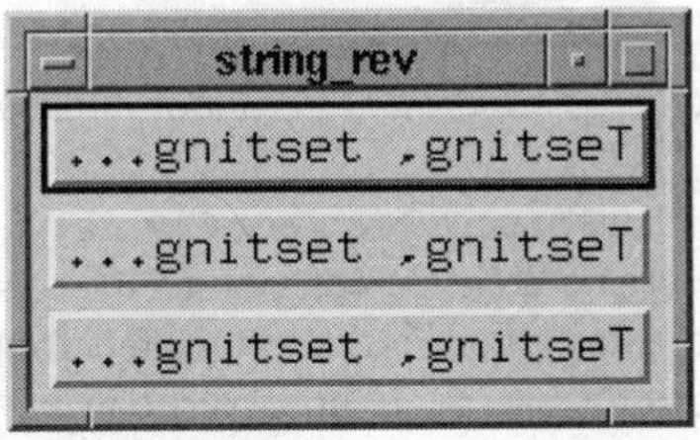

Figure 19-4. Output of string.c using a right-to-left string direction

You can also use the function XmStringDirectionCreate() to create a compound string segment that contains only directional information. This routine takes the following form:

```
XmString
XmStringDirectionCreate(direction)
    XmStringDirection direction;
```

The routine returns a compound string segment that can be concatenated with another compound string to cause a directional change.

String Separators

Separators are used to break compound strings into multiple lines, in much the same way that a newline character does in a character string. To demonstrate separators, we can change the string creation line in Example 19-1 to the following:

```
text = XmStringCreateLtoR ("Testing,\ntesting...", "MY_TAG");
```

In this case, we use XmStringCreateLtoR() not because we need to specify the left-to-right direction explicitly, but because this function interprets embedded newline characters (\n) as separators. The effect of this change is shown in Figure 19-5, where the Push-Buttons display multiple lines of text.

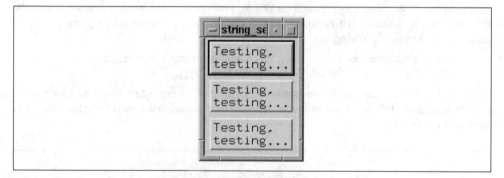

Figure 19-5. Output of string.c using separators to render multiple lines

XmStringCreate() and XmStringSegmentCreate() do not interpret newline characters as separators; they create a single compound string segment in which the '\n' is treated just like any other character value in the associated font or font set, as shown in Figure 19-6. XmStringSegmentCreate(), however, can be told to append a separator to the compound string it creates.

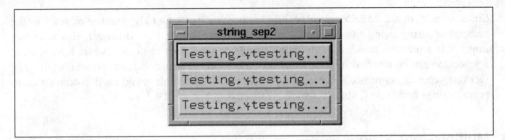

Figure 19-6. Output of string.c with \n not interpreted as a separator

Most applications need newline characters to be interpreted as separators. For example, if you are using `fgets()` or `read()` to read the contents of a file, and newlines are read into the buffer, you should use `XmStringCreateLtoR()` to convert the buffer into a compound string that contains separators. Example 19-2 shows a function that reads the contents of a file into a buffer and then converts that buffer into a compound string.†

Example 19-2. The ConvertFileToXmString() routine

```
XmString
ConvertFileToXmString(filename, &lines)
char *filename;
int *lines;
{
    struct stat  statb;
    int          fd, len, lines;
    char         *text;
    XmString     str;

    *lines = 0;
    if (!(fd = open (filename, O_RDONLY))) {
        XtWarning ("Internal error -- can't open file");
        return NULL;
    }
    if (fstat (fd, &statb) == -1 ||
            !(text = XtMalloc ((len = statb.st_size) + 1))) {
        XtWarning ("Internal error -- can't show text");
        close (fd);
        return NULL;
    }
    (void) read (fd, text, len);
    text[len] = 0;

    str = XmStringCreateLtoR (text, XmFONTLIST_DEFAULT_TAG);

    XtFree (text);
    close (fd);

    *lines = XmStringLineCount (str);
    return str;
}
```

---

† XmFONTLIST_DEFAULT_TAG replaces XmSTRING_DEFAULT_CHARSET in Motif 1.2.

Since separators are considered to be line breaks, we can count the number of lines in the compound string using the function XmStringLineCount(). However, this does not imply that separators terminate compound strings or cause font changes. As we have shown, a separator can be inserted into the middle of a compound string without terminating it. The fact that separate segments are created has little significance unless you need to convert compound strings back into C strings, which we discuss in Section 19.3.3.

19.2.4 Multiple-font Strings

Once multiple font list tags are specified in a font list, you can use the list to display more than one font or font set in a single compound string. You can create a multi-font string in one of two ways: create the compound text in segments or create separate compound strings. Either way, once the segments or strings have been created, they must be concatenated together to form a new compound string that has font-change information embedded in it. Example 19-3 demonstrates the creation of a compound string that uses three fonts.†

Example 19-3. The multi_font.c program

```
/* multi_font.c -- create three compound strings using 12, 14 and 18
 * point fonts.  The user can specify resources so that each of the strings
 * use different fonts by setting resources similar to that shown
 * by the fallback resources.
 */
#include <Xm/Label.h>

String fallbacks[] = {
    "multi_font*fontList:\
-*-courier-*-r-*--12-*=TAG1,\
-*-courier-bold-o-*--14-*=TAG2,\
-*-courier-medium-r-*--18-*=TAG3",
    NULL
};

main(argc, argv)
int argc;
char *argv[];
{
    Widget          toplevel;
    XtAppContext    app;
    XmString        s1, s2, s3, text, tmp;
    String          string1 = "This is a string ",
                    string2 = "that contains three ",
                    string3 = "separate fonts.";

    XtSetLanguageProc (NULL, NULL, NULL);

    toplevel = XtVaAppInitialize (&app, "String", NULL, 0,
        &argc, argv, fallbacks, NULL);

    s1 = XmStringCreate (string1, "TAG1");
    s2 = XmStringCreate (string2, "TAG2");
    s3 = XmStringCreate (string3, "TAG3");
```

---

†XtSetLanguageProc() is only available in X11R5; there is no corresponding function in X11R4.

Example 19-3. The multi_font.c program (continued)

```
    /* concatenate the 3 strings on top of each other, but we can only
     * do two at a time.  So do s1 and s2 onto tmp and then do s3.
     */
    tmp = XmStringConcat (s1, s2);
    text = XmStringConcat (tmp, s3);

    XtVaCreateManagedWidget ("widget_name",
        xmLabelWidgetClass, toplevel,
        XmNlabelString,     text,
        NULL);

    XmStringFree (s1);
    XmStringFree (s2);
    XmStringFree (s3);
    XmStringFree (tmp);
    XmStringFree (text);

    XtRealizeWidget (toplevel);
    XtAppMainLoop (app);
}
```

The output of this program is shown in Figure 19-7.

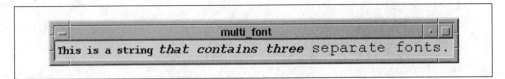

Figure 19-7. Output of multi_font.c

The XmNfontList resource is specified using three fonts, each with a distinct font list tag. We create each string using XmStringCreate() with the appropriate text and tag. Then we concatenate the strings using XmStringConcat(), two at a time until we have a single compound string that contains all the text. XmStringConcat() does not work like strcat() in C. The Motif function creates a new compound string that is composed of the two existing strings, rather than appending one string to the other string. Details of this function and other related functions are discussed in Section 19.3.1.

It is possible to specify compound string resource values, such as the XmNlabelString resource of the Label widget, in a resource file as normal C strings. Motif provides a resource converter that converts the character string into a compound string. However, this resource converter does not allow you to specify font list tags in the character string. If you need font changes within a compound string, you need to create the compound strings explicitly in your application as we have done in Example 19-3.

19.3 Manipulating Compound Strings

Most C programmers are used to dealing with functions such as strcpy(), strcmp(), and strcat() to copy, compare, and modify strings. However, these functions do not work with compound strings, as they are not based on a byte-per-character format, and they may have NULL characters as well as other types of information embedded in them. In order to perform these common tasks, you can either convert the compound string into a character string, or you can use the compound string manipulation functions provided by Motif. The method you choose depends largely on the complexity of the compound strings you have and/or the complexity of the manipulation you need to do.

19.3.1 Compound String Functions

Motif provides a number of functions that allow you to treat compound strings in much the same way that you treat C-style character arrays. The toolkit provides the following routines:

```
XmStringByteCompare()
XmStringCompare()
XmStringConcat()
XmStringCopy()
XmStringEmpty()
XmStringHasSubstring()
XmStringLength()
XmStringNConcat()
XmStringNCopy()
```

Both XmStringCompare() and XmStringByteCompare() compare two compound strings. These routines take the following form:

```
Boolean
XmStringCompare(string1, string2)
    XmString string1, string2;

Boolean
XmStringByteCompare(string1, string2)
    XmString string1, string2;
```

XmStringCompare() simply checks if the strings have the same text components, directions, and separators; it returns True if they do. This routine is simpler and more frequently used than XmStringByteCompare(), which performs a byte-by-byte comparison of the two compound strings. If each string uses the same font list tags, has the same direction, and contains the same embedded char string internally, the function returns True. The mapping between font list tags and fonts does not happen until a compound string is rendered by a widget, so whether or not the same font list tag actually maps to two different fonts does not affect the results of this function.

`XmStringConcat()` and `XmStringNConcat()` can be used to concatenate compound strings. These functions take the following form:

```
XmString
XmStringConcat(string1, string2)
    XmString string1, string2;
```

```
XmString
XmStringNConcat(string1, string2, n)
    XmString string1, string2;
    int n;
```

Both of these routines create a new compound string and copy the concatenation of *string1* and *string2* into the newly allocated string. `XmStringNConcat()` copies all of *string1*, but only *n* bytes from *string2*, into the new string. The original strings are preserved, and you are responsible for freeing the string returned by the routines using `XmStringFree()`.

You can copy a compound string using either `XmStringCopy()` or `XmStringNCopy()`, which take the following forms:

```
XmString
XmStringCopy(string)
    XmString string;
```

```
XmString
XmStringNCopy(string, n)
    XmString string;
    int n;
```

Both functions copy *string* into a newly-allocated compound string; `XmStringNCopy()` only copies *n* bytes from *string*.

`XmStringHasSubstring()` determines whether or not a compound string contains a particular substring. The routine has the following form:

```
Boolean
XmStringHasSubstring(string, substring)
    XmString string, substring;
```

For this function, *substring* must be a single-segment compound string. If its text is completely contained within any single segment of *string*, the function returns `True`. The two strings must use the same font list tags for the routine to return `True`.

To get the length of a compound string, use `XmStringLength()`, which has the following form:

```
int
XmStringLength(string)
    XmString string;
```

This function returns the number of bytes in the compound string including all tags, direction indicators, and separators. If the structure of *string* is invalid, the routine returns zero. This function cannot be used to get the length of the text represented by the compound string; it is not the same as `strlen()`).

You can determine whether or not a compound string contains any segments using Xm-StringEmpty(), which takes the following form:

```
Boolean
XmStringEmpty(string)
    XmString string;
```

This function returns True if there are no segments in the specified *string* and False, otherwise. If the routine is passed NULL, it returns True.

19.3.2 Compound String Retrieval

You can retrieve a compound string from a Motif widget using XtVaGetValues(). However, the way XtVaGetValues() is used for compound string resources is different than how it is used for most other resources. The value returned by XtVaGetValues() for a compound string resource is a copy of the internal data, so the compound string must be freed by the application, as shown in the following code fragment:

```
XmString str;
extern Widget pushbutton;
char *text;

XtVaGetValues (pushbutton, XmNlabelString, &str, NULL);
...
/* do whatever you want with the compound string */
...
XmStringFree (str);  /* must free compound strings from GetValues */
```

To avoid memory leaks in your application, you must remember to free any compound strings that you retrieve from a widget using XtVaGetValues().

19.3.3 Compound String Conversion

If the Motif routines described in the previous section are inadequate for your needs, you can convert compound strings back into C strings and manipulate them using the conventional C functions. This process can be simple or complicated depending on the complexity of the compound string to be converted. If the compound string only has one tag associated with it and has a left-to-right orientation, the process is quite simple. In this case, which is quite common, you can use the following function to make the conversion:

```
Boolean
XmStringGetLtoR(string, tag, text)
    XmString         string;
    XmStringCharSet  tag;
    char             **text;
```

XmStringGetLtoR() takes a compound string and a tag and converts it back into a C character string. If successful, the function returns True, and the text parameter points to a newly-allocated string. Since the routine allocates storage for the character string, you must free this pointer when you are done using it, as shown in the following code fragment:

```
XmString  string;
char      *text;

if (XmStringGetLtoR (string, "MY_TAG", &text)) {
    printf ("Text = %s\n", text);
    XtFree (text);
}
```

As its name implies, `XmStringGetLtoR()` only gets left-to-right oriented text. Additionally, the function only gets the first text segment from the compound string that is associated with the specified *tag*. If the string contains multiple tags or has a right-to-left direction, you need to traverse the compound string and retrieve each segment individually in order to obtain the entire string. Motif defines a new type, `XmStringContext`, that is used to identify and maintain the position within the compound string being scanned. To cycle through a compound string, you need to use the following sequence of operations:

1. Initialize a string context for the compound string using `XmStringInitContext()`.

2. Iterate through the string by calling `XmStringGetNextSegment()` to get the character set, C string, direction, and separator associated with each segment.

3. Free the string context using `XmStringFreeContext()`.

`XmStringInitContext()` initializes a string context that allows an application to read the contents of a compound string segment by segment. This routine takes the following form:

```
Boolean
XmStringInitContext(context, string)
    XmStringContext  *context;
    XmString         string;
```

The function allocates a new `XmStringContext` type and sets the pointer that is passed by the calling function in the *context* parameter to this data. If the allocation is successful and the compound string is valid, the function returns `True`.

Once the string context has been initialized, the contents of the string can be scanned using `XmStringGetNextSegment()`:

```
Boolean
XmStringGetNextSegment(context, text, tag, direction, separator)
    XmStringContext     context;
    char                **text;
    XmStringCharSet     *tag;
    XmStringDirection   *direction;
    Boolean             *separator;
```

The routine does not take an `XmString` parameter because the *context* parameter is used to keep track of the compound string. The function reads the next segment; it stops when it encounters a new tag or a directional change. The values for *text*, *tag*, and *direction* are filled in, and if a separator is found at the end of the segment, *separator* is set to

True. The *text* parameter points to allocated data that should be freed by the caller using `XtFree()`.

When you are through scanning the compound string, you need to free the string context using `XmStringFreeContext()`, which takes the following form:

```
void
XmStringFreeContext (context)
    XmStringContext context;
```

Example 19-4 shows a routine that uses these functions to print a compound string used as the label for a widget.

Example 19-4. The PrintLabel() routine

```
void
PrintLabel(widget)
Widget widget;
{
    XmString            str;
    XmStringContext     context;
    char                *text, *tag, buf[128], *p;
    XmStringDirection   direction;
    Boolean             separator;

    XtVaGetValues (widget, XmNlabelString, &str, NULL);

    if (!XmStringInitContext (&context, str)) {
        /* compound strings from GetValues still need to be freed! */
        XmStringFree (str);
        XtWarning ("Can't convert compound string.");
        return;
    }

    /* p keeps a running pointer thru buf as text is read */
    p = buf;

    while (XmStringGetNextSegment (context, &text, &tag,
            &direction, &separator)) {
        /* copy text into p and advance to the end of the string */
        p += (strlen (strcpy (p, text)));
        if (separator == True) { /* if there's a separator ... */
            *p++ = '\n';
            *p = 0;   /* add newline and null-terminate */
        }
        XtFree (text);    /* we're done with the text; free it */
    }

    XmStringFreeContext (context);
    XmStringFree (str);

    printf ("Compound string:\n%s\n", buf);
}
```

19.4 Working With Font Lists

As we have demonstrated, font lists can be set in a resource file. If your application is robust enough to handle any particular font that the user may specify, you are encouraged to use fallback resources and the application defaults files for all font list specifications. This technique simplifies maintenance for your application, as you do not have to open fonts, maintain handles to them, and free them. If you are writing an internationalized application, you should only specify font lists in resource files so that you can specify different fonts and/or font sets in the resource files for different locales.

However, if you specifically don't want the user to override your font specifications, you can hard-code fonts within the application using various Motif routines to create a font list. In this case, you are taking on the responsibility of creating, maintaining, and destroying fonts as necessary. Motif also provides routines that allow you to retrieve information about a font list.

19.4.1 Creating Font Lists

All of the font list creation functions deal with a font list object of type XmFontList. This type is intended to be opaque, so you should not attempt to access the internal fields of the data structure. If you need information about the fonts in a font list, you can use the routines for querying a font list that we are going to describe.

The Motif API for font lists has changed significantly in Motif 1.2 to support the new XFontSet abstraction. The Motif 1.1 routines exist for backwards compatibility, but they are now obsolete. In Motif 1.2, each item in a font list specifies an XmFontListEntry and an associated tag, while in Motif 1.1 each item specifies a font and a character set tag. The XmFontListEntry type is an opaque type that can specify either a font or a font set.

The process for creating a font list involves creating individual font list entries and then appending these entries to a font list. Example 19-5 shows a program that produces the same output as Example 19-3, but now the font list is hard-coded in the program.†

Example 19-5. The fontlist.c program

```
/* fontlist.c -- demonstrate how to create, add to, and destroy
 * font lists.  The fonts and text displayed are hardcoded in
 * this program and cannot be overriden by user resources.
 */
#include <Xm/Label.h>

main(argc, argv)
int argc;
char *argv[];
```

---

†XtSetLanguageProc() is only available in X11R5; there is no corresponding function in X11R4. XmFont-ListEntryCreate() is only available in Motif 1.2; there is no corresponding function in Motif 1.1. XmFont-ListAppendEntry() is only available in Motif 1.2; XmFontListCreate() and XmFontListAdd() are the corresponding functions in Motif 1.1.

Example 19-5. The fontlist.c program (continued)

```
{
    Widget              toplevel;
    XtAppContext        app;
    XmString            s1, s2, s3, text, tmp;
    XmFontListEntry     entry1, entry2, entry3;
    XmFontList          fontlist;
    String              string1 = "This is a string ",
                        string2 = "that contains three ",
                        string3 = "separate fonts.";

    XtSetLanguageProc (NULL, NULL, NULL);

    toplevel = XtVaAppInitialize (&app, "Demos", NULL, 0,
        &argc, argv, NULL, NULL);

    entry1 = XmFontListEntryLoad (XtDisplay (toplevel),
        "-*-courier-*-r-*--*-120-*", XmFONT_IS_FONT, "TAG1");
    entry2 = XmFontListEntryLoad (XtDisplay (toplevel),
        "-*-courier-bold-o-*--*-140-*", XmFONT_IS_FONT, "TAG2");
    entry3 = XmFontListEntryLoad (XtDisplay (toplevel),
        "-*-courier-medium-r-*--*-180-*", XmFONT_IS_FONT, "TAG3");
    fontlist = XmFontListAppendEntry (NULL, entry1);
    fontlist = XmFontListAppendEntry (fontlist, entry2);
    fontlist = XmFontListAppendEntry (fontlist, entry3);
    XmFontListEntryFree (&entry1);
    XmFontListEntryFree (&entry2);
    XmFontListEntryFree (&entry3);

    s1 = XmStringCreate (string1, "TAG1");
    s2 = XmStringCreate (string2, "TAG2");
    s3 = XmStringCreate (string3, "TAG3");

    /* concatenate the 3 strings on top of each other, but we can only
     * do two at a time.  So do s1 and s2 onto tmp and then do s3.
     */
    tmp = XmStringConcat (s1, s2);
    text = XmStringConcat (tmp, s3);

    XtVaCreateManagedWidget ("label", xmLabelWidgetClass, toplevel,
        XmNlabelString,     text,
        XmNfontList,        fontlist,
        NULL);

    XmStringFree (s1);
    XmStringFree (s2);
    XmStringFree (s3);
    XmStringFree (tmp);
    XmStringFree (text);
    XmFontListFree (fontlist);

    XtRealizeWidget (toplevel);
    XtAppMainLoop (app);
}
```

This program creates font list entries for three fonts, appends the entries to a font list, and uses the resulting font list to specify the XmNfontList resource of a Label widget. The compound strings are created using the same tags as the font list entries, so they are displayed in the appropriate fonts.

In Example 19-5, we create the font list entries using `XmFontListEntryLoad()`, which takes the following form:

```
XmFontListEntry
XmFontListEntryLoad(display, font_name, type, tag)
    Display     *display;
    char        *font_name;
    XmFontType  type;
    char        *tag;
```

This routine loads the font or creates the font set specified by *font_name*. The function uses Xt resource converters to convert the string name of the font to the appropriate type. The *type* parameter specifies whether the font name is a font or a font set; it can have the value `XmFONT_IS_FONT` or `XmFONT_IS_FONT_SET`. The *tag* is associated with the font list entry. If the routine can load or create the specified font, it allocates and returns an `XmFontListEntry`, which the application must free using `XmFontListEntryFree()`. If the routine cannot find the specified font, it returns NULL.

Once we have created the font list entries, we can use them to make a font list. `XmFontListAppendEntry()` appends a font list entry to a font list. We call this routine three times to add the three entries. `XmFontListAppendEntry()` takes the following form:

```
XmFontList
XmFontListAppendEntry(oldlist, entry)
    XmFontList     oldlist;
    XmFontListEntry entry;
```

The routine adds the specified *entry* to the old font list and returns a new font list. If *oldlist* is NULL, the routine simply creates a font list using the font list entry. Motif caches font lists, so when we add a font list entry to a font list, the routine searches the cache for a font list that matches the new font list. If the routine finds a matching font list, it returns that font list and increments its reference count. Otherwise, `XmFontListAppendEntry()` allocates space for the new font list and caches it. The routine deallocates the storage for the old font list, but the application is responsible for freeing the storage for the new font list using `XmFontListFree()`.

After we add the font list entries to the font list, we don't need the individual entries, so we free them using `XmFontListEntryFree()`. Notice that this routine takes an address of a font list entry, not the actual font list entry. When Motif creates a font list entry, it does not copy the `XFontStruct` or `XFontSet`, so these items must not be freed. If you pass a font list entry, instead of its address, to `XmFontListEntryFree()`, you end up freeing the font or font set, which results in an X protocol error.

The *fontlist.c* program creates compound strings just like our previous examples. The strings are associated with the same tags as the font list entries, so the strings are rendered using the appropriate fonts. The program sets the `XmNfontList` resource of the Label widget, so the fonts are hard-coded in the application and cannot be modified using a resource file. When a font list is assigned to a widget, the widget copies the list using `XmFontListCopy()`. After the resource has been specified, the program no longer needs the font list, so it frees it using `XmFontListFree()`.

We used XmFontListEntryLoad() to both load the font and create a font list entry. Alternatively, we could have loaded the fonts using a routine like XLoadQueryFont() and then called XmFontListEntryCreate() to create the font list entries. This routine takes the following form:

```
XmFontListEntry
XmFontListEntryCreate(tag, type, font)
    char        *tag
    XmFontType  type;
    XtPointer   font;
```

The *type* parameter specifies whether the specified *font* is an XFontStruct or an XFontSet. You can load a font using XLoadQueryFont(). Use XCreateFontSet() to create a font set. (See Volume One, *Xlib Programming Manual*, for more information on these routines.) XmFontListEntryCreate() allocates and returns a font list entry; the application is responsible for freeing this entry using XmFontListEntryFree().

It is purely a matter of preference whether you use XmFontListEntryCreate() or XmFontListEntryLoad(). In Example 19-5, we could replace our calls to XmFontListEntryLoad() with the following code:

```
XFontStruct     *font1, *font2, *font3;
XmFontListEntry  entry1, entry2, entry3;

font1 = XLoadQueryFont (XtDisplay (toplevel),
    "-*-courier-*-r-*--*-120-*");
font2 = XLoadQueryFont (XtDisplay (toplevel),
    "-*-courier-bold-o-*--*-140-*");
font3 = XLoadQueryFont (XtDisplay (toplevel),
    "-*-courier-medium-r-*--*-180-*");

entry1 = XmFontListEntryCreate ("TAG1", XmFONT_IS_FONT, font1);
entry2 = XmFontListEntryCreate ("TAG2", XmFONT_IS_FONT, font2);
entry3 = XmFontListEntryCreate ("TAG3", XmFONT_IS_FONT, font3);
```

The functionality of the program is the same in either case, so which method you use really depends on whether you want to load the fonts yourself or let the routine handle it for you.

In Motif 1.1, there are two routines for dealing with font lists. XmFontListCreate() creates a new font list with one entry, while XmFontListAdd() adds a font to an existing font list. These routines take the following form:

```
XmFontList
XmFontListCreate(font, charset)
    XFontStruct      *font;
    XmStringCharSet  charset;


XmFontList
XmFontListAdd(oldlist, font, charset);
    XmFontList       oldlist;
    XFontStruct      *font;
    XmStringCharSet  charset;
```

The routines both take an XFontStruct, so you have to load the font yourself using XLoadQueryFont(). The functions both allocate and return a font list that the application must free when it is done using it. These routines exist for backwards compatibility purposes only, so you should not use them with Motif 1.2.

19.4.2 Retrieving Font Lists

You can retrieve a font list directly from a widget using XtVaGetValues() no matter whether the font list is specified in a resource file or created programatically. The following code fragment demonstrates this technique:

```
XmFontList fontlist;

XtVaGetValues (widget, XmNfontList, &fontlist, NULL);
```

The font list returned by XtVaGetValues() is a pointer to internal data, so it should be considered read-only. You should not alter this font list or free it. This is in direct contrast to how Motif uses XtVaGetValues() for compound strings, where a copy of the string is returned. If you need to manipulate the font list, you can make a copy of it using XmFont-ListCopy().

Once you have obtained a font list from a widget, you can use it to specify the font list for another widget, as shown in the following code:

```
XtVaSetValues (another_widget, XmNfontList, fontlist, NULL);
```

Since the font list was obtained through a call to XtVaGetValues(), we do not free it after setting the XmNfontList resource.

19.4.3 Querying Font Lists

The XmFontList type is opaque to the programmer, so if you need to get information about a font list, you have to use Motif-specific functions that access font list information. This internal information can be useful if you need the font handles or tags for any reason. Motif provides a number of routines to cycle through the font list. The XmFontContext type is used to identify and maintain the position within the font list being queried. To query a font list, you need to use the following sequence of operations:

1. Initialize a font context for the font list using XmFontListInitFontContext().

2. Iterate through the font list by calling XmFontListNextEntry() and access whatever information is desired.

3. Free the font context using XmFontListFreeFontContext().

XmFontListInitContext() initializes a font context that lets an application get the individual font list entries from the font list. This routine takes the following form:

```
Boolean
XmFontListInitFontContext(context, fontlist)
    XmFontContext   *context;
    XmFontList      fontlist;
```

The routine is passed the address of an XmFontContext variable and a font list. It allocates a new font context structure based on the font list and returns True. If the font list is not valid or there is not enough memory available to allocate a new context, False is returned.

Once the font context has been initialized, the entries in the font list can be retrieved using `XmFontListNextEntry()`:

```
XmFontListEntry
XmFontListNextEntry(context)
    XmFontContext context;
```

This routine cycles through all of the font list entries in the font list. The first call returns the first entry in the font list; repeated calls using the same font context access successive entries. Since the `XmFontListEntry` type is also opaque, you have to use `XmFontListEntry-GetFont()` and `XmFontListEntryGetTag()` to retrieve the actual font or font set and tag for the font list entry. These routines take the following form:

```
XtPointer
XmFontListEntryGetFont(entry, type_return)
    XmFontListEntry  entry;
    XmFontType       *type_return;


char *
XmFontListEntryGetTag(entry)
    XmFontListEntry entry;
```

`XmFontListEntryGetFont()` returns an `XFontStruct` or an `XFontSet` depending on the value of *type_return*. The routine does not copy the data structure, so the application must not free it. `XmFontListEntryGetTag()` retrieves the tag for the font list entry. This routine allocates storage for the tag, so the application must free it.

In Motif 1.1, you call `XmFontListGetNextFont()` to cycle through the fonts in a font list. This routine has the following form:

```
Boolean
XmFontListGetNextFont(context, charset, font)
    XmFontContext    context;
    XmStringCharSet  *charset;
    XFontStruct      **font;
```

If the function returns `True`, the character set and font pointers are set to the appropriate values. The *charset* returned is a pointer to allocated data that must be freed when no longer needed. The value for *font* points to the actual `XFontStruct` data used in the font list, so it must not be freed. If the end of the list has been reached, the function returns `False`. This routine exists for backwards compatibility and should not be used with Motif 1.2.

When you are done querying the font list, you need to free the font context using `XmFont-ListFreeFontContext()`, which takes the following form:

```
void
XmFontListFreeFontContext(context)
    XmFontListFontContext context;
```

If you are searching through a font list and need to back up, you must restart the entire process by freeing the current font context and creating a new one.

19.5 Rendering Compound Strings

Motif always renders compound strings automatically within its widgets, so you should never find yourself in a situation where you need to render a compound string manually. However, if you are writing your own widget, you may need to incorporate the same type of functionality. Motif provides three functions that render compound strings:

```
XmStringDraw()
XmStringDrawImage()
XmStringDrawUnderline()
```

In Motif 1.2, all of these routines use the X11R5 text output routines when necessary, to ensure that the text is rendered correctly for the current locale.

The most basic rendering function is `XmStringDraw()`, which takes the following form:

```
XmStringDraw(display, window, fontlist, string, gc, x, y, width,
            alignment, layout_direction, clip);
    Display       *display;
    Window        window;
    XmFontList    fontlist;
    XmString      string;
    GC            gc;
    Position      x, y;
    Dimension     width;
    unsigned char alignment;
    unsigned char layout_direction;
    XRectangle    *clip;
```

As you can see, the function requires a great deal of information to actually render the string. If you are rendering into a widget, you can specify the *display* and *window* using Xt-Window() and XtDisplay(). Since a gadget does not have a window, you must use XtWindowOfObject() with a gadget. The *fontlist* parameter can be constructed using any of the functions described in Section 19.4, or you can retrieve a font list from a widget using XtVaGetValues().

The function also requires a graphics context (GC) so that certain rendering attributes such as color can be applied. A graphics context is generally not available through a widget, so you have to get one at the Xlib level. If you are writing your own widget, you can probably use a GC that is cached by Xt and returned by XtGetGC() (see Volume Four, *X Toolkit Intrinsics Programming Manual*). Also, if you are writing your own widget, you may want to consider exposing the GC to the programmer in the form of a resource.

The *x*, *y*, and *width* parameters specify the coordinates and width of the rectangle that contains the compound string. The *width* parameter is used only for alignment purposes. There is no height parameter because the font list may specify fonts that are unknown in size and whose heights are too variable. The *clip* parameter defines the drawing boundary; you can pass NULL to indicate that the rendering should not be clipped.

The *alignment* parameter can be set to one of the following values:

```
XmALIGNMENT_BEGINNING
XmALIGNMENT_CENTER
XmALIGNMENT_END
```

The value identifies the justification for the text. The effect of the value is modified by the value of the *layout_direction* parameter, which can be set to XmSTRING_DIRECTION_L_TO_R or XmSTRING_DIRECTION_R_TO_L.

The function XmStringDrawImage() is to XmStringDraw() as XDrawString() is to XDrawImageString(). The difference is that the image routines overwrite the background even in places where the font does not set bits in the character image, while the other routines only render foreground pixels.

The XmStringDrawUnderline() routine takes the same parameters as XmStringDraw() with one addition. The last parameter specifies the portion of the compound string that should be underlined. A compound string can be wholly or partially underlined depending on whether the last parameter specifies the entire compound string or only a substring of the *string* parameter.

It may be necessary to get dimensional information about a compound string in order to know where to place it within the window when it is drawn. You may also want this data to determine the optimal or desired width and height of a widget in case you have to provide a geometry callback method. When a call to XtQueryGeometry is made, a widget that contains compound strings may need to tell the calling function the dimensions it needs to render its compound strings adequately. Motif provides the following routines to help you determine compound string dimensions:

```
XmStringBaseLine()
XmStringExtent()
XmStringHeight()
XmStringWidth()
```

Each of these functions takes *fontlist* (XmFontList) and *string* (XmString) parameters. The font list is dependent on the widget associated with the string, but there is no requirement that you must use a string that is associated with a widget. If you just want to get the dimensions of a particular compound string rendered using an arbitrary font or font set, you can create a font list manually, as described in Section 19.4.

XmStringBaseline() returns the number of pixels between the top of the character box and the baseline of the first line of text in the compound string. XmStringWidth() and XmStringHeight() return the width and height, respectively, for the specified compound string. XmStringExtent() takes two additional parameters, *width* and *height*. These arguments return the width and height in pixels of the smallest rectangle that encloses the compound string specified in *string*.

19.6 Summary

Compound strings can be useful for creating multi-line or multi-font text for widgets such as Labels, PushButtons, and ToggleButtons. Compound strings were also designed to help in making internationalized applications, but this functionality has basically been made obsolete by the addition of internationalization features in X11R5. Since Motif applications have to use compound strings to display most textual data, the trick to developing an internationalized application is to use compound strings without interfering with lower-level X internationalization functionality.

The best practice is to specify compound string and font list resources in resource files, so that you can have a separate file for each language that is supported by your application. If you have to create compound strings in an application, you should use `XmStringCreate-Localized()` or specify the `XmFONTLIST_DEFAULT_TAG` font list tag to ensure that the strings are interpreted and rendered in the current locale.

Compound Strings

20

Signal Handling

This chapter describes the problems that can occur when UNIX signals are mixed with X applications. It explains how signals work, and why they can wreak havoc with X. The chapter also suggests some workarounds that can help an application to minimize the damage. Since the technology is not well thought-through in this area and signals are a fact of life for UNIX applications, something must be done. The techniques described here can be thought of as a practical starting point until the problems are addressed by UNIX and X system developers at a more fundamental level.

In This Chapter:

Signal Handling

When writing an X-based application, programmers sometimes run into one of the most frustrating stumbling blocks of development: how to handle UNIX signals appropriately for an X client application. The problem is difficult to identify because there are rarely any adverse effects to the improper handling of signals. When problems do arise, the unwitting developer may spend weeks trying to unravel the mystery. Symptoms include spurious X protocol errors, lost X events, incomplete window redraws, or even core dumps. These problems arise because many people fail to understand the relationship between UNIX signals and the X protocol design.

To make an analogy for the type of behavior associated with UNIX signals, let's examine a telephone feature most of us are familiar with: call waiting. We start with a situation where you're on the phone talking to someone while someone else is trying to call you. When you have call waiting and another caller is trying to get through, an audio tone is sent to your receiver. (In most modern telephone systems, the other party doesn't hear the tone, but in older systems, they may hear a click.) Quite literally, you've been interrupted by another call, and you have to handle it. What you do next is what UNIX programmers would call interrupt handling.

In the UNIX operating system, signals are delivered to an application (a process) when an abnormal condition occurs. The difference between call waiting and UNIX signals is that there is more than one signal that can be delivered by UNIX, but there is only one tone that call waiting would deliver. These signals may be generated by the user at the keyboard, by another process using the `kill` system call (which sends a signal to a process ID), by the operating system itself, and so on. For example, job control typically involves one signal that indicates when the process has stopped (SIGTSTP), and another that indicates when the process has continued (SIGCONT). Another signal is generated when an application has spawned a new process with `fork()` and this child process dies. The operating system notifies the parent about the child's death, so that the parent can reap the child. In this case, the operating system delivers a SIGCHLD (SIGCLD for System V) to the parent. Still another signal is SIGFPE (floating point exception), which indicates a division by 0 error. A final example is a segmentation fault (SIGSEGV), where the application has exceeded some internal boundary, like an array index that is out of range.

In all these cases, the signal that the operating system sends to the application is like the tone that you hear when call waiting is activated. The programmer has the ability to specify how these signals should be serviced by trapping them using *signal handlers*. A signal handler is a function installed for a signal type using the `signal()` system call, which takes the following form:

```
signal(sig_number, function)
```

The `sig_number` is the signal identifier, which is a defined symbol like those described above, while `function` is a routine that you write. If the signal is delivered, the routine is called automatically. What the signal handler function actually does is up to you. For example, if you trap the `SIGCHLD` signal, when a previously forked process terminates, your signal handler should probably call the `wait()` system call to reap the child. With `SIGFPE`, you may want to notify the user that he has entered an invalid value. For `SIGSEGV`, your program should assume that the application is no longer in a runnable state and clean up after itself by removing temporary files, making backup copies of unfinished files, flushing buffers, or whatever.

Now, what does all this have to do with X applications? Let's say that you want to display an ErrorDialog upon receipt of a signal. Here is where the problem with X and UNIX signals arises. To elaborate, we return to the call-waiting analogy. The original telephone conversation that you were having before call waiting interrupted represents the X protocol communication between an X client and the X server. Now, let's assume that instead of hearing a tone that indicates there is an incoming call, you are immediately transferred to the new call without any notification. In mid-conversation, the original caller can no longer hear you. Furthermore, when you are transferred back to the original caller, the discussion may have progressed without your knowledge. Whatever you were saying would now be completely confusing to anyone listening.

This situation is analogous to what happens when a UNIX signal interrupts a program that might be communicating with the X server via the X protocol. When a UNIX signal is delivered, the operating system immediately branches to your signal handler without notice. If you are in the middle of an X protocol message (an Xlib call) at the time of the signal delivery, and your signal handler also calls an Xlib routine that generates another protocol message, the X server is sent a garbled message. Basically, you started to say something and got interrupted, so now you are saying something completely different. The result is an X protocol error.

What are the chances of this happening? Most of the time, it's pretty slim, especially when you're dealing with signals that are delivered infrequently. An application doesn't spawn a new process or find a floating point exception very often, and it certainly should never find a segmentation fault. It is unlikely that an Xlib call will be interrupted by a UNIX signal, and many people get away with using the `signal()` system call without programming around potential problems. However, this kind of sloppy programming can lead to problems that are extremely difficult to decipher. The fact is, these problems do occur, so a robust program needs to be ready in case the improbability machine is turned on.

Now that we've explained the problem, let's address the solution. We can learn something from the design of the telephone call waiting system. Fortunately, call waiting doesn't disconnect you from the original caller and transfer you to the new one; it just beeps and lets you switch over when you've had a chance to announce what you're going to do. We'd like to handle UNIX signals this way, but unfortunately, that's not how they work. Signals do interrupt the application without notice.† Instead, we can emulate the behavior of the beep by writing a signal handler that notes the signal's delivery, but does not actually do anything that involves X. Later, when we know it's safe, we can do what we originally intended to do. Now all we have to do is determine when it is safe to take action.

20.1 Handling Signals in Xlib

An application that uses Xlib gets events from the server using a function like XNext-Event(). This function reads the next event in the queue and fills an XEvent data structure that describes various things about the event, such as the window associated with it, the time it took place, the event type, and so on. When the function returns, the event has been delivered and it is up to the application to decide what to do next. The following code fragment demonstrates a simplified view of Xlib event handling:

```
void sigchld_handler();

main_event_loop()
{
    . . .
    signal (SIGCHLD, sigchld_handler);

    while (1) {
        XNextEvent (display, &event);
        switch (event.type) {
            case ConfigureNotify: /*...*/ break;
            case Expose: /*...*/ break;
            case ButtonPress: /*...*/ break;
            case EnterWindow: /*...*/ break;
            case LeaveWindow: /*...*/ break;
            case MapNotify: /*...*/ break;
            . . .
        }
    }
}
```

If the operating system decides to deliver a SIGCHLD signal, the signal can arrive at any time, possibly inside any of the case statements or even inside the call to XNextEvent(). The signal handler for the signal is called automatically by the operating system. If the signal handler makes any Xlib calls, you have no way of knowing if it is doing so at a time when another Xlib call is being sent to the X server. The solution is to have the signal handler do nothing but set a flag to indicate that the signal has been delivered. Then, just before the call to XNextEvent(), the event loop can check the flag to determine whether or not to call another function that actually processes the signal. This new design is shown in the following code fragment:

```
static int sigchld_delivered;
void sigchld_handler(), real_sigchld_handler();
```

---

† It should be noted that BSD-style UNIX systems do provide a system call that effectively suspends signal delivery, but it would be too costly to invoke this routine for each Xlib call. Furthermore, it is inappropriate for X, a windowing system that is completely independent of the operating system, to use this technique.

```
main_event_loop()
{
    ...
    signal(SIGCHLD, real_sigchld_handler);

    while (1) {
        /* it's safe to handle signals that may have been delivered */
        if (sigchld_delivered > 0) {
            sigchld_handler (SIGCHLD); /* add other params as necessary */
            sigchld_delivered--;
        }

        XNextEvent (display, &event);
        switch (event.type) {
            case ConfigureNotify: /*...*/ break;
            case Expose: /*...*/ break;
            case ButtonPress: /*...*/ break;
            case EnterWindow: /*...*/ break;
            case LeaveWindow: /*...*/ break;
            case MapNotify: /*...*/ break;
            ...
        }
    }
}
```

All that `real_sigchld_handler()` does is increment the `sigchld_delivered` flag,
as shown in the following fragment:

```
void
real_sigchld_handler(sig)
int sig;
/* additional parameters differ between BSD and SYSV */
{
    sigchld_delivered++;
}
```

The actual `sigchld_handler()` routine can do whatever it needs to do, including call
Xlib routines, since it is only called when it is safe to do so. You should note that `XNext-
Event()` waits until it reads an event from the X server before it returns, so handling the
signal may take a long time if the program is waiting for the user to do something.

These code fragments demonstrate the general design for handling signals in a rudimentary
way. In a real application, the actual signal handler would probably need access to all of the
parameters passed to the original signal handling function. One example of this situation
would be a signal handler that displays the values of all its parameters in a dialog box. You
can't change anything on the display using the original signal handler because it would
require making Xlib calls, so you have to save the parameters until the real signal handler is
called. To save the parameters, you could define a data structure that contains fields for all of
the parameters. The original signal handler could allocate a new structure and fill it in each
time a signal is delivered.† When the real signal handler is called, it can access the data
structure and create a dialog using the appropriate Xlib calls.

---

† As we will discuss later, there can also be problems with memory allocation in a signal handler.

20.2 Handling Signals in Xt

Since this is a book on Motif and Motif is based on Xt, the next step is to find a solution that is appropriate for Xt-based applications. In Xt, you typically don't read events directly from the X server using XNextEvent() and then branch on the event type to decide what to do next. Instead, Xt provides XtAppMainLoop(); the code for this function is below:

```
void
XtAppMainLoop(app_context)
XtAppContext app_context;
{
    XEvent event;

    for (;;) {
        XtAppNextEvent (app_context, &event);
        XtDispatchEvent (&event);
    }
}
```

Since the event processing loop is internal to the Xt toolkit, we don't have the opportunity to insert a check to see if any signals have been delivered, as we did with Xlib. There are various ways to handle this problem. We could write our own event processing loop and include code that tests for the delivery of a signal. One problem with this solution is that it bypasses a standard library routine. We want to ensure upwards compatibility with future versions of Xt, and if we write our own routine, we risk losing any functionality that might be introduced later.

Even though it is unlikely that XtAppMainLoop() will change in the future, we should find another way to solve the problem. Clearly, the desired effect is to get Xt to notify us just before it's going to call XNextEvent(), since this is the window of opportunity where it is safe for a signal handler to make Xlib or Xt calls. It just so happens that Xt provides two methods that do what we want: work procedures and timers.

A work procedure is a function that is called by Xt when it does not have any events to process. Although an application can register multiple work procedures, the procedures are processed one at a time, with the most recent one being invoked first. We can solve the signal handler problem using a work procedure because most applications spend a fair bit of time waiting for the user to generate events. In the signal handler, we register a work procedure using XtAppAddWorkProc(). When the application is idle, Xt invokes the work procedure, which does the real work of handling the signal. The following code fragment uses this approach:

```
XtAppContext app;
static void real_reset(), reset();

main(argc, argv)
int argc;
char *argv[];
{
    . . .
    signal (SIGCHLD, real_reset);
    . . .
}
```

```
/* reset() -- a program died... */
static void
real_reset()
{
    int pid, i;
#ifdef SYSV
    int status;
#else
    union wait status;
#endif /* SYSV */

    if ((pid = wait (&status)) == -1)
        /* an error of some kind (fork probably failed); ignore it */
        return;

    (void) XtAppAddWorkProc (app, reset, NULL);
}

static Boolean
reset(client_data)
XtPointer client_data;
{
    /* handle anything Xt/Xlib-related that needs to be done now */

    return True;  /* remove the work procedure from the list */
}
```

This example assumes that the application forks off a new process at some point. When the child eventually exits, the parent is sent a SIGCHLD signal, at which point the application branches directly to the real_reset() signal handler. This routine reaps the child using wait() and then adds a work procedure using XtAppAddWorkProc(). (The function normally returns a work procedure ID, but we're not interested in it here.) When Xt does not have any events to process, it calls reset(). This routine can perform any other tasks necessary for handling the signal, such as calling Xlib routines, popping up dialogs, or anything it likes.

If the application is waiting for events when it receives the signal, the work procedure is invoked almost immediately after the actual signal handler. However, if the application is in a callback routine handling an event, the work procedure is not called until control is passed back to the event loop. While it's true that there may be some delay between the time that the signal is delivered and the time that it is actually processed, the delay is usually small enough that an application doesn't need to worry about it. If timing is critical, you can always set a global signal flag when the signal is received, and then test that variable in critical sections of your code to see if the signal has been delivered.

20.3 An Example

The signal handling problem can also be solved with a timer, using the same approach as with a work procedure. Example 20-1 demonstrates the use of a timer in a more realistic application. The program displays an array of DrawnButtons that start application programs. While an application is running, the associated button is insensitive, so that the user can only run one instance of the application. When the application exits, the button is reactivated, so that the user can select it again.†

Example 20-1. The app_box.c program

```
/* app_box.c -- make an array of DrawnButtons that, when activated,
 * executes a program.  When the program is running, the drawn button
 * associated with the program is insensitive.  When the program dies,
 * reactivate the button so the user can select it again.
 */
#include <Xm/DrawnB.h>
#include <Xm/RowColumn.h>
#include <signal.h>

#ifndef SYSV
#include <sys/wait.h>
#else
#define SIGCHLD SIGCLD
#endif /* SYSV */

#define MAIL_PROG "/bin/mail"

typedef struct {
    Widget drawn_w;
    char *pixmap_file;
    char *exec_argv[6]; /* 6 is arbitrary, but big enough */
    int pid;
} ExecItem;

ExecItem prog_list[] = {
    { NULL, "terminal",   { "xterm", NULL },                   0 },
    { NULL, "flagup",     { "xterm", "-e", MAIL_PROG, NULL }, 0 },
    { NULL, "calculator", { "xcalc", NULL },                   0 },
    { NULL, "xlogo64",    { "foo", NULL },                     0 },
};

XtAppContext app;     /* application context for the whole program */
GC gc;                /* used to render pixmaps in the widgets */
void reset(), reset_btn(), redraw_button(), exec_prog();

main(argc, argv)
int argc;
char *argv[];
{
    Widget toplevel, rowcol;
    Pixmap pixmap;
    Pixel fg, bg;
    int i;
```

---

†XtSetLanguageProc() is only available in X11R5; there is no corresponding function in X11R4.

Example 20-1. The app_box.c program (continued)

```
    /* we want to be notified when child programs die */
    signal (SIGCHLD, reset);

    XtSetLanguageProc (NULL, NULL, NULL);

    toplevel = XtVaAppInitialize (&app, "Demos",
        NULL, 0, &argc, argv, NULL, NULL);

    rowcol = XtVaCreateWidget ("rowcol",
        xmRowColumnWidgetClass, toplevel,
        XmNorientation, XmHORIZONTAL,
        NULL);

    /* get the foreground and background colors of the rowcol
     * so the gc (DrawnButtons) will use them to render pixmaps.
     */
    XtVaGetValues (rowcol,
        XmNforeground, &fg,
        XmNbackground, &bg,
        NULL);
    gc = XCreateGC (XtDisplay (rowcol),
        RootWindowOfScreen (XtScreen (rowcol)), NULL, 0);
    XSetForeground (XtDisplay (rowcol), gc, fg);
    XSetBackground (XtDisplay (rowcol), gc, bg);

    for (i = 0; i < XtNumber (prog_list); i++) {
        /* the pixmap is taken from the name given in the structure */
        pixmap = XmGetPixmap (XtScreen (rowcol),
            prog_list[i].pixmap_file, fg, bg);

        /* Create a drawn button 64x64 (arbitrary, but sufficient)
         * shadowType has no effect till pushButtonEnabled is false.
         */
        prog_list[i].drawn_w = XtVaCreateManagedWidget ("dbutton",
            xmDrawnButtonWidgetClass, rowcol,
            XmNwidth,               64,
            XmNheight,              64,
            XmNpushButtonEnabled, True,
            XmNshadowType,          XmSHADOW_ETCHED_OUT,
            NULL);
        /* if this button is selected, execute the program */
        XtAddCallback (prog_list[i].drawn_w,
            XmNactivateCallback, exec_prog, &prog_list[i]);

        /* when the resize and expose events come, redraw pixmap */
        XtAddCallback (prog_list[i].drawn_w,
            XmNexposeCallback, redraw_button, pixmap);
        XtAddCallback (prog_list[i].drawn_w,
            XmNresizeCallback, redraw_button, pixmap);
    }

    XtManageChild (rowcol);
    XtRealizeWidget (toplevel);
    XtAppMainLoop (app);
}

/* redraw_button() -- draws the pixmap into its DrawnButton
 * using the global GC.  Get the width and height of the pixmap
 * being used so we can either center it in the button or clip it.
```

Example 20-1. The app_box.c program (continued)

```
 */
void
redraw_button(button, client_data, call_data)
Widget button;
XtPointer client_data;
XtPointer call_data;
{
    Pixmap pixmap = (Pixmap) client_data;
    XmDrawnButtonCallbackStruct *cbs =
        (XmDrawnButtonCallbackStruct *) call_data;
    int srcx, srcy, destx, desty, pix_w, pix_h;
    int drawsize, border;
    Dimension bdr_w, w_width, w_height;
    short hlthick, shthick;
    Window root;

    /* get width and height of the pixmap. don't use srcx and root */
    XGetGeometry (XtDisplay (button), pixmap, &root, &srcx, &srcx,
        &pix_w, &pix_h, &srcx, &srcx);

    /* get the values of all the resources that affect the entire
     * geometry of the button.
     */
    XtVaGetValues (button,
        XmNwidth,              &w_width,
        XmNheight,             &w_height,
        XmNborderWidth,        &bdr_w,
        XmNhighlightThickness, &hlthick,
        XmNshadowThickness,    &shthick,
        NULL);

    /* calculate available drawing area, width 1st */
    border = bdr_w + hlthick + shthick;

    /* if window is bigger than pixmap, center it; else clip pixmap */
    drawsize = w_width - 2 * border;
    if (drawsize > pix_w) {
        srcx = 0;
        destx = (drawsize - pix_w) / 2 + border;
    }
    else {
        srcx = (pix_w - drawsize) / 2;
        pix_w = drawsize;
        destx = border;
    }

    drawsize = w_height - 2 * border;
    if (drawsize > pix_h) {
        srcy = 0;
        desty = (drawsize - pix_h) / 2 + border;
    }
    else {
        srcy = (pix_h - drawsize) / 2;
        pix_h = drawsize;
        desty = border;
    }

    XCopyArea (XtDisplay (button), pixmap, cbs->window, gc,
```

Example 20-1. The app_box.c program (continued)

```
            srcx, srcy, pix_w, pix_h, destx, desty);
}

/* exec_proc() -- the button has been pressed; fork() and call
 * execvp() to start up the program.  If the fork or the execvp
 * fails (program not found?), the sigchld catcher will get it
 * and clean up.  If the program is successful, set the button's
 * sensitivity to False (to prevent the user from execing again)
 * and set pushButtonEnabled to False to allow shadowType to work.
 */
void
exec_prog(drawn_w, client_data, call_data)
Widget drawn_w;
XtPointer client_data;
XtPointer call_data;
{
    ExecItem *program = (ExecItem *) client_data;
    XmDrawnButtonCallbackStruct *cbs =
        (XmDrawnButtonCallbackStruct *) call_data;

    switch (program->pid = fork ()) {
        case 0:   /* child */
            execvp (program->exec_argv[0], program->exec_argv);
            perror (program->exec_argv[0]); /* command not found? */
            _exit (255);
        case -1:
            printf ("fork() failed.\n");
    }

    /* The child is off executing program... parent continues */
    if (program->pid > 0) {
        XtVaSetValues (drawn_w,
            XmNpushButtonEnabled, False,
            NULL);
     XtSetSensitive (drawn_w, False);
    }
}

/* reset() -- a program died, so find out which one it was and
 * reset its corresponding DrawnButton widget so it can be reselected
 */
void
reset ()
{
    int pid, i;
#ifdef SYSV
    int status;
#else
    union wait status;
#endif /* SYSV */

    if ((pid = wait (&status)) == -1)
        /* an error of some kind (fork probably failed); ignore it */
        return;

    for (i = 0; i < XtNumber (prog_list); i++)
        if (prog_list[i].pid == pid) {
            /* program died -- now reset item.  But not here! */
```

Example 20-1. The app_box.c program (continued)

```
            XtAppAddTimeOut (app, 0, reset_btn, prog_list[i].drawn_w);
            return;
        }

    printf ("Pid #%d ???\n", pid); /* error, but not fatal */
}

/* reset_btn() -- reset the sensitivity and pushButtonEnabled resources
 * on the drawn button.  This cannot be done within the signal
 * handler or we might step on an X protocol packet since signals are
 * asynchronous.  This function is safe because it's called from a timer.
 */
void
reset_btn(drawn_w)
Widget drawn_w;    /* client_data from XtAppAddTimeOut() */
{
    XtVaSetValues(drawn_w,
        XmNpushButtonEnabled, True,
        NULL);
    XtSetSensitive (drawn_w, True);
}
```

The output of the program is shown in Figure 20-1.

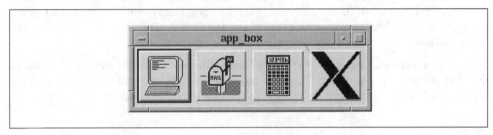

Figure 20-1. Output of app_box.c

The program in Example 20-1 is almost identical in design to the code fragment that used a work procedure, but it is more like something you might actually write. The program uses DrawnButtons to represent different application programs. The idea is that when a button is pressed, the program corresponding to the image drawn on the button is run. The button turns insensitive for as long as the application is alive. When the user exits the program, the button's state is restored so the user can select it again.

Each button has a data structure associated with it that specifies the file that contains the icon bitmap, an `argv` that represents the program to be run, the process ID associated with the program's execution, and a handle to the button itself. The callback routine for each button spawns a new process, sets the button to insensitive, and immediately returns control to the main event loop. The process ID is saved in the button's data structure. When the external process terminates, a `SIGCHLD` signal is sent to the main program and the button is reset.

As a general note, it is crucial that you understand that the new process does not attempt to interact with the widgets in its parent application or read events associated with the same display connection as its parent process. Even though the child has access to the same data structures as the parent, it cannot use its parent's connection to the X server because multiple processes cannot share an X server connection. If a child process intends to interact with the X server, it must close its existing connection and open a new one.

In our application, we play it safe by running a completely new application using `execvp()`. This system call executes a program provided it can be found in the user's PATH, so we don't need to specify full pathnames to the applications. If the program cannot be found for whatever reason, the child process dies immediately and the `reset()` signal handler is called by the operating system.

The `reset()` signal handler is called whenever a child process dies. At this point, the child needs to be reaped and the state of the button needs to be reset. The `wait()` system call is used to reap the child; this routine can be called from within `reset()` because it doesn't make any Xlib calls. However, we cannot reset the button's state by calling `XtVaSet-Values()` and `XtSetSensitive()` because these routines would ultimately result in Xlib calls. Therefore, rather than actually resetting the button in `reset()`, we call `XtApp-AddTimeOut()` to install a timer routine. This Xt call is safe in a signal handler because it does not make any calls to Xlib; the timer is handled entirely on the client side.

`XtAppAddTimeOut()` registers a timer procedure that is called after a specified amount of time. Xt's main event processing loop takes care of calling the timer routine after the appropriate time interval. Since we have specified an interval of 0 for the `reset_btn()` timer, the routine is called immediately after the signal is received and control is passed back to the main event loop. The `reset_btn()` routine handles restoring the state of the Drawn-Button, so that the user can run the associated application again.

In terms of signal handling, there is really one main difference between using a work procedure and using an interval timer. The work procedure is called as soon as the application is idle and waiting for input, while the timer is called after a specified interval.

20.4 Additional Issues

There are several loose ends that we need to address. One issue involves the way timers are implemented. You may be thinking, "Isn't a timer another signal in UNIX?" While the answer is yes, what is important is that Xt-timers are not implemented using UNIX signals, but instead using a feature of the `select()` system call. In this context, `select()` is used to determine if the X server is sending events to the application (although this function does not actually read any events). The last parameter to `select()` is a time interval that specifies how long the routine waits before returning whether there is anything to read. Setting this time interval allows Xt to implement what appears to be a timer. As long as there are events to read from the server, however, the timer is inactive, which is why a timer in Xt can only be set in terms of an interval, rather than as a real-time value. It is also why you should never rely on the accuracy of these timers.

Timers are not implemented using UNIX signals for the same reasons that we did not call `Xt-VaSetValues()` from within the SIGCHLD signal handler. It is also for this reason that you should not use UNIX-based functions such as `sleep()` or `setitimer()` to modify widgets or make Xlib calls. We don't mean to imply that you should not use these functions at all;

it's just that the same restrictions apply to UNIX timers as they do to other UNIX signals. If you need to do any X or Xt-related function calls, don't do it from a signal handler. You should install a zero-length interval timeout function using `XtAppAddTimeOut()` and, when the toolkit invokes your function, call whatever X routines are necessary. Timers of this type are used frequently with clock programs and text widgets. In the case of a clock, the timer advances the second hand, while for a text widget, it causes the insertion cursor to flash.

Another loose end that needs to be tied up involves System V's handling of signals. In most modern versions of UNIX (derived from BSD UNIX), when a signal is delivered to an application, any system call that might be going on is interrupted, the signal handler is called, and when it returns, the system call is allowed to continue. For example, if you are reading in the text of a file using `read()` and a signal is sent to the application, the `read()` is suspended while the signal handler is called. After your signal handler returns, the `read()` is restarted and it returns the actual number of bytes read as if no signal had ever occurred. Under System V, all system calls are interrupted and return an error (with errno set to `EINTR`). In this case, all of the data read by the `read()` call is lost.

This situation is a problem in X because `read()` is used to read events from the X server. If `read()` fails because a signal is delivered, then the protocol that was being sent by the server is lost, as would be anything we were sending to the server, since the same is true for calls to `write()`. There really isn't anything you can do about this problem, except, perhaps, for upgrading to a more modern version of UNIX. This problem does not exist with SVR4 or Solaris.

Even system calls in BSD-derived UNIX systems may have problems. If, for example, you call `read()` from a signal handler that interrupted another `read()`, you still might not get what you expected because `read()` is not *re-entrant*. A function that is re-entrant is one that can be called at any time, even while the function is already being executed.

We're pretty safe with the advice we've given so far, with one exception: calling `XtApp-AddTimeOut()` or `XtAppAddWorkProc()` eventually requires the allocation of memory to add the new timer or work procedure to the respective list. If your application happens to be allocating memory when a signal is delivered and you try to add a timer or a work procedure, you could make another call to `alloc()`, which is the lowest-level routine that allocates memory from the system. Unless your version of UNIX has a re-entrant memory allocation system call, your memory stack may be corrupted.† There really isn't anything that you can do about these problems, and there are no official specifications anywhere in the X documents that even address these issues, so the best tactic is to minimize the exposure using timers or work procedures as described here.

---

† The GNU version of `malloc()` is re-entrant, so it is safe from this problem.

20.5 Summary

The official advice of the X Consortium staff is that you should not mix signals with X applications. However, there are cases where you must choose the lesser of two evils. The need for signal handling exists and cannot simply be ignored. In X11R6, Xt will have support for signal handlers, so this problem should no longer exist. Until then, however, the approaches given in this chapter should serve you well most of the time.

The most important lesson to learn from this chapter may well be that UNIX signals are dangerous to X applications, or any sort of program that relies on a client-server protocol. They can also be a problem for system calls in an extremely sensitive or real-time environment. Whenever the operating system can interrupt the client side (or the server side, for that matter), you should be prepared to consider those cases where the protocol may be breached.

21

Advanced Dialog Programming

This chapter describes some Motif features that have not been described, or at least not completely, in earlier chapters. The topics, which all deal with dialogs, include the creation of multi-stage help systems, the development of WorkingDialogs that allow the user to interrupt long-running tasks, and a method for dynamically changing the pixmaps displayed in a dialog.

In This Chapter:

21
Advanced Dialog Programming

In one sense, this chapter isn't about dialogs at all, but about various aspects of X programming that become most evident when working with dialogs. Here we address some issues involved in creating multi-stage help systems, we show you how to create a WorkingDialogs that allows the user to interrupt a long-running task, and we describe a method for dynamically changing the pixmaps that are displayed in a dialog. These topics explore some of the most interesting problems in this book.

These topics take us deeper into the lower layers of X than anything we've discussed so far in this book. You should have a good basic understanding of X event-processing, as implemented both in Xlib and Xt. Otherwise, be prepared to refer frequently to Volume One, *Xlib Programming Manual*, and Volume Four, *X Toolkit Intrinsics Programming Manual*, when faced with references to lower-level functions.

21.1 Help Systems

The *Motif Style Guide* doesn't have much to say about how help is presented to the user, although it does discuss the ways in which the user can request help from an application. The user can request help by selecting the **Help** button in a dialog box, by choosing help items from the **Help** menu in the MenuBar, or by pressing the HELP or F1 key on the keyboard. Help information should be presented clearly, so that it is accessible and beneficial to users. You should also maintain consistency in a help system, so that the user can become familiar with the style of help that you provide.

The easiest and most straightforward method of presenting help information involves creating an InformationDialog with the necessary text displayed as the XmNmessageString. Example 21-1 demonstrates how to display a help dialog when the user presses the **Help** button in another dialog box.†

---

†XtSetLanguageProc() is only available in X11R5; there is no corresponding function in X11R4. XmStringCreateLocalized() is only available in Motif 1.2; XmStringCreateSimple() is the corresponding function in Motif 1.1. XmFONTLIST_DEFAULT_TAG replaces XmSTRING_DEFAULT_CHARSET in Motif 1.2.

Example 21-1. The simple_help.c program

```
/* simple_help.c -- create a PushButton that posts a dialog box
 * that entices the user to press the help button.  The callback
 * for this button displays a new dialog that gives help.
 */
#include <Xm/MessageB.h>
#include <Xm/PushB.h>

main(argc, argv)
int argc;
char *argv[];
{
    Widget toplevel, button;
    XtAppContext app;
    XmString label;
    void pushed();

    XtSetLanguageProc (NULL, NULL, NULL);

    toplevel = XtVaAppInitialize (&app, "Demos", NULL, 0,
        &argc, argv, NULL, NULL);

    label = XmStringCreateLocalized ("Push Me");
    button = XtVaCreateManagedWidget ("button",
        xmPushButtonWidgetClass, toplevel,
        XmNlabelString,          label,
        NULL);
    XtAddCallback (button, XmNactivateCallback,
        pushed, "You probably need help for this item.");
    XmStringFree (label);

    XtRealizeWidget (toplevel);
    XtAppMainLoop (app);
}

#define HELP_TEXT "This is the help information.\nNow press 'OK'"

/* pushed() -- the callback routine for the main app's pushbutton. */
void
pushed(w, client_data, call_data)
Widget w;
XtPointer client_data;
XtPointer call_data;
{
    char *text = (char *) client_data;
    Widget dialog;
    XmString t = XmStringCreateLocalized (text);
    Arg args[5];
    int n;
    void help_callback(), help_done();

    n = 0;
    XtSetArg (args[n], XmNautoUnmanage, False); n++;
    XtSetArg (args[n], XmNmessageString, t); n++;
    dialog = XmCreateMessageDialog (XtParent(w), "notice", args, n);
    XmStringFree (t);

    XtUnmanageChild (
        XmMessageBoxGetChild (dialog, XmDIALOG_CANCEL_BUTTON));

    XtAddCallback (dialog, XmNokCallback, help_done, NULL);
```

Example 21-1. The simple_help.c program (continued)

```
    XtAddCallback (dialog, XmNhelpCallback, help_callback, HELP_TEXT);

    XtManageChild (dialog);
    XtPopup (XtParent (dialog), XtGrabNone);
}
/*
 * help_callback() -- callback routine for the Help button in the
 * original dialog box that displays an InformationDialog based on the
 * help_text parameter.
 */
void
help_callback(parent, client_data, call_data)
Widget parent;
XtPointer client_data;
XtPointer call_data;
{
    char *help_text = (char *) client_data;
    Widget dialog;
    XmString text;
    void help_done();
    Arg args[5];
    int n;

    n = 0;
    text = XmStringCreateLtoR (help_text, XmFONTLIST_DEFAULT_TAG);
    XtSetArg (args[n], XmNmessageString, text); n++;
    XtSetArg (args[n], XmNautoUnmanage, False); n++;
    dialog = XmCreateInformationDialog (parent, "help", args, n);
    XmStringFree (text);

    XtUnmanageChild (   /* no need for the cancel button */
        XmMessageBoxGetChild (dialog, XmDIALOG_CANCEL_BUTTON));
    XtSetSensitive (    /* no more help is available. */
        XmMessageBoxGetChild (dialog, XmDIALOG_HELP_BUTTON), False);
    /* the OK button will call help_done() below */
    XtAddCallback (dialog, XmNokCallback, help_done, NULL);

    /* display the help text */
    XtManageChild (dialog);
    XtPopup (XtParent (dialog), XtGrabNone);
}

/* help_done() -- called when user presses "OK" in dialogs. */
void
help_done(dialog, client_data, call_data)
Widget dialog;
XtPointer client_data;
XtPointer call_data;
{
    XtDestroyWidget (dialog);
}
```

The main window contains a PushButton that posts a simple MessageDialog. This dialog, as you can tell from Figure 21-1, contains a **Help** button, that pops up an InformationDialog. This dialog is intended to provide help text for the user.

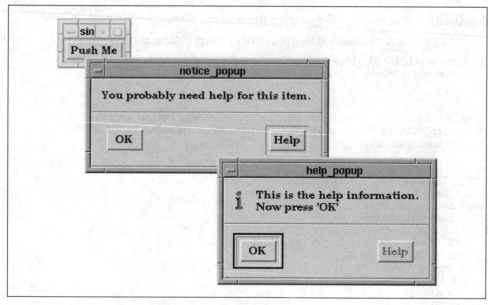

Figure 21-1. Output of simple_help.c

The callback routine for the **Help** button is installed using the XmNhelpCallback. This routine pops up an InformationDialog that contains some predefined text. Obviously, this text is for demonstration purposes only. We used XmStringCreateLtoR() to display the text, instead of XmStringCreateLocalized(), since the help message contains newline characters. You could also use XmStringCreateLtoR() to specify an alternate font for use in your help system, but we are not taking advantage of this feature. See Chapter 19, *Compound Strings*, for more information on how you can use compound strings to display text using different fonts.

The XmNhelpCallback resource serves as the callback for any widget that wishes to provide help information; every Motif widget has an XmNhelpCallback resource associated with it. Whenever the user presses the HELP key on the keyboard (if one exists and the X server is set up correctly†), the XmNhelpCallback is invoked for the widget that has the keyboard focus. The F1 key also serves as a help key for compatibility with Microsoft Windows and to compensate for any computer that may not have a HELP key.‡

If a widget does not have an XmNhelpCallback function installed, Motif climbs the widget tree, searching for the nearest ancestor that has a help callback. If you assign help callbacks to widgets, we recommend that you provide specific help information for individual interface components, such as PushButtons, Lists, and Text widgets, and more general information for manager widgets. It is possible to design an elaborate context-sensitive help

---

† By default, Sun workstations do not generate the proper event when the HELP key is pressed, and your mileage may vary for other computers.

‡ The F1 key works by default, but it may be remapped to perform another function in the user's *.mwmrc* file.

system for an application by installing help callback routines for the widgets in the interface and providing relevant help information throughout the hierarchy.

Although *simple_help.c* is rather contrived, we can use it to examine the different actions the user might take within a help system. You can think of the **Push Me** button as any widget in an application on which the user might want help. When the button is activated, the user is presented with a MessageDialog that undoubtedly requires help. The user can select the **Help** button or press the F1 or HELP keys to access the help information. Since the InformationDialog is modeless, as it should be, the user can either close the Information-Dialog or the original MessageDialog.

Since the InformationDialog is a child of the MessageDialog, if the MessageDialog is destroyed, the InformationDialog is also destroyed. Similarly, if the MessageDialog is unmapped, so is the InformationDialog. In general, when you display an InformationDialog, you should remove it if the user unmanages, destroys, or otherwise disables the dialog from which it was posted because if the help dialog remains posted, it could confuse the user. By making the InformationDialog the child of the original dialog, you can let the parent-child interaction handle this behavior.

21.1.1 Multi-level Help

Developing a help system may involve providing multiple levels of help information. If the user has already posted an InformationDialog, it is possible to display an additional dialog if the user requests help in the original dialog. However, multiple help windows can confuse the user, so they should be avoided. A better solution is to display the new help text in the same InformationDialog, so that all of the help information is displayed in the same place. Example 21-2 shows new `help_callback()` and `help_done()` routines that implement this technique.†

Example 21-2. The help_callback() and help_done() routines for multi-level help

```
#define MAX_HELP_STAGES 3
char *help_text[3][5] = {
    {
        "You have reached the first stage of the help system.",
        "If you need additional help, select the 'More Help' button.",
        "You may exit help at any time by pressing 'Done'.",
        NULL,
    },
    {
        "This is the second stage of the help system.  There is",
        "more help available.  Press 'More Help' to see more.",
        "Press 'Previous' to return to the previous help message,",
        "or press 'Done' to exit the help system.",
        NULL,
    },
```

---

†XmStringCreateLocalized() is only available in Motif 1.2; XmStringCreateSimple() is the corresponding function in Motif 1.1. XmFONTLIST_DEFAULT_TAG replaces XmSTRING_DEFAULT_CHARSET in Motif 1.2.

```
    {
        "This is the last help message you will see on this topic.",
        "You may either press 'Previous' to return to the previous",
        "help level, or press 'Done' to exit the help system.",
        NULL,
    }
};

/* help_callback() -- callback routine for the Help button in the
 * original dialog box.  The routine also serves as its own help
 * callback for displaying multiple levels of help messages.
 */
void
help_callback(parent, client_data, call_data)
Widget parent;
XtPointer client_data;
XtPointer call_data;
{
    static Widget dialog; /* prevent multiple help dialogs */
    XmString text;
    char buf[BUFSIZ], *p;
    static int index;
    int i;
    void help_done();
    int index_incr = (int) client_data;

    if (dialog && index_incr == 0) {
        /* user pressed Help button in MesageDialog again.  We're
         * already up, so just make sure we're visible and return. */
        XtPopup (XtParent (dialog), XtGrabNone);
        XMapRaised (XtDisplay (dialog), XtWindow (XtParent (dialog)));
        return;
    }

    if (dialog)
        index += index_incr; /* more/previous help; change index */
    else {
        /* We're not up, so create new Help Dialog */
        Arg args[5];
        int n;

        /* Action area button labels. */
        XmString done = XmStringCreateLocalized ("Done");
        XmString cancel = XmStringCreateLocalized ("Previous");
        XmString more = XmStringCreateLocalized ("More Help");

        n = 0;
        XtSetArg (args[n], XmNautoUnmanage, False); n++;
        XtSetArg (args[n], XmNokLabelString, done); n++;
        XtSetArg (args[n], XmNcancelLabelString, cancel); n++;
        XtSetArg (args[n], XmNhelpLabelString, more); n++;
        dialog = XmCreateInformationDialog (parent, "help", args, n);

        /* pass help_done() the address of "dialog" so it can reset */
        XtAddCallback (dialog, XmNokCallback, help_done, &dialog);

        /* if more/previous help, recall ourselves with increment */
        XtAddCallback (dialog, XmNcancelCallback, help_callback, -1);
        XtAddCallback (dialog, XmNhelpCallback, help_callback, 1);
```

```
            /* If our parent dies, we must reset "dialog" to NULL! */
            XtAddCallback (dialog, XmNdestroyCallback, help_done, &dialog);

            XmStringFree (done);   /* once dialog is created, these */
            XmStringFree (cancel); /* strings are no longer needed. */
            XmStringFree (more);

            index = 0; /* initialize index--needed for each new help stuff */
        }

    /* concatenate help text into a single string with newlines */
    for (p = buf, i = 0; help_text[index][i]; i++) {
        p += strlen (strcpy (p, help_text[index][i]));
        *p++ = '\n';
        *p = 0;
    }

    text = XmStringCreateLtoR (buf, XmFONTLIST_DEFAULT_TAG);
    XtVaSetValues (dialog, XmNmessageString, text, NULL);
    XmStringFree (text); /* after set-values, free unneeded memory */

    /* If no previous help msg, set "Previous" to insensitive. */
    XtSetSensitive (
        XmMessageBoxGetChild (dialog,XmDIALOG_CANCEL_BUTTON), index > 0);
    /* If no more help, set "More Help" insensitive. */
    XtSetSensitive (XmMessageBoxGetChild (
        dialog, XmDIALOG_HELP_BUTTON), index < MAX_HELP_STAGES-1);

    /* display the dialog */
    XtManageChild (dialog);
    XtPopup (XtParent (dialog), XtGrabNone);
}

/* help_done () -- callback used to set the dialog pointer
 * to NULL so it can't be referenced again by help_callback().
 * This function is called from the Done button in the help dialog.
 * It is also our XmNdestroyCallback, so reset our dialog_ptr to NULL.
 */
void
help_done(dialog, client_data, call_data)
Widget dialog;
XtPointer client_data;
XtPointer call_data;
{
    Widget *dialog_ptr;

    if (!client_data) { /* destroy original MessageDialog */
        XtDestroyWidget (dialog);
        return;
    }

    dialog_ptr = (Widget *) client_data;
    if (!*dialog_ptr) /* prevent unnecessarily destroying twice */
        return;
    XtDestroyWidget (dialog); /* this might call ourselves.. */
    *dialog_ptr = NULL;
}
```

In our help system, each level has a new help string that needs to be displayed. All of the help text is displayed in the same InformationDialog. The dialog for the first level of help is shown in Figure 21-2.

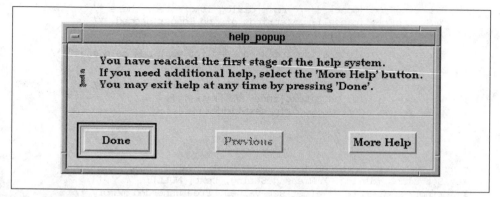

Figure 21-2. Displaying multiple levels of help text

The `help_callback` routine addresses several problems that arise when dealing with the added complexity of a multi-level help system. Since many dialogs may be trying to pop up the same InformationDialog, the routine uses a static variable for the dialog to prevent multiple instances of the dialog. This variable allows the routine to keep track of when the dialog is active and when it is dormant.

The routine is conceptually recursive, in that it is used as the callback routine for the buttons in the help dialog. The `client_data` is used as an index into the `help_text` array. When this parameter is 0, the routine was called by the original MessageDialog. Otherwise, the routine was invoked as a result of the user pressing the **Previous** button or the **More Help** button. In this case, the `index` is changed so that the help text changes.

If the InformationDialog has already been created and the user presses the **Help** button anyway, the dialog is remapped and raised to the top of the screen using `XMapRaised()`. If the parent dialog is unmapped or destroyed, the InformationDialog is also unmapped or destroyed. In order to maintain the correct state information, we install an `XmNdestroyCallback` to monitor the destruction of the InformationDialog. When the dialog is destroyed, we need to reset the handle to the dialog to NULL so that we cannot reference the destroyed dialog again from `help_callback()` the next time help is requested.

All of our help text is fairly short, but if you need to provide help text that longer, you may want to use a ScrolledText object in your help dialog. With a ScrolledText object, you can display text of an arbitrary length without worrying about screen real estate. This technique is explained in Chapter 7, *Custom Dialogs*.

21.1.2 Context-sensitive Help

Although the user can access the help system by using the HELP or F1 keys, this interface is somewhat cumbersome and it doesn't work for widgets like Labels that do not process input events. You can provide a more intuitive interface that allows the user to point-and-click directly on a widget to obtain help. The *Motif Style Guide* refers to this style of help as *context-sensitive* help.

Context-sensitive help is make possible by the XmTrackingEvent() routine, which takes the following form:

```
Widget
XmTrackingEvent(widget, cursor, confine_to, event)
    Widget  widget;
    Cursor  cursor;
    Boolean confine_to;
    XEvent *event;
```

The routine invokes a server-grab on the pointer, changes the pointer shape to that specified by the *cursor* parameter, and waits until the user presses a mouse button. The routine returns the widget on which the user pressed the button. If the *confine_to* parameter is True, the cursor is confined to the window of the specified *widget*. This window is also used as the owner of the pointer grab. The *event* parameter returns the actual event performed by the user.

XmTrackingEvent() is new in Motif 1.2; it replaces the existing XmTracking-Locate() routine. XmTrackingEvent() should be used in place of the older routine because it works for all widgets, regardless of whether they handle input events. For example, if the user presses the mouse button over a Label widget, XmTrackingEvent() returns the Label, while XmTrackingLocate() would return the parent of the Label.

An application usually provides context-sensitive help through an item on the **Help** menu. Example 21-3 shows the query_for_help() callback routine that could be used for such a menu item.†

Example 21-3. The query_for_help() routine

```
#include <X11/cursorfont.h>

Widget toplevel;

void
query_for_help(widget, client_data, call_data)
Widget          widget;
XtPointer       client_data;
XtPointer       call_data;
{
    Cursor              cursor;
    Display             *display;
    Widget              help_widget;
    XmAnyCallbackStruct *cbs, *newcbs;
```

---

†XmTrackingEvent() is only available in Motif 1.2; XmTrackingLocate() is the corresponding function in Motif 1.1.

Example 21-3. The query_for_help() routine (continued)

```
    XEvent                *event;

    cbs = (XmAnyCallbackStruct *) call_data;
    display = XtDisplay (toplevel);
    cursor = XCreateFontCursor (display, XC_hand2);

    help_widget = XmTrackingEvent (toplevel, cursor, True, &event);
    while (help_widget != NULL) {
        if (XtHasCallbacks (help_widget, XmNhelpCallback) ==
            XtCallbackHasSome ) {
            newcbs->reason = XmCR_HELP;
            newcbs->event = event;
            XtCallCallbacks (help_widget, XmNhelpCallback,
                (XtPointer) newcbs);
            help_widget = NULL;
        }
        else
            help_widget = XtParent (help_widget);
    }
    XFreeCursor (display, cursor);
}
```

When the user selects the menu item for context-sensitive help, query_for_help() is invoked. This routine calls XmTrackingEvent() to allow the user to specify a widget on which to see help information. The confine_to parameter is set to True, so the pointer is constrained to the window of the toplevel widget. We use toplevel so that the user can select any component in the entire application.

XmTrackingEvent() changes the pointer to the specified cursor to provide visual feedback that the application is in a new state. Since the user is expected to click on a object, the routine uses the XC_hand2 glyph that shows a pointing hand. The cursor is created using XCreateFontCursor(). See Volume One, *Xlib Programming Manual*, for more information.

If the user clicks on any valid widget within the application, XmTrackingEvent() returns the ID for that widget. The widget itself is not activated and it does not receive any events that indicate that anything has happened at all. If the user does not click on a valid widget, the function returns NULL. If XmTrackingEvent() returns a widget ID, we use XtCallCallbacks() to activate the XmNhelpCallback for the widget. If the widget does not have a help callback, query_for_help() climbs the widget tree looking for an ancestor widget with a help callback.

While the confine_to flag makes XmTrackingEvent() useful for constraining mouse movement, you should use this feature with caution. Once the cursor is confined to the window, the server grab is not released until the user presses the mouse button. We also advise caution if you are using a debugger while working with this function. If the debugger stops at a breakpoint while the function is invoked, you will have to log in remotely and kill the debugger process to release the pointer grab. If you kill the process, you will have to shut down the computer.

21.2 Working Dialogs

The Motif WorkingDialog is used to inform the user that an application is busy processing, so that it doesn't have the time to handle other actions the user may take. For example, if your application is busy trying to figure out the complete value of *pi*, the user is probably going to have to wait for the application to respond to her next action. The delay occurs because the application code has control, rather than Xt. When Xt has control, it processes events and dispatches them to the appropriate widgets in the application. If a widget has a callback installed for an event, Xt returns control to the application. While the application has control, there is no way for the window system to service any requests the user may happen to make.

In the meantime, the application is faced with the dilemma of how it is going to process events that happen in the interim. While your application is busy number-crunching, the user is frantically pounding on the **Stop** button and hoping that the application will figure out that she really didn't want it to figure out the complete value of *pi*, but instead to print out the recipe for *cherry pie*.

What the application needs to do is to find a way to do the necessary work for callback routine and process events at the same time. The solution is conceptually simple: the application should periodically check to see if there are any events in the input queue, and if there are, process and dispatch them. The implementation of this solution, on the other hand, is quite a different story. There are a number of different approaches you can take, depending on the nature of the work you are trying to do. Let's examine four of the options:

- If the task can be broken down into tiny chunks, you can set up *work procedures* that are invoked automatically by Xt when there are no events on the event queue. Since events are very infrequent in terms of processor time, this type of processing goes quite quickly. This technique works best for tasks that are not critical to the application; the tasks can be done in the background and not interfere with the normal event-processing loop. To minimize the effect on system performance, you should be sure to break the task into small components time-wise.

- You can set timer event handlers to go off periodically using XtAppAddTimeOut(). As each timer fires, another chunk of work is done before control is returned to Xt. While this method is similar to using work procedures, the time intervals may be more in tune with the type of processing you are doing. Timers are typically used when the work being done is synchronous with the system clock or some other regular interval. However, timers are not associated directly with the system clock, so a task should not rely on their accuracy.

- You can choose to maintain control and use Xlib and Xt functions to process events yourself. In this case, your application checks for events in the queue and processes them. This technique is appropriate for applications that need to perform complex operations, as it is possible to handle sophisticated looping constructs, process recursively, or manage complex state information.

- You can simply choose to ignore events entirely. In this case, it is best to set the cursor to a stopwatch or hour glass shape, and/or post a message that indicates that the user must wait. This solution is sometimes the only one available if the task is dependent on some outside entity. Examples include device driver communication (printer, disk drives), network communications (NFS), interprocess activity (forks and pipes), or anything that puts the application in a state where it has no control over the object with which it is communicating.

You can mix and match some of these techniques. Say the user wants to send a large PostScript file to a laser printer. When she clicks on the **Print** button, you can post a WorkingDialog that reports that the file is being printed and the user must wait. Additionally, you could provide an option that allows the user to send the file to the printer in the background. In this case, you can send the file to the printer in small chunks using work procedures.

The four methods fall into two basic categories:

- Xt maintains control, processes events as normal, and periodically calls application routines

- The application takes control, performs the necessary tasks, and periodically calls Xlib functions to check the event queue

Work procedures and timers return control to Xt and allow it to process events as normal. In turn, Xt gives control back to the application for short intervals every now and then. When the application maintains control, it can query and process X events whenever it wants. While this process is more complicated, it does make it easier for the application to control its own processing.

In all four situations, you can decide whether or not to display a WorkingDialog. If you want to give the user the ability to terminate the work in progress, you can provide a **Stop** button in the dialog. Otherwise, you can simply display the dialog for informational purposes. If you do not want the user to interact with other windows in the application while the WorkingDialog is being displayed, you can make the dialog modal as described in Section 5.7.1.

21.2.1 Using Work Procedures

Work procedures in Xt are extremely simple in design. They are typically used by applications that can process tasks in the background. When a work procedure is used in conjunction with a WorkingDialog, the application can provide feedback on the status of the task. Say the user wants to load a large bitmap into a window. The nature of your application requires you to load the file from disk into client-side memory, perform some bitmap manipulation, and then send the bitmap to the X server to be loaded into a pixmap. If you suspect that this task might take a long time and you want to allow the user to interrupt it, you can use work procedures and a WorkingDialog.

Unfortunately, demonstrating such a task is difficult, due to its extremely complex nature. The bitmap loading operation requires a great deal of image-handling code that is a distraction from the issue at hand, which is installing a work procedure. To get around this problem, we present a short, abstract program that demonstrates the use of a work procedure. In Example 21-4, we represent a time-consuming task by counting from 0 to 20000.†

Example 21-4. The working.c program

```
/* working.c -- represent a complicated, time-consuming task by
 * counting from 0 to 20000 and provide feedback to the user about
 * how far we are in the process.  The user may terminate the process
 * at any time by selecting the Stop button in the WorkingDialog.
 * This demonstrates how a WorkingDialog can be used to allow the
 * user to interrupt lengthy procedures.
 */
#include <Xm/MessageB.h>
#include <Xm/PushB.h>

#define MAXNUM 20000

void done();

/* Global variables */
static int         i = 0;
static XtWorkProcId work_id;

main(argc, argv)
int argc;
char *argv[];
{
    XtAppContext   app;
    Widget         toplevel, button;
    XmString       label;
    void           pushed();

    XtSetLanguageProc (NULL, NULL, NULL);

    toplevel = XtVaAppInitialize (&app, "Demos",
        NULL, 0, &argc, argv, NULL, NULL);

    label = XmStringCreateLocalized ("Press Here To Start A Long Task");
    button = XtVaCreateManagedWidget ("button",
        xmPushButtonWidgetClass, toplevel,
        XmNlabelString,           label,
        NULL);
    XtAddCallback (button, XmNactivateCallback, pushed, app);
    XmStringFree (label);

    XtRealizeWidget (toplevel);
    XtAppMainLoop (app);
}

/* pushed() -- the callback routine for the main app's pushbutton. */
void
pushed(w, client_data, call_data)
Widget w;
XtPointer client_data;
XtPointer call_data;
```

†XtSetLanguageProc() is only available in X11R5; there is no corresponding function in X11R4. Xm-StringCreateLocalized() is only available in Motif 1.2; XmStringCreateSimple() is the corresponding function in Motif 1.1.

Example 21-4. The working.c program (continued)

```
{
    XtAppContext  app = (XtAppContext) client_data;
    Widget        dialog;
    XmString      stop_txt;
    Arg           args[5];
    int           n;
    Boolean       count();

    /* Create the dialog -- the "cancel" button says "Stop" */
    n = 0;
    stop_txt = XmStringCreateLocalized ("Stop");
    XtSetArg(args[n], XmNcancelLabelString, stop_txt); n++;
    dialog = XmCreateWorkingDialog (w, "working", args, n);
    XmStringFree (stop_txt);

    work_id = XtAppAddWorkProc (app, count, dialog);

    XtUnmanageChild (XmMessageBoxGetChild (dialog, XmDIALOG_OK_BUTTON));
    XtUnmanageChild (XmMessageBoxGetChild (dialog, XmDIALOG_HELP_BUTTON));

    /* Use cancel button to stop counting. True = remove work proc */
    XtAddCallback (dialog, XmNcancelCallback, done, True);

    XtManageChild (dialog);
    XtPopup (XtParent (dialog), XtGrabNone);
}

/* count() -- work procedure that counts to MAXNUM.  When we get there,
 * change the "Stop" button to say "Done".
 */
Boolean
count(client_data)
XtPointer client_data;
{
    Widget dialog = (Widget) client_data;
    char buf[64];
    XmString str, button;
    Boolean finished = False;

    /* If we printed every number, the flicker is too fast to read.
     * Therefore, just print every 1000 ticks for smoother feedback.
     */
    if (++i % 1000 != 0)
        return finished;

    /* display where we are in the counter. */
    sprintf (buf, "Counter: %d", i);
    str = XmStringCreateLocalized (buf);
    XtVaSetValues (dialog, XmNmessageString, str, NULL);
    XmStringFree (str);

    if (i == MAXNUM) {
        i = 0;
        finished = True;
        button = XmStringCreateLocalized ("Done");
        XtVaSetValues (dialog, XmNcancelLabelString, button, NULL);
        XmStringFree (button);
        XtRemoveCallback (dialog, XmNcancelCallback, done, True);
        XtAddCallback (dialog, XmNcancelCallback, done, False);
        XMapRaised (XtDisplay (dialog), XtWindow (XtParent (dialog)));
```

Example 21-4. The working.c program (continued)

```
    }

    /* Return either True, meaning we're done and remove the work proc,
     * or False, meaning continue working by calling this function.
     */
    return finished;
}

/* done () -- user pressed "Stop" or "Done" in WorkingDialog. */
void
done(dialog, client_data, call_data)
Widget dialog;
XtPointer client_data;
XtPointer call_data;
{
    Boolean remove_work_proc = (Boolean) client_data;

    if (remove_work_proc) {
        i = 0;
        XtRemoveWorkProc (work_id);
    }
    XtDestroyWidget (dialog);
}
```

The main application simply displays a button. When the user presses the button, the application starts counting and displays a WorkingDialog. The user can press **Stop** at any time during the process. If the user allows the application to finish counting, the button is changed from **Stop** to **Done**. Figure 21-3 shows both states of the WorkingDialog.

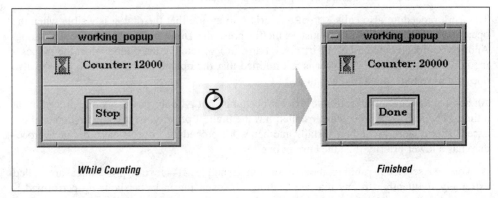

Figure 21-3. Output of working.c

This program is designed to demonstrate how a work procedure and a WorkingDialog can interact. The callback for the button in the application creates a WorkingDialog using

`XmCreateWorkingDialog()`. The callback routine also installs a work procedure using `XtAppAddWorkProc()`. This function takes the following form:

```
XtWorkProcId
XtAppAddWorkProc(app_context, proc, client_data)
    XtAppContext  app_context;
    XtWorkProc    proc;
    XtPointer     client_data;
```

The WorkingDialog is used as the client data for the `count()` work procedure, so that the procedure can update the dialog. To allow the user to interrupt the counting operation, we install `done()` as the `XmNcancelCallback` resource. If the user presses the **Stop** button, this routine is invoked. The routine stops the counting operation by removing the work procedure using `XtRemoveWorkProc()`.

During the counting operation, Xt calls the work procedure when there are no events that need to be processed. The work procedure increments the global counter variable, i. Each time i reaches an increment of `1000`, the `XmNmessageString` for the WorkingDialog is updated to inform the user about the progress of the operation. The work procedure returns `True` when the task is complete, which causes Xt to remove the procedure from the list of work procedures being called. When `count()` returns `False`, Xt continues to call the routine when the application is idle.

If the user allows the task to complete, the work procedure changes the action button to say **Done** and removes the `XmNcancelCallback`. The procedure then reinstalls the callback in order to change the client data from `True` to `False`. The client data must be set to `False` so that `done()` does not try to remove the work procedure. Since the work procedure returns `True` in this case, Xt removes the procedure for us.

The work procedure also calls `XMapRaised()` to ensure that the dialog is visible when the operation completes. The user must explicitly press the **Done** button to remove the dialog. Another approach is to call `XtDestroyWidget()` to remove the dialog when the processing is done. In this case, the user is not notified that the operation has finished, but she also does not have to respond to the dialog.

An application can install multiple work procedures, but Xt only processes one procedure at a time. The last work procedure installed has the highest priority, so it is the first one called, except if one work procedure installs another work procedure. In this case, the new procedure has a lower priority than the current one.

As you can see from running the program in Example 21-4, work procedures are called extremely frequently. In any real application, however, the task that is being performed is going to be more sophisticated and time-consuming than our example here. It is important that the operations you perform in a work procedure do not take too much time, or response time will suffer. A work procedure should return frequently enough to allow Xt to process user events, so that the operation of the entire application flows smoothly.

21.2.2 Using Timers

Using timers to process a task is very similar to using work procedures. Timers are not called as frequently as work procedures, so Xt can wait longer for user events to be generated and processed when the application uses timers. An application can add a timer using `XtApp-AddTimeOut()`, which takes the following form:

```
XtIntervalId
XtAppAddTimeOut(app_context, interval, proc, client_data)
    XtAppContext          app_context;
    unsigned long         interval;
    XtTimerCallbackProc   proc;
    XtPointer             client_data;
```

The *interval* parameter specifies how long Xt waits before invoking the timer specified by *proc*. The main difference between using a timer and a work procedure is that a timer is called once and then automatically unregistered. To have a timer called at a regular interval, an application must call `XtAppAddTimeOut()` again from within the timer callback. With this exception, using timers is similar to using work procedures, so we aren't going to present a separate example here. See Chapter 11, *Labels and Buttons*, for some examples that use timers in various contexts.

21.2.3 Processing Events

If your application needs to start a lengthy process that is difficult to break into small pieces, you probably don't want to return control to Xt. In this case, you never lose control of your own processing loop, but you need to check for X events that need to be processed every once in a while. This technique is more convenient than work procedures for certain algorithms, since the application doesn't have to break out of its processing loop unless the user terminates the operation or the task completes naturally.

Processing events is somewhat complicated, but not because of the function calls involved or the design required to support the processing. The complications involve the decisions about which events you want to process, which you want to ignore, and which you want to put off handling until later. Say you are rendering a complicated graphic directly into a Drawing-Area. While you are busy processing, you need to decide what to do if you get an incoming `ButtonPress`, `Expose`, or `ConfigureNotify` event, among others. In many cases, what you do depends on the widget or the window that receives the event.

When an application starts a lengthy task, it should post a WorkingDialog that displays an appropriate message. The WorkingDialog can also provide a **Stop** button to allow the user to terminate the task. During the operation, the user should not be interacting with other windows in the application. It is a good idea to change the cursor that is used in these windows, to make it clear that the windows will not respond to user input. When the operation is finished, the application needs to remove the WorkingDialog and reset the cursor.

If you are going to process events yourself, you probably want to write a routine that checks the event queue for relevant events. This routine would process all of the important events, such as those that cause widgets to be repainted. The routine should also handle events for the **Stop** button in the WorkingDialog, so the user can terminate the task.

The program listed in Example 21-5 supports the requirements that we have laid out for an application that processes its own events.†

Example 21-5. The busy.c program

```
/* busy.c -- demonstrate how to use a WorkingDialog and to process
 * only important events.  e.g., those that may interrupt the
 * task or to repaint widgets for exposure.  Set up a simple shell
 * and a widget that, when pressed, immediately goes into its own
 * loop.  Set a timeout cursor on the shell and pop up a WorkingDialog.
 * Then enter loop and sleep for one second ten times, checking between
 * each interval to see if the user clicked the Stop button or if
 * any widgets need to be refreshed.  Ignore all other events.
 *
 * main() and get_busy() are stubs that would be replaced by a real
 * application; all other functions can be used as is.
 */
#include <Xm/MessageB.h>
#include <Xm/PushB.h>
#include <X11/cursorfont.h>

Widget shell;
void TimeoutCursors();
Boolean CheckForInterrupt();

main(argc, argv)
int argc;
char *argv[];
{
    XtAppContext app;
    Widget button;
    XmString label;
    void get_busy();

    XtSetLanguageProc (NULL, NULL, NULL);

    shell = XtVaAppInitialize (&app, "Demos",
        NULL, 0, &argc, argv, NULL, NULL);

    label = XmStringCreateLocalized ("Press Here To Start A Long Task");
    button = XtVaCreateManagedWidget ("button",
        xmPushButtonWidgetClass, shell,
        XmNlabelString,          label,
        NULL);
    XmStringFree (label);
    XtAddCallback (button, XmNactivateCallback, get_busy, NULL);

    XtRealizeWidget (shell);
    XtAppMainLoop (app);
}

void
```

---

†`XtSetLanguageProc()` is only available in X11R5; there is no corresponding function in X11R4. `Xm-StringCreateLocalized()` is only available in Motif 1.2; `XmStringCreateSimple()` is the corresponding function in Motif 1.1.

Example 21-5. The busy.c program (continued)

```
get_busy(widget, client_data, call_data)
Widget widget;
XtPointer client_data;
XtPointer call_data;
{
    int n;

    TimeoutCursors (True, True);
    for (n = 0; n < 10; n++) {
        sleep (1);
        if (CheckForInterrupt ()) {
            puts ("Interrupt!");
            break;
        }
    }
    if (n == 10)
        puts ("Done");
    TimeoutCursors (False, False);
}

/* The interesting part of the program -- extract and use at will */

static Boolean stopped;   /* True when user wants to stop task */
static Widget dialog;     /* WorkingDialog displayed */

/* TimeoutCursors() -- turns on the watch cursor over the application
 * to provide feedback for the user that she's going to be waiting
 * a while before she can interact with the application again.
 */
void
TimeoutCursors(on, interruptable)
Boolean on, interruptable;
{
    static int locked;
    static Cursor cursor;
    extern Widget shell;
    XSetWindowAttributes attrs;
    Display *dpy = XtDisplay (shell);
    XEvent event;
    Arg args[5];
    int n;
    XmString str;
    extern void stop();

    /* "locked" keeps track if we've already called the function.
     * This allows recursion and is necessary for most situations.
     */
    if (on)
        locked++;
    else
        locked--;
    if (locked > 1 || locked == 1 && on == 0)
        return; /* already locked and we're not unlocking */

    stopped = False;
    if (!cursor)
        cursor = XCreateFontCursor (dpy, XC_watch);

    /* if on is true, then turn on watch cursor, otherwise, return
```

Example 21-5. The busy.c program (continued)

```
     * the shell's cursor to normal.
     */
    attrs.cursor = on ? cursor : None;

    /* change the main application shell's cursor to be the timeout
     * cursor or to reset it to normal.  If other shells exist in
     * this application, they will have to be listed here in order
     * for them to have timeout cursors too.
     */
    XChangeWindowAttributes (dpy, XtWindow (shell), CWCursor, &attrs);

    XFlush (dpy);

    if (on) {
        /* we're timing out, put up a WorkingDialog.  If the process
         * is interruptable, allow a "Stop" button.  Otherwise, remove
         * all actions so the user can't stop the processing.
         */
        n = 0;
        str = XmStringCreateLocalized ("Busy -- Please Wait.");
        XtSetArg (args[n], XmNmessageString, str); n++;
        dialog = XmCreateWorkingDialog (shell, "busy", args, n);
        XmStringFree (str);
        XtUnmanageChild (XmMessageBoxGetChild (dialog, XmDIALOG_OK_BUTTON));
        XtUnmanageChild (XmMessageBoxGetChild (dialog, XmDIALOG_HELP_BUTTON));
        if (interruptable) {
            str = XmStringCreateLocalized ("Stop");
            XtVaSetValues (dialog, XmNcancelLabelString, str, NULL);
            XmStringFree (str);
            XtAddCallback (dialog, XmNcancelCallback, stop, NULL);
        }
        else
            XtUnmanageChild (XmMessageBoxGetChild
                (dialog, XmDIALOG_CANCEL_BUTTON));
        XtManageChild (dialog);
    }
    else {
        /* get rid of all button and keyboard events that occured
         * during the time out.  The user shouldn't have done anything
         * during this time, so flush for button and keypress events.
         * KeyRelease events are not discarded because accelerators
         * require the corresponding release event before normal input
         * can continue.
         */
        while (XCheckMaskEvent (dpy,
                ButtonPressMask | ButtonReleaseMask | ButtonMotionMask
                | PointerMotionMask | KeyPressMask, &event)) {
            /* do nothing */;
        }
        XtDestroyWidget (dialog);
    }
}

/* stop() -- user pressed the "Stop" button in dialog. */
void
stop(dialog, client_data, call_data)
Widget dialog;
XtPointer client_data;
```

Motif Programming Manual

Example 21-5. The busy.c program (continued)

```
XtPointer call_data;
{
    stopped = True;
}

/* CheckForInterrupt() -- check events in event queue and process
 * the interesting ones.
 */
Boolean
CheckForInterrupt()
{
    extern Widget shell;
    Display *dpy = XtDisplay (shell);
    Window win = XtWindow (dialog);
    XEvent event;

    /* Make sure all our requests get to the server */
    XFlush (dpy);

    /* Let Motif process all pending exposure events for us. */
    XmUpdateDisplay (shell);

    /* Check the event loop for events in the dialog ("Stop"?) */
    while (XCheckMaskEvent (dpy,
        ButtonPressMask | ButtonReleaseMask | ButtonMotionMask |
        PointerMotionMask | KeyPressMask, &event)) {
        /* got an "interesting" event. */
        if (event.xany.window == win)
            XtDispatchEvent (&event); /* it's in our dialog.. */
        else /* uninteresting event--throw it away and sound bell */
            XBell (dpy, 50);
    }
    return stopped;
}
```

This program is obviously for demonstration purposes only. To keep to the subject matter, we have made the main part of the program quite unrealistic and only use it to support the functions we are about to discuss. The application displays a single button that starts a "long task." The get_busy() callback routine is trivial, but it demonstrates the use of the TimeoutCursors() and CheckForInterrupt() routines.

The TimeoutCursors() routine is used to change the cursor for the main application shell and to post the WorkingDialog. The cursor is changed to a watch shape to give the user visual feedback that the main window is not responding to input. The routine uses the static variable locked to keep track of how many times it has been called with on set to True. The function does not reset the cursor and remove the WorkingDialog until a matching number of calls has been made with on set to False. This technique makes it possible for a low-level function in an application to call TimeoutCursors() at its beginning and end, without affecting higher-level loops that also call the function.

The routine stores the XC_watch cursor in the static cursor variable. The cursor is created using XCreateFontCursor(), which is why *<X11/cursorfont.h>* is included. TimeoutCursors() uses XChangeWindowAttributes() to change the cursor to the watch shape and to reset it to its normal shape when on is False. The cursor is modified for the window of the shell widget, which is the main window for the application. If your application uses multiple ApplicationShells or TopLevelShells, you will need to modify the function to change the cursor shape for all of the shells.

At this point, we call XFlush() to make sure that all of our requests have been sent to the server. The TimeoutCursors() function may be called from deep within an application, so there may be a number of server requests that are waiting and we want to be sure that the server knows about them now. If the are turning off the timeout cursor, we may also need to read any resulting events.

Now we determine whether we are locking or unlocking the application. If we are locking it, we create and post a WorkingDialog. The dialog is created with a standard message. If the interruptable parameter is True, we provide a **Stop** button by changing the label of the **Cancel** button. We also add a callback routine for button, so that we can actually stop the task in progress.

We should note that an application does not necessarily have to post a WorkingDialog, as long as it changes the cursor. The watch cursor provides enough feedback to indicate that the application is in a busy state. The decision about whether or not to post a dialog really depends on the length of the task being performed. For relatively short tasks, it typically doesn't make sense to provide a WorkingDialog, as it takes some time to actually create and post the dialog.

Now the application is in a busy state. However, the user has yet to see anything; events need to be processed in order for the dialog to be mapped to the screen. At this point, the CheckForInterrupt() routine takes over. This routine handles Expose events by calling XmUpdateDisplay(). This Motif function processes all of the **Expose** events in the event queue by causing the server to flush these events for all of the windows on the display. This processing may cause redrawing event handlers to be called for various widgets. If you have installed your own exposure routines for any widgets, be sure that they are not too time consuming, or you may find yourself in a bind. You can check to see which windows are going to be repainted before it actually happens by using XCheckMaskEvent() to process Expose events.

After any possible repainting has occurred, we check for any button or keyboard events in the event queue. If one has been generated, we extract it from the input queue using XCheck-MaskEvent(). The function takes the following form:

```
Bool
XCheckMaskEvent(display, event_mask, event_return)
    Display  *display;
    long      event_mask;
    XEvent   *event_return;
```

This Xlib function looks for events in the queue that match *event_mask*. If there is a matching event, the *event_return* parameter is filled in with the event and the routine returns True. Otherwise, the function returns False and we can return. The event is processed only if it occurred within the WorkingDialog window. Since the application is busy, events in other windows are not processed. If the user did something in the WorkingDialog, we process the event because she may have activated the **Stop** button. If the button is not provided for the dialog, it does not affect the code here.

You should be aware that XCheckMaskEvent() removes the event from the queue. If you choose not to process an event, you cannot stick it back in the queue. If you retrieve an event out of the queue and don't want to process it, you should set an application-defined variable or flag that notifies the application that it must eventually deal with the event. Another alternative is to save the event by allocating a new XEvent structure and copying the data. Then you dispatch the event later, when you are prepared to handle it.

We do not check for KeyRelease events in CheckForInterrupt() for a very important reason that concerns how the X Toolkit Intrinsics handles accelerators. Say your application has a menu item that initiates a long, complicated process. The callback function for this menu item calls both TimeoutCursors() and CheckForInterrupt(), just like the get_busy() routine. Let's say that ALT-X is the accelerator for the menu item. When the user types this key sequence, the callback routine for the menu item is activated by the KeyPress events. At this time, the KeyRelease events associated with the accelerator are still in the event queue. If we checked for KeyRelease events in CheckFor-Interrupt(), the ones for the accelerator would get thrown away, since they did not occur in the WorkingDialog.

Throwing away these events is a problem because Xt uses an internal state machine to determine whether or not any particular sequence of keyboard events is an accelerator or a prefix for one. Since Xt would never get the accompanying KeyRelease events, it would think that the user is still entering a keyboard accelerator. Xt would not get out of that state until the matching events were given, with the result that no other keyboard events would work in the application until the user happened to type the same accelerator sequence. This situation is not a bug in Xt; Xt is simply doing what it must to handle acclerators. However, the situation does demonstrate the intricacies of handling events in X.

Getting back to CheckForInterrupt(), if the user presses the **Stop** in the dialog, the event is processed and the stop() callback routine is invoked. This routine simply sets the global variable stopped to True. By the time that CheckForInterrupt() is ready to return, stopped has been set, so the function returns True. If the WorkingDialog does not have a **Stop** button, the callback routine is not installed, so stopped is never set to True.

After the get_busy() routine finishes processing, it calls TimeoutCursors() again to unlock the application. When on is set to False, the routine uses XCheckMaskEvent() to look in the event queue for button and keyboard events. In this case, the events are thrown away, since the input is no longer useful. The routine also destroys the WorkingDialog. In one sense, TimeoutCursors() implements a kind of modality, similar to that discussed in Section 5.7.1. However, modality alone cannot provide the functionality necessary to handle long-running tasks.

21.2.4 Updating the Display

As discussed earlier, XmUpdateDisplay() checks the event queue for all Expose events and processes them immediately. However, there are some circumstances under which the routine does not work as you might expect. For example, let's say that your application creates and posts a dialog that contains a DrawingArea widget. You call XSync() and Xm-UpdateDisplay() to make sure that the dialog is on the screen and fully exposed. After you call XClearWindow() to make sure the window is clear, you begin drawing. Unfortunately, you may find that nothing is drawn.

The problem is due to the redirection of events from the window manager and the way events are processed and queued. When a dialog is posted using XtManageChild() or Xt-Popup(), the toolkit calls XMapRaised() to raise the window to the top of the window stack. The call to XSync() sends the MapRequest event to the server, which redirects it to the window manager (e.g., *mwm*). A bottleneck can occur if the window manager is swapped out, which is a side effect of multi-tasking operating systems such as UNIX.

In this case, *mwm* may not react immediately to the redirection and can take an indeterminate amount of time to respond. The X server doesn't take this delay into account. It thinks that the event has been delivered properly, so your application believes that the window has been mapped. As a result, XmUpdateDisplay() doesn't get the Expose event that you were expecting and drawing does no good because the window still hasn't been mapped. When *mwm* gets around to mapping the window to the screen, the server generates the Expose event, but by now your application is off doing something else.

One solution to this problem is to change the design of your application so that it doesn't start drawing until the server actually generates the Expose events. In this case, you should post the dialog and immediately return control to the main event-processing loop (XtApp-MainLoop()). If you have installed an event handler or a translation for the Expose event, the routine is called at the appropriate time. Another advantage to this design is that the drawing procedure is called anytime an Expose event occurs, which ensures that the window is always up-to-date.

In Example 21-6, we show another solution. This solution should be used only if you need to create, pop up, or manage a dialog and then immediately draw into the window. The ForceUpdate() routine ensures that the specified widget is visible before it returns.

Example 21-6. The ForceUpdate() routine

```
/* ForceUpdate() -- a superset of XmUpdateDisplay() that ensures
 * that a window's contents are visible before returning.
 * The monitoring of window states is necessary because an attempt to
 * map a window is subject to the whim of the window manager, which can
 * introduce a significant delay before the window is actually mapped
 * and exposed.  This function is intended to be called after XtPopup(),
 * XtManageChild() or XMapRaised().  Don't use it in other situations
 * as it may sit and process other unrelated events until the widget
 * becomes visible.
 */
void
ForceUpdate(w)
Widget w; /* This widget must be visible before the function returns */
{
    Widget diashell, topshell;
    Window diawindow, topwindow;
    XtAppContext cxt = XtWidgetToApplicationContext (w);
    Display *dpy;
    XWindowAttributes xwa;
    XEvent event;

    /* Locate the shell we are interested in */
```

Example 21-6. The ForceUpdate() routine (continued)

```
for (diashell = w; !XtIsShell (diashell); diashell = XtParent (diashell))
    ;

/* Locate its primary window's shell (which may be the same) */
for (topshell = diashell; !XtIsTopLevelShell (topshell);
        topshell = XtParent (topshell))
    ;

/* If the dialog shell (or its primary shell window) is not realized,
 * don't bother ... nothing can possibly happen.
 */
if (XtIsRealized (diashell) && XtIsRealized (topshell)) {
    dpy = XtDisplay (topshell);
    diawindow = XtWindow (diashell);
    topwindow = XtWindow (topshell);

    /* Wait for the dialog to be mapped.  It's guaranteed to become so */
    while (XGetWindowAttributes (dpy, diawindow, &xwa) &&
        xwa.map_state != IsViewable) {

        /* ...if the primary is (or becomes) unviewable or unmapped,
         * it's probably iconic, and nothing will happen.
         */
        if (XGetWindowAttributes (dpy, topwindow, &xwa) &&
            xwa.map_state != IsViewable)
            break;

        /* we are guaranteed there will be an event of some kind. */
        XtAppNextEvent (cxt, &event);
        XtDispatchEvent (&event);
    }
}

/* The next XSync() will get an expose event. */
XmUpdateDisplay (topshell);
}
```

This routine makes sure that a dialog is visible by waiting for the window of the dialog to be mapped to the screen.

21.2.5 Avoiding Forks

Before we close out this section, there is one more method of of executing tasks in the background that we should discuss. Beginning programmers tend to use library functions and system calls such as system(), popen(), fork(), and exec() to invoke external commands. Although these functions are perfectly reasonable, they can backfire quite easily on virtually any error condition. Recovering from these errors is the GUI programmer's nightmare, since there are so many different possible conditions to deal with.

The purpose of using these functions, of course, is to call another UNIX program and have it run concurrently with the main application. The system() and popen() functions fork a new process using the fork() system call. They also use some form of exec() so the new child process can invoke the external UNIX program. If the new process cannot fork, if there is something wrong with the external UNIX command, if there is a communications protocol error, or any one of a dozen other possible error conditions, there is no way for the external program to display an error message as a part of the main application.

It is unlikely that the external program would display a dialog box or any sort of reasonable user-interface element. It is illegal for a new process to use any of the widgets or windows in the main application because only one connection to the server is allowed per process. If the child process wants to post a dialog, it must establish a new connection to the X server and create an entirely new widget tree, as it is a separate application. Since most system utilities do not have graphical user interface front ends, this scenario is very unlikely. It is also entirely unreasonable to have any expectations of the external process, especially since other solutions are much easier.

If a separate process is necessary in order to accomplish a particular task, setting up pipes between the child application and the parent is usually the best alternative. The popen() function uses this method superficially, but it is not the most elegant solution. The routine only handles forking the new process and setting up half of a two-way pipe. The popen() function is used in several places throughout the book; check the index for those uses.

To really handle external processes and pipes properly, an application should do the following:

1. The parent process calls pipe() to set up entry points for the expected child process' input and output channels. Two pipes for both input and output are usually needed.

2. The parent process calls fork() to spawn the new child process.

3. The child uses dup2() to redirect its own stdin, stdout, and stderr to the other ends of the pipes set up by the parent. The communication pipeline between the parent and the child is now established.

4. The parent calls XtAppAddInput() to tell Xt to monitor an additional file descriptor while it is waiting for input events from the X server.

5. The parent can read data (e.g., output, error conditions, etc.) sent by the child using read() on the appropriate pipe.

6. The parent can display the output from the pipe to a dialog, a ScrolledText object, or some other widget because it is still in connection with the X server.

If the parent calls XtAppAddInput(), Xt can see the data the child sends through the pipe and invoke the callback routine associated with the file descriptor. XtAppAddInput() takes the following form:

```
XtInputId
XtAppAddInput(app_context, source, mask, proc, client_data)
    XtAppContext        app_context;
    int                 source;
    XtPointer           mask;
    XtInputCallbackProc proc;
    XtPointer           client_data;
```

The *source* parameter should be the side of the pipe that the parent uses to read data sent by the child process. The *proc* function is called when there is data to read on the pipe. When the function is called, the *client_data* is passed to the callback. For example, you can pass the process ID returned by `fork()`, so you can see if the process is still alive and read the data using `read()`.

This discussion is merely presented as an overview, since the implementation details are beyond the scope of this book. For example, UNIX signals cause problems in a number of ways. The parent process is sent signals when the child dies or its process state changes. The child is also sent signals that are delivered to the parent by the user or other outside forces. Different forms of UNIX require that process groups be set up in different ways to avoid other problems with signals.

Another problem involves file descriptors that are set up as non-blocking files. If `read()` returns 0 with one of these descriptors, you may not know whether there is nothing to read or the end of the file has been reached, which means that the child process has terminated. Incidentally, `popen()` does not deal with any of these issues correctly, so building a new solution is the best thing to do in the long run.

You should really consult the programmer's guide for your UNIX system for more information on the techniques used to spawn new processes and communicate with them appropriately. Once you have a handle on those issues, it should be relatively easy to redirect text from file descriptors using the toolkit. For more information on `XtAppAddInput()`, including examples of how it can be used, see Volume Four, *X Toolkit Intrinsics Programming Manual*.

21.3 Dynamic Message Symbols

The MessageDialog is used to display many different types of messages; the image in the dialog helps the user identify the purpose of the dialog. The pixmaps used by the standard MessageDialogs are predefined by the Motif toolkit. When you are using the standard dialogs, you typically change the dialog's type rather than its symbol, since changing its type effectively changes the symbol that it displays. However, you can change the Message-Dialog's symbol to a customized image using the `XmNsymbolPixmap` resource.

The resource takes a pixmap value that must be created before the resource is set. When the resource is set, the pixmap is not copied by the dialog widget. If the dialog is destroyed, you should be sure to free the pixmap unless you are using it elsewhere. If you are going to destroy the dialog using `XtDestroyWidget()` directly, you should get the pixmap by calling `XtVaGetValues()`, so that you can free it. However, the dialog can also be destroyed automatically, so you should also specify an `XmNdestroyCallback` procedure that is called whenever the dialog is destroyed.

Example 21-7 shows an example of using a custom image in a standard MessageDialog. The program also demonstrates how the dialog should clean up after itself.†

---

† `XtSetLanguageProc()` is only available in X11R5; there is no corresponding function in X11R4. `XmStringCreateLocalized()` is only available in Motif 1.2; `XmStringCreateSimple()` is the corresponding function in Motif 1.1. `XmFONTLIST_DEFAULT_TAG` replaces `XmSTRING_DEFAULT_CHARSET` in Motif 1.2.

Example 21-7. The warn_msg.c program

```
/* warn_msg.c -- display a very urgent warning message.
 * Really catch the user's attention by flashing an urgent-
 * looking pixmap every 250 milliseconds.
 * The program demonstrates how to set the XmNsymbolPixmap
 * resource, how to destroy the pixmap and how to use timers.
 */
#include <Xm/MessageB.h>
#include <Xm/PushB.h>

#include "bang0.symbol"
#include "bang1.symbol"

#define TEXT "Alert!\n\
The computer room is ON FIRE!\n\
All of your e-mail will be lost."

/* define the data structure we need to implement flashing effect */
typedef struct {
    XtIntervalId    id;
    int             which;
    Pixmap          pix1, pix2;
    Widget          dialog;
    XtAppContext    app;
} TimeOutClientData;

main(argc, argv)
int argc;
char *argv[];
{
    XtAppContext app;
    Widget toplevel, button;
    XmString label;
    void warning();

    XtSetLanguageProc (NULL, NULL, NULL);

    toplevel = XtVaAppInitialize (&app, "Demos",
        NULL, 0, &argc, argv, NULL, NULL);

    label = XmStringCreateLocalized (
        "Don't Even Think About Pressing This Button");
    button = XtVaCreateManagedWidget ("button",
        xmPushButtonWidgetClass, toplevel,
        XmNlabelString,         label,
        NULL);
    XmStringFree (label);

    /* set up callback to popup warning */
    XtAddCallback (button, XmNactivateCallback, warning, NULL);

    XtRealizeWidget (toplevel);
    XtAppMainLoop (app);
}

/* warning() -- callback routine for the button.  Create a message
 * dialog and set the message string.  Allocate an instance of
 * the TimeOutClientData structure and set a timer to alternate
 * between the two pixmaps.  The data is passed to the timeout
 * routine and the callback for when the user presses "OK".
 */
```

Example 21-7. The warn_msg.c program (continued)

```
void
warning(parent, client_data, call_data)
Widget parent;
XtPointer client_data;
XtPointer call_data;
{
    Widget        dialog;
    XtAppContext  app = XtWidgetToApplicationContext (parent);
    XmString      text;
    extern void   done(), destroy_it(), blink();
    Display       *dpy = XtDisplay (parent);
    Screen        *screen = XtScreen (parent);
    Pixel         fg, bg;
    Arg           args[5];
    int           n, depth;
    TimeOutClientData *data = XtNew (TimeOutClientData);

    /* Create the dialog */
    n = 0;
    XtSetArg (args[n], XmNdeleteResponse, XmDESTROY); n++;
    dialog = XmCreateMessageDialog (parent, "danger", args, n);

    XtUnmanageChild (XmMessageBoxGetChild (dialog, XmDIALOG_CANCEL_BUTTON));
    XtUnmanageChild (XmMessageBoxGetChild (dialog, XmDIALOG_HELP_BUTTON));

    XtAddCallback (dialog, XmNokCallback, done, NULL);
    XtAddCallback (dialog, XmNdestroyCallback, destroy_it, data);

    /* now that dialog has been created, it's colors are initialized */
    XtVaGetValues (dialog,
        XmNforeground, &fg,
        XmNbackground, &bg,
        XmNdepth, &depth,
        NULL);

    /* Create pixmaps that are going to be used as symbolPixmaps.
     * Use the foreground and background colors of the dialog.
     */
    data->pix1 = XCreatePixmapFromBitmapData (dpy, XtWindow (parent),
        bang0_bits, bang0_width, bang0_height, fg, bg, depth);
    data->pix2 = XCreatePixmapFromBitmapData (dpy, XtWindow (parent),
        bang1_bits, bang1_width, bang1_height, fg, bg, depth);
    /* complete the timeout client data */
    data->dialog = dialog;
    data->app = app;

    /* Add the timeout for blinking effect */
    data->id = XtAppAddTimeOut (app, 1000L, blink, data);

    /* display the help text and the appropriate pixmap */
    text = XmStringCreateLtoR (TEXT, XmFONTLIST_DEFAULT_TAG);
    XtVaSetValues (dialog,
        XmNmessageString,     text,
        XmNsymbolPixmap,      data->pix2,
        NULL);
    XmStringFree (text);

    XtManageChild (dialog);
    XtPopup (XtParent (dialog), XtGrabNone);
```

Example 21-7. The warn_msg.c program (continued)

```
}

/* blink() -- visual blinking effect for dialog's symbol.  Displays
 * flashing ! symbol, restarts timer and saves timer id.
 */
void
blink(client_data, id)
XtPointer client_data;
XtIntervalId *id;
{
    TimeOutClientData *data = (TimeOutClientData *) client_data;

    data->id = XtAppAddTimeOut (data->app, 250L, blink, data);
    XtVaSetValues (data->dialog,
        XmNsymbolPixmap,   (data->which = !data->which) ?
            data->pix1 : data->pix2,
        NULL);
}

/* done() -- called when user presses "OK" in dialog or
 * if the user picked the Close button in system menu.
 * Remove the timeout id stored in data, free pixmaps and
 * make sure the widget is destroyed (which is only when
 * the user presses the "OK" button.
 */
void
done(dialog, client_data, call_data)
Widget dialog;
XtPointer client_data;
XtPointer call_data;
{
    XtDestroyWidget(dialog);
}

/* destroy_it() -- called when dialog is destroyed.  Removes
 * timer and frees allocated data.
 */
void
destroy_it(dialog, client_data, call_data)
Widget dialog;
XtPointer client_data;
XtPointer call_data;
{
    TimeOutClientData *data = (TimeOutClientData *) client_data;
    Pixmap symbol;

    XtRemoveTimeOut (data->id);
    XFreePixmap (XtDisplay (data->dialog), data->pix1);
    XFreePixmap (XtDisplay (data->dialog), data->pix2);
    XtFree (data);
}
```

The dialog is created in warning(), the callback routine for the PushButton in the main window. We create a simple MessageDialog that does not have a predefined symbol so we can specify a custom image. The dialog actually uses two symbols that are exchanged every 250 milliseconds by a timer callback routine. The output of this program is shown in Figure 21-4. To implement the flashing symbol, we must associate certain information with the

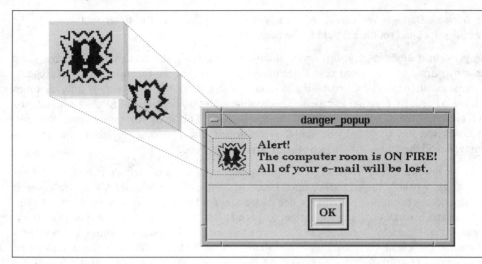

Figure 21-4. Output of warn_msg.c

dialog. Basically, we need to keep track of the two pixmaps and the timer routine. All of the information is placed in a single data structure, so we can pass the structure around as client data. We can also use multiple structure variables to store information about multiple dialogs. The `TimeOutClientData` is defined as follows:

```
typedef struct {
    XtIntervalId    id;
    int             which;
    Pixmap          pix1, pix2;
    Widget          dialog;
    XtAppContext    app;
} TimeOutClientData;
```

The `warning()` routine allocates a new instance of the structure using `XtNew()`, since it is going to create a new dialog and it needs a unique structure for the dialog. The routine uses `XmCreateMessageDialog()` to create the dialog. We unmanage the **Cancel** and **Help** buttons and specify a callback for the **OK** button. The `done()` callback simply calls `XtDestroyWidget()`, which causes the `XmNdestroyCallback` to be called. We also set the `XmNdeleteResponse` resource for the dialog to `XmDESTROY`. This setting causes the Motif toolkit to destroy the dialog if the user dismisses it using the **Close** button on the window menu,

Since we are not reusing the dialog or its data, we must be sure to free the pixmaps, release the timer, and free the allocated data structure when the dialog is destroyed. To be sure that these tasks take place, we install a callback function for the `XmNdestroyCallback` resource. The `destroy_it()` routine handles all of the cleanup for the dialog.

Before we create the pixmaps that are used in the dialog, we retrieve the dialog's foreground and background colors using `XtVaGetValues()` so that the new pixmaps can use the same colors. Once the colors are known, we can create the pixmaps and finish initializing the fields in the `TimeOutClientData` structure. The `dialog` field of the structure points to the MessageDialog. We call XtAppAddTimeOut() to start the timer that controls the flashing effect and set the id field to the timer ID.

We perform a final bit of setup for the dialog by specifying the XmNsymbolPixmap and XmNmessageString resources. Once everything is set up, the function returns, Xt regains control, and normal event processing resumes. After the initial one-second interval times out, the blink() function is called. This routine adds another timeout for 250 milliseconds and switches the pixmaps displayed in the dialog. This loop continues until the user dismisses the dialog, at which time it is destroyed, the pixmaps are freed, the timer is removed, and the TimeOutClientData structure is freed.

Since we created a simple MessageDialog that does not have a predefined image, we did not have to get a handle to the XmNsymbolPixmap for the dialog and destroy it. However, if you decide to change the pixmap for one of the standard dialogs that has a predefined symbol, like the ErrorDialog, you should get its pixmap and free it. In this case, you should use XmDestroyPixmap() rather than XFreePixmap(). The Motif dialogs use XmGet-Pixmap() to create their images, so the pixmaps must be freed with the companion routine XmDestroyPixmap(). See Section 3.4.5 in Chapter 3, *Overview of the Motif Toolkit*, for a discussion on XmGetPixmap().

Although changing the symbol pixmap in a dialog is quite simple, using the feature effectively requires a careful design to make sure that all of the pointers and data structures are destroyed appropriately. Being meticulous about cleaning up after destroyed widgets and other objects is sometimes a difficult task because of the many ways in which the user can destroy them. However, eliminating these possible memory leaks enables a program to run longer and more efficiently.

21.4 Summary

Developing a real application often involves a lot of work to get the details just right. Some of the most interesting problems in designing an interface cannot be solved by Motif alone. Motif provides the basic user interface, but you must make it work with your application. A solid understanding of the fundamentals of the X Window System and the X Toolkit Intrinsics makes it easier to fine-tune the interface for an application. This chapter has presented some solutions to common problems that require using both Xlib and Xt routines in conjunction with the Motif toolkit.

22

Introduction to UIL

This chapter provides a basic introduction to the User Interface Language (UIL) and the Motif Resource Manager (Mrm). The chapter describes UIL and Mrm, talks about how to use them, and discusses the advantages and disadvantages of using them to create a user interface. It also presents a "Hello, World" application that is meant to provide you with a basic understanding of how to use both UIL and Mrm to develop an application with Motif.

In This Chapter:

22

Introduction to UIL

In this chapter, we introduce the OSF/Motif User Interface Language (UIL) and the Motif Resource Manager (Mrm). We begin by explaining the purpose and capabilities of UIL and Mrm. Then we describe the structure of both a UIL module and a program that uses Mrm by walking through the traditional "Hello World" application. The example gives you an overview of how a user interface is described with UIL and created with Mrm. For the most part we concentrate on the big picture and leave the discussion of low-level details until Chapter 24, *Creating a User Interface With UIL*.

In all of these chapters on UIL, we assume that you are familiar with the basics of the X Toolkit (Xt) and the concepts of Motif programming discussed earlier in this book. At the very least, you must understand the process of widget creation and the concept of widget resources. (Xt programming is covered in Volume Four, *X Toolkit Intrinsics Programming Manual*, and you can find references for Xt and Motif in Volume Five, *X Toolkit Intrinsics Reference Manual*; and Volume Six B, *Motif Reference Manual* respectively.)

22.1 Overview of UIL and Mrm

UIL is a text-based language used to describe a user interface that consists of Motif (and other) widgets. Like a C program, a UIL description is a plain text file that you can edit with a standard editor. However, unlike a structured programming language, which supports dynamic constructs like loops and conditional statements, UIL is strictly a static description language. It is designed to work with the Motif widget set and data types, although you can incorporate other Xt-based widgets as well. UIL files look vaguely C-like, as curly braces are used extensively for grouping.

Mrm is a library of C routines that reads compiled UIL files to create a user interface at runtime. Mrm consists of functions for opening and closing compiled UIL files, creating widgets, retrieving values (such as strings and icons), and declaring callbacks. Loosely speaking, the UIL description is a "resource" that Mrm "manages," hence the name.

22.1.1 Using UIL and Mrm

An application that uses UIL consists of one or more UIL source modules and the application source code. A UIL module contains widget declarations that describe the application's user interface. The application source code, which is usually written in C or another high-level language, creates the user interface and implements the application's behavior. Depending on its needs, an application may also use other types of files.

The process of using UIL and Mrm consists of three main steps:

1. Describe a user interface in one or more UIL files. The description is written using a text editor. Writing the description involves defining the widget hierarchy of the interface and specifying resources and callback settings. (Some user interface builder tools also generate interface descriptions in UIL, but their operation is beyond the scope of this book.)

2. Compile the files with the UIL compiler. The compiler parses and validates the files. If there are no errors, the compiler writes out a user interface description (UID) file for each UIL source file. A UID file is analogous to an object file in a programming language; it contains a binary description of the interface which is read by Mrm.

3. Create the user interface at run-time with Mrm. After making the standard Xt initialization calls, an application only needs to make a few calls to Mrm to create and display the interface. Mrm handles nearly all of the work of creating an interface by calling routines in the Xm, Xt, and X libraries.

Figure 22-1 illustrates how UIL and Mrm fit in with your application and the Xm, Xt, and X libraries.

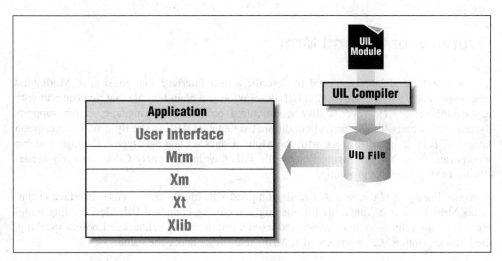

Figure 22-1. User interface creation with UIL and Mrm

22.1.2 Advantages and Disadvantages of UIL

Before you decide whether or not to use UIL in an application, consider the advantages and disadvantages of the language. The next two sections discuss the arguments for and against using UIL.

Advantages

UIL provides a relatively simple syntax for specifying a user interface in terms of a widget hierarchy. Both novice and experienced Motif programmers can quickly learn the UIL syntax. In contrast, it is more difficult and time consuming to learn all of the Motif and Xt function calls needed to create an interface in code. In addition, since a UIL module is only a static interface description, it is not subject to the ordering constraints of widget creation that typically affect the layout of programmatically-created widgets.

The extensive error checking provided by the UIL compiler can also speed up development and help ensure a more robust application. The compiler knows the resources and callbacks supported by each widget, the type of value each resource can be set to, and the children, if any, that are allowed for each widget. Any mistakes you make are caught prior to run-time. Much of this error checking is not available for interfaces created in C code. Although an ANSI C compiler checks the syntax of each function call, you can set an unsupported widget resource or create a child under a widget parent that doesn't support that child (or any children). Some of these errors are caught at run-time, but in most cases, it is up to you to notice when the interface doesn't look or act correctly.

UIL is considerably less complex than a dynamic language like C. As a result, you can compile an interface description in UIL in a fraction of the time it would take to compile and link a comparable interface created strictly in code. The time needed for the design-compile-test cycle is greatly reduced. By using UIL as a prototyping tool, you can try out several alternative interfaces without wasting too much time on those you don't use.

Many of the graphical user interface builders (UIBs) available today can read and write UIL files, which can be an advantage if you're currently using such a builder or might use one in the future. The syntax of UIL is simple enough that these products can read any UIL file, including one written without the builder. However, there are currently no tools that can read an interface created with arbitrary C code. Most builders can generate application code, but unlike UIL files, you cannot make changes to the generated C code and have a UIB import it.

Internationalizing applications with UIL is often easier than internationalizing applications written only in C because nearly all the strings used in an interface are stored in the application's associated UIL modules. Internationalizing the application is simply a matter of isolating language-dependent strings in a single module and writing separate versions of that module for each language supported by the application. (An example of this technique is presented in Section 26.2.3 in Chapter 26.)

Disadvantages

If you decide to work with UIL, you must spend some time learning how to use it. This is mainly a problem for experienced Motif and Xt programers who already know how to create an interface in C. People entirely new to Motif can usually get started faster with UIL, as there is less to learn than with the corresponding C language interface. While UIL attempts to be C-like, working with the UIL syntax can be difficult because in some instances it is overly verbose and requires unnecessary keywords and delimiters. For example, C programmers who begin using UIL often forget the required semicolon after a closed curly brace. The syntax is apparently designed to make UIL easy for the compiler to parse, rather than easy for a person to use.

In exchange for its simplicity, UIL lacks many of the advantages of a dynamic programming language. As a result, the more dynamic an interface, the less useful UIL is for describing it. Dynamic aspects of the interface, such as changing the sensitivity of widgets, performing drag and drop operations, or creating and destroying parts of the interface "on the fly" must be dealt with in application code. In these situations, it may not be possible to completely externalize an interface description. Therefore, you can expect more dependencies between the code and the interface description. Changing either one may require changing the other as well. These limitations can make dynamic interfaces more complicated to work with when UIL is involved.

Until Motif 1.2, the biggest disadvantage of using UIL was instability, which was caused by a number of bugs. While most of these bugs have now been fixed, UIL still has a bad reputation. As of Motif 1.2, UIL continues to have problems with some of the more complicated features, but with each new Motif release more of these outstanding bugs are resolved. To help you along, we point out many of these bugs, and whenever possible, explain how to work around them. If you are using an earlier version of UIL, you may encounter additional bugs that are not mentioned here.

22.2 The "Hello, World" Application

A good way to gain an understanding of the basic UIL and Mrm programming model is to examine a simple application. The one we present here is a version of the classic "Hello, World" program, which illustrates the three steps we listed earlier. We'll concentrate on the first and third steps: describing the interface in UIL and creating it at run-time using Mrm. We'll also take a quick look at how to compile the UIL module, but we'll leave the detailed discussion of the UIL compiler for Chapter 23, *Using the UIL Compiler*.

The "Hello, World" application requires only a few of the basic UIL constructs to describe the interface and a few Mrm function calls to create it. The application consists of a single UIL module that contains the interface description and a C program that initializes Xt, creates the interface with Mrm, and implements one callback. The output of the application is shown in Figure 22-2. It consists of an earth icon Label and a PushButton that contains the string `Hello, World!`.

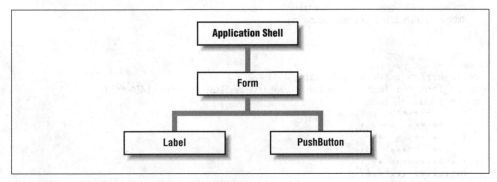

Figure 22-2. The Hello, World user interface

The icon Label and the PushButton are contained in a Form, which manages their positions. As in a typical Motif program, an ApplicationShell at the root of the hierarchy contains the Form. A diagram of the hierarchy appears in Figure 22-3.

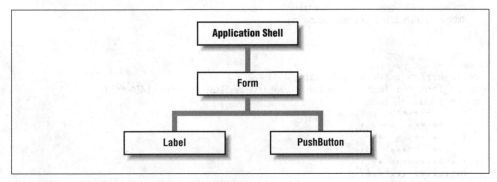

Figure 22-3. The Hello, World widget hierarchy

22.3 Describing an Interface With UIL

An interface description in a UIL module consists of three things:

- The widget hierarchy

- The initial resource settings of the individual widgets, which define the "look" of the interface

- The callbacks invoked in response to user actions, which define the "feel" of the application

The UIL module for the "Hello, World" application is shown in Example 22-1. This module defines the widget hierarchy starting at the Form. Its parent ApplicationShell is created by the C program, which we'll examine later. This division is typical for an application that creates its interface with UIL because at least one widget must be created by the program to be used as a parent for the UIL-defined widgets.

Example 22-1. The hello_world.uil module

```
/* hello_world.uil -- Illustrate basic UIL programming concepts */

module hello_world
  objects = { XmPushButton = gadget; }

value
  form_margin : 3;       ! Value for all-around form margins.

object hello_main : XmForm {
  controls {
    XmLabel        world;
    XmPushButton  hello;
  };
  arguments {
    XmNshadowThickness = 0;
    XmNresizePolicy = XmRESIZE_GROW;
    XmNmarginHeight = form_margin;
    XmNmarginWidth  = form_margin;
  };
};

value
  hello_string : "Hello, World!";
  hello_font   : font ('-adobe-helvetica-medium-r-*-*-*-140-*');
  world_icon   : icon (
    '      ******      ',
    '    ** *** **      ',
    '   *** **  *  *    ',
    '  ****     ***  *  ',
    '  * ********* **   ',
    ' * ****** *** ***  ',
    ' * ********    **  ',
    ' * ********    **  ',
    ' * ********    **  ',
    ' *   ****  *    *  ',
    ' *    **      *  * ',
    ' *    **      *  * ',
    '  *    **      *   ',
    '  *   *****    *   ',
    '   *  ******* *    ',
    '    **********     ',
    '       ******     '  );

procedure
  quit (string);

object world : XmLabel {
  arguments {
    XmNlabelType        = XmPIXMAP;
    XmNlabelPixmap      = world_icon;

    ! Form constraint resources
    XmNleftAttachment   = XmATTACH_FORM;
    XmNtopAttachment    = XmATTACH_FORM;
    XmNbottomAttachment = XmATTACH_FORM;
  };
};

object hello : XmPushButton {
  arguments {
```

Example 22-1. The hello_world.uil module (continued)

```
        XmNlabelString      = hello_string;
        XmNfontList         = hello_font;
        XmNmarginHeight     = 2;
        XmNmarginWidth      = 3;

        ! Form constraint resources
        XmNleftAttachment   = XmATTACH_WIDGET;
        XmNleftWidget       = world;
        XmNtopAttachment    = XmATTACH_FORM;
        XmNbottomAttachment = XmATTACH_FORM;
        XmNrightAttachment  = XmATTACH_FORM;
      };
      callbacks {
        XmNactivateCallback = procedure quit ("Goodbye!");
      };
    };

end module;
```

The overall structure of a UIL module is fairly simple. A module begins with a name, which is followed immediately by a number of optional settings. The bulk of a module typically consists of one or more sections that describe the user interface. This structure is depicted in Figure 22-4.

22.3.1 Starting and Ending a Module

Excluding blank lines and comments, every UIL module must begin with a `module` statement that names the module. Essentially, the statement is a syntactic formality required by the UIL compiler. It consists of the string `module` followed by a name of your choosing. The name has no special significance, but it must be a UIL identifier. (The syntax of UIL identifiers is explained in Section 22.3.5.) Our example begins with the following module statement:

```
    module hello_world
```

The name is usually the same as the module's filename without the *.uil* suffix. When choosing the name for a module, keep in mind that the name cannot be reused to name anything else in the module, such as a variable or a widget. If you should accidentally reuse the module name, the UIL compiler generates an error message.

Likewise, you must explicitly indicate the end of every UIL module with the following statement:

```
    end module;
```

Like the `module` statement at the start of the module, this statement is required for the sake of the UIL compiler.†

---

† In early versions of Motif 1.2 and previous releases, the compiler generates an error if you do not place a newline after the `end module` statement. Although this problem has been fixed, you should try to include the final newline to keep all versions of the compiler happy.

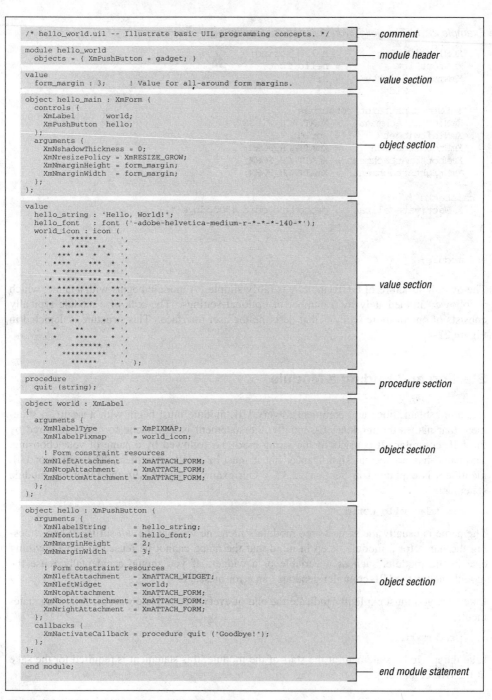

```
/* hello_world.uil -- Illustrate basic UIL programming concepts. */
```
— comment

```
module hello_world
  objects = { XmPushButton = gadget; }
```
— module header

```
value
  form_margin : 3;      ! Value for all-around form margins.
```
— value section

```
object hello_main : XmForm {
  controls {
    XmLabel       world;
    XmPushButton  hello;
  };
  arguments {
    XmNshadowThickness = 0;
    XmNresizePolicy = XmRESIZE_GROW;
    XmNmarginHeight = form_margin;
    XmNmarginWidth  = form_margin;
  };
};
```
— object section

```
value
  hello_string : 'Hello, World!';
  hello_font   : font ('-adobe-helvetica-medium-r-*-*-*-140-*');
  world_icon : icon (
    '    ******      ',
    '   ** *** **    ',
    '  *** **  *  *  ',
    ' ****    ***  * ',
    ' *  *********  **',
    '** ****** *** ***',
    '** *********   **',
    '** *********   **',
    '** *******    **',
    '** ****  *    * ',
    ' *    **     * *',
    ' *      *****   * ',
    '  *  *******  *  ',
    '   **********    ',
    '     ******      '  );
```
— value section

```
procedure
  quit (string);
```
— procedure section

```
object world : XmLabel
{
  arguments {
    XmNlabelType      = XmPIXMAP;
    XmNlabelPixmap    = world_icon;

    ! Form constraint resources
    XmNleftAttachment   = XmATTACH_FORM;
    XmNtopAttachment    = XmATTACH_FORM;
    XmNbottomAttachment = XmATTACH_FORM;
  };
};
```
— object section

```
object hello : XmPushButton {
  arguments {
    XmNlabelString    = hello_string;
    XmNfontList       = hello_font;
    XmNmarginHeight   = 2;
    XmNmarginWidth    = 3;

    ! Form constraint resources
    XmNleftAttachment   = XmATTACH_WIDGET;
    XmNleftWidget       = world;
    XmNtopAttachment    = XmATTACH_FORM;
    XmNbottomAttachment = XmATTACH_FORM;
    XmNrightAttachment  = XmATTACH_FORM;
  };
  callbacks {
    XmNactivateCallback = procedure quit ('Goodbye!');
  };
};
```
— object section

```
end module;
```
— end module statement

Figure 22-4. Structure of the hello_world.uil module

22.3.2 Specifying Module-wide Options

Options for the module, if present, immediately follow the module name. The options allow you to tell the UIL compiler how it should deal with certain information it encounters in the module. The Motif 1.2 compiler supports the following three options: `names` for setting case sensitivity, `character_set` for setting the default character set, and `object` for indicating whether the widget or gadget variants of certain objects are used by default.†

Case Sensitivity

The `names` option can be set to `case_sensitive` or `case_insensitive`. As these settings imply, the option determines how the UIL compiler interprets both programmer-defined names (like widget names) and built-in keywords. If you don't set this option, it defaults to `case_sensitive`. For example, with the `case_sensitive` setting in effect, the names snowball, SnowBall, and SNOWBALL are considered different by the compiler. However, the same names are considered to be equal when `case_insensitive` is specified. When names are `case_sensitive`, built-in keywords must appear in lowercase, but when names are `case_insensitive` they may appear in lowercase, uppercase, or mixed case. Note, however, that the `module`, `names`, `case_sensitive`, and `case_insensitive` keywords must always appear in lowercase.

We suggest that you stick with the default `case_sensitive` setting for a couple of reasons. First, case insensitivity can easily lead to confusion for C programmers who are accustomed to case sensitivity. Second, when `case_insensitive` is set, all programmer-defined names are converted to and saved in uppercase, which in turn requires the inconvenient use of uppercase references in an application program. If you decide to use the `case_sensitive` setting, it must be the first option set after the module name, as this example illustrates:

```
module bookmark_dialog
  names = case_insensitive
  . . .
```

Keeping with our suggestion, the *hello_world.uil* module does not set the `names` option, so it uses the default `case_sensitive` setting.

---

† You may see the `version` option in older UIL modules. This option is supported in Motif 1.2 for backwards compatibility but may be dropped from future versions. Unlike the other options, the `version` setting does not affect the interpretation of the module. It is used to associate a version string with the module. Instead of using the `version` option, you should place version information in a comment or in a variable in a `value` section.

Character Set

The `character_set` option allows you to set the default character set of compound strings, fonts, and font sets that appear in a UIL module. (We talk about defining these values and how the default character set affects them in Section 24.3.4.) This option is normally used when you are developing an interface for a language that uses a character set different from the one used by your native language.

Our example application uses the English language. Since this is the same language as our computing environment, it isn't necessary to specify the `character_set` option in our module. If we were building the application in a non-English environment, but wanted it to run in an English environment, the module would begin:

```
module hello_world
  character_set = iso_latin1
  . . .
```

When the `character_set` option is not set, the character set defaults to the codeset portion of the LANG environment variable if it is set, or to the vendor-specific Xm-FALLBACK_CHARSET otherwise. Because the default character set is dependent on the environment and on vendor settings, you should ensure that the proper character set is chosen for modules that may be compiled in a different environment.

On the surface, it would appear that you can always set the default character set using the `character_set` option and not worry about the setting of LANG. Unfortunately, setting this option has the side-effect of disabling locale-specific parsing of compound strings, which is important for modules containing strings with multi-byte characters. Currently, the only way to avoid this problem is to specify the character set in the LANG environment variable. In this example, we can safely set the character set in the module because we haven't used any multi-byte strings. (For more information about multi-byte string parsing see Sections 23.1.4 and 24.3.4.)

Widgets or Gadgets

The `objects` option allows you to choose whether the gadget or widget version of the Label, PushButton, ToggleButton, CascadeButton, and Separator objects is used by default. The widget or gadget variant is specified independently for each type of object. In our example, we use the following setting to get the gadget version PushButton:

```
module paint
  objects = { XmPushButton = gadget; }
```

The default value for each object is `widget`, so you need to specify the `objects` option only if you want to create gadgets by default instead. Setting this option does not prevent you from explicitly using the widget or gadget variant of a control in an `object` definition. We recommend setting the `objects` option when you know that you are going to be using gadgets for all or most of a certain type of object.

22.3.3 Include Files

As in C, it is possible to include other files in a UIL module. However, the syntax of an include directive in UIL is different. Our example application isn't large enough to make it worth using include files, but to include a file named *procedures.uih* we would use the following line in a module:

```
include file "procedures.uih";
```

The *.uih* suffix is not required; it is a convention that we've chosen to distinguish a UIL module from a UIL include file. Nested include files are supported, so an include file may itself contain include directives. Unlike a module, an include file must not begin with the module name statement or end with the `end module` statement. In addition, an include file may contain only one or more *complete* UIL sections. You cannot start a section in one UIL file and continue it in an include file.

Since you've probably used C include files before, you should already have a good idea of how to use UIL include files. You can avoid repetitive and time-consuming declarations of variables, procedures, and widgets that are referenced in multiple modules by placing them in a single include file. Then you simply include the appropriate file if you need to reference any of its declarations. Include files can also be used to obtain definitions of commonly used user interface components. (Chapter 26, *Advanced UIL Programming*, discusses using include files in more detail and contains several examples of their use.)

22.3.4 Adding Comments

There are two different types of comments that you can add to a UIL module. The first type of comment can span one or more lines; it begins with the character sequence /* and ends with */. This style is the same as a C comment. The second type of comment begins with an exclamation mark and ends at the end of the line. Both comment styles appear in Example 22-1.

You can place comments anywhere in a UIL module except, of course, within a quoted string. Comments are the only text that can occur before the module name statement or after the end module statement. For example, the first line of the *hello_world.uil* module is a C-style comment.

22.3.5 Overview of UIL Language Syntax

UIL, like C, is a free-form language, which means that the compiler doesn't care about the spacing and positioning of symbols within a UIL module. The only requirements are that one or more whitespace characters (space, newline, etc.) must appear between successive symbols, and lines cannot exceed 132 characters in length.

A symbol is a string of characters, like `module` or `age`. Single character operators and separators, such as +, =, and :, are not considered symbols. Most UIL modules contain both predefined and programmer-defined symbols.

Predefined symbols, or keywords, are built into the UIL compiler. The built-in symbols are categorized as either reserved or unreserved keywords. The difference between the two is that you can redefine unreserved keywords, while the meaning of reserved keywords is fixed. The complete list of UIL reserved keywords appears in Table 22-1, and the complete list of unreserved keywords is shown in Table 22-2. We suggest you avoid redefining unreserved keywords, as this practice can easily lead to confusion and programming errors.

Table 22-1. UIL Reserved Keywords

Type	Reserved Keywords
General	module, end, widget, gadget
Section and list names	arguments, callbacks, controls, identifier, include, list, object, procedure, procedures, value
Storage classes	exported, private
Boolean constants	on, off, true, false

Table 22-2. UIL Unreserved Keywords

Type	Unreserved Keywords
Resource names	XmNaccelerators, XmNactivateCallback, et al.
Character set names	iso_latin1, iso_greek, et al.
Enumerated values	XmATTACH_FORM, XmSHADOW_ETCHED_IN, et al.
Widget class names	XmPushButton, XmSeparator, et al.
Option names and values	background, case_insensitive, case_sensitive, file, foreground, imported, managed, names, objects, right_to_left, unmanaged, user_defined
Type names	any, argument, asciz_table, asciz_string_table, boolean, character_set, color, color_table, compound_string, compound_string_table, float, font, font_table, fontset, icon, integer, integer_table, keysym, reason, rgb, single_float, string, string_table, translation_table, wide_character, xbitmapfile

Programmer-defined symbols, also called *identifiers*, are used to name the variables, procedures, lists, and widgets that you define in a UIL module. For the most part, you can choose any name that you like for these items, although the UIL compiler imposes three rules:

• A name must be unique within a module.

- A name must begin with one of the characters A–Z, a–z, $, or _ and may contain these characters as well as the digits 0–9.

- A name must be no longer than 32 characters.

Based on these rules, you can see that Alpha, $money, _tab, and moon44 are legal identifiers, while the following symbols are not: 1993, 3DogNight, next-char, and ask_the_user_to_save_her_work_callback.

22.3.6 Sections of a UIL Module

The main body of a UIL module is divided into several sections that group the different types of definitions and declarations. Each section begins with the section name and ends at the start of the next section. The list below gives a brief overview of the five sections supported by UIL: object, value, identifier, procedure, and list.

- An object section defines the widget hierarchy and widgets in a user interface. The widget definitions may include initial resource and callback settings. The other four sections are used to define named items that you use for these settings. The object section is covered in detail in Section 24.2.

- A value section contains definitions of variables used as resource settings in an object section or as the client_data argument to callbacks specified in the module. You can also retrieve most values directly from an application. UIL supports value types for almost every type of resource that can be specified in a widget definition. The value section is described in Section 24.3.

- An identifier section contains declarations of variables defined in the application program. Identifiers can represent values that do not have a corresponding UIL type or cannot be determined until run-time. The identifier section is explained in Section 24.6.

- A procedure section contains declarations of callback procedures that are used in the application program. Any routine specified as a callback in an object section must be declared in a procedure section. The procedure section is covered in Section 24.4.

- A list section defines lists of resource settings, callback settings (for different callbacks), callback procedures (for a single callback), and widget children. It is often convenient to define lists of commonly used settings. The list section is described in Section 24.5.

These different sections help to organize a UIL module and make it easier for the UIL compiler to parse a module. Unlike larger applications, Example 22-1 only contains value, procedure, and object sections. Without describing the syntax of these sections in detail, we'll look at how they are used in this module.

Defining Constants

The first section in Example 22-1 is a `value` section that defines a symbolic constant:

```
value
    form_margin : 3;
```

This section defines `form_margin`, whose value is the integer 3. You can place more than one definition in a `value` section. As you can see in the module, the second `value` section defines three more constants: the string `hello_string`, the font `hello_font`, and the pixmap `world_icon`. Although we've only defined integer, string, font, and pixmap values, UIL supports a number of additional data types. The complete set is described in Section 24.3.

You gain a couple of benefits by defining symbolic constants instead of always using literal values. First, the name of a value helps document your UIL module by making its purpose more clear. Second, you can easily change values that are used in more than one place, which is useful for changing strings or adjusting the layout of your interface.

Declaring Procedures

In UIL, a callback procedure is just a specialized type of value used to set a widget's callback resource. Like other constant values, you need to declare callbacks in a UIL module, but these declarations go in a `procedure` section instead. We say that callbacks are declared instead of defined (like values) because the callback definitions really occur in the application's source code. The following `procedure` section appears in our example:

```
procedure
    quit (string);
```

This section declares a callback named `quit` that takes a `string` argument. The actual callback is defined in the *hello_world.c* program. The argument in a procedure declaration specifies the type of the expected argument, similar to a function prototype in C. In some cases, the UIL compiler can convert a compatible value to the expected type. This capability is explained in Section suilarg. As with `value` sections, single `procedure` sections may contain multiple declarations. Section 24.4 describes the syntax of a `procedure` section in further detail.

Defining Widgets

Although constants and procedures are important, widget definitions usually constitute the majority of a UIL module. In UIL, you can define almost the entire widget hierarchy of your application, including top-level windows, dialog boxes, and menu systems. As we mentioned earlier, only the ApplicationShell widget of an application must be created with application code.

A widget definition occurs in an `object` section of a UIL module. While an `object` section can contain more than one widget definition, we have adopted the style of putting each widget definition in its own `object` section. This practice causes widget definitions to stand out, making UIL modules easier to read and modify. The widget hierarchy of our example application starts with the following definition:

```
object hello_main : XmForm
{
  controls {
    XmLabel       world;
    XmPushButton  hello;
  };
  arguments {
    XmNshadowThickness = 0;
    XmNresizePolicy = XmRESIZE_GROW;
    XmNmarginHeight = form_margin;
    XmNmarginWidth  = form_margin;
  };
};
```

This `object` section defines the Form widget `hello_main`, which is the parent of the other widgets in the module. A definition consists of a name, which is just a UIL identifier, and a widget type. You can use the name of any Motif widget or widget variant as a type name. For example, both `XmRowColumn` and `XmPulldownMenu` are legal widget types. (For a complete list of UIL widget types see Volume Six B, *Motif Reference Manual*.)

Widget definitions can contain three optional subsections that specify different widget attributes: `controls`, which specify a widget's children; `arguments`, which set the widget's initial resource settings; and `callbacks`, which specify the widget's callback procedures. Each subsection can occur only once per widget definition.

Our definition of the `hello_main` Form contains two of these subsections. The `controls` subsection indicates that the Form has two children: a Label and a PushButton. These two widgets are defined later in the module. The UIL compiler knows if a widget allows children, and for those that do, which widget types can be created as their children. If you try to include a child widget where it isn't allowed or supported, the UIL compiler generates an error message and the compilation fails, which is one of the advantages of describing a user interface in UIL rather than with a programming language like C.

You set widget resources, with the exception of callbacks, in a widget's `argument` subsection. This subsection in the `hello_main` widget illustrates several typical resource settings. We used a symbolic constant to set the last two resources so that it is easy to adjust the Form margins by changing the constant definition.

Callback resource settings are specified separately from other resources in the `callbacks` subsection of a widget definition. The `hello_main` widget does not have any callbacks, but the PushButton does. Here's the relevant part of its definition:

```
object hello : XmPushButton
{
  ! ... arguments ...
  callbacks {
    XmNactivateCallback = procedure quit ("Goodbye!");
  };
};
```

This subsection sets the PushButton's activate callback to the `quit()` procedure declared earlier in the module. The string argument `"Goodbye!"` is passed as `client_data` to the procedure when the callback is invoked. You'll see how this value is used later when we explain registering callback procedures with Mrm.

The widget definitions, along with the value definitions and procedure declaration, are all there is to the "Hello, World" module. As a whole, they form the interface description, which is the first step in developing an application with UIL. Our interface is quite simple; the interface for a real application would obviously be much more complex. The UIL modules for a real application are presented in Chapter 25, *Building an Application With UIL*.

22.4 Compiling the UIL Module

The UIL module must be compiled to produce a user interface description (UID) file. This compiled file is read at run-time by Mrm to obtain the interface description and create the widgets. The UID file is generated only if the source module is free of errors. On a UNIX system, we use the following command to compile our module:

```
uil -o hello_world.uid hello_world.uil
```

The -o option specifies the name of the output file. (This option, along with the rest of the compiler options, is explained in Chapter 23, *Using the UIL Compiler*). The name of the module to compile, in this case *hello_world.uil*, always follows the options. If the compilation is successful, the compiler generates a UID file. But if the compilation fails, the compiler prints one or more error messages and does not generate a UID file. Warning and informational messages can also be printed in either situation. The *hello_world.uil* module is free of errors and warnings, so this compilation does not print anything.

22.5 Structure of an Mrm Application

The structure of an application that uses Mrm and UIL is similar in most respects to that of an application that uses only Xt. The main difference is that you create the user interface with calls to Mrm procedures that encapsulate the Xt widget creation routines. Mrm also takes care of setting up any callbacks for your widgets. Other aspects of an Xt application, including toolkit initialization and event processing, are the same for both types of applications. Figure 22-5 illustrates the structure of an Mrm application.

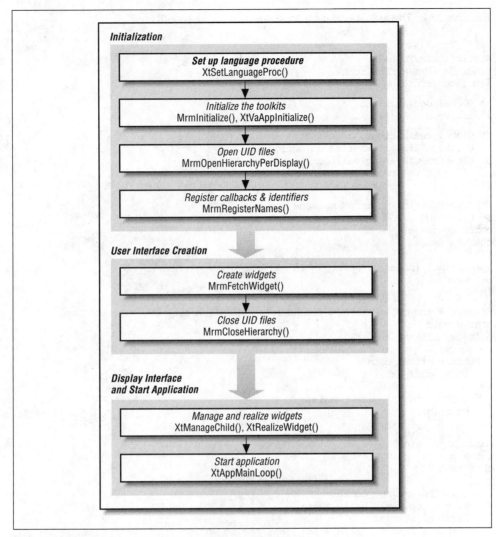

Figure 22-5. Structure of the hello_world.c Mrm application

In the remainder of this section, we take a closer look at each of these steps by examining the *hello_world.c* program shown in Example 22-2. In our explanation of this program, we concentrate only on how it differs from a standard Motif application. If you are unfamiliar with the details of a particular function call, see Chapter 2, *The Motif Programming Model*, in this book or see Volume Four, *X Toolkit Intrinsics Programming Manual*, and Volume Five, *X Toolkit Intrinsics Reference Manual*.

Example 22-2. The hello_world.c application program

```
/* hello_world.c --
 * Initialize X Toolkit creating ApplicationShell widget, then create
 * the user interface described in the hello_world.uid file.
```

Example 22-2. The hello_world.c application program (continued)

```c
 */

#include <Xm/Xm.h>
#include <Mrm/MrmPublic.h>
#include <stdio.h>

/* Global declarations. */
static void quit();

/* Global definitions. */
/* Callback list looks like an action list: */
static MrmRegisterArg callback_list[] = {
    { "quit", (XtPointer) quit },
};

/* error - Print an error message and exit. */
static void
error (message)
char *message;
{
    fprintf (stderr, "hello_world: %s\n", message);
    exit (1);
}

/* quit - The quit callback procedure.  Exits the program. */
static void
quit (w, client_data, call_data)
Widget w;
XtPointer client_data;
XtPointer call_data;
{
    puts ((char *) client_data);
    exit (0);
}

main (argc, argv)
int argc;
char *argv[];
{
    XtAppContext app_context;
    Widget toplevel, hello_main;
    Cardinal status;
    static String uid_file_list[] = { "hello_world" };
    MrmHierarchy hierarchy;
    MrmType class_code;

    XtSetLanguageProc (NULL, NULL, NULL);

    MrmInitialize();

    toplevel =
        XtVaAppInitialize (&app_context,   /* application context    */
                           "Demos",        /* application class name */
                           NULL, 0,        /* command line options   */
                           &argc, argv,    /* argc and argv          */
                           NULL,           /* fallback resources     */
                           NULL);          /* arg list               */

    status =
```

Example 22-2. The hello_world.c application program (continued)

```
                MrmOpenHierarchyPerDisplay (XtDisplay (toplevel),      /* display   */
                                            XtNumber (uid_file_list), /* num files */
                                            uid_file_list,            /* file list */
                                            NULL,                     /* OS data   */
                                            &hierarchy);              /* hierarchy */

        if (status != MrmSUCCESS)
            error ("Unable to open hello_world.uid file.");

        status = MrmRegisterNames (callback_list, XtNumber (callback_list));

        if (status != MrmSUCCESS)
            error ("Unable to register callback functions with Mrm.");

        status = MrmFetchWidget (hierarchy,             /* hierarchy to search */
                                 "hello_main",          /* object name         */
                                 toplevel,              /* parent              */
                                 &hello_main,           /* widget created      */
                                 &class_code);          /* widget's class code */

        if (status != MrmSUCCESS)
            error ("Unable to create interface from UID file");

        MrmCloseHierarchy (hierarchy);

        XtManageChild (hello_main);
        XtRealizeWidget (toplevel);

        XtAppMainLoop (app_context);
    }
```

Compiling this program is similar to any other Motif application—we just need to add the Mrm library to the link line. Because the program consists of a single file, we can use the following command to compile it on most UNIX systems:

```
    cc -o hello_world hello_world.c -lMrm -lXm -lXt -lX11
```

You should note that this program, like any program that uses Mrm, includes the file *<Mrm/MrmAppl.h>*. This file contains the function prototypes and constant definitions necessary to use Mrm. It also includes the *<Xm/Xm.h>* file, which contains the necessary declarations and definitions for the Motif library. When you use Mrm, there's no need to include a header file for each type of widget in the interface because the interface is not created directly in C. However, if your application uses any widget convenience functions, you do need to include the appropriate widget header file(s).

22.5.1 Initializing the Application

The first step for any Motif application is the initialization of the library components. The addition of Mrm doesn't change this—the initialization process is just a little more involved. As you can see in Figure 22-5, initialization is the most involved step in an Mrm application.

Initializing Mrm and Xt

Before initializing any of the libraries, the *hello_world.c* program calls XtSetLanguage-Proc(). This function sets the default procedure used to establish the run-time language environment. In X11R5 you should be sure to include this call before any other X-related initialization since other libraries depend on the language setting.

Next, we initialize the Mrm library by calling MrmInitialize(). This routine sets up internal data structures that Mrm needs to create widgets and should be called prior to initializing Xt.† You should call this function only once, preferably when your application is starting up. Unlike the other Mrm functions, MrmInitialize() does not return a status value.

After initializing Mrm, we're ready to initialize Xt with the following call:

```
toplevel =
  XtVaAppInitialize (&app_context,        /* application context    */
                     "Hello",             /* application class name */
                     NULL, 0,             /* command line options   */
                     &argc, argv,         /* argc and argv          */
                     NULL,                /* fallback resources     */
                     NULL);               /* arg list               */
```

This convenience function initializes the toolkit, creates an application context, opens the display, and creates the top-level ApplicationShell. This call is used by most Xt and Motif applications.

Opening the UID Files

Once both Mrm and Xt are initialized, we must open the UID files. We use the MrmOpen-HierarchyPerDisplay() function to do this.‡ The form of this function is:

```
Cardinal
MrmOpenHierarchyPerDisplay(display, num_files, file_list, os_data,
                           hierarchy)
    Display          *display;
    MrmCount         num_files;
    String           file_list[];
    MrmOsOpenParmPtr os_data[];
    MrmHierarchy     hierarchy;
```

The first argument is the Display; the second and third are the number of UID files and an array of filenames to open; the fourth is an operating system-dependent structure that should always be NULL (it is used internally by the UIL compiler); and the fifth is the address of an

---

† You may run across some code that initializes Mrm after Xt. While the order doesn't matter currently, the OSF documentation specifically states that you should initialize Mrm before Xt, so you should probably follow their advice.

‡ The Motif 1.2 MrmOpenHierarchyPerDisplay() function supersedes the Motif 1.1 MrmOpen-Hierarchy() function that you may encounter in older applications. Motif 1.2 still supports the older version to remain backwards compatible, but you shouldn't use it.

`MrmHierarchy` value that is filled in by the routine. Here's the call used by the "Hello, World" application to open its UID file:

```
String uid_file_list[] = { "hello_world" };
...
status =
  MrmOpenHierarchyPerDisplay (XtDisplay (toplevel),      /* display   */
                              XtNumber (uid_file_list),  /* num files */
                              uid_file_list,             /* file list */
                              NULL,                      /* OS data   */
                              &hierarchy);               /* hierarchy */
```

Although we need to open only one UID file in this situation, we use the `XtNumber()` macro so that we can easily add filenames to the `uid_file_list` array. While the "Hello World" interface is described in a single UID file, the interface of a more complex application is often broken into multiple UID files for organizational and internationalization purposes. (See Section 26.2 for a discussion on UIL module organization.)

Note that the *hello_world* filename is missing the *.uid* extension. We don't need to add it because Mrm supplies the extension by default. The filenames you pass to this function may be either full pathnames that begins with a slash or partial pathnames. Full pathnames are opened directly, while partial names like *hello_world* are located using a search path. Mrm gets the path from the UIDPATH environment variable if it is set. Otherwise, the following default path is used:†

%U%S
$XAPPLRESDIR/%L/uid/%N/%U%S
$XAPPLRESDIR/%l/uid/%N/%U%S
$XAPPLRESDIR/uid/%N/%U%S
$XAPPLRESDIR/%L/uid/%U%S
$XAPPLRESDIR/%l/uid/%U%S
$XAPPLRESDIR/uid/%U%S
$HOME/uid/%U%S
$HOME/%U%S
/usr/lib/X11/%L/uid/%N/%U%S
/usr/lib/X11/%l/uid/%N/%U%S
/usr/lib/X11/uid/%N/%U%S
/usr/lib/X11/%L/uid/%U%S
/usr/lib/X11/%l/uid/%U%S
/usr/lib/X11/uid/%U%S
/usr/include/X11/uid/%U%S

If XAPPLRESDIR is not set, Mrm uses HOME instead in the default search path. You might recognize some of the substitution characters in the default path, as they are also used in Xt resource file paths like XFILESEARCHPATH. In the path above, *%L* represents the LANG environment variable, *%N* represents the application class name, *%U* represents the UID filename in question, *%S* represents the filename suffix *.uid*, and *%l* represents the language part LANG. You can find a complete listing of substitutions in the `XtResolve-Pathname()` reference in Volume Five, *X Toolkit Intrinsics Reference Manual*.

---

†*/usr/lib/X11* and */usr/include/X11* are vendor specific and may therefore differ in some implementations.

Mrm may actually search the UID path twice for each partial pathname that you specify in the *file_list*. If Mrm cannot find the file with the suffix (%S) set to *.uid*, it tries again with no suffix, which is why we did not need to use the *.uid* suffix in our file list.

If MrmOpenHierarchyPerDisplay() successfully opens the specified files, it returns an MrmHierarchy value in the *hierarchy* argument and returns the status MrmSUCCESS. The *hierarchy* value, which is analogous to a FILE pointer, is used as an argument to other Mrm routines that read information from UID files. If Mrm fails to open a UID file, it prints an error message with XtAppWarning() and returns one of the following:

- MrmNOT_FOUND, if the file cannot be opened

- MrmNOT_VALID, if the file version is incorrect

- MrmDISPLAY_NOT_OPENED, if the display argument is NULL and the display has not been opened

- MrmFAILED, for any other failure

When a failure occurs, none of the UID files remain open and a valid *hierarchy* is not returned. If our example application detects an error, it simply prints an error message and exits.

We suggest that you always check the status value returned by MrmOpenHierarchyPerDisplay() and the other Mrm functions against MrmSUCCESS, as opposed to checking against one or more error values. By using this approach, you avoid the possibility of accidentally forgetting to check for one or more errors. If necessary, you can check for a specific error status value after checking against MrmSUCCESS.

Registering Callback Procedures

Recall that we set the XmNactivateCallback of the PushButton to quit() in the UIL module. The UIL compiler stores the name quit in the compiled UID file, but Mrm needs the address of the quit() procedure to add the callback to the widget at run-time. This raises the question, "Why not store the procedure's address in the UID file, instead of its name?" While this sounds like a reasonable solution, it would impose two undesirable restrictions. First, the UIL module would need to be recompiled any time we relink the application, and second, the compiled UID file would be usable only with that specific application on that particular host architecture.

By calling MrmRegisterNames(), the application provides Mrm with the information it needs to map the procedure names stored in the UID files to procedure addresses. Here is the call and associated data from Example 22-2:

```
static MrmRegisterArg callback_list[] = {
    { "quit", (XtPointer) quit },
};
    . . .
MrmRegisterNames (callback_list, XtNumber (callback_list));
```

MrmRegisterNames() has two arguments: an array of callbacks and the number of elements in that array. The callback_list is an array of mappings from procedure names to procedure addresses. The list is of type `MrmRegisterArg`, which takes the following form:

```
typedef struct {
    String name;
    XtPointer value;
} MrmRegisterArg, *MrmRegisterArglist;
```

When the button is created and Mrm encounters the `quit` procedure, Mrm can find the address associated with the name and add the callback in the usual Xt fashion as long as `MrmRegisterNames()` has been called. If the mappings are successfully registered, the routine returns `MrmSUCCESS` A value of `MrmFAILURE` is returned otherwise. This function only fails if it cannot allocate memory.

You can also register callbacks using `MrmRegisterNamesInHierarchy()`. This function is similar to `MrmRegisterNames()` and takes the following form:

```
Cardinal
MrmRegisterNamesInHierarchy(hierarchy, callback_list, num_callbacks)
    MrmHierarchy         hierarchy;
    MrmRegisterArglist   callback_list;
    MrmCount             num_callbacks;
```

The difference between the two routines is that this function takes an `MrmHierarchy` as an additional argument. An application may open more than one set of UID files; `MrmRegisterNamesInHierarchy()` allows you to limit the availability of callbacks to a particular set of UID files. In contrast, callbacks registered with `MrmRegisterNames()` can be referenced from any open hierarchy. As most applications open only a single hierarchy, `MrmRegisterNamesInHierarchy()` is rarely used. Even if you are working with an application that opens multiple hierarchies, you only need to use this function if two different callbacks are referenced by the same name in two separate hierarchies.

22.5.2 Creating the Interface

After the initialization is complete, it is time to create the user interface. Unlike a plain Motif application in which we need to create each widget individually, with Mrm we only need to make a single call to `MrmFetchWidget()`. The form of this function is:

```
Cardinal
MrmFetchWidget(hierarchy, widget_name, parent, widget_return,
                class_return)
    MrmHierarchy    hierarchy;
    String          widget_name;
    Widget          parent;
    Widget          *widget_return;
    MrmType         *class_return;
```

Mrm looks in the UID files specified by *hierarchy* for a widget named *widget_name* and creates it as a child of *parent*. The *parent* argument required in this call is the reason that we had to create the top-level ApplicationShell in our program before fetching any widgets. Mrm also recursively creates and manages all of the descendents of the specified widget, which is why only a single call is needed to create the entire widget hierarchy.

If all goes well, the routine puts the ID of the newly created widget in *widget_return* and returns a status of MrmSUCCESS. The other return parameter, *class_return*, holds the internal UIL class code of the widget. Note that the *class_return* value is not a pointer to the widget's class record.† If MrmFetchWidget() fails, it returns the following: MrmBAD_HIERARCHY, if the *hierarchy* argument is invalid; MrmNOT_FOUND, if the widget description cannot be found in the UID files; or Mrm_FAILURE for any other type of failure. To avoid crashing your application, you should always check the return status against MrmSUCCESS after fetching a widget hierarchy, as illustrated in Example 22-2. Although our example simply exits when an error occurs, a more robust application should attempt to recover from the problem.

The MrmFetchWidget() routine takes the place of all the widget calls needed in an application that doesn't use UIL and Mrm. As it creates widgets, Mrm automatically sets the resources and callbacks that are specified in the UIL module. Without Mrm, the interface would require many more function calls to create the individual widgets and resource values, set the resources, and add the callbacks. We fetch a Form named hello_main and create it as a child of the ApplicationShell with the following call:

```
status =
   MrmFetchWidget (hierarchy,        /* hierarchy to search */
                   "hello_main",     /* object name         */
                   toplevel,         /* parent              */
                   &hello_main,      /* widget created      */
                   &class_code);     /* widget's class      */
```

To keep this introduction easy to understand, we've only touched on the basics of the Mrm widget creation process. If you plan on doing any serious application development with UIL and Mrm, you need to understand the details of the entire process, which are discussed in Section 24.2.3.

Once an application has finished creating its interface, it should close the UID files by calling MrmCloseHierarchy(). This routine frees memory and closes the files that are associated with the Mrm hierarchy. Once you close a hierarchy, it cannot be used again. The function takes the MrmHierarchy to close as its only argument. The call from *hello_world.c* is simply:

```
MrmCloseHierarchy (hierarchy);
```

Although the function returns a status code like most of the other Mrm routines, failure to close the hierarchy usually doesn't have a negative impact on an application, so you can generally ignore the return status.‡ Technically, closing the hierarchy doesn't have much to do with creating the user interface, but it makes sense to free up some resources before entering the event loop. Larger applications that do not create the entire user interface at the start of the program should not close the hierarchy until the program exits. By using this technique, your program can avoid the extra time it would take to reopen the hierarchy when creating additional user interface components on demand.

---

† As of Motif 1.2, the *class_return* value is useless because the possible return values are not publicly defined in the Mrm header files. If you need to determine the type of the returned widget, you can use the appropriate XtIs*() or XmIs*() macro. For example, to verify that hello_main is really a Form, you would use XmIsForm (hello_main).

‡ Interestingly, MrmCloseHierarchy() unconditionally returns MrmSUCCESS in Motif 1.2.

22.5.3 Displaying the Interface

Now that the interface has been created, the remaining steps are the same as any other Motif application. When Mrm is creating the hierarchy with `MrmFetchWidget()`, it manages all of the widgets except the widget at the top of the hierarchy. To make the hierarchy visible, you must manage the widget that you fetch. The following line from Example 22-2 takes care of managing the widget:

```
XtManageChild (hello_main);
```

The widget management process in an Mrm application is different from the one used in a C code interface, where you must use the widget creation convenience routines that create and manage the widgets, or explicitly call `XtManageChild()` on each widget. However, Mrm makes one exception—it does not manage shell widgets in order to prevent menus and dialogs from popping up unexpectedly.

After managing the top-level widget, all that's left to do is realize the widgets and hand off control to Xt's event processing loop. The following two calls make these steps happen:

```
XtRealizeWidget (toplevel);
XtAppMainLoop (app_context);
```

Again, these calls are part of any Xt application, whether or not you use UIL and Mrm to create the interface. The call to `XtRealizeWidget()` creates windows for the widgets, initiates geometry management, and maps the windows. The call to `XtAppMainLoop()` causes the application to begin processing events from the X server.

22.6 Summary

The basic purpose of UIL and Mrm is to provide a way to describe and create a Motif user interface. UIL is a static user interface description language that allows you to define widget hierarchies and specify the resource and callback settings of those widgets. Mrm is a run-time library that provides the application interface for creating the widgets described in a UIL module. We considered some of the advantages and disadvantages of programming with UIL and Mrm. Understanding these tradeoffs can help you decide when UIL and Mrm are worth using.

Using UIL and Mrm involves writing the interface description, compiling the UIL module, and creating the interface with Mrm. Using a simple "Hello World" application, we looked at the process of writing an interface description in UIL to help you understand the structure and content of a UIL module. Likewise, we looked at the C code of the application to illustrate how a program that uses Mrm differs from a typical Motif application.

23

Using the UIL Compiler

This chapter explains how to use the UIL compiler. The chapter describes all of the different compiler options and looks at the different types of messages that the compiler can generate.

In This Chapter:

23
Using the UIL Compiler

The job of the UIL compiler is to turn a UIL module (or UIL source file) into a user interface description (UID) file, which contains a compact, Mrm-readable form of your UIL source module. The compiler checks the module for coding errors and potential problems and reports what it finds. As with any compilation process, the source module must be free of errors before the compiler can successfully generate a UID file.

The UIL compiler is invoked with the *uil* command, followed by the name of the file to be compiled. You may also provide a number of options. A typical compilation command looks like this:

```
uil interface.uil
```

In this simple invocation, the compiler outputs a file named *a.uid*, assuming there are no errors in *interface.uil*. (This default output name is similar to the *a.out* file generated by most C compilers.) For obvious reasons, the standard suffix for a UIL source module is *.uil* and the suffix for UID files is *.uid*. In addition, we use the suffix *.uih* for UIL include files.†

23.1 Compiler Options

The UIL compiler supports a number of options that affect the compilation process. These options are summarized in Table 23-1.

Table 23-1. UIL Compiler Options

Option	Description
-o *filename*	Name the UID output file
-I *path*	Specify an include file directory name
-v *filename*	Generate a listing file
-s	Set the locale when parsing strings
-w	Suppress warning and informational messages

---

† The OSF/Motif documentation uses *.uil* for both main modules and include files, but we feel that using *.uil* and *.uih* is easier to work with, as well as being more C-like.

Table 23-1. UIL Compiler Options (continued)

Option	Description
-m	Generate machine (UID) code in the listing
-wmd *filename*	Use the widget descriptions from *filename*

23.1.1 Output File

The -o option names the UID output file. The format of this option is -o *filename*. As we just mentioned, the default output filename is *a.uid*. You probably don't want a file named *a.uid*, just like you usually don't want an executable named *a.out*. The following command line shows the use of this option:

```
uil -o interface.uid interface.uil
```

Under Motif 1.2.x and earlier releases, the generated UID file is platform dependent. This means that you must recompile your UIL modules under each operating system that your application runs under. For OSF/Motif release 2.0 and later, UID files are platform independent, so you can use one instance of a UID file under any operating system that supports Motif 2.0.

23.1.2 Include Path

The -I option tells the UIL compiler where to look for include files. By default, the compiler looks in the same directory as the UIL source module and then in */usr/include*. You can use this option repeatedly to specify more than one include directory. Any directories you specify with the -I option are searched after the directory that contains the source module and before */usr/include*. Consider the following command:

```
uil -o menus.uid -I../uil_headers -I/global/uil menus.uil
```

The search path is . (the current directory), *../uil_headers*, */global/uil*, and */usr/include*. This path applies to all included files, even nested includes. The current directory always refers to the directory in which the compiler was invoked and does not change to the directory of include files.

23.1.3 Generate Listing

The -v option tells the compiler to generate a printable listing from the compiled module. The syntax for the option is -v *filename*. On UNIX systems, a filename of */dev/tty* can be used to send the listing to the terminal. The output contains a listing of the source module and all included files. A header with the compiler version, the date, the page number, and the module name appear on the top of each page. Here's an example of a listing generated using the –v option with a small module:

```
Motif Uil Compiler V2.0-000     Sat Apr 17 12:12:22 1993     Page 1
Module: listme
    1 (0)          /* listme.uil -- Test module for the -v option. */
    2 (0)
    3 (0)          module listme
    4 (0)
    5 (0)          include file 'listme.uih';
    1 (1)          procedure
    2 (1)            exit();
    6 (0)
    7 (0)          object lister : XmList { };
    8 (0)
    9 (0)          end module;

    File (0)     listme.uil
    File (1)     listme.uih
```

The first column of the listing is the line number, and the second column is a number representing the file that contains the line. There is a key of file names and numbers at the end of the listing. If the compiler detects any errors or warnings, the messages appear interspersed with the lines in the listing, and a summary of the number of each type of message is printed at the end.

23.1.4 Set Locale

The –s option causes the compiler to set the locale based on the LANG environment variable. The setting affects how the compiler parses multibyte string values. On ANSI-C systems, the locale is set with a call to `setlocale` (`LC_ALL`, `""`). Note, however, that if the module-wide `character_set` option is set, then the –s option has no effect. (The `character_set` option is described in Chapter 22, *Introduction to UIL*.) If you are going to use the –s option, you should specify the character set in the codeset portion of the LANG environment variable.†

23.1.5 Suppress Warnings

The –w option suppresses the printing of warning and informational messages. Normally the compiler prints errors, warnings, and informational messages. Error messages are always printed and cannot be suppressed. This option can be useful if your module has a lot of errors and warnings and you want to concentrate the on errors only. Section 23.2 describes the different types of messages in more detail.

---

† In early releases of Motif 1.2, the UIL compiler may crash if you use the –s option when LANG is set to a value that is not supported by the operating system. This problem is fixed as of release 1.2.3.

Using the
UIL Compiler

23.1.6 Machine Listing

The -m option tells the compiler to print the information written to the UID file along with the module listing. This option has no effect unless the -v option is also used. The option was probably intended to help debug the compiler. It is useful for determining exactly how the compiler interprets a particular statement and approximately how much storage is used for each definition in the module. If a module contains errors, the compiler cannot generate a machine listing because it doesn't generate a UID file.

23.1.7 Use WML Description

The -wmd option directs the compiler to load an alternate widget set description from a compiled Widget Meta-Language (WML) description file. The format of this option is -wmd *filename*. By default, the compiler uses a set of built-in tables that describe the OSF/Motif widget set. This option is rarely used because few people write widget set descriptions in WML. Recently, however, some companies have started to ship Widget Meta-Language Database (WMD) files with their custom widget sets, so use of this option will probably increase.

23.2 Errors, Warnings, and Informational Messages

As we mentioned, the UIL compiler can generate several different types of messages: severe errors, regular errors, warnings, and informational messages. The type of each message is indicated by a prefix of either Severe, Error, Warning, or Info. When a message is generated as a result of a problem in the module (as opposed to, say, a system error), the message is printed with the line number and source line that triggered the problem. When a compilation results in one or more of these messages, a summary of the number of occurrences of each type is output at the end of the compilation.

23.2.1 Severe Error Messages

Severe errors occur when something prevents the UIL compiler from continuing. Severe errors commonly occur when an input or output file cannot be opened or an internal compiler error is detected. Severe errors can also occur after too many regular errors are encountered. Unlike the other types of problems, severe errors never contain an associated line number, even when the error occurs because an include file cannot be found. For example, if you attempt to compile a nonexistent file or write a listing to a non-writable directory, UIL generates the following errors:

```
% uil bogus.uil
Severe: error opening source file: bogus.uil

% uil -v /cant-write listme.uil
Severe: error opening listing file: /cant-write
```

23.2.2 Regular Error Messages

The most common causes of other errors are syntax mistakes, type mismatch problems, and identifier redefinitions. Regular errors are almost always associated with a specific source line. Example 23-1 shows a UIL module with one of each of these types of errors.

Example 23-1. The buggy.uil module

```
module buggy

object button : XmPushButton { };;

value
  duplicate : 10;
  duplicate : "whoops!";

object label : XmLabel {
  arguments {
    XmNlabelString = button;
  };
};

end module;
```

An attempt to compile this module results in the following output:

```
        object button : XmPushButton { };;
                                         *
Error: unexpected SEMICOLON token seen - parsing resumes after ";"
              line: 3  file: buggy.uil
          duplicate : "whoops!";
          *
Error: name duplicate previously defined as integer
              line: 7  file: buggy.uil
          XmNlabelString = button;
          *
Error: found widget_ref widget when expecting compound_string value
              line: 11  file: buggy.uil
Info: no UID file was produced
Info: errors: 3  warnings: 0  informationals: 1
```

The compiler prints an asterisk (*) under the offending line to show you exactly where the error occurred. Note that because errors were detected, the compiler did not produce a UID file.

23.2.3 Warning Messages

Warning messages turn up most often when part of a widget definition does not make sense to the compiler. Since warnings are not critical problems, a UID file is still produced when they occur. You shouldn't ignore warnings, as they typically indicate a misunderstanding of some kind. For example, in Example 23-2 we incorrectly try to create a List gadget and use the XmNset resource in a Label widget.

Example 23-2. The mistakes.uil module

```
module mistakes

object files : XmList gadget { };

object label : XmLabel {
  arguments {
    XmNset = true;
  };
};

end module;
```

Running this module through the compiler produces the following warnings:

```
        object files : XmList gadget { };
                              *
Warning: XmList gadget is not supported - XmList widget will be used instead
                line: 3  file: warn.uil
          XmNset = true;
                 *
Warning: the XmNset argument is not supported for the XmLabel object
                line: 7  file: warn.uil
Info: errors: 0  warnings: 2  informationals: 0
```

Warning messages are usually associated with a line in the source module. Warnings are also generated if you specify an unknown option to the *uil* command or when the compiler cannot close a file.

23.2.4 Informational Messages

The UIL compiler uses informational messages to let you know about the state of the compilation. The compiler also generates an informational message if you set the same resource or callback more than once. You've already seen two of the three possible informational messages in the example output from above. The module in Example 23-3 demonstrates the third situation.

Example 23-3. The infos.uil module

```
module infos

list base : arguments {
  XmNlabelString = "original";
};

object main_widget : XmLabel {
  arguments {
    arguments base;
    XmNlabelString = "actual";
  };
};
end module;
```

Motif Programming Manual

The compiler output for this module is as follows:†

```
        XmNlabelString = "original";
                              *
Info: this XmNlabelString argument supersedes a previous definition in this
argument list
                   line: 4  file: info.uil
Info: errors: 0  warnings: 0  informationals: 1
```

Although you may set the same resource twice by mistake, you may want to do it intentionally. This technique can be used (as above) to override the value of a resource obtained from a reusable list of resources, as described in Section 24.5.

23.3 Summary

The UIL compiler is needed to convert a UIL source module into a UID file that can be read at run-time by Mrm. The *uil* command invokes the compiler; it is typically used with the −o *filename* option to specify the output UID file name. The compiler also supports a number of other options that affect the output of the compilation. A compilation can result in messages that report severe errors, regular errors, warnings, and informational messages. A UID file is never produced when one or more errors occur, but can still be generated when only warnings or informational messages occur.

---

† These informational messages were generated by an early version of the Motif 1.2 compiler, which incorrectly outputs the line of the original resource rather than the line that superseded it.

24

Creating a User Interface With UIL

This chapter expands upon the overview of UIL and Mrm presented earlier.
The syntax and usage of UIL are described in detail, along with the Mrm
functions associated with the various UIL constructs.

In This Chapter:

Creating a User Interface With UIL

Now that you have a basic understanding of how UIL and Mrm are used to define and create a user interface, we can turn to the details of using UIL and Mrm. Recall that a UIL module can contain five different types of sections: the `object` section for defining widgets; the `value` section for defining resource values and callback arguments; the `identifier` section for declaring application variables exported to UIL; the `procedure` section for declaring callbacks; and the `list` section for defining lists·of widgets, resource settings, callback settings, and callback routines.

An application accesses UIL definitions using the Mrm library. Mrm functions serve three basic purposes: file handling, importing information from UIL, and exporting information to UIL. Examples of each of these types of functionality appear in the *hello_world.c* program in Chapter 22, *Introduction to UIL*. The functions that import information create widgets that are defined in `object` sections and retrieve data that is defined in `value` sections. The functions that export information register callbacks that are declared in `procedure` sections and application data that is declared in `identifier` sections. There are no Mrm functions that work with UIL lists, because unlike other UIL entities, lists are strictly internal to a module.

In this chapter, we describe the role of UIL in each major step of creating an application:

- Defining and creating the widgets that make up an interface

- Defining and fetching values (resources)

- Working with widget callbacks

We also talk about two other related topics:

- Using lists of widgets, resources, and callbacks

- Exporting application-created data to UIL

The vast amount of information that is covered in this chapter makes it impractical to illustrate all of the UIL and Mrm concepts with a single UIL module or application. Such an application would be quite large and unrealistic. Therefore, we demonstrate the features of UIL and Mrm with many small, self-contained examples. To facilitate this approach, we've put together a small C program that you can use to try out the various UIL modules and callback functions we discuss.

24.1 Viewing UIL Examples

The *showuid.c* program is designed to display a portion of a user interface that is defined in a UID file. The idea is to allow you to examine the output of different UIL modules without needing a separate program for every module. The complete source code of this program appears in Example 24-1.

Example 24-1. The showuid.c program

```
/* showuid.c --
 * Program to show the interface defined in a UID file.
 */

#include <stdio.h>
#include <Mrm/MrmAppl.h>

void quit();
void print();

static MrmRegisterArg callback_list[] = {
    { "quit",       (XtPointer) quit },
    { "print",      (XtPointer) print },
  /* Add additional callback procedures here... */
};

typedef struct {
    String root_widget_name;
} app_data_t;

static app_data_t app_data;

static XtResource resources[] = {
    { "root", "Root", XmRString, sizeof(String),
        XtOffsetOf (app_data_t,root_widget_name), XmRString,
        (XtPointer) "root" },
};

static XrmOptionDescRec options[] = {
    { "-root", "root", XrmoptionSepArg, NULL },
};

void
quit (w, client_data, call_data)
Widget     w;
XtPointer client_data;
XtPointer call_data;
{
    exit (0);
}

void
print (w, client_data, call_data)
Widget     w;
XtPointer client_data;
XtPointer call_data;
{
    char *message = (char *) client_data;
    puts (message);
}
```

Example 24-1. The showuid.c program (continued)

```
main (argc, argv)
int    argc;
char *argv[ ];
{
    XtAppContext    app_context;
    Widget          toplevel;
    Widget          root_widget;
    Cardinal        status;
    MrmHierarchy    hierarchy;
    MrmType         class_code;

    XtSetLanguageProc (NULL, NULL, NULL);

    MrmInitialize();

    toplevel = XtVaAppInitialize (&app_context, "Demos", options,
        XtNumber(options), &argc, argv, NULL, NULL);

    XtGetApplicationResources (toplevel, &app_data, resources,
        XtNumber(resources), NULL, 0);

    /* Check number of args after Xt and App have removed their options. */
    if (argc < 2) {
        fprintf (stderr,
            "usage: showuid [Xt options] [-root name] uidfiles ...\n");
        exit (1);
    }

    /* Use argc and arv to obtain UID file names from the command line.
       (Most applications use an internal static array of names.) */
    status = MrmOpenHierarchyPerDisplay (XtDisplay (toplevel), argc - 1,
        argv + 1, NULL, &hierarchy);

    if (status != MrmSUCCESS) {
        XtAppError (app_context, "MrmOpenHierarchyPerDisplay failed");
        exit (1);
    }

    MrmRegisterNames (callback_list, XtNumber (callback_list));

    status = MrmFetchWidget (hierarchy, app_data.root_widget_name,
        toplevel, &root_widget, &class_code);

    if (status != MrmSUCCESS) {
        XtAppError (app_context, "MrmFetchWidget failed");
        exit (1);
    }

    MrmCloseHierarchy (hierarchy);

    XtManageChild (root_widget);
    XtRealizeWidget (toplevel);

    XtAppMainLoop (app_context);
}
```

This program is similar to the *hello_world.c* program in Chapter 22, *Introduction to UIL*. However, we've made a few small changes to make the program flexible enough to accommodate our needs in this chapter. The main() procedure follows the steps required of any

Mrm program except that the UID files containing the interface description and the name of the widget to be created are not hard-coded in the program. This information is now specified on the command line, so the program can be used to display different UID files and widget trees.

The list of UID files passed to `MrmOpenHierarchyPerDisplay()` is taken directly from the command line. Since `argv` is in the format expected by the routine, we pass it directly to the routine, after adding 1 to skip the name of program in `argv[0]`; We then subtract 1 from `argc` to account for the difference. `MrmOpenHierarchyPer-Display()` is called after the other command-line arguments have been removed by `Xt-VaAppInitialize()` and `XtGetApplicationResources()`.

You can specify the name of the widget hierarchy created by the program with the `-root` option. Xt takes care of parsing the command-line switch and putting the value into the `app_data` structure. (See Volume Four, *X Toolkit Intrinsics Programming Manual*, for detailed information on this process.) If you do not specify the `-root` option, the application uses `root` as the default name. In most of the modules in this chapter, we use the default name `root` for the top-level widget.

The following command compiles the *showuid* program:

```
cc -o showuid showuid.c -lMrm -lXm -lXt -lX11
```

To display a UID file, use the following command:

```
showuid -root form hello_world.uid
```

The command-line options tell the command to open a description file named *hello_world.uid* and create the widget hierarchy rooted at the widget named `form`. Mrm searches for the UID files specified on the command line using the UIDPATH environment variable if it is set, or the default path described in Chapter 22. It is easy to run the command on a file in the current directory, since the current directory is included in the default search path. Remember that you can also specify an absolute path to a UID file.

We recommend that you use the *showuid* program for trying out our examples as well as experimenting on your own. In addition, the program is an excellent starting point for your own Mrm programs. The basic Mrm framework is already in place. You only need to add the callbacks that implement your application's functionality and provide an array of UID files, instead of taking them from the command line.

24.2 Defining and Creating Widgets

As you know, the main purpose of a UIL module is to define the widgets of a user interface. We mentioned earlier that widget definitions always occur in an `object` section of a UIL module, which begins with the keyword `object` followed by one or more widget definitions. The complete form of a widget definition is shown in Figure 24-1.

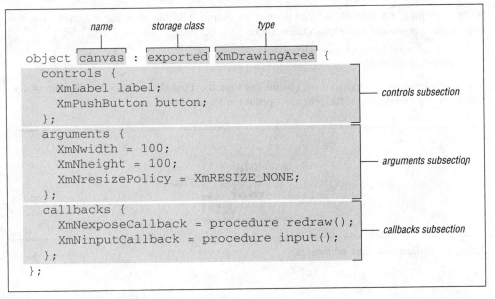

Figure 24-1. Structure of a widget definition

The figure may seem a little imposing at first, but if we ignore all the optional parts of the definition, it is really quite simple. Example 24-2 defines a PushButton widget named `root` using only the required parts of a definition. This module, along with the `showuid.c` program, comprise all the source necessary for a complete application.

Example 24-2. The trivial.uil module

```
/* trivial.uil -- Illustrate a minimal widget declaration. */

module trivial

object root : XmPushButton { };

end module;
```

The widget definition in Example 24-2 consists of three parts, not including the `object` keyword. The definition begins with the widget name, which is a programmer-defined identifier. The name of the widget in this example is `root`. The type of widget follows the name; a colon separates the name and the type. Legal widget types include all of the standard Motif widgets as well as the names of specific instances of Motif widgets, such as `XmMenuBar` (a RowColumn) or `XmQuestionDialog` (a MessageBox).† The last, and usually largest, part of a widget definition is made up of the widget attributes. In our simple definition, we do not specify any attributes, but even so, we must include the curly braces that would surround them. Widget definitions always end with a semicolon.

---

† You can find a complete list of widget type names in Appendix D, *Table of UIL Objects*, of Volume Six B, *Motif Reference Manual*. UIL also supports non-Motif widgets with the `user_defined` type, which we explain later in Chapter 26, *Advanced UIL Programming*.

After compiling the module, we can display its output with the *showuid* program. The following two commands accomplish these steps:

```
uil -o trivial.uid trivial.uil
showuid trivial
```

You don't need to use the -root option because the PushButton uses the default widget name root. The output of the program appears in Figure 24-2.

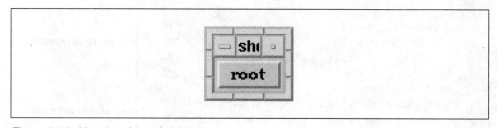

Figure 24-2. User interface of trivial.uil

24.2.1 Specifying Widget Attributes

A bare-bones widget definition like the one in the previous example is rare in even the simplest Motif applications. To create a useful interface, you need a hierarchy of customized widgets, which is where widget attributes enter the picture. When you define a widget in UIL, you can specify children and resources in subsections of its attribute section. The controls subsection contains a list of a manager widget's children, and the arguments and callbacks subsections contain lists of the widget's resource and callback settings. Each subsection begins with the subsection name followed by a list of children, resources, or callback settings. Each subsection can occur only once in a single widget definition, but they can occur in any order.

Children

The controls subsection of a widget definition is where you specify the children of the widget. The name of this subsection was chosen because the parent widget manages, or *controls*, the child widgets. The module in Example 24-3 shows a typical usage of the controls subsection.

Example 24-3. The kids.uil module

```
/* kids.uil -- Simple demonstration of the controls subsection. */
module kids
object top : XmTextField { };
object bottom : XmPushButton { };
object root : XmPanedWindow {
  controls {
```

Example 24-3. The kids.uil module (continued)

```
    XmTextField top;
    XmPushButton bottom;
  };
};

end module;
```

In this example, we define three widgets: a TextField, a PushButton, and a PanedWindow. The `controls` subsection of the PanedWindow specifies that the TextField and the Push-Button are its children. The example illustrates the form of an entry in a `controls` subsection, where the widget type is followed by the name of a widget and a semicolon. Even though the type of the widget has already been specified in a separate widget definition, you must specify it again here. In this example, we define the children before their parent, but widgets referenced in a `controls` subsection can be defined anywhere in the UIL module because UIL allows forward references. The output of the module is shown in Figure 24-3, where we typed some text in the TextField.

Figure 24-3. User interface of kids.uil

Each of the three widget definitions begins with `object`, which means that each of them is in a separate object section. Technically, you only need the `object` keyword before the first widget in consecutive definitions. Although the convention of placing an `object` keyword before each definition requires a bit more typing, it makes definitions easier to recognize and move around in a module.

One advantage of defining your interface with UIL is that the compiler always makes sure that the children listed in a `controls` subsection are allowed for that parent. If you try to use an unsupported widget, the UIL compiler issues an error message, and the compilation fails.† In contrast, when you create widgets directly with Xt, there is no compile-time checking that makes sure the widget hierarchy is valid. Many of the Motif manager widgets provide some form of run-time checking, but we don't recommend relying on this behavior.

The presence of a widget definition in a UIL module does not necessarily mean that the widget is created at run-time. A widget is not created until you fetch it directly with `Mrm-FetchWidget()` or `MrmFetchWidgetOverride()`, or it appears in a widget hierarchy fetched with one of these routines. By referencing a widget in a `controls` subsection, you make it part of a widget hierarchy. When the hierarchy is fetched, all of the widgets in the

---

† Appendix D, *Table of UIL Objects*, in Volume Six B, *Motif Reference Manual*, contains a complete listing of the Motif widgets and the children that they support.

hierarchy are created. (The widget creation process is described in Section 24.2.3.) If a widget is defined, but never referenced or fetched from an application, it is never created.

When a widget is created based on a UIL definition, you are not limited to creating a single instance of it. Every call to `MrmFetchWidget()` or `MrmFetchWidgetOverride()` results in the creation of a new widget, assuming a definition is found. In addition, each widget reference in a `controls` subsection results in the creation of an instance of that widget when the enclosing hierarchy is fetched. This behavior lets you reuse a widget as often as necessary. You can reuse widgets at any level, from a single widget to an entire hierarchy.

24.2.1.0.1 In-line widget definitions.

You can place a complete widget definition inside a `controls` subsection, instead of referencing a widget defined elsewhere. For example, we can move the child widget definitions from Example 24-3 into the body of the PanedWindow definition, as shown in the following fragment:

```
object root : XmPanedWindow {
  controls {
    top : XmText { };
    bottom : XmPushButton { };
  };
};
```

The form of an in-line widget definition is the same as a widget definition in an `object` section. In-line definitions are most useful for specifying widget children that have few or no attributes. While larger definitions are allowed, they tend to clutter up the parent definition, which makes both reading and editing the module more difficult.

Unlike widgets defined in an object section, the name of an in-line widget is optional. This feature is most frequently used in menu definitions, as the following fragment illustrates:

```
object file_menu : XmPulldownMenu {
  controls {
    XmPushButton open;
    XmPushButton print;
    XmSeparator { };
    XmPushButton quit;
  };
};
```

This definition contains an unnamed Separator, along with references to three PushButtons that are defined elsewhere. In this situation, it is worthwhile to create a stand-alone definition for the Separator because it doesn't have any attributes. The UIL compiler automatically generates a name when you don't provide one. The format of these names is not documented and can vary from one compilation to the next. If a widget does not have a well-defined name, neither you nor the users of your application can customize it using X resource files. If you want to allow such customizations, you must explicitly name the widget.

24.2.1.0.2 Widget or gadget. When you define an object of a class that has both a widget and a gadget variant, you can specify in the definition which type is created. Motif supports widget and gadget variants of the Label, PushButton, ToggleButton, ArrowButton, CascadeButton, and Separator objects. As we explained in Section 22.3.2, you can specify the default type for each class in the `objects` option setting at the top of a module. If you do not set this option, widgets are used by default. The following code fragment demonstrates how to define a PushButtonGadget, regardless of the default PushButton type setting:

```
object push_me : XmPushButton gadget { };
```

UIL also supports the type names with `Gadget` appended, so the following definition is also legal:

```
object toggle_me : XmToggleButtonGadget { };
```

You can use the `widget` keyword to ensure that the widget version of an object is created, as shown in the following fragment:

```
object this_way : XmArrowButton widget { };
```

This syntax is the only way to specify a widget variant; the UIL compiler does not recognize type names such as `XmArrowButtonWidget`.

24.2.1.0.3 Automatically-created children. Several Motif widgets are compound objects, which means that they are composed of one or more simpler widgets. For example, the File-SelectionBox is a complete dialog box packaged as a widget; it contains Lists, TextFields, Labels and PushButtons. As of Motif 1.2, UIL lets you access and customize the automatically-created children of a compound object. Like other child widgets, you reference automatically-created children in the `controls` subsection of their parent, although the syntax is slightly different. The following code fragment illustrates this syntax:

```
object yes_or_no : XmQuestionDialog {
  controls {
    Xm_OK {
      arguments {
        XmNlabelType = XmPIXMAP;
        XmNlabelPixmap = xbitmapfile ('thumb_up.xbm');
      };
    };
  };
};
```

This fragment shows how to make the **OK** PushButtons in a QuestionDialog display an icon instead of the usual text string. The name of this button is Xm_OK. The name is followed by attribute settings, just like any other widget definition. Table 24-1 lists the names of all the automatically-created children of each of the Motif composite widgets.

Table 24-1. Automatically-created Children of Motif Widgets

Widget	Child Names
XmScale	Xm_Title
XmScrolledWindow	Xm_VertScrollBar, Xm_HorScrollBar
XmOptionMenu	Xm_OptionLabel, Xm_OptionButton
XmPopupMenu	Xm_TearOffControl
XmPulldownMenu	Xm_TearOffControl
XmMainWindow	Xm_Separator1, Xm_Separator2, Xm_Separator3
XmMessageBox	Xm_Symbol, Xm_Separator, Xm_Message, Xm_OK, Xm_Cancel, Xm_Help
XmSelectionBox	Xm_Items, Xm_ItemsList, Xm_Selection, Xm_Text, Xm_Separator, Xm_OK, Xm_Apply, Xm_Cancel, Xm_Help
XmFileSelectionBox	Xm_Items, Xm_ItemsList, Xm_Separator, Xm_OK, Xm_Cancel, Xm_Help, Xm_FilterLabel, Xm_Filter, Xm_FilterText, Xm_DirList, Xm_Dir

Remember that the Motif compound objects provide resources that allow you to set the commonly-used resources of their children. For example, the XmNmessageString resource of the QuestionDialog is the same as the XmNlabelString resource of its Xm_Message child. It is better to set the resource on the compound object rather than on the child, so we suggest that before you set a resource on an automatically-created child, you make sure that the resource cannnot be set in the arguments subsection of the parent.

24.2.1.0.4 Unmanaged children. Mrm automatically manages all of the widgets that you fetch with the exception of dialogs, menus, and the widget at the top of the fetched hierarchy. You can prevent Mrm from managing individual widgets by preceding their controls subsection entry with the unmanaged keyword, as shown in the following fragments:

```
object panel : XmRowColumn {
  controls {
    XmPushButton visible;
    unmanaged XmPushButton invisible;
  };
};

object error : XmErrorDialog {
  controls {
    Xm_Help unmanaged { };
  };
};
```

When the panel RowColumn widget is created, both PushButtons are created, but only the first one is managed. When you want to manage the other button, your application code must handle it, just like it must manage dialogs and popup menus. You can also unmanage automatically-created children as shown in the second object definition above. In this case, the unmanaged keyword follows the name of the automatically-created widget instead of pre-ceding it.

Resources

In UIL, you specify resources (with the exception of callbacks) in the `arguments` subsec-tion of a widget definition. The UIL module in Example 24-4 shows several examples of resource settings.

Example 24-4. The resource.uil module

```
/* resource.uil - Basic example of setting widget resources. */

module resource

object root : XmPushButton {
  arguments {
    XmNlabelString = "Candy-Gram!";
    XmNmarginWidth = 350;
    XmNmarginHeight = 350;
    XmNunitType = Xm100TH_MILLIMETERS;
    XmNforeground = color ('SlateGrey');
    XmNbackground = color ('LemonChiffon');
    XmNfontList = font ('*times-bold-r-normal*180-100-100*');
  };
};

end module;
```

In this example, we set several PushButton resources. These settings demonstrate the use of a number of UIL data types. However, we're not going to discuss the data types right now, as they are covered later in Section 24.3. The basic format of each setting is the same. Each consists of a resource name, an equal sign (=), a value, and a semicolon. Figure 24-4 shows the output of this example, which is quite different from the simple PushButtons in our ear-lier examples.

Figure 24-4. User interface of resource.uil

Creating a PushButton with the same resource settings in application code requires a lot more work. You need to declare variables for the `XmString`, `Color`, and `XmFontList` values and then you must create or allocate each of these values by calling various Xm, Xt, and X routines. After the values are created, you can create the widget. Any values copied by the widget should be freed. When you use UIL and Mrm, all of this work boils down to the much simpler widget definition shown above and a single call to `MrmFetchWidget()`.

The UIL compiler checks resource names, so if you specify a resource that is not supported by a widget, the compiler generates an error message. In contrast, if you try to set an unsupported resource with `XtSetValues()`, Xt ignores the resource and does not generate an error. By using UIL, you can also avoid setting a resource to the wrong type of value because the UIL compiler ensures that the type of resource matches the type of the value you assign to it. (Appendix C, *Table of Motif Resources*, in Volume Six B, *Motif Reference Manual*, contains a complete list of Motif widget resources and their associated types.) Once again, this type of error is not caught in C code when you use `XtSetValues()` or `XtVaSet-Values()`. Unrecognized resource names are also ignored in X resource files.

The disadvantages of specifying resource values in code and in resource files may give you the impression that you should always set resources from a UIL module. However, there are also disadvantages to setting resources in UIL. The main disadvantage is that users of your application cannot override UIL settings with their own resource settings. In Section 26.3 we take a closer look at the issues involved in deciding whether to set a resource in UIL, application code, or an X resource file.

24.2.1.0.5 Automatic conversions. The type of a value you assign to a resource must match the type of the resource. However, there are a few cases in which the UIL compiler automatically converts a value to the appropriate type. The supported conversions are shown in Table 24-2.

Table 24-2. Automatic Type Conversions Performed by UIL

Value Type	Automatically Converted To
string	compound_string
asciz_string_table	compound_string_table
font	font_list
fontset	font_list
icon	pixmap
xbitmapfile	pixmap
rgb	color

This feature is most useful when you are working with string and font values. Example 24-4 relies on the `string` to `compound_string` (`XmString`) conversion for setting the `XmNlabelString` resource.

24.2.1.0.6 Coupled resources. Several of the Motif widgets have array resources for which there is an associated count resource that indicates the size of the table. These resource pairs are given special treatment by the UIL compiler. Whenever you set one of the resources listed in Table 24-3, UIL automatically sets the corresponding count resource for you.

Table 24-3. Coupled Resources in UIL

Widget	Table Resource	Coupled Count Resource
XmList	XmNitems	XmNitemCount
XmList	XmNselectedItems	XmNselectedItemCount
XmSelectionBox	XmNlistItems	XmNlistItemCount
XmCommand	XmNhistoryItems	XmNhistoryItemCount
XmFileSelectionBox	XmNdirListItems	XmNdirListItemCount
XmFileSelectionBox	XmNfileListItems	XmNfileListItemCount
XmText	XmNselectionArray	XmNselectionArrayCount
XmTextField	XmNselectionArray	XmNselectionArrayCount

The following code fragment illustrates this feature:

```
object toppings : XmScrolledList {
    arguments {
        XmNitems = string_table ("Anchovies", "Extra Cheese", "Ham",
            "Mushroom", "Pepperoni", "Peppers", "Pineapple", "Sausage");
        XmNselectedItems = string_table ("Ham", "Pineapple");
        XmNvisibleItemCount = 6;
    };
};
```

This fragment sets two `XmStringTable` resources in a List widget. We do not have to set the `XmNitemCount` or `XmNselectedItemCount` resources because the UIL compiler sets them automatically.

Callbacks

Although callbacks are really just another type of resource, you specify them separately in the `callbacks` subsection of a widget definition. Since callback functions are implemented in application code, the process of setting up callbacks involves a few more steps than the specification of other attributes. We explained the basics of this process in Chapter 22, *Introduction to UIL*. In this section, we describe how to add a callback procedure to a widget. In Section 24.4, we discuss declaring callbacks, specifying callback arguments, and registering callbacks with Mrm.

Setting a callback in a UIL module requires two steps. First, you declare the callback in a `procedure` section, and then you specify the callback in a widget definition. The module in Example 24-5 illustrates this process.

Example 24-5. The cb.uil module

```
/* cb.uil - Plain and simple callback setting example. */

module cb

procedure
    print (string);
    quit();

object Hello : XmPushButton {
```

Example 24-5. The cb.uil module (continued)

```
    callbacks {
      XmNactivateCallback = procedure print ("hello!");
    };
};

object Goodbye : XmPushButton {
  callbacks {
    XmNactivateCallback = procedures {
      print ("goodbye!");
      quit();
    };
  };
};

object root : XmRowColumn {
  controls {
    XmPushButton Hello;
    XmPushButton Goodbye;
  };
};

end module;
```

The callback declarations in the `procedure` section tell the UIL compiler that the procedures are defined externally in the application program. A callback setting looks similar to a resource setting; it always begins with the name of a callback, such as `XmNactivate-Callback`, and is followed by an equal sign. The right-hand side of the setting varies depending on the number of callback procedures you are specifying. A single callback is specified with the keyword `procedure` followed by the callback invocation. Multiple callbacks are specified with the keyword `procedures` followed by a list of callback invocations.

In Example 24-5, the `XmNactivateCallback` of the **Hello** PushButton is set to the single callback procedure `print()`, while the `XmNactivateCallback` of the **Goodbye** PushButton is set to the two callbacks `print()` and `quit()`. You cannot specify multiple callbacks by setting the same callback more than once because when you set the same resource or callback multiple times, only the last setting is used. The Xt specification doesn't guarantee the order in which callbacks are called, as widgets can reorder callback lists internally. In nearly all cases, however, callbacks are called in the order that they are listed.

As with resource settings in an `arguments` section, the UIL compiler makes sure that the callbacks you set in a `callbacks` subsection exist and are supported by the widget. When you add callbacks in application code, there is nothing to prevent you from setting a callback on a widget that does not support it. This problem is not caught at compile-time or run-time by Xt.

24.2.2 Sharing Widgets Among Modules

When the source code for an application grows beyond a certain size, you normally split it into multiple source files. You can use the same technique to divide an interface description among multiple UIL modules. When you use this technique, one module must often reference a widget that is defined in another module. UIL supports this technique by allowing you to export a widget definition from one module and import, or reference, the definition in another module. A widget definition is exported by using the optional `exported` storage specifier before the widget type name in the definition, as shown in Example 24-6.

Example 24-6. The first.uil module
```
/* first.uil - First half of a two-module interface description. */
module first

object top : exported XmText { };

end module;
```

An `exported` definition looks and acts just like a regular definition. The difference is that you can access an exported widget in another module by declaring it with the `imported` storage class specifier. This technique is illustrated in Example 24-7, which imports the `top` widget from Example 24-6.

Example 24-7. The second.uil module
```
/* second.uil - Second half of a two-module interface description. */
module second

object top : imported XmText;

object bottom : XmPushButton { };

object root : XmPanedWindow {
  controls {
    XmText top;
    XmPushButton bottom;
  };
};

end module;
```

Since the `imported` declaration refers to a widget defined elsewhere, you cannot specify attributes for the widget and must end the declaration immediately after the type name, as shown in this example. You can think of an `imported` widget declaration as having the same meaning as an `extern` variable declaration in C. Collectively, the two modules describe the same interface as Example 24-3. After compiling these two modules, you can view the interface with the following command:

```
showuid first second
```

Placing a single widget in a separate file, as we've done in this example, is clearly a trivial example of sharing widgets. This technique makes more sense when you are creating a larger interface for a real application. You can see a more realistic example of sharing widgets in Chapter 25, *Building an Application With UIL.*

Widget definitions, like top-level variable definitions in C, are global by default, which means that you really don't need to use the `exported` storage specifier. However, we recommend using it when you plan to reference a widget in another module because it clearly indicates which widget definitions you expect to use elsewhere. When you import a widget, UIL assumes that the widget class in the `imported` declaration matches the class of the widget definition. If you make a mistake and import a widget that is different from its declared class, you defeat the compiler's type-checking of the imported widget and may run into problems at run-time. Although some of the Motif managers can detect an attempt to create an unsupported child, you should ensure that your widget definitions and declarations match rather than relying on possible run-time detection.

UIL also supports the `private` storage specifier. This specifier allows you to restrict the use of a widget definition to the module in which it occurs. The `static` storage class specifier in C has the same effect on C functions and variables. As of Motif 1.2, however, widgets defined as `private` can still be accessed from other modules. Although the `private` storage specifier is rarely used, you can specify it if you want to protect access to private widgets (assuming the problem will be fixed), or if you want to explicitly indicate that a widget should not be referenced elsewhere.

24.2.3 The Widget Creation Process

Now that you know how to define widgets in a UIL module, we can take a closer look at how to create widgets at run-time using `MrmFetchWidget()`. In Chapter 22, *Introduction to UIL*, we showed you the basics of using `MrmFetchWidget()` to create a widget or a widget hierarchy. As a reminder, this function takes the following form:

```
Cardinal
MrmFetchWidget(hierarchy, widget_name, parent, widget_return,
               class_return)
    MrmHierarchy    hierarchy;
    String          widget_name;
    Widget          parent;
    Widget          *widget_return;
    MrmType         *class_return;
```

The *hierarchy* argument is an `MrmHierarchy` that has been opened with `MrmOpenHierarchyPerDisplay()`. The *widget_name* parameter is the name of the widget to fetch. The *parent* argument is the parent of the widget that is to be created. On success, *widget_return* contains the widget ID of the widget and *class_return* contains the internal UIL class code for the widget.

You can also fetch a widget by calling `MrmFetchWidgetOverride()`, which lets you override resource settings in the application. This routine takes the following form:

```
Cardinal
MrmFetchWidgetOverride(hierarchy, widget_name, parent, override_name,
                       arg_list, num_args, widget_return, class_return)
    MrmHierarchy    hierarchy;
    String          widget_name;
    Widget          parent;
    String          override_name;
```

```
ArgList      arg_list;
Cardinal     num_args;
Widget       *widget_return;
MrmType      *class_return;
```

The *override_name* argument lets you specify a name for the widget that differs from *widget_name*. *widget_name* is used only to look up the widget definition. If *override_name* is NULL, *widget_name* is used for the name. The *arg_list* and *num_arg* parameters specify a standard array of Xt resource name-value pairs. Any resources specified in this list override those specified in the widget definition from the UIL module. The rest of the parameters are the same as for MrmFetchWidget().

For each of these functions, Mrm first makes sure that the *hierarchy* specified is valid and open. If you supply an invalid *hierarchy* to a function, it immediately fails and returns MrmBAD_HIERARCHY. Assuming the *hierarchy* is valid, the two routines use the widget creation algorithm illustrated in Figure 24-5 and described in the following sections.

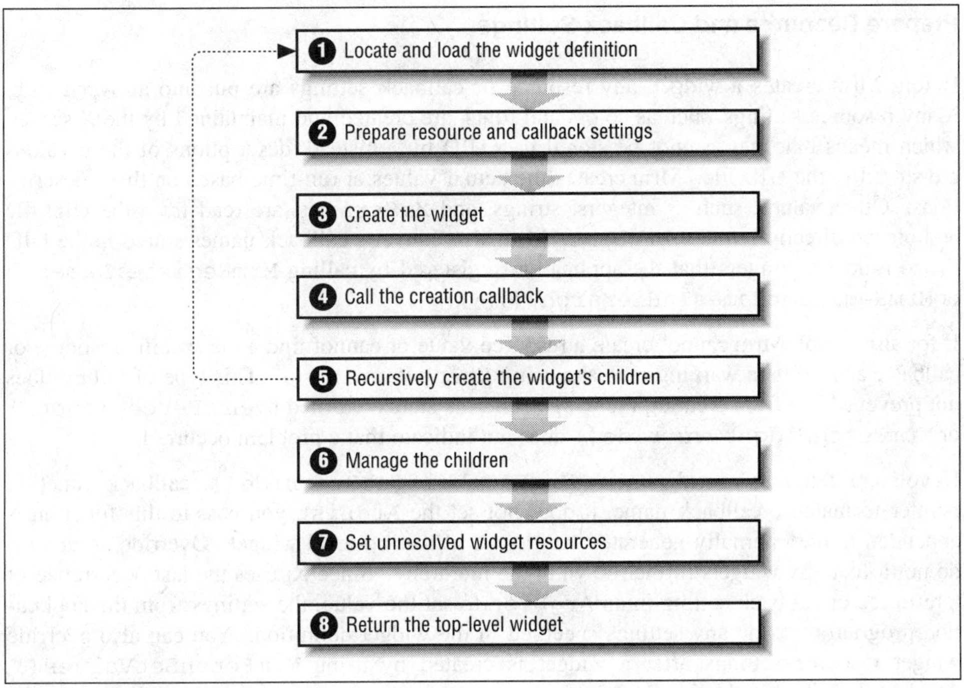

Figure 24-5. Widget creation algorithm

Locate and Load the Widget Definition

Mrm begins the widget creation process by searching for the widget definition in the UID files associated with the hierarchy. The files are searched in the same order as they appear in the array passed to `MrmOpenHierarchyPerDisplay()`. The search order matters when two widgets with the same name are defined in different files, as Mrm uses the first definition that it finds. Once Mrm locates the widget definition, it reads it from the UID file and moves on to the next step. If Mrm cannot find the widget after looking in each file, it prints a warning message by calling `XtAppWarning()`.

If the missing widget is at the root of the hierarchy that the application is fetching, `MrmFetchWidget()` returns a status of `MrmNOT_FOUND`. But if the missing widget is one of its descendents, the widget hierarchy creation process continues, minus one widget. While a failure to create a child widget is bound to cause problems for your application, `MrmFetchWidget()` unfortunately returns `MrmSUCCESS` as long as the top-level widget is created.

Prepare Resource and Callback Settings

Before Mrm creates a widget, any resource or callback settings are put into an `ArgList`. Many resource settings, such as colors and fonts, are created and maintained by the X server, which means that they cannot be stored in a UID file. Instead, descriptions of these values are stored in the UID file. Mrm creates the actual values at run-time based on these descriptions. Other values, such as integers, strings, and `XmStrings`, are read from the UID file and placed directly into the `ArgList`. Mrm also converts callback names stored in the UID file to function pointers that the application registered by calling `MrmRegisterNames()` or `MrmRegisterNamesInHierarchy()`.

If for any reason Mrm cannot create a resource value or cannot find a the specific resource or callback and prints a warning message using `XtAppWarning()`. This type of failure does not prevent Mrm from creating the widget, and the status returned by `MrmFetchWidget()` or `MrmFetchWidgetOverride()` does not indicate that a problem occurred.

If you are fetching a widget with `MrmFetchWidgetOverride()`, callback function pointer to match a callback name, it does not set the `ArgList` you pass to this function is appended to the internally generated `ArgList` of the top-level widget. Override arguments do not affect any widgets further down in the hierarchy. Since Xt uses the last occurrence of a resource or callback setting in an `ArgList` to set the value, the settings from the application program override any settings specified in the widget definition. You can also override widget resource settings after a widget is created by using `MrmFetchSetValues()`, which is described in Section 24.3.2.

Create the Widget

Now Mrm calls the widget creation function corresponding to the class of the widget. For the built-in Motif widgets, Mrm uses the Motif convenience functions, such as `XmCreatePushButton()`. Some widgets, like the FileSelectionBox, create their own children at the time they themselves are created. Mrm is aware of these children, but is not responsible for their creation. For `user_defined` widgets, Mrm calls the creation procedure that you specified when registering the widget. (User-defined widgets are described in Section 26.1.) Mrm does not manage the widget at this point in the procoess.

Call the Creation Callback

In addition to the callbacks that are part of each widget, Mrm and UIL support a special creation callback, `MrmNcreateCallback`, which is invoked by Mrm immediately after the widget is created. In the case of an automatically-created child, the callback is invoked after its resources are set. The widgets are not aware of the callback, since it is handled directly by Mrm. The `MrmNcreateCallback` takes the same form as any other callback and is specified in the `callbacks` subsection of a widget definition. The `client_data` argument is an `XmAnyCallbackStruct`, which is defined in *<Xm/Xm.h>* as follows:

```
typedef struct {
    int        reason;
    XEvent *event;
} XmAnyCallbackStruct;
```

The `reason` field is always set to `MrmCR_CREATE`, and the `event` pointer is always `NULL`. You can use this callback to handle almost anything you would normally do in a standard Xt program after creating a widget.

Recursively Create the Widget's Children

At this point, the widget creation process becomes recursive. If the newly-created widget has any children specified in its `controls` subsection, Mrm creates them now. Mrm uses the process just described to create each of the children. Automatically-created children are also processed recursively so that Mrm can handle any resources or callbacks specified in the UIL file. Instead of creating an automatically-created child in the widget creation step, Mrm just sets the resources and callbacks using the `XtArgList` for the child.

The recursive nature of the widget creation process allows you to create, with a single function call, a user interface that consists of an arbitrarily large widget hierarchy. This behavior is what makes `MrmFetchWidget()` and `MrmFetchWidgetOverride()` so powerful. As we mentioned earlier, if Mrm cannot create a child widget, it prints a warning message using `XtAppWarning()` and continues with the next child. In general, both fetch functions continue working through just about any type of failure, short of not finding the definition of the top-level widget in the hierarchy.

Manage the Children

If any children have been created, Mrm now manages them. Mrm manages all non-Shell children that are part of the `controls` subsection of the parent widget, unless they are declared as `unmanaged`. Since the creation process is recursive, any children of the widgets that are being managed have been managed previously. The top-level widget that is being fetched is not managed by Mrm because the management step only applies to the children of a widget.

Set Unresolved Widget Resources

After all of the widgets in the hierarchy have been created, there may still be some resources that Mrm needs to set because UIL allows you to make forward references to widgets. As a result, you can specify widgets in resource settings and as callback arguments without worrying about the creation order of the widgets involved. If you reference a widget before it is defined, Mrm cannot resolve the reference when it is encountered. To handle this situation, Mrm remembers the reference and resolves it once all of the widgets in the hierarchy have been created.

The ability to use forward references makes UIL quite flexible. One situation where this feature is useful is when you create an interface that uses the Form widget. With UIL, you can specify complex Form attachments without having to worry about the creation order of the widgets. The one limitation to this feature is that it only works within a single call to `Mrm-FetchWidget()`. During a call to `MrmFetchWidget()`, Mrm maintains a list of the widgets that have been created, which means that you can only reference a widget that is part of the hierarchy created by the current call. If you need to set a resource to a widget in another hierarchy, you can set it using the `MrmNcreateCallback` or set it after the hierarchy has been created.

Return Top-level Widget

After the entire hierarchy has been created, Mrm returns the widget ID of the top-level widget to the application. The top-level widget is the one that you name in the `MrmFetch-Widget()` or `MrmFetchWidgetOverride()` function call. Remember that Mrm does not manage this widget, so an application must explicitly call `XtManageChild()` on the widget. Although the widget creation process is rather involved, all you really need is a general understanding of the process. If you encounter problems with Mrm widget creation, you can return to this section to brush up on the details.

24.3 Defining and Fetching Values

UIL supports over 20 different data types, which gives you the ability to specify values for nearly every Motif resource. In addition, most types of values can be passed as the `client_data` argument to your callbacks or retrieved on demand from a UID file by Mrm. Each of the types has its own syntax so that the UIL compiler can distinguish between them. But before we describe the syntax of each value, we need to look at defining symbolic variables and retrieving variables at run-time using Mrm.

Variables provide a convenient and descriptive way to refer to values. Variables are defined in a `value` section of a UIL module. This section begins with the keyword `value` and consists of one or more variable definitions. Most `value` sections define variables for familiar values like integers and strings, as shown in the following fragment:

```
value
    spacing : 10;
    warning : "Aviso";
```

A value definition consists of an identifier followed by a colon, the value assigned to the identifier, and a semicolon.

UIL supports forward references to variables, so you don't need to declare or define a variable before you reference it. However, we recommend that you avoid forward references for a couple of reasons. The first reason is purely stylistic. Programmers expect to see a definition or declaration before a reference, since it is required by many programming languages. A module is also easier to read if variables are defined or declared before they are used. Another reason has to do with the UIL compiler. While forward references tend to work most of the time, problems with the compiler may cause unexpected errors depending on the context in which you use a forward-referenced variable.

24.3.1 Sharing Values Between Modules

Like widgets, you can share most values between modules by defining an `exported` value in one module and declaring it `imported` in another module. This feature is commonly used to maintain strings in a separate module from the interface definition for internationalization purposes. (This style of internationalization is illustrated in Section 26.2.3.) You can specify a storage class of `private` (the default) or `exported` just before the value in a declaration, as shown in the following fragment:

```
value
    ducks : private 7;
    swans : 3;
    geese : exported 5;
```

The variables `ducks` and `swans` are accessible only in the module in which they are defined, while the variable `geese` is accessible from any module.† You can also retrieve

---

†Unlike `private` widget definitions, `private` variables really are private, so you cannot access them from another module.

exported values from an application, as you'll see shortly. You can use a variable from another module by declaring it as an imported variable. The syntax is similar to an imported widget declaration, as shown below:

```
value
    geese : imported integer;
```

Like imported widgets, you need to make sure that the type of an imported variable matches the type in its definition. If they do not match, there's a good chance you'll run into problems when you create a widget that references the imported value.

24.3.2 Fetching Values

As we mentioned earlier, an application can read all types of exported variables from a UIL module, with the exception of character_set and color_table values. You retrieve most exported variables using MrmFetchLiteral(). However, pixmap and color are retrieved with special routines that we'll describe later. Fetching values from a UIL module is useful for obtaining internationalized strings or widget resource values that change dynamically based on the state of the program. MrmFetchLiteral() takes the following form:

```
Cardinal
MrmFetchLiteral(hierarchy, name, display, value_return, type_return)
    MrmHierarchy   hierarchy;
    String         name;
    Display        *display;
    XtPointer       *value_return;
    MrmCode        *type_return)
```

Mrm looks for the variable specified by *name* in the UID files associated with the *hierarchy* parameter. The files are searched in the same order as they appeared in the array of files passed to MrmOpenHierarchyPerDisplay(), so if two variables with the same name occur in separate files, you'll get the value from the first file in the list. When a value is fetched successfully, the function returns MrmSUCCESS, fills in *value_return* with a pointer to the value, and fills in *type_return* with a constant from *<Mrm/MrmPublic.h>* indicating the type of value. If MrmFetchLiteral() cannot find the variable in any of the UID files, it returns MrmNOT_FOUND.

The *value_return* parameter usually contains a pointer to the value that you fetched, even for types such as integer and boolean. You can check the type by examining *type_return*. Table 24-4 lists each UIL data type, the type of the value placed in *value_return*, and the associated type identifier placed in *type_return*.

Table 24-4. UIL Data Types and Their Return Types

Type	Mrm Return Type	C Return Type	Free Routine
asciz_table	MrmRtypeChar8Vector	String*	XtFree()
boolean†	MrmRtypeBoolean	int*	XtFree()
class_rec_name	MrmRtypeClassRecName	WidgetClass	N/A
color	N/A‡	Pixel	XFreeColors()
compound_string	MrmRtypeCString	XmString	XmStringFree()
compound_ string_table	MrmRtypeCStringVector	XmStringTable	XtFree()
float	MrmRtypeFloat	double*	XtFree()
font	MrmRtypeFont	XFontStruct*	N/A
fontset	MrmRtypeFontSet	XFontSet	N/A
font_table	MrmRtypeFontList	XmFontList	XmFonyListFree()
icon	N/A‡	Pixmap	XFreePixmap()
integer	MrmRtypeInteger	int*	XtFree()
integer_table	MrmRtypeIntegerVector	int*	XtFree()
keysym	MrmRtypeKeysym	char	N/A
rgb	N/A‡	Pixel	XFreeColors()
single_float	MrmRtypeSingleFloat	float*	XtFree()
string	MrmRtypeChar8	String	XtFree()
translation_table	MrmRtypeTransTable	XtTranslations	N/A
wide_character	MrmRtypeWideCharacter	wchar_t*	XtFree()
xbitmapfile	N/A‡	Pixmap	XFreePixmap()

† Mrm allocates an int for boolean values, so you cannot use the Xt Boolean type because on some machines it is defined as a char. However, you can still assign the int that is returned to a Boolean.
‡ The specialized routines MrmFetchBitmapLiteral(), MrmFetchColorLiteral(), and MrmFetch-IconLiteral() do not have an MrmType argument. If the named value is not the right type, a status of Mrm-WRONG_TYPE is returned.

Mrm allocates storage for most of the values returned by MrmFetchLiteral(). The application is responsible for freeing the storage; it uses the routine indicated in Table 24-4. However, note that you should not free font or fontset values because they are cached by Mrm and are reused as needed. There is no need to free class_rec_name or keysym values because they are returned by value, and you cannot free translation_table values because Xt does not provide a way to free them. In addition, Mrm allocates asciz_string_table, compound_string_table, and integer_table values in a single chunk of memory, which means you should free them with a single call, rather than freeing the individual elements.

The following code fragment illustrates using MrmFetchLiteral() to fetch a string and an integer:

```
extern MrmHierarchy hierarchy;
extern Widget toplevel;
Cardinal status;
MrmCode type;
String animal;
int *count;

status = MrmFetchLiteral (hierarchy, "animal", XtDisplay(toplevel),
    (XtPointer) &animal, &type);
if (status != MrmSUCCESS || type != MrmRtypeChar8)
    error ();

status = MrmFetchLiteral (hierarchy, "count", XtDisplay(toplevel),
    (XtPointer) &count, &type);
if (status != MrmSUCCESS || type != MrmRtypeInteger)
    error ();

printf ("There are %d %s\n", *count, animal);

XtFree (count);
XtFree (animal);
```

Mrm fills in the string pointer and the integer pointer with the values from the UID file. The integer value is returned as a pointer to an integer. We check the types of the values returned just in case the values are not a string and an integer as expected. The two values can be defined in a UIL module as follows:

```
value
    animal : exported "frogs";
    count  : 7;
```

With MrmFetchLiteral(), you can retrieve values from a UIL module that are not necessarily part of the user interface, such as printed error messages and program configuration values.

Since values fetched from a UIL module are often used to set resources of existing widgets, Mrm provides a function that handles this situation. If you use MrmFetchLiteral(), you still have to call XtVaSetValues() to set the values. MrmFetchSetValues() handles both fetching the values and setting the resources. This routine takes the following form:

```
Cardinal
MrmFetchSetValues(hierarchy, widget, args, num_args)
    MrmHierarchy  hierarchy;
    Widget        widget;
    ArgList       args;
    Cardinal      num_args;
```

The *hierarchy* argument specifies the Mrm hierarchy, and *widget* specifies the widget on which to set the values. The *args* parameter is an array of resource settings, and *num_args* specifies the size of the array. Each array element is an `Arg` structure, which is defined as follows:

```
typedef struct {
    String    name;
    XtArgVal  value;
} Arg, *ArgList;
```

This structure is the same one used with `XtSetValues()`, but it is used in a slightly different way. When you call `MrmFetchSetValues()`, the name field still specifies the name of a resource, but the `value` field names a UIL variable that contains the value instead of specifying the value directly. The function and its structure are demonstrated in the `Message()` routine shown in Example 24-8.

Example 24-8. The Message() routine

```
extern Widget message_dialog;
...
void
Message(hierarchy, name)
MrmHierarchy hierarchy;
String name;
{
    char msg_buf[33], type_buf[3];
    Arg args[2];

    sprintf (type_buf, "%s_type", name);
    sprintf (msg_buf, "%s_msg", name);

    args[0].name = XmNdialogType;
    args[0].value = (XtArgVal) type_buf;

    args[1].name = XmNmessageString;
    args[1].value = (XtArgVal) msg_buf;

    MrmFetchSetValues (hierarchy, message_dialog, args, XtNumber (args));
    XtManageChild (message_dialog);
}
```

This function uses its name argument to form two UIL variable names and calls `Mrm-FetchSetValues()` to fetch the values and set the resources of a MessageDialog. The string buffers are only 33 characters long because a UIL variable name can be at most 32 characters long. The corresponding variable definitions in a UIL module might look like the following:

```
value
    fnf_msg  : exported compound_string ("File not found!");
    fnf_type : exported XmDIALOG_ERROR;
    dsl_msg  : exported compound_string ("Almost out of disk space.");
    dsl_type : exported XmDIALOG_WARNING;
```

An application could use the following function calls to display the MessageDialog with these messages:

```
Message (hierarchy, "fnf");
Message (hierarchy, "dsl");
```

Each message string is explicitly defined as a `compound_string` in the UIL module. The UIL compiler only converts a `NULL`-terminated `string` to a `compound_string` when it is assigned to an `XmString` resource.

24.3.3 Numeric Values

UIL supports several numeric value types, specifically integers, booleans, floating point values, and integer arrays. In addition, UIL understands C-like numeric expressions and lets you explicitly convert numeric values from one type to another. Let's begin by looking at UIL integer values. The following fragment illustrates how you can define integer variables and set widget resources to integer values:

```
value
    spacing : 5;
    font_size : exported -2;

object rc : XmRowColumn {
    arguments {
        XmNmarginWidth = 3;
        XmNspacing = spacing;
    };
};
```

Unlike in C, the `boolean` type is built into UIL. You represent `boolean` values with the the reserved keywords `true`, `false`, `on` and `off`, as shown in the following code fragment:

```
value
    alive : true;
    debug : exported true;

object button : XmPushButton {
    arguments {
        XmNwidth = 100;
        XmNrecomputeSize = false;
        XmNsensitive = alive;
        XmNtraversalOn = off;
    };
};
```

The keywords `true` and `on` both represent true values, while `false` and `off` are both false values.

Although none of the Motif widgets use floating point resources, UIL provides support for floating point values. Floating point values must contain a decimal point so that the UIL compiler can distinguish them from integers. The following code fragment shows a `value` section that defines several floating point variables:

```
value
    pi : 3.14159;
    Avogadro: exported 6.023e23;
    slope : -3.3337;
    millisecond: 1e-3;
```

Floating point values can be defined both with and without exponents. A floating point value defined in UIL is stored as a C `double`. Although you probably won't use floats very often, some potential uses include setting resources of user-defined widgets, exporting them back to the application, and passing them as callback arguments.

Numeric Expressions

Even though UIL is a static description language, you can use numeric expressions that are very similar to C expressions. Expressions in UIL are evaluated at compile-time, not at run-time. UIL supports the standard operators for use with integer, floating point, and boolean values. Table 24-5 summarizes these operators and their precedence order. As with C, you can add parentheses to change the order of evaluation.

Table 24-5. UIL Numeric Expression Operators

Operator	Type	Operand Types	Operation	Precedence
~	unary	boolean	NOT	1 (highest)
		integer	One's complement	1
−	unary	integer	Negation	1
		float	Negation	1
+	unary	integer	None	1
		float	None	1
*	binary	integer	Multiplication	2
		float	Multiplication	2
/	binary	integer	Division	2
		float	Division	2
+	binary	integer	Addition	3
		float	Addition	3
−	binary	integer	Subtraction	3
		float	Subtraction	3
>>	binary	integer	Shift right	4
<<	binary	integer	Shift left	4
&	binary	boolean	AND	5
		integer	Bitwise AND	5
|	binary	boolean	OR	6
		integer	Bitwise OR	6
^	binary	boolean	XOR	6
		integer	Bitwise XOR	6 (lowest)

You can use a numeric expression just about anywhere that a numeric value is expected.† However, the UIL compiler does place some restrictions on expressions. An expression must evaluate to a known value when you compile a module, which means that you cannot use

---

† In early releases of Motif 1.2, if you use an expression in an `rgb` definition, the result is always zero.

imported numeric values in an expression since the unknown value prevents the compiler from evaluating the expression.

Like C, UIL lets you mix values of different types in an expression. In this situation, the result of the expression is the type of the most complex type in the expression. The order of complexity, from lowest to highest, is `boolean`, `integer`, and `float`. For example, the result of the expression 2 * 2.71828 is the `float` value 5.43656, and the result of the expression 15 & `true` is the `integer` value 1.

You can explicitly cast any numeric value or numeric expression to a specific type. UIL allows casts to `integer`, `float`, and `single_float` values, but not to `boolean` values. The UIL `float` type is a C `double`, while the UIL `single_float` type is a C `float`. Here are several examples of casting:

```
value
    one      : integer (true);
    zero     : integer (false);
    result   : integer (2 * 2.71828);
    five_oh  : float (5);
    g        : single_float (9.8);
    round    : float (integer (2.71828 + 0.5));
```

When you cast a `float` value to an `integer`, the fractional part is always truncated, so the value of `result` is 5. A cast to `float` simply converts an `integer` or a `boolean` into a C `double`. A cast to a `single_float` is the only way you can define a C `float` value, since a floating point literal is always stored as a C `double`. You must use a `single_float` to set a user-defined resource that is a C `float`.

Integer Arrays

In addition to individual integer values, UIL supports integer arrays. The compiler does not currently support boolean or floating point arrays, however. The following code fragment illustrates an array definition:

```
value
    primes : exported integer_table (2, 3, 5, 7, 11, 13);
```

An integer array consists of the keyword `integer_table` followed by a list of integer values. Like most other UIL values, you can export integer arrays from a UIL module or pass them as callback arguments. UIL does not provide a way to indicate the end of an integer array, so an application must know the length or obtain it somehow. You can define integer arrays as `exported` values and fetch them from your application or use them to set the Text and TextField `XmNselectionArray` resource. Unfortunately, setting this resource does not work in early releases of Motif 1.2 because the possible values for the array elements are not defined. Even if you define the values yourself, based on the definitions in *<Xm/Xm.h>*, an incompatibility between the two widgets and Mrm prevents an `XmNselectionArray` setting from working properly.†

---

† This problem has been fixed as of Motif Release 1.2.3.

24.3.4 Text-related Values

Text is almost always an important part of a graphical user interface. UIL supports string, character set, and font values, all of which are related to the display of text in your interface. A string consists of displayable text. A string only makes sense in the context of a character set, which defines the supported characters in a string and the encoding (or mapping from values to glyphs) of the string. A font contains the actual glyphs that visually represent a character on the screen or on paper. These three elements are closely related as all are necessary to display text. Figure 24-6 illustrates the relationships among these types under UIL.

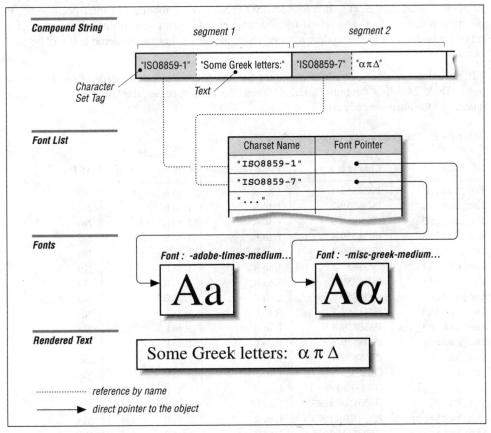

Figure 24-6. Relationships among strings, character sets, and fonts in UIL

This figure may look complicated, but UIL and Motif provide default values for character sets and fonts. You don't have to worry about these values unless you are customizing or internationalizing an application. Of course, you must always provide the strings, but that's the easy part.

Character Sets

Before we can explain strings or fonts, you need to understand character sets, because both strings and fonts depend on them. The character set of a string determines the string's parsing direction, writing direction, and the number of bytes per character. For example, character sets for Latin-based languages like English are read from left to right, are written from left to right, and are typically encoded using one byte per character.

When a string is displayed, it must be drawn with a font that uses the same character set as the string because a character set defines a mapping from character codes to character glyphs. For example, in the ISO 8859-1 character set (ISO Latin-1), the value 65 represent an A, the value 66 represents a B, etc. In a font for ISO 8859-1, the symbol A occupies position 65, B occupies position 66, and so on. If the character set of a string doesn't match the character set of the font with which it is drawn, there's a good chance that the rendered text will be gibberish.

UIL provides a number of built-in character sets that should meet the needs of most applications. Table 24-6 lists the built-in UIL character sets and specifies the UIL name, the official name, and the attributes of each.

Table 24-6. The Built-in UIL Character Sets

UIL Name	Character Set	Parse Direction	Writing Direction	16 Bit
iso_latin1	ISO8859-1	L to R	L to R	No
iso_latin2	ISO8859-2	L to R	L to R	No
iso_latin3	ISO8859-3	L to R	L to R	No
iso_latin4	ISO8859-4	L to R	L to R	No
iso_latin5	ISO8859-5	L to R	L to R	No
iso_cyrillic	ISO8859-5	L to R	L to R	No
iso_arabic	ISO8859-6	L to R	L to R	No
iso_greek	ISO8859-7	L to R	L to R	No
iso_latin8	ISO8859-8	R to L	R to L	No
iso_latin8_lr	ISO8859-8	L to R	R to L	No
iso_hebrew	ISO8859-8	R to L	R to L	No
iso_hebrew_lr	ISO8859-8	L to R	R to L	No
gb_hanzi	GB2313.1980-0	L to R	L to R	Yes
gb_hanzi_gr	GB2313.1980-1	L to R	L to R	Yes
jis_kanji	JISX0208.1983-0	L to R	L to R	Yes
jis_kanji_gr	JISX0208.1983-1	L to R	L to R	Yes
jis_katakana	JISX0201.1976-0	L to R	L to R	No
ksc_hangul	KSC5601.1987-0	L to R	L to R	Yes
ksc_hangul_gr	KSC5601.1987-1	L to R	L to R	Yes

If you need to use a character set that is not built into UIL, you can define your own character set. UIL allows user-defined character sets anywhere a built-in is expected, except in the

Motif Programming Manual

`character_set` option at the beginning of a module. The specification of a user-defined character set takes the following form:

```
character_set ('string_expression'
               [, right_to_left = boolean_expression]
               [, sixteen_bit = boolean_expression] )
```

The *string_expression* that is used to name a user-defined character set is the key that links a string to a font, as you'll see shortly. The name is followed by two optional character set properties that only affect string values. When the `right_to_left` property is set to `false`, strings that use the character set are parsed and written from left to right. When the property is set to `true`, strings are parsed and written from right to left. When the `sixteen_bit` property is set to `false`, each character in a string that uses the character set is one byte long, but when it is set to `true`, each character is two bytes long. Since both properties default to `false`, you do not need to specify them in most cases. Here are a few specifications of user-defined character sets:

```
character_set ('bold');
character_set ('italic');
character_set ('hieroglyphic', sixteen_bit = true);
character_set ('xnaye, right_to_left = true);
```

UIL does not allow the definition of character set variables. You can only specify a character set by using the `character_set` option in the module header or by explicitly specifying the character set of a string. We describe how to specify the character set for a string in the next section. While a character set traditionally represents the characters of a language, you can also represent different font styles with user-defined character sets.

Strings

UIL supports several different types of strings so that it can represent the various string values used for Motif widget resources. The `asciz_string_table` type is the only type that is not associated with a widget resource. Table 24-7 lists all of the UIL string types and their corresponding C types.

Table 24-7. UIL String Types

UIL Type Name	C/Xt/Motif Type Name
string	char *, String
compound_string	XmString
wide_character	char_t *
asciz_string_table	char **, String *
asciz_table	char **, String *
compound_string_table	XmString *, XmStringTable
string_table	XmString *, XmStringTable

The basic representation of all strings in UIL is a sequence of zero or more characters within single or double quotes. In Motif 1.1, quoted strings are limited to 2000 characters, but later releases allow greater lengths. The exact type of a string can be determined implicitly by the context in which it appears or explicitly when it is used in a named-string definition. All of the string types except `string` have an explicit form.

Both single and double-quoted strings can contain any of the printable single-byte characters. These are the characters with decimal values in the ranges 32 to 126 and 160 to 255. Characters with values outside of the ranges can only be entered using the *value*\\ escape sequence, where *value* represents the character code desired. In addition, you must escape a single quote (') in a single-quoted string and a double quote (") in a double-quoted string. To allow the easy specification of commonly used nonprinting characters, UIL recognizes the escape sequences shown in Table 24-8.

Table 24-8. UIL String Escape Sequences

Escape Sequence	Meaning
\b	Backspace
\f	Formfeed
\n	Newline
\r	Carriage return
\t	Horizontal tab
\v	Vertical tab
\\	Backslash
\'	Single quote
\"	Double quote

The following code fragment shows some examples of quoted string variable definitions that include escape sequences:

```
value
   bell : 'Beep\7\';
   quote : "\"You don't believe me?\" asked the lawyer.";
```

The first string includes some normal text and an escaped control character, decimal 7, which is the bell character on most terminals. The second string contains a couple of double quotes that must be escaped because the string itself is double-quoted. Alternatively, we could have made it a single-quoted string, thereby eliminating the need for escaping the double quotes within it. In general, non-printable escape characters only make sense in the context of NULL-terminated strings and may produce strange results if you use them within compound strings (which we'll discuss shortly).

You can continue a single-quoted string over multiple lines by adding the backslash character as the last character on a continued line. The string continues with the first character on the following line and does not include a newline. If you want a newline in a string, you must use the \n escape sequence. Double-quoted strings cannot span multiple lines. The following definition shows an example of a multi-line single-quoted string:

```
value
   sentence : 'TRUE! -- NERVOUS -- VERY, very dreadfully nervous \
I had been and am; but why will you say that I am mad?';
```

24.3.4.0.1 **NULL-terminated strings**. UIL NULL-terminated strings are the same as C strings. While most Motif text resources are XmString values, there are a few strings that are NULL-terminated. The most common is the XmNvalue resource of the Text and TextField widgets. You also use NULL-terminated strings in the literal syntax of many UIL variable definitions, and you can use a NULL-terminated string as the argument to a callback. The following fragment demonstrates the use of NULL-terminated strings:

```
procedure
  verify (string);

object phone : XmTextField {
  arguments {
    XmNvalue = '(512) 555-1212';
    XmNbackground = color ('wheat');
  };
  callbacks {
    XmNmodifyVerifyCallback = procedure verify ('(###) ###-####');
  };
};
```

In this widget definition, we assign a NULL-terminated string to the XmNvalue resource, we use one in the definition of a UIL color value, and we pass one as a callback argument. The callback is declared as taking a string value, which is the UIL type for NULL-terminated strings. We recommend using the convention of writing NULL-terminated strings as single-quoted strings. This distinguishes them from compound strings, which we recommend writing as double-quoted strings.

You can concatenate two or more NULL-terminated strings with the ampersand (&), which is the UIL string concatenation operator. It is a binary operator that creates a new string consisting of the left operand followed by the right operand. You can use this operand with NULL-terminated strings that are used for resource settings, callback arguments, and variable definitions. However, using string concatenation in the literal syntax of a UIL value definition may crash the UIL compiler or result in an incorrect definition. The following fragment shows an example of string concatenation:

```
value
  first : 'Bilbo';
  last  : 'Baggins';
  full  : first & ' ' & last;
```

The full variable is defined as the concatenation of the variables first and last, separated by a space. The resulting string is 'Bilbo Baggins'. You can use both variables and NULL-terminated string literals as the operands for string concatenation.

24.3.4.0.2 **Compound strings**. Most text values in the Motif widget set are handled as XmString values, or compound strings. Compound strings differ from NULL-terminated strings in that they contain information about the character set and writing direction of the string along with the textual information. This additional information is necessary for displaying text in different languages and fonts. Essentially, a compound string is a string that comes with all of the information that is needed to render it. In most situations, you can simply specify the text, and the UIL compiler provides the character set, as in the following familiar example:

```
object hello : XmLabel
{
  arguments {
    XmNlabelString = "Hello, World!";
  };
};
```

XmNlabelString is an XmString resource, but in this definition we only specify the text portion of the compound string. This specification works because there is a default character set associated with every UIL module. As we explained in Chapter 22, *Introduction to UIL*, you can specify the default character set by setting the LANG environment variable or by setting the character_set option at the beginning of the module. If you do not specify the default character set, the UIL compiler uses a built-in default which is vendor specific. In any event, you can use a single or double-quoted string wherever a compound string is expected, and the UIL compiler will automatically convert it to a compound string. Figure 24-7 illustrates how the UIL compiler determines the character set for compound strings.

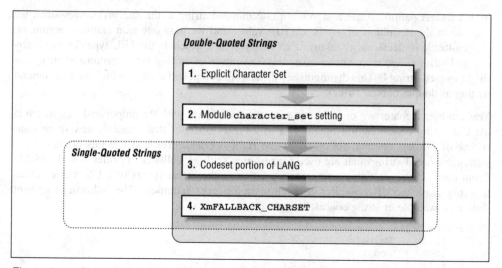

Figure 24-7. Character set determination for compound strings

The character set of an individual string can also be specified explicitly. You do so by preceding a string with the pound sign (#) and specifying the name of a built-in or user-defined character set. This syntax only works with double-quoted strings, however, which is why we

Motif Programming Manual

recommend using double-quoted strings to represent compound strings.† The following code fragment demonstrates how to set the character set of a string explicitly:

```
object hello : XmLabel {
  arguments {
    XmNlabelString = #iso_greek"χαιρε";
  };
};
```

In this example, we explicitly set the character set to iso_greek, which is one of the built-in UIL character sets. At run-time, the string is displayed in Greek as long as the font list of the Label is set correctly. (We explain font lists later in this section.) It is rare for an application to specify a character set explicitly, as most applications only display text using one language for a given invocation, although the language may vary between invocations.

You can also specify different font styles using character sets, although that is not their primary purpose. You can define your own character set to represent a different style, as shown in the following fragment:

```
object title : XmLabel {
  arguments {
    XmNlabelString = #character_set('italic')"Elsinore";
  };
};
```

The XmNlabelString resource is set to a compound string that contains the text "Elsinore" and uses the character set named italic. Displaying the string in italics requires that the font list of the Label contain an italic character set.

Unlike other UIL values, you cannot define a character set variable, which means that you must always specify a user-defined character set explicitly, as shown in this example. Specifying font styles with character sets is most useful when you want to display a compound string that contains text in several different styles, as we'll show you in an example later in this section.

Although automatic string conversion can handle the creation of most compound strings, there are still a few situations when you need to define compound strings explicitly. If you want to declare an exported compound string variable or override one of the properties of a compound string, you need to use the compound string literal syntax. An explicit compound string definition takes the following form:

```
compound_string (string_expression,
                [, right_to_left = boolean_expression ]
                [, separate = boolean_expression ] )
```

A compound_string literal begins with the compound_string keyword and is followed by a single or double-quoted string and the optional properties. You can set the writing direction of the compound string with the right_to_left property; the default value of this property is taken from the writing direction string's character set. The separate

---

† In early releases of Motif 1.2, the UIL compiler does not generate an error if you specify a character set for a single-quoted string. The compiler silently ignores the specification, so you should be careful to always use double-quoted strings when specifying a character set.

property specifies whether or not a separator component is added to the end of the compound string. The default value is `false`, which means that a separator is not added.

Unlike with NULL-terminated strings, placing a newline character in a compound string does not produce a multi-line string. A line break in a compound string is indicated by a separator component, which you add by setting the `separate` property to `true` in an explicit compound string definition. You can create a multi-line compound string by concatenating compound strings with the & operator, as shown in Example 24-9.

Example 24-9. The multiline.uil module

```
module multiline

value
  file  : compound_string ("/vmunix", separate=true);
  owner : compound_string ("root", separate=true);
  desc  : compound_string ("The UNIX kernel.");
  all   : "File: " & file & "Owner: " & owner & "Desc: " & desc;

object root : XmLabel {
  arguments {
    XmNlabelString = all;
  };
};

end module;
```

Both `file` and `owner` are defined as compound string values that contain a compound string separator. The concatenation of the strings in this example produces a three-line compound string, which is shown in Figure 24-8.

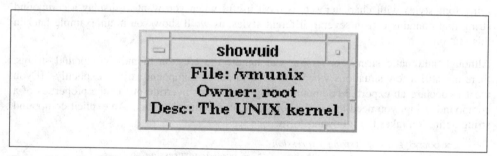

Figure 24-8. User interface of multiline.uil

As Example 24-9 shows, you can mix NULL-terminated strings and compound strings with the & concatenation operator. When you concatenate two strings, the result is a compound string if either one of the strings is a compound string, or if the character sets of the two strings are different.

24.3.4.0.3 Wide-characters. The `wide_character` string type was added in Motif 1.2 to support the definition of user interfaces that contain Asian language text.† The form of a wide-character definition is:

```
wide_character (string_expression)
```

The *string_expression* contains a multibyte string. Asian language text must be represented with multibyte or wide-character strings because the number of different characters in these languages cannot be encoded in single bytes. In a multibyte character string, the length in bytes of each individual character varies, but in a wide-character string, the length of each character is the same. Most programs, including the Motif widgets, work with wide-character strings internally because the fixed character size makes them easier to use than multibyte characters.

The `wide_character` type converts a multibyte character string into an equivalent wide-character string. The conversion is based on the locale that is set when you run the UIL compiler. When compiling a module that contains wide-character strings, you must use the `-s` compiler option or multibyte string conversions may be incorrect. See Section 23.1.4 for more information about this option.

The only wide-character resource in the Motif widget set is the `XmNvalueWcs` resource of the Text and TextField widgets. In addition to setting this resource, you can also fetch exported wide-character strings from an application program and use them as callback arguments.

24.3.4.0.4 String tables. In addition to single, NULL-terminated strings and compound strings, UIL supports arrays of both types. The `XmNitems` and `XmNselectedItems` resources of the List widget are both `XmStringTable` values, or compound string arrays. Even though there are no NULL-terminated string array resources in the Motif widget set, you can still pass these arrays as callback arguments and fetch exported arrays with `MrmFetchLiteral()`, just as you can with compound string arrays. The form of each type of array is similar, as shown in the following fragment:

```
value
    seasons : asciz_string_table ('winter', 'spring', 'summer', 'autumn');
    fruits : compound_string_table ("apple", "banana", "grape", "cherry");
```

You can also use the keywords `asciz_table` and `string_table` when defining NULL-terminated and compound string tables, respectively. The UIL compiler terminates both types of arrays with a NULL pointer. Quoted strings in the `compound_string_table` are converted automatically to compound strings by the UIL compiler. However, unlike with individual string values, the UIL compiler does not convert an `asciz_string_table` to a `compound_string_table`. Remember that when you set a Motif `XmStringTable` resource, the UIL compiler sets the associated count resource automatically.

---

† Unfortunately, the UIL compiler flags a wide-character definition as an error in early releases of Motif 1.2.

Fonts

Fonts are the last piece of the textual information picture that we need to examine. As we explained earlier, you cannot display a compound string without an associated font; a character set links a string to a particular font. You specify the fonts used by Motif widgets with font list resources. The simplest case involves setting the `XmNfontList` resource of a widget to a single font. A font list can also specify a list of fonts or font sets and their associated character sets. For more information on Motif font lists, see Chapter 19, *Compound Strings*.

UIL provides support for font, font set, and font list values. These types correspond to the `XFontStruct`, `XFontSet`, and `XmFontList` types in C. The UIL font set type was added in Motif 1.2 to support the `XFontSet` type that was added in X11R5. A font list can contain both fonts and font sets, so we'll look at these two types first. The following code fragment shows a value of each type:

```
value
    menu_font : font
        ('-adobe-times-bold-r-normal--12-120-75-75-p-67-iso8859-1');
    label_font : fontset ('-*-fixed-medium-r-normal-*-*-130-*');
```

As these definitions illustrate, fonts and font sets are defined using X Logical Font Description (XLFD) names and patterns. Xlib may load one or more fonts in a font set, which is why you must always specify a pattern instead of a single font name. Xlib determines the exact fonts that are needed based on the locale setting. For example, drawing Japanese text typically requires a Kanji font, a Kana font, and a Latin font. For additional information about fonts and font sets, see Volume One, *Xlib Programming Manual*, and Volume Two, *Xlib Reference Manual*.

Fonts and font sets are loaded at run-time because they are resources maintained by the X server. UIL simply stores the font names or patterns that you specify in the UID output file without checking to see if the fonts exist. The `font` and `fontset` types are typically used to set a Motif font list resource. Mrm also creates a `XFontStruct` or `XFontSet` value for you when you pass a `font` or `fontset` value as a callback argument or when you fetch one of the values from an application program.

Each Motif widget that displays text has a `XmFontList` resource associated with it. UIL provides the `font_table` type so you can define font lists directly in UIL. A font list is simply an array of font and/or font set values, each of which has an associated character set. The following fragment illustrates the definition of a font list:

```
value
    latin1 : font ('*-iso8859-1', character_set = iso_latin1);
    hebrew : font ('*-iso8859-8')
    fonts : font_table (latin1, iso_hebrew = font ('*-iso8859-8'));
```

You define a font list using the `font_table` keyword followed by a list of fonts. This example demonstrates the two ways of associating a character set with a font or font set. You can specify the character set in the font or font set definition by adding a `character_set` property setting, or you can specify the character set directly in the `font_table` definition. The character set specified in a font table definition takes precedence over a character set specified in a font or font set definition.

If you do not specify a character set for a font or a font set, it defaults to the codeset portion of the LANG environment variable if it is set, or to XmFALLBACK_CHARSET otherwise. Unlike with string definitions, the default character set of the module has no effect on the character set used for font and font set definitions. If a font list contains only a single font or font set, you can set the XmNfontList resource to the font or font set directly, and the UIL compiler creates a font list that contains the entry automatically. Motif obtains the font or font set needed to render a compound string by matching the character set of the string with a font or font set in a font list that has the same character set.

An Example

Now we can take a look at an example that uses strings, character sets, fonts, and font lists. The module in Example 24-10 shows how these values work together.†

Example 24-10. The joel.uil module

```
/* joel.uil - Example of strings, character sets, and fonts, and font sets. */

module joel

value
    artist : #iso_latin1 "Billy Joel";
    title  : #iso_cyrillic "186\\222\\221\\230\\213\\224\\226\";
    album  : #character_set('latin1-bold') "Album";

value
    normal  : font ('*fixed-medium-r-normal-*-*-140-*-iso8859-1');
    bold    : font ('*fixed-medium-r-bold-*-*-140-*-iso8859-1');
    russian : font ('*fixed-medium-r-normal-*-*-140-*-iso8859-5');

value
    styles : font_table (iso_latin1 = normal,
                         iso_cyrillic = russian,
                         character_set('latin1-bold') = bold);

object root : XmLabel {
    arguments {
        XmNlabelString =  album & " : " & artist & " - " & title;
        XmNfontList = styles;
    };
};

end module;
```

The module begins with the definition of three strings, each with a different character set. Two of the character sets are built-in and one is user-defined. The built-in ones represent two different languages, while the user-defined character set represents both a language and a font style. The characters in the second string are shown in their decimal form, as we are unable to print the corresponding characters in this book. You could enter the actual characters directly with a Cyrillic editor, as they are not control characters. We've specified the character sets explicitly because we are using more than one language and don't want to worry about the setting of the LANG environment variable.

---

† In early releases of Motif 1.2, the user-defined character set in this module may cause a compilation error or it may crash the UIL compiler.

The font definitions for the text come next. We define three fonts, one for each string. Each font is defined using an XLFD font name. We combine the fonts in the `styles` font list definition, which is where we establish the connection between the character sets used by the strings and the fonts. The character set names in the compound string definitions must match the character set names used in the `font_table`. Finally, we define a Label that displays the concatenated string. The output of this module is shown in Figure 24-9.

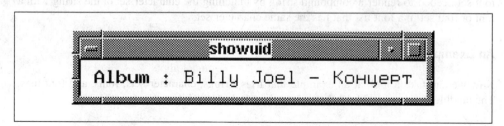

Figure 24-9. User interface of joel.uil

In early releases of Motif 1.2, the user-defined character set in the font list definition may cause a compilation error, or it may cause the UIL compiler to crash. You can work around this problem by specifying the font list in an X resource file. In this case, you must specify the character set names of the built-in character sets using the names shown in the second column of Table 24-6. The proper resource specification for this module is:

```
Demos*XmLabel.fontList: \
    *fixed-medium-r-normal-*-*-140-*-iso8859-1=ISO8859-1, \
    *fixed-medium-r-normal-*-*-140-*-iso8859-5=ISO8859-5, \
    *fixed-bold-r-normal-*-*-140-*-iso8859-1=latin1-bold
```

The name of the user-defined character set is the same as the name we used in the module. In general, placing font list definitions in an app-defaults file is a good idea anyway, since it lets the users of an application customize the font settings.

24.3.5 Colors

The UIL compiler supports color values, which means that you can set all of the different Motif color resources in a UIL module. In addition, UIL color values play an important role in the specification of color pixmaps in UIL.

Specifying Colors

Color values in UIL can be specified by the name of the color or by the amount of red, green, and blue (RGB) that compose the color. Both types of color values are easy to define, as shown in the following fragment:

```
object button : XmPushButton {
  arguments {
    XmNbackground = color ('wheat');
```

```
        XmNforeground = rgb (500, 0, 65535);
    };
};
```

A named color value is specified with the keyword `color` followed by a color name. Mrm converts the color name to the corresponding RGB value at run-time using Xlib.† You specify RGB values with the keyword `rgb` and the amount of red, green, and blue present in the color. Each amount can range from 0 to 65535, which represents 0 to 100 percent of a color.

Like other values, you can assign both `color` and `rgb` values to UIL variables, pass them as arguments to callback functions, and use them to specify resources. If Mrm cannot allocate a color at run-time for setting a resource, the resource is simply not set, and Mrm prints a warning message by calling `XtAppWarning()`. If Mrm cannot allocate a color that you use as a callback argument, your application may crash when the callback is invoked. As a result, you should avoid passing color arguments from UIL and allocate or fetch colors directly in application code instead.

For the most part, we recommend that you avoid setting color resources in a UIL module because users cannot override UIL resource settings using a resource file. Color is one of the most frequently customized aspects of an application, so you should not hard-code color values. However, colors do have their place in UIL. They are still useful for defining color pixmaps, where you don't have to worry about allowing users to change the colors.

Fetching Colors

Color values are one of the types that cannot be fetched with `MrmFetchLiteral()` because Mrm requires a colormap in which to allocate the color. The `MrmFetchColorLiteral()` function exists to allow the retrieval of color values. This function takes the following form:

```
Cardinal
MrmFetchColorLiteral(hierarchy, name, display, colormap, pixel_return)
    MrmHierarchy    hierarchy;
    String          name;
    Display         *display;
    Colormap        colormap;
    Pixel           *pixel_return;
```

As with `MrmFetchLiteral()`, the *hierarchy* and *name* arguments specify the Mrm hierarchy to search and the exported color variable to fetch. Mrm allocates the color in the colormap specified by the *colormap* parameter. If this argument is NULL, Mrm allocates the color in the colormap returned by the `DefaultColormap()` macro.

When Mrm successfully fetches the color, the *pixel_return* argument contains the allocated color, and the function returns MrmSUCCESS. If Mrm cannot find a variable by the specified name, the routine returns MrmNOT_FOUND. If Mrm finds a variable with the specified name, but it isn't a color value, the function returns MrmWRONG_TYPE. The routine can also return MrmBAD_HIERARCHY if the *hierarchy* argument is invalid or MrmFAILURE

---

† On most UNIX systems, Xlib converts colors from names to values using the mappings defined in the file */usr/lib/X11/rgb.txt*. You can find more details on this process in Volume Two, *Xlib Reference Manual*.

if anything else goes wrong. As usual, you should check the return value against Mrm-SUCCESS before testing for a specific failure. If MrmFetchColorLiteral() fails to allocate a color, Mrm should substitute black or white and print a warning message by calling XtAppWarning(). However, in early releases of Motif 1.2 this fallback mechanism does not take place, and the function returns MrmNOT_FOUND instead. When you are finished using a color retrieved with this function, you must free it with a call to XFreeColors().

24.3.6 Pixmaps

The UIL compiler supports pixmap values so that the various pixmap resources can be set in a UIL module. These resources include icon-type resources such as XmNsymbolPixmap and shading-type resources such as XmNbackgroundPixmap. There are two different forms of pixmap values that you can use in a UIL module. The first type is an xbitmapfile, which is a reference to a bitmap defined in a separate file.† The second type is an icon, which is defined entirely within a UIL module.

Specifying Bitmaps

The xbitmapfile type is used to specify a bitmap file. The contents of the file are used to create the actual bitmap. The module in Example 24-11 shows the use of this type.

Example 24-11. The bomb.uil module

```
/* bomb.uil -- Example using xbitmapfile type */
module bomb

procedure quit;

object root : XmMessageDialog {
  arguments {
    XmNmessageString = compound_string ("Segmentation Fault", separate=true) &
                       compound_string ("(Dumping Core)");
    XmNsymbolPixmap = xbitmapfile ('bomb.xbm');
    XmNdialogTitle = "Fatal Error";
  };
};

end module;
```

This example creates a MessageDialog that uses a customized icon instead of one of the standard Motif symbols. The output of the module is shown in Figure 24-10.

---

† For details on the X bitmap file format, see Volume One, *Xlib Programming Manual*.

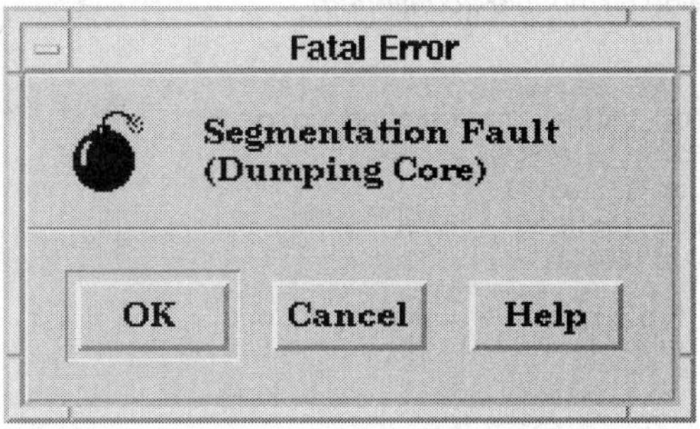

Figure 24-10. User interface of bomb.uil

The xbitmapfile value is a bitmap whose contents are defined in the file *bomb.xbm*. X bitmaps are a convenient format since they can be edited and created with the standard *bitmap* client. Bitmaps are monochrome images, which means that each pixel is either on or off. When you use a bitmap in a Motif widget, the "on" pixels are set to the foreground color of the widget, and the "off" pixels are set to the background color. You can only adjust the colors of a bitmap by changing the foreground and background color of a widget.

When you compile a module that contains an xbitmapfile value, the UIL compiler does not verify the contents or existence of the file. The file name is saved in the UID file, and Mrm handles loading the bitmap at run-time by calling XmGetPixmap(). (For details on this routine, see Section 3.4.5 in Chapter 3, *Overview of the Motif Toolkit*.) If Mrm cannot find or load a bitmap file, it prints a warning message by calling XtAppWarning(). If the bitmap file is used as a resource setting, the resource is not set. When an xbitmapfile is used as a callback argument in early releases of Motif 1.2, the application crashes when the callback is invoked. We recommend that you only use xbitmapfile values for resource settings.

Specifying Icons

You can also represent pixmaps with the UIL icon type, which supports full color images. You define icon values entirely within a UIL module, instead of referencing an external file. The UIL icon type is a useful feature, as neither Motif, Xt, or Xlib provides any support for defining color pixmaps. The only drawback is that you may have to edit the icon manually using a text editor.† The *Hello, World* example in Chapter 22, *Introduction to UIL*, used an icon value to create the earth image. We've taken the image from that example and colorized it to illustrate the complete syntax of an icon, as shown in Example 24-12.

Example 24-12. The globe.uil module

```
/* globe.uil --  colorize the world icon */

module globe
```

---

† Several third-party vendors sell color pixmap editors that can save images using the UIL icon format; many of these editors are part of a user interface builder (UIB) tool.

Example 24-12. The globe.uil module (continued)

```
value
    world_colors : color_table (background color = ' ',
                color ('black') = '*',
                color ('blue') = '.',
                color ('green') = 'x',
                color ('white') = '=');

    world_icon : icon (color_table = world_colors,
        '      ******       ',
        '    **.===..**     ',
        '   *xx.==..x..*    ',
        '  *xxx....xxx..*   ',
        '  *.xxxxxxxxx.x*   ',
        ' *.xxxxxx.xxx.xx*  ',
        ' *.xxxxxxxxx...x*  ',
        ' *.xxxxxxxxx...x*  ',
        ' *..xxxxxxxxx...x* ',
        ' *...xxxx..x....* ',
        ' *....xx.....x..* ',
        ' *....xx......* ',
        ' *....xxxxx...* ',
        '  *..xxxxxxx.* ',
        '   **xxxxxx**    ',
        '     ******       ' );
object root : XmLabel {
    arguments {
        XmNlabelType = XmPIXMAP;
        XmNlabelPixmap = world_icon;
        XmNmarginWidth = 10;
        XmNmarginHeight = 10;
    };
};

end module;
```

An `icon` definition specifies a UIL `color_table`, which maps characters to color values, and a number of strings, where each character represents an individual pixel in the resulting pixmap. The output of this module is shown in Figure 24-11. Obviously, the output is not in color, but you can tell from the different degrees of shading that the pixels are different colors.

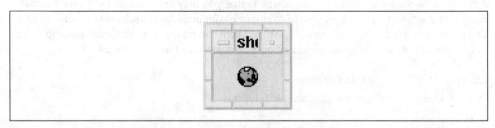

Figure 24-11. User interface of globe.uil

Although `color_table` is a distinct UIL type, a `color_table` value is only useful in the context of an `icon` definition. A `color_table` value consists of the keyword `color_table` followed by a parenthesized list of color mappings. The form of each mapping is a `color` or `rgb` value followed by an equal sign and a single character, which is used to represent that color in an icon definition. You can also use the special colors `foreground color` and `background color`. These colors are taken from the widget in which an `icon` appears. We use the `background color` around the earth so that it blends in smoothly with the Label.

When you use a `color` value in a `color_table`, you can specify how the color appears on a monochrome display, or when Mrm cannot allocate color, you can specify either `foreground` or `background` after the color name. For example, we can ensure that our earth icon looks reasonable on a monochrome display by using the following `color_table` definition:

```
world_colors : color_table (background color = ' ',
                color ('black', foreground) = '*',
                color ('blue', background) = '.',
                color ('green', foreground) = 'x',
                color ('white', foreground) = '=');
```

Without these attributes, each color is mapped to white on a monochrome display. We recommend specifying the `foreground` and `background` attributes in a `color_table`, as they ensure that an icon looks reasonable. These attributes only affect colors that are allocated as part of a `color_table`; if you specify the attribute in a color that is used as a resource or a callback argument, the UIL compiler quietly ignores the attribute.

The UIL compiler does not support the `foreground` and `background` attributes with `rgb` values. However, unlike a `color` value, an `rgb` value maps predictably to black or white based on its intensity. The mapping of a monochrome `color` value depends on the X server's color database, which varies from server to server. If you must use `rgb` values in a `color_table`, you should use `rgb` values for all of the mappings and be sure to view the resulting icon on a monochrome screen. Avoid mixing `color` and `rgb` values in the same `color_table`, since the mapping of a `color` value depends on the foreground and background colors of a widget, while the mapping of an `rgb` value is always the same.

An `icon` definition consists of the keyword `icon` followed by an optional `color_table` setting and a list of equal-length strings that define the rows of the pixmap. If you leave out the `color_table` setting, as we did in the original `world_icon` definition, the following default `color_table` is used:

```
color_table (background color = ' ',
             foreground color = '*');
```

If you specify a `color_table`, it must be the first entry in the `icon` definition, as in Example 24-12. The pixmap definition consists of an arbitrary number of comma-separated strings that correspond to the rows of the pixmap. Each pixel in the pixmap is defined using one of the characters from the `color_table`. Any other characters are illegal and are flagged as such by the UIL compiler. The compiler also verifies that all of the strings in an `icon` definition are the same length.

Fetching Pixmaps

Pixmap values are another one of the types that cannot be fetched with `MrmFetch-Literal()` because Mrm needs a `Screen` pointer, as well as background and foreground colors, in order to create a pixmap. Mrm provides two specialized functions for fetching pixmap values: `MrmFetchBitmapLiteral()` and `MrmFetchIconLiteral()`. `Mrm-FetchBitmapLiteral()` is new in Motif 1.2; it takes the following form:

```
Cardinal
MrmFetchBitmapLiteral(hierarchy, name, screen, display, pixmap_return,
                      width_return, height_return)
    MrmHierarchy    hierarchy;
    String          name;
    Screen          *screen;
    Display         *display;
    Pixmap          *pixmap_return;
    Dimension       *width_return;
    Dimension       *height_return;
```

This routine fetches an `icon` value in the form of a `Bitmap`, which is a `Pixmap` with a depth of 1. The *hierarchy* argument specifies the Mrm hierarchy that contains the exported `icon` value specified by the *name* argument. If Mrm finds the `icon`, it creates the bitmap on the *screen* of the *display* and returns it in *pixmap_return*. The width and height of the pixmap are returned in *width_return* and *height_return*. A return value of `MrmSUCCESS` indicates that the pixmap has been fetched and created successfully. In this case, the application is responsible for freeing the pixmap with `XFreePixmap()`.

The `icon` that is specified can only use the colors `foreground color` and `background color`. These colors represent the values of 1 and 0, respectively, in the resulting bitmap. If you use any other colors, the function fails and returns `MrmNOT_VALID`. The function can also return `MrmBAD_HIERARCHY` if the *hierarchy* argument is not a valid Mrm hierarchy, `MrmNOT_FOUND` if Mrm cannot find the `icon` in the hierarchy, `MrmWRONG_TYPE` if Mrm finds a value but it is not an `icon`, or `MrmFAILURE` if anything else goes wrong.

You can use the bitmap returned by `MrmFetchBitmapLiteral()` anywhere that a bitmap or a bit mask is needed. Common uses include setting the window manager icon of an application or defining a cursor by calling `XCreatePixmapCursor()`.

You can also fetch pixmaps with `MrmFetchIconLiteral()`. This function can retrieve both `icon` and `xbitmapfile` values. The routine returns a `Pixmap` whose depth is the default depth of the screen as returned by the `DefaultDepthOfScreen()` macro. It takes the following form:

```
Cardinal
MrmFetchIconLiteral(hierarchy, name, screen, display, foreground,
                    background, pixmap_return);
    MrmHierarchy    hierarchy;
    String          name;
    Screen          *screen;
    Display         *display;
    Pixel           foreground;
    Pixel           background;
    Pixmap          *pixmap_return;
```

The first four arguments are the same as for `MrmFetchBitmapLiteral()`. The *foreground* and *background* arguments specify the colors of the pixmap. When you fetch an `xbitmapfile`, "on" pixels are set to the foreground color and "off" pixels are set to the background color. When you fetch a UIL `icon`, it specifies the colors for `foreground color` and `background color` pixels. Mrm allocates the other colors that are used in the default colormap of the *display*. For this reason, you should not use this function to fetch icons for a visual class other than the default.

On success, `MrmFetchIconLiteral()` fills in *pixmap_return* with the pixmap and returns `MrmSUCCESS`. An application is responsible for freeing the pixmap using `XFreePixmap()`. The routine can also return `MrmBAD_HIERARCHY` if the specified *hierarchy* is not valid, `MrmNOT_FOUND` if Mrm cannot find the `icon` or `xbitmapfile` in the hierarchy, `MrmWRONG_TYPE` if Mrm finds a value but it is not an `icon` or `xbitmapfile`, or `MrmFAILURE` if anything else goes wrong.

When `MrmFetchIconLiteral()` cannot allocate a color for an `icon`, it should substitute either black or white. However, in early releases of Motif 1.2 this substitution does not take place, and the function returns `MrmNOT_FOUND` when a color allocation fails. To avoid this problem, you should set pixmap-type widget resources, such as `XmNlabelPixmap`, in a UIL module widget definition or by calling `MrmFetchSetValues()`.

24.3.7 Widget Classes

The widget class type, or `class_rec_name` as it is called in UIL, is new in Motif 1.2. (This feature may have been present in earlier versions, but was not documented until Motif 1.2) The type mainly supports the `XmNentryClass` resource, which restricts the allowable children of a RowColumn widget. You can also use a widget class value as a callback argument or with a user-defined widget. The `XmNentryClass` resource is usually set automatically by RowColumn when you create a MenuBar or RadioBox. You can also set the resource manually, as the following fragment illustrates:

```
object root_widget : XmRowColumn {
  arguments {
    ! Must set isHomogeneous for entryClass to take effect.
    XmNisHomogeneous = true;
    XmNentryClass = class_rec_name ('XmLabel');
  };
};
```

You specify a widget class value with the keyword `class_rec_name` followed by the name of the widget class. You can use the name of an actual widget class, such as XmPushButtonGadget, or the name of a compound object, such as XmPulldownMenu. When you use a name that is not really a widget class, the `class_rec_name` value represents the name of the actual class. For example, the real class of an XmPulldownMenu object is XmRowColumn.

24.3.8 Keysyms

In UIL, you define key mnemonics with the `keysym` type. The `XmNmnemonic` resource is the only `keysym` resource in the Motif widget set. The following widget definition illustrates the use of this type:

```
object open : XmPushButton {
  arguments {
    XmNlabelString = "Open...";
    XmNmnemonic = keysym ('O');
  };
};
```

A `keysym` definition is specified with the `keysym` keyword followed by a single character. In early releases of Motif 1.2, the UIL compiler does not report an error if you specify more than one character, but Mrm does catch the mistake at run-time.

24.3.9 Translation Tables

The UIL `translation_table` type corresponds to the `XtTranslations` type. A translation table maps events to action procedures. The format of a UIL translation table looks like an `asciz_table` in that it contains a list of strings, but the individual entries in the table must contain valid translations. (See Volume Four, *X Toolkit Intrinsics Programming Manual*, for a description of the Xt translation table syntax.) The following fragment shows the definition of a `translation_table` value:

```
value
  actions : translation_table ('#override',
                    'Ctrl<Key>A: beginning-of-line()',
                    'Ctrl<Key>E: end-of-line()',
                    'Ctrl<Key>space: set-anchor()');
```

The first entry of a `translation_table` can be used to control how the table affects the existing translations of a widget. If the first entry is not a translation, the string must be one of `#augment`, `#override`, or `#replace`. Each of the remaining entries in the table must be a `NULL`-terminated string containing a single translation. If you specify a translation in a UIL module, a user cannot override it from a resource file. You should consider placing translations in an *app-defaults* file so that users can customize them if they wish.

24.4 Working With Callbacks

Setting up a callback with UIL and Mrm involves four steps: writing the callback in application code, registering the callback with Mrm, declaring the callback in the UIL module, and setting the callback in a UIL widget definition. A callback that you write for use in an Mrm application is no different from a callback in a plain Xt application. However, as we explained in Chapter 22, *Introduction to UIL*, you need to register the routine with Mrm before creating any widgets that call it. The following code fragment from *showuid.c* shows how to register callbacks:

```
static MrmRegisterArg callback_list[] = {
    { "quit",     (XtPointer) quit },
    { "print",    (XtPointer) print },
    /* Add additional callback procedures here... */
};
    ...
MrmRegisterNames (callback_list, XtNumber (callback_list));
    ...
```

You're already familiar with the basics of declaring a callback procedure in a UIL module and using it in the `callbacks` subsection of a widget definition. Now we are going to look at how you can pass a UIL value as a callback argument. As you know, callbacks are declared in a `procedure` section of a UIL module. The purpose of the declaration is to let the compiler know that the callback exists and to give it enough information to verify that the callback is being used correctly. A callback declaration consists of the name of the callback followed by an optional argument type enclosed in parentheses.† Here are the procedure declarations that correspond to the callback functions from *showuid.c*:

```
procedure
    quit();
    print (string);
```

When no argument type is specified, as with the `quit()` declaration, the callback is declared as taking no arguments. When a UIL type name is present, as with the `print()` declaration, you must specify a value that matches the type when you use the callback. You can use any of the built-in UIL types. In addition, you can also specify the name of a Motif widget class such as `XmPushButton` or `XmForm` in a callback declaration.‡ Finally, you can indicate that an argument is expected, but not restrict its type, by specifying the special type-name `any`. If you use the `any` specifier, you should take extra care to ensure that references to the procedure elsewhere in the UIL module do not pass values to the callback that might crash your application.

The UIL compiler makes sure that the use of a callback is consistent with its declaration. If you declare a callback as taking no arguments, you cannot pass an argument to the callback when you use it. Likewise, when a callback does take an argument, you must provide one when you use the routine, and the argument must match the type in the declaration. You can pass an argument whose type does not match the declaration if the UIL automatic type

---

† The parentheses are optional as well, but because the compiler does not perform argument type-checking when this style of declaration is used, we recommend against using it.

‡ This problem has been fixed as of Motif Release 1.2.3.

conversions described earlier provide for it. For example, you can pass a `string` to a call-back that is declared as taking a `compound_string`. If the use of a callback does not agree with its declaration, the UIL compiler generates an error, and the module is not compiled successfully. The following code fragment shows how you might use the `print` and `quit` callbacks:

```
object close : XmPushButton {
  callbacks {
    XmNarmCallback = procedure print ("Armed!");
    XmNactivateCallback = procedure quit();
  };
};
```

When a callback specified in a UIL module is invoked at run-time, the argument, if any, is passed to the callback as the `client_data` parameter. In this example, the string "Armed!" is passed to the `print()` callback when the PushButton is armed. The callback simply prints the argument that is passed to it. This routine is shown in the following code fragment:

```
void
print (w, client_data, call_data)
Widget    w;
XtPointer client_data;
XtPointer call_data;
{
    char *message = (char *) client_data;
    puts (message);
}
```

You should always cast the `client_data` argument to the appropriate type before using it, as this fragment illustrates. The argument type depends on the UIL value passed to a callback. Table 24-5 contains a complete listing of the UIL data types and the corresponding C types. In particular, you should note that the `integer`, `float`, and `boolean` numeric types are passed as pointers to the values, not the values themselves.

24.5 Using Lists

A UIL list is a group of widget children, resource settings, callback settings, or callback procedures. Although we didn't mention it earlier, the `controls`, `arguments`, and `callbacks` subsections of a widget definition are all in-line lists. The `procedures` syntax for specifying multiple callbacks is also an in-line list. You can also define a list outside of a widget definition and name it, so that you can use the list later in a widget definition or in another list.

You define named lists in a `list` section of a UIL module, which begins with the `list` keyword. A list definition consists of the name of the list, followed by a colon, the type of the list, and its contents. Unlike variable and widget definitions, list definitions are always private to a module, so you cannot export them. If you want to use a list in more than one module, you should place its definition in a UIL include file. The list name is a programmer-specified identifier; the list type is one of `controls`, `arguments`, `callbacks`, or procedures. The content of a list depends on its type.

Lists of `controls`, `arguments`, and `callbacks`, like the widget subsections by the same name, contain widget children, resource settings, and callback settings, respectively. The format of each of these lists is the same as the format of the corresponding subsection of a widget definition. A procedures list is used to specify multiple callback routines for a particular callback reason, as we explained earlier. Once you define a named list, you can use it in a widget definition. Example 24-13 shows a UIL module that uses all four types of lists.

Example 24-13. The simple_lst.uil module

```
/* simple_lst.uil -- simple example of lists */

module simple_lst

procedure
  quit();
  print (string);

list buttons : controls {
  XmPushButton OK;
  XmPushButton Help;
};

list size : arguments {
  XmNwidth = 50;
  XmNheight = 50;
};

list funcs : callbacks {
  XmNactivateCallback = procedure print ("Help!");
  XmNhelpCallback = procedure print ("Help!");
};

list ok_cbs : procedures {
  print ("Okee-dokee");
  quit();
};

object OK : XmPushButton {
  arguments size;
  callbacks {
    XmNactivateCallback = procedures ok_cbs;
  };
};

object Help : XmPushButton {
  arguments size;
  callbacks funcs;
};

object root : XmRowColumn {
  controls buttons;
};

end module;
```

As with the object definition, we use the convention of placing each list definition in its own `list` section, even though it is not necessary for consecutive definitions. This example defines the `buttons`, `size`, `funcs`, and `ok_cbs` lists, and then uses the lists in defining the widget hierarchy. To use a list in a widget definition, you specify the subsection followed by the name of a list. The named list replaces the in-line list definition that you have seen previously. The UIL compiler makes sure that the type of each named list matches the name of the subsection, which means that you cannot specify a named `controls` list for an `arguments` subsection, for example.

A named `list` definition lets you separate the contents of each list type from a widget definition. One advantage of this approach is that you can abstract commonly-used settings and define them in one place. However, the ability to factor out duplicate widget subsections and procedure lists is not that big of an advantage. The feature of lists that makes them more useful is the ability to reference other lists of the same type. You include one list in another by including an entry that consists of the type of the included list, followed by the name of the list to include.

Each reference to a list includes a copy of that list, which has different results depending on the type of the list. When you include a `controls` or `procedures` list in another list, the widgets or callbacks in the included list are added to the existing list, even if the same widget or callback is already there. Therefore, you can create multiple instances of the same widget or call the same callback multiple times. When you include an `arguments` or `callbacks` list in another list, the resources or callback settings in the included list are added to the existing list, but any duplicate setting supersedes the earlier setting. The advantage of this behavior is that you can selectively override resource or callback settings that have already been specified.† Example 24-14 illustrates the use of nested lists.

Example 24-14. The station.uil module

```
/* station.uil -- Example of using lists in lists */

module dialog

list basic_buttons : controls {
  OK     : XmPushButton { };
  Cancel : XmPushButton { };
};

list extended_buttons : controls {
  controls basic_buttons;
  Help : XmPushButton { };
};

list attach_all : arguments {
  XmNtopAttachment    = XmATTACH_FORM;
  XmNbottomAttachment = XmATTACH_FORM;
  XmNleftAttachment   = XmATTACH_FORM;
  XmNrightAttachment  = XmATTACH_FORM;
};
```

† When you override a resource or callback setting, the UIL compiler generates an informational message. You can turn off these messages with the -w compiler option, but you should be careful to do so only if you know that a module does not generate any other warnings.

Example 24-14. The station.uil module (continued)

```
object stations : XmRadioBox {
  controls {
    WAQY : XmToggleButton { };   KLBJ : XmToggleButton { };
    WPLR : XmToggleButton { };   KRCK : XmToggleButton { };
    WHCN : XmToggleButton { };   KPEZ : XmToggleButton { };
  };
  arguments {
    XmNorientation = XmHORIZONTAL;
    XmNnumColumns = 3;
    XmNmarginWidth = 20;
    arguments attach_all;
    XmNbottomAttachment = XmATTACH_NONE;
  };
};

object panel : XmRowColumn {
  controls extended_buttons;
  arguments {
    XmNorientation = XmHORIZONTAL;
    XmNentryAlignment = XmALIGNMENT_CENTER;
    XmNpacking = XmPACK_COLUMN;
    arguments attach_all;
    XmNtopAttachment = XmATTACH_WIDGET;
    XmNtopWidget = stations;
  };
};

object root : XmFormDialog {
  controls {
    XmRadioBox stations;
    XmRowColumn panel;
  };
  arguments {
    XmNdialogTitle = "Station Chooser";
  };
};

end module;
```

This module describes a simple user interface that uses two different types of lists. The output of the module is shown in Figure 24-12.

The `basic_buttons` list is a `controls` list that consists of two PushButtons: **OK** and **Cancel**. The `extended_buttons` list builds on the first list by adding a **Help** PushButton. This list is used as part of the dialog later in the module. The `attach_all` list is an `arguments` list that contains several Form attachment resource settings. We reference this list in the definition of both the RadioBox and the RowColumn, instead of reproducing the same settings in both widget definitions. In both cases, we override one of the resource settings from the list in the widget definition. This section only covers the basic use of lists in a UIL module. For more information on using lists, see Section 26.4 in Chapter 26, *Advanced UIL Programming*.

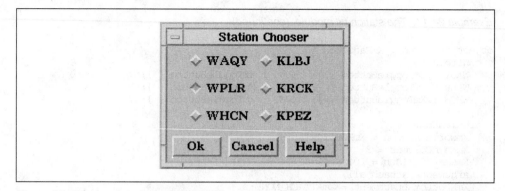

Figure 24-12. User interface of station.uil

24.6 Exporting Application Data

A value that is created or defined in an application can be used in a UIL module by declaring the value as a UIL `identifier` and registering it with Mrm. In this context, the term identifier means a value that is imported from the application, not a programmer-defined symbol. You can use an identifier as the value of a resource or as a callback argument. Unlike other values in a UIL module, identifiers are not typed, which means that the UIL compiler cannot perform type checking on identifiers. You should be careful to avoid type-mismatch problems in your use of identifiers.

24.6.1 Declaring Identifiers in UIL

You can use a registered application-defined value in a UIL module by declaring it an `identifier` section. This section begins with the keyword `identifier` and is followed by a list of declarations. Identifiers can be used like any other values, as illustrated in the following code fragment:

```
identifier
  home_directory;
  complex_data;

procedure
  open (any);

object fsb : XmFileSelectionBox {
  controls {
    Xm_OK {
      callbacks {
        XmNactivateCallback = procedure open (complex_data);
      };
    };
  };
  arguments {
    XmNdirectory = home_directory;
    XmNpattern = '*.uil';
```

```
    };
  };
```

In this fragment, we use the identifier `complex_data` as the argument to the `open()` callback. The identifier represents a value of type `ComplexStructure` that is declared in the application program, as you will see shortly. We declare the callback as taking an argument of type `any` because there is no UIL type that correspondes to the `ComplexStructure` type. The `any` type indicates that the callback function takes an argument, but that the argument can be of any type. We recommend that you only use the `any` type for identifier arguments, since the UIL compiler cannot perform type-checking when you use a callback that takes an `any` argument. We also use the identifier `home_directory` as the value of a resource setting. This setting is not type-checked either, so it is up to the application to make sure that `home_directory` is a string.

24.6.2 Exporting Identifiers From Application Code

When Mrm creates a widget that uses an identifier, it must convert the identifier name to the corresponding application-defined value. Similar to callback procedures, you must register the names of identifiers and their associated values with Mrm by calling `MrmRegisterNames()` or `MrmRegisterNamesInHierarchy()` before fetching widgets that reference the exported values. These routines are the same ones that are used to register callback procedures, as described in Chapter 22, *Introduction to UIL*. These functions take the following form:

```
Cardinal
MrmRegisterNames(identifier_list, num_identifiers)
    MrmRegisterArglist    identifier_list;
    MrmCount              num_identifiers;


Cardinal
MrmRegisterNamesInHierarchy(hierarchy, identifier_list,
                            num_identifiers)
    MrmHierarchy          hierarchy;
    MrmRegisterArglist    identifier_list;
    MrmCount              num_identifiers;
```

A call to `MrmRegisterNames()` makes the identifiers accessible from any open Mrm hierarchy, while a call to `MrmRegisterNamesInHierarchy()` makes the identifiers accessible from the Mrm hierarchy passed to the function. Identifiers that are registered in a specific Mrm hierarchy take precedence over those that are registered globally. The *identifier_list* argument specifies an array of `MrmRegisterArg` structures, and *num_identifiers* indicates the size of the array. The `MrmRegisterArg` structure indicates the mapping from an identifier name to an application value and is defined as follows:

```
typedef struct {
    String     name;
    XtPointer  value;
} MrmRegisterArg, *MrmRegisterArglist;
```

The name field is the name of the identifier as used in the UIL module. The name is case-sensitive, unless it is being referenced from a module that has the names option set to case_insensitive, in which case the name must be upper case. The value field is a pointer to an application variable. Since value is an XtPointer, you should only register values that are pointers. If you use a value whose size is not the same as an XtPointer, part of the value may be lost or corrupted. The size of certain C values, such as int and float, are not necessarily the same size as an XtPointer on all architectures. You can ensure the portability of an application by using the address of non-pointer types as the value of an identifier.

The following code fragment shows how MrmRegisterNames() can be used to register the identifier values used in the UIL fragment of the previous section:

```
char *home_directory;
ComplexStructure complex_data;
static MrmRegisterArg identifiers[] = {
    { "home_directory", (XtPointer) directory },
    { "complex_data", (XtPointer) &complex_data },
};
    ...
MrmRegisterNames (identifiers, XtNumber (identifiers));
    ...
```

This code registers the home_directory and complex_data identifiers globally, so that they are accessible from any Mrm hierarchy. The home_directory identifier is a string, while complex_data is a value of type ComplexStructure. Identifiers provide a mechanism for exporting arbitrarily complex data to a UIL module.

24.7 Summary

A UIL module may contain five types of sections, whose usage and syntax we have explained and demonstrated in detail.

An object section contains definitions of the widgets in an interface. An application creates these widgets at run-time by using the MrmFetchWidget() routine in the Mrm library.

A value section consists of declarations and definitions of UIL values that are used as resource settings and callback arguments in the widget definitions. Values can be fetched from a UIL module using a number of different Mrm routines.

A procedure section contains the declarations of callback procedures that are defined in the application program. Any callbacks that are specified in a UIL module must be declared in this section. Callback procedures are registered with the application program using Mrm-RegisterNames().

A list section is used to define controls, arguments, or callbacks lists that are used in the corresponding subsections of widget definitions, and to define procedures lists that specify the functions that are called when a single callback is invoked. The use of lists is private to a UIL module.

An identifier section contains declarations of application variables that are exported to UIL. The names and values of identifiers are registered with the application program using MrmRegisterNames().

25

Building an Application With UIL

This chapter draws on many of the features of UIL in developing a fully functional text editor application. It shows how the various components of UIL and Mrm come together in a real application.

In This Chapter:

25

Building an Application With UIL

In this chapter, we examine a real application that uses UIL. Although we have shown you a simple application and a number of UIL modules in the preceding chapters, we have not put everything together yet. This chapter provides some examples of common uses of UIL in an application, including the definition of a menu system and some dialogs.

Rather than start from scratch, we are going to use the simple text editor application from Chapter 14, *Text Widgets*. This program reads and writes text files, provides the usual cut, copy, and paste operations on the **Edit** menu, and performs search and replace operations from the **Search** menu. The interface of the editor program appears in Figure 25-1.

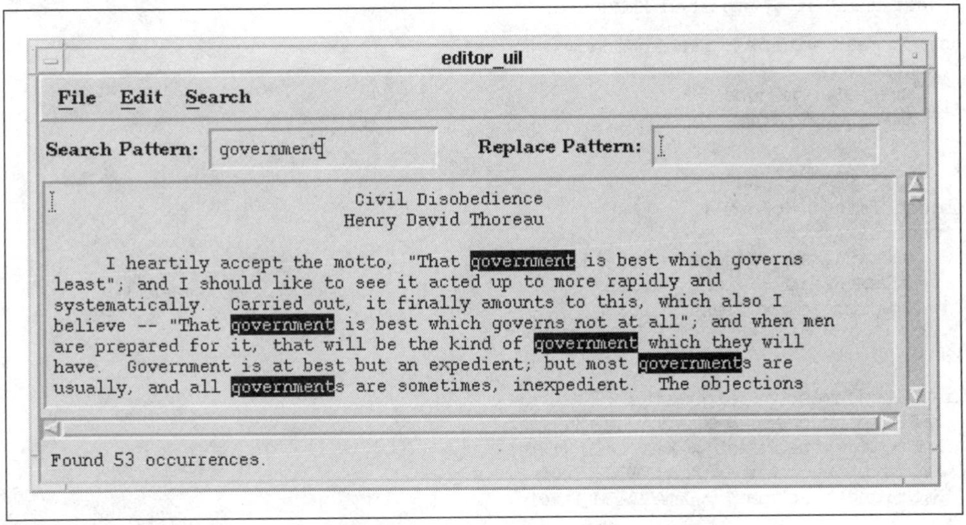

Figure 25-1. The editor_uil application

The UIL version of the text editor differs from the non-UIL version in several ways. The most obvious change is that the user interface must be described in UIL, instead of C. The program code also needs to be modified to create the interface with Mrm. The application callbacks need to be connected to procedures in UIL, and some global variables need to be initialized when widgets are created. We have also enhanced the program so that it distinguishes between status and error messages. Status messages are still displayed in the message area below the Text widget, while error messages are displayed in an ErrorDialog.

25.1 Defining the User Interface

Since we are going to create the user interface in UIL, we can remove many of the Motif and Xt function calls from the application code. We can break the interface description into three modules, so that the modules are smaller and easier to manage. The logical division is to describe the main application in one module, the menu system in another, and the dialogs in a third module.

25.1.1 The Main Application Window

The main application window for the editor consists of a MainWindow widget that contains a MenuBar, the text-editing area, TextFields for entering search and replace text, and a message area. Example 25-1 shows the UIL module that describes this interface.

Example 25-1. The editor.uil module

```
! editor.uil - editor application main user interface definition
module editor
include file 'procedures.uih';
include file 'identifiers.uih';

object menubar : imported XmMenuBar;

object main_window : XmMainWindow {
  controls {
    XmMenuBar menubar;
    XmForm    form;
  };
};

object form : XmForm {
  controls {
    XmRowColumn    search_panel;
    XmTextField    text_output;
    XmScrolledText text_edit;
  };
};

list attachments : arguments {
  XmNtopAttachment = XmATTACH_FORM;
  XmNbottomAttachment = XmATTACH_FORM;
  XmNleftAttachment = XmATTACH_FORM;
  XmNrightAttachment = XmATTACH_FORM;
};

object search_panel : exported XmRowColumn {
  controls {
    search_prompt : XmLabel gadget {
      arguments {
        XmNlabelString = "Search Pattern:";
      };
    };
    search_text : XmTextField {
      callbacks {
```

Example 25-1. The editor.uil module (continued)

```
                MrmNcreateCallback = procedure register_widget (w_search_text);
        };
    };
    replace_prompt : XmLabel gadget {
        arguments {
            XmNlabelString = "      Replace Pattern:";
        };
    };
    replace_text : XmTextField {
        callbacks {
            MrmNcreateCallback = procedure register_widget (w_replace_text);
        };
    };
  };
  arguments {
    XmNorientation = XmHORIZONTAL;
    XmNpacking = XmPACK_TIGHT;
    arguments attachments;
    XmNbottomAttachment = XmATTACH_NONE;
  };
};
object text_edit : XmScrolledText {
  arguments {
    XmNrows = 10;
    XmNcolumns = 80;
    XmNeditMode = XmMULTI_LINE_EDIT;
    arguments attachments;
    XmNtopAttachment = XmATTACH_WIDGET;
    XmNtopWidget = search_panel;
    XmNbottomAttachment = XmATTACH_WIDGET;
    XmNbottomWidget = text_output;
  };
  callbacks {
    MrmNcreateCallback = procedure register_widget (w_text_edit);
  };
};
object text_output : XmTextField {
  arguments {
    XmNeditable = false;
    XmNcursorPositionVisible = false;
    XmNshadowThickness = 0;
    arguments attachments;
    XmNtopAttachment = XmATTACH_NONE;
  };
  callbacks {
    MrmNcreateCallback = procedure register_widget (w_text_output);
  };
};

end module;
```

The module begins by including two files: *procedures.uih* and *identifiers.uih*. The *procedures.uih* file contains the callback declarations for the interface. The file also defines some arguments for the callback routines. This file is shown in Example 25-2.

Example 25-2. The procedures.uih include file

```
! procedures.uih - declarations of editor callbacks and their arguments
procedure
    register_widget (any);
procedure
    file_cb (integer);
    file_select_cb (integer);
value
    FILE_OPEN : 0;
    FILE_SAVE : 1;
    FILE_EXIT : 2;
procedure
    edit_cb (integer);
value
    EDIT_CUT   : 0;
    EDIT_COPY  : 1;
    EDIT_PASTE : 2;
    EDIT_CLEAR : 3;
procedure
    search_cb (integer);
value
    SEARCH_FIND_NEXT : 0;
    SEARCH_SHOW_ALL  : 1;
    SEARCH_REPLACE   : 2;
    SEARCH_CLEAR     : 3;
procedure
    popdown_cb();
```

The callback routines for the menu items and the FileSelectionDialog take `integer` arguments. The file defines the possible argument values for each of the callback routines. These values correspond to enumeration values in the application code; they indicate which action the callback should perform when it is invoked. We could write a separate procedure for each callback, but instead we use a single callback for each menu because the actions are similar. The callbacks that use these definitions are in the *menubar.uil* and *dialogs.uil* modules described later in this chapter.

The *identifiers.uih* file contains the declarations for several global widget variables. These variables are set in the UIL module by `MrmNcreateCallback`. This file is listed in Example 25-3.

Example 25-3. The identifiers.uih include file

```
! identifiers.uih - declarations of application defined data
identifier
  w_search_text;
  w_replace_text;
  w_text_edit;
  w_text_output;
```

After the include directives at the top of *editor.uil*, the module declares the MenuBar, because it is used in this module but defined in another. You must declare a widget that is defined in another module before you can use it. The declaration of the MainWindow portion of the interface comes next. The MainWindow is at the top of the hierarchy; it manages the MenuBar and a Form. The Form is the work area. It contains the other main sections of the window, which are a RowColumn that contains the search and replace TextFields, the ScrolledText editing area, and the TextField message area.

We specify the Form attachments using the `attachments` list, which specifies an attachment for each side of a widget. In the individual widget definitions, we override the necessary attachments to arrange the components properly. Since UIL allows forward references, we should be able to list the three children in the Form's `controls` subsection in the same order that they appear in the user interface. However, forward references may not always work correctly in early releases of Motif 1.2 due to an Mrm bug. To work around this problem we need to specify the children in a particular order. If one child is attached to another, the child that specifies the attachment should be listed after the widget to which it is attached. For example, in the *editor.uil* module, the `text_edit` contains attachments to both of its siblings, so we list it after the other two widgets in the `controls` subsection of the form. The actual widget definitions can occur in any order in the UIL module.

In addition to the Form attachments, each widget definition contains other resource settings that are necessary for the interface. The `search_panel` RowColumn contains two Labels and two TextField widgets. Since the definitions of these widgets are short, they are defined in the body of the `search_panel` definition instead of in separate `object` sections. In contrast, the size of the `search_panel` itself makes it too large to place in the Form parent without making the module unreadable.

25.1.2 The Menu System

Even though the MenuBar for this application contains only a few entries, there are still enough widgets to make it worthwhile to define the menu system in a separate UIL module. This technique makes sense for most applications. The general widget hierarchy for a Menu-Bar is basically the same for all applications. The top-level widget is the MenuBar; it contains a CascadeButton for each menu. The editor application provides **File**, **Edit**, and **Search** menus. A PulldownMenu is associated with each CascadeButton and contains the individual menu entries. The definition of the menu system for the editor program is shown in Example 25-4.

Example 25-4. The menubar.uil module

```
! menubar.uil - editor application main window MenuBar definitions

module editor_menubar
  objects = {
    XmLabel          = gadget;
    XmCascadeButton  = gadget;
    XmPushButton     = gadget;
    XmToggleButton   = gadget;
    XmSeparator      = gadget;
  }

include file 'procedures.uih';

object menubar : exported XmMenuBar {
  controls {
    XmCascadeButton  file;
    XmCascadeButton  edit;
    XmCascadeButton  search;
  };
};

object file : XmCascadeButton {
  controls {
    file_menu : XmPulldownMenu {
      controls {
        XmPushButton  open;
        XmPushButton  save;
        XmSeparator   { };
        XmPushButton  exit;
      };
    };
  };
  arguments {
    XmNlabelString = "File";
    XmNmnemonic    = keysym ('F');
  };
};

object open : XmPushButton {
  arguments {
    XmNlabelString = "Open...";
    XmNmnemonic    = keysym ('O');
  };
  callbacks {
    XmNactivateCallback = procedure file_cb (FILE_OPEN);
  };
};

object save : XmPushButton {
  arguments {
    XmNlabelString = "Save...";
    XmNmnemonic    = keysym ('S');
  };
  callbacks {
    XmNactivateCallback = procedure file_cb (FILE_SAVE);
  };
};

object exit : XmPushButton {
```

Example 25-4. The menubar.uil module (continued)

```
    arguments {
      XmNlabelString     = "Exit";
      XmNmnemonic        = keysym ('x');
      XmNaccelerator     = 'Ctrl<Key>c';
      XmNacceleratorText = "Ctrl+C";
    };
    callbacks {
      XmNactivateCallback = procedure file_cb (FILE_EXIT);
    };
};

object edit : XmCascadeButton {
  controls {
    edit_menu : XmPulldownMenu {
      controls {
        XmPushButton   cut;
        XmPushButton   copy;
        XmPushButton   paste;
        XmSeparator    { };
        XmPushButton   eclear;
      };
    };
  };
  arguments {
    XmNlabelString = "Edit";
    XmNmnemonic    = keysym ('E');
  };
};

object cut : XmPushButton {
  arguments {
    XmNlabelString     = "Cut";
    XmNmnemonic        = keysym ('t');
    XmNaccelerator     = 'Shift<Key>Delete';
    XmNacceleratorText = "Shift+Del";
  };
  callbacks {
    XmNactivateCallback = procedure edit_cb (EDIT_CUT);
  };
};

object copy : XmPushButton {
  arguments {
    XmNlabelString     = "Copy";
    XmNmnemonic        = keysym ('C');
    XmNaccelerator     = 'Ctrl<Key>Insert';
    XmNacceleratorText = "Ctrl+Ins";
  };
  callbacks {
    XmNactivateCallback = procedure edit_cb (EDIT_COPY);
  };
};

object paste : XmPushButton {
  arguments {
    XmNlabelString     = "Paste";
    XmNmnemonic        = keysym ('P');
    XmNaccelerator     = 'Shift<Key>Insert';
```

Example 25-4. The menubar.uil module (continued)

```
      XmNacceleratorText = "Shift+Ins";
   };
   callbacks {
      XmNactivateCallback = procedure edit_cb (EDIT_PASTE);
   };
};

object eclear : XmPushButton {
   arguments {
      XmNlabelString = "Clear";
      XmNmnemonic    = keysym ('l');
   };
   callbacks {
      XmNactivateCallback = procedure edit_cb (EDIT_CLEAR);
   };
};

object search : XmCascadeButton {
   controls {
      search_menu : XmPulldownMenu {
         controls {
            XmPushButton   find_next;
            XmPushButton   show_all;
            XmPushButton   replace;
            XmSeparator    { };
            XmPushButton   sclear;
         };
      };
   };
   arguments {
      XmNlabelString = "Search";
      XmNmnemonic    = keysym ('S');
   };
};

object find_next : XmPushButton {
   arguments {
      XmNlabelString     = "Find Next";
      XmNmnemonic        = keysym ('N');
      XmNaccelerator     = 'Ctrl<Key>N';
      XmNacceleratorText = "Ctrl+N";
   };
   callbacks {
      XmNactivateCallback = procedure search_cb (SEARCH_FIND_NEXT);
   };
};

object show_all : XmPushButton {
   arguments {
      XmNlabelString     = "Show All";
      XmNmnemonic        = keysym ('A');
      XmNaccelerator     = 'Ctrl<Key>A';
      XmNacceleratorText = "Ctrl+A";
   };
   callbacks {
      XmNactivateCallback = procedure search_cb (SEARCH_SHOW_ALL);
   };
};
```

Example 25-4. The menubar.uil module (continued)

```
object replace : XmPushButton {
  arguments {
    XmNlabelString       = "Replace Text";
    XmNmnemonic          = keysym ('R');
  };
  callbacks {
    XmNactivateCallback = procedure search_cb (SEARCH_REPLACE);
  };
};
object sclear : XmPushButton {
  arguments {
    XmNlabelString = "Clear";
    XmNmnemonic    = keysym ('C');
  };
  callbacks {
    XmNactivateCallback = procedure search_cb (SEARCH_CLEAR);
  };
};

end module;
```

We set the `objects` option at the beginning of this module so that all of the menu entries
are created as gadgets. Setting this option at the top of the module saves you from accidentally forgetting to use the gadget version of one of the buttons in a widget definition. Even
though our menus do not include Labels or ToggleButtons, these objects are included in the
option setting in case we decide to add some later.

Once again, the widget definitions in this module are organized in a top-down manner. The
first widget definition is the MenuBar, which contains a CascadeButton for each menu. In
UIL, you declare the PulldownMenu associated with a CascadeButton as a child of the but-
ton, instead of as a child of the MenuBar, like in C code. The UIL method is more intuitive.
At run-time, Mrm creates each menu as a child of the MenuBar and sets the `XmNsubMenu-
Id` resource of the appropriate CascadeButton to satisfy the Motif requirements.

For each menu, we define PulldownMenu in-line, since it only contains a list of child widgets. This convention makes the definitions easier to read and modify. We define the buttons
separately, however, since the definitions are longer, and they would be too large in-line.
Since there are no resource settings for the Separators, we define these components in-line
and do not name them, as it is unlikely that users will specify resources for them.

There is a single callback routine associated with each PulldownMenu, so the callback
resource for each menu item is set to the appropriate routine. The action taken by the callback procedure when it is invoked is determined by the argument passed to the callback. The
possible arguments are defined in *procedures.uih* along with the callback procedures. The
arguments correspond to enumeration values defined in the application source code.

25.1.3 Dialog Boxes

The *editor_uil* interface uses some predefined Motif dialogs that are defined in the *dialogs.uil* module. Unlike the MenuBar definition, these dialogs are not imported by the main *editor.uil* module. Instead, the dialogs are fetched by the application when they are needed. The application uses two FileSelectionDialogs, one for opening files and one for saving files. It also uses an ErrorDialog for displaying error messages. The definitions of these widgets are shown in Example 25-5.

Example 25-5. The dialogs.uil module

```
! dialogs.uil - editor application dialog definitions

module editor_dialogs

include file 'procedures.uih';

object open_dialog : XmFileSelectionDialog {
  arguments {
    XmNdialogTitle = "Open File";
    XmNokLabelString = "Open";
  };
  callbacks {
    XmNcancelCallback = procedure popdown_cb();
    XmNokCallback = procedure file_select_cb (FILE_OPEN);
  };
};

object save_dialog : XmFileSelectionDialog {
  arguments {
    XmNdialogTitle = "Save File";
    XmNokLabelString = "Save";
  };
  callbacks {
    XmNcancelCallback = procedure popdown_cb();
    XmNokCallback = procedure file_select_cb (FILE_SAVE);
  };
};

object error_dialog : XmErrorDialog {
  controls {
    Xm_Cancel unmanaged { };
    Xm_Help unmanaged { };
  };
  arguments {
    XmNdialogTitle = "Error";
    XmNdialogStyle = XmDIALOG_FULL_APPLICATION_MODAL;
  };
};

end module;
```

Each FileSelectionDialog has the same form. The titles and the labels and callbacks for the **OK** buttons are set for the different purposes of each dialog. Both dialogs use the same **Cancel** callback, `file_select_cb()`. This routine uses the same arguments as the `file_cb()` callback.

The definition of the ErrorDialog is quite simple, since specifying an ErrorDialog causes most of the necessary MessageBox resources to be set appropriately. We make the dialog modal, so the user is forced to acknowledge an error before continuing, and we unmanage the Cancel and Help buttons so the user can only acknowledge an error message. The dialog needs a few other changes, but they cannot be made in UIL. The XmNmessageString must be set each time an error is displayed. This change is handled in the application code, which we explain in the next section.

25.2 Creating the Application

The original *editor.c* program needs several changes before it can work with the UIL user interface we have defined. Like any application that uses UIL, the widget creation is now handled by Mrm. The callbacks also need a few minor changes that are related to the use of Mrm. We have added a new callback that lets the application obtain the widget IDs of Mrm-created widgets. The new version of the application is shown in Example 25-6. Compared to the original version, the *editor_uil.c* program is about 50 lines shorter. Most of the shrinkage comes from main(), in which the Motif widget creation calls are replaced by Mrm calls.

Example 25-6. The editor_uil.c application

```
/* editor_uil.c -- create a full-blown Motif editor application complete
 * with a menubar, facilities to read and write files, text search
 * and replace, clipboard support and so forth.
 */

#include <Mrm/MrmAppl.h>
#include <Xm/Text.h>
#include <Xm/MessageB.h>

#include <stdio.h>
#include <sys/types.h>
#include <sys/stat.h>

MrmHierarchy   hierarchy;
Cardinal       status;
MrmType        class_code;
static char    buf[256];

static String uid_files[] = { "editor", "menubar", "dialogs" };

XtAppContext   app_context;
Widget toplevel, text_edit, search_text, replace_text, text_output;

static MrmRegisterArg widgets_list[] = {
    { "w_text_edit",      (XtPointer) &text_edit },
    { "w_search_text",    (XtPointer) &search_text },
    { "w_replace_text",   (XtPointer) &replace_text },
    { "w_text_output",    (XtPointer) &text_output },
};

void register_widget(), file_cb(), edit_cb(), search_cb(), file_select_cb();
void popdown_cb();

/* These definitions depend on the order of the menu entries and are
   also defined in the procedures.uih file with the callback decls. */
```

Example 25-6. The editor_uil.c application (continued)

```
typedef enum { FILE_OPEN, FILE_SAVE, FILE_EXIT } FileOp;
typedef enum { EDIT_CUT, EDIT_COPY, EDIT_PASTE, EDIT_CLEAR } EditOp;
typedef enum { SEARCH_FIND_NEXT, SEARCH_SHOW_ALL, SEARCH_REPLACE,
               SEARCH_CLEAR } SearchOp;

static MrmRegisterArg callbacks_list[] = {
    { "register_widget", (XtPointer) register_widget },
    { "file_cb",         (XtPointer) file_cb },
    { "edit_cb",         (XtPointer) edit_cb },
    { "search_cb",       (XtPointer) search_cb },
    { "file_select_cb",  (XtPointer) file_select_cb },
    { "popdown_cb",      (XtPointer) popdown_cb },
};

main(argc, argv)
int   argc;
char *argv[];
{
    Widget main_window;

    XtSetLanguageProc (NULL, NULL, NULL);

    MrmInitialize();

    toplevel = XtVaAppInitialize (&app_context, "Demos", NULL, 0,
        &argc, argv, NULL, NULL);

    status = MrmOpenHierarchyPerDisplay (XtDisplay(toplevel),
        XtNumber(uid_files), uid_files, NULL, &hierarchy);

    if (status != MrmSUCCESS) {
        XtAppError (app_context, "MrmOpenHierarchyPerDisplay failed");
        exit (1);
    }

    MrmRegisterNames (widgets_list, XtNumber (widgets_list));
    MrmRegisterNames (callbacks_list, XtNumber (callbacks_list));

    status = MrmFetchWidget (hierarchy, "main_window", toplevel,
        &main_window, &class_code);

    if (status != MrmSUCCESS) {
        XtAppError (app_context, "MrmFetchWidget failed");
        exit (1);
    }

    XtManageChild (main_window);
    XtRealizeWidget (toplevel);

    XtAppMainLoop (app_context);
}

/* routine to display an error dialog */
void
show_error (message)
char *message;
{
    static Widget dialog;
    XmString s;

    if (dialog == NULL) {
```

Example 25-6. The editor_uil.c application (continued)

```
            MrmFetchWidget (hierarchy, "error_dialog", toplevel,
                &dialog, &class_code);
        if (dialog == NULL || ! XmIsMessageBox (dialog)) {
            XtAppError (app_context, "Creation of error dialog failed.");
            exit (1);
        }
    }

    s = XmStringCreateLocalized (message);
    XtVaSetValues (dialog, XmNmessageString, s, NULL);
    XmStringFree (s);

    XtManageChild (dialog);
}
/* callback routine for "OK" button in FileSelectionDialogs */
void
file_select_cb (dialog, client_data, call_data)
Widget dialog;
XtPointer client_data;
XtPointer call_data;
{
    char   *filename, *text;
    struct stat statb;
    long len;
    FILE *fp;
    FileOp reason = *((FileOp *) client_data);
    XmFileSelectionBoxCallbackStruct *cbs =
      (XmFileSelectionBoxCallbackStruct *) call_data;

    XmTextSetString (text_output, NULL);   /* clear the message area */

    if (!XmStringGetLtoR (cbs->value, XmFONTLIST_DEFAULT_TAG, &filename))
        return; /* must have been an internal error */

    if (*filename == NULL) {
        XtFree (filename);
        XBell (XtDisplay (text_edit), 50);
        XmTextSetString (text_output, "Choose a file.");
        return; /* nothing typed */
    }

    if (reason == FILE_SAVE) {
        long bytes_written;
        if (!(fp = fopen (filename, "w"))) {
            perror (filename);
            sprintf (buf, "Can't save to %s.", filename);
            show_error (buf);
            XtFree (filename);
            return;
        }
        /* saving -- get text from Text widget... */
        text = XmTextGetString (text_edit);
        len = XmTextGetLastPosition (text_edit);
        /* write it to file (check for error) */

        bytes_written = fwrite (text, sizeof (char), len, fp);
        if (bytes_written != len) {
            strcpy (buf, "Warning: did not write entire file!");
```

Example 25-6. The editor_uil.c application (continued)

```
                show_error (buf);
            }
        else {
                /* make sure a newline terminates file */
                if (text[len-1] != '\n')
                    fputc ('\n', fp);
                sprintf (buf, "Saved %ld bytes to %s.", len, filename);
                XmTextSetString (text_output, buf);
            }
        }
        else {   /* reason == FILE_OPEN */
            /* make sure the file is a regular text file and open it */
            if (stat (filename, &statb) == -1 ||
                (statb.st_mode & S_IFMT) != S_IFREG ||
             !(fp = fopen (filename, "r"))) {
                perror (filename);
                sprintf (buf, "Can't read %s.", filename);
                show_error (buf);
                XtFree (filename);
                return;
            }
        /* put the contents of the file in the Text widget by
         * allocating enough space for the entire file, reading the
         * file into the space, and using XmTextSetString() to show
         * the file.
         */
        len = statb.st_size;
        if (!(text = XtMalloc ((unsigned)(len+1)))) { /* +1 for NULL */
            sprintf (buf, "%s: XtMalloc(%ld) failed.", len, filename);
            show_error (buf);
            }
        else {
            long bytes_read = fread (text, sizeof(char), len, fp);
            if (bytes_read != len) {
                sprintf (buf, "Did not read entire file!");
                    show_error (buf);
            }

                sprintf (buf, "Loaded %ld bytes from %s.", bytes_read, filename);
                XmTextSetString (text_output, buf);
                text[len] = 0; /* NULL-terminate */
                XmTextSetString (text_edit, text);
            }
        }

    /* free all allocated space. */
    XtFree (text);
    XtFree (filename);
    fclose (fp);
    XtUnmanageChild (dialog);
}

/* a menu item from the "File" pulldown menu was selected */
void
file_cb (w, client_data, call_data)
Widget w;
XtPointer client_data;
```

Example 25-6. The editor_uil.c application (continued)

```
XtPointer call_data;
{
    static Widget open_dialog, save_dialog;
    FileOp reason = *((FileOp *) client_data);

    if (reason == FILE_EXIT) {
        MrmCloseHierarchy (hierarchy);
        exit (0);
    }

    XmTextSetString (text_output, NULL);   /* clear the message area */

    if (reason == FILE_OPEN) {
        if (open_dialog == NULL)
            MrmFetchWidget (hierarchy, "open_dialog", toplevel,
                &open_dialog, &class_code);
        if (open_dialog)
            XtManageChild (open_dialog);
        else
            show_error ("Creation of the open dialog failed.");
    }
    else {  /* reason == FILE_SAVE */
        if (save_dialog == NULL)
            MrmFetchWidget (hierarchy, "save_dialog", toplevel,
                &save_dialog, &class_code);
        if (save_dialog)
            XtManageChild (save_dialog);
        else
            show_error ("Creation of the save dialog failed.");
    }
}

/* a menu item from the "Search" pulldown menu was selected */
void
search_cb (w, client_data, call_data)
Widget w;
XtPointer client_data;
XtPointer call_data;
{
    char *search_pat, *p, *string, *new_pat;
    XmTextPosition pos = 0;
    int len, nfound = 0;
    int search_len, pattern_len;
    SearchOp reason = *((SearchOp *) client_data);
    Boolean found = False;

    XmTextSetString (text_output, NULL);   /* clear the message area */

    if (reason == SEARCH_CLEAR) {
        pos = XmTextGetLastPosition (text_edit);
        XmTextSetHighlight (text_edit, 0, pos, XmHIGHLIGHT_NORMAL);
        return;
    }

    if (!(string = XmTextGetString (text_edit)) || !*string) {
        show_error ("No text to search.");
        return;
    }
```

Example 25-6. The editor_uil.c application (continued)

```
    if (!(search_pat = XmTextGetString (search_text)) || !*search_pat) {
        XmTextSetString (text_output, "Specify a search pattern.");
        XtFree (string);
        return;
    }

    new_pat = XmTextGetString (replace_text);
    search_len = strlen (search_pat);
    pattern_len = strlen (new_pat);

    if (reason == SEARCH_FIND_NEXT) {
        pos = XmTextGetCursorPosition (text_edit) + 1;
        found = XmTextFindString (text_edit, pos, search_pat,
            XmTEXT_FORWARD, &pos);
        if (!found)
            found = XmTextFindString (text_edit, 0, search_pat,
                XmTEXT_FORWARD, &pos);
        if (found)
            nfound++;
    }
    else {   /* reason == SHOW_ALL || reason == SEARCH_REPLACE */
        do {
            found = XmTextFindString (text_edit, pos, search_pat,
                XmTEXT_FORWARD, &pos);
            if (found) {
                nfound++;
                if (reason == SEARCH_SHOW_ALL)
                    XmTextSetHighlight (text_edit, pos, pos + search_len,
                        XmHIGHLIGHT_SELECTED);
                else
                    XmTextReplace (text_edit, pos, pos + search_len, new_pat);
                pos++;
            }
        }
        while (found);
    }

    if (nfound == 0) {
        XmTextSetString (text_output, "Pattern not found");
    } else {
        switch (reason) {
            case SEARCH_FIND_NEXT :
                sprintf (buf, "Pattern found at position %ld.", pos);
                XmTextSetInsertionPosition (text_edit, pos);
                break;
            case SEARCH_SHOW_ALL :
                sprintf (buf, "Found %d occurrences.", nfound);
                break;
            case SEARCH_REPLACE :
                sprintf (buf, "Made %d replacements.", nfound);
        }
        XmTextSetString (text_output, buf);
    }
    XtFree (string);
    XtFree (search_pat);
    XtFree (new_pat);
}
```

Example 25-6. The editor_uil.c application (continued)

```
/* the callback routine for the items in the edit menu */
void
edit_cb (widget, client_data, call_data)
Widget widget;
XtPointer client_data;
XtPointer call_data;
{
    Boolean result = True;
    EditOp reason = *((EditOp *) client_data);
    XEvent *event = ((XmPushButtonCallbackStruct *) call_data)->event;
    Time when;

    XmTextSetString (text_output, NULL);   /* clear the message area */

    if (event != NULL &&
        reason == EDIT_CUT || reason == EDIT_COPY || reason == EDIT_CLEAR) {
        switch (event->type) {
            case ButtonRelease :
                when = event->xbutton.time;
                break;
            case KeyRelease :
                when = event->xkey.time;
                break;
            default:
                when = CurrentTime;
                break;
        }
    }

    switch (reason) {
        case EDIT_CUT :
            result = XmTextCut (text_edit, when);
            break;
        case EDIT_COPY :
            result = XmTextCopy (text_edit, when);
            break;
        case EDIT_PASTE :
            result = XmTextPaste (text_edit);
        case EDIT_CLEAR :
            XmTextClearSelection (text_edit, when);
            break;
    }

    if (result == False)
        XmTextSetString (text_output, "There is no selection.");
}

void
popdown_cb (w, client_data, call_data)
Widget w;
XtPointer client_data;
XtPointer call_data;
{
    XtUnmanageChild (w);
}

void
register_widget (w, client_data, call_data)
```

Example 25-6. The editor_uil.c application (continued)

```
Widget w;
XtPointer client_data;
XtPointer call_data;
{
    Widget *w_ptr = (Widget *) client_data;
    *w_ptr = w;
}
```

In order to create the interface that we defined in UIL, the application must use Mrm. Like any other application that uses Mrm, this application calls `MrmInitialize()`, `MrmOpenHierarchyPerDisplay()`, and `MrmFetchWidget()`. It also registers its callbacks and some global widget variables with `MrmRegisterNames()`. While it is possible to register both types of data with one call, we use two separate calls to distinguish between the two types of data. We create the main window of the application in `main()` and leave the creation of the dialogs until they are needed.

25.2.1 Widget IDs

When you create an interface by calling the Motif creation functions directly, you get the ID of each widget that you create. With Mrm, many widgets are created with a single call, and all you get back is the ID of the widget at the top of the hierarchy. In most cases, application programs need the IDs of other widgets in the hierarchy; the *editor_uil* program is no exception. It is easy to get the necessary widget IDs by using an `MrmNcreateCallback`. The `register_widget()` routine is used as the creation callback for all of the widgets for which we need an ID.

The `register_widget()` callback takes a pointer to a widget as its `client_data`. The routine assigns the ID of the widget that was just created to this pointer. The `widget_list` array declared at the beginning of the program specifies a list of UIL identifiers and global widget pointers. The application registers these identifiers with Mrm, so they are available in the UIL modules for use as callback arguments. Each identifier is prefixed with `w_`, so that the name does not conflict with the actual widget name defined in the UIL module. The identifiers are declared in *identifiers.uih*, which is included by *editor.uil*.

25.2.2 Callbacks

The *editor_uil* application registers its callbacks with Mrm by calling `MrmRegisterNames()` with the `callbacks_list` array. As with identifiers, you must declare any exported callbacks that you use in a UIL module. We use the convention of placing these declarations in a file named *procedures.uih*, which is included by all of our UIL modules.

The application uses a single callback for each PulldownMenu. The `client_data` argument to each callback specifies the action that the callback should perform. The *procedures.uih* file contains the callback declarations, as well as value definitions for the callback arguments. These values are defined with the same values used in the application, so if any changes are made to the values in the application program, the UIL definitions must be updated as well.

Most of the callbacks in our application are the same as in the original. Only the `file_cb()` callback has been changed; it now includes code that creates part of the user interface, namely the FileSelectionDialogs. The creation routines are replaced by calls to `MrmFetchWidget()`. The application creates each dialog the first time it is needed and keeps the widget pointer in a static variable so the dialog can be reused. This type of delayed widget creation can make a program start up faster and it can save memory. In order to allow delayed widget creation, the application does not close the `MrmHierarchy` before calling `XtAppMainLoop()`. The hierarchy is closed when the user exits the program, which is an action that is also handled by `file_cb()`.

25.2.3 The Error Dialog

Originally, the TextField message area at the bottom of the main application window displayed both status and error messages. However, we believe making error messages as explicit as possible is a good idea. As an enhancement to the original *editor* program, we have added an ErrorDialog to display error messages. The `show_error()` routine creates and displays the ErrorDialog shown in Figure 25-2.

Figure 25-2. The editor_uil ErrorDialog

The `show_error()` routine creates the ErrorDialog with a call to `MrmFetchWidget()` the first time an error occurs. The standard Motif ErrorDialog includes three PushButtons: **OK**, **Cancel**, and **Help**. Since the **OK** button is sufficient for our purposes, the routine unmanages the other two PushButtons after fetching the dialog. Unfortunately, you cannot unmanage automatically-created children directly in UIL, which means that the program must handle this step.

The program also updates the `XmNmessageString` of the ErrorDialog each time it is used to display an error message. The error strings are hard-coded into this application. You can make your programs more open to internationalization if you place the strings in a UIL module. Then you can easily set string resources by replacing calls to `XtVaSetValues()` with calls to `MrmFetchSetValues()`.

25.3 Summary

Creating an application that uses UIL and Mrm is very similar to creating an application that just uses Motif. The main difference is that the user interface of the application is defined in one or more UIL modules, instead of being created in application code by Motif and Xt creation procedures. Using UIL tends to simplify the application code by separating the interface from the code itself. In some situations, provisions must be made to pass widget IDs from a UIL module to the application, so that the application can modify a widget dynamically while it is running. While using UIL certainly affects the creation of a user interface, application callbacks and other internal operations remain much the same.

26

Advanced UIL Programming

This chapter describes advanced concepts and programming techniques in UIL. It builds on the UIL material explained in the previous chapters.

In This Chapter:

Advanced UIL Programming

This chapter introduces and examines ways that you can make the most of UIL's more advanced features. In the following sections, we describe how to add non-Motif widgets to an interface description, discuss methods and ideas for organizing UIL files, and examine the considerations that you face when setting resources in UIL. Finally, we present material on advanced uses of UIL lists and user-interface prototyping.

26.1 Using Non-Motif Widgets

With UIL, it is easy to define instances of any of the Motif widgets, because their type names are built into the compiler. However, you may need to use your own widget or a third-party widget in an application to provide functionality that is not available in the Motif widget set. Fortunately, it is possible to include other widgets using the special `user_defined` widget class along with the `argument` and `reason` value types.

OSF/Motif also supports non-Motif widget descriptions using the widget meta-language (WML). These widgets are written into a separate WML description file which is run through the WML compiler. WML is typically used for describing alternative widget sets; many third party widget sets include compiled WML description files. The use of compiled WML description files is covered in 23.1.7, but a complete description of WML syntax and usage is beyond the scope of this book.

Getting back to UIL, here are the steps involved in defining and creating a user-defined widget:

1. Write a widget creation procedure for the new widget.

2. Register the creation procedure with Mrm using `MrmRegisterClass()`.

3. Declare the creation procedure in UIL.

4. Declare the widget's resources and callbacks in UIL.

5. Define one or more instances of the widget.

To illustrate these steps, we are going to present an example that uses the Athena (Xaw) Tree and Panner widgets. The Tree widget is a constraint widget that arranges its children in a tree, while the Panner is a two-dimensional scroll bar.

26.1.1 The Widget Creation Procedure

In order to create a non-Motif widget, you must write a creation procedure and register it with Mrm. A user-defined widget creation procedure takes the same form as the Motif widget creation routines. The *parent* argument specifies the parent of the widget to create, and the *name* argument is the widget's name. The *args* and *num_args* parameters supply the initial resource settings for the widget. Most creation procedures create a widget simply by calling XtCreateWidget().

Mrm must know about a new creation function before you can create widgets with it. Widget creation functions are registered with MrmRegisterClass(), which must be called before any user-defined widgets are created. This function takes the following form:

```
Cardinal
MrmRegisterClass(class_code, class_name, proc_name, create_proc,
                 widget_class)
    MrmType     class_code;
    String      class_name;
    String      proc_name;
    Widget      (*create_proc)();
    WidgetClass widget_class;
```

The first two arguments, *class_code* and *class_name*, are obsolete but remain to preserve backwards compatibility. You should always pass 0 and NULL for these arguments, respectively. The *proc_name* parameter specifies the name of the creation procedure as it appears in a UIL module. To avoid confusion, it is a good idea to use the same name in both application code and UIL. The *create_proc* argument is the address of the creation procedure, and *widget_class* is a pointer to the class structure of the widget. The function indicates the result of the operation by returning either MrmSUCCESS or MrmFAILURE. A failure only occurs when the function cannot allocate memory.

MrmRegisterClass() does not take an MrmHierarchy argument like many of the Mrm routines, which means that any user-defined widgets that you register with this function are accessible from all open hierarchies. Mrm does not provide a way to register a widget class with an individual hierarchy. Example 26-1 demonstrates the use of MrmRegister-Class().

Example 26-1. The tree.c program

```
/* tree.c --
 * Program to show the Tree and Panner widgets.
 */

#include <stdio.h>
#include <X11/Intrinsic.h>
#include <X11/Xaw/Tree.h>
#include <X11/Xaw/Panner.h>
#include <X11/StringDefs.h>
#include <Mrm/MrmAppl.h>

void pan();

static MrmRegisterArg callback_list[] = {
    { "pan",            (XtPointer) pan },
    /* Add additional callback procedures here... */
```

Example 26-1. The tree.c program (continued)

```
};
Widget
XawCreateTreeWidget (parent, name, args, num_args)
Widget parent;
String name;
ArgList args;
Cardinal num_args;
{
    return (XtCreateWidget (name, treeWidgetClass, parent, args, num_args));
}

Widget
XawCreatePannerWidget (parent, name, args, num_args)
Widget parent;
String name;
ArgList args;
Cardinal num_args;
{
    return (XtCreateWidget (name, pannerWidgetClass, parent, args, num_args));
}

void
pan (panner, client_data, call_data)
Widget panner;
XtPointer client_data;
XtPointer call_data;
{
    Widget tree = (Widget) client_data;
    XawPannerReport *report = (XawPannerReport *) call_data;

    /* Should use XtSetValues, but DrawingArea bug prevents us */
    XtMoveWidget (tree, -report->slider_x, -report->slider_y);
}

int
main (argc, argv)
int    argc;
char *argv[];
{
    XtAppContext   app_context;
    Widget         toplevel, root_widget;
    Cardinal       status;
    static String uid_file_list[] = { "tree" };
    MrmType        class_code;
    MrmHierarchy   hierarchy;

    XtSetLanguageProc (NULL, NULL, NULL);

    MrmInitialize();

    toplevel = XtVaAppInitialize (&app_context, "Demos", NULL, 0,
        &argc, argv, NULL, NULL);

    status = MrmOpenHierarchyPerDisplay (XtDisplay (toplevel),
        XtNumber (uid_file_list), uid_file_list, NULL, &hierarchy);

    if (status != MrmSUCCESS) {
        XtAppError (app_context, "MrmOpenHierarchyPerDisplay failed");
        exit (1);
```

Example 26-1. The tree.c program (continued)

```
    }

    MrmRegisterNames (callback_list, XtNumber (callback_list));
    MrmRegisterClass (0, NULL, "XawCreateTreeWidget",
        XawCreateTreeWidget, treeWidgetClass);
    MrmRegisterClass (0, NULL, "XawCreatePannerWidget",
        XawCreatePannerWidget, pannerWidgetClass);

    status = MrmFetchWidget (hierarchy, "root", toplevel, &root_widget,
        &class_code);

    if (status != MrmSUCCESS) {
        XtAppError (app_context, "MrmFetchWidget failed");
        exit (1);
    }

    XtManageChild (root_widget);
    XtRealizeWidget (toplevel);

    XtAppMainLoop (app_context);
}
```

This program defines widget creation functions for the Tree and Panner widgets and registers the routines with Mrm. The program also defines the pan() callback routine for the Panner widget. This routine is specified for the XtNreportCallback, as we'll show you shortly.

26.1.2 Widget Include Files

It usually makes sense to place the declarations for a user-defined widget in an include file so that they can be used in more than one module. The include file for the Tree widget is shown in Example 26-2.

Example 26-2. The XawTree.uih include file

```
/* UIL declarations for the Xaw Tree widget. */

! Declare the creation procedure
procedure
    XawCreateTreeWidget ();

! Declare resources
value
    XtNautoReconfigure : argument ('autoReconfigure', boolean);
    XtNhSpace          : argument ('hSpace',          integer);
    XtNlineWidth       : argument ('lineWidth',       integer);
    XtNvSpace          : argument ('vSpace',          integer);
    XtNgravity         : argument ('gravity',         integer);
        NorthGravity : 2;
        WestGravity  : 4;
        EastGravity  : 6;
        SouthGravity : 8;

    ! Constraint resources
    XtNtreeGC          : argument ('treeGC',          any);
    XtNtreeParent      : argument ('treeParent',      widget);
```

The Tree creation procedure is declared in a `procedure` section, even though the application registers a widget creation procedure differently from a callback procedure. Creation procedures should be declared as taking no arguments.

The resources for the Tree widget are defined using the UIL `argument` type. The syntax is the same as for any other value, although `argument` values cannot be imported or exported. The `argument` literal specifies the internal name of the widget resource and the type of the resource. If a widget follows the Xt coding conventions, the internal resource name is the name of the resource minus the `XtN` prefix. The UIL compiler uses the type argument for type checking the resource, just like the built-in resources. UIL does not support a type that corresponds to a GC (graphics context), so the type of the `XtNtreeGC` argument is specified as `any`. This resource can only be set correctly using a GC imported from the application as an `identifier`. The file also contains constraint resource definitions for the children of the Tree.

The include file also defines variables for the possible values of the `XtNgravity` resource. These values are merely a convenience, as there is no way to make the UIL compiler check the setting of the resource for these values. (This type of checking is possible for widget descriptions written with WML, however.) Once the resources are defined, the UIL compiler allows you to set user-defined resources, such as `XtNtreeGC` and `XtNtreeParent`, in the `arguments` subsection of any widget, including the built-in Motif widgets. You can also use the built-in Motif resources in a user-defined widget definition, which is why we did not define the Tree widget's `XtNbackground` or `XtNforeground` resources.†

We use a separate include file for the Panner widget. The UIL definitions for the Panner appear in Example 26-3.

Example 26-3. The XawPanner.uih include file

```
/* UIL declarations for thw Xaw Panner widget. */

! Declare the creation procedure
procedure
  XawCreatePannerWidget();

! Declare resources
value
  XtNallowOff          : argument ('allowOff',          boolean);
  XtNbackgroundStipple : argument ('backgroundStipple', string);
  XtNcanvasWidth       : argument ('canvasWidth',       integer);
  XtNcanvasHeight      : argument ('canvasHeight',      integer);
  XtNdefaultScale      : argument ('defaultScale',      integer);
  XtNinternalSpace     : argument ('internalSpace',     integer);
  XtNresize            : argument ('resize',            boolean);
  XtNrubberBand        : argument ('rubberBand',        boolean);
  XtNshadowThickness   : argument ('shadowThickness',   integer);
  XtNsliderX           : argument ('sliderX',           integer);
  XtNsliderY           : argument ('sliderY',           integer);
  XtNsliderWidth       : argument ('sliderWidth',       integer);
  XtNsliderHeight      : argument ('sliderHeight',      integer);
```

---

† These resources are the same as the Motif `XmNbackground` and `XmNforeground` resources, even though the prefix is different. The names can be used interchangeably.

Example 26-3. The XawPanner.uih include file (continued)

```
! Declare callbacks
value
    XtNreportCallback    : reason    ('reportCallback');
```

This file declares the widget creation function and defines a number of resources. The Panner also has a callback, so the include file declares the callback using the UIL reason type. The reason literal simply specifies the string name of the callback resource. Unlike the argument literal, no type is necessary because the type is always a callback.

26.1.3 Creating User-defined Widgets

A module can create instances of the user-defined Tree and Panner widgets by including the two files shown above. Example 26-4 illustrates a typical application of these widgets.

Example 26-4. The tree.uil module

```
module tree

include file 'XawTree.uih';
include file 'XawPanner.uih';

procedure
    pan (widget);

object root : XmForm {
    controls {
        user_defined panner;
        XmDrawingArea viewport;
    };
    arguments {
        XmNdialogTitle = "Motif Widget Classes";
    };
};

object panner : user_defined procedure XawCreatePannerWidget {
    arguments {
        XtNdefaultScale   = 10;
        XtNcanvasWidth    = 325;
        XtNcanvasHeight   = 300;
        XtNsliderWidth    = 200;
        XtNsliderHeight   = 200;
        XmNleftAttachment = XmATTACH_FORM;
        XmNtopAttachment  = XmATTACH_FORM;
    };
    callbacks {
        XtNreportCallback = procedure pan (motif_widgets);
    };
};

object viewport : XmDrawingArea {
    arguments {
        XmNmarginWidth    = 0;
        XmNmarginHeight   = 0;
        XmNwidth          = 200;
        XmNheight         = 200;
```

Example 26-4. The tree.uil module (continued)

```
    XmNtopAttachment     = XmATTACH_FORM;
    XmNbottomAttachment  = XmATTACH_FORM;
    XmNleftAttachment    = XmATTACH_FORM;
    XmNrightAttachment   = XmATTACH_FORM;
  };
  controls {
    user_defined motif_widgets;
  };
};
object motif_widgets : user_defined procedure XawCreateTreeWidget {
  controls {
    Primitive : XmLabel { };
    ArrowButton : XmLabel {
      arguments {
        XtNtreeParent = Primitive;
      };
    };
    Label : XmLabel {
      arguments {
        XtNtreeParent = Primitive;
      };
    };
    CascadeButton : XmLabel {
      arguments {
        XtNtreeParent = Label;
      };
    };
    DrawnButton : XmLabel {
      arguments {
        XtNtreeParent = Label;
      };
    };
    PushButton : XmLabel {
      arguments {
        XtNtreeParent = Label;
      };
    };
    ToggleButton : XmLabel {
      arguments {
        XtNtreeParent = Label;
      };
    };
    List : XmLabel {
      arguments {
        XtNtreeParent = Primitive;
      };
    };
    Sash : XmLabel {
      arguments {
        XtNtreeParent = Primitive;
      };
    };
    ScrollBar : XmLabel {
      arguments {
        XtNtreeParent = Primitive;
```

Example 26-4. The tree.uil module (continued)

```
      };
    };
    Separator : XmLabel {
      arguments {
        XtNtreeParent = Primitive;
      };
    };
    Text : XmLabel {
      arguments {
        XtNtreeParent = Primitive;
      };
    };
    TextField: XmLabel {
      arguments {
        XtNtreeParent = Primitive;
      };
    };
  };
  arguments {
    XtNlineWidth = 2;
    XmNborderWidth = 0;
    XtNhSpace = 22;
    XtNvSpace = 10;
  };
};

end module;
```

This module defines a Form that contains a DrawingArea and a Panner widget. The DrawingArea contains a Tree widget that depicts the class hierarchy of the Motif primitive widgets. The Panner scrolls the Tree, so that the user can view the entire hierarchy. The output of this example is shown in Figure 26-1.

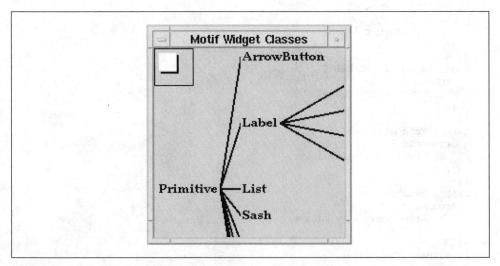

Figure 26-1. User interface of tree.uil

The syntax of the Panner and Tree widget definitions is almost the same as the many Motif widget definitions that you've already seen. The main difference is that you replace the Motif widget class name with `user_defined procedure` followed by the name of the widget creation procedure. To reference a user-defined widget in the `controls` subsection of a widget, you just use the keyword `user_defined` followed by the name of the widget.

You can mix user-defined resources and built-in resources as in the Panner definition, which contains some of its own resource settings as well as a couple of Form constraint resource settings. You can also specify user-defined resource names in the `arguments` subsection of a built-in widget definition. For example, the Label widget children of the Tree contain resource settings for the user-defined `XtNtreeParent` resource. The Panner widget contains a user-defined callback setting; the `pan()` callback routine is invoked when the user adjusts the Panner. The syntax of using user-defined resources and callbacks is the same as that for built-in resources and callbacks. The main drawback of user-defined widgets is that, unlike with the built-in Motif widgets, the compiler does not know which resources are valid for the widget, so it lets you set any resources. This generally is not a problem when you are only working with a few user-defined widgets, but as the number of user-defined widget instances increases, so does the probability of making an error that the UIL compiler cannot catch. You can avoid this problem by describing user-defined widgets with WML, at the expense of learning a more complicated widget description format.

26.2 Organizing UIL Modules

When developing an application with UIL, it is important to think about the organization of the modules that make up the interface. There are a number of benefits to be gained from careful organization, such as code that is easier to edit, test, and maintain, interface components that are reusable, and applications that are easier to internationalize. While these benefits are not all unique to UIL, there are specific organizational strategies that make it easier to realize the benefits. This section presents some organizational techniques for UIL modules. Since there are no rules when it comes to organization, you should consider these techniques as guidelines.

You should adhere to the general principal of grouping things by purpose or function. Some of the things you should consider grouping in UIL are interface components, procedures, lists and strings. Basically, it makes sense to group any collection of UIL declarations or definitions that you consider to be logically related. You can organize aspects of an application both in separate files and by sections within a file.

26.2.1 Using Separate Modules

When an application uses multiple top-level windows, such as a main window and various dialog boxes, it makes sense to describe each window in a separate UIL module. When a window is especially complex, you may want to describe the interface using several modules. For example, the menu system of an application could be described in a separate module, as illustrated by the example in Chapter 25, *Building an Application With UIL*.

When you divide an application into separate modules, it is easier to find specific declarations or definitions because the modules map directly to the appearance of the interface. Multiple files also help to reduce editing conflicts when you are working on a project with a team of programmers. Breaking components into separate files helps to eliminate dependencies between logically separate parts of the interface. For example, if you make a change to a dialog, it shouldn't affect any other parts of the interface. Another benefit is rapid prototyping and testing. With a few modifications, you can use the *showuid* program from Chapter 24, *Creating a User Interface With UIL*, to preview a component without needing to have a complete application program. We'll take a closer look at prototyping a user interface later in this chapter.

26.2.2 Organizing Within a Module

Within a UIL module, one organizational decision involves whether widgets are declared from the top-down or from the bottom-up. Top-down organization means that you define the parent widgets first, followed by their children. Bottom-up is the opposite, in that you define the child widgets and then define their parents. We recommend using the top-down approach, since it is an extension of the organization at the file level. In addition, it is more natural for developers who are accustomed to creating an interface in application code. Whichever approach you choose, you should be sure to use it consistently in all of your modules.

Using `value` and `list` sections to define settings for widget resources that you use or change often is another useful practice. This technique makes a module easier to read and maintain. As you know, UIL lets you define variables that can be fetched by an application. It makes sense to place values that you intend to fetch in the same module as the part of the interface to which they correspond. Although UIL allows forward references to most variables, you should try to define or declare variables before using them, as it is a more familiar style. Grouping variables together at the beginning of a module is another common practice that we recommend.

In some cases, you may need to share a variable or a list among several modules. For most types of variables, you can place the definition in one module and include declarations in any other modules that use the value. For lists and for values that cannot be exported, you must place the values directly in an include file. This kind of reuse frees you from trying to maintain the same information in more than one place.

26.2.3 Supporting Internationalization

Although it is a good idea to put variable definitions in the module where you use them, we need to make an exception to this guideline for internationalization purposes. To support internationalization, an application should not use literal values for strings, compound strings, character sets, fonts, and font sets in a UIL module that contains widget declarations. You should consolidate these values into one module per language and define a variable for each value. Then, you can use the variables in widget declarations instead of literal values. You can create a single include file that contains declarations of all of these values and include it anywhere you need to use one of the values. Example 26-5 illustrates this technique.

Example 26-5. The i18n_dialog.uil module

```
! i18n_dialog.uil - Dialog used to prompt the user for a filename

module savebox

include file 'strings.uih';

object root : XmPromptDialog {
  arguments {
    XmNokLabelString = ok_text;
    XmNcancelLabelString = cancel_text;
    XmNhelpLabelString = help_text;
    XmNselectionLabelString = save_prompt_text;
    XmNdialogTitle = save_title_text;
  };
};

end module;
```

As you can see, a variable is used everywhere that we needed to set a language-dependent resource string. Example 26-6 shows the corresponding *strings.uih* declaration file.

Example 26-6. The strings.uih include file

```
! strings.uih - Interface string declarations

value
  ok_text          : imported compound_string;
  cancel_text      : imported compound_string;
  help_text        : imported compound_string;
  save_title_text  : imported compound_string;
  save_prompt_text : imported compound_string;
```

The declaration file is the same for every module that uses the strings, so you don't have to declare them in each module. Each string variable is declared as an `imported` value, which we explained in Section 24.3.1. All you need is a string definition file for each language that is supported by the application. Example 26-7 contains the English version of the strings for this dialog.

Example 26-7. The strings.uil module

```
! strings.uil - English version of interface strings

module strings

value
  ok_text          : exported compound_string ("Ok");
  cancel_text      : exported compound_string ("Cancel");
  help_text        : exported compound_string ("Help");
  save_title_text  : exported compound_string ("Save Dialog");
  save_prompt_text : exported compound_string ("File Name:");

end module;
```

To support another language, we only need to create a new version of *strings.uil* for that language. The English version of the dialog is shown in Figure 26-2.

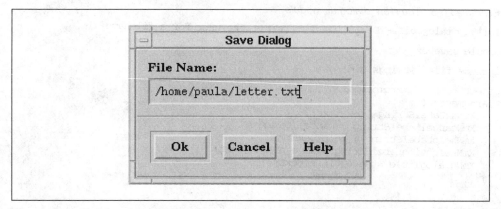

Figure 26-2. User interface of i18n_dialog.uil using an English strings.uil

A separate subdirectory in the development environment is typically created for each supported language. If the directory names correspond to possible values of the LANG environment variable, it is easy to test the interface for each language by setting the LANG and UID-PATH variables, which are described in Chapter 22, *Introduction to UIL*.

At run-time, language-dependent UID files are normally installed in */usr/lib/X11/%L/uid/%N*, where %L stands for the LANG environment variable and %N is the application class name. For example, if the class name of the application that uses the save dialog is Demos, you install the English version of the strings in */usr/lib/X11/C/uid/Demos/strings.uid*. Likewise, you install the French version in */usr/lib/X11/Fr/uid/Demos/strings.uid*. The language-dependent files, such as *strings.uid*, are the only ones for which we need to have multiple versions; the rest of the UID files are installed in the */usr/lib/X11/uid/Demos* directory.

26.2.4 Organizing With Include Files

UIL include files are quite useful for organizing a user interface. You can use include files that declare or define values and define lists, as shown in Section 26.4. You can also use include files for information defined in the application program, namely callback procedures and identifiers. Include files provide a convenient place to organize these declarations by functioning like C header files. If you use an include file, there is no need to declare the same procedure or identifier in more than one module. Another advantage of keeping callback declarations and identifiers in an include file is that you can make any changes and additions in a single file.

26.2.5 Creating Reusable Components

Reusability is another benefit of proper organization. You can organize for reusability at a number of levels, from complete dialogs to individual widgets. You may not have recognized it at the time, but you've already seen an example of reusable components in the guise of user-defined widgets. Widgets are generally designed to be reusable items. You can extend this notion in UIL by creating a separate include file for any user-defined widgets that you use, as Section 26.1 illustrated. The other alternative is to place the necessary definitions and declarations directly in the module where the widget is used. Clearly, using an include file is the more flexible of the two techniques.

If you are developing several different applications, you may find that there are a number of common components such as help windows, print dialogs, and various menus. While the Motif widget set provides some reusable components, such as the FileSelectionBox, you can create your own reusable user-interface components using UIL. For example, if you create a reusable context-sensitive help facility using UIL, it is easy to add help to all of your applications. This use of UIL not only saves you time, but it also promotes a common look and feel across your set of applications.

You can also reuse callbacks to a certain degree. While most callbacks are specific to the task at hand, it is possible to write generic callbacks that you can use in multiple applications. Section 26.5 describes several such callbacks. You are not limited to a single callback procedure for a callback action, so it is possible to split the behavior of a certain action over more than one callback. For example, a typical **Cancel** button on a dialog might reset the dialog contents and then pop down the dialog. These two actions can be handled by two callbacks. Other dialogs can have their own reset callback, but can reuse the pop down callback. If you have a group of related callbacks, it may make sense to put the callbacks into a single source code file and write one UIL include file for all of the callbacks.

26.3 Specifying Resource Values

Even though all of the UIL examples in this book specify widget resource settings directly in UIL modules, it is important to realize that this approach is not always the best, especially for real-world applications. With any application, you have the choice of setting resources in a UIL module, in an X resource file, or directly in application code. This section looks at the advantages and disadvantages of setting resources in each of these places.

26.3.1 Resource Name Checking

When it comes to error checking of resource settings, UIL comes out on top. Anytime you attempt to set a built-in resource or callback, the UIL compiler makes sure that the resource exists and that it is supported by the widget in which you are setting it. If you make a typing error or mistakenly set an unsupported resource, the compiler issues an error message.

Neither one of these errors is caught in an X resource file because the X resource manager waits until run-time to perform a search of the resource database. Since resource files are not validated, it is up to you to notice mistakes at run-time when a widget doesn't look or act as you expect.

When you set a resource in application code, you only get partial error checking. The C preprocessor or the C compiler generates an undefined symbol error if you use a resource name that does not exist, but this mechanism does not prevent you from using a resource in the wrong context, as the compiler cannot detect this error.

26.3.2 Resource Type Checking

Type checking takes place for resources set in both UIL modules and X resource files. The UIL compiler knows the expected type for each built-in resource as well as the type of a value, so it is able to produce an error message if you try to set a resource to a value of an incompatible type. However, there are a few cases in which UIL doesn't perform complete type checking. The UIL compiler only checks resources that can be set to enumerated values, such as XmNalignment and XmNleftAttachment, for integer assignments. In addition, no type checking is performed on user-defined resources of the type any or on resources that are set to identifier variables.

The type checking in X resource files is similar, but has slightly different limitations. The string is the only recognized type in an X resource file. At run-time, Xt automatically calls the appropriate resource converter, which creates a value of the type the widget expects for a particular resource. If you specify a string that cannot be converted, the converter function generates a warning message. The Motif library includes a separate converter for each of the enumerated types, so you cannot accidentally use an incorrect value. There is no type checking for string-typed resources, however, as their values are taken literally. For example, if you set a string resource to False thinking that its type is Boolean, you won't get a warning. The biggest weakness of setting resources in an X resource file is that type checking does not occur until the widgets are created at run-time.

There is essentially no type checking when you set resources in application code because of the general nature of the Xt resource-setting API. The XtSetValues() macro takes an array of generic structures, and all of the values are represented by the XtArgVal type. Therefore, the compiler cannot perform its usual type checking. You can get partial type checking in C by using convenience functions, but only a few exist compared to the total number of resources. If you set a resource to the wrong type in application code, the results are unpredictable. Nothing may happen, but more likely the error will cause strange behavior and/or crash the application. Unfortunately, the source of this kind of error is usually difficult to track down.

26.3.3 Resource Type Support

You can set every resource of a Motif widget from either a UIL module or application source code, while X resource files allow you to set nearly every type. In source code, resource type support is almost inherent. As long as you include the right header file and know the format of a resource type, you can create a value. Creating values for types in non-Motif widget sets is no different, since you can use X, Xt, or Motif functions to create complex types.

Type support in UIL is built into the compiler; each type is specified with a unique literal syntax. Because UIL is designed to support Motif, the built-in types are limited to the types used by the Motif widget set, and there is no way to add a new type short of modifying the UIL compiler. You can work with new types imported from the application using identifiers, but that's not quite the same as being able to define the values directly in a module.

As we just mentioned, type support in resource files is limited to the available resource converters. Without adding any new converters, you can set most Motif resources. Two notable exceptions are resources that specify widget and color pixmap values. You can add new type converters, but in order to do so you must have a strong knowledge about the workings of Xt. Even then, perfecting a converter takes a good deal of work. See Volume Four, *X Toolkit Intrinsics Programming Manual*, for more information on resource converters.

26.3.4 Callback Specifications

You can set callbacks in both UIL and application source code, but not in X resource files. You might think of callbacks differently because they determine the behavior of an interface, while most other resources affect the appearance. As far as a widget is concerned, however, a callback is just another resource whose type is an array of function pointers. In UIL you use the `callbacks` subsection to set a callback resource. With Xt, you normally use `Xt-AddCallback()` or `XtAddCallbacks()`. The situation is different in a resource file, where all values are considered equal. In order to set a callback in a resource file, you need a callback resource converter, but such a converter is not available by default.†

26.3.5 Wildcard Specification

Only X resource files give you the ability to set resources by widget class and to represent one or more widgets in the hierarchy with wildcards. Neither of these powerful features are available from UIL or application source code. In both UIL and application code, you are limited to setting resources on a specific widget instance. In an X resource file, you can write a single resource setting that applies to a single widget, to widgets of a specific class, or to all of the widgets in a hierarchy. This feature is particularly useful for specifying a common appearance for a group of widgets. Doing the same thing in UIL or source code requires a lot

---

† Several third-party software packages provide this functionality. Most notable is the Widget Creation Language (Wcl), which also supports complete interface specifications with capabilities similar to UIL. For more information on Wcl, see Issue 2 of *The X Resource*.

of repetition. You can use a list in UIL or a convenience routine in source code to factor out common settings, but at some point you still need an explicit list reference or function call.

26.3.6 User Customization

Another difference between the three methods of specifying resources is the freedom that they give a user to customize or override a resource setting. Any settings that you place in an X resource file can be overridden by the user. Settings made in UIL or in source code are fixed and cannot be changed by the user.† Neither behavior is any better or worse than the other. Allowing or disallowing user customization is just something for you to consider when deciding where to set a resource, rather than a limitation of the method.

26.3.7 Dynamic Updating

Many resource settings are not just set at widget creation time and left alone, but are continually updated to indicate the state of the application in response to user actions. You can make dynamic resource changes in source code using `XtSetValues()` or `XtVaSetValues()` and application-created values. The `MrmFetchSetValues()` function is the counterpart for UIL. Instead of using application-defined values, the routine automatically loads the data from exported values in a UIL module. (For more information on `MrmFetchSetValues()` see Section 24.3.2.) With X resource files, the resource settings are loaded and applied only when a widget is created. Once again, it is possible to write code to dynamically fetch and convert a value from a resource file, but the Xt library does not provide this functionality.

26.3.8 Guidelines for Setting Resources

Now that we have explained the capabilities and limitations of each method of specifying resources, we can look at where to place resource settings in some common situations. The first thing to think about for a resource setting is whether you want to let the user change it. If so, using an X resource file is the only way to go. You should try to allow the user to override settings that affect the appearance of widgets, such as colors and fonts. On the other hand, you normally do not want to let the user change layout or behavior settings, such as form attachments and widget sensitivity. It is fairly common to allow changes to translation tables, however.

You should also consider which specification methods support the resource in question, and how much work is involved in creating the value. If you want to set a color pixmap resource, UIL is clearly the best choice, as the values are not supported in X resource files or application code. Compound strings are good candidates for resource files or UIL. It is easier to specify a compound string in one of these than it is in C code, where you must worry about

---

† This fact is generally true about UIL. A user could conceivably replace a compiled UID module with a new version that contains different settings, but it is rather unlikely.

creating and freeing the values. However, X resource files only handle 8-bit left-to-right strings, so if you need to do anything beyond that, look to UIL. Callbacks present yet another choice where you can go with source code or UIL.

When it is an option, UIL is generally the best method for setting resources, as it provides the most comprehensive error-checking capabilities. The most common reason for not using UIL is to allow user customization. Dynamically-computed or complex resource settings are best made in application source code. Sometimes a combined approach is possible, in which the values are defined in UIL, but manipulated and set within the application.

These are only a few guidelines. When you encounter a new situation and have a choice, try to determine the consequences of using a particular method. Table 26-1 summarizes the features supported by each method. Finally, don't forget to think about ease of use and reliability for both you and the people using your application.

Table 26-1. Comparison of Resource Setting Options

Feature	UIL	Resource File	Application
Existence Checking	Yes	No	Yes
Validity Checking	Yes	No	No
Type Checking	Yes	Yes	No
Motif Types Supported	Yes	No	Yes
New Types Supported	No	Yes	Yes
Callbacks Supported	Yes	No	Yes
Wildcard Specifications	No	Yes	No
User Customization	No	Yes	No
Dynamic Updating	Yes	No	Yes

26.4 Using Lists Effectively

Lists are a powerful feature of UIL because they give you an alternative to specifying widget children, callbacks, and arguments directly in a widget definition. Lists also let you specify multiple procedures for a specific callback resource. The ability to include lists in other lists makes them even more useful, as we'll show you in this section.

26.4.1 Specifying Common Resources

We talked about reusing interface components and callbacks earlier. By using lists, you can take this technique one step further to the level of widget children, resources, and callbacks. You can reduce the size of your modules by using lists to factor out common sets of resources. This technique is particularly useful for dealing with Form resource settings, as this fragment illustrates:

```
list attachments : arguments {
   XmNleftAttachment = XmATTACH_FORM;
   XmNleftOffset = 3;
   XmNrightAttachment = XmATTACH_FORM;
   XmNrightOffset = 3;
};
```

The `attachments` list defines some attachments that we can apply to a group of widgets in a Form, as shown in the following definitions:

```
object name : XmTextField {
   arguments {
      arguments attach_args;
      XmNtopAttachment = XmATTACH_FORM;
   };
};
```

```
object phone : XmTextField {
   arguments {
      arguments attach_args;
      XmNtopAttachment = XmATTACH_WIDGET;
      XmNtopWidget = name;
      XmNbottomAttachment = XmATTACH_FORM;
   };
```

Each TextField definition includes its own attachments and the list, instead of restating the common settings. Although some of the resources are specified twice, only the last setting has any effect.

An extension of this concept gives us another interesting and useful way of working with lists. By including one or more lists in another list, you can create a flexible hierarchy of resource or callback settings. For example, you might use a list to specify a base style for all widgets, as in the following fragment:

```
list base_style : arguments {
   XmNforeground = color ('black');
   XmNbackground = color ('magenta');
   XmNtraversalOn = true;
};
```

When you add components to the interface, you can build on this base style. The following fragment shows how you might handle defining a ToggleButton-specific style:

```
list toggle_btn_style : arguments {
   arguments base_style;
   XmNindicatorSize = 10;
   XmNindicatorType = XmN_OF_MANY;
   XmNselectColor = color ('yellow');
};
```

Unfortunately, it turns out that most of the resource settings that work well in these situations are best left to resource files, as we discussed in the previous section. This use of lists can still be useful, however, when you are prototyping an application and don't feel like using an X resource file. When you are done prototyping, be sure to move the resource settings that affect appearance to a resource file, so that they can be modified by the user.

You can also use a hierarchy of lists to specify callback resources. If you are developing an application that supports context sensitive help, the root of your callback hierarchy might be specified as in the following list:

```
list help_cbs : callbacks {
   XmNhelpCallback = procedure help();
};
```

You can include this list in each widget that supports help. For a group of ToggleButtons, you can augment the list as follows:

```
list toggle_cbs : callbacks {
   callbacks help_cbs;
   XmNvalueChangedCallback = procedure toggle_changed();
};
```

The following widget definition illustrates how both the style and callback lists might be used:

```
object hot_fudge : XmToggleButton {
   arguments {
      arguments attach_args;
      arguments toggle_args;
      XmNlabelString = "Hot Fudge";
   };
   callbacks toggle_cbs;
};
```

You gain a couple of advantages by using lists this way. First, if you decide to change a color or a callback, you only need to make the change in one place, not in every widget definition. Second, each widget definition is considerably shorter than it would be without the list, which saves typing and generally makes a module shorter and easier to read.

26.4.2 Reusing Components

You can also use lists to help create reusable components. Earlier in this chapter, we talked about reusing components for top-level windows and dialogs. Although reusing parts of a dialog is not very common, reusing the panel of buttons that compose the action area of a dialog makes some sense. An application may use the definitions of **OK**, **Cancel**, and **Help** PushButtons repeatedly. Using lists, you can create a hierarchy of include files that allows you to reuse the same definitions for each dialog that needs them.

The first thing that needs to be defined is a container widget to hold the buttons. We keep this example simple by using a RowColumn manager widget. Example 26-8 shows the definition of the RowColumn.

Example 26-8. The btn_panel.uih include file

```
! btn_panel.uih -- Button panel container

object button_panel : XmRowColumn {
   controls buttons;
   arguments {
      XmNorientation = XmHORIZONTAL;
```

Example 26-8. The btn_panel.uih include file (continued)

```
        XmNpacking = XmPACK_COLUMN;
        XmNentryAlignment = XmALIGNMENT_CENTER;
        !  Assume bottom of form placement
        XmNleftAttachment = XmATTACH_FORM;
        XmNrightAttachment = XmATTACH_FORM;
        XmNbottomAttachment = XmATTACH_FORM;
        ! Provide a hook for additional arguments
        arguments button_panel_args;
    };
};
```

The `button_panel` RowColumn is an open-ended definition, as the children are specified as an undefined list. The definition also contains an undefined list in its `arguments` subsection, which allows the specification of additional resources. The next step is to add the **OK, Cancel,** and **Help** buttons to the panel using another include file, which is shown in Example 26-9.

Example 26-9. The three_btn.uih include file

```
! three_btn.uih -- OK, Cancel, Help button definitions

list buttons : controls {
  OK : XmPushButton {
    arguments ok_args;
    callbacks ok_cbs;
  };
  Cancel : XmPushButton {
    arguments cancel_args;
    callbacks cancel_cbs;
  };
  Help : XmPushButton {
    arguments help_args;
    callbacks help_cbs;
  };
  ! Hook for additional buttons
  controls more_buttons;
};

include file 'btn_panel.uih';
```

So far, all of the widget definitions have been placed in include files. This technique is necessary because UIL does not support imported list values, so the only way you can reuse lists is by placing them in include files. We also define the PushButtons in an include file because they reference callback and argument lists. These lists must be defined by the module that includes the `button` definition. If the buttons were defined in a separate module, there would be no way to specify their behavior from within UIL.

The *three_btn.uih* file defines the three buttons for the panel and defines the `controls` list referenced in *btn_panel.uih*. An important feature of this example is that we have incorporated undefined lists in each of the widget's `callbacks` and `arguments` subsections. These lists work like macros in that they allow a module to use customized versions of the standard definitions. We also keep the list of buttons open-ended by including another undefined `controls` list named `more_buttons`. The file ends by including the button panel definition so that the main module does not need to include it. We normally recommend putting the include directives at the top of a file, but in early releases of Motif 1.2, a forward reference to a list causes the UIL compiler to crash. Therefore, it is necessary to include object definitions after the lists that they reference.

Now that the button panel and button definitions are complete, we can create a dialog that uses them. Example 26-10 demonstrates the creation of such a dialog.

Example 26-10. The dialog.uil module

```
/* dialog.uil - a simple dialog that contains reusable PushButtons */
module dialog
include file 'procedures.uih';
object root : XmForm {
  controls {
    XmRowColumn dialog_contents;
    XmSeparator separator;
    XmRowColumn button_panel;
  };
  arguments {
    XmNdialogTitle = "Login";
    XmNdefaultButton = OK;
  };
};
object dialog_contents : XmRowColumn {
  controls {
    User     : XmLabel { };
    Password : XmLabel { };
    XmTextField user_field;
    XmTextField pw_field;
  };
  arguments {
    XmNnumColumns = 2;
    XmNpacking = XmPACK_COLUMN;
    XmNtopAttachment = XmATTACH_FORM;
    XmNleftAttachment = XmATTACH_FORM;
    XmNrightAttachment = XmATTACH_FORM;
    XmNbottomAttachment = XmATTACH_WIDGET;
    XmNbottomWidget = separator;
  };
};
object user_field : XmTextField {
  arguments {
    XmNcolumns = 2;
  };
};
object pw_field : XmTextField {
  arguments {
    XmNcolumns = 2;
  };
};
object separator : XmSeparator {
  arguments {
    XmNrightAttachment  = XmATTACH_FORM;
```

Example 26-10. The dialog.uil module (continued)

```
     XmNleftAttachment    = XmATTACH_FORM;
     XmNbottomAttachment  = XmATTACH_WIDGET;
     XmNbottomWidget      = button_panel;
   };
};

! Button specific settings.
list ok_args : arguments { };
list ok_cbs : callbacks {
  XmNactivateCallback = procedure do_it();
};

list cancel_args : arguments { };
list cancel_cbs : callbacks {
  XmNactivateCallback = procedure forget_it();
};

list help_args : arguments { };
list help_cbs : callbacks {
  XmNactivateCallback = procedure help_me();
};

! No additional button panel arguments
list button_panel_args : arguments { };

! No more buttons
list more_buttons : controls { };

! Include the button panel definition
include file 'three_btn.uih';

end module;
```

The module starts by including the files that contain the callback procedure declarations. The top-level Form of the dialog contains the work area, a separator, and the `button_panel`. The work area consists of two labeled TextFields in a RowColumn. We complete the `button_panel` by defining the lists referenced in the include files. The `arguments` and `callbacks` lists for the **OK**, **Cancel**, and **Help** buttons are defined. There are no additional arguments for the buttons, the `arguments` lists are empty. Since there are no additional `button_panel` arguments and the dialog only has three buttons, the `button_panel_args` and `more_buttons` lists are also empty. With these list definitions in place, the module finally includes the file that defines the buttons and the button panel. The output of the dialog is shown in Figure 26-3.

You can reuse the button panel in as many dialogs as you want by following the model used in Example 26-10. Although we did not use many of the undefined lists, they make the button panel more flexible and configurable. These techniques can also be applied in a number of other situations throughout an application. This method of using lists and include files can help to reduce redundancy in an interface definition.

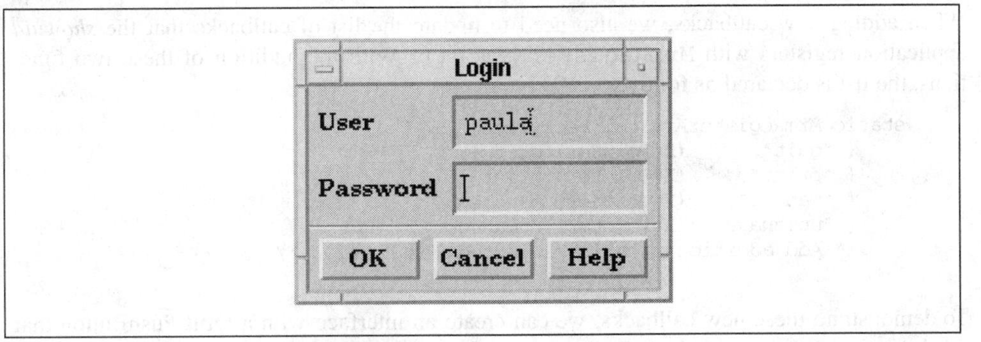

Figure 26-3. User interface of dialog.uil

26.5 Prototyping an Interface With UIL

The *showuid* program in Chapter 24, *Creating a User Interface With UIL*, provides a useful foundation for prototyping a user interface. The program contains two simple callbacks: one for printing a message and one for exiting the program. By adding a few more callbacks, we can make the program even more useful as a building block for developing interfaces.

26.5.1 Managing Widgets

Most user interfaces consist of a main application window and several support windows or dialogs. Since dialogs are frequently posted and unposted, we can make prototyping easier by writing callbacks that manage and unmanage widgets. Example 26-11 shows these routines.

Example 26-11. The manage() and unmanage() routines

```
void
manage (w, client_data,call_data)
Widget w;
XtPointer client_data;
XtPointer call_data;
{
    Widget target = (Widget) client_data;
    XtManageChild (target);
}

void
unmanage (w, client_data, call_data)
Widget w;
XtPointer client_data;
XtPointer call_data;
{
    Widget target = (Widget) client_data;
    XtUnmanageChild (target);
}
```

When adding new callbacks, we also need to update the list of callbacks that the *showuid* application registers with `MrmRegisterNames()`. With the addition of these two functions, the list is declared as follows:

```
static MrmRegisterArg callback_list[] = {
    { "quit",     (XtPointer) quit },
    { "print",    (XtPointer) print },
    { "manage",   (XtPointer) manage },
    { "unmanage", (XtPointer) unmanage },
    /* Add additional callback procedures here... */
};
```

To demonstrate these new callbacks, we can create an interface with a **Quit** PushButton that displays a confirmation dialog. This example is realistic, as many applications bring up a confirmation dialog to prevent you from quitting accidentally or making irreversible changes. A module that uses the `manage()` callback is shown in Example 26-12.

Example 26-12. The quitbox.uil module

```
module quitbox

procedure
  quit();
  manage (widget);
  unmanage (widget);

object quit_dialog : XmQuestionDialog {
  controls {
    Xm_Help {
      ! Disable the help button for now.
      arguments {
        XmNsensitive = false;
      };
    };
  };
  callbacks {
    XmNokCallback = procedure quit();
  };
  arguments {
    XmNmessageString = "Really Quit?";
    XmNdialogTitle = "Confirm Quit";
    XmNdialogStyle = XmDIALOG_FULL_APPLICATION_MODAL;
  };
};

object quitb : XmPushButton {
  arguments {
    XmNlabelString = "Quit";
  };
  callbacks {
    XmNactivateCallback = procedure manage (quit_dialog);
  };
};

object root : XmMainWindow {
  controls {
    XmPushButton quitb;
    unmanaged XmQuestionDialog quit_dialog;
  };
```

Motif Programming Manual

Example 26-12. The quitbox.uil module (continued)

```
};
end module;
```

The output of this example is shown in Figure 26-4.

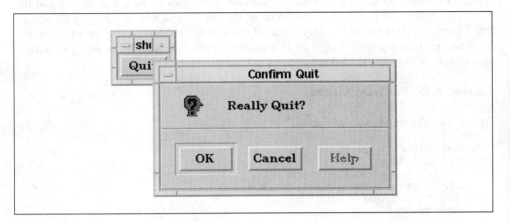

Figure 26-4. User interface of quitbox.uil

The **Quit** PushButton manages the dialog, which causes it to be displayed. Pressing the **OK** PushButton exits the application. There is no need to use the unmanage() callback in this example, as the **Cancel** PushButton unmanages the dialog by default. You can easily apply the manage() and unmanage() callbacks to other dialogs in an interface.

26.5.2 Creating Widgets

In Example 26-12, the entire user interface is defined in a single widget hierarchy. This technique is fine for a small application, but for performance reasons it is not practical in a larger application. Creating a separate hierarchy for each window allows you to divide an interface into separate modules, as discussed earlier in this chapter. The only drawback to distributing dialog creation is that it takes longer for a dialog to appear the first time it is displayed. Since this delay is typically not noticeable, we still recommend this approach.

You can support the as-needed dialog creation policy in UIL by adding another callback that creates a widget hierarchy. A new widget hierarchy is created by calling MrmFetch-Widget(). As a reminder, this function takes the following form:

```
Cardinal
MrmFetchWidget(hierarchy, widget_name, parent, widget_return,
               class_return)
    MrmHierarchy    hierarchy;
    String          widget_name;
    Widget          parent;
    Widget          *widget_return;
    MrmType         *class_return;
```

A creation callback needs three values to be able to create a new widget hierarchy. These values are the first three arguments to `MrmFetchWidget()`. The `MrmHierarchy` is already available in the application program, so we only need to make it a global variable instead of a local variable in `main()`. Since the callback accesses the hierarchy repeatedly, we also need to remove the call to `MrmCloseHierarchy()`. In order to get the other two arguments, we use an `asciz_table` that contains the names of the parent widget and the widget to create. We can convert the name of the parent to a widget ID using `XtName-ToWidget()`. This technique only works if we specify a unique name for each widget. Since we need the top-level widget as an argument to this routine, it becomes a global variable as well. The complete callback appears in Example 26-13.

Example 26-13. The create() routine

```
void
create (w, client_data, call_data)
Widget w;
XtPointer client_data;
XtPointer call_data;
{
    String *args = (String *) client_data;
    String parent_name = args[0];
    Widget parent;

    /* Get a widget id for the parent widget. */
    if (strcmp (parent_name, "toplevel") != 0)
        parent = XtNameToWidget (toplevel, parent_name);
    else
        parent = toplevel;

    /* If the parent was found try to create the hierarchy. */
    if (parent == NULL)
        fprintf (stderr, "Create: No such widget `%s'\n", args[0]);
    else {
        String child_name = args[1];
        Widget new_w;
        Cardinal status;
        MrmType class;

        status = MrmFetchWidget (hierarchy, child_name, parent,
            &new_w, &class);
        if (status != MrmSUCCESS)
            fprintf (stderr, "Failed to create hierarchy `%s'\n", child_name);
    }

    /* After the widget is created, this callback can be removed. */
    XtRemoveCallback (w, XmNactivateCallback, create, client_data);
}
```

The callback assigns the `client_data` argument to a `String` array, since that is appropriate for the UIL `asciz_table` type. The routine also converts the name of the parent widget to a widget ID using `XtNameToWidget()`. Since that routine does not consider the top-level widget in its search, the callback performs a special test for that widget. If the routine finds the ID for the parent widget, it attempts to create the new widget hierarchy. Once the hierarchy is created, the callback is removed so that the widget hierarchy is not created more than once. We make the assumption that if the creation fails once, subsequent attempts will also fail.

With the addition of the `create()` callback, we can split Example 26-12 into two modules. Unfortunately, breaking up the module into two introduces a new problem. Now that we have two separate widget hierarchies, the `manage()` callback can no longer reference the `quit_dialog` widget because it is defined in another hierarchy. One solution to this problem is to export the widget ID of the dialog as a UIL identifier, using the `MrmNcreate-Callback` (illustrated in Chapter 25, *Building an Application With UIL*). The problem with this approach is that you must maintain a list of identifiers for all of the exported widgets. Another solution, which avoids this problem, uses `XtNameToWidget()` in the `manage()` and `unmanage()` callbacks to obtain a widget ID given a widget name. The revised callbacks are shown in Example 26-14.

Example 26-14. The modified manage() and unmanage() routines

```
void
manage (w, client_data,call_data)
Widget w;
XtPointer client_data;
XtPointer call_data;
{
    String name = (String) client_data;
    Widget target = XtNameToWidget (toplevel, name);
    if (target != NULL)
        XtManageChild (target);
    else
        fprintf (stderr, "Cannot manage widget named %s\n", name);
}

void
unmanage (w, client_data, call_data)
Widget w;
XtPointer client_data;
XtPointer call_data;
{
    String name = (String) client_data;
    Widget target = XtNameToWidget (toplevel, name);
    if (target != NULL)
        XtUnmanageChild (target);
    else
        fprintf (stderr, "Cannot unmanage widget named %s\n", name);
}
```

Now we can rewrite the *quitbox* example using two modules. The main window definition is listed in Example 26-15.

Example 26-15. The quitmain.uil module

```
module mainwindow

procedure
  manage (string);
  create (asciz_table);

list confirm_quit : procedures {
  create (asciz_table ("toplevel", "quit_dialog"));
  manage ("*quit_dialog");
};
```

Example 26-15. The quitmain.uil module (continued)

```
object quitb : XmPushButton {
  arguments {
    XmNlabelString = "Quit";
  };
  callbacks {
    XmNactivateCallback = procedures confirm_quit;
  };
};

object root : XmMainWindow {
  controls {
    XmPushButton quitb;
  };
};

end module;
```

The `XmNactivateCallback` of the **Quit** PushButton now creates the confirmation dialog and manages it. The parent and widget to be created are passed to the creation callback in an `asciz_table`. Because the `create()` callback removes itself, subsequent invocations of the callback only manage the dialog. `XtNameToWidget()` expects a qualified widget name, much like resource specifications, so we must precede the name passed to the `manage()` callback with an asterisk. The `quit_dialog` is now defined in a separate module, shown in Example 26-16.

Example 26-16. The quitdialog.uil module

```
module quitbox

procedure
  quit();

object quit_dialog : XmQuestionDialog {
  controls {
    Xm_Help {
      ! Disable the help button for now.
      arguments {
        XmNsensitive = false;
      };
    };
  };
  callbacks {
    XmNokCallback = procedure quit();
  };
  arguments {
    XmNmessageString = "Really Quit?";
    XmNdialogTitle = "Confirm Quit";
    XmNdialogStyle = XmDIALOG_FULL_APPLICATION_MODAL;
  };
};

end module;
```

The only potential disadvantage of this method of creating dialogs is that string-to-widget lookup is slightly slower than using a widget pointer directly. For most moderately-sized widget trees, the difference should not be noticeable. The creation callback is a useful tool that can be especially helpful when you are prototyping an interface.

26.6 Summary

Once you've learned the basics of UIL, you can begin to take full advantage of its features. Some advanced techniques include: defining non-Motif widgets; using lists to shorten modules and create reusable interface components, and using UIL to rapidly prototype the interface for an application. As UIL modules grow, it is important to pay attention to their organization. A well-organized set of modules can ease the task of editing and maintaining an interface. When you develop a real-world application with UIL, it is also important to consider the best location for resource settings. While most fixed resources can be set in UIL and possibly modified in application code, it is usually best to specify values that a user might want to change in an app-defaults file.

Appendix

Additional Example Programs

This appendix provides some additional example programs that illustrate techniques not discussed in the body of the book.

In This Appendix:

Appendix
Additional Example Programs

This appendix contains a number of programs that provide more realistic examples of how the Motif toolkit is used. Most of the examples are also intended to encourage further investigation into other X-related topics, such as the use of app-defaults files, fallback resources, and command-line option parsing. Our discussion of the examples is fairly limited; see the comments in the code for explanations of various implementation details.

A.1 A Postcard Interface for Mail

The first example provides a GUI wrapper for a mail program. The user-interface model is that of a postcard. The program does not provide any facilities for reading mail messages; it simply allows the user to compose and send one message at a time. Before compiling the program shown in Example A-1, check the definition of MAIL_CMD. If you don't have *zmail* on your system, set the value to the name of the mail agent you normally use.†

Example A-1. The zcard.c program

```
/* Written by Dan Heller.  Copyright 1991, 1993, Z-Code Software Corp.
 * This program is freely distributable without licensing fees and
 * is provided without guarantee or warrantee expressed or implied.
 * This program is -not- in the public domain.
 */

/* zcard.c -- a postcard interface for zmail.
 */
#include <stdio.h>
#include <Xm/List.h>
#include <Xm/LabelG.h>
#include <Xm/PushB.h>
#include <Xm/MessageB.h>
#include <Xm/RowColumn.h>
#include <Xm/Form.h>
#include <Xm/Text.h>
```

---

†XtSetLanguageProc() is only available in X11R5; there is no corresponding function in X11R4. Xm-StringCreateLocalized() is only available in Motif 1.2; XmStringCreateSimple() is the corresponding function in Motif 1.1. XmFONTLIST_DEFAULT_TAG replaces XmSTRING_DEFAULT_CHARSET in Motif 1.2.

```
#include "zcard.icon"

/* redefine to "mush" or "Mail" if you don't have Z-Mail */
#define MAIL_CMD      "mush"

extern char *strcpy();
Widget list_w, text_w, to_w, subj_w;
Widget CreateLabeledTextForm();
void add_user(), send_it(), add_to_to(), move();

/* These only take effect if the app-defaults file is not found */
String fallback_resources[] = {
    "*XmText.fontList: -*-courier-medium-r-*--12-*",
    "*XmText.translations: #override \
        Ctrl<Key>D: activate() \n\
        Ctrl<Key>U: kill-to-start-of-line() \n\
        Ctrl<Key>W: delete-previous-word() \n\
        <Key>osfDelete: delete-previous-character()",
    "*msg-text.rows: 15",
    "*msg-text.columns: 35",
    "*XmPushButton.fontList: -*-new century schoolbook-bold-r-*--12-*",
    "*XmPushButtonGadget.fontList: -*-new century schoolbook-bold-r-*--12-*",
    "*XmLabelGadget.fontList: -*-new century schoolbook-bold-r-*--12-*",
    "*XmList.fontList: -*-courier-medium-r-*--12-*",
    "*zcard.labelString: Z-Card",
    "*title.labelString: Quick Message Sender",
    "*actions*leftAttachment: attach_position",
    "*actions*rightAttachment: attach_position",
    "*to-label.labelString: To:",
    "*to-list.visibleItemCount: 6",
    "*subject-label.labelString: Subject:",
    "*add-btn.labelString: Add",
    "*delete-btn.labelString: Delete",
    "*send-btn.labelString: Send",
    "*quit-btn.labelString: Quit",
    "*error.messageString: You must provide at least one message recipient.",
    NULL
};

main(argc, argv)
int argc;
char *argv[];
{
    Widget toplevel, label, left, heading, icon, titles;
    Widget actions, rc, w, send_w;
    XtAppContext app;
    Arg args[5];
    int n;
    Pixel fg, bg;
    Pixmap pixmap;
    extern void exit();

    XtSetLanguageProc (NULL, NULL, NULL);

    toplevel = XtVaAppInitialize (&app, "Zcard", NULL, 0,
        &argc, argv, fallback_resources,
        XmNallowShellResize,  True,
        NULL);
```

```
/* The form is the general layout manager for the application.
 * It contains two main widgets: a rowcolumn and a scrolled text.
 */
rc = XtVaCreateWidget ("rc",
    xmRowColumnWidgetClass, toplevel,
    XmNorientation, XmHORIZONTAL,
    NULL);

/* left side is a RowColumn -- a child of the bigger RowColumn */
left = XtVaCreateWidget ("left", xmRowColumnWidgetClass, rc, NULL);

/* start the left side with a Form to hold the heading */
heading = XtVaCreateWidget ("heading", xmFormWidgetClass, left, NULL);

/* create an icon to make things pretty */
XtVaGetValues (heading,
    XmNforeground, &fg,
    XmNbackground, &bg,
    NULL);
pixmap = XCreatePixmapFromBitmapData (XtDisplay (heading),
    RootWindowOfScreen (XtScreen (heading)),
    /* these values are defined in "zcard.icon" */
    zcard_logo_bits, zcard_logo_width, zcard_logo_height,
    fg, bg, DefaultDepthOfScreen (XtScreen (heading)));
icon = XtVaCreateManagedWidget ("zcard_icon",
    xmLabelGadgetClass, heading,
    XmNleftAttachment,  XmATTACH_FORM,
    XmNlabelType,       XmPIXMAP,
    XmNlabelPixmap,     pixmap,
    XmNalignment,       XmALIGNMENT_END,
    NULL);

/* identify the program */
titles = XtVaCreateWidget ("titles",
    xmRowColumnWidgetClass, heading,
    XmNrightAttachment,  XmATTACH_FORM,
    XmNleftAttachment,   XmATTACH_WIDGET,
    XmNleftWidget,       icon,
    XmNtopAttachment,    XmATTACH_FORM,
    XmNbottomAttachment, XmATTACH_FORM,
    NULL);
XtVaCreateManagedWidget ("zcard", xmLabelGadgetClass, titles, NULL);
XtVaCreateManagedWidget ("title", xmLabelGadgetClass, titles, NULL);
XtManageChild (titles);
XtManageChild (heading);

/* provide the "To:" prompt (see the resources above) */
to_w = CreateLabeledTextForm (left, "to-label", "to");

/* prompt for the subject (see the resources above) */
subj_w = CreateLabeledTextForm (left, "subject-label", "subject-text");

/* when user hits <Return>, advance caret to next input item */
XtAddCallback (subj_w, XmNactivateCallback, move, NULL);

/* right side is a scrolled text region for letter input. */
n = 0;
XtSetArg (args[n], XmNeditMode,      XmMULTI_LINE_EDIT); n++;
XtSetArg (args[n], XmNscrollVertical,    True); n++;
```

```
    XtSetArg (args[n], XmNscrollHorizontal,  True); n++;
    text_w = XmCreateScrolledText (rc, "msg-text", args, n);
    XtManageChild (text_w);

    /* Ctrl-D in text_w causes activate() which calls send_it() */
    XtAddCallback (text_w, XmNactivateCallback, send_it, send_w);

    /* Create a ScrolledList of all the recipients entered in To: */
    n = 0;
    XtSetArg (args[n], XmNscrollingPolicy, XmAUTOMATIC); n++;
    XtSetArg (args[n], XmNselectionPolicy, XmEXTENDED_SELECT); n++;
    XtSetArg (args[n], XmNlistSizePolicy, XmRESIZE_IF_POSSIBLE); n++;
    list_w = XmCreateScrolledList (left, "to-list", args, n);
    XtAddCallback (list_w, XmNdefaultActionCallback, add_to_to, to_w);
    XtManageChild (list_w);

    /* Any command line args are recipients */
    while (argc-- > 1) {
        XmString str = XmStringCreateLocalized (*++argv);
        XmListAddItemUnselected (list_w, str, 0);
        XmStringFree (str);
    }

    /* Add, Delete, Send and Quit buttons -- space equally */
    actions = XtVaCreateWidget ("actions", xmFormWidgetClass, left, NULL);

    send_w = XtVaCreateManagedWidget ("send-btn",
        xmPushButtonWidgetClass, actions,
        XmNleftAttachment, XmATTACH_POSITION,
        XmNleftPosition, 0,
        XmNrightAttachment, XmATTACH_POSITION,
        XmNrightPosition, 23,
        NULL);
    XtAddCallback (send_w, XmNactivateCallback, send_it, NULL);

    w = XtVaCreateManagedWidget ("add-btn",
        xmPushButtonWidgetClass, actions,
        XmNleftAttachment, XmATTACH_POSITION,
        XmNleftPosition, 26,
        XmNrightAttachment, XmATTACH_POSITION,
        XmNrightPosition, 46,
        NULL);
    /* clicking on Add user adds user to scrolled list */
    XtAddCallback (w, XmNactivateCallback, add_user, (XtPointer) 1);

    /* Make it appear as tho hitting return in To: text widget
     * is just like clicking on the Add button.
     */
    XtAddCallback (to_w, XmNactivateCallback, add_user, w);

    w = XtVaCreateManagedWidget ("delete-btn",
        xmPushButtonWidgetClass, actions,
        XmNleftAttachment, XmATTACH_POSITION,
        XmNleftPosition, 49,
        XmNrightAttachment, XmATTACH_POSITION,
        XmNrightPosition, 75,
        NULL);
    /* clicking on delete calls add_user() with a 0 client_data */
    XtAddCallback (w, XmNactivateCallback, add_user, (XtPointer) 0);
```

```
    w = XtVaCreateManagedWidget ("quit-btn",
        xmPushButtonWidgetClass, actions,
        XmNleftAttachment, XmATTACH_POSITION,
        XmNleftPosition, 78,
        XmNrightAttachment, XmATTACH_POSITION,
        XmNrightPosition, 100,
        NULL);
    XtAddCallback (w, XmNactivateCallback, exit, NULL);
    XtManageChild (actions);

    XtManageChild (left);
    XtManageChild (rc);

    /* specify tab groups in the order we'd like tabbing to follow */
    XtVaSetValues (to_w, XmNnavigationType, XmEXCLUSIVE_TAB_GROUP, NULL);
    XtVaSetValues (subj_w, XmNnavigationType, XmEXCLUSIVE_TAB_GROUP, NULL);
    XtVaSetValues (text_w, XmNnavigationType, XmEXCLUSIVE_TAB_GROUP, NULL);
    XtVaSetValues (actions, XmNnavigationType, XmEXCLUSIVE_TAB_GROUP, NULL);
    XtVaSetValues (list_w, XmNnavigationType, XmEXCLUSIVE_TAB_GROUP, NULL);

    XtRealizeWidget (toplevel);
    XtAppMainLoop (app);
}

/* add_user() -- add an address to the list of recipients.
 * The user clicked on either Add or Delete buttons, or he hit return in
 * the To: text field.  In the latter case, client data is the add_btn,
 * so call that widget's ArmAndActivate() action proc.
 */
void
add_user(w, client_data, call_data)
Widget w;
XtPointer client_data;
XtPointer call_data;
{
    int data = (int) client_data;
    XmAnyCallbackStruct *cbs = (XmAnyCallbackStruct *) call_data;

    if (w == to_w) {
        /* User hit return... make it look as tho he clicked on Add */
        XtCallActionProc (data, "ArmAndActivate", cbs->event, NULL, 0);
        return;
    }

    /* User clicked on Add if data == 1, or delete otherwise */
    if (data) {
        /* get the value of the To: text widget */
        char *text = XmTextGetString (to_w);
        XmString str = XmStringCreateLocalized (text);
        if (text && *text) /* if not a null string, add to List */
            XmListAddItemUnselected (list_w, str, 0);
        XmStringFree (str);
        XtFree (text);
        XmTextSetString (to_w, NULL); /* reset so user can add more */
    }
    else {
        /* user clicked on Delete; delete all selected names */
        int *sel, n;
```

```
        if (!XmListGetSelectedPos (list_w, &sel, &n))
            return;
        /* Must delete in reverse order or positions get messed up! */
        while (n--)
            XmListDeletePos (list_w, sel[n]);
        XtFree (sel);
    }
}

/* add_to_to() -- callback for double-clicking a list item that
 * causes the selected item to be added to To: text.  Now
 * the user can edit the address.
 */
void
add_to_to(list_w, client_data, call_data)
Widget list_w;
XtPointer client_data;
XtPointer call_data;
{
    Widget to_w = (Widget) client_data;
    XmListCallbackStruct *cbs = (XmListCallbackStruct *) call_data;
    char *text;

    XmStringGetLtoR (cbs->item, XmFONTLIST_DEFAULT_TAG, &text);
    XmTextSetString (to_w, text);
    XmTextSetInsertionPosition (to_w, strlen(text));
    XtFree (text);
    XmListDeletePos (list_w, cbs->item_position);
    /* it's a long way, but traverse to To: text field */
    XmProcessTraversal (list_w, XmTRAVERSE_NEXT_TAB_GROUP);
}

/* send_it() -- callback for when user clicked on Send.  Build
 * a command line, use popen() to open pipe to mail command, send
 * text data to it and then exit.  The message is sent to all
 * of the addresses that have been specified and are shown in the
 * list.
 */
void
send_it(w, client_data, call_data)
Widget w;
XtPointer client_data;
XtPointer call_data;
{
    Widget send_w;
    XmAnyCallbackStruct *cbs = (XmAnyCallbackStruct *) call_data;
    char *text, *subj, cmd[BUFSIZ], *p, *dummy, *getenv();
    int n, i, status;
    XmString *list;
    FILE *pp, *popen();

    if (w == text_w) {
        send_w = (Widget) client_data;
        XtCallActionProc (send_w, "ArmAndActivate", cbs->event, NULL, 0);
        return;
    }

    /* if something was left in the To: field, grab it */
```

```
    text = XmTextGetString (to_w);
    if (text != 0 && *text != 0) {
        XmString str = XmStringCreateLocalized (text);
        XmListAddItemUnselected (list_w, str, 0);
        XmTextSetString (to_w, "");
        XmStringFree (str);
        XtFree (text);
    }

    /* Get the list of users entered */
    XtVaGetValues (list_w,
        XmNitems, &list,
        XmNitemCount, &n,
        NULL);
    if (n == 0) {
        static Widget dialog;
        /* user goofed -- must provide at least one recipient */
        if (!dialog) {
            Arg args[5];
            n = 0;
            XtSetArg (args[n], XmNdialogStyle,
                XmDIALOG_APPLICATION_MODAL); n++;
            dialog = XmCreateErrorDialog (to_w, "error", args, n);
            XtUnmanageChild (
                XmMessageBoxGetChild (dialog, XmDIALOG_HELP_BUTTON));
            XtUnmanageChild (
                XmMessageBoxGetChild (dialog, XmDIALOG_CANCEL_BUTTON));
        }
        XtManageChild (dialog);
        return;
    }

    /* get the subject (may be empty) */
    subj = XmTextGetString (subj_w);

    /* build command line */
    if (!(p = getenv ("MAIL_CMD")))
        p = MAIL_CMD;
    p = strcpy (cmd, p);
    p += strlen (cmd);
    *p++ = ' ';
    if (subj && *subj) {
        /* if subject not empty, add to mail command */
        sprintf (p, "-s \"%s\" ", subj);
        p += strlen (p);
    }

    /* Add each user in the List to the command line */
    for (i = 0; i < n; i++) {
        XmStringGetLtoR (list[i], XmFONTLIST_DEFAULT_TAG, &dummy);
        p += strlen (strcpy (p, dummy));
        if (i < n-1) /* more to come yet... */
            *p++ = ',', *p++ = ' '; /* separate addresses w/commas */
    }

    /* open pipe to mail command */
    if (!(pp = popen (cmd, "w"))) {
        fprintf (stderr, "Can't execute");
```

```
            perror (cmd);
            return;
    }
    /* give it the text user typed (may be empty) */
    text = XmTextGetString (text_w);
    fputs (text, pp);
    fputc ('\n', pp); /* make sure there's a terminating newline */
    status = pclose (pp); /* close mail program */

    XtFree (text);
    XtFree (subj);
    if (status == 0) {
        XmTextSetString (to_w, NULL);
        XmTextSetString (text_w, NULL);
        XmTextSetString (subj_w, NULL);
        XmListDeleteAllItems (list_w);
    }
    /* send complete -- start back at beginning */
    XmProcessTraversal (w, XmTRAVERSE_HOME);
}

/* move() -- callback for when the user hits return in the Text widget */
void
move(text_w, client_data, call_data)
Widget text_w;
XtPointer client_data;
XtPointer call_data;
{
    XmProcessTraversal (text_w, XmTRAVERSE_NEXT_TAB_GROUP);
}

/* CreateLabeledTextForm() -- create a Form widget that has a label on
 * the left and a Text widget to the right.  Attach perimeter edges to
 * form.  We use it twice in the program, so make a function out of it.
 */
Widget
CreateLabeledTextForm(parent, label_name, text_name)
Widget parent;
char *label_name, *text_name;
{
    Widget form, label, ret;

    form = XtVaCreateWidget ("form",
        xmFormWidgetClass, parent,
        XmNorientation,         XmHORIZONTAL,
        NULL);
    label = XtVaCreateManagedWidget (label_name,
        xmLabelGadgetClass, form,
        XmNleftAttachment,    XmATTACH_FORM,
        XmNtopAttachment,     XmATTACH_FORM,
        XmNbottomAttachment,  XmATTACH_FORM,
        NULL);
    ret = XtVaCreateManagedWidget (text_name,
        xmTextWidgetClass, form,
        XmNleftAttachment,    XmATTACH_WIDGET,
        XmNleftWidget,        label,
        XmNtopAttachment,     XmATTACH_FORM,
        XmNrightAttachment,   XmATTACH_FORM,
```

Example A-1. The zcard.c program (continued)

```
        XmNbottomAttachment, XmATTACH_FORM,
        NULL);
    XtManageChild (form);

    return ret;
}
```

Figure A-1 shows the output of the program.

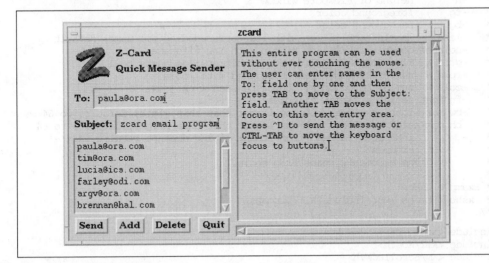

Figure A-1. Output of zcard.c

A.2 A Bitmap Display Utility

The *xshowbitmap* program is a useful utility for reviewing a group of bitmap files. The filenames for the bitmaps can be specified on the command line, sent through a pipe, or typed into `stdin`. All of the bitmaps are drawn into a pixmap, which is rendered into a Drawing-Area widget. The DrawingArea is used as the work window for a ScrolledWindow, so that we can demonstrate application-defined scrolling for the Motif ScrolledWindow. The bitmaps are displayed in an equal number of rows and columns if possible. Alternatively, you can specify either the number of rows or the number of columns using the `-rows` or `-columns` command-line option, respectively.

The example in Example A-2 demonstrates the use of Xt mechanisms for adding command-line options and application-level resources in an application. For an explanation of these Xt features, see Volume Four, *X Toolkit Intrinsics Programming Manual*. For details on the Xlib functions for reading and manipulating bitmaps, see Volume One, *Xlib Programming Manual*.†

---

† `XtSetLanguageProc()` is only available in X11R5; there is no corresponding function in X11R4.

```
/* xshowbitmap.c -- displays a set of bitmaps specified on the command
 * line, from a pipe, or typed into stdin.  Bitmaps must be specified
 * as file names.
 *
 * Usage: xshowbitmap
 *    -s       sorts the bitmaps in order of size with largest first
 *    -v       verbose mode for when input is redirected to stdin
 *    -w       width of viewport window
 *    -h       height of viewport window
 *    -fg      foreground color
 *    -bg      background color
 *    -label   labels each bitmap with its corresponding filename; default
 *    -nolabel doesn't label each bitmap with its filename
 *    -grid N  line width for grid between bitmaps; defaults to 1
 *    -rows N  number of rows; cannot be used with -cols
 *    -cols N  number of columns; cannot be used with -rows
 *    -fn font font for bitmap filenames
 *    -bw max-width  excludes bitmaps larger than this width; defaults to 64
 *    -bh max-height excludes bitmaps larger than this height; defaults to 64
 *    -        indicates to read from stdin; piping doesn't require the '-'
 *             argument
 *             no arguments reads from stdin
 *
 * Example usage:
 *   xshowbitmaps /usr/include/X11/bitmaps/*
 */

#include <stdio.h>
#include <X11/Xos.h>
#include <Xm/ScrolledW.h>
#include <Xm/DrawingA.h>
#include <Xm/ScrollBar.h>

#ifdef max
#undef max
#endif
#define max(a,b)  ((int)(a)>(int)(b)?(int)(a):(int)(b))
#define min(a,b)  ((int)(a)<(int)(b)?(int)(a):(int)(b))

typedef struct {
    char *name;
    int len;
    unsigned int width, height;
    Pixmap bitmap;
} Bitmap;

/* Resrcs is an object that contains global variables that we want the
 * user to be able to initialize through resources or command line options.
 * XtAppInitialize() initializes the fields in this data structure to values
 * indicated by the XrmOptionsDescRec structure defined later.
 */
struct _resrcs {
    Boolean      sort;                      /* sort the bitmaps */
    Boolean      verbose;                   /* loading bitmaps verbosely */
    Boolean      label_bitmap;              /* whether to label bitmaps */
    int          max_width, max_height;     /* largest allowable bitmap */
    unsigned int grid;                      /* line width between bitmaps */
    Pixel        fg, bg;                    /* colors of bitmaps */
```

```
    XFontStruct *font;                          /* font for bitmap labels */
    Dimension   view_width, view_height; /* initial clip window size */
    int         rows, cols;                     /* forcefully set #rows/cols */
} Resrcs;

/* .Xdefaults or app-defaults resources.  The last field in each structure
 * is used as the default values for the field in the Resrcs struct above.
 */
static XtResource resources[] = {
    { "sort", "Sort", XmRBoolean, sizeof (Boolean),
        XtOffsetOf (struct _resrcs, sort), XmRImmediate, False },
    { "verbose", "Verbose", XmRBoolean, sizeof (Boolean),
        XtOffsetOf (struct _resrcs,verbose), XmRImmediate, False },
    { "labelBitmap", "LabelBitmap", XmRBoolean, sizeof (Boolean),
        XtOffsetOf (struct _resrcs, label_bitmap), XmRImmediate,
        (char *) True },
    { "grid", "Grid", XmRInt, sizeof (int),
        XtOffsetOf (struct _resrcs, grid), XmRImmediate, (char *) 1 },
    { "bitmapWidth", "BitmapWidth", XmRInt, sizeof (int),
        XtOffsetOf (struct _resrcs, max_width), XmRImmediate, (char *) 64 },
    { "bitmapHeight", "BitmapHeight", XmRInt, sizeof (int),
        XtOffsetOf (struct _resrcs, max_height), XmRImmediate, (char *) 64 },
    { XmNfont, XmCFont, XmRFontStruct, sizeof (XFontStruct *),
        XtOffsetOf (struct _resrcs, font), XmRString, XtDefaultFont },
    { XmNforeground, XmCForeground, XmRPixel, sizeof (Pixel),
        XtOffsetOf (struct _resrcs, fg), XmRString, XtDefaultForeground },
    { XmNbackground, XmCBackground, XmRPixel, sizeof (Pixel),
        XtOffsetOf (struct _resrcs, bg), XmRString, XtDefaultBackground },
    { "view-width", "View-width", XmRDimension, sizeof (Dimension),
        XtOffsetOf (struct _resrcs, view_width), XmRImmediate,
        (char *) 500 },
    { "view-height", "View-height", XmRDimension, sizeof (Dimension),
        XtOffsetOf (struct _resrcs, view_height), XmRImmediate,
        (char *) 300 },
    { "rows", "Rows", XmRInt, sizeof (int),
        XtOffsetOf (struct _resrcs, rows), XmRImmediate, 0 },
    { "cols", "Cols", XmRInt, sizeof (int),
        XtOffsetOf (struct _resrcs, cols), XmRImmediate, 0 },
};

/* If the following command line args (1st field) are found, set the
 * associated resource values (2nd field) to the given value (4th field).
 */
static XrmOptionDescRec options[] = {
    { "-sort", "sort", XrmoptionNoArg, "True" },
    { "-v", "verbose", XrmoptionNoArg, "True" },
    { "-fn", "font", XrmoptionSepArg, NULL },
    { "-fg", "foreground", XrmoptionSepArg, NULL },
    { "-bg", "background", XrmoptionSepArg, NULL },
    { "-w", "view-width", XrmoptionSepArg, NULL },
    { "-h", "view-height", XrmoptionSepArg, NULL },
    { "-rows", "rows", XrmoptionSepArg, NULL },
    { "-cols", "cols", XrmoptionSepArg, NULL },
    { "-bw", "bitmapWidth", XrmoptionSepArg, NULL },
    { "-bh", "bitmapHeight", XrmoptionSepArg, NULL },
    { "-bitmap_width", "bitmapWidth", XrmoptionSepArg, NULL },
    { "-bitmap_height", "bitmapHeight", XrmoptionSepArg, NULL },
```

```
    { "-label", "labelBitmap", XrmoptionNoArg, "True" },
    { "-nolabel", "labelBitmap", XrmoptionNoArg, "False" },
    { "-grid", "grid", XrmoptionSepArg, NULL },
};

/* size_cmp() -- used by qsort to sort bitmaps into alphabetical order
 * This is used when the "sort" resource is true or when -sort is given.
 */
size_cmp(b1, b2)
Bitmap *b1, *b2;
{
    int n = (int) (b1->width * b1->height) - (int) (b2->width * b2->height);
    if (n)
        return n;
    return strcmp (b1->name, b2->name);
}

/* int_sqrt() -- get the integer square root of n.  Used to put the
 * bitmaps in an equal number of rows and colums.
 */
int_sqrt(n)
register int n;/
{
    register int i, s = 0, t;
    for (i = 15; i >= 0; i--) {
        t = (s | (1L << i));
        if (t * t <= n)
            s = t;
    }
    return s;
}

/* global variables that are not changable thru resources or command
 * line options.
 */
Widget drawing_a, vsb, hsb;
Pixmap pixmap; /* used the as image for Label widget */
GC gc;
Display *dpy;
unsigned int cell_width, cell_height;
unsigned int pix_hoffset, pix_voffset, sw_hoffset, sw_voffset;
void redraw();

main(argc, argv)
int argc;
char *argv[];
{
    extern char *strcpy();
    XtAppContext app;
    Widget toplevel, scrolled_w;
    Bitmap *list = (Bitmap *) NULL;
    char buf[128], *p;
    XFontStruct *font;
    int istty = isatty(0), redirect = !istty, i = 0, total = 0;
    unsigned int bitmap_error;
    int j, k;
    void scrolled(), expose_resize();
```

```
    XtSetLanguageProc (NULL, NULL, NULL);

    toplevel = XtAppInitialize (&app, "XShowbitmap",
        options, XtNumber (options), &argc, argv, NULL, NULL, 0);
    dpy = XtDisplay (toplevel);

    XtGetApplicationResources (toplevel, &Resrcs,
        resources, XtNumber (resources), NULL, 0);

    if (Resrcs.rows && Resrcs.cols)
        XtWarning ("You can't specify both rows *and* columns.");

    font = Resrcs.font;

    /* check to see if we have to load the bitmaps from stdin */
    if (!argv[1] || !strcmp(argv[1], "-")) {
        printf ("Loading bitmap names from standard input. ");
        if (istty) {
            puts ("End with EOF or .");
            redirect++;
        }
        else
            puts ("Use -v to view bitmap names being loaded.");
    }
    else if (!istty && strcmp(argv[1], "-")) {
        printf ("%s: either use pipes or specify bitmap names.\n",
            argv[0]);
        exit (1);
    }

    /* Now, load the bitmap file names */
    while (*++argv || redirect) {
        if (!redirect)
            /* this may appear at the end of a list of filenames */
            if (!strcmp (*argv, "-"))
                redirect++; /* switch to stdin prompting */
            else
                (void) strcpy (buf, *argv);
        if (redirect) {
            if (istty)
                printf ("Bitmap file: "), fflush(stdout);
            if (!fgets (buf, sizeof buf - 1, stdin) || !strcmp (buf, ".\n"))
                break;
            buf[strlen (buf) - 1] = 0; /* plug a null at the newline */
        }
        if (!buf[0])
            continue;
        if (Resrcs.verbose)
            printf ("Loading \"%s\"...", buf), fflush(stdout);
        if (i == total) {
            total += 10; /* allocate bitmap structures in groups of 10 */
            if (!(list = (Bitmap *) XtRealloc
                    (list, total * sizeof (Bitmap))))
                XtError ("Not enough memory for bitmap data");
        }
        if ((bitmap_error = XReadBitmapFile (dpy, DefaultRootWindow(dpy),
                buf, &list[i].width, &list[i].height, &list[i].bitmap,
                &j, &k)) == BitmapSuccess) {
```

```
        if (p = rindex (buf, '/'))
            p++;
        else
            p = buf;
        if (Resrcs.max_height && list[i].height > Resrcs.max_height ||
            Resrcs.max_width && list[i].width > Resrcs.max_width) {
            printf ("%s: bitmap too big\n", p);
            XFreePixmap (dpy, list[i].bitmap);
            continue;
        }
        list[i].len = strlen (p);
        list[i].name = strcpy (XtMalloc (list[i].len + 1), p);
        if (Resrcs.verbose)
            printf ("size: %dx%d\n", list[i].width, list[i].height);
        i++;
    }
    else {
        printf ("Couldn't load bitmap: ");
        if (!istty && !Resrcs.verbose)
            printf("\"%s\": ", buf);
        switch (bitmap_error) {
            case BitmapOpenFailed : puts ("open failed."); break;
            case BitmapFileInvalid : puts ("bad file format."); break;
            case BitmapNoMemory : puts ("not enough memory."); break;
        }
    }
}
if ((total = i) == 0) {
    puts ("couldn't load any bitmaps.");
    exit (1);
}
printf ("Total bitmaps loaded: %d\n", total);
if (Resrcs.sort) {
    printf ("Sorting bitmaps...");
    fflush (stdout);
    qsort (list, total, sizeof (Bitmap), size_cmp);
    putchar ('\n');
}

/* calculate size for pixmap by getting the dimensions of each bitmap. */
printf ("Calculating sizes for pixmap...");
fflush (stdout);
for (i = 0; i < total; i++) {
    if (list[i].width > cell_width)
        cell_width = list[i].width;
    if (list[i].height > cell_height)
        cell_height = list[i].height;
    if (Resrcs.label_bitmap && (j = XTextWidth
            (font, list[i].name, list[i].len)) > cell_width)
        cell_width = j;
}

/* Compensate for vertical font height if label_bitmap is true.
 * Add value of grid line weight and a 6 pixel padding for aesthetics.
 */
cell_height += Resrcs.grid + 6 +
    Resrcs.label_bitmap * (font->ascent + font->descent);
```

```
    cell_width += Resrcs.grid + 6;

    /* if user didn't specify row/column layout figure it out ourselves.
     * optimize layout by making it "square".
     */
    if (!Resrcs.rows && !Resrcs.cols) {
        Resrcs.cols = int_sqrt (total);
        Resrcs.rows = (total + Resrcs.cols - 1) / Resrcs.cols;
    }
    else if (Resrcs.rows)
        /* user specified rows -- figure out columns */
        Resrcs.cols = (total + Resrcs.rows - 1) / Resrcs.rows;
    else
        /* user specified cols -- figure out rows */
        Resrcs.rows = (total + Resrcs.cols - 1) / Resrcs.cols;

    printf ("Creating pixmap area of size %dx%d (%d rows, %d cols)\n",
        Resrcs.cols * cell_width, Resrcs.rows * cell_height,
        Resrcs.rows, Resrcs.cols);

    if (!(pixmap = XCreatePixmap (dpy, DefaultRootWindow(dpy),
            Resrcs.cols * cell_width, Resrcs.rows * cell_height,
            DefaultDepthOfScreen (XtScreen (toplevel)))))
        XtError ("Can't Create pixmap.");

    if (!(gc = XCreateGC (dpy, pixmap, NULL, 0)))
        XtError ("Can't create gc.");
    XSetForeground (dpy, gc, Resrcs.bg); /* init GC's foreground to bg */
    XFillRectangle (dpy, pixmap, gc, 0, 0,
        Resrcs.cols * cell_width, Resrcs.rows * cell_height);
    XSetForeground (dpy, gc, Resrcs.fg);
    XSetBackground (dpy, gc, Resrcs.bg);
    XSetFont (dpy, gc, font->fid);
    if (Resrcs.grid) {
        if (Resrcs.grid != 1)
            /* Line weight of 1 is faster when left as 0 (the default) */
            XSetLineAttributes (dpy, gc, Resrcs.grid, 0, 0, 0);
        for (j = 0; j <= Resrcs.rows * cell_height; j += cell_height)
            XDrawLine (dpy, pixmap, gc, 0, j, Resrcs.cols * cell_width, j);
        for (j = 0; j <= Resrcs.cols * cell_width; j += cell_width)
            XDrawLine (dpy, pixmap, gc, j, 0, j, Resrcs.rows * cell_height);
    }

    /* Draw each of the bitmaps into the big picture */
    for (i = 0; i < total; i++) {
        int x = cell_width * (i % Resrcs.cols);
        int y = cell_height * (i / Resrcs.cols);
        if (Resrcs.label_bitmap)
            XDrawString (dpy, pixmap, gc,
                x + 5 + Resrcs.grid / 2, y + font->ascent + Resrcs.grid / 2,
                list[i].name, list[i].len);
        if (DefaultDepthOfScreen (XtScreen (toplevel)) > 1)
            XCopyPlane (dpy, list[i].bitmap, pixmap, gc,
                0, 0, list[i].width, list[i].height,
                x + 5 + Resrcs.grid / 2,
                y + font->ascent + font->descent + Resrcs.grid / 2, 1L);
        else
            XCopyArea (dpy, list[i].bitmap, pixmap, gc,
```

```
                     0, 0, list[i].width, list[i].height,
                     x + 5 + Resrcs.grid / 2,
                     y + font->ascent + font->descent + Resrcs.grid / 2);
        XFreePixmap (dpy, list[i].bitmap);
        XtFree (list[i].name);
    }
    XtFree (list);

    /* Now we get into the Motif stuff */

    /* Create automatic Scrolled Window */
    scrolled_w = XtVaCreateManagedWidget ("scrolled_w",
        xmScrolledWindowWidgetClass, toplevel,
        XmNscrollingPolicy, XmAPPLICATION_DEFINED,
        XmNvisualPolicy,    XmVARIABLE,
        XmNshadowThickness, 0,
        NULL);

    /* Create a drawing area as a child of the ScrolledWindow.
     * The DA's size is initialized (arbitrarily) to view_width and
     * view_height.  The ScrolledWindow will expand to this size.
     */
    drawing_a = XtVaCreateManagedWidget ("drawing_a",
        xmDrawingAreaWidgetClass, scrolled_w,
        XmNwidth,          Resrcs.view_width,
        XmNheight,         Resrcs.view_height,
        NULL);
    XtAddCallback (drawing_a, XmNexposeCallback, expose_resize, NULL);
    XtAddCallback (drawing_a, XmNresizeCallback, expose_resize, NULL);

    /* Application-defined ScrolledWindows won't create their own
     * ScrollBars.  So, we create them ourselves as children of the
     * ScrolledWindow widget.  The vertical ScrollBar's maximum size is
     * the number of rows that exist (in unit values).  The horizontal
     * ScrollBar's maximum width is represented by the number of columns.
     */
    vsb = XtVaCreateManagedWidget ("vsb",
        xmScrollBarWidgetClass, scrolled_w,
        XmNorientation,    XmVERTICAL,
        XmNmaximum,        Resrcs.rows,
        XmNsliderSize,     min (Resrcs.view_height / cell_height, Resrcs.rows),
        NULL);
    if (Resrcs.view_height / cell_height > Resrcs.rows)
        sw_voffset = (Resrcs.view_height - Resrcs.rows * cell_height) / 2;
    hsb = XtVaCreateManagedWidget ("hsb",
        xmScrollBarWidgetClass, scrolled_w,
        XmNorientation,    XmHORIZONTAL,
        XmNmaximum,        Resrcs.cols,
        XmNsliderSize,     min (Resrcs.view_width / cell_width, Resrcs.cols),
        NULL);
    if (Resrcs.view_width / cell_width > Resrcs.cols)
        sw_hoffset = (Resrcs.view_width - Resrcs.cols * cell_width) / 2;

    /* Allow the ScrolledWindow to initialize itself accordingly...*/
    XmScrolledWindowSetAreas (scrolled_w, hsb, vsb, drawing_a);

    XtAddCallback (vsb, XmNvalueChangedCallback, scrolled, XmVERTICAL);
    XtAddCallback (hsb, XmNvalueChangedCallback, scrolled, XmHORIZONTAL);
```

```
    XtAddCallback (vsb, XmNdragCallback, scrolled, XmVERTICAL);
    XtAddCallback (hsb, XmNdragCallback, scrolled, XmHORIZONTAL);

    XtRealizeWidget (toplevel);
    XtAppMainLoop (app);
}

/* scrolled() -- react to scrolling actions; cbs->value is ScrollBar's
 * new position.
 */
void
scrolled(scrollbar, client_data, call_data)
Widget scrollbar;
XtPointer client_data;
XtPointer call_data;
{
    int orientation = (int) client_data;
    XmScrollBarCallbackStruct *cbs =
        (XmScrollBarCallbackStruct *) call_data;

    if (orientation == XmVERTICAL)
        pix_voffset = cbs->value * cell_height;
    else
        pix_hoffset = cbs->value * cell_width;
    redraw (XtWindow (drawing_a));
}

/* expose_resize() -- handles both expose and resize (configure) events.
 * For XmCR_EXPOSE, just call redraw() and return.  For resizing,
 * we must calculate the new size of the viewable area and possibly
 * reposition the pixmap's display and position offset.  Since we
 * are also responsible for the ScrollBars, adjust them accordingly.
 */
void
expose_resize(drawing_a, client_data, call_data)
Widget drawing_a;
XtPointer client_data;
XtPointer call_data;
{
    XmDrawingAreaCallbackStruct *cbs =
        (XmDrawingAreaCallbackStruct *) call_data;
    Dimension view_width, view_height, oldw, oldh;
    int do_clear = 0;

    if (cbs->reason == XmCR_EXPOSE) {
        redraw (cbs->window);
        return;
    }
    oldw = Resrcs.view_width;
    oldh = Resrcs.view_height;

    /* Unfortunately, the cbs->event field is NULL, we have to have
     * get the size of the drawing area manually.
     */
    XtVaGetValues (drawing_a,
        XmNwidth, &Resrcs.view_width,
        XmNheight, &Resrcs.view_height,
        NULL);
```

```
    /* Get the size of the viewable area in "units lengths" where
     * each unit is the cell size for each dimension.  This prevents
     * rounding error for the {vert,horiz}_start values later.
     */
    view_width = Resrcs.view_width / cell_width;
    view_height = Resrcs.view_height / cell_height;

    /* When the user resizes the frame bigger, expose events are generated,
     * so that's not a problem, since the expose handler will repaint the
     * whole viewport.  However, when the window resizes smaller, then no
     * expose event is generated.  In this case, the window does not need
     * to be redisplayed if the old viewport was smaller than the pixmap.
     * (The existing image is still valid--no redisplay is necessary.)
     * The window WILL need to be redisplayed if:
     * 1) new view size is larger than pixmap (pixmap needs to be centered).
     * 2) new view size is smaller than pixmap, but the OLD view size was
     *    larger than pixmap.
     */
    if ( (int) view_height >= Resrcs.rows) {
        /* The height of the viewport is taller than the pixmap, so set
         * pix_voffset = 0, so the top origin of the pixmap is shown,
         * and the pixmap is centered vertically in viewport.
         */
        pix_voffset = 0;
        sw_voffset = (Resrcs.view_height - Resrcs.rows * cell_height) / 2;
        /* Case 1 above */
        do_clear = 1;
        /* scrollbar is maximum size */
        view_height = Resrcs.rows;
    }
    else {
        /* Pixmap is larger than viewport, so viewport will be completely
         * redrawn on the redisplay.  (So, we don't need to clear window.)
         * Make sure upper side has origin of a cell (bitmap).
         */
        pix_voffset = min (pix_voffset,
            (Resrcs.rows-view_height) * cell_height);
        sw_voffset = 0; /* no centering is done */
        /* Case 2 above */
        if (oldh > Resrcs.rows * cell_height)
            do_clear = 1;
    }
    XtVaSetValues (vsb,
        XmNsliderSize,    max (view_height, 1),
        XmNvalue,         pix_voffset / cell_height,
        XmNpageIncrement, max (view_height - 1, 1),
        NULL);

    /* identical to vertical case above */
    if ( (int) view_width >= Resrcs.cols) {
        /* The width of the viewport is wider than the pixmap, so set
         * pix_hoffset = 0, so the left origin of the pixmap is shown,
         * and the pixmap is centered horizontally in viewport.
         */
        pix_hoffset = 0;
        sw_hoffset = (Resrcs.view_width - Resrcs.cols * cell_width) / 2;
```

```
            /* Case 1 above */
            do_clear = 1;
            /* scrollbar is maximum size */
            view_width = Resrcs.cols;
        }
        else {
            /* Pixmap is larger than viewport, so viewport will be completely
             * redrawn on the redisplay.  (So, we don't need to clear window.)
             * Make sure left side has origin of a cell (bitmap).
             */
            pix_hoffset = min (pix_hoffset,
                (Resrcs.cols - view_width) * cell_width);
            sw_hoffset = 0;
            /* Case 2 above */
            if (oldw > Resrcs.cols * cell_width)
                do_clear = 1;
        }
        XtVaSetValues (hsb,
            XmNsliderSize,    max (view_width, 1),
            XmNvalue,         pix_hoffset / cell_width,
            XmNpageIncrement, max (view_width - 1, 1),
            NULL);

        if (do_clear)
            /* XClearWindow() doesn't generate an ExposeEvent */
            XClearArea (dpy, cbs->window, 0, 0, 0, 0, True);
    }

void
redraw(window)
Window window;
{
    XCopyArea (dpy, pixmap, window, gc, pix_hoffset, pix_voffset,
        Resrcs.view_width, Resrcs.view_height, sw_hoffset, sw_voffset);
}
```

The output of the example is shown in Figure A-2.

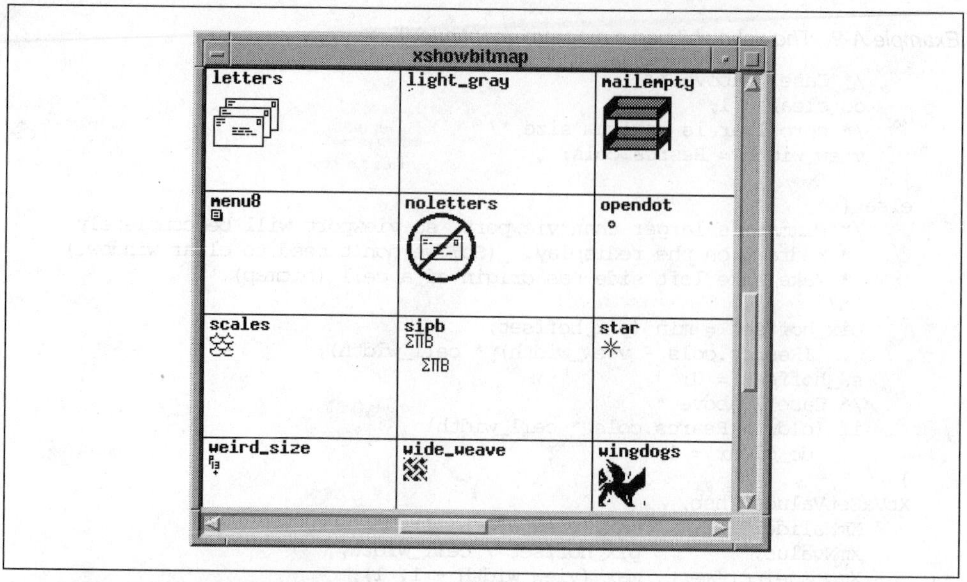

Figure A-2. Output of xshowbitmap.c

A.3 A Memo Calendar

The *xmemo* program creates a main application window that contains a calendar and a list of months. Selecting a month changes the calendar, while selecting a day causes that date to become activated. When a date is activated, the application displays another window that contains a Text widget. The Text widget could be used to keep a memo for that day if you were to add code to save and retrieve the contents of the memo. If you select the same day a second time, the window is popped down. Figure A-3 shows the output of the program.

The program shown in Example A-3 demonstrates a number of very subtle quirks about X and Motif programming. What separates simple programs from sophisticated ones is how well you get around quirks like the ones demonstrated in this example. For example, the way the dates in the calendar are handled is not as simple as it might appear. Unlike the *xcal* example in Chapter 11, *Labels and Buttons*, which used a single Label widget as the calendar, here each date in a month is a separate PushButton widget. To give the appearance that the calendar is a single flat area, the XmNShadowThickness of each PushButton is initialized to 0. When a date is selected, the shadow thickness for that PushButton is reset to 2 (the default) to provide visual feedback that there is a memo associated with it.†

---

†XtSetLanguageProc() is only available in X11R5; there is no corresponding function in X11R4. Xm-StringCreateLocalized() is only available in Motif 1.2; XmStringCreateSimple() is the corresponding function in Motif 1.1.

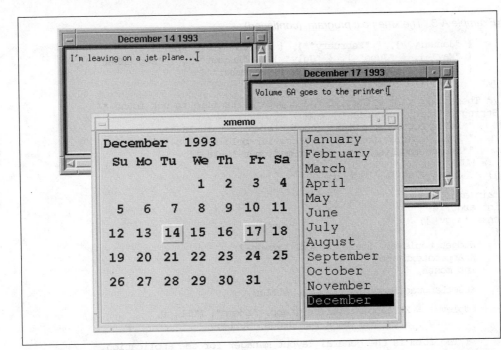

Figure A-3. Output of xmemo.c

Example A-3. The xmemo.c program

```
/* xmemo.c -- a memo calendar program that creates a calendar on the
 * left and a list of months on the right.  Selecting a month changes
 * the calendar.  Selecting a day causes that date to become activated
 * and a popup window is displayed that contains a text widget.  This
 * widget is presumably used to keep memos for that day.  You can pop
 * up and down the window by continuing to select the date on that month.
 */
#include <stdio.h>
#include <X11/Xos.h>
#include <Xm/List.h>
#include <Xm/Frame.h>
#include <Xm/LabelG.h>
#include <Xm/PushB.h>
#include <Xm/RowColumn.h>
#include <Xm/Form.h>
#include <Xm/Text.h>

int year;
void XmStringFreeTable(), date_dialog(), set_month();
Widget list_w, month_label;

typedef struct _month {
    char *name;
    Widget form, dates[6][7];
} Month;

Month months[] = { /* only initialize "known" data */
```

```
      { "January" }, { "February" }, { "March" }, { "April" },
      { "May" }, { "June" }, { "July" }, { "August" }, { "September" },
      { "October" }, { "November" }, { "December" }
};

/* These only take effect if the app-defaults file is not found */
String fallback_resources[] = {
    "*XmPushButton.fontList: -*-courier-bold-r-*--18-*",
    "*XmLabelGadget.fontList: -*-courier-bold-r-*--18-*",
    "*XmList.fontList: -*-courier-medium-r-*--18-*",
    NULL
};

main(argc, argv)
int argc;
char *argv[];
{
    Widget toplevel, frame, rowcol, rowcol2;
    XtAppContext app;
    int month;

    XtSetLanguageProc (NULL, NULL, NULL);

    toplevel = XtVaAppInitialize (&app, "XMemo", NULL, 0,
        &argc, argv, fallback_resources, NULL);

    /* The form is the general layout manager for the application.
     * It will contain two widgets (the calendary and the list of months).
     * These widgets are laid out horizontally.
     */
    rowcol = XtVaCreateWidget ("rowcol",
        xmRowColumnWidgetClass, toplevel,
        XmNorientation, XmHORIZONTAL,
        NULL);

    /* Place a frame around the calendar... */
    frame = XtVaCreateManagedWidget ("frame1",
        xmFrameWidgetClass, rowcol, NULL);
    /* the calendar is placed inside of a RowColumn widget */
    rowcol2 = XtVaCreateManagedWidget ("rowcol2",
        xmRowColumnWidgetClass, frame, NULL);
    /* the month label changes dynamically as each month is selected */
    month_label = XtVaCreateManagedWidget ("month_label",
        xmLabelGadgetClass, rowcol2, NULL);
    XtVaCreateManagedWidget (" Su Mo Tu  We Th  Fr Sa",
        xmLabelGadgetClass, rowcol2, NULL);

    /* Create a ScrolledText that contains the months.  You probably won't
     * see the ScrollBar unless the list is resized so that not all of
     * the month names are visible.
     */
    {
        XmString strs[XtNumber (months)];
        for (month = 0; month < XtNumber (months); month++)
            strs[month] = XmStringCreateLocalized (months[month].name);
        list_w = XmCreateScrolledList (rowcol, "list", NULL, 0);
        XtVaSetValues (list_w,
            XmNitems,     strs,
            XmNitemCount, XtNumber (months),
```

```
            NULL);
        for (month = 0; month < XtNumber (months); month++)
            XmStringFree (strs[month]);
        XtAddCallback (list_w, XmNbrowseSelectionCallback, set_month, NULL);
        XtManageChild (list_w);
    }

    /* Determine the year we're dealing with and establish today's month */
    if (argc > 1)
        year = atoi (argv[1]);
    else {
        long time(), t = time (0);
        struct tm *today = localtime (&t);
        year = 1900 + today->tm_year;
        month = today->tm_mon + 1;
    }
    XmListSelectPos (list_w, month, True);

    XtManageChild (rowcol);

    XtRealizeWidget (toplevel);
    XtAppMainLoop (app);
}

/* set_month() -- callback routine for when a month is selected.
 * Each month is a separate, self-contained widget that contains the
 * dates as PushButton widgets.  New months do not overwrite old ones,
 * so the old month must be "unmanaged" before the new month is managed.
 * If the month has not yet been created, then figure out the dates and
 * which days of the week they fall on using clever math computations...
 */
void
set_month(w, client_data, call_data)
Widget w;
XtPointer client_data;
XtPointer call_data;
{
    XmListCallbackStruct *list_cbs = (XmListCallbackStruct *) call_data;
    char text[BUFSIZ];
    register char *p;
    int i, j, m, tot, day;
    static int month = -1;

    if (list_cbs->item_position == month + 1)
        return; /* same month, don't bother redrawing */

    if (month >= 0 && months[month].form)
        XtUnmanageChild (months[month].form); /* unmanage last month */
    month = list_cbs->item_position - 1; /* set new month */
    sprintf (text, "%s  %d", months[month].name, year);
    XtVaSetValues (month_label,
        XtVaTypedArg, XmNlabelString, XmRString, text, strlen (text) + 1,
        NULL);
    if (months[month].form) {
        /* it's already been created -- just manage and return */
        XtManageChild (months[month].form);
        return;
    }
```

Additional
Example Programs

```
/* Create the month Form widget and dates PushButton widgets */
months[month].form = XtVaCreateWidget ("month_form",
    xmRowColumnWidgetClass, XtParent (month_label),
    XmNorientation,     XmHORIZONTAL,
    XmNnumColumns,      6,
    XmNpacking,         XmPACK_COLUMN,
    NULL);

/* calculate the dates of the month using science */
/* day_number() takes day-of-month (1-31), returns day-of-week (0-6) */
m = day_number (year, month + 1, 1);
tot = days_in_month (year, month + 1);

/* We are creating a whole bunch of PushButtons, but not all of
 * them have dates associated with them.  The buttons that have
 * dates get the number sprintf'ed into it.  All others get two blanks.
 */
for (day = i = 0; i < 6; i++) {
    for (j = 0; j < 7; j++, m += (j > m && --tot > 0)) {
        char *name;
        if (j != m || tot < 1)
            name = "  ";
        else {
            sprintf(text, "%2d", ++day);
            name = text;
        }
        months[month].dates[i][j] =
            XtVaCreateManagedWidget (name,
                xmPushButtonWidgetClass, months[month].form,
                /* this is where we will hold the dialog later. */
                XmNuserData,        NULL,
                XmNsensitive,       (j % 7 == m && tot > 0),
                XmNshadowThickness, 0,
                NULL);
        XtAddCallback (months[month].dates[i][j],
            XmNactivateCallback, date_dialog, day);
    }
    m = 0;
}
XtManageChild (months[month].form);

/* The RowColumn widget creates equally sized boxes for each child
 * it manages.  If one child is bigger than the rest, all children
 * are that big.  If we create all the PushButtons with a 0 shadow
 * thickness, as soon as one PushButton is selected and its thickness
 * is set to 2, the entire RowColumn resizes itself.  To compensate
 * for the problem, we need to set the shadow thickness of at least
 * one of the buttons to 2, so that the entire RowColumn is
 * initialized to the right size.  But this will cause the button to
 * have a visible border and make it appear preselected, so, we have
 * to make it appear invisible.  If it is invisible then it cannot be
 * selected, but it just so happens that the last 5 days in
 * the month will never have selectable dates, so we can use any one
 * of those.  To make the button invisible, we need to unmap the
 * widget.  We can't simply unmanage it or the parent won't consider
 * its size, which defeats the whole purpose.  We can't create the
 * widget and then unmap it because it has not been realized, so it
```

```
            * does not have a window yet.  We don't want to realize and manage
            * the entire application just to realize this one widget, so we
            * set XmNmappedWhenManaged to False along with the shadow thickness
            * being set to 2.  Now the RowColumn is the right size.
            */
        XtVaSetValues (months[month].dates[5][6],
            XmNshadowThickness, 2,
            XmNmappedWhenManaged, False,
            NULL);
    }

/* date_dialog() -- when a date is selected, this function is called.
 * Create a dialog (toplevel shell) that contains a multiline text
 * widget for memos about this date.
 */
void
date_dialog(w, client_data, call_data)
Widget w;
XtPointer client_data;
XtPointer call_data;
{
    int date = (int) client_data;
    Widget dialog;
    XWindowAttributes xwa;

    /* the dialog is stored in the PushButton's XmNuserData */
    XtVaGetValues (w, XmNuserData, &dialog, NULL);
    if (!dialog) {
        /* it doesn't exist yet, create it. */
        char buf[32];
        Arg args[5];
        int n, n_pos, *list;

        /* get the month that was selected -- we just need it for its name */
        if (!XmListGetSelectedPos (list_w, &list, &n_pos))
            return;
        sprintf (buf, "%s %d %d", months[list[0]-1].name, date, year);
        XtFree (list);
        dialog = XtVaCreatePopupShell ("popup",
            topLevelShellWidgetClass, XtParent (w),
            XmNtitle,               buf,
            XmNallowShellResize, True,
            XmNdeleteResponse,      XmUNMAP,
            NULL);
        n = 0;
        XtSetArg (args[n], XmNrows,       10); n++;
        XtSetArg (args[n], XmNcolumns,    40); n++;
        XtSetArg (args[n], XmNeditMode, XmMULTI_LINE_EDIT); n++;
        XtManageChild (XmCreateScrolledText (dialog, "text", args, n));
        /* set the shadow thickness to 2 so user knows there is a memo
         * attached to this date.
         */
        XtVaSetValues (w,
            XmNuserData, dialog,
            XmNshadowThickness, 2,
            NULL);
    }
```

```
    /* See if the dialog is realized and is visible.  If so, pop it down */
    if (XtIsRealized (dialog) && XGetWindowAttributes
            (XtDisplay (dialog), XtWindow (dialog), &xwa) &&
         xwa.map_state == IsViewable)
       XtPopdown (dialog);
    else
       XtPopup (dialog, XtGrabNone);
}

/* the rest of the file is junk to support finding the current date. */

static int mtbl[] = { 0,31,59,90,120,151,181,212,243,273,304,334,365 };

int
days_in_month(year, month)
int year, month;
{
    int days;

    days = mtbl[month] - mtbl[month - 1];
    if (month == 2 && year % 4 == 0 && (year % 100 != 0 || year % 400 == 0))
        days++;
    return days;
}

int
day_number(year, month, day)
int year, month, day;
{
    /* Lots of foolishness with casts for Xenix-286 16-bit ints */

    long days_ctr;       /* 16-bit ints overflowed Sept 12, 1989 */

    year -= 1900;
    days_ctr = ((long)year * 365L) + ((year + 3) / 4);
    days_ctr += mtbl[month - 1] + day + 6;
    if (month > 2 && (year % 4 == 0))
        days_ctr++;
    return (int) (days_ctr % 7L);
}
```

Index

cursor, callbacks, 506
   insertion, 469-475;
      bugs, 506
   position, 469
custom dialogs, 76, 195-232
cut and paste, and Text widgets, 479
   clipboard, 595-611
   example, 479, 597

D

data formats, clipboard, 611
data types, supported in UIL, 819
   UIL, 809, 821
deactivating menu titles, 534
default action, in list selection, 430
default button, dialog, 138
default font list tag, 687
default language procedure, 23
DefaultDepthOfScreen, 329
defining constants in UIL, 774
delayed widget creation, 877
delete key, remapping, 36
deleting items from a list, 420
deselecting items from a list, 422
destination cursor, 89, 455
dialog actions, 128
dialog boxes, example using, 868
   (see also dialogs)
dialog callbacks, adding, 144
   routine for, 197
dialog shells, BulletinBoard, 239
   versus dialog widgets, 126
dialog widgets, (see dialogs)
dialogs, 72-76, **123**, 167-191
   accessing internal widgets, 150
   action areas, 127, 205-207, 219-227;
      buttons in, 128
   anatomy of, 127-128
   and BulletinBoards, 125
   and manager widgets, 205
   and shell widgets, 71
   and the window manager, 136
   buttons; default, 138;
      fonts, 142;
      keyboard focus, 140;
      sizes, 141
   callback reasons, 144
   callback routines, 143, 197, 220;
      example, 145-146
   closing, 135-138
   CommandDialog, 75, 178-180

control areas, 127, 205-207
creating, 128-138, 137, 203-221;
   disadvantages, 905, 908
custom, 76, 195-232
defining fonts in, 730
definition, 8
destroying, 753
ErrorDialog, 72, 877
example, 133
FileSelectionDialog, 74, 180
fonts, 142, 688
full-application-modal, 151
function of, 124-126
header files, 128
help, 727-736;
   context-sensitive, 735;
   example, 209, 727, 731;
   point-and-click, 735
InformationDialog, 72
interacting with other windows, 151
labels; fonts, 142
layout of, 205
managing, 131-135, 905
MessageDialog, 72-73
modality, 76, 151-163;
   example, 157-162;
   implementing, 154;
   setting, 154
modifying, 195-203
popping down, 132
popping up, 132, 221, 231
positioning, 229-232
pre-defined, 123, 127
primary-application-modal, 151
PromptDialog, 74
QuestionDialog, 73
relation to manager widgets, 125
resizing, 142
resources; setting, 130, 215
reusable components, 899
reusing, 136, 159, 877
SelectionDialog, 74, 167-175
system-modal, 151
TemplateDialog, 73, 198
terminology, 126
text; fonts, 142
titlebar, 141, 215
TopLevelShells, using with, 228-229
transient, 123
unmanaging, 135-138, 905
unmapping, 136
versus dialog shells, 126
WarningDialog, 73

Index

examples (cont'd)

InformationDialog, 133

keyboard traversal; in ScrolledWindows, 331-333;
  processing manually, 292

list types, 849

lists; adding items to, 415;
  creating, 410;
  nested, 850-851;
  selecting items, 423, 433-434

mail interface, postcard, 921

MainWindow, 95, 209, 860-862;
  displaying bitmaps in, 105;
  using a ScrolledList in, 98

menu of common editing actions, 479

MenuBars, 105, 209, 532

menus; cascading, 547-550, 558-562;
  help, 537;
  option, 529, 558-562;
  popup, 551, 558-562;
  pulldown, 544, 547-551, 558-562

MessageDialog, 159, 196, 753

Motif 1.2 changes, 90

MrmFetchLiteral( ), 822

MrmRegisterClass( ), 882-884

multi-font strings, creating, 692

nested lists, 850-851

of UIL in an application, 859-878

PanedWindow, 278-283

password, prompting for, 501

position attachments, 256

postcard interface for mail, 921

PromptDialog; creating, 175

protocols, 585, 588

PushButton callbacks, 376

RadioBoxes, 387, 393

RowColumn, 264, 266, 268, 272

Scales, 440, 445

ScrolledText, 114

scrolling; application-defined, 317-330;
  automatic, 303

SelectionDialog, 169

shell, resizing, 571-572

strings, character sets, fonts, font lists, 837

text editor, 485;
  dropping files into, 658-666, 671-674

Text widgets, preventing text modification in, 500

text; converting to uppercase, 496;
  pattern, searching for, 469

tic-tac-toe, 256

timers, using, 753

ToggleButtons, 383

UIL for widget creation, 869-876

updating an existing drag source, 653-655

user interface in UID file, 800-801

using manage( ) callback, 904

window manager functions, 580

work areas, 209

WorkDialog, 739, 744

XmCreateSimpleMenuBar( ), 102

XmNentryCallback, 272

XmNfileSearchProc, 189

XmNsymbolPixmap, 753

XtAppAddTimeOut( ), 753

exec( ) system call, 751

execvp( ), system call, 722

exported defintion, 813

exported value, 819

exporting, application data, 852-854

callbacks, 876

identifiers to UIL, 853-854

information to UIL, 799

list definitions, 848

widgets, 813

Expose events, 749

processing, 748

expose_resize( ), 328

extended selection mode, 434

external commands, executing, 751-753

F

fallback resources, 25

fetching, color values, 839

dialogs, 868

pixmap values, 844-845

string and integer with MrmFetchLiteral( ), 822

values, 819-846;
  and internationalization, 820;
  to set widget resources, 822

widgets, 805, 814;
  with MrmFetchWidgetOverride( ), 816

file browser, 463

file descriptors, and running external processes, 753

file handling, in Mrm, 799

file manager with draggable files, 641-647

file objects, 658

file type masks, 190

XmFILE_REGULAR, 190

files, searching with FileSelectionDialog, 184-189

selecting with FileSelectionDialog, 180

FileSB.h, 129
FileSelectionBox, 89, 167
FileSelectionDialog, **74**, 89, 105, 180, 463, 862, 868
    callback routines, 184
    creating, 181-183
    searching directories, 189
filesystem searches, 184-189
filter buttons, and FileSelectionDialog, 181
floating point values, 824
    float value, 826
FMT16BIT, 499
FMT8BIT, 499
focus callbacks, 508
font list entries, appending, 701
    creating, 701-702
    freeing, 701
font list resources, 836
font list tags, 683-688
font lists, 683-688
    and BulletinBoard, 240
    caching, 701
    creating, 699-703
    description, 836
    entries, 699
    freeing, 701
    internationalization, 687, 699
    querying, 703-704
    retrieving, 703
font styles, specifying with character sets, 833
fonts, and compound strings, 681
    and dialogs, 688
    and Labels, 371
    defining in dialogs, 730
    dialogs, 142
    font sets, 836
    fonts lists, 836
    used by widgets, 688
    used in UIL, 827, 836-838
ForceUpdate( ), 750
foreground and background colors, 843
fork( ) system call, 751
Form, 60, **236**, 244-263
    and geometry management, 249
    attachments, 218, 245, 863
    circular dependencies, 261
    common problems with, 261
    creating user interface with, 818
    positions, 255
    resizing, 246
forward references, 818
    in Motif 1.2, 863
    to lists in Motif 1.2, 901

to variables, 819
Frame, 60, 86, 236, 274-278
fread( ), 468
freehand drawing, 347-348
full-application-modal dialogs, 151
function overloading, 342
functions, callbacks, 34;
    (see also callback routines.)
    popen, 751
    system, 751

G

gadgets, **55**, 62
    and DrawingArea widgets, 343
    and widget variants, 807
    class hierarchy, 56
    coloring, 62, 80
    creating, 62
    definition, 16, 27
    header files, 21
    Label; (see LabelGadget)
    managing, 62
    option in UIL, 770
    pointers, 365
    ToggleButtonGadget, 381
    translation tables, 291
GC (graphics context), 343
geometry management, 61-62, 235-294
    and BulletinBoard, 240-244
    and DrawingArea, 343
    and Form, 244, 249
    and RowColumn, 264
getpwent( ), 306
global variables, and drawing, 343
graphical user interface builder, 763
graphics context, 343
grips, 60, 278
GUI buttons, and menus, 521

H

hard-coded resources, 29
header files, 21, 83
    dialog, 128
    private, 21
hello world program, Motif-style, 19
    UIL module for, 765-767
    used to illustrate UIL and Mrm, 764
help, and drop sites, 622
    and Labels, 287

help dialogs, 727-736
   context-sensitive, 735
   example, 209, 727, 731
   multi-level, 731
   point-and-click, 735
help keys, 730
help menus, 537-539
HOME, 80
hooks, (see attachments)
horizontal alignment of widgets, 259
horizontal scrollbars, 54
   and scrolled lists, 412

I

-I (include path) UIL compiler option, 790
ICCCM, and clipboard functions, 596
   and drag and drop, 624
   and window managers, 71
icons, 574-577
   creating, 576
   defining, 843
   naming, 577
   setting pixmap, 575
   setting position, 577
   specifying, 841-843
identifier section, in UIL module, 773, 852-854
   overview, 855
identifiers, 852-854
   exporting, 853-854
   (see also identifier section.)
IDs, widget, 876
images, and Label widgets and gadgets, 367
   installing personalized, 79
   names, 79
   uninstalling, 79
imported declaration, 813
imported value, 819, 891
importing, information to UIL, 799
   widgets, 813
include directives to lists, 901
include files, and using lists, 899
   for Panner widget, 885
   for Tree widget, 884
   in UIL, 771
   used for organizing user interface, 892
InformationDialog, **72**, 128
   as help dialog, 727
   example, 133
   for help about drag and drop, 671, 674
initializing Mrm and Xt, 779
initializing the toolkit, 23-26

in-line lists, 848
in-line widget definitions, 806
input context, 513
input focus, setting, 293
input manager, 512
input method, 511
insertion cursor, 89, 455, 469-475
   bugs, 506
instantiating widgets, 16
integer arrays, 826
interactivePlacement, 231
Inter-Client Communications Conventions Manual (ICCCM), drag and drop, 624
   target types, 624, 649
   window sizing and placement, 567
interface description, in UIL module, 765-776;
   adding comments, 771;
   include files, 771;
   module statement, 767;
   options, 769-770;
   sections of UIL module, 773-776;
   UIL language syntax, 771-773
interface design, 10-12
   basic concepts, 6
internationalization, 22, 83, 89, 370, 509-514, 679-680, 819
   and compound strings, 681, 707
   and fetching values, 820
   and hard-coding error strings, 877
   font lists, 687, 699
   in UIL modules, 890-892;
      language-dependent resource strings, 891
   of applications with UIL, 763
int_sqrt( ), 367

J

Japanese text fonts, 836
justification, and Label widgets, 370

K

key mnemonics, 846
keyboard traversal, **63**, 85, 284-294
   and DrawingAreas, 347
   and ScrolledWindows, 331-333
   processing manually, 292
   translation table, 290
KeyPress events, 35
KeyRelease events, 749
keysym type, 846

keysyms, 35
keywords, (see predefined symbols)
kill, system call, 711

L

Label, 49, 87, 363-404
aligning, 370
and color, 82
and PushButton, 375
and scrolled windows, 317
and Text widgets, 364
creating, 365
desensitizing, 369
dragging and dropping, 50, 623, 635
fonts, 371, 688
help, 287
images, 367
justification, 370
multi-colored, 82
text, 365
widget and gadget variants of, 807
LabelGadget, 365
LANG environment variable, 23, 80, 837, 892
language procedure, 23, 509, 679
language-dependent, resource strings, 891
UID files, 892
libraries, Xlib, 21
Xm, 21
Xt, 21
line wrapping, and Text widgets, 468
linear search, and lists, 417
linking data via drag and drop, 622
List, 53, 87, 407-435
and color, 82
and tab groups, 64
callback routines, 430-435;
installing, 431
CheckBox, compared to, 381
creating, 409-411
dragging and dropping, 53, 623, 636
RadioBox, compared to, 381
selection policies, 408, 410, 430;
browse, 408, 430;
extended, 408, 434;
multiple, 408, 433;
single, 408, 430
(see also lists.)
list section, in UIL module, 773, 848
overview, 855
used to set widget resources, 890

lists, 848-851
adding items to, 414-417;
example, 415
and hierarchy of include files, 899-900
attachment, 863
definition, 848
deleting items from, 420
deselecting items from, 422
displaying, 407
double-clicking on an item, 430
finding items in, 417
forward references to, 901
in-line, 848
making items visible, 411
nested, 850-851
positioning items in, 427
replacing items in, 418
scrolled; (see scrolled lists)
searching; binary, 417;
linear, 417
selecting items from, 413, 421, 430;
default action, 430;
example, 423
undefined, 900
using in UIL, 897-903;
to reduce size of modules, 897-899
(see also list section.)
loading pixmaps, 112
locale, 22, 509, 679
localization, 23, 509, 679
locking, clipboards, 599, 602, 610

M

-m (machine listing) UIL compiler option, 792
main application window, example using,
860-862
main() procedure, 801
main windows, 65, 93-120
command areas, 114
configurability, 118
example, 209
message areas, 114
suggested layout, 93
using resources with, 118
(see also MainWindow.)
MainWindow, 59, 65, **237**, 482
and ScrolledWindows, 95
creating, 94
default size, 97
example, 95, 860-862

Index

Index

values (cont'd)
    floating point, 824
    font, 836
    identifier, 852
    imported, 891
    numeric, 824-826;
        and integer arrays, 826;
        and numeric expressions, 825-826
    scrollbar, 308
    sharing, 819
    specifying for Motif resources, 819
    text-related, 827-838
varargs, 26
    and dialogs, 130
VarargsI.h, 477
VendorShell, **71**, 89, 148, 513, 568
    resources, 577-580
vertical scrollbars, 54
    and scrolled lists, 412
vertically tiled format, and PanedWindows, 278
vi, and Text widgets, 455
view length, scrollbars, 308
view_height, and scrolled windows, 328
view_width, and scrolled windows, 328
virtual bindings, 35, 86
virtual keysyms, 35
vsprintf( ), 477

W

-w (suppress warnings) UIL compiler option, 791
WarningDialog, **73**, 128
wide-character strings, 509, 680, 835
widget attributes, 804-806
    and in-line definitions, 806
widget class, setting resources by, 895
widget class type, class_rec_name, 845
widget definition, arguments subsection of, 809-810
    callbacks subsection of, 811-812
    controls subsection, 804
    exporting and importing, 813
    in menu system, 867
    in-line, 806
    searching for, 816
    structure of, 802-804
    syntax, 803
widget hierarchy, fetching, 805
widget IDs, 876
widget management, and Mrm, 808
Widget Meta-Language (WML), 792

widget_name, 814
widget_return, 814
widgets, and color, 80
    and delayed widget creation, 877
    and gadget variants, 807
    attachment list for, 863
    attributes of; (see widget attributes)
    children of, 804-806
    class type, 845
    container, 899
    creating, 16, 26-28;
        algorithm, 815;
        and searching for widget definition, 816;
        by Mrm calls vs. Motif widget calls, 869;
        hierarchy for, 905;
        recursively, 817;
        user-defined widgets, 881-884;
        with MrmFetchWidget( ), 814-818;
        with UIL vs. Xt, 805
    defining in UIL, 774, 802-818
    definition, 15
    drag and drop, 623
    event handling, 34-40
    fetching, 814;
        with MrmFetchWidgetOverride( ), 816
    foreground and background colors of, 843
    instantiating, 16
    MainWindow, 860-862
    manager, 27, 56, 56-64;
        (see also manager widgets.)
    managing, 903
    Motif; list of automatically-created children, 807
    naming, 33
    naming in-line, 806
    option in UIL, 770
    overview, 45-90
    parent-child relationships, 58
    protocol, 583
    realizing, 40
    redrawing, 400
    returning top-level, 818
    setting unresolved resources, 818
    sharing among UIL modules, 813-814
    user-defined, 817
    using non-Motif in UIL programs, 881
wildcard specification, for X resource files, 895
window manager, 567-592
    and dialogs, 136
    and ICCCM, 71
    and shell widgets, 68
    borders, 577
    bugs, 575

Index

Index

About the Authors

Dan Heller is President of Z-Code Software Corp., makers of electronic messaging software for UNIX, Mac, and PC/Windows platforms. His history with the X Window System dates back to 1987, when he developed some of the first toolkits to use Xt. In 1990, he developed Z-Code's first product, Z-Mail, using the Motif toolkit, concurrent with the writing of the first edition of Volume 6A, *Motif Programming Manual*.

Dan has a degree in Computer and Information Sciences from the University of California, Santa Cruz, and has since developed and brought to market many applications that integrate various well-known user-interface styles from SunView to Motif to Open Look.

Dan is also the author of O'Reilly & Associates' *XView Programming Manual*.

Paula Ferguson is a writer for O'Reilly & Associates. In addition to co-authoring this book, she has written articles for *The X Resource*, helped update other volumes in the X series, and authored Volume 6B, *Motif Reference Manual*. Paula has also developed and taught courses on Motif for the Open Software Foundation and worked on interface-design and software development projects.

Paula graduated from the Massachusetts Institute of Technology in 1990 with a B.S. in Computer Science and Engineering. She lives in Somerville, Massachusetts with her two cats, but spends as much time outside of the city as possible. When she can escape, Paula likes to go rock climbing, cycling, hiking, backpacking, and mountaineering.

 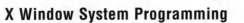

More Titles from O'Reilly

X Window System Programming

Volume 1: Xlib Programming Manual

By Adrian Nye
3rd Edition July 1992
824 pages, ISBN 1-56592-002-3

Covering X11 Release 5, the *Xlib Programming Manual* is a complete guide to programming the X library (Xlib), the lowest level of programming interface to X. It includes introductions to internationalization, device-independent color, font service, and scalable fonts.

Includes chapters on:

- X Window System concepts
- A simple client application
- Window attributes
- The graphics context
- Graphics in practice
- Color
- Events
- Interclient communication
- Internationalization
- The Resource Manager
- A complete client application
- Window management
- Other programming techniques

This manual is a companion to Volume 2, *Xlib Reference Manual*.

Volume 2: Xlib Reference Manual

By Adrian Nye
3rd Edition June 1992
1138 pages, ISBN 1-56592-006-6

Volume 2, *Xlib Reference Manual*, is a complete programmer's reference for Xlib. Covers X11 Release 4 and Release 5.

Contents Include:

- Reference pages for Xlib functions
- Reference pages for event types
- Permuted index to Xlib functions
- Description of macros and reference pages for their function versions
- Listing of the server-side color database
- Alphabetical index and description of structures
- Alphabetical index and description of defined symbols
- KeySyms and their meaning
- Illustration of the standard cursor font
- Function group index to the right routine for a particular task
- Reference pages for Xlib-related Xmu functions (miscellaneous utilities)
- Four single-page reference aids for the GC and window attributes
- Index

New features in the third edition include:

- Over 100 new man pages covering Xcms, internationalization, and the function versions of macros.
- Updating to the R5 spec.
- New "Returns" sections on all the functions which return values, making this information easier to find.

Volume 4M: X Toolkit Intrinsics Programming Manual

Motif Edition, By Adrian Nye & Tim O'Reilly
2nd Edition August 1992
674 pages, ISBN 1-56592-013-9

A complete guide to programming with the X Toolkit Intrinsics, the library of C language routines that facilitates the design of user interfaces with reusable components called widgets. This book provides concepts and examples that show how to use the various X Toolkit routines. The first few chapters are devoted to using widgets; the remainder of the book covers the more complex task of writing new widgets.

Uses the Motif 1.2 widget set in examples and covers X11 Release 5.

X Window System Programming

Volume 5: X Toolkit Intrinsics Reference Manual

VOLUME 5 Edited by David Flanagan
3rd Edition April 1992
916 pages, ISBN 1-56592-007-4

The *X Toolkit Intrinsics Reference Manual* is a complete programmer's reference for the X Toolkit. This volume is based on Xt documentation from the X Consortium and has been reorganized and expanded for X11 Release 5. It provides reference pages for each of the Xt functions, as well as the widget classes defined by Xt and the Athena widgets, and many useful appendices.

This manual is a companion to Volume 4M, *X Toolkit Intrinsics Programming Manual*.

Volume 6B: Motif Reference Manual

VOLUME 6B By Paula Ferguson & David Brennan
1st Edition June 1993
920 pages, ISBN 1-56592-038-4

The *Motif Reference Manual* is a complete programmer's reference for the Motif toolkit from the Open Software Foundation (OSF). Motif has become the standard user interface for X Window System applications, and the Motif toolkit makes it easy for programmers to build applications that conform with the Motif "look and feel."

This book provides reference pages for the Motif functions and macros, the Motif and Xt widget classes, the Mrm functions, the Motif clients, and the UIL file format, data types, and functions. The reference material has been expanded from the appendices of the first edition of Volume 6 and covers Motif 1.2. This book is designed to be used with Volume 6A, *Motif Programming Manual*, which describes how to build applications using the Motif toolkit and provides a complete tutorial with programming examples.

Java

Java Power Reference

By David Flanagan
1st Edition March 1999
64 pages, Features CD-ROM
ISBN 1-56592-589-0

Java Power Reference is a searchable, browser-based resource that documents all the packages and classes of the Java 2™ platform on a single CD-ROM. Based on the clear, concise quick-reference style of the bestselling *Java in a Nutshell*, the *Java Power Reference* provides a unique view of the functionality of the Java APIs. In addition to the CD-ROM, the package contains a concise printed overview of the newly released Java 2 platform.

Java 2D Graphics

By Jonathan Knudsen
1st Edition May 1999
366 pages, ISBN 1-56592-484-3

Java 2D Graphics describes the 2D API from top to bottom, demonstrating how to set line styles and pattern fills as well as more advanced techniques of image processing and font handling. You'll see how to create and manipulate the three types of graphics objects: shapes, text, and images. Other topics include image data storage, color management, font glyphs, and printing.

Java Swing

By Robert Eckstein, Marc Loy & Dave Wood
1st Edition September 1998
1252 pages, ISBN 1-56592-455-X

The Swing classes eliminate Java's biggest weakness: its relatively primitive user interface toolkit. *Java Swing* helps you to take full advantage of the Swing classes, providing detailed descriptions of every class and interface in the key Swing packages. It shows you how to use all of the new components, allowing you to build state-of-the-art user interfaces and giving you the context you need to understand what you're doing. It's more than documentation; *Java Swing* helps you develop code quickly and effectively.

O'REILLY®

TO ORDER: **800-998-9938** • **order@oreilly.com** • **http://www.oreilly.com/**
OUR PRODUCTS ARE AVAILABLE AT A BOOKSTORE OR SOFTWARE STORE NEAR YOU.
FOR INFORMATION: **800-998-9938** • **707-829-0515** • **info@oreilly.com**

Java

Java Cryptography

By Jonathan B. Knudsen
1st Edition May 1998
362 pages, ISBN 1-56592-402-9

Java Cryptography teaches you how to write secure programs using Java's cryptographic tools. It includes thorough discussions of the java.security package and the Java Cryptography Extensions (JCE), showing you how to use security providers and even implement your own provider. It discusses authentication, key management, public and private key encryption, and includes a secure talk application that encrypts all data sent over the network. If you work with sensitive data, you'll find this book indispensable.

Java Distributed Computing

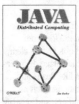

By Jim Farley
1st Edition January 1998
384 pages, ISBN 1-56592-206-9

Java Distributed Computing offers a general introduction to distributed computing, meaning programs that run on two or more systems. It focuses primarily on how to structure and write distributed applications and discusses issues like designing protocols, security, working with databases, and dealing with low bandwidth situations.

Java Network Programming

By Elliotte Rusty Harold
1st Edition February 1997
442 pages, ISBN 1-56592-227-1

The network is the soul of Java. Most of what is new and exciting about Java centers around the potential for new kinds of dynamic networked applications. *Java Network Programming* teaches you to work with Sockets, write network clients and servers, and gives you an advanced look at the new areas like multicasting, using the server API, and RMI. Covers Java 1.1.

Java Security

By Scott Oaks
1st Edition May 1998
474 pages, ISBN 1-56592-403-7

This essential Java 2 book covers Java's security mechanisms and teaches you how to work with them. It discusses class loaders, security managers, access lists, digital signatures, and authentication and shows how to use these to create and enforce your own security policy.

Java Threads, 2nd Edition

By Scott Oaks & Henry Wong
2nd Edition January 1999
336 pages, ISBN 1-56592-418-5

Revised and expanded to cover Java 2, *Java Threads, 2nd Edition* shows you how to take full advantage of Java's thread facilities: where to use threads to increase efficiency, how to use them effectively, and how to avoid common mistakes. It thoroughly covers the Thread and ThreadGroup classes, the Runnable interface, and the language's synchronized operator. The book pays special attention to threading issues with Swing, as well as problems like deadlock, race condition, and starvation to help you write code without hidden bugs.

Java I/O

By Elliotte Rusty Harold
1st Edition March 1999
596 pages, ISBN 1-56592-485-1

All of Java's Input/Output (I/O) facilities are based on streams, which provide simple ways to read and write data of different types. Java I/O tells you all you need to know about the four main categories of streams and uncovers less-known features to help make your I/O operations more efficient. Plus, it shows you how to control number formatting, use characters aside from the standard ASCII character set, and get a head start on writing truly multilingual software.

Java

Java Fundamental Classes Reference

By Mark Grand & Jonathan Knudsen
1st Edition May 1997
1114 pages, ISBN 1-56592-241-7

The *Java Fundamental Classes Reference*
provides complete reference documentation
on the core Java 1.1 classes that comprise the
java.lang, java.io, java.net, java.util, java.text,
java.math, java.lang.reflect, and java.util.zip
packages. Part of O'Reilly's Java documentation series, this edition
describes Version 1.1 of the Java Development Kit. It includes
easy-to-use reference material and provides lots of sample code
to help you learn by example.

Java Language Reference, 2nd Edition

By Mark Grand
2nd Edition July 1997
492 pages, ISBN 1-56592-326-X

This book helps you understand the subtle
nuances of Java – from the definition of
data types to the syntax of expressions and
control structures – so you can ensure
your programs run exactly as expected.
The second edition covers the language features that have
been added in Java 1.1, such as inner classes, class literals,
and instance initializers.

Java Virtual Machine

By Jon Meyer & Troy Downing
1st Edition March 1997
452 pages, Includes diskette
ISBN 1-56592-194-1

This book is a comprehensive programming
guide for the Java Virtual Machine (JVM). It
gives readers a strong overview and reference
of the JVM so that they may create their own
implementations or write their own compilers that create Java
object code.

Java AWT Reference

By John Zukowski
1st Edition April 1997
1074 pages, ISBN 1-56592-240-9

The *Java AWT Reference* provides complete
reference documentation on the Abstract
Window Toolkit (AWT), a large collection of
classes for building graphical user interfaces
in Java. Part of O'Reilly's Java documentation
series, this edition describes both Version 1.0.2 and Version 1.1
of the Java Development Kit, includes easy-to-use reference
material on every AWT class, and provides lots of sample code.

Exploring Java, 2nd Edition

By Pat Niemeyer & Josh Peck
2nd Edition September 1997
614 pages, ISBN 1-56592-271-9

Whether you're just migrating to
Java or working steadily in the forefront
of Java development, this book gives a clear,
systematic overview of the language. It covers
the essentials of hot topics like Beans and
RMI, as well as writing applets and other applications, such as
networking programs, content and protocol handlers, and security
managers.

Developing Java Beans

By Robert Englander
1st Edition June 1997
316 pages, ISBN 1-56592-289-1

Developing Java Beans is a complete
introduction to Java's component architecture.
It describes how to write Beans, which are
software components that can be used in
visual programming environments. This
book discusses event adapters, serialization, introspection,
property editors, and customizers, and shows how to use Beans
within ActiveX controls.

Java

Enterprise JavaBeans

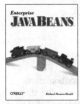

By Richard Monson-Haefel
1st Edition June 1999
336 pages, ISBN 1-56592-605-6

Enterprise JavaBeans is a thorough introduction to EJB for the enterprise software developer. It shows how to get started developing enterprise Beans, how to deploy those Beans in a server, and how to use those Beans to create applications that do useful tasks. The end result is a highly flexible system built from components that can easily be reused and that can be changed to suit your needs without upsetting other parts of the system.

Java Servlet Programming

By Jason Hunter with William Crawford
1st Edition November 1998
528 pages, ISBN 1-56592-391-X

Java servlets offer a fast, powerful, portable replacement for CGI scripts. *Java Servlet Programming* covers everything you need to know to write effective servlets. Topics include: serving dynamic Web content, maintaining state information, session tracking, database connectivity using JDBC, and applet-servlet communication.

How to stay in touch with O'Reilly

1. Visit Our Award-Winning Web Site

http://www.oreilly.com/

★ "Top 100 Sites on the Web" —*PC Magazine*
★ "Top 5% Web sites" —*Point Communications*
★ "3-Star site" —*The McKinley Group*

Our web site contains a library of comprehensive product information (including book excerpts and tables of contents), downloadable software, background articles, interviews with technology leaders, links to relevant sites, book cover art, and more. File us in your Bookmarks or Hotlist!

2. Join Our Email Mailing Lists

New Product Releases

To receive automatic email with brief descriptions of all new O'Reilly products as they are released, send email to:
listproc@online.oreilly.com
Put the following information in the first line of your message (*not* in the Subject field):
subscribe oreilly-news

O'Reilly Events

If you'd also like us to send information about trade show events, special promotions, and other O'Reilly events, send email to:
listproc@online.oreilly.com
Put the following information in the first line of your message (*not* in the Subject field):
subscribe oreilly-events

3. Get Examples from Our Books via FTP

There are two ways to access an archive of example files from our books:

Regular FTP

- ftp to:
  ftp.oreilly.com
  (login: anonymous
  password: your email address)
- Point your web browser to:
  ftp://ftp.oreilly.com/

FTPMAIL

- Send an email message to:
  ftpmail@online.oreilly.com
  (Write "help" in the message body)

4. Contact Us via Email

order@oreilly.com
To place a book or software order online. Good for North American and international customers.

subscriptions@oreilly.com
To place an order for any of our newsletters or periodicals.

books@oreilly.com
General questions about any of our books.

software@oreilly.com
For general questions and product information about our software. Check out O'Reilly Software Online at **http://software.oreilly.com/** for software and technical support information. Registered O'Reilly software users send your questions to: **website-support@oreilly.com**

cs@oreilly.com
For answers to problems regarding your order or our products.

booktech@oreilly.com
For book content technical questions or corrections.

proposals@oreilly.com
To submit new book or software proposals to our editors and product managers.

international@oreilly.com
For information about our international distributors or translation queries. For a list of our distributors outside of North America check out:
http://www.oreilly.com/www/order/country.html

O'Reilly & Associates, Inc.
101 Morris Street, Sebastopol, CA 95472 USA
TEL   707-829-0515 or 800-998-9938
         (6am to 5pm PST)
FAX   707-829-0104

Titles from O'Reilly

International Distributors

UK, EUROPE, MIDDLE EAST AND AFRICA (EXCEPT FRANCE, GERMANY, AUSTRIA, SWITZERLAND, LUXEMBOURG, LIECHTENSTEIN, AND EASTERN EUROPE)

INQUIRIES
O'Reilly UK Limited
4 Castle Street
Farnham
Surrey, GU9 7HS
United Kingdom
Telephone: 44-1252-711776
Fax: 44-1252-734211
Email: josette@oreilly.com

ORDERS
Wiley Distribution Services Ltd.
1 Oldlands Way
Bognor Regis
West Sussex PO22 9SA
United Kingdom
Telephone: 44-1243-779777
Fax: 44-1243-820250
Email: cs-books@wiley.co.uk

FRANCE

ORDERS
GEODIF
61, Bd Saint-Germain
75240 Paris Cedex 05, France
Tel: 33-1-44-41-46-16 (French books)
Tel: 33-1-44-41-11-87 (English books)
Fax: 33-1-44-41-11-44
Email: distribution@eyrolles.com

INQUIRIES
Éditions O'Reilly
18 rue Séguier
75006 Paris, France
Tel: 33-1-40-51-52-30
Fax: 33-1-40-51-52-31
Email: france@editions-oreilly.fr

GERMANY, SWITZERLAND, AUSTRIA, EASTERN EUROPE, LUXEMBOURG, AND LIECHTENSTEIN

INQUIRIES & ORDERS
O'Reilly Verlag
Balthasarstr. 81
D-50670 Köln
Germany
Telephone: 49-221-973160-91
Fax: 49-221-973160-8
Email: anfragen@oreilly.de (inquiries)
Email: order@oreilly.de (orders)

CANADA (FRENCH LANGUAGE BOOKS)

Les Éditions Flammarion ltée
375, Avenue Laurier Ouest
Montréal (Québec) H2V 2K3
Tel: 00-1-514-277-8807
Fax: 00-1-514-278-2085
Email: info@flammarion.qc.ca

HONG KONG

City Discount Subscription Service, Ltd.
Unit D, 3rd Floor, Yan's Tower
27 Wong Chuk Hang Road
Aberdeen, Hong Kong
Tel: 852-2580-3539
Fax: 852-2580-6463
Email: citydis@ppn.com.hk

KOREA

Hanbit Media, Inc.
Sonyoung Bldg. 202
Yeksam-dong 736-36
Kangnam-ku
Seoul, Korea
Tel: 822-554-9610
Fax: 822-556-0363
Email: hant93@chollian.dacom.co.kr

PHILIPPINES

Mutual Books, Inc.
429-D Shaw Boulevard
Mandaluyong City, Metro
Manila, Philippines
Tel: 632-725-7538
Fax: 632-721-3056
Email: mbikikog@mnl.sequel.net

TAIWAN

O'Reilly Taiwan
No. 3, Lane 131
Hang-Chow South Road
Section 1, Taipei, Taiwan
Tel: 886-2-23968990
Fax: 886-2-23968916
Email: taiwan@oreilly.com

CHINA

O'Reilly Beijing
Room 2410
160, FuXingMenNeiDaJie
XiCheng District
Beijing, China PR 100031
Tel: 86-10-66412305
Fax: 86-10-86631007
Email: beijing@oreilly.com

INDIA

Computer Bookshop (India) Pvt. Ltd.
190 Dr. D.N. Road, Fort
Bombay 400 001 India
Tel: 91-22-207-0989
Fax: 91-22-262-3551
Email: cbsbom@giasbm01.vsnl.net.in

JAPAN

O'Reilly Japan, Inc.
Kiyoshige Building 2F
12-Bancho, Sanei-cho
Shinjuku-ku
Tokyo 160-0008 Japan
Tel: 81-3-3356-5227
Fax: 81-3-3356-5261
Email: japan@oreilly.com

ALL OTHER ASIAN COUNTRIES

O'Reilly & Associates, Inc.
101 Morris Street
Sebastopol, CA 95472 USA
Tel: 707-829-0515
Fax: 707-829-0104
Email: order@oreilly.com

AUSTRALIA

WoodsLane Pty., Ltd.
7/5 Vuko Place
Warriewood NSW 2102
Australia
Tel: 61-2-9970-5111
Fax: 61-2-9970-5002
Email: info@woodslane.com.au

NEW ZEALAND

Woodslane New Zealand, Ltd.
21 Cooks Street (P.O. Box 575)
Waganui, New Zealand
Tel: 64-6-347-6543
Fax: 64-6-345-4840
Email: info@woodslane.com.au

LATIN AMERICA

McGraw-Hill Interamericana
Editores, S.A. de C.V.
Cedro No. 512
Col. Atlampa
06450, Mexico, D.F.
Tel: 52-5-547-6777
Fax: 52-5-547-3336
Email: mcgraw-hill@infosel.net.mx

O'REILLY®

O'REILLY™

O'Reilly & Associates, Inc.
101 Morris Street
Sebastopol, CA 95472-9902
1-800-998-9938

Visit us online at:
http://www.ora.com/
orders@ora.com

O'REILLY WOULD LIKE TO HEAR FROM YOU

Which book did this card come from?

_____

Where did you buy this book?
- ❏ Bookstore
- ❏ Direct from O'Reilly
- ❏ Bundled with hardware/software
- ❏ Other _____
- ❏ Computer Store
- ❏ Class/seminar

What operating system do you use?
- ❏ UNIX
- ❏ Windows NT
- ❏ Other _____
- ❏ Macintosh
- ❏ PC(Windows/DOS)

What is your job description?
- ❏ System Administrator
- ❏ Network Administrator
- ❏ Web Developer
- ❏ Other _____
- ❏ Programmer
- ❏ Educator/Teacher

❏ Please send me O'Reilly's catalog, containing a complete listing of O'Reilly books and software.

Name _____ Company/Organization _____

Address _____

City _____ State _____ Zip/Postal Code _____ Country _____

Telephone _____ Internet or other email address (specify network)

Nineteenth century wood engraving
of a bear from the O'Reilly &
Associates Nutshell Handbook®
Using & Managing UUCP.

BUSINESS REPLY MAIL
FIRST CLASS MAIL   PERMIT NO. 80   SEBASTOPOL, CA

Postage will be paid by addressee

O'Reilly & Associates, Inc.
101 Morris Street
Sebastopol, CA 95472-9902